A Heritage Of
GREAT
Evangelical
Teaching

A HERITAGE OF
GREAT
EVANGELICAL
TEACHING

Featuring the Best of Martin Luther, John Wesley,
Dwight L. Moody, C. H. Spurgeon and others

THOMAS NELSON PUBLISHERS
Nashville • Atlanta • Vancouver • London

Published in Nashville, Tennessee, by Thomas Nelson, Inc. Distributed in Canada by Nelson/Word Canada.

Library of Congress Cataloging-in-Publication Data

Heritage of great evangelical teaching.
    p. cm.
  ISBN 0-7852-1161-6
  1. Evangelicalism.
BR1640.H45 1996
230'.044—dc20

96–8958
CIP

Manufactured in the United States of Amercica.
1 2 3 4 5 6 — 01 00 99 98 97 96

Contents

Publisher's Preface

Eight outstanding Christian leaders from the past are brought together to minister to you in the present. The books they've written have changed the landscape of the Christian mind. Now the best from their classic works is brought together in one volume, *A Heritage of Great Evangelical Teaching.*

Featuring the best from the works of Dwight Moody, Martin Luther, Charles Finney, John Wesley, George MacDonald, F. B. Meyer, C. H. Spurgeon, and Andrew Murray, this collection will help you nurture your own spiritual life and appreciate the riches of your Christian heritage.

Each work is prefaced with an introduction and timeline to help you understand the world these leaders lived in and why these works are still important today. Recommendations for further reading are also included.

A Heritage of Great Evangelical Teaching offers you the timeless relevance and solid, accessible wisdom of eight of Christianity's most influential spiritual leaders. With it, you can enhance your own spiritual growth and strengthen your connection to the heritage of faith that joins the people of God from all times into one body.

MARTIN LUTHER

Martin Luther

Abridged and edited by Stephen Rost

Contents

MARTIN LUTHER 1483–1546

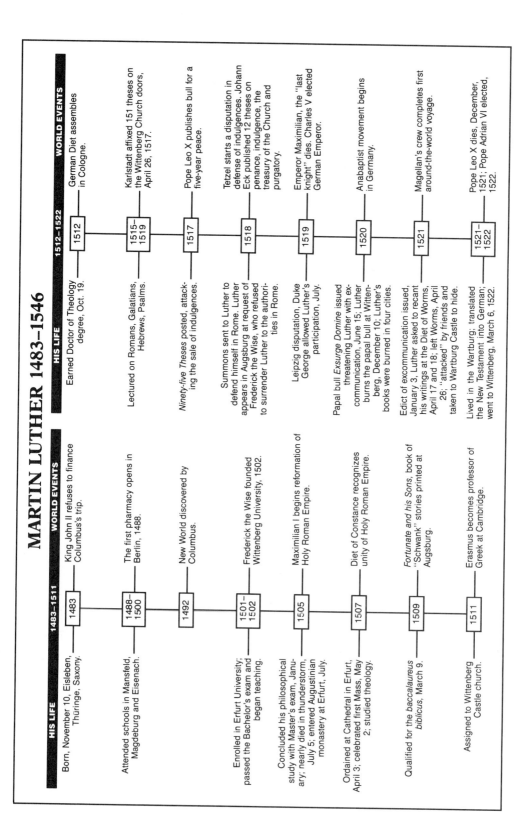

1483–1511

HIS LIFE

1483 — Born, November 10, Eisleben, Thüringe, Saxony.

1488–1500 — Attended schools in Mansfeld, Magdeburg and Eisenach.

1492 — New World discovered by Columbus.

1501–1502 — Enrolled in Erfurt University; passed the Bachelor's exam and began teaching.

1505 — Concluded his philosophical study with Master's exam, January; nearly died in thunderstorm, July 5; entered Augustinian monastery at Erfurt, July.

1507 — Ordained at Cathedral in Erfurt, April 3; celebrated first Mass, May 2; studied theology.

1509 — Qualified for the *baccalaureus biblicus*, March 9.

1511 — Assigned to Wittenberg Castle church.

WORLD EVENTS

King John II refuses to finance Columbus's trip.

The first pharmacy opens in Berlin, 1488.

Frederick the Wise founded Wittenberg University, 1502.

Maximilian I begins reformation of Holy Roman Empire.

Diet of Constance recognizes unity of Holy Roman Empire.

Fortunate and his Sons, book of "Schwank" stories printed at Augsburg.

Erasmus becomes professor of Greek at Cambridge.

1512–1522

HIS LIFE

1512 — Earned Doctor of Theology degree, Oct. 19.

1515–1519 — Lectured on Romans, Galatians, Hebrews, Psalms.

1517 — *Ninety-five Theses* posted, attacking the sale of indulgences.

1518 — Summons sent to Luther to defend himself in Rome. Luther appears in Augsburg at request of Frederick the Wise, who refused to surrender Luther to the authorities in Rome.

1519 — Leipzig disputation, Duke George allowed Luther's participation, July.

1520 — Papal bull *Exsurge Domine* issued threatening Luther with excommunication, June 15; Luther burns the papal bull at Wittenberg, December 10; Luther's books were burned in four cities.

1521 — Edict of excommunication issued, January 3, Luther asked to recant his writings at the Diet of Worms, April 17 and 18; left Worms, April 26; "attacked" by friends and taken to Wartburg Castle to hide.

1521–1522 — Lived in the Wartburg; translated the New Testament into German; went to Wittenberg, March 6, 1522.

WORLD EVENTS

German Diet assembles in Cologne.

Karlstadt affixed 151 theses on the Wittenberg Church doors, April 26, 1517.

Pope Leo X publishes bull for a five-year peace.

Tetzel starts a disputation in defense of indulgences. Johann Eck published 12 theses on penance, indulgence, the treasury of the Church and purgatory.

Emperor Maximilian, the "last knight" dies. Charles V elected German Emperor.

Anabaptist movement begins in Germany.

Magellan's crew completes first around-the-world voyage.

Pope Leo X dies, December, 1521; Pope Adrian VI elected, 1522.

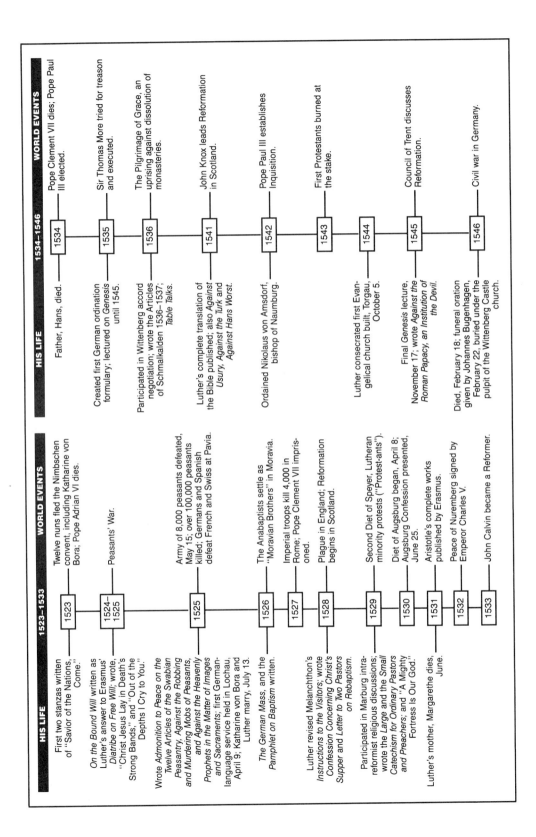

1534–1546

Year	WORLD EVENTS	HIS LIFE
1534	Pope Clement VII dies; Pope Paul III elected.	Father, Hans, died.
1535	Sir Thomas More tried for treason and executed.	Created first German ordination formulary; lectured on *Genesis* until 1545.
1536	The Pilgrimage of Grace, an uprising against dissolution of monasteries.	Participated in Wittenberg accord negotiation; wrote the Articles of Schmalkalden 1536–1537; *Table Talks*.
1541	John Knox leads Reformation in Scotland.	Luther's complete translation of the Bible published; also *Against Usury, Against the Turk and Against Hans Worst*.
1542	Pope Paul III establishes Inquisition.	Ordained Nikolaus von Amsdorf, bishop of Naumburg.
1543	First Protestants burned at the stake.	
1544	Council of Trent discusses Reformation.	Luther consecrated first Evangelical church built, Torgau, October 5.
1545		Final *Genesis* lecture, November 17; wrote *Against the Roman Papacy, an Institution of the Devil*.
1546	Civil war in Germany.	Died, February 18; funeral oration given by Johannes Bugenhagen, February 22, buried under the pulpit of the Wittenberg Castle church.

1523–1533

Year	WORLD EVENTS	HIS LIFE
1523	Twelve nuns fled the Nimbschen convent, including Katharine von Bora; Pope Adrian VI dies.	First two stanzas written of "Savior of the Nations, Come."
1524–1525	Peasants' War.	*On the Bound Will* written as Luther's answer to Erasmus' *Diatribe on Free Will*; wrote, "Christ Jesus Lay in Death's Strong Bands," and "Out of the Depths I Cry to You."
1525	Army of 8,000 peasants defeated, May 15; over 100,000 peasants killed; Germans and Spanish defeat French and Swiss at Pavia.	Wrote *Admonition to Peace on the Twelve Articles of the Swabian Peasantry, Against the Robbing and Murdering Mobs of Peasants*, and *Against the Heavenly Prophets in the Matter of Images and Sacraments*; first German-language service held in Lochau, April 9; Katharine von Bora and Luther marry, July 13.
1526	The Anabaptists settle as "Moravian Brothers" in Moravia.	*The German Mass*, and the *Pamphlet on Baptism* written.
1527	Imperial troops kill 4,000 in Rome; Pope Clement VII imprisoned.	
1528	Plague in England; Reformation begins in Scotland.	Luther revised Melanchthon's *Instructions to the Visitors*; wrote *Confession Concerning Christ's Supper and Letter to Two Pastors on Rebaptism*.
1529	Second Diet of Speyer, Lutheran minority protests ("Protest-ants").	Participated in Marburg intra-reformist religious discussions; wrote the *Large* and the *Small Catechism for Ordinary Pastors and Preachers*; and "A Mighty Fortress Is Our God."
1530	Diet of Augsburg began, April 8; Augsburg Confession presented, June 25.	
1531	Aristotle's complete works published by Erasmus.	Luther's mother, Margarethe dies, June.
1532	Peace of Nuremberg signed by Emperor Charles V.	
1533	John Calvin became a Reformer.	

MARTIN LUTHER

Introduction

The study of church history is one of the greatest intellectual endeavors to be undertaken by man. No doubt those who hate the church or are ignorant of church history will contest the importance of this particular branch of study. Yet one need only examine history beginning with Rome to see the tremendous impact the church has had on philosophy, theology, politics, law, science, and even war. Some of the greatest minds to be found, men who gave rise to great movements, or moved nations, were connected with the church in some way.

Martin Luther is the epitome of such greatness. It is difficult to fully express the importance of this man, for church history has many competitors for such a reputation: Augustine, Anselm, Aquinas, Calvin, Schliermacher, and Barth, to name a few. While these men excelled in their own ways above their contemporaries, Martin Luther stands as possibly the most influential figure since Jesus Christ. One historian has stated that no other man in history apart from Christ has had more written about him and his thought than Martin Luther.

What has made Luther such a vital link in the chain of history? One should examine his life for the answer. Born in 1483 in Eisleben, Germany, Luther grew up in a period when the intellectual climate was at a high point. The works of great men such as Augustine, Anselm, Aquinas, Peter the Lombard, Abelard, Ockham, Aristotle, and Plato, were among the primary sources of study. Logic, philosophy, science, theology, law, classical literature and languages (Greek, Latin, Hebrew), and political theory dominated the curriculum of the universities. The intellectual environment in the universities challenged young scholars to reach far and above what the typical twentieth-century student must achieve. Luther grew up in this stimulating world.

Luther attended the University of Erfurt (considered one of the most influential schools of the fifteenth century), earning the bachelor of arts degree in 1502 and the master of arts degree in 1505. In 1505 he began to study law, but his heart was really drawn to theological matters. Soon he gave up the study of law and joined an Augustinian monastery in Erfurt. There he became fully immersed in the traditional Catholic faith. His great intellectual bent enabled him to master Greek and Hebrew and to commit to memory most of the New Testament. Ordained as a priest in 1507, he began his career as a university professor at Wittenberg and Erfurt, and he acquired his doctorate in 1512.

Luther became distressed at the selling of indulgences by the pope, so in 1517 he nailed his "Ninety-five Theses" to the door of the Wittenberg church. This noncombative act was the acceptable means for seeking a public discussion on the issues in dispute. The conflicts that resulted eventually led Luther to see the Bible, not the pope, as the sole authority over man. Later he became a true Christian, and from there his relationship with the Catholic church became so strained that he was excommunicated. This separation led to greater conflict, and Luther became the recognized leader of what became the Reformation. Luther's outspokenness signaled the beginning of a new movement—Protestantism—and a new period in history—the Reformation.

Luther wrote extensively on such matters as politics and theological issues in his commentaries on the Bible, sermons, devotional material, and hymns. He also translated the Bible into German. Luther died in 1546, but he left a tremendous mark on history.

His influence truly reaches beyond the sixteenth century. His clear teaching on the authority of the Bible and salvation by faith alone have relevance for Christians today and always.

What started out as a peaceful challenge to the selling of indulgences initiated one of the greatest religious movements in history. Luther's "Ninety-five Theses" (posted October 31, 1517 in Wittenberg) indirectly gave rise to Protestantism. The dominance of the Catholic church was for the first time challenged with such force that she couldn't stop it.

In the "Ninety-five Theses" Luther challenged the selling of indulgences by the Catholic church. Luther merely sought a peaceful means to communicate with Catholic authorities, but a great schism resulted, leading to Luther's excommunication and the beginning of the Reformation.

In the Theses Luther points out that, according to canon law, the pope cannot remit penalties upon souls in purgatory. Luther attacked the greed and avarice found in the church, as well as the false teaching that men could buy their way into heaven. Luther ended the Theses by stating that Christ was the only source of salvation from hell, and that all men should cast their hope upon Him. It is no wonder that these and other charges were not taken well by the Catholic authorities.

CHAPTER ONE

Ninety-five Theses

Out of love and zeal for truth and the desire to bring it to light, the following theses will be publicly discussed at Wittenberg under the chairmanship of the Reverend Father Martin Luther, Master of Arts and Sacred Theology and regularly appointed Lecturer on these subjects at that place. He requests that those who cannot be present to debate orally with us will do so by letter.[1]

In the Name of Our Lord Jesus Christ. Amen.

1. When our Lord and Master Jesus Christ said, "Repent" (Matt. 4:17), he willed the entire life of believers to be one of repentance.

2. This word cannot be understood as referring to the sacrament of penance, that is, confession and satisfaction, as administered by the clergy.

3. Yet it does not mean solely inner repentance; such inner repentance is worthless unless it produces various outward mortifications of the flesh.

4. The penalty of sin[2] remains as long as the hatred of self, that is, true inner repentance, until our entrance into the kingdom of heaven.

5. The pope neither desires nor is able to remit any penalties except those imposed by his own authority or that of the canons.[3]

6. The pope cannot remit any guilt, except by declaring and showing that it has been remitted by God; or, to be sure, by remitting guilt in cases reserved to his [the pope's] judgment. If his right to grant remission in these cases were disregarded, the guilt would certainly remain unforgiven.

7. God remits guilt to no one unless at the same time he humbles him in all things and makes him submissive to his vicar, the priest.

8. The penitential canons are imposed only on the living, and, according to the canons themselves, nothing should be imposed on the dying.

9. Therefore, the Holy Spirit through the pope is kind to us insofar as the pope in his decrees always makes exception of the article of death and of necessity.[4]

10. Those priests act ignorantly and wickedly who, in the case of the dying, reserve canonical penalties for purgatory.

11. Those tares of changing the canonical penalty to the penalty of purgatory were evidently sown while the bishops slept (Matt. 13:25).

12. In former times canonical penalties were imposed, not after, but before absolution, as tests of true contrition.

---

1. There was actually no debate, for no one responded to the invitation. The contents of the ninety-five theses were soon widely disseminated by word of mouth and by the printers, and in effect a vigorous debate took place that lasted for a number of years.

2. Catholic theology distinguishes between the "guilt" and the "penalty" of sin.

3. The canons, or decrees of the church, have the force of law. Those referred to here and in Theses 8 and 85 are the so-called penitential canons.

4. Commenting on this thesis in the *Explanations of the Ninety-five Theses*, Luther distinguishes between temporal and eternal necessity. "Necessity knows no law." "Death is the necessity of necessities."

13. The dying are freed by death from all penalties, are already dead as far as the canon laws are concerned, and have a right to be released from them.

14. Imperfect piety or love on the part of the dying person necessarily brings with it great fear; and the smaller the love, the greater the fear.

15. This fear or horror is sufficient in itself, to say nothing of other things, to constitute the penalty of purgatory, since it is very near the horror of despair.

16. Hell, purgatory, and heaven seem to differ the same as despair, fear, and assurance of salvation.

17. It seems as though for the souls in purgatory fear should necessarily decrease and love increase.

18. Furthermore, it does not seem proved, either by reason or Scripture, that souls in purgatory are outside the state of merit, that is, unable to grow in love.

19. Nor does it seem proved that souls in purgatory, at least not all of them, are certain and assured of their own salvation, even if we ourselves may be entirely certain of it.

20. Therefore, the pope, when he uses the words "plenary remission of all penalties," does not actually mean "all penalties," but only those imposed by himself.

21. Thus those indulgence preachers are in error who say that a man is absolved from every penalty and saved by papal indulgences.

22. As a matter of fact, the pope remits to souls in purgatory no penalty which, according to canon law, they should have paid in this life.

23. If remission of all penalties whatsoever could be granted to anyone at all, certainly it would be granted only to the most perfect, that is, to very few.

24. For this reason most people are necessarily deceived by that indiscriminate and high-sounding promise of release from penalty.

25. That power which the pope has in general over purgatory corresponds to the power which any bishop or curate has in a particular way in his own diocese or parish.

26. The pope does very well when he grants remission to souls in purgatory, not by the power of the keys, which he does not have,[5] but by way of intercession for them.

27. They preach only human doctrines who say that as soon as the money clinks into the money chest, the soul flies out of purgatory.

28. It is certain that when money clinks in the money chest, greed and avarice can be increased; but when the church intercedes, the result is in the hands of God alone.

29. Who knows whether all souls in purgatory wish to be redeemed, since we have exceptions in Saint Severinus and Saint Paschal,[6] as related in a legend.

30. No one is sure of the integrity of his own contrition, much less of having received plenary remission.

31. The man who actually buys indulgences is as rare as he who is really penitent; indeed, he is exceedingly rare.

32. Those who believe that they can be certain of their salvation because they have indulgence letters will be eternally damned, together with their teachers.

---

5. This is not a denial of the power of the keys, that is, the power to forgive and to retain sin, but merely an assertion that the power of the keys does not extend to purgatory.

6. The legend is to the effect that these saints, Pope Severinus (638–640) and Pope Paschal I (817–824), preferred to remain longer in purgatory that they might have greater glory in heaven.

33. Men must especially be on their guard against those who say that the pope's pardons are that inestimable gift of God by which man is reconciled to him.

34. For the graces of indulgences are concerned only with the penalties of sacramental satisfaction[7] established by man.

35. They who teach that contrition is not necessary on the part of those who intend to buy souls out of purgatory or to buy confessional privileges[8] preach unchristian doctrine.

36. Any truly repentant Christian has a right to full remission of penalty and guilt,[9] even without indulgence letters.

37. Any true Christian, whether living or dead, participates in all the blessings of Christ and the church; and this is granted him by God, even without indulgence letters.

38. Nevertheless, papal remission and blessing are by no means to be disregarded, for they are, as I have said [Thesis 6], the proclamation of the divine remission.

39. It is very difficult, even for the most learned theologians, at one and the same time to commend to the people the bounty of indulgences and the need of true contrition.

40. A Christian who is truly contrite seeks and loves to pay penalties for his sins; the bounty of indulgences, however, relaxes penalties and causes men to hate them—at least it furnishes occasion for hating them.

41. Papal indulgences must be preached with caution, lest people erroneously think that they are preferable to other good works of love.

42. Christians are to be taught that the pope does not intend that the buying of indulgences should in any way be compared with works of mercy.

43. Christians are to be taught that he who gives to the poor or lends to the needy does a better deed than he who buys indulgences.

44. Because love grows by works of love, man thereby becomes better. Man does not, however, become better by means of indulgences but is merely freed from penalties.

45. Christians are to be taught that he who sees a needy man and passes him by, yet gives his money for indulgences, does not buy papal indulgences but God's wrath.

46. Christians are to be taught that, unless they have more than they need, they must reserve enough for their family needs and by no means squander it on indulgences.

47. Christians are to be taught that the buying of indulgences is a matter of free choice, not commanded.

48. Christians are to be taught that the pope, in granting indulgences, needs and thus desires their devout prayer more than their money.

49. Christians are to be taught that papal indulgences are useful only if they do not put their trust in them, but very harmful if they lose their fear of God because of them.

---

7. Satisfaction is that act on the part of the penitent, in connection with the sacrament of penance, by means of which he pays the temporal penalty for his sins. If at death he is in arrears in paying his temporal penalty for venial sins, he pays this penalty in purgatory. Indulgences are concerned with this satisfaction of the sacrament of penance—they permit a partial or complete (plenary) remission of temporal punishment. According to Roman Catholic theology, the buyer of an indulgence still has to confess his sins, be absolved from them, and be truly penitent.

8. These are privileges entitling the holder of indulgence letters to choose his own confessor and relieving him, the holder, of certain satisfactions.

9. To justify the placing of absolution before satisfaction, contrary to the practice of the early church, theologians distinguished between the guilt and the penalty of sins.

50. Christians are to be taught that if the pope knew the exactions of the indulgence preachers, he would rather that the basilica of Saint Peter were burned to ashes than built up with the skin, flesh, and bones of his sheep.

51. Christians are to be taught that the pope would and should wish to give of his own money, even though he had to sell the basilica of Saint Peter, to many of those from whom certain hawkers of indulgences cajole money.

52. It is vain to trust in salvation by indulgence letters, even though the indulgence commissary, or even the pope, were to offer his soul as security.

53. They are enemies of Christ and the pope who forbid altogether the preaching of the Word of God in some churches in order that indulgences may be preached in others.

54. Injury is done the Word of God when, in the same sermon, an equal or larger amount of time is devoted to indulgences than to the Word.

55. It is certainly the pope's sentiment that if indulgences, which are a very insignificant thing, are celebrated with one bell, one procession, and one ceremony, then the gospel, which is the very greatest thing, should be preached with a hundred bells, a hundred processions, a hundred ceremonies.

56. The treasures of the church,[10] out of which the pope distributes indulgences, are not sufficiently discussed or known among the people of Christ.

57. That indulgences are not temporal treasures is certainly clear, for many indulgence sellers do not distribute them freely but only gather them.

58. Nor are they the merits of Christ and the saints, for, even without the pope, the latter always work grace for the inner man, and the cross, death, and hell for the outer man.

59. Saint Laurence said that the poor of the church were the treasures of the church, but he spoke according to the usage of the word in his own time.

60. Without want of consideration we say that the keys of the church,[11] given by the merits of Christ, are that treasure;

61. For it is clear that the pope's power is of itself sufficient for the remission of penalties and cases reserved by himself.

62. The true treasure of the church is the most holy gospel of the glory and grace of God.

63. But this treasure is naturally most odious, for it makes the first to be last (Matt. 20:16).

64. On the other hand, the treasure of indulgences is naturally most acceptable, for it makes the last to be first.

65. Therefore, the treasures of the gospel are nets with which one formerly fished for men of wealth.

66. The treasures of indulgences are nets with which one now fishes for the wealth of men.

67. The indulgences which the demagogues acclaim as the greatest graces are actually understood to be such only insofar as they promote gain.

68. They are nevertheless in truth the most insignificant graces when compared with the grace of God and the piety of the cross.

69. Bishops and curates are bound to admit the commissaries of papal indulgences with all reverence.

70. But they are much more bound to strain their eyes and ears lest these

---

10. The treasury of merits is a reserve fund of good works accumulated by Christ and the saints upon which the pope could draw when he remitted satisfaction in indulgences.

11. The office of the keys: the preaching of the gospel, the celebrating of the sacraments, the remitting of sins to the penitent, and the excommunicating of impenitent sinners.

men preach their own dreams instead of what the pope has commissioned.

71. Let him who speaks against the truth concerning papal indulgences be anathema and accursed;

72. But let him who guards against the lust and license of the indulgence preachers be blessed;

73. Just as the pope justly thunders against those who by any means whatsoever contrive harm to the sale of indulgences.

74. But much more does he intend to thunder against those who use indulgences as a pretext to contrive harm to holy love and truth.

75. To consider papal indulgences so great that they could absolve a man even if he had done the impossible and had violated the mother of God is madness.

76. We say on the contrary that papal indulgences cannot remove the very least of venial sins as far as guilt is concerned.

77. To say that even Saint Peter, if he were now pope, could not grant greater graces is blasphemy against Saint Peter and the pope.

78. We say on the contrary that even the present pope, or any pope whatsoever, has greater graces at his disposal, that is, the gospel, spiritual powers, gifts of healing, etc., as it is written in 1 Corinthians 12:28.

79. To say that the cross emblazoned with the papal coat of arms, and set up by the indulgence preachers, is equal in worth to the cross of Christ is blasphemy.

80. The bishops, curates, and theologians who permit such talk to be spread among the people will have to answer for this.

81. This unbridled preaching of indulgences makes it difficult even for learned men to rescue the reverence which is due the pope from slander or from the shrewd questions of the laity,

82. Such as, "Why does not the pope empty purgatory for the sake of holy love and the dire need of the souls that are there if he redeems an infinite number of souls for the sake of miserable money with which to build a church? The former reasons would be most just; the latter is most trivial."

83. Again, "Why are funeral and anniversary masses for the dead continued and why does he not return or permit the withdrawal of the endowments founded for them, since it is wrong to pray for the redeemed?"

84. Again, "What is this new piety of God and the pope that for a consideration of money they permit a man who is impious and their enemy to buy out of purgatory the pious soul of a friend of God and do not rather, because of the need of that pious and beloved soul, free it for pure love's sake?"

85. Again, "Why are the penitential canons, long since abrogated and dead in actual fact and through disuse, now satisfied by the granting of indulgences as though they were still alive and in force?"

86. Again, "Why does not the pope, whose wealth is today greater than the wealth of the richest Crassus,[12] build this one basilica of Saint Peter with his own money rather than with the money of poor believers?"

87. Again, "What does the pope remit or grant to those who by perfect contrition already have a right to full remission and blessings?"[13]

88. Again, "What greater blessing

---

12. Marcus Licinius Crassus (115–53 B.C.), also called Dives ("the Rich"), was noted for his wealth and luxury by the classical Romans. Crassus means "the Fat."
13. See Theses 36 and 37.

could come to the church than if the pope were to bestow these remissions and blessings on every believer a hundred times a day, as he now does but once?"[14]

89. "Since the pope seeks the salvation of souls rather than money by his indulgences, why does he suspend the indulgences and pardons previously granted when they have equal efficacy?"[15]

90. To repress these very sharp arguments of the laity by force alone, and not to resolve them by giving reasons, is to expose the church and the pope to the ridicule of their enemies and to make Christians unhappy.

91. If, therefore, indulgences were preached according to the spirit and intention of the pope, all these doubts would be readily resolved. Indeed, they would not exist.

92. Away then with all those prophets who say to the people of Christ, "Peace, peace," and there is no peace! (Jer. 6:14).

93. Blessed be all those prophets who say to the people of Christ, "Cross, cross," and there is no cross!

94. Christians should be exhorted to be diligent in following Christ, their head, through penalties, death, and hell;

95. And thus be confident of entering into heaven through many tribulations rather than through the false security of peace (Acts 14:22).

---

14. The indulgence letter entitled its possessor to receive absolution once during his lifetime and once at the approach of death.

15. During the time when the jubilee indulgences were preached, other indulgences were suspended.

With the possible exception of John 3:16, no other passage in the Bible is better known than Psalm 23. This popular passage has brought hope even to the unregenerate.

Luther cited this passage as a source of comfort to Christians in the midst of struggles. Because Christ is the Shepherd who cares for His flock, He seeks to provide what is best for His sheep. A child of God can rely on the fresh provisions the Shepherd supplies. Protection from would-be destroyers provides peace for the soul. Even the discipline of the rod is indicative of the Shepherd's great love and care. Without these benefits, the sheep would be hopelessly lost.

CHAPTER TWO

Psalm 23

The Lord is my Shepherd, I shall not want.

First of all the prophet, and every believing heart, calls God his Shepherd. Scripture gives God many friendly names, but especially dear and charming is the one that the prophet gives God here in calling Him a Shepherd and saying, "The Lord is my Shepherd." It is most comforting when Scripture calls God our refuge, our strength, our rock, our fortress, shield, hope, our comfort, Savior, King. For by His actions and without ceasing, He truly demonstrates in His people that He is exactly as Scripture portrays Him. It is exceedingly comforting to know, however, that here and in other places in Scripture He is frequently called a Shepherd. For in this single little word "shepherd" there are gathered together in one almost all the good and comforting things that we praise in God.

The prophet therefore uses these words with a happy, secure heart—a heart that is filled with faith and overflows with great joy and comfort. He does not say, "The Lord is my strength, fortress," which would also be very comforting, but "my Shepherd"; as though he would say, "If the Lord is my Shepherd and I am His sheep, then I am very well supplied both in body and soul. He will feed me well, protect and preserve me from misfortune, care for me, help me out of all troubles, comfort me, and strengthen me. In short, He will do for me what a good shepherd can be expected to do." All of these blessings, and more, are comprehended in the single little word "shepherd"; and so he himself soon interprets it when he says, "I shall not want." Some of the other names which Scripture gives God sound almost too splendid and majestic and at once arouse awe and fear when we hear them mentioned; for example, when Scripture calls God our Lord, King, Creator. The little word "shepherd," however, is not of that kind but has a very friendly sound. When the devout read or hear it, it immediately grants them a confidence, a comfort, and a sense of security that the word "father" and others grant when they are attributed to God.

Therefore this metaphor is one of the most beautiful and comforting and yet most common of all in Scripture, when it compares His Divine Majesty to a pious, faithful, or as Christ says, "good shepherd" (John 10:14), and compares us poor, weak, miserable sinners to sheep. One can, however, understand this comforting and beautiful picture best when one goes to nature, from which the prophets have taken this picture and similar ones, and carefully learns from it the traits and characteristics of a natural sheep and the office, the work, and the care of a pious shepherd. Whoever does this carefully will not only readily understand this comparison and others in Scripture concerning the shepherd and the sheep, but will also find the comparisons exceedingly sweet and comforting.

A sheep must live entirely by its shepherd's help, protection, and care. As soon as it loses him, it is surrounded by all kinds of dangers and must perish, for it is quite unable to help itself. The reason? It is a poor, weak, simple little beast that can neither feed nor rule itself, nor find the right way, nor protect itself against any kind of danger or misfortune. Moreover, it is by nature timid, shy, and likely to go astray. When it does go a bit astray and leaves its shepherd, it is unable to find its way back to him; indeed, it merely runs farther away from him. Though it may find other shepherds and sheep, that does not help it, for it does not know the voices of strange shepherds. Therefore it flees them and strays about until the wolf seizes it or it perishes some other way.

Still, however weak and small an animal a sheep may be, it nevertheless has this trait about it: it is very careful to stay near its shepherd, take comfort in his help and protection, and follow him however and wherever he may lead it. And if it can only so much as be near him, it worries about nothing, fears no one, and is secure and happy; for it lacks absolutely nothing. It also has this virtue—and this is to be marked well, because Christ praises it especially in His sheep (John 10:4)—that it very carefully and surely hears and knows its shepherd's voice, is guided by it, does not let itself be turned away from it, but follows it without swerving. On the other hand, it pays no attention at all to the voices of strange shepherds. Though they may tempt and lure it in the most friendly manner, it does not heed them, much less does it follow them.

It is the function of a faithful shepherd not only to supply his sheep with good pasture and other related things, but also to keep them from suffering harm. Moreover, he takes good care not to lose any of them. But if one of them should go astray, he goes after it, seeks it, and returns it (Luke 15:4). He looks after the young, the weak, and the sick very carefully, waits on them, lifts them up and carries them in his arms (Is. 40:11) until they are grown and are strong and well.

Just so it is in spiritual shepherding, that is, in Christendom. As little as a natural sheep can feed, direct, guide itself, or guard and protect itself against danger and misfortune—for it is a weak and quite defenseless little animal—just so little can we poor, weak, miserable people feed and guide ourselves spiritually, walk and remain on the right path, or by our own power protect ourselves against all evil and gain help and comfort for ourselves in anxiety and distress.

How shall a man be able to govern himself in a God-pleasing manner when he knows nothing of God, is born and conceived in sin (Ps. 51:5), as we all are, and is by nature a child of wrath (Eph. 2:3) and an enemy of God? How shall we find the right path and stay on it when, as Isaiah says (Is. 63:6), we cannot do otherwise than go astray? How is it possible for us to defend ourselves against the devil, who is a prince and ruler of this world and whose captives we all are, when with all our strength and power we cannot keep even a little leaf from hurting us or even command a weak fly? Why should we poor, miserable people desire to boast loudly of great comfort, help, and counsel against the judgments of God, the wrath of God, and eternal death, when every day and every hour we experience in ourselves and in others that even in trivial, bodily needs we can neither counsel and help ourselves nor seek comfort?

Let us therefore conclude freely [that] as little as a natural sheep can help itself in even the slightest degree but must simply depend on its shepherd for all benefits, just so little—and much less—can a man govern himself and find comfort, help, and counsel in himself in the things that pertain to his salvation. He must depend on God, his Shepherd, for all of that. And God is a thousand times more willing to do everything that is to be done for His sheep than is any faithful human shepherd.

This Shepherd, however, of whom the prophet foretold so long before, is Christ, our dear Lord, who is a Shepherd much different from Moses. Moses is harsh and unfriendly toward his sheep. He drives them away into the desert, where they will find neither pasture nor water but only want (Ex. 3:1). Christ, however, is the good, friendly Shepherd, who goes after a famished and lost sheep in the wilderness, seeks it there, and, when He has found it, lays it on His shoulder rejoicing (Luke 15:4). He even "gives His life for His sheep" (John 10:12). He is a friendly Shepherd. Who would not be happy to be His sheep?

The voice of this Shepherd, however, with which He speaks to His sheep and calls them, is the holy Gospel. It teaches us how we may win grace, forgiveness of sins, and eternal salvation: not by the law of Moses, which makes us even more shy, unstable, and discouraged, though even in times past we were excessively timid, shy, and frightened; but by Christ, who is "the Shepherd and Bishop of our souls" (1 Pet. 2:25). For Christ has sought us miserable, lost sheep and has brought us back from the wilderness. That is, He has redeemed us from the law, sin, death, the power of the devil, and eternal damnation. By giving His life for us He has obtained for us grace, forgiveness of sin, comfort, help, strength, and eternal life against the devil and all misfortune. To the sheep of Christ this is a dear, sweet voice. They are sincerely glad to hear it, for they know it well and let themselves be guided by it. But a strange voice they

neither know nor hear, because it sounds unfamiliar; they avoid it and flee from it (John 10:5).

The pasture with which Christ feeds His sheep is also the dear gospel, by which our souls are fed and strengthened, preserved from error, comforted in all temptations and sorrows, protected against the devil's wile and power, and finally saved from all need. But His sheep are not all equally strong; in part they are still lost, scattered hither and yon, wounded, sick, young, and weak. He does not reject them for that reason but actually gives more attention to them and also cares for them more diligently than He does for the others who have no faults. As the prophet Ezekiel says in his thirty-fourth chapter (Ezek. 34:16), He seeks the lost, brings back the strayed, binds up the crippled, strengthens the sick. And the young lambs that have just been born, says Isaiah (40:11), He will gather in His arms and carry them so that they may not grow tired, and will gently lead those that are with young. All of this, Christ, our dear Shepherd, effects through the office of preaching and the holy sacraments, as is taught elsewhere frequently and with many words. It would take too long and require too many words to emphasize all these things adequately at this place. Besides, the prophet will indicate them later in the psalm.

From these words we can also see clearly how shamefully we have been led astray under the papacy. It did not depict Christ in so friendly a fashion as did the dear prophets, apostles, and Christ Himself, but portrayed Him so horribly that we were more afraid of Him than of Moses and thought that the teaching of Moses was much easier and more friendly than the teaching of Christ. Therefore, we knew Christ only as an angry judge, whose anger we had to reconcile with our good works and holy life and whose grace we had to obtain through the merit and intercession of the dear saints. That is a shameful lie that not only deceives poor consciences miserably but also profanes God's grace to the extreme, denies Christ's death, resurrection, ascension into heaven, together with all His inexpressible blessings, blasphemes and damns His holy gospel, destroys faith, and sets up in its place nothing but horror, lies, and error.

If that is not darkness, then I do not know what darkness is. Up to now no one was able to notice it, but everyone considered it the pure truth. To the present day our papists wish to have it preserved as right and hence shed much innocent blood. Dear friend, if we can feed and rule ourselves, protect ourselves against error, gain grace and forgiveness of sins through our own merit, resist the devil and all misfortune, conquer sin and death—then all Scripture must be a lie when it testifies of us that we are lost, scattered, wounded, weak, and defenseless sheep. Then we do not need a Christ either as a Shepherd who would seek, gather, and direct us, bind up our wounds, watch over us, and strengthen us against the devil. Then He has also given His life for us in vain. For as long as we can do and gain all these things through our own powers and piety, we do not need the help of Christ at all.

But here at once you hear the opposite, namely, that you lost sheep cannot find your way to the Shepherd yourself but can only roam around in the wilderness. If Christ, your Shepherd, did not seek you and bring you back, you would simply have to fall prey to the wolf. But now He comes, seeks, and finds you. He takes you into His flock, that is, into Christendom, through the Word and the sacrament. He gives His life for you, keeps you always on the right path, so that you may not fall into error. You hear

nothing at all about your powers, good works, and merits—unless you would say that it is strength, good works, merit when you run around in the wilderness and are defenseless and lost. No, Christ alone is active here, merits things, and manifests His power. He seeks, carries, and directs you. He earns life for you through His death. He alone is strong and keeps you from perishing, from being snatched out of His hand (John 10:28). And for all of this you can do nothing at all but only lend your ears, hear, and with thanksgiving receive the inexpressible treasure, and learn to know well the voice of your Shepherd, follow Him, and avoid the voice of the stranger.

If you wish, therefore, to be richly supplied in both body and soul, then, above all, give careful attention to the voice of this Shepherd; listen to His words, let Him feed, direct, lead, protect, and comfort you. That is, hold fast to His Word, hear and learn it gladly, for then you will be well supplied in both body and soul.

From what has been said until now, I hope one can easily understand these words, "The Lord is my Shepherd," and indeed the whole psalm. The words "The Lord is my Shepherd" are brief but also very impressive and apt. The world glories and trusts in honor, power, riches, and the favor of men. Our psalm, however, glories in none of these, for they are all uncertain and perishable. It says briefly, "The Lord is my Shepherd." Thus speaks a sure, certain faith that turns its back on everything temporal and transitory, however noble and precious it may be, and turns its face and heart directly to the Lord, who alone is Lord and is and does everything. "He and none other, be he a king or an emperor, is my Shepherd," the psalmist says. Therefore he speaks out freely and with all boldness and says,

I shall not want

Thus the prophet speaks, in a general way, of the various kinds of bodily and spiritual blessings that we receive through the office of preaching. It is as though he would say, "If the Lord is my Shepherd, then of course I shall not want. I shall have an abundance of meat, drink, clothing, food, protection, peace, and of all the necessities that pertain to the preservation of this life. For I have a rich Shepherd who will not let me suffer want." Chiefly, however, he speaks of the spiritual possessions and gifts that God's Word provides and says, "Because the Lord has taken me into His flock and provides me with His pasture and care, that is, because He has richly given me His holy Word, He will not let me want anywhere. He will bless His Word so that it may be effective and bring forth fruit in me. He will also give me His Spirit, who will assist and comfort me in all temptations and distresses and will also make my heart safe and sure. My heart, therefore, will not doubt that I am my Lord's dear sheep and that He is my faithful Shepherd. He will treat me gently as His poor, weak sheep. He will strengthen my faith and provide me with other spiritual gifts; comfort me in all my troubles; hear me when I call upon Him; keep the wolf, that is, the devil, from being able to do me harm; and finally redeem me from all misfortune." This is what the psalmist has in mind when he says, "I shall not want."

"Yes," you may say, "but how shall I know that the Lord is my Shepherd? I have not experienced that He is as friendly toward me as the psalm says; in fact, I have experienced the opposite. David was a holy prophet and a man dear and precious to God, so it was easy for him to speak of the matter and to believe what he spoke. But I cannot emulate him, for I am a poor sinner."

Answer: I have shown above that in itself a sheep has chiefly this good attribute and fine virtue, that it knows the voice of its shepherd well and is guided more by its ears than its eyes. The same virtue Christ also praises in His sheep, when He says, "My sheep know My voice" (John 10:4), His voice, however, speaks thus, "I am the Good Shepherd . . . and lay down My life for My sheep. . . . And I give them eternal life. And they shall never perish, and no man shall snatch them out of My hand" (John 10:14, 15, 28). Give careful attention to this voice and be guided by it. If you do, then firmly believe that you are Christ's sheep and that He is your Shepherd, who knows you well and is also able to call you by your name. But when you have Him as your Shepherd, you will surely not want. Yes, you already have what you shall have—eternal life. Nor will you ever perish. Nor shall any power be so great and mighty that it could snatch you out of His hand. Of that you can be sure. For this Shepherd's voice will surely not lead you astray. What more could you want?

But if you ignore this voice and are guided by what your eyes see and your old Adam feels, then you will lose the faith and the confidence that you ought, as a sheep, to have in Him as your Shepherd. Sometimes this thought, sometimes that one comes to you, so that you cannot be content but must argue with yourself and say, "If the Lord is my Shepherd, why does He impose this upon me, that the world torments and persecutes me so cruelly through no fault of mine? I am sitting in the midst of the wolves, I am not sure of my life for a moment; but I do not see any shepherd who would protect me." Again, "Why does He permit the devil to harm me so greatly with terrors and doubts? Besides, I find myself quite unfit, weak, impatient, still laden with many sins. I feel no security but only doubt, no comfort but only fear and trembling because of God's wrath. When will He ever begin to manifest in me that He is my Shepherd?"

Such strange thoughts and many others will come to you if you fail to heed His voice and Word. But if you hold fast to them, you will be tempted neither by the devil's wile, the world's disfavor and raging, nor by your own weakness and unworthiness. You will go straight forward to speak freely, "Let the devil, the world, or my own conscience oppose me as violently as they may. I will not for that reason grieve myself to death. It must be so and it shall be so, that whoever is the Lord's sheep will surely be assailed by the wolves. Be it with me as it may, let them boil or roast me, it shall be my comfort that my Shepherd has given His life for me. Moreover, He has a sweet, kind voice with which He comforts me and says that I shall never perish, neither shall any man snatch me out of His hand; I shall have eternal life (John 10:28). And He will keep this promise, no matter what happens to me. If because of my weakness some sin or other fault by chance is still found in me, he will not reject me on that account. For He is a friendly Shepherd, who watches over the weak sheep, binds up their wounds, and heals them. And so that I may be all the more sure and not doubt, He has given me, as a token, His holy sacraments."

Just so it was with the prophet. He was not always happy, nor was he at all times able to sing, "The Lord is my Shepherd, I shall not want." At times he wanted much, almost too much. He would feel neither justice nor God's comfort and help, but only sin, God's wrath, terror, doubt, and the fear of hell, as he laments in many psalms. Nevertheless he abandons his feelings and holds God to His promise of a coming Messiah and thinks, "Be it with me as it may. This is still the comfort of my heart, that I have a gracious, merciful Lord, who is my Shepherd, whose Word and promise strengthen and comfort me. Therefore I shall not want." For this reason also he wrote this psalm and others, that we might be sure that in real temptation we can find counsel and comfort nowhere else, and that this alone is the golden art: to cling to God's Word and promise, to make judgments on the basis of this Word and not on the basis of the feelings of the heart. Then help and comfort will surely follow, and absolutely nothing will be wanting. The second verse follows.

He feeds me in a green pasture and leads me to the fresh water.

In the first verse the prophet briefly gathered together the meaning of the whole psalm, namely, that whoever has the Lord as a Shepherd will not want. He does not teach anything more in this psalm, but he does emphasize the thought further by means of fine figurative words and pictures and shows how it comes about that those who are the Lord's sheep want nothing, and says, "He feeds me." Through almost the entire psalm, as he often does elsewhere, he uses words with a meaning different from their literal one. When he mentions the shepherd, the pasture, the green meadow, the fresh water, the rod, and the staff, therefore, we may well conclude that he wants something else to be understood by these words than we human beings are in the habit of saying with them. Such a way of speaking is very common in Scripture, and therefore we should make every effort to get accustomed to it and learn to understand it.

But see how beautifully he can speak! "I am," he says, "the Lord's sheep; He feeds me in a green pasture." For a natural sheep nothing can be better than when its shepherd feeds it in pleasant green pastures and near fresh water. Where that happens to it, it feels that no one on earth is richer and more blessed than it is. For it finds there whatever it might desire: fine, lush, heavy grass, from which it will grow strong and fat; fresh water, with which it can refresh and restore itself whenever it likes; and it has its joy and pleasure there too. At this point David would also say that God had shown him no greater grace and blessing on earth than this, that he was permitted to be at a place and among people where God's Word and dwelling place and the right worship were to be found. There these treasures are found, there things prosper well, both in the spiritual and in the secular realm. It is as if he were saying, "All people and kingdoms on earth are nothing. They may be richer, more powerful, and more splendid than we Jews, and they may also boast mightily of what they have. Moreover, they may glory in their wisdom and holiness, for they, too, have gods whom they serve. But with all their glory and splendor they are a mere desert and wilderness. For they have neither shepherd nor pasture, and therefore, the sheep must go astray, famish, and perish. But though we are surrounded by many deserts, we can sit and rest here, safe and happy in paradise and in a pleasant green pasture, where there is an abundance of grass and of fresh water and where we have our Shepherd near us, who feeds us, leads us to the watering place, and protects us. Therefore, we cannot want."

That man had spiritual eyes and therefore saw plainly what is the best and noblest thing on earth. He does not glory in his royal splendor and power, for he knows well that such possessions are gifts of God. He does not run away

from them either and let them lie idle, but uses them to the glory of God and thanks God for them. Above all he glories in this, that the Lord is his Shepherd and that he is in His pasture and in His care, that is, that he has God's Word. This blessing he can never forget, but speaks about it very beautifully and with great joy, and praises it far above all possessions on earth, as he also does in many other psalms. Thus he says, "The word of Thy mouth is dearer to me than thousands of gold and silver pieces" (Ps. 119:72), and, also, "It is more precious than gold, even much fine gold; sweeter also than honey and drippings of the honeycomb" (Ps. 19:11).

We too should learn this art, namely, to let the world glory forever in great riches, honor, and power. For these are indeed loose, uncertain, perishable wares that God lets men scramble for. It is a simple thing for Him to give to a scoundrel—who in turn blasphemes and slanders Him—a kingdom, a principality, or other honors and possessions on this earth. These are His chaff and His husks, with which He fills the bellies of His sows that He is about to slaughter (Luke 15:16). To His children, however, as David says here, He gives the genuine treasure. Therefore, as the dear children and heirs of God, we ought to glory in neither our wisdom, nor strength, nor riches, but in this, that we have the "pearl of great value" (Matt. 13:46), the dear Word, through which we know God, our dear Father, and Jesus Christ, whom He has sent (John 17:3). That is our treasure and heritage, and it is sure and eternal and better than all worldly possessions. Whoever has this treasure may let others gather money, live riotously, be proud and haughty. Let him not be troubled by such things, though he be despised and poor in the eyes of the world. But let him thank God for His inexpressible gift (2 Cor. 9:15) and pray that he may abide by it.

It does not matter how rich and glorious we are here on earth; if we keep this treasure, we are exceedingly rich and sufficiently honored. Saint Paul was an unworthy, miserable man on earth, and the devil and the world assailed him most violently. To God he was a dear, worthy man. He was so poor, too, that he had to provide for himself with the work of his hands. And yet, despite such great poverty, he was richer than the emperor in Rome, though he had no other riches than the knowledge of Christ, in comparison with which, he says, "I count all things (nothing on earth is excluded) but loss and refuse" (Phil. 3:8).

May our dear God grant us grace that we, too, like David, Paul, and other saints, regard our treasure, which is the very same one they had, as something great and exalt it above all possessions on earth and thank God sincerely for having honored us with it above many other thousands. He might just as well have let us go astray as the Turks, Tartars, Jews, and other infidels, who know nothing of the treasure. He might have let us remain hardened like the papists, who blaspheme and damn our treasure. It is only because of His grace, however, that He has placed us into His green pastures and has provided us so richly with good food and fresh water. Therefore we should thank Him all the more.

The prophet, however, calls God's people and the holy Christian church a "green pasture," for it is God's pleasure ground, decorated and adorned with all kinds of spiritual gifts. The pasture, however, or the grass in it, is God's Word, with which our consciences are strengthened and restored. Into this green pasture our Lord God gathers His sheep, feeds them in it with precious grass, and restores them with fresh water. That is, He commits to the holy Christian church the office of a shepherd, entrusts and gives to it the holy gospel and the sacraments, so that by means of these it may care for and watch over His sheep and so that these sheep may be richly provided with instruction, comfort, strength, and protection against all evil. But those who preach the law of Moses or the ordinances of men do not feed the sheep in a green pasture but in the desert, where they famish, and lead them to foul, smelly water, which will cause them to decay and die.

By means of the allegory of the green pasture, however, the prophet wants to indicate the great abundance and the riches of the holy gospel and of the knowledge of Christ among the believers. For just as the grass in a green pasture stands very thick and full and grows more and more, so it is with the believers: they not only have God's Word richly, but the more they use and apply it, the more it increases and grows among them. Therefore, the psalmist expresses himself very plainly. He does not say, "He leads me once, or often, in a green pasture," but, "He leads me in them without ceasing, so that amid the grass and in the pasture I may lie, rest, and dwell securely and never suffer hunger or any other want." The word that he uses here means "lie" and "rest," as a four-footed animal lies and rests. In the same manner Solomon also speaks in the seventy-second psalm, where he prophesies that the kingdom of God and the gospel will prevail with might and go to all places, and says, "In the land, on the tops of the mountains, may the grain wave and blossom forth in the cities like the grass of the field" (Ps. 72:16). David shows that he is speaking of the gospel also in this psalm when he says later, "He restores my soul"; and "Thy rod and Thy staff, they comfort me."

This then, is the first fruit of the dear Word: that the Christians are instructed through it in such a way that they grow in faith and hope, learn to commit all their doings and ways unto God, and hope in Him for everything they need in soul and body.

He leads me to the fresh water

This is the second fruit of the dear Word. It is not only the believers' pasture and grass, with which they are satisfied and grow strong in the faith; to them it is also pleasantly cool, fresh water, through which they gain refreshment and comfort. The psalmist therefore does not stop with saying, "He makes me lie down in green pastures," but also adds, "He leads me to the fresh water." It is as though he would say, "In great heat, when the sun smites hard (Ps. 121:6) and I can have no shade, He leads me to fresh water, gives me to drink, and refreshes me." That is, in all kinds of afflictions, anxieties, and distresses—spiritual and physical—when I cannot find help and comfort anywhere, I cling to the Word of grace. There alone, and nowhere else, do I find the right comfort and refreshment, and find it richly. What he says here in figurative language he expresses elsewhere in sober, clear words and says, "If Thy Law had not been my delight, I should have perished in my affliction. I will never forget it, for with it Thou doest restore me" (Ps. 119:92).

But he still retains the metaphor of the shepherd and the sheep, which is a common thing among all the prophets. For the Jews had their best food from sheep and other animals and commonly were shepherds, even as David himself and also the dear patriarchs were shep-

herds. Therefore this metaphor is often employed in Scripture. David, however, speaks of this matter in keeping with the nature of the country; the Promised Land is a hot, dry, sandy, stony land that has many deserts and little water. Therefore the book of Genesis reports more than once how the shepherds of the heathen quarreled with the shepherds of the patriarchs about water.[1] They accordingly considered it a special treasure in that land when they could have water for their cattle. In our countries this is unknown, for there is enough water everywhere. David has looked at his land and cites it as a special blessing that he is under the protection of the Lord, who not only feeds him in a green pasture but during the heat also leads him to the fresh water.

In brief, he wishes to say this: as little as one can come to the knowledge of God and the truth and to the right faith without the Word of God, just so little can one find comfort and peace of conscience without it. The world has its comfort and joy, too, but these last only a moment; when anxiety and distress and especially the last hour comes, then it is as Solomon says, "After laughter the heart is sad; and after joy comes grief" (Prov. 14:13). But those who drink of this fresh and living water may indeed suffer affliction and distress in the world, but they will never lack genuine comfort. Especially when the moment of crisis comes, the page turns for them to the place where it says, "After brief weeping comes eternal laughter; after a small sorrow comes glorious joy" (2 Cor. 4:17). For they shall not weep and be sorrowful both here and there, but it will be as Christ says, "Blessed are you that weep here, for you shall laugh" (Luke 6:21).

---

1. Cf. Gen. 21:25, 26:19–22.

He restores my soul, He leads me in the right path for His name's sake.

Here the prophet himself explains what kind of pasture and fresh water he has been discussing, namely, that kind by which the soul is strengthened and restored. That, however, can be nothing else than God's Word. But because our Lord God has a twofold Word, the law and the gospel, the prophet makes it sufficiently clear that he is speaking here not of the law but of the gospel when he says, "He restores my soul." The law cannot restore the soul, for it is a Word that makes demands on us and commands us that we shall love God with all our hearts and our neighbors as ourselves (Matt. 22:37, 39). It damns him that does otherwise and pronounces this sentence upon him, "Cursed be everyone who does not do all the things written in the Book of the Law" (Gal. 3:10; Deut. 27:26). Now, it is certain that nobody on earth does that; therefore the law comes in due time with its sentence and only grieves and frightens the souls. Where no help is provided, it presses them so that they must despair and be lost forever. Saint Paul therefore says, "By the law comes only knowledge of sin" (Rom. 3:20), and, "The law brings only wrath" (Rom. 4:15).

The gospel, however, is a blessed Word. It demands nothing of us, but announces everything that is good, namely, that God has given us poor sinners His only Son and that He is to be our Shepherd. He will seek us famished and scattered sheep and give His life for us, to redeem us from sin, from eternal death, and from the power of the devil. That is the green grass and the fresh water with which the Lord restores our souls. Thus we are rid of our bad consciences and sad thoughts. More of that in the fourth verse.

He leads me in the right path

"The Lord," he says, "does not stop with feeding me in a green pasture and leading me to the fresh water and thus restoring my soul. He also leads me in the right paths so that I may not go astray, get into the wilderness, and thus perish. That is, He keeps me in pure doctrine, that I may not be misled by false spirits nor fall away from it because of temptation or offense; that I may know how I am to walk and live outwardly and not take offense at the holiness and the strict lives of hypocrites; and that I may also know what is the right doctrine, faith, and worship."

Another fine fruit and power of the dear Word is this: those who cling to it firmly not only receive from it strength and comfort for their souls, but are also protected against false doctrine and false holiness. Many, it is true, receive this treasure but without being able to keep it. For when a man becomes smug and presumptuous and thinks he is safe, he will soon be lost; before he can look about, he has been led astray. The devil can also assume holiness and disguise himself, as Saint Paul says, as "an angel of light" (2 Cor. 11:14). His servants, then, pretend to be preachers of righteousness and enter the flock of Christ in sheep's clothing but inwardly are ravenous wolves (Matt. 7:15). Therefore we should watch and pray, as the prophet does in the last verse, that our Shepherd would keep us true to the treasure He has given us. Those who fail in this surely lose the treasure, and, as Christ says, their last state becomes worse than the first (Luke 11:26). For later they become the most venomous foes of Christianity and do much more harm with their false doctrine than the tyrants do with the sword. Saint Paul indeed learned this from the false prophets who led his Corinthians and

Galatians astray for a time and later carried off all of Asia (2 Tim. 1:15). In our days we see this, too, in the Anabaptists and other schismatic spirits.

For His name's sake

The name of God is the preaching of God, by which He is glorified and made known as the gracious, merciful, patient, truthful, and faithful one. Although we are the children of wrath (Eph. 2:3) and are guilty of eternal death, He forgives us all our sins and receives us as His children and heirs. That is His name, and that name He causes to be proclaimed through the Word. He wants to be known, glorified, and honored by these means; and, according to the first commandment, He will also reveal Himself to us exactly as He has men preach of Him (Ex. 20:5, 6). Thus, without ceasing, He strengthens and restores our souls spiritually and keeps us from falling into error, and also feeds us bodily and wards off all misfortune. But only those who cling to His Word, and who believe and confess boldly that all the gifts and possessions of body and soul that they own, they have received from God purely out of grace and kindness, that is, solely for His name's sake and not because of their own deeds and merits—only they give Him the honor of being exactly as we have just been told. They thank Him for His blessings and also proclaim these blessings to others. No haughty saints, such as heretics, schismatic spirits, or enemies and blasphemers of the Word of God, can give Him this honor, for they glorify not His name but their own.

Even though I walk through the valley of the shadow, I fear no evil; for Thou art with me; Thy rod and Thy staff, they comfort me.

Until now the prophet has shown that those who have and love God's Word do not want, for the Lord is their Shepherd. This Shepherd not only feeds them in a green pasture and leads them to the fresh water so that they may become quite fat and strong and restored spiritually and physically; He also keeps them from becoming weary of the good pasture and the fresh water, and from leaving the green pasture and straying from the right path into the desert. That is the first part of this psalm. Now he goes on to teach that those who are this Lord's sheep are surrounded by much danger and misfortune. But the Lord, he says, not only protects them but also saves them from all temptations and distresses, for He is with them. He also shows beautifully in what way He is with them.

Here you can see that as soon as the Word is preached and as soon as there are people that accept and confess it, the devil quickly appears with all his angels and arouses the world with all its might against this Word, to stifle it and completely destroy those that have and confess it. Whatever our Lord God says or does must be swept clean and pass through the fire. It is very important for Christians to know this, else they may become perplexed and think, "How can this be harmonized? The prophet has said above, 'The Lord is my Shepherd, I shall not want,' and here he says the very opposite: that he must walk through the valley of the shadow. And in the following verse he admits that he has enemies. With these words he surely lets us know well enough that he does want—too much, yes, practically everything. For he who has enemies and wanders through the valley of the shadow can see no light, that is, he has neither comfort nor hope but is forsaken by everybody. Everything is black and dark before his eyes, even the beautiful, bright sun. How, then, can it be true that he does not want?"

Here you must not be guided by your eyes or follow your reason, as the world does. The world cannot see this rich, splendid comfort of the Christians, that they want nothing. Yes, the world considers it quite certain that the opposite is true, namely, that on earth there are no poorer, more miserable, and more unhappy people than these same Christians. And [the world] helps very faithfully and boldly in having them most cruelly persecuted, exiled, reviled, and killed. And when the world does this, it thinks that thereby it has offered service to God (John 16:2). Outwardly, then, it appears as if the Christians were the scattered sheep, forsaken by God and surrendered to the very jaws of the wolves, and that they wanted absolutely everything.

But those who serve the great god mammon or belly appear to the world to be the dear sheep which do not want and which, as the psalm says, God richly supports, comforts, and guards against all danger and misfortune. For they have what their hearts desire: honor, possessions, joy, pleasure, and everyone's favor. Nor do they have to fear that because of their faith they will be persecuted and killed. As long as they do not believe in Christ or confess Him, the only true Shepherd, they believe in the devil and his mother.[2] Otherwise, too, they do as they will, for example, in covetousness. Not only do they prosper therein, but they also appear to be living saints, who are holding fast to the old faith and are not misled by any such heresy as this, that, as David teaches here, the Lord alone is a Shepherd. It is so horrible, great, and deadly a sin to believe in this shepherd[3] and to confess him that there has never been anything

on earth like it. Even his Holiness the Pope, who otherwise grants dispensation from all sins and even forgives them, is unable to grant forgiveness in the case of this sin only.

Therefore, I say, do not follow the world in this matter, nor your reason which, because it judges according to outward appearances, becomes a fool and considers the prophet a liar for saying, "I shall not want." You, however, cling to God's Word and promise, as was also said before. Listen to your Shepherd, however, and whatever He speaks to you. Judge according to His voice and not according to what your eyes see and your heart feels. Then you have gained the victory. That is how the prophet acts in his own case. He confesses that he is walking through the valley of the shadow, that is, that he is surrounded by distresses, sadness, anxiety, and trouble, as can also be seen from his life's history and from other psalms. His need of comfort is indicated sufficiently by the fact that he is grieved and has enemies. Nevertheless, he says, "Though my temptations were even more numerous and great, and though my lot were even worse, and though I were already in the jaws of death, yet I will fear no evil. Not that I could assist myself through my own care, efforts, work, or help. Nor do I depend on my own wisdom, piety, royal power, or riches. Here all human help, counsel, comfort, and power are far too weak. This, however, avails for me, that the Lord is with me."

It is as if he would say, "As for me, I am indeed weak, sad, anxious, and surrounded by all kinds of danger and misfortune. Because of my sin, my heart and my conscience are not satisfied either. I experience such horrible terrors

---

2. This is perhaps a variation on Luther's more customary metaphor of the world as the devil's bride.

3. Either Luther is speaking ironically here, or by the term "shepherd" he means the devil.

of death and hell that I almost despair. Yet though the whole world and also the gates of hell should oppose me, that will not dismay me (Matt. 16:18). Yes, I will not be afraid of all the evil and sorrow that they may be able to lay on me, for the Lord is with me. The Lord is my counselor, comforter, protector, and helper—the Lord, I say, who has created heaven and earth and everything that is in it out of a more trifling thing than a speck of dust, that is, out of nothing. To Him all creation is subject: angels, devils, men, sin, death. In brief, He has everything in His power. And therefore I fear no evil."

Asaph also speaks thus in the seventy-third psalm. There he comforts the Christians because of the great offense that the wicked prosper so greatly on earth, while the dear saints of God are constantly tormented, and says, "If only I have Thee, Lord, I will ask nothing of heaven and earth. Even though my body and soul should fail, Thou, O God, art the strength of my heart and my portion forever" (Ps. 73:23). But how the Lord is with him, he now goes on to show, and says,

Thy rod and Thy staff, they comfort me

"The Lord," he says, "is with me, but not bodily so that I might see or hear Him. This presence of the Lord of which I am speaking is not to be grasped by the five senses. But faith sees it and believes surely that the Lord is nearer to us than we are to ourselves." How? Through His Word. He says therefore, "Thy rod and Thy staff, they comfort me." It is as though he would say, "In all of my anxieties and troubles I find nothing on earth that might help to satisfy me. But then God's Word is my rod and my staff. To that Word I will cling, and by it I raise myself up again. I will also learn for sure that the Lord is with me and

that He not only strengthens and comforts me with this same Word in all distresses and temptations, but that He also redeems me from all my enemies, contrary to the will of the devil and the world."

With the words, "Thy rod and Thy staff, they comfort me," he returns to the metaphor of the shepherd and the sheep. He would speak thus, "Even as a bodily shepherd guides his sheep with his rod or staff and leads them to fresh water where they find food and drink and protects them with his staff against all danger, so the Lord, the real Shepherd, leads and guides me also with His staff, that is, with His Word, so that I may walk before Him with a good faith and a happy conscience, remain in the right path, and be able to protect myself against false doctrine and fictitious holiness. He also protects me against all danger and evil of spirit and of body and saves me from all my enemies with His staff. That is, with the same Word He strengthens and comforts me so richly that no evil can be so great, be it of spirit or body, that I cannot endure and overcome it."

You see, then, that the prophet is not speaking here of any human help, protection, and comfort. He does not draw a sword. Everything is done here in a hidden and mysterious manner through the Word, so that no one becomes aware of any protection and comfort but the believers alone. Here David lays down a common rule for all Christians, and it is to be well noted: that there is no other way or counsel on earth to get rid of all kinds of temptation than this, that a man cast all his cares upon God, take Him at His Word of grace, hold fast to it, and not let it be taken from him in any way. Whoever does that can be satisfied, whether he prospers or fails, whether he lives or dies. And in the end he can also stand and must succeed against all devils, the world, and evil. That is the way, I feel, to magnify the dear Word and to credit it with much greater power than the power of all angels and men. And that is the way in which also Saint Paul magnifies it, "The gospel," he says, "is a power of God that saves all who believe in it" (Rom. 1:16).

Here the prophet also touches upon the office of preaching. For through the oral preaching of the Word, which enters the ears and touches the heart by faith, and through the holy sacraments our Lord God accomplished all these things in His Christendom, namely, that men are brought to faith, are strengthened in faith, are kept in pure doctrine, and in the end are enabled to withstand all the assaults of the devil and the world. Without these means, Word and sacrament, we obtain none of these things. For since the beginning of the world God has dealt with all the saints through His Word and, in addition, has given them external signs of grace. This I say so that no one may venture to deal with God without these means or build for himself a special way to heaven, lest he fall and break his neck, as the pope has done to his followers and still does, and as today the Anabaptists and other schismatic spirits do.

But with the words "Thy rod and Thy staff, they comfort me," the prophet wishes to say something special. It is as though he would say, "Moses is also a shepherd and also has a rod and a staff. But he does nothing with them but drive and plague and burden his sheep with an unbearable burden (Acts 15:10; Is. 9:3.) Therefore, he is a terrible, horrible shepherd, whom the sheep only fear and from whom they flee. But Thou, O Lord, do not drive and frighten Thy sheep with Thy rod and Thy staff, nor burden them, but only comfort them."

Therefore, he is speaking here about the office of preaching in the New Testa-ment, which proclaims to the world that "Christ came into the world to save sinners" (1 Tim. 1:15) and that He has gained this salvation for sinners by giving His life for them. Whoever believes this should not perish but have eternal life (John 3:16). That is the rod and the staff by which the souls obtain rest, comfort, and joy. In spiritual shepherding, that is, in the kingdom of Christ, one should, therefore, preach to the sheep of Christ—the goats one must govern with Moses and the emperor's rod and staff—not the law of God, much less the ordinances of men, but the gospel, which the prophet with metaphorical words calls a rod of comfort and a staff of comfort. For through the Gospel, Christ's sheep obtain strength in their faith, rest in their hearts, and comfort in all kinds of anxieties and perils of death.

Those who preach this way conduct the office of a spiritual shepherd properly, feed the sheep of Christ in a green pasture, lead them to the fresh water, restore their souls, keep them from being led astray, and comfort them with Christ's rod and staff. Where men hear such preachers, they should believe for certain that they are hearing Christ Himself. They should also acknowledge such preachers as right shepherds, that is, as servants of Christ and stewards of God (1 Cor. 4:1), and pay no attention at all to the fact that the world proclaims and damns them as heretics and seducers. Those who preach something else than the gospel, who guide men to works, merit, and self-appointed holiness, may indeed praise themselves ten times over as the followers of the apostles, adorn themselves with the name and title of the Christian Church, and even raise the dead. Actually they are horrible wolves and murderers that do not spare the flock of Christ, but scatter, torture, and slaughter it not only spiritually but also bodily, as is now clearly and plainly to be seen.

Earlier the prophet called God's Word, or the Gospel, grass, water, the right path, a rod, a staff. In the fifth verse he calls it a table that is prepared for us, an oil, and a cup that is filled to overflowing. He takes these metaphors of the table, oil, and cup from the Jews' Old Testament worship of God, and says practically the same thing he had said before—namely, that those who have God's Word are richly supplied with all things of body and soul—except that here he indicates these blessings with other figures and allegories. First he presents the picture of the table on which the showbread had to be set at all times (Ex. 25:30; 40:23). And he also shows what that means, and says:

Thou preparest a table before me against my enemies; Thou anointest my head with oil, Thou pourest my cup full.

Here the prophet confesses frankly that he has enemies. He says, however, that he defends himself against them and drives them back in this way, that the Lord has prepared a table before him against these same enemies of his. Is not that a wonderful protector? I should think He would prepare before him a mighty wall, a strong rampart, a deep moat, an armor, and other arms and weapons that have to do with battle, through which he might be safe from his enemies or put them to flight. But He prepares a table before him, at which he is to eat and to drink and in this way to defeat his enemies. I, too, would like to wage war if, without any danger, care, trouble, and work, one could conquer one's enemies by doing nothing more than sitting at a table and eating, drinking, and making merry.

By means of these words, "Thou pre-

parest a table before me in the presence of my enemies," the prophet wishes to indicate the great, splendid, and wonderful power of the dear Word. It is as though he would say, "Thou, O Lord, dost offer me so many good things and feed me so splendidly and richly at the table that Thou hast prepared for me. That is, Thou dost overwhelm me so greatly with the boundless knowledge of Thy dear Word, that through this Word I not only have rich comfort inwardly, in my heart, despite my guilty conscience, despite sin, fear, the terror of death, and God's wrath and judgment; through it I also become outwardly so courageous and invincible a hero that all my enemies cannot prevail against me. The more raging and raving and insane they are toward me, the less I worry about them; yes, instead, I am secure, happy, and cheerful. And that is true only because I have Thy Word. It gives me such strength and comfort in the presence of all my enemies, so that even when they rage and rave most violently, I feel more at ease than when I am sitting at a table and have all that my heart desires: food, drink, joy, pleasures, music, and the like."

Here you shall hear how highly blessed David exalts and praises the dear Word, namely, by telling us that by means of it the believers gain the victory over the devil, the world, the flesh, sin, conscience, and death. When one has the Word and in faith clings to it firmly, these enemies, who otherwise are invincible, must all yield and let themselves be taken captive. It is, however, a wonderful victory and power, also a very proud and haughty boast on the part of the believers, that they may compel and conquer all of these horrible and, as it were, almighty enemies, not by raging, biting, resisting, striking back, avenging, seeking counsel and help here and there, but by eating, drinking, rejoicing, sitting, being happy, and resting. All of this, as we have said, is accomplished through the Word. For in Scripture "eating and drinking" means believing and clinging firmly to the Word, and from this proceed peace, joy, comfort, strength, and the like.

Reason cannot accommodate itself to this wonderful victory of the believers. Here everything happens in a contradictory way. The world always persecutes and murders the Christians as the most harmful people on earth. When reason sees that, it must think that the Christians are succumbing and their enemies are supreme and victorious. Thus the Jews dealt with Christ, the apostles, and the believers, and executed them. When they had murdered, or at least exiled them, they cried, "On to victory! Those who have done us harm no longer can confound us. Now we shall act according to our own pleasure." But when they felt most secure, our Lord sent the Romans against them, who treated them so horribly that it frightens one to hear it. Several hundred and more years later He also gave the Romans their reward, who had killed many thousands of martyrs throughout the Roman Empire. He had the city of Rome conquered by the Goths and Wends four times within a few years, and finally had it burned down and leveled, and let the empire perish. Who was victorious now? The Jews and the Romans, who had shed the blood of the dear saints like water? Or the poor Christians, who had been killed like sheep led to the slaughter, and had no other defense and weapons than the dear Word?

David is not speaking here only about his own person, but by means of these words he shows how the holy Christian church fares. He gives it the proper coloration and paints a fine picture of it.

Before God it is a pleasant green meadow, on which there is grass and water in abundance. That is, it is God's paradise and pleasure garden, adorned with all His gifts, and it has His inexpressible treasure: the holy sacraments and the dear Word, with which [He] instructs, governs, restores, and comforts His flock. To the world, however, it has a different appearance. It is a black, gloomy valley where neither joy nor pleasure is to be seen, but only distress, anxiety, and trouble. The devil assails it with all his might because of its treasure. Inwardly he tortures it with his venomous, fiery arrows (Eph. 6:16); outwardly he separates it with schisms and offenses (Rom. 16:17). And he also incites his bride, the world,[4] against it, which imposes upon it all misery and heartache through persecution, slander, blasphemy, damnation, and murder. It would not be surprising, therefore, if the dear Christian church were completely destroyed in a moment's time through the great craft and might of both the devil and the world. For it cannot defend itself against its enemies; they are much too strong, crafty, and powerful for it. So it is, as the prophet depicts it here, an innocent, simple, defenseless lamb, which neither will nor can do anyone any harm, but at all times is ready not only to do good but to receive evil in return.

How, then, does it happen that Christendom, which is so weak, can withstand the craft and the tyranny of the devil and the world? The Lord is its Shepherd; therefore, it does not want. He feeds and restores it spiritually and physically. He keeps it in the right path. He also gives it His rod and His staff as a sword. [The church] does not, however, wield this sword with its hand but with its mouth. With it, it not only comforts

---

4. A favorite metaphor of Luther's for the world.

the sad but also puts the devil and all his apostles to flight, no matter how craftily and shrewdly they may defend themselves. Moreover, the Lord has prepared a table or paschal lamb before it, in order to destroy its enemies completely when they rage greatly, gnash their teeth against it, become mad, insane, raging, and raving, and call to their aid all their craft, strength, and power. Thus the dear bride of Christ can sit down at the table of her Lord, eat of the paschal lamb, drink of the fresh water, be happy and sing, "The Lord is my Shepherd, I shall not want." These are her weapons and guns, with which she has defeated and conquered all her foes until now. With these she will also retain the victory until Judgment Day. The more the devil and the world plague and torture her, the better she fares. For her betterment and growth come in persecution, suffering, and dying. Therefore, one of the old fathers has said, "The blood of the martyrs is a seed."[5] Where one is executed, a hundred others rise again. Of this wonderful victory several psalms sing; for example, the ninth, the tenth, and others.

In this way I also have been preserved by the grace of God [for] the past eighteen years. I have let my enemies rage, threaten, slander, and damn me, take counsel against me without ceasing, invent many evil devices, and practice many a piece of knavery. I have let them worry anxiously how they might kill me and destroy my teaching, or rather God's. Moreover, I have been happy and of good cheer—at one time better than at another—have not worried greatly about their raving and raging, but have clung to the staff of comfort and found my way to the Lord's table. That is, I have committed my cares to our Lord God, into which He had led me abso-lutely without my will or counsel; and meanwhile I spoke an Our Father or a psalm. That is all of the armor with which until now I have not only held off all my enemies, but by the grace of God have also accomplished so much that, when I look behind me and consider how matters stand in the papacy, I really must be surprised that things have gone so far. I should never have dared to imagine that even one tenth of what is now evident would happen. He that has begun the good work will also bring it to completion (Phil. 1:6), even though nine more hells and worlds were gathered together in a heap. Therefore, let every Christian thoroughly learn this art: to cling to this rod and this staff and to find his way to this table when sorrow or other misfortune appears. Then he will surely gain strength and comfort for everything that worries him.

The second metaphor is that of the oil, which is often employed in Holy Writ. It was, however, a precious oil, such as a balsam or other sweet-smelling liquid. The priests and the kings were customarily anointed with it. Furthermore, when the Jews had their festivals and wished to be happy, they would anoint or sprinkle themselves with such precious oil, as Jesus also mentions when He says, "When you fast, anoint your head, and wash your face" (Matt. 6:17). This custom, then, of using oil was common among these people when they wanted to be merry and happy (John 12:3). Magdalene also wished to make the Lord happy when she poured precious ointment of pure perfume on His head, for she saw that He was sad (Luke 7:38). The third metaphor is that of a cup, which they used in their worship when they brought drink offerings and rejoiced before the Lord.

With these words, "Thou anointest

---

5. An allusion to Tertullian, *Apologeticus*, 50, which had become proverbial.

my head with oil, Thou pourest my cup full," the prophet, then, wishes to indicate the great, rich comfort that the believers have through the Word, that their consciences are sure, happy, and well satisfied amid all temptations and distresses, even death. It is as though he would say, "The Lord indeed makes an unusual warrior of me and arms me quite wonderfully against my enemies. I thought that He would have put armor on me, placed a helmet on my head, put a sword into my hand, and warned me to be cautious and give careful attention to the business at hand lest I be surprised by my enemies. But instead He places me at a table and prepares a splendid meal for me, anoints my head with precious balm or (after the fashion of our country) puts a wreath on my head as if, instead of going out to do battle, I were on my way to a party or a dance. And so that I may not want anything now, He fills my cup to overflowing so that at once I may drink, be happy and of good cheer, and get drunk. The prepared table, accordingly, is my armor, the precious balm my helmet, the overflowing cup my sword; and with these I shall conquer all my enemies." But is that not a wonderful armor and an even more wonderful victory?

David wishes to say, "Lord, Thy guests who are sitting at Thy table, the believers, not only become strong and bold giants in the presence of all their enemies, but they also become happy and drunk. That is due to the fact that Thou dost treat them well, as a rich man usually treats his guests. Thou dost feed them splendidly, make them happy and gay, and serve them so well with wine that they get drunk." All of that is done through the Word of grace. Through it the Lord, our Shepherd, feeds and strengthens the hearts of His believers, so that they defy all of their enemies and say with the prophet, "I am not afraid

of the many hundreds of thousands of people who have set themselves against me round about" (Ps. 3:6). And above, in the fourth verse, he said, "I fear no evil; for Thou, Lord, art with me." He accordingly gives them the Holy Spirit together with the Word, yes, through this same Word. The Holy Spirit makes them not only courageous and bold, but also so secure and happy that they get drunk with a great and boundless joy.

David is thus speaking here of spiritual power, joy, and intoxication—the power of God (Rom. 1:16); and a joy in the Holy Spirit, as Saint Paul calls it (Rom. 14:17); and a blessed intoxication, in which the people are filled not with wine, for that is debauchery, but with the Holy Spirit (Eph. 5:18). And this is the armor and the weapons with which our Lord God equips His believers against the devil and the world; that is, He puts the Word into their mouths and puts courage, that is, the Holy Spirit, into their hearts. Unafraid and cheerful, they attack all their enemies with that equipment. They smite and conquer them despite all their [enemies'] power, wisdom, and holiness. Such warriors were the apostles on the day of Pentecost (Acts 2:1ff.). They stood up in Jerusalem against the command of the emperor and the high priest and acted as though they were veritable gods and all the others mere locusts. And they pressed forward with all strength and joy, as though they were intoxicated, as some actually mocked them and said they were filled with new wine. But Saint Peter showed from the prophet Joel that they were not filled with wine but with the Holy Spirit. Afterward he flayed about with his sword; that is, he opened his mouth and preached, and with one stroke he rescued three thousand souls from the devil.

But such power, joy, and blissful intoxication are manifested in the believers not only when they prosper and have peace, but also when they suffer and die. When the council at Jerusalem, therefore, had the apostles flogged, they rejoiced that they had been counted worthy to suffer dishonor for the name of Christ (Acts 5:41). And in Romans 5:3 Saint Paul says, "We also rejoice in our sufferings." Later on many martyrs, men and women went to their deaths with happy hearts and laughing mouths as though they were going to a happy festival or dance. So we read of Saint Agnes and Saint Agatha,[6] who were virgins of thirteen or fourteen years, and of many others. They not only boldly and confidently conquered the devil and the world through their deaths, but were also cheerful with all their hearts, just as if they had been drunk with great joy. And it does vex the devil beyond measure when one can so confidently despise his great might and guile. In our times, too, many have died cheerfully because they have confessed Christ. Similarly, we learn that many die in their beds with a fine understanding and faith and say with Simeon, "With peace and joy I now depart," so that it is a pleasure to behold, as I myself have often beheld it. And all this because, as the prophet says, they are anointed with the oil which the psalm calls an oil of gladness (Ps. 45:7), and have drunk from the overflowing cup which the Lord has filled.

"Good!" you say, "but I do not yet find myself sufficiently well equipped to die cheerfully." That does not matter. As mentioned earlier, David did not always have the ability either; indeed, at times he complained that he had been cast away from the presence of God. Nor did other saints at all times have full confidence in God and an eternal pleasure and patience in their distresses and afflictions. Saint Paul at times trusted so securely and surely in Christ that he would not have bothered even to stand up because of the law, sin, death, and the devil. "It is no longer I who live," he says, "but Christ who lives in me" (Gal. 2:20). And, "My desire is to depart and to be with Christ" (Phil. 1:23). And, "Who shall separate us from the love of God? He did not spare His own Son, but gave Him up for us all. Will He not also give us all things with Him? Shall tribulation, or distress, or persecution, or the sword separate us from Him?" (Rom. 8:32, 35). When he speaks here of death, the devil, and all misfortune, he is as sure as though he were the strongest and greatest saint, for whom death would be pure joy. Elsewhere, then, he speaks as though he were the weakest and greatest sinner on earth. First Corinthians 2:3: "I was with you in weakness and in much fear and trembling." Romans 7:14: "I am carnal, sold under sin," which brings me into captivity. Romans 7:24: "Wretched man that I am! Who will deliver me from the body of this death?" And in Galatians 5:17, he teaches that in the saints there is an eternal struggle of the flesh against the spirit. Therefore, you ought not despair so soon, though you find yourself weak and fainthearted, but pray diligently that you might remain with the Word and grow in the faith and knowledge of Christ. This is what the prophet is doing here, teaching others to do by saying:

Goodness and mercy shall follow me all the days of my life; and I shall dwell in the house of the Lord forever.

Because the devil never stops tormenting the believers—inwardly with

---

6. Luther seems to be thinking primarily of Saint Agnes here, combining with the details of her martyrdom the story of another virgin martyr, Saint Agatha.

terror, outwardly with the wiles of false teachers and the power of the tyrants—the prophet here at the end earnestly asks that God, who has given him this treasure, would also keep him in it to the end. He says, "Oh, may the dear God grant His grace that goodness and mercy might follow me all the days of my life and that He might soon make manifest what He calls goodness and mercy," that is, that he might dwell in the house of the Lord forever. It is as though he would say, "Lord, Thou hast begun the matter. Thou hast given me Thy holy Word and received me among those who are Thy people, who know Thee, praise and magnify Thee. Continue to give Thy grace, that I may remain with the Word and nevermore be separated from Thy holy Christendom." Thus, he also prays in the twenty-seventh psalm, "One thing I ask of the Lord," he says, "that will I seek after; that I may dwell in the house of the Lord all the days of my life, to behold the beautiful worship of the Lord, and to visit His temple" (Ps. 27:4).

Thus, the prophet here teaches and admonishes all believers by his example not to become smug, proud, or presumptuous, but to fear and pray that they may not lose their treasure. Such an earnest admonition, however, should truly arouse us and awaken us to pray diligently. Blessed David, a prophet enlightened with all kinds of divine wisdom and knowledge and endowed with so many kinds of great and splendid gifts of God, prayed often and very earnestly that he might remain in possession of the blessings of God. We, then, who surely must be considered as nothing at all in comparison with David and who, besides, live at the end of the world—and that, as Christ and the apostles tell us, is a horrible and dangerous time—ought much more to awaken and to pray with all earnestness and diligence that we may remain in the house of the Lord all the days of our life, that is, that we may hear God's Word, through it receive the many kinds of blessings and fruits that were shown us above, and endure therein unto the end. May Christ, our only Shepherd and Savior, grant us this! Amen.

Isaiah's "suffering servant" chapter is one of the Old Testament's great Messianic prophecies. This prophecy was given hundreds of years before the birth of Jesus and was repeated as the Jews awaited the Messiah. It illustrates God's redemptive plan, describing the one who would come to suffer in the place of mankind. But Isaiah's message of the coming justification often fell on deaf ears.

Isaiah 53 describes the punishment of Christ in such detail that there was no excuse for the Jewish leaders, who were familiar with the Old Testament, to misinterpret his identity. Jesus himself made it clear that his mission was prophesied in the Old Testament and the Jewish leaders of his day should have understood who he was.

Luther spoke to Christians who were removed from the sufferings of Christ, who were perhaps unfamiliar with the prophecy. His recurring theme of faith as a gift of the Holy Spirit and of the Word is evident here.

CHAPTER THREE

Isaiah 53

Who has believed what we have heard?

Seeing the greatness of Christ, the prophet thinks of his fellow Jews, how few there will be to believe this. He had said that almost all would regard Him as an offense. Many Gentiles would receive Him but only a few Jews. For that reason he says here, "Who will ever believe this?" The Jews were indeed disgusted, as we see in the narratives of the Gospels and the Acts of the Apostles. This is what the prophet is bemoaning here, that so offensive an appearance of Christ must be received and respected by the kings. This reception takes place not by reason and its research facilities, but it is brought about solely by the Holy Spirit and the Word. To believe that Christ, so exceedingly disgraced and dying between robbers, is the Savior—this reason cannot believe. No more loathsome kind of death can be read about than that which Christ suffered, and to believe in Him under that form as the Messiah and to die in that faith—this is the office of the Holy Spirit. So far the prophet has completed one [verse] concerning Christ as the Servant hanging on the cross, and concerning His completely absurd appearance, and concerning His exalted kingdom, so that the kings will shut their mouths. Therefore I conclude that after His death, Christ will have an eternal kingdom.

He grew up like a young plant.

Here the prophet is still dealing with his prophecy concerning Christ's suffering. He grew up *like a young plant and like a root*. This is remarkable. *Before Him*, he says. Indeed, he grows up before God, but not in the eyes of the world. This is a metaphor, as if to say, a root does not grow in parched ground. It strikes me as if a lovely sprout were to grow up out of parched earth, that is, a dry Christ cannot possibly accomplish anything good. Trying to draw water from a rock and oil from iron is just as believable as saying that Christ must be splendid and glorious.

He had no form or comeliness. Not having form or comeliness means simply to deprive Him of everything, since no robber was completely without form. But here there is to be no form or adornment whatever.

We look at Him, because He was crucified publicly.

There was no beauty that we should desire Him. "There was nothing to attract us, nothing that we might care for. Everything about Him was repulsive." See how the prophet toils as he describes His contemptible appearance. It is as if he were saying, "The people treated Him in a most horrible way."

He was despised and rejected by men; a man of sorrows, and acquainted with grief.

For *rejected by men* the Hebrew has "one for whom there is no concern whatever; one from whom all turn away." This is not an easy suffering. These words cannot be understood as referring to the glory of the kingdom, nor do they speak of a simple and spiritual suffering. They speak rather of a physical, open, and extremely shameful suffering. Away with the Jews who refuse to admit that this refers to Christ! They imagine two Messiahs. They say that one has come already and is walking around in the world in the garb of a beggar and that a second one is to come in earthly glory. Thus this text compelled them.

A man of sorrows. This does not denote weaknesses but many sicknesses and griefs. He is a man wounded and beaten, as the following shows.

As one from whom men hide their faces.

Faces must be referred to others who saw Him; that is, as often as they saw Christ, they turned away from His wretched face. There was a revulsion of seeing. Here are two [verses] in which the prophet depicts both the glory of Christ and the lack of glory and His suffering. Now follows a third [verse] which shows what Christ would do.

We have heard that in these paragraphs there was a description of Christ's person with respect to His suffering and His glorification. This passage forms the basis for the Church's faith that Christ's kingdom is not of this world. Now follows what He would accomplish by His suffering, whether He suffered for His own sake or for the sake of others. And this is the second part of our understanding and justification, to know that Christ suffered and was cursed and killed, but FOR US. It is not enough to know the matter, the suffering, but it is necessary to know its function. The pope retained the matter but denied the function. The Anabaptists deny both.

Surely He has borne our griefs and carried our sorrows; yet we esteemed Him stricken, smitten by God, and afflicted.

This states the purpose of Christ's suffering. It was not for Himself and His own sins, but for our sins and griefs. He bore what we should have suffered. Here you see the fountain from which Saint Paul draws countless dreams of the suffering and merits of Christ, and he condemns all religions, merits, and endeavors in the whole world through which men seek salvation. Note the countless sects who to this day are toiling to obtain salvation. But here the prophet says, "He for us." It is difficult for the flesh to repudiate all its resources, to turn away from self, and to be carried over to Christ. It is for us who have merited nothing not to have regard for our merits but simply to cling to the Word between heaven and earth, even though we do not feel it. Unless we have been instructed by God, we will not understand this. Therefore I delight in this text as if it were a text of the New Testament. This new teaching which demolishes the righteousness of the law clearly appeared absurd to the Jews. For that reason the apostles needed Scripture, *Surely He has borne our griefs.* His suffering was nothing else than our sin. These words, OUR, US, FOR US, must be written in letters of gold. He who does not believe this is not a Christian. *Yet we esteemed Him [stricken].* We thought that He was suffering because of His own sin, as it were. In the eyes of the world and of the flesh, Christ does not suffer for us, since He seemed to have deserved it Himself. This is what the prophet says here too, that He was judged guilty in the eyes of the world. It is therefore difficult to believe that such a one suffered for us. The law is that everybody dies for his own sins. Natural reason, and divine as well, argues that everybody must bear his own sin. Yet He is struck down contrary to all law and custom. Hence, reason infers that He was smitten by God for His own sake. Therefore, the prophet leads us so earnestly beyond all righteousness and our rational capacity and confronts us with the suffering of Christ to impress upon us that all that Christ has is mine. This is the preaching of the whole gospel, to show us that Christ suffered for our sake contrary to law, right, and custom. He expounds more fully what His suffering for us means.

He was wounded.

The prophet is eloquent in describing the suffering of Christ. Word by word he expounds it in opposition to the hardened Jews. Do you want to know what it is to bear our sins, that is, what it means that *He was wounded?* Here you have Christ delineated perfectly and absolutely, since this chapter speaks of Him. Christ was a man, a servant of the Word, who by means of suffering bore our sins. What will the unrestrained Jew answer in opposition to this delineation? From this you must infer how far apart are the teachings of Paul and the pope. Paul clings to Christ alone as the sin bearer. By means of this one [name], "Lamb of God" (John 1:29), John the Baptist understands this levitical sacrifice, that He suffered for the sins of all. It follows, then, that the Law and merits do not justify. Away with the antichrist pope with his traditions, since Christ has borne all these things! I marvel that this text was so greatly obscured in the church. They note the concern of Scripture that faith without works is dead, and we say the same thing. In public argument, however, we say that works are indeed necessary, but not as justifying elements. Thus, anyone may

privately come to the conclusion, "It is all the same whether I have sinned or whether I have done well." This is hard for the conscience to believe, that it is the same and in fact something angelic and divine. Therefore, this text draws the following conclusion: "Christ alone bears our sins. Our works are not Christ. Therefore, there is no righteousness of works." Surely none of the papists can escape this fact when he sees Scripture as a whole, that Christ has accomplished all things for justification and therefore we have not done it. Appeal to works, rewards, and merits and make much of them in the realm of outward recompense. Only do not make them responsible for justification and the forgiveness of sins. We can preach and uphold this passage in public, but we can only believe it with difficulty in private. If we preserve this article, "Jesus Christ is the Savior," all other articles concerning the Holy Spirit and of the church and of Scripture are safe. Thus Satan attacks no article so much as this one. He alone is a Christian who believes that Christ labors for us and that He is the Lamb of God slain for our sins. While this article stands, all the monasteries of righteousness are struck down by lightning. In the light of this text read all the epistles of Paul with regard to redemption, salvation, and liberation, because they are all drawn from this fountain. A blind papacy read and chanted these and similar words as in a dream, and no one really considered them. If they had, they would have cast off all righteousness from themselves. Hence, it is not enough to know and accept the fact. One must also accept the function and the power of the fact. If we have this, we stand unconquered on the royal road, and the Holy Spirit is present in the face of all sects and deceptions. When this doctrine is safe, we firmly stand up to all people, but where this article is lost, we proceed from one error to the next, as we observe in the babbling Enthusiasts and in Erasmus. Our nature is opposed to the function and power of Christ's Passion. As far as the fact itself is concerned, both the pope and the Turk believe it and proclaim it, but they do not accept its function. As for you, lift up this article and extol it above every law and righteousness, and let it be to you a measureless sea over against a little spark. The sea is Christ who has suffered. Your works and your righteousness are the little spark. Therefore, beware as you place your sins on your conscience that you do not panic, but freely place them on Christ, as this text says, "He has borne our iniquities." We must clearly transfer our sins from ourselves to Christ. If you want to regard your sin as resting on you, such a thought in your heart is not of God, but of Satan himself, contrary to Scripture, which by God's will places your sin on Christ. Hence, you must say, "I see my sin in Christ, therefore, my sin is not mine but another's. I see it in Christ." It is a great thing to say confidently, "My sin is not mine." However, it is a supreme conflict with a most powerful beast, which here becomes most powerful, "I behold sins heaped on Christ." Thus, a certain hermit who was extremely harassed by Satan could not evade him, but said, "I have not sinned. Everybody must look upon his conscience as free." He did not answer well because he did have sin. This is what he should have said, "My sins have been transferred to Christ; He has them." This is the grafting of the wild olive into the olive tree. It is not without purpose that the prophet uses so many words in this article, since it is necessary for a Christian to know that these are his own sins, whatever they are, and that they have been borne by Christ, by whom we have been redeemed and saved. This is the Savior from eternal damnation, from death, and from sin. So by this thunderbolt the law and its righteousness are struck down, as you see Paul treat this matter in detail.

Something further must be noted, [so that] those who do not feel this [assurance of salvation] despair. There Satan can turn the antidote into poison and the hope into despair. For when a Christian hears these supreme consolations and then sees how weak he is with regard to his faith in them, he soon thinks that they do not apply to him. In this way Satan can turn consolation into distress. But as for you, however weak you are, know that you are a Christian, whether you believe perfectly or imperfectly, even while weakness and a feeling of death and sin remain with you. To such a person we must say, "Brother, your situation is not desperate, but pray together with the apostles for the perfection of your faith." Paul also struggled with this problem and was deeply disturbed. A Christian is not yet perfect, but he is a Christian who has, that is, who begins to have, the righteousness of God. I say this for the sake of the weak, so that they will not despair when they feel the bite of sin within themselves. They should not yet be masters and doctors but disciples of Christ, people who learn Christ, not perfect teachers. Let it suffice for us to remain with that Word as learners. Therefore, however perfect and absolute the teaching of Christ is that affirms that all our sins belong to Christ, it is not perfect in our life. It is enough for us to have begun and to be in the state of reaching after what is before us. Hence, a Christian man must be especially vexed in his conscience and heart by Satan, and yet he must remain in the Word and not seek peace anywhere else than in Christ. We must not make a log or a rock out of the Christian as one who does not feel sin in himself. This is the claim of the exceedingly spiritual Enthusiasts.

The chastisement of peace. Peter treats this passage (1 Pet. 2:24). Christ is not so much a judge and an angry God but one who bears and carries our sins, a mediator. Away with the papists, who have set Christ before us as a terrible judge and have turned the saints into intercessors! There they have added fuel to the fire. By nature we are already afraid of God. Blessed therefore are those who as uncorrupted young people arrived at this understanding, that they can say, "I only knew Jesus Christ as the bearer of my sins." The name of Christ, then, is most agreeable. *The chastisement, or punishment, of our peace,* that is, His chastisement is the remedy that brings peace to our conscience. [Apart from] Christ there is nothing but disorder. But He was chastised for the sake of our peace. Note the wonderful exchange: one man sins, another pays the penalty; one deserves peace, the other has it. The one who should have peace has chastisement, while the one who should have chastisement has peace. It is a difficult thing to know what Christ is. Would that our Enthusiasts saw this clearly!

And with His stripes we are healed. See how delightfully the prophet sets Christ before us. It is a remarkable plaster. His stripes are our healing. The stripes should be ours and the healing in Christ. Hence this is what we must say to the Christian, "If you want to be healed, do not look at your own wounds, but fix your gaze on Christ."

All we like sheep have gone astray.

This is the conclusion and confutation of the preceding. There he calls all our labors and endeavors errors. Christ alone was without sin. In this text all the apostles have attacked the religions

and the law itself. *All we have gone astray.* The religions through their own rules and their own way want to load our sins on us and say, "If you will observe these things, you will be free from your sins." Yet the prophet says that "our sins" and the sins "of all men" have been placed on Christ.

All we like sheep have gone astray. As I said [before], This is the supreme and chief article of faith, that our sins, placed on Christ, are not ours; again, that the peace is not Christ's but ours. Once this foundation is established, all will be well with the superstructure. If we do not bump against this rock, other teachings will not harm us. This article alone Satan cannot but attack by means of tyrants and sects. The whole world can put up with every sectarian teaching and even support it in peace. But it cannot bear this faith and the rejection of all works and merits. Because self-glory is brought to naught and the world likes to hear its own glory, it is not willing to reject its own. [Thus,] the head of self-righteousness must be lopped off. I grant that the works of the godly are good and right, but they do not justify. This Satan cannot bear, and because of this we are persecuted and we suffer to the present day, since we have taught all things in peace, tranquility, patience, and purity, certainly more than he. By this text we have cast down every foreign righteousness and hypocrisy. Therefore, write this text on the foundation in golden letters or in your own blood. That is why he says *all we,* and no one is excepted.

Each one of us all, because Christ has nothing from us but death and labor (cf. chapter 43) and we have righteousness and life from Him.

And the Lord has laid. This confirms our conscience that Christ did not take our sins by His own will but by the will of the Father who had mercy on us. *On*

Him, not on us, contrary to every law and order, where whoever sins is punished. Here, however, we have the punishment of our sins on Christ Himself. In public life, however, if anyone sins openly, let him be punished by the magistrate.

He was offered because He Himself wanted it.

This is noted and sung everywhere against the scandal of the cross over against Jews and Gentiles who say, "How does He wish to save others when He could not save Himself?" (cf. Matt. 27:42). For that reason this text responds to this slander, *Because He Himself wanted it*. This is a good thought, but it is different in Hebrew. *He was oppressed, and He was afflicted, yet He opened not His mouth, like a lamb that is led to the slaughter.* That text about His suffering is treated by Peter in this way, "When He suffered, He did not threaten" (1 Pet. 2:23).

[Thus,] that [verse] expresses the will and the patience of Christ as He suffers, that He does not even think of vengeance. This is the way for Christians to suffer, that they endure very patiently without threats and curses, yea, that they pray for and bless their tormentors. Therefore, he depicts Christ's patience by comparing Him in a most felicitous way with a sheep. This is the force of that crucifixion, that such a Christ will suffer who is described as overflowing in suffering like that of sheep, with His whole heart filled with love.

Led to the slaughter. The sheep that is to be shorn and slaughtered is silent. So Christ, keeping silence, always sympathizes with their ills. Thus, you have Christ undergoing most shameful suffering in His person and yet suffering with a most patient heart. Having completed the first aspect, the prophet begins the second one, regarding the resurrection.

By oppression and judgment He was taken away.

Now he begins to treat His glorification. Behold, here he declares that He whom he had until now depicted as a sheep to be killed and whom he had described as destined for a most shameful death for the sins of others is to be raised again. Now he describes Him again. He is not dead but taken away from oppression. Here he says that His *oppression and judgment* is finished. This cannot be said of a dead person remaining in the grave, but it can be said of one liberated and revived. The text says that He was oppressed and in judgment but has now been removed from them, hence resurrected.

As for His generation, who will tell it? Who can relate its duration, since His life and duration is eternal? Note the two contrary statements: someone dying and yet enduring forever. *Generation* properly means age, era, a lifetime. It is a proverbial statement that "a generation goes, and a generation comes, but the earth remains forever" (Eccl. 1:4). This must be understood as referring not to generation but to age. Here, then, the prophet established Christ in an eternal age, something that cannot be expressed, namely, that He has been transposed into eternal life. Peter expounds this passage in Acts, where he says, "God raised Him up, having loosed the pangs of death, because it was not possible for Him to be held by it" (Acts 2:24), and led Him into generation, that is, into length of life and eternity. Christ has such length of life that it cannot be expressed. Unless we believe it by faith, eternity is beyond expression.

That He was cut off out of the land of the living, stricken for the transgression of My people. Again he says that Christ was stricken *for the transgression of My people*. Ever and again he says *for the sins of My people*. Let us not simply pass over Christ's suffering, but we must always look to its function, that it was for the sake of our sins. He says that He was separated and brought into another life, something no one understands from the perspective of this life. Therefore, the Jews are in error when they hope that He will reign in this life. No, in this life He served, preached, and suffered, and then He passed out of this world to another place.

From the land of the living, from this world where we live. Through this suffering He was transported from a mortal existence to an immortal one.

And they made His grave with the wicked.

If the Jews and we, in our weakness, should hitherto have been in doubt about the suffering Christ, the following proves it even more, as if to say, He not only died, but He was also buried. *His grave will be given Him with the ungodly and with a rich man in His death*. It is clearly evident that Christ was buried and dead. The Jews read "lifted up," not "buried." Here, however, the text clearly states that He was buried. No one is said to be buried unless he were dead, and so He was buried as an ungodly man. In this way this text refutes the slanders which deny that Christ died, and it is a strengthening of our faith.

Let us here look at the grammar. We are dealing with a Hebraism. In Scripture "rich man" is used instead of "ungodly" through a certain figure of speech. This is so since it often happens that the rich of this world are ungodly and their riches are often used for un-

godly purposes. Therefore, he says here that He died like an ungodly man and was buried like a rich man, just as the gospel reports that He was put to death as a rebel and was buried with this name and disgrace attached to Him. The Jews, who might here dispute that Christ is king, cannot quibble, since He was to die in this way according to Scripture.

Although He had done no violence, and there was no deceit in His mouth. The most innocent Christ was judged by the Jews to be the most guilty, He who was most innocent and guiltless in His teaching and His life. They had not a word to say to Him. Although He was innocent, yet the Lord willed it that He should take upon Himself to be the most criminal of men. Therefore, he compares Him with all other men, and they, even though most holy, are guilty. This one Christ alone is the exception; He alone is righteous and holy. For that reason death could not hold Him.

If He gave His soul as the measure.

You now have the person suffering and a description of His death and resurrection. Now he describes the fruit of His Passion, and this is His fruit, that He will have His future kingdom according to the statement, "He sits at the right hand of the Father, from thence He shall come."[1] *If He gave His soul*, that is, He Himself gave His life as an offering for the transgression. "Transgression" is properly called "guilt" in Psalm 32:5. And they do not commit sin. "To commit sin" properly means that someone has done something and remains guilty. Thus, we are unable to remove our guilt. Therefore, only Christ can do it.

Since, therefore, *He gave His life for sin*, it follows that *He shall see His seed*

1. From the Apostles' Creed.

and His days shall be prolonged. Thus, he wants to say, "We hope that the Messiah, of whom you say that He is dead, will be the completely unconquerable King." And we say to them, "He will be a king both ancient and eternal and will see His offspring for a very long time. None of your kings will forever and eternally see his offspring, as He will." A king of the world does not see his offspring for long. In fact, when he dies, he leaves them behind. Here you see what *the will of the Lord* is. He placed all our iniquities upon Him, freeing us from death and giving us eternal life. This is *the will of God.*

The travail of His soul.

So far he has especially talked about His soul being in toil, in misfortune. Hence, He must now receive His reward. *He shall see the fruit and be satisfied.* He shall have His delight in all things and have a full measure of pleasures. Everything will go just as He wants it.

By His knowledge He will justify. As to the manner in which the course of the kingdom will proceed, how will this King progress? This will be the manner: *by His knowledge.* This is a very lovely text. *By His knowledge He will justify many, because He shall bear their iniquities.* Those who confess that their sins have been borne by Him are the righteous. The definition of righteousness is wonderful. The sophists say that righteousness is the fixed will to render to each his own. Here he says that righteousness is the knowledge of Christ, who bears our iniquities. Therefore whoever will know and believe in Christ as bearing his sins will be righteous.

Many servants. Thus the Gospel is the means or vehicle by which the knowledge of God reaches us. Hence the kingdom of Christ does not consist in works

or endeavors, since no rule and no law, not even the law of Moses, can lead us to that knowledge, but we arrive at it through the Gospel. A Christian cannot arrive at this knowledge by means of any laws, either moral or civil, but he must ascend to heaven by means of the Gospel. Therefore, he says here *by His knowledge.* There is no other plan or method of obtaining liberty than the knowledge of Christ. For that reason Peter and Paul are constantly saying that we must increase in this knowledge, since we can never be perfect in it (cf. 2 Pet. 3:18; Col. 1:10). The knowledge of Christ must be construed in a passive sense. It is that by which He is known, the proclamation of His suffering and death. You must therefore note this new definition of righteousness. Righteousness is the knowledge of Christ. What is Christ? He is the person who bears all our sins. These are unspeakable gifts and hidden and unutterable kinds of wisdom.

We have heard this outstanding passage *by His knowledge* and *iniquities.* I have said that the individual words must be pondered in supreme faith, and they must be read and considered with the most watchful eyes, so that it is not simply any kind of knowledge or understanding but a knowledge that justifies, in opposition to other kinds of knowledge. Thus, you see this remarkable definition of righteousness through the knowledge of God. It sounds ridiculous to call righteousness a speculative knowledge. Therefore, it is said in Jeremiah 9:24: "Let him who glories glory in this, that he understands and knows Me." Therefore, this knowledge is the formal and substantial righteousness of the Christians, that is, faith in Christ, which I obtain through the Word. The Word I receive through the intellect, but to assent to that Word is the work of the Holy Spirit. It is not the work of reason, which always seeks its own kinds of righteousness. The Word, however, sets forth another righteousness through the consideration and the promises of Scripture, which causes this faith to be accounted for righteousness. This is our glory to know for certain that our righteousness is divine in that God does not impute our sins. Therefore, our righteousness is nothing else than knowing God. Let the Christian who has been persuaded by these words cling firmly to them, and let him not be deceived by any pretense of works or by his own suffering, but rather let him say, "It is written that the knowledge of God is our righteousness, and therefore no monk, no celibate, is justified."

And He shall bear their iniquities. Here he repeats, as it were, the foundation. To bring Christ, this is righteousness. Another part is, Who is Christ? He answers, "Christ is not a judge and tormentor and tyrant, as reason apart from the Word fashions Him, but He is the bearer of our iniquities." Yet He will become judge and tyrant to those who refused to believe in Him. It is, however, the office of Christ to bear our sins. Hence, we must conclude from this text, "If Christ bears my iniquities, then I do not bear them." All teachings which say that our sins must be borne by us are ungodly. Thus, from such a text countless thunderbolts have come forward against an ungodly self-righteousness. So Paul by this article of justification struck down every kind of self-righteousness. Therefore, we must diligently observe this article. I see that there are many snorers treating this article. They are the ones who consider these words the way a man does who looks at his face in a mirror (as James says, 1:23f.). The moment they come upon another object or business, they are overwhelmed, and they forget the grace of God. For that reason you must most diligently consider this article and not allow yourself to be led astray by other teachings, occupations, or persecutions.

Therefore I will divide Him a portion with the great, and He shall divide the spoil with the strong.

Here he repeats as if by an exclamation. Since *He poured out His soul in death* and was not simply dead but *was numbered with the transgressors,* the prophet in these words repeats the suffering of Christ. Here he says, *He gave His life into death.* With that battering ram he strikes the stubbornness of the Jews, who do not want to hear about the Christ who dies but who look for a Christ who never dies. Here the prophet in a very simple and expressive way depicts the manner of His death. He says He will die and then points with the fingers, *He will be numbered with the transgressors,* as if to say, "You Jews want to acknowledge your Christ. He will appear in such a form that He will die the most despised kind of death in the midst of robbers." The Jews, who look for a glorious Christ before they will believe in a crucified one, did not want to see this text. This is the way it happens to us who are blind, although as for us, let us believe in the crucified One.

Yet He bore the sins of many. He has described the death. Now he delineates the force and power of His sufferings. He says, "He did not die in vain, but all promises of Scripture have been fulfilled, and all our sins have been taken away. No, He did not toil in vain by His death, but He died to fulfill the promises and to set us free.

And made intercession for the transgressors. There he commends His patience to us. He was heartily glad to do it. First, He depicts the suffering, second, the kind of suffering, third, the power of the suffering, and fourth, His patience. Thus, He compassionately prayed for transgressors and crucifiers, shed tears for them, and did not deal with them with threats. Who can place the Christ thus depicted in love into his heart, as He is here described? Oh, we would be blessed people if we could believe this most noble text, which must be magnified. I would wish it to be honored in the church, so that we might accustom ourselves to an alert study of this text, to bring us to see Christ as none other than the One who bears and shoulders the burden of our sins. This figure is a solace to the afflicted, but to snoring readers these are nothing but idle words.

Luther regards the Sermon on the Mount as a source of comfort for Christians and a source of irritation for the Jews. By reading it Christians understand the love of God and learn to depend on Him for comfort. He renounces the idol mammon, which is money or whatever source of comfort the nonbeliever seeks to depend on.

For Luther the Beatitudes represent the antithesis to what the world says will bring success. The secular realm depends on such temporal items as the possession of money, property, power, and the like for its feeble support. This dependence is inappropriate for the Christian, whose true happiness rests on God and what He alone provides. While it is true that the Christian has to endure hardship in this life, Luther encourages the Christian to keep his eyes on the glory of heaven.

In this sermon Luther does an exceptional job of contrasting the insubstantial, useless wares of the world with the hope that is to be found only in Christ. All that one need do is exercise patience; peace will come soon enough. To live in this life means possible hunger, thirst, oppression, and poverty. But for those who come to Christ, all these problems will be resolved.

CHAPTER FOUR

Sermon on the Mount: The Beatitudes

Blessed are the spiritually poor, for theirs is the kingdom of heaven.

This is a fine, sweet, and friendly beginning for His instruction and preaching. He does not come like Moses or a teacher of the law, with demands, threats, and terrors, but in a very friendly way, with enticements, allurements, and pleasant promises. In fact, if it were not for this report which has preserved for us all the first dear words that the Lord Christ preached, curiosity would drive and impel everyone to run all the way to Jerusalem, or even to the end of the world, just to hear one word of it. You would find plenty of money to build such a road well! And everyone would proudly boast that he had heard or read the very word that the Lord Christ had preached. How wonderfully happy the man would seem who succeeded in this! That is exactly how it would really be if we had none of this in written form, even though there might be a great deal written by others. Everyone would say, "Yes, I heard what Saint Paul and His other apostles have taught, but I would much rather hear what He Himself spoke and preached."

But now since it is so common that everyone has it written in a book and can read it every day, no one thinks of it as anything special or precious. Yes, we grow sated and neglect it, as if it had been spoken by some shoemaker rather than the High Majesty of heaven. Therefore, it is in punishment for our ingratitude and neglect that we get so little

out of it and never feel nor taste what a treasure, power, and might there is in the words of Christ. But whoever has the grace to recognize it as the Word of God rather than the word of man, will also think of it more highly and dearly, and will never grow sick and tired of it.

Friendly and sweet as this sermon is for Christians, who are His disciples, just so irksome and unbearable it is for the Jews and their great saints. From the very beginning He hits them hard with these words, rejecting and condemning their teaching, preaching the exact opposite, yes, pronouncing woe upon their life and teaching, as Luke 6:24–26 shows. The essence of their teaching was, "If a man is successful here on earth, he is blessed and well off." That was all they aimed for, that if they were pious and served God, He should give them plenty upon earth and deprive them of nothing. Thus, David says of them in Psalm 144:13–15, "This is their teaching, that all their corners and garners should be full of grain and their fields full of sheep that bear often and much, and of cattle that labor much, with no harm or failure or mischance or distress coming upon them. Happy are such people!"

In opposition to this, Christ opens His mouth here and says that something is necessary other than the possession of enough on earth, as if He were to say, "My dear disciples, when you come to preach among the people, you will find out that this is their teaching and belief: 'Whoever is rich or powerful is completely blessed; on the other hand, whoever is poor and miserable is rejected and condemned before God.'" The Jews were firmly persuaded that if a man was successful, this was a sign that he had a gracious God, and vice versa. The reason for this was the fact that they had many great promises from God regarding the temporal, physical goods that He would grant to the pious. They counted upon these, in the opinion that if they had this, they were right with Him. The book of Job is addressed to this theory. His friends argue and dispute with him about this and insist that he is being punished this way because of some great sin he must have knowingly committed against God. Therefore he ought to admit it, be converted, and become pious, that God might lift the punishment from him.

At the outset, therefore, it was necessary for [Christ's] sermon to overthrow this delusion and to tear it out of their hearts as one of the greatest obstacles to faith and a great support for the idol mammon in their heart. Such a doctrine could have no other consequence than to make people greedy, so that everyone would be interested only in amassing plenty and in having a good time, without need or trouble. And everyone would have to conclude, "If that man is blessed who succeeds and has plenty, I must see to it that I do not fall behind."

This is still what the whole world believes today, especially the Turks, who draw their reliance and strength from it, coming to the conclusion that they could not have had so much success and victory if they had not been the people of God to whom He was gracious in preference to all others. Among us, too, the whole papacy believes this. Their

doctrine and life are founded only upon their having enough; therefore, they have assembled all the goods of the world, as everyone can see. In short, this is the greatest and most universal belief or religion on earth. On it all men depend according to their flesh and blood, and they cannot regard anything else as blessedness. That is why He preaches a totally new sermon here for the Christians: if they are a failure, if they have to suffer poverty and do without riches, power, honor, and good days, they will still be blessed and have not a temporal reward, but a different, eternal one; they will have enough in the kingdom of heaven.

Physical poverty and spiritual poverty

But you say, "What? Must all Christians, then, be poor? Dare none of them have money, property, popularity, power, and the like? What are the rich to do, people like princes, lords, and kings? Must they surrender all their property and honor, or buy the kingdom of heaven from the poor, as some have taught?" Answer: No. It does not say that whoever wants to have the kingdom of heaven must buy it from the poor, but that he must be poor himself and be found among the poor. It is put clearly and candidly, "Blessed are the poor." Yet the little word "spiritually" is added, so that nothing is accomplished when someone is physically poor and has no money or goods. Having money, property, land, and retinue outwardly is not wrong in itself. It is God's gift and ordinance. No one is blessed, therefore, because he is a beggar and owns nothing of his own. The command is to be "spiritually poor." I said at the very beginning that Christ is not dealing here at all with the secular realm and order, but that He wants to discuss only the spiritual—

how to live before God, above and beyond the external.

Having money, property, honor, power, land, and servants belongs to the secular realm; without these it could not endure. Therefore a lord or prince should not and cannot be poor, because for his office and station he must have all sorts of goods like these. This does not mean, therefore, that one must be poor in the sense of having nothing at all of his own. The world could not endure if we were all to be beggars and to have nothing. The head of a household could not support his household and servants if he himself had nothing at all. In short, physical poverty is not the answer. There is many a beggar getting bread at our door more arrogant and wicked than any rich man, and many a miserly, stingy peasant who is harder to get along with than any lord or prince.

So be poor or rich physically and externally, as it is granted to you—God does not ask about this—and know that before God, in his heart, everyone must be spiritually poor. That is, he must not set his confidence, comfort, and trust on temporal goods, nor hang his heart upon them and make mammon his idol. David was an outstanding king, and he really had his wallet and treasury full of money, his barns full of grain, his land full of all kinds of goods and provisions. In spite of all this he had to be a poor beggar spiritually, as he sings of himself, "I am poor, and a guest in the land, like all my fathers" (Ps. 39:12). Look at the king, sitting amid such possessions, a lord over land and people; yet he does not dare to call himself anything but a guest or a pilgrim, one who walks around on the street because he has no place to stay. This is truly a heart that does not tie itself to property and riches; but though it has [possessions],

it behaves as if it had nothing, as Saint Paul boasts of the Christians, "As poor, yet making many rich; as having nothing, and yet possessing everything" (2 Cor. 6:10).

All this is intended to say that while we live here, we should use all temporal goods and physical necessities, the way a guest does in a strange place, where he stays overnight and leaves in the morning. He needs no more than bed and board and dare not say, "This is mine, here I will stay." Nor dare he take possession of the property as though it belonged to him by right; otherwise he would soon hear the host say to him, "My friend, don't you know that you are a guest here? Go back where you belong." That is the way it is here too. The temporal goods you have, God has given to you for this life. He does permit you to use them and with them to fill the bag of worms[1] that you wear around your neck. But you should not fasten or hang your heart on them as though you were going to live forever. You should always go on and consider another, higher, and better treasure, which is your own and which will last forever.

This is said coarsely for the common man. Thus, he will learn to understand what it means in scriptural language to be "spiritually poor" or poor before God. We should not evaluate things externally, on the basis of money and property or of deficits and surpluses. For, as we have said above, we see that the poorest and most miserable beggars are the worst and most desperate rascals and dare to commit every kind of mischief and evil tricks, which fine, upstanding people, rich citizens or lords and princes, do not do. On the other hand, many saintly people who had plenty of money and property, honor, land, and retinue, still were poor amid all this

---

1. A frequent designation of the body in Luther.

property. We should evaluate things on the basis of the heart. We must not be overly concerned whether we have something or nothing, much or little. And whatever we do have in the way of possessions, we should always treat it as though we did not have it, being ready at any time to lose it and always keeping our hearts set on the kingdom of heaven (Col. 3:2).

Then, too, a man is called "rich" in Scripture, even though he does not have any money or property, if he scrambles and scratches for them and can never get enough of them. These are the very ones whom the Gospel calls "rich bellies,"[2] who in the midst of great wealth have the very least and are never satisfied with what God grants them. That is so because the Gospel looks into the heart, which is crammed full of money and property, and evaluates on the basis of this, though there may be nothing in the wallet or the treasury. On the other hand, it also calls a man "poor" according to the condition of his heart, though he may have his treasury, house, and hearth full. Thus the Christian faith goes straight ahead. It looks at neither poverty nor riches, but only at the condition of the heart. If there is a greedy belly there, the man is called "spiritually rich"; on the other hand, he is called "spiritually poor" if he does not depend upon these things and can empty his heart of them. As Christ says elsewhere, "He who forsakes houses, land, children, or wife, will receive a hundredfold, and besides he will inherit eternal life" (Matt. 19:29). By this He seeks to rescue their hearts from regarding property as their treasure, and to comfort His own who must forsake it; even in this life they will receive more than they leave behind.

We are not to run away from property, house, home, wife, and children, wandering around the countryside as a burden to other people. This is what the Anabaptist sect does, and they accuse us of not preaching the gospel rightly because we keep house and home and stay with wife and children. No, He does not want such crazy saints! This is what it means: in our hearts we should be able to leave house and home, wife and children. Even though we continue to live among them, eating with them and serving them out of love, as God has commanded, still we should be able, if necessary, to give them up at any time for God's sake. If you are able to do this, you have forsaken everything, in the sense that your heart is not taken captive but remains pure of greed and of dependence, trust, and confidence in anything. A rich man may properly be called "spiritually poor" without discarding his possessions. But when the necessity arises, then let him do so in God's name, not because he would like to get away from wife and children, house and home, but because, as long as God wills it, he would rather keep them and serve Him thereby, yet is also willing to let Him take them back.

The promise of the kingdom

So you see what it means to be "poor" spiritually and before God, to have nothing spiritually and to forsake everything. Now look at the promise which Christ appends when He says, "For of such is the kingdom of heaven." This is certainly a great, wonderful, and glorious promise. Because we are willing to be poor here and pay no attention to temporal goods, we are to have a beautiful, glorious, great, and eternal possession in heaven. And because you have

---

2. It is not clear which passage of the Gospels Luther has in mind here; possibly it is Luke 12:16–21.

given up a crumb, which you still may use as long and as much as you can have it, you are to receive a crown, to be a citizen and a lord in heaven. This would stir us if we really wanted to be Christians and if we believed that His words are true. But no one cares who is saying this, much less what He is saying. They let it go in one ear and out the other, so that no one troubles himself about it or takes it to heart.

With these words [Christ] shows that no one can understand this unless he is already a real Christian. This point and all the rest that follow are purely fruits of faith, which the Holy Spirit Himself must create in the heart. Where there is no faith, there the kingdom of heaven also will remain outside; nor will spiritual poverty, meekness, and the like follow, but there will remain only scratching and scraping, quarrels and riots over temporal goods. Therefore, it is all over for such worldly hearts, so that they never learn or experience what spiritual poverty is, and neither believe nor care what He says and promises about the kingdom of heaven.

Yet for their sakes He so arranges and orders things that whoever is not willing to be spiritually poor in God's name and for the sake of the kingdom of heaven, must still be poor in the devil's name and not have any thanks for it. God has so hung the greedy to their bellies that they are never satisfied or happy with their greedily gained goods. Sir Greed is such a jolly guest that he does not let anyone rest. He seeks, pushes, and hunts without stopping, so that he cannot enjoy his precious property for a single hour. Thus Solomon the preacher wonders and says, "Is it not a sore affliction that God gives a man wealth and possessions, land and retinue, and yet he is not capable of enjoying them?"

(Eccl. 6:2). He must always be afraid, troubled, and concerned about how he is going to keep it and expand it, lest it disappear or diminish. He is so completely its prisoner that he cannot enjoy spending a [coin] of it. But if there were a heart that could be content and satisfied, it would have rest and the kingdom of heaven besides. Otherwise, amid great possessions and with its greed, it must have purgatory here and hell-fire hereafter. As they say, "Here you travel in a wheelbarrow, but there on one wheel,"[3] that is, you have trouble and anxiety here, but bitter grief hereafter.

This is the way God always works, so that His Word remains true and no one is saved or satisfied except the Christian. Though the others have everything, their lot is never any better; indeed, it is never as good, and they must still remain poor beggars as far as their heart is concerned. The difference is that the former are glad to be poor and depend upon an imperishable, eternal possession, that is, upon the kingdom of heaven, and are the blessed children of God; but the latter are greedy for temporal goods, and yet they get what they want, but must eternally be the victims of the devil's tortures besides. In short, there is no difference between a beggar before the door and such a miserable belly, except that the one has nothing and lets himself be put off with a crust of bread, while the other, the more he has, the less satisfied he is, even though he were to get all the goods and money in the world in one pile.

As I have said, therefore, this sermon does the world no good and accomplishes nothing for it. The world stubbornly insists upon being right. It refuses to believe a thing, but must have it before its very eyes and hold it in its hand, saying, "A bird in the hand is

---

3. The reference is to a German proverb.

worth two in the bush."[4] Therefore, Christ also lets them go. He does not want to force anyone or drag him in by the hair. But He gives His faithful advice to all who will let Him advise them, and He holds before us the dearest promises. If you want it, you have peace and quiet in your heart here, and hereafter whatever your heart desires forever. If you do not want it, have your own way, and rather have sorrow and misfortune both here and hereafter. For we see and experience that everything depends upon being content and not clinging to temporal goods. There are many people whose hearts God can fill so that they may have only a morsel of bread and yet are cheerful and more content than any prince or king. In brief, such a person is a rich lord and emperor, and he need have no worry, trouble, or sorrow. This is the first point of this sermon: whoever wants to have enough here and hereafter, let him see to it that he is not greedy or grasping. Let him accept and use what God gives him, and live by his labor in faith. Then he will have paradise and even the kingdom of heaven here, as Saint Paul also says, "Godliness is of value in every way, as it holds promise for the present life and also for the life to come" (1 Tim. 4:8).

Blessed are those who mourn, for they shall be comforted.

He began this sermon against the doctrine and belief of the Jews—in fact, not only of the Jews but of the whole world which, even at its best, sticks to the delusion that it is well off if it just has property, popularity, and its mammon here, and which serves God only for this purpose. In the same way He now continues, overturning even what

they thought was the best and most blessed life on earth, one in which a person would attain to good and quiet days and would not have to endure discomfort, as Psalm 73:5 describes it: "They are not in trouble as other men are; they are not stricken like other men."

For that is the highest thing that men want, to have joy and happiness and to be without trouble. Now Christ turns the page and says exactly the opposite; He calls "blessed" those who sorrow and mourn. Thus throughout, all these statements are aimed and directed against the world's way of thinking, the way it would like to have things. It does not want to endure hunger, trouble, dishonor, unpopularity, injustice, and violence; and it calls "blessed" those who can avoid all these things.

So He wants to say here that there must be another life than the life of their quests and thoughts, and that a Christian must count on sorrow and mourning in the world. Whoever does not want to do this may have a good time here and live to his heart's desire, but hereafter he will have to mourn forever. As He says, "Woe unto you that laugh and have a good time now! For you shall have to mourn and weep" (Luke 6:25). This is how it went with the rich man in Luke 16. He lived luxuriously and joyfully all his life, decked out in expensive silk and purple. He thought he was a great saint and well off in the sight of God because He had given him so much property. Meanwhile, he let poor Lazarus lie before his door daily, full of sores, in hunger and trouble and great misery. But what kind of judgment did he finally hear when he was lying in hell? "Remember that in your lifetime you received good things, but Lazarus, evil things. Therefore you are now in an-

---

4. The original phrasing of the proverb which Luther cites is "It is better to hold a sparrow in your hand than to stare at a crane in the air."

guish, but he is comforted" (Luke 16:25).

See, this is the same text as "Blessed are those who mourn, for they shall be comforted," which is as much as saying, "Those who seek [to] have nothing but joy and fun here shall weep and howl forever."

You may ask again, "What are we to do, then? Is everyone to be damned who laughs, sings, dances, dresses well, eats, and drinks? After all, we read about kings and saints who were cheerful and lived well. Paul is an especially wonderful saint; he wants us to be cheerful all the time (Phil. 4:4), and he says, 'Rejoice with those who rejoice,' and again, 'Weep with those who weep' (Rom. 12:15). That sounds contradictory, to be joyful all the time and yet to weep and mourn with others."

Answer: I said before that having riches is not sinful, nor is it forbidden. So also being joyful, eating and drinking well, is not sinful or damnable; nor is having honor and a good name. Still I am supposed to be "blessed" if I do not have these things or can do without them, and instead suffer poverty, misery, shame, and persecution. So both of these things are here and must be—being sad and being happy, eating and going hungry, as Paul boasts about himself, "I have learned the art, wherever I am, to be content. I know how to be abased, and I know how to abound; in any and all circumstances I have learned the secret of facing plenty and hunger, abundance and want" (Phil. 4:11, 12). And in 2 Corinthians 6:8–10: "In honor and dishonor, in ill repute and good repute; as dying, and, behold, we live; as sorrowful, yet always rejoicing."

So this is what it means: a man is called "spiritually poor," not because he has no money or anything of his own, but because he does not covet it or set his comfort and trust upon it as though it were his kingdom of heaven. So also a man is said to "mourn and be sorrowful"—not if his head is always drooping and his face is always sour and never smiling; but if he does not depend upon having a good time and living it up, the way the world does, which yearns for nothing but having sheer joy and fun here, revels in it, and neither thinks nor cares about the state of God or men.

Joy in perspective

In this way many great and outstanding people, kings and others, who were Christians, have had to mourn and be sorrowful, though in the eyes of the world they lived a glorious life. Thus, throughout the Psalter David complains about his weeping and sorrow. Now, too, I could easily cite examples of great men, lords and princes, who have experienced and learned this about the gracious Gospel, at the recent Diet of Augsburg and elsewhere. Externally they lived well, dressed in princely fashion in silk and gold, and looked like people for whom life was a bed of roses.[5] But daily they had to be right in the midst of poisonous snakes; and in their heart they had to experience such unheard of arrogance, insolence, and shame, so many evil tricks and words from the vile papists, who delighted in embittering their hearts and, as far as possible, in denying them a single happy hour. Thus, they had to stew within themselves and do nothing but lament before God with sighs and tears. Such people know something of what the statement means: "Blessed are those who mourn and are sorrowful," though they do not always show it. They eat and drink with other people and sometimes laugh and joke with them, to forget their sorrow. You must not suppose that "to

---

5. The original expression is "People who were traveling on sheer roses."

mourn" means only to weep and cry and scream, like women and children. It is not the real and most profound mourning when it has come over the heart and breaks forth through the eyes, but when really great shocks come, which strike and shake the heart so that one cannot cry and dare not complain to anyone.

Therefore, mourning and sorrow are not a rare plant among Christians, in spite of outward appearances. They would like to be joyful in Christ, outwardly, too, as much as they can. Daily, whenever they look at the world, they must see and feel in their heart so much wickedness, arrogance, contempt, and blasphemy of God and His Word, so much sorrow and sadness, which the devil causes in both the spiritual and the secular realm. Therefore, they cannot have many joyful thoughts, and their spiritual joy is very weak. If they were to look at this continually and did not turn their eyes away from time to time, they could not be happy for a moment. It is bad enough that this really happens oftener than they would like, so that they do not have to go out looking for it.

Therefore, simply begin to be a Christian, and you will soon find out what it means to mourn and be sorrowful. If you can do nothing else, then get married, settle down, and make a living in faith. Love the Word of God, and do what is required of you in your station. Then you will experience, both from your neighbors and in your own household, that things will not go as you might wish. You will be hindered and hemmed in on every side, so that you will suffer enough and see enough to make your heart sad. But especially the dear preachers must learn this well and be disciplined daily with all sorts of envy, hatred, scorn, ridicule, ingratitude, contempt, and blasphemy. In addition, they have to stew inside, so that their hearts and souls are pierced through and continually tormented.

Because the world does not want to have such mourning and sorrow, it seeks out those stations and ways of life where it can have fun and does not have to suffer anything from anyone, as the monks' and priests' station used to be. It cannot stand the idea that in a divine station it should serve other people with nothing but care, toil, and trouble, and get nothing as a reward for this but ingratitude, contempt and other malicious treatment. Therefore, when things do not go with it as it wishes and one person looks at another with a sour face, all they can do is to batter things with cursing and swearing, and with their fists too, and be ready to put up property and reputation, land and servants. But God arranges things so that they still cannot get off too easily, without seeing or suffering any trouble at all. What He gives them as a reward for not wanting to suffer is this: they still have to suffer, but by their anger and impatience they make it twice as great and difficult, and without finding any comfort or a good conscience. The Christians have the advantage that though they mourn too, they shall be comforted and be blessed both here and hereafter.

Therefore, whoever wants to have fellowship with Christians and does not want to be an outright child of the world, let him be on the list of those who are willing to sigh and mourn, so that he may be comforted, as this promise says. We have an instance of this in Ezekiel 9. God sent out six men with "destroying weapons" against the city of Jerusalem, but one of them He sent with a writing case; he was to go through the middle of the city and put a mark upon the foreheads of those who sighed and groaned over the shameful situation and who had to watch it with sorrow in their hearts. Whoever was marked this way was to live, but all the others were to be killed. You see, this is the Christians' advantage. In the world they have to see nothing but sorrow and trouble. Yet when the world is at its smuggest and is riding along on sheer joy, suddenly the wheel turns, and a misfortune comes upon them in which they have to stay and perish. But the Christians are rescued and saved, the way Lot was saved in Sodom; for as Saint Peter says, they had long vexed and distressed his heart with their licentiousness (2 Pet. 2:7, 8). Let the world, therefore, laugh now and live riotously in its delights and pleasures. Though you have to mourn and be sorrowful and daily see your heart troubled, take it in stride and hold fast to this saying. Let it satisfy and comfort you. Outwardly, too, refresh yourself and be as cheerful as possible.

The promise of comfort

Those who mourn this way are entitled to have fun and to take it wherever they can so that they do not completely collapse for sorrow. Christ also adds these words and promises this consolation so that they do not despair in their sorrow nor let the joy of their heart be taken away and extinguished altogether, but mix this mourning with comfort and refreshment. Otherwise, if they never had any comfort or joy, they would have to languish and wither away. No man can stand continual mourning. It sucks out the very strength and savor of the body, as the wise man says, "Sadness has killed many people" (Ecclesiasticus 30:25); and again, "A downcast spirit dries up the marrow in the bones" (Prov. 17:22). Therefore, we should not neglect this but should command and urge such people to have a good time once in a while if possible, or at least to temper their sorrow and forget it for a while.

Thus Christ does not want to urge continual mourning and sorrow. He wants to warn against those who seek to escape all mourning and to have nothing but fun and all their comfort here. And He wants to teach His Christians, when things go badly for them and they have to mourn, to know that it is God's good pleasure and to make it theirs as well, not to curse or rage or despair as though their God did not want to be gracious. When this happens, the bitter draft should be mixed and made milder with honey and sugar. He promises here that this is pleasing to Him; and He calls them "blessed," comforting them here, and hereafter taking the sorrow away from them completely. Therefore, say good-bye to the world and to all those who harm us, in the name of their lord, the devil. And let us sing this song and be joyful in the name of God and Christ. Their outcome will surely not be the one they want. Now they take pleasure in our misfortune and do much to harm us. Still we take heart, and we shall live to see that at the last they will have to howl and weep when we are comforted and happy.

Blessed are the meek, for they shall inherit the earth.

This statement fits the first one well, when He said, "Blessed are the spiritually poor." For as He promises the kingdom of heaven and an eternal possession there, so here He also adds a promise about this temporal life and about possessions here on earth. But how does being poor harmonize with inheriting the land? It might seem that the preacher has forgotten how He began. Whoever is to inherit land and possessions cannot be poor. By "inheriting the land" here and having all sorts of possessions here on earth, He does not mean that everyone is to inherit a whole country; otherwise God would have to create more worlds. But God confers possessions upon everyone in such a way that He gives a man wife, children, cattle, house, and home, and whatever pertains to these, so that he can stay on the land where he lives and have dominion over his possessions. This is the way Scripture customarily speaks, as Psalm 37 says several times, "Those who wait for the Lord will inherit the land"; and again, "His blessed ones inherit the land." Therefore, He adds His own gloss here: to be "spiritually poor," as He used the expression before, does not mean to be a beggar or to discard money and possessions. For here He tells them to live and remain in the land and to manage earthly possessions, as we shall hear later.

What does it mean, then, to be meek? From the outset you must realize that Christ is not speaking at all about the government and its work, whose property it is not to be meek, as we use the word in German, but to bear the sword (Rom. 13:4) for the punishment of those who do wrong (1 Pet. 2:14), and to wreak a vengeance and a wrath that are called the vengeance and wrath of God. He is only talking about how individuals are to live in relation to others, apart from official position and authority—how father and mother are to live, not in relation to their children nor in their official capacity as father and mother, but in relation to those for whom they are not father and mother, like neighbors and other people. I have often said that we must sharply distinguish between these two, the office and the person. The man who is called Hans or Martin is a man quite different from the one who is called elector or doctor or preacher. Here we have two different persons in one man. The one is that in which we are created and born, according to which we are alike—man or woman or child, young or old. But once you are born, God adorns and dresses you up as another person. He makes you a child and me a father, one a master and another a servant, one a prince and another a citizen. Then this one is called a divine person, one who holds a divine office and goes about clothed in its dignity—not simply Hans or Nick, but the Prince of Saxony, father, or master. He is not talking about this person here, letting it alone in its own office and rule, as He has ordained it. He is talking merely about how each individual, natural person is to behave in relation to others.

Living together reasonably

Therefore, if we have an office or a governmental position, we must be sharp and strict, we must get angry and punish; for here we must do what God puts into our hand and commands us to do for His sake. In other relations, in what is unofficial, let everyone learn for himself to be meek toward everyone else, that is, not to deal with his neighbor unreasonably, hatefully, or vengefully, like the people whom they call "Headlong Hans." They refuse to put up with anything or to yield an inch, but they tear up the world and the hills and want to uproot the trees. They never listen to anyone nor excuse him for anything. They immediately buckle on their armor, thinking of nothing but how to take vengeance and hit back. This does not forbid the government to punish and to wreak vengeance in the name of God. But neither does it grant license to a wicked judge, burgomaster, lord, or prince to confuse these two persons and to reach beyond his official authority through personal malice or envy or hate or hostility, as commonly happens, under the cloak and cover of his office and legal right. This would be as though, in the name of the government, our neighbors wanted to take some action against us which they could not get away with otherwise.

He is talking here especially to His Jews, as He had begun. They always insisted that they were not supposed to suffer anything from a Gentile or stranger and that they had a right to avenge themselves immediately. For this purpose they cited sayings from Moses, such as Deuteronomy 28:13: "The Lord will make you the head, and not the tail; and you shall tend upward only, and not downward." There would be nothing wrong with this. But it means that if God Himself does this, then it is well done. It is one thing if He commands it and says, "I will do it," and quite another thing if we do it ourselves, without authorization. What He says should and must happen; what we say happens if it can, or maybe it does not happen at all. So you have no right to lay claim to this promise for yourself and to count on it when you want to do something which He ought to do, and you refuse to wait until He commands you to do it.

You see, then, that here Christ is rebuking those crazy saints who think that everyone is master of the whole world and is entitled to be delivered from all suffering, to roar and bluster and violently to defend his property. And He teaches us that whoever wants to rule and possess his property, his possessions, house, and home in peace, must be meek, so that he may overlook things and act reasonably, putting up with just as much as he possibly can. It is inevitable that your neighbor will sometimes do you injury or harm, either accidentally or maliciously. If he did it accidentally, you do not improve the situation by refusing or being unable to endure anything. If he did it maliciously, you only irritate him by your violent scratching and pounding; meanwhile he is laughing at you and enjoying

the fact that he is baiting and troubling you, so that you still cannot have any peace or quietly enjoy what is yours.

So select one of the two, whichever you prefer: either to live in human society with meekness and patience and to hold on to what you have with peace and a good conscience; or boisterously and blusterously to lose what is yours, and to have no peace besides. There stands the decree, "The meek shall inherit the earth." Just take a look for yourself at the queer characters who are always arguing and squabbling about property and other things. They refuse to give in to anybody, but insist on rushing everything through headlong, regardless of whether their quarreling and squabbling costs them more than they could ever gain. Ultimately they lose their land and servants, house and home, and get unrest and a bad conscience thrown in. And God adds His blessing to it, saying, "Do not be meek, then, so that you may not keep your precious land, nor enjoy your morsel in peace."

Inheriting the land

But if you want to do right and have rest, let your neighbor's malice and viciousness smother and burn itself out. Otherwise you can do nothing more pleasing to the devil or more harmful to yourself than to lose your temper and make a racket. Do you have a government? Then register a complaint, and let it see to it. The government has the charge not to permit the harsh oppression of the innocent. God will also overrule so that His Word and ordinance may abide and you may inherit the land according to this promise. Thus you will have rest and God's blessing, but your neighbor will have unrest together with God's displeasure and curse. This sermon is intended only for those who are Christians, who believe and know that they have their treasure in heaven, where it is secure for them and cannot be taken away. Hence, they must have enough here, too, even though they do not have treasuries and pockets full of [money]. Since you know this, why let your joy be disturbed and taken away? Why cause yourself disquiet and rob yourself of this magnificent promise?

See now that you have three points with three rich promises. Whoever is a Christian must have enough of both the temporal and the eternal, though here he must suffer much both outwardly and inwardly, in the heart. On the other hand, because the worldlings refuse to endure poverty or trouble or violence, they neither have the kingdom of heaven nor enjoy temporal goods peacefully and quietly. You can read more about this in Psalm 37, which is the right gloss on this passage, richly describing how the meek are to inherit the land while the ungodly are to be exterminated.

Blessed are those who hunger and thirst for righteousness, for they shall be satisfied.

"Righteousness" in this passage must not be taken in the sense of that principal Christian righteousness by which a person becomes pious and acceptable to God. I have said before that these eight items are nothing but instruction about the fruits and good works of a Christian. Before these must come faith, as the tree and chief part or summary of a man's righteousness and blessedness, without any work or merit of his; out of which faith these items all must grow and follow. Therefore, take this in the sense of the outward righteousness before the world, which we maintain in our relations with each other. Thus, the short and simple meaning of these words is this: that man is righteous and blessed who continually works and strives with all his might to promote the general welfare and the proper behavior of everyone and who helps to maintain and support this by word and deed, by precept and example.

Now, this is also a precious point, embracing very many good works, but by no means a common thing. Let me illustrate with an example. If a preacher wants to qualify under this point, he must be ready to instruct and help everyone to perform his assigned task properly and to do what it requires. And when he sees that something is missing and things are not going right, he should be on hand to warn, rebuke, and correct by whatever method or means he can. Thus, as a preacher I dare not neglect my office. Nor dare the others neglect theirs, which is to follow my teaching and preaching. In this way the right thing is done on both sides. Now, where there are people who earnestly take it upon themselves to do right gladly and to be found engaged in the right works and ways, such people "hunger and thirst for righteousness." If this were the situation, there would be no rascality or injustice, but sheer righteousness and blessedness on earth. What is the righteousness of the world except that in his station everyone should do his duty? That means that the rights of every station should be respected—those of the man, the woman, the child, the manservant, and the maid in the household, the citizen of the city in the land. And it is all contained in this, that those who are charged with overseeing and ruling other people should execute this office diligently, carefully, and faithfully, and that the others should also render their due service and obedience to them faithfully and willingly.

A holy passion

It is not by accident that he uses the term "hunger and thirst for righteousness." By it He intends to point out that this requires great earnestness, longing, eagerness, and unceasing diligence and that where this hunger and thirst [are] lacking, everything will fail. The reason is that there are too many great hindrances. They come from the devil, who is blocking and barricading the way everywhere. They also come from the world—that is, his children—which is so wicked that it cannot stand a pious man who wants to do right himself or to help other people do so, but plagues him in every way, [so] that he finally becomes tired and perplexed over the whole business. It is painful to see how shamefully people behave, and to get no reward for pure kindness except ingratitude, contempt, hate, and persecution. For this reason, many people who could not stand the sight of such evil conduct finally despaired over it, ran away from human society into the desert, and became monks, so that the saying has repeatedly been verified: "Despair makes a man a monk."[6] A person may not trust himself to make his own living and run into the monastery for his belly's sake, as the great crowd has done; otherwise a person may despair of the world and not trust himself in it, either to remain pious or to help people.

But this is not hungering and thirsting for righteousness. Anyone who tries to preach or rule in such a way that he lets himself become tired and impatient and be chased into a corner will not be of much help to other people. The command to you is not to crawl into a corner or into the desert, but to run out, if that is where you have been, and to offer your hands and your feet and your whole body, and to wager everything you have and can do. You should be the kind of man who is firm in the face of firmness, who will not let himself be frightened off or dumbfounded or overcome by the world's ingratitude or malice, who will always hold on and push with all the might he can summon. In short, the ministry requires a hunger and thirst for righteousness that can never be curbed or stopped or sated, one that looks for nothing and cares for nothing except the accomplishment and maintenance of the right, despising everything that hinders this end. If you cannot make the world completely pious, then do what you can. It is enough that you have done your duty and have helped a few, even if there be only one or two. If others will not follow, then in God's name let them go. You must not run away on account of the wicked, but rather conclude, "I did not undertake this for their sakes, and I shall not drop it for their sakes. Eventually some of them might come around; at least there might be fewer of them, and they may improve a little."

A promise of satisfaction

Here you have a comforting and certain promise, with which Christ allures and attracts His Christians: "Those who hunger and thirst for righteousness shall be filled." That is, they will be recompensed for their hunger and thirst by seeing that their work was not in vain and that at last a little flock has been brought around who have been helped. Although things are not going now as they would like and they have almost despaired over it, all this will become manifest, not only here on earth, but even more in the life hereafter, when everyone will see what sort of fruit such people have brought by their diligence and perseverance. For example, a pious preacher has snatched many souls out of the jaws of the devil and brought

---

6. Part of a medieval proverb: "Despair makes a man three things—a monk, a physician, or a soldier."

them to heaven; or a pious, faithful ruler has helped many lands and people, who testify that he has done so and who praise him before the whole world.

The counterfeit saints are exactly the opposite. Because of their great sanctity they forsake the world and run into the desert, or they sneak away into a corner somewhere to escape the trouble and worry that they would otherwise have to bear. They do not want to pay attention to what is going on in the world. Never once do they think of the fact that they should help or advise other people with teaching, instruction, warning, reproof, correction, or at least with prayers and sighs to God. Yes, it even disgusts and grieves them when other people become pious; for they want to be thought of as the only ones who are holy so that anyone who wants to get to heaven has to buy their good works and merits from them. In brief, they are so full of self-righteousness that they look down their noses at other poor sinners. Just so in Luke 18:11 the great pharisee in his intoxication looks down at the poor publican and spits on him. He is so much in love with himself that he pays court to God and thanks Him that he alone is pious and other people are bad.

Note that these are the people against whom Christ is speaking here, the shameful, proud, and self-sufficient spirits, who are tickled, pleased, and overjoyed over the fact that other people are not pious, whereas they ought to pity them, sympathize with them, and help them. All they can do is to despise, slander, judge, and condemn everyone else; everything must be stench and filth except what they themselves do. But going out to admonish and help a poor, frail sinner—this they avoid as they would avoid the devil. Hence they will have to hear again what Christ cries out against them in Luke 6:25, "Woe to you that are full, for you shall hunger." As those who now hunger and thirst shall be filled, so these others must hunger forever; though they are full and sated now, no one has ever got any benefit from them or been able to praise them for ever helping anyone or setting him aright. There you have a summary of the meaning of this passage, which, as I have said, embraces many good works, indeed, all the good works by which a man may live right by himself in human society and help to give success to all sorts of offices and stations.

Blessed are the merciful, for they shall obtain mercy.

This is also an outstanding fruit of faith, and it follows well upon what went before. Anyone who is supposed to help other people and to contribute to the common weal and success should also be kind and merciful. He should not immediately raise a rumpus and start a riot if something is missing or if things do not go as they should, as long as there is still some hope for improvement. One of the virtues of counterfeit sanctity is that it cannot have pity or mercy for the frail and weak, but insists on the strictest enforcement and the purest selection; as soon as there is even a minor flaw, all mercy is gone, and there is nothing but fuming and fury. Saint Gregory also teaches us how to recognize this when he says, "True justice shows mercy, but false justice shows indignation." True holiness is merciful and sympathetic, but all that false holiness can do is to rage and fume. Yet it does so, as they boast, "out of zeal for justice"; that is, it is done through love and zeal for righteousness.

The whole world is being forced to the conclusion that they have been carrying on their mischief and violence under the lovely and excellent pretext and cover of doing it for the sake of righteousness. In the same way, both in the past and in the present, they have been exercising their enmity and treachery against the Gospel under the guise of defending the truth and exterminating heresy. For this they want God to crown them and to elevate them to heaven, as a reward for those who out of great thirst and hunger for righteousness persecute, strangle, and burn His saints.

They want to make the claim and to give the impression, even more than the true saints, that they hunger and thirst for righteousness. They put up such a good front and use such beautiful words that they think even God Himself will not know any better. But the noble tree is known by its fruits. When they should demand justice, that is, the proper administration of both the spiritual and the temporal realm, they do not do so. It never enters their mind to instruct and improve anyone. They themselves live in continual vice; and if anyone denounces their behavior or does not praise it and do as they want, he must be a heretic and let himself be damned. You see, that is how it is with every counterfeit saint. His self-made holiness makes him so proud that he despises everyone else and cannot have a kind and merciful heart.

Therefore, this is a necessary warning against such abominable saints. If a man deals with his neighbor in an effort to help and correct him in his station and way of life, he should still take care to be merciful and to forgive. In this way people will see that your aim really is righteousness and not the gratification of your own malice and anger; for you are righteous enough to deal in a friendly and gentle manner with the man who is willing to forsake his unrighteousness and improve himself, and you tolerate and endure his fault or weakness until he comes around. But if you try all this and find no hope for improvement, then you may give him up and turn him over to those whose duty it is to punish.

A spirit of forgiveness and helpfulness

Now, this is the one aspect of mercy, that one gladly forgives the sinful and the frail. The other is to do good also to those who are outwardly poor or in need of help; on the basis of Matthew 25:35 we call these "works of mercy." The arrogant Jewish saints knew nothing about this aspect either. There was nothing in them but ice and frost—yes, a heart as hard as a block of stone—and not a single loving drop of blood that took pleasure in doing good for a neighbor, nor any mercy that forgave sin. All they were concerned about and thought about was their own belly, even though another man might have been starving to death. Thus, there is much more mercy among public sinners than there is in such a saint. This is how it has to be; for they praise only themselves and regard only themselves as holy, despising everyone else as worthless. They suppose that the whole world must serve them and give them plenty, while they are under no obligation to render anyone any service.

Hence, this sermon and exhortation seems contemptible and useless to such saints. The only pupils it finds are those who already cling to Christ and believe in Him. They know of no holiness of their own. On the basis of the preceding items they are poor, miserable, meek, really hungry and thirsty; they are inclined not to despise anyone, but to assume and to sympathize with the need of everyone else. To them applies the comforting promise, "It is well with you who are merciful. For you will find pure mercy in turn, both here and hereafter, and a mercy which inexpressibly surpasses all human kindness and mercy." There is no comparison between our mercy and God's, nor between our possessions and the eternal possessions in the kingdom of heaven. So pleased is He with our kindness to our neighbor that for one [small coin] He promises us a hundred thousand [pieces of gold] if we have need of them, and for a drink of water, the kingdom of heaven (Matt. 10:42).

Receiving what we give

Now, if anyone will not let himself be moved by this wonderful and comforting promise, let him turn the page and hear another judgment: "Woe and curses upon the unmerciful, for no mercy shall be shown to them." At the present time the world is full of people, among the nobles and city people and peasants, who sin very grievously against the dear Gospel. Not only do they refuse to give support or help to poor ministers and preachers, but besides they commit theft and torment against it wherever they can, and act as if they meant to starve it out and chase it out of the world. Meanwhile they go along quite smugly, supposing that God must keep quiet about it and approve of everything they do. But it will hit them someday. I am afraid that someone will come along who will make a prophet out of me—for I have given ample warning—and treat them mercilessly, taking away their reputation and their property, their body and their life, so that the Word of God might remain true and so that he who refuses to show or to have mercy might experience endless wrath and eternal displeasure. As Saint James also says, "Judgment without mercy will be spoken over the one who has shown no mercy" (James 2:13). At the Last Day, therefore, Christ will also cite this lack of mercy as the worst injury done to Him, whatever we have done out of a lack of mercy. He Himself will utter the curse, "I was hungry and thirsty, and you gave Me no food, you gave Me no drink. Depart from Me, therefore, you cursed, into eternal hell-fire" (Matt. 25:41, 42). He warns and exhorts us faithfully, out of sheer grace and mercy. Whoever does not want to accept this, let him choose the curse and eternal damnation. Think of the rich man in Luke 16; daily he saw poor Lazarus lying before his door full of sores, yet he did not have enough mercy to give him a bundle of straw or to grant him the crumbs under his table. But look how terribly he was requited; in hell he would gladly have given a hundred thousand guldens [pieces of gold] for the privilege of boasting that he had given him a thread.

Blessed are those of a pure heart, for they shall see God.

This item is rather obscure, and not very intelligible to us who have such coarse, carnal hearts and minds. It is also hidden from all the sophists, who have the reputation of being most learned, none of them can say what it means to have a "pure heart," much less what it means to "see God." With mere dreams and random thoughts they walk around things of which they have no experience. Therefore, we must look at these words according to the Scriptures and learn to understand them correctly.

They have imagined that having a pure heart means for a man to run away from human society into a corner, a monastery, or a desert, neither thinking about the world nor concerning himself with worldly affairs and business, but amusing himself only with heavenly thoughts. By this delusive doctrine they have not only beguiled and dangerously deceived themselves and other people, but have even committed the murderous crime of calling "profane" the act and stations which the world requires and which, as a matter of fact, God Himself has ordained. But Scripture speaks of this pure heart and mind in a manner that is completely consistent with being a husband, loving wife and children, thinking about them and caring for them, and paying attention to other matters involved in such a relationship. For God has commanded all of this. Whatever God has commanded cannot be profane (Acts 10:15); indeed it must be the very purity with which we see God. For example, when a judge performs his official duty in sentencing a criminal to death, that is not *his* office and work but God's. If he is a Christian, therefore, this is a good, pure, and holy work, one he could not do if he did not already have a pure heart. In the same way it must be regarded as a pure work and pure heart when a servant in the household does a dirty and repulsive job, like hauling manure or washing and cleaning children. Hence, it is a shameful perversion to disparage the relationships covered by the Ten Commandments this way and to gape at other special and showy works. As though God did not have as pure a mouth or eyes as we, or as pure a heart and hand when He creates both man and woman! Then how can such works and thoughts make a heart impure? This is the blindness and foolishness that comes upon men who despise the Word of God and who determine purity only by the outward mask and the show of works. Meanwhile, they are causing trouble with their own wandering thoughts . . . as though they wanted to climb up to heaven and grope for God, until they break their own necks in the process.

Let us understand correctly, then, what Christ calls a "pure heart." Note again that the target and object of this sermon were principally the Jews. They did not want to suffer, but sought a life of ease, pleasure, and joy; they did not want to hunger nor to be merciful, but to be smug in their exclusive piety while they judged and despised other people. In the same way, their holiness also consisted in outward cleanliness of body, skin, hair, clothes, and food, so that they did not dare to have even a speck on their clothing; if anyone touched a dead body, or had a scab or a rash on his body, he did not dare to approach other people. This is what they called "purity." "But that does not do it," says Christ, "the ones I praise are those who take pains to have a pure heart." So He says in Matthew 23:25, "You cleanse the outside of the cup and of the plate, but inside you are full of extortion and rapacity." Again, "You are like whitewashed tombs, which outwardly appear beautiful, but within they are full of dead men's bones and all uncleanness" (Matt. 23:27). This is the way it is with our clergy today. Outwardly they lead a decent life, and in the churches everything is conducted with such excellent taste and formality that it is beautiful to behold. But He does not ask for such purity. He wants to have the heart pure, though outwardly the person may be a drudge in the kitchen, black, sooty, and grimy, doing all sorts of dirty work.

Then what is a pure heart? In what does it consist? The answer can be given quickly, and you do not have to climb up to heaven or run to a monastery for it, establishing it with your own ideas. You should be on your guard against any ideas that you call your own, as if they were just so much mud and filth. And you should realize that when a monk in the monastery is sitting in deepest contemplation, excluding the world from his heart altogether, and thinking about the Lord God the way he himself paints and imagines Him, he is actually sitting—if you will pardon the expression—in the dung, not up to his knees but up to his ears. For he is proceeding on his own ideas without the Word of God; and that is sheer deception and delusion, as Scripture testifies everywhere.

Following God's standard

What is meant by a "pure heart" is this: one that is watching and pondering what God says and replacing its own ideas with the Word of God. This alone is pure before God, yes, purity itself, which purifies everything that it includes and touches. Therefore, though a common laborer, a shoemaker, or a blacksmith may be dirty and sooty or may smell because he is covered with dirt and pitch, still he may sit at home and think, "My God has made me a man. He has given me my house, wife, and child and has commanded me to love them and to support them with my work." Note that he is pondering the Word of God in his heart; and though he stinks outwardly, inwardly he is pure incense before God. But if he attains the highest purity so that he also takes hold of the gospel and believes in Christ—without this, that purity is impossible—then he is pure completely, inwardly in his heart toward God and outwardly toward everything under him on earth. Then everything he is and does, his walking, standing, eating, and drinking, is pure for him; and nothing can make him impure. So it is when he looks at his own wife or fondles her, as the patriarch Isaac did (Gen. 26:8), which a monk regards as disgusting and defiling. For here he has the Word of God, and he knows that God has given her to him. But if he were to desert his wife and take up another, or neglect his job or duty to harm or bother other people, he would no longer be pure; for that would be contrary to God's commandment.

But so long as he sticks to these two—namely, the Word of faith toward God, which purifies the heart, and the Word of understanding, which teaches him what he is to do toward his neighbor in his station—everything is pure for him, even if with his hands and the rest of his body he handles nothing but dirt. If a poor housemaid does her duty and is a Christian in addition, then before God in heaven she is a lovely and pure beauty, one that all the angels admire and love to look at. On the other hand, if the most austere Carthusian fasts and whips himself to death, if he does nothing but weep out of sheer devotion, if he never gives the world a thought, and yet lacks faith in Christ and love for his neighbor, he is nothing but a stench and a pollution, inwardly and outwardly, so that both God and the angels find him abhorrent and disgusting.

So you see that everything depends on the Word of God. Whatever is included in that and goes in accordance with it, must be called clean, pure, and white as snow before both God and man. Therefore, Paul says, "To the pure all things are pure"; and again, "To the corrupt and unbelieving nothing is pure" (Titus 1:15). Why is this so? Because both their minds and their consciences are impure. How does this happen? Because "they profess to know God, but with their deeds they deny it" (Titus 1:16). These are the people who are abominable in the sight of God. Look how horribly the apostle paints and denounces these great Jewish saints. Take, for example, a Carthusian monk. He thinks that if he lives according to his strict rule of obedience, poverty, and celibacy, if he is isolated from the world, he is pure in every way. What is this but his own way of thinking, growing up in his own heart without the Word of God and faith? In this way monks think that they alone are pure and that other people are impure. Saint Paul calls this an "impure mind," that is, everything they think and imagine. Since this delusion and idea is impure, everything they do on the basis of it must also be impure for them. As their mind is, so is their conscience too. Though they should and could be of help to other people, they have a conscience that functions on the basis of their ideas and is bound to their cowls, cloisters, and rules. They think that if they neglected this routine even for a moment to serve their neighbor and had relations with other people, they would be committing a most grievous sin and defiling themselves altogether. The cause of all this is that they do not acknowledge God's Word and creatures, although, as Saint Paul says, "With their mouths they profess that they do" (Titus 1:16). If they knew the means and the purpose of their creation by God, they would not despise these other stations nor exalt their own so highly; they would recognize the purity of these as the works and creatures of God, and would honor them, willingly remain in them, and be of service to their neighbor. That would be the true recognition of God, both in His Word and in His creatures, and the true purity of both heart and conscience, which comes to this faith and conclusion: whatever God does and ordains must be pure and good. For He makes nothing impure, and He consecrates everything through the Word which He has attached to every station and creature.

Avoiding humanity's false ideas

Therefore, be on guard against all your own ideas if you want to be pure before God. See to it that your heart is founded and fastened on the Word of God. Then you will be purer than all the Carthusians and saints in the world. When I was young, people used to take pride in this proverb: "Enjoy being alone, and your heart will stay pure."[7] In support of it they would cite a quotation from Saint Bernard, who said that whenever he was among people, he defiled himself. In the lives of the fathers we read about a hermit who would not let anyone come near him or talk to him, because, he said, "The angels cannot come to anyone who moves around in human society." We also read about two others, who would not let their mother see them. She kept watch, and once she caught them. Immediately they closed the door and let her stand outside for a long time crying; finally they persuaded her to go away and to wait until they would see each other in the life hereafter.

This is what they call a noble deed, the highest kind of sanctity and the most perfect kind of purity. But what was it really? Here is the Word of God: "Honor your father and your mother" (Ex. 20:12). If they had regarded this as holy and pure, they would have shown their mother and their neighbor all honor, love, and friendship. On the contrary, they followed their own ideas and a holiness they chose for themselves; hence they isolated themselves from them, and by their very effort to be most pure they most shamefully profaned themselves before God. As though even the most desperate scoundrels could not have such thoughts and put on such a show that people would have to say, "These are living saints! They can despise the world and have to do only with angels." With angels all right—from the abyss of hell! The angels like nothing more than to watch us deal with the Word of God; with such people they

---

7. This proverb is the first half of a medieval rhyme that Luther was fond of quoting in his criticisms of monasticism.

enjoy dwelling. Therefore, leave the angels up there in heaven undisturbed. Look for them here on earth below, in your neighbor, father and mother, children, and others. Do for these what God has commanded, and the angels will never be far away from you.

I have said this to help people evaluate this matter correctly and not go so far away to look for it as the monks do. They have thrown it out of the world altogether and stuck it into a corner or a cowl. All this is stench and filth and the devil's real dwelling. Let it be where God has put it, in a heart that clings to God's Word and that regards its tasks and every creature on the basis of it. Then the chief purity, that of faith toward God, will also manifest itself outwardly in this life. Everything will proceed from obedience to the Word and command of God, regardless of whether it is physically clean or unclean. I spoke earlier of a judge who has to condemn a man to death, who thus sheds blood and defiles himself with it. A monk would regard this as an abominably impure act, but Scripture says it is the service of God. In Romans 13:4 Paul calls the government, which bears the sword, "God's servant." This is not its own work and command, but His, which He imposes on it and demands from it.

A promise of perception

Now you have the meaning of "pure heart": it is one that functions completely on the basis of the pure Word of God. What is their reward; what does He promise to them? "They shall see God." A wonderful title and an excellent treasure! But what does it mean to "see God"? Here again the monks have their own dreams. To them it means sitting in a cell and elevating your thoughts heavenward, leading a "contemplative life," as they call it in the many books

they have written about it. That is still a far cry from seeing God, when you come marching along on your own ideas and scramble up to heaven, the way the sophists, schismatic spirits, and crazy saints insist on using their own brains to measure and master God together with His Word and works. But if you have a true faith that Christ is your Savior, then you see immediately that you have a gracious God. For faith leads you up and opens up the heart and will of God for you. There you see sheer, superabundant grace and love. That is exactly what it means "to see God," not with physical eyes, with which no one can see Him in this life, but with faith, which sees His fatherly, friendly heart, where there is no anger or displeasure. Anyone who regards Him as angry is not seeing Him correctly, but has pulled down a curtain and cover, more, a dark cloud over His face. But in scriptural language "to see His face" means to recognize Him correctly as a gracious and faithful Father, on whom you can depend for every good thing. This happens only through faith in Christ.

Therefore, if according to God's Word and command you live in your station with your husband, wife, child, neighbor, or friend, you can see God's intention in these things; and you can come to the conclusion that they please Him, since this is not your own dream, but His Word and command, which never deludes or deceives us. It is a wonderful thing, a treasure beyond every thought or wish, to know that you are standing and living in the right relation to God. In this way not only can your heart take comfort and pride in the assurance of His grace, but you can know that your outward conduct and behavior is pleasing to Him. From this it follows that cheerfully and heartily you can do and suffer anything, without letting it make you fearful or despondent. None of this is possible for those who lack this faith and pure heart guided only by God's Word. Thus, all the monks have publicly taught that no one can know whether or not he is in a state of grace.[8] It serves them right that because they despise faith and true godly works and seek their own purity, they must never see God or know how they stand in relation to Him.

Ask one who has most diligently observed his canonical hours of prayer, celebrated Mass and fasted daily, whether he is also sure that this is pleasing to God. He must say he does not know, that he is doing it all as a risk: "If it succeeds, let it succeed." It is impossible for anyone to say anything else. None of them can make a boast and say, "God gave me this cowl, He commanded me to wear it, He ordered me to celebrate this Mass." Until now we have all been groping in such blindness as this. We performed many works, contributed, fasted, prayed our rosaries; and yet we never dared to say, "This work is pleasing to God; of this I am sure, and I would be willing to die for it." Hence, no one can boast that in all his life and activity he has ever seen God. Or if in his pride someone glorifies such works and thinks that God must be well disposed to them and reward him for them, he is not seeing God but the devil in place of God. There is no word of God to support him; it is all the invention of men, grown up in their own hearts. That is why it can never assure or pacify any heart, but remain hidden by pride until it comes to its final gasps, when it all disappears and brings on despair, so that one never gets around to seeing the face of God. But anyone who takes hold of the Word of God and who remains in faith can take his stand before God and look at Him as his gracious Father. He does not have to be afraid that He is standing behind him with a club; and he is sure that He is looking at him and smiling graciously, together with all the angels and saints in heaven.

You see, that is what Christ means by this statement, that only those who have such a pure heart see God. By this He cuts off and puts aside every other kind of purity. Where this kind is absent, everything else in a man may be pure; but it is worth nothing before God, and he can never see God. Where the heart is pure, on the other hand, everything is pure; and it does not matter if outwardly everything is impure, yes, if the body is full of sores, scabs, and leprosy.

Blessed are the peacemakers, for they shall be called the children of God.

With an excellent title and wonderful praise the Lord here honors those who do their best to try to make peace, not only in their own lives but also among other people, who try to settle ugly and involved issues, who endure squabbling and try to avoid and prevent war and bloodshed. This is a great virtue, too, but one that is very rare in the world and among the counterfeit saints. Those who are not Christians are both liars and murderers, as is their father, the devil (John 8:44). Therefore, they have no other goal than to stir up unrest, quarrels, and war. Thus, among the priests, bishops, and princes nowadays practically all we find are bloodhounds. They have given many evidences that there is

---

8. At the Council of Trent (Session VI, Canon 16), this was to become the official teaching of the Roman Catholic church, but in the following form: "If anyone says with absolute and infallible certainty that he will certainly have that great gift of perseverance until the end, unless he teaches this on the basis of special revelation, let him be anathema."

nothing they would rather see than all of us swimming in blood. If a prince loses his temper, he immediately thinks he has to start a war. Then he inflames and incites everyone, until there has been so much war and bloodshed that he regrets it and gives a few thousand [gold coins] for the souls that were killed. These are bloodhounds, and that is what they remain. They cannot rest until they have taken revenge and spent their anger, until they have dragged their land and people into misery and sorrow. Yet they claim to bear the title "Christian princes" and to have a just cause.

You need more to start a war than having a just cause. As we have said, this does not prohibit the waging of war; for Christ has no intention here of taking anything away from the government and its official authority, but is only teaching individuals who want to lead a Christian life. Still it is not right for a prince to make up his mind to go to war against his neighbor, even though, I say, he has a just cause and his neighbor is in the wrong. The command is "Blessed are the peacemakers." Therefore, anyone who claims to be a Christian and a child of God, not only does not start war or unrest; but he also gives help and counsel on the side of peace wherever he can, even though there may have been a just and adequate cause for going to war. It is sad enough if one has tried everything and nothing helps, and then he has to defend himself, to protect his land and people. Therefore, not "Christians" but "children of the devil" is the name for those quarrelsome young noblemen who immediately draw and unsheathe their sword on account of one word. Even worse are the ones that are now persecuting the Gospel and ordering the burning and murder of innocent

preachers of the Gospel, who have done them no harm but only good and have served them with body and soul. We are not talking about these right now, but only about those who claim that they are in the right and have a just cause, thinking that as high and princely personages they ought not to suffer, even though other people do.

This also means that if you are the victim of injustice and violence, you have no right to take the advice of your own foolish head and immediately start getting even and hitting back; but you are to think it over, try to bear it and have peace. If that is impossible and you cannot stand it, you have law and government in the country, from which you can seek legitimate redress. It is ordained to guard against such things and to punish them. Therefore, anyone who does violence to you sins not only against you but also against the government itself; for the order and command to maintain peace was given to the government and not to you. Therefore, leave the vengeance and punishment to your judge, who has the command; it is against him that your enemy has done wrong. If you take it upon yourself to wreak vengeance, you do an even greater wrong. You become guilty of the same sin as he who sins against the government and interferes with its duties, and by doing so you invalidate the justice of your own righteous cause. For the proverb says, "The one who strikes back is in the wrong, and striking back makes a quarrel."[9]

Making peace among others

Note that this is one demand that Christ makes here in opposition to those who are vengeful and violent. He gives the name "peacemakers," in the first place, to those who help make peace

---

9. A proverb cited by Luther.

among lands and people, like pious princes, counselors, or jurists, to people in government who hold their rule and reign for the sake of peace; and in the second place, to pious citizens and neighbors, who with their salutary and good tongues adjust, reconcile, and settle quarrels and tensions between husband and wife or between neighbors, brought on by evil and poisonous tongues. Thus, Saint Augustine boasts that when his mother Monica saw two people at odds, she would always speak the best to both sides. Whatever good she heard about the one, she brought to the other; but whatever evil she heard, that she kept to herself or mitigated as much as possible. In this way she often brought on a reconciliation. It is especially among womenfolk that the shameful vice of slander is prevalent, so that great misfortune is often caused by an evil tongue. This is the work of those bitter and poisonous brides of the devil, who when they hear a word about another, viciously make it sharper, more pointed, and more bitter against the others, so that sometimes misery and murder are the result.

All this comes from the shameful, demonic filth which naturally clings to us, that everyone enjoys hearing and telling the worst about his neighbor and it tickles him to see a fault in someone else. If a woman were as beautiful as the sun but had one little spot or blemish on her body, you would be expected to forget everything else and to look only for that spot and to talk about it. If a lady were famous for her honor and virtue, still some poisonous tongue would come along and say that she had once been seen laughing with some man and defame her in such a way as to eclipse all her praise and honor. These are really poisonous spiders that can suck out nothing but poison from a beautiful, lovely rose, ruining both the flower and

the nectar, while a little bee sucks out nothing but honey, leaving the roses unharmed. That is the way some people act. All they can notice about other people are the faults or impurities which they can denounce, but what is good about them they do not see. People have many virtues which the devil cannot destroy, yet he hides or disfigures them to make them invisible. For example, even though a woman may be full of faults and have no other virtue, she is still a creature of God. At least she can carry water and wash clothes. There is no person on earth so bad that he does not have something about him that is praiseworthy. Why is it, then, that we leave the good things out of sight and feast our eyes on the unclean things? It is as though we enjoyed only looking at—if you will pardon the expression—a man's behind, while God has covered the unpresentable parts of the body and, as Paul says, has given them "greater honor" (1 Cor. 12:24). We are so filthy that we only look for what is dirty and stinking, and wallow in it like pigs.

Children of our Father

You see, these are also real children of the devil, who gets his name from doing this. He is called *diabolus,* that is, a slanderer and reviler, who takes pleasure in shaming us most miserably and embittering us among ourselves, causing nothing but murder and misery and tolerating no peace or concord between brothers, between neighbors, or between husband and wife. I once heard of a case where a married couple lived together in such love and harmony that it was the talk of the whole town. When the devil was unable to undermine this in any other way, he sent an old hag to the wife, to tell her that her husband was having an affair with another woman and planned to kill her. Thus, she embittered the wife against her husband and advised her to hide a knife on her person in order to beat him to it. When the hag had done this, she went to the husband and told him the same, that his wife planned to murder him; and as proof of it, she said, he would find a knife next to her in bed at night. He found it, and he cut her head off with it. Whether this story is fact or fiction, it does show what such wicked and poisonous mouths can do, even to people who love each other deeply. Thus, they may rightly be called "the devil's mouths" or she-devils; for the devil, *diabolus*, means nothing else than a bitter, poisonous, evil mouth.

So be on your guard against such people, and neither listen nor pay attention to them. Learn to put the best interpretation on what you hear about your neighbor, or even to conceal it, so that you may establish and preserve peace and harmony. Then you can honorably bear the title "child of God" before the whole world and before the angels in heaven. You should let this honor draw and attract you; in fact, you should chase it to the end of the world, if need be, and gladly surrender everything you have for it. Now you have it offered to you here and spread out in front of you for nothing. There is nothing that you have to do or give for it, except that if you want to be a child of God, you must also show yourself to be one and do your Father's works toward your neighbor. This is what Christ, our Lord, has done for us by reconciling us to the Father, bringing us into His favor, daily representing us, and interceding on our behalf.

You do the same. Be a reconciler and a mediator between your neighbors. Carry the best to both sides; but keep quiet about the bad, which the devil has inspired, or explain it the best way you can. If you come to Margaret, do what is said of Monica, Augustine's mother,

and say, "My dear Margaret, why are you so bitter? Surely she does not intend it so badly. All I notice about her is that she would like to be your dear sister." In the same way, if you meet Catherine, do the same thing. Then, as a true child of God, you will have made peace on both sides as far as possible.

But if you will or must talk about an evil deed, do as Christ has taught you. Do not carry it to others, but go to the one who has done it, and admonish him to improve. Do not act ostentatiously when you come and expose the person involved, speaking when you ought to be quiet and being quiet when you ought to speak. This is the first method: you should discuss it between yourself and your neighbor alone (Matt. 18:15). If you must tell it to others, however, when the first method does not work, then tell it to those who have the job of punishing, father and mother, master and mistress, burgomaster and judge. That is the right and proper procedure for removing and punishing a wrong. Otherwise, if you spread it among other people, the person remains unimproved; and the wrong remains unpunished, besides being broadcast by you and by others, so that everyone washes out his mouth with it. Look what a faithful physician does with a sick child. He does not run around among the people and broadcast it; but he goes to the child and examines his pulse or anything else that is necessary, not to gratify his pleasure at the cost of the child, nor to make fun of him, but with the good, honest intention of helping him. So we read about that holy patriarch Joseph in Genesis 37. He was tending the cattle with his brothers; and when he heard an evil report about them, he went and brought it to their father as their superior, whose task it was to investigate and to punish them because they would not listen to him.

But you may say, "Then why do you

yourself publicly attack the pope and others, instead of keeping the peace?" Answer: A person must advise and support peace while he can and keep quiet as long as possible. But when the sin is evident and becomes too widespread or does public damage, as the pope's teaching has, then there is no longer time to be quiet but only to defend and attack, especially for me and others in public office whose task it is to teach and to warn everyone. I have the commission and charge, as a preacher and a doctor, to see to it that no one is misled, so that I may give account of it at the Last Judgment (Heb. 13:17). So Saint Paul commands the preachers to watch and guard their whole flock against the wolves that were to appear among them (Acts 20:28). Thus, it is my duty to chastise public sinners so that they may improve, just as a judge must publicly condemn and punish evildoers in the performance of his office. As we have said often enough, Christ is not talking here about public office, but in general about all Christians insofar as we are all alike before God.

Blessed are those who are persecuted for righteousness' sake, for theirs is the kingdom of heaven.

I have said earlier that all these items and promises must be understood by faith in reference to things that are neither seen nor heard and that they are not talking about outward appearances. How can the poor and the mourners be said to look outwardly successful and blessed when, in addition, they have to suffer all sorts of persecution—all things that the whole world and our reason calls trouble and that they say should be avoided? Therefore whoever wants to have the blessedness and the possessions that Christ is talking about

here, must lift up his heart far above all senses and reason. He must not evaluate himself on the basis of his feelings, but he must argue this way, "If I am poor, then I am not poor. I am poor outwardly, according to the flesh; but before God, in faith, I am rich." Thus when he feels sad, troubled, and worried, he must not use this standard and say that he is not a blessed man. But he must turn himself over and say, "I feel sorrow, misery, and sadness of heart; but still I am blessed, happy, and settled on the basis of the Word of God." The situation in the world is the exact counterpart of this, for those who are called rich and happy are not. Christ calls out His "Woe!" against them and calls them unhappy (Luke 6:24, 25), although it appears that they are well off and having the greatest possible success. Therefore, they should lift up their thoughts above the riches and fun which they are having and say, "Yes, I am rich and living in the midst of pure fun. But too bad for me if I have nothing else; for there must certainly be plenty of trouble, misery, and sorrow in all this that will come over me before I feel it or know it." This applies to all these items; every one of them looks different before the world from the way it looks according to these words.

So far we have been treating almost all the elements of a Christian's way of life and the spiritual fruits under these two headings: first, that in his own person he is poor, troubled, miserable, needy, and hungry; second, that in relation to others he is a useful, kind, merciful, and peaceable man, who does nothing but good works. Now [Christ] adds the last: how he fares in all this. Although he is full of good works, even toward his enemies and rascals, for all this he must get this reward from the world: he is persecuted and runs the risk of losing his body, his life, and everything.

The world's reward

If you want to be a Christian, therefore, consider this well, lest you be frightened, lose heart, and become impatient. But be cheerful and content, knowing that you are not badly off when this happens to you. [Christ] and all the saints had the same experience, as He says a little later. For this reason He issues a warning beforehand to those who want to be Christians, that they should and must suffer persecution. Therefore you may take your choice. You have two ways before you—either to heaven and eternal life or to hell; either with Christ or with the world. But this you must know: if you live in order to have a good time here without persecution, then you will not get to heaven with Christ, and vice versa. In short, you must either surrender Christ and heaven, or make up your mind that you are willing to suffer every kind of persecution and torture in the world. Briefly, anyone who wants to have Christ must put in jeopardy his body, life, goods, reputation, and popularity in the world. He dare not let himself be scared off by contempt, ingratitude, or persecution.

The reason is this: the devil is a wicked and angry spirit. He will not and cannot stand seeing a man enter the kingdom of God. And if the man undertakes to do so, he blocks the way himself, arousing and attempting every kind of opposition he can summon. If you want to be God's child, therefore, prepare yourself for persecution, as the wise man says.[10] Paul says in 2 Timothy 3:12, "All who desire to live a godly life in Christ Jesus will be persecuted." And Christ Himself says, "The disciple should not be better off than his master. If they persecuted Me, they will also persecute you" (John 15:20). There is no other way out, and therefore, "Blessed are those who are persecuted for the sake of the kingdom of heaven," to let us know how to console ourselves. Otherwise, this would look outwardly like a troubling and unhappy situation, and it wears us down to be sitting constantly amid danger to life and property. But when faith takes over, we can lift ourselves up above this and think, "Nevertheless, Christ has said that I am blessed and well off. Because He has said so, I let it be my comfort and pleasure. The Word will make my heart great, yes, greater than heaven and earth. What are all my persecutors in comparison with this Man or His Word? If there are one or two persecuting us, there are many more (2 Kings 6:16) defending us, cheering us up, consoling us, and blessing us—yes, ten thousand angels over against one of them, together with all the saints, who act in concert with Christ and with God Himself." Hence, we must not be so coarse and cold, letting this Word lie around, but blow it up and magnify it, pitting it against every persecution. Then we shall see and learn that we should despise all our suffering as nothing at all when compared with this great consolation and eternal blessing.

But it is significant that He should add the phrase, "for righteousness' sake," to show that where this condition is absent, persecution alone will not accomplish this. The devil and wicked people also have to suffer persecution. Rascals often get into each other's hair, and there is no love lost between them. So one murderer persecutes another, and the Turk battles against the Tartar; but this does not make them blessed. This statement applies only to those who are persecuted for righteousness'

---

10. This appears to be a reference to John 15:20, which is explicitly quoted a few lines further; of course, the passage itself may have had a proverbial background.

sake. So also 1 Peter 4:15 says, "Let none of you suffer as a murderer or a thief or a wrongdoer." Therefore, bragging and yelling about great suffering is worthless without this condition. So the godless monks have deceived the poor people whom they have led away to be punished, consoling them with the statement that with their death they were paying for their sins. Beware of any death that is supposed to pay for your sin, for it belongs in the abyss of hell. First there must come righteousness and the death of Christ the Lord.

See to it, therefore, that you have a genuine divine cause for whose sake you suffer persecution, and that you are really convinced of it so that your conscience can take a stand and stick by it, even though the whole world should stand up against you. The primary thing is that you grasp the Word of God firmly and surely so that there can be no doubt or hesitation there. Suppose that the emperor, the bishops, or the princes were to forbid marriage, freedom in the choice of food, the use of both kinds in the sacrament, and the like, and were to persecute you for these things. Then you would have to see to it that your heart is convinced and persuaded that the Word of God has made these things free and unprohibited, that it even commands us to take them seriously and to stake our lives upon them. Then you can have the confidence to say, "This cause does not belong to me but to Christ, my Lord. For I have not concocted it out of my own head. I have not assumed or begun it on my own or at the advice or suggestion of any man. But it has been brought and announced to me from heaven through the mouth of Christ, who never deludes or deceives me but is Himself sheer truth and righteousness. At this Man's Word I will take the risk of suffering, of doing and forsaking whatever I should. All by itself, His Word will accomplish more to comfort and strengthen my heart than the raging and threatening of all the devils and of the world can accomplish to frighten me."

The Lord's reward

Who cares if a crazy prince or foolish emperor fumes in his rage and threatens me with sword, fire, or the gallows! Just as long as my Christ is talking dearly to my heart, comforting me with the promises that I am blessed, that I am right with God in heaven, and that all the heavenly host and creation called me blessed. Just let my heart and mind be ready to suffer for the sake of His Word and work. Then why should I let myself be scared by these miserable people, who rage and foam in their hostility to God but suddenly disappear like a puff of smoke or a bubble, as the prophet Isaiah says, "I, I am He that comforts you; who are you that you are afraid of man who dies, of the son of man who is made like grass, and have forgotten the Lord, who made you, who stretched out the heavens and laid the foundations of the earth?" (Is. 51:12, 13). That is to say, "He who comforts you and takes pleasure in you is almighty and eternal. When it is all over with them, He will still be sitting up there, and so will you. Why, then, let the threatening and fuming of a miserable, stinking bag of worms concern you more than this divine comfort and approval? Be grateful to God and happy in your heart that you are worthy of suffering this, as the apostles went forth leaping for joy over the fact that they were disgraced and beaten down (Acts 5:41).

You see, these words are a great blessing to us if only we receive them with love and thanks, since we have no shortage of persecution. But our great advantage is that our enemies themselves cannot condemn our cause and must acknowledge—no thanks to them!—that it is right and true. What is wrong is the fact that we are teaching it, for they refuse to learn or accept it from us. Such a thing is unprecedented and unheard of. What we suffer on this account, therefore, is a holy and blessed suffering, as they themselves must testify. This is no longer a human persecution, but a truly demonic one, when they say that we must not and dare not call it the Word of God but must keep our mouths shut and not preach unless first we go and fall at the pope's feet, asking for approval from him and from his masks.

So let us be all the more willing and happy to suffer everything they can do against us, since we have the strong and certain comfort and the great and glorious satisfaction that their own mouth confirms our teaching and our cause. In addition, we hear the wonderful and delightful promise here that we shall be well rewarded in heaven and that we should be happy and rejoice over this, as people who do not have to yearn for heaven but already have it. All they do by their persecution is to further this, actually driving and chasing us to heaven. Now tell me whether these simple, short words do not encourage you as much as the whole world can, and provide more comfort and joy than all the suffering and torture our enemies can inflict on us. We should not listen to them with only *half* an ear, but take them to heart and ponder them.

This applies to persecution with deeds and fists, involving person or property, when Christians are seized and tortured, burned, hanged, and massacred, as happens nowadays and has happened before. There is, in addition, another kind of persecution. It is called defamation, slander, or disgrace, involving our reputation and good name. In this way Christians have to suffer more than others. Now Christ discusses this.

Blessed are you when men revile you and persecute you and utter all kinds of evil against you falsely on My account.

This, too, is a great persecution and, as I have said, the real suffering of Christians, that they endure bitter slander and poisonous defamation. Though other people must also suffer persecution, violent and unjust treatment, still men are willing to let them keep their reputation and good name. So this is not yet really Christian suffering, which requires not merely all sorts of tortures and troubles, but more; their good name must be spit upon and slandered, and the world must boast loudly that in murdering the Christians it has executed the worst kind of criminal, whom the earth could no longer carry, and that it has done God the greatest and most acceptable service, as Christ says (John 16:2). Thus no name has ever appeared on earth so slanderous and disreputable as the name "Christian." No nation has ever experienced so much bitter opposition and attack by wicked and poisonous tongues as have the Christians.

Right now they are proving this in the slander, defamation, lies, deceit, vicious tricks, and wicked misinterpretations they have perpetrated against the dear Gospel and its preachers, such that one would die many times rather than endure these poisonous, malicious darts (Eph. 6:16). Along comes the pope with his thunderbolts, damning us to the ninth hell as the children of the devil. In the same way his retinue, the bishops and princes, rage and roar with such terrible blasphemies and slanders that our whole body trembles, and we would soon tire and give up if we did not have a comfort stronger and more powerful than all their malice and rage. Thus, we let them rage and blaspheme. They will only plague themselves, and their poisonous hatred and insatiable envy will give them a burning pain. But we are content and courageous. If they want to rage and storm, we can still laugh and be joyful.

Therefore, I say it again: anyone who wants to be a Christian should learn to expect such persecution from poisonous, evil, slanderous tongues, especially when they cannot do anything with their fists. He should let the whole world sharpen its tongue on him, aim at him, sting and bite. Meanwhile, he should regard all this with defiant contempt and laughter in God's name, letting them rage in the name of their god, the devil, and being firmly persuaded, as we have said above, that our cause is the right cause and is God's own cause. [Even] they [must] confirm [this]; even though they condemn us, they have to say it is the truth. Besides, before God our hearts and consciences are sure that our teaching is right. We are not teaching on the basis of our own brains, reason, or wisdom, or using this to gain advantage, property, or reputation for ourselves before the world. We are preaching only God's Word and praising only His deeds. Our enemies, on the other hand, brag about nothing but their own deeds, merits, and holiness. They persecute us for refusing to join them in this.

They do not persecute us for being adulterers, robbers, or thieves. In fact, they can tolerate the most desperate scoundrels and criminals in their midst. But they are raising such a hue and cry because we refuse to approve their teaching and life, because we praise nothing but the Gospel, Christ, faith, and truly good works, and because we do not suffer for ourselves but suffer everything for the sake of Christ the Lord. Therefore, we will sing it to the end with them. No matter how hard their head, ours is still harder. In short,

they must let that Man alone, whether they like it or not.

Rejoice and be glad, for your reward is great in heaven.

These are really sweet and comforting words. They should gladden and encourage our hearts against all kinds of persecution. Should not the dear Lord's Word and comfort be dearer and more important to us than that which comes from a helpless bag of worms, or the rage, threats, excommunication, curses, and lightning of the miserable pope, even though he deluged us with the very dregs and the whole hell of his wrath and cursing? For I hear my Lord Christ telling me that He is truly delighted, and commanding me to be happy about it. In addition, He promises me such a wonderful reward: the kingdom of heaven shall be mine and everything that Christ has, together with all the saints and all Christendom—in short, such a treasure and comfort that I should not trade it for all the possessions, joy, and music in the whole world, even though all the leaves and all the blades of grass were tongues singing my praises. This is not a Christian calling me "blessed," nor even an angel, but the Lord of all the angels, before whom they and all the creatures must kneel and adore. With all the other creatures, therefore, with the leaves and the grass, they must cheerfully sing and dance in my honor and praise.

And those who slander and curse me, what are they by comparison but nits and lousy paunches—if you will pardon the expression—so shameful that there is no name for them. If every creature, the leaves and the blades of grass in the forest, and the sand on the shore were all tongues to accuse and destroy them, what would all that be in comparison with a single word of this Man? His voice sounds clear enough to fill heaven and earth and to echo through them, silencing the slobbering coughs and the hoarse scratching of His enemies.

You see, that is how we should learn something about using these words for our benefit. They are not put here for nothing but were spoken and written for our strengthening and comfort. By them our dear Master and faithful Shepherd, or Bishop, arms us. Then we shall be unafraid and ready to suffer if for His sake they lay all kinds of torment and trouble upon us in both words and deeds, and we shall despise whatever is offensive to us, even though contrary to our own reason and heart.

For if we cling to our own thoughts and feelings, we are dismayed and hurt to learn that for our service, help, counsel, and kindness to the world and to everyone we should get no thanks except the deepest and bitterest hatred and cursed, poisonous tongues. If flesh and blood were in charge here, it would soon say, "If I am to get nothing else out of this, then let anyone who wants to, stick with the gospel and be a Christian! The world can go to the devil for help if that is what it wants!" This is the reason for the general complaint and cry that the gospel is causing so much conflict, strife, and disturbance in the world and that everything is worse since it came than it was before, when things moved along smoothly, when there was no persecution, and when the people lived together like good friends and neighbors.

But it says, "If you do not want to have the gospel or be a Christian, then go out and take the world's side. Then you will be its friend, and no one will persecute you. But if you want to have the gospel and Christ, then you must count on having trouble, conflict, and persecution wherever you go." The devil cannot bear it otherwise, nor will he stop egging people on against the gospel, so that all the world is incensed against it. Thus, at the present time peasants, city people, nobles, princes, and lords oppose the gospel from sheer cussedness, and even they do not know why.

So I say in reply to these idle talkers and grumblers, "Things neither can nor should run peacefully and smoothly. How could things run smoothly, when the devil is in charge, and is a mortal enemy of the gospel? There is good reason for this, too, since it hurts him in his kingdom, where he can feel it. If he were to let it go ahead unhindered, it would soon be all over and his kingdom would be utterly destroyed. But if he is to resist it and hinder it, he must rally all his art and power and arouse everything in his might against it. So do not hope for any peace and quiet so long as Christ and His gospel are in the midst of the devil's kingdom. And woe upon the peaceful and smooth situation that used to be, and upon those who would like to have it back! This is a sure sign that the devil is ruling with all his might and that no Christ is there. I am worried that it may be this way again and that the gospel may be taken away from us Germans all too soon, which is just what these rioters are struggling for now."

But we have the assurance that it is not our fault when there is trouble. It would give us heartfelt joy if everything went right. We have done our share. We have been teaching, warning, pleading, beseeching, and giving in, even to our enemies, offering them peace, and doing everything we should do. We have given help and counsel with all our might, at our own risk and disadvantage, tolerating what we should. Yet all we accomplish is shameful and poisonous persecution, slander, and abuse from men who will not stop till they have cooled their rage in our blood. Since the situation will never be different, we let them go ahead with their threatenings, fury, and blasphemy, and hold on to the comfort we have heard. We are sure that they cannot accomplish what they desire until they first topple Christ from heaven and make a liar out of Him, with all that He has said.

For Martin Luther the message of the gospel is the most glorious of all messages. It is the promise of God's love for man and His provision for his salvation. Luther's sermon on John 3:16 is rich in content. Any reader who desires to know the essence of the gospel will find an unsurpassed explanation in this fine message. Luther describes clearly the Incarnation, showing that Jesus was not two persons, but two natures—one human and one divine—in one person. He emphasizes that Christ was sent as the sacrifice for our sins and through His death the curse of death has been defeated. We appropriate the gift of God by believing in the Lord Jesus Christ. This, as Luther explains, is the gospel: We are made sons of God by faith alone.

CHAPTER FIVE

John 3:16

For God so loved the world.

Shortly before, Christ had said, "The Son of man must be lifted up, that whoever believes in Him may have eternal life." Now He says, "God so loved the world that He gave His only Son, that whoever believes in Him should not perish but have eternal life." What Christ said about the Son of man—that He must be lifted up—He now also says about the Son of God. He tells us that God's great love prompted Him to give His only Son. Earlier He said that Mary had given her Son, and now He says, "God the Father gave His Son to be crucified." God's Son and Mary's Son is only one Person. He appropriates both natures for the work of salvation and redemption from eternal death. John the evangelist always links the two natures, deity and humanity, together.

Two natures

Someone may ask, "How is it possible for the Son of man to save and to give eternal life?" Or, "How can it be that God's Son should be delivered to be crucified?" It sounds plausible that the Son of man might be crucified, but that He should bestow eternal life does not seem reasonable. And it seems just as incongruous that God's Son should die and give His life for the life of the world. But we must bear in mind that when we speak of Christ, we are thinking of His two natures in one person and that what is ascribed to the two natures is really comprehended in one person. Thus, I can very properly say that the Son of man created heaven and earth, just as I say that the Son of God is the Creator of heaven and earth. We dare not follow those heretics, the Nestorians, the ancestors of the Turks,[1] who alleged that only Mary's Son, not God's Son, died for us. For here we find it clearly stated and written, "God gave His Son for the world." And this Son is assuredly not only Mary's Son, born of Mary, but also the Son of God. And when Christ was delivered to Pilate to be crucified, and when Pilate led Him from the judgment hall, he took hold of the hand not only of the man Jesus but also of the Son of God, whom he crucified. Therefore, Saint Paul said, "If they had understood, they would not have crucified the King of glory" (1 Cor. 2:8), whom all creatures usually adore. Thus, it was God's Son who was conceived by the Virgin Mary, who suffered and died, was buried, descended into hell, and rose again from the dead.

This is the way to interpret expressions of the apostles, bishops, and ancient teachers, "Oh, Thou Son of David!" Or, "Thou Son of Mary, have mercy on me!" "Oh, dear Jesus, born of the Virgin Mary, be gracious to me!" The words are a prayer to God and are the equivalent of, "Oh, Jesus, Thou Son of God, have mercy on me!" In these words you also

---

1. Nestorian Christians were indeed among those with whom Mohammed came into contact in his formative years. The Moslems also came into contact with Nestorians in Persia in the seventh century.

worship the Son of Mary, because the two natures are united in the one Christ.

One Son

Thus, the words of this text indicate that God gave His Son for us and that the Son of man died for us. There are not two Jesuses, the one coming from the Father and the other born of Mary. No, there is only one Jesus. Therefore, the ancient fathers said that the attributes of both natures are ascribed and imputed to the whole person of Christ "in the concrete," creating a "communication of properties," a union in which the attributes of the one nature are imparted to the other. Each nature, of course, has its own peculiar character. For instance, it is peculiar to the human nature of Christ to be born of the Virgin Mary. The divine nature has different attributes. But since the person of Christ cannot be divided, there is a communion, which enables one to say, "The infant Christ, who lies in the cradle and is suckled by the Virgin Mary, created heaven and earth." Also, "The Son of God who is with the Father from eternity nurses at His mother's breasts, is crucified, and dies." "For the communion of the natures also effects a communication of properties." The ancient fathers diligently taught this and wrote about it.

God incarnate

But now we have to make the practical application and learn why the person who is God and man came into the world. The Lord Christ teaches us this too, when He says that any believer in Him shall be delivered from eternal death and be assured of eternal life. It was not an angel, a principality, or any of the world's mighty who became incarnate and died for us—no, both the angelic and the human nature would have been too weak—but it was the divine nature that assumed humanity. It was Christ who adopted our flesh and blood that we might be saved through Him.

Now we see how gloriously the evangelist John speaks of Christ and of the sublime doctrine of our Christian faith: that Christ is both God and man. This is what John stresses in his Gospel. He says nothing about the necessity of good works for salvation, as the wicked pope does.

The Lord informed Nicodemus in an excellent sermon that no one will go to heaven or enter the kingdom of God unless he is born anew and believes in the serpent hanging on the cross, that is, believes in the Son of man, who was lifted up that all who believe in Him should not perish but have everlasting life. This is the new spiritual birth, the way to eternal life, namely, faith in the crucified Son of man. Now Christ stresses, and enlarges on, this theme in the fine sermon delivered to only one man, Nicodemus. It seems surprising that He should preach so beautifully to him. Yet His sermon is not in vain; it awakens in Nicodemus a love for Christ which does not only endure during the lifetime of Christ but lives on after His death (John 19:39). The end and aim of this sermon by Christ is the conversion of Nicodemus. The words, "For God so loved the world" do not need a lengthy commentary and exposition, for we preach on this text every year. Therefore our discussion will be brief.

After Christ has said, "As Moses lifted up the serpent in the wilderness, so must the Son of man be lifted up," He continues with the words, "For God so loved the world, that He gave His only Son, that whoever believes in Him should not perish but have eternal life." To astound Nicodemus, He repeats what He had said before. As though He wanted to say, "Dear Nicodemus, is it not wonderful that the Son of man is hanged on the cross and lifted up, and that the Son of man, born of the Virgin Mary, true man with body and soul, is also the Son of God? Is it not a miracle that the Son of man and the Son of God are both one Son? (For Christ relates the statement that whosoever believes in Him should not perish but have everlasting life to the Son of man and to the Son of God; this refers to both.) Thus, Nicodemus, I am preaching to you about very important matters which may well astonish you; for instance, about the necessity of the new birth. But still more amazing than this is the process of the new birth." It is, of course, out of the question for a man to re-enter his mother's womb to be born again. No, this is the procedure: God gave His only Son into death for us; that is how we are reborn. Does it not surprise you that for the sake of this rebirth God adopts such a wonderful plan and chooses His only Son—for He has no other—and lets Him become man, instead of selecting some angel or some patriarch? God does not confine Himself to giving us His Son in His incarnation, but He also delivers Him into death for us. He has Him lifted up as Moses lifted up the serpent. Isn't that wonderful? Isn't that medicine effective enough? Who would ever have had the boldness to ask for such a cure for death and sin? But such strong help and powerful medicine will work this for you.

Now you do not understand all this, and you are wondering about this demand for a new birth and about this deliverance from sin. You know full well that we are sinners and are lodged in the jaws of death. Hence, it must sound odd and strange to you that we are to conquer sin and death and need not fear God's stern judgment and His wrath. Yes indeed, it is strange. But now behold! What is God's plan? The answer would never have occurred to you.

He gave His Son.

Because of His divine wisdom, counsel, and mercy God gives His only begotten Son, who is also the Son of man, as a remedy against sin, death, and your old nature and birth. The Son is "given" to us by dying for us and being buried for us. That, I take it, is another miracle and one far greater. If you are astonished and regard it as incredible that a man must be born anew, this greater wonder must amaze you still more. God loved a poor sinner so much that He gave him, not an angel or a prophet but His only Son. The way of His giving was that His Son became man, and the purpose of His giving was that He might be crucified. This you must learn; and after you have learned it and beheld these wonderful things, your heart will feel constrained to say, "This is truly miraculous! How is it possible?" But if you can accept and believe it, you will conclude, "After all, if God's Son is the cure and remedy for sin and death, why should I be surprised, since I know that God's Son is greater than sin, the devil, and my death?" Just believe it, and you will experience that He is greater. It is surely true that by my own strength I cannot banish death but must die even if I don a monk's cowl, join all the monastic orders and abide by their rules, go on pilgrimages, and perform all those good works on which they place their reliance. None of this is the correct prescription or medicine. But if I can believe in and accept this remedy, that God gives us His Son—not an ordinary son like Abraham, Isaac, and David, of whom God has many, but His only begotten Son—it is certain that this Son can effect a new birth in us and can, therefore, be a victor and conqueror of the devil. This is because God's Son is vastly greater than death, far stronger than sin and the devil. Through Him we have the grace of God rather than wrath, and whatever else we may need besides. If it puzzles you how a man is to be transferred from the devil's realm to the kingdom of God, God's gift of His Son must surprise you still more. And if you accept this in faith, you will no longer be puzzled about the other. If we have the Son of God, who faces death and opposes the devil on our behalf, on our side, let the devil rage as he will. If the Son of God died for me, let death consume and devour me; for he will surely have to return and restore me, and I will stand my ground against him. Christ died; death devoured the Son of God. But in doing so death swallowed a thorn and had to get rid of it. It was impossible for death to hold Him. For this person is God; and since both God and man in one indivisible person entered into the belly of death and the devil, death ate a morsel that ripped [its] stomach open.

Defeating death

It was the counsel of God the Father from eternity to destroy death, ruin the kingdom of the devil, and give the devil a little pill which he would gleefully devour, but which would create a great rumpus in his belly and in the world. Now the Lord wants to say, "Dear Nicodemus, it is miraculous, as you see, that God should spend such a great and precious treasure for our rebirth. For is it a miracle that I, the Son of man and the Son of God in one person, am sacrificed to death and enter the jaws of death and the devil? But I shall not remain there. Not only will I come forth again, but I will also rip open death's belly; for the poison is too potent, and death itself must die."

Christ wants to prevent us from thinking of Him as separate from the Father. Therefore He again directs our mind from Himself to the Father and says that the Father's love for us is just as strong and profound as His own, which is reflected in His sacrificial death. He wants to say, "Whoever beholds the Father's love also beholds Mine; for Our love is identical. I love you with a love that redeems you from sin and death. And the Father's love, which gave you His only Son, is just as miraculous."

Furthermore, Christ tells us how He destroys death and how I am rescued from death. He will be death's venom. Death and [the] law, to be sure, will condemn Him. Therefore, He will have to die and be buried. But He will rise again from the dead. And where He is now, the devil will have to retreat. But how do I approach this Savior and Redeemer? By means of cowls or monastic orders and rules? No! Just cling to the Son in faith. He conquered death and the devil, and He slit the devil's belly open. He will reign and rule again, even though He was crucified under Annas and Caiaphas. Therefore, attach yourself to Him, and you will tear through death and devil; for this text assures us, "Whoever believes in Him shall have eternal life." Accept the truth of this miracle of God's love for the world, and say, "I believe in the Son of God and of Mary, who was lifted up and nailed to the cross." Then you will experience the new birth; for death and sin will no longer accuse, harm, and injure you. Whoever believes in the Son will have eternal life. Cling to His neck or to His garment; that is, believe that He became man and suffered for you. Cross yourself and say, "I am a Christian and will conquer." And you will find that death is vanquished. In Acts 2:24 Saint Peter says that death was not able to hold Christ, since deity and humanity were united in one person. In the same way we, too, shall not remain in death; we shall destroy death, but only if we remain steadfast in faith and cling to death's Destroyer.

In John 17:11 Christ prays, "That they may be one in Me, as I and the Father are one." If I cling to Christ in true faith and remain in Him, it is impossible for sin and death to accuse and condemn me; for Christ has conquered them. This, however, is accomplished, not by our strength but by faith in Him. In this way we, like pious lambs, remain resting in the arms of Christ, the faithful Shepherd.

Overcoming fear by faith

Therefore, whoever is a Christian and takes hold of Christ by faith is not terrified by the devil; nor is he cowed by sin and death. Even though he feels his sins and is frightened and saddened by them, he nevertheless overcomes this feeling and is not subdued; for he will be quick to say, "I believe in the Son of God and of Mary. He is the devil's venom and death; but at the same time He is my salvation, my remedy, and my life."

We read an excellent story about a certain nun. (In every station of life God preserves some, keeps them in faith, and saves them.) This nun was very much troubled and assaulted by thoughts of the devil and of sin. Of course, all but those who serve their own belly feel God's wrath and judgment; this accounts for the fact that people will take refuge in the saints. Now, since this little nun was filled with terror at the thought of the wrath of God and wanted to be saved, she made it a habit to say whenever the devil troubled her, "Devil, let me alone. I am a Christian!" And the devil had to leave her. On the surface this seems to be a simple technique and easy to learn. But it is necessary that the words be inspired by faith, as those of this little nun were. For the devil did not particularly fear the words, "I am a Christian." No, it was her faith, the fact that she firmly relied on Christ and said, "I am baptized on Christ, and I entrust myself solely to Him; for He is my life, salvation, and wisdom." Wherever such words proceed from faith, they generate a completely fiery atmosphere, which burns and pains the devil so that he cannot tarry. But if a person speaks without warmth about matters pertaining to God and salvation, as the common man does, then the devil merely laughs. But if your words are aglow in your heart, you will put the devil to flight. For then Christ is present. As we read in Hosea 13:14, "He devours death and destroys it"; and here He declares, "Whoever believes in Me shall not perish but have everlasting life." If the believer is to have eternal life, it is implied that he is also free from sin and death. When the devil hears the name of Christ, he flees, because he cannot bear it. But if he does not feel the presence of Him who has destroyed him, he casts man into hell.

I am saying this for the sake of those who think that the mere recital of the words suffices, without any faith in the heart. Thus, many hear these words spoken and also resolve to use them on occasion. I want to tell you a story about this. An ungodly medical doctor in Italy was once asked to stand as godfather for an infant. During the rite of baptism he heard the beautiful words of institution, how the infant became an heir of salvation through Christ, and how the church implored God that Christ would accept this infant. After the baptism, when he pondered these words at home, he became very sad and depressed. As it happened, he had invited guests to dine with him that evening. When the guests noticed his melancholy mood, they asked him why he sighed and why he seemed so troubled in his mind. Then he revealed his feelings and said, "I stood as godfather today and heard some great and wonderful words. If I had the assurance that I was baptized in the same way, I would never again be terrified by the devil." One of the guests was an old man who had actually been godfather at this doctor's baptism. He spoke up, "Now my dear doctor, my dear doctor, you need not be in doubt on that score. For I was present in your baptism. I stood as godfather for you, and I can testify that you, too, were baptized this way." This made the doctor very happy. A little later he rose from the table and went to his room. There he noticed two large, long goat's horns projecting from a wall that had previously been bare. In an attempt to torment the doctor, the devil had assumed the guise of these horns. Now, when the doctor saw this, the thought flashed to him, "But I am baptized; I am a Christian. So why should I fear the devil?" Armed with that faith, he rushed to the wall and broke off one of the horns. Then he hurried back to his guests and joyfully related to them what had happened in the room. The guests all arose from the table and hurried into his room to see whether the one horn was still visible. Lo and behold, they found two horns again protruding from the wall. One of the guests wanted to show off and imitate his host. He said, "Well, I am a Christian too!" And with these words he dashed toward the wall, intending to break off one of the horns. The devil broke his neck and killed him. This guest [had] tried to make light of the whole matter to deck himself with glory. In consequence, his head was torn off, whereas the doctor, who took recourse to faith in the hour of trial, suffered no harm.

This story is undoubtedly credible. My purpose in narrating it is to impress the fact that one must learn not only to recite the words of holy Scripture by rote but also to believe them with one's heart and to remain steadfast in times of peril and in the hour of death. For there are many who speak the words, "I am a Christian," with their mouth but do not believe this in their heart. When trouble besets you, you will find out whether you take these words seriously. In days of sorrow take hold of the Word of God and of faith; pray, and say very fervently, "I am a Christian!" Then you will discover whether you really believe. When a person is not oppressed by sorrow, he has no occasion to perceive this. Callous people, who are not assailed by trouble or temptation, know nothing of this. The rebirth of which Christ speaks here is not acquired while dozing idly and comfortably behind the stove. If you are a Christian and really believe, join the nun in her words, "I am a Christian!" What is the result? You will find relief, and your mind will be at ease; and you will be able to thank God that the devil had to take to his heels. For he cannot withstand these words of fire.

Believing in God's miracle

Thus, it all depends on this great and grand miracle, that I believe that God gave His Son for us. If I do not doubt this, then I am able to say in the midst of my trials, "I concede, devil, that I am a sinner burdened with the old Adam and subject to the wrath of God. But what do you, devil, say about this: God so loved the world that He gave His only Son that all who believe in Him might not perish but have eternal life? These words I believe!" And you must speak these words in sincere faith. For Christ has passed through death and sin, and death was powerless to hold Him. And now Christ says, "If you believe in Me, death shall not devour you either. Even if death should hold you for three days or so, as he detained Me for three days in the earth and Jonah for three days in the belly of the whale, he shall nonetheless spew you out again." You might have reason to be surprised about all this—not only that you must be born anew but also that God so loved the world that He gave us a potent plaster, remedy, and syrup against sin, death, the devil, and hell, so that whoever lays that on his heart will not perish.

On the other hand, consider the abominable error of those who directed us to other methods, telling people, for instance, that they should retire into the desert, enter cloisters, or go on pilgrimages—and all this so that we might not perish but have eternal life. I, too, entered the monastery that I might not perish but have eternal life.[2] I wanted to follow my own counsel and help myself by means of the cowl. Truly, it is a vexing and troublesome business. In Turkey and in the papacy this doctrine is still rampant; the Jews teach the same thing. But it really comes from the mouth of the devil.

One might be tempted to ask, "Is it possible that so many can be mistaken about this?" The answer is that the Son of God is stronger than all the gates of hell (Matt. 16:18), also greater than all the monks and their cowls. Nicodemus, too, was curious to hear how he was to be reborn and saved from death. He asked how this was to happen. Jesus told him, "This is the way: the Son of man must be lifted up, and God's Son must be given into death, and man must believe in Him." Even if the world were to teem with monk's cowls and with monastic rules, even if the world were full of the ordinances of the pope, the Turks' Koran, or the Jews' laws, Christ would still be greater than all these. For He is still the Creator of heaven and earth and Lord over all creatures. His sacrifice for me was not Saint Francis or any other monk or the mother of Christ or Saint Peter or an angel or cowls and tonsures; it was a far more precious treasure. Salvation and deliverance from death call for a greater service than any human or any angel could render. Only God's only begotten Son can render it. The Son swallows up death.

Relying on Christ's merit

Our adversaries also read this text, but they do not understand it. We also had these words in the papacy, but we failed to comprehend them. Instead, our thoughts were directed solely to our works. And yet some took hold of these words in faith and were saved, like the nun who said, "I am a Christian." I once saw a monk who took a cross into his hands and remarked while the other monks were boasting of their good works, "I know of no merit of my own but only of the merit of Him who died for me on the cross." And in reliance on that merit he also died. In the papacy it was customary to admonish a dying monk to be mindful of his own merits and works and of those of others. And in that faith they died. But just as the pious monk died a blessed death, relying solely on the merit of Jesus Christ, so many a wretched criminal on the gallows has been delivered from sin and saved through faith.

That is how Saint Bernard was saved. He was an exemplary monk; he observed the rules of his order scrupulously, and he fasted so assiduously that his breath stank and no one could abide his presence. But on the threshold of death he exclaimed, "Oh, I have lived damnably! But heavenly Father, Thou hast given me Thy Son, who has a two-fold claim to heaven: first, from eternity, by reason of the fact that He is Thy Son; secondly, He earned heaven as the Son

---

2. Luther entered the monastery on July 17, 1505.

of man with His suffering, death, and resurrection. And thus He has also given and bestowed heaven on me." Thereby, Saint Bernard dropped out of the monastic role, forsook cowl and tonsure and rules, and turned to Christ; for he knew that Christ conquered death, not for Himself but for us men, that all who believe in the Son should not perish but have eternal life. And so Saint Bernard was saved.

These are golden words which must be preserved in Christendom; they alone make a person a Christian. You see how woefully those err who try to escape eternal damnation by means of their monkeries, cowls, and tonsures. Moreover, such people even offer their supererogatory works for sale and transfer them to others. This, I regret to say, is how we lived in the papacy. You young people, be grateful to God for your better insight, and learn these words well. For death and the devil are in league with the pope and with the Turks' Koran to delude the people into relying on their foul works for salvation. But salvation demands more than our good works; for not even the holiness of the angels sufficed. God's own Son had to be given to conquer death. Now heaven and the victory over death are not Christ's alone; whoever believes in Him is not to perish but shall have eternal life. On the other hand, whoever refuses to believe is eternally beyond help and rescue, as Christ points out later when He says, "He who does not believe is condemned already" (John 3:18).

Christ said to Nicodemus, "God so loved the world." Furthermore, He assured him that God did not send His Son to condemn the world. From these words we learned that God's Son and the Son of man are one person. We learned that the Son of man was hanged and lifted up as the serpent in the wilderness had been lifted up. This applies properly only to His human nature, since God cannot suffer and be crucified. And yet Christ says here that the Son of God was given into death and was crucified. From this we learn about the "communication of properties," the fact that the attributes of both natures pertain to the one person, that the attributes of both natures inhere in the one person. Despite the fact that Creator and creature are two disparate beings, as different from each other as nothing is from something or from everything, or as different as heaven and earth, still it is true that here they are united.

Accepting the testimony of Scripture

I am stressing this for a very good reason. Many heretics have arisen—and still more schismatic spirits will appear—who have assailed this article of faith and have been offended at the thought that God should suffer. The Godhead, they argued, is an eternal majesty, while humankind is only a temporal creature. They toyed with this article regarding the two natures in Christ most adroitly and alleged that Mary was not the mother of the Son of God, and that Christ, Mary's Son, is not the Son of God. They were offended by the two natures found in Christ. In place of the two natures they contrived to find two persons. According to holy Scripture, however, we declare that there are two natures in Christ but only one person and not two, and that this one person, God and man, suffered, that the Son of God and of Mary was crucified. A schismatic spirit may contradict this and say, "Ah, God cannot be crucified!" But tell them that this person, who is God and man, was crucified. Since God manages to harmonize this, we, of course, must harmonize it too and declare that Mary is Christ's mother not only according to His humanity, but that she is also the mother of the Son of God and that her Son is both God and man. This is the language Saint Paul employs in Hebrews 6:6, when he speaks of the false Christians who "crucify the Son of God on their own account and hold Him up to contempt." And in 1 Corinthians 2:8 he says, "If they had understood, they would not have crucified the Lord of glory." Since it is the language of Saint Paul and of holy Scripture that the Son of God and the King of glory was crucified, we can accept it without hesitation. Anyone who believes the Bible will not mutter a sound against it. We can also reverse the picture and say, "This Infant, born of Mary and suckled by her or lying in her lap, created heaven and earth." If someone were to interpose, "Well, what, after all, could such a little child create?" I reply, "This is what holy Scripture says." For instance, in Luke 2:11 we hear the dear angels sing at Christmas time, "To you is born this day in the city of David a Savior, who is Christ the Lord." That angelic song, in which Christ was called the Lord, was sung at a time when the Infant still clung to His mother's breast.

The fathers contended fervidly for this, maintaining against the heretics that there are two natures in Christ but not two persons, that there is only one Son. This is how Scripture speaks and how we, too, must speak. To be sure, Christ was crucified according to His humanity, and He created heaven and earth according to His divinity; but since this one person is God and man, it is proper to say that God's Son is the Creator of heaven and earth, and God's Son was also crucified. One dare not divide the person, leaving only the human nature; one must bear in mind that this person is also God. Thus Saint Hilary says, "When Christ suffered, the Logos was quiescent." If we fail to hold that the person who was crucified was both

God and man, we are eternally damned and lost. We must have a Savior who is more than a saint or an angel. If He were not superior to these, we would get no help from Him. But if He is God, then the treasure is so heavy that it not only outweighs and cancels sin and death but also gives eternal life. No mere human could acquire eternal life for us or overcome devil and death.

This is our Christian creed, and in conformity with it we confess, "I believe in Jesus Christ, His only Son, our Lord, who was born of the Virgin Mary, suffered and died." Let heathen and heretics be ever so smart; hold firmly to this faith, and you will be saved. It follows, then, that whoever believes in the Son of man, who was born of Mary, who suffered and was buried, will not be lost but is a son of God in possession of eternal life. Devil, sin, and death will not be able to harm him, for he has eternal life.

Whosoever believes on Him will not perish but have everlasting life.

The text has good reason for adding that God gave His *only* Son and that believers in Him will not perish but have eternal life. For God has many other sons. We, for instance, glory in the fact that God is our Father, as we pray in the Our Father. And Saint Paul declares that God "destined us in love to be His sons through Jesus Christ" (Eph. 1:5). But the evangelist identifies these sons when he says, "These are sons who believe in the Son." It is logical that the Son in whom we believe must be distinct and different and greater than we, the sons of God who believe in Him. Others are also sons of God, but they are not such sons as is He in whom we must believe. He is not a Son of God by reason of His believing in us; we, however, become sons of God through our believing in Him. Therefore, His divine sonship is vastly different from yours or mine.

The heretics garbled holy Scripture terribly. They claimed that Christ is called a Son of God by a metaphor, as we, too, are called sons of God. In Job 38:4, 7 the angels are also termed sons of God. We read, "Where were you when the sons of God [that is, all the angels] worshiped Me in heaven?" They claim that Christ was a son of God in that sense too. But scrutinize this text. Here we learn that He is the Son in whom we must believe. We holy people and the angels are not sons of God such as He is; for we all become sons of God through our faith in Him. The angels, too, were made sons of God through Him; for they were all created by the Son, as we read in Colossians 1:16. We human beings were also created by Him, but we lost and condemned sinners become sons of God through our faith in Him. Christ, however, is God and the Son of God; for there is a great difference between the one who believes and the one in whom one believes. If someone deserves the honor that men believe in Him and through that faith become children of God and achieve the new birth, such a person must be very God. Again, if He created the angels and if the angels take first rank among the creatures, then Christ must be Lord of all creatures. Likewise, since He created us men, He cannot be a son of God in the sense in which we or John the Baptist are sons of God.

God's unique Son

This is the real difference between the other sons of God and this Son of God. He is God Himself, whereas we are made sons of God through Him; He gives us eternal life and through Himself overcomes death. These are essential differences. This is how you must interpret holy Scripture, not only for your own sake but also to enable you to cope with the schismatic spirits, who twist and interpret Scripture according to their own ideas. You must realize that this Son is holy, safe from devil and death, and is not subject to damnation as we humans are. Nor does He require salvation for Himself; for He has always been, and still is, salvation and life personified. He is very God not only in His person but also in His office and His works. These bear witness to His divinity, as He says in John, "Even though you do not believe Me, believe Me for the sake of the works" (John 14:11). Therefore, it is a definition of His essence when this text says, "Whoever believes in Him has eternal life." It is He who bestows eternal life, kills death through Himself, and saves all who believe in Him. Such a work only God can do.

Your faith finds its vindication in the fact that Christ is very God in view not only of His essence and nature but also of His work. He is God in person, but He also performs the work of God: He saves those who believe in Him. Nowhere do we find it recorded that faith in any angel, whether Gabriel or Michael, or in John the Baptist or in the Virgin Mary, will make a person a child of God. Only of the Son is it said that He rescues from death and gives eternal life. Thus, Christ is established in the Godhead not only according to His person and majesty but also according to His work.

Therefore, it is fitting for us to write this text on every wall, and also in our hearts, with large, yes, with golden letters; for these are words of life and salvation. They teach us how to escape death and defend ourselves against all heretics, also against the pope and the Turk, all of whom read this text, but with drowsy eyes and deaf ears. For if they had heard, comprehended, and believed these words, they would not have fallen into such folly but would have said, "I am saved by Christ alone, who gave Himself into death for me." And if this is true, I am quick to add, "Well then, what am I doing in the cloister? Why did I run to Rome or to Saint James?" I did all this for the purpose of gaining salvation. And henceforth, I adjudge all religions and faiths false and heretical, whether of the Turk, of Mohammed, of the pope, or of the Jew, who also read and recite these words, but in the same indolent and indifferent manner in which the nuns read the Psalter without paying heed to its content. They, too, speak these words, but they only repeat them by rote like a parrot. But you must reflect on these words and impress them on your heart. And after you have gained a good understanding of them, you are in a position to examine and judge faith and to stand your ground against the attacks of the schismatic spirits.

Christ says further, "Ponder this, dear Nicodemus: that God so loved the world that He gave His only Son, that [you] should be saved by Him." As if He were to say, "I Myself perform the work of redemption from sin and death." And this work performed by Him, He gives or transfers to the Father, so that the Father's work and the Son's work are one and the same. The evangelist John consistently distinguishes between the persons, but he identifies the work. For the Father is not the son of the Virgin Mary, nor was He crucified, but only the Son; and yet Father and Son remain true God, and the Son draws us to the Father through Himself.

God's wrath and God's love

We heard Christ say, "That which is born of the flesh is flesh, and that which is born of the Spirit is spirit" (John 3:6); and, "No one has ascended into heaven but He who descended from heaven" (John 3:13). This is a hard and terrifying speech; it reflects nothing but the wrath of God. It condemns the whole world, deprives it of God, and leaves it lost and condemned. Yes, God is a real tyrant. You have heard of God's anger and judgment; you have heard that we all were conceived and born in sin. But now hear of the love of God, that He looks with favor on you and loves you. If you wish to have a gracious God and Father and know of His love for you, you must realize that you come to God by believing in the Son, whom the Father gave for you and who had Himself crucified for you. If this is your faith, it will be impossible for you not to feel the ineffable love of God manifested when He saved you from eternal doom and gave His Son that you might live. Hold firmly to this if you wish to be saved. For if you believe this, you ascend to heaven through Christ. Then you will not confront an angry judge but a dear Father, who is so kindly disposed toward you that He gave His Son for you; otherwise you would be lost. Now I can confidently say, "If God loved me so that He gave His only Son for my salvation, why should I fear His anger?"

In the papacy many sermons dealt with sin, death, and hell, and also with the wrath of God. But what did they say about deliverance from all this? They insisted that we render satisfaction for our sins with our good works and atone for them with monastic life, pilgrimages, and masses. But here we read, "Whoever does not believe in the Son has the wrath of God abiding over him." The pope, on the other hand, demands that I wear a cowl, be tonsured, and perform other tomfoolery to appease God's wrath. The Turk, the pope, and the Jews depict God as an angry God, but as one whose anger can be allayed and whose favor can be won if I humble myself, fast, sacrifice, perform good works, and expiate my sins with an ascetic life. It is the devil himself who directs people to their good works and not to Christ, the Son of God. God forbids us to rely on ourselves and boast of our good works, no matter how good they may be; and He insists that we approach the Son, take hold of Him, cleave to Him, believe in Him, and say, "I believe in Jesus Christ, the only Son of God, who was born of the Virgin Mary, who suffered and died for me."

The papists sang this in their churches daily, and they also taught this creed to their children. However, no one understood it; otherwise no one would have said, "I want to escape hell with my monkery and my order." The Lord demands here that we refrain from all thoughts of finding God and attaining salvation by means of good works and seek refuge solely in Christ the Lord. For to seek God outside Christ leads to eternal damnation.

Much could still be said on this subject if time permitted. At all times there have been many schismatic spirits who ignored Christ and wanted to climb up into heaven and seek God with their clever thoughts and their good works. All the heresies that were rampant among the Jews can be traced back to the hermits or Levites, who erected altars in their gardens, in beautiful fields, in bright meadows, under a pretty linden tree, or on a hill, whither they lured the people. Occasionally the devil would lend a hand with a miracle, and thus the people were miserably seduced. The prophets earnestly warned against this practice and condemned this self-devised zeal and worship of God. But when the clerics declared that this or that was to be done in these places be-

cause it was pleasing to God, the devil supported the suggestion. And the people flocked there in droves and established their own worship of God, just as though God were in agreement with them. He, however, had made it known through Moses where He wanted to be worshiped—not in any attractive spot, under a beautiful tree, in a gay meadow or field, or on a mountain, but at the place where the Ark of the Covenant rested. Thus, God was to be found only in the temple in Jerusalem. But the schismatic spirits retorted, "Why should God not also be found on this mountain or on the spot where Abraham, Isaac, and Jacob worshiped? God can hear us here as well as in Jerusalem." This meant climbing to God with one's own zeal.

Trying to climb into heaven

We did the same thing. We were not content with God's plan, "No one ascends into heaven but He who descends from heaven," and, "To escape damnation and to attain eternal life, one must believe in the crucified Son." No, we replied, "You must assuredly perform good works, not only the good works prescribed in the Ten Commandments—oh, no, these do not suffice! You must also do the good works commanded by the pope, such as fasting, observing holidays, etc." And now these people mock us when we preach about faith. They say, "Faith? Nonsense! No, whoever joins this or that order is saved." This is the trouble. This means seeking God in our own arbitrary way and trying to climb into heaven on the self-invented ladder of our own ideas. We must be on our guard against that devil whose name is Enthusiasm.[3] People who follow him disparage the oral Word and de-

---

3. Luther uses the word *enthusiasmus* as a Latin translation of the German *Schwermerey,* his favorite name for the left wing of the Reformation.

clare, "The Spirit must do it!" All they ever talk about is the Spirit. Of course, Nicodemus might have received the Spirit in this way too, but he gives ear to the Word of truth preached to him here by Christ, "No one ascends into heaven." The Word must still be preached and read orally, and the burden of our message must be, "I believe in the only Son of God, who died for me." We must seal our faith with the confession that we know of no other God than Him of whom we read here, "Whoever believes in the Son of man has everlasting life." No other thoughts or works will achieve this for me; the only way and the true way to God is to believe in the Son. Therefore, God has also commanded us to preach this diligently. That is why He established the ministry of oral preaching, instituted the sacraments, and commanded absolution. He wanted this message to remain alive among Christians that faith might be preserved in wakeful hearts, a faith which confesses, "I believe in the Son, who was given into death for me."

The papists, to be sure, hear these words too; for they possess the Bible as we do. But they slumber and snore over them; they have eyes and do not see, ears and do not hear. They say, "Oh, if only I had done what Saint Augustine or Saint Francis commanded!" The laity call upon the Virgin Mary to intercede for them with her Son. During my twenty years in the cloister I was obsessed with the one thought of observing the rules of my order. We were so drowned in the stupor of our own good works that we did not see and understand these words. But if you want to find God, then inscribe these words in your heart. Don't sleep, but be vigilant. Learn and ponder these words diligently, "God so loved the world that He gave His only Son, that whoever believes in Him should not perish but have eternal life." Let him who

can write, write these words. Furthermore, read them, discuss them, meditate and reflect on them in the morning and in the evening, whether awake or asleep! For the devil will sorely assail your faith in an effort to make you doubt that Christ is the Son of God and that your faith is pleasing to God. He will torture you with thoughts of predestination, with the wrath and the judgment of God. Then you must say, "I don't want to hear or know anything else about God than that He loves me. I don't want to know anything about a wrathful God, about His judgment and anger, about hell, about death, and about damnation. But if I do see God's wrath, I know that this drives me to the Son, where I find refuge; and if I come to the Son, I also have a merciful Father." For Saint John tells us in his epistle that the Father loved me before I ever loved Him or knew Him, that He remitted my sin and gave me salvation (1 John 4:10).

Words of eternal life

Hearing these words and believing them makes a person a true Christian. But if one loses these words, all is lost, be you a Carthusian or whatever you will.

The words "not perish" are inexpressibly glorious. They mean to be rid of sin, to have a good conscience, and not to be under the law. Otherwise the law punishes sin; but now, even if someone feels sin and the wrath of God, sin will not give him a bad conscience, because his sin is forgiven. The law will not accuse him, sin will not bite or plague him, death will not devour him; for if he believes these words, he is safe and secure.

This is what we preach and believe. And let anyone who does not share this faith pray God that it may be imparted also to him. But see to it that you do not resist this faith or violate and blaspheme it, as the pope does when he says,

"Of course, I know that Christ saves; but He does not save me." Well, the devil, too, knew that Christ saved Peter. Faith is not a paltry and petty matter as the pope's contempt of it would make it appear; but it is a heartfelt confidence in God through Christ that Christ's suffering and death pertain to you and should belong to you. The pope and the devil have a faith too, but it is only a "historical faith." True faith does not doubt; it yields its whole heart to the conviction that the Son of God was given into death for us, that sin is remitted, that death is destroyed, and that these evils have been done away with—but, more than this, that eternal life, salvation, and glory, yes, God Himself have been restored to us, and that through the Son God has made us His children.

These are living words which Christ addresses to us, to you and to me, when He says that he who accepts the Son shall be saved and that death, devil, and hell shall be disposed of for him. These words comfort us when we are frightened and troubled or when we contend against the schismatic spirits. They extinguish the flaming darts of the devil (Eph. 6:16). They assure us that we retain the glory that God's Son is our gift and our treasure. This conviction cannot be imparted to us by any monastic order or rule, whether it be named for Saint Augustine or anyone else. No, you must say, "I believe in Christ, in whom Saint Augustine also believed." But if I were to say, "Oh, you dear Virgin Mary, you are holier than I. And you, Saint Francis, have many merits; transfer some of them to my credit!" it would all be vain. The same answer would be given to you that, according to Matthew 25:9, was given to the five foolish virgins when they wished to borrow from the wise virgins, who had their lamps full of oil: "Go to the dealers and buy for yourselves"; that is, go to your preachers and teachers, who misinformed you so.

Thus, we find rich, excellent, and salutary words in this text. They should be diligently heeded.

The theme of Romans 5 is justification by faith. This concept was the key to Luther's own awakening, and he expounded this message with great fervor during the Reformation.

Luther witnessed the Catholic church's sale of indulgences, as people paid the church for the hope of gaining eternal life. As he teaches, Romans 5 makes it clear that the gospel is not for sale, nor is it limited to a particular group. Salvation is a free gift of God made available to all who believe.

Luther's exposition is thorough and practical. He deals directly with important theological issues such as God's wrath and love, and Christ's death and resurrection. The impact of this message is a crucial factor in understanding the gospel.

CHAPTER SIX

Romans 5

Therefore since we are justified by faith, we have peace with God.

This is the spiritual peace of which all the prophets sing. And because this is the case, he adds the words *with God*. And this peace is prefigured in every peace which the children of Israel enjoyed in days of old.

And this is the real peace of conscience and trust in God. Just as on the contrary a spiritual disturbance is the lack of a quiet conscience and a mistrust of God. Thus Hosea says, "For they sow the wind, and they shall reap the whirlwind" (Hos. 8:7). For the penalty of a bad conscience is stated in Psalm 1:4 to be "like the chaff which the wind drives away."

Thus Christ is also called the Prince of Peace and a Solomon (cf. Is. 9:6; 1 Chr. 22:9). Ephesians 2:14, 17 reads, "He is our peace, who has made us both one. . . . And He came and preached peace to you who were far off and peace to those who were near." The same idea is expressed in Isaiah 57:19, and in John 16:33, "That in Me you may have peace; in the world you have tribulation." The other kind of peace is carnal, of which He says, "I have not come to bring peace, but a sword" (Matt. 10:34). By contrast there is the carnal disturbance and temporal quietness. Hence also Psalm 72:7, "In His days shall righteousness flourish, and peace abound," must not be understood in the sense of the temporal peace which existed under Augustus, as many think, but of this spiritual peace "with God."

But note how the apostle places this spiritual peace only after righteousness has preceded it. For first he says, "since we are justified by faith," and then, "we have peace." Thus also in Psalm 85:10, "Righteousness and peace have kissed," the term "righteousness" precedes the word "peace." And again, "In His days shall righteousness flourish, and peace abound" (Ps. 72:7). And here the perversity of men seeks peace before righteousness, and for this reason they do not find peace. Thus the apostle creates a very fine antithesis in these words, namely,

The righteous man has peace with God but affliction in the world, because he lives in the Spirit.
The unrighteous man has peace with the world but affliction and tribulation with God, because he lives in the flesh.
But as the Spirit is eternal, so also will be the peace of the righteous man and the tribulation of the unrighteous.
And as the flesh is temporal, so will be the tribulation of the righteous and the peace of the unrighteous.

Hence we read in Isaiah 57:21 and 48:22, "There is no peace for the wicked, says the Lord," that is, spiritually, for there surely is a peace for the wicked; in Psalm 73:3, "For I was envious of the arrogant when I saw the prosperity of the wicked"; and in Psalm 28:3, "Who speak peace with their neighbor while mischief (that is, not peace, but disturbance and restlessness toward God) is in their hearts."

Through whom we have obtained access by faith.

In a most useful manner the apostle joins together these two expressions, "through Christ" and "by faith," as he did also above in the expression "since we are justified by faith . . . through our Lord." In the first place, the statement is directed against those who are so presumptuous as to believe that they can approach God without Christ, as if it were sufficient for them to have believed by faith alone, not through Christ, but beside Christ, as if after accepting the grace of justification they no longer needed Him. And now there are many people who from the works of faith make for themselves works of the law and of the letter, when having received faith by baptism and penitence, they now think that they are personally pleasing to God even without Christ, when actually both are necessary, namely, to have faith and also always to possess Christ as our mediator in this faith. Hence we read in Psalm 91:1, "He who dwells in the shelter of the Most High shall abide in the shadow of God in heaven." Faith makes the dwelling place, but Christ the protection and the aid. And later we read, "He will cover you with His [feathers], and under His wings you will trust" (Ps. 91:4); and in Malachi 4:2, "But for you who fear My name the Sun of righteousness shall rise with healing in His wings"; and in Psalm 31:2, "Be Thou unto me a God, a protector and a house of refuge"; and again in Psalm 90:1, "Lord, Thou hast been our dwelling place." Thus, the apostle is interpreting these and all similar authoritative expressions of Scripture, together with many other figurative expressions of the law.

But in our day the hypocrites and legalists swell up with horrifying pride and think that they are now saved and sufficiently righteous because they believe in Christ, but they are unwilling to be considered unrighteous or regarded as fools. And what is this except the rejection of Christ's protection and a desire to approach God only from faith but not through Christ? Indeed, then there is not faith at all, but only the appearance. So at sunset the rays of the sun and the light of the sun go down together. But he who is wise does not set such high value on the light that he no longer needs the sun, rather he wants to have both the sun and the light at the same time. Therefore, those who approach God through faith and not at the same time through Christ actually depart from Him.

Second, the apostle is speaking against those who rely too heavily on Christ and not enough on faith, as if they were to be saved through Christ in such a way that they themselves had to do nothing and show no evidence of faith. These people have too much faith, or actually none at all. For this reason it is necessary to emphasize both points: "through faith" and "through Christ," so that we do and suffer everything which we possibly can in faith in Christ. And yet in all of these activities we must confess that we are unprofitable servants, believing that only through Christ are we made worthy to approach God.

For in all works of faith we must strive to make ourselves worthy of Christ and His righteousness as our protection and refuge. "Therefore, since we are justified by faith" and our sins are forgiven, "we have access and peace," but only "through our Lord Jesus Christ." This also applies to those who follow the mystical theology and struggle in inner darkness, omitting all pictures of Christ's suffering, wishing to hear and contemplate only the uncreated Word Himself, but not having first been justified and purged in the eyes of their heart through the incarnate Word. For the incarnate Word is first necessary for the purity of the heart, and only when one has this purity, can he through this Word be taken up spiritually into the uncreated Word. But who is there who thinks that he is so pure that he dares aspire to this level unless he is called and led into the rapture by God, as was the case with the apostle Paul, or unless he is "taken up with Peter, James, and John, his brother" (Matt. 17:1)? In brief, this rapture is not called an "access."

We rejoice in our sufferings.

From this text we clearly see the distinction of a twofold wrath and a twofold mercy of God and also of a twofold suffering. For there is a kind of suffering that comes from His severity and another from His kindness. That suffering which comes from His kindness, because of its nature, works only things which are very good, although by an accident something different may take place. But this is not His fault but the fault of him to whom it happens because of his weakness; for he does not know the true nature of his suffering and its power and working. He judges and esteems it according to its outward appearance, that is, in a wrong way, since it ought to be adored as the very cross of Christ.

Of whatever quality suffering finds characteristics and people to be, it makes them even more [so]. Thus if a person is carnal, weak, blind, evil, irascible, arrogant, when trial comes, he becomes more carnal, weaker, blinder, more evil, more irascible, more arrogant. And on the other hand, if he is spiritual, brave, wise, good, meek, and humble, he becomes more spiritual, braver, wiser, better, meeker, and humbler. In Psalm 4:1 we read, "Thou hast given me room when I was in distress." But concerning the other kind of people, Matthew 7:27 says, "The floods came and the winds blew and beat against that house, and great was the fall thereof."

Those people talk nonsense who attribute their bad temper or their impatience to that which causes them offense or suffering. For suffering does not make a person impatient but merely shows that he has been or is still impatient. Thus, a person learns in suffering what kind of man he is, just as the glutton does when he itches.

Rude, puerile, and even hypocritical are those people who venerate the relics of the holy cross with the highest outward honor and then flee from and curse their sufferings and adversities. This is obvious, for in Scripture tribulations are expressly called the cross of Christ, as in 1 Corinthians 1:17, "Lest the cross of Christ be emptied of its power"; "And he who does not take his cross and follow Me" (Matt. 10:38); and, "Why am I still persecuted? In that case the stumbling block of the cross has been removed" (Gal. 5:11); and, "I tell you with tears that they live as enemies of the cross of Christ" (Phil. 3:18). But our theologians and priests today think of nothing else in the term "enemies of the cross of Christ" but Turks and Jews, as the theologians of Cologne did against John Reuchlin, and as the papal bulls and the glosses of the lawyers do.

But they themselves are actually "the enemies of the cross of Christ." For it is true that only the friends of the cross are its enemies, according to the statement in Psalm 38:11, "My friends and companions have stood against Me." "And they who praised Me swore against Me" (Ps. 102:8). For who hates tribulation and suffering more than the priests and the lawyers? Indeed, who seeks riches, pleasures, leisure, honors, and glories more than they do?

Whoever is unwilling to suffer tribulation should never think that he is a Christian, but rather a Turk and an enemy of Christ. For here he is speaking about all of us when he says: "We rejoice in our sufferings." In Acts 14:22 we read, "Through many tribulations we must . . ." "We must," he says, not "it just happens" or "it may be the case" or "we are disposed to." And in 1 Peter 1:6 we read, "Though now for a little while you may have to suffer various trials." "Have to," he says, that is, it absolutely cannot take place in any other way.

But we must note this: there are two kinds of enemies of the cross of Christ. The first kind is the violent type, and the second is the cunning. The violent are those who want to make the cross of no effect by force, and they attack it with all their forces; they are the ones who seek vengeance against anyone who offends them, and they are neither willing nor able to be at rest until they have been vindicated. They fall into many evils, such as hatred, detractions, abuses, rejoicing at the evils which befall their neighbor and sorrow over his good fortune.

But the cunning enemies are those who desert the cross in flight, that is, those who do not want to speak or perform the truth for anyone but are always trying to please, to wheedle, to flatter everyone and to offend no one, or else they withdraw into solitude (at least for this reason). The apostle refers to such people in Galatians 6:12, when he says, "It is those who want to make a good showing in the flesh that would compel you to be circumcised, and only that they may not be persecuted for the cross of Christ."

We must note that this climax or gradation is also contrary to those who do not stand in this grace, namely, that suffering works impatience, and impatience rejection, and rejection despair, and despair eternal confounding. And thus finally the hatred of God will be poured out (that is, it will be recognized that it has been poured out whenever this hatred reaches its completion) in their hearts through the wicked spirit under whose dominion they have been delivered. Therefore I said that the impatient man is not yet a Christian, at least before God, because he is found to have been rejected through suffering.

Hence, since the Lord in many passages is given the name of Savior and Helper in suffering, he who is unwilling to suffer as much as he can deprives Him of His true titles and names. Thus to this man there will be no Jesus, that is, no Savior, because he is unwilling to be damned; for him there will be no God the Creator because he is unwilling to be nothing, so that He may be his Creator. God will be no power, wisdom, or good to him, because he does not want Him to uphold him in his weakness, his foolishness, or his punishment.

Endurance and trial.

The different degrees of impatience are known from the degrees of anger which the Lord shows in Matthew 5:21–22, when He is explaining the commandment "You shall not kill." For because impatience is the cause of anger, the effect of both is the same, unless someone should separate impatience from anger. Then its degrees are more intensive than extensive. For an impatient man is patient in nothing. But the apostle here clearly indicates the degrees of endurance. Baptista Mantuanus distinguishes very carefully among these degrees. The lowest is to bear sufferings only with difficulty and with a mind which prefers to be delivered from the trial. The second and medium degree is to bear it with joy to be sure and willingly, but not to seek it. The highest degree is to long for suffering, to seek it like a treasure and to bring it about. This is the meaning of the words "we rejoice in our sufferings" and also of the statement in Galatians 6:14, "We must glory in the cross of our Lord."

The expression "trial" in this passage must be understood in a good sense, namely, as the goal of suffering, as that which is sought through tribulation. For God accepts no one as righteous whom He has not first tested, and He proves him through no other means than through the fire of tribulation, as we read in Psalm 17:3, "Thou hast tried me by fire, and iniquity has not been found in me." And there is this statement of Ecclesiasticus 44:16–17, "He pleased God, . . . and he was found perfect"; and again, ". . . he who is found without blemish" (Ecclesiasticus 31:8); also, "The Lord tests the righteous and the wicked" (Ps. 11:5). Thus one comes to this testing in no other way than through endurance. And this testing takes place in order that each person may see his own state of mind, that is, that each may know himself, whether he really loves God for the sake of God, which God of course knows even without any testing. Thus we read, "Search me, O God, and know my heart" (that is, make it known also to me). "Try me and know my paths. And see if there be any wicked way in me, and lead me in the way everlasting" (Ps. 139:23–24). This passage very beautifully expresses the reason why God brings tribulations to men, in order that He might test them, that is, make them approved through en-

durance. For if God should not test us by tribulation, it would be impossible for any man to be saved.

The reason is that our nature has been so deeply curved in upon itself because of the viciousness of original sin that it not only turns the finest gifts of God in upon itself and enjoys them (as is evident in the case of legalists and hypocrites), indeed, it even uses God Himself to achieve these aims. It also seems to be ignorant of this very fact, that in acting so iniquitously, so perversely, and in such a depraved way, it is even seeking God for its own sake. Thus the prophet Jeremiah says, "The heart is perverse above all things, and desperately corrupt; who can understand it?" (Jer. 17:9); that is, it is so curved in on itself that no man, no matter how holy (if a testing is kept from him) can understand it. Thus Psalm 19:12 reads: "Who can discern his errors? Clear Thou me from hidden faults," and, "Therefore, let everyone who is godly offer prayer to Thee at a proper time" (Ps. 32:6). And the Scripture calls this viciousness by a name most proper to it, that is, iniquity, depravity, or crookedness. The doctor of *The Sentences*[1] deals with this subject in a discussion of enjoyment and use and of the love of friendship and the love of concupiscence. Therefore, if we have said that iniquity is this very impatience, or at least the cause of this impatience, then this crookedness is also iniquity, which of necessity is hostile to the cross. The cross puts to death everything we have, but our iniquity tries to keep itself and its possessions alive. Therefore, our good God, after He has justified us and given us His spiritual gifts, quickly brings tribulation upon us, exercises us, and tests us so that this

---

1. This is a reference to the great medieval theologian, Peter the Lombard. His classic work *The Sentences* became the required theological text in the major medieval universities.

godless nature of ours does not rush in upon these enjoyable sins, lest in his ignorance man should die the eternal death. For they are very lovely and vigorously excite enjoyment. Thus man learns to love and worship God purely for Himself, and not just because of His grace and His gifts; but he worships God for His own sake alone. Thus, "He chastises every son whom He receives" (Heb. 12:6). And unless He did this, the son would quickly be drawn away by the sweetness of his new inheritance, he would luxuriate in his enjoyment of the grace which he had received and would offend his Father more deeply than before. Therefore, in very good order the apostle says, "Suffering produces endurance, and endurance trial," that is, a proving or a testing.

And hope does not disappoint us.

Without a testing of this sort, as I have said, hope would founder, indeed, it would no longer be hope, but presumptuousness; in fact, it would be worse, for it would be the enjoyment of the creature instead of the Creator. And if a person remained in this state, he would be confounded for all eternity. Therefore suffering comes, through which a man is made patient and tested; it comes and takes away everything he has and leaves him naked and alone, allowing him no help or safety in either his physical or spiritual merits. It makes a man despair of all created things, to turn away from them and from himself, to seek help outside of himself and all other things, in God alone, and thus to sing in the words of Psalm 3:3, "But Thou, O Lord, art my Protector and my Glory." This is what it means to hope, and that hope is created in times of testing, while of necessity the ungodly, who are accustomed to trust in their own powers, are unwilling

to remain calm and to endure their tribulations in order that they may be tested. In the final test, since they do not know how to trust solely in God, after their substance has been ruined and the mountains of their own achievements have fallen down, then they themselves fall into ruin for eternity. "Then they will begin to say to the mountains, 'Fall upon us'" (Luke 23:30; cf. Hos. 10:8). For their hope was not a real hope, but a perverse presumptuousness, a confidence in their own works and their own righteousness.

But yet we must know that suffering is of two kinds. The first is physical, in which men who are carnal are overcome; they fail because of their concern for physical goods, for things, for the body, for reputation, and they depart from God, lose hope because of their impatience, and thus deliver themselves up to the flesh and forsake God. Of such people the apostle says, "They have become callous and have given themselves up to licentiousness" (Eph. 4:19). The second is the suffering of conscience and spirit, wherein all of one's self-righteousness and wisdom in which people trust are devoured and done away. Of these the Savior says, in a mystical way, "When a strong man fully armed . . . but when one stronger than he assails him and overcomes him, he takes away his armor and binds him and divides his spoils" (Luke 11:21–22), that is, he will strip a man who is fortified with his own righteousnesses and will teach him that they are to be used for the common good and not for his own pleasure.

For God's love has been poured into our hearts through the Holy Spirit who has been given to us.

This expression ought to be understood as instruction in the Holy Spirit, as to why and how we can glory in our sufferings, namely, that we might learn that of ourselves and of our own powers it is impossible, but that it is a gift of the love which is given by the Holy Spirit.

Therefore, "God's love," which is the purest feeling toward God and alone makes us right at heart, alone takes away iniquity, alone extinguishes the enjoyment of our own righteousness. For it loves nothing but God alone, not even His gifts, as the hypocritical self-righteous people do. Therefore, when physical and spiritual blessings flow in, it does not get excited. Again, when they disappear, and physical and spiritual evils deluge us, it is not crushed. But "Knowledge puffs up" (1 Cor. 8:1), and so does righteousness. Again, ignorance humbles us, and so does sin. "But love bears all things" (1 Cor. 13:7), even glorying in its tribulations. Therefore we must note that; it is called "God's love" because by it we love God alone, where nothing is visible, nothing experiential, either inwardly or outwardly, in which we can trust or which is to be loved or feared. It is carried away beyond all things into the invisible God, who cannot be experienced, who cannot be comprehended, that is, into the midst of the shadows, not knowing what it loves, only knowing what it does not love; turning away from everything which it has known and experienced, and desiring only that which it has not yet known, saying, "I am sick with love" (Song 2:5), that is, I do not want what I have and I do not have what I want. But this gift is far removed from those who still look at their own righteousnesses, trust in them, feel secure in them, and thus do

not "rejoice in sufferings," are not tested, and thus have no hope.

Thus the apostle asserts that this sublime power which is in us is not from ourselves, but must be sought from God. Thus it follows that it *is poured* into us, not born in us or originated in us. And this takes place *through the Holy Spirit;* it is not acquired by moral effort and practice, as our moral virtues are. *Into our hearts,* that is, into the depths and the midst and center of our hearts, not on the surface of the heart, as foam lies on water. This is the kind of love that the hypocrites have, who imagine and pretend that they have love. But a period of testing only proves the pride and impatience which lies deep within them.

Who has been given to us, that is, whom we do not deserve, rather we deserve the direct opposite. But he proves that this is true, because now follows, "He is really given" and not deserved. For Christ "died for the weak" (v. 6) and not for the strong and the deserving. Thus it is called *love* to indicate the difference between this and the unworthy and low kind of love by which a creature is loved; for the term "love" means to love something very dearly and preciously and to regard as very precious the thing that is loved. For this is what it means to love God above all things and to esteem Him with a rich love, that is, to love Him with a precious love. But to love Him for the sake of His gifts or for some advantage is the lowest kind of love, that is, to love Him with a selfish desire. This is using God but not enjoying Him.[2] *God's* love is used because only God is loved in this way, not even

---

2. Luther is no doubt indebted to Augustine's discussion of the difference between "using" and "enjoying" in *De doctrina Christiana,* where Augustine compares the Christian pilgrim to a traveler far from home who "uses" a conveyance to return home but does not "enjoy" the journey for its own sake. In the same way, says Augustine, "if we wish to return to our Father's home, this world must be used, not enjoyed. . . . The true objects of enjoyment are the Father and the Son and the Holy Spirit, who are at the same time the Trinity, one Being."

the neighbor, except for the sake of God, that is, because God so wills, and one loves His will above all things.

We must also note that love dwells nowhere but in the heart, indeed, in the innermost center of the heart, and for this reason there is that difference between sons and bond servants. The sons serve Him happily, willingly, and freely, not in fear of punishment or desire for glory, but only to fulfill the will of God; but the bond servants are forced by the fear of punishment, and they serve Him unwillingly and with great difficulty, or they are desirous of a reward, in which case they serve Him willingly enough but with a mercenary intent, but never absolutely out of a desire to fulfill His will. Particularly in time of tribulation does the servant and the hireling run away, but the son perseveres, as John 10:12 says: "But the hireling flees." Thus He says to them, "Oh, that there were one among you who would shut the doors, that you might not kindle fire on my altar in vain!" (Mal. 1:10). And then He continues, "I have no pleasure in you, says the Lord of Hosts," for they are actually very presumptuous and believe that they are carrying out the will of God. This is the reason why in the same place, when the Lord has said, "You offer polluted bread upon My altar," they reply as if they could not imagine this to be possible, saying, "How have we polluted it?" (Mal. 1:7–8) which is to say, "In our opinion we have done everything which Thou has commanded." The Lord replies, "When you offer blind animals for sacrifice, is that no evil? And when you offer those that are lame or sick, is that no evil?" That is, they worship God without true love but with a desire for their own advantage, like hirelings, not having the single eye of the bride, with which she sees only the invisible God and nothing of her own things or those of any other creature.

Note again how the apostle unites the spring with the river. He speaks of the "love . . . through the Holy Spirit, who is given to us." For it is not enough to have the gift unless the giver also be present, as Moses also begged in Exodus 33:15, "If Thy presence will not go with me, do not carry us up from here." Indeed, properly it is to love alone that the apostle attributes the presence and at the same time the giving of the Spirit. For all other gifts, as he says in 1 Corinthians 12:7ff., are given by the same Spirit but are not the Spirit Himself. Just so he says here regarding love that it is not given unless the Spirit Himself has first been given, who then spreads this love abroad in our hearts. But in that passage he says, "But all these gifts are inspired by one and the same Spirit" (v. 11). Hence he goes on to say in the same chapter, "I will show you a still more excellent way" (v. 31). Or at least, even if He is given in all the gifts, yet He does not pour forth love in all.

At the right time.

Some refer this expression to the statement which follows, so that the meaning is "When we were still weak, He died for the ungodly according to time," as if to say that, although He is eternal and immortal, yet He died in time. He died because of His humanity which lived in time, but He is alive forever because of His deity, which lives in eternity. Others interpret it thus, "He died at the time when we were weak," that is, He died at the time when we were not yet righteous and whole, but rather weak and sickly, so that the meaning is, "at the right time," namely, at that time when we were still weak. And this interpretation is the better one, as becomes evident in what follows: *For if, while we were enemies we were reconciled to God by the death of His Son*

(v. 10). But others refer the expression to the preceding sentence, so that the meaning is when we were weak according to time, even though before God we were already righteous through His predestination. For in the predestination of God all things have already taken place, even things which in our reality still lie in the future.

Therefore, as sin through one man.

That the apostle is in this passage talking about original sin and not actual sin is proved in many passages, and we assume this to be so from these points:

First, because he says, "through one man." Thus Augustine says in his work *On the Merits of Sins and Their Remission*, "If the apostle had wanted to point out that sin came into this world not by propagation but by imitation, he would not have spoken of Adam as the one who originated it, but rather of the devil, . . . of whom it is said in Wisdom of Solomon 2:24, 'And they follow him who are of his side.'" In this sense Adam also imitated him and thus had the devil as the originating cause of his sin. But here the apostle says, "through a man." All actual sins enter and have entered the world through the devil, but original sin came through this one man. Blessed Augustine also says, "Thus, when the apostle mentions that sin and the death which passed from this one man to all men through propagation, he makes him the originating cause from whom the propagation of the human race took its beginning." Chrysostom says regarding this passage, "It is clear that it is not the sin which comes from the transgression of the law but the sin which derives from the disobedience of Adam, which contaminates all things."

Second, he says, "Through one man," because actual sin is committed by many, since every man brings his own sin into the world.

Third, he says, "Sin came into the world." But no actual sin enters the world, for each man's sin hangs over him, as we read in Ezekiel 18:20, that each will carry his own sin. Therefore, it does not come upon others but remains on each person individually. And that the term "world" does not mean heaven and earth in this passage but only the men in the world is clear from Romans 3:6, "How could God judge the world?" and 1 John 5:19, "The whole world is in the power of the evil one." In John 3:16 we read, "God so loved the world"; and later on, "If the world hates you . . ." (John 15:18); again, "I chose you out of the world" (John 15:19). And the reason is that the physical world is insensitive and incapable of sinning, so that sin and death could not enter it. For it neither dies nor sins, but man both sins and dies; therefore, for sin to enter the world means that the world becomes guilty and sinful because of one man. As we read below, "As by one man's disobedience many were made sinners" (v. 19).

Fourth, *death through sin*, because it is certain that the death of the world (that is, of all men) does not come from the personal sin of each man, since even those who have not sinned die. Therefore, if death comes by sin and if without sin there would be no death, then sin is in all of us. Thus it is not personal sin that he is talking about here. Otherwise it would be false to say that death had entered by sin, but rather we ought to say that it came by the will of God.

Fifth, because he says *death spread to all men*, even if death came because of our personal sin, yet it comes upon only him who commits it, as the Law says: "The fathers shall not be put to death for the children" (Deut. 24:16).

Sixth, he uses the term "sin" in the

singular, referring to one. But if he had wanted us to understand this passage of actual sin, he would use the plural, as he does below, when he speaks of "many trespasses" (v. 16), where he is clearly comparing that one particular sin with many others, and from this he concludes that the efficacy of grace is greater than that of sin.

Seventh, *in which all men sinned.* There is nothing else "in which all men sinned," but each sins his own.

Eighth, *sin was in the world before the Law was given* (v. 13). Actual sin also was in the world before Moses, and it was imputed, because it was also punished by men; but original sin was unknown until Moses revealed it in Genesis 3.

Ninth, he says here that their *sins were not like the transgressions of Adam* (v. 14), that is, an exact simulation of his sin; but nevertheless they all sin with actual sin who commit sin.

Tenth, *Adam is a type of the One who was to come,* but not by actual sin; for otherwise all men would be a figure of Christ, but now only Adam is that figure, because of the extension of his one sin to all men.

But now in order to confound and overturn the perversity of future heretics, whom he foresaw in spirit, the apostle in explaining how Adam is the figure of Christ speaks only in the singular, for fear that some impudent sophist might reduce it to nonsense by saying: "He is taking the word 'sin' in a collective sense, using it in the singular rather than the plural, as the Scripture frequently does." Thus he says expressly, "through one man who sinned" (v. 12), and, "the effect of that one man's sin unto condemnation" (v. 16), and again, "because of one man's trespass" (v. 17), again, "by one man's trespass" (v. 18), and "by one man's disobedience" (v. 19). This point of comparison is particularly

strong, "For the judgment following one trespass brought condemnation, but the free gift following many trespasses brings justification" (v. 16). For "judgment (as blessed Augustine says) leads from many offenses unto justification." But since he does not say this, however, but rather "by one," it is easy to see that he is speaking of original sin. Likewise, he denies that many sinned, but only the one, when he says "through one man's trespass" (v. 15) and "one man's sin" (v. 18) and "one man's sin" (v. 16). Note how at the same time it is true that only one man sinned, that only one sin was committed, that only one person was disobedient, and yet because of him many were made sinners and disobedient.

What, therefore, is original sin?

First, according to the subtle distinctions of the scholastic theologians, original sin is the privation or lack of original righteousness. And righteousness, according to these men, is only something subjective in the will, and therefore also the lack of it, its opposite. This comes under the category of a quality, according to the *Logic* and *Metaphysics* of Aristotle.

Second, however, according to the apostle and the simplicity of meaning in Christ Jesus, it is not only a lack of a certain quality in the will, nor even only a lack of light in the mind or of power in the memory, but particularly it is a total lack of uprightness and of the power of all the faculties both of body and soul and of the whole inner and outer man. On top of all this, it is a propensity toward evil. It is a nausea toward the good, a loathing of light and wisdom, and a delight in error and darkness, a flight from and an abomination of all good works, a pursuit of evil, as it is written in Psalm 14:3, "They are all gone astray, they are all alike corrupt"; and, "For the imagination and thought of man's heart are evil from his youth" (Gen. 8:21). For God hates and imputes not only this lack (even as many forget their own sin and no longer acknowledge it) but also this universal concupiscence by which we become disobedient to the commandment "You shall not covet" (Ex. 20:17; Deut. 5:21). As the apostle most clearly argues later on in chapter 7, this commandment shows us our sin: "I should not have known what it is to covet if the Law had not said, 'You shall not covet.'"

Therefore, as the ancient holy fathers[3] so correctly said, this original sin is the very tinder of sin, the law of the flesh, the law of the members, the weakness of our nature, the tyrant, the original sickness. For it is like a sick man whose mortal illness is not only the loss of health of one of his members, but it is, in addition to the lack of health in all his members, the weakness of all of his senses and powers, culminating even in his disdain for those things which are healthful and in his desire for those things which make him sick. Thus, this is Hydra,[4] a many-headed and most tenacious monster, with which we struggle in the Lernean Swamp of this life till the very day of our death. It is Cerberus,[5] that irrepressible barker, and Antaeus,[6] who cannot be overcome while loose here on the earth. I have not found so clear a discussion of the subject of original sin as in Gerard Groote's treatise *Blessed Is the Man,*[7] in which he speaks not as an arrogant philosopher but as a sound theologian.

Therefore, to think that original sin is merely the lack of righteousness in the will is merely to give occasion for lukewarmness and a breakdown of the whole concept of penitence, indeed, to implant pride and presumptuousness, to eradicate the fear of God, to outlaw humility, to make the command of God invalid, and thus condemn it completely. At least, this is the situation if these theologians are taken at their word! And as a result, one can easily become proud over against another man, when he thinks that he himself is free from a sin in which he sees his neighbor still struggling.

This is why many people, in order that they may have a reason for humility, busy themselves with exaggerating their past sins and those that they possibly could have committed, and they do the same thing regarding their present sins, so that they may appear humble because of their attention to them. Here is good instruction. But there obviously are also present sins, and they permit no hint of superiority or complacency to gain the upper hand in us at the condemnation of someone else (which often is the case). For the real reason for humility is obvious, namely, that sin remains in us, but "it has no dominion over us" (Rom. 6:14), but it is subject to the Spirit, so that a person may destroy what formerly ruled over him.

3. The formulation is mainly that of Peter Lombard, but this is heavily dependent on Augustine. For Luther ancient fathers often means Augustine.

4. In Greek mythology a monster that inhabited the swamps of Lerna in the Peloponnesus. When one of its nine heads was cut off, it was immediately replaced by two new ones, unless cauterized. Hercules slew this dragon.

5. The surly, three-headed dog that guarded the gates to Hades. In his most difficult "twelfth labor" Hercules subdued this formidable beast. Cf. Virgil, *Aeneid,* VI, 698.

6. The giant whose strength was constantly renewed so long as he remained in contact with his mother, Earth. Hercules crushed him while holding him aloft.

7. Gerard Groote wrote no such tract. Luther must be thinking of Gerard Zerbolt of Zütphen, whose tract *De spiritualibus ascensionibus* begins with these words of Ps. 84:6.

Therefore, if anyone looks down on another man as a sinner, sin still rules him doubly. For since he himself is a sinner, he compares himself as a righteous man to the other person and thus makes himself a liar and does not realize as a sinner that he is a sinner. Properly speaking, this is iniquity. For it is prohibited to judge, and yet he judges. But a man cannot judge unless he is superior and better. Therefore in this very act he is proudly preferring himself to the other, and in this way he sins, although he has committed no other sin than that he has forgotten that he himself is a sinner and that he has considered himself to be righteous. Therefore, whoever realizes that sin is in him, which he must govern, this man will surely fear to become a servant of sin, especially will he be afraid of judging. For if he judges, he knows that the Lord will say to him, Why do you judge like a righteous man, when you are unrighteous? And even if you have been righteous, yet because you trust in your own righteousness, you have already polluted it and have created a twofold unrighteousness, since you set up your sin as righteousness and then boast of it as righteousness."

Sin came into the world. The apostle uses this particular expression to indicate that original sin does not come from men but rather that it comes to them. For it is the nature of actual sin that it comes out of us, as the Lord says, "For out of the heart come evil thoughts" (Matt. 15:19). But this sin enters into men, and they do not commit it but suffer it, as Moses says, "And there came out this calf" (Ex. 32:24).

In which all have sinned. This is unclear in the Greek as to whether it is masculine or neuter. Thus it seems that the apostle wants it understood in both senses. Hence blessed Augustine also interprets it in both ways . . . saying, "'in that all have sinned.' It surely is clear and obvious that personal sins, in which only those who have committed them are involved, are one thing and that this one sin in which all have taken part insofar as all were in this one man is something quite different." From this statement of Augustine it would seem to follow that original sin is the very first sin, namely, the transgression of Adam. For he interprets the expression "all men sinned" with reference to a work which has actually been committed and not only with reference to the transmission of guilt. He continues, "But if that one man and not sin is referred to, in that all have sinned in this one man, what can be clearer than this clear expression?" But the first interpretation is better in view of what follows. For later on the apostle says, "For as by one man's disobedience many were made sinners" (v. 19), and this is the same as saying that all have sinned in the sin of the one man. But even so the second interpretation can be advanced, that is, while one man sinned, all men sinned. Thus, in Isaiah 43:26f., "Set forth your case, that you may be proved right. Your first father sinned," which is to say, you cannot be justified, because you are the son of Adam, who sinned first. Therefore, you also are a sinner, because you are the son of a sinner; but a sinner can beget nothing but another sinner like himself.

Sin indeed was in the world before the law was given.

In regard to this verse Augustine has this to say, "This means that the law, either natural or written, could not take away sin. For by the works of the law no one can be justified." And elsewhere, in his *Exposition of Certain Propositions*, he says, "The expression 'before the law was given, sin was in the world' must be understood in the sense 'until grace should come.' For he is speaking against those who think that sin can be taken away by the law. And he says that sins are made manifest by the law but are not taken away, since the Scripture says, 'Sin was not counted where there was no law.' For it does not say that sin did not exist but that it was not imputed. Nor was sin taken away when the law was given; rather it began to be imputed, that is, to be made manifest. Therefore we should not think that the expression 'before the law' is to be understood as if there were no sin under the law, for the term 'before the law' is spoken in the sense that he counts the entire time of the law until the end of the law, which is Christ."

And in this way blessed Augustine ties the expression "before the law" to the expression "sin was in the world." But then it becomes necessary to say, as he himself does say, that sin was not only until the law, but much more so under the law, which entered that the offense might abound. But if one takes the expression in connection with the negative phrase "sin was not counted," then it is not necessary to take such a harsh interpretation of the phrase "before the law," which in any case indicates the end. The meaning then is [that] before the law, sin (which, however, was always in the world) was not imputed, which is to say, it was not counted or known until the law came, which brought it forth, not in actual being, for it already was in existence, but in the sense that it became known. Or thus, "Before the law, sin was in the world," that is, it was merely there, only insofar as it existed, but beyond the fact that it was there and remained, sin was also acknowledged through the law. And thus it is not understood to mean that sin existed until the law came and then ceased to exist, but that sin received an

understanding of itself which it did not possess before. And the words of the apostle clearly indicate this interpretation: "But sin was not counted where there was no law," as if to say that through the law, which it had preceded, sin was not abolished but imputed.

Yet death reigned.

It is as if he were saying that the penalty of sin, which was death, was known and recognized experientially by all men, but the cause of death, which is sin, was not recognized. Here again we ought not to understand this passage to mean that death reigned only until Moses, since Moses also died and all men do until the end of the world; and the rule of death hangs especially over those who are lost. But the expression "death reigned to Moses" means that until the time of Moses it was not understood why and whence death reigned. But Augustine understands this reign in the work cited previously, "When the guilt of sin so rules over men that it does not permit them to come to the eternal life, which is the only true life, but drags them down even to the second death (which is eternal punishment)."

In the likeness
of the transgression of Adam.

Blessed Augustine interprets this passage as applying to those who had not yet sinned in their own volition, as the other man had. Also blessed Ambrose understands the phrase "in the likeness" to refer to the preceding words "who have not sinned," for otherwise if the apostle had not defined the expression "who have not sinned" in this way, he would have contradicted his earlier statement "in which all have sinned" (v. 12). For how can it be that all have sinned and yet that some have not sinned, unless it means that all have sinned in Adam and in Adam's sin, but not all have sinned in the likeness of Adam's sin or transgression? For sin is one thing and transgression is another; for sin remains as guilt, while transgression is an act which passes on. Thus all have not sinned in action, but they are all in the same guilt; but only Adam sinned by both action and guilt insofar as he committed the first sin.

Faber Stapulensis, however, . . . understands this passage in a different way and reconciles the contradiction between the phrases "in which all have sinned" (v. 12) and "who have not sinned" (v. 14) in a different way. But I doubt, in fact, I fear, that he has not reconciled them correctly. For he refers the phrase "in the likeness" to the term "reigned," and I will accept this because of John Chrysostom, who in explaining this passage says, "How did death reign? In the likeness of Adam's transgression." And thus the phrase "even over them who have not sinned" he takes as being in a parenthetical position. And then the expression "who have not sinned" must be understood as referring to personal sin in a stricter sense than he used above when he said "in which all have sinned." The same doctor speaks thus also of little children, "For this reason we baptize infants, even though they do not have sin," that is, actual sins of their own.

Who is a type of the One who was to come.

Chrysostom, as quoted by blessed Augustine, says concerning this passage: " 'In the likeness of the transgression of Adam, who is a type of the One who was to come,' because Adam is also a figure of Christ. And how is he a figure? they ask. The answer is that just as Adam has become a cause of death to those who

are born of him, even though they have not eaten of the tree, the death brought on by the eating, so also Christ was made a provider of righteousness for those who belong to Him, even though they are entirely lacking in righteousness, and He has given it to us all through His cross."

Thus the likeness of Adam's transgression is in us, because we die, as if we had sinned in the same way he did. And the likeness of Christ's justification is in us, because we live, as if we had produced the same kind of righteousness that He did. Therefore, because of this likeness, Adam is "the type of the One who was to come," that is, Christ, who came after him. Indeed, in order that Christ might take away this likeness and give us His own, "He was born in the likeness of men" (Phil. 2:7) and sent by the Father "in the likeness of sinful flesh" (Rom. 8:3). And thus, "as in Adam all die, so also in Christ shall all be made alive" (1 Cor. 15:22). Hence I lean toward Chrysostom's view that the expression "in the likeness" ought to be connected with the word "reigned."

The free gift is not like the trespass.

Chrysostom says, "If a Jew should say to you: 'How has the world been saved by the power of the one man Christ?' you can say to him: 'How has the world been condemned by the disobedience of one man Adam?' Yet grace and sin are not equal, nor are death and life, nor God and the devil. For if sin, even the sin of one man, had such power, how can it be that the grace of God and the grace of one Man will not have greater power? For this is much more reasonable. For it certainly does not seem reasonable that one person be damned for another, but it appears much more proper and reasonable that one person be saved for another."

The grace of God and the free gift in the grace of that one Man.

The apostle joins together grace and the gift, as if they were different, but he does so in order that he may clearly demonstrate the type of the One who was to come which he has mentioned, namely, that although we are justified by God and receive His grace, yet we do not receive it by our own merit, but it is His gift, which the Father gave to Christ to give to men, according to the statement in Ephesians 4:8, "When He ascended on high, He led a host of captives, and He gave gifts to men." Therefore, these are the gifts of God's grace, which Christ received from the Father through His merit and His personal grace, in order that He might give them to us, as we read in Acts 2:33, "Having received from the Father the promise of the Holy Spirit, He has poured out this gift which you see." Thus the meaning is "the grace of God" (by which He justifies us, which actually is in Christ as in its origin, just as the sin of man is in Adam) "and the free gift," namely, that which Christ pours out from His Father upon those who believe in Him. This gift is "by the grace of that one Man," that is, by the personal merit and grace of Christ, by which He was pleasing to God, so that He might give this gift to us. This phrase "by the grace of that one Man" should be understood of the personal grace of Christ, corresponding to the personal sin of Adam which belonged to him, but the "gift" is the very righteousness which has been given to us. Thus also original sin is a gift (if I may use the term) in the sin of the one man Adam. But "the grace of God" and "the gift" are the same thing, namely, the very righteousness

which is freely given to us through Christ. And He adds this grace because it is customary to give a gift to one's friends. But this gift is given even to His enemies out of His mercy, because they were not worthy of this gift unless they were made worthy and accounted as such by the mercy and grace of God.

The law came in.

He uses a very appropriate word, "came in" as if he were saying that sin entered in and the law came in on the side, that is, after sin it also entered in, and thus sin was not abolished by the law. That the law came in on the side indicates that sin, which had come in first, still remained and was even increased. For sin entered, and the law followed sin, arousing it by prescribing things against it and prohibiting the things which sin wished to do. Therefore, he says *that sin might abound*. This expression is not causal but consecutive, because the conjunction "that" refers to what follows and not to the final cause of the law. For the law did not come because of sin, although he also says this in Galatians 3:19, "Why then the law? It was added because of transgressions, till the seed should come to whom He made the promise." So here he uses the expression "that sin might abound," that is, for the sake of sin. Thus, the meaning is that through the transgression of the law the first sin is made known, therefore, for the sake of transgression, not in order that transgression should take place but because it necessarily followed upon the establishment of the law, so that through this transgression of the law we might learn the sinfulness of our own weakness, our blindness, and our evil desire. For it was not necessary to establish the law because of the transgression of it, inasmuch as, even if this was not the intention and if the law was not established because of transgression, yet the transgression of the law would follow, since without grace it is impossible to overcome concupiscence and to destroy the body of sin.

And this affirmative statement, "the law came in, that sin might abound," is trying to show nothing else than the negative expression: the law did not make alive, the law did not take away sin, or the law did not come in to take away sin or to make alive. Thus, this affirmative statement necessarily follows: therefore the law did come in to increase sin. And this is true, so that the meaning is [that] the law came and without any fault on the part of the law or in the intentions of the Lawgiver, it happened that it came for the increasing of sin, and this happened because of the weakness of our sinful desire, which was unable to fulfill the law. Hence blessed Augustine says, "By this very word he has shown that the Jews did not understand the purpose for which the law was given. For it was not given that it might give life—for grace alone through faith gives life—but it was given to show by how many tight bonds of sin they are held who presume to fulfill the law by their own powers." This is a common method of speaking, as when a doctor comes to a sick man to console him and cannot help him because the sick man's hopes are in vain; then the sick man can say: "You have come not to comfort me but to make my despair greater." The same is the case with the law, which the human race most anxiously desires (as is evident in all the philosophers and seekers after truth), but the law is not a help and a cure; it only serves to increase the disease, as is typified by the woman in the Gospel who had the issue of blood. She had spent all her substance on doctors and yet had been made worse (Luke 8:43ff.). Hence he has used a most significant word when he says, "The law came in that sin might abound," that is, God did not establish the law for this purpose, but it became so when the law entered "that sin might abound."

During the Reformation, crucial theological debate was fiercely active. Men were put to the test as to their devotion to Christ. Luther emphasizes the need for cross-bearing, and readily acknowledges that the cross is a source of pain for those who take it up. The people of God are called upon to engage in conflict not only with flesh-and-blood adversaries, but also with the spiritual realm, that is, the devil. The world and the devil hate the Cross and seek to diminish its power in our lives. Luther teaches in this brief treatise the necessity of bearing with patience the cross that God bestows on an individual.

CHAPTER SEVEN

That a Christian Should Bear His Cross with Patience

The ancient and saintly fathers and theologians have contrasted the living wood with dead and have allegorized that contrast this way: From the living wood[1] came sin and death; from the dead wood,[2] righteousness and life. They conclude: do not eat from that living tree, or you will die, but eat of this dead tree; otherwise, you will remain in death.

You do indeed desire to eat and enjoy [the fruit] of some tree. I will direct you to a tree so full that you can never eat it bare. But just as it was difficult to stay away from that living tree, so it is difficult to enjoy eating from the dead tree. The first was the image of life, delight, and goodness, while the other is the image of death, suffering, and sorrow because one tree is living, the other dead. There is in man's heart the deeply rooted desire to seek life where there is certain death and to flee from death where one has the sure source of life.

Taking up the cross is by nature something that causes pain. It must not be self-imposed (as the Anabaptists and all the work-righteous teach); it is something that is imposed upon a person.

The Need for It

We must be conformed to the image of the Son of God (Rom. 8:29).

"All who desire to live a godly life in Christ Jesus will be persecuted" (2 Tim. 3:12).

"In the world you have tribulation" (John 16:33). Likewise, "You will be sorrowful; you will weep and lament, but the world will rejoice" (John 16:20).

"If we share in [Christ's] sufferings we shall also be glorified with Him" (Rom. 8:17).

"If you are left without discipline, in which all have participated, then you are illegitimate children and not sons" (Heb. 12:8). Otherwise, what is the purpose of so many comforting passages of Scripture?

The Source of It

The devil, a mighty, evil, deceitful spirit, hates the children of God. For them the holy cross serves for learning the faith, for [learning] the power of the Word, and for subduing whatever sin and pride remain. Indeed, a Christian can no more do without the cross than without food or drink.

The Entreaty

The touch of Christ sanctifies all the sufferings and sorrows of those who believe in Him. Whoever does not suffer shows that he does not believe that Christ has given him the gift of sharing in His own passion. But if anyone does not wish to bear the cross which God

---

1. I.e., the tree in the Garden of Eden, Gen. 2:17.
2. I.e., the tree of the Cross on Golgotha.

places upon him, he will not be compelled to do so by anyone—he is always free to deny Christ. But in so doing he must know that he cannot have fellowship with Christ or share in any of His gifts.

For example, a merchant, a hunter, a soldier risk so much pain for the sake of an uncertain gain and victory, while here, where it is certain that glory and blessedness will be the result, it is a disagreeable thing to suffer even for a bit, as Isaiah 54:7, Christ in John 16:20–22, Peter in 1 Peter 1:6, and Paul in 2 Corinthians 4:17 usually put it, "for a little while," and momentarily.

Notice how our adversaries, those torturers from the devil, are torn and divided in their teachings in so many ways that they fail to realize their hopes, since they must be concerned with so much peril and misfortune that they can never act for a moment with certainty or confidence.[3] And these penalties and punishments are only temporal! How can I comprehend their guilt, namely, that without God and through the devil's craftiness they, beset by an evil conscience, are eternally lost? Even though they are uncertain as to the outcome of their endeavor, they keep on rejoicing in a hope that is completely and absolutely lost, while we, on the other hand, have God's unfailing promises for our comfort.

In short, since God is the same and the cause is the same, in which He has upheld the faith of all the saints so that He might be vindicated, God will not now, just for our own sake, be found a liar; nor are we to make a liar of Him. God grant, whether we do or do not believe, that He will yet defend His word and surely help [us]. This demands great effort and care so that, in the first place, we turn our eyes from the might [of this world] and second, hold fast to the Word. Eve disregarded the Word and relied on what was visible, but a Christian, in contrast, disregards what he can see and holds to the Word. The godless do not do so but rely upon the emperor to uphold them in this world, but because they neglect the Word, they will be ruined and lost to eternity.

---

3. Luther alludes here to the intrigue and cross-purposes at the Diet of Augsburg and preceding it which hindered the Roman parties from taking decisive action to root out the Lutheran heresy as they had hoped to do.

In this devotional piece Luther examines the passion of Christ. Some think about the evil of the Jews; others feel pity for the suffering Christ. Luther felt that Christ's passion paid the penalty for sin. His suffering in our place not only delivered us from torment, but also reconciled all believers to God.

When one contemplates the work of Christ, he is made aware of his great sin. He is confronted with the guilt that has rightly been his, and with God's grace, which has paid the penalty for sin. The sins of mankind were nailed to the cross, making it possible for all men to be saved if they would only believe. The passion represents God's great effort to reach the people who were created in His image.

CHAPTER EIGHT

A Meditation on Christ's Passion

Some people meditate on Christ's passion by venting their anger on the Jews.[1] This singing and ranting about wretched Judas satisfies them, for they are in the habit of complaining about other people, of condemning and reproaching their adversaries. That might well be a meditation on the wickedness of Judas and the Jews, but not on the sufferings of Christ.

Some point to the manifold benefits and fruits that grow from contemplating Christ's passion. There is a saying ascribed to Albertus[2] about this, that it is more beneficial to ponder Christ's passion just once than to fast a whole year or to pray a psalm daily. These people follow this saying blindly and, therefore, do not reap the fruit of Christ's passion, for in so doing they are seeking their own advantage. They carry pictures and booklets, letters and crosses on their person. Some who travel afar do this in the belief that they thus protect themselves against water and sword, fire, and all sorts of perils.[3] Christ's suffering is thus used to effect in them a lack of suffering contrary to His being and nature.

Some feel pity for Christ, lamenting and bewailing His innocence. They are like the women who followed Christ from Jerusalem and were chided and told by Christ that it would be better to weep for themselves and their children (Luke 23:27–28). They are the kind of people who go far afield in their meditation on the passion, making much of Christ's farewell from Bethany and of the Virgin Mary's anguish, but never progressing beyond that, which is why so many hours are devoted to the contemplation of Christ's passion. Only God knows whether that is invented for the purpose of sleeping or of waking.

Also to this group belong those who have learned what rich fruits the holy Mass offers. In their simplemindedness they think it enough simply to hear Mass. In support of this several teachers are cited to us who hold that the Mass is effective in itself without our merit and worthiness, and that this is all that is needed. Yet the Mass was not instituted for its own worthiness, but to make us worthy and to remind us of the passion of Christ. Where that is not done, we make of the Mass a physical and unfruitful act, though even this is of some good. Of what help is it to you that God is God, if He is not God to you? Of what benefit is it to you that food and drink are good and wholesome in themselves if they are not healthful for

---

1. Luther's attitude toward the Jews finds frequent expression in his works. At the beginning of his career his position was one of benevolent hope of converting them to Christianity. This is reflected in this treatise, as well as in his *That Christ Was Born a Jew*, 1523. Over the years his position changed, due largely to the adamant refusal of the Jews to accept his invitation to acknowledge Christ. This is evidenced in his treatise of 1547, *On the Jews and Their Lies*.

2. Albert Magnus (1193–1280) was a scholastic theologian, often called *"Doctor universalis,"* and a teacher of Thomas Aquinas.

3. Luther here directs his criticism at those who carry holy pictures, prayer books, rosaries, etc., as amulets to ward off harm and danger, as well as those who undertake pilgrimages.

you? And it is to be feared that many Masses will not improve matters as long as we do not seek the right fruit in them.

An Occasion for Fear and Despair

They contemplate Christ's passion aright who view it with a terror-stricken heart and a despairing conscience. This terror must be felt as you witness the stern wrath and the unchanging earnestness with which God looks upon sin and sinners, so much so that He was unwilling to release sinners even for His only and dearest Son without His payment of the severest penalty for them. Thus He says in Isaiah 53:8, "I have chastised Him for the transgressions of My people." If the dearest child is punished thus, what will be the fate of sinners?[4] It must be an inexpressible and unbearable earnestness that forces such a great and infinite person to suffer and die to appease it. And if you seriously consider that it is God's very own Son, the eternal wisdom of the Father, who suffers, you will be terrified indeed. The more you think about it, the more intensely will you be frightened.

You must get this thought through your head and not doubt that you are the one who is torturing Christ thus, for your sins have surely wrought this. In Acts 2:36–37 Saint Peter frightened the Jews like a peal of thunder when he said to all of them, "You crucified Him." Consequently three thousand alarmed and terrified Jews asked the apostles on that one day, "O dear brethren, what shall we do now?" Therefore, when you see the nails piercing Christ's hands, you can be certain that it is your work. When you behold His crown of thorns,

you may rest assured that these are your evil thoughts.

For every nail that pierces Christ, more than one hundred thousand should in justice pierce you, yes, they should prick you forever and ever more painfully! When Christ is tortured by nails penetrating His hands and feet, you should eternally suffer the pain they inflict and the pain of even more cruel nails, which will in truth be the lot of those who do not avail themselves of Christ's passion. This earnest mirror,[5] Christ, will not lie or trifle, and whatever it points out will come to pass in full measure.

Saint Bernard[6] was so terrified by this that he declared, "I regarded myself secure; I was not aware of the eternal sentence that had been passed on me in heaven until I saw that God's only Son had compassion upon me and offered to bear this sentence for me. Alas, if the situation is that serious, I should not make light of it or feel secure." We read that Christ commanded the women not to weep for Him but for themselves and their children (Luke 23:28). And He adds the reason for this, saying, "For if they do this to the green wood, what will happen when it is dry?" (Luke 23:31). He says, as it were, "From My martyrdom you can learn what it is that you really deserve and what your fate should be." Here the saying applies that the small dog is whipped to frighten the big dog. Thus the prophet[7] said that all the generations on earth will bewail themselves over Him; he does not say that they will bewail Him, but that they will bewail themselves because of Him. In like manner the people of whom we heard in Acts 2:36–37 were so frightened that they

---

4. Cf. Luke 23:31.

5. I.e., the one in and through whom we see our sin in its starkness.

6. St. Bernard of Clairvaux (1090–1153), Cistercian monk, mystic, and founder of the abbey of Clairvaux, was held in high regard and frequently quoted by Luther.

7. Cf. Jer. 4:31.

said to the apostles, "O brethren, what shall we do?" This is also the song of the church: "I will ponder this diligently and, as a result, my soul will languish within me."

We must give ourselves wholly to this matter, for the main benefit of Christ's passion is that man sees into his own true self and that he be terrified and crushed by this. Unless we seek that knowledge, we do not derive much benefit from Christ's passion. The real and true work of Christ's passion is to make man conformable to Christ, so that man's conscience is tormented by his sins in like measure as Christ was pitiably tormented in body and soul by our sins. This does not call for many words but for profound reflection and a great awe of sins. Take this as an illustration: a criminal is sentenced to death for the murder of the child of a prince or a king. In the meantime you go your carefree way, singing and playing, until you are cruelly arrested and convicted of having inspired the murderer. Now the whole world closes in upon you, especially since your conscience also deserts you. You should be terrified even more by the meditation on Christ's passion. For the evildoers, the Jews, whom God has judged and driven out, were only the servants of your sin; you are actually the one who, as we said, by his sin killed and crucified God's Son.

He who is so hardhearted and callous as not to be terrified by Christ's passion and led to a knowledge of self, has reason to fear. For it is inevitable, whether in this life or in hell, that you will have to become conformable to Christ's image and suffering.[8] At the very least, you will sink into this terror in the hour of death and in purgatory[9] and will tremble and quake and feel all that Christ suffered on the cross. Since it is horrible to lie waiting on your deathbed, you should pray God to soften your heart and let you now ponder Christ's passion with profit to you. Unless God inspires our heart, it is impossible for us of ourselves to meditate thoroughly on Christ's passion. No meditation or any other doctrine is granted to you that you might be boldly inspired by your own will to accomplish this. You must first seek God's grace and ask that it be accomplished by His grace and not by your own power. That is why the people we referred to above fail to view Christ's passion aright. They do not seek God's help for this, but look to their own ability to devise their own means of accomplishing this. They deal with the matter in a completely human but also unfruitful way.

From Suffering to New Birth

We say without hesitation that he who contemplates God's sufferings for a day, an hour, yes, only a quarter of an hour, does better than to fast a whole year, pray a psalm daily, yes, better than to hear a hundred Masses. This meditation changes man's being and, almost like baptism, gives him a new birth. Here the passion of Christ performs its natural and noble work, strangling the old Adam and banishing all joy, delight, and confidence which man could derive from other creatures, even as Christ was forsaken by all, even by God.

Since this [strangling of the old Adam] does not rest with us, it happens that we occasionally pray for it, and yet do not attain it at once. Nevertheless we should neither despair nor desist. At times this happens because we do not pray for it as God conceives of it and

8. Cf. 1 Cor. 15:49.
9. At this point in his career Luther did not question the doctrine of purgatory.

wishes it, for it must be left free and unfettered. Then man becomes sad in his conscience and grumbles to himself about the evil in his life. It may well be that he does not know that Christ's passion, to which he gives no thought, is effecting this in him, even as the others who do think of Christ's passion still do not gain this knowledge of self through it. For these the passion of Christ is hidden and genuine, while for those it is only unreal and misleading. In that way God often reverses matters, so that those who do not meditate on Christ's passion do meditate on it, and those who do not hear Mass do hear it, and those who hear it do not hear it.

Deliverance Through Christ

Until now we have sojourned in Passion Week and rightly celebrated Good Friday. Now we come to the resurrection of Christ, to the day of Easter. After man has thus become aware of his sin and is terrified in his heart, he must watch that sin does not remain in his conscience, for this would lead to sheer despair. Just as [our knowledge of] sin flowed from Christ and was acknowledged by us, so we must pour this sin back on Him and free our conscience of it. Therefore, beware, lest you do as those perverse people who torture their hearts with their sins and strive to do the impossible, namely, get rid of their sins by running from one good work or penance to another, or by working their way out of this by means of indulgences. Unfortunately such false confidence in penance and pilgrimages is widespread.

You cast your sins from yourself and onto Christ when you firmly believe that His wounds and sufferings are your sins, to be borne and paid for by Him, as we read in Isaiah 53:6, "The Lord has laid on Him the iniquity of us all." Saint Peter says, "In His body has He borne our sins on the wood of the cross" (1 Pet. 2:24). Saint Paul says, "God has made Him a sinner for us, so that through Him we would be made just" (2 Cor. 5:21). You must stake everything on these and similar verses. The more your conscience torments you, the more tenaciously must you cling to them. If you do not do that, but presume to still your conscience with your contrition and penance, you will never obtain peace of mind, but will have to despair in the end. If we allow sin to remain in our conscience and try to deal with it there, or if we look at sin in our heart, it will be much too strong for us and will live on forever. But if we behold it resting on Christ and [see it] overcome by His resurrection, and then boldly believe this, even it is dead and nullified. Sin cannot remain on Christ, since it is swallowed up by His resurrection. Now you see no wounds, no pain in Him, and no sign of sin. Thus Saint Paul declares that "Christ died for our sin and rose for our justification" (Rom. 4:25). That is to say, in His suffering Christ makes our sin known and thus destroys it, but through His resurrection He justifies us and delivers us from all sin, if we believe this.

If, as was said before, you cannot believe, you must entreat God for faith. This too rests entirely in the hands of God. What we said about suffering also applies here, namely, that sometimes faith is granted openly, sometimes in secret.

However, you can spur yourself on to believe. First of all, you must no longer contemplate the suffering of Christ (for this has already done its work and terrified you), but pass beyond that and see His friendly heart and how this heart beats with such love for you that it impels Him to bear with pain your conscience and your sin. Then your heart will be filled with love for Him, and the confidence of your faith will be strengthened. Now continue and rise beyond Christ's heart to God's heart and you will see that Christ would not have shown this love for you if God in His eternal love had not wanted this, for Christ's love for you is due to His obedience to God. Thus you will find the divine and kind paternal heart, and, as Christ says, you will be drawn to the Father through Him. Then you will understand the words of Christ, "For God so loved the world that He gave His only Son" (John 3:16). We know God aright when we grasp Him not in His might or wisdom (for then He proves terrifying), but in His kindness and love. Then faith and confidence are able to exist, and then man is truly born anew in God.

A Pattern for Life

After your heart has thus become firm in Christ, and love, not fear of pain, has made you a foe of sin, then Christ's passion must from that day on become a pattern for your entire life. Henceforth you will have to see His passion differently. Until now we regarded it as a sacrament which is active in us while we are passive, but now we find that we too must be active, namely, in the following. If pain or sickness afflicts you, consider how paltry this is in comparison with the thorny crown and the nails of Christ. If you are obliged to do or to refrain from doing things against your wishes, ponder how Christ was bound and captured and led hither and yon. If you are beset by pride, see how your Lord was mocked and ridiculed along with criminals. If unchastity and lust assail you, remember how ruthlessly Christ's tender flesh was scourged, pierced, and beaten. If hatred, envy, and vindic-

tiveness beset you, recall that Christ, who indeed had more reason to avenge Himself, interceded with tears and cries for you and for all His enemies. If sadness or any adversity, physical or spiritual, distresses you, strengthen your heart and say, "Well, why should I not be willing to bear a little grief, when agonies and fears caused my Lord to sweat blood in the Garden of Gethsemane? He who lies abed while his master struggles in the throes of death is indeed a slothful and disgraceful servant."

So then, this is how we can draw strength and encouragement from Christ against every vice and feeling. That is a proper contemplation of Christ's passion, and such are its fruits. And he who exercises himself in that way does better than to listen to every story of Christ's passion or to read all the Masses. This is not to say that Masses are of no value, but they do not help us in such meditation and exercise.

Those who thus make Christ's life and name a part of their own lives are true Christians. Saint Paul says, "Those who belong to Christ have crucified their flesh with all its desires" (Gal. 5:24). Christ's passion must be met not with words or forms, but with life and truth. Thus, Saint Paul exhorts us, "Consider Him who endured such hostility from evil people against Himself, so that you may be strengthened and not be weary at heart" (Heb. 12:3). And Saint Peter, "Since therefore Christ suffered in the flesh, strengthen and arm yourselves by meditating on this" (2 Pet. 4:1). However, such meditation has become rare, although the letters of Saint Paul and Saint Peter abound with it. We have transformed the essence into semblance and painted our meditations on Christ's passion on walls and made them into letters.

Before Luther's conversion, he was a teacher and priest who was trained in theology, yet lacked a clear understanding of God's saving grace. At best he was a religious laborer whose efforts were of no redemptive value.

In this message Luther points to the flaw in thinking that the duties of religion bring salvation. He cites those who dress and act in good conscience, expecting this to lead to eternal bliss. As Luther realized for himself, it is not the outward expression of religion that makes one truly religious, nor does such conduct earn God's salvation. It is not our works that save us, but the work of Christ. He is the only means of salvation.

CHAPTER NINE

A Sermon on the Three Kinds of Good Life for the Instruction of Consciences

It should be noted first of all how God Almighty commanded through Moses in the Old Testament that a tabernacle be built and divided into three parts. The first part was the holiest part of all and was called the Holy of Holies. It was ten cubits in length, breadth, and height and cubical in shape. The next was called the Holy Place, and that was the same height and width and twenty cubits long. These two parts were joined together in one building made of wooden boards so one could go into one from the other as easily as going from one room into another. The third part was called the atrium, the courtyard, which was one hundred cubits long, fifty wide, and five high, and there was a white curtain, transparent like a net, hanging around the tabernacle. No doubt our churches have developed from this pattern. We divide them into three parts too: the churchyard, the nave, and the sanctuary. The sanctuary is the holiest, then the nave, and after that the churchyard. The same three parts are to be found in a house. First there is the yard, second the house, and third the study or bedchamber.

In this way the Holy Spirit shows that there are three kinds of preaching or teaching which make for three kinds of conscience and three kinds of sin, as well as three kinds of the good life with three kinds of good works. All these differences are helpful, and a Christian needs to know them lest he confuse one

with the other and do nothing properly. He must not mistake the sanctuary for the churchyard, nor the churchyard for the nave. To understand these things better we propose to call the Holy of Holies the sanctuary, the Holy Place the nave, and the court the churchyard.

A Preoccupation with Externals

We start with the churchyard. It is preaching or teaching which is concerned only with outward works which are bound up with time and place. These matters are the ceremonies, the outward performances and techniques in matters of dress or food which cause severe damage to the conscience if a preacher does not alert his people about them. As a result of this kind of teaching, people become hardened and blind, and in this state you can tell them nothing. Let us give a few examples. Priests, monks, nuns, bishops, and all the clergy wear clothes different from the general run of people. They also do other kinds of jobs, wear sacred vestments in church, pray, sing, and so on. These are all outward works linked to dress and occasion. Now he who does these things holds that such teaching has been established by law and that they are called good works, the good life, the spiritual office. When he has done them he believes that he has most certainly earned a good conscience (for what it is worth) and that he has done the right thing. The opposite is true too—if he overlooks one of them or neglects to do it, for example, if he does not wear his garb properly or does not observe the [canonical] hours, he gets a bad conscience like a man who has not kept the commandments.

We act the same way when we observe or break the prescribed commandments, fasts, and feasts, until, through the neglect of the clergy, who are asleep on the job, we reach the point where we make it a more serious matter of conscience for someone to eat a morsel of bread on the eve of a fast than to soak himself in drink, or curse and swear, lie, deceive, or commit adultery or some other serious sin, so inseparably does this kind of teaching bind life and conscience to food and external things. In fact today there are many clergy who would have pangs of conscience ten times worse if they were to celebrate the Mass without a maniple or a chasuble or an altar stone[1] or a silver chalice and things like that, than if they had spoken five times in a scurrilous and scandalous fashion or told lies or spoken behind somebody's back, or otherwise injured their neighbor, so inseparably bound up with these external things is their conscience and so far removed from the things that matter. And what layman or man in the street does not endure worse pangs of conscience if he eats eggs or butter or meat on the eve of a saint's day or other fast day than if he had killed or been unchaste by word or deed? Yes, things are in such a state, owing to certain blind teachers, that no layman dare touch the chalice or corporal. A great fuss and matter of conscience is made of it if anybody unwittingly does touch it. It is worse than that! If an ordinary man were incau-

tiously to touch the holy sacrament with his finger, they skin that finger for him. They make such a matter of conscience out of this affair that there is not a command or prohibition that I regard, they have become so ridiculous.

Just think it over. Such a view of conscience and such error arise from the fact that people have got everything confused and do not differentiate one thing from another in the right way. Then sound instruction and the capacity to differentiate are gone, and before we know where we are, we have reached the stage where the worst is upheld as the best, and the best as the worst. Then the fear of God goes out, human presumption takes over, and the hardening and blinding of men to their sins goes on apace. This is easy to see everywhere in the world. Is it not true that everybody, spiritual and secular estate alike, is unfaithful, prideful, avaricious, hateful, unchaste, and commits all the sins there are, and that nobody takes the slightest notice of them? They have the audacity to think that they live in the fear of the Lord and do His works, although they do not seek to improve themselves in these particular items. They think that they are in a right relationship with God, and that they are doing quite well so long as they exercise their office, pray the canonical hours, wear their clerical garb, and do the right thing in church.

The laity think the same, that all they have to do is to keep their fasts and feasts. As if our God were bothered in the slightest whether you drink beer or water, whether you eat fish or meat, whether you keep the feasts or fasts! It was of people like this that Christ spoke in Matthew 23:23–24, "Woe to you, scribes and Pharisees, hypocrites! for

---

1. Luther is referring to the marble tablets carried about by clergy, on which Mass was celebrated when no episcopally consecrated altar was available, e.g., on military expeditions.

you tithe mint and dill and cummin, and have neglected the weightier matters of the law, justice and mercy and faith; these you ought to have done, without neglecting the others. You blind guides, straining out a gnat and swallowing a camel!"

Has our Lord Himself not depicted here the foolish, perverted conscience which offends God by making important matters trifles and trifles important? How is it that a man can take such a careful sip of outward works that he even strains out a gnat, and can take such a gulp of the right works that he even swallows a camel? It is because he makes things which matter little if at all into strict matters of conscience, but has a very free and easy conscience in things of great importance on which everything depends. People who do this are all churchyard saints. They are only five cubits high. This means that their holiness is circumscribed by their five senses and their bodily existence. And yet, this very holiness shines brighter in the eyes of the world than does real holiness. That is why many stand in this court, for the churchyard is more than three times the length of the nave and ten times as long as the sanctuary. Further, the fact that there are such vast numbers in the courtyard constitutes a great inducement to follow such erroneous, perverted ideas of conscience, works, and life. Indeed, the office of the preacher and pastor is a very serious matter, for the clergy will have to render a solemn account of their failure here if they are not vigilant and active now, and are not striving against such a state of affairs and giving their people true instruction in these matters. But there is another side to it. If they resolve to do this, they will have to suffer persecution from the pope, the bishops, and the prelates. For that gang is itself in such a "churchyardish" state of spiritual life,

utterly drowned in grave sin, that they will not let anyone teach anything different. They want to strain gnats and swallow camels.

Anybody can see for himself that such a "churchyardish" external system betters nobody, and that all the performances bound up with food and clothes, occasion and place, make nobody righteous. For everybody can see that such people continue to be unfaithful, avaricious, impatient, proud, unchaste, angry, and envious. In fact, nobody is more deeply involved in those sins than these very people who have equated righteousness with matters of food, clothing, and observances of time and place. We can see this all around us. Is it not time we called a halt and thought things over? This cannot be the right road to become righteous. There must be another way somewhere. And because these people take such a light view of transgressing in very serious matters, we ought to be wise enough to despise the transgressions of their external pomposities in which we see so much that is corrupt. We must get into the habit of looking in the right direction.

Imagine you were to meet a slanderer or a vulgar gossip, and then you were to meet another man who happened not to have kept the fast or feast or who had eaten nonprescribed food. Would you not be ten times more shocked by the first man than by the second? Would you not regard the second man as one who had swallowed a gnat, and the first a camel? It is grievous and aggravating that the pope is so concerned about eating butter and eggs that people have to buy letters from him, and yet at the same time he is not bothered about whether a man sins against God. The bishops and the prelates follow suit in this, and aid and abet him. If they themselves confuse these matters and get them upside-down, strain gnats and swallow camels, how shall the poor people extricate themselves? How indeed, when their rulers and teachers fight against them in this by their doctrine, example, and authority?

The Proper Road to Piety

Let us now leave the atrium or churchyard and proceed into the Holy Place, the nave. This means teaching, works, and concepts of conscience which are really good. These are humility, meekness, gentleness, peace, fidelity, love, propriety, purity, and the like. These are not bound up with food and clothing, or with place, time, or person. For in these matters a layman may do more of value than a priest, a priest more than a pope, a woman more than a man, a boy more than an adult, a poor man more than a rich man, a naked man more than a man richly clad; more of value may be done in the field than in the home, more in the secret chamber than in the church. This is what God looks for. He who takes this course is traveling on the right road to heaven, apart from what he does or leaves undone in the atrium, for God does not ask him about what happened there, so long as he journeys rightly in this holy place. On the other hand, it is in the nave that we ought to make it a matter of conscience if anybody blasphemes, swears, or speaks uncleanly, or if anybody hears, sees, does, or thinks anything improper. That constitutes the true conscience. It is here that a man strains camels and swallows gnats. It is here that a man gathers up the corn and casts away the chaff. It is here that Abel sacrifices a lamb and lets Cain sacrifice his straw. It is here that a man must fight against pride, avarice, immodesty, anger, hatred, and the like. Here must we keep ourselves fully occupied as long as we live, so as to forget the churchyard altogether and not want it. Here we see what is the proper road to piety and holiness, for we see for ourselves that those who practice this become truly righteous, but those who practice "churchyard" piety do not. That proves that this way and not the other must be the right way.

Some do these works in a living and selfless way. Others, however, set about them in the wrong way. They drag their dead works in with them on their backs and bury them. These are the ones who maintain a pious posture not of their own desire, but because they fear disgrace, punishment, or hell. For many a man is chaste. But if there were no shame or punishment attached to unchastity, then they would go in for it just like those who pay no regard to shame or punishment. In a similar way, many a man controls his anger or temper not gladly or because he loves gentleness, but because he could not very well vent his anger and does not like to confess it. Many a man even gives to the church and endows services, not from generosity but for the sake of glory or to satisfy his vanity. And this false ground is so deep that no saint has ever fathomed its bottom, but shows uncertainty about it and says, "Lord God, create in me a clean heart, and renew a right spirit or will in my inmost being" (Ps. 51:10). Or again in Psalm 19:12, "Lord, who can know all his faults? Cleanse me from secret sins." God does not just want such works by themselves. He wants them to be performed gladly and willingly. And when there is no joy in doing them, and the right will and motive are absent, then they are dead in God's eyes. Such work is riddled with errors; it is service under compulsion, necessity, and duress and is not pleasing to God. As Saint Paul says, "God loves a cheerful giver" (2 Cor. 9:7).

Such gladness, love, joy, and willingness are not found in the heart of any man on earth. As far as our nature goes, we are all sinners. We do not really want to be righteous; we only pretend because we are afraid of being punished or disgraced, or because we seek our own ends and pleasure in these works. And no one is righteous solely and alone for God's sake, the way it ought to be. The natural man wants to and has to seek something whereby he may be righteous; he is not able and has no desire to be righteous for righteousness' sake. He does not allow himself to be content with righteousness, as he ought to do, but is determined by means of it either to earn something or escape something. But that is wrong in God's sight. As Saint Paul concludes in Romans 3:10, quoting Psalm 14:1, "Therefore no man is righteous in God's sight." We ought not be good to earn something or avoid something, for that is to behave no better than a hireling, a bondsman, a journeyman, and not as willing children and heirs who are righteous for the sake of righteousness itself. Children and heirs are righteous only for righteousness' sake, that is, for God's own sake alone, for God Himself is righteousness, truth, goodness, wisdom, holiness. He who seeks nothing other than holiness is the one who seeks God Himself, and he will find Him. He who seeks reward, however, and avoids pain, never finds Him at all and makes reward his god. Whatever it is that makes a man do something, that motive is his god.

A Holy Altar

For these reasons man has to go down on his knees for grace and deny himself. To this end, then, God has built the sanc-

tuary and *Sanctum sanctorum*[2] for us. Here He has set Christ before us and promised that he who believes in Him and calls on His name shall at once receive the Holy Spirit. As He says in John 16, "The Father will send the Holy Spirit in My name."[3] A man who denies himself and calls upon Christ in genuine trust is certain to receive the Holy Spirit. Where Christ's name is, there the Holy Spirit follows. He who calls on Christ in faith, however, possesses His name, and the Holy Spirit most certainly comes to Him. When the Spirit comes, however, He makes a pure, free, cheerful, glad, and loving heart, a heart which is simply gratuitously, righteous, seeking no reward, fearing no punishment. Such a heart is holy for the sake of holiness and righteousness alone and does everything with joy. Look! Here is really sound doctrine! This shows what a conscience is and what good works are! It is to go into the *Sanctum sanctorum*,[4] to pass into the sanctuary. That is the last thing on earth that any man can do. This is the road to heaven. No man remains wicked; on the contrary, all become righteous. This road is quite the opposite of the atrium, for it has no regard for the external things of the churchyard. Indeed, one sees only what enemies of this road they are and how dangerous they are.

Christ referred to this when he said in Mark 16:16, "He that believes shall be saved." Faith alone saves. Why? Faith brings with it the Spirit, and He performs every good work with joy and love. In this way the Spirit fulfills God's commandments, and brings a man his salvation, all of which is signified by the sanctuary and the nave (the *Sanctum* and the *Sanctum sanctorum*)[5] be-

2. Holy of Holies.
3. A conflation of John 16:7 and 26.
4. Holy of Holies.
5. "Holy" and "Holy of Holies."

ing built in one and the same structure. But the atrium, the churchyard that lies apart, is to show that good works without faith cannot happen, and that faith without works cannot endure. A preacher should not try to separate the two, although he should push faith to the fore. Further, faith and good works may well exist without the continuance of those external things, such as sacred foods, sacred garments, sacred times, sacred places. It is for this reason that it is written in the Apocalypse that in the new dispensation the court would be handed over to the heathen (Rev. 11:2), because in the new covenant external matters of this kind should rest with the free and unfettered choice of each individual. Consequently, only the nave and the sanctuary would really be used.

Tragically has it come to pass that there has never been a people on the face of the earth that has had a better atrium, more holy foods, more holy garments, more holy days, more holy places, than Christians now have! It is the fault of the pope and of his canon law, in which so many worthless, dangerous, and aggravating regulations are laid down to the unspeakable detriment and obscuring of faith and good works. May God redeem us from them and protect us with His grace. Amen.

The letters of Martin Luther serve as windows to the heart of a man who on the outside seemed hard but who, inwardly, had a deep sense of tenderness toward his loved ones. His letters reveal a side of Luther many have never seen. These letters show us Martin Luther as husband, father, and child.

Luther the husband is shown to be loving and deeply appreciative of his wife. It is clear that she played an important role in his life as counselor, sounding board, and comforter. Such letters are good examples of how a minister should involve his wife in his life and ministry.

Luther the father is deeply concerned about the welfare of his children. He is constantly encouraging them to love God and never lose sight of His importance. We also find him involved in their education. He praises them for good study habits and conduct. This age is unaccustomed to seeing Christian men so involved with their children.

Finally, Luther the son never lost his love for his parents and always sought to keep them informed of his activities. He honored his parents and saw to it that they knew how important they were to him.

Luther's letters illustrate how Christians should regulate their domestic lives. In doing so they develop a heritage that will either be a curse or blessing.

CHAPTER TEN

Letters

TO HANS LUTHER

This book[1] I have decided to dedicate to you, dearest father. [I do not intend to make] your name famous in the world and to glory in the flesh, which would be contrary to the teaching of Saint Paul.[2] Rather my purpose is to recall, in a short preface, what took place between you and me in order to indicate to the pious reader the argument and the content of this book, together with an example.

To begin with, I wish you to know that your son has reached the point where he is altogether persuaded that there is nothing holier, nothing more important, nothing more scrupulously to be observed than God's commandment.[3] But here you will say, "Have you been so unfortunate as ever to doubt this, and have you only now learned that this is so?" Most unfortunately indeed, I not only doubted it, but I did not at all know that it is so; and if you will permit me, I am ready to show you that this ignorance was common to both of us.

It is now almost sixteen years since I became a monk,[4] taking the vow without your knowledge and against your will.

In your paternal love you were fearful about my weakness because I was then a youth, just entering my twenty-second year (that is, to use Saint Augustine's words, I was still "clothed in hot youth"),[5] and you had learned from numerous examples that this way of life turned out sadly for many. You were determined, therefore, to tie me down with an honorable and wealthy marriage.[6] This fear of yours, this care, this indignation against me was for a time implacable. [Your] friends tried in vain to persuade you that if you wished to offer something to God, you ought to give your dearest and your best. The Lord, meanwhile, was dinning in your ears that Psalm verse: "God knows the thoughts of men, that they are vain";[7] but you were deaf. At least you desisted and bowed to the will of God, but your fears for me were never laid aside. For I remember very well[8] that after we were reconciled and you were [again] talking with me, I told you that I had been called by terrors from heaven and that I did not become a monk of my own free will and desire, still less to gain any gratification of the flesh, but that I was walled in by the terror and the agony of

---

1. *Martin Luther's Opinion on Monastic Vows* (Wittenberg: M. Lotther, February, 1522).
2. Gal. 6:13.
3. In this case the Fourth Commandment.
4. Luther entered the monastery in July of 1505.
5. St. Augustine's *Confessions* (see *Patrology*, pp. 499f.), II, 3.
6. As far as this editor can see, this seems to be the only reference from which the marriage plans his father had for Luther can be deduced. These plans seem to be quite in agreement with the father's ambition to see young Martin in the important and influential position of a legally-trained administrator.
7. Ps. 94:11 (Vulgate).
8. The following is a recollection of what took place between father and son at the celebration of Luther's first mass.

sudden death and forced by necessity to take the vow. Then you said, "Let us hope that it was not an illusion and a deception." That word penetrated to the depths of my soul and stayed there, as if God had spoken by your lips, though I hardened my heart against you and your word as much as I could. You said something else too. When in filial confidence I upbraided you for your wrath, you suddenly retorted with a reply so fitting and so much to the point that I have hardly ever in all my life heard any man say anything which struck me so forcibly and stayed with me so long. "Have you not also heard," you said, "that parents are to be obeyed?" But I was so sure of my own righteousness that in you I heard only a man and boldly ignored you; though in my heart I could not ignore your word.

See now, whether you too were not unaware that the commandments of God are to be put before all things. If you had known that I was then in your power, would you not have used your paternal authority to pull me out of the cowl? On the other hand, had I known it, I would never have attempted to become a monk without your knowledge and consent, even though I had to die many deaths. For my vow was not worth a fig, since by taking it I withdrew myself from the authority and guidance of the parent [to whom I was subject] by God's commandment; indeed, it was a wicked vow and proved that it was not of God not only because it was a sin against your authority, but because it was not absolutely free and voluntary.[9] In short it was taken in accordance with the doctrines of men and the superstition of hypocrites, none of which God

has commanded. But behold how much good God (whose mercies are without number and whose wisdom is without end)[10] has made to come out of all these errors and sins! Would you now not rather have lost a hundred sons than not have seen this good?

I think that from [the days of] my childhood Satan must have foreseen something in me [which is the cause] of his present suffering. He has therefore raged against me with incredible contrivings to destroy or hinder me, so that I have often wondered whether I was the only man in the whole world whom he was seeking. But it was the Lord's will, as I now see, that the wisdom of the schools and the sanctity of the monasteries should become known to me by my own actual experience, that is, through many sins and impieties, so that wicked men might not have a chance, when I became their adversary, to boast that I condemned something about which I knew nothing. Therefore, I lived as a monk, indeed not without sin but without reproach. For in the kingdom of the pope, impiety and sacrilege pass for supreme piety; still less are they considered matters for reproach.

What do you think now? Will you still take me out of the monastery? You are still my father, and I am still your son, and all the vows are worthless. On your side is the authority of God; on my side there is nothing but human presumption. For that continence of which they boast with puffed-up cheeks is valueless without obedience to God's commandments. Continence is not commanded but obedience is, yet the mad and silly papists will not allow any virtue to be

---

9. I.e., the vow was said under the pressure of external circumstances (the lightning near Stotternheim) and thus with the wrong motivation.
10. Ps. 147:5.

equal to continence and virginity. They extol both these virtues with such prodigious lies that their very craze for lying and the greatness of their ignorance, singly or together, ought to cast suspicion on all they do or think.

What kind of intelligence do they show when they distort the word of the sage, "No balance can weigh the value of a continent mind," to mean that virginity and continence are to be preferred to everything else and that vows of virginity cannot be commuted or dispensed with? It was a Jew who wrote these words to Jews about a chaste wife; among the Jews virginity and continence were condemned. Thus, too, they apply to virgins that eulogy of a modest wife: "This is she who has not known a sinful bed."[11] In a word, although the Scriptures do not laud virginity but only approve it, these men,[12] who are so ready to inflame men's souls to lives that endanger their salvation, dress it up in borrowed plumes, so to speak, by applying to it the praises the Scriptures bestow on a chaste marriage.

But isn't [the value] of an obedient soul also beyond all measure? For that reason indeed a continent soul (that is, a chaste wife) defies every measure, not only because [such a soul] is commanded by God but also because, as the well-known proverb says, there is nothing in the world more desirable than a chaste wife.[13] But these "faithful" interpreters of Scripture [take] everything that is said about the continence which is commanded [and] apply it to that type of continence which is not commanded and make a human evaluation the measure of God's judgment. Thus, they grant dispensations from everything, even from obedience to God, [but they grant no dispensation from continence],[14] even from that forbidden continence which is entered upon against the authority of one's parents. O worthy and truly picayunish papistic doctors and teachers! Virginity and chastity are to be praised, but in such a way that by their very greatness men are frightened off from them rather than led to them. This was Christ's way. When the disciples praised continence and said, "If such is the case of a man with his wife, it is expedient not to marry," He at once set their minds straight on the matter and said, "Not all men can receive this precept."[15] The precept must be accepted, but it was Christ's will that only a few should understand it.

But to come back to you, my father; would you still take me out of the monastery? But that you would not boast of it, the Lord has anticipated you and taken me out Himself. What difference does it make whether I retain or lay aside the cowl and tonsure? Do [they] make the monk? "All things are yours, and you are Christ's," says Paul.[16] Shall I belong to the cowl, or shall not the cowl rather belong to me? My conscience has been freed, and that is the most complete liberation. Therefore, I am still a monk and yet not a monk. I am a new creature, not of the pope but of Christ. The pope also has his creatures, but he creates puppets and straw-men, that is, masks and idols of himself. I myself was formerly one of them, led astray by the various usages

11. Wisdom of Solomon 3:13.
12. I.e., the papists.
13. This is either a popular saying (which could not be traced) or an allusion to Prov. 12:4; 31:10, 30.
14. I.e., the monastic and clerical vow of celibacy.
15. Matt. 19:10–11.
16. 1 Cor. 3:22–23.

of words, by which even the sage confesses that he was brought into the danger of death but by God's grace was delivered.[17]

But am I not robbing you again of your right and authority? No, for your authority over me still remains, so far as the monastic life is concerned; but this is nothing to me anymore, as I have said. Nevertheless, [God], who has taken me out of the monastery, has an authority over me that is greater than yours; you see that He has placed me now not in a pretended monastic service but in the true service of God. Who can doubt that I am in the ministry of the Word? And it is plain that the authority of parents must yield to this service, for Christ says, "He who loves father or mother more than Me is not worthy of Me."[18] Not that this word destroys the authority of parents, for the Apostle [Paul] often insists that children should obey their parents;[19] but if the authority of parents conflicts with the authority or calling of Christ, then Christ's authority must reign alone.

Therefore—so I am now absolutely persuaded—I could not have refused to obey you without endangering my conscience unless [Christ] had added the ministry of the Word to my monastic profession. This is what I meant when I said that neither you nor I realized that God's commandments must be put before everything else. But almost the whole world is now laboring under this same ignorance, for under the papal abomination error rules. So Paul also predicted when he said that men would become disobedient to parents. This fits the monks and priests exactly, especially those who under the pretense of piety and the guise of serving God withdraw themselves from the authority of their parents, as though there were any other service of God except the keeping of His commandments, which includes obedience to parents.

I am sending [you] this book, then, in which you may see by what signs and wonders Christ has absolved me from the monastic vow and granted me such great liberty. Although He has made me the servant of all men, I am, nevertheless, subject to no one except to Him alone. He is Himself (as they say) my immediate bishop,[20] abbot, prior, lord, father, and teacher; I know no other. Thus, I hope that He has taken from you one son in order that He may begin to help the sons of many others through me. You ought not only to endure this willingly, but you ought to rejoice with exceeding joy—and this I am sure is what you will do. What if the pope should slay me or condemn me to the depths of hell! Having once slain me, he will not raise me up again to slay me a second and third time, and now that I have been condemned I have no desire ever to be absolved. I trust that the day is at hand when that kingdom of abomination and perdition will be destroyed. Would that we were worthy to be burned or slain by him[21] before that time, so that our blood might cry out against him all the more and hasten the day of his judgment! But if we are not worthy to bear testimony with our blood, then let us at least pray and implore mercy that we may testify with deed and word that Jesus Christ alone is the Lord our God, who is praised forever. Amen.

---

17. Ecclesiasticus 34:12–13.
18. Matt. 10:37.
19. Eph. 6:1; Col. 3:20.
20. I.e., the diocesan bishop to whom the individual church member was subordinate.
21. I.e., the pope, or Satan.

Farewell, [in the Lord], my dearest father, and greet in Christ my mother, your Margaret, and our whole family.

From the wilderness, Wartburg,
November 21, 1521
Dedication of On Monastic Vows

TO JOHN LUTHER

Grace and peace in Christ! My beloved son, I am pleased to learn that you are doing well in your studies, and that you are praying diligently. Continue to do so, my son, [and] when I return home I shall bring you a nice present from the fair.

I know of a pretty, beautiful, [and] cheerful garden where there are many children wearing little golden coats. [They] pick up fine apples, pears, cherries, [and] yellow and blue plums under the trees; they sing, jump, and are merry. They also have nice ponies with golden reins and silver saddles. I asked the owner of the garden whose children they were. He replied, "These are the children who like to pray, study, and be good." Then I said, "Dear sir, I also have a son, whose name is Hänschen Luther. Might he not also [be permitted] to enter the garden, so that he too could eat such fine apples and pears, and ride on these pretty ponies, and play with these children?" Then the man answered, "If he too likes to pray, study, and be good, he too may enter the garden, and also Lippus and Jost. And when they are all together [there], they will also get whistles, drums, lutes, and all kinds of other stringed instruments; and they will also dance and shoot with little crossbows."

And he showed me there a lovely lawn in the garden, all prepared for dancing, where many gold whistles and drums and fine silver crossbows were hanging. But it was still so early [in the morning] that the children had not yet eaten; therefore, I couldn't wait for the dancing. So I said to the man, "Dear sir, I shall hurry away and write about all this to my dear son Hänschen so that he will certainly study hard, pray diligently, and be good in order that he too may get into this garden. But he has an Aunt Lena, whom he must bring along." "By all means," said the man, "go and write him accordingly."

Therefore, dear son Hänschen, do study and pray diligently, and tell Lippus and Jost to study and pray too; then you [boys] will get into the garden together. Herewith, I commend you to the dear Lord ['s keeping]. Greet Aunt Lena, and give her a kiss for me.

June 19, 1530   Your loving father,
Coburg   MARTIN LUTHER

TO MRS. MARGARET LUTHER

My dearly beloved[22] mother! I have received my brother James's[23] letter concerning your illness. Of course this grieves me deeply, especially because I cannot be with you in person, as I certainly would like to be. Yet I am coming to you personally through this letter, and I, together with all the members of my family, shall certainly not be absent from you in spirit.

I trust that you have long since been abundantly instructed, without any help from me, that (God be praised) you have taken [God's] comforting Word into [your heart], and that you are ade-

---

22. Literally: "Beloved from the heart [or: heartily beloved]."
23. James Luther.

quately provided with preachers and comforters. Nevertheless, I shall do my part too and, according to my duty, acknowledge myself to be your child, and you to be my mother, as our common God and Creator has made us and bound us to each other with mutual ties, so that I shall in this way increase the number of your comforters.

First, dear mother, by God's grace you well know by now that this sickness of yours is [God's] fatherly, gracious chastisement.[24] It is a quite small chastisement in comparison with that which He inflicts upon the godless and, sometimes, even His own dear children, when one person is beheaded, another burned, a third drowned, and so on.[25] And so all of us must sing, "For Thy sake we are being daily killed and regarded as sheep to be slaughtered."[26] This sickness, therefore, should not distress or depress you. On the contrary, you should accept it with thankfulness as being sent by God's grace; [you should] recognize how slight a suffering it is— even if it be a sickness unto death—compared with the sufferings of His own dear Son, our Lord Jesus Christ, who did not have to suffer on behalf of Himself, as we have to do, but who suffered for us and for our sins.

Second, dear mother, you also know the true center and foundation of your salvation from whom you are to seek comfort in this and all troubles, namely, Jesus Christ, the cornerstone.[27] He will not waver or fail us, nor allow us to sink or perish, for He is the Savior and is called the Savior of all poor sinners, and of all who are caught in tribulation and

death, and rely on Him, and call on His name.

[Christ] says, "Be of good cheer; I have overcome the world."[28] If He has overcome the world, surely He has also overcome the sovereign of this world[29] with all his power. But what else is [the devil's] power but death, by which he has made us subject to himself, [and] held us captives on account of our sin? But now that death and sin are overcome, we may joyfully and cheerfully listen to the sweet words: "Be of good cheer; I have overcome the world." We certainly are not to doubt that these words are indeed true. More than that, we are commanded to accept this comfort with joy and thanksgiving. Whoever would be unwilling to be comforted by these words would do the greatest injustice and dishonor to the dear Comforter, as if it were not true that He bids us to be of good cheer, or as if it were not true that He has overcome the world. [If we acted thus,] we would only restore within ourselves the tyranny of the vanquished devil, sin and death, and oppose the dear Savior. From this may God preserve us.

Let us, therefore, now rejoice with all assurance and gladness, and should any thought of sin or death frighten us, let us in opposition to this lift up our hearts and say, "Behold, dear soul, what are you doing? Dear death, dear sin, how is it that you are alive and terrify me? Do you not know that you have been overcome? Do you, death, not know that you are quite dead? Do you not know the One who says of you, 'I have overcome the world'? It does not behoove me either to listen to your terrifying sugges-

24. See Heb. 12:6, 11; Rev. 3:19.
25. This is perhaps a reference to the persecutions suffered by some of the evangelicals.
26. Ps. 44:22; Rom. 8:36.
27. See 1 Pet. 2:6; Is. 28:16.
28. John 16:33.
29. See John 12:31.

tions, or heed them. Rather [I should listen] to the comforting words of my Savior: 'Be of good cheer, be of good cheer; I have overcome the world.' He is the victor, the true hero, who gives and appropriates to me His victory with this word: 'Be of good cheer!' I shall cling to Him, and to His words and comfort I shall hold fast; regardless whether I remain here or go yonder, I shall live by [this word, for] He does not lie to me. You would like to deceive me with your terrors, and with your lying thoughts you would like to tear me away from such a victor and Savior. But they are lies, as surely as it is true that He has overcome you and commanded us to be comforted.

"Saint Paul also boasts likewise and defies the terrors of death: 'Death is swallowed up in victory. O death, where is thy victory? O hell, where is thy sting?'[30] Like a wooden image of death, you can terrify and challenge, but you have no power to strangle. For your victory, sting, and power have been swallowed up in Christ's victory. You can show your teeth, but you cannot devour, for God has given us the victory over you through Christ Jesus our Lord, to whom be praise and thanks. Amen."

By such words and thoughts, and by none other, let your heart be moved, dear mother. Above all be thankful that God has brought you to such knowledge and not allowed you to remain caught in papistic error, by which we were taught to rely on our own works and the holiness of the monks, and to consider this only comfort of ours, our Savior, not as a comforter but as a severe judge and

tyrant, so that we had to flee from Him to Mary and the saints, and not expect of Him any grace or comfort. But now we know it differently; [we know] about the unfathomable goodness and mercy of our heavenly Father: that Jesus Christ is our mediator,[31] our throne of grace,[32] and our bishop[33] before God in heaven, who daily intercedes for us and reconciles all who believe in Him alone, and who call upon Him;[34] that He is not a judge, nor cruel, except for those who do not believe in Him, or who reject His comfort and grace; [and] that He is not the man who accuses and threatens us, but rather the man who reconciles us [with God], and intercedes for us with His own death and blood shed for us so that we should not fear Him, but approach Him with all assurance and call Him dear Savior, sweet Comforter, faithful bishop of our souls.

To such knowledge (I say) God has graciously called you. You possess God's seal and letter of this [calling], namely, the gospel you hear preached, baptism, and the sacrament of the altar,[35] so that you should have no trouble or danger. Only be of good cheer and thank [God] joyfully for such great grace! For He who has begun [His work] in you will also graciously complete it,[36] since we are unable to help ourselves in such matters. We are unable to accomplish anything against sin, death, and the devil by our own works. Therefore, another appears for us and in our stead who definitely can do better; He gives us His victory, and commands us to accept it and not to doubt it. He says, "Be of good cheer; I have overcome the

---

30. See 1 Cor. 15:54f.
31. 1 Tim. 2:5.
32. Rom. 3:25 (Luther Bible); Heb. 4:16.
33. 1 Pet. 2:25 (Luther Bible).
34. Rom. 8:34; 1 Tim. 4:10; Heb. 7:25.
35. Literally: "the gospel, baptism, and sacrament, which you hear being preached."
36. Phil. 1:6.

world"; and again: "I live, and you will live also, and no one will take your joy from you."[37]

The Father and God of all consolation[38] grant you, through His holy Word and Spirit, a steadfast, joyful, and grateful faith blessedly to overcome this and all other trouble, and finally to taste and experience that what He Himself says is true: "Be of good cheer; I have overcome the world." And with this I commend your body and soul to His mercy. Amen.

All your children and my Katie pray for you; some weep, others say at dinner, "Grandmother is very sick." God's grace be with us all. Amen.

May 20, 1531   Your loving son,
Wittenberg   MARTIN LUTHER

TO MRS. KATHARINE LUTHER

God in Christ be with you! My dearly beloved Katie! As soon as Doctor Brück is granted permission to leave the court—he puts me off with this prospect—I hope to come along with him tomorrow or the next day. Pray God to bring us home chipper and healthy! I am sleeping very well, about six or seven hours without interruption, and then thereafter again for two or three hours. It's the beer's fault, I think. But, just as in Wittenberg, I am sober.

Doctor Caspar[39] says that the gangrene in our Gracious Lord's[40] foot will spread no further.[41] But neither Dobitzsch[42] nor any prisoner on the stretching rack in jail suffers such agony from John the jailer as His Electoral Grace suffers from the surgeons. His Sovereign Grace is, in his whole body, as healthy as a little fish, but the devil has bitten and pierced His Grace's foot. Pray, and continue to pray! I trust God will listen to us, as He has begun. For Doctor Caspar too thinks that in this case God has to help.

Since John[43] is moving away, it is both necessary and honorable that I let him go honorably from me. For you know that he has served me faithfully and diligently and conducted himself with humility, and [he has] done and endured all [he was required to do], according to the gospel. Remember how often we have given something to bad boys and ungrateful students, in which cases all that we did was lost. Now, therefore, reach into your wallet[44] and let nothing be lacking for this fine fellow, since you know that it is well used and God-pleasing. I certainly know that little is available; yet if I had them I wouldn't mind giving him ten gulden. But you shouldn't give him less than five gulden, since we didn't give him a new suit of clothes [upon his departure]. Whatever you might be able to do beyond this, do it, I beg you for it. The Common Chest might, of course, make a present to my servant in my honor, in view of the fact that I am forced to maintain my ser-

37. John 14:19; 16:22.
38. Rom. 15:5 (Luther Bible).
39. I.e., Dr. Caspar Lindemann, the Elector's personal physician.
40. I.e., Elector John.
41. Literally: "that our Gracious Lord's foot will not eat further."
42. This is a reference to an infamous outlaw knight who had been executed on November 30, 1531.
43. I.e., John Rischmann of Brunswick. He had studied in Wittenberg since 1527, had been Luther's *famulus*, and had lived with the Luther family. With Luther's fine letter of recommendation, dated February 27, 1532, Rischmann became assistant principal of a school in Husum (Schleswig-Holstein) in 1533; soon thereafter he was appointed deacon and archdeacon there. In 1544 he visited Luther again in order to get advice on a marital problem of one of his parishioners.
44. Literally: "So, now touch yourself here [i.e., in this case]."

vants at my expense for the service and benefit of the local congregation.[45] But they may do as they please. Yet under no circumstances should you let anything be lacking as long as there is still a fine goblet [in the house]. Figure out from where you will take the money. God certainly will provide more; this I know. With this I commend you to God. Amen.

Tell the pastor of Zwickau he really ought to be pleased and content with the quarters. Upon my return I shall tell you how Mühlpfort and I have been guests of Rietesel, and how Mühlpfort has demonstrated much wisdom to me. But I wasn't eager for his wisdom.

Kiss young Hans for me,[46] keep after Hänschen, Lenchen,[47] and Aunt Lena to pray for the dear Sovereign and for me. I am unable to find anything to buy for the children in this town even though there is now a fair here. If I am unable to bring anything special along, please have something ready for me!

February 27, 1532   DOCTOR
Torgau   MARTIN LUTHER

TO JOHN LUTHER

Thus far, my dearest son, your studies and the letters you have written to me have been a pleasure for me. If you continue this way then not only will you please me, your father who loves you, but you also will very much benefit yourself, so that you will not seem to have stained yourself with dishonor. Therefore, take care to pursue diligently what you started. For God, who has commanded children to be obedient to their parents, has also promised His blessing to obedient children. See to it that you have only this blessing before your eyes and that you do not let yourself be diverted from it by any evil example. For that same God has also threatened disobedient children with a curse. Therefore, fear God who blesses and curses, who even though He delays with His promises and threats, a fact which leads to the ruin of the evil, nevertheless, quite quickly implements them for the well-being of the good. Fear God, therefore, and listen to your parents— who certainly want nothing but the best for you—and run from disgraceful and disreputable conversations.

Your mother cordially greets you; so do Aunt Lena and your sisters and brothers, all of whom are looking forward to a successful progress and conclusion of your studies. Mother requests that you greet your teacher and his wife. Further, should they wish to be with you here during this Shrovetide, or these happy days, while I am gone from here, then this is fine with us. Aunt Lena very much asks for this.

Farewell, my son; listen to and learn for the exhortations given to you by good men. The Lord be with you.

January 27, 1537   MARTIN LUTHER,
Wittenberg   your Father according
to the flesh and spirit

---

45. Literally: "benefit of their [i.e., the citizens of Wittenberg] church."
46. John Luther
47. Magdalen Luther

The Table Talks represent the best of Luther's small talk. They were collected by friends of his as they met together to enjoy moments of light conversation. It is not hard to see these brief statements as passing thoughts shared around a table of good food with good friends. They are those off-the-record private thoughts not easily preserved for posterity.

These talks offer a more intimate look at Luther as he lived his life from day to day. Especially touching are his thoughts on the death of his daughter. Any parent who has lost a child will find great comfort in his comments.

It is important that we see Luther as more than an academic or reformer. He was a human being subject to the same feelings as the rest of us. His methods of expression may seem at times inappropriate, but then that was Martin Luther, a man with a heart of gold and feet of clay.

CHAPTER ELEVEN

Table Talks

LUTHER'S EVALUATION OF HIS WIFE

"I wouldn't give up my Katie[1] for France or Venice—first, because God gave her to me and gave me to her; second, because I have often observed that other women have more shortcomings than my Katie (although she too has some shortcomings, they are outweighed by many great virtues); and third, because she keeps faith in marriage, that is, fidelity and respect.

"A wife ought to think the same way about her husband."

Summer or Fall, 1531

THE GREATEST THING IN DEATH IS FEAR

"Fear of death is death itself and nothing else. Anybody who has torn death from deep down in his heart does not have death or taste it."

Somebody inquired about the pains of death, and Martin Luther replied, "Ask my wife if she felt anything when she was really dead."[2]

She herself responded, "Nothing at all, doctor."

Thereupon, Dr. Martin Luther continued, "For this reason I say that the greatest thing in death is the fear of death. It is written in the epistle to the Hebrews

[2:9], 'that by the grace of God He might taste death for every one.' We are blessed if we don't taste death, which is very bitter and sharp. How great the pain of tasting death is we can discern in Christ when He said, 'My soul is very sorrowful, even to death' [Matt. 26:38]. I regard these as the greatest words in all the Scriptures, although it is also a great and inexplicable thing that Christ cried out on the cross, 'Eli, Eli' [Matt. 27:46]. No angel comprehends how great a thing it was that He sweated blood [Luke 22:44]. This was tasting and fearing death. Creation consoles the Creator,[3] and the disciples noticed nothing of these things."

September 1542

DESCRIPTION OF THE DEATH OF MAGDALENE LUTHER

When his daughter was in the agony of death, he [Martin Luther] fell on his knees before the bed and, weeping bitterly, prayed that God might will to save her. Thus, she gave up the ghost in the arms of her father. Her mother was in the same room, but farther from the bed on account of her grief. It was after the ninth hour on the Wednesday after the fifteenth Sunday after Trinity, in the year 1542.

September 20, 1542

---

1. Luther was married to Katharine von Bora (1499–1552), a former nun, on June 13, 1525. See Clara S. Schreiber, *Katharine, Wife of Luther* (Philadelphia: Muhlenberg Press, 1954).
2. The reference is to the grave illness of Luther's wife Katharine in 1540.
3. Cf. Luke 22:43.

THE LOVE OF PARENTS FOR THEIR CHILDREN

Often he [Martin Luther] repeated the words given above: "I'd like to keep my dear daughter because I love her very much, if only our Lord God would let me. However, His will be done! Truly nothing better can happen to her, nothing better."

While she was still living he often said to her, "Dear daughter, you have another Father in heaven. You are going to go to Him."

Philip Melanchthon said, "The feelings of parents are a likeness of divinity impressed upon the human character. If the love of God for the human race is as great as the love of parents for their children, then it is truly great and ardent."[4]

September 1542

LUTHER'S DAUGHTER MAGDALENE PLACED IN COFFIN

When his dead daughter was placed in a coffin, he [Martin Luther] said, "You dear little Lena! How well it has turned out for you!"

He looked at her and said, "Ah, dear child, to think that you must be raised up and will shine like the stars, yes, like the sun!"

The coffin would not hold her, and he said, "The little bed is too small for her."

[Before this,] when she died, he said, "I am joyful in spirit, but I am sad according to the flesh. The flesh doesn't take kindly to this. The separation [caused by death] troubles me above measure. It's strange to know that she is surely at peace and that she is well

off there, very well off, and yet to grieve so much!"

September 1542

THE COFFIN IS ESCORTED FROM THE HOME

When people came to escort the funeral, and friends spoke to him according to custom and expressed to him their sympathy, he [Martin Luther] said, "You should be pleased! I've sent a saint to heaven—yes, a living saint. Would that our death might be like this! Such a death I'd take this very hour."

The people said, "Yes, this is quite true. Yet everybody would like to hold on to what is his."

Martin Luther replied, "Flesh is flesh, and blood is blood. I'm happy that she's safely out of it. There is no sorrow except that of the flesh."

Again, turning to others, he said, "Do not be sorrowful. I have sent a saint to heaven. In fact, I have now sent two of them."[5]

Among other things, he said to those who had come to escort the funeral as they were singing the verse in the psalm, "Lord, remember not against us former iniquities" (Ps. 79:8), "O Lord, Lord, Lord, not only former iniquities but also present ones! We are usurers, gougers, and for fifteen years I read Mass and conducted the abominations of the Mass."

September 1542

WHAT IT TAKES TO UNDERSTAND THE SCRIPTURES

"I wonder whether Peter, Paul, Moses, and all the saints fully and thoroughly

---

4. Cf. Isa. 49:15.
5. Luther's eight-month-old daughter Elizabeth had died August 3, 1528.

understood a single word of God so that they had nothing more to learn from it, for the understanding of God is beyond measure.[6] To be sure, the saints understood the Word of God and could also speak about it, but their practice did not keep pace with it. Here one forever remains a learner. The scholastics illustrated this with a ball which only at one point touches the table on which it rests, although the whole weight of the ball is supported by the table.

"Though I am a great doctor, I haven't yet progressed beyond the instruction of children in the Ten Commandments, the Creed, and the Lord's Prayer. I still learn and pray these every day with my Hans and my little Lena.[7] Who understands in all of its ramifications even the opening words,[8] 'Our Father who art in heaven'? For if I understood these words in faith—that the God who holds heaven and earth in His hand is my Father—I would conclude that, therefore, I am lord of heaven and earth, therefore Christ is my brother, therefore, all things are mine, Gabriel is my servant, Raphael is my coachman, and all the other angels are ministering spirits[9] sent forth by my Father in heaven to serve me in all my necessities, lest I strike my foot against a stone. In order that this faith should not remain untested, my Father comes along and allows me to be thrown into prison or to be drowned in water. Then it will finally become apparent how well we understand these words. Our faith wavers.

Our weakness gives rise to the question, 'Who knows if it is true?' So this one word 'your' or 'our' is the most difficult of all in the whole Scripture. It's like the word 'your' in the First Commandment, 'I am the Lord your God' (Ex. 20:2)."

Fall 1531

THE STUDY OF THE BIBLE DEMANDS HUMILITY

"The Holy Scriptures require a humble reader who shows reverence and fear toward the Word of God and constantly says, 'Teach me, teach me, teach me!' The Spirit resists the proud. Though they study diligently and some preach Christ purely for a time, nevertheless, God excludes them from the church if they're proud. Wherefore, every proud person is a heretic, if not actually, then potentially. However, it's difficult for a man who has excellent gifts not to be arrogant. Those whom God adorns with great gifts He plunges into the most severe trials in order that they may learn that they're nothing. Paul got a thorn in the flesh to keep him from being haughty.[10] And if Philip were not so afflicted he would have curious notions. When on the other hand Jacob[11] and Agricola[12] are haughty and despise their teachers and learning, I fear it may be done with them. I knew the spirit of Münzer,[13] Zwingli, and Karlstadt. Pride drove the angel out of heaven and spoils

---

6. Cf. Ps. 147:5.
7. Luther's son John was born in 1526 and his daughter Magdalene was born in 1529.
8. Of the Lord's Prayer. Cf. Matt. 6:9.
9. Cf. Heb. 1:14.
10. Cf. 2 Cor. 12:7.
11. Jacob Schenk, an Antinomian.
12. John Agricola was Luther's chief Antinomian opponent.
13. Thomas Münzer was a radical religious leader in the Peasants' War.

many preachers. Accordingly it's humility that's needed in the study of sacred literature."

May or June 1540

WHERE THE WORD IS THERE IS CONTEMPT

"When the Word comes, contempt for it is there too. This is certain. One can see it in the case of the Jews. God sent them the prophets Isaiah, Jeremiah, Amos, sent them Christ Himself, even divided the Holy Spirit among the apostles, who cried out together, 'Be penitent!' But nothing helped. They all had to endure much. Soon Jerusalem lay in ruin, and it remains so to this day. The same thing will happen in Germany. I think a great darkness will follow the present light, and after that the Judgment Day will come."

Winter 1542–43

MAN'S ARROGANCE AND SELF-ASSURANCE

"It's remarkable that men should be so arrogant and secure when there are so many, indeed countless, evidences around us to suggest that we ought to be humble. The hour of our death is uncertain. The grain on which we live is not in our hands. Neither the sun nor the air, on which our life depends, lies in our power, and we have no control over our sleeping and waking. I shall say nothing of spiritual things, such as the private and public sins which press upon us. Yet our hearts are hard as steel and pay no attention to such evidence."

November 1531

GOD'S PUNISHMENT OF THE GODLESS

"While I was in Erfurt I once said to Dr. Staupitz,[14] 'Dear doctor, our Lord God treats people too horribly. Who can serve Him as long as He strikes people down right and left, and we see He does in many cases involving our adversaries?' Then Dr. Staupitz answered, 'Dear fellow, learn to think of God differently. If He did not treat them this way, how could God restrain those blockheads? God strikes us for our own good, in order that He might free us who would otherwise be crushed.'

"When I was in Coburg[15] these comments about adversaries taught me the meaning of the words in the Decalogue, 'I the Lord your God am a jealous God.'[16] It is not so much a cruel punishment of adversaries as it is a necessary defense of ourselves. They say that Zwingli recently died thus;[17] if his error had prevailed, we would have perished, and our church with us. It was a judgment of God. That was always a proud people. The others, the papists, will probably also be dealt with by our Lord God. They invoked the bread[18] as God, and

---

14. Luther was recalling this conversation which he had with John Staupitz (d. 1524), then vicar-general of the Augustinian Observantists in Germany, while Luther was still in the Augustinian monastery in Erfurt.

15. During the Diet of Augsburg in 1530 Luther was in Castle Coburg.

16. Ex. 20:5. In Luther's *Small Catechism* these words appear at the conclusion of the Ten Commandments.

17. Huldreich Zwingli, the Swiss reformer, died in battle on October 11, 1531.

18. I.e., the transubstantiated bread of the Roman Mass.

now He will become as hard as iron toward them. Oecolampadius[19] called our Lord's Supper a Thyestian banquet[20] [and ridiculed participants in it as] flesh-eaters and blood-drinkers. Now we say to them "Here you have what you asked for." God has spoken once for all: He will not hold him guiltless who takes His name in vain.[21] Surely they blasphemed when they invoked God in the bread or called us flesh-eaters, blood-drinkers, God-devourers. The same will happen to our papists who have burdened themselves with the blood of the godly. God grant that by Pentecost they may be destroyed root and branch! They themselves say that they want either to smother doctrine or leave nothing behind. Amen. Let it be as they wish! How can our Lord God repay them better than by giving them what they want?"

November 1531

THE TRIALS OF A PREACHER AND REFORMER

"If I were to write about the burdens of the preacher as I have experienced them and as I know them, I would scare everybody off. For a good preacher must be committed to this, that nothing is dearer to him than Christ and the life to come, and that when this life is gone Christ will say to all, 'Come to me, son. [You have been my dear and faithful servant].'[22] I hope that on the last day He'll speak to me too in this way, for here He speaks to me in a very unfriendly way. I bear [the hatred of] the whole world, the

emperor, and the pope, but since I got into this I must stand my ground and say, 'It's right.' Afterward the devil also speaks to me about this, and he has often tormented me with this argument, 'You haven't been called,' as if I had not been made a doctor."[23]

Early in the year 1533

DO NOT DEBATE WITH SATAN WHEN ALONE

"Almost every night when I wake up, the devil is there and wants to dispute with me. I have come to this conclusion: when the argument that the Christian is without the law and above the law doesn't help, I instantly chase him away. The rogue wants to dispute about righteousness although he is himself a knave, for he kicked God out of heaven and crucified His Son. No man should be alone when he opposes Satan. The church and the ministry of the Word were instituted for this purpose, that hands may be joined together and one may help another. If the prayer of one doesn't help, the prayer of another will."

Spring 1533

WHAT IS INVOLVED IN A CALL TO THE MINISTRY

"First of all, this is certain: young people must be brought up to learn the Scriptures. Later they will know that they are to be educated to be pastors.

---

19. John Oecolampadius, co-laborer of Zwingli in Switzerland, died in Basel on November 24, 1531, shortly after this conversation in Wittenberg.
20. Thyestes was a mythological figure who was served his own son to eat.
21. Cf. Ex. 20:7.
22. Cf. Matt. 25:21.
23. Luther often appealed to his doctor's degree as the ground for his authority to instruct and reform the church.

Afterward they will offer their services when some position is unoccupied. That is to say, they will not force their way in but will indicate that they are prepared, in case anybody should ask for them; thus, they will know whether they should go. It is like a girl who is trained for marriage; if anybody asks her, she gets married. To force one's way in is to push somebody else out. But to offer one's service is to say, 'I'll be glad to accept if you can use me in this place.' If he is wanted, it is a true call. So Isaiah said, 'Here I am. Send me' (Isa. 6:8). He went when he heard that a preacher was needed. This ought to be done.

"A young man should find out whether somebody is wanted, and then whether *he* is wanted. The latter must also be. What is to be said about talents is touched upon in the text that speaks about servants who are called.[24] It is written by Paul, 'If anyone aspires to the office of bishop, do not hinder him, for he desires a noble task' (1 Tim. 3:1). But to force one's way in is to do as Karlstadt did; during my absence he abandoned his citadel (that is, his pulpit), occupied my pulpit, and changed the Mass.[25] All this he did on his own authority. So he did also in Orlamünde,[26] and he said he wanted to give the theologians some trouble.

Spring 1533

EVERY SEVENTH YEAR BRINGS A CHANGE

"My Hans is about to enter upon his seventh year,[27] which is always climacteric, that is, a time of change. People always change every seventh year. The first period of seven years is childhood, and at the second change—say, in the fourteenth year—boys begin to look out into the world; this is the time of boyhood, when the foundations are laid in the arts. At the age of twenty-one youths desire marriage, in the twenty-eighth year young men are householders and heads of families, while at the age of thirty-five men have civil and ecclesiastical positions. This continues to the age of forty-two, when we are kings. Soon after this men begin to lose their sense. So every seventh year always brings to man some new condition and way of life. This has happened to me, and it happens to everybody."

June 5, 1532

WHY GOD PLACES CHRISTIANS IN THE WORLD

"God placed His church in the midst of the world, among countless external activities and callings, not in order that Christians should become monks but so that they may live in fellowship and that our works and the exercises of our faith may become known among men. For human society, as Aristotle[28] said, is not an end in itself but a means [to an end]; and the ultimate end is to teach one another about God. Accordingly Aristotle said that society isn't made by a physician and a physician or by a farmer and a farmer. There are three kinds of life: labor must be engaged in, warfare must be carried on, governing must be done.

---

24. Cf. Luke 19:12–27.
25. While Luther was absent in the Wartburg Castle in the fall of 1521 and the spring of 1522, Andrew Karlstadt took it upon himself to introduce changes in Wittenberg that confused the people.
26. In 1524 Karlstadt introduced even more radical changes in the church in Orlamünde, near Wittenberg, and was expelled on account of them.
27. Luther's oldest son, John, was born June 7, 1526.
28. Greek philosopher (384–322 B.C.) who had great influence on medieval theology.

The state consists of these three. Consequently Plato[29] said that just as oxen aren't governed by oxen and goats by goats, so men aren't governed by men but by heroic persons."

August 31, 1538

---

29. Greek philosopher (d. 347 B.C.) who was the teacher of Aristotle.

Alex, Ben. *Martin Luther.* Wheaton, Illinois. Victor Books, SP Publications, 1995.

Althaus, Paul. *The Ethics of Martin Luther.* Robert C. Schultz, translator, Minneapolis, Augsburg Fortress Press, 1972.

Atkinson, James. *Martin Luther: Prophet to the Catholic Church.* Reprint edition, Books on Demand, n.d.

Bainton, Roland H. *Here I Stand: A Life of Martin Luther.* Nashville, Abingdon Press, 1991.

Beard, Charles. *Martin Luther and the Reformation in Germany until the Close of the Diet of Worms.* Reprint edition, New York. AMS Press, n.d.

Boehmer, Heinrich. *Luther and the Reformation in the Light of Modern Research.* Reprint edition, New York. AMS Press, n.d.

Brecht, Martin. *Martin Luther: Shaping and Defining the Reformation.* Minneapolis, Augsburg Fortress, 1994.

Friedenthal, Richard. *Luther, His Life and Times.* English Translation by John Nowell, New York, Harcourt, Brace, Jovanovich, 1970.

Kolb, Robert. *Luther: Pastor of God's People.* 10 vols. St. Louis, Concordia, 1990.

Luther, Martin. *Luther's Ninety-five Theses.* C. M. Jacobs, translator, Minneapolis, Fortress Press, 1957.

Manns, Peter. *Martin Luther, An Illustrated Biography.* New York, Crossroad Pub. Co., 1983.

Nohl, Frederick. *Martin Luther: Hero of Faith.* (Juvenile Literature) St. Louis, Concordia, 1982.

Olivier, D. *Luther's Faith: The Cause of the Gospel in the Church.* St. Louis, Concordia, 1982.

Plass, Ewald. *This is Luther.* St. Louis, Concordia, 1984.

————. *What Luther Says: A Practical-in-Home Anthology for the Active Christian.* St. Louis, Concordia, 1995.

Simon-Netto, Uwe. *The Fabricated Luther: The Rise & Fall of the Shirer Myth.* St. Louis, Concordia, 1995.

Van de Weyer, Robert. *Luther.* New York, Revell, 1991.

Zachman, Randall C. *The Assurance of Faith: Conscience in the Theology of Martin Luther & John Calvin.* Minneapolis, Augsburg Fortress, 1992.

JOHN WESLEY

John Wesley

Abridged and edited by Stephen Rost

Contents

JOHN WESLEY 1703–1791

1703–1729

His Life	Year	World Events
Born June 17, Epworth, Lincolnshire, England.	1703	Peter the Great founds St. Petersburg.
Father, Samuel, imprisoned for 4 months.	1705	Twinings Tea Company founded in London.
Brother Charles, born.	1708	First Colonial newspaper issued in Boston.
John is rescued from fire in Epworth rectory, February 9.	1709	Copyright Act enacted in Britain.
Entered Charterhouse boarding school, January 28.	1714	Queen Anne dies, King George I takes throne.
Entered Christ Church, Oxford, B.A. degree.	1720–1724	Old Haymarket Theater opens in London.
Ordained deacon, September 19; preached at S. Leigh, near Oxford, September 26.	1725	Homer's *Odyssey* and *Iliad* translated by Alexander Pope.
At Epworth transcribing Samuel's work on the Book of Job; experienced the "Ghost of Epworth"; preached at St. Michael's on September 29.	1726	Jonathan Swift writes *Gulliver's Travels*.
M.A. degree from Lincoln College, February 14; assists father as curate at Wroot, August 1727—November 1729; first and last experience as a parish clergyman.	1727	Defoe's *The Complete English Tradesman* published.
Ordained to Priest's Orders, September 22.	1728	William Law publishes *A Serious Call to Devout and Holy Life*.
Visited Oxford and Charles' "Holy Club," later known as "Methodists," June; returned to Oxford as Junior Fellow, joined "Holy Club," November.	1729	James and Benjamin Franklin begin a newspaper, later to become *The Saturday Evening Post*.

1730–1739

His Life	Year	World Events
Appointed moderator in philosophy; temporary curacy at Pyrton, February; publishes *A Collection of Forms of Prayer for Every Day in the Week*, his first book; held services for prisoners at Oxford Castle and Bocardo, 1730–1732.	1730–1732	In 1732, Benjamin Franklin publishes *Poor Richard's Almanac*.
"Holy Club" member, William Morgan, died after fasting; John and Charles blamed for his death.	1732	Moravian Brethren start missionary work.
Preached "Circumcision of the Heart" for the first time.	1733	Savannah, Georgia founded by James Oglethorpe.
Father, Samuel, died; began keeping *Journal*; sent to America as chaplain; Charles ordained as a deacon; brothers set sail.	1735	The Bible is first translated into Lithuanian.
Arrived at Tyree Island; visited by Indians on board ship, February 14; preached first sermon in Savannah, "On Love," March 7.	1736	English repeal statutes against witchcraft.
Translated many German hymns; departed America; "Psalms and Hymns'" published.	1737	Richmond, Virginia founded by William Byrd.
First convert to salvation by faith alone was a death-row prisoner, March; preached at St. Ann's; Aldersgate "heart strangely warmed" experience, May 24; preached "By Grace You Are Saved Through Faith" at St. Mary's; went to Germany to be with Moravians, June.	1738	George Whitefield goes to Georgia as "Leader of the Great Awakening."
First sermon preached outdoors; cornerstone for first Methodist chapel laid in Bristol; preached to more than 2,000 outside at Bristol in May; by June preaching to 50,000 a week; *Hymns and Sacred Poems* published as first hymnbook; school begun in Kingswood.	1739	Moravian Church founded in America.

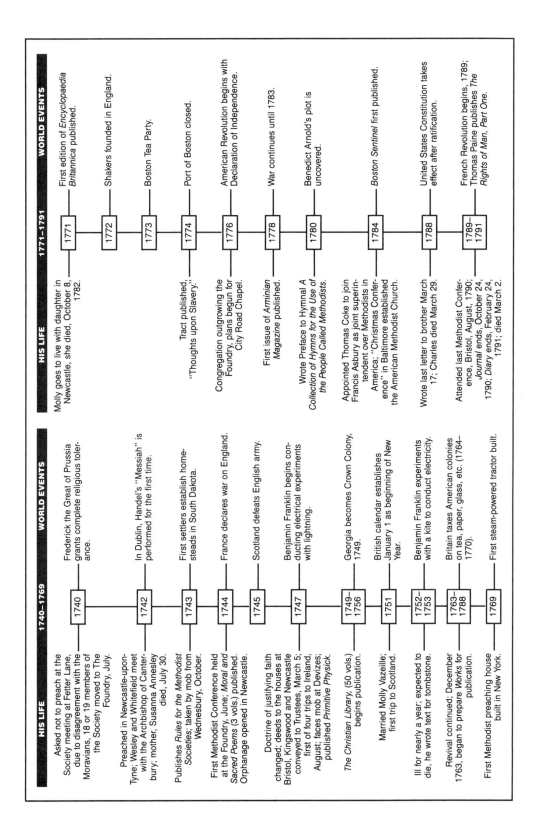

1740–1769

HIS LIFE

Asked not to preach at the Society meeting at Fetter Lane, due to disagreement with the Moravians, 18 or 19 members of the Society moved to The Foundry, July.

Preached in Newcastle-upon-Tyne; Wesley and Whitefield meet with the Archbishop of Canterbury; mother, Susanna Annesley died, July 30.

Publishes *Rules for the Methodist Societies;* taken by mob from Wednesbury, October.

First Methodist Conference held at the Foundry, June; *Moral and Sacred Poems* (3 vols.) published. Orphanage opened in Newcastle.

Doctrine of justifying faith changed; deeds to the houses at Bristol, Kingswood and Newcastle conveyed to Trustees, March 5; first of four trips to Ireland, August; faces mob at Devizes; published *Primitive Physick.*

The Christian Library, (50 vols.) begins publication.

Married Molly Vazeille; first trip to Scotland.

Ill for nearly a year; expected to die, he wrote text for tombstone.

Revival continued; December 1763, began to prepare *Works* for publication.

First Methodist preaching house built in New York.

WORLD EVENTS

Frederick the Great of Prussia grants complete religious tolerance.

In Dublin, Handel's "Messiah" is performed for the first time.

First settlers establish homesteads in South Dakota.

France declares war on England.

Scotland defeats English army.

Benjamin Franklin begins conducting electrical experiments with lightning.

Georgia becomes Crown Colony, 1749.

British calendar establishes January 1 as beginning of New Year.

Benjamin Franklin experiments with a kite to conduct electricity.

Britain taxes American colonies on tea, paper, glass, etc. (1764–1770).

First steam-powered tractor built.

Timeline years: 1740 · 1742 · 1743 · 1744 · 1745 · 1747 · 1749–1756 · 1751 · 1752–1753 · 1763–1788 · 1769

1771–1791

WORLD EVENTS

First edition of *Encyclopaedia Britannica* published.

Shakers founded in England.

Boston Tea Party.

Port of Boston closed.

American Revolution begins with Declaration of Independence.

War continues until 1783.

Benedict Arnold's plot is uncovered.

Boston Sentinel first published.

United States Constitution takes effect after ratification.

French Revolution begins, 1789; Thomas Paine publishes *The Rights of Man, Part One.*

Timeline years: 1771 · 1772 · 1773 · 1774 · 1776 · 1778 · 1780 · 1784 · 1788 · 1789–1791

HIS LIFE

Molly goes to live with daughter in Newcastle, she died, October 8, 1782.

Tract published, "Thoughts upon Slavery."

Congregation outgrowing the Foundry, plans begun for City Road Chapel.

First issue of *Arminian Magazine* published.

Wrote Preface to Hymnal *A Collection of Hymns for the Use of the People Called Methodists.*

Appointed Thomas Coke to join Francis Asbury as joint superintendent over Methodists in America; "Christmas Conference" in Baltimore established the American Methodist Church.

Wrote last letter to brother March 17; Charles died March 29.

Attended last Methodist Conference, Bristol, August, 1790; *Journal* ends, October 24, 1790; *Diary* ends, February 24, 1791; died March 2.

JOHN WESLEY

Introduction

A church historian once observed that some successful church movements of profound historical significance resulted from the vision, leadership, and resources of wealthy, well-educated men. Such men found that the less affluent segments of society were particularly ripe for the gospel message. The marriage of good leadership with willing followers brought about great institutions that are still going strong.

John Wesley exemplified the sort of leadership mentioned. Born in 1703 in England, Wesley was the son of the Anglican rector of Epworth in Lincolnshire. Under this influence, John and his brother Charles grew to manhood embracing religion.

John Wesley attended Oxford University and later became a lecturer at Lincoln College. Yet Wesley's niche in life was not in the classroom. His brother Charles had formed a group called the Holy Club, and John became deeply involved with it, eventually engaging in ministry very similar to that of a pastor. Visiting poor, needy people in the streets and prisons, John discovered the place he felt God wanted him. Thus began the long, fruitful life of Methodism's greatest leader.

Wesley's spiritual development took an interesting course. It is clear that he earnestly sought involvement in religious activity, be it education or street ministry. Yet he never seemed to have the assurance of salvation shown by other religious workers with whom he came into contact. In the American colonies some Moravian Christians challenged John and Charles Wesley to find the assurance they desperately wanted. On May 21, 1738, Charles Wesley experienced genuine conversion as a result of reading Martin Luther's commentary on Galatians. Three days later John Wesley, after hearing the reading of Luther's preface to Romans, also experienced real conversion. How remarkable that these two great works of the German reformer should be the instruments in the conversions of two great leaders.

John Wesley became a powerful preacher of the gospel throughout England and America. He established Methodist societies as a means of bringing together the converts from his meetings. They were cared for by other Methodist preachers, with Wesley maintaining overall control. Because of his deep concern for the welfare of disadvantaged people, he invested much time and energy in combating poverty and slavery. He opposed the American Revolution and wrote letters to both sides in an effort to dispel the obvious animosity between the two factions.

Wesley died in 1791. A statue in his honor stands in Bristol, England, as a reminder to all of the influence of one of England's last great evangelists.

A selection of John Wesley's writings are presented with pleasure for the spiritual benefit of all who read them and may be inspired to study Wesley further. Even more, that it will have the influence on spiritually searching readers that Luther's works had on John and Charles Wesley.

PART ONE

The Conversion
of John Wesley

─────────────

The conversion of John Wesley was remarkable because it came during a time when he was already very active in ministry. It appears that he associated salvation with works, a common problem among some Christian groups today. Yet he acknowledged an emptiness in himself that he couldn't explain or resolve.

Like many who have had similar experiences, Wesley had his moments of peace as well as turmoil. His involvement in sin was, as he put it, one of unwillingness, but of inability to conquer. Sin was like a hound on his trail and he could not do anything in and of himself to shake the pursuit.

Eventually, he met a man named Peter Böhler in London who labored with him until finally his persistence paid off and Wesley became a Christian.

Wesley's conversion illustrates powerfully how one can be deeply religious but at the same time thoroughly lost spiritually. Had John Wesley died in his sins he would undoubtedly have said, "Lord, Lord, did I not prophesy in your name . . . ?"

The testimony that follows is a reminder to all that the external qualities of a person do not necessarily reveal the truth.

─────────────

CHAPTER ONE

Beating the Air

Being ignorant of the righteousness of Christ, which, by a living faith in him, bringeth salvation "to every one that believeth," I sought to establish my own righteousness, and so labored in the fire all my days. I was now properly "under the law"; I knew that "the law" of God was "spiritual; I consented to it, that it was good." Yea, "I delighted in it, after the inner man." Yet was I "carnal, sold under sin." Every day was I constrained to cry out, "What I do, I allow not: for what I would, I do not; but what I hate that I do. To will is" indeed "present with me; but how to perform that which is good, I find not. For the good which I would, I do not; but the evil which I would not, that I do. I find a law, that when I would do good, evil is present with me": Even "the law in my members, warring against the law of my mind," and still "bringing me into captivity to the law of sin."

In this vile, abject state of bondage to sin, I was indeed fighting continually, but not conquering. Before, I had willingly served sin; now it was unwillingly, but still I served it. I fell, and rose, and fell again. Sometimes I was overcome and in heaviness; sometimes I overcame and was in joy. For as in the former state I had some foretastes of the terrors of the law, so had I in this of the comforts of the gospel. During this whole struggle between nature and grace, which had now continued above ten years, I had many remarkable returns to prayer, especially when I was in trouble. I had many sensible comforts, which are, indeed, no other than short anticipations

of the life of faith. But I was still "under the law," not "under grace" (the state most who are called Christians are content to live and die in): for I was only striving with, not freed from, sin: neither had I the witness of the Spirit with my spirit and, indeed, could not; for I "sought it not by faith, but, as it were, by the works of the law."

In my return to England, January, 1738, being in imminent danger of death and very uneasy on that account, I was strongly convinced that the cause of that uneasiness was unbelief; and that gaining a true, living faith, was the "one thing needful" for me. But still I fixed not this faith on its right object: I meant only faith in God, not faith in or through Christ. Again, I knew not that I was wholly void of this faith, but only thought I had not enough of it. So that when Peter Böhler, whom God prepared for me as soon as I came to London, affirmed of true faith in Christ (which is but one), that it had those two fruits inseparably attending it, "Dominion over sin, and constant peace from a sense of forgiveness," I was quite amazed, and looked upon it as a new gospel. If this was so, it was clear I had not faith. But I was not willing to be convinced of this. Therefore, I disputed with all my might and labored to prove that faith might be where these were not; especially where the sense of forgiveness was not, for, all the Scriptures relating to this, I had been long since taught to construe away; and to call all who spoke otherwise Presbyterians. Besides, I well saw no one could in the nature of things have such a sense of forgiveness and not *feel* it. But I felt it not. If then there was no faith without this, all my pretensions to faith dropped at once.

When I met Peter Böhler again, he consented to put the dispute upon the issue which I desired, namely, Scripture and experience. I first consulted the Scripture. But when I set aside the glosses of men, and simply considered the words of God, comparing them together, endeavoring to illustrate the obscure by the plainer passages; I found they all made against me and was forced to retreat to my last hold, "that experience would never agree with the *literal interpretation* of those Scriptures. Nor could I, therefore, allow it to be true, till I found some living witnesses of it." He replied [that] he could show me such at any time; if I desired it, the next day. And accordingly, the next day he came again with three others, all of whom testified of their own personal experience, that a true living faith in Christ is inseparable from a sense of pardon for all past, and freedom from all present, sins. They added with one mouth that this faith was the gift, the free gift of God; and that he would surely bestow it upon every soul who earnestly and perseveringly sought it. I was now thoroughly convinced; and by the grace of God I resolved to seek it unto the end by absolutely renouncing all dependence, in whole or in part, upon *my own* works or righteousness, on which I had really grounded my hope of salvation, though I knew it not, from my youth up; by adding to the constant use of all the other means of grace, continual prayer for

this very thing, justifying, saving faith, a full reliance on the blood of Christ shed for *me;* a trust in him, as *my* Christ, as *my* sole justification, sanctification, and redemption.

I continued thus to seek it (though with strange indifference, dullness, and coldness, and unusually frequent relapses into sin), till Wednesday, May 24. I think it was about five this morning that I opened my Testament on those words, "There are given unto us exceeding great and precious promises, even that ye should be partakers of the Divine nature," 2 Peter 1:4. Just as I went out, I opened it again on those words, "Thou art not far from the kingdom of God." In the afternoon I was asked to go to Saint Paul's. The anthem was "Out of the deep have I called unto thee, O Lord: Lord, hear my voice. O let thine ears consider well the voice of my complaint. If thou, Lord, wilt be extreme to mark what is done amiss, O Lord, who may abide it? For there is mercy with thee; therefore, shalt thou be feared. O Israel, trust in the Lord: for with the Lord there is mercy, and with him is plenteous redemption. And he shall redeem Israel from all his sins."

In the evening I went very unwillingly to a society in Aldersgate Street, where one was reading Luther's preface to the epistle to the Romans. About a quarter before nine, while he was describing the change which God works in the heart through faith in Christ, I felt my heart strangely warmed. I felt I did trust in Christ, Christ alone for salvation; and an assurance was given me that he had taken away *my* sins, even *mine,* and saved *me* from the law of sin and death.

PART TWO

The Sermons of John Wesley

The doctrine of original sin is an attempt to define the nature and extent of man's fall in Adam. Both topics have been hotly debated for centuries.

Wesley sought to explain the doctrine of original sin by describing God's understanding of man before the flood. In his opinion, God clearly considered that man was dead in sin. Wesley saw original sin as the source of spiritual blindness afflicting all mankind. While it is true that man could use reason to gain an incomplete knowledge of God, such reason never enabled any man apart from God's intervention to come to him. Only by God's initiative does man have the opportunity to go beyond the blindness of sin and become a Christian.

CHAPTER TWO

Original Sin

"And God saw that the wickedness of man was great in the earth, and that every imagination of the thoughts of his heart was only evil continually" (Gen. 6:5).

How widely different is this from the fair pictures of human nature, which men have drawn in all ages! The writings of many of the ancients abound with gay descriptions of the dignity of man; whom some of them paint as having all virtue and happiness in his composition, or at least, entirely in his power, without being beholden to any other being; yea, as self-sufficient; able to live on his own stock, and little inferior to God himself.

Nor have heathens alone, men who were guided in their researches by little more than the dim light of reason, but many likewise of them that bear the name of Christ, and to whom are entrusted the oracles of God, spoken as magnificently concerning the nature of man, as if it were all innocence and perfection. Accounts of this kind have particularly abounded in the present century; and perhaps in no part of the world more than in our own country. Here not a few persons of strong understanding, as well as extensive learning, have employed their utmost abilities to show what they termed, "the fair side of human nature." And it must be acknowledged that if their accounts of him be just man is still but "a little lower than the angels," or, as the words may be more literally rendered, "a little less than God."

Is it any wonder, that these accounts are very readily received by the gener-

ality of men? For who is not easily persuaded to think favorably of himself? Accordingly, writers of this kind are most universally read, admired, applauded. And innumerable are the converts they have made, not only in the gay, but the learned world. So that it is now quite unfashionable to talk otherwise, to say anything to the disparagement of human nature, which is generally allowed, notwithstanding a few infirmities, to be very innocent and wise and virtuous!

But, in the mean time, what must we do with our Bibles? For they will never agree with this. These accounts, however pleasing to flesh and blood, are utterly irreconcilable with the scriptural. The Scripture avers that "by one man's disobedience all men were constituted sinners"; that "in Adam all died," spiritually died, lost the life and the image of God; that fallen, sinful Adam then "begat a son in his own likeness." Nor was it possible he should beget him in any other; for "who can bring a clean thing out of an unclean?" Consequently we, as well as other men, were by nature "dead in trespasses and sin," "without hope, without God in the world," and therefore "children of wrath"; that every man may say, "I was shapen in wickedness, and in sin did my mother conceive me"; that "there is no difference," in that "all have sinned and come short of the glory of God," of that glorious image of

God, wherein man was originally created. And hence, when "the Lord looked down from heaven upon the children of men, he saw they were all gone out of the way; they were altogether become abominable, there was none righteous, no, not one," none that truly sought after God. Just agreeable [is] this to what is declared by the Holy Ghost, in the words above recited, "God saw," when he looked down from heaven before, "that the wickedness of man was great in the earth"; so great, that "every imagination of the thoughts of his heart was only evil continually."

This is God's account of man: from which I shall take occasion, first, to show what men were before the Flood; secondly, to inquire whether they are not the same now; and, thirdly, to add some inferences.

Mankind Before the Flood

I am, first, by opening the words of the text to show what men were before the Flood. And we may fully depend on the account here given: for God saw it, and he cannot be deceived. He "saw that the wickedness of man was great"—not of this or that man; not of a few men only; not barely of the greater part, but of man in general, of men universally. The word includes the whole human race, every partaker of human nature. And it is not easy for us to compute their numbers, to tell how many thousands and millions they were. The earth then retained much of its primeval beauty and original fruitfulness. The face of the globe was not rent and torn as it is now, and spring and summer went hand in hand. It is therefore probable, it afforded sustenance for far more inhabitants than it is now capable of sustaining; and these must be immensely multiplied, while men begat sons and daughters for seven or eight hundred

years together. Yet, among all this inconceivable number, only "Noah found favor with God." He alone (perhaps including part of his household) was an exception from the universal wickedness, which, by the just judgment of God, in a short time after brought on universal destruction. All the rest were partakers in the same guilt as they were in the same punishment.

"God saw all the imaginations of the thoughts of his heart," of his soul, his inward man, the spirit within him, the principle of all his inward and outward motions. He "saw all the imaginations"—it is not possible to find a word of a more extensive signification. It includes whatever is formed, made, fabricated within; all that is or passes in the soul; every inclination, affection, passion, appetite; every temper, design, thought. It must of consequence include every word and action as naturally flowing from these fountains and being either good or evil, according to the fountain from which they severally flow.

Now God saw that all this, the whole thereof, was evil, contrary to moral rectitude; contrary to the nature of God, which necessarily includes all good; contrary to the divine will, the eternal standard of good and evil; contrary to the pure, holy image of God, wherein man was originally created, and wherein he stood when God, surveying the works of his hands, saw them all to be very good; contrary to justice, mercy, and truth, and to the essential relations which each man bore to his Creator and his fellow creatures.

But was there not good mingled with the evil? Was there not light intermixed with the darkness? No; none at all: "God saw that the whole imagination of the heart of man was only evil." It cannot indeed be denied, but many of them, perhaps all, had good motions put into their hearts, for the Spirit of God did then also "strive with man," if haply he might repent, more especially during that gracious reprieve, the hundred and twenty years, while the ark was preparing. But still "in his flesh dwelt no good thing"; all his nature was purely evil. It was wholly consistent with itself and unmixed with anything of an opposite nature.

However, it may still be matter of inquiry, "Was there no intermission of this evil? Were there no lucid intervals, wherein something good might be found in the heart of man?" We are not here to consider what the grace of God might occasionally work in his soul; and abstracted from this, we have no reason to believe there was any intermission of that evil. For God, who "saw the whole imagination of the thoughts of his heart to be *only* evil," saw likewise, that it was always the same, that it "was only evil *continually*"; every year, every day, every hour, every moment. He never deviated into good.

Such is the authentic account of the whole race of mankind, which he who knoweth what is in man, who searcheth the heart and trieth the reins, hath left upon record for our instruction. Such were all men before God brought the Flood upon the earth. We are, secondly, to inquire, whether they are the same now?

Mankind Since the Flood

And this is certain, the Scripture gives us no reason to think any otherwise of them. On the contrary, all the above cited passages of Scripture refer to those who lived after the Flood. It was above a thousand years after, that God declared by David concerning the children of men, "They are all gone out of the way, [of truth and holiness,] there is none righteous, no, not one." And to this bear all the prophets witness, in their

several generations. So Isaiah, concerning God's peculiar people (and certainly the heathens were in no better condition), "The whole head is sick, and the whole heart faint. From the sole of the foot even unto the head there is no soundness in it; but wounds, and bruises, and putrefying sores." The same account is given by all the apostles, yea, by the whole tenor of the oracles of God. From all these we learn concerning man in his natural state, unassisted by the grace of God, that "every imagination of the thoughts of his heart is [still] evil, only evil [and that] continually."

And this account of the present state of man is confirmed by daily experience. It is true, the natural man discerns it not: and this is not to be wondered at. So long as a man, born blind, continues so, he is scarce sensible of his want: much less, could we suppose a place where all were born without sight, would they be sensible of the want of it. In like manner, so long as men remain in their natural blindness of understanding, they are not sensible of their spiritual wants, and of this in particular. But as soon as God opens the eyes of their understanding, they see the state they were in before; they are then deeply convinced, that "every man living," themselves especially, are, by nature, "altogether vanity"; that is, folly and ignorance, sin and wickedness.

We see, when God opens our eyes, that we were before *without God*, or rather, *atheists in the world*. We had, by nature, no knowledge of God, no acquaintance with him. It is true, as soon as we came to the use of reason, we learned "the invisible things of God, even his eternal power and Godhead, from the things that are made." From the things that are seen we inferred the existence of an eternal powerful being, that is not seen. But still, although we acknowledged his being, we had no acquaintance with him. As we know there is an emperor of China, whom yet we do not know; so we knew there was a king of all the earth, yet we knew him not. Indeed, we could not, by any of our natural faculties. By none of these could we attain the knowledge of God. We could no more perceive him by our natural understanding, than we could see him with our eyes. For "no one knoweth the Father but the Son, and he to whom the Son willeth to reveal him. And no one knoweth the Son but the Father, and he to whom the Father revealeth him."

We read of an ancient king, who, being desirous to know what was the *natural language* of men, in order to bring the matter to a certain issue, made the following experiment: he ordered two infants, as soon as they were born, to be conveyed to a place prepared for them, where they were brought up without any instruction at all, and without ever hearing a human voice. And what was the event? Why, that when they were at length brought out of their confinement, they spake no language at all, they uttered only inarticulate sounds, like those of other animals. Were two infants in like manner to be brought up from the womb without being instructed in any religion, there is little room to doubt, but (unless the grace of God interposed) the event would be just the same. They would have no religion at all: they would have no more knowledge of God than the beasts of the field, than the wild ass's colt. Such is natural religion, abstracted from traditional, and from the influences of God's Spirit!

A Nature Against God

And having no knowledge, we can have no love of God: we cannot love him we know not. Most men *talk* indeed of loving God, and perhaps imagine they

do; at least few will acknowledge they do not love him: but the fact is too plain to be denied. No man loves God by nature, any more than he does a stone, or the earth he treads upon. What we love we delight in: but no man has naturally any delight in God. In our natural state we cannot conceive how any one should delight in him. We take no pleasure in him at all; he is utterly tasteless to us. To love God! It is far above, out of our sight. We cannot, naturally, attain unto it.

We have, by nature, not only no love, but no fear of God. It is allowed, indeed, that most men have, sooner or later, a kind of senseless, irrational fear, properly called superstition, though the blundering Epicureans give it the name of religion. Yet even this is not natural, but acquired; chiefly by conversation or from example. By nature "God is not in all our thoughts": we leave him to manage his own affairs, to sit quietly, as we imagine, in heaven, and leave us on earth to manage ours; so that we have no more of the fear of God before our eyes, than of the love of God in our hearts.

Thus are all men "atheists in the world." But atheism itself does not screen us from idolatry. In his natural state every man born into the world is a rank idolater. Perhaps, indeed, we may not be such in the vulgar sense of the word. We do not, like the idolatrous heathens, worship molten or graven images. We do not bow down to the stock of a tree, to the work of our own hands. We do not pray to the angels or saints in heaven, any more than to the saints that are upon the earth. But what then? We have set up our idols in our hearts; and to these we bow down, and worship them: we worship ourselves, when we pay that honor to ourselves, which is due to God only. Therefore all pride is idolatry; it is ascribing to ourselves what is due to God alone. And although pride was not made for man, yet where is the man that is born without it? But hereby we rob God of his unalienable right, and idolatrously usurp his glory.

But pride is not the only sort of idolatry which we are all by nature guilty of. Satan has stamped his own image on our heart in self-will also. "I will," said he, before he was cast out of heaven, "I will sit upon the sides of the north; I will do my own will and pleasure, independently of that of my Creator." The same does every man born into the world say, and that in a thousand instances; nay, and avow it too, without ever blushing upon the account, without either fear or shame. Ask the man, "Why did you do this?" He answers, "Because I had a mind to it." What is this but, "Because it was my will"; that is, in effect, because the devil and I are agreed; because Satan and I govern our actions by one and the same principle. The will of God, meantime, is not in his thoughts, is not considered in the least degree; although it be the supreme rule of every intelligent creature, whether in heaven or earth, resulting from the essential, unalterable relation, which all creatures bear to their Creator.

Lovers of the World

So far we bear the image of the devil, and tread in his steps. But at the next step we leave Satan behind; we run into an idolatry whereof he is not guilty: I mean, love of the world; which is now as natural to every man, as to love his own will. What is more natural to us than to seek happiness in the creature, instead of the Creator? To seek that satisfaction in the works of his hands, which can be found in God only? What more natural than "the desire of the flesh"? That is, of the pleasure of sense in every kind? Men indeed talk magnifi-

cently of despising these low pleasures, particularly men of learning and education. They affect to sit loose to the gratification of those appetites wherein they stand on a level with the beasts that perish. But it is mere affectation; for every man is conscious to himself that in this respect he is, by nature, a very beast. Sensual appetites, even those of the lowest kind, have, more or less, the dominion over him. They lead him captive; they drag him to and fro, in spite of his boasted reason. The man, with all his good breeding and other accomplishments, has no preeminence over the goat: nay, it is much to be doubted, whether the beast has not the preeminence over him. Certainly he has, if we may hearken to one of their modern oracles, who very decently tells us,

Once in a season, beasts too taste
   of love;
Only the beast of reason is its
   slave,
And in that folly drudges all the
   year.

A considerable difference indeed, it must be allowed, there is between man and man, arising (beside that wrought by preventing grace) from difference of constitution and of education. But, notwithstanding this, who, that is not utterly ignorant of himself, can here cast the first stone at another? Who can abide the test of our blessed Lord's comment on the seventh commandment? "He that looketh on a woman to lust after her, hath committed adultery with her already in his heart"? So that one knows not which to wonder at most, the ignorance or the insolence of those men, who speak with such disdain of them that are overcome by desires which every man has felt in his own breast; the desire of every pleasure of sense, innocent or not, being natural to every child of man.

And so is "the desire of the eye," the desire of the pleasures of the imagination. These arise either from great, or beautiful, or uncommon objects—if the two former do not coincide with the latter; for perhaps it would appear upon a diligent inquiry, that neither grand nor beautiful objects please, any longer than they are new; that when the novelty of them is over, the greatest part, at least, of the pleasure they give, is over; and in the same proportion as they become familiar, they become flat and insipid. But let us experience this ever so often, the same desire will remain still. The inbred thirst continues fixed in the soul; nay, the more it is indulged, the more it increases, and incites us to follow after another, and yet another object; although we leave every one with an abortive hope, and a deluded expectation. Yea,

> The hoary fool, who many days
>   Has struggled with continued
>   sorrow,
> Renews his hope, and fondly lays
>   The desperate bet upon to-
>   morrow!
> Tomorrow comes: 'Tis noon; 'Tis
>   night;
> This day, like all the former
>   flies:
> Yet, on he goes, to seek delight
>   Tomorrow, till tonight he dies!

A third symptom of this fatal disease, the love of the world, which is so deeply rooted in our nature, is "the pride of life"; the desire of praise, of the honor that cometh of men. This the greatest admirers of human nature allow to be strictly natural; as natural as the sight, or hearing, or any other of the external senses. And are they ashamed of it, even men of letters, men of refined and improved understanding? So far from it, that they glory therein! They applaud themselves for their love of applause!

Yea, eminent Christians, so called, make no difficulty of adopting the saying of the old, vain heathen, "Not to regard what men think of us, is the mark of a wicked and abandoned mind." So that to go calm and unmoved through honor and dishonor, through evil report and good report, is with them a sign of one that is, indeed, not fit to live: "Away with such a fellow from the earth." But would one imagine that these men had ever heard of Jesus Christ or his apostles; or that they knew who it was that said, "How can ye believe who receive honor one of another, and seek not the honor which cometh of God only"? But if this be really so, if it be impossible to believe, and consequently to please God, so long as we receive or seek honor one of another, and seek not the honor which cometh of God only; then in what a condition are all mankind! The Christians as well as heathens! Since they all seek honor one of another! Since it is as natural for them so to do, themselves being the judges, as it is to see the light which strikes upon their eye, or to hear the sound which enters their ear; yea, since they account it a sign of a virtuous mind, to seek the praise of men, and of a vicious one, to be content with the honor that cometh of God only!

Three Inferences

I proceed to draw a few inferences from what has been said. And first, from hence we learn one grand fundamental difference between Christianity, considered as a system of doctrines, and the most refined heathenism. Many of the ancient heathens have largely described the vices of particular men. They have spoken much against their covetousness, or cruelty; their luxury or prodigality. Some have dared to say, that "no man is born without vices of one kind or another." But still, as none of them were apprised of the fall of man, so none of them knew of his total corruption. They knew not that all men were empty of all good, and filled with all manner of evil. They were wholly ignorant of the entire depravation of the whole human nature, of every man born into the world, in every faculty of his soul, not so much by those particular vices which reign in particular persons, as by the general flood of atheism and idolatry, of pride, self-will, and love of the world. This, therefore, is the first, grand, distinguishing point between heathenism and Christianity. The one acknowledges that many men are infected with many vices, and even born with a proneness to them; but supposes withal, that in some the natural good much overbalances the evil: the other declares that all men are "conceived in sin," and "shapen in wickedness"—that hence there is in every man a "carnal mind, which is enmity against God, which is not, cannot be subject to [his], law"; and which so infects the whole soul, that "there dwelleth in [him] in his flesh," in his natural state, "no good thing"; but "every imagination of the thoughts of his heart is evil," only evil, and that "continually."

Hence we may, secondly, learn, that all who deny this, call it original sin, or by any other title, are but heathens still, in the fundamental point which differences heathenism from Christianity. They may, indeed, allow, that men have many vices; that some are born with us; and that, consequently, we are not born altogether so wise or so virtuous as we should be; there being few that will roundly affirm, "We are born with as much propensity to good as to evil, and that every man is, by nature, as virtuous and wise as Adam was at his creation." But here is the *shibboleth:* Is man by nature filled with all manner of evil? Is he void of all good? Is he wholly fallen? Is his soul totally corrupted? Or, to come back to the text, is "every imagination of the thoughts of his heart evil continually"? Allow this, and you are so far a Christian. Deny it, and you are but a heathen still.

We may learn from hence, in the third place, what is the proper nature of religion, of the religion of Jesus Christ. It is God's method of *healing a soul* which is thus diseased. Hereby the great physician of souls applies medicines to heal this sickness; to restore human nature, totally corrupted in all its faculties. God heals all our atheism by the knowledge of himself, and of Jesus Christ whom he hath sent; by giving us faith, a divine evidence and conviction of God, and of the things of God; in particular, of this important truth, "Christ loved *me*, and gave himself for *me*." By repentance and lowliness of heart, the deadly disease of pride is healed; that of self-will by resignation, a meek and thankful submission to the will of God; and for the love of the world in all its branches, the love of God is the sovereign remedy. Now this is properly religion, "faith [thus] working by love"; working the genuine meek humility, entire deadness to the world, with a loving, thankful acquiescence in, and conformity to, the whole will and word of God.

Indeed, if man were not thus fallen, there would be no need of all this. There would be no occasion for this work in the heart, this renewal in the spirit of our mind. The superfluity of godliness would then be a more proper expression than the "superfluity of naughtiness." For an outside religion, without any godliness at all, would suffice to all rational intents and purposes. It does accordingly suffice, in the judgment of those who deny this corruption of our nature. They make very little more of religion than the famous Mr. Hobbes did of reason. According to him, reason is only "a well-ordered train of words": according to them, religion is only a well-ordered train of words and actions. And they speak consistently with themselves; for if the inside be not full of wickedness, if this be clean already, what remains, but to "cleanse the outside of the cup"? Outward reformation, if their supposition be just, is indeed the one thing needful.

But ye have not so learned the oracles of God. Ye know, that he who seeth what is in man gives a far different account both of nature and grace, of our fall and our recovery. Ye know that the great end of religion is to renew our hearts in the image of God, to repair that total loss of righteousness and true holiness, which we sustained by the sin of our first parents. Ye know that all religion which does not answer this end, all that stops short of this, the renewal of our soul in the image of God, after the likeness of him that created it, is no other than a poor farce, and a mere mockery of God, to the destruction of our own soul. Oh, beware of all those teachers of lies, who would palm this upon you for Christianity! Regard them not, although they should come unto you with all the deceivableness of unrighteousness; with all smoothness of language, all decency, yea, beauty and elegance of expression, all professions of earnest good will to you, and reverence for the holy Scriptures. Keep to the plain, old faith, "once delivered to the saints," and delivered by the Spirit of God to our hearts. Know your disease! Know your cure! Ye were born in sin: therefore "ye must be born again," born of God. By nature ye are wholly corrupted: by grace ye shall be wholly renewed. In Adam ye all died: in the second Adam, in Christ, ye all are made alive. "You that were dead in sins hath he quickened": he hath already given you a principle of life, even faith in him who loved you, and gave himself for you! Now, "go on from faith to faith," until your whole sickness be healed, and all that "mind be in you, which was also in Christ Jesus"!

The heart of man to Wesley was a great deceiver for it failed to reveal to man his true condition before God. The heart convinced men that they were really not so bad. The heart even convinced many that good actions are sufficient for salvation. The heart was also the seat of innumerable evils, evils that did not require the work of the devil to be activated.

Wesley's sermon reflects his belief in the futility of depending on the unchecked murmurings of the heart. For him only a fool trusted his heart, and the wise man never looked to himself for an honest evaluation of his condition.

CHAPTER THREE

The Deceitfulness of the Human Heart

"The heart of man is deceitful above all things, and desperately wicked: who can know it?" (Jer. 17:9).

The most eminent of the ancient heathens have left us many testimonies of this. It was indeed their common opinion, that there was a time when men in general were virtuous and happy: this they termed the "golden age." And the account of this was spread through almost all nations. But it was likewise generally believed, that this happy age had expired long ago; and that men are now in the midst of the "iron age." At the commencement of this, says the poet:

> Immediately broke in,
> With a full tide, all wickedness
>   and sin:
> Shame, truth, fidelity, swift fled
>   away,
> And cursed thirst of gold bore
>   unresisted sway.

But how much more knowing than these old pagans are the present generation of Christians! How many labored panegyrics do we now read and hear on the dignity of human nature! One eminent preacher, in one of his sermons, preached and printed a few years ago, does not scruple to affirm; first, that men in general (if not every individual) are very wise: secondly, that men in general are very virtuous: and thirdly, that they are very happy—and I do not know, that anyone yet has been so hardy as to controvert the assertion.

Nearly related to them, were the sentiments of an ingenious gentleman, who

being asked, "My lord, what do you think of the Bible?" answered, "I think it is the finest book I ever read in my life. Only that part of it which indicates the mediatorial scheme, I do not understand: for I do not conceive there is any need of a mediator between God and man. If indeed," continued he, "I was a sinner, then I should need a mediator: but I do not conceive I am. It is true, I often act wrong, for want of more understanding; and I frequently *feel* wrong tempers, particularly proneness to anger: but I cannot allow this to be a sin; for it depends on the motion of my blood and spirits, which I cannot help. Therefore it cannot be a sin: or if it be, the blame must fall not on *me*, but on him that made me." The very sentiments of pious lord Kames, and modest Mr. Hume!

Some years ago a charitable woman discovered, that there was no sinner in the world, but the devil. "For," said she, "he *forces* men to act as they do; therefore they are unaccountable: the blame lights on Satan." But these more enlightened gentlemen have discovered, that there is no sinner in the world but God! For he *forces* men to think, speak, and act as they do; therefore the blame lights on God alone. Satan, avaunt! It may be doubted, whether he himself ever uttered so foul a blasphemy as this!

But whatever unbaptized or baptized infidels may say concerning the innocence of mankind, he that made man, and that best knows what he has made, gives a very different account of him. He informs us, that "the heart of man," of all mankind, of every man born into the world, "is desperately wicked"; and that it is "deceitful above all things": so that we may well ask, "Who can know it?"

Wicked to the Core

To begin with this: "The heart of man is desperately wicked." In considering this, we have no need to refer to any particular sins; (these are no more than the leaves, or, at most, the fruits, which spring from that evil tree); but rather to the general root of all. See how this was first planted in heaven itself, by "Lucifer, son of the morning"; till then undoubtedly "one of the first, if not the first archangel": "Thou saidst, I will sit upon the side of the north." See self-will; the first-born of Satan! "I will be like the Most High." See pride the twin sister of self-will. Here was the true origin of evil. Hence came the inexhaustible flood of evils upon the lower world. When Satan had once transfused his own self-will and pride into the parents of mankind, together with a new species of sin—love of the world, the loving the creature above the Creator—all manner of wickedness soon rushed in; all ungodliness and unrighteousness; shooting out into crimes of every kind; soon covering the whole face of the earth with all manner of abominations. It would be an endless task, to enumerate all the enormities that broke out. Now the fountains of the great deep were broken up. The earth soon became a field of blood: revenge, cruelty, ambition, [and] all sorts of injustice, every species of public and private wrongs, were diffused through every part of the earth. Injustice, in ten thousand forms, hatred, envy, malice, bloodthirstiness, with

every species of falsehood, rode triumphant; till the Creator, looking down from heaven, would be no more entreated for an incorrigible race; but swept them off from the face of the earth. But how little were the following generations improved by the severe judgment! They that lived after the Flood do not appear to have been a whit better than those that lived before it. In a short time, probably before Noah was removed from the earth, all unrighteousness prevailed as before.

But is there not a God in the world? Doubtless there is: and it is "he that hath made us, not we ourselves." He made us gratuitously; of his own mere mercy: for we could merit nothing of him before we had a being. It is of his mercy that he made us at all; that he hath made us sensible, rational creatures; and, above all, creatures capable of God. It is this, and this alone, which puts the essential difference between men and brutes. But if he has made us, and given us all we have; if we owe all we are and have to him; then surely he has a right to all we are and have—to all our love and obedience. This has been acknowledged by almost all who believed themselves to be his creatures, in all ages and nations. But a few years ago a learned man frankly confessed, "I could never apprehend, that God's having created us, gave him any title to the government of us: or, that his having created us laid us under any obligation to yield him our obedience." I believe that Dr. Hutcheson was the first man that ever made any doubt of this. Or that ever doubted, much less denied, that a creature was obliged to obey his Creator. If Satan ever entertained this thought (but it is not probable he ever did), it would be no wonder he should rebel against God, and raise war in heaven. And hence would enmity against God arise in the hearts of men also; together with all the branches of ungodliness, which abound therein at this day. Hence would naturally arise the neglect of every duty which we owe to him as our Creator, and all the passions and hopes which are directly opposite to every such duty.

From the devil the spirit of independence, self-will, and pride, productive of all ungodliness and unrighteousness, quickly infused themselves into the hearts of our first parents in paradise. After they had eaten of the tree of knowledge, wickedness and misery of every kind rushed in with a full tide upon the earth, alienated us from God, and made way for all the rest: atheism (now fashionably termed dissipation) and idolatry, love of the world, seeking happiness in this or that creature, covered the whole earth.

> Upright both in heart and will,
>   We by our God were made:
> But we turn'd from good to ill,
>   And o'er the creature stray'd:
> Multiplied our wand'ring
>   thought,
> Which first was fixed on God
>   alone;
> In ten thousand objects sought
>   The bliss we lost in One.

It would be endless to enumerate all the species of wickedness, whether in thought, word, or action, that now overspread the earth, in every nation, and city, and family. They all center in this—atheism, or idolatry: pride; either thinking of themselves more highly than they ought to think, or glorying in something which they have received, as though they had not received it: independence and self-will—doing their own will, not the will of him that made them. Add to this, seeking happiness out of God; in gratifying the desire of the flesh, the desire of the eye, and the pride of life. Hence, it is a melancholy truth, that (unless when the Spirit of God has made

the difference) all mankind now, as well as four thousand years ago, "have corrupted their ways before the Lord; and every imagination of the thought of man's heart is evil, only evil, and that continually." However, therefore, men may differ in their outward ways (in which undoubtedly there are a thousand differences), yet in the inward root, the enmity against God, atheism, pride, self-will, and idolatry, it is true of all, that "the heart of man," of every natural man, "is desperately wicked."

Deceiving Even Ourselves

But if this be the case, how is it that every one is not conscious of it? For who should "know the things of a man, like the spirit of a man that is in him"? Why is it that so few know themselves? For this plain reason, because the heart is not only "desperately wicked, but deceitful above all things." So deceitful, that we may well ask, "Who can know it?" Who indeed, save God that made it? By his assistance we may, in the second place, consider this: the deceitfulness of man's heart.

"It is deceitful above all things"; that is, in the highest degree, above all that we can conceive. So deceitful, that the generality of men are continually deceiving both themselves and others. How strangely do they deceive themselves; not knowing either their own tempers or characters; imagining themselves to be abundantly better and wiser than they are. The ancient poet supposes there is no exception to this rule; that no man is willing to know his own heart.

And if men thus deceive themselves, is it any wonder, that they deceive others also, and that we so seldom find "an Israelite indeed, in whom there is no guile"! In looking over my books some years ago, I found the following memorandum: "I am this day thirty years old; and till this day I know not that I have met with one person of that age, except in my father's house, who did not use guile more or less."

This is one of the sorts of desperate wickedness, which cleaves to the nature of every man, proceeding from those fruitful roots, self-will, pride, and independence of God. Hence springs every species of vice and wickedness; hence every sin against God, our neighbor, and ourselves. Against God—forgetfulness and contempt of God, of his name, his day, his word, his ordinances; atheism on the one hand, and idolatry on the other; in particular, love of the world, the desire of the flesh, the desire of the eyes, and the pride of life; the love of money, the love of power, the love of ease, the love of the "honor that cometh of men," the love of the creature more than the Creator, the being lovers of pleasure more than lovers of God—against our neighbor—ingratitude, revenge, hatred, envy, malice, uncharitableness.

Hence there is in the heart of every child of man an inexhaustible fund of ungodliness and unrighteousness, deeply and strongly rooted in the soul, that nothing less than Almighty grace can cure it. From hence naturally arises a plentiful harvest of all evil words and works; and to complete the whole, that complex of all evils:

> That foul monster, War, that we
>   meet,
> Lays deep the noblest work of the
>   creation;
> Which wears in vain its Maker's
>   glorious image,
> Unprivileg'd from thee!

In the train of this fell monster are murder, adultery, rape, violence, and cruelty of every kind. And all these abominations are not only found in Mo-hammedan or Pagan countries, where their horrid practice may seem to be the natural result of equally horrid principles; but in those that are called Christian countries, yea, in the most knowing and civilized states and kingdoms. And let it not be said, this is only the case in Roman Catholic countries. Nay, we that are called reformed, are not one whit behind them in all manner of wickedness. Indeed no crime ever prevailed among the Turks or Tartars, which we here cannot parallel in every part of Christendom. Nay, no sin ever appeared in heathen or papal Rome, which is not found, at this day, in Germany, France, Holland, England, and every other Protestant as well as popish country. So that it might now be said, with as much truth, and as few exceptions, of every court in Europe, as it was formerly in the court of Saul; "There is none righteous, no, not one: they are altogether become abominable: there is none that understandeth, and seeketh after God."

The Divine Exception

But, is there no exception as to the wickedness of man's heart? Yes, in those that are born of God. "He that is born of God, keepeth himself, and that wicked one toucheth him not." God has "purified his heart by faith," so that his wickedness is departed from him. "Old things are passed away, and all things [in him] are become new." So that his heart is no longer desperately wicked, but "renewed in righteousness and true holiness." Only let it be remembered, that the heart, even of a believer, is not wholly purified when he is justified. Sin is then overcome, but it is not rooted out; it is conquered, but not destroyed. Experience shows him, first, that the root of sin, self-will, pride, and idolatry, remain still in his heart. But as long as he continues to watch and pray, none of them can prevail against him. Experience teaches him, secondly, that sin (generally pride or self-will) cleaves to his best actions. So that even with regard to these, he finds an absolute necessity for the blood of atonement.

But how artfully does this conceal itself, not only from others, but even from ourselves. Who can discover it in all the disguises it assumes, or trace it through all its latent mazes? And if it be so difficult to know the heart of a good man, who can know the heart of a wicked one, which is far more deceitful? No unregenerate man, however sensible, ever so experienced, ever so wise in his generation. And yet these are they who pique themselves upon "knowing the world"; and imagine, they see through all men. Vain men! One may boldly say, they "know nothing yet as they ought to know." Even that politician in the late reign neither knew the heart of himself or of other men, whose favorite saying was, "Do not tell me of your virtue, or religion: I tell you, every man has his price"; yes, sir R———, every man like you; everyone that sells himself to the devil.

Did that right honorable wretch, compared to whom sir R——— was a saint, know the heart of man? He that so earnestly advised his own son, "never to speak the truth? To lie or dissemble as often as he speaks? To wear a mask continually?" That earnestly counseled him, "not to debauch *single women* (because some inconveniences might follow) but always married women." Would one imagine this groveling animal ever had a wife or a married daughter of his own? Oh rare Lord C———! Did ever man so well deserve, though he was a peer of the realm, to die by the side of Newgate? Or did ever book so well deserve to be burned by the common hangman, as his letters? Did Mr. David Hume, lower, if possible, than either of the former, know the heart of man? No more than a worm or a beetle does. After "playing so idly with the darts of death," do you now find it a laughing matter? What think you now of Charon? Has he ferried you over Styx? At length he has taught you to know a little of your own heart! At length you know it is a fearful thing to fall into the hands of the living God!

One of the ablest champions of infidelity (perhaps the most elegant and the most decent writer, that ever produced a system of religion, without being in the least obliged to the Bible for it) breaks out in the fullness of his heart; "Who would not wish that there was full proof of the Christian revelation; since it is undoubtedly the most benevolent system that ever appeared in the world!" Might he not add a reason of another kind; because without this, man must be altogether a mystery to himself. Even with the help of revelation, he knows exceedingly little: but without it, he would know abundantly less; and nothing with any certainty. Without the light which is given us by the oracles of God, how could we reconcile his greatness with his meanness? While we acknowledged with Sir John Davis:

I know my soul has power to
    know all things;
  Yet is she blind, and ignorant of
    all:
I know I'm one of nature's little
    kings;
  Yet to the least and vilest things
    in thrall.

Who then knoweth the hearts of all men? Surely none but he that made them. Who knoweth his own heart? Who can tell the depth of its enmity against God? Who knoweth how deeply it is sunk into the nature of Satan?

Three Proverbs

From the preceding considerations, may we not learn, first, "He that trusteth in his own heart is a fool"? For who that is wise would trust one whom he knows to be "desperately wicked"? Especially, whom he hath known by a thousand experiments to be "deceitful above all things"? What can we expect, if we still trust a known liar and deceiver, but to be deceived and cheated to the end?

We may, hence, in the second place, infer the truth of that other reflection of Solomon: "Seest thou a man that is wise in his own eyes; there is more hope of a fool than of him." For at what distance from wisdom must that man be, who never suspected his want of it? And will not his thinking so well of himself, prevent his receiving instruction from others? Will he not be apt to be displeased at admonition, and to construe reproof into reproach? Will he not, therefore, be less ready to receive instruction, than even one that has little natural understanding? Surely no fool is so incapable of amendment, as one that imagines himself to be wise. He that supposes himself not to need a physician, will hardly profit by his advice.

May we not learn hence, thirdly, the wisdom of that caution: "Let him who thinketh he standeth, take heed lest he fall": Or, (to render the text more properly) "Let him that assuredly standeth, take heed lest he fall." How firmly soever he may stand, he has still a deceitful heart. In how many instances has he been deceived already! And so he may again. Suppose he be not deceived now, does it follow that he never will? Does he not stand upon slippery ground? And is he not surrounded with snares into which he may fall and rise no more?

Is it not wisdom for him that is now standing, continually to cry to God, "Search me, oh Lord, and prove me; try out my reins and my heart? Look well, if there be any way of wickedness in me, and lead me in the way everlasting." Thou alone, oh God, "knowest the hearts of all the children of men": Oh show thou me what spirit I am of and let me not deceive my own soul! Let me not "think of myself more highly than I ought to think." But let me always "think soberly, according as thou hast given me the measure of faith"!

Halifax, April 21, 1790.

The willingness of modern preaching to address hell is seemingly at an all time low. Many reasons for this deficiency could be given, but the general view seems to be that such a topic is unpopular.

In the tradition of great preaching, Wesley did not hesitate to acquaint the people of England with this obvious but difficult doctrine. He considered Jesus very clear on the matter of hell and noted that Jesus regularly reminded his audiences of the reality of hell. If our Lord displayed such evident concern over man's understanding of such an awful place, how much more should preachers address it?

This sermon presents hell literally as a place of eternal punishment for those who have rejected the gospel. Wesley did not see hell as a fright tactic used by God to scare men and women into the kingdom, but as a place of punishment for wickedness. Detailing the various torments that accompany hell such as the fire, worms, and the company of wicked inhabitants, he described it as a place of perpetual unrest for the damned and a cause for praise to God from those who have been delivered from it.

CHAPTER FOUR

Of Hell

"Where their worm dieth not, and the fire is not quenched" (Mark 9:48).

Every truth which is revealed in the oracles of God is undoubtedly of great importance. Yet it may be allowed, that some of those which are revealed therein, are of greater importance than others; as being more immediately conducive to the grand end of all, the eternal salvation of men. And we may judge of their importance, even from this circumstance: that they are not mentioned once only in the sacred writings, but are repeated over and over. A remarkable instance of this we have, with regard to the awful truth which is now before us. Our blessed Lord, who uses no superfluous words, who makes no "vain repetitions," repeats it over and over in the same chapter, and, as it were, in the same breath. So, verses 43, 44, "If thy hand offend thee"; if a thing or persons as useful as a hand, be an occasion of sin, and there is no other way to shun that sin; "cut it off: it is better for thee to enter into life maimed, than having two hands to go into hell, into the fire that never shall be quenched: where their worm dieth not, and the fire is not quenched." So again, verses 45, 46, "If thy foot offend thee, cut it off: it is better for thee to enter halt into life, than having two feet to be cast into hell, into the fire that never shall be quenched; where their worm dieth not, and the fire is not quenched." And yet again, verses 47, 48, "If thine eye"; a person or thing as dear as thine eye; "offend thee"; hinder thy running the race which is set before thee; "pluck it out: it is better for thee

to enter into the kingdom of God with one eye, than having two eyes to be cast into hell fire; where their worm dieth not, and the fire is not quenched."

And let it not be thought, that the considerations of these terrible truths is proper only for enormous sinners. How is this supposition consistent with what our Lord speaks to those who were then, doubtless, the holiest men upon earth? When innumerable multitudes were gathered together, he said to his disciples, [the apostles,] "First of all, I say unto you, my friends, fear not them that can kill the body, and after that have no more that they can do. But I say unto you, Fear him, who after he hath killed hath power to cast into hell; yea, I say unto you, Fear him!" Luke 12:1–5. Yea, fear him under this very notion, of having power to cast into hell: that is, in effect, fear, lest he should cast you into the place of torment. And this very fear, even in the children of God, is one excellent means of preserving them from it.

It behooves, therefore, not only the outcasts of men, but even *you, his friends;* you that fear and love God; deeply to consider what is revealed in the oracles of God concerning the future state of punishment. How widely distant is this from the most elaborate accounts which are given by the heathen authors! Their accounts are (in many particulars at least) childish, fanciful, and self-inconsistent. So that it is no wonder they did not believe themselves, but only related the tales of the vulgar.

So Virgil strongly intimates, when, after the labored account he had given of the shades beneath, he sends him that had related it out at the ivory gate, through which (as he tells us) only *dreams* pass: thereby giving us to know, that all the preceding account is no more than a dream. This he only insinuates; but his brother poet, Juvenal, speaks out flat and plain:

> Even our children do not believe a word of the tales concerning another world.

Here, on the contrary, all is worthy of God, the Creator, the Governor of mankind. All is awful and solemn; suitable to his wisdom and justice, by whom "Tophet was ordained of old": although originally prepared, not for the children of men, but "for the devil and his angels."

The punishment of those who, in spite of all the warnings of God, resolve to have their portion with the devil and his angels, will, according to the ancient and not improper division, be either what they lose or what they feel. After considering these separately, I shall touch on a few additional circumstances, and conclude with two or three inferences.

The Punishment of Loss

And, first, let us consider what they lose; the punishment of loss. This commences in that very moment, wherein the soul is separated from the body; in that instant, the soul loses all those pleasures, the enjoyment of which depends on the outward senses. The smell, the taste, the touch, delight no more: the organs that ministered to them are spoiled, and the objects that used to gratify them, are removed far away. In the dreary regions of the dead, all these things are forgotten; or, if remembered, are only remembered with pain; seeing they are gone forever. All the pleasures

of the imagination are at an end. There is no grandeur in the infernal regions; there is nothing beautiful in those dark abodes; no light but that of livid flames. And nothing new, but one unvaried scene of horror upon horror! There is no music but that of groans and shrieks; of weeping, wailing, and gnashing of teeth; of curses and blasphemies against God, or cutting reproaches of one another. Nor is there anything to gratify the sense of honor: no; they are the heirs of shame and everlasting contempt.

Thus are they totally separated from all the things they were fond of in the present world. At the same instant will commence another loss; that of all the *persons* whom they loved. They are torn away from their nearest and dearest relations; their wives, husbands, parents, children; and (what to some will be worse than all this) the friend which was as their own soul. All the pleasure they ever enjoyed in these, is lost, gone, vanished away: for there is no friendship in hell. Even the poet who affirms, (though I know not on what authority,) "Devil with devil damn'd firm concord holds"; does not affirm that there is any concord among the human fiends, that inhabit the great abyss.

But they will then be sensible of a greater loss, than all they have enjoyed on earth. They have lost their place in Abraham's bosom; in the paradise of God. Hitherto, indeed, it hath not entered into their hearts to conceive what holy souls enjoy in the garden of God, in the society of angels, and of the wisest and best men that have lived from the beginning of the world (not to mention the immense increase of knowledge which they will then, undoubtedly, receive); but they will then fully understand the value of what they have vilely cast away.

But as happy as the souls in paradise are, they are preparing for far greater happiness. For paradise is only the porch of heaven, and it is there the spirits of just men are made perfect. It is in heaven only that there is the fullness of joy; the pleasures that are at God's right hand forevermore. The loss of this, by those unhappy spirits, will be the completion of their misery. They will then know and feel, that God alone is the center of all created spirits; and, consequently, that a spirit made for God, can have no rest out of him. It seems that the apostle had this in his view, when he spoke of those "who shall be punished with everlasting destruction from the presence of the Lord." Banishment from the presence of the Lord is the very essence of destruction to a spirit that was made for God. And if that banishment last forever, it is "everlasting destruction."

The Punishment of Sense

Such is the loss sustained by those miserable creatures, on whom that awful sentence will be pronounced: "Depart from me, ye cursed!" What an unspeakable curse, if there were no other! But, alas! This is far from being the whole: for, to the punishment of loss, will be added the punishment of sense. What they lose implies unspeakable misery, which yet is inferior to what they feel. This it is which our Lord expresses in those emphatical words: "Where their worm dieth not, and the fire is not quenched."

From the time that sentence was pronounced upon man; "Dust thou art, and unto dust thou shalt return"; it was the custom of all nations, so far as we can learn, to commit dust to dust: it seemed natural to restore the bodies of the dead to the general mother earth. But, in process of time, another method obtained, chiefly among the rich and great, of burning the bodies of their relations,

and frequently in a grand magnificent manner: for which purpose they erected huge funeral piles with immense labor and expense. By either of these methods the body of man was soon restored to its parent dust. Either the worm or the fire soon consumed the well-wrought frame; after which the worm itself quickly died, and the fire was entirely quenched. But there is, likewise, a worm that belongs to the future state, and that is a worm that never dieth! And there is a fire hotter than that of the funeral pile, and it is a fire that will never be quenched!

The first thing intended by the worm that never dieth, seems to be a guilty conscience; including self-condemnation, sorrow, shame, remorse, and a sense of the wrath of God. May not we have some conception of this by what is sometimes felt, even in the present world? Is it not of this, chiefly, that Solomon speaks, when he says, "The spirit of a man may bear his infirmities"; his infirmities, or griefs, of any other kind; "but a wounded spirit who can bear?" Who can bear the anguish of an awakened conscience, penetrated with a sense of guilt, and the arrows of the Almighty sticking in the soul, and drinking up the spirit! How many of the stouthearted have sunk under it and chose strangling rather than life! And yet what are these wounds, what is all this anguish of a soul while in this present world, in comparison [to] those they must suffer when their souls are wholly awakened to feel the wrath of an offended God! Add to these all unholy passions: fear, horror, rage, evil desires; desires that can never be satisfied. Add all unholy tempers: envy, jealousy, malice, and revenge; all of which will incessantly gnaw the soul, as the vulture was supposed to do the liver of Tityus. To these if we add hatred of God and all his creatures, all these united together may serve to give us some little, imperfect idea of the worm that never dieth.

A Variety of Punishment

We may observe a remarkable difference in the manner wherein our Lord speaks concerning the two parts of the future punishment. He says, "Where *their* worm dieth not," of the one; "where *the* fire is not quenched," of the other. This cannot be by chance. What then is the reason for this variation of the expression?

Does it not seem to be this? *The fire* will be the same, essentially the same, to all that are tormented therein; only perhaps more intense to some than others, according to their degree of guilt; but *their worm* will not, cannot be the same: it will be infinitely varied, according to their various kinds, as well as degrees, of wickedness. This variety will arise partly from the just judgment of God, "rewarding every man according to his works": for we cannot doubt but this rule will take place, no less in hell than in heaven. As in heaven, "every man shall receive his own reward"; incommunicably his, according to his own labors; that is, the whole tenor of his tempers, thoughts, words, and actions. So, undoubtedly, every man, in fact, will receive his own bad reward, according to his own bad labor. And this, likewise, will be incommunicably *his own;* even as his labor was. Variety of punishment will, likewise, arise from the very nature of the thing. As they that bring most holiness to heaven will find most happiness there; so, on the other hand, it is not only true that the more wickedness a man brings to hell, the more misery he will find there, but that this misery will be infinitely varied according to the various kinds of his wickedness. It was, therefore, proper to say, *the fire,* in general; but *their worm,* in particular.

But it has been questioned by some, "Whether there be any fire in hell," that is, any material fire. Nay, if there be any fire, it is, unquestionably, material. For what is immaterial fire? The same as immaterial water or earth! Both the one and the other is absolute nonsense; a contradiction in terms. Either, therefore, we must affirm it to be material, or we deny its existence. But if we granted them, there is no fire at all there, what would they gain thereby? Seeing this is allowed, on all hands, that it is either fire or something worse. And consider this: does not our Lord speak as if it were real fire? No one can deny or doubt of this. Is it possible then to suppose, that the God of truth would speak in this manner if it were not so? Does he design to fright his poor creatures? What, with scarecrows? With vain shadows of things that have no being? Oh, let not anyone think so! Impute no such folly to the Most High!

But others aver, "it is not possible that fire should burn always. For by the immutable law of nature, it consumes whatever is thrown into it. And, by the same law, as soon as it has consumed its fuel, it is itself consumed; it goes out."

It is most true that in the present constitution of things, during the present laws of nature, the element of fire does dissolve and consume whatever is thrown into it. But here is the mistake: the present laws of nature are not immutable. When the heavens and the earth shall flee away the present scene will be totally changed; and, with the present constitution of things, the present laws of nature will cease. After this great change, nothing will be dissolved, nothing will be consumed anymore. Therefore, if it were true, that fire consumes all things now, it would not follow that it would do the same after the whole frame of nature has undergone that vast, universal change.

I say, if it were true, that "fire consumes all things now." But, indeed, it is not true. Has it not pleased God to give us already some proof of what will be hereafter? Is not the incombustible flax known in most parts of Europe? If you take a towel or handkerchief made of this (one of which may now be seen in the British Museum), you may throw it into the hottest fire, and when it is taken out again, it will be observed, upon the nicest experiment, not to have lost one grain of its weight. Here, therefore, is a substance before our eyes which, even in the present constitution of things (as if it were an emblem of things to come), may remain in fire without being consumed.

Many writers have spoken of other bodily torments, added to the being cast into the lake of fire. One of these, even pious Kempis, supposes that misers, for instance, have melted gold poured down their throats; and he supposes many other particular torments to be suited to men's particular sins. Nay, our great poet himself supposes the inhabitants of hell to undergo a variety of tortures; not to continue always in the lake of fire, but to be frequently, "By harpy-footed furies, hauled" into regions of ice; and then back again through "Extremes, by change more fierce." But I find no word, no tittle of this, not the least hint of it in all the Bible. And surely this is too awful a subject, to admit of such play of imagination. Let us keep to the written Word. It is torment enough, to dwell with everlasting burnings.

This is strongly illustrated by a fabulous story, taken from one of the eastern writers, concerning a Turkish king, who, after he had been guilty of all manner of wickedness, once did a good thing. Seeing a poor man falling into a pit, wherein he must have inevitably perished, and kicking him from it, he saved his life. The story adds, that when he was cast into hell for his enormous wickedness, that foot wherewith he had saved the man's life was permitted to lie out of the flames. But allowing this to be a real case, what a poor comfort would it be? What if both feet were permitted to lie out of the flames, yea, and both hands, how little would it avail! Nay, if all the body were taken out, and placed where no fire touched it, and only one hand or one foot kept in a burning fiery furnace, would the man, meantime, be much at ease? Nay, quite the contrary. Is it not common to say to a child, "Put your finger into that candle: can you bear it even for one minute? How then will you bear hell fire?" Surely it would be torment enough to have the flesh burned off from only one finger. What then will it be, to have the whole body plunged into a lake of fire burning with brimstone!

It remains now only to consider two or three circumstances attending the never-dying worm and the unquenchable fire.

Company of the Condemned

And, first, consider the company wherewith everyone is surrounded in that place of torment. It is not uncommon to hear even condemned criminals in our public prisons say, "Oh I wish I was hanged out of the way, rather than to be plagued with these wretches that are round about me." But what are the most abandoned wretches upon earth, compared to the inhabitants of hell? None of these are, as yet, perfectly wicked, emptied of every spark of good; certainly not till this life is at an end; probably not till the day of judgment. Nor can any of these exert, without control, their whole wickedness on their fellow creatures. Sometimes they are restrained by good men; sometimes even by bad. So even the tortures in the

Romish inquisition are restrained by those that employ them when they suppose the sufferer cannot endure any more. They then order the executioners to forbear because it is contrary to the rules of the house that a man should die upon the rack. And very frequently, when there is no human help, they are restrained by God, who hath set them their bounds which they cannot pass and saith, "Hitherto shall ye come, and no farther." Yea, so mercifully hath God ordained that the very extremity of pain causes a suspension of it. The sufferer faints away; and so, for a time at least, sinks into insensibility. But the inhabitants of hell are perfectly wicked, having no spark of goodness remaining. And they are restrained by none from exerting to the uttermost their total wickedness. Not by *men:* none will be restrained from evil by his companions in damnation; and not by *God:* for he hath forgotten them, hath delivered them over to the tormentors. And the devils need not fear, like their instruments upon earth, lest they should expire under the torture. They can die no more: they are strong to sustain whatever the united malice, skill, and strength of angels can inflict upon them. And their angelic tormentors have time sufficient to vary their torments a thousand ways. How infinitely may they vary one single torment—horrible appearances! Whereby, there is no doubt, an evil spirit, if permitted, could terrify the stoutest man upon earth to death.

Torment Without Intermission

Consider, secondly, that all these torments of body and soul are without intermission. They have no respite from pain, but "the smoke of their torment ascendeth up day and night." Day and night! That is, speaking according to the constitution of the present world, wherein God has wisely and graciously ordained that day and night should succeed each other: so that in every four and twenty hours there comes a

Daily sabbath, made to rest
Toiling man and weary beast.

Hence we seldom undergo much labor, or suffer much pain, before "Tired nature's sweet restorer, balmy sleep," steals upon us by insensible degrees and brings an interval of ease. But although the damned have uninterrupted night, it brings no interruption of their pain. No sleep accompanies that darkness: whatever ancient or modern poets, either Homer or Milton, dream, there is no sleep either in hell or heaven. And be their suffering ever so extreme, be their pain ever so intense, there is no possibility of their fainting away; no, not for a moment.

Again: the inhabitants of earth are frequently diverted from attending to what is afflictive by the cheerful light of the sun, the vicissitudes of the seasons, "the busy hum of men," and a thousand objects that roll around them in endless variety. But the inhabitants of hell have nothing to divert them from their torments, even for a moment: "Total eclipse: no sun, no moon!" No change of seasons, or of companions. There is no business, but [only] one uninterrupted scene of horror to which they must be all attention. They have no interval of inattention or stupidity: they are all eye, all ear, all sense. Every instant of their duration, it may be said of their whole frame that they are "tremblingly alive all o'er, / And smart and agonize at every pore!"

And of this duration there is no end! What a thought is this! Nothing but eternity is the term of their torment! And who can count the drops of rain, or the sands of the sea, or the days of eternity?

Every suffering is softened, if there is any hope, though distant, of deliverance from it. But here, "Hope never comes, that comes to all" the inhabitants of the upper world! What! Sufferings *never* to end!

> NEVER!—Where sinks the soul at that dread sound?
> Into a gulf how dark, and how profound!

Suppose millions of days, of years, of ages elapsed, still we are only on the threshold of eternity! Neither the pain of body or of soul is any nearer an end, than it was millions of ages ago. When they are cast into the fire, the unquenchable,—all is concluded: their worm dieth not, and the fire is not quenched!

Such is the account which the Judge of all gives of the punishment which he has ordained for impenitent sinners. And what a counterbalance may the consideration of this be, to the violence of any temptation! In particular to the fear of man; the very use to which it is applied by our Lord himself: "Be not afraid of them that kill the body, and after that have no more that they can do. But fear him, who after he hath killed hath power to cast into hell," Luke 7:4, 5.

What a guard may these considerations be against any temptation from pleasure! Will you lose, for any of these poor, earthly pleasures, which perish in the using (to say nothing of the present substantial pleasures of religion), the pleasures of paradise, such "as eye hath not seen, nor ear heard, neither hath it entered into our hearts to conceive"? Yea, the pleasures of heaven, the society of angels, and of the spirits of just men made perfect; the conversing face to face with God your Father, your Savior, your Sanctifier; and the drinking of those rivers of pleasure that are at God's right hand forevermore?

Are you tempted by pain, either of body or mind? Oh, compare present things with future! What is the pain of body which you do or may endure, to that of lying in a lake of fire burning with brimstone? What is any pain of mind; any fear, anguish, sorrow, compared to the "worm that never dieth"? *That never dieth!* This is the sting of all! As for our pains on earth, blessed be God, they are not eternal. There are some intervals to relieve, and there is some period to finish them. When we ask a friend that is sick, how he does: "I am in pain now," says he, "but I hope to be easy soon." This is a sweet mitigation of the present uneasiness. But how dreadful would his case be if he should answer, "I am all over pain, and I shall be never eased of it. I lie under exquisite torment of body and horror of soul, and I shall feel it *forever!*" Such is the case of the damned sinners in hell. Suffer any pain, then, rather than come into that place of torment!

I conclude with one more reflection, taken from Dr. Watts: "It demands our highest gratitude, that we, who have long ago deserved this misery, are not plunged into it. While there are thousands that have been adjudged to this place of punishment before they had continued so long in sin as many of us have done, what an instance is it of divine goodness that we are not under this fiery vengeance! Have we not seen many sinners on our right and our left cut off in their sins? And what but the tender mercy of God hath spared us week after week, month after month, and given us space for repentance? What shall we render unto the Lord for all his patience and longsuffering, even to this day? How often have we incurred the sentence of condemnation by our repeated rebellion against God? And yet we are still alive in his presence and are hearing the words of hope and salvation. Oh, let us look back and shudder at the thoughts of that dreadful precipice on the edge of which we have so long wandered! Let us fly for refuge to the hope that is set before us, and give a thousand thanks to the divine mercy that we are not plunged into this perdition!"

In the history of the church, no doctrine has caused greater debate than the doctrine of predestination. Even John Wesley and George Whitefield disagreed over this matter.

Wesley sought to understand this doctrine as explaining the method by which God operates and as setting forth the order in which the various aspects of salvation operate. In his discussion of foreknowledge, he sought to dispel a possible misconception concerning the nature of God's knowledge of things.

For Wesley the concept of predestination followed a progression in which God foreknew, predestined, called, justified, and finally glorified. The ultimate answer was God's absolute control of all existence, so total that nothing could escape His directing hand.

CHAPTER FIVE

On Predestination

"Whom he did foreknow, he also did predestinate to be conformed to the image of his Son:—whom he did predestinate, them he also called: and whom he called, them he also justified: and whom he justified, them he also glorified" (Rom. 8:29, 30).

"Our beloved brother Paul," says Saint Peter, "according to the wisdom given unto him, hath written unto you; as also in all his epistles, speaking in them of these things; in which are some things hard to be understood, which they that are unlearned and unstable wrest, as they do also the other Scriptures, unto their own destruction," 2 Peter 3:15, 16.

It is not improbable, that among those things spoken by Saint Paul, which are hard to be understood, the apostle Peter might place what he speaks on this subject, in the eighth and ninth chapters of his epistle to the Romans. And it is certain not only the unlearned, but many of the most learned men in the world, and not the "unstable" only, but many who seemed to be well established in the truths of the gospel, have, for several centuries, "wrested" these passages "to their own destruction."

"Hard to be understood," we may well allow them to be, when we consider how men of the strongest understanding, improved by all the advantages of education, have continually differed in judgment concerning them. And this very consideration that there is so wide a difference upon the head, between men of the greatest learning, sense, and piety, one might imagine would make all who now speak upon the subject exceedingly wary and self-diffident. But I know not how it is that just the reverse is observed in every part of the Christian world. No writers upon earth appear more positive than those who write on this difficult subject. Nay, the same men who, writing upon any other subject, are remarkably modest and humble, on this alone lay aside all self distrust, "And speak *ex cathedrâ* infallible."

This is peculiarly observable of almost all those who assert the absolute decrees. But surely it is possible to avoid this: whatever we propose may be proposed with modesty and with deference to those wise and good men who are of a contrary opinion; and the rather, because so much has been said already on every part of the question, so many volumes have been written, that it is scarcely possible to say anything which has not been said before. All I would offer at present, not to the lovers of contention, but to men of piety and candor, are a few short hints which perhaps may cast some light on the text above recited.

The more frequently and carefully I have considered it, the more I have been inclined to think that the apostle is not here (as many have supposed) describing a chain of causes and effects (this does not seem to have entered into his heart); but simply showing *the method in which God works, the order* in which the several branches of salvation constantly follow each other. And this, I apprehend, will be clear to any serious and impartial inquirer surveying the work of God either forwards or backwards, either from the beginning to the end, or from the end to the beginning.

Salvation from Beginning to End

And first, let us look forward on the whole work of God, in the salvation of man; considering it from the beginning, the first point, till it terminates in glory. The first point is the foreknowledge of God. God *foreknew* those in every nation who would believe, from the beginning of the world to the consummation of all things. But in order to throw light upon this dark question, it should be well observed, that when we speak of God's foreknowledge we do not speak according to the nature of things, but after the manner of men. For if we speak properly there is no such thing as either foreknowledge or after knowledge in God. All time, or rather all eternity (for time is only that small fragment of eternity which is allotted to the children of men), being present to him at once, he does not know one thing before another, or one thing after another; but [he] sees all things in one point of view, from everlasting to everlasting. As all time, with everything that exists therein, is present with him at once, so he sees at once whatever was, is, or will be, to the end of time. But observe: we must not think they are, because he knows them. No; he knows them, because they are. Just as I (if one may be allowed to compare the things of men with the deep things of God) now know the sun shines: yet the sun does not shine because I know it; but I know it, because he shines. My knowledge supposes the sun to shine, but does not in any wise cause it. In like manner, God knows that man sins for he knows all things: yet we do not sin because he knows it, but he knows it because we sin; and his knowledge sup-

poses our sin, but does not in any wise cause it. In a word, God, looking on all ages, from the creation to the consummation, as a moment, and seeing at once whatever is in the hearts of all the children of men, knows every one that does or does not believe, in every age or nation. Yet what he knows, whether faith or unbelief, is in no wise caused by his knowledge. Men are as free in believing or not believing as if he did not know it at all.

Indeed, if man were not free, he could not be accountable either for his thoughts, words, or actions. If he were not free, he would not be capable either of reward or punishment; he would be incapable either of virtue or vice, of being either morally good or bad. If he had no more freedom than the sun, the moon, or the stars, he would be no more accountable than they. On supposition that he had no more freedom than they, the stones of the earth would be as capable of reward, and as liable to punishment, as man: one would be as accountable as the other. Yea, and it would be as absurd to ascribe either virtue or vice to him as to ascribe it to the stock of a tree.

But to proceed: "Whom he did foreknow, them he did predestinate to be conformed to the image of his Son." This is the second step (to speak after the manner of men: for in fact, there is nothing *before* or *after* in God): in other words, God decrees, from everlasting to everlasting, that all who believe in the Son of his love, shall be conformed to his image; shall be saved from all inward and outward sin, into all inward and outward holiness. Accordingly, it is a plain, undeniable fact, all who truly believe in the name of the Son of God do now "receive the end of their faith, the salvation of their souls"; and this in virtue of the unchangeable, irreversible, irresistible decree of God: "He that believeth shall be saved"; "he that believeth not shall be damned."

"Whom he did predestinate, them he also called." This is the third step (still remembering that we speak after the manner of men), to express it a little more largely: according to his fixed decree that believers shall be saved, those whom he foreknows as such, he calls both outwardly and inwardly—*outwardly* by the word of his grace, and *inwardly* by his Spirit. This inward application of his Word to the heart seems to be what some term "effectual calling": and it implies the calling them children of God, the accepting them "in the Beloved," the justifying them freely by his grace, through the redemption that is in Jesus Christ."

"Whom he called, them he justified." This is the fourth step. It is generally allowed that the word "justified" here is taken in a peculiar sense; that it means he made them just or righteous. He executed his decree, "conforming them to the image of his Son"; or, as we usually speak, sanctified them.

It remains, "whom he justified, them he also glorified." This is the last step. Having made them "meet to be partakers of the inheritance of the saints in light," he gives them "the kingdom which was prepared for them before the world began." This is the order wherein, "according to the counsel of his will," the plan he has laid down from eternity, he saves those whom he foreknew, the true believers in every place and generation.

Salvation from the End to the Beginning

The same great work of salvation by faith, according to the foreknowledge and decree of God, may appear in a still clearer light, if we view it backward, from the end to the beginning. Suppose then you stood with the "great multitude which no man can number, out of every nation, and tongue, and kindred and people," who "give praise unto him that sitteth upon the throne, and unto the lamb forever and ever"; you would not find one among them all that were entered into glory who was not a witness of that great truth, "without holiness no man shall see the Lord"; not one of all that innumerable company, who was not sanctified before he was glorified. By holiness he was prepared for glory, according to the invariable will of the Lord, that the crown, purchased by the blood of his Son, should be given to none but those who are renewed by his Spirit. He is become "the author of eternal salvation" only "to them that obey him"; that obey him inwardly and outwardly; that are holy in heart, and holy in all manner of conversation.

And could you take a view of all those upon earth who are now sanctified, you would find not one of these had been sanctified till after he was called. He was first called, not only with an outward call, by the word and the messengers of God, but, likewise, with an inward call, by his Spirit applying his Word enabling him to believe in the only begotten Son of God, and bearing testimony with his spirit that he was a child of God. And it was by this very means they were all sanctified. It was by a sense of the love of God shed abroad in his heart, that every one of them was enabled to love God. Loving God, he loved his neighbor as himself and had power to walk in all his commandments blameless. This is a rule which admits of no exception. God calls a sinner his own, that is, justifies him, before he sanctifies. And by this very thing, the consciousness of his favor, he works in him that grateful, filial affection, from which spring every good temper and word and work.

And who are they that are thus called of God, but those whom he had before predestined, or decreed to "conform to the image of his Son"? This decree (still speaking after the manner of men) precedes every man's calling: every believer was predestined before he was called. For God calls none but "according to the counsel of his will," according to this plan of acting which he had laid down before the foundation of the world.

Once more: as all that are called were predestinated, so all whom God has predestinated he foreknew. He knew, he saw them as believers, and as such predestinated them to salvation according to his eternal decree: "He that believeth shall be saved." Thus we see the whole process of the work of God, from the end to the beginning. Who are glorified? None but those who were first sanctified. Who are sanctified? None but those who were first justified. Who are justified? None but those who were first predestinated. Who are predestinated? None but those whom God foreknew as believers. Thus the purpose and Word of God stand unshaken as the pillars of heaven: "He that believeth shall be saved; he that believeth not shall be damned." And thus God is clear from the blood of all men; since whoever perishes, perishes by his own act and deed. "They will not come unto me," says the Savior of men; and "there is no salvation in any other." They "will not believe"; and there is no other way either to present or eternal salvation. Therefore, their blood is upon their own heads; and God is still "justified in his saying," that he "willeth all men to be saved, and to come to the knowledge of his truth."

The Eternal Now

The sum of all is this: the almighty, all-wise God sees and knows, from everlasting to everlasting, all that is, that was, and that is to come, through one eternal now. With him nothing is either past or future, but all things equally present. He has, therefore, if we speak according to the truth of things, no foreknowledge, no after knowledge. This would be ill consistent with the apostle's words, "With him is no variableness or shadow of turning"; and with the account he gives of himself by the prophet, "I the Lord change not." Yet when he speaks to us, knowing whereof we are made, knowing the scantiness of our understanding, he lets himself down to our capacity and speaks of himself after the manner of men. Thus, in condescension to our weakness, he speaks of his own purpose, counsel, plan, foreknowledge. Not that God has any need of counsel, of purpose, or of planning his work beforehand. Far be it from us to impute these to the Most High, to measure him by ourselves! It is merely in compassion to us, that he speaks thus of himself, as foreknowing the things in heaven or earth, and as predestinating or foreordaining them. But can we possibly imagine that these expressions are to be taken literally? To one who was so gross in his conceptions, might he not say, "Thinkest thou I am such a one as thyself"? Not so: "As the heavens are higher than the earth, so are my ways higher than thy ways. I know, decree, work, in such a manner as it is not possible for thee to conceive: but to give thee some faint, glimmering knowledge of my ways, I use the language of men, and suit myself to thy apprehensions, in this thy infant state of existence."

What is it then that we learn from this whole account? It is this, and no more: God knows all believers, wills that they should be saved from sin, to that end justifies them, sanctifies, and takes them to glory.

Oh, that men would praise the Lord for this his goodness; and that they would be content with this plain account of it, and not endeavor to wade into those mysteries which are too deep for angels to fathom!

For Wesley, faith was the divine evidence and conviction of unseen things. It began with God and ended with God. It was this doctrine that caused such confusion for Wesley until he accepted the message of saving faith after a reading of Luther's work on Romans.

For Wesley, faith came in a variety of forms. The materialist expressed faith in science, the empirical evidences. The deist had faith in a supreme being, but not the Bible. He trusted that he came to be as a result of the work of a Creator, but now must depend on the progress of man. Heathens expressed a faith similar to deists. God was not available so they were left with what was around them. The faith of a Jew was directed at the Messiah, but unfortunately the identity of the Messiah was unknown. The faith expressed by Protestants was the saving faith revealed in the Bible.

Wesley drew a distinction between a servant of God and a son of God, in which the former was not necessarily the latter. Wesley would have seen himself in his pre-conversion days as a servant who, upon hearing Romans, became a son of God.

CHAPTER SIX

On Faith

"Without faith it is impossible to please him" (Heb. 11:6).

But what is faith? It is a divine "evidence and conviction of things not seen": of things which are not seen now, whether they are visible or invisible in their own nature. Particularly, it is a divine evidence and conviction of God, and of the things of God. This is the most comprehensive definition of faith that ever was or can be given; as including every species of faith, from the lowest to the highest. And yet I do not remember any eminent writer that has given a full and clear account of the several sorts of it, among all the verbose and tedious treatises which have been published upon the subject.

Something indeed of a similar kind has been written by that great and good man, Mr. Fletcher, in his Treatise on the Various Dispensations of the Grace of God. Herein, he observes that there are four dispensations that are distinguished from each other by the degree of light which God vouchsafes to them that are under each. A small degree of light is given to those that are under the heathen dispensation. These generally believed, "that there was a God, and that he was a rewarder of them that diligently seek him." But a far more considerable degree of light was vouchsafed to the Jewish nation, in as much as to them "were entrusted" the grand means of light, "the oracles of God." Hence many of these had clear and exalted views of the nature and attributes of God, of their duty to God and man, yea, and of the great promise made to our first parents, and transmitted by them to their posterity, that "the seed of the woman should bruise the serpent's head."

But above both the heathen and Jewish dispensation was that of John the Baptist. To him a still clearer light was given; and he was himself "a burning and a shining light." To whom it was given to "behold the Lamb of God, that taketh away the sin of the world." Accordingly our Lord himself affirms that "of all which had been born of women," there had not till that time arisen "a greater than John the Baptist." But, nevertheless, he informs us, "He that is least in the kingdom of God," the Christian dispensation, "is greater than he." By one that is under the Christian dispensation, Mr. Fletcher means, one that has received the Spirit of adoption, that has the Spirit of God witnessing "with his spirit, that he is a child of God."

In order to explain this still further, I will endeavor, by the help of God, first, to point out the several sorts of faith; and, secondly, to draw some practical inferences.

Varieties of Faith

In the first place, I will endeavor to point out the several sorts of faith. It would be easy, either to reduce these to a smaller number, or to divide them into a greater. But it does not appear that this would answer any valuable purpose.

The lowest sort of faith, if it be any faith at all, is that of a materialist: a man who, like the late Lord Kames, believes there is nothing but matter in the universe. I say, if it be any faith at all; for, properly speaking, it is not. It is not "an evidence or conviction of God," for they do not believe there is any; neither is it "a conviction of things not seen"; for they deny the existence of such. Or if, for decency's sake, they allow there is a God, yet they suppose even him to be material. For one of their maxims is, "Whatever you see, is God." *Whatever you see!* A visible, tangible god! Excellent divinity! Exquisite nonsense!

The second sort of faith, if you allow a materialist to have any, is the faith of a deist. I mean one who believes there is a God, distinct from matter, but does not believe the Bible. Of these we may observe two sorts: one sort are mere beasts in human shape, wholly under the power of the basest passions, and having "a downright appetite to mix with mud." Other deists are, in most respects, rational creatures, though unhappily prejudiced against Christianity. Most of these believe the being and attributes of God: they believe that God made and governs the world; and that the soul does not die with the body, but will remain forever in a state of happiness or misery.

The next sort of faith is the faith of heathens, with which I join that of Mohammedans. I cannot but prefer this before the faith of the deists; because though it embraces nearly the same objects, yet they are rather to be pitied than blamed for the narrowness of their faith. And their not believing the whole truth is not owing to want of sincerity, but merely to want of light. When one asked Chicali, an old Indian chief, "Why do not you, red men, know as much as us, white men?" he readily answered, "Because you have the great Word, and we have not!"

It cannot be doubted but this plea will avail for millions of modern heathens. In-as-much as to them little is given, of them little will be required. As to the ancient heathens, millions of them likewise were savages. No more, therefore, will be expected of them than the living up to the light they had. But many of them, especially in the civilized nations, we have great reason to hope, although they lived among heathens, yet were quite of another spirit, being taught of God, by his inward voice, all the essentials of true religion. Yea, and so was that Mohammedan, an Arabian, who, a century or two ago, wrote the life of Hai Ebn Yokdan. The story seems to be feigned; but it contains all the principles of pure and undefiled religion.

But, in general, we may surely place the faith of a Jew above that of a heathen or Mohammedan. By Jewish faith I mean the faith of those who lived between the giving of the Law and the coming of Christ. These, that is, those that were serious and sincere among them, believed all that is written in the Old Testament. In particular, they believed that, in the fullness of time, the Messiah would appear, "to finish the transgression, to make an end of sin, and bring in everlasting righteousness."

It is not so easy to pass any judgment concerning the faith of our modern Jews. It is plain, "the veil is still upon their hearts," when Moses and the prophets are read. The god of this world still hardens their hearts and still blinds their eyes, "lest at any time the light of the glorious gospel" should break in upon them. So that we may say of this people, as the Holy Ghost said to their forefathers, "The heart of this people is waxed gross, and their ears are dull of hearing, and their eyes have they closed, lest they should see with their eyes, and hear with their ears, and understand with their hearts, and should be converted, and I should heal them," Acts 28:27. Yet it is not our part to pass sentence upon them, but to leave them to their own Master.

I need not dwell upon the faith of John the Baptist, any more than the dispensation which he was under; because these, as Mr. Fletcher well describes them, were peculiar to himself. Setting him aside, the faith of the Roman Catholics in general, seems to be above that of the ancient Jews. If most of these are volunteers in faith, believing more than God has revealed, it cannot be denied that they believe all which God has revealed, as necessary to salvation. In this we rejoice on their behalf: we are glad that none of those new articles which they added at the Council of Trent to "the faith once delivered to the saints," does so materially contradict any of the ancient articles as to render them of no effect.

The faith of the Protestants, in general, embraces only those truths as necessary to salvation, which are clearly revealed in the oracles of God. Whatever is plainly declared in the Old and New Testament, is the object of their faith. They believe neither more nor less, than what is manifestly contained in, and provable by the holy Scriptures. The Word of God is "a lantern to their feet, and a light in all their paths." They dare not, on any pretense, go from it to the right hand or to the left. The written Word is the whole and sole rule of their faith, as well as practice. They believe whatsoever God has declared, and profess to do whatsoever he hath commanded. This is the proper faith of Protestants: by this they will abide and no other.

Hitherto faith has been considered chiefly as an evidence and conviction of such or such truths. And this is the sense wherein it is taken at this day in every part of the Christian world. But in the meantime let it be carefully observed (for eternity depends upon it),

that neither the faith of a Roman Catholic, nor that of a Protestant, if it contains no more than this, no more than the embracing such and such truths, will avail any more before God, than the faith of a Mohammedan or a heathen; yea, of a deist or materialist. For can this "faith save him"? Can it save any man either from sin or from hell? No more than it could save Judas Iscariot; no more than it could save the devil and his angels, all of whom are convinced, that every tittle of holy Scripture is true.

A Saving Faith

But what is the faith which is properly saving; which brings eternal salvation to all those that keep it to the end? It is such a divine conviction of God, and the things of God, as, even in its infant state, enables everyone that possesses it to "fear God and work righteousness." And whosoever in every nation believes thus far, the apostle declares, is "accepted of him." He actually is, at that very moment, in a state of acceptance. But he is at present only a *servant* of God, not properly a *son*. Meantime let it be well observed that "the wrath of God" no longer "abideth on him."

Indeed nearly fifty years ago, when the preachers commonly called Methodists began to preach that grand scriptural doctrine, salvation by faith, they were not sufficiently apprised of the difference between a servant and a child of God. They did not clearly understand, that even one "who feareth God, and worketh righteousness, is accepted of him." In consequence of this, they were apt to make sad the hearts of those whom God had not made sad. For they frequently asked those who feared God, "Do you know that your sins are forgiven?" And upon their answering, "No," immediately replied, "Then you are a child of the devil." No; that does not follow. It might have been said (and it is all that can be said with propriety), "Hitherto you are only a *servant*, you are not a *child* of God. You have already great reason to praise God that he has called you to his honorable service. Fear not. Continue crying unto him, 'and you shall see greater things than these.'"

And indeed, unless the servants of God halt by the way, they will receive the adoption of sons. They will receive the *faith* of the children of God by his *revealing* his only begotten Son in their hearts. Thus, the faith of a child is, properly and directly, a divine conviction whereby every child of God is enabled to testify, "The life that I now live, I live by faith in the Son of God, who loved me, and gave himself for me." And whosoever hath this, "the Spirit of God witnesseth with his spirit, that he is a child of God." So the apostle writes to the Galatians: "Ye are the sons of God by faith. And because ye are sons, God hath sent forth the Spirit of his Son into your hearts, crying, Abba, Father"; that is, giving you a childlike confidence in him, together with a kind affection toward him. This then it is (if Saint Paul was taught of God, and wrote as he was moved by the Holy Ghost) that properly constitutes the difference between a servant of God and a child of God. "He that believeth" as a child of God, "hath the witness in himself." This the servant hath not. Yet let not man discourage him: rather, lovingly exhort him to expect it every moment!

It is easy to observe that all the sorts of faith which we can conceive, are reducible to one or other of the preceding. But let us covet the best gifts and follow the most excellent way. There is no reason why you should be satisfied with the faith of a materialist, a heathen, or a deist, nor indeed with that of a servant. I do not know that God requires it at your hands. Indeed, if you have received this, you ought not to cast it away: you ought not in any wise to undervalue it, but to be truly thankful for it. Yet in the meantime, beware how you rest here: press on till you receive the Spirit of adoption. Rest not, till that Spirit clearly witnesses with your spirit that you are a child of God.

Implications of Faith

I proceed, in the second place, to draw a few inferences from the preceding observations.

And I would first infer in how dreadful a state, if there be a God, is a materialist: one who denies not only the "Lord that bought him," but also the Lord that made him. "Without faith it is impossible to please God." But it is impossible *he* should have any faith at all—any conviction of any invisible world; for he believes there is no such thing—any conviction of the being of a God, for a material God is no God at all. For you cannot possibly suppose the sun or skies to be God, any more than you can suppose a god of wood or stone. And further, whosoever believes all things to be mere matter must of course believe that all things are governed by dire necessity! Necessity that is as inexorable as the winds; as ruthless as the rocks; as merciless as the waves that dash upon them or the poor shipwrecked mariners! Who then shall help thee, thou poor desolate wretch, when thou art most in need of help? Winds, and seas, and rocks, and storms! Such are the best helpers, which the materialists can hope for!

Almost equally desperate is the case of the poor deist, how learned, yea, [however] moral he be. For you, likewise, though you may not advert to it, are really "without God in the world." See your religion, the "religion of nature, delineated" by the ingenious Mr. Wollaston (whom I remember to have seen when I was at school, attending the public service at the Charterhouse chapel). Does he found his religion upon God? Nothing less. He founds it upon truth, abstract truth. But does he not by that expression mean God? No: he sets him out of the question and builds a beautiful castle in the air, without being beholden either to him or his Word. See your smooth-tongued orator of Glasgow, one of the most pleasing writers of the age! Has he any more to do with God, on his system, than Mr. Wollaston? Does he deduce his "idea of virtue," from him as the Father of lights, the source of all good? Just the contrary. He not only plans his whole theory without taking the least notice of God, but toward the close of it proposes that question, "Does the having an eye to God in an action, enhance the virtue of it?" He answers, "No; it is so far from this, that if in doing a virtuous, that is, a benevolent action, a man mingles a desire to please God, the more there is of this desire, the less virtue there is in that action." Never before did I meet with either Jew, Turk, or heathen, who so flatly renounced God, as this Christian professor.

But with heathens, Mohammedans, and Jews, we have at present nothing to do: only we may wish that their lives did not shame many of us that are called Christians. We have not much more to do with the members of the church of Rome. But we cannot doubt that many of them, like the excellent archbishop of Cambray, still retain (notwithstanding many mistakes) that faith that worketh by love. And how many of the Protestants enjoy this, whether members of the church, or of other congregations? We have reason to believe a considerable number, both of one and the other (and, blessed be God, an increasing number), in every part of the land.

Once more I exhort you that fear God and work righteousness, you that are *servants* of God, first, flee from all sin, as from the face of a serpent; being,

> Quick as the apple of an eye,
> The slightest touch of sin to feel;

and to work righteousness, to the utmost of the power you now have; to abound in works both of piety and mercy: and, secondly, continually to cry to God that he would reveal his Son in your hearts to the intent you may be no more *servants* but *sons;* having his love shed abroad in your hearts and walking in "the glorious liberty of the children of God."

I exhort you, lastly, who already feel the Spirit of God witnessing with your spirit that you are the children of God, follow the advice of the apostle: "Walk in all the good works whereunto ye are created in Christ Jesus." And then, "leaving the principles of the doctrine of Christ, and not laying again the foundation of repentance from dead works, and of faith toward God," go on to perfection. Yea, and when ye have attained a measure of perfect love, when God has circumcised your hearts, and enabled you to love him with all your heart and with all your soul, think not of resting there. That is impossible. You cannot stand still: you must either rise or fall; rise higher or fall lower. Therefore, the voice of God to the children of Israel, to the children of God, is, "Go forward!" "Forgetting the things that are behind, and reaching forward unto those that are before, press on to the mark for the prize of your high calling of God in Christ Jesus!"

Faith is not a belief in what God is, or knowing about God by means of natural revelation as found in Romans 1. Nor is faith the same as the belief expressed by devils who know who God is.

Faith that saves is centered on the person of Christ and what Christ did on the cross. It is an acknowledgment of man's inability in and of himself to accomplish his own salvation. Christ is the basis of salvation and faith is the means by which man appropriates Christ.

Saving faith delivers man from eternal destruction in hell. It unites him to God, thereby restoring a previously severed relationship. This faith may be to some a means of escaping good works. Wesley denied this and answered that whereas works cannot save, saving faith compels the believer to do good works. Whereas belief merely acknowledges the validity of facts, true faith activates the desire to do what is pleasing to the object of faith.

CHAPTER SEVEN

Salvation by Faith

Preached at St. Mary's, Oxford, before the University, June 18, 1738

"By grace are ye saved, through faith" (Eph. 2:18).

All the blessings which God hath bestowed upon man, are of his mere grace, bounty, or favor; his free, undeserved favor; favor altogether undeserved; man having no claim to the least of his mercies. It was free grace that "formed man of the dust of the ground, and breathed into him a living soul," and stamped on that soul the image of God, and "put all things under his feet." The same free grace continues to us at this day, life and breath, and all things. For there is nothing we are, or have, or do, which can deserve the least thing at God's hand. "All our works, thou, O God, hast wrought in us." These, therefore, are so many more instances of free mercy: and, whatever righteousness may be found in man, this is also the gift of God.

Wherewithal then shall a sinful man atone for any the least of his sins? With his own works? No. Were they ever so many or holy, they are not his own, but God's. But, indeed, they are all unholy and sinful themselves, so that everyone of them needs a fresh atonement. Only corrupt fruit grows on a corrupt tree. And his heart is altogether corrupt and abominable, being "come short of the glory of God," the glorious righteousness at first impressed on his soul after the image of his great Creator. Therefore, having nothing, neither righteousness nor works to plead, his mouth is utterly stopped before God.

If then sinful men find favor with God it is "grace upon grace"! If God vouchsafe still to pour fresh blessings upon us—yea, the greatest of all blessings, salvation—what can we say to these things, but, "Thanks be unto God for his unspeakable gift!" And thus it is. Herein "God commendeth his love toward us, in that while we were yet sinners, Christ died" to save us. "By grace, then, are ye saved, through faith." Grace is the source, faith the condition, of salvation.

Now, [so] that we fall not short of the grace of God, it concerns us carefully to inquire, first, what faith it is through which we are saved; second, what is the salvation which is through faith; third, how we may answer some objections.

The Nature of Saving Faith

First, what faith is it through which we are saved?

It is not barely the faith of a heathen. Now God requireth of a heathen to believe, "That God is; that he is a rewarder of them that diligently seek him"; and that he is to be sought by glorifying him as God, by giving him thanks for all things, and by a careful practice of moral virtue, of justice, mercy and truth toward their fellow creatures. A Greek or Roman, therefore, yea, a Scythian or Indian, was without excuse if he did not believe thus much: the being and attributes of God, a future state of reward and punishment, and the obligatory nature of moral virtue. For this is barely the faith of a heathen.

Nor is it the faith of a devil, though he goes much farther than that of a heathen. For the devil believes not only that there is a wise and powerful God, gracious to reward and just to punish, but also that Jesus is the Son of God, the Christ, the Savior of the world. So we find him declaring in express terms, Luke 4:34, "I know thee, who thou art; the Holy One of God." Nor can we doubt but that unhappy spirit believes all those words which came out of the mouth of the Holy One; yea, and whatsoever else was written by those holy men of old, of two of whom he was compelled to give that glorious testimony, "These men are the servants of the Most High God, who show unto you the way of salvation. Thus much, then, the great enemy of God and man believes, and trembles in believing, that God was made manifest in the flesh; that he will "tread all enemies under his feet"; and that "all Scripture was given by inspiration of God." Thus far goeth the faith of a devil.

The faith through which we are saved, in that sense of the word which will hereafter be explained, is not barely that which the apostles themselves had while Christ was yet upon earth; though they so believed on him as to "leave all and follow him"; although they had then power to work miracles, to "heal all manner of sickness, and all manner of disease"; yea, they had then "power and authority over all devils"; and, which is beyond all this, were sent by their Master to "preach the kingdom of God."

What faith is it then through which we are saved? It may be answered, first, in general, it is a faith in Christ; Christ, and God through Christ, are the proper objects of it. Herein, therefore, it is sufficiently, absolutely distinguished from the faith either of ancient or modern heathens. And from the faith of a devil, it is fully distinguished by this: it is not barely a speculative, rational thing, a cold, lifeless assent, a train of ideas in the head, but also a disposition of the heart. For thus saith the Scripture, "With the heart man believeth unto righteousness." And, "If thou shalt confess with thy mouth the Lord Jesus, and shalt believe with thy heart, that God hath raised him from the dead, thou shalt be saved."

And herein does it differ from that faith which the apostles themselves had while our Lord was on earth, that it acknowledges the necessity and merit of his death and the power of his resurrection. It acknowledges his death as the only sufficient means of redeeming man from death eternal, and his resurrection as the restoration of us all to life and immortality; inasmuch as he "was delivered for our sins, and rose again for our justification." Christian faith is then, not only an assent to the whole gospel of Christ, but also a full reliance on the blood of Christ; a trust in the merits of his life, death, and resurrection; a recumbency upon him as our atonement and our life, *as given for us*, and *living in us*. It is a sure confidence which a man hath in God that, through the merits of Christ, *his* sins are forgiven and *he* [is] reconciled to the favor of God; and, in consequence hereof, a closing with him, and cleaving to him, as our "wisdom, righteousness, sanctification, and redemption," or, in one word, our salvation.

The Nature of Salvation Through Faith

What is the salvation which is through faith?

And first, whatsoever else it imply, it is a present salvation. It is something attainable, yea, actually attained on earth, by those who are partakers of this faith. For thus saith the apostle to the believers at Ephesus, and in them to the believers of all ages, not *ye shall be* (though that also is true), but *"ye are saved* through faith."

Ye are saved (to comprise all in one word) from sin. This is the salvation which is through faith. This is that great salvation foretold by the angel, before God brought his first-begotten into the world: "Thou shall call his name Jesus, for he shall save his people from their sins." And neither here, nor in other parts of Holy Writ, is there any limitation or restriction. All his people, or as it is elsewhere expressed, "all that believe in him," he will save from all their sins; from original and actual, past and present sin, "of the flesh and of the spirit." Through faith that is in him, they are saved both from the guilt and from the power of it.

First from the guilt of all past sin: for, whereas all the world is guilty before God, insomuch that should he "be extreme to mark what is done amiss there is none that could abide it"; and whereas, "by the law is" only "the knowledge of sin," but no deliverance from it, so that, "by fulfilling the deeds of the law, no flesh can be justified in his sight"; now, "the righteousness of God, which is by faith [in] Jesus Christ, is manifested unto all [who] believe." Now, "they are justified freely by his grace, through the redemption that is in Jesus Christ." "Him God hath set forth to be a propitiation, through faith in his blood; to declare his righteousness for (or by) the remission of the sins that are past." Now hath Christ taken away "the curse of the Law, being made a curse for us." He hath "blotted out the handwriting that was against us, taking it out of the way, nailing it to his cross." "There is,

therefore, no condemnation now, to them which" believe in Christ Jesus.

And being saved from guilt, they are saved from fear. Not, indeed, from a filial fear of offending, but, from all servile fear; from that fear which hath torment; from fear of punishment; from fear of the wrath of God, whom they now no longer regard as a severe master, but as an indulgent Father. "They have not received again the spirit of bondage, but the spirit of adoption, whereby they cry Abba, Father: the Spirit itself also bearing witness with their spirits, that they are the children of God." They are also saved from the fear, though not from the possibility, of falling away from the grace of God and coming short of the great and precious promises: they are "sealed with the Holy Spirit of promise, which is the earnest of their inheritance," Ephesians 1:13. Thus have they "peace with God through our Lord Jesus Christ. They rejoice in hope of the glory of God. And the love of God is shed abroad in their hearts through the Holy Ghost, which is given unto them." And hereby they are persuaded (though perhaps not at all times, nor with the same fullness of persuasion), that "neither death, nor life, nor things present, nor things to come, nor height, nor depth, nor any other creature, shall be able to separate them from the love of God, which is in Christ Jesus our Lord."

Again, through this faith they are saved from the power of sin, as well as from the guilt of it. So the apostle declares, "Ye know that he was manifested to take away our sins, and in him is no sin. Whosoever abideth in him, sinneth not," 1 John 3:5. Again, "Little children, let no man deceive you. He that committeth sin is of the devil. Whosoever believeth is born of God. And whosoever is born of God doth not commit sin for his seed remaineth in him: and he cannot sin, because he is born of God." Once more, "We know, that whosoever is born of God sinneth not: but he that is begotten of God, keepeth himself, and that wicked one toucheth him not," 1 John 5:18.

He that is born of God by faith sinneth not by any habitual sin; for all habitual sin, is sin reigning: but sin cannot reign in any that believeth. Nor by any willful sin, for his will, while he abideth in the faith, is utterly set against all sin, and abhorreth it as deadly poison. Nor by any sinful desire; for he continually desireth the holy and perfect will of God; and any tendency to an unholy desire, he, by the grace of God, stifleth in the birth. Nor doth he sin by infirmities, whether in act, word, or thought: for his infirmities have no concurrence of his will; and without this they are not properly sins. Thus, "He that is born of God doth not commit sin." And though he cannot say he hath not sinned, yet, now "he sinneth not."

This then is the salvation which is through faith, even in the present world: a salvation from sin and the consequences of sin, both often expressed in the word justification; which, taken in the largest sense, implies a deliverance from guilt and punishment by the atonement of Christ actually applied to the soul of the sinner now believing on him, and a deliverance from the whole body of sin, through Christ, formed in his heart. So that he who is thus justified, or saved by faith, is indeed born again. He is born again of the Spirit unto a new life "which is hid with Christ in God." "He is a new creature: old things are passed away: all things in him are become new." And as a new born babe he gladly receives the "sincere milk of the word, and grows thereby," going on in the might of the Lord his God, from faith to faith, from grace to grace, until at length he comes unto "a perfect man, unto the measure of the stature of the fullness of Christ."

Confronting Objections to This Doctrine

Objections and answers to them.

That to preach salvation, or justification, by faith only, is to preach against holiness and good works. To which a short answer might be given: It would be so, if we spake, as some do, of a faith which was separate from these: but we speak of a faith which is not so, but necessarily productive of all good works and all holiness.

But it may be of use to consider it more at large, especially since it is no new objection, but as old as Saint Paul's time: for even then it was asked, "Do we not make void the law through faith?" We answer, first, all who preach not faith, do manifestly make void the law; either directly and grossly by limitations and comments, that eat out all the spirit of the text; or, indirectly, by not pointing out the only means whereby it is possible to perform it. Whereas, secondly, "we establish the law," both by showing its full extent and spiritual meaning; and by calling all to that living way, whereby "the righteousness of the law may be fulfilled in them." These, while they trust in the blood of Christ alone, use all the ordinances which he hath appointed, do all the "good works which he had before prepared that they should walk therein," and enjoy and manifest all holy and heavenly tempers, even the same mind that was in Christ Jesus.

But does not preaching this faith lead men into pride? We answer, accidentally it may: therefore ought every believer to be earnestly cautioned, in the words of the great apostle, "Because of unbelief, the first branches were broken off; and thou standest by faith. Be not highminded, but fear. If God spared not the natural branches, take heed lest he spare not thee. Behold, therefore, the goodness and severity of God! On them which fell, severity; but toward thee, goodness, if thou continue in his goodness; otherwise thou also shalt be cut off." And while he continues therein, he will remember those words of Saint Paul, foreseeing and answering this very objection, Romans 3:27, "Where is boasting then? It is excluded. By what law? Of works? Nay, but by the law of faith. If a man were justified by his works, he would have whereof to glory." But there is no glorying for him "that worketh not, but believeth on him that justifieth the ungodly," Romans 4:5. To the same effect are the words both preceding and following the text: Ephesians 2:4, "God, who is rich in mercy, even when we were dead in sins, hath quickened us together with Christ (by grace ye are saved), that he might show the exceeding riches of his grace, in his kindness toward us through Christ Jesus. For, by grace are ye saved, through faith; and that not of yourselves." Of yourselves cometh neither your faith nor your salvation: "It is the gift of God"; the free, undeserved gift; the faith through which ye are saved, as well as the salvation, which he of his own good pleasure, his mere favor, annexes thereto. That ye believe, is one instance of his grace; that believing ye are saved, another. "Not of works, lest any man should boast." For all our works, all our righteousness, which were before our believing, merited nothing of God but condemnation. So far were they from deserving faith, which, therefore, whenever given, is not *of works*. Neither is salvation of the works we do when we believe: for *it is then God that worketh in us*, and, therefore, that he giveth us a reward for what he himself worketh, only commendeth the riches of his

mercy, but leaveth us nothing whereof to glory.

However, may not the speaking thus of the mercy of God, as saving or justifying freely by faith only, encourage men in sin? Indeed, it may and will. Many will "continue in sin that grace may abound." But their blood is upon their own head. The goodness of God ought to lead them to repentance; and so it will those who are sincere of heart. When they know there is yet forgiveness with him, they will cry aloud that he would blot out their sins also, through faith which is in Jesus. And if they earnestly cry and faint not; if they seek him in all the means he hath appointed; if they refuse to be comforted till he come; "he will come and will not tarry." And he can do much work in a short time. Many are the examples in the Acts of the Apostles of God's shedding abroad this faith in men's hearts, even like lightning falling from heaven. So in the same hour that Paul and Silas began to preach, the jailer "repented, believed, and was baptized," as were three thousand by Saint Peter, on the day of Pentecost, who all repented and believed at his first preaching. And blessed be God, there are now many living proofs that he is still "mighty to save."

Yet to the same truth placed in another view, a quite contrary objection is made: "If a man cannot be saved by all that he can do, this will drive men to despair." True, to despair of being saved by their own works, their own merits, or righteousness. And so it ought; for none can trust in the merits of Christ till he has utterly renounced his own. He that "goeth about to establish his own righteousness," cannot receive the righteousness of God. The righteousness which is of faith cannot be given him while he trusteth in that which is of the law.

But this, it is said, is an uncomfortable doctrine. The devil spoke like himself, that is, without either truth or shame, when he dared to suggest to men that it is such. It is the only comfortable one, it is "very full of comfort," to all self-destroyed, self-condemned sinners. That "whosoever believeth on him shall not be ashamed, that the same Lord over all is rich unto all that call upon him." Here is comfort high as heaven, stronger than death! What! Mercy for all? For Zaccheus, a public robber? For Mary Magdalene, a common harlot? Methinks I hear one say, "Then I, even I, may hope for mercy!" And so thou mayest, thou afflicted one, whom none hath comforted! God will not cast out thy prayer. Nay, perhaps he may say the next hour, "Be of good cheer, thy sins are forgiven thee"; so forgiven, that they shall reign over thee no more; yea, and that "the Holy Spirit shall bear witness with thy spirit that thou art a child of God." O glad tidings! Tidings of great joy which are sent unto all people! "Ho, every one that thirsteth, come ye to the waters: Come ye, and buy, without money and without price." Whatever your sins be, "though red, like crimson," though more than the hairs of your head, "return ye unto the Lord, and he will have mercy upon you; and to our God, for he will abundantly pardon."

Universal Application

When no more objections occur, then we are simply told that salvation by faith only ought not to be preached as the first doctrine or, at least, not to be preached to all. But what saith the Holy Ghost? "Other foundation can no man lay than that which is laid, even Jesus Christ." So then, that "whosoever believeth on him, shall be saved" is, and must be, the foundation of all our preaching, that is, must be preached first. "Well, but not to all." To whom then are we not to preach it? Whom shall we except? The poor? Nay; they have a peculiar right to have the gospel preached unto them. The unlearned? No. God hath revealed these things unto unlearned and ignorant men from the beginning. The young? By no means. Suffer these, in any wise, to come unto Christ, and forbid them not. The sinners? Least of all. "He came not to call the righteous, but sinners to repentance." Why then, if any, we are to except the rich, the learned, the reputable, the moral men. And, it is true, they too often except themselves from hearing; yet we must speak the words of our Lord. For thus the tenor of our commission runs, "Go and preach the gospel to every creature." If any man wrest it, or any part of it, to his destruction, he must bear his own burden. But still, "as the Lord liveth, whatsoever the Lord saith unto us, that we will speak."

At this time, more especially, will we speak that "by grace ye are saved, through faith," because never was the maintaining this doctrine more seasonable than it is at this day. Nothing but this can effectually prevent the increase of the Romish delusion among us. It is endless to attack, one by one, all the errors of that church. But salvation by faith strikes at the root, and all fall at once where this is established. It was this doctrine, which our church justly calls *the strong rock and foundation of the Christian religion*, that first drove popery out of these kingdoms, and this alone can keep it out. Nothing but this can give a check to that immorality which hath "overspread the land as a flood." Can you empty the great deep, drop by drop? Then you may reform us by dissuasives from particular vices. But let the "righteousness which is of God by faith" be brought in, and so shall its proud waves be stayed. Nothing but this can stop the mouths of those who "glory in their shame and openly deny the Lord that bought them." They can talk as sublimely of the Law as he that hath it written, by God, in his heart. To hear them speak on this head, might incline one to think they were not far from the kingdom of God. But take them out of the Law into the gospel; begin with the righteousness of faith, with Christ, "the end of the law, to every one that believeth"; and those who but now appeared almost, if not altogether Christians, stand confessed the sons of perdition; as far from life and salvation (God be merciful unto them!) as the depth of hell from the height of heaven.

For this reason the adversary so rages whenever "salvation by faith" is declared to the world; for this reason did he stir up earth and hell: to destroy those who first preached it. And for the same reason, knowing that faith alone could overturn the foundations of his kingdom, did he call forth all his forces and employ all his arts of lies and calumny to affright that champion of the Lord of hosts, Martin Luther, from reviving it. Nor can we wonder thereat; for as that man of God observes, "How would it enrage a proud strong man armed to be stopped and set at nought by a little child coming against him with a reed in his hand?" Especially, when he knew that little child would surely overthrow him and tread him under foot. Even so, Lord Jesus! Thus hath thy strength been ever "made perfect in weakness!" Go forth then, thou little child that believest in him, and "his right hand shall teach thee terrible things!" Though thou art helpless and weak as an infant of days, the strong man shall not be able to stand before thee. Thou shalt prevail over him, and subdue him, and overthrow him, and trample him under thy feet. Thou shalt march on, under the great Captain of thy salvation, "conquering, and to conquer," until all thine enemies are destroyed and "death is swallowed up in victory."

"Now, thanks be to God, which giveth us the victory through our Lord Jesus Christ," to whom with the Father and the Holy Ghost, be blessing, and glory, and wisdom, and thanksgiving, and honor, and power, and might, forever. Amen.

In his discussion of the Holy Spirit, Wesley examined the fall of Adam, the person of Christ, and the works and operations of the Spirit.

In Adam man became a fallen creature. His fellowship with God was severed. Before the Fall, Adam and Eve enjoyed the presence of God through the guidance of his Spirit. With the Fall, the guidance and communion were lost, resulting in man's separation from God.

Christ represents the coming of salvation for mankind, the means by which man's redemption would be secured. The Holy Spirit participated in this process as the instrument of the incarnation and, following Christ's ascension, the source of power in the redeemed. He would assume responsibility as the comforter of Christians.

Finally, the work of the Spirit is what has enabled Christians to perform various miracles, discern false spirits, and grow in the faith. He has also been a source of comfort and guidance.

CHAPTER EIGHT

On the Holy Spirit

Preached at St. Mary's, Oxford, on Whitsunday, 1736

"Now the Lord is that Spirit" (2 Cor. 3:17).

The apostle had been showing, how the gospel ministry was superior to that of the law, the time being now come when types and shadows should be laid aside, and we should be invited to our duty by the manly and ingenuous motives of a clear and full revelation, open and free on God's part, and not at all disguised by his ambassadors. But what he chiefly insists upon is not the *manner*, but the *subject* of their ministry: "Who hath made us able ministers," saith he, "of the New Testament, not of the letter, but of the Spirit, for the letter killeth, but the Spirit giveth life." Here lies the great difference between the two dispensations: that the law was indeed *spiritual* in its demands, requiring a life consecrated to God in the observance of many rules but not conveying spiritual assistance, its effect was only to kill and mortify man by giving him to understand that he must needs be in a state of great depravity, since he found it so difficult to obey God; and that, as particular deaths were by that institution inflicted for particular sins, so death, in general, was but the consequence of his universal sinfulness. But the ministration of the New Testament was that of a "Spirit which giveth life," a Spirit not only promised, but actually conferred, which should both enable Christians now to live unto God, and fulfill precepts even more spiritual than the former, and restore them hereafter to

perfect life, after the ruins of sin and death. The incarnation, preaching, and death of Jesus Christ were designed to represent, proclaim, and purchase for us this gift of the Spirit; and, therefore, says the apostle, "The Lord is that Spirit," or *the* Spirit.

This description of Christ was a proper inducement to Jews to believe on him, and it is still a necessary instruction to Christians, to regulate their expectations from him. But I think this age has made it particularly necessary to be well assured [of] what Christ is to us. When that question is so differently resolved by the pious but weak accounts of some pretenders to *faith* on one hand, and by the clearer but not perfectly Christian accounts of some pretenders to *reason* on the other: while some derive from him a "righteousness of God," but in a sense somewhat improper and figurative; and others, no more than a charter of pardon, and a system of morality; while some so interpret the gospel, as to place the holiness they are to be saved by, in something divine but exterior to themselves; and others, so as to place it in things really within themselves but not more than human. Now the proper cure of what indistinctness there is one way and what infidelity in the other, seems to be contained in the doctrine of my text: "The Lord is that Spirit."

In treating of which words, I will consider, first, the nature of our fall in

Adam, by which it will appear that if "the Lord" were not "that Spirit" he could not be said to save or redeem us from our fallen condition; second, I will consider the person of Jesus Christ: by which it will appear, that "the Lord is that Spirit"; and, third, I will inquire into the nature and operations of the Holy Spirit, as bestowed upon Christians.

The Spirit and Adam

First, I am to consider the nature of our fall in Adam.

Our first parents did enjoy the presence of the Holy Spirit, for they were created in the image and likeness of God, which was no other than his Spirit. By that he communicates himself to his creatures, and by that alone they can bear any likeness to him. It is, indeed, his life in them; and so properly divine, that upon this ground, angels and regenerate men are called his children.

But when man would not be guided by the Holy Spirit, it left him. When he would be wise in his own way and in his own strength and did not depend in simplicity upon his heavenly Father, the seed of a superior life was recalled from him. For he was no longer fit to be formed into a heavenly condition when he had so unworthy a longing for, or rather dependence upon, an earthly fruit, which he knew God would not bless to him; no longer fit to receive supernatural succors, when he could not be content with his happy state toward God, without an overcurious examination into it.

Then he found himself forsaken of God and left to the poverty, weakness, and misery of his own proper nature. He was now a mere animal like unto other creatures made of flesh and blood, but only possessed of a larger understanding, by means of which he should either be led into greater absurdities than they could be guilty of, or else be made sensible of his lost happiness and put into the right course for regaining it. That is, if he continued a careless apostate, he should love and admire the goods of this world, the adequate happiness only of animals; and to recommend them and dissemble their defects, add all the ornament to them that his superior wit could invent. Or else (which is, indeed, more above brutes, but no nearer the perfection of man as a partaker of God, than the other) he should frame a new world to himself in theory; sometimes by warm imaginations, and sometimes by cool reasonings, endeavor to aggrandize his condition and defend his practice, or at least divert himself from feeling his own meanness and disorder.

If, on the other hand, he should be willing to find out the miseries of his fall, his understanding might furnish him with reasons for constant mourning, for despising and denying himself; might point out the sad effects of turning away from God and losing his Spirit, in the shame and anguish of a nature at variance with itself; thirsting after immortality and yet subject to death; approving righteousness and yet taking pleasure in things inconsistent with it; feeling an immense want of something to perfect and satisfy all its faculties and yet neither able to know what that mighty thing is, otherwise than from its present defects, nor how to attain it, otherwise than by going contrary to its present inclinations.

Well might Adam now find himself *naked*: nothing less than God was departed from him. Till then he had experienced nothing but the goodness and sweetness of God; a heavenly life spread itself through his whole frame as if he were not made of dust; his mind was filled with angelic wisdom; a direction from above took him by the hand; he walked and thought uprightly and seemed not to be a child or novice in divine things. But now he had other things to experience; something in his soul, that he did not find, nor need to fear, while he was carried on straightforward by the gentle gale of divine grace; something in his body, that he could not see nor complain of, while that body was covered with glory. He feels there a self-displeasure, turbulence, and confusion such as is common to other spirits who have lost God. He sees here causes of present shame, and a future dissolution, and a strong engagement to that groveling life which is common to animals that never enjoyed the divine nature.

The general character, therefore, of man's present state is death, a death from God whereby we no longer enjoy any intercourse with him, or happiness in him; we no longer shine with his glory or act with his powers. It is true, while we have a being, *"in him* we must live, and move, and have our being": but this we do now, not in a *filial* way, but only in a *servile* one, as all, even the meanest creatures, exist in him. It is one thing to receive from God an ability to walk and speak, eat and digest, to be supported by his hand as a part of this earthly creation and upon the same terms with it, for further trial or vengeance; and another, to receive from him a life which is his own likeness, to have within us something which is not of this creation and which is nourished by his own immediate Word and power.

Yet this is not the whole that is implied in man's sin. For he is not only inclined himself to all the sottishness of appetite and all the pride of reason, but he is fallen under the tutorage of the *evil* one, who mightily furthers him in both. The state he was at first placed in was a state of the most simple subjection to

God, and this entitled him to drink of his Spirit. But when he, not content to be actually in paradise, under as full a light of God's countenance as he was capable of, must know good and evil, and be satisfied upon rational grounds whether it was best for him to be as he was, or not; when disdaining to be directed as a child, he must weigh everything himself and seek better evidence than the voice of his Maker and the seal of the Spirit in his heart; then he not only obeyed but became like to that eldest son of pride, and was unhappily entitled to frequent visits, or rather a continued influence from him. As life was annexed to his keeping the command, and accordingly that Spirit, which alone could *form* it unto true life, dwelt in his body; so being sentenced to death for his transgression, he was now delivered unto "him who has the power of death, that is, the devil," whose hostile and unkindly impressions promote death and sin at once.

This being the state of man, if God should send him a Redeemer, what must that Redeemer do for him? Will it be sufficient for him to be the promulger of a new law, to give us a set of excellent precepts? No: if we could keep them, that alone would not make us happy. A good conscience brings a man the happiness of being consistent with himself, but not that of being raised above himself into God, which every person will find, after all, is the thing he wants. Shall he be the fountain of an *imputed* righteousness and procure the tenderest favor to all his followers? This is also not enough. Though a man should be allowed to be righteous and be exempt from all punishment, yet if he is as really enslaved to the corruptions of nature as endued with these privileges of redemption, he can hardly make himself easy; and whatever favor he can receive from God, here or hereafter, without a communication of himself, it is neither the cure of a spirit fallen, nor the happiness of one reconciled. Must not then our Redeemer be (according to the character which Saint John his forerunner gave of him) one that "baptizeth with the Holy Ghost," the Fountain and Restorer of that to mankind, whereby they are restored to their first estate and the enjoyment of God? And this is a presumptive argument that "the Lord is that Spirit."

The Spirit and Christ

But it will appear more plainly that he is so from the second thing proposed, which was the consideration of the person of Jesus Christ.

He was one to whom "God gave not the Spirit by measure; but in him dwelt all the fullness of the Godhead bodily; and of his fullness we have all received, and grace for grace." Indeed, all the communications of the Godhead, which any creatures could receive, were always from him as the Word of God. But all that mankind now in an earthly state were to receive must be from him by means of that body, at first mortal like unto theirs, and then glorious "in the likeness of God," which he took upon him for their sake.

In the beginning, the heavenly Word—being a Spirit that issued from the Father, and the Word of his power—made man an image of immortality, according to the likeness of the Father. But he who had been made in the image of God, afterward became mortal when the more powerful Spirit was separated from him. To remedy this, the Word became man, that man, by receiving the adoption, might become a son of God once more, that the light of the Father might rest upon the flesh of our Lord and come bright from thence unto us; and so man, being encompassed with the

light of the Godhead, might be carried into immortality. When he was incarnate and became man, he recapitulated in himself all generations of mankind, making himself the center of our salvation, that what we lost in Adam, even the image and likeness of God, we might receive in Christ Jesus. By the Holy Ghost coming upon Mary, and the power of the Highest overshadowing her, the incarnation of Christ was wrought, and a new birth, whereby man should be born of God, was shown, that as by our first birth we did inherit death, so by this birth we might inherit life.

This is no other than what Saint Paul teaches us: "The first man, Adam, was made a living soul, but the second Adam was made a quickening Spirit." All that the first man possessed of himself, all that he has transmitted to us, is "a living soul," a nature endued with an animal life and receptive of a spiritual. But the second Adam is, and was made to us, "a quickening Spirit"; by a strength from him as our Creator, we were at first raised above ourselves; by a strength from him as our Redeemer, we shall again live unto God.

In him is laid up for us that supplement to our nature which we shall find the need of sooner or later; and that it cannot be countervailed by any assistance from the creatures or any improvement of our own faculties. For we were made to be happy only in God; and all our labors and hopes, while we do not thirst after our deified state—to partake as truly of God as we do of flesh and blood, to be glorified in his nature, as we have been dishonored in our own—are the labors and hopes of those who utterly mistake themselves.

The Divine Wisdom knew what was our proper consolation though we did not. What does more obviously present itself in the Savior of the world than a union of man with God? A union attended with all the propriety of behavior that *we* are called to as candidates of the Spirit, such as walking with God in singleness of heart, perfect self-renunciation, and a life of sufferings. A union which submitted to the necessary stages of our progress, where the divine life was hid for the most part in the secret of the soul till death, in the state of separation, comforted the soul but did not raise it above the intermediate region of paradise; at the Resurrection, clothed the body with heavenly qualities and the powers of immortality; and at last raised it to the immediate presence and right hand of the Father.

Christ is not only God above us—which may keep us in awe, but cannot save—but he is Immanuel, God with us and in us. As he is the Son of God, God must be where he is; and as he is the Son of man, he will be with mankind. The consequence of this is that in the future age, "the tabernacle of God will be with men," and he will show them his glory; and at present he will *dwell* in their hearts by faith in his Son.

I hope it sufficiently appears that "the Lord is that Spirit." Considering what we are, and what we have been, nothing less than the receiving that Spirit again would be redemption to us; and considering who that heavenly person was that was sent to be our Redeemer, we can expect nothing less from him.

The Spirit and the Believer

I proceed now to the third thing proposed: to inquire into the nature and operations of the Holy Spirit, as bestowed upon Christians.

And here I shall pass by the particular extraordinary gifts—vouchsafed to the first ages for the edification of the church—and only consider what the Holy Spirit is to every believer for his personal sanctification and salvation. It is not granted to everyone to raise the dead and heal the sick. What is most necessary is to be sure, as to ourselves, that we are "passed from death unto life"; to keep our bodies pure and undefiled, and let them reap that health which flows from a magnanimous patience and the serene joys of devotion. The Holy Spirit has enabled men to speak with tongues and to prophesy, but the light that most necessarily attends it is a light to discern the fallacies of flesh and blood, to reject the irreligious maxims of the world, and to practice those degrees of trust in God and love to men, whose foundation is not so much in the present appearances of things, as in some that are yet to come. The object which this light brings us most immediately to know is ourselves; and by virtue of this, one that is born of God and has a lively hope may, indeed, see far into the ways of providence, and farther yet into the holy Scriptures. For the holy Scriptures, excepting some accidental and less necessary parts, are only a history of that new man which he himself is; and providence is only a wise disposal of events for the awakening of particular persons, and ripening the world in general for the coming of Christ's kingdom.

But I think the true notion of the Spirit is that it is some portion of, as well as preparation for, a life in God, which we are to enjoy hereafter. The gift of the Holy Spirit looks full to the resurrection; for then is the life of God completed in us.

Then, after man has passed through all the *penalties* of sin, the drudgery and vanity of human life, the painful reflections of an awakened mind, the infirmities and dissolution of the body, and all the sufferings and mortifications a just God shall lay in his way; when, by this means he is come to know God and himself, he may safely be entrusted with true life, with the freedom and ornaments of a child of God; for he will no more arrogate anything to himself. Then shall the Holy Spirit be fully bestowed, when the flesh shall no longer resist it but be itself changed into an angelical condition, being clothed with the incorruption of the Holy Spirit; when the body, which by being born with the soul and living through it, could only be called an animal one, shall now become spiritual whilst by the Spirit it rises into eternity.

Everything in Christianity is some kind of anticipation of something that is to be at the end of the world. If the apostles were to preach by their Master's command "that the kingdom of God drew nigh"; the meaning was that from henceforth all men should fix their eyes on that happy time foretold by the prophets, when the Messiah should come and restore all things; that by renouncing their worldly conversation and submitting to the gospel institution they should fit themselves for and hasten that blessing. "Now are we the sons of God," as Saint John tells us. And yet what he imparts to us at present will hardly justify that title without taking in that fullness of his image, which shall then be displayed in us when we shall be "the children of God, by being the children of the resurrection."

True believers, then, are entered upon a life, the *sequel* of which they know not; for it is "a life hid with Christ in God." He, the forerunner, hath attained the end of it, being gone unto the Father; but we can know no more of it than appeared in him while he was upon earth. And even that, we shall not know but by following his steps; which if we do, we shall be so strengthened and renewed day by day in the inner man, that we shall desire no comfort from the present world through a sense of "the

joy set before us"; though as to the outward man, we shall be subject to distresses and decays and treated as the offscouring of all things.

Well may a man ask his own heart, whether it is able to admit the Spirit of God. For where that Divine Guest enters, the laws of another world must be observed. The body must be given up to martyrdom, or spent in the Christian warfare as unconcernedly, as if the soul were already provided of its house from heaven. The goods of this world must be parted with as freely as if the last fire were to seize them tomorrow. Our neighbor must be loved as heartily as if he were washed from all his sins and demonstrated to be a child of God by the resurrection from the dead. The fruits of this Spirit must not be mere moral virtues calculated for the comfort and decency of the present life, but holy dispositions, suitable to the instincts of a superior life already begun.

Thus to press forward, whither the promise of life calls him; to turn his back upon the world and comfort himself in God, everyone that has faith perceives to be just and necessary, and forces himself to do it; everyone that has hope does it gladly and eagerly, though not without difficulty; but he that has love does it with ease and singleness of heart.

The state of love being attended with "joy unspeakable and full of glory," with rest from the passions and vanities of man, with the integrity of an unchangeable judgment and an undivided will, is in a great measure its own reward, yet not so as to supersede the desire of another world. For though such a man, having a free and insatiable love of that which is good, may seldom have need formally to propose to himself the hopes of retribution, in order to overcome his unwillingness to his duty; yet surely he must long for that which is best of all and feel a plain attraction toward that country in which he has his place and station already assigned him; and join in the earnest expectation of all creatures, which wait for the manifestation of the sons of God. For now we obtain but some part of his Spirit, to model and fit us for incorruption, that we may by degrees be accustomed to receive and carry God within us; and, therefore, the apostle calls it, "the earnest of the Spirit"; that is, a part of that honor which is promised us by the Lord. If, therefore, the earnest, abiding in us, makes us spiritual even now, and that which is mortal is, as it were, swallowed up [in] immortality, how shall it be when, rising again, we shall see him face to face? When all our members shall break forth into songs of triumph, and glorify him who hath raised them from the dead and granted them everlasting life? For if this earnest or pledge, embracing man into itself, makes him now cry, "Abba, Father," what shall the whole grace of the Spirit do, when being given at length to believers, it shall make us like unto God and perfect us through the will of the Father?

And thus I have done what was at first proposed: I have considered the nature of our fall in Adam, the person of Jesus Christ, and the operations of the Holy Spirit in Christians.

The Believer's Opportunity of Suffering

The only inference I will draw from what has been said, and principally from the account of man's fall, shall be the reasonableness of those precepts of self-denial, daily suffering, and renouncing the world, which are so peculiar to Christianity, and which are the only foundation whereon the other virtues recommended in the New Testament can be practiced or attained, in the sense there intended.

This inference is so natural that I could not help anticipating it in some measure all the while. One would think it should be no hard matter to persuade a creature to abhor the badges of his misery; to dislike a condition or mansion which only banishment and disgrace have assigned him; to trample on the grandeur, refuse the comforts, and suspect the wisdom of a life whose nature it is to separate him from his God.

Your Savior bids you "hate your own life." If you ask the reason, enter into your heart; see whether it be holy and full of God, or whether, on the other hand, many things that are contrary to him are wrought there, and it is become a plantation of the enemy. Or if this be too nice an inquiry, look upon your body. Do you find there the brightness of an angel and the vigor of immortality? If not, be sure your soul is in the same degree of poverty, nakedness, and absence from God. It is true, your soul may sooner be readmitted to some rays of the light of God's countenance than your body can; but if you would take any step at all toward it, to dislike your present self must be the first.

You want a reason why you should renounce the world? Indeed, you cannot see the prince of it walking up and down, "seeking whom he may devour"; and you may be so far ignorant of his devices, as not to know that they take place, as well in the most specious measures of business and learning as in the wildest pursuits of pleasure. But this, however, you cannot but see, that the world is not still a paradise of God, guarded and ennobled with the light of glory; it is, indeed, a place where God has determined he will not appear to you at best, but leave you in a state of hope, that you shall see his face when this world is dissolved.

However, there is a way to rescue ourselves, in great measure, from the ill consequences of our captivity, and our Savior has taught us that way. It is by suffering. We must not only "suffer many things," as he did, and so enter into our glory, but we must also suffer many things that we may get above our corruption at present and enjoy the Holy Spirit.

The world has no longer any power over us than we have a quick relish of its comforts, and suffering abates that. Suffering is, indeed, a direct confutation of the pretenses which the flattering tempter gains us by. For I am in human life, and if that life contains such soft ease, ravishing pleasure, glorious eminence, as you promise, why am I thus? Is it because I have not yet purchased riches to make me easy, or the current accomplishments to make me considerable? Then I find that all the comfort you propose is by leading me off from myself; but I will rather enter deep into my own condition, bad as it is. Perhaps I shall be nearer to God, the Eternal Truth, in feeling sorrows and miseries that are personal and real, than in feeling comforts that are not so. I begin already to find that all my grievances center in one point: there is always at the bottom one great loss or defect, which is not the want of friends or gold, of health or philosophy. And the abiding sense of this may possibly become a prayer in the ears of the Most High: a prayer not resulting from a set of speculative notions, but from the real, undissembled state of all that is within me; nor, indeed, so explicit a prayer as to describe the thing I want; but, considering how strange a want mine is, as explicit a one as I can make. Since then suffering opens me a door of hope, I will not put it from me as long as I live. It helps me to a true discovery of one period of my existence, though it is a low

one, and bids fairer for having some connection with a more glorious period that may follow, than the arts of indulgence, the amusements of pride and sloth, and all the dark policy of this world, which wage war with the whole truth, that man must know and feel before he can look toward God. It may be, while I continue on the cross, I shall, like my Savior, put off "principalities and powers," recover myself more and more from the subjection I am, indeed, in (which he only seemed to be) to those wicked rulers, and to "triumph over them in it." At least, it shall appear, in the day when God shall visit, that my heart, though grown unworthy of his residence, was too big to be comforted by any of his creatures; and was kept for him as a place originally sacred, though for the present unclean.

But supposing that our state does require of us to "die daily," to sacrifice all that this present life can boast of or is delighted with, before we give up life itself. Supposing also, that in the hour we do somewhat of this kind, we receive light and strength from God to grow superior to our infirmities, and are carried smoothly toward him in the joy of the Holy Ghost. Yet how can a man have such frequent opportunities of suffering? Indeed, martyrdoms do not happen in every age, and some days of our lives may pass without reproaches from men; we may be in health and not want food to eat and raiment to put on (though health itself and nutrition itself, oblige us to the pain of a constant correction of them), yet still, the love of God and heavenly hope will not want something to oppress them in this world.

Let a man descend calmly into his heart and see if there be no root of bitterness springing up; whether at least his thoughts, which are ever in motion, do not sometimes sally out into projects suggested by pride, or sink into indolent trifling, or be entangled in mean anxiety. Does not he find a motion of anger, or of gaiety, leavening him in an instant throughout, depriving him of the meekness and steady discernment he labored after? Or, let him but conceive at any time, that unfeigned obedience, and watchful zeal, and dignity of behavior, which is suitable, I do not say to an angel, but to a sinner that has "a good hope through grace," and endeavor to work himself up to it. And if he find no sort of obstacle to this within him, he has, indeed then, no opportunity of suffering. In short, if he is such an abject sort of creature as will, unless grace should do him a perpetual violence, relapse frequently into a course of thinking and acting entirely without God, then he can never want occasions of suffering, but will find his own nature to be the same burden to him as that "faithless and perverse generation" was to our Savior, of whom he said, "How long shall I be with you? How long shall I suffer you?"

I will conclude all with that excellent collect of our church: "Oh, God, who in all ages hast taught the hearts of thy faithful people by sending to them the light of thy Holy Spirit; grant us by the same Spirit to have a right judgment in all things, and evermore to rejoice in his holy comfort, through the merits of Jesus Christ our Savior, who liveth and reigneth with thee, in the unity of the same Spirit, one God, world without end. Amen."

The witness of the Spirit is of great importance because of the mounting influence of mysticism. Christians are becoming more and more attracted to the idea of "let go and let God" without recognizing that a purely subjective approach to the faith can result in confusion and extreme error.

In this sermon Wesley addressed the problem from two perspectives. First, what is the witness of the Spirit? How does it work? Wesley indicated that the Spirit witnesses to our spirits by means of Scripture and inner urgings. The Scripture teaches us what is expected of us, and the Spirit therefore moves us to act upon what we have learned. The inner urgings do not appear to work independently of the Scripture. However, once we become changed through salvation we are united with God and that produces a means by which His Spirit can move us.

The means by which we discern the Holy Spirit from some other influence is clearly the Scripture. For Wesley this seemed to be the sole means for preventing deception. The Scripture teaches what is expected of true believers and anything contrary is suspect.

CHAPTER NINE

The Witness of the Spirit

"The Spirit itself beareth witness with our spirit, that we are the children of God" (Rom. 8:16).

How many vain men, not understanding what they spake neither whereof they affirmed, have wrested this Scripture to the great loss, if not the destruction, of their souls? How many have mistaken the voice of their own imagination for this "witness of the Spirit of God," and thence idly presumed they were the children of God, while they were doing the works of the devil? These are truly and properly enthusiasts and, indeed, in the worst sense of the word. But with what difficulty are they convinced thereof, especially if they have drunk deep into that spirit of error! All endeavors to bring them into the knowledge of themselves they will then account fighting against God; and that vehemence and impetuosity of spirit which they call "contending earnestly for the faith" sets them so far above all the usual methods of conviction, that we may well say, "With men it is impossible."

Who can then be surprised if many reasonable men, seeing the dreadful effects of this delusion and laboring to keep at the utmost distance from it, should sometimes lean toward another extreme? If they are not forward to believe any who speak of having this witness, concerning which others have so grievously erred? If they are almost ready to set all down for enthusiasts, who use the expressions which have been so terribly abused? Yea, if they should question whether the witness or testimony here spoken of be the privilege of *ordinary* Christians, and not rather one of those *extraordinary* gifts, which they suppose belonged only to the apostolic age?

But is there any necessity laid upon us of running either into one extreme or the other? May we not steer a middle course—keep a sufficient distance from the spirit of error and enthusiasm—without denying the gift of God, and giving up the great privilege of his children? Surely we may. In order thereto, let us consider in the presence and fear of God,

First, what is this witness or testimony of our spirit; what is the testimony of God's Spirit; and, how does he "bear witness with our spirit that we are the children of God"?

Secondly, how is this joint testimony of God's Spirit and our own clearly and solidly distinguished from the presumption of a natural mind and from the delusion of the devil?

The Witness of Our Spirit

Let us first consider what is the witness or testimony of our spirit. Here I cannot but desire all those who are for swallowing up the testimony of the Spirit of God in the rational testimony of our own spirit, to observe that in this text the apostle is so far from speaking of the testimony of our own spirit *only*, that it may be questioned whether he speaks of it *at all*, whether he does not speak *only* of the testimony of God's Spirit? It does not appear but the original text may be fairly understood thus. The apostle had just said, in the preceding verse, "Ye have received the spirit of adoption, whereby we cry, Abba, Father," and immediately subjoins, "The same Spirit beareth witness to our spirit, that we are the children of God."

The foundation is laid in those numerous texts of Scripture which describe the marks of the children of God, and that so plainly that he which runneth may read them. These are also collected together and placed in the strongest light, by many both ancient and modern writers. If any need further light, he may receive it by attending on the ministry of God's Word, by meditating thereon before God in secret, and by conversing with those who have the knowledge of his ways. And by the reason or understanding that God has given him, which religion was designed not to extinguish, but to perfect, according to that of the apostle, "Brethren, be not children in understanding; in malice [or wickedness] be ye children; but in understanding be ye men"; 1 Corinthians 14:20. Every man applying those scriptural marks to himself may know whether he is a child of God. Thus, if he know, first, "As many as are led by the Spirit of God," into all holy tempers and actions, "they are the sons of God" (for which he has the infallible assurance of Holy Writ); secondly, I am thus "led by the Spirit of God"; he will easily conclude, "Therefore, I am a son of God."

Agreeable to this are all those plain declarations of Saint John in his first epistle: "Hereby we know, that we do know him, if we keep his commandments," chapter 2:3. "Whoso keepeth his word, in him verily is the love of God perfected: hereby know we that we are in him," that we are indeed the children of God, verse 5. "If ye know that he is righteous, ye know that every one that doeth righteousness is born of him," verse 29. "We know that we have passed from death unto life, because we love the brethren," chapter 3:14. "Hereby we know that we are of the truth, and shall assure our hearts before him," verse 19; namely, because we "love one another, not in word, neither in tongue; but in deed and in truth." "Hereby we know that we dwell in him, because he hath given us of his [loving] Spirit," chapter 4:13. And, "Hereby we know that he abideth in us by the [obedient] Spirit which he hath given us," chapter 3:24.

It is highly probable there never were any children of God, from the beginning of the world unto this day, who were farther advanced in the grace of God and the knowledge of our Lord Jesus Christ than the apostle John at the time when he wrote these words, and the fathers in Christ to whom he wrote. Notwithstanding which, it is evident, both the apostle himself and all those pillars in God's temple, were very far from despising these marks of their being the children of God, and that they applied them to their own souls for the confirmation of their faith. Yet all this is no other than rational evidence, the witness of our spirit, our reason or understanding. It all resolves into this: those who have these marks are the children of God. We have these marks: therefore, we are children of God.

But how does it appear that we have these marks? This is a question which still remains. How does it appear that we do love God and our neighbor and that we keep his commandments? Observe that the meaning of the question is, how does it appear to *ourselves*? (not to *others*.) I would ask him, then, that proposes this question, How does it appear to you, that you are alive? And that you are now in ease and not in pain? Are you not immediately conscious of it? By the same immediate consciousness you will know if your soul is alive to God; if you are saved from the pain of proud wrath and have the ease of a meek and quiet spirit. By the same means you cannot but perceive if you love, rejoice, and delight in God. By the same you must be directly assured, if you love your neighbor as yourself; if you are kindly affectioned to all mankind, and full of gentleness and long-suffering. And with regard to the outward mark of the children of God, which is, according to Saint John, the keeping his commandments, you undoubtedly know in your own breast, if by the grace of God it belongs to you. Your conscience informs you from day to day if you do not take the name of God within your lips, unless with seriousness and devotion, with reverence and godly fear; if you remember the sabbath day to keep it holy; if you honor your father and mother; if you do to all as you would they should do unto you; if you possess your body in sanctification and honor; and if, whether you eat or drink, you are temperate therein and do all to the glory of God.

Now this is properly the testimony of our own spirit; even the testimony of our own conscience, that God hath given us to be holy of heart, and holy in outward conversation. It is a consciousness of our having received, in and by the spirit of adoption, the tempers mentioned in the word of God, as belonging to his adopted children; even a loving heart toward God, and toward all mankind; hanging with childlike confidence on God our Father, desiring nothing but him, casting all our care upon him, and embracing every child of man with earnest, tender affection; so as to be ready to lay down our life for our brother, as

Christ laid down his life for us: a consciousness, that we are inwardly conformed by the Spirit of God to the image of his Son, and that we walk before him in justice, mercy, and truth, doing the things which are pleasing in his sight.

The Witness of God's Spirit

But what is that testimony of God's Spirit which is superadded to and conjoined with this? How does he "bear witness with our spirit that we are the children of God"? It is hard to find words in the language of men to explain "the deep things of God." Indeed, there are none that will adequately express what the children of God experience. But perhaps one might say (desiring any who are taught of God to correct, to soften, or strengthen the expression) the testimony of the Spirit is an inward impression on the soul, whereby the Spirit of God directly witnesses to my spirit that I am a child of God; that Jesus Christ hath loved me, and given himself for me; and that all my sins are blotted out, and I, even I, am reconciled to God.

That this testimony of the Spirit of God must needs, in the very nature of things, be antecedent to the testimony of our own spirit, may appear from this single consideration: we must be holy of heart and holy in life before we can be conscious that we are so, before we can have the testimony of our spirit that we are inwardly and outwardly holy. But we must love God before we can be holy at all, this being the root of all holiness. Now we cannot love God, till we know he loves us. "We love him, because he first loved us." And we cannot know his pardoning love to us, till his Spirit witnesses it to our spirit. Since, therefore, this testimony of his Spirit must precede the love of God and all holiness, of consequence it must precede our inward consciousness thereof, or

our inward consciousness thereof, or the testimony of our spirit concerning them.

Then, and not till then—when the Spirit of God beareth that witness to our spirit, "God hath loved thee, and given his own Son to be the propitiation for thy sins; the Son of God hath loved thee, and hath washed thee from thy sins in his blood"—"we love God, because he first loved us"; and, for his sake, we love our brother also. And of this we cannot but be conscious to ourselves: we "know the things that are freely given to us of God." We know that we love God and keep his commandments, and "hereby also we know that we are of God." This is that testimony of our own spirit, which, so long as we continue to love God and keep his commandments, continues joined with the testimony of God's Spirit "that we are the children of God."

Not that I would by any means be understood, by anything which has been spoken concerning it, to exclude the operation of the Spirit of God, even from the testimony of our own spirit. In no wise. It is he that not only worketh in us every manner of thing that is good, but also shines upon his own work and clearly shows what he has wrought. Accordingly, this is spoken of by Saint Paul, as one great end of our receiving the Spirit, "That we may know the things which are freely given to us of God"; that he may strengthen the testimony of our conscience, touching our "simplicity and godly sincerity"; and give us to discern in a fuller and stronger light that we now do the things which please him.

A Unified Witness

Should it still be inquired, how does the Spirit of God "bear witness with our spirit, that we are the children of God,"

so as to exclude all doubt and evince the reality of our sonship, the answer is clear from what has been observed above. And first, as to the witness of our spirit: the soul as intimately and evidently perceives when it loves, delights, and rejoices in God, as when it loves and delights in anything on earth. And it can no more doubt whether it loves, delights, and rejoices or no, than whether it exists or no. If, therefore, this be just reasoning, he that now loves God, that delights and rejoices in him with an humble joy, and holy delight, and an obedient love, is a child of God. But I thus love, delight, and rejoice in God; therefore, I am a child of God.

Then a Christian can in no wise doubt of his being a child of God. Of the former proposition he has as full an assurance as he has that the Scriptures are of God. And of his thus loving God, he has an inward proof, which is nothing short of self-evidence. Thus, the testimony of our own spirit is with the most intimate conviction manifested to our hearts, in such a manner as beyond all reasonable doubt to evince the reality of our sonship.

The manner how the *divine* testimony is manifested to the heart, I do not take upon me to explain. Such knowledge is too wonderful and excellent for me: I cannot attain unto it. The wind bloweth, and I hear the sound thereof; but I cannot tell how it cometh or whither it goeth. As no one knoweth the things of a man save the spirit of a man that is in him, so the *manner* of the things of God knoweth no one, save the Spirit of God. But the fact we know: namely, that the Spirit of God does give a believer such a testimony of his adoption, that while it is present to the soul, he can no more doubt the reality of his sonship than he can doubt of the shining of the sun, while he stands in the full blaze of his beams.

A Distinctive Witness

How this joint testimony of God's Spirit and our spirit, may be clearly and solidly distinguished from the presumption of a natural mind and from the delusion of the devil, is the next thing to be considered. And it highly imports all who desire the salvation of God, to consider it with the deepest attention, as they would not deceive their own souls. An error in this is generally observed to have the most fatal consequences; the rather, because he that errs seldom discovers his mistake till it is too late to remedy it.

And first, how is this testimony to be distinguished from the presumption of a natural mind? It is certain, one who was never convinced of sin is always ready to flatter himself and to think of himself, especially in spiritual things, more highly than he ought to think. And hence, it is in no wise strange, if one who is vainly puffed up by his fleshly mind, when he hears of this privilege of true Christians, among whom he undoubtedly ranks himself, should soon work himself up into a persuasion that he is already possessed thereof. Such instances now abound in the world and have abounded in all ages. How then may the real testimony of the Spirit with our spirit be distinguished from this damning presumption?

I answer, the holy Scriptures abound with marks whereby the one may be distinguished from the other. They describe in the plainest manner the circumstances which go before, which accompany, and which follow, the true, genuine testimony of the Spirit of God with the spirit of a believer. Whoever carefully weighs and attends to these will not need to put darkness for light. He will perceive so wide a difference with respect to all these between the real and the pretended witness of the Spirit, that there will be no danger—I might say, no possibility—of confounding the one with the other.

By these, one who vainly presumes on the gift of God might surely know, if he really desired it, that he hath been hitherto "given up to a strong delusion" and suffered to believe a lie. For the Scriptures lay down those clear, obvious marks, as preceding, accompanying, and following that gift, which a little reflection would convince him beyond all doubt were never found in his soul. For instance, the Scripture describes repentance, or conviction of sin, as constantly going before this witness of pardon. So, "Repent: for the kingdom of heaven is at hand," Matthew 3:2. "Repent ye, and believe the gospel," Mark 1:15. "Repent, and be baptized every one of you, for the remission of sins," Acts 2:38. "Repent ye therefore and be converted, that your sins may be blotted out," Acts 3:19. In conformity whereto, our church also continually places repentance before pardon, or the witness of it. "He pardoneth and absolveth all them that truly repent, and unfeignedly believe his holy gospel." "Almighty God hath promised forgiveness of sins to all them who, with hearty repentance and true faith, turn unto him." But he is a stranger even to this repentance: he hath never known a broken and a contrite heart. "The remembrance of his sins" was never "grievous unto him," nor "the burden of them intolerable." In repeating those words he never meant what he said; he merely paid a compliment to God. And were it only from the want of this previous work of God, he hath too great reason to believe, that he hath grasped a mere shadow and never yet known the real privilege of the sons of God.

Again, the Scriptures describe the being born of God, which must precede the witness that we are his children, as a vast and mighty change; a change "from darkness to light," as well as "from the power of Satan unto God"; as a "passing from death unto life," a resurrection from the dead. Thus, the apostle to the Ephesians: "You hath he quickened who were dead in trespasses and sins," chapter 2:1. And again, "When we were dead in sins, he hath quickened us together with Christ; and hath raised us up together, and made us sit together in heavenly places in Christ Jesus," verses 5, 6. But what knoweth he, concerning whom we now speak, of any such change as this? He is altogether unacquainted with this whole matter. This is a language which he does not understand. He tells you He always was a Christian. He knows no time when he had need of such a change. By this also, if he give himself leave to think, may he know that he is not born of the Spirit, that he has never yet known God but has mistaken the voice of nature for the voice of God.

But waiving the consideration of whatever he has or has not experienced in time past, by the present marks may we easily distinguish a child of God from a presumptuous self-deceiver. The Scriptures describe that joy in the Lord which accompanies the witness of his Spirit as an humble joy, a joy that abases to the dust; that makes a pardoned sinner cry out, "I am vile! What am I, or my father's house? Now mine eye seeth Thee, I abhor myself in dust and ashes!" And wherever lowliness is, there is meekness, patience, gentleness, longsuffering. There is a soft, yielding spirit, a mildness and sweetness, a tenderness of soul which words cannot express. But do these fruits attend that *supposed* testimony of the Spirit in a presumptuous man? Just the reverse. The more confident he is of the favor of God, the more is he lifted up, the more does he exalt himself, the more haughty and assuming is his whole behavior. The stronger witness he imagines himself to have, the

more overbearing is he to all around him, the more incapable of receiving any reproof, the more impatient of contradiction. Instead of being more meek, and gentle, and teachable, more "swift to hear, and slow to speak," he is more slow to hear, and swift to speak, more unready to learn of anyone, more fiery and vehement in his temper and eager in his conversation. Yea, perhaps, there will sometimes appear a kind of fierceness in his air, his manner of speaking, his whole deportment, as if he were just going to take the matter out of God's hands, and "devour the adversaries" himself.

Once more the Scriptures teach, "This is the love of God," the sure mark thereof, "that we keep his commandments," 1 John 5:3. And our Lord himself saith, "He that keepeth my commandments, he it is that loveth me," John 14:21. Love rejoices to obey; to do, in every point, whatever is acceptable to the Beloved. A true lover of God hastens to do his will on earth as it is done in heaven. But is this the character of the presumptuous pretender to the love of God? Nay, but his love gives him a liberty to disobey—to break, not keep—the commandments of God. Perhaps, when he was in fear of the wrath of God, he did labor to do his will. But now, looking on himself as "not under the law," he thinks he is no longer obliged to observe it. He is, therefore, less zealous of good works, less careful to abstain from evil, less watchful over his own heart, less jealous over his tongue. He is less earnest to deny himself and to take up his cross daily. In a word, the whole form of his life is changed, since he has fancied himself to be *at liberty*. He is no longer "exercising himself unto godliness," "wrestling not only with flesh and blood, but with principalities and powers," enduring hardships, "agonizing to enter in at the straight gate." No, he has found an easier way to heaven; a broad, smooth, flowery path in which he can say to his soul, "Soul, take thy ease; eat, drink, and be merry." It follows with undeniable evidence that he has not the true testimony of his own spirit. He cannot be conscious of having those marks which he hath not, that lowliness, meekness, and obedience; nor yet can the Spirit of the God of Truth bear witness to a lie or testify that he is a child of God when he is manifestly a child of the devil.

Discover thyself, thou poor self-deceiver! Thou who are confident of being a child of God; thou who sayest, "I have the witness in myself," and, therefore, defiest all thy enemies. Thou art weighed in the balance and found wanting, even in the balance of the sanctuary. The word of the Lord hath tried thy soul and proved thee to be reprobate silver. Thou art not lowly of heart, therefore, thou hast not received the Spirit of Jesus unto this day. Thou art not gentle and meek, therefore, thy joy is nothing worth; it is not joy in the Lord. Thou dost not keep his commandments, therefore, thou lovest him not, neither art thou partaker of the Holy Ghost. It is consequently as certain and as evident, as the oracles of God can make it, his Spirit doth not bear witness with thy spirit that thou art a child of God. Oh, cry unto him that the scales may fall off thine eyes; that thou mayest know thyself as thou art known; that thou mayest receive the sentence of death in thyself, till thou hear the voice that raises the dead, saying, "Be of good cheer: thy sins are forgiven; thy faith hath made thee whole."

Spiritual Discernment

"But how may one who has the real witness in himself distinguish it from presumption?" How, I pray, do you distinguish day from night? How do you distinguish light from darkness, or the light of a star or a glimmering taper from the light of the noonday sun? Is there not an inherent, obvious, essential difference between the one and the other? And do you not immediately and directly perceive that difference, provided your senses are rightly disposed? In like manner, there is an inherent, essential difference between spiritual light and spiritual darkness, and between the light wherewith the Sun of righteousness shines upon our heart and that glimmering light which arises only from "sparks of our own kindling." And this difference also is immediately and directly perceived if our spiritual senses are rightly disposed.

To require a more minute and philosophical account of the manner whereby we distinguish these and of the *criteria*, or intrinsic marks, whereby we know the voice of God, is to make a demand which can never be answered; no, not by one who has the deepest knowledge of God. Suppose when Paul answered before Agrippa, the wise Roman had said, "Thou talkest of hearing the voice of the Son of God. How dost thou know it was his voice? By what *criteria*, what intrinsic marks, dost thou know the voice of God? Explain to me the *manner* of distinguishing this from a human or angelic voice?" Can you believe the apostle himself would have once attempted to answer so idle a demand? And yet, doubtless, the moment he heard that voice, he knew it was the voice of God. But *how* he knew this, who is able to explain? Perhaps neither man nor angel.

To come yet closer: suppose God were now to speak to any soul, "Thy sins are forgiven thee." He must be willing that soul should know his voice; otherwise he would speak in vain. And he is able to effect this; for, whenever he wills, to do is present with him. And he does effect it: that soul is absolutely assured, "This voice is the voice of God." But yet he who hath that witness in himself, cannot explain it to one who hath it not, nor, indeed, is it to be expected that he should. Were there any natural medium to prove, or natural method to explain, the things of God to unexperienced men, then the natural man might discern and know the things of the Spirit of God. But this is utterly contrary to the assertion of the apostle that "he cannot know them because they are spiritually discerned," even by spiritual senses, which the natural man hath not.

"But how shall I know that my spiritual senses are rightly disposed?" This also is a question of vast importance; for if a man mistake in this, he may run on in endless error and delusion. "And how am I assured that this is not my case; and that I do not mistake the voice of the Spirit?" Even by the testimony of your own spirit; by "the answer of a good conscience toward God." By the fruits which he hath wrought in your spirit you shall know the testimony of the Spirit of God. Hereby you shall know that you are in no delusion, that you have not deceived your own soul. The immediate fruits of the Spirit ruling in the heart are "love, joy, peace, bowels of mercies, humbleness of mind, meekness, gentleness, longsuffering." And the outward fruits are: the doing good to all men, the doing no evil to any, and the walking in the light—a zealous, uniform obedience to all the commandments of God.

By the same fruits shall you distinguish this voice of God from any delusion of the devil. That proud spirit cannot humble thee before God. He neither can nor would soften thy heart and melt it first into earnest mourning after God and then into filial love. It is not the adversary of God and man that enables thee to love thy neighbor or to put on meekness, gentleness, patience, temperance, and the whole armor of God. He is not divided against himself or a destroyer of sin, his own work. No; it is none but the Son of God who cometh "to destroy the works of the devil." As surely, therefore, as holiness is of God, and as sin is the work of the devil, so surely the witness thou hast in thyself is not of Satan but of God.

Well then mayest thou say, "Thanks be unto God for his unspeakable gift!" Thanks be unto God, who giveth me to "know in whom I have believed"; who hath "sent forth the Spirit of his Son into my heart, crying, Abba, Father," and even now, "bearing witness with my spirit that I am a child of God!" And see, that not only thy lips, but thy life show forth his praise. He hath sealed thee for his own; glorify him then in thy body and thy spirit, which are his. Beloved, if thou hast this hope in thyself, purify thyself as he is pure. While thou beholdest what manner of love the Father hath given thee, that thou shouldest be called a child of God, cleanse thyself "from all filthiness of flesh and spirit, perfecting holiness in the fear of God"; and let all thy thoughts, words, and works be a spiritual sacrifice, holy, acceptable to God through Christ Jesus!

For Wesley, the condition of being in Christ brought a radical change in conduct and affections. Those who are in Christ, he indicated in this sermon, seek to do those things that are pleasing to Christ and that reflect the outlook of a child of God. The Christian abstains from the works of the flesh that characterize the former life, such as idolatry, witchcraft, and hatred. The lordship of Christ is clearly reflected in the lives of the saints. He is their sole focus, and the Holy Spirit enables them to live upright, virtuous lives.

According to Wesley, the blood of Christ has cleansed the lives of the saints and delivered them from the condemnation demanded by their sins. Because Christ bore his transgressions, the Christian stands before God as if he had never sinned. This is an important aspect of the Christian life.

CHAPTER TEN

The First Fruits of the Spirit

"There is therefore now no condemnation to them which are in Christ Jesus, who walk not after the flesh, but after the Spirit" (Rom. 8:1).

By "them which are in Christ Jesus," Saint Paul evidently means, those who truly believe in him; those who, "being justified by faith, have peace with God, through our Lord Jesus Christ." They who thus believe do no longer "walk after the flesh," no longer follow the motions of corrupt nature, but "after the Spirit"; their thoughts, words and works, are under the direction of the blessed Spirit of God.

"There is therefore now no condemnation to" these. There is no condemnation to them from God; for he hath *justified* them "freely by his grace, through the redemption that is in Jesus." He hath forgiven all their iniquities, and blotted out all their sins. And there is no condemnation to them from within; for they "have received not the spirit of the world, but the Spirit which is of God; that they might know the things which are freely given to them of God," 1 Corinthians 2:12; which Spirit "beareth witness with their spirits, that they are the children of God." And to this is added the testimony of their conscience, "that in simplicity and godly sincerity, not with fleshly wisdom, but by the grace of God, they have had their conversation in the world," 2 Corinthians 1:12.

But because this Scripture has been so frequently misunderstood, and that in so dangerous a manner, because such multitudes of "unlearned and unstable men," have wrested it to their own destruction; I propose to show as clearly as I can, first, who those are "which are in Christ Jesus, and walk not after the flesh, but after the Spirit"; and, secondly, how "there is no condemnation to" these. I shall conclude with some practical inferences.

Living in Christ

First I am to show who those are that "are in Christ Jesus." And are they not those who believe in his name? Those who are "found in him, not having their own righteousness, but the righteousness which is of God by faith"? These, who "have redemption through his blood," are properly said to be *in him*. For they dwell in Christ, and Christ in them. They are joined unto the Lord in one Spirit. They are ingrafted into him as branches into the vine. They are united as members to their head in a manner which words cannot express, nor could it before enter into their hearts to conceive.

Now "whosoever abideth in him, sinneth not," "walketh not after the flesh." The flesh, in the usual language of Saint Paul, signifies corrupt nature. In this sense he uses the word, writing to the Galatians, "The works of the flesh are manifest," Galatians 5:19; and a little before, "Walk in the Spirit, and ye shall not fulfill the lust (or desire) of the flesh," chapter 5:16. To prove which, namely, that those who "walk by the Spirit, do not fulfill the lusts of the flesh," he immediately adds, "For the flesh lusteth against the Spirit; and the Spirit lusteth against the flesh (for these are contrary to each other), that ye may not do the things which ye would."

They who are of Christ, who abide in him, "have crucified the flesh with its affections and lusts." They abstain from all those works of the flesh: from "adultery and fornication," from "uncleanness and lasciviousness," from "idolatry, witchcraft, hatred, variance," from "emulations, wrath, strife, sedition, heresies, envyings, murders, drunkenness, revellings," from every design, and word, and work to which the corruption of nature leads. Although they feel the root of bitterness in themselves, yet are they endued with power from on high to trample it continually underfoot so that it cannot "spring up to trouble them," insomuch that every fresh assault which they undergo only gives them fresh occasion of praise, of crying out, "Thanks be unto God, who giveth us the victory, through Jesus Christ our Lord."

They now "walk after the Spirit," both in their hearts and lives. They are taught of him to love God and their neighbor with a love which is as "a well of water, springing up into everlasting life." And by him they are led into every holy desire, into every divine and heavenly temper, till every thought which arises in their heart is holiness unto the Lord.

They who "walk after the Spirit" are also led by him into all holiness of conversation. Their "speech is always in grace, seasoned with salt": with the love and fear of God. "No corrupt communication comes out of their mouth, but only that which is good," that which is "to the use of edifying," which is "meet to minister grace to the hearers." And herein likewise do they exercise themselves day and night, to do only the things which please God; in all their outward behavior to follow him "who left us an example that we might tread in his steps"; in all their intercourse with their neighbor to walk in justice, mercy, and truth; and "whatsoever they do," in every circumstance of life, to "do all to the glory of God."

These are they who, indeed, "walk after the Spirit." Being filled with faith and with the Holy Ghost, they possess in their hearts, and show forth in their lives, in the whole course of their words and actions, the genuine fruits of the Spirit of God, namely, "love, joy, peace, longsuffering, gentleness, goodness, fidelity, meekness, temperance," and whatsoever else is lovely or praiseworthy. They "adorn in all things the gospel of God our Savior"; and give full proof to all mankind that they are indeed actuated by the same Spirit "which raised up Jesus from the dead."

Escaping Condemnation

I proposed to show, in the second place how "there is no condemnation to them which are thus in Christ Jesus," and thus "walk, not after the flesh, but after the Spirit."

And, first, to believers in Christ walking thus, "there is no condemnation" on account of their past sins. God condemneth them not for any of these; they are as though they had never been; they are cast "as a stone into the depth of the sea, and he remembereth them no more. God having set forth his Son to be a propitiation" for them, "through faith in his blood," "hath declared unto them his righteousness, for the remission of the sins that are past." He layeth, therefore, none of these to their charge; their memorial is perished with them.

And there is no condemnation in their own breast; no sense of guilt, or dread of the wrath of God. They "have the witness in themselves": they are conscious of their interest in the blood of sprinkling. "They have not received again the spirit of bondage unto fear," unto doubt and racking uncertainty; but they "have received the spirit of adoption," crying in their hearts, "Abba, Father." Thus being "justified by faith," they have the peace of God ruling in their hearts, flowing from a continual sense of his pardoning mercy and "the answer of a good conscience toward God."

If it be said, "but sometimes a believer in Christ may lose his sight of the mercy of God, sometimes such darkness may fall upon him that he no longer sees him that is invisible, no longer feels that witness in himself of his part in the atoning blood. And then he is inwardly condemned; he hath again the sentence of death in himself": I answer, supposing it so to be, supposing him not to see the mercy of God, then he is not a believer: for faith implies light, the light of God shining upon the soul. So far, therefore, as anyone loses this light, he, for the time, loses his faith. And, no doubt, a true believer in Christ may lose the light of faith; and so far as this is lost, he may, for a time, fall again into condemnation. But this is not the case of them who now "are in Christ Jesus," who now believe in his name. For so long as they believe and walk after the Spirit, neither God condemns them nor their own heart.

They are not condemned, secondly, for any present sins, for now transgressing the commandments of God. For they do not transgress them; they do not "walk after the flesh, but after the Spirit." This is the continual proof of their "love of God, that they keep his commandments." Even as Saint John bears witness, "Whosoever is born of God doth not commit sin. For his seed remaineth in him, and he cannot sin, because he is born of God." He cannot so

long as that seed of God, that loving, holy faith, remaineth in him. So long as "he keepeth himself" herein, "that wicked one toucheth him not." Now, it is evident he is not condemned for the sins which he doth not commit at all. They, therefore, who are thus "led by the Spirit, are not under the law," Galatians 5:18. Not under the curse or condemnation of it; for it condemns none but those who break it. Thus, the law of God, "Thou shalt not steal," condemns none but those who do steal. Thus, "Remember the sabbath day to keep it holy," condemns those only who do not keep it holy. But against the fruits of the Spirit, "there is no law," chapter 5:23; as the apostle more largely declares, in those memorable words of his [first] epistle to Timothy: "We know that the law is good, if a man use it lawfully; knowing this, that the law does not lie against a righteous man"; it has no force against him, no power to condemn him. "But against the lawless and disobedient, against the ungodly and sinners, against the unholy and profane; according to the glorious gospel of the blessed God," 1 Timothy 1:8, 9, 11.

They are not condemned, thirdly, for inward sin, even though it does now remain. That the corruption of nature does still remain, even in those who are the children of God by faith—that they have in them the seeds of pride and vanity, of anger, lust and evil desire, yea, sin of every kind—is too plain to be denied, being matter of daily experience. And on this account it is that Saint Paul, speaking to those whom he had just before witnessed to be "in Christ Jesus," 1 Corinthians 1:2, 9, to have been "called of God into the fellowship (or participation) of his Son Jesus Christ"; yet declares, "Brethren, I could not speak unto you as unto spiritual, but as unto carnal, even as unto babes in Christ"; 1 Corinthians 3:1; "Babes in Christ"; so we see they were "in Christ"; they were believers in a low degree. And yet how much of sin remained in them! Of that "carnal mind, which is not subject to the law of God!"

And yet, for all this, they are not condemned. Although they feel the flesh, the evil nature in them; although they are more sensible, day by day, that their "heart is deceitful and desperately wicked"; yet, so long as they do not yield thereto; so long as they give no place to the devil; so long as they maintain a continual war with all sin, with pride, anger, desire, so that the flesh hath not dominion over them, but they still "walk after the Spirit"; there is "no condemnation to them which are in Christ Jesus." God is well pleased with their sincere, though imperfect, obedience. And they "have confidence towards God," knowing they are his, "by the Spirit which he hath given them," 1 John 3:24.

Nay, fourthly, although they are continually convinced of sin cleaving to all they do; although they are conscious of not fulfilling the perfect law, either in their thoughts, or words, or works; although they know they do not love the Lord their God with all their heart, and mind, and soul, and strength; although they feel more or less of pride, or self-will, stealing in and mixing with their best duties; although even in their more immediate intercourse with God, when they assemble themselves with the great congregation, and when they pour out their souls in secret to him who seeth all the thoughts and intents of the heart, they are continually ashamed of their wandering thoughts, or of the deadness and dullness of their affections; yet there is no condemnation to them still, either from God or from their own heart. The consideration of these manifold defects only gives them a deeper sense that they have always need of the blood of sprinkling which speaks for

them in the ears of God, and that Advocate with the Father, "who ever liveth to make intercession for them." So far are these from driving them away from him, in whom they have believed, that they rather drive them the closer to him, whom they feel the want of every moment. And, at the same time, the deeper sense they have of this want, the more earnest desire do they feel, and the more diligent they are, as they "have received the Lord Jesus, so to walk in him."

They are not condemned, fifthly, for sins of infirmity, as they are usually called. Perhaps it were advisable rather to call them *infirmities*, that we may not seem to give any countenance to sin, or to extenuate it in any degree by thus coupling it with infirmity. But (if we must retain so ambiguous and dangerous an expression) by sins of infirmity I would mean such involuntary failings as the saying a thing we believe true, though, in fact, it prove to be false; or the hurting our neighbor without knowing or designing it, perhaps when we designed to do him good. Though these are deviations from the holy, and acceptable, and perfect will of God, yet they are not properly sins, nor do they bring any guilt on the conscience of "them which are in Christ Jesus." They separate not between God and them, neither intercept the light of his countenance; as being no ways inconsistent with their general character of "walking not after the flesh, but after the Spirit."

Lastly, "There is no condemnation" to them for anything whatever which it is not in their power to help, whether it be of an inward or outward nature, and whether it be doing something or leaving something undone. For instance, the Lord's supper is to be administered, but you do not partake thereof. Why do you not? You are confined by sickness; therefore, you cannot help omitting it; and for the same reason you are not condemned. There is no guilt because there is no choice. As there "is a willing mind, it is accepted according to that a man hath, not according to that he hath not."

Special Situations

A believer indeed may sometimes be *grieved* because he cannot do what his soul longs for. He may cry out when he is detained from worshiping God in the great congregation, "Like as the hart panteth after the water brooks, so panteth my soul after thee, O God. My soul is athirst for God, yea, even for the living God: when shall I come to appear in the presence of God?" He may earnestly desire (only still saying in his heart, "Not as I will, but as thou wilt") to "go again with the multitude, and bring them forth into the house of God." But still if he cannot go, he feels no condemnation, no guilt, no sense of God's displeasure; but can cheerfully yield up those desires with, "Oh, my soul! Put thy trust in God. For I will yet give him thanks who is the help of my countenance and my God."

It is more difficult to determine concerning those which are usually styled sins of surprise: as when one who commonly in patience possesses his soul, on a sudden and violent temptation, speaks or acts in a manner not consistent with the royal law, "Thou shalt love thy neighbor as thyself." Perhaps it is not easy to fix a general rule concerning trangressions of this nature. We cannot say either that men are or that they are not condemned for sins of surprise in general. But it seems whenever a believer is by surprise overtaken in a fault, there is more or less condemnation, as there is more or less concurrence of his will. In proportion as a sinful desire or word or action is more or less voluntary, so we may conceive God is more or less displeased, and there is more or less guilt upon the soul.

But if so, then there may be some sins of surprise, which bring much guilt and condemnation. For, in some instances our being surprised is owing to some willful and culpable neglect, or to a sleepiness of soul which might have been prevented or shaken off before the temptation came. A man may be previously warned either of God or man that trials and dangers are at hand, and yet may say in his heart, "A little more slumber, a little more folding of the hands to rest." Now, if such a one afterward falls, though unaware, into the snare which he might have avoided, that he fell unaware is no excuse; he might have foreseen and have shunned the danger. The falling even by surprise, in such an instance as this is, in effect, a willful sin; and, as such, must expose the sinner, to condemnation both from God and his own conscience.

On the other hand, there may be sudden assaults, either from the world or the god of this world and frequently from our own evil hearts, which we did not, and hardly could, foresee. And by these even a believer, while weak in faith, may possibly be borne down, suppose into a degree of anger or thinking evil of another, with scarce any concurrence of his will. Now, in such a case the jealous God would undoubtedly show him that he had done foolishly. He would be convinced of having swerved from the perfect law, from the mind which was in Christ, and consequently *grieved* with a godly sorrow and lovingly *ashamed* before God. Yet he need not come into condemnation. God layeth not folly to his charge, but hath compassion upon him "even as a father pitieth his own children." And his heart condemneth him not. In the midst of that sorrow and shame he can still say, "I will trust and not be afraid; for the Lord Jehovah is my strength and my song; he also is become my salvation."

It remains only to draw some practical inferences from the preceding considerations.

Abolishing Fear

And, first, if there be "no condemnation to them which are in Christ Jesus, and walk not after the flesh, but after the Spirit," on account of their past sin; then, why art thou fearful, O thou of little faith? Though thy sins were once more in number than the sand, what is that to thee, now thou art in Christ Jesus? "Who shall lay anything to the charge of God's elect? It is God that justifieth; who is he that condemneth?" All the sins thou hast committed from thy youth up, until the hour when thou wast "accepted in the Beloved," are driven away as chaff, are gone, are lost, swallowed up, remembered no more. Thou art now "born of the Spirit": wilt thou be troubled or afraid of what is done before thou wert born? Away with thy fears! Thou art not called to fear, but to the "spirit of love and of a sound mind." Know thy calling! Rejoice in God thy Savior, and give thanks to God thy Father through him!

Wilt thou say, "But I have again committed sin, since I had redemption through his blood? And, therefore, it is that 'I abhor myself, and repent in dust and ashes.'" It is meet thou shouldest abhor thyself; and it is God who hath wrought thee to this self-same thing. But, dost thou now believe? Hath he again enabled thee to say, "I know that my Redeemer liveth," "and the life which I now live, I live by faith in the Son of God"? Then that faith again cancels all that is past, and there is no condemnation to thee. At whatsoever time thou truly believest in the name of the Son of God, all thy sins, antecedent to that hour, vanish away as the morning dew. Now then, "Stand thou fast in the liberty wherewith Christ hath made thee free." He hath once more made thee free from the power of sin, as well as from the guilt and punishment of it. Oh, "be not entangled again with the yoke of bondage"—neither the vile, devilish bondage of sin, of evil desires, evil tempers, or words, or works, the most grievous yoke on this side of hell; nor the bondage of slavish, tormenting fear, of guilt and self-condemnation.

Avoiding Sin

But, secondly: do all they which abide "in Christ Jesus, walk not after the flesh, but after the Spirit"? Then we cannot but infer, that whosoever now committeth sin, hath no part or lot in this matter. He is even now condemned by his own heart. But, "if our heart condemn us," if our own conscience beareth witness that we are guilty, undoubtedly God doth; for "he is greater than our heart, and knoweth all things"; so that we cannot deceive him, if we can ourselves. And think not to say, "I was justified once; my sins were once forgiven me." I know not that; neither will I dispute whether they were or no. Perhaps at this distance of time it is next to impossible to know with any tolerable degree of certainty whether that was a true, genuine work of God, or whether thou didst only deceive thy own soul. But this I know with the utmost degree of certainty, "He that committeth sin is of the devil." Therefore, thou art of thy father the devil. It cannot be denied: for the works of thy father thou doest. Oh, flatter not thyself with vain hopes. Say not to thy soul, "Peace, peace!" For there is no peace. Cry aloud! Cry unto God out of the deep; if haply he may hear thy voice. Come unto him as at first, as wretched and poor, as sinful, miserable, blind, and naked! And beware thou suffer thy soul to take no rest, till his pardoning love be again revealed; till he "heal thy backslidings" and fill thee again with the "faith that worketh by love."

Thirdly, there is no condemnation to them which "walk after the Spirit," by reason of *inward sin* still remaining, so long as they do not give way thereto; nor by reason of *sin cleaving* to all they do. Then fret not thyself because of ungodliness, though it still remain in thy heart. Repine not, because thou still comest short of the glorious image of God; nor yet because praise, self-will, or unbelief cleave to all thy words and works. And be not afraid to know all this evil of thy heart, to know thyself as also thou art known. Yea, desire of God that thou mayest not think of thyself more highly than thou oughtest to think. Let thy continual prayer be:

Show me, as my soul can bear,
The depth of inbred sin:
All the unbelief declare,
The pride that lurks within.

But when he heareth thy prayer and unveils thy heart, when he shows thee thoroughly what spirit thou art of, then beware that thy faith fail thee not, that thou suffer not thy shield to be torn from thee. Be abased. Be humbled in the dust. See thyself nothing, less than nothing and vanity. But still "let not thy heart be troubled, neither let it be afraid." Still hold fast, "I, even I, have an Advocate with the Father, Jesus Christ the righteous." "And as the heavens are higher than the earth, so is his love higher than even my sins." Therefore, God is merciful to thee a sinner! Such a sinner as thou art! God is love; and Christ hath died! Therefore, the Father himself loveth thee! Thou art his child! Therefore, he will withhold from thee no manner of thing that is good. Is it good that the whole body of sin, which is now crucified in thee, should be de-

stroyed? It shall be done! Thou shalt be "cleansed from all filthiness, both of flesh and spirit." Is it good that nothing should remain in thy heart but the pure love of God alone? Be of good cheer! "Thou shalt love the Lord thy God, with all thy heart, and mind, and soul, and strength." "Faithful is he that hath promised, who also will do it." It is thy part, patiently to continue in the work of faith, and in the labor of love; and in cheerful peace, in humble confidence, with calm and resigned, and yet earnest expectation, to wait till the zeal of the Lord of hosts shall perform this.

Fourthly, if they that "are in Christ, and walk after the Spirit," are not condemned for *sins of infirmity,* as neither for *involuntary failings,* nor for anything whatever which they are not able to help; then beware, O thou that hast faith in his blood, that Satan herein "gain no advantage over thee." Thou art still foolish and weak, blind and ignorant; more weak than any words can express; more foolish than it can yet enter into thy heart to conceive; knowing nothing yet as thou oughtest to know. Yet let not all thy weakness and folly, or any fruit thereof, which thou art not yet able to avoid, shake thy faith, thy filial trust in God, or disturb thy peace or joy in the Lord. The rule which some give, as to willful sins, and which, in that case, may perhaps be dangerous, is undoubtedly wise and safe if it be applied only to the case of weakness and infirmities. Art thou fallen, O man of God? Yet, do not lie there, fretting thyself and bemoaning thy weakness; but meekly say, "Lord, I shall fall thus every moment, unless thou uphold me with thy hand." And then arise! Leap and walk! Go on thy way! "Run with patience the race set before thee."

Lastly, since a believer need not come into condemnation, even though he be *surprised* into what his soul abhors (suppose his being surprised is not owing to any carelessness or willful neglect of his own); if thou who believest, art thus overtaken in a fault, then grieve unto the Lord; it shall be a precious balm. Pour out thy heart before him, and show him of thy trouble. And pray with all thy might to him who is "touched with the feeling of thy infirmities," that he would establish, and strengthen, and settle thy soul, and suffer thee to fall no more. But still he condemneth thee not. Wherefore shouldest thou fear? Thou hast no need of any "fear that hath torment." Thou shalt love him that loveth thee, and it sufficeth: more love will bring more strength. And, as soon as thou lovest him with all thy heart, thou shalt be "perfect and entire, lacking nothing." Wait in peace for that hour when "the God of peace shall sanctify thee wholly, so that thy whole spirit, and soul, and body, may be preserved blameless unto the coming of our Lord Jesus Christ!"

Wesley saw scriptural Christianity as a logical progression spreading from the individual throughout the entire world.

The New Testament clearly describes the spread of Christianity from Christ to various individuals to whom he preached his message. It is a personal relationship that requires a decision by each individual, not a passive, crowd-following approach. Every person must decide whether to accept or reject the gospel.

From the individual Christianity spreads to others by means of good works, preaching Christ, and warning all of condemnation if they reject the message. Like the Old Testament prophets, the Christian loudly proclaims the message of the gospel to those around him in the hope that they will come to Christ.

Finally, as others believe the message and spread it in their turn, the gospel begins to spread throughout the world, finding converts in every culture and social stratum. Thus we find the essence of scriptural Christianity.

CHAPTER ELEVEN

Scriptural Christianity

Preached at Saint Mary's, Oxford, before the University, on August 24, 1744

"Whosoever heareth the sound of the trumpet, and taketh not warning; if the sword come, and take him away, his blood shall be upon his own head" (Ezek. 33:4).

"And they were all filled with the Holy Ghost" (Acts 4:31).

The same expression occurs in the second chapter, where we read, "When the day of pentecost was fully come, they were all," (the apostles, with the women, and the mother of Jesus, and his brethren) "with one accord, in one place. And suddenly there came a sound from heaven, as of a rushing mighty wind. And there appeared unto them cloven tongues, like as of fire, and it sat upon each of them. And they were all filled with the Holy Ghost." One immediate effect thereof was "they began to speak with other tongues," insomuch that the Parthians, Medes, Elamites, and the other strangers who "came together when this was noised abroad, heard them speak in their several tongues the wonderful works of God," Acts 2:1–6.

In this chapter we read that when the apostles and brethren had been praying and praising God, "the place was shaken where they were assembled together, and they were all filled with the Holy Ghost," Acts 4:31. Not that we find any visible appearance here such as had been in the former instance; nor are we informed that the *extraordinary gifts* of the Holy Ghost were then given to all or any of them; such as the "gift of healing, of working other miracles, of prophecy, of discerning spirits, the speaking with divers kinds of tongues, and the inter-

pretation of tongues," 1 Corinthians 12:9, 10.

Whether these gifts of the Holy Ghost were designed to remain in the church throughout all ages, and whether or no they will be restored at the nearer approach of the "restitution of all things," are questions which it is not needful to decide. But it is needful to observe this, that, even in the infancy of the church, God divided them with a sparing hand. Were all even then prophets? Were all workers of miracles? Had all the gifts of healing? Did all speak with tongues? No, in no wise. Perhaps not one in a thousand. Probably none but the teachers in the church, and only some of them, 1 Corinthians 12:28–30. It was, therefore, for a more excellent purpose than this that "they were all filled with the Holy Ghost."

It was to give them (what none can deny to be essential to all Christians in all ages) the mind which was in Christ, those holy fruits of the Spirit, which whosoever hath not, is none of his; to fill them with "love, joy, peace, longsuffering, gentleness, goodness," Galatians 5:22–24; to endue them with faith (perhaps it might be rendered, *fidelity*), with meekness and temperance; to enable them to crucify the flesh, with its affections and lusts, its passions and desires, and, in consequence of that inward change, to fulfill all outward righteousness, to "walk as Christ also walked" "in the work of faith, in the patience of hope, the labor of love," 1 Thessalonians 1:3.

Without busying ourselves then in curious, needless inquiries, touching those *extraordinary* gifts of the Spirit, let us take a nearer view of these his *ordinary* fruits, which we are assured will remain throughout all ages—of that great work of God among the children of men, which we are used to express by one word, Christianity, not as it implies a set of opinions, a system of doctrines, but as it refers to men's hearts and lives. And this Christianity it may be useful to consider under three distinct views: first, as beginning to exist in individuals; second, as spreading from one to another; third, as covering the earth.

I design to close these considerations with a plain practical application.

Christianity As It Began

1. Let us consider Christianity in its rise, as beginning to exist in individuals.

Suppose, then, one of those who heard the apostle Peter preaching repentance and remission of sins was pricked to the heart, was convinced of sin, repented, and then believed in Jesus. By this faith of the operation of God, which was the very substance, or subsistence of things hoped for, Hebrews 11:1; the demonstrative evidence of invisible things, he instantly received the spirit of adoption, whereby he now cried, "Abba, Father," Romans 8:15. Now first it was that he could call Jesus Lord, by the Holy Ghost, 1 Corinthians 3, the Spirit itself bearing witness with his spirit that he was a child of God, Romans 8:15. Now it was that he could truly say, "I live not, but Christ liveth in me; and the life which I now live in the flesh, I live by faith in the Son of God, who loved me and gave himself for me," Galatians 2:20.

This, then, was the very essence of his faith, a divine *evidence or conviction* of the love of God the Father, through the Son of his love, to him a sinner, now accepted in the Beloved. And, "being justified by faith, he had peace with God," Romans 5:1, yea, "the peace of God ruling in his heart"; a peace which, passing all understanding, kept his heart and mind from all doubt and fear through the knowledge of him in whom he had believed. He could not, therefore, "be afraid of any evil tidings"; for his "heart stood fast believing in the Lord." He feared not what man could do unto him, knowing the very hairs of his head were all numbered. He feared not all the powers of darkness whom God was daily bruising under his feet. Least of all was he afraid to die; nay, he desired to "depart and to be with Christ," Philippians 1:23; who, "through death, had destroyed him that had the power of death, even the devil, and delivered them who, through fear of death, were all their lifetime (till then) subject to bondage," Hebrews 2:15.

His soul, therefore, magnified the Lord, and his spirit rejoiced in God his Savior. "He rejoiced in him with joy unspeakable, who had reconciled him to God, even the Father," "in whom he had redemption through his blood, the forgiveness of sins." He rejoiced in that witness of God's Spirit with his spirit that he was a child of God, and more abundantly, "in hope of the glory of God"; in hope of the glorious image of God, and full renewal of his soul in righteousness and true holiness; and in hope of that crown of glory, that "inheritance, incorruptible, undefiled, and that fadeth not away."

"The love of God was also shed abroad in his heart, by the Holy Ghost which was given unto him," Romans 5:5. "Because he was a son, God had sent forth the Spirit of his Son into his heart, crying, Abba, Father!" Galatians 4:6. And that filial love of God was continually increased by the witness he had in himself (1 John 5:10) of God's pardoning love to him; by "beholding what manner of love it was which the Father had bestowed upon him that he should be called a child of God," 1 John 3:1. So that God was the desire of his eyes and the joy of his heart, his portion in time and in eternity.

He that thus *loved* God could not but love his brother also, and "not in word only, but in deed and in truth." "If God," said he, "so loved us, we ought also to love one another," 1 John 4:11; yea, every soul of man as "the mercy of God is over all his works," Psalm 145:9. Agreeably hereto, the affection of this lover of God embraced all mankind for his sake, not excepting those whom he had never seen in the flesh or those of whom he knew nothing more than that they were "the offspring of God," for whose souls his Son had died; not excepting the *evil* and *unthankful*, and least of all his enemies, those who hated, or persecuted, or despitefully used him for his Master's sake. These had a peculiar place both in his heart and in his prayers. He loved them "even as Christ loved us."

And "love is not puffed up," 1 Corinthians 13:4. It abases to the dust every soul wherein it dwells: accordingly, he was lowly of heart, little, mean, and vile in his own eyes. He neither sought, nor received the praise of men, but that which cometh of God only. He was meek and longsuffering, gentle to all, and easy to be entreated. Faithfulness and truth never forsook him; they were "bound about his neck, and wrote on the table of his heart." By the same Spirit he was enabled to be temperate in all things, refraining his soul even as a weaned

child. He was "crucified to the world, and the world crucified to him"; superior to "the desire of the flesh, the desire of the eye, and the pride of life." By the same almighty love was he saved from both passion and pride, from lust and vanity, from ambition and covetousness, and from every temper which was not in Christ.

It may easily be believed, he who had this love in his heart would work no evil to his neighbor. It was impossible for him knowingly and designedly to do harm to any man. He was at the greatest distance from cruelty and wrong, from any unjust or unkind action. With the same care did he "set a watch before his mouth, and keep the door of his lips," lest he should offend in tongue against justice or against mercy or truth. He put away all lying, falsehood, and fraud; neither was guile found in his mouth. He spake evil of no man; nor did an unkind word ever come out of his lips.

And, as he was deeply sensible of the truth of that word, "without me ye can do nothing," and, consequently, of the need he had to be watered of God every moment, so he continued daily in all the ordinances of God, the stated channels of his grace to man: "in the apostles' doctrine," or teaching, receiving that food of the soul with all readiness of heart; in "the breaking of bread," which he found to be the communion of the body of Christ; and "in the prayers" and praises offered up by the great congregation. And thus, he daily "grew in grace," increasing in strength, in the knowledge and love of God.

But it did not satisfy him barely to abstain from doing evil. His soul was athirst to do good. The language of his heart continually was, "My Father worketh hitherto, and I work. My Lord went about doing good, and shall not I tread in his steps?" As he had opportunity, therefore, if he could do no good of a higher kind, he fed the hungry, clothed the naked, helped the fatherless or stranger, visited and assisted them that were sick or in prison. He gave all his goods to feed the poor. He rejoiced to labor or to suffer for them; and wheresoever he might profit another, there especially to "deny himself." He counted nothing too dear to part with for them, as well remembering the word of his Lord, "Inasmuch as ye have done it unto one of the least of these my brethren, ye have done it unto me," Matthew 25:40.

Such was Christianity in its rise. Such was a Christian in ancient days. Such was every one of those, who, when they heard the threatenings of the chief priests and elders, "lifted up their voice to God with one accord, and were all filled with the Holy Ghost. The multitude of them that believed were of one heart and of one soul." (So did the love of him in whom they had believed constrain them to love one another!) "Neither said any of them that aught of the things which he possessed was his own; but they had all things common." So fully were they crucified to the world, and the world crucified to them! "And they continued steadfastly with one accord in the apostles' doctrine, and in the breaking of bread, and in prayer," Acts 2:42. "And great grace was upon them all; neither was there any among them that lacked: for as many as were possessors of lands or houses, sold them, and brought the prices of the things that were sold, and laid them down at the apostles' feet, and distribution was made unto every man according as he had need," Acts 4:31–35.

Christianity in Dissemination

2. Let us take a view of this Christianity, as spreading from one to another, and so gradually making its way into the world: for such was the will of God concerning it, who did not "light a candle to put it under a bushel, but that it might give light to all that were in the house." And this our Lord had declared to his first disciples, "Ye are the salt of the earth," "the light of the world"; at the same time that he gave that general command, "Let your light so shine before men, that they may see your good works, and glorify your Father which is in heaven," Matthew 5:13–16.

And, indeed, supposing a few of these lovers of mankind to see "the whole world lying in wickedness," can we believe they would be unconcerned at the sight, at the misery of those for whom their Lord died? Would not their bowels yearn over them, and their hearts melt away for very trouble? Could they then stand idle all the day long, even were there no command from him whom they loved? Rather would they not labor, by all possible means to pluck some of these brands out of the burning? Undoubtedly they would: they would spare no pains to bring back whomsoever they could of those poor "sheep that had gone astray, to the great Shepherd and Bishop of their souls," 1 Peter 2:25.

So the Christians of old did. They labored, having opportunity, "to do good unto all men," Galatians 6:10, warning them to flee from the wrath to come; now, to escape the damnation of hell. They declared, "The times of ignorance God winked at; but now he calleth all men everywhere to repent," Acts 17:30. They cried aloud, turn ye, turn ye from your evil ways; "so iniquity shall not be your ruin," Ezekiel 18:30. They reasoned with them of temperance and righteousness, of justice, of the virtues opposite to their reigning sins, and of judgment to come; of the wrath of God, which would surely be executed on evildoers in that day when he should judge the world, Acts 24:25.

They endeavored herein to speak to every man severally as he had need. To the careless, to those who lay unconcerned in darkness and in the shadow of death, they thundered, "Awake, thou that sleepest: arise from the dead, and Christ shall give thee light." But to those who were already awakened out of sleep and groaning under a sense of the wrath of God, their language was, "We have an Advocate with the Father; he is the propitiation for our sins." Meantime, those who had believed they provoked to love and to good works, to patient continuance in doing well, and to abound more and more in that holiness without which no man can see the Lord, Hebrews 12:14.

And their labor was not in vain in the Lord. His Word ran and was glorified. It grew mightily and prevailed. But so much the more did offenses prevail also. The world in general were offended, "because they testified of it, that the works thereof were evil," John 7:7. The men of pleasure were offended, not only because these men were made, as it were, to reprove their thoughts—"He professeth," said they, "to have the knowledge of God; he calleth himself the child of the Lord; his life is not like other men's; his ways are of another fashion; he abstaineth from our ways, as from filthiness; he maketh his boast, that God is his Father," Wisdom of Solomon 2:13–16—but much more, because so many of their companions were taken away, and would no more run with them to the same excess of riot, 1 Peter 4:4. The men of reputation were offended because, as the gospel spread, they declined in the esteem of the people, and because many no longer dared to give them flattering titles, or to pay man the homage due to God only. The men of trade called one another together and said, "Sirs, ye know that by this craft we have our wealth. But ye see and hear

that these men have persuaded and turned away [many] people. So that this our craft is in danger to be set at nought," Acts 19:25. Above all, the so-called men of religion, the men of *outside* religion, "the saints of the world," were offended and ready at every opportunity to cry out, "Men of Israel, help! We have found these men pestilent fellows, movers of sedition throughout the world," Acts 24:5. "These are the men that teach all men everywhere against the people and against the Law," Acts 21:28.

Thus it was that the heavens grew black with clouds, and the storm gathered amain. For the more Christianity spread, the more hurt was done in the account of those who received it not; and the number increased of those who were more and more enraged at these "men who thus turned the world upside down," Acts 17:6; insomuch that more and more cried out, "Away with such fellows from the earth. It is not fit that they should live"; yea, and sincerely believed, that whosoever should kill them would do God service.

Meanwhile they did not fail to cast out their name as evil, Luke 6:22, so that this "sect was everywhere spoken against," Acts 28:22. Men said all manner of evil of them, even as had been done of the prophets that were before them, Matthew 5:11. And whatsoever any would affirm, others would believe. So that offenses grew as the stars of heaven for multitude. And hence arose, at the time foreordained of the Father, persecution in all its forms. Some, for a season, suffered only shame and reproach; some, "the spoiling of their goods"; "some had trial of mocking and scourging; some of bonds and imprisonment"; and others "resisted unto blood," Hebrews 10:34; 11:36.

Now it was that the pillars of hell were shaken and the kingdom of God spread more and more. Sinners were everywhere "turned from darkness to light, and from the power of Satan unto God." He gave his children "such a mouth, and such wisdom, as all their adversaries could not resist," and their lives were of equal force with their words. But above all, their sufferings spake to all the world. They "approved themselves the servants of God, in afflictions, in necessities, in distresses, in stripes, in imprisonments, in tumults, in labors; in perils in the sea, in perils in the wilderness, in weariness and painfulness, in hunger and in thirst, in cold and nakedness," 2 Corinthians 6:4. And when, having fought the good fight, they were led as sheep to the slaughter, and offered up on the sacrifice and service of their faith, then the blood of each found a voice, and the heathen owned, "He being dead yet speaketh."

Thus did Christianity spread itself in the earth. But how soon did the tares appear with the wheat and the *mystery of iniquity* work as well as the *mystery of godliness!* How soon did Satan find a seat, even *in the temple of God*, "till the woman fled into the wilderness" and "the faithful were again minished from the children of men!" Here we tread a beaten path: the still increasing corruptions of the succeeding generations have been largely described from time to time, by those witnesses God raised up, to show that he had "built his church upon a Rock, and the gates of hell should not (wholly) prevail against her," Matthew 16:18.

Pervasive Christianity

3. But shall we not see greater things than these? Yea, greater than have been yet from the beginning of the world. Can Satan cause the truth of God to fail or his promises to be of none effect? If not, the time will come when Christianity will prevail over all and cover the earth. Let us stand a little and survey (the third thing which was proposed) this strange sight, a *Christian world*. Of this the prophets of old inquired and searched diligently, 1 Peter 1:10, 11. Of this the Spirit which was in them testified, "It shall come to pass in the last days, that the mountain of the Lord's house shall be established on the top of the mountains, and shall be exalted above the hills, and all nations shall flow unto it. And they shall beat their swords into ploughshares, and their spears into pruning hooks. Nation shall not lift up sword against nation; neither shall they learn war any more," Isaiah 2:1–4. "In that day there shall be a root of Jesse, which shall stand for an ensign of the people. To it shall the Gentiles seek, and his rest shall be glorious. And it shall come to pass in that day, that the Lord shall set his hand again to recover the remnant of his people; and he shall set up an ensign for the nations, and shall assemble the outcasts of Israel, and gather together the dispersed of Judah, from the four corners of the earth," Isaiah 11:10–12. "The wolf shall then dwell with the lamb, and the leopard shall lie down with the kid, and the calf, and the young lion, and the fatling together; and a little child shall lead them. They shall not hurt nor destroy, saith the Lord, in all my holy mountain. For the earth shall be full of the knowledge of the Lord, as the waters cover the sea," Isaiah 11:6–9.

To the same effect are the words of the great apostle, which it is evident have never yet been fulfilled. "Hath God cast away his people? God forbid." "But through their fall salvation is come to the Gentiles." "And if the diminishing of them be the riches of the Gentiles, how much more their fullness?" "For I would not, brethren, that ye should be ignorant of this mystery, That blindness in part is happened to Israel, until the fullness of the Gentiles be come in; and so all Israel shall be saved," Romans 11:1, 11, 25, 26.

Suppose now the fullness of time to be come, and the prophecies to be accomplished. What a prospect is this! All is "peace, quietness, and assurance forever." Here is no din of arms, no "confused noise," no "garments rolled in blood." "Destructions are come to a perpetual end"; wars are ceased from the earth. Neither are there any intestine jars remaining; no brother rising up against brother; no country or city divided against itself and tearing out its own bowels. Civil discord is at an end forevermore, and none is left either to destroy or hurt his neighbor. Here is no oppression to make even the wise man mad; no extortion to grind the face of the poor; no robbery or wrong; no rapine or injustice; for all are "content with such things as they possess." Thus "righteousness and peace have kissed each other," Psalm 85:10; they have "taken root and filled the land": "righteousness flourishing out of the earth," and "peace looking down from heaven."

And with righteousness or justice, mercy is also found. The earth is no longer full of cruel habitations. The Lord hath destroyed both the bloodthirsty and malicious, the envious and revengeful man. Were there any provocation, there is none that now knoweth to return evil for evil; but indeed there is none that doeth evil, no, not one; for all are harmless as doves. And being filled with peace and joy in believing, and united in one body, by one spirit, they all love as brethren, they are all of one heart, and of one soul. "Neither saith any of them, that aught of the things which he possesseth is his own." There is none among them that lacketh; for every man loveth his neighbor as himself. And all walk by one rule, "Whatever ye would that men should do unto you even so do unto them."

It follows that no unkind word can ever be heard among them, no strife of tongues, no contention of any kind, no railing or evil speaking; but everyone "opens his mouth with wisdom, and in his tongue there is the law of kindness." Equally incapable are they of fraud or guile: their love is without dissimulation: their words are always the just expression of their thoughts, opening a window into their breast, that whosoever desires may look into their hearts and see that only love and God are there.

Thus, where the Lord omnipotent taketh to himself his mighty power and reigneth doth he "subdue all things to himself," cause every heart to overflow with love, and fill every mouth with praise. "Happy are the people that are in such a case: yea, blessed are the people who have the Lord for their God," Psalm 144:15. "Arise, shine (saith the Lord), for thy light is come, and the glory of the Lord is risen upon thee." "Thou hast known that I, the Lord, am thy Savior, and thy Redeemer, the mighty God of Jacob. I have made thy officers peace, and thy exacters righteousness. Violence shall no more be heard in the land, wasting nor destruction within thy borders; but thou shalt call thy walls, salvation, and thy gates, praise." "Thy people are all righteous; they shall inherit the land forever; the branch of my planting, the work of my hands, that I may be glorified." "The sun shall be no more thy light by day; neither for brightness shall the moon give light unto thee: but the Lord shall be unto thee an everlasting light, and thy God thy glory," Isaiah 61:1, 16–19.

In Quest of Vital Christianity

4. Having thus briefly considered Christianity, as beginning, as going on, and as covering the earth; it remains

only that I should close the whole with a plain, practical application.

And first, I would ask, where does this Christianity now exist? Where, I pray, do the Christians live? Which is the country, the inhabitants whereof are all thus filled with the Holy Ghost? Are all of one heart and of one soul? Cannot suffer one among them to lack anything but continually give to every man as he hath need? Who, one and all, have the love of God filling their hearts and constraining them to love their neighbor as themselves? Who have all "put on bowels of mercy, humbleness of mind, gentleness, longsuffering"? Who offend not in any kind, either by word or deed, against justice, mercy, or truth; but in every point do unto all men, as they would these should do unto them. With what propriety can we term any a Christian country, which does not answer this description? Why then, let us confess we have never yet seen a Christian country upon earth.

I beseech you, brethren, by the mercies of God, if ye do account me a madman or a fool, yet, *as a fool bear with me.* It is utterly needful that someone should use great plainness of speech toward you. It is more especially needful at *this* time; for who knoweth but it is the *last.* Who knoweth how soon the righteous Judge may say, "I will no more be entreated for this people." "Though Noah, Daniel, and Job were in this land, they should but deliver their own souls." And who will use this plainness, if I do not? Therefore I, even I, will speak. And I adjure you, by the living God, that ye steel not your breasts against receiving a blessing at *my* hands. Do not say in your hearts, Lord, thou shalt not *send by whom thou wilt send;* let me rather perish in my blood, than be saved by this man!

Brethren, "I am persuaded better things of you, though I thus speak." Let me ask you then, in tender love and in the spirit of meekness, is this city a Christian city? Is Christianity, scriptural Christianity, found here? Are we considered as a community of men so "filled with the Holy Ghost" as to enjoy in our hearts and show forth in our lives the genuine fruits of that Spirit? Are all the magistrates, all heads and governors of colleges and halls, and their respective societies (not to speak of the inhabitants of the town), "of one heart and one soul"? Is "the love of God shed abroad in our hearts"? Are our tempers the same that were in him? And are our lives agreeable thereto? Are we "holy as He who hath called us is holy, in all manner of conversation"?

I entreat you to observe that here are no peculiar notions now under consideration: that the question moved is not concerning *doubtful opinions* of one kind or another, but concerning the undoubted, fundamental branches (if there be any such) of our common Christianity. And for the decision thereof, I appeal to your own consciences, guided by the Word of God. He, therefore, that is not condemned by his own heart let him go free.

In the fear, then, and in the presence of the great God before whom both you and I shall shortly appear, I pray you that are in authority over us, whom I reverence for your office's sake, to consider (and not after the manner of dissemblers with God), are you "filled with the Holy Ghost"? Are you lively portraitures of him whom ye are appointed to represent among men? "I have said ye are gods," ye magistrates and rulers; ye are by office so nearly allied to the God of heaven! In your several stations and degrees, ye are to show forth unto us "the Lord our Governor." Are all the thoughts of your hearts, all your tempers and desires suitable to your high calling? Are all your words like unto those which come out of the mouth of God? Is there in all your actions dignity and love? A greatness which words cannot express, which can flow only from a heart full of God, and yet consistent with the character of "man that is a worm and the son of man that is a worm"!

Ye venerable men, who are more especially called to form the tender minds of youth, to dispel thence the shades of ignorance and error and train them up to be wise unto salvation, are you "filled with the Holy Ghost"? With all those "fruits of the Spirit," which your important office so indispensably requires? Is your heart whole with God? Full of love and zeal to set up his kingdom on earth? Do you continually remind those under your care that the one rational end of all our studies is to know, love, and serve "the only true God, and Jesus Christ whom he hath sent"? Do you inculcate upon them day by day that love alone never faileth (whereas, whether there be tongues, they shall fail, or philosophical knowledge, it shall vanish away); and that without love, all learning is but splendid ignorance, pompous folly, vexation of spirit? Has all you teach an actual tendency to the love of God and of all mankind for his sake? Have you an eye to this end in whatever you prescribe, touching the kind, the manner, and the measure of their studies; desiring and laboring that, wherever the lot of these young soldiers of Christ is cast, they may be so many burning and shining lights, adoring the gospel of Christ in all things? And permit me to ask, do you put forth all your strength in the vast work you have undertaken? Do you labor herein with all your might? Exerting every faculty of your soul? Using every talent which God hath lent you, and that to the uttermost of your power?

Let it not be said that I speak here as if all under your care were intended to be clergymen. Not so: I only speak as if they were all intended to be Christians. But what example is set them by us who enjoy the beneficence of our forefathers? By fellows, students, scholars; more especially those who are of some rank and eminence? Do ye, brethren, abound in the fruits of the Spirit, in lowliness of mind, in self-denial and mortification, in seriousness and composure of spirit, in patience, meekness, sobriety, temperance, and in unwearied, restless endeavors to do good in every kind unto all men, to relieve their outward wants and to bring their souls to the true knowledge and love of God? Is this the general character of fellows of colleges? I fear it is not. Rather, have not pride and haughtiness of spirit, impatience and peevishness, sloth and indolence, gluttony and sensuality, and even proverbial uselessness, been objected to us, perhaps not always by our enemies, nor wholly without ground? Oh, that God would roll away this reproach from us, that the very memory of it might perish forever!

Many of us are more immediately consecrated to God, called to minister in holy things. Are we then patterns to the rest, "in word, in conversation, in charity, in spirit, in faith, in purity"? 2 Corinthians 4:2. Is there written on our forehead and on our heart, "Holiness to the Lord"? From what motives did we enter upon this office? Was it indeed with a single eye "to serve God, trusting that we were inwardly moved by the Holy Ghost, to take upon this ministration, for the promoting of his glory, and the edifying of his people"? And have we "clearly determined, by God's grace, to give ourselves wholly to this office"? Do we forsake and set aside, as much as in us lies, all worldly cares and studies? Do we apply ourselves wholly to this one thing and draw all our cares and studies this way? Are we apt to teach? Are we taught of God that we may be able to teach others also? Do we know God? Do we know Jesus Christ? Hath "God revealed his Son in us"? And hath he made us able ministers of the new covenant"? Where then are the "seals of our apostleship"? Who, that were dead in trespasses and sins, have been quickened by our word? Have we a burning zeal to save souls from death, so that for their sake we often forget even to eat our bread? Do we speak plain, "by manifestation of the truth commending ourselves to every man's conscience in the sight of God"? 2 Corinthians 4:2. Are we dead to the world and the things of the world, "laying up all our treasure in heaven"? Do we lord over God's heritage? Or are we the least, the servants of all? When we bear the reproach of Christ, does it sit heavy upon us? Or do we rejoice therein? When we are smitten on the one cheek, do we resent it? Are we impatient of affronts? Or do we turn the other also; not resisting the evil, but overcoming evil with good? Have we a bitter zeal, inciting us to strive sharply and passionately with them that are out of the way? Or is our zeal the flame of love, so as to direct all our words with sweetness, lowliness, and meekness of wisdom?

Once more, what shall we say concerning the youth of this place? Have you either the form or the power of Christian godliness? Are you humble, teachable, advisable; or stubborn, self-willed, heady, and high-minded? Are you obedient to your superiors as to parents? Or do you despise those to whom you owe the tenderest reverence? Are you diligent in your easy business, pursuing your studies with all your strength? Do you redeem the time, crowding as much work into every day as it can contain? Rather, are ye not conscious to yourselves, that you waste away day af-

ter day, either in reading what has no tendency to Christianity, or in gaming, or in—you know not what? Are you better managers of your fortune than of your time? Do you, out of principle, take care to owe no man anything? Do you "remember the sabbath day to keep it holy"; to spend it in the more immediate worship of God? When you are in his house, do you consider that God is there? Do you behave, "as seeing him that is invisible"? Do you know how to "possess your bodies in sanctification and honor"? Are not drunkenness and uncleanness found among you? Yea, are there not of you who "glory in their shame"? Do not many of you "take the name of God in vain," perhaps habitually, without either remorse or fear? Yea, are there not a multitude of you that are forsworn? I fear, a swiftly increasing multitude. Be not surprised, brethren. Before God and this congregation, I own myself to have been of the number, solemnly swearing to observe all those customs which I then knew nothing of; and those statutes which I did not so much as read over, either then or for some years after. What is perjury if this is not? But if it be, oh, what a weight of sin, yea, sin of no common dye, lieth upon us! And doth not the Most High regard it?

May it not be one of the consequences of this that so many of you are a generation of triflers; triflers with God, with one another and with your own souls? For how few of you spend from one week to another a single hour in private prayer? How few have any thought of God in the general tenor of your conversation? Who of you is in any degree acquainted with the work of his Spirit, his supernatural work in the souls of men? Can you bear, unless now and then in a church, any talk of the Holy Ghost? Would not you take it for granted if one began such a conversation that it was either hypocrisy or enthusiasm? In the name of the Lord God Almighty, I ask, what religion are you of? Even the talk of Christianity, ye cannot, will not bear. Oh, my brethren! what a Christian city is this! "It is time for thee, Lord, to lay to thine hand!"

For, indeed, what probability, what possibility rather (speaking after the manner of men), is there that Christianity, scriptural Christianity, should be again the religion of this place? That all orders of men among us should speak and live as men "filled with the Holy Ghost"? By whom should this Christianity be restored? By those of you that are in authority? Are you convinced then that this is scriptural Christianity? Are you desirous it should be restored? And do ye not count your fortune, liberty, life, dear unto yourselves so ye may be instrumental in the restoring of it? But, suppose ye have this desire, who hath any power proportioned to the effect? Perhaps some of you have made a few faint attempts, but with how small success! Shall Christianity then be restored by young, unknown, inconsiderable men? I know not whether ye yourselves could suffer it. Would not some of you cry out, "Young man, in so doing thou reproachest us"? But there is no danger of your being put to the proof, so hath iniquity overspread us like a flood. Whom then shall God send? The famine, the pestilence (the last messengers of God to a guilty land), or the sword? The armies of the Romish aliens to reform us into our first love? Nay, "rather let us fall into thy hand, O Lord, and let us not fall into the hand of man."

Lord, save, or we perish! Take us out of the mire that we sink not! Oh, help us against these enemies! for vain is the help of man. Unto thee all things are possible. According to the greatness of thy power preserve thou those that are appointed to die, and preserve us in the manner that seemeth to thee good; not as we will, but as thou wilt!

Justification began in Eden, when Adam's fall brought the curse of death upon the human race. Because man was made in the image of God, he was unique, the object of God's great love. Even after the Fall the love of God was not diminished; God provided a remedy for man's fallen condition. Only by being justified could mankind be restored to grace.

Justification is the means by which God pardons man from the penalty for sin. With such a pardon comes the blotting out of the sins committed in the past. The shedding of Christ's blood provided man's justification. The only requirement for receiving justification through the gospel is that every person must accept it by faith. God justifies the ungodly in accordance with their decision for Christ. All mankind has sinned and fallen under condemnation, and all mankind is offered the pardon. The sole requirement is "a sure trust and confidence that God both hath and will forgive our sins, that he hath accepted us again into His favor, for the merits of Christ's death and passion."

CHAPTER TWELVE

Justification by Faith

"To him that worketh not, but believeth on him that justifieth the ungodly, his faith is counted to him for righteousness" (Rom. 4:5).

How a sinner may be justified before God, the Lord and Judge of all, is a question of no common importance to every child of man. It contains the foundation of all our hope, inasmuch as while we are at enmity with God, there can be no true peace, no solid joy, either in time or in eternity. What peace can there be, while our own heart condemns us; and much more, he that is "greater than our heart and knoweth all things"? What solid joy, either in this world or that to come, while "the wrath of God abideth on us"?

And yet how little hath this important question been understood! What confused notions have many had concerning it! Indeed, not only confused, but often utterly false; contrary to the truth, as light to darkness; notions absolutely inconsistent with the oracles of God and with the whole analogy of faith. And hence, erring concerning the very foundation, they could not possibly build thereon; at least, not "gold, silver, or precious stones," which would endure when tried as by fire, but only "hay and stubble," neither acceptable to God nor profitable to man.

In order to do justice, as far as in me lies, to the vast importance of the subject, to save those that seek the truth in sincerity from "vain jangling and strife of words," to clear the confusedness of thought into which so many have already been led thereby, and to give them true and just conceptions of this great mystery of godliness, I shall endeavor to show: first, what is the general ground of this whole doctrine of justification; secondly, what justification is; thirdly, who are they that are justified; and fourthly, on what terms they are justified.

The Basis of Justification

1. I am first to show, what is the general ground of this whole doctrine of justification.

In the image of God was man made, holy as he that created him is holy; merciful as the Author of all is merciful; perfect as his Father in heaven is perfect. As God is love, so man dwelling in love dwelt in God, and God in him. God made him to be an "image of his own eternity," an incorruptible picture of the God of glory. He was accordingly pure, as God is pure, from every spot of sin. He knew not evil in any kind or degree but was inwardly and outwardly sinless and undefiled. He "loved the Lord his God with all his heart, and with all his mind, and soul, and strength."

To man thus upright and perfect, God gave a perfect Law, to which he required full and perfect obedience. He required full obedience in every point, and this to be performed without any intermission from the moment man became a living soul till the time of his trial should be ended. No allowance was made for any falling short. As, indeed, there was no need of any, man being altogether equal to the task assigned, and thoroughly furnished for every good word and work.

To the entire law of love which was written in his heart (against which, perhaps, he could not sin directly), it seemed good to the sovereign wisdom of God to superadd one positive law: "Thou shalt not eat of the fruit of the tree that groweth in the midst of the garden"; annexing that penalty thereto, "In the day that thou eatest thereof, thou shalt surely die."

Such then was the state of man in paradise. By the free, unmerited love of God, he was holy and happy. He knew, loved, enjoyed God, which is, in substance, life everlasting. And in this life of love he was to continue forever, if he continued to obey God in all things; but, if he disobeyed in any, he was to forfeit all. "In that day," said God, "thou shalt surely die."

Man did disobey God. He "ate of the tree, of which God commanded him, saying, thou shalt not eat of it." And in that day he was condemned by the righteous judgment of God. Then also the sentence whereof he was warned before began to take place upon him. For the moment he tasted that fruit he died. His soul died, was separated from God; separate from whom the soul has no more life than the body has when separate from the soul. His body, likewise, became corruptible and mortal, so that death then took hold on this also. And being already dead in spirit, dead to God, dead in sin, he hastened on to death everlasting, to the destruction both of body and soul in the fire never to be quenched.

Thus "by one man sin entered into the world, and death by sin. And so death passed upon all men," as being contained in him who was the common father and representative of us all. Thus, "through the offense of one," all are dead, dead to God, dead in sin, dwelling in a corruptible, mortal body, shortly to be dissolved, and under the sentence of death eternal. For as, "by one man's disobedience," all "were made sinners"; so, by that offense of one "judgment came upon all men to condemnation," Romans 5:12.

In this state we were, even all mankind, when "God so loved the world that he gave his only begotten Son, to the end we might not perish, but have everlasting life." In the fullness of time he was made man, another common head of mankind, a second general parent and representative of the whole human race. And as such it was that "he bore our griefs," "the Lord laying upon him the iniquities of us all." Then was he "wounded for our transgressions, and bruised for our iniquities." "He made his soul an offering for sin": he poured out his blood for the transgressors; he "bore our sins in his own body on the tree," that by his stripes we might be healed, and by that one oblation of himself once offered, he hath redeemed me and all mankind; having thereby "made a full, perfect, and sufficient sacrifice and satisfaction for the sins of the whole world."

In consideration of this, that the Son of God hath "tasted death for every man," God hath now "reconciled the world to himself, not imputing to them their former trespasses." And thus, "as, by the offense of one, judgment came upon all men to condemnation, even so by the righteousness of one, the free gift came upon all men unto justification." So that for the sake of his well-beloved Son of what he hath done and suffered for us, God now vouchsafes, on only one condition (which himself also enables us to perform), both to remit the punishment due to our sins, to reinstate us in his favor, and to restore our dead souls to spiritual life, as the earnest of life eternal.

This, therefore, is the general ground of the whole doctrine of justification. By the sin of the first Adam, who was not only the father, but likewise the representative, of us all, we all fell short of the favor of God; we all became children of wrath, or, as the apostle expresses it, "judgment came upon all men to condemnation." Even so, by the sacrifice for sin made by the second Adam, as the representative of us all, God is so far reconciled to all the world that he hath given them a new covenant; the plain condition whereof being once fulfilled, "there is no more condemnation" for us, but "we are justified freely by his grace, through the redemption that is in Jesus Christ."

The Nature of Justification

2. But what is it to be justified? What is justification? This was the second thing which I proposed to show. And it is evident, from what has been already observed, that it is not the being made actually just and righteous. This is sanctification; which is, indeed, in some degree the immediate fruit of justification; but, nevertheless, is a distinct gift of God and of a totally different nature. The one implies what God "does for us" through his Son, the other, what he "works in us" by his Spirit. So that, although some rare instances may be found wherein the term justified or justification is used in so wide a sense as to include sanctification also, yet, in general use, they are sufficiently distinguished from each other by Saint Paul and the other inspired writers.

Neither is that far-fetched conceit, that justification is the clearing us from accusation, particularly that of Satan, easily provable from any clear text of Holy Writ. In the whole scriptural account of this matter, as above laid down, neither that accuser, nor his accusation, appears to be at all taken in. It cannot indeed be denied, that he is the "accuser" of men, emphatically so called. But it does in no wise appear, that the great apostle hath any reference to this, more or less, in all that he hath written touching justification, either to the Romans or the Galatians.

It is also far easier to take for granted than to prove from any clear Scripture testimony, that justification is the clearing us from the accusation brought against us by the law: at least, if this forced, unnatural way of speaking mean either more or less than this, that whereas we have transgressed the law of God, and thereby deserved the damnation of hell, God does not inflict on those who are justified the punishment which they had deserved.

Least of all does justification imply that God is deceived in those whom he justifies; that he thinks them to be what in fact they are not; that he accounts them to be otherwise than they are. It does by no means imply that God judges concerning us contrary to the real nature of things; that he esteems us better than we really are or believes us righteous when we are unrighteous. Surely no. The judgment of the all-wise God is always according to truth. Neither can it ever consist with his unerring wisdom to think that I am innocent, to judge that I am righteous or holy, because another is so. He can no more, in this manner, confound me with Christ, than with David or Abraham. Let any man to whom God hath given understanding weigh this without prejudice; and he cannot but perceive that such a notion of justification is neither reconcilable to reason nor Scripture.

The plain scriptural notion of justification is pardon, the forgiveness of sins. It is that act of God the Father, whereby, for the sake of the propitiation made by the blood of his Son, he "showeth forth his righteousness (or mercy) by the remission of the sins that are past." This is the easy, natural account of it given by Saint Paul, throughout this whole epistle. So he explains it himself more particularly in this and in the following chapter. Thus, in the next verses but one to the text, "Blessed are they," saith he, "whose iniquities are forgiven, and whose sins are covered: blessed is the man to whom the Lord will not impute sin." To him that is justified or forgiven, God "will not impute sin" to his condemnation. He will not condemn him on that account, either in this world, or in that which is to come. His sins, all his past sins, in thought, word, and deed, are covered, are blotted out, shall not be remembered or mentioned against him any more than if they had not been. God will not inflict on that sinner what he deserved to suffer because the Son of his love hath suffered for him. And from the time we are "accepted through the beloved," "reconciled to God through his blood," he loves and blesses and watches over us for good, even as if we had never sinned.

Indeed the apostle in one place seems to extend the meaning of the word much farther, where he says, "Not the hearers of the law, but the doers of the law, shall be justified." Here he appears to refer our justification to the sentence of the great day. And so our Lord himself unquestionably doth, when he says, "By thy words thou shalt be justified"; proving thereby that "for every idle word men shall speak, they shall give an account in the day of judgment." But perhaps we can hardly produce another instance of Saint Paul's using the word in that distant sense. In the general tenor of his writings it is evident he doth not, and least of all in the text before us, which undeniably speaks, not of those who have already "finished their course," but of those who are now just *setting out*, just beginning to "run the race which is set before them."

The Objects of Justification

3. But this is the third thing which was to be considered, namely, who are they that are justified? And the apostle tells us expressly, the ungodly: "He (that is, God), justifieth the ungodly," the ungodly of every kind and degree, and none but the ungodly. As "they that are righteous need no repentance," so they need no forgiveness. It is only sinners that have any occasion for pardon: it is sin alone which admits of being forgiven. Forgiveness therefore has an immediate reference to sin, and, in this respect, to nothing else. It is our *unrighteousness* to which the pardoning God is merciful; it is our *iniquity* which he "remembereth no more."

This seems not to be at all considered by those who so vehemently contend that a man must be sanctified, that is, holy, before he can be justified; especially by such of them as affirm that universal holiness or obedience must precede justification (unless they mean, that justification at the last day, which is wholly out of the present question). So far from it that the very supposition is not only flatly impossible (for where there is no love of God, there is no holiness, and there is no love of God but from a sense of his loving us), but also grossly, intrinsically absurd, contradictory to itself. For it is not a saint but a sinner that is forgiven and under the notion of a sinner. God justifieth not the godly, but the ungodly; not those that are holy already, but the unholy. Upon what condition he doth this will be considered quickly: but whatever it is, it cannot be holiness. To assert this is to say the Lamb of God takes away only those sins which were taken away before.

Does then the Good Shepherd seek and save only those that are found already? No: he seeks and saves that which is lost. He pardons those who need his pardoning mercy. He saves from the guilt of sin (and, at the same time, from the power), sinners of every kind, of every degree; men who, till then, were altogether ungodly; in whom the love of the Father was not; and, consequently, in whom dwelt no good thing, no good or truly Christian temper, but all such as were evil and abominable: pride, anger, love of the world, the genuine fruits of that *carnal mind* which is "enmity against God."

These who are sick, the burden of whose sins is intolerable, are they that need a physician. These who are guilty, who groan under the wrath of God, are they that need a pardon. These who are *condemned already*, not only by God, but also by their own conscience, as by a thousand witnesses of all their ungodliness, in thought and word and work, cry aloud for him that "justifieth the ungodly" through the redemption that is in Jesus—the ungodly, and "him that worketh not," that worketh not before he is justified, anything that is good, that is truly virtuous or holy but only evil continually. For his heart is necessarily, essentially evil till the love of God is shed abroad therein. And while the tree is corrupt so are the fruits, "for an evil tree cannot bring forth good fruit."

If it be objected, "Nay, but a man before he is justified may feed the hungry or clothe the naked, and these are good works"; the answer is easy. He may do these even before he is justified. And these are in one sense "good works"; they are "good and profitable to men." But it does not follow that they are, strictly speaking, good in themselves or good in the sight of God. All truly *good works* (to use the words of our church) *follow after justification.* And they are, therefore, good and "acceptable to God in Christ" because they "spring out of a true and living faith." By a parity of reason, all *works done before justification are not good*, in the Christian sense, *forasmuch as they spring not of faith in Jesus Christ* (though often from some kind of faith in God they may spring); "yea, rather, for that they are not done as God hath willed and commanded them to be done, we doubt not" ([however] strange it may appear to some) "but they have the nature of sin."

Perhaps those who doubt of this have not duly considered the weighty reason which is here assigned, why no works done before justification can be truly and properly good. The argument plainly runs thus:

No works are good, which are not done as God hath willed and commanded them to be done. But no works done before justification are done as God hath willed and commanded them to be done. Therefore, no works done before justification are good.

The first proposition is self-evident. And the second, that no works done before justification are done as God hath willed and commanded them to be done, will appear equally plain and undeniable if we only consider God hath willed and commanded that *all our works* should *be done in charity*, in love, in that love to God which produces love to all mankind. But none of our works can be done in this love while the love of the Father (of God as our Father) is not in us. And this love cannot be in us till we receive the "Spirit of adoption crying in our hearts Abba, Father." If, therefore, God doth not *justify the ungodly*, and him that (in this sense) *worketh not*, then hath Christ died in vain; then, notwithstanding his death, can no flesh living be justified.

The Terms of Justification

4. But, on what terms, then, is he justified who is altogether *ungodly* and till that time *worketh not?* On one alone; which is faith: he "believeth in him that justifieth the ungodly." And "he that believeth is not condemned"; yea, he is "passed from death unto life." "For the righteousness (or mercy) of God is by faith of Jesus Christ unto all and upon all them that believe: whom God hath set forth for a propitiation through faith in his blood; that he might be just and (consistently with his justice) the justifier of him which believeth in Jesus." "Therefore, we conclude, that a man is justified by faith, without the deeds of the law," without previous obedience to the moral law, which, indeed, he could not till now perform. That it is the moral law, and that alone, which is here intended appears evidently from the words that follow. "Do we then make void the law through faith? God forbid! Yea, we establish the law." What law do we establish by faith? Not the ritual law, not the ceremonial law of Moses. In no wise; but the great unchangeable law of love, the holy love of God and of our neighbor.

Faith in general is a divine, supernatural *evidence* or *conviction,* "of things not seen," not discoverable by our bodily senses, as being either past, future, or spiritual. Justifying faith implies not only a divine evidence or conviction that "God was in Christ reconciling the world unto himself," but a sure trust and confidence that Christ died for *my* sins, that he loved *me,* and gave himself for *me.* And at [whatever] time a sinner thus believes, be it in early childhood, in the strength of his years, or when he is old and hoary-haired, God justifieth that ungodly one. God for the sake of his Son pardoneth and absolveth him, who had in him till then no good thing.

Repentance, indeed, God had given him before; but that repentance was neither more nor less than a deep sense of the want of all good and the presence of all evil. And whatever good he hath or doth from that hour when he first believes in God through Christ, faith does not *find* but *bring.* This is the fruit of faith. First the tree is good, and then the fruit is good also.

I cannot describe the nature of this faith better than in the words of our own church. "The only instrument of salvation" (whereof justification is one branch), "is faith: that is, a sure trust and confidence that God both hath and will forgive our sins, that he hath accepted us again into his favor, for the merits of Christ's death and passion. But here we must take heed that we do not halt with God through an inconstant, wavering faith. Peter coming to Christ upon the water, because he fainted in faith, was in danger of drowning. So we, if we begin to waver or doubt, it is to be feared that we shall sink as Peter did, not into the water, but into the bottomless pit of hell fire."

"Therefore, have a sure and constant faith, not only that the death of Christ is available for all the world, but that he hath made a full and sufficient sacrifice for *thee,* a perfect cleansing of *thy* sins, so that thou mayest say with the apostle he loved *thee,* and gave himself for *thee.* For this is to make Christ *thine own,* and to apply his merits unto *thyself.*"

By affirming that this faith is the term or condition of justification, I mean, first, that there is no justification without it. "He that believeth not, is condemned already. And so long as he believeth not, that condemnation cannot be removed, but "the wrath of God abideth on him."

As "there is no other name given under heaven" than that of Jesus of Nazareth, no other merit whereby a condemned sinner can ever be saved from the guilt of sin, so there is no other way of obtaining a share in his merit than *by faith in his name.* So that as long as we are without this faith, we are "strangers to the covenant of promise," we are "aliens from the commonwealth of Israel, and without God in the world." Whatsoever virtues (so called) a man may have—I speak of those unto whom the gospel is preached; for "what have I to do to judge them that are without?"— whatsoever good works (so accounted) he may do, it profiteth not; he is still a *child of wrath,* still under the curse, till he believes in Jesus.

The Condition of Justification

Faith, therefore, is the *necessary* condition of justification. Yea, and the *only necessary* condition thereof. This is the second point carefully to be observed: that the very moment God giveth faith (for *it is the gift of God*) to the "ungodly" that "worketh not," that "faith is counted to him for righteousness." He hath no righteousness at all antecedent to this, not so much as negative righteousness, or innocence. But "faith is imputed to him for righteousness" the very moment that he believeth. Not that God (as was observed before) thinketh him to be what he is not. But as "he made Christ to be sin for us," that is, treated him as a sinner, punishing him for our sins; so he counteth us righteous from the time we believe in him. That is, he doth not punish us for our sins, yea, treats us as though we were guiltless and righteous.

Surely the difficulty of assenting to the proposition that faith is the *only condition* of justification must arise from not understanding it. We mean thereby thus much, that it is the only thing without which no one is justified; the only thing that is immediately, indispensably, absolutely requisite in order

to pardon. As on the one hand, though a man should have everything else without faith, yet he cannot be justified; so on the other, though he be supposed to want everything else, yet if he hath faith, he cannot but be justified. For suppose a sinner of any kind or degree, in a full sense of his total ungodliness, of his utter inability to think, speak, or do good, and his absolute meetness for hell fire; suppose, I say, this sinner, helpless and hopeless, casts himself wholly on the mercy of God in Christ (which indeed he cannot do but by the grace of God), who can doubt but he is forgiven in that moment? Who will affirm that any more is *indispensably required* before that sinner can be justified?

Now, if there ever was one such instance from the beginning of the world (and have there not been, and are there not, ten thousand times ten thousand?) it plainly follows that faith is, in the above sense, the sole condition of justification.

It does not become poor, guilty, sinful worms, who receive whatsoever blessings they enjoy (from the least drop of water that cools our tongue to the immense riches of glory in eternity) of grace, of mere favor, and not of debt, to ask of God the reasons of his conduct. It is not meet for us to call him in question, "who giveth account to none of his ways"; to demand, "Why didst thou make faith the condition, the only condition of justification? Wherefore didst thou decree, *He that believeth,* and he only, *shall be saved*"? This is the very point on which Saint Paul so strongly insists in the ninth chapter of this epistle, that the terms of pardon and acceptance must depend not on us, but on him that calleth us; that there is no unrighteousness with God in fixing his own terms, not according to ours, but his own good pleasure; who may justly say, "I will have mercy on whom I will have mercy," namely, on him who believeth in Jesus. "So then, it is not of him that willeth, nor of him that runneth," to choose the condition on which he shall find acceptance, "but of God that showeth mercy," that accepteth none at all but of his own free love, his unmerited goodness. "Therefore, hath he mercy on whom he will have mercy," on those who believe on the Son of his love; "and whom he will," that is, those who believe not, "he hardeneth," leaves at last to the hardness of their hearts.

One reason, however, we may humbly conceive of God's fixing this condition of justification, "If thou believest in the Lord Jesus Christ, thou shalt be saved," was to *hide pride from man*. Pride had already destroyed the very angels of God, had cast down "a third part of the stars of heaven." It was, likewise, in great measure owing to this when the tempter said, "Ye shall be as gods," that Adam fell from his own steadfastness and brought sin and death into the world. It was, therefore, an instance of wisdom worthy of God to appoint such a condition of reconciliation for him and all his posterity as might effectually humble, might abase them to the dust. And such is faith. It is peculiarly fitted for this end; for he that cometh unto God by this faith must fix his eye singly on his own wickedness, on his guilt and helplessness, without having the least regard to any supposed good in himself, to any virtue or righteousness whatsoever. He must come as a *mere sinner*, inwardly and outwardly, self-destroyed and self-condemned, bringing nothing to God but ungodliness only, pleading nothing of his own but sin and misery.

Thus it is, and thus alone, when his *mouth is stopped* and he stands utterly *guilty before* God that he can look unto Jesus as the whole and sole propitiation for his sins. Thus only can he be "found in him" and receive the "righteousness which is of God by faith."

Thou ungodly one, who hearest or readest these words, thou vile, helpless, miserable sinner, I charge thee before God, the Judge of all, go straight unto him with all thy ungodliness. Take heed thou destroy not thy own soul by pleading thy righteousness more or less. Go as altogether ungodly, guilty, lost, destroyed, deserving, and dropping into hell; and thou shalt then find favor in his sight and know that he justifieth the ungodly. As such thou shalt be brought unto the blood of sprinkling, as an undone, helpless, damned sinner. Thus look unto Jesus! There is the Lamb of God who taketh away thy sins! Plead thou no works, no righteousness of thine own! No humility, contrition, sincerity! In no wise. That were, in very deed, to deny the Lord that bought thee. No: plead thou, singly, the blood of the covenant, the ransom paid for thy proud, stubborn, sinful soul. Who art thou, that now seest and feelest both thine inward and outward ungodliness? Thou art the man! I want thee for my Lord! I challenge *thee* for a child of God by faith! The Lord hath need of thee. Thou who feelest thou art just fit for hell, art just fit to advance his glory; the glory of his free grace, justifying the ungodly and him that worketh not. Oh, come quickly! Believe in the Lord Jesus; and thou, even thou, art reconciled to God.

Wesley's discussion of sin in believers opened a difficult and controversial aspect of his theology. Historically, this issue and the question of perfection gradually developed into holiness theology. In this sermon Wesley attempted to find a balance between what he perceived to be two extremes: the view that man is utterly and hopelessly in bondage to sin no matter what his state, and the other extreme, which teaches that sin no longer resides in man following regeneration.

For Wesley, the problem of sin in believers centered on inward sin—wrongs such as lust, greed, and pride. He acknowledged that inward sin is not eradicated from the believer and noted Paul's recognition that the flesh and Spirit are in conflict in the believer. For Wesley, the biblical evidence overwhelmingly refutes the notion that believers are without sin.

CHAPTER THIRTEEN

On Sin in Believers

"If any man be in Christ, he is a new creature" (2 Cor. 5:17).

Is there then sin in him that is in Christ? Does sin *remain* in one that believes in him? Is there any sin in them that are born of God or are they wholly delivered from it? Let no one imagine this to be a question of mere curiosity; or, that it is of little importance whether it be determined one way or the other. Rather it is a point of the utmost moment to every serious Christian; the resolving of which very nearly concerns both his present and eternal happiness.

And yet I do not know that ever it was controverted in the primitive church. Indeed, there was no room for disputing concerning it, as all Christians were agreed. And so far as I have ever observed, the whole body of ancient Christians, who have left us anything in writing, declare with one voice, that even believers in Christ, till they are "strong in the Lord and in the power of his might," have need to "wrestle with flesh and blood," with an evil nature, as well as "with principalities and powers."

And herein our own church (as indeed in most points) exactly copies after the primitive, declaring in her ninth article, "Original sin is the corruption of the nature of every man, whereby man is in his own nature inclined to evil, so that the flesh lusteth contrary to the spirit. And this infection of nature doth remain, yea in them that are regenerated; whereby the lust of the flesh is not subject to the law of God. And although

there is no condemnation for them that believe, yet this lust hath of itself the nature of sin."

The same testimony is given by all other churches, not only by the Greek and Romish church, but by every reformed church in Europe, of whatever denomination. Indeed, some of these seem to carry the thing too far, so describing the corruption of heart in a believer as scarce to allow that he has dominion over it, but rather is in bondage thereto. And, by this means, they leave hardly any distinction between a believer and an unbeliever.

To avoid this extreme, many well-meaning men, particularly those under the direction of the late Count Zinzendorf, ran into another, affirming, that "all true believers are not only saved from the *dominion* of sin, but from the *being* of inward as well as outward sin, so that it no longer *remains* in them." And from them, about twenty years ago, many of our countrymen imbibed the same opinion, that even the corruption *is no more* in those who believe in Christ.

It is true that when the Germans were pressed upon this head, they soon allowed (many of them at least), that "sin did still remain *in the flesh,* but not *in the heart* of a believer." And after a time, when the absurdity of this was shown, they fairly gave up the point, allowing that sin did still remain, though not reign, in him that is born of God.

But the English, who had received it

from them (some directly, some at second- or third-hand), were not so easily prevailed upon to part with a favorite opinion. And even when the generality of them were convinced it was utterly indefensible, a few could not be persuaded to give it up, but maintain it to this day.

For the sake of those who really fear God and desire to know "the truth as it is in Jesus," it may not be amiss to consider the point with calmness and impartiality. In doing this, I use indifferently the words *regenerate, justified,* or *believers.* Since, though they have not precisely the same meaning (the first implying an inward, actual change, the second a relative one, and the third, the means whereby both the one and the other are wrought), yet they come to one and the same thing, as everyone that believes is both justified and born of God.

By sin, I here understand inward sin; any sinful temper, passion, or affection such as pride, self-will, love of the world in any kind or degree; such as lust, anger, peevishness, [or] any disposition contrary to the mind which was in Christ.

The question is not concerning *outward sin,* whether a child of God *commit sin* or no. We all agree and earnestly maintain, "He that committeth sin is of the devil." We agree, "Whosoever is born of God doth not commit sin." Neither do we now inquire, whether inward sin will *always* remain in the children of God; whether sin will continue in the soul, as long as it continues in the body: nor yet do we inquire, whether a justified person may *relapse* either into inward or outward sin; but simply this, Is a justified or regenerate man freed from *all sin* as soon as he is justified? Is there then no sin in his heart?—nor ever after, unless he fall from grace?

The State of the Believer

We allow that the state of a justified person is inexpressibly great and glorious. He is born again, "not of blood, nor of the flesh, nor of the will of man, but of God." He is a child of God, a member of Christ, an heir of the kingdom of heaven. "The peace of God, which passeth all understanding, keepeth his heart and mind in Christ Jesus." His very body is a "temple of the Holy Ghost," and a "habitation of God through the Spirit." He is "created anew in Christ Jesus": he is *washed,* he is *sanctified.* His heart is purified by faith; he is cleansed "from the corruption that is in the world"; "the love of God is shed abroad in his heart by the Holy Ghost which is given unto him." And so long as he "walketh in love" (which he may always do), he worships God in spirit and in truth. He keepeth the commandments of God, and doeth those things that are pleasing in his sight; so exercising himself as to "have a conscience void of offence, toward God and toward man"; and he has power both over outward and inward sin, even from the moment he is justified.

But was he not then freed from all sin, so that there is no sin in his heart? I cannot say this; I cannot believe it; because Saint Paul says the contrary. He is speaking to believers, and describing the state of believers in general, when he says, "The flesh lusteth against the Spirit, and the Spirit against the flesh: these are contrary the one to the other," Galatians 5:17. Nothing can be more express. The apostle here directly affirms that the flesh, evil nature, opposes the Spirit even in believers; that even in the regenerate there are two principles "contrary the one to the other."

Again: when he writes to the believers at Corinth, to those who were sanctified in Christ Jesus, he says, "I, brethren, could not speak unto you as unto spiritual, but as unto carnal, as unto babes in Christ. Ye are yet carnal: for whereas there is among you envying and strife, are ye not carnal?" 1 Corinthians 3:1–3. Now here, the apostle speaks unto those who were unquestionably believers— whom in the same breath he styles his brethren in Christ—as being still, in a measure, carnal. He affirms there was envying (an evil temper), occasioning strife among them, and yet does not give the least intimation that they had lost their faith. Nay, he manifestly declares they had not, for then they would not have been babes in Christ. And (what is most remarkable of all) he speaks of being carnal, and babes in Christ, as one and the same thing; plainly showing that every believer is (in a degree) carnal while he is only a babe in Christ.

Two Contrary Principles

Indeed, this grand point, that there are two contrary principles in believers, nature and grace, the flesh and the Spirit, runs through all the epistles of Saint Paul, yea, through the holy Scriptures, almost all the directions and exhortations therein are founded on this supposition, pointing at wrong tempers or practices in those who are, notwithstanding, acknowledged by the inspired writers to be believers. And they are continually exhorted to fight with and conquer these [carnal temptations] by the power of the faith which was in them.

And who can doubt but there was faith in the angel of the church of Ephesus when our Lord said to him, "I know thy works, and thy labor, and thy patience: thou hast patience, and for my name's sake hast labored and hast not fainted," Revelation 2:2–4. But was there, meantime, no sin in his heart? Yea, or Christ would not have added,

"Nevertheless, I have somewhat against thee, because thou hast left thy first love." This was a real sin which God saw in his heart; of which, accordingly, he is exhorted to *repent*. And yet we have no authority to say that even then he had no faith.

Nay, the angel of the church at Pergamos also is exhorted to *repent*, which implies sin, though our Lord expressly says, "Thou hast not denied my faith," verses 13 and 16. And to the angel of the church in Sardis he says, "Strengthen the things which remain, that are ready to die." The good which remained was *ready to die* but was not actually dead, chapter 3:2. So there was still a spark of faith even in him which he is accordingly commanded to *hold fast*, verse 3.

Once more: when the apostle exhorts believers to "cleanse themselves from all filthiness of flesh and spirit," 2 Corinthians 7:1, he plainly teaches, that those believers were not yet cleansed therefrom.

Will you answer, "He that abstains from all appearance of evil," does *ipso facto* "cleanse himself from all filthiness"? Not in any wise. For instance: a man reviles me; I feel resentment, which is filthiness of spirit, yet I say not a word. Here, I "abstain from all appearance of evil," but this does not cleanse me from that filthiness of spirit as I experience to my sorrow.

And as this position—there is no sin in a believer, no carnal mind, no bent to backsliding—is thus contrary to the Word of God, so it is to the experience of his children. These continually feel a heart bent to backsliding, a natural tendency to evil, a proneness to depart from God and cleave to the things of earth. They are daily sensible of sin remaining in their heart—pride, self-will, unbelief—and of sin cleaving to all they speak and do, even their best actions and holiest duties. Yet at the same time they "know that they are of God"; they cannot doubt of it for a moment. They feel his Spirit clearly "witnessing with their spirit, that they are the children of God." They "rejoice in God through Christ Jesus, by whom they have now received the atonement," so that they are equally assured that sin is in them, and that "Christ [is] in them the hope of glory."

"But can Christ be in the same heart where sin is?" Undoubtedly he can. Otherwise, it never could be saved therefrom. Where the sickness is, there is the physician:

> Carrying on his work within,
> Striving till he cast out sin.

Christ indeed cannot *reign* where sin *reigns;* neither will he *dwell* where any sin is *allowed.* But he *is* and *dwells* in the heart of every believer, who is *fighting against* all sin; although it be not yet purified, according to the purification of the sanctuary.

A New Doctrine Refuted

It has been observed before, that the opposite doctrine, that there is no sin in believers, is quite new in the church of Christ; that it was never heard of for seventeen hundred years; never till it was discovered by Count Zinzendorf. I do not remember to have seen the least intimation of it, either in any ancient or modern writer; unless perhaps in some of the wild, ranting Antinomians. And these likewise say and unsay, acknowledging there is sin *in their flesh,* although no *sin in their heart.* But whatever doctrine is *new* must be *wrong;* for the *old* religion is the only *true* one; and no doctrine can be right, unless it is the very same "which was from the beginning."

One argument more against this new, unscriptural doctrine, may be drawn from the dreadful consequences of it. One says, "I felt anger today." Must I reply, "Then you have no faith"? Another says, "I know what you advise is good, but my will is quite averse to it." Must I tell him, "Then you are an unbeliever, under the wrath and the curse of God"? What will be the natural consequence of this? Why, if he believe what I say, his soul will not only be grieved and wounded, but perhaps utterly destroyed; inasmuch as he will "cast away" that "confidence which hath great recompense of reward": and having cast away his shield, how shall he "quench the fiery darts of the wicked one"? How shall he overcome the world? Seeing "this is the victory that overcometh the world, even our faith." He stands disarmed in the midst of his enemies, open to all their assaults. What wonder then if he be utterly overthrown; if they take him captive at their will; yea, if he fall from one wickedness to another, and never see good anymore? I cannot therefore by any means receive this assertion, that there is no sin in a believer from the moment he is justified. First, because it is contrary to the whole tenor of Scripture. Secondly, because it is contrary to the experience of the children of God. Thirdly, because it is absolutely new, never heard of in the world till yesterday. And, lastly, because it is naturally attended with the most fatal consequences; not only grieving those whom God hath not grieved, but perhaps dragging them into everlasting perdition.

However, let us give a fair hearing to the chief arguments of those who endeavor to support it. And it is, first, from Scripture they attempt to prove that there is no sin in a believer. They argue thus: "The Scripture says every believer is born of God, is clean, is holy, is sanctified, is pure in heart, has a new heart, is a temple of the Holy Ghost. Now, as 'that which is born of the flesh is flesh,' is altogether evil, so 'that which is born of the Spirit is spirit,' is altogether good. Again; a man cannot be clean, sanctified, holy, and at the same time unclean, unsanctified, unholy. He cannot be pure and impure, or have a new and an old heart together. Neither can his soul be unholy, while it is a temple of the Holy Ghost."

I have put this objection as strongly as possible, that its full weight may appear. Let us now examine it, part by part. "That which is born of the Spirit is spirit, is altogether good." I allow the text, but not the comment. For the text affirms this and no more, that every man who is "born of the Spirit" is a spiritual man. He is so. But so he may be and yet not be altogether spiritual. The Christians at Corinth were spiritual men, else they had been no Christians at all; and yet they were not altogether spiritual: they were still, in part, carnal—"But they were fallen from grace." Saint Paul says, no. They were even then babes in Christ. "But a man cannot be clean, sanctified, holy, and at the same time unclean, unsanctified, unholy." Indeed, he may. So the Corinthians were. "Ye are washed," says the apostle, "ye are sanctified"; namely, cleansed from "fornication, idolatry, drunkenness," and all other outward sin, 1 Corinthians 6:9–11. And yet, at the same time, in another sense of the word, they were unsanctified; they were not washed, not inwardly cleansed from envy, evil surmising, partiality. "But sure they had not a new heart and an old heart together." It is most sure they had; for at that very time, their hearts were *truly*, yet not *entirely* renewed. Their carnal mind was nailed to the cross; yet it was not wholly destroyed. "But could they

be unholy while they were 'temples of the Holy Ghost'?" Yes; that they were temples of the Holy Ghost is certain, 1 Corinthians 6:19; and it is equally certain, they were, in some degree, carnal, that is, unholy.

The New Man and the Old

"However, there is one Scripture [verse] more which will put the matter out of question: 'If any man be [a believer] in Christ, he is a new creature. Old things are passed away; behold all things are become new,' 2 Corinthians 5:17. Now, certainly, a man cannot be a new creature and an old creature at once." Yes, he may: he may be partly renewed, which was the very case with those at Corinth. They were doubtless "renewed in the spirit of their mind," or they could not have been so much as "babes in Christ"; yet they had not the whole mind which was in Christ, for they *envied* one another. "But it is said expressly, old things are passed away: all things are become new." But we must not so interpret the apostle's words, as to make him contradict himself. And if we will make him consistent with himself, the plain meaning of the words is this: his old judgment concerning justification, holiness, happiness, indeed concerning the things of God in general, is now passed away; so are his old desires, designs, affections, tempers, and conversation. All these are undeniably become new, greatly changed from what they were. And yet, though they are new, they are not wholly new. Still he feels, to his sorrow and shame, remains of the old man, too manifest taints of his former tempers and affections, though they cannot gain any advantage over him, as long as he watches unto prayer.

This whole argument, "If he is clean, he is clean"; "if he is holy, he is holy" (and twenty more expressions of the same kind may easily be heaped together); is really no better than playing upon words: it is the fallacy of arguing from a *particular* to a *general;* of inferring a general conclusion from particular premises. Propose the sentence entire, and it runs thus: "If he is holy *at all,* he is holy *altogether.*" That does not follow: every babe in Christ is holy, and yet not altogether so. He is saved from sin, yet not entirely; it *remains,* though it does not *reign.* If you think it does not *remain* (in babes at least, whatever be the case with young men, or fathers), you certainly have not considered the height, and depth, and length, and breadth of the law of God (even the law of love, laid down by Saint Paul in the thirteenth chapter of Corinthians), and that *every* disconformity to, or deviation from this law, *is sin.* Now, is there no disconformity to this in the heart or life of a believer? What may be in an adult Christian, is another question; but what a stranger must he be to human nature, who can possibly imagine that this is the case with every babe in Christ!

"But believers walk after the Spirit, Romans 8:1, and the Spirit of God dwells in them; consequently they are delivered from the guilt, the power, or in one word, the being of sin."

These are coupled together, as if they were the same thing. But they are not the same thing. The *guilt* is one thing, the *power* another, and the *being* yet another. That believers are delivered from the *guilt* and *power* of sin we allow; that they are delivered from the *being* of it we deny. Nor does it in any wise follow from these texts. A man may have the Spirit of God dwelling in him and may "walk after the Spirit," though he still feels "the flesh lusting against the Spirit."

"But the 'church is the body of Christ,' Colossians 1:24; this implies that its members are washed from all filthiness; otherwise, it will follow that Christ and Belial are incorporated with each other."

Nay, it will not follow from hence, "Those who are the mystical body of Christ still feel the flesh lusting against the Spirit," that Christ has any fellowship with the devil, or with that sin which he enables them to resist and overcome.

"But are not Christians 'come to the heavenly Jerusalem,' where 'nothing defiled can enter'?" Hebrews 12:22. Yes; "and to an innumerable company of angels, and to the spirits of just men made perfect." That is:

> Earth and heaven all agree;
> All is one great family.

And they are likewise holy and undefiled while they "walk after the Spirit," although sensible there is another principle in them and that "these are contrary to each other."

"But Christians are reconciled to God. Now this could not be, if any of the carnal mind remained; for this is enmity against God: consequently, no reconciliation can be effected, but by its total destruction."

We are "reconciled to God through the blood of the cross." And in that moment the corruption of nature, which is enmity with God, is put under our feet; the flesh has no more dominion over us. But it still *exists,* and it is still in its nature enmity with God, lusting against his Spirit.

"But 'they that are Christ's have crucified the flesh, with its affections and lusts,'" Galatians 5:24. They have so; yet it remains in them still, and often struggles to break from the cross. "Nay, but they have 'put off the old man with his deeds,'" Colossians 3:9. They have; and, in the sense above described, "old things are passed away; all things are become new." A hundred texts may be cited to the same effect, and they will all admit of the same answer: "But to say all in one word, 'Christ gave himself for the church, that it might be holy, and without blemish,'" Ephesians 5:25, 27. And so it will be in the end, but it never was yet from the beginning to this day.

"But let experience speak: all who are justified do at that time find an absolute freedom from all sin." That I doubt. But, if they do, do they find it ever after? Else you gain nothing. "If they do not, it is their own fault." That remains to be proved.

"But in the very nature of things, can a man have pride in him and not be proud; anger, and yet not be angry?"

A man may have *pride* in him, may think of himself in some particulars above what he ought to think (and so be proud in that particular), and yet not be a proud man in his general character. He may have *anger* in him, yea, and a strong propensity to furious anger, without *giving way* to it. "But can anger and pride be in that heart, where *only* meekness and humility are felt?" No: but *some* pride and anger may be in that heart where there is much humility and meekness.

"It avails not to say these tempers are there, but they do not *reign:* for sin cannot, in any kind or degree, exist where it does not reign, for *guilt* and *power* are essential properties of sin. Therefore, where one of them is, all must be."

An Appeal to Experience and Scripture

Strange indeed! "Sin cannot, in any kind or degree, *exist* where it does not *reign*." Absolutely contrary this to all experience, all Scripture, all common

sense. Resentment of an affront is sin; it is disconformity to the law of love. This has existed in me a thousand times. Yet it did not, and does not *reign.* "But *guilt* and *power* are essential properties of sin; therefore, where one is, all must be." No: in the instance before us, if the resentment I feel is not yielded to, even for a moment, there is no guilt at all, no condemnation from God upon that account. And in this case, it has no *power;* though it "lusteth against the Spirit," it cannot prevail. Here, therefore, as in ten thousand instances, there is *sin* without either *guilt* or *power.*

"But the supposing sin in a believer is pregnant with everything frightful and discouraging. It implies the contending with a power that has the possession of our strength, maintains his usurpation of our hearts, and there prosecutes the war in defiance of our Redeemer." Not so: the supposing sin is in us, does not imply that it has the possession of our strength, no more than a man crucified has the possession of those that crucify him. As little does it imply that "sin maintains its usurpation of our hearts." The usurper is dethroned. He remains, indeed, where he once reigned, but remains *in chains.* So that he does, in some sense, "prosecute the war," yet he grows weaker and weaker while the believer goes on from strength to strength, conquering and to conquer.

"I am not satisfied yet: he that hath sin in him is a slave to sin. Therefore, you suppose a man to be justified while he is a slave to sin. Now if you allow men may be justified while they have pride, anger, or unbelief in them; nay, if you aver, these are (at least for a time) in all that are justified; what wonder that we have so many proud, angry, unbelieving believers?"

I do not suppose any man who is justified is a slave to sin. Yet I do suppose sin remains (at least for a time) in all that are justified.

"But, if sin remains in a believer, he is a sinful man: if pride, for instance, then he is proud; if self-will, then he is self-willed; if unbelief, then he is an unbeliever, [and] consequently, no believer at all. How then does he differ from unbelievers, from unregenerate men?" This is still mere playing upon words. It means no more than if there is sin, pride, self-will, in him, then there is sin, pride, self-will. And this nobody can deny. In that sense, then, he is proud, or self-willed. But he is not proud or self-willed in the same sense that unbelievers are, that is, *governed* by pride or self-will. Herein he differs from unregenerate men. They *obey* sin; he does not. Flesh is in them both. But they *walk after the flesh;* he *walks after the Spirit.*

"But how can *unbelief* be in a believer?" That word has two meanings. It means either no faith or little faith; either the *absence* of faith or the *weakness* of it. In the former sense, unbelief is not in a believer; in the latter, it is in all babes. Their faith is commonly mixed with doubt or fear, that is, in the latter sense, with unbelief. "Why are ye fearful (says our Lord), o ye of little faith?" Again, "Oh, thou of little faith, wherefore didst thou doubt?" You see here was *unbelief* in *believers;* little faith and much unbelief.

"But this doctrine—that sin remains in a believer, that a man may be in the favor of God while he has sin in his heart—certainly tends to encourage men in sin." Understand the proposition right and no such consequence follows. A man may be in God's favor though he feel sin, but not if he *yields* to it. *Having sin,* does not forfeit the favor of God; *giving way to sin* does. Though the flesh in you "lust against the Spirit," you may still be a child of God; but if you "walk after the flesh," you are a child of the

devil. Now this doctrine does not encourage to *obey* sin, but to resist it with all your might.

The sum of all is this: there are in every person, even after he is justified, two contrary principles, nature and grace, termed by Saint Paul, the *flesh* and the *Spirit*. Hence, although even babes in Christ are *sanctified*, yet it is only in part. In a degree, according to the measure of their faith, they are spiritual; yet, in a degree they are carnal. Accordingly, believers are continually exhorted to watch against the flesh, as well as the world and the devil. And to this agrees the constant experience of the children of God. While they feel this witness in themselves, they feel a will not wholly resigned to the will of God. They know they are in him, and yet find a heart ready to depart from him, a proneness to evil in many instances, and a backwardness to that which is good. The contrary doctrine is wholly new, never heard of in the church of Christ, from the time of his coming into the world till the time of Count Zinzendorf; and it is attended with the most fatal consequences. It cuts off all watching against our evil nature, against the Delilah which we are told is gone, though she is still lying in our bosom. It tears away the shield of weak believers, deprives them of their faith, and so leaves them exposed to all the assaults of the world, the flesh, and the devil.

Let us, therefore, hold fast the sound doctrine "once delivered to the saints," and delivered down by them with the written Word to all succeeding generations; that although we are renewed, cleansed, purified, sanctified the moment we truly believe in Christ, yet we are not then renewed, cleansed, purified altogether. The flesh, the evil nature, still *remains* (though subdued) and wars against the Spirit. So much the more let us use all diligence in "fighting the good fight of faith." So much the more earnestly let us "watch and pray" against the enemy within. The more carefully let us take to ourselves and "put on the whole armor of God"; that, although "we wrestle" both "with flesh and blood, and with principalities, and powers, and wicked spirits in high places," we "may be able to withstand in the evil day, and having done all, to stand."

Are Christians perfect or imperfect? This question has caused much debate over the last several hundred years. Even as Wesley presented this message, he acknowledged the controversial nature of the topic. For him it was a both/and, not either/or, matter.

Christians are properly designated as imperfect in attributes. The regenerate man does not possess perfect knowledge or freedom from error. The very state of finiteness constitutes imperfection, or better, limitation. Man is not perfect in physical constitution for he eventually becomes ill or suffers injury.

Christians achieve perfection, according to Wesley, by virtue of the fact that they are born again (Rom. 6:1, 2). Regeneration brings the ability to put away outward sin. (Wesley acknowledged that Christians still maintain inward sin. See his sermon On Sin in Believers*). Yet, as the sermon progresses, we find Wesley strongly suggesting that both outward and inward sin is eradicated.*

CHAPTER FOURTEEN

On Christian Perfection

"Not as though I had already attained, either were already perfect" (Phil. 3:12).

There is scarce any expression in Holy Writ, which has given more offense than this. The word *perfect* is what many cannot bear. The very sound of it is an abomination to them. And whosoever *preaches perfection* (as the phrase is), asserts that it is attainable in this life, runs great hazard of being accounted by them worse than a heathen man or a publican.

And hence, some have advised wholly to lay aside the use of those expressions "because they have given so great offense." But are they not found in the oracles of God? If so, by what authority can any messenger of God lay them aside, even though all men should be offended? We have not so learned Christ, neither may we thus give place to the devil. Whatsoever God hath spoken, that will we speak, whether men will hear, or whether they will forbear, knowing that then alone can any minister of Christ be "pure from the blood of all men," when he hath "not shunned to declare unto them all the counsel of God."

We may not, therefore, lay these expressions aside, seeing they are the words of God and not of man. But we may and ought to explain the meaning of them, that those who are sincere of heart may not err to the right hand or left from the mark of the prize of their high calling. And this is the more needful to be done because, in the verse already repeated, the apostle speaks of himself as not perfect, "Not," saith he, "as though I were already perfect." And

yet immediately after, in the fifteenth verse, he speaks of himself, yea, and many others, as perfect: "Let us," saith he, "as many as be perfect, be thus minded."

In order, therefore, to remove the difficulty arising from this seeming contradiction, as well as to give light to them who are pressing forward to the mark, and that those who are lame be not turned out of the way, I shall endeavor to show, first, in what sense Christians *are not*, and secondly, in what sense they *are*, *perfect*.

Imperfect in Knowledge

In the first place, I shall endeavor to show in what sense Christians are *not perfect*. And both from experience and Scripture it appears, first, that they are not perfect in knowledge: they are not *so* perfect in this life, as to be free from ignorance. They know, it may be, in common with other men, many things relating to the present world; and they know, with regard to the world to come, the general truths which God hath revealed. They know, likewise (what the natural man receiveth not; for these things are spiritually discerned), "what manner of love" it is wherewith "the Father" hath loved them, "that they should be called the sons of God." They know the mighty working of his Spirit in their hearts and the wisdom of his providence, directing all their paths and causing all things to work together for their good. Yea, they know in every circumstance of life what the Lord requireth of them, and how to keep a conscience void of offense both toward God and toward man.

But innumerable are the things which they know not. Touching the Almighty himself, they cannot search him out to perfection. "Lo, these are but a part of his ways; but the thunder of his power, who can understand?" They cannot understand, I will not say, how "there are three that bear record in heaven, the Father, the Son, and the Holy Spirit, and these three are one"; or how the eternal Son of God "took upon himself the form of a servant"; but not any one attribute, not any one circumstance of the divine nature. Neither is it for them to know the times and seasons when God will work his great works upon the earth; no, not even those which he hath in part revealed by his servants and prophets since the world began. Much less do they know when God, having "accomplished the number of his elect, will hasten his kingdom"; when "the heavens shall pass away with a great noise and the elements shall melt with fervent heat."

They know not the reasons even of many of his present dispensations with the sons of men, but are constrained to rest here: though "clouds and darkness are round about him, righteousness and judgment are the habitation of his seat." Yea, often with regard to his dealings with themselves, doth their Lord say unto them, "What I do, thou knowest not now; but thou shalt know hereafter." And how little do they know of what is ever before them, of even the visible works of his hands? How "he spreadeth the north over the empty place, and hangeth the earth upon nothing"? How he unites all the parts of this vast machine by a secret chain which cannot be broken? So great is the ignorance, so

very little the knowledge of even the best of men!

Imperfect Through Error

No one, then, is so perfect in this life as to be free from ignorance, nor from mistake which, indeed, is almost an unavoidable consequence of it, seeing those who "know but in part," are ever liable to err, touching the things which they know not. It is true, the children of God do not mistake as to the things essential to salvation. They do not "put darkness for light, or light for darkness"; neither "seek death in the error of their life." For they are "taught of God"; and the way which he teaches them, the way of holiness, is so plain that "the wayfaring man, though a fool, need not err therein." But in things unessential to salvation they do err, and that frequently. The best and wisest of men are frequently mistaken, even with regard to facts; believing those things not to have been which really were, or those to have been done which were not. Or, suppose they are not mistaken as to the fact itself; they may be, with regard to its circumstances, believing them, or many of them, to have been quite different from what, in truth, they were. And hence cannot but arise many further mistakes. Hence, they may believe either past or present actions which were or are evil to be good, and such as were or are good to be evil. Hence also, they may judge not according to truth with regard to the characters of men, and that, not only by supposing good men to be better or wicked men to be worse than they are, but by believing them to have been or to be good men, who were or are very wicked; or perhaps those to have been or to be wicked men, who were or are holy and unreprovable.

Nay, with regard to the holy Scriptures themselves, as careful as they are to avoid it, the best of men are liable to mistake and do mistake day by day, especially with respect to those parts thereof which less immediately relate to practice. Hence, even the children of God are not agreed as to the interpretation of many places in Holy Writ; nor is their difference of opinion any proof that they are not the children of God on either side. But it is a proof, that we are not more to expect any living man to be infallible than to be omniscient.

If it be objected to what has been observed under this and the preceding head, that Saint John, speaking to his brethren in the faith, says, "Ye have an unction from the Holy One, and know all things," 1 John 2:20; the answer is plain: "Ye know all things that are needful for your souls' health." That the apostle never designed to extend this farther, that he could not speak it in an absolute sense, is clear, first, from hence; that otherwise he would describe the disciple as "above his Master," seeing Christ himself, as man, knew not all things. "Of that hour," saith he, "knoweth no man; no, not the Son, but the Father only." It is clear, secondly, from the apostle's own words that follow: "These things have I written unto you concerning them that deceive you"; as well as from his frequently repeated caution, "Let no man deceive you," which had been altogether needless, had not those very persons who had that unction from the Holy One been liable not to ignorance only, but mistake also.

Imperfect Due to Infirmities

Even Christians, therefore, are not *so* perfect as to be free either from ignorance or error. We may, thirdly, add, nor from infirmities. Only let us take care to understand this word aright; only let us not give that soft title to known sins as the manner of some is. So one man tells us, "Every man has his infirmity, and mine is drunkenness"; another has the infirmity of uncleanness; another, that of taking God's holy name in vain; and yet another has the infirmity of calling his brother, "Thou fool," or returning "railing for railing." It is plain that all you who thus speak, if ye repent not, shall, with your infirmities, go quick into hell! But I mean hereby not only those which are properly termed *bodily infirmities*, but all those inward or outward imperfections which are not of a moral nature. Such are weakness or slowness of understanding, dullness or confusedness of apprehension, incoherency of thought, irregular quickness or heaviness of imagination. Such (to mention no more of this kind) is the want of a ready or retentive memory. Such, in another kind, are those which are commonly, in some measure, consequent upon these; namely, slowness of speech, impropriety of language, ungracefulness of pronunciation; to which one might add a thousand nameless defects, either in conversation or behavior. These are the infirmities which are found in the best of men, in a larger or smaller proportion. And from these none can hope to be perfectly freed, till the spirit returns to God that gave it.

Imperfect Due to Temptation

Nor can we expect till then to be wholly free from temptation. Such perfection belongeth not to this life. It is true there are those who, being given up to work all uncleanness with greediness, scarce perceive the temptations which they resist not, and so seem to be without temptation. There are also many, whom the wise enemy of souls seeing to be fast asleep in the dead form of godliness, will not tempt to gross sin, lest they should awake before they drop into everlasting burnings. I know there are also children of God who, being now justified freely, having found redemption in the blood of Christ, for the present feel no temptation. God hath said to their enemies, "Touch not mine anointed, and do my children no harm." And for this season, it may be for weeks or months, he causeth them to ride on high places, he beareth them as on eagles' wings above all the fiery darts of the wicked one. But this state will not last always, as we may learn from that single consideration that the Son of God himself, in the days of his flesh, was tempted even to the end of his life. Therefore, so let his servant expect to be; for "it is enough that he be as his Master."

Christian perfection, therefore, does not imply (as some men seem to have imagined) an exemption from ignorance, or mistake, or infirmities, or temptations. Indeed, it is only another term for holiness. They are two names for the same thing. Thus, everyone that is holy is, in the Scripture sense, perfect. Yet we may, lastly, observe that neither in this respect is there any absolute perfection on earth. There is no *perfection of degrees,* as it is termed; none which does not admit of a continual increase. So that [no matter] how much any man has attained or in how high a degree he is perfect, he hath still need to "grow in grace" and daily to advance in the knowledge and love of God his Savior.

Growing Toward Perfection

In what sense, then, are Christians perfect? This is what I shall endeavor, in the second place, to show. But it should be premised that there are several stages in Christian life as in natural; some of the children of God being but newborn babes; others having attained to more maturity. And accordingly Saint John, in his first epistle, chapter 2:12 [and following], applies himself severally to those he terms little children, those he styles young men, and those whom he entitles fathers. "I write unto you, little children," saith the apostle, "because your sins are forgiven you": because thus far you have attained; being "justified freely," you "have peace with God, through Jesus Christ." "I write unto you, young men, because ye have overcome the wicked one," or (as he afterwards addeth) "because ye are strong, and the word of God abideth in you." Ye have quenched the fiery darts of the wicked one, the doubts and fears wherewith he disturbed your first peace; and the witness of God that your sins are forgiven now abideth in your heart. "I write unto you, fathers, because ye have known him that is from the beginning." Ye have known the Father, and the Son, and the Spirit of Christ in your inmost soul. Ye are "perfect men," being grown up to "the measure of the stature of the fullness of Christ."

It is of these chiefly I speak in the latter part of this discourse. For these only are perfect Christians. But even babes in Christ are in such a sense perfect, or born of God (an expression taken also in divers senses), as first not to commit sin. If any doubt of this privilege of the sons of God, the question is not to be decided by abstract reasonings, which may be drawn out into an endless length and leave the point just as it was before. Neither is it to be determined by the experience of this or that particular person. Many may suppose they do not commit sin, when they do; but this proves nothing either way. To the Law and to the testimony we appeal. "Let God be true, and every man a liar." By his Word will we abide and that alone. Hereby we ought to be judged.

Now, the Word of God plainly declares, that even those who are justified, who are born again in the lowest sense, "do not continue in sin"; that they cannot "live any longer therein," Romans 6:1, 2; that they are "planted together in the likeness of the death" of Christ, verse 5; that their "old man is crucified with him," the body of sin being destroyed so that henceforth they do not serve sin; that being dead with Christ they are free from sin, verses 6 and 7; that they are "dead unto sin and alive unto God," verse 11; that "sin hath no more dominion over them," who are "not under the law, but under grace"; but that these, "being free from sin, are become the servants of righteousness," verses 14 and 18.

Free from Outward Sin

The very least which can be implied in these words is that the persons spoken of therein, all real Christians or believers in Christ, are made free from outward sin. And the same freedom which Saint Paul here expresses in such variety of phrases, Saint Peter expresses in that one, 1 Peter 4:1, 2, "He that hath suffered in the flesh, hath ceased from sin, that he no longer should live to the desires of men, but to the will of God." For this *ceasing from sin*, if it be interpreted in the lowest sense, as regarding only the outward behavior, must denote the ceasing from the outward act, from any outward transgression of the Law.

But most express are the well-known words of Saint John, in the third chapter of his first epistle, verse 8, "He that committeth sin is of the devil; for the devil sinneth from the beginning. For this purpose the Son of God was manifested, that he might destroy the works of the devil. Whosoever is born of God, doth not commit sin; for his seed remaineth in him: and he cannot sin, because he is born of God." And those in the fifth, verse 18, "We know that whosoever is born of God, sinneth not; but he that is begotten of God keepeth himself, and that wicked one toucheth him not."

Indeed, it is said, this means only he sinneth not *willfully;* or he doth not commit sin *habitually;* or *not as other men do;* or *not as he did before.* But by whom is this said? By Saint John? No: there is no such word in the text; nor in the whole chapter; nor in all this epistle; nor in any part of his writings whatsoever. Why then, the best way to answer a bold assertion is simply to deny it. And if any man can prove it from the Word of God, let him bring forth his strong reasons.

And a sort of reason there is, which has been frequently brought to support these strange assertions, drawn from the examples recorded in the Word of God: "What!" say they, "did not Abraham himself commit sin, prevaricating, and denying his wife? Did not Moses commit sin, when he provoked God at the waters of strife? Nay, to produce one for all, did not even David, "the man after God's own heart," commit sin, "in the matter of Uriah the Hittite; even murder and adultery"? It is most sure he did. All this is true. But what is it you would infer from hence? It may be granted, first, that David, in the general course of his life, was one of the holiest men among the Jews; and, secondly, that the holiest men among the Jews did sometimes commit sin. But if you would hence infer that all Christians do and must commit sin as long as they live, this consequence we utterly deny; it will never follow from those premises.

A Different Dispensation

Those who argue thus seem never to have considered that declaration of our Lord, Matthew 11:11, "Verily, I say unto you, Among them that are born of women, there hath not risen a greater than John the Baptist: notwithstanding, he that is least in the kingdom of heaven is greater than he." I fear, indeed, there are some who have imagined "the kingdom of heaven," here to mean the kingdom of glory; as if the Son of God had just discovered to us that the least glorified saint in heaven is greater than any man up on earth! To mention this is sufficiently to refute it. There can, therefore, no doubt be made, but "the kingdom of heaven" here (as in the following verse, where it is said to be taken by force), or "the kingdom of God," as Saint Luke expresses it, is that kingdom of God on earth, whereunto all true believers in Christ, all real Christians, belong. In these words, then, our Lord declares two things: first, that before his coming in the flesh, among all the children of men there had not been one greater than John the Baptist; whence it evidently follows that neither Abraham, David, nor any Jew, was greater than John. Our Lord, secondly, declares that he which is least in the kingdom of God (in that kingdom which he came to set upon earth, and which the violent now began to take by force), is greater than he—not a greater prophet, as some have interpreted the word, for this is palpably false in fact; but greater in the grace of God and in the knowledge of our Lord Jesus Christ. Therefore, we cannot measure the privileges of real Christians, by those formerly given to the Jews. Their "ministration" (or dispensation) we allow "was glorious," but ours "exceeds in glory." So that whosoever would bring down the Christian dispensation to the Jewish standard, whosoever gleans up the examples of weakness recorded in the Law and the prophets, and thence infers that they who have "put on Christ" are endued with no greater strength, doth greatly err, neither "knowing the Scriptures, nor the power of God."

"But are there not assertions in Scripture which prove the same thing, if it cannot be inferred from those examples? Does not the Scripture say expressly, 'Even a just man sinneth seven times a day'?" I answer, no: the Scripture says no such thing. There is no such text in all the Bible. That which seems to be intended is the sixteenth verse of the twenty-fourth chapter of Proverbs, the words of which are these: "A just man falleth seven times, and riseth up again." But this is quite another thing. For, first, the words *a day*, are not in the text. So that if a just man falls seven times in his life, it is as much as is affirmed here. Secondly, here is no mention of *falling into sin* at all; what is here mentioned is *falling into temporal affliction*. This plainly appears from the verse before, the words of which are these: "Lay not wait, O wicked man, against the dwelling of the righteous; spoil not his resting place." It follows, "For a just man falleth seven times, and riseth up again: but the wicked shall fall into mischief." As if he had said, "God will deliver him out of his trouble; but when thou fallest, there shall be none to deliver thee."

"But however, in other places," continue the objectors, "Solomon does assert plainly, 'There is no man that sinneth not,' 1 Kings 8:46; 2 Chronicles 6:36; yea, 'there is not a just man upon earth that doeth good, and sinneth not,'" Ecclesiastes 7:20. I answer without doubt, thus it was in the days of Solomon. Yea, thus it was from Adam to Moses, from Moses to Solomon, and from Solomon to Christ. There was then no man that sinned not. Even from the day that sin entered into the world, there was not a just man upon earth that did good and sinned not, until the Son of God was manifested to take away our sins. It is unquestionably true that "the heir, as long as he is a child, differeth nothing from a servant." And that even so they (all the holy men of old who were under the Jewish dispensation) were, during that infant state of the church, "in bondage under the elements of the world." "But when the fullness of the time was come, God sent forth his Son, made under the Law, to redeem them that were under the Law, that they might receive the adoption of sons"—that they might receive that "grace which is now made manifest by the appearing of our Savior Jesus Christ; who hath abolished death, and brought life and immorality to light through the gospel," 2 Timothy 1:10. Now, therefore, they "are no more servants, but sons." So that whatsoever was the case of those under the law, we may safely affirm with Saint John that since the gospel was given, "He that is born of God sinneth not."

It is of great importance to observe, and that more carefully than is commonly done, the wide difference that is between the Jewish and the Christian dispensation; and that ground of it, which the same apostle assigns in the seventh chapter of his gospel, verse 38. After he had there related those words of our blessed Lord, "He that believeth on me, as the Scripture hath said, out of his belly shall flow rivers of living water," he immediately subjoins, "This spake he of the Spirit, *which they who should believe on him, were afterward to receive.* For the Holy Ghost was not yet given because Jesus was not yet glorified." Now the apostle cannot mean here (as some have taught) that the miracle-working power of the Holy Ghost was not yet given. For this was given; our Lord had given it to all his apostles when he first sent them forth to preach the gospel. He then gave them power over unclean spirits to cast them out; power to heal the sick; yea, to raise the dead. But the Holy Ghost was not yet given in his sanctifying graces as he was after Jesus was glorified. It was, then,

when "he ascended up on high, and led captivity captive" that he "received [those] gifts for men, yea, even for the rebellious, that the Lord God might dwell among them." And when the day of Pentecost was fully come, then first it was that they who "waited for the promise of the Father" were made more than conquerors over sin by the Holy Ghost given unto them.

That this great salvation from sin was not given till Jesus was glorified, Saint Peter also plainly testifies, where, speaking of his brethren in the flesh as now "receiving the end of their faith, the salvation of their souls," he adds, 1 Peter 1:9, 10, "Of which salvation the prophets have inquired and searched diligently, who prophesied of the grace [the gracious dispensation] that should come unto you: searching what, or what manner of time the Spirit of Christ which was in them did signify, when it testified beforehand the sufferings of Christ, and the glory [the glorious salvation] that should follow. Unto whom it was revealed, that not unto themselves, but unto us they did minister the things, which are now reported unto you by them that have preached the gospel unto you with the Holy Ghost sent down from heaven"; at the day of Pentecost and so unto all generations into the hearts of all true believers. On this ground, even "the grace which was brought unto them by the revelation of Jesus Christ," the apostle might well build that strong exhortation, "Wherefore girding up the loins of your mind, as he which hath called you is holy, so be ye holy in all manner of conversation."

Those who have duly considered these things must allow that the privileges of Christians are in no wise to be measured by what the Old Testament records concerning those who were under the Jewish dispensation; seeing the fullness of time is now come, the Holy

Ghost is now given; the great salvation of God is brought unto men by the revelation of Jesus Christ. The kingdom of heaven is now set up on earth; concerning which the Spirit of God declared of old (so far is David from being the pattern or standard of Christian perfection), "He that is feeble among them at that day shall be as David; and the house of David shall be as God, as the angel of the Lord before them," Zechariah 12:8.

New Testament Examples

If, therefore, you would prove that the apostle's words, "He that is born of God sinneth not," are not to be understood according to their plain, natural, obvious meaning, it is from the New Testament you are to bring your proofs; else you will fight as one that beateth the air. And the first of these which is usually brought is taken from the examples recorded in the New Testament. "The apostles themselves," it is said, "committed sin; nay, the greatest of them, Peter and Paul: Saint Paul, by his sharp contention with Barnabas, and Saint Peter, by his dissimulation at Antioch." Well, suppose both Peter and Paul did then commit sin; what is it you would infer from hence? That all the other apostles committed sin sometimes? There is no shadow of proof in this. Or would you thence infer that all the other Christians of the apostolic age committed sin? Worse and worse: this is such an inference as one would imagine a man in his senses could never have thought of. Or will you argue thus: "If two of the apostles did once commit sin, then all other Christians, in all ages, do and will commit sin as long as they live"? Alas, my brother! A child of common understanding would be ashamed of such reasoning as this. Least of all can you with any color of argument infer that any man *must* commit sin at all.

No; God forbid we should thus speak! No necessity of sinning was laid upon them. The grace of God was surely sufficient for them. And it is sufficient for us at this day. With the temptation which fell on them, there was a way to escape, as there is to every soul of man in every temptation. So that whosoever is tempted to any sin need not yield; for no man is tempted above that he is able to bear.

"But Saint Paul besought the Lord thrice, and yet he could not escape from his temptation." Let us consider his own words literally translated, "There was given to me a thorn in the flesh, an angel [or messenger] of Satan to buffet me. Touching this, I besought the Lord thrice, that it [or *he*] might depart from me. And he said unto me, my grace is sufficient for thee. For my strength is made perfect in weakness. Most gladly, therefore, will I rather glory in [these] my weaknesses, that the strength of Christ may rest upon me. Therefore I take pleasure in weaknesses; for when I am weak, then am I strong."

As this Scripture is one of the strongholds of the patrons of sin, it may be proper to weigh it thoroughly. Let it be observed, then, first, it does by no means appear that this thorn, whatsoever it was, occasioned Saint Paul to commit sin, much less laid him under any necessity of doing so. Therefore, from hence it can never be proved that any Christian must commit sin. Secondly, the ancient fathers inform us it was bodily pain—a violent headache, saith Tertullian; to which both Chrysostom and Saint Jerome agree. Saint Cyprian expresses it a little more generally in these terms: "Many and grievous torments of the flesh and of the body." Thirdly, to this exactly agree the apostle's own words: "A thorn to the flesh, to smite, beat, or buffet me"; "My strength is made perfect in weakness," which same word occurs no less than four times in these two verses only. But, fourthly, whatsoever it was, it could not be either inward or outward sin. It could no more be inward stirrings, than outward expressions, of pride, anger, or lust. This is manifest beyond all possible exception from the words that immediately follow: "Most gladly will I glory in [these] my weaknesses, that the strength of Christ may rest upon me." What! did he glory in pride, in anger, in lust? Was it through these *weaknesses* that the strength of Christ rested upon him? He goes on: "Therefore, I take pleasure in weaknesses; for when I am weak, then am I strong"; when I am weak *in body,* then am I strong *in spirit.* But will any man dare to say, when I am weak by pride or lust, then am I strong in spirit? I call you all to record this day, who find the strength of Christ resting upon you, can you glory in anger, or pride, or lust? Can you take pleasure in these infirmities? Do these weaknesses make you strong? Would you not leap into hell, were it possible, to escape them? Even by yourselves, then, judge whether the apostle could glory and take pleasure in them? Let it be lastly observed that this thorn was given to Saint Paul above fourteen years before he wrote this epistle, which itself was written several years before he finished his course. So that he had, after this, a long course to run, many battles to fight, many victories to gain, and great increase to receive in all the gifts of God and the knowledge of Jesus Christ. Therefore, from any spiritual weakness (if such had been) which he at that time felt, we could by no means infer, that he was never made strong; that Paul the aged, the father in Christ, still labored under the same weaknesses; that he was in no higher state till the day of his death. From all which it appears that this instance of Saint Paul is quite foreign to the question, and does in no wise clash with the assertion of Saint John, "He that is born of God sinneth not."

"But does not Saint James directly contradict this? His words are, 'In many things we offend all,' chapter 3:2: and is not offending the same as committing sin?" In this place, I allow it is: I allow the persons here spoken of did commit sin; yea, that they all committed many sins. But who are the persons here spoken of? Why, those many masters or teachers, whom God had not sent (probably the same vain men who taught that faith without works, which is so sharply reproved in the preceding chapter), not the apostle himself, nor any real Christian. That in the word *we* (used by a figure of speech common in all other, as well as the inspired writings), the apostle could not possibly include himself or any other true believer appears evident, first, from the same word in the ninth verse: "Therewith," said he, "bless we God, and therewith curse we men. Out of the same mouth proceedeth blessing and cursing." True, but not out of the mouth of the apostle, nor of anyone who is in Christ a new creature. Secondly, from the verse immediately preceding the text and manifestly connected with it: "My brethren, be not many masters *(or teachers),* knowing that we shall receive the greater condemnation. For in many things *we* offend all." *We!* Who? Not the apostles, nor true believers; but they who knew they should *receive the greater condemnation* because of those many offenses. But this could not be spoken of the apostle himself or of any who trod in his steps, seeing "there is no condemnation to them who walk not after the flesh, but after the Spirit." Nay, thirdly, the very verse itself proves that "we offend all," cannot be spoken either of all men or of all Christians: for in it there immediately follows the mention

offends not, as the *we* first mentioned did; from whom, therefore, he is professedly contradistinguished, and pronounced *a perfect man.*

So clearly does Saint James explain himself and fix the meaning of his own words. Yet, lest any one should still remain in doubt, Saint John, writing many years after Saint James, puts the matter entirely out of dispute, by the express declarations above recited. But here a fresh difficulty may arise: how shall we reconcile Saint John with himself? In one place he declares, "Whosoever is born of God doth not commit sin"; and again, "We know that he which is born of God sinneth not"; and yet in another, he saith, "If we say that we have no sin, we deceive ourselves, and the truth is not in us"; and again, "If we say that we have not sinned, we make him a liar, and his word is not in us."

As great a difficulty as this may at first appear, it vanishes away, if we observe, first, that the tenth verse fixes the sense of the eighth: "If we say we have no sin," in the former, being explained by, "If we say we have not sinned," in the latter verse. Secondly, that the point under present consideration is not, whether we *have or have not sinned heretofore;* and neither of these verses asserts, that we *do sin, or commit sin now.* Thirdly, that the ninth verse explains both the eighth and tenth: "If we confess our sins, he is faithful and just to forgive us our sins, and to cleanse us from all unrighteousness": as if he had said, "I have before affirmed, 'the blood of Jesus Christ cleanseth us from all sin'; but let no man say, I need it not; I have no sin to be cleansed from. If we say, that we have no sin, that we have not sinned, we deceive ourselves and make God a liar. But 'if we confess our sins, he is faithful and just,' not only 'to forgive our sins,' but also 'to cleanse us

from all unrighteousness,' that we may 'go and sin no more.'"

Saint John, therefore, is well consistent with himself, as well as with the other holy writers, as will yet more evidently appear if we place all his assertions touching this matter in one view: he declares, first, the blood of Jesus Christ cleanseth us from all sin. Secondly, no man can say, I have not sinned; I have no sin to be cleansed from. Thirdly, but God is ready both to forgive our past sins and to save us from them for the time to come. Fourthly, "These things write I unto you," saith the apostle, "that you may not sin. But if any man [should] sin," or *have sinned* (as the word might be rendered), he need not continue in sin; seeing "we have an Advocate with the Father, Jesus Christ the righteous." Thus far, all is clear. But lest any doubt should remain in a point of so vast importance, the apostle resumes this subject in the third chapter and largely explains his own meaning: "Little children," saith he, "let no man deceive you" [as though I had given any encouragement to those that continue in sin]. "He that doeth righteousness is righteous, even as he is righteous. He that committeth sin is of the devil; for the devil sinneth from the beginning. For this purpose the Son of God was manifested, that he might destroy the works of the devil. Whosoever is born of God doth not commit sin: for his seed remaineth in him; and he cannot sin, because he is born of God. In this the children of God are manifest, and the children of the devil," verses 7–10. Here the point, which till then might possibly have admitted of some doubt in weak minds, is purposely settled by the last of the inspired writers and decided in the clearest manner. In conformity, therefore, both to the doctrine of Saint John and to the whole tenor of the New Testament, we fix this conclusion:

a Christian is so far perfect as not to commit sin.

The Christian's Glorious Privilege

This is the glorious privilege of every Christian; yea, though he be but *a babe in Christ*. But it is only of those who *are strong* in the Lord "and have overcome the wicked one," or rather of those who "have known him that is from the beginning" that it can be affirmed they are in such a sense perfect as, secondly, to be freed from evil thoughts and evil tempers. First, from evil or sinful thoughts. But here let it be observed that thoughts concerning evil are not always evil thoughts; that a thought concerning sin and a sinful thought are widely different. A man, for instance, may think of a murder which another has committed, and yet this is no evil or sinful thought. So our blessed Lord himself doubtless thought of, or understood, the thing spoken by the devil when he said, "All these things will I give thee, if thou wilt fall down and worship me." Yet had he no evil or sinful thought nor, indeed, was capable of having any. And even hence it follows that neither real Christians: for "everyone that is perfect is as his Master," Luke 6:40. Therefore, if he was free from evil or sinful thoughts, so are they likewise.

And, indeed, whence should evil thoughts proceed in the servant who is *as his Master?* "Out of the heart of man [if at all] proceed evil thoughts," Mark 7:21. If, therefore, his heart be no longer evil, then evil thoughts can no longer proceed out of it. If the tree were corrupt, so would be the fruit: but the tree is good; the fruit, therefore, is good also," Matthew 12:33; our Lord himself bearing witness, "Every good tree bringeth forth good fruit. A good tree cannot bring forth evil fruit, [as] a cor-

rupt tree cannot bring forth good fruit," Matthew 7:17, 18.

The same happy privilege of real Christians Saint Paul asserts from his own experience. "The weapons of our warfare," saith he, "are not carnal, but mighty through God to the pulling down of strong holds; casting down imaginations" [or all the reasonings of pride and unbelief against the declarations, promises or gifts of God], "and every high thing that exalteth itself against the knowledge of God and bringing into captivity every thought to the obedience of Christ," 2 Corinthians 10:4.

And as Christians, indeed, are freed from evil thoughts, so are they, secondly, from evil tempers. This is evident from the above-mentioned declaration of our Lord himself: "The disciple is not above his Master; but everyone that is perfect shall be as his Master." He had been delivering, just before, some of the sublimest doctrines of Christianity and some of the most grievous to flesh and blood. "I say unto you, love your enemies, do good to them which hate you; and unto him that smiteth thee on the one cheek, offer also the other." Now these he well knew the world would not receive and, therefore, immediately adds, "Can the blind lead the blind? Will they not both fall into the ditch?" As if he had said, "Do not confer with flesh and blood, [concerning] these things— with men void of spiritual discernment, the eyes of whose understanding God hath not opened—lest they and you perish together." In the next verse he removes the two grand objections with which these wise fools meet us at every turn—"These things are too grievous to be borne"; or, "They are too high to be attained"—[by] saying, "The disciple is not above his Master"; therefore, if I have suffered, be content to tread in my steps. And doubt ye not then, but I will fulfill my Word: "For everyone that is perfect, shall be as his Master." But his Master was free from all sinful tempers. So, therefore, is his disciple, even every real Christian.

"Christ Liveth in Me"

Everyone of these can say with Saint Paul, "I am crucified with Christ, nevertheless I live; yet not I, but Christ liveth in me"—words that manifestly describe a deliverance from inward, as well as from outward sin. This is expressed both negatively, *I live not* (my evil nature, the body of sin, is destroyed); and positively, *Christ liveth in me* and, therefore, all that is holy, and just, and good. Indeed, both these, *Christ liveth in me* and *I live not*, are inseparably connected: for "what communion hath light with darkness, or Christ with Belial?"

He, therefore, who liveth in true believers, hath "purified their hearts by faith," insomuch that everyone that hath Christ in him, the hope of glory, "purifieth himself, even as he is pure," 1 John 3:3. He is purified from pride, for Christ was lowly of heart. He is pure from self-will or desire, for Christ desired only to do the will of his Father, and to finish his work. And he is pure from anger, in the common sense of the word, for Christ was meek and gentle, patient and longsuffering. I say, in the common sense of the word, for all anger is not evil. We read of our Lord himself, Mark 3:5, that he once "looked round with anger." "Grieved for the hardness of their hearts." So then he was angry at the sin, and in the same moment grieved for the sinners; angry or displeased at the offense, but sorry for the offenders. With anger, yea, hatred, he looked upon the thing; with grief and love upon the persons. Go, thou that art perfect, and do likewise. Be thus angry, and thou sinnest not, feeling a displacency at every offense against God, but only love and tender compassion to the offender.

Thus doth Jesus "save his people from their sins." And not only from outward sins, but also from the sins of their hearts; from evil thoughts and from evil tempers. "True," say some, "we shall thus be saved from our sins; but not till death; not in this world." But how are we to reconcile this with the express words of Saint John: "Herein is our love made perfect, that we may have boldness in the day of judgment: because as he is, so are we in this world"? The apostle here, beyond all contradiction, speaks of himself and other living Christians, of whom (as though he had foreseen this very evasion and set himself to overturn it from the foundation) he flatly affirms that not only at or after death but *in this world* they are as their Master, 1 John 4:17.

Exactly agreeable to this are his words in the first chapter of this epistle, verse 5: "God is light, and in him is no darkness at all. If we walk in the light, we have fellowship one with another, and the blood of Jesus Christ his Son cleanseth us from all sin." And again: "If we confess our sins, he is faithful and just to forgive us our sins, and to cleanse us from all unrighteousness." Now, it is evident the apostle here also speaks of a deliverance wrought *in this world*. For he saith not the blood of Christ will cleanse at the hour of death or in the day of judgment, but it "cleanseth" at the time present, "us" living Christians, "from all sin." And it is equally evident, that if *any sin* remain we are not cleansed from *all sin;* if *any* unrighteousness remain in the soul it is not cleansed from *all* unrighteousness. Neither let any sinner against his own soul say that this relates to justification only or the cleansing us from the guilt of sin; first, because this is confounding together what the apostle clearly distinguishes, who mentions first *to forgive us our sins,* and then *to cleanse us from all unrighteousness.* Secondly, because this is asserting justification by works in the strongest sense possible; it is making all inward as well as outward holiness necessarily previous to justification. For, if the cleansing here spoken of is no other than the cleansing us from the guilt of sin, then we are not cleansed from guilt, are not justified, unless on condition of *walking in the light, as he is in the light.* It remains then, that Christians are saved in this world from all sin, from all unrighteousness; that they are now in such a sense perfect as not to commit sin and to be freed from evil thoughts and evil tempers.

Thus hath the Lord fulfilled the things he spoke by his holy prophets which have been since the world began—by Moses in particular, saying, Deuteronomy 30:6, I "will circumcise thine heart, and the heart of thy seed, to love the Lord thy God with all thy heart, and with all thy soul"; by David, crying out, "Create in me a clean heart, and renew a right spirit within me"; and most remarkably by Ezekiel, in those words: "Then will I sprinkle clean water upon you, and ye shall be clean: from all your filthiness, and from all your idols, will I cleanse you. A new heart also will I give you, and a new spirit will I put within you, and cause you to walk in my statutes, and ye shall keep my judgments, and do them. Ye shall be my people, and I will be your God. I will also save you from all your uncleannesses. Thus saith the Lord God, in the day that I shall have cleansed you from all your iniquities, the heathen shall know that I the Lord build the ruined places; I the Lord have spoken it, and I will do it," Ezekiel 36:25.

"Having, therefore, these promises, dearly beloved," both in the Law and in the prophets, and having the prophetic words confirmed unto us in the Gospel by our blessed Lord and his apostles; "let us cleanse ourselves from all filthiness of flesh and spirit, perfecting holiness in the fear of God." "Let us fear, lest [so many] promises being made us of entering into his rest [which he that hath entered into, has ceased from his own works], any of us should come short of it." "This one thing let us do, forgetting those things which are behind, and reaching forth unto those things which are before, let us press toward the mark, for the prize of the high calling of God in Christ Jesus"; crying unto him day and night till we also are "delivered from the bondage of corruption, into the glorious liberty of the sons of God!"

Of all the recorded words spoken by Christ, none seem to achieve the familiarity among Christians and non-Christians as those found in the Sermon on the Mount, especially the Beatitudes.

This selection demonstrates Wesley at his best as an expositor of the Scripture. As he makes his way through the Beatitudes, the reader is rewarded with the care of interpretation and application. Wesley handles the passages as if he, being a spiritual surgeon, were performing an operation on the heart of each reader, cutting away at the infection that diminishes the Christian's ability to live a life pleasing to God.

For Wesley, the Beatitudes were essential instruction for Christian behavior, instructing us on the proper response to the most difficult situations, promising us ultimate victory over the ills of this world, and instructing us for now to tolerate the rules of conduct imposed upon us and to respond in the same manner as our example, Jesus Christ, responded.

CHAPTER FIFTEEN

Upon Our Lord's Sermon on the Mount

Part 1

"Blessed are the meek: for they shall inherit the earth.
"Blessed are they which do hunger and thirst after righteousness: for they shall be filled.
"Blessed are the merciful: for they shall obtain mercy" (Matt. 5:5–7).

When "the winter is past," when "the time of singing is come, and the voice of the turtle is heard in the land"; when he that comforts the mourners is now returned, "that he may abide with them forever"; when, at the brightness of his presence, the clouds disperse, the dark clouds of doubt and uncertainty, the storms of fear flee away, the waves of sorrow subside, and their spirit again rejoiceth in God their Savior; then is it that this word is eminently fulfilled; then those whom he hath comforted can bear witness, "Blessed," or happy, "are the meek, for they shall inherit the earth."

On Meekness

But who are the meek? Not those who grieve at nothing, because they know nothing; who are not discomposed at the evils that occur, because they discern not evil from good. Not those who are sheltered from the shocks of life by a stupid insensibility, who have either by nature or art the virtue of stocks and stones and resent nothing, because they feel nothing. Brute philosophers are wholly unconcerned in this matter. Apathy is as far from meekness as from humanity. So that one would not easily conceive how any Christians of the purer ages, especially any of the fathers of the church, could confound these and mistake one of the foulest errors of heathenism for a branch of true Christianity.

Nor does Christian meekness imply the being without zeal for God any more than it does ignorance or insensibility. No; it keeps clear of every extreme, whether in excess or defect. It does not destroy but balance the affections which the God of nature never designed should be rooted out by grace, but only brought and keep under due regulations. It poises the mind aright. It holds an even scale without regard to anger, and sorrow, and fear; reserving the mean in every circumstance of life, and not declining either to the right hand or the left.

Meekness therefore seems properly to relate to ourselves, but it may be referred either to God or our neighbor. When this due composure of mind has reference to God, it is usually termed resignation, a calm acquiescence in whatsoever is his will concerning us, even though it may not be pleasing to nature; saying continually, "It is the Lord; let him do what seemeth him good." When we consider it more strictly with regard to ourselves, we style it patience or contentedness. When it is exerted toward other men, then it is mildness to the good and gentleness to the evil.

They who are truly meek can clearly discern what is evil, and they can also suffer it. They are sensible of everything of this kind, but still meekness holds the reins. They are exceeding "zealous for the Lord of Hosts," but their zeal is always guided by knowledge, and tempered in every thought, word, and work with the love of man as well as the love of God. They do not desire to extinguish any of the passions which God has for wise ends implanted in their nature, but they have the mastery of all; they hold them all in subjection and employ them only in subservience to those ends. And thus even the harsher and more unpleasing passions are applicable to the noblest purposes; even hatred, anger, and fear, when engaged against sin and regulated by faith and love, are as walls and bulwarks to the soul so that the wicked one cannot approach to hurt it.

It is evident this divine temper is not only to abide but to increase in us day by day. Occasions of exercising, and thereby increasing it, will never be wanting while we remain upon earth. "We have need of patience, that after we have done [and suffered] the will of God, we may receive the promise." We have need of resignation, that we may in all circumstances say, "Not as I will, but as thou wilt." And we have need of "gentleness toward all men"; but especially toward the evil and unthankful. Otherwise, we shall be overcome of evil instead of overcoming evil with good.

On Anger

Nor does meekness restrain only the outward act, as the scribes and Pharisees taught of old, and the miserable teachers who are not taught of God will

not fail to do in all ages. Our Lord guards against this and shows the true extent of it in the following words: "Ye have heard, that it was said by them of old time, thou shalt not kill; and whosoever shall kill shall be in danger of the judgment," verse 21; "But I say unto you, that whosoever is angry with his brother without a cause, shall be in danger of the judgment: and whosoever shall say to his brother, Raca, shall be in danger of the council: but whosoever shall say, Thou fool, shall be in danger of hell fire."

Our Lord here ranks under the head of murder even that anger which goes no farther than the heart, which does not show itself by any outward unkindness, no, not so much as a passionate word. "Whosoever is angry with his brother," with any man living, seeing we are all brethren; whosoever feels any unkindness in his heart, any temper contrary to love; whosoever is angry without a cause, without a sufficient cause, or farther than that cause requires, "shall be in danger of the judgment"; *shall*, in that moment, *be obnoxious to* the righteous judgment of God.

But would not one be inclined to prefer the reading of *without a cause?* Is it not entirely superfluous? For if *anger at persons* be a temper contrary to love, how can there be a cause, a sufficient cause for it, any that will justify it in the sight of God?

Anger at sin we allow. In this sense, we may be angry and yet we sin not. In this sense our Lord himself is once recorded to have been angry. "He looked round about upon them with anger, being grieved for the hardness of their hearts." He was grieved at the sinners and angry at the sin. And this is undoubtedly right before God.

"And whosoever shall say to his brother, Raca," whosoever shall give way to anger, so as to utter any contemptuous word. It is observed by commentators, that "raca" is a Syriac word, which properly signifies, *empty, vain, foolish;* so that it is as inoffensive an expression as can well be used toward one at whom we are displeased. And yet, whosoever shall use this, as our Lord assures us, "shall be in danger of the council"; rather, shall be obnoxious thereto: he shall be liable to a severer sentence from the Judge of all the earth.

"But whosoever shall say, Thou fool," whosoever shall so give place to the devil, as to break out into reviling, into designedly reproachful and contumelious language, "shall be obnoxious to hell fire": shall, in that instant, be liable to the highest condemnation. It should be observed that our Lord describes all these as obnoxious to capital punishment. The first to strangling, usually inflicted on those who were condemned in one of the inferior courts; the second to stoning, which was frequently inflicted on those who were condemned by the great council at Jerusalem; the third to burning alive, inflicted only on the highest offenders in the "valley of the sons of Hinnom."

And whereas men naturally imagine that God will excuse their defect in some duties for their exactness in others, our Lord next takes care to cut off that vain though common imagination. He shows that it is impossible for any sinner to *commute* with God, who will not accept one duty for another nor take a part of obedience for the whole. He warns us that the performing our duty to God will not excuse us from our duty to our neighbor; that works of piety, as they are called, will be so far from commending us to God, if we are wanting in charity, that, on the contrary, that want of charity will make all those works an abomination to the Lord.

"Therefore, if thou bring thy gift to the altar, and there rememberest that thy brother hath aught against thee,"—

on account of thy unkind behavior toward him, of thy calling him, Raca, or Thou fool; think not that thy gift will atone for thy anger; or that it will find any acceptance with God, so long as thy conscience is defiled with the guilt of unrepented sin. "Leave there thy gift before the altar, and go thy way, first be reconciled to thy brother" (at least do all that in thee lies toward being reconciled), "and then come and offer thy gift," verses 23 and 24.

And let there be no delay in what so nearly concerneth thy soul. "Agree with thine adversary quickly"; now, upon the spot; "while thou art in the way with him"; if it be possible, before he go out of thy sight, "lest at any time the adversary deliver thee to the judge," lest he appeal to God, the Judge of all; "and the judge deliver thee to the officer," to Satan, the executioner of the wrath of God; "and thou be cast into prison," into hell, there to be reserved to the judgment of the great day. "Verily, I say unto thee, Thou shalt by no means come out thence, till thou hast paid the uttermost farthing." But this it is impossible for thee ever to do, seeing thou hast nothing to pay. Therefore, if thou art once in that prison, the smoke of thy torment must "ascend up forever and ever."

Meanwhile, "The meek shall inherit the earth." Such is the foolishness of worldly wisdom! The wise of the world had warned them again and again, "That if they did not resent such treatment, if they would tamely suffer themselves to be thus abused, there would be no living for them upon earth; that they would never be able to procure the common necessaries of life, nor to keep even what they had; that they could expect no peace, no quiet possession, no enjoyment of anything." Most true. Suppose there were no God in the world, or, suppose he did not concern himself with the children of men; but "when God ariseth to judgment, and to help all the meek upon earth," how doth he laugh all this heathen wisdom to scorn, and turn the "fierceness of man to his praise"! He takes a peculiar care to provide them with all things needful for life and godliness; he secures to them the provision he hath made, in spite of the force, fraud, or malice of men; and what he secures he gives them richly to enjoy. It is sweet to them, be it little or much. As in patience they possess their souls, so they truly possess whatever God hath given them. They are always content, always pleased with what they have: it pleases them, because it pleases God: so that while their heart, their desire, their joy is in heaven, they may truly be said to "inherit the earth."

But there seems to be a yet further meaning in these words, even that they shall have a more eminent part in "the new earth, wherein dwelleth righteousness"; in that inheritance, a general description of which (and the particulars we shall know hereafter) Saint John hath given in the twentieth chapter of the Revelation: "And I saw an angel come down from heaven, and he laid hold on the dragon, that old serpent, and bound him a thousand years. And I saw the souls of them that were beheaded for the witness of Jesus, and for the Word of God, and of them which had not worshipped the beast, neither his image, neither had received his mark upon their foreheads or in their hands; and they lived and reigned with Christ a thousand years. But the rest of the dead lived not again, until the thousand years were finished. This is the first resurrection. Blessed and holy is he that hath part in the first resurrection: on such the second death hath no power, but they shall be priests of God and of Christ, and shall reign with him a thousand years."

Pursuing Righteousness

Our Lord has hitherto been more immediately employed in removing the hindrances of true religion: such is pride, the first grand hindrance of all religion, which is taken away by poverty of spirit; levity and thoughtlessness, which prevent any religion from taking root in the soul till they are removed by holy mourning; such are anger, impatience, discontent, which are all healed by Christian meekness. And when once these hindrances are removed, these evil diseases of the soul, which were continually raising false cravings therein, and filling it with sickly appetites, the native appetite of a heaven-born spirit returns; it hungers and thirsts after righteousness. And, "Blessed are they which do hunger and thirst after righteousness; for they shall be filled."

Righteousness, as was observed before, is the image of God, the mind which was in Christ Jesus. It is every holy and heavenly temper in one, springing from, as well as terminating in, the love of God as our Father and Redeemer and the love of all men for his sake.

"Blessed are they which do hunger and thirst after" this. In order fully to understand which expression, we should observe, first, that hunger and thirst are the strongest of all our bodily appetites. In like manner this hunger in the soul, this thirst after the image of God, is the strongest of all our spiritual appetites, when it is once awakened in the heart: yea, it swallows up all the rest in that one great desire—to be renewed after the likeness of him that created us. We should, secondly, observe that from the time we begin to hunger and thirst, those appetites do not cease but are more and more craving and importunate, till we either eat and drink or die. And even so, from the time that we begin to hunger and thirst after the whole mind which was in Christ, these spiritual appetites do not cease but cry after their food with more and more importunity; nor can they possibly cease before they are satisfied, while there is any spiritual life remaining. We may, thirdly, observe that hunger and thirst are satisfied with nothing but meat and drink. If you would give to him that is hungry all the world beside, all the elegance of apparel, all the trappings of state, all the treasure upon earth, yea, [much] gold and silver; if you would pay him ever so much honor, he regards it not: all these things are then of no account with him. He would still say, "These are not the things I want: give me food, or else I die." The very same is the case with every soul that truly hungers and thirsts after righteousness. He can find no comfort in anything but this: he can be satisfied with nothing else. Whatever you offer besides, it is lightly esteemed: whether it be riches, or honor, or pleasure, he still says, "This is not the thing which I want! Give me love, or else I die!"

And it is as impossible to satisfy such a soul, a soul that is athirst for God, the living God, with what the world accounts religion, as with what they account happiness. The religion of the world implies three things: (1) the doing no harm, the abstaining from outward sin; at least from such as is scandalous, as robbery, theft, common swearing, drunkenness, (2) the doing good, the relieving the poor; the being charitable, as it is called, (3) the using the means of grace; at least the going to church and to the Lord's supper. He in whom these three marks are found is termed by the world a religious man. But will this satisfy him who hungers after God? No: it is not food for his soul. He wants a religion of a nobler kind, a religion higher and deeper than this. He can no more feed on this poor, shallow, formal thing

than he can "fill his belly with the east wind." True, he is careful to abstain from the very appearance of evil; he is zealous of good works; he attends all the ordinances of God; but all this is not what he longs for. This is only the outside of that religion which he insatiably hungers after. The knowledge of God in Christ Jesus—"the life which is hid with Christ in God"; the being "joined unto the Lord in one spirit"; the having "fellowship with the Father and the Son"; the "walking in the light as God is in the light"; the being "purified even as he is pure"—this is the religion, the righteousness he thirst after. Nor can he rest, till he thus rests in God.

"Blessed are they who [thus] hunger and thirst after righteousness: for they shall be filled." They shall be filled with the things which they long for; even with righteousness and true holiness. God shall satisfy them with the blessings of his goodness, with the felicity of his chosen. He shall feed them with the bread of heaven, with the manna of his love. He shall give them to drink of his pleasures as out of the river which he that drinketh of shall never thirst, only for more and more of the water of life. This thirst shall endure forever.

> The painful thirst, the fond desire,
>   Thy joyous presence shall remove:
> But my full soul shall still require
>   A whole eternity of love.

Whosoever then thou art, to whom God hath given to "hunger and thirst after righteousness," cry unto him that thou mayest never lose that inestimable gift, that this divine appetite may never cease. If many rebuke thee and bid thee hold thy peace, regard them not; yea, cry so much the more, "Jesus, Master, have mercy on me!" "Let me not live, but to be holy as thou art holy!" No more "spend thy money for that which is not bread, nor thy labor for that which satisfieth not." Canst thou hope to dig happiness out of the earth, to find it in the things of the world? O trample underfoot all its pleasures, despise its honors, count its riches as dung and dross, yea, and all the things which are beneath the sun, "for the excellency of the knowledge of Christ Jesus," for the entire renewal of thy soul in that image of God wherein it was originally created. Beware of quenching that blessed hunger and thirst by what the world calls religion; a religion of form, of outside show which leaves the heart as earthly and sensual as ever. Let nothing satisfy thee but the power of godliness, but a religion that is spirit and life; thy dwelling in God and God in thee; the being an inhabitant of eternity; the entering in by the blood of sprinkling "within the veil," and sitting "in heavenly places with Christ Jesus."

And the more they are filled with the life of God, the more tenderly will they be concerned for those who are still without God in the world, still dead in trespasses and sins. Nor shall this concern for others lose its reward. "Blessed are the merciful, for they shall obtain mercy."

On Love

The word used by our Lord more immediately implies the compassionate, the tenderhearted; those who, far from despising, earnestly grieve for those that do not hunger after God. This eminent part of brotherly love is here, by a common figure, put for the whole; so that "the merciful," in the full sense of the term, are they who love their neighbors as themselves.

Because of the vast importance of this love—without which, "though we spake with the tongues of men and angels, though we had the gift of prophecy, and understood all mysteries, and all knowledge, though we had all faith so as to remove mountains; yea, though we gave all our goods to feed the poor, and our very bodies to be burned, it would profit us nothing,"—the wisdom of God has given us by the apostle Paul, a full and particular account of it; by considering which we shall most clearly discern who are the merciful that shall obtain mercy.

"Charity," or love (as it were to be wished it had been rendered throughout, being a far plainer and less ambiguous word), the love of our neighbor as Christ hath loved us "suffereth long"; is patient toward all men: it suffers all the weakness, ignorance, errors, infirmities, all the frowardness and littleness of faith of the children of God; all the malice and wickedness of the children of the world. And it suffers all this, not only for a time, for a short season, but to the end; still feeding our enemy when he hungers; if he thrists, still giving him drink; thus, continually "heaping coals of fire," of melting love "upon his head."

And in every step toward this desirable end, the "overcoming evil with good," "Love is kind." It is *soft, mild, benign*. It stands at the utmost distance from moroseness, from all harshness or sourness of spirit, and inspires the sufferer at once with the most amiable sweetness and the most fervent and tender affection.

Consequently, "Love envieth not." It is impossible it should; it is directly opposite to that baneful temper. It cannot be that he who has this tender affection to all, who earnestly wishes all temporal and spiritual blessings, all good things in this world and the world to come, to every soul that God hath made, should be pained at his bestowing any good gift on any child of man. If he has himself received the same, he does not grieve but rejoices that another partakes of the common benefit. If he has not, he blesses God that his brother at least has, and is herein happier than himself. And the greater his love, the more does he rejoice in the blessings of all mankind, the farther is he removed from every kind and degree of envy toward any creature.

Love *is not rash* or *hasty* in judging; it will not hastily condemn anyone. It does not pass a severe sentence on a slight or sudden view of things. It first weighs all the evidence, particularly that which is brought in favor of the accused. A true lover of his neighbor is not like the generality of men who, even in cases of the nicest nature, "see a little, presume a great deal, and so jump to the conclusion." No: he proceeds with wariness and circumspection, taking heed to every step; willingly subscribing to that rule of the ancient heathen, (Oh, where will the modern Christian appear!) "I am so far from lightly believing what one man says against another, that I will not easily believe what a man says against himself. I will always allow him second thoughts, and many times counsel too."

It follows, love "is not puffed up." It does not incline or suffer any man "to think more highly of himself than he ought to think"; but rather to think soberly: yea, it humbles the soul unto the dust. It destroys all high conceits engendering pride, and makes us rejoice to be as nothing, to be little and vile, the lowest of all, the servant of all. They who are "kindly affectioned one to another with brotherly love," cannot but "in honor prefer one another." Those who, having the same love, are of one accord, do in lowliness of mind "each esteem others better than themselves."

"It doth not behave itself unseemly": it is not rude or willingly offensive to any. It "renders to all their due: fear to whom fear, honor to whom honor";

courtesy, civility, humanity to all the world; in their several degrees "honoring all men." A late writer defines good breeding, the highest degree of it, [as] politeness, "a continual desire to please appearing in all the behavior." But if so, there is none so well bred as a Christian, a lover of all mankind. For he cannot but desire to "please all men for their good to edification"; and this desire cannot be hid; it will necessarily appear in all his intercourse with men. For his "love is without dissimulation": it will appear in all his actions and conversations, yea, and will constrain him, though without guile, to "become all things to all men, if by any means he may save some."

And in becoming all things to all men, "love seeketh not her own." In striving to please all men, the lover of mankind has no eye at all to his own temporal advantage. He covets no man's silver, or gold, or apparel. He desires nothing but the salvation of their souls. Yea, in some sense, he may be said *not to seek his own* spiritual any more than temporal advantage; for while he is on the full stretch to save their souls from death, he, as it were, forgets himself. He does not think of himself so long as that zeal for the glory of God swallows him up. Nay, at sometimes he may almost seem, through an excess of love, to give up himself, both his soul and his body; while he cries out with Moses, "Oh! this people have sinned a great sin; yet now, if thou wilt, forgive their sin; and if not, blot me out of the book which thou hast written!" Exodus 32:32, 33. Or with Saint Paul: "I could wish that myself were accursed from Christ, for my brethren, my kinsmen according to the flesh!" Romans 9:3.

No marvel that such "love is not provoked." Let it be observed, the word *easily,* strangely inserted in the translation, is not in the original. Saint Paul's words are absolute. "Love is not provoked"; it is not provoked to unkindness toward anyone. Occasions, indeed, will frequently occur, outward provocations of various kinds. But love does not yield to provocation; it triumphs over all. In all trials it looketh unto Jesus and is more than conqueror in his love.

It is not improbable that our translators inserted that word, as it were, to *excuse* the apostle; who, as they supposed, might otherwise appear to be wanting in the very love which he so beautifully describes. They seem to have supposed this from a phrase in the Acts of the Apostles, which is likewise very inaccurately translated. When Paul and Barnabas disagreed concerning John, the translation runs thus, "And the contention was so sharp between them that they departed asunder," Acts 15:39. This naturally induces the reader to suppose that they were equally sharp therein: that Saint Paul, who was undoubtedly right, with regard to the point in question (it being quite improper to take John with them again, who had deserted them before), was as much provoked as Barnabas, who gave such a proof of his anger as to leave the work for which he had been set apart by the Holy Ghost. In consequence of which Barnabas left Saint Paul, took John, and went his own way. Paul then "chose Silas, and departed, being recommended by the brethren to the grace of God" (which is not said concerning Barnabas); "and he went through Syria and Cilicia," as he had proposed, "confirming the churches." But to return.

Love prevents a thousand provocations which would otherwise arise, because it "thinketh no evil." Indeed the merciful man cannot avoid knowing many things that are evil; he cannot but see them with his own eyes, and hear them with his own ears; for love does not put out his eyes, so that it is impossi-

ble for him not to see that such things are done. Neither does it take away his understanding any more than his senses, so that he cannot but know that they are evil. For instance: when he sees a man strike his neighbor, or hears him blaspheme God, he cannot either question the thing done or the words spoken, or doubt of their being evil. The word *thinketh* does not refer either to our seeing and hearing, or to the first and involuntary acts of our understanding, but to our *willingly thinking* what we need not, our *inferring* evil where it does not appear; to our *reasoning* concerning things which we do not see; our *supposing* what we have neither seen nor heard. This is what true love absolutely destroys. It tears up, root and branch, all *imagining* what we have not known. It casts out all jealousies, all evil surmisings, all readiness to believe evil. It is frank, open, unsuspicious; and, as it cannot design, so neither does it fear evil.

It "rejoiceth not in iniquity," common as this is, even among those who bear the name of Christ, who scruple not to rejoice over their enemy when he falleth either into affliction, or error, or sin. Indeed, how hardly can they avoid this who are zealously attached to any party? How difficult is it for them not to be pleased with any fault which they discover in those of the opposite party, with any real or supposed blemish either in their principles or practice? What warm defender of any cause is clear of these? Yea, who is so calm as to be altogether free? Who does not rejoice when his adversary makes a false step which he thinks will advantage his own cause? Only a man of love. He alone weeps over either the sin or folly of his enemy, takes no pleasure in hearing or in repeating it, but rather desires that it may be forgotten forever.

But he "rejoiceth in the truth," wheresoever it is found; in "the truth which is after godliness"; bringing forth its proper fruit: holiness of heart and holiness of conversation. He rejoices to find that even those who oppose him, whether with regard to opinions or some points of practice, are nevertheless lovers of God, and in other respects unreprovable. He is glad to hear good of them and to speak all he can consistently with truth and justice. Indeed, good in general is his glory and joy, wherever diffused throughout the race of mankind. As a citizen of the world he claims a share in the happiness of all the inhabitants of it. Because he is a man, he is not unconcerned in the welfare of any man, but enjoys whatsoever brings glory to God, and promotes peace and good will among men.

This "love covereth all things" because the merciful man rejoiceth not in iniquity, neither does he willingly make mention of it. Whatever evil he sees, hears, or knows, he nevertheless conceals, so far as he can, without making himself "partaker of other men's sins." Wheresoever or with whomsoever he is, if he sees anything which he approves not, it goes not out of his lips unless to the person concerned, if haply he may gain his brother. So far is he from making the faults or failings of others the matter of his conversation that of the absent he never does speak at all, unless he can speak well. A tale bearer, a back-biter, a whisperer, an evil speaker is to him all one as a murderer. He would just as soon cut his neighbor's throat as thus murder his reputation. Just as soon would he think of diverting himself by setting fire to his neighbor's house as of thus "scattering abroad arrows, fire brands, and death," and saying, "Am I not in sport?"

He makes one only exception. Sometimes he is convinced that it is for the glory of God or (which comes to the same) the good of his neighbor, that an evil should not be covered. In this case, for the benefit of the innocent, he is constrained to declare the guilty. But even here, he will not speak at all till love, superior love, constrains him. He cannot do it from a general confused view of doing good, or promoting the glory of God, but from a clear sight of some particular end, some determinate good which he pursues. Still he cannot speak unless he be fully convinced that this very means is necessary to that end; that the end cannot be answered, at least not so effectually, by any other way. He then doeth it with the utmost sorrow and reluctance; using it as the last and worst medicine, a desperate remedy in a desperate case, a kind of poison never to be used but to expel poison. Consequently, he uses it as sparingly as possible. And this he does with fear and trembling, lest he should transgress the law of love by speaking too much, more than he would have done by not speaking at all.

Love "believeth all things." It is always willing to think the best, to put the most favorable construction on everything. It is ever ready to believe whatever may tend to the advantage of anyone's character. It is easily convinced of (what it earnestly desires) the innocence or integrity of any man, or, at least, of the sincerity of his repentance, if he had once erred from the way. It is glad to excuse whatever is amiss; to condemn the offender as little as possible; and to make all the allowance for human weakness which can be done without betraying the truth of God.

And when it can no longer believe, then love "hopeth all things." Is any evil related of any man? Love hopes that the relation is not true, that the thing related was never done. Is it certain it was? "But perhaps it was not done with such circumstances as are related; so that allowing the fact, there is room to hope it was not so ill as it is represented." Was the action apparently, undeniably evil? Love hopes the intention was not so. Is it clear the design was evil too? "Yet might it not spring from the settled temper of the heart, but from a start of passion, or from some vehement temptation, which hurried the man beyond himself?" And even when it cannot be doubted, but all the actions, designs, and tempers are equally evil; still love hopes that God will at last make bare his arm, and get himself the victory; and that there shall be "joy in heaven over [this] one sinner that repenteth, more than over ninety and nine just persons that need no repentance."

Lastly, it "endureth all things." This completes the character of him that is truly merciful. He endureth not some, not many things only, not most, but absolutely *all things*. Whatever the injustice, the malice, the cruelty of men can inflict, he is able to suffer. He calls nothing intolerable; he never says of anything, "This is not to be borne." No: he can not only do but suffer all things through Christ which strengtheneth him. And all he suffers does not destroy his love, nor impair it in the least. It is proof against all. It is a flame that burns even in the midst of the great deep. "Many waters cannot quench" his "love, neither can the floods drown it." It triumphs over all. It "never faileth," either in time or in eternity:

> Thus in obedience to what Heaven
>   decrees,
> Knowledge shall fail, and prophecy
>   shall cease;
> But lasting charity's more ample
>   sway,
> Nor bound by time, nor subject to
>   decay,
> In happy triumph shall forever live,
> And endless good diffuse, and
>   endless praise receive.

So shall "the merciful obtain mercy"; not only by the blessing of God upon all their ways, by his now repaying the love they bear to their brethren a thousand-fold into their own bosom; but likewise by "an exceeding and eternal weight of glory," in the "kingdom prepared for them from the beginning of the world."

For a little while you may say, "Woe is me that I am constrained to dwell with Mesech, and to have my habitation among the tents of Kedar!" You may pour out your soul and bemoan the loss of true, genuine love in the earth. Lost, indeed! You may well say (but not in the ancient sense), "See how *these Christians* love one another!" These Christian kingdoms that are tearing out each other's bowels, desolating one another with fire and sword! These Christian armies that are sending each other by thousands, by ten thousands, quick into hell! These Christian nations that are all on fire with intestine broils, party against party, faction against faction! These Christian cities where deceit and fraud, oppression and wrong, yea, robbery and murder, go not out of their streets! These Christian families torn asunder with envy, jealousy, anger, domestic jars, without number, without end! Yea, what is most dreadful, most to be lamented of all, these Christian churches! Churches ("tell it not in Gath," but, alas! how can we hide it, either from Jews, Turks, or Pagans?) that bear the name of Christ, the Prince of Peace, and wage continual war with each other! That convert sinners by burning them alive! That are "drunk with the blood of the saints!" Does this praise belong only to "Babylon the great, the mother of harlots and abominations of the earth"? Nay, verily, but reformed churches (so called) have fairly learned to tread in her steps. Protestant churches, too, know to persecute when they have power in their hands, even unto blood. And meanwhile, how do they also anathematize each other! Devote each other to the nethermost hell! What wrath, what contention, what malice, what bitterness, is everywhere found among them, even where they agree in essentials and only differ in opinions, or in the circumstantials of religion! Who follows after *only* the "things that make for peace, and things wherewith one may edify another"? O God! how long? Shall thy promise fail? Fear it not, ye little flock! Against hope, believe in hope! It is your Father's good pleasure yet to renew the face of the earth. Surely all these things shall come to an end, and the inhabitants of the earth shall learn righteousness. "Nation shall not lift up sword against nation, neither shall they know war any more."

"The mountain of the Lord's house shall be established on the top of the mountains"; and "all the kingdoms of the world shall become the kingdoms of our God." "They shall not [then] hurt or destroy in all his holy mountain"; but they shall call [their] "walls salvation, and [their] gates praise." They shall all be without spot or blemish, loving one another, even as Christ hath loved us. Be thou part of the first fruits, if the harvest is not yet. Do thou love thy neighbor as thyself. The Lord God fill thy heart with such a love to every soul, that thou mayest be ready to lay down thy life for his sake! May thy soul continually overflow with love, swallowing up every unkind and unholy temper, till he calleth thee up into the region of love, there to reign with him forever and ever!

Part 2

"Blessed are the pure in heart: for they shall see God.
"Blessed are the peacemakers: for they shall be called the children of God.
"Blessed are they which are persecuted for righteousness' sake: for theirs is the kingdom of heaven.
"Blessed are ye, when men shall revile you, and persecute you, and shall say all manner of evil against you falsely, for my sake.
"Rejoice, and be exceeding glad: for great is your reward in heaven: for so persecuted they the prophets which were before you" (Matt. 5:8–12).

How excellent things are spoken of the love of our neighbor! It is "the fulfilling of the law," "the end of the commandment." Without this, all we have, all we do, all we suffer, is of no value in the sight of God. But it is that love of our neighbor which springs from the love of God: otherwise it is worth nothing. It behooves us, therefore, to examine well upon what foundation our love of our neighbor stands; whether it is really built upon the love of God, whether we do "love him because he first loved us"; whether we are pure in heart: for this

is the foundation which shall never be moved. "Blessed are the pure in heart: for they shall see God."

On Purity of Heart

"The pure in heart," are they whose hearts God hath "purified even as he is pure"; who are purified through faith in the blood of Jesus from every unholy affection; who, being "cleansed from all filthiness of flesh and spirit, perfect holiness in the [loving] fear of God." They are, through the power of his grace, purified from pride by the deepest poverty of spirit; from anger, from every unkind or turbulent passion by meekness and gentleness; from every desire but to please and enjoy God, to know and love him more and more by that hunger and thirst after righteousness, which now engrosses their whole soul, so that now they love the Lord their God with all their heart, and with all their soul, and mind, and strength.

But how little has this purity of heart been regarded by the false teachers of all ages! They have taught men barely to abstain from such outward impurities as God hath forbidden by name; but they did not strike at the heart, and by not guarding against, they in effect countenanced inward corruptions.

A remarkable instance of this, our Lord has given us in the following words: "Ye have heard, that it was said by them of old time, Thou shalt not commit adultery," verse 27; and, in explaining this, those blind leaders of the blind only insisted on men's abstaining from the outward act. "But I say unto you, that whosoever looketh on a woman to lust after her hath committed adultery with her already in his heart," verse 28; for God requireth truth in the inward parts; he searcheth the heart, and trieth the reins; and if thou incline unto iniquity with thy heart, the Lord will not hear thee.

And God admits no excuse for retaining anything which is an occasion of impurity. Therefore, "If thy right eye offend thee, pluck it out, and cast from thee: for it is profitable for thee that one of thy members should perish, and not that thy whole body should be cast into hell," verse 29. If persons as dear to thee as thy right eye be an occasion of thy thus offending God, a means of exciting unholy desire in thy soul, delay not: forcibly separate from them. "And if thy right hand offend thee, cut it off and cast [it] from thee: for it is profitable for thee that one of thy members should perish and not that thy whole body should be cast into hell," verse 30. If any who seem as necessary to thee as thy right hand be an occasion of sin, of impure desire, even though it were never to go beyond the heart, never to break out in word or action; constrain thyself to an entire and final parting: cut them off at a stroke, give them up to God. Any loss, whether of pleasure, or substance, or friends, is preferable to the loss of thy soul.

Two steps only it may not be improper to take before such an absolute and final separation. First, try whether the unclean spirit may not be driven out by fasting and prayer and by carefully abstaining from every action, and word, and look, which thou hast found to be an occasion of evil. Secondly, if thou art not by this means delivered, ask counsel of him that watcheth over thy soul, or, at least, of some who have experience in the ways of God, touching the time and manner of that separation; but confer not with flesh and blood, lest thou be "given up to a strong delusion to believe a lie."

Nor may marriage itself, holy and honorable as it is, be used as a pretense for giving [way] to our desires. Indeed, "It hath been said, whosoever will put away his wife, let him give her a writing of divorcement," and then all was well, though he alleged no cause but that he did not like her or liked another better. "But I say unto you, That whosoever shall put away his wife, saving for the cause of fornication, causeth her to commit adultery," if she marry again: "and whosoever shall marry her that is put away committeth adultery," verses 31 and 32.

All polygamy is clearly forbidden in these words, wherein our Lord expressly declares that for any woman who has a husband alive, to marry again is adultery. By parity of reason, it is adultery for any man to marry again, so long as he has a wife alive, yea, although they were divorced; unless that divorce had been for the cause of adultery: in that only case there is no Scripture which forbids the innocent person to marry again.

Such is the purity of heart which God requires and works in those who believe on the Son of his love. And "blessed are" they who are thus "pure in heart, for they shall see God." He will "manifest himself unto them," not only "as he doth not unto the world," but as he doth not always to his own children. He will bless them with the clearest communications of his Spirit, the most intimate "fellowship with the Father and with the Son." He will cause his presence to go continually before them and the light of his countenance to shine upon them. It is the ceaseless prayer of their heart, "I beseech thee, show me thy glory"; and they have the petition they ask of him. They now see him by faith (the veil of flesh being made, as it were, transparent), even in these his lowest works, in all that surrounds them, in all that God has created and made. They see him in the height above and in the depth beneath; they see him filling all in all. The pure in heart see all things full of God. They see him in the firmament of heaven; in the moon, walking in brightness; in the sun, when he rejoiceth as a giant to run his course. They see him "making the clouds his chariots, and walking upon the wings of the wind." They see him, "preparing rain for the earth, and blessing the increase of it; giving grass for the cattle, and green herb for the use of man." They see the Creator of all wisely governing all and "upholding all things by the word of his power." "O Lord, our Governor, how excellent is thy name in all the world!"

In all his providences relating to themselves, to their souls or bodies, the pure in heart do more particularly see God. They see his hand ever over them for good; giving them all things in weight and measure, numbering the hairs of their head, making a hedge round about them and all that they have, and disposing all the circumstances of their life, according to the depth both of his wisdom and mercy.

But in a more especial manner they see God in his ordinances. Whether they appear in the great congregation to "pay him the honor due unto his name," "and worship him in the beauty of holiness," or "enter into their closets," and there pour out their souls before their "Father which is in secret"; whether they search the oracles of God, or hear the ambassadors of Christ proclaiming glad tidings of salvation; or by eating of that bread, and drinking of that cup, "show forth his death till he come" in the clouds of heaven—in all these his appointed ways they find such a near approach as cannot be expressed. They see him, as it were, face to face and "talk with him as a man talketh with his friend," a fit preparation for those mansions above wherein they shall see him as he is.

On Seeing God

But how far were they from seeing God, who having heard, "that it had been said by them of old time, verse 33, Thou shalt not forswear thyself, but shalt perform unto the Lord thine oaths"; interpreted it thus, Thou shalt not forswear thyself, when thou swearest by the Lord Jehovah. Thou "shalt perform unto the Lord [these] thine oaths"; but as to other oaths, he regardeth them not.

So the Pharisees taught. They not only allowed all manner of swearing in common conversation, but accounted even forswearing a little thing, so they had not sworn by the peculiar name of God.

But our Lord here absolutely forbids all common swearing, as well as all false swearing, and shows the heinousness of both by the same awful consideration, that every creature is God's, and he is everywhere present, in all, and over all. "I say unto you, Swear not at all; neither by heaven, for it is God's throne," verse 34; and, therefore, this is the same as to swear by him who sitteth upon the circle of the heavens. "Nor by the earth; for it is his footstool," verse 35; and he is as intimately present in earth as heaven. "Neither by Jerusalem; for it is the city of the great King," and God is well known in her palaces. "Neither shalt thou swear by thy head; because thou canst not make one hair white or black," verse 36, because even this, it is plain, is not thine, but God's, the sole disposer of all in heaven and earth. "But let your communication," verse 37, your conversation, your discourse with each other, "be yea, yea; nay, nay"; a bare, serious affirming or denying; "for whatsoever is more than these cometh of evil."

That our Lord does not here forbid the "swearing in judgment and truth," when we are required so to do by a magistrate, may appear from the occasion of this part of his discourse, the abuse he was here reproving, which was false swearing and common swearing; the swearing before a magistrate being quite out of the question. From the very words wherein he forms the general conclusion: "Let your communication," or discourse, "be yea, yea; nay, nay." From his own example; for he answered himself upon oath when required by a magistrate. When the high priest said unto him, "I adjure thee by the living God, that thou tell us, whether thou be the Christ, the Son of God"; Jesus immediately answered in the affirmative,

"Thou hast said" (the truth); "nevertheless" (or rather, *moreover*), "I say unto you, hereafter shall ye see the Son of man sitting on the right hand of power, and coming in the clouds of heaven," Matthew 26:63, 64. From the example of God, even the Father who, "willing more abundantly to show unto the heirs of promise the immutability of his counsel, confirmed it by an oath," Hebrews 6:17. From the example of Saint Paul, who we think had the Spirit of God and well understood the mind of his Master. "God is my witness," saith he to the Romans, "that without ceasing, I make mention of you always in my prayers," Romans 1:9; to the Corinthians, "I call God to record upon my soul, that to spare you, I came not as yet unto Corinth," 2 Corinthians 1:23; and to the Philippians, "God is my record, how greatly I long after you, in the bowels of Jesus Christ," Philippians 1:8. Hence, it undeniably appears that if the apostle knew the meaning of his Lord's words, they do not forbid swearing on weighty occasions, even to one another; how much less before a magistrate! And lastly, from that assertion of the great apostle concerning solemn swearing in general (which it is impossible he could have mentioned without any touch of blame, if his Lord had totally forbidden it): "Men verily swear by the greater [by one greater than themselves]: and an oath for confirmation is to them the end of all strife," Hebrews 6:16.

But the great lesson which our blessed Lord inculcates here, and which he illustrates by this example, is that God is in all things, and that we are to see the Creator in the glass of every creature; that we should use and look upon nothing as separate from God, which, indeed, is a kind of practical atheism; but with a true magnificence of thought survey heaven and earth and all that is therein, as contained by God in the hollow of his hand, who by his intimate presence holds them all in being, who pervades and actuates the whole created frame, and is, in a true sense, the soul of the universe.

Thus far our Lord has been more directly employed in teaching the religion of the heart. He has shown what Christians are to be. He proceeds to show what they are to do also, how inward holiness is to exert itself in our outward conversation. "Blessed," saith he, "are the peacemakers: for they shall be called the children of God."

The Role of Peacemakers

The *peacemakers.* Accordingly when Saint Paul, in the titles of his epistles, wishes grace and peace to the Romans or the Corinthians, it is as if he had said, "As a fruit of the free, undeserved love and favor of God, may you enjoy all blessings, spiritual and temporal; all the good things which God hath prepared for them that love him."

Hence we may easily learn in how wide a sense the term peacemakers is to be understood. In its literal meaning it implies those lovers of God and man who utterly detest and abhor all strife and debate, all variance and contention, and accordingly labor with all their might, either to prevent this fire of hell from being kindled, or, when it is kindled, from breaking out, or, when it is broken out, from spreading any farther. They endeavor to calm the stormy spirits of men, to quiet their turbulent passions, to soften the minds of contending parties, and, if possible, reconcile them to each other. They use all innocent arts and employ all their strength, all the talents which God has given them, as well to preserve peace where it is, as to restore it where it is not. It is the joy of their heart to promote, to confirm, to increase, mutual good will among men,

but more especially among the children of God, however distinguished by things of smaller importance; that as they have all "one Lord, one faith," as they are all "called in one hope of their calling," so they may all "walk worthy of the vocation wherewith they are called; with all lowliness and meekness, with longsuffering, forbearing one another in love; endeavoring to keep the unity of the Spirit in the bond of peace."

But, in the full extent of the word, a peacemaker is one that, as he hath opportunity, "doeth good unto all men"; one that, being filled with the love of God and of all mankind, cannot confine the expressions of it to his own family, or friends, or acquaintance, or party, or to those of his own opinions, no, nor those who are partakers of like precious faith; but steps over all these narrow bounds that he may do good to every man, that he may, some way or other, manifest his love to neighbors and strangers, friends and enemies. He doeth good to them all, as he hath opportunity, that is, on every possible occasion; "redeeming the time," in order thereto; buying up every opportunity, improving every hour, losing no moment wherein he may profit another. He does good, not of one particular kind, but good in general, in every possible way; employing herein all his talents of every kind, all his powers and faculties of body and soul, all his fortune, his interest, his reputation; desiring only that when his Lord cometh, he may say, "Well done, good and faithful servant!"

He doeth good, to the uttermost of his power, even to the bodies of all men. He rejoices to "deal his bread to the hungry," and to "cover the naked with a garment." Is any a stranger? He takes him in and relieves him according to his necessities. Are any sick or in prison? He visits them and administers such help as they stand most in need of. And all this he does, not as unto man; but remembering him that hath said, "Inasmuch as ye have done it unto one of the least of these my brethren, ye have done it unto me."

How much more does he rejoice, if he can do any good to the soul of any man! This power, indeed, belongeth unto God. It is he only that changes the heart, without which every other change is lighter than vanity. Nevertheless, it pleases him who worketh all in all, to help man chiefly by man; to convey his own power, and blessing, and love, through one man to another. Therefore, although it be certain that "the help which is done upon earth, God doeth it himself"; yet has no man need, on this account, to stand idle in his vineyard. The peacemaker cannot: he is ever laboring therein, and, as an instrument in God's hand, preparing the ground for his Master's use, or sowing the seed of the kingdom, or watering what is already sown, if haply God may give the increase. According to the measure of grace which he has received, he uses all diligence to reprove the gross sinner, to reclaim those who run on headlong in the broad way of destruction; or "to give light to them that sit in darkness," and are ready to "perish for lack of knowledge"; or to "support the weak, to lift up the hands that hang down, and the feeble knees"; or to bring back and heal that which was lame and turned out of the way. Nor is he less zealous to confirm those who are already striving to enter in at the straight gate; to strengthen those that stand, that they may "run with patience the race which is set before them"; to build up in their most holy faith those that know in whom they have believed; to exhort them to stir up the gift of God which is in them, that, daily growing in grace, "an entrance may be ministered unto them abun-dantly into the everlasting kingdom of our Lord and Savior Jesus Christ."

"Blessed" are they who are thus continually employed in the work of faith and the labor of love; "for they shall be called," that is, *shall be* (a common Hebraism) "the children of God." God shall continue unto them the spirit of adoption, yea, shall pour it more abundantly into their hearts. He shall bless them with all the blessings of his children. He shall acknowledge them as sons before angels and men; "and, if sons, then heirs; heirs of God, and joint heirs with Christ."

One would imagine such a person as has been above described, so full of genuine humility, so unaffectedly serious, so mild and gentle, so free from all selfish design, so devoted to God, and such an active lover of men, should be the darling of mankind. But our Lord was better acquainted with human nature in its present state. He, therefore, closes the character of this man of God, with showing him the treatment he is to expect in the world. "Blessed," saith he, "are they which are persecuted for righteousness' sake: for theirs is the kingdom of heaven."

On Facing Persecution

In order to understand this thoroughly, let us first inquire, who are they that are persecuted? And this we may easily learn from Saint Paul: "As of old, he that was born after the flesh persecuted him that was born after the Spirit, even so it is now," Galatians 4:29. "Yea," saith the apostle, "and all that will live godly in Christ Jesus, shall suffer persecution," 2 Timothy 3:12. The same we are taught by Saint John: "Marvel not, my brethren, if the world hate you. We know that we have passed from death unto life, because we love the brethren," 1 John 3:13, 14. As if he had said, the brethren, the Christians cannot be loved, but by them who have passed from death unto life. And most expressly, by our Lord: "If the world hate you, ye know that it hated me before it hated you. If ye were of the world, the world would love his own; but because ye are not of the world, therefore the world hateth you. Remember the word that I said unto you, The servant is not greater than his lord. If they have persecuted me, they will also persecute you," John 15:18.

By all these Scriptures it manifestly appears who they are that are persecuted: namely, the righteous; he "that is born of the Spirit"; "all that will live godly in Christ Jesus"; they that are "passed from death unto life"; those who are "not of the world"; all those who are meek and lowly in heart, that mourn for God, that hunger after his likeness; all that love God and their neighbor, and therefore as they have opportunity do good unto all men.

If it be, secondly, inquired, why they are persecuted, the answer is equally plain and obvious. It is "for righteousness' sake"; because they are righteous; because they are born after the Spirit; because they "will live godly in Christ Jesus"; because they "are not of the world." Whatever may be pretended, this is the real cause: be their infirmities more or less, still, if it were not for this, they would be borne with, and the world would love its own. They are persecuted because they are *poor in spirit*, that is, says the world, "Poor-spirited, mean, dastardly souls, good for nothing, not fit to live in the world"—because they *mourn*. "They are such dull, heavy, lumpish creatures, enough to sink anyone's spirit that sees them! They are mere death heads; they kill innocent mirth, and spoil company wherever they come"—because they are *meek:* "Tame, passive fools, must fit to be trampled

upon"—because they *hunger and thirst after righteousness:* "a parcel of hot-brained enthusiasts, gaping after they know not what, not content with rational religion, but running mad after raptures and inward feelings"—because they are *merciful,* lovers of all, lovers of the evil and unthankful: "Encouraging all manner of wickedness, nay, tempting people to do mischief by impunity; and men who, it is to be feared, have their own religion still to seek; very loose in their principles"—because they are *pure in heart:* "Uncharitable creatures, that damn all the world but those that are of their own sort! Blasphemous wretches, that pretend to make God a liar, to live without sin!"—Above all, because they are *peacemakers:* because they take all opportunities of doing good to all men. This is the grand reason why they have been persecuted in all ages, and will be till the restitution of all things: "If they would but keep their religion to themselves it would be tolerable. But it is this spreading their errors, this infecting so many others, which is not to be endured. They do so much mischief in the world that they ought to be tolerated no longer. It is true, the men do some things well enough; they relieve some of the poor. But this, too, is only done to gain the more to their party; and so, in effect, to do the more mischief!" Thus the men of the world sincerely think and speak. And the more the kingdom of God prevails, the more the peacemakers are enabled to propagate lowliness, meekness, and all other divine tempers, the more mischief is done in their account. Consequently, the more are they enraged against the authors of this, and the more vehemently will they persecute them.

Let us, thirdly, inquire, who are they that persecute them? Saint Paul answers, "He that is born after the flesh"—everyone who is not "born of the Spirit," or at least desirous so to be; all that do not at least labor to "live godly in Christ Jesus"; all that are not "passed from death unto life," and, consequently, cannot "love the brethren"; "the world," that is, according to our Savior's account, "they who know not him that sent me"; they who know not God, even the loving, pardoning God, by the teaching of his own Spirit.

The reason is plain: the spirit which is in the world is directly opposite to the Spirit which is of God. It must, therefore, needs be that those who are of the world, will be opposite to those who are of God. There is the utmost contrariety between them in all their opinions, their desires, designs, and tempers. And hitherto the leopard and the kid cannot lie down in peace together. The proud, because he is proud, cannot but persecute the lowly; the light and airy, those that mourn; and so in every other kind, the unlikeness of disposition (were there no other) being a perpetual ground of enmity. Therefore, were it only on this account, all the servants of the devil will persecute the children of God.

Should it be inquired, fourthly, how they will persecute them, it may be answered in general, just in that manner and measure which the wise Disposer of all sees will be most for his glory, will tend most to his children's growth in grace and the enlargement of his own kingdom. There is no one branch of God's government of the world which is more to be admired than this. His ear is never heavy to the threatenings of the persecutor or the cry of the persecuted. His eye is ever open, and his hand stretched out to direct even the minutest circumstance. When the storm shall begin, how high it shall rise, which way it shall point its course, when and how it shall end, are all determined by his unerring wisdom. The ungodly are only a sword of his, an instrument which he uses as it pleaseth him, and which itself, when the gracious ends of his providence are answered, is cast into the fire.

At some rare times, as when Christianity was first planted, and while it was taking root in the earth; as also when the pure doctrine of Christ began to be planted again in our nation; God permitted the storm to rise high, and his children were called to resist unto blood. There was a peculiar reason why he suffered this with regard to the apostles, that their evidence might be the more unexceptionable. But from the annals of the church we learn another and a far different reason why he suffered the heavy persecutions which arose in the second and third centuries; namely, because the mystery of iniquity did so strongly work because of the monstrous corruptions which even then reigned in the church. These God chastised, and at the same time strove to heal, by those severe but necessary visitations.

Perhaps the same observation may be made, with regard to the grand persecution in our own land. God had dealt very graciously with our nation. He had poured out various blessings upon us. He had given us peace abroad and at home, and a king, wise and good beyond his years. And, above all, he had caused the pure light of his gospel to arise and shine among us. But what return did he find? "He looked for righteousness, but behold a cry!"—a cry of oppression and wrong, of ambition and injustice, of malice, and fraud, and covetousness. Yea, the cry of those who even then expired in the flames entered into the ears of the Lord of Sabaoth. It was then God arose to maintain his own cause against those that held the truth in unrighteousness. Then he sold them into the hands of their persecutors, by a judgment mixed with mercy; an affliction to punish, and yet a medicine to heal, the grievous backslidings of his people.

But it is seldom that God suffers the storm to rise so high as torture, or death, or bonds, or imprisonment. Whereas his children are frequently called to endure the lighter kinds of persecution, they frequently suffer the estrangement of kinsfolk [and] the loss of the friends that were as their own soul. They find the truth of their Lord's Word (concerning the *event*, though not the *design* of his coming), "Suppose ye that I am come to give peace upon earth? I tell you, Nay; but rather division," Luke 7:51. And hence will naturally follow loss of business or employment, and consequently of substance. But all these circumstances, likewise, are under the wise direction of God, who allots to everyone what is most expedient for him.

The Badge of Discipleship

But the persecution which attends *all* the children of God is that our Lord describes in the following words: "Blessed are ye when men shall revile you, and persecute you [shall persecute by reviling you], and say all manner of evil against you, falsely, for my sake." This cannot fail; it is the very badge of our discipleship; it is one of the seals of our calling; it is a sure portion entailed on all the children of God: if we have it not, we are bastards and not sons. Straight through evil report, as well as good report, lies the only way to the kingdom. The meek, serious, humble, zealous lovers of God and man are of good report among their brethren; but of evil report with the world, who count and treat them "as the filth and offscouring of all things."

Indeed, some have supposed that before the fullness of the Gentiles shall come in, the scandal of the cross will cease; that God will cause Christians to be esteemed and loved even by those who are as yet in their sins. Yea, and sure it is that even now he at some times suspends the contempt as well as the fierceness of men; "he makes a man's enemies to be at peace with him" for a season, and gives him favor with his bitterest persecutors. But setting aside this exempt case, the scandal of the cross is not yet ceased; but a man may say still, "If I please men, I am not the servant of Christ." Let no man, therefore, regard that pleasing suggestion (pleasing doubtless to flesh and blood), "That bad men only *pretend* to hate and despise them that are good, but do indeed love and esteem them in their hearts." Not so: they may employ them sometimes, but it is for their own profit. They may put confidence in them, for they know their ways are not like other men's. But still they love them not, unless so far as the Spirit of God may be striving with them. Our Savior's words are express: "If ye were of the world, the world would love its own; but because ye are not of the world, therefore, the world hateth you." Yea (setting aside what exceptions may be made by the preventing grace, or the peculiar providence of God), it hateth them as cordially and sincerely as ever it did their Master.

It remains only to inquire, how are the children of God to behave with regard to persecution? And, first, they ought not knowingly or designedly to bring it upon themselves. This is contrary both to the example and advice of our Lord and all his apostles, who teach us not only not to seek, but to avoid it as far as we can without injuring our conscience; without giving up any part of that righteousness which we are to prefer before life itself. So our Lord expressly saith, "When they persecute you in this city, flee ye into another"; which is, indeed, when it can be taken, the most unexceptionable way of avoiding persecution.

Yet think not that you can always avoid it, either by this or any other means. If ever that idle imagination steals into your heart, put it to flight by that earnest caution, "Remember the word that I said unto you, The servant is not greater than his lord. If they have persecuted me, they will also persecute you." "Be ye wise as serpents, and harmless as doves." But will this screen you from persecution? Not unless you have more wisdom than your Master, or more innocence than the Lamb of God.

Neither desire to avoid it, to escape it wholly; for if you do, you are none of his. If you escape the persecution, you escape the blessing, the blessing of those who are persecuted for righteousness' sake. If you are not persecuted for righteousness' sake, you cannot enter into the kingdom of heaven. "If we suffer with him, we shall also reign with him. But if we deny him, he will also deny us."

Nay, rather, "Rejoice and be exceeding glad," when men persecute you for his sake; when they persecute you by reviling you, and by saying all manner of evil against you falsely"; which they will not fail to mix with every kind of persecution; they must blacken you to excuse themselves: "For so persecuted they the prophets which were before you," those who were most eminently holy in heart and life, yea, and all the righteous which ever have been from the beginning of the world. Rejoice, because by this mark also ye know unto whom ye belong; and "because great is your reward in heaven," the reward purchased by the blood of the covenant, and freely bestowed in proportion to your sufferings, as well as to your holiness of heart and life. "Be exceeding glad," knowing that these "light afflictions, which are but for a moment, work out for you a far more exceeding and eternal weight of glory."

Meantime, let no persecution turn you out of the way of lowliness and meekness, of love and beneficence. "Ye have heard [indeed] that it hath been said, an eye for an eye, and a tooth for a tooth"; and your miserable teachers have hence allowed you to avenge yourselves, to return evil for evil; "But I say unto you that ye resist not evil," not thus, not by returning it in kind. "But," rather than do this, "whosoever smiteth thee on thy right cheek, turn to him the other also. And if any man will sue thee at the law, and take away thy coat, let him have thy cloak also. And whosoever shall compel thee to go a mile, go with him twain."

So invincible let thy meekness be. And be thy love suitable thereto. "Give to him that asketh thee, and from him that would borrow of thee turn not thou away." Only, give not away that which is another man's, that which is not thine own. Therefore, take care to owe no man anything: for what thou owest is not thy own, but another man's. Provide for those of thine own household: this also God hath required of thee, and what is necessary to sustain them in life and godliness is also not thine own. Then, give or lend all that remains, from day to day, or from year to year: only first, seeing thou canst not give or lend to all, remember the household of faith.

Living the Lesson

The meekness and love we are to feel, the kindness we are to show, to them which persecute us for righteousness' sake, our blessed Lord describes further in the following verses: Oh, that they were engraven upon our hearts! "Ye have heard that it hath been said, Thou shalt love thy neighbor, and hate thy enemy": God indeed had said only the former part, "Thou shalt love thy neigh-

added the latter, "and hate thy enemy." "But I say unto you," Love your enemies": see that you bear a tender good will to those who are most bitter of spirit against you, who wish you all manner of evil. "Bless them that curse." Are there any whose bitterness of spirit breaks forth in bitter words? who are continually cursing and reproaching you when you are present, and "saying all evil against you" when absent? So much the rather do you bless; in conversing with them, use all mildness and softness of language. Reprove them by repeating a better lesson before them, by showing them how they ought to have spoken. And in speaking of them say all the good you can, without violating the rules of truth and justice. "Do good to them that hate you": let your actions show that you are as real in love as they in hatred. Return good for evil. "Be not overcome of evil, but overcome evil with good." If you can do nothing more, at least "Pray for them that despitefully use you and persecute you." You can never be disabled from doing this; nor can all their malice or violence hinder you. Pour out your souls to God, not only for those who did this once but now repent: this is a little thing. "If thy brother, seven times a day, turn and say unto thee, I repent"; Luke 17:3; that is, if after ever so many relapses he give thee reason to believe that he is really and thoroughly changed, then thou shalt forgive him, so as to trust him, to put him in thy bosom, as if he had never sinned against thee at all. But pray for, wrestle with God for those that do not repent, that now despitefully use thee and persecute thee. Thus far forgive them, "not until seven times only, but until seventy times seven," Matthew 18:22. Whether they repent or no, yea, though they appear farther and farther from it, yet show them this instance of kindness, "That ye may be the children,"

that ye may approve yourselves the genuine children "of your Father which is in heaven," who shows his goodness by giving such blessings as they are capable of, even to his stubbornest enemies; "who maketh the sun to rise on the evil and on the good, and sendeth rain on the just and on the unjust." "For if ye love them which love you, what reward have ye? Do not even the publicans the same?" Matthew 5:46—who pretend to no religion; whom ye yourselves acknowledge to be without God in the world. "And if ye salute," show kindness in word or deed, to "your brethren," your friends or kinsfolk "only; what do ye more than others," than those who have no religion at all? "Do not even the publicans so?" Nay, but follow ye a better pattern than them. In patience, in longsuffering, in mercy, in beneficence of every kind, to all, even to your bitterest persecutors; "Be ye [Christians] perfect (in kind, though not in degree], even as your Father which is in heaven, is perfect," verse 48.

Behold Christianity in its native form, as delivered by its great Author! This is the genuine religion of Jesus Christ! Such he presents it to him whose eyes are opened. See a picture of God, so far as he is imitable by man! A picture drawn by God's own hand! "Behold, ye despisers, and wonder, and perish!" Or rather, wonder and adore! Rather cry out, is this the religion of Jesus of Nazareth? The religion which I persecuted? Let me no more be found even to fight against God. Lord, what wouldest thou have me to do? What beauty appears in the whole! How just a symmetry! What exact proportion in every part! How desirable is the happiness here described! How venerable, how lovely the holiness! This is the spirit of religion, the quintessence of it. These are, indeed, the fundamentals of Christianity. Oh, that we may not be hearers of it only "like a man beholding his own face in a glass, who goeth his way, and straightway forgetteth what manner of man he was." Nay, but let us steadily "look into this perfect law of liberty, and continue therein." Let us not rest until every line thereof is transcribed into our own hearts. Let us watch, and pray, and believe, and love, and "strive for the mastery," till every part of it shall appear in our soul, graven there by the finger of God; till we are "holy as He which hath called us is holy, perfect as our Father which is in heaven is perfect!"

PART THREE

Miscellaneous Correspondence

Neither the single life nor the married life can be held up as absolutely better. Both make contributions to mankind that are honorable and necessary. Wesley explored this matter and offered sound advice for those in both situations.

For the single person, freedom of movement is the great advantage. Spatial, financial, or emotional boundaries do not exist to the same degree that they do within marriage. The single person can serve God in a capacity that is less distracting. Having more time the single person must be a good steward of each moment, using it with great care.

Wesley emphasizes that being single is not an abnormality. It has its place in God's program and therefore should never be looked upon with contempt. The great apostle Paul was single by choice and God used him greatly. To be single or married is a freedom God gives humans, and neither in excess is beneficial to the human race.

CHAPTER SIXTEEN

Thoughts on a Single Life

The forbidding to marry, as it is well known the Church of Rome does and has done for several ages (in which marriage is absolutely forbidden, not only to all religious orders, but to the whole body of clergy), is numbered by the great apostle among "the doctrines of devils." And among the same we need not scruple to number the despising or condemning marriage, as do many of those in the Romish Church who are usually termed Mystic writers. One of these does not scruple to affirm, "Marriage is only licensed fornication." But the Holy Ghost says, "Marriage is honorable in all and the bed undefiled." Nor can it be doubted but persons may be as holy in a married as in a single state.

In the latter clause of the sentence, the apostle seems to guard against a mistake into which some sincere Christians have fallen, particularly when they have just found such a liberty of spirit as they had not before experienced. They imagine a defilement where there is none, "and fear where no fear is." And it is possible this very fear of sin may betray them into sin. For it may induce persons to defraud each other, forgetting the express determination of the apostle: "The wife hath not power of her own body, but the husband; and the husband hath not power of his own body, but the wife," 1 Corinthians 7:14.

And yet we must not forget what the apostle subjoins in the following verses: "I say to the unmarried and widows, It is good for them, if they abide even as I. Art thou bound unto a wife? Seek not to be loosed. Art thou loosed from a wife?

Seek not a wife. But if thou marry, thou hast not sinned. Nevertheless, such shall have trouble in the flesh. I would have you without carefulness. He that is unmarried careth for the things of the Lord, how he may please the Lord; but he that is married careth for the things of the world, how he may please his wife. The unmarried woman careth for the things of the Lord," that she may be holy both in body and spirit; "but she that is married careth for the things of the world, how she may please her husband. And this I speak for your own profit, that you may attend upon the Lord without distraction," verses 8, 27, 28, 32, and 35.

Not for All

But though "it is good for a man not to touch a woman," verse 1, yet this is not a universal rule. "I would," indeed, says the apostle, "that all men were as myself," verse 7. But that cannot be; for "every man hath his proper gift of God, one after this manner, another after that." "If," then, "they cannot contain, let them marry; for it is better to marry than to burn," verse 9. "To avoid fornication, let every man have his own wife, and let every woman have her own husband." Exactly agreeable to this are the words of our Lord. When the apostles said, "If the case be so, it is good not to marry; he said unto them, All men cannot receive this saying, but they to whom it is given. For there are some eunuchs, who were so born from their mother's womb; there are some, who were made eunuchs by men; and there are eunuchs, who have made themselves eunuchs for the kingdom of heaven's sake. He that is able to receive it, let him receive it," Matthew 19:11, 12.

But who is able to "receive this saying," to abstain from marriage, and yet not burn? It behooves everyone here to judge for himself; none is called to judge for another. In general, I believe every man is able to receive it when he is first justified. I believe everyone then receives this gift; but with most it does not continue long. Thus much is clear; it is a plain matter of fact, which no man can deny. It is not so clear whether God withdraws it of his own good pleasure or for any fault of ours. I incline to think it is not withdrawn without some fault on our part. But, be that as it may, I have now only to do with those who are still able to "receive this saying."

Specific Advantages

To this happy few I say know the advantages you enjoy, many of which are pointed out by the apostle himself. You may be without carefulness. You are under no necessity of "caring for the things of the world." You have only to "care for the things of the Lord, how you may please the Lord." One care alone lies upon you, how you "may be holy both in body and spirit."

You may "attend upon the Lord without distraction"; while others, like Martha, are cumbered with much serving and drawn hither and thither by many things, you may remain centered in God, sitting, like Mary, at the Master's feet and listening to every word of his mouth.

You enjoy a blessed liberty from the "trouble in the flesh," which must more or less attend a married state, from a thousand nameless domestic trials which are found sooner or later in every

family. You are exempt from numberless occasions of sorrow and anxiety, with which heads of families are entangled; especially those who have sickly, or weak, or unhappy, or disobedient children. If your servants are wicked, you may put them away, and your relation to them ceases. But what could you do with a wicked son or daughter? How could you dissolve that relation?

Above all, you are at liberty from the greatest of all entanglements, the loving one creature above all others. It is possible to do this without sin, without any impeachment of our love to God. But how inconceivably difficult to give God our whole heart while a creature has so large a share of it! How much more easily may we do this, when the heart is tenderly, indeed, but equally attached to more than one; or, at least, without any great inequality! What angelic wisdom does it require to give enough of our affection, and not too much, to so near a relation!

And how much easier is it (just to touch on one point more) wholly to conquer our natural desires than to gratify them exactly so far as Christian temperance allows! Just so far as every pleasure of sense prepares us for taking pleasure in God.

You have leisure to improve yourself in every kind, to wait upon God in public and private, and to do good to your neighbor in various ways, as Christian prudence shall suggest; whereas those who are married are necessarily taken up with the things of the world. You may give all your time to God without interruption and need ask leave of none but yourself so to do. You may employ every hour in what you judge to be the most excellent way. But if you were married, you may ask leave of your companion; otherwise what complaints or disgust would follow! And how hard is it even to know (how much more to act suitably to that knowledge) how far you ought to give way, for peace's sake, and where to stop! What wisdom is requisite in order to know how far you can recede from what is most excellent, particularly with regard to conversation that is not "to the use of edifying," in order to please your good-natured or ill-natured partner, without displeasing God!

You may give all your worldly substance to God; nothing need hinder. You have no increasing family; you have no wife or children to provide for which might occasion a thousand doubts whether you had done either too much or too little for them. You may "make yourself friends of" all "the mammon of unrighteousness" which God entrusts you with; having none that has any right to complain, or to charge you with unkindness for so doing. You may lay out all your talents of every kind entirely for the glory of God; as you have none else to please, none to regard but him that lived and died for you.

I say, prize the advantages you enjoy; know the value of them. Esteem them as highly while you have them as others do after they have lost them. Pray constantly and fervently for this very thing, that God would teach you to set a due value upon them. And let it be matter of daily thanksgiving to God, that he has made you a partaker of these benefits. Indeed, the more full and explicit you are herein, the more sensible you will be of the cause you have to be thankful; the more lively conviction you will have of the greatness of the blessing.

Resisting Temptations

If you know and duly prize the advantages you enjoy, then be careful to keep them. But this (as easy as it may seem) it is impossible you should do by your own strength, so various, so frequent, and so strong, are the temptations which you will meet with to cast them away. Not only the children of the world, but the children of God, will undoubtedly tempt you thereto; and that partly by the most plausible reasons, partly by the most artful persuasions. Meantime, the old deceiver will not be wanting to give an edge to all those reasons and persuasions, and to recall the temptation again and again, and press it close upon your heart. You have need, therefore, to use every help, and the first of these is earnest prayer. Let no day pass without this, without praying for this very thing, that God would work what with men is impossible; that he would vouchsafe to preserve his own gift, and that you may not suffer any loss this day, either by the subtlety or power of devils or men, or the deceitfulness of your own heart.

A second help may be the conversing frequently and freely with those of your own sex who are like-minded. It may be of infinite service to disclose to these the very secrets of your hearts; especially the weaknesses springing from your natural constitution, or education, or long-contracted habit, and the temptations which from time to time most easily beset you. Advise with them on every circumstance that occurs; open your heart without reserve. By this means a thousand devices of Satan will be brought to nought; innumerable snares will be prevented; or you will pass through them without being hurt. Yea, and if at some time you should have suffered a little, the wound will speedily be healed.

I say, it will be highly expedient to avoid all needless conversation, much more all intimacy, with those of the other sex; so expedient, that unless you observe this, you will surely cast away the gift of God. Say not, "But they have much grace and much understanding." So much the greater is the danger. There would be less fear of your receiving hurt from them if they had less grace or less understanding. And whenever any of these are thrown in your way, "make a covenant with your eyes," your ears, your hands, that you do not indulge yourself in any that are called innocent freedoms. Above all, "keep your heart with all diligence." Check the first rising of desire. Watch against every sally of imagination, particularly if it be pleasing. If it is darted in, whether you will or no, yet let no "vain thought lodge within you." Cry out, "My God and my all, I am thine, thine alone! I will be thine forever! O save me from setting up an idol in my heart! Save me from taking any step toward it. Still bring my 'every thought into captivity to the obedience of Christ.' "

"But how shall I attain to, or how preserve this strength and firmness of spirit?" In order to [do] this, I advise you (need I say, to avoid the sin of Onan, seeing Satan will not cast out Satan? or rather) avoid, with the utmost care, all softness and effeminacy; remembering the express denunciation of an inspired writer, the *soft* or *effeminate*, whether poor or rich (the apostle does not make any difference upon that account), "shall not inherit the kingdom of God." Avoid all delicacy, first in spirit, then in apparel, food, lodging, and a thousand nameless things; and this the more speedily and the more resolutely if you have been long-accustomed thereto. Avoid all needless self-indulgence, as well as delicacy and softness. All these tend to breed or cherish those appetites and passions which you have renounced for Christ's sake. They either create or increase those desires which, "for the kingdom of heaven's sake," you are determined not to gratify. Avoid all sloth, inactivity, indolence. Sleep no more than nature requires. Be never idle; and use as much bodily exercise as your strength will allow. I dare not add Monsieur Pascal's rule: avoid all pleasure. It is not possible to avoid all pleasure, even of sense, without destroying the body. Neither doth God require it at our hands; it is not his will concerning us. On the contrary, he "giveth us all things to enjoy," so we enjoy them to his glory. But I say, avoid all that pleasure which any way hinders you from enjoying him; yea, all such pleasure as does not prepare you for taking pleasure in God. Add to this constant and continued course of universal self-denial, the taking up your cross daily, the enduring "hardship as a good soldier of Jesus Christ." Remember, "the kingdom of heaven suffers violence, and the violent take it by force." This is the way; walk therein; think not of a smoother path. Add to your other exercises constant and prudent fasting, and the Lord will uphold you with his hand.

Putting Singleness to Work

I advise you, if you desire to keep them, use all the advantages you enjoy. Indeed, without this, it is utterly impossible to keep them; for the mouth of the Lord hath spoken the word which cannot be broken, which must be fulfilled with regard to all the good gifts of God: "To him that hath," uses what he hath, "shall be given; and he shall have more abundantly: but from him that hath not," uses it not, "shall be taken even that which he hath." Would you, therefore, retain what you now have, what God hath already given? If so, "giving all diligence," use it to the uttermost. "Stand fast in" every instance of "the liberty wherewith Christ hath made you free." Be not "entangled" again in the "cares of this life"; but "cast all your care on Him that careth for you. Be careful for nothing, but in everything make your requests known unto God with thanksgiving."

See that you "wait upon the Lord without distraction": let nothing move you from your center. "One thing is needful"; to see, love, follow Christ, in every thought, word, and work.

Flee the "sorrow of this world"; it "worketh death." Let not your heart be troubled. In all circumstances, let your soul magnify the Lord and your spirit rejoice in God your Savior. Preserve a constant serenity of mind, an even cheerfulness of spirit.

Keep at the utmost distance from foolish desires, from desiring any happiness but in God. Still let all your "desire be to him, and to the remembrance of his name."

Make full use of all the leisure you have; never be unemployed, never triflingly employed; let every hour turn to some good account. Let not a scrap of time be squandered away; "gather up the fragments, that nothing be lost." Give all your time to God; lay out the whole as you judge will be most to his glory. In particular, see that you waste no part of it in unprofitable conversation; but let all your discourse "be seasoned with salt, and meet to minister grace to the hearers."

Give all your money to God. You have no pretense for laying up treasure upon earth. While you "gain all you can," and "save all you can," "give all you can," that is, all you have.

Lay out all your talents of every kind in doing all good to all men; knowing that "every man shall receive his own reward, according to his own labor."

Upon the whole, without disputing whether the married or single life be the more perfect state (an idle dispute; since perfection does consist in any outward state whatever, but in an absolute devotion of all our heart and all our life to God), we may safely say, blessed are "they who have made themselves eunuchs for the kingdom of heaven's sake," who abstain from things lawful in themselves in order to be more devoted to God. Let these never forget those remarkable words: "Peter said, Lo, we have left all and followed thee. And Jesus answered and said, Verily I say unto you" (a preface denoting both the certainty and importance of what is spoken), "There is no man that hath left" (either by giving them up, or by not accepting them) "house, or brethren, or sisters, or father, or mother, or wife, or children, or lands, for my sake and the gospel's, but he shall receive a hundredfold now in this time; and in the world to come eternal life," Mark 10:28–30.

FOR ADDITIONAL INFORMATION

Cannon, William R. *The Theology of John Wesley*. New York, University Press of America, 1984.

Coleman, Robert E. *Nothing to Do But to Save Souls; John Wesley's Charge to His Preachers*. Nappanee, New Jersey. Evangel Indiana.

Curnock, Nehemiah, ed. *The Journal of the Rev. John Wesley, A.M.* 8 Vols. London, Epworth Press, 1938.

Harper, Steve. *John Wesley's Message for Today*. Grand Rapids, Michigan, Francis Asbury Press, Zondervan, 1983.

Heitzenrater, Richard P. *The Elusive Mr. Wesley*. Vol. One. Nashville, Tennessee, Abingdon Press, 1984.

———. *Wesley and the People Called Methodists*. Nashville, Tennessee, Abingdon Press, 1995.

———. Heitzenrater, ed. *The Works of John Wesley*, Nashville, Tennessee, Abingdon Press, 1988, et al.

Oden, Thomas C. *John Wesley's Scriptural Christianity*. Grand Rapids, Michigan, Zondervan Pub. House, 1994.

Outler, Albert C., ed. *John Wesley*. New York, Oxford University Press, 1964.

———. *The Works of John Wesley*. Nashville, Abingdon Press, 1984, et al.

Pellowe, Susan, ed. *A Wesley Family Book of Days*. Illustrated. Aurora, Illinois, Renard Prod., 1994.

Rogal, Samuel J. *John Wesley in Ireland, 1747–1789*. Studies in the History of Missions: Vol. 9, Illustrated, Lewiston, New York, E. Mellen Publishers, 1993.

———. *John Wesley's Mission to Scotland*. Illustrated, Vol. 2, Lewiston, New York, E. Mellen Publishers, 1988.

———. *John Wesley in Wales, 1739–1790: Lions and Lambs*. Vol. 11, Lewiston, New York, E. Mellen, 1993.

Spurgeon, C. H. *The Two Wesleys*. New York, Pilgrim Press, 1975.

Sugden, Edward H., ed. *John Wesley's Fifty-Three Sermons*. Nashville, Abingdon Press, 1983.

Taylor, Blaine. *John Wesley: A Blueprint for Church Renewal*. Champaign, Illinois. C-Four Resources, 1984.

Telford, John, ed. *The Letters of the Rev. John Wesley*. 8 Vols. London, Epworth Press, 1931.

Tuttle, Robert G., Jr. *John Wesley, His Life and Theology*. Grand Rapids, Michigan, Zondervan Pub. House, 1978.

Vernon, Louise. *A Heart Strangely Warmed: The Life of John Wesley*. (Juvenile literature, grades 4–8) Greenleaf, Tennessee, 1994.

Weems, Lovett H., Jr. *John Wesley's Message Today*. Nashville, Abingdon Press, 1991.

Wesley, John, ed. *Christian Library*. 50 Vols. Bristol, England, 1749–55.

———. *Explanatory Notes Upon the New Testament, Vol. 1, Matthew to Acts, Vol. 2 Romans to Revelation*. Grand Rapids, Michigan, Baker Book House, 1981, reprinted.

———. *A Plain Account of Christian Perfection*. New York, Emory and Waugh, 1829.

Wilder, Franklin. *John Wesley Rides Again!* New York, Vantage Press, 1995.

Williams, Colin W. *John Wesley's Theology Today*. Nashville, Abingdon Press, 1972.

CHARLES FINNEY

Charles Finney

Abridged and edited by Stephen Rost

Contents

CHARLES GRANDISON FINNEY 1792-1875

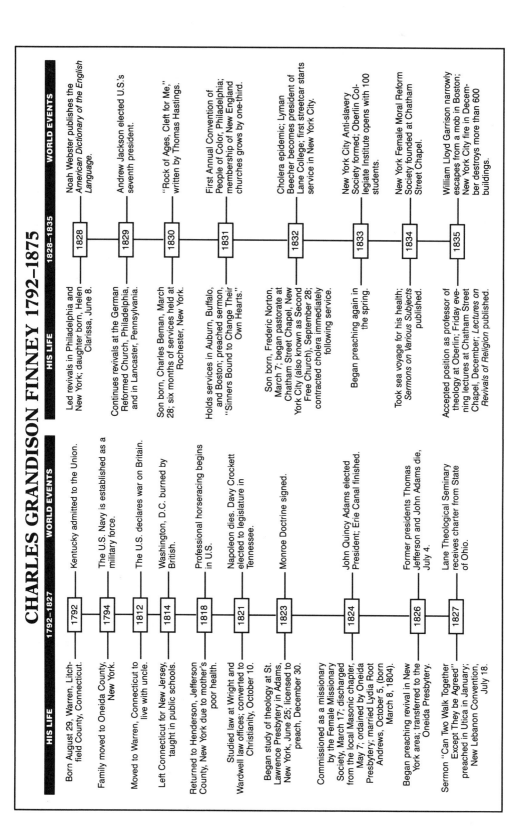

1792–1827

HIS LIFE

Born August 29, Warren, Litchfield County, Connecticut.

Family moved to Oneida County, New York.

Moved to Warren, Connecticut to live with uncle.

Left Connecticut for New Jersey, taught in public schools.

Returned to Henderson, Jefferson County, New York due to mother's poor health.

Studied law at Wright and Wardwell law offices; converted to Christianity, October 10.

Began study of theology at St. Lawrence Presbytery in Adams, New York, June 25; licensed to preach, December 30.

Commissioned as a missionary by the Female Missionary Society, March 17; discharged from the local Masonic chapter, May 7; ordained by Oneida Presbytery; married Lydia Root Andrews, October 5, (born March 8, 1804).

Began preaching revival in New York area; transferred to the Oneida Presbytery.

Sermon "Can Two Walk Together Except They be Agreed" preached in Utica in January; New Lebanon Convention, July 18.

WORLD EVENTS

1792 — Kentucky admitted to the Union.

1794 — The U.S. Navy is established as a military force.

1812 — The U.S. declares war on Britain.

1814 — Washington, D.C. burned by British.

1818 — Professional horseracing begins in U.S.

1821 — Napoleon dies. Davy Crockett elected to legislature in Tennessee.

1823 — Monroe Doctrine signed.

1824 — John Quincy Adams elected President; Erie Canal finished.

1826 — Former presidents Thomas Jefferson and John Adams die, July 4.

1827 — Lane Theological Seminary receives charter from State of Ohio.

1828–1835

HIS LIFE

Led revivals in Philadelphia and New York; daughter born, Helen Clarissa, June 8.

Continues revivals at the German Reformed Church, Philadelphia, and in Lancaster, Pennsylvania.

Son born, Charles Beman, March 28; six months of services held at Rochester, New York.

Holds services in Auburn, Buffalo, and Boston; preached sermon, "Sinners Bound to Change Their Own Hearts."

Son born, Frederic Norton, March 7; began pastorate at Chatham Street Chapel, New York City (also known as Second Free Church), September 28; contracted cholera immediately following service.

Began preaching again in the spring.

Took sea voyage for his health; Sermons on Various Subjects published.

Accepted position as professor of theology at Oberlin; Friday evening lectures at Chatham Street Chapel, December; Lectures on Revivals of Religion published.

WORLD EVENTS

1828 — Noah Webster publishes the American Dictionary of the English Language.

1829 — Andrew Jackson elected U.S.'s seventh president.

1830 — "Rock of Ages, Cleft for Me," written by Thomas Hastings.

1831 — First Annual Convention of People of Color, Philadelphia; membership of New England churches grows by one-third.

1832 — Cholera epidemic; Lyman Beecher becomes president of Lane College; first streetcar starts service in New York City.

1833 — New York City Anti-slavery Society formed; Oberlin Collegiate Institute opens with 100 students.

1834 — New York Female Moral Reform Society founded at Chatham Street Chapel.

1835 — William Lloyd Garrison narrowly escapes from a mob in Boston; New York City fire in December destroys more than 600 buildings.

1849–1875

HIS LIFE	Year	WORLD EVENTS
Preached in Britain with brief rest time in France, November 1849—April 1851.	1849	British defeat Sikhs and annex Punjab.
Elected President of Oberlin College, August 26; preached at Broadway Tabernacle, in Hartford, Connecticut and Brooklyn Plymouth Congregational Church, Fall 1851—April 1852.	1851	*The New York Daily Times* begins publication; fire destroys 30,000 volumes at Library of Congress.
Rochester revival, Fall.	1855	Crimean War.
Elizabeth died November 27.	1863	Emancipation Proclamation issued.
Married Rebecca Rayl, she died September 12, 1907.	1864	Sherman's march through Georgia.
Resigned as president of Oberlin, August.	1865	Abraham Lincoln assassinated.
The Character, Claims and Practical Workings of Freemasonry published.	1869	First national Woman's Suffrage Convention held.
Spoke to the National Congregational Council at Oberlin, November.	1871	Chicago fire.
Retired as pastor of First Congregational Church in May.	1872	Ulysses S. Grant elected to second term.
Spoke to the National Congregational Council.	1874	Society for the Prevention of Cruelty to Children founded.
Taught last pastoral theology course, July; died on August 16.	1875	Alexander Graham Bell invents the telephone.

1836–1848

HIS LIFE	Year	WORLD EVENTS
Resigned as pastor of Chatham Street Chapel, March 13; first services held at Broadway Tabernacle Church, April 10; returned to Oberlin and Broadway Tabernacle in the fall.	1836	Davy Crockett dies in Mexican attack on the Alamo; Arkansas becomes a state; Oberlin graduates first class.
Daughter born, Julia, March 16; resigned as pastor of Broadway Tabernacle, April 6.	1837	Panic of 1837; all New York City banks closed.
Lectures to Professing Christians published.	1839	"Trail of Tears" to relocate the Cherokees kills 4,000 of the Indians along the way.
Skeletons of a Course of Theological Lectures by the Rev. Charles G. Finney and *Views of Sanctification* published.	1840	*World Anti-Slavery Convention* in London; William Henry Harrison elected president.
Daughter born, Sarah, died March 9, 1843.	1841	John Tyler becomes tenth president.
Preached revivals at Rochester, Marlborough Chapel in Boston and in Providence, Rhode Island; Sylvester Finney died June 26.	1842	Massachusetts enacts child labor law limiting children's workdays to 10 hours.
Preached at Marlborough Chapel, December—March 1844.	1843	William Miller predicted the return of Christ.
Daughter born, Delia, died September 1, 1852; held first services as the pastor of the First Congregational Church of Christ at Oberlin.	1844	YMCA founded in England; October 22 Miller's second date for return of Christ.
Lectures on Systematic Theology written.	1846	U.S. and Mexico at war; sewing machine invented by Elias Howe.
Lydia died, December 17.	1847	Congress authorizes postage stamps.
Wed Mrs. Elizabeth Ford Atkinson of Rochester, November 13.	1848	Gold Rush begins in California; Wisconsin becomes a state.

CHARLES FINNEY

Introduction

Charles G. Finney (1792–1875) goes down in history as one of the greatest American evangelists, who influenced many of the leaders of nineteenth-century America.

Law was Finney's chosen profession. In order to prepare for his career Finney became an apprentice in the law offices of Judge Benjamin Wright and argued cases in the local court of Adams, New York. Although his legal career was getting off to a good start, the Lord had other plans. After his conversion on October 12, 1821, Finney engaged in theological studies under Princeton graduate George Gale in 1823 and was licensed to preach several months later.

Finney excelled as a preacher, drawing huge crowds and multiple conversions. Being progressive in style, Finney built a ministry that established him as the new leader of revivalism. New York City, Philadelphia, Boston, and Rochester, as well as cities in England were touched in a mighty way by his work.

In 1832, illness caused Finney to slow down and seek ministry in other areas. A successful pastoral career in New York and Ohio began, later followed by a professorship at Oberlin Collegiate Institute (Oberlin College) in Ohio. On August 16, 1875, Finney died in Oberlin, Ohio, leaving behind a wife and eight children. He was a devoted family man as well as a gifted minister.

Divine teaching is essential to aiding men in understanding spiritual things. Most men are able to comprehend the historical facts of religion. This is not unusual, for historical facts are apprehended by reason. Even doctrinal issues can be understood without the aid of divine help. Many non-Christians are able to articulate the gospel clearly even though it means nothing to them personally.

While Jesus was alive on earth, he aided the disciples and others in understanding the gospel and other doctrinal matters. With his ascension, the Holy Spirit became the illuminator of divine truth. Men are given the ability to receive great depths of truth according to their needs.

CHAPTER ONE

The Necessity of Divine Teaching

Nevertheless I tell you the truth; It is expedient for you that I go away; for if I go not away: the Comforter will not come unto you; but if I depart, I will send him unto you. And when he is come, he will reprove the world of sin, and of righteousness, and of judgment; of sin, because they believe not on me; of righteousness, because I go to my Father, and ye see me no more; of judgment, because the prince of this world is judged. I have yet many things to say unto you, but ye cannot bear them now. Howbeit when he, the Spirit of truth, is come, he will guide you into all truth; for he shall not speak of himself, but whatsoever he shall hear, that shall he speak: and he will show you things to come (John 16:7–13).

The doctrine of the necessity of divine influence to enlighten and sanctify the minds of men is very abundantly taught in the Bible and is generally maintained, as a matter of opinion at least, in all orthodox churches. But, as a matter of fact, there seems to be very little available knowledge of the gospel among mankind, so little that it exerts comparatively little influence. The great ends of the gospel have hardly begun to be realized in the production of holiness on the earth. It is a grand question whether we do need divine influence to attain the ends of the gospel; and if we do need it, then in what degree do we need it, and why? If our minds are unsettled on this question, we shall be unsettled on all the subjects that practically concern our sanctification.

In discoursing on this subject tonight, I design to pursue the following order: (1) Inquire how far the reason of man, unaided by divine illumination, is capable of understanding the things of religion; (2) Show wherein the reason of man is defective in regard to the capacity of gaining any available knowledge of the gospel; (3) That the Spirit of God alone can supply the illumination that is needed; (4) That everyone may have the influence of the Spirit, according to his necessities; (5) The reasons why any individual fails to receive this divine aid to the extent of his necessities; (6) That men are responsible for the light which they might have, as well as for that which they actually enjoy.

Reason Without Illumination

I shall inquire how far the reason of man, unaided by divine illumination, is capable of apprehending the things of religion.

The mind of man is capable of understanding the historical facts of religion, just as it comprehends any other historical facts. It is capable of understanding the doctrinal propositions of the gospel. That is, it can understand those abstractions which make up the skeleton of the gospel, such as the being and character of God, the divine authority and inspiration of the Scriptures, and other fundamental doctrines which make up the framework of the gospel. That is, it can understand them as propositions and see the evidence that supports them as true, just as it can understand any propositions in science.

For instance, to enter a little into detail, a man, by his reason, may understand the law of God. He can understand that it requires him to exercise perfect love toward God and all other beings. He can see the ground of his obligation to do this because he is a moral being. He knows by experience what love is, for he has exercised love toward different objects. And he can, therefore, form or comprehend the idea of love so far as to see the reasonableness of the requirement. He can understand the foundation and the force of moral obligation and see, in some measure, the extent of his obligation to love God.

So, likewise, he can see that he is a sinner and that he cannot be saved by his own works. He has broken the law, so that the law can never justify him. He can see that if he is ever saved, he must be justified through mere mercy, by an act of pardon.

I might go through the whole circle of theology and show that the human understanding is capable of knowing it, in the abstract, as a system of propositions, to be received and believed on evidence like any other science. I do not mean to be understood as saying that unaided reason can attain any available knowledge of the things of religion or any such knowledge as will be effectual to produce a sanctifying change.

Humanity's Defective Knowledge

I am to show wherein our knowledge of the things of religion is necessarily defective without the aids of the Holy Spirit. In other words, I am to show what our knowledge of the gospel lacks to make it available to salvation.

And here it is necessary to distinguish between knowledge which might be available to one that was himself disposed to love and obey God and what will be available, in fact, to a sinner, who is wholly indisposed to holiness. It is easy to see that one who is disposed to do right would be influenced to duty by a far less amount of illumination, or a far less clear and vivid view of motives, than one who is disposed to do wrong. What we are now inquiring after respects the matter of fact in this world. Whether the knowledge attainable by our present faculties would be available to influence us to do right were there no sin in the world is more than I can say. As a matter of fact, the knowledge which Adam had when in a state of innocence did not avail to influence him to do right. But we are now speaking of things as they are in their world and to show what is the reason that men, as sinners, can have no available knowledge of divine things; no such knowledge as will, as a matter of fact, influence them to love and serve God.

Knowledge, to avail anything toward effecting its object, must be such as will influence the mind. The will must be controlled. And to do this, the mind must have such a view of things as to excite emotion, corresponding to the object in view. Mere intellect never will move the soul to act. A pure scientific abstraction of the intellect that does not touch the feelings or excite any emotion is wholly unavailable to move the will. It is so everywhere. It would be so in heaven. You must bring the mind under a degree of excitement to influence the will in any case. In the case of sinners, to influence sinners to love God, you must have a great degree of light such as will powerfully excite the mind and produce strong emotions. The reasons for obedience must be made to appear with great strength and vividness so as to subdue their rebellious hearts and bring them voluntarily to obey God. This is available knowledge. This men never have, and never can have, without the Spirit of God. If men were disposed to do right, I know not how far their knowledge, attainable by unaided reason, might avail. But, as they are universally and totally indisposed, this knowledge will never do it. I will mention some of the reasons.

All the knowledge we can have here of spiritual things is by analogy or comparison. Our minds are here shut up in the body, and we derive all our ideas from external objects, through the senses. Now, we never can of ourselves obtain knowledge of spiritual or eternal things in this way sufficient to rightly influence our wills. Our bodily powers were not created for this. All the ideas we can have of the spiritual world is by analogy, or comparing them with the things around us. It is easily seen that all ideas conveyed to our minds in this way must be extremely imperfect, and that we do not, after all, get the true idea in our minds. The Jewish types were probably the most forcible means which God could then use for giving to the Jews a correct idea of the gospel. Considering how the eastern nations were accustomed by their education to the use of figures and parables and types, probably the system of types was the most impressive and happy mode that could be devised to gain a more ready access for the truth to their minds and give them a more full idea of the plan of redemption than could be communicated in any other way. And yet it is manifest that the ideas which were communicated in this way were extremely imperfect; and that, without divine illumination to make them see the reality more fully than they could by unaided reason, they never would have got any available knowledge in this way.

So words are merely signs of ideas. They are not the ideas but the representatives of ideas. It is often very difficult and sometimes impossible to convey ideas by words. Take a little child and attempt to talk with him, and how difficult it is on many subjects to get your ideas into his little mind. He must have some experience of the things you are trying to teach before you can convey ideas to him by words.

Suppose this congregation were all blind and had never seen colors. Then suppose that on that wall hung a most grand and beautiful painting and that I was a perfect master of the subject and should undertake to describe it to you. No language that I could use would give you such an idea of the painting as to enable you to form a picture of it in your minds. Where on any subject we are obliged from the nature of the case to use figurative language, analogies, and resemblances, the knowledge we communicate is necessarily defective and inadequate. Who of you have not heard descriptions of persons and places till you thought you had an accurate knowledge of them; but when you come to see them you find you had no true idea of the reality?

Suppose an individual were to visit this world from another planet where all things are constituted on the most opposite principles from those which are adopted here; suppose him to remain here long enough to learn our language and that then he should undertake to give us a description of the world he had left. We should understand it according to our ideas and experience. Now, if the analogy between the two worlds is very imperfect, it is plain that our knowledge of things there, from his description, must be imperfect in proportion. So, when we find in the Bible descriptions of heaven and hell or anything in the invisible world, it is plain that from mere words we can get no true ideas at all adequate to the reality.

The wickedness of our hearts is so

great as to pervert our judgment and shut out from our minds much that we might understand of the things of religion. When a man's mind is so perverted on any subject that he will not take up the evidence concerning it, he cannot, of course, come at the knowledge of the truth on that subject. This is our case in regard to religion. Perverseness of heart so shuts out the light that the intellect does not, and from the nature of things *cannot*, get even the ideas it might otherwise gain respecting divine things.

Prejudice is a great obstacle to the reception of correct knowledge concerning religion. Take the case of the disciples of Christ. They had strong Jewish prejudices respecting the plan of salvation, so strong that all the instructions of Christ himself could not make them understand the truth. After teaching them personally for three years with all the talent and simplicity and skill he was master of, he could never get their minds in possession of the first principle of the gospel. Up to his very death he could not make them see that he should die and rise from the dead. Therefore, he says in his last conversation, "If I go not away, the Comforter will not come unto you; but if I depart, I will send him unto you." This was the very design of his going away from them that the Spirit of truth might come and put them in possession of the things which he meant by the words he had used in teaching them.

The general truth is this: that without divine illumination men can understand from the Bible enough to convict and condemn them, but not enough to sanctify and save them.

Some may ask, What, then, is the use of revelation?

It is of much use. The Bible is as plain as it can be. Who doubts that our Lord Jesus Christ gave instructions to his dis-

ciples as plainly as he could? See the pains which he took to illustrate his teaching—how simple his language, how he brings it down to the weakest comprehension as a parent would to a little child. And yet it remains true that without divine illumination the unaided reason of man never did and never will attain any available knowledge of the gospel. The difficulty lies in the subject. The Bible contains the gospel as plain as it can be made. That is, it contains the signs of the ideas as far as language can represent the things of religion. No language but figurative language can be used for this purpose. And this will forever be inadequate to put our minds in real possession of the things themselves. The difficulty is in our ignorance and sin and in the nature of the subject. This is the reason why we need divine illumination to get any available knowledge of the gospel.

Illumination from God's Spirit

The Spirit of God alone can give us this illumination. The Bible says, "No man can say that Jesus Christ is Lord, but by the Holy Ghost." Now the abstract proposition of the deity of Christ can be proved as a matter of science so as to gain the assent of any unbiased mind to the truth, that Jesus is Lord. But nothing but the Holy Ghost can so put the mind in possession of the idea of Christ as God as to fix the soul in the belief of the fact and make it available to sanctify the heart.

Again, it is said that, "No man can come to me, except the Father which hath sent me draw him; and I will raise him up at the last day. It is written in the prophets and they shall be all taught of God. Every man, therefore, that hath heard, and hath learned of the Father, cometh unto me." Here it is evident that the drawing spoken of is the teaching of the Holy Spirit. They must be taught of God and learn of the Father before they can ever have such a knowledge of the things of religion as actually to come to Christ.

Christ says, "It is expedient for you that I go away: for if I go not away, the Comforter will not come unto you." The word *paracletos*, here translated Comforter, properly means a Helper or Teacher. "When he is come, he will reprove the world of sin, and of righteousness, and of judgment: Of sin, because they believe not on me; of righteousness, because I go to my Father, and ye see me no more; of judgment, because the prince of this world is judged. I have yet many things to say unto you, but ye cannot bear them now. Howbeit, when he, the Spirit of Truth, is come, he will guide you into all truth; for he shall not speak of himself; but whatsoever he shall hear, that shall he speak; and he will show you things to come."

So in the fourteenth chapter the Savior says, "I will pray the Father and he shall give you another Comforter, that he may abide with you forever; even the Spirit of Truth, whom the world cannot receive, because it seeth him not, neither knoweth him; but ye know him, for he dwelleth with you, and shall be in you." And again, in the twenty-sixth verse, "But the Comforter, which is the Holy Ghost, whom the Father will send in my name, he shall teach you all things, and bring all things to your remembrance, whatsoever I have said unto you." Here you see the office of the Spirit of God is to instruct mankind in regard to the things of religion.

Now, it is manifest that none but the Spirit of God can supply this defect from a single consideration, that all teaching by words, whether by Jesus Christ or by apostles or by any inspired or uninspired teacher coming merely through the senses, can never put the mind in possession of the idea of spiritual things. The kind of teaching that we need is this: we want someone to teach us the things of religion, who is not obliged to depend on words or to reach our minds through the medium of the senses. We want some way in which the ideas themselves can be brought to our minds and not merely the signs of the ideas. We want a teacher who can directly approach the mind itself and not through the senses, and who can exhibit the ideas of religion without being obliged to use words. This the Spirit of God can do.

The manner in which the Spirit of God does this is what we can never know in this world. But the fact is undeniable that he can reach the mind without the use of words and can put our minds in possession of the ideas themselves, of which the types or figures or words of the human teacher are only the signs or imperfect representatives. The human teacher can only use words to our senses and finds it impossible to possess us of the ideas of that which we have never experienced. But the Spirit of God, having direct access to the mind, can through the outward sign possess us of the actual idea of things. What Christian does not know this as a matter of fact? What Christian does not know from his own experience that the Spirit of God does lead him instantly to see that in a passage of Scripture which all his study and effort of mind to know the meaning of could never have given him in the world?

Take the case again of a painting on the wall there and suppose that all the congregation were blind and I was trying to describe to them this painting. Now, suppose while I was laboring to make them understand the various distinctions and combinations of colors and they are bending their minds to understand it, all at once their eyes are opened! You can then see for yourselves the very things which I was vainly trying to bring to your minds by words. Now, the office of the Spirit of God, and what he alone can do, is to open the spiritual eye and bring the things which we try to describe by analogy and signs, in all their living reality before the mind, so as to put the mind in complete possession of the thing as it is.

It is evident, too, that no one but the Spirit of God so knows the things of God as to be able to give us the idea of those things correctly. "What man knoweth the things of a man, save the spirit of man that is in him?" What can a beast know of the things of a man, of a man's character, designs, etc.? I can speak to your consciousness, being a man and knowing the things of a man. But I cannot speak these things to the consciousness of a beast, neither can a beast speak of these things because he has not the spirit of a man in him and cannot know them. In like manner the Bible says, "The things of God knoweth no man, but the Spirit of God." The Spirit of God, knowing from consciousness the things of God, possesses a different kind of knowledge of these things from what other beings can possess and, therefore, can give us the kind of instruction we need and such as no other being can give.

Availability of the Spirit's Influence

The needed influences of the Spirit of God may be possessed by all men freely and under the gospel. A few passages from the Bible will show this.

Jesus Christ says God is more willing to give his Holy Spirit to them that ask him than parents are to give their children bread. "Ask, and it shall be given you; seek, and ye shall find; knock, and it shall be opened unto you." "And all things whatsoever ye shall ask in prayer, believing, ye shall receive." "Therefore I say unto you, What things soever ye desire when ye pray, believe that ye receive them, and ye shall have them." James says, "If any of you lack wisdom, let him ask of God, that giveth to all men liberally, and upbraideth not; *and it shall be given him*." If it be true that God has made these unlimited promises, that *all men* who will ask of him may have divine illumination as much as they will ask for, then it is true that all men may have as much of divine illumination as they need.

Why Many Are in Darkness

I will show the reasons why many do not have as much divine illumination as they need:

They do not ask for it in such a manner or degree as they need it.

They ask amiss or from selfish motives. The apostle James says, "Ye ask and receive not, because ye ask amiss, that ye may consume it on your lusts." When an individual has a selfish motive for asking or some other reason than a desire to glorify God, he need not expect to receive divine illumination. If his object in asking for the Holy Ghost is that he may always be happy in religion or that he may be very wise in the Scriptures or be looked upon as an eminent Christian or have his experience spoken of as remarkable or any other selfish view, that is a good reason why he should not receive even what he asks.

They do not use the proper means to attain what they ask. Suppose a person neglects his Bible and yet asks God to give him a knowledge of the things of religion: that is tempting God. The manner in which God gives knowledge is through the Bible and the other appointed means of instruction. If a person will not use these means when they are in his power, however much he may pray, he need not expect divine instruction. "Faith cometh by hearing, and hearing by the word of God."

There is an important difference to be observed between the cases of those who possess these means and those who do not. I suppose that a person may hear the gospel and receive all the illumination he needs under any circumstances of privation of means. As if he [were] on a desolate island, he might receive direct illumination from the Spirit of God. And so he might in any other circumstances where he absolutely could not have access to any means of instruction. Some very remarkable cases of this kind have occurred within a few years. I have known one case, which I looked upon at the time as miraculous, and for that reason have seldom mentioned it, feeling that even the church was not prepared to receive it. When I was an evangelist I labored once in a revival in a neighborhood where there were many Germans. They had received but little instruction and many of them could not read. But when the gospel was preached among them, the Spirit of God was poured out and a most powerful revival followed. In the midst of the harvest if a meeting was appointed at any place, the whole neighborhood would come together and fill the house and hang upon the preacher's lips while he tried to possess their minds with the truth of the gospel. One poor German woman naturally intelligent, but who could not read, in relating her experience in one of these meetings told this fact which was certified to by her neighbors. With many tears and a heart full of joy she said, "When I loved God I longed to read the Bible, and I prayed to Jesus Christ, I said and felt, O Jesus! thou canst teach me to read thy Holy Bible, and the Lord taught me to read. There was a Bible in the house and when I had prayed, I

thought I could read the Bible, and I got the book and opened it and the words were just what I had heard people read. I said, 'O Lord Jesus Christ, thou canst teach me to read,' and I believed he could, and I thought I did read, but I went and asked the school-madam if I read and she said I read it right and the Lord has taught me to read my Bible, blessed be his name for it." I do not know but the school-madam to whom she referred was in the house and heard her relation. At all events she was a woman of good character among her neighbors, and some of the most respectable of them afterward told me they did not doubt the truth of what she said. I have no doubt it was true.

At the time, I thought it was a miracle; but since the facts which have been developed within a few years respecting the indestructibleness of the memory, I have thought this case might be explained in that way; and that she had probably been told the names of letters and their powers when young and now the Spirit of God, in answer to her prayer, had quickened her mind and brought it all to her remembrance so that she could read the Bible.

Some of you will recollect the facts which were stated here one evening by President Mahan, which shows that every impression which is made on the mind of man remains there forever indelible. One case that he mentioned was that of an old lady who, when she was young, had read some lines of poetry relating a little story; and afterward, when old, she wished to tell the story to some children to whom she thought it would be useful, and to her surprise the whole of the lines came up fresh in her memory and she repeated them word for word although she had never committed them to memory at all, but only read them when she was young. Another was the case of an ignorant servant girl.

She had once lived with a learned minister who was accustomed to read aloud the Hebrew Bible in his study which was in hearing of the place where this girl did her work. Of course, she understood nothing of the words, but only heard the sounds. Long afterward when she was on her deathbed, she astonished the bystanders by reciting whole chapters of Hebrew and Chaldaic. The neighbors at first thought it was a miracle, but at length learned the explanation. It is plain from this that even unintelligible sound may be so impressed on the memory as afterward to recur with entire distinctness. I suppose that was the case with this poor German woman and that the Spirit of God, in answer to her fervent prayer, so refreshed her memory as to recall the sounds and forms of letters she had been told when a child, and thus enable her at once to read the Bible.

I say, therefore, that while those who do not possess any outward means of instruction may obtain directly from the Spirit of God whatever degree or kind of illumination they need in the things of religion, those who possess or can obtain the outward means, and do not use them, tempt God when they pray for divine illumination and neglect the use of means for obtaining knowledge. To those who have the opportunity, "faith cometh by hearing, and hearing by the word of God." If any man keeps away from the means within his reach, he can expect illumination in no other way. Whereas, if he is shut out from the use of means as God is true to his promises, we must believe that he can be illuminated without means to any extent he needs.

Another reason why many do not receive that illumination from the Spirit of God which they need is because they grieve the Spirit in many ways. They live in such a manner as to grieve or offend the Holy Spirit so that he cannot consistently grant them his illuminating grace.

Another reason is that they *depend* on the instructions and means as available without divine influence. How many rely on the instructions they receive from ministers or commentaries or books or their own powers of inquiry, not feeling that all these things without the Spirit of God will only kill, but can never make alive; can only damn, but never save. It seems as though the whole church was in error on this point: depending on means for divine knowledge without feeling that no means are available without the Spirit of God. Oh! if the church felt this—if they really felt that all the means in creation are unavailing without the teaching of the Holy Ghost, how they would pray and cleanse their hands and humble their hearts, until the Comforter would descend to teach them all things that they need to know of religion.

Self-confidence is another reason why so little is experienced of divine illumination. So long as professing Christians place confidence in learning or criticism or their natural ingenuity to learn the things of religion, rely on it, they are not likely to enjoy much of the illumination of the Spirit of God.

The Extent of Human Responsibility

I am to show that men are responsible for what they might have of divine illumination. This is a universal truth and is acknowledged by all mankind, that a man is just as responsible for what light he might have, as for that he actually has. The common law, which is the voice of common reason, adopts it as a maxim that no man who breaks the law is to be excused for ignorance of the law because all are held bound to know what the law is. So it is with your children. In a case where they might know your will, you consider them so much the more blameworthy if they offend. So it is in religion: where men have both the outward means of instruction and the inward teachings of the Holy Spirit absolutely within their reach, if they sin ignorantly, they are not only without excuse on that score, but their ignorance is itself a crime and is an aggravation of their guilt. And all men are plainly without excuse for not possessing all the knowledge which would be available for their perfect and immediate sanctification.

REMARKS

You see what is the effect of all other instructions on a congregation where no divine influence is enjoyed. It may convince the church of duty, but will never produce sanctification. It may harden the heart, but will never change it. Without divine influence it is but a savor of death unto death.

You see that it is important to use all the appropriate means of religious instruction in our power as the medium through which the Spirit of God conveys divine illumination to the mind. There is no reason why we should not use the means in our power and apply our natural faculties to acquire knowledge of religion as faithfully as if we could understand the whole subject without divine influence. And if we do not use means, when within our power, we have no reason to expect divine aid. When we help ourselves God helps us. When we use our natural faculties to understand these things, we may expect God will enlighten us. To turn our eyes away from the light and then pray that we may be made to see is to tempt God.

They are blind leaders of the blind who attempt to teach the things of religion without being themselves taught of God. No degree of learning or power of discrimination as to the didactics of theology will ever make a man a successful teacher of religion unless he enjoys the illuminating powers of the Holy Ghost. He is blind if he supposes he understands the Bible without this, and if he undertakes to teach religion, he deceives himself and all who depend on him, and both will fall into the ditch together.

Taught by the Spirit

If an individual teaches the gospel with the Holy Ghost sent down from heaven, he will be understood. He may understand the gospel himself and yet not make his hearers understand it because the Holy Ghost is not sent on them as well as on himself. But if the Spirit of God is on them, precisely in proportion as he understands the real meaning of the gospel, he will make his hearers understand it.

In preaching the gospel, ministers should never use texts, the meaning of which they have not been taught by the Spirit of God. They should not attempt to explain passages of which they are not confident they have been taught the meaning of by the Holy Spirit. It is presumption. And they need not do it for they may always have the teachings of the Spirit, by asking. God is always more ready to bestow divine illumination than an earthly parent is to give bread to his child and if they ask as a child when he is hungry asks its mother for bread, they may always receive all the light they need. This is applicable both to preachers and to teachers in Sabbath schools and Bible classes. If any of them attempt to teach the Scriptures without being themselves taught, they are no more fit to teach without divine teaching than the most ignorant person in the streets is fit to teach astronomy. I fear both ministers and teachers generally have understood very little of their *need* of this divine teaching and have felt very little of the necessity of praying over their sermons and Bible lessons till they feel confident that the Spirit of God has possessed their minds with the true idea of the word of God. If this was done as it ought to be, their instructions would be far more effectual than we now see them. Do you who are teachers of Bible and Sabbath school classes in this church believe this? Are you in the habit, conscientiously and uniformly, of seeking the true idea of every lesson on your knees? Or do you go to some commentary and then come and peddle out your dry stuff to your classes that you get out of the commentaries and books without any of the Holy Ghost in your teaching? If you do this, let me tell you that you had better be doing something else. What would you say of a minister if you knew he never prayed over his texts? You might as well have Balaam's ass for a minister, and even the dumb beast in such a case might speak with man's voice and rebuke the madness of such a man. He could give just as much available instruction to reach the deep fountains of the heart as such a preacher. Well now, this is just as important for a Sunday school teacher as for a minister. If you do not pray over your lesson until you feel that God has taught you the idea contained in it, *beware!* How dare you go and teach that for religion which you do not honestly suppose you have been taught of God?

The Folly of Independent Learning

It is a vast error in theological students when they study to get the views of all the great teachers, the tomes of the fathers and doctors, and everybody's opinion as to what the Bible means, but the opinion of the Holy Ghost. With hearts as cold as marble instead of going right to the source of light, they go and gather up the husks of learning and peddle it out among the churches as religious instruction. Horrible! While they do thus, we never shall have an efficient ministry. It is right they should get all the help they can from learning to understand the word of God. But they ought never to rest in anything they get from book learning until they are satisfied that God has put them in possession of the very idea which *he* would have them receive.

I have tried hard to make this impression and I believe I have succeeded in some degree on the theological students under my care. And if I had done it more, I have no doubt I might have succeeded better. And I can say that when I studied theology, I spent many hours on my knees, and perhaps I might say weeks, often with the Bible before me laboring and praying to come at the very mind of the Spirit. I do not say this boastingly, but as a matter of fact to show that the sentiment here advanced is no novel opinion with me. And I have always got my texts and sermons on my knees. And yet I am conscious that I have gained very little knowledge in religion compared with what I might have had if I had taken right hold of the source of light as I ought to have done.

How little knowledge has the great body of the church respecting the word of God! Put them, for instance, to read the epistles and other parts and probably they will not have knowledge enough to give an opinion as to the real meaning of one-tenth of the Bible. No wonder the church is not sanctified! They need *more truth.* Our Savior says, "Sanctify them through thy truth." This grand means of sanctification must be more richly enjoyed before the church will know what entire sanctification means.

The church do not understand the Bible. And the reason is *they have not gone to the author* to explain it. Although they have this blessed privilege every day and just as often as they choose of carrying the book right to the author for his explanation, yet how little, how very little, do the church know of the Bible which they are conscious they have been taught to know by the Holy Ghost! Read the text again, read other similar passages, and then say if Christians are not exceedingly to blame for not understanding the Bible.

You see the necessity that we should all give ourselves up to the study of the Bible, under divine teaching. I have recently recommended several books to you to read such as Wesley's *Thoughts on Christian Perfection*, the Memoirs of Brainerd Taylor, Payson, Mrs. Rogers, and others. I have found that, in a certain state of mind, such books are useful to read. But I never pretend to make but *one book* my study. I read them occasionally, but have little time or inclination to read other books much while I have so much to learn of my Bible. I find

it like a deep mine; the more I work it, the richer it grows. We must read that more than any or all other books. We must pause and pray over it, verse after verse, and compare part with part, dwell on it, digest it, and get it into our minds till we feel that the Spirit of God has filled us with the spirit of holiness.

Will you do it? Will you lay your hearts open to God and not give him rest till he has filled you with divine knowledge? Will you *search* the Scriptures? I have often been asked by young converts and young men preparing for the ministry what they should read. *Read the Bible.* I would give the same answer five hundred times. Over and above all other things, study the Bible. It is a sad fact that most young men when they enter the ministry often know less of the Bible than of any other book they study. Alas! alas! Oh, if they had the spirit of James Brainerd Taylor, his love for the Scriptures, his prayer for divine teaching, we should no longer hear the groans of the churches over the barrenness of so many young preachers who come out of our seminaries full of book-learning and almost destitute of the Holy Ghost.

The doctrine of justification is of vital importance to the development of a proper understanding of salvation. From a legal standpoint, the term refers to being acquitted of a crime in light of the fact that the incident was committed under justified conditions. Biblical justification is when God pardons a person and accepts him as if he or she were righteous. This means that the sins of every justified person are no longer held against him or her. The account is clear and the saint stands before God in a state of guiltlessness.

CHAPTER TWO

Justification by Faith

Knowing that a man is not justified by works of the law, but by the faith of Jesus Christ, even we have believed in Jesus Christ, that we might be justified by the faith of Christ, and not by the works of the law; for by the works of the law shall no flesh be justified (Gal. 2:16).

This last sentiment is expressed in the same terms in the third chapter of Romans. The subject of the present lecture, as I announced last week, is justification by faith. The order which I propose to pursue in the discussion is this: (1) Show what justification by law or legal justification is; (2) Show that by the deeds of the law no flesh can be justified; (3) Show what gospel justification is; (4) Show what is the effect of gospel justification or the state into which it brings a person that is justified; (5) Show that gospel justification is by faith; (6) Answer some inquiries which arise in many minds on this subject.

Justification by Law

I am to show what legal justification is. In its general, legal sense it means not guilty. To justify an individual in this sense is to declare that he is not guilty of any breach of the law. It is affirming that he has committed no crime. It is pronouncing him innocent. More technically, it is a form of pleading to a charge of crime where the individual who is charged admits the fact, but brings forward an excuse on which he claims that he had a right to do as he did or that he is not blameworthy. Thus, if a person is charged with murder, the plea of justification admits that he killed the man, but alleges either that it was done in self-defense and he had a right to kill him or that it was by unavoidable accident and he could not help it. In either case, the plea of justification admits the fact, but denies the guilt on the ground of a sufficient excuse.

No Justification by Deeds of the Law

I am to show that by the deeds of the law there shall no flesh be justified. And this is true under either form of justification.

Under the first or general form of justification . . . the burden of proof is on the accuser, who is held to prove the facts charged. And in this case he only needs to prove that a crime has been committed once. If it is proved once, the individual is guilty. He cannot be justified in this way by the law. He is found guilty. It is not available for him to urge that he has done more good than hurt or that he has kept God's law longer than he has broken it, but he must make it out that he has fulfilled every jot and tittle of the law. Who can be justified by the law in this way? No one.

Nor under the second or technical form of justification . . . the burden of proof lies on him who makes the plea. When he pleads in justification he admits the fact alleged, and therefore he must make good his excuse or fail. There are two points to be regarded. The thing pleaded as an excuse must be *true*, and it must be a good and sufficient excuse or justification, not a frivolous apology or one that does not meet the case. If it is not true or if it is insufficient, and especially if it reflects on the court or government, it is an infamous aggravation of his offense. You will see the bearing of this remark by and by.

I will now mention some of the prominent reasons which sinners are in the habit of pleading as a justification and will show what is the true nature and bearing of these excuses and the light in which they stand before God. I have not time to name all these pleas, but will only refer to two of each of the classes I have described, those which are good if true and those which are true but unavailing.

Sinners often plead their sinful nature as a justification. This excuse is a good one, if it is true. If it is true, as they pretend, that God has given them a nature which is itself sinful and the necessary actings of their nature are sin, it is a good excuse for sin and in the face of heaven and earth and at the day of judgment will be a good plea in justification. God must annihilate the reason of all the rational universe before they will ever blame you for sin if God made you sin or if he gave you a nature that is itself sinful. How can your nature be sinful? What is sin? Sin is a transgression of the law. There is no other sin but this. Now, does the law say you must not have such a nature as you have? Nothing like it.

The fact is, this doctrine overlooks the distinction between sin and the occasion of sin. The bodily appetites and constitutional susceptibilities of body and mind, when strongly excited, become the occasion of sin. So it was with Adam. No one will say that Adam had a sinful nature. But he had, by his constitution, an appetite for food and a desire for knowledge. These were not sinful, but were as God made them and were necessary to fit him to live in this world as a subject of God's moral government; but being strongly excited, as you know, led to prohibited indulgence and thus became the occasions of his sinning against God. They were innocent in themselves, but he yielded to them in a sinful manner, and that was his sin. When the sinner talks about this sinful nature as a justification, he confounds these innocent appetites and susceptibilities with sin itself. By so doing, he in fact charges God foolishly and accuses him of giving him a sinful nature, when in fact his nature, in all its elements, is essential to moral agency; God has made it as well as it could be made and perfectly adapted it to the circumstances in which he lives in this world. The truth is, man's nature is all right and is as well fitted to love and obey God as to hate and disobey him. Sinner! the day is not far distant when it will be known whether this is a good excuse or not. Then you will see whether you can face your Maker down in this way; and when he charges you with sin, turn round and throw the blame back upon him.

Do you inquire what influence Adam's sin has then had in producing the sin of his posterity? I answer it has subjected them to aggravated temptation, but has by no means rendered their nature in its sinful.

Another excuse coming under the same class is inability. This also is a good excuse if it is true. If sinners are really unable to obey God, this is a good plea in justification. When you are charged with sin, in not obeying the laws of God, you have only to show, if you can, by good proof that God has required what you were not able to perform, and the whole intelligent universe will resound with the verdict of "not guilty." If you have not natural power to obey God, they must give this verdict or cease to be reasonable beings. For it is a first law of reason that no being has a right to do what he has no power to do.

Suppose God should require you to undo something which you have done. This, everyone will see, is a natural impossibility. Now, are you to blame for not doing it? God requires repentance of past sins and not that you should undo them. Now, suppose it was your duty on the first of January to warn a certain individual who is now dead. Are you under obligation to warn that individual? No. That is an impossibility. All that God can now require is that you should repent. It never can be your duty, now, to warn that sinner. God may hold you responsible for not doing your duty to him when it was in your power. But it would be absurd to make it your duty to do what is not in your power to do.

This plea being false and throwing the blame of tyranny on God is an infamous aggravation of the offense. If God requires you to do what you have no power to do, it is tyranny. And what God requires is on penalty of eternal death—he threatens an infinite penalty for not doing what you have no power to do and so he is an infinite tyrant. This plea, then, charges God with infinite tyranny and is not only insufficient for the sinner's justification, but is a horrible aggravation of his offense.

Let us vary the case a little. Suppose God requires you to repent for not doing what you never had natural ability to do. You must either repent, then, of not doing what you had no natural power to do or you must go to hell. Now, you can neither repent of this nor can he make you repent of it. What is repentance? It is to blame yourself and justify God. But if you had no power, you can do neither.

It is a natural impossibility that a rational being should ever blame himself for not doing what he is conscious he had not power to do. Nor can you justify God. Until the laws of mind are reversed, the verdict of all intelligent beings must pronounce it infinite tyranny to require that which there is no power to perform.

Suppose God should call you to account and require you to repent for not flying. By what process can he make you blame yourself for not flying when you are conscious that you have no wings and no power to fly? If he could cheat you into the belief that you had the power and make you believe a lie, then you might repent. But what sort of a way is that for God to take with his creatures?

What do you mean, sinner, by bringing such an excuse? Do you mean to have it go that you have never sinned? It is a strange contradiction you make when you admit that you ought to repent and in the next breath say you have no power to repent. You ought to take your ground one way or the other. If you mean to rely on this excuse, come out with it in full and take your ground before God's bar and say, "Lord, I am not going to repent at all—I am not under any obligation to repent for I have no power to obey thy law, and therefore, I plead not guilty absolutely, for I have never sinned!"

In which of these ways can any one of you be justified? Will you, dare you, take ground on this excuse and throw back the blame upon God?

Another excuse which sinners offer for their continued impenitence is their wicked heart. This excuse is true, but it is not sufficient. The first two that I mentioned, you recollect, were good if they had been true, but they were false. This is true but is no excuse. What is a wicked heart? It is not the bodily organ which we call the heart, but the affection of the soul, the wicked disposition, the wicked feelings, the actings of the mind. If these will justify you, they will justify the devil himself. Has he not as wicked a heart as you have? Sup pose you have committed murder and you should be put on trial and plead this plea. "It is true," you would say, "I killed the man, but then I have such a thirst for blood and such a hatred of mankind that I cannot help committing murder whenever I have an opportunity." "Horrible!" the judge would exclaim, "Horrible! Let the gallows be set up immediately and let this fellow be hung before I leave the bench; such a wretch ought not to live an hour. Such a plea! Why, that is the very reason he ought to be hung if he has such a thirst for blood that no man is safe." Such is the sinner's plea of a wicked heart in justification of sin. "Out of thine own mouth will I condemn thee, thou wicked servant."

Another great excuse which people make is the conduct of Christians. Ask many a man among your neighbors why he is not religious and he will point you at once to the conduct of Christians as his excuse. "These Christians," he will say, "are no better than anybody else; when I see them live as they profess I shall think it time for me to attend to religion." Thus he is hiding behind the sins of Christians. He shows that he knows how Christians ought to live, and therefore he cannot plead that he has sinned through ignorance. But what does it amount to as a ground of justification? I admit the fact that Christians behave very badly and do much that is entirely contrary to their profession. But is that a good excuse for you? So far from it, this is itself one of the strongest reasons why you ought to be religious. You know so well how Christians ought to live, you are bound to show an example. If you had followed them ignorantly

because you did not know any better and had fallen into sin in that way, it would be a different case. But the plea, as it stands, shows that you knew they [were] wrong, which is the very reason why you ought to be right and exert a better influence than they do. Instead of following them and doing wrong because they do, you ought to break off from them and rebuke them and pray for them and try to lead them in a better way. This excuse, then, is true in fact but unavailing in justification. You only make it an excuse for charging God foolishly, and instead of clearing you, it only adds to your dreadful, damning guilt. A fine plea this, to get behind some deacon or some elder in the church and there shoot your arrows of malice and cavilling at God!

Who among you, then, can be justified by the law? Who has kept it? Who has got a good excuse for breaking it? Who dares go to the bar of God on these pleas and face his Maker with such apologies?

The Nature of Gospel Justification

I am to show what gospel justification is.

First—negatively: Gospel justification is not the imputed righteousness of Jesus Christ. Under the gospel, sinners are not justified by having the obedience of Jesus Christ set down to their account, as if he had obeyed the law for them or in their stead. It is not an uncommon mistake to suppose that when sinners are justified under the gospel, they are accounted righteous in the eye of the law by having the obedience or righteousness of Christ imputed to them. I have not time to enter into an examination of this subject now. I can only say this idea is absurd and impossible, for this reason, that Jesus Christ was bound to obey the law for himself and could no more perform works of supererogation or obey on our account than anybody else. Was it not his duty to love the Lord his God with all his heart and soul and mind and strength, and to love his neighbor as himself? Certainly; and if he had not done so it would have been sin. The only work of supererogation he could perform was to submit to sufferings that were not deserved. This is called his obedience unto death and this is set down to our account. But if his obedience of the law is set down to our account, why are we called on to repent and obey the law ourselves? Does God exact double service, yes, triple service—first to have the law obeyed by the surety for us, then that he must suffer the penalty for us, and then that we must repent and obey ourselves? No such thing is demanded. It is not required that the obedience of another should be imputed to us. All we owe is perpetual obedience to the law of benevolence. And for this there can be no substitute. If we fail of this, we must endure the penalty or receive a free pardon.

Justification by faith does not mean that faith is accepted as a substitute for personal holiness or that by an arbitrary constitution, faith is imputed to us instead of personal obedience to the law. Some suppose that justification is this, that the necessity of personal holiness is set aside and that God arbitrarily dispenses with the requirement of the law and imputes faith as a substitute. But this is not the way. Faith is accounted for just what it is, and not something else that it is not. Abraham's faith was imputed unto him for righteousness because it was itself an act of righteousness and because it worked by love, and thus produced holiness. Justifying faith is holiness, so far as it goes, and produces holiness of heart and life and is imputed to the believer as holiness, not instead of holiness.

Nor does justification by faith imply that a sinner is justified by faith without good works or personal holiness. Some suppose that justification by faith only is without any regard to good works or holiness. They have understood this from what Paul has said where he insists so largely on justification by faith. But it should be borne in mind that Paul was combating the error of the Jews who expected to be justified by obeying the law. In opposition to this error, Paul insists on it that justification is by faith without works of law. He does not mean that good works are unnecessary to justification, but that works of law are not good works because they spring from legal considerations, from hope and fear, and not from faith that works by love.

But inasmuch as a false theory had crept into the church on the other side, James took up the matter and showed them that they had misunderstood Paul. And to show this, he takes the case of Abraham our father [who was] justified by works when he had offered Isaac his son upon the altar. Seest thou how faith wrought with his works and by works was faith made perfect? And the Scripture was fulfilled which saith, "Abraham believed God, and it was imputed unto him for righteousness: and he was called the Friend of God. Ye see then how that by works a man is justified, and not by faith only." This epistle was supposed to contradict Paul, and some of the ancient churches rejected it on that account. But they overlooked the fact that Paul was speaking of one kind of works and James of another. Paul was speaking of works performed from legal motives. But he has everywhere insisted on good works springing from faith or the righteousness of faith as indispensable to salvation. All that he denies is that works of law, or works grounded on legal motives, have anything to do in the matter of justification. And James teaches the same thing when he teaches that men are justified not by works nor by faith alone, but by faith together with the works of faith, or as Paul expresses it, faith that works by love. You will bear in mind that I am speaking of gospel justification which is very different from legal justification.

Secondly—positively: Gospel justification or justification by faith consists in pardon and acceptance with God. When we say that men are justified by faith and holiness, we do not mean that they are accepted on the ground of law, but that they are treated as if they were righteous on account of their faith and works of faith. This is the method which God takes in justifying a sinner. Not that faith is the foundation of justification. The foundation is in Christ. But this is the manner in which sinners are pardoned and accepted and justified, that if they repent, believe, and become holy, their past sins shall be forgiven for the sake of Christ.

Here it will be seen how justification under the gospel differs from justification under the law. Legal justification is a declaration of actual innocence and freedom from blame. Gospel justification is pardon and acceptance as if he [were] righteous, but on other grounds than his own obedience. When the apostle says, "By deeds of law shall no flesh be justified," he uses justification as a lawyer, in a strictly legal sense. But when he speaks of justification by faith, he speaks not of legal justification but of a person's being treated as if he were righteous.

The Effect of Gospel Justification

I will now proceed to show the effect of this method of justification or the state into which it brings those who are justified. The first item to be observed is that when an individual is pardoned, the penalty of the law is released. The first effect of a pardon is to arrest and set aside the execution of the penalty. It admits that the penalty was deserved but sets it aside. Then, so far as punishment is concerned, the individual has no more to fear from the law than if he had never transgressed. He is entirely released. Those, then, who are justified by true faith, as soon as they are pardoned, need no more be influenced by fear or punishment. The penalty is as effectually set aside as if it had never been incurred.

The next effect of pardon is to remove all the liabilities incurred in consequence of transgression, such as forfeiture of goods or incapacity for being a witness or holding any office under government. A real pardon removes all these and restores the individual back to where he was before he transgressed. So, under the government of God, the pardoned sinner is restored to the favor of God. He is brought back into a new relation and stands before God and is treated by him, so far as the law is concerned, as if he were innocent. It does not suppose or declare him to be really innocent, but the pardon restores him to the same state as if he were.

Another operation of pardon under God's government is that the individual is restored to sonship. In other words, it brings him into such a relation to God that he is received and treated as really a child of God. Suppose the son of a sovereign on the throne had committed murder and was convicted and condemned to die. A pardon, then, would not only deliver him from death but restore him to his place in the family. God's children have all gone astray and entered into the service of the devil; but the moment a pardon issues to them, they are brought back; they receive a spirit of adoption, are sealed heirs of

God, and restored to all the privileges of children of God.

Another thing effected by justification is to secure all needed grace to rescue themselves fully out of the snare of the devil and all the innumerable entanglements in which they are involved by sin. Beloved, if God were merely to pardon you and then leave you to get out of sin as you could by yourselves, of what use would your pardon be to you? None in the world. If a child runs away from his father's house and wanders in a forest and falls into a deep pit and the father finds him and undertakes to save him; if he merely pardons him for running away, it will be of no use unless he lifts him up from the pit and leads him out of the forest. So in the scheme of redemption, whatever helps and aids you need are all guaranteed, if you believe. If God undertakes to save you, he pledges all the light and grace and help that are necessary to break the chains of Satan and the entanglements of sin and leads you back to your Father's house.

I know when individuals are first broken down under a sense of sin and their hearts gush out with tenderness, they look over their past lives and feel condemned and see that it is all wrong, and then they break down at God's feet and give themselves away to Jesus Christ; they rejoice greatly in the idea that they have done with sin. But in a little time they begin to feel the pressure of old habits and former influences and they see so much to be done before they overcome them all that they often get discouraged and cry, "Oh, what shall I do, with so many enemies to meet and so little strength of resolution or firmness of purpose to overcome them?" Let me tell you, beloved, that if God has undertaken to save you, you have only to keep near to him and he will carry you through. You need not fear your ene-

mies. Though the heavens should thunder and the earth rock and the elements melt, you need not tremble nor fear for enemies without or enemies within. God is for you and who can be against you? "Who is he that condemneth? It is Christ that died, yea, rather that is risen again, who is even at the right hand of God, who also maketh intercession for us."

Justification enlists all the divine attributes in your favor as much as if you had never sinned. See that holy angel, sent on an errand of love to some distant part of the universe. God's eye follows him and if he sees him likely to be injured in any way, all the divine attributes are enlisted at once to protect and sustain him. Just as absolutely are they all pledged for you, if you are justified, to protect, and support, and save you. Notwithstanding, you are not free from remaining sin and are so totally unworthy of God's love, yet if you are truly justified, the only wise and eternal God is pledged for your salvation. And shall you tremble and be faint-hearted with such support?

If a human government pardons a criminal, it is then pledged to protect him as a subject, as much as if he had never committed a crime. So it is when God justifies a sinner. The apostle says, "Being justified by faith, we have peace with God." Henceforth, God is on his side and pledged as his faithful and eternal Friend.

Gospel justification differs from legal justification in this respect: If the law justifies an individual, it holds no longer than he remains innocent. As soon as he transgresses once, his former justification is of no more avail. But when the gospel justifies a sinner, it is not so; but "if any man sin, we have an Advocate with the Father, Jesus Christ the righteous." A new relation is now constituted entirely peculiar. The sinner is now brought out from under the covenant of works and placed under the covenant of grace. He no longer retains God's favor by the tenure of absolute and sinless obedience. If he sins, now, he is not thrust back again under the law but receives the benefit of the new covenant. If he is justified by faith and so made a child of God, he receives the treatment of a child and is corrected and chastised and humbled and brought back again. "The gifts and callings of God are without repentance." The meaning of that is not that God calls and saves the sinner without his repenting, but that God never changes his mind when once he undertakes the salvation of a soul.

I know this is thought by some to be very dangerous doctrine, to teach that believers are perpetually justified—because, say they, it will embolden men to sin. Indeed. To tell a man that has truly repented of sin and heartily renounced sin and sincerely desires to be free from sin that God will help him and certainly give him the victory over sin will embolden him to commit sin! Strange logic that! If this doctrine emboldens any man to commit sin, it only shows that he never did repent; that he never hated sin and never loved God for his own sake, but only feigned repentance, and if he loved God it was only a selfish love because he thought God was going to do him a favor. If he truly hated sin, the consideration that notwithstanding all his unworthiness, God had received him as a child and would give him a child's treatment is the very thing to break him down and melt his heart in the most godly sorrow. Oh, how often has the child of God melted in adoring wonder at the goodness of God in using means to bring him back, instead of sending him to hell as he deserved! What consideration is calculated to bring him lower in the dust than the thought that notwithstanding all God had done for him and the gracious help God was always ready to afford him, he should wander away again when his name was written in the Lamb's book of life!

It secures the discipline of the covenant. God has pledged himself that if any who belong to Christ go astray, he will use the discipline of the covenant and bring them back. In Psalm 89:30–34 God says, putting David for Christ,

If his children forsake my law, and walk not in my judgments: if they break my statutes, and keep not my commandments; then will I visit their transgression with the rod, and their iniquity with stripes. Nevertheless my loving kindness will I not utterly take from him, nor suffer my faithfulness to fail. My covenant will I not break, nor alter the thing that is gone out of my lips.

Thus, you see that professors of religion may always expect to be more readily visited with God's judgments, if they get out of the way, than the impenitent. The sinner may grow fat and live in riches and have no bands in his death, all according to God's established principles of government. But let a child of God forsake his God and go after riches or any other worldly object, and as certain as he is a child, God will smite him with his rod. And when he is smitten and brought back, he will say with the psalmist, "It is good for me that I have been afflicted, that I might learn thy statutes. Before I was afflicted, I went astray, but now have I kept thy word." Perhaps some of you have known what it is to be afflicted in this way and to feel that it was good.

Another effect of gospel justification is to insure sanctification. It not only insures all the means of sanctification, but the actual accomplishment of the work so that the individual who is truly converted will surely persevere in obedience till he is fitted for heaven and actually saved.

Gospel Justification and Faith

I am to show that this is justification by faith. Faith is the medium by which the blessing is conveyed to the believer. The proof of this is in the Bible. The text declares it expressly. "Knowing that a man is not justified by the works of the law, but by the faith of Jesus Christ, even we have believed in Jesus Christ, that we might be justified by the faith of Christ, and not by the works of the law: for by the works of the law shall no flesh be justified." The subject is too often treated in the New Testament to be necessary to go into a labored proof. It is manifest, from the necessity of the case, that if men are saved at all, they must be justified in this way and not by works of law, for "by the deeds of the law shall no flesh be justified."

Responses to Natural Questions

I will now answer several inquiries which may naturally arise in your minds growing out of this subject.

"Why is justification said to be by faith rather than by repentance or love or any other grace?"

Answer: It is nowhere said that men are justified or saved *for* faith, as the ground of their pardon, but only that they are justified *by* faith, as the medium or instrument. If it is asked why faith is appointed as the instrument rather than any other exercise of the mind, the answer is, because of the nature and effect of faith. No other exercise could be appointed. What is faith? It is that confidence in God which leads us to love and obey him. We are, therefore, justified by faith *because* we are

sanctified by faith. Faith is the appointed instrument of our justification because it is the natural instrument of sanctification. It is the instrument of bringing us back to obedience and therefore is designated as the means of obtaining the blessings of that return. It is not imputed to us by an arbitrary act *for* what it is not, but for what it is as the foundation of all real obedience to God. This is the reason why faith is made the medium through which pardon comes. It is simply set down to us for what it really is because it first leads us to obey God from a principle of love to God. We are forgiven our sins on account of Christ. It is our duty to repent and obey God and when we do so, this is imputed to us as what it is, holiness or obedience to God. But for the forgiveness of our past sins we must rely on Christ. And therefore justification is said to be by faith in Jesus Christ.

The second query is of great importance: "What is justifying faith? What must I believe in order to be saved?"

Answer: Negatively, justifying faith does not consist in believing that your sins are forgiven. If that were necessary, you would have to believe it before it was done or to believe a lie. Remember your sins are not forgiven *until* you believe. But if saving faith is believing that they are already forgiven, it is believing a thing before it takes place, which is absurd. You cannot believe your sins are forgiven before you have the evidence that they are forgiven; and you cannot have the evidence that they are forgiven until it is true that they are forgiven, and they cannot be forgiven until you exercise saving faith. Therefore saving faith must be believing something else. Nor does saving faith consist in believing that you shall be saved at all. You have no right to believe that you shall be saved at all until after you have exercised justifying or saving faith. But justifying faith consists in believing the atonement of Christ or believing the record which God has given of his Son.

The correctness of this definition has been doubted by some; and I confess my own mind has undergone a change on this point. It is said that Abraham believed God and it was imputed to him for righteousness. But what did Abraham believe? He believed that he should have a son. Was this all? By no means. But his faith included the great blessing that depended on that event, that the Messiah, the Savior of the world, should spring from him. This was the great subject of the Abrahamic covenant, and it depended on his having a son. Of course, Abraham's faith included the "Desire of all Nations," and was faith in Christ. The apostle Paul has showed this, at full length, in the third chapter of Galatians, that the sum of the covenant was, "In thee shall all nations be blessed." In verse 16, he says, "Now to Abraham and his seed were the promises made. He saith not, And to seeds, as of man; but as of one: And to thy seed, which is Christ."

It is said that in the eleventh [chapter] of Hebrews, the saints are not all spoken of as having believed in Christ. But if you examine carefully, you will find that in all cases, faith in Christ is either included in what they believe or fairly implied by it. Take the case of Abel. "By faith Abel offered unto God a more excellent sacrifice than Cain, by which he obtained witness that he was righteous, God testifying of his gifts: and by it he being dead yet speaketh." Why was his sacrifice more excellent? Because by offering the firstlings of his flock, he recognized the necessity of the atonement and that "without the shedding of blood there is no remission." Cain was a proud infidel and offered the fruits of the ground as a mere thank offering for the blessings of Providence, without any admission that he was a sinner and needed an atonement as the ground on which he could hope for pardon.

Some suppose that an individual might exercise justifying faith while denying the divinity and atonement of Jesus Christ. I deny this. The whole sum and substance of revelation, like converging rays, all center on Jesus Christ, his divinity and atonement. All that the prophets and other writers of the Old Testament say about salvation comes to him. The Old Testament and the New, all the types and shadows, point to him. All the Old Testament saints were saved by faith in him. Their faith terminated in the coming Messiah, as that of the New Testament saints did in the Messiah already come. In the fifteenth chapter of First Corinthians, the apostle Paul shows what place [he] would assign to this doctrine: "For I delivered unto you first of all that which I also received, how that Christ died for our sins according to the scriptures; and that he was buried, and that he rose again the third day according to the scriptures." Mark that expression, "first of all." It proves that Paul preached that Christ died for sinners, as the "first," or primary, doctrine of the gospel. And so you will find it from one end of the Bible to the other, that the attention of men was directed to this new and living way as the only way of salvation. This truth is the only truth that can sanctify men. They may believe a thousand other things, but this is the great source of sanctification, "God in Christ, reconciling the world unto himself." And this alone can, therefore, be justifying faith.

There may be many other acts of faith that may be right and acceptable to God. But nothing is justifying faith but believing the record that God has given of his Son. Simply believing what God has revealed on any point is an act of faith;

but justifying faith fastens on Christ, takes hold of his atonement, and embraces him as the only ground of pardon and salvation. There may be faith in prayer, the faith that is in exercise in offering up prevailing prayer to God. But that is not properly justifying faith.

"When are men justified?" This is also an inquiry often made.

Answer: Just as soon as they believe in Christ with the faith which worketh by love. Sinner, you need not go home from this meeting under the wrath of Almighty God. You may be justified here, on the spot, now, if you will only believe in Christ. Your pardon is ready, made out and sealed with the broad seal of heaven; and the blank will be filled up, and the gracious pardon delivered, as soon as by one act of faith you receive Jesus Christ as he is offered in the gospel.

"How can I know whether I am in a state of justification or not?"

Answer: You can know it in no way except by inference. God has not revealed it in the Scriptures that you or any other individuals are justified; but he has set down the characteristics of a justified person and declared that all who have these characteristics are justified.

Have you the witness of the Spirit? All who are justified have this. They have intercourse with the Holy Ghost; he explains the Scriptures to them and leads them to see their meaning, he leads them to the Son and to the Father, and reveals the Son in them, and reveals the Father. Have you this? If you have, you are justified. If not, you are yet in your sins.

Have you the fruits of the Spirit? They are love, joy, peace, and so on. These are matters of human conscious-

ness; have you them? If so, you are justified.

Have you peace with God? The apostle says, "Being justified by faith, we have peace with God." Christ says to his disciples, "My peace I give unto you; not as the world giveth give I unto you." And again, "Come unto me, all ye that labor and are heavy laden, and I will give you rest." Do you find *rest* in Christ? Is your peace like a river, flowing gently through your soul and filling you with calm and heavenly delight? Or do you feel a sense of condemnation before God?

Do you feel a sense of acceptance of God, of pardoned sin, of communion with God? This must be a matter of experience, if it exists. Don't imagine you *can be in* a justified state and yet have no evidence of it. You may have great peace in reality, filling your soul, and yet not draw the inference that you are justified. I remember the time when my mind was in a state of such sweet peace that it seemed to me as if all nature was listening for God to speak; but yet I was not aware that this was the peace of God or that it was evidence of my being in a justified state. I thought I had lost all my conviction and actually undertook to bring back the sense of condemnation that I had before. I did not draw the inference that I was justified till after the love of God was shed abroad in my soul by the Holy Ghost that I was compelled to cry out, "Lord, it is enough, I can bear no more." I do not believe it possible for the sense of condemnation to remain where the act of pardon is already past.

Have you the spirit of adoption? If you are justified, you are also adopted as one of God's dear children and he has sent forth his Spirit into your heart so that you naturally cry, "Abba, Father!" He seems to you just like a father and you want to call him father. Do you know anything of this? It is one thing to *call* God your father in heaven and another thing to *feel* toward him as a father. This is one evidence of a justified state when God gives the spirit of adoption.

REMARKS

I would go around to all my dear hearers tonight and ask them one by one, "Are you in a state of justification? Do you honestly think you are justified?" I have briefly run over the subject and showed what justification is not and what it is, how you can be saved, and the evidences of justification. Have you it? Would you dare to die now? Suppose the loud thunders of the last trumpet were now to shake the universe and you should see the Son of God coming to judgment—are you ready? Could you look up calmly and say, "Father, this is a solemn sight, but Christ has died and God has justified me and who is he that shall condemn me?"

If you think you ever [were] justified and yet have not at present the evidence of it, I want to make an inquiry. Are you under the discipline of the covenant? If not, have you any reason to believe you were justified? God's covenant with you, if you belong to Christ, is this: "If they backslide, I will visit their iniquity with the rod, and chasten them with stripes." Do you feel the stripes? Is God awakening your mind and convicting your conscience, is he smiting you? If not, where are the evidences that he is dealing with you as a son? If you are not walking with God and at the same time are not under chastisement, you cannot have any good reason to believe you are God's children.

Those of you who have evidence that you are justified should maintain your relation to God and live up to your real privileges. This is immensely important. There is no virtue in being distrustful and unbelieving. It is important to your growth in grace. One reason why many Christians do not grow in grace is that they are afraid to claim the privileges of God's children which belong to them. Rely upon it, beloved, this is no virtuous humility, but criminal unbelief. If you have the evidence that you are justified, take the occasion from it to press forward to holiness of heart and come to God with all the boldness that an angel would and know how near you are to him. It is your duty to do so. Why should you hold back? Why are you afraid to recognize the covenant of grace in its full extent? Here are the provisions of your Father's house, all ready and free; and are you converted and justified and restored to his favor and yet afraid to sit down at your Father's table? Do not plead that you are so unworthy. This is nothing but self-righteousness and unbelief. True, you are so unworthy. But if you are justified, that is no longer a bar. It is now your duty to take hold of the promises as belonging to you. Take any promise you can find in the Bible that is applicable and go with it to your Father and plead it before him, believing. Do you think he will deny it? These exceeding great and precious promises were given you for this very purpose, that you may become a partaker of the divine nature. Why then should you doubt? Come along, beloved, come along up to the privileges that belong to you and take hold of the love and peace and joy offered to you in this holy gospel.

If you are not in a state of justification, however much you have done and prayed and suffered, you are nothing. If you have not believed in Christ, if you have not received and trusted in him, as he is set forth in the gospel, you are yet in a state of condemnation and wrath.

You may have been, for weeks and months, and even for years, groaning with distress, but for all that you are still in the gall of bitterness. Here you see the line drawn; the moment you pass this, you are in a state of justification.

Dear hearer, are you now in a state of wrath? Now believe in Christ. All your waiting and groaning will not bring you any nearer. Do you say you want more conviction? I tell you to come now to Christ. Do you say you must wait till you have prayed more? What is the use of praying in unbelief? Will the prayers of a condemned rebel avail? Do you say you are so unworthy? But Christ died for such as you. He comes right to you now, on your seat. Where do you sit? Where is that individual I am speaking to? Sinner, you need not wait. You need not go home in your sins with that heavy load on your heart. Now is the day of salvation. Hear the word of God. "If thou believe in thine heart in the Lord Jesus Christ, and if thou confess with thy mouth that God raised him from the dead, thou shalt be saved."

Do you say, "What must I believe?" Believe just what God says of his Son; believe any of those great fundamental truths which God has revealed respecting the way of salvation and rest your soul on it, and you shall be saved. Will you now trust Jesus Christ to dispose of you? Have you confidence enough in Christ to leave yourself with him, to dispose of your body and your soul, for time and eternity? Can you say,

"Here, Lord, I give myself away;
'Tis all that I can do?"

Perhaps you are trying to pray yourself out of your difficulties before coming to Christ. Sinner, it will do no good. Now, cast yourself down at his feet and leave your soul in his hands. Say to him, "Lord, I give myself to thee, with all my powers of body and of mind; use me and dispose of me as thou wilt, for thine own glory, I know thou wilt do right, and that is all I desire." Will you do it?

Worldliness is an age-old problem that preachers of every generation have had to deal with. Unfortunately, many have misunderstood the command to avoid worldliness. It does not mean that Christians are to avoid contact with the lost. Nor does it demand an avoidance of art, culture, improvements, wealth, etc. What it does communicate is that Christians are to avoid acting in ways that reflect worldly standards. In business, fashion, and politics, worldliness consists of selfish ambitions, immodesty, and crooked dealings. Such attitudes and actions constitute conformity, not the situations that give rise to those problems.

CHAPTER THREE

Conformity to the World

Be not conformed to this world (Rom. 12:2).

It will be recollected by some who are present that, some time since, I made use of this text in preaching in this place, but the object of this evening's discourse is so far different that it is not improper to employ the same text again. The following is the order in which I design to discuss the subject of conformity to the world: to show what is *not* meant by the command of the text; show what is meant by the command, "Be not conformed to this world"; to mention some of the reasons why this requirement is made upon all who will live a godly life; to answer some objections that are made to the principles laid down.

I am to show what is not meant by the requirement, "Be not conformed to this world." I suppose it is not meant that Christians should refuse to benefit by the useful arts, improvements, and discoveries of the world. It is not only the privilege but the duty of the friends of God to avail themselves of these and to use for God all the really useful arts and improvements that arise among mankind.

I am to show what is meant by the requirement. It is meant that Christians are bound not to conform to the world in the three following things. I mention only these three, not because there are not many other things in which conformity to the world is forbidden, but because these three classes are all that I have had time to examine tonight, and further, because these three are pecu-

liarly necessary to be discussed at the present time. The three things are three departments of life in which it is required that you be not conformed to this world. They are business, fashion, and politics.

In all these departments it is required that Christians should not do as the world [does], they should neither receive the maxims, nor adopt the principles, nor follow the practices of the world.

I am to mention some reasons for the command, "Be not conformed to this world." You are by no means to act on the same principles nor from the same motives nor pursue your object in the same manner that the world [does], either in the pursuits of business or of fashion or of politics. I shall examine these several departments separate[ly].

Nonconformity in Business

In regard to business: The first reason why we are not to be conformed to this world in business is that the principle of the world is that of supreme selfishness. This is true universally in the pursuit of business. The whole course of business in the world is governed and regulated by the maxims of supreme and unmixed selfishness. It is regulated without the least regard to the commands of God or the glory of God or the welfare of their fellow men. The maxims of business generally current among businessmen and the habits and usages of businessmen are all based upon supreme selfishness. Who does not know that in making bargains, the business-men of the world consult their own interest and seek their own benefit and not the benefit of those they deal with? Who has ever heard of a worldly man of business making bargains and doing business for the benefit of those he dealt with? No, it is always for their own benefit. And are Christians to do so? They are required to act on the very opposite principle to this: "Let no man seek his own, but every man another's wealth." They are required to copy the example of Jesus Christ. Did he ever make bargains for his own advantage? And may his followers adopt the principle of the world—a principle that contains in it the seeds of hell! If Christians are to do this, is it not the most visionary thing on earth to suppose the world is ever going to be converted to the gospel?

They are required not to conform to the world because conformity to the world is totally inconsistent with the love of God or man. The whole system recognizes only the love of self. Go through all the ranks of businessmen, from the man that sells candy on the sidewalk at the corner of the street to the greatest wholesale merchant or importer in the United States, and you will find that one maxim runs through the whole, to "buy as cheap as you can, and sell as dear as you can, to look out for number one," and to do always, as far as the rules of honesty will allow, all that will advance your own interests, let what will become of the interest of others. Ungodly men will not deny that these are the maxims on which business is done in the world. The man who pursues this course is universally regarded as doing business on business principles. Now, are these maxims consistent with holiness, with the love of God or the love of man, with the spirit of the gospel or the example of Jesus Christ?

Can a man conform to the world in these principles and yet love God? Impossible! No two things can be more unlike. Then Christians are by no means to conform to the business maxims of the world.

These maxims, and the rules by which business is done in the world, are directly opposite to the gospel of Jesus Christ and the spirit he exhibited, and the maxims he inculcated, and the rules which he enjoined that all his followers should obey, on pain of hell. What was the spirit Jesus Christ exemplified on earth? It was the spirit of self-denial, of benevolence, of sacrificing himself to do good to others. He exhibited the same spirit that God does, who enjoys his infinite happiness in going out of himself to gratify his benevolent heart in doing good to others. This is the religion of the gospel to be like God, not only doing good, but enjoying it, joyfully going out of self to do good. This is the gospel maxim: "It is more blessed to give than to receive." And again, "Look not every man on his own things, but every man also on the things of others." What says the businessman of the world? "Look out for number one." These very maxims were made by men who knew and cared no more for the gospel than the heathen do. Why should Christians conform to such maxims as these?

To conform to the world in the pursuits of business is a flat contradiction of the engagements that Christians make when they enter the church. What is the engagement that you make when you enter the church? Is it not to renounce the world and live for God and to be actuated by the Spirit of Jesus Christ and to possess supreme love to God and to renounce self and to give yourself to glorify God and do good to men? You profess not to love the world, its honors, or its riches. Around the communion table, with your hand on the broken body of your Savior, you avouch these to be your principles and pledge yourself to live by these maxims. And then what do you do? Go away and follow maxims and rules gotten up by men whose avowed principle is the love of the world and whose avowed object is to get the world? Is this your way? Then, unless you repent, let me tell you, you will be damned. It is not more certain that any infidel or any profligate wretch will go to hell than that all such professing Christians will go there who conform to the world. They have double guilt. They are sworn before God to a different course, and when they pursue the business principles of the world, they show that they are perjured wretches.

Conformity to the world is such a manifest contradiction of the principles of the gospel that sinners, when they see it, do not and cannot understand from it the true nature and object of the gospel itself. How can they understand that the object of the gospel is to raise men above the love of the world and above the influence of the world and place them on higher ground, to live on totally different principles? When they see professing Christians acting on the same principles with other men, how can they understand the true principles of the gospel or know what it means by heavenly-mindedness, self-denial, benevolence, and so on?

It is this spirit of conformity to the world that has already eaten out the love of God from the church. Show me a young convert, while his heart is warm and the love of God glows out from his lips. What does he care for the world? Call up his attention to it, point him to its riches, its pleasures or its honors, and try to engage him in their pursuit, and he loathes the thought. But let him now go into business and do business on the principles of the world one year

and you no longer find the love of God glowing in his heart, and his religion has become the religion of conscience, dry, meager, uninfluential—anything but the glowing love of God moving him to acts of benevolence. I appeal to every man in this house, and if my voice was loud enough I would appeal to every professor of religion in this city, if it is not. And if anyone should say, "No, it is not so," I should regard it as proof that he *never* knew what it was to feel the glow of a convert's first love.

This conformity to the world in business is one of the greatest stumbling blocks in the way of the conversion of sinners. What do wicked men think when they see professing Christians, with such professions on their lips and pretending to believe what the Bible teaches, and yet driving after the world as eager as anybody, making the best bargains and dealing as hard as the most worldly? What do they think? I can tell you what they say. They say, "I do not see but these Christians do just as the rest of us do; they act on the same principles, look out as sharp for number one, drive as hard bargains, and get as high interest as anybody." And it must be said that these are not things of which the world accuses Christians slanderously. It is a notorious fact that most of the members of the church pursue the world, as far as appears, in the same spirit, by the same maxims, and to the same degree that the ungodly do who maintain a character for uprightness and humanity. The world says, "Look at the church. I don't see as they are any better than I am; they go to the full length that I do after the world." If professing Christians act on the same principles with worldly men, and the Lord liveth, they shall have the same reward. They are set down in God's book of remembrance as black hypocrites, pretending to be the friends of God while they love the world. For whoso loveth the world is the enemy of God. They profess to be governed by principles directly opposite to the world, and if they do the same things with the world, they are hypocrites.

Another reason for the requirement, "Be not conformed to this world," is the immense, salutary, and instantaneous influence it would have if everybody would do business on the principles of the gospel. Just turn the tables over and let Christians do business one year on gospel principles. It would shake the world. It would ring louder than thunder. Let the ungodly see professing Christians, in every bargain, consulting the good of the person they are trading with—seeking not their own wealth, but every man another's wealth—living above the world—setting no value on the world any farther than it can be a means of glorifying God. What do you think would be the effect? What effect *did* it have in Jerusalem when the whole body of Christians gave up their business and turned out in a body to pursue the salvation of the world? They were only a few ignorant fishermen and a few humble women, but they turned the world upside down. Let the church live so now and it would cover the world with confusion of face and overwhelm them with convictions of sin. Only let them see the church living above the world and doing business on gospel principles, seeking not their own interests but the interests of their fellow men, and infidelity would hide its head, heresy would be driven from church, and this charming, blessed spirit of love would go over the world like the waves of the sea.

Nonconformity in Fashion

In regard to fashion: Why are Christians required not to follow the fashions of the world? Because it is directly at war with the spirit of the gospel and is minding earthly things. What is minding earthly things if it is not to follow the fashions of the world that like a tide are continually setting to and fro and fluctuating in their forms and keeping the world continually changing? There are many men of large business in the world and men of wealth who think they care nothing for the fashion. They are occupied with something else and they trust the fashions altogether with their tailor, taking it for granted that he will make all right. But mind, if he should make a garment unfashionable, you would see that they do care about the fashions and they never would employ that tailor again. Still, at present their thoughts are not much on the fashions. They have a higher object in view. And they think it beneath the dignity of a minister to preach about fashions. They overlook the fact that with the greater part of mankind, fashion is everything. The greater part of the community are not rich and never expect to be, but they look to the world to enable them to make a "respectable" appearance and to bring up their families in a "respectable" manner; that is, to "follow the fashions." Nine-tenths of the population never look at anything higher than to do as the world does or to follow the fashions. For this they strain every nerve. And this is what they set their hearts on and what they live for.

The merchant [or] the rich man deceives himself, therefore, if he supposes that fashion is a little thing. The great body of the people mind this, their minds are set upon it, the thing which they look for in life is to have their dress, equipage, furniture, and so on, like other people in the fashion, or "respectable" as they call it.

To conform to the world is contrary to their profession. When people join the church, they profess to give up the spirit that gives rise to the fashions. They profess to renounce the pomps and vanities of the world, to repent of their pride, to follow the meek and lowly Savior, to live for God. And now, what do they do? You often see professors of religion go to the extreme of the fashion. Nothing will satisfy them that is not in the height of fashion. And a Christian female dressmaker who is conscientiously opposed to the following of fashions cannot get her bread. She cannot get employment even among professing Christian ladies, unless she follows the fashions in all their countless changes. God knows it is so, and they must give up their business if their conscience will not permit them to follow the changes of fashion.

This conformity is a broad and complete approval of the spirit of the world. What is it that lies at the bottom of all this shifting scenery? What is the cause that produces all this gaudy show and dash and display? It is the love of applause. And when Christians follow the changes of fashion, they pronounce all this innocent. All this waste of money and time and thought, all this feeding and cherishing of vanity and the love of applause, the church sets her seal to, when she conforms to the world.

Nay, further, another reason is that following the fashions of the world, professing Christians show that they do in fact love the world. They show it by their conduct, just as the ungodly show it by the same conduct. As they act alike, they give evidence that they are actuated by one principle, the love of fashion.

When Christian professors do this, they show most clearly that they love the praise of men. It is evident that they love admiration and flattery, just as sinners do. Is not this inconsistent with Christian principle, to go right into the very things that are set up by the pride and fashion and lust of the ungodly?

Conforming to the world in fashion, you show that you do not hold yourself accountable to God for the manner in which you lay out money. You practically disown your stewardship of the money that is in your possession. By laying out money to gratify your own vanity and lust, you take off the keen edge of that truth which ought to cut that sinner in two who is living to himself. It is practically denying that the earth is the Lord's, with the cattle on a thousand hills and all to be employed for his glory.

You show that reputation is your idol. When the cry comes to your ears on every wind from the ignorant and the lost of all nations, "Come over and help us, come over and help us," and every week brings some call to send the gospel, to send tracts and Bibles and missionaries to those who are perishing for lack of knowledge, if you choose to expend money in following the fashions, it is demonstration that reputation is your idol. Suppose now, for the sake of argument that it is not prohibited in the word of God to follow the fashions and that professing Christians, if they will, may *innocently* follow the fashions: (I deny that it is innocent, but suppose it were,) does not the fact that they do follow them when there are such calls for money and time and thought and labor to save souls prove conclusively that they do not love God nor the souls of men?

Take the case of a woman whose husband is in slavery and she is trying to raise money enough for his redemption. There she is, toiling and saving, rising up early and sitting up late, and eating the bread of carefulness because her husband, the father of her children, the friend of her youth, is in slavery. Now go to that woman and tell her that it is innocent for her to follow the fashions and dress and display like her neighbors—will she do it? Why not? She does not desire to do it. She will scarcely buy a pair of shoes for her feet; she grudges almost the bread she eats—so intent is she on her great object.

Now suppose a person loved God and the souls of men and the kingdom of Christ; does he need an express prohibition from God to prevent him from spending his money and his life in following the fashion? No, indeed, he will rather need a positive injunction to take what is needful for his own comfort and the support of his own life. Take the case of Timothy. Did he need a prohibition to prevent him from indulging in the use of wine? So far from it, he was so cautious that it required an express injunction from God to make him drink a little as a medicine. Although he was sick, he would not drink it till he had the word of God for it, he saw the evils of it so clearly. Now, show me a man or woman, I care not what their professions are, that follows the fashions of the world and I will show you what spirit they are of.

Now, do not ask me why Abraham and David and Solomon, who were so rich, did not lay out their money in spreading the kingdom of God. Ah, tell me, did they enjoy the light that professors now enjoy? Did they even know so much as this, that the world can be converted as Christians now see clearly that it can? But suppose it were as allowable in you as it was in Abraham or David to be rich and to lay out the property you possess in display and pomp and fashion; suppose it were perfectly innocent. Who that loves the Lord Jesus Christ would wish to lay out money in fashion when they could lay it out to gratify the *all-absorbing* passion to do good to the souls of men?

By conforming to the world in fashion, you show that you differ not at all from ungodly sinners. Ungodly sinners say, "I don't see but that these Christian men and women love to follow the fashions as well as I do." Who does not know that this leads many to infidelity.

By following the fashions you are tempting God to give you up to a worldly spirit. There are many now that have followed the world and followed the fashions till God seems to have given them over to the devil for the destruction of the flesh. They have little or no religious feeling, no spirit of prayer, no zeal for the glory of God or the conversion of sinners: the Holy Spirit seems to have withdrawn from them.

You tempt the church to follow the fashions. Where the principle members, the elders and leaders in the church and their wives and families, are fashionable Christians, they drag the whole church along with them into the train of fashion, and everyone apes them as far as they can, down to the lowest servant. Only let a rich Christian lady come out to the house of God in full fashion and the whole church are set agog to follow as far as they can, and it is a chance if they do not run in debt to do it.

You tempt yourself to pride and folly and a worldly spirit. Suppose a man that had been intemperate and was reformed should go and surround himself with wine and brandy and every seductive liquor, keeping the provocatives of appetite always under his eye, and from time to time tasting a little; does he not tempt himself? Now see that woman that has been brought up in the spirit of pride and show and that has been reformed and has professed to abandon them all; let her keep these trappings and continue to follow the fashions and pride will drag her backward as sure[ly] as she lives. She tempts herself to sin and folly.

You are tempting the world. You are setting the world into a more fierce and hot pursuit of these things. The very things that the world loves and that they are sure to have scruples about their being right, professing Christians fall in with and follow and thus tempt the world to continue in the pursuit of what will destroy their souls in hell.

By following the fashions, you are tempting the devil to tempt you. When you follow the fashions, you open your heart to him. You keep it for him, empty, swept, and garnished. Every woman that suffers herself to follow the fashions may rely upon it, she is helping Satan to tempt her to pride and sin.

You lay a great stumbling block before the greatest part of mankind. There are a few persons who are pursuing greater objects than fashion. They are engaged in the scramble for political power or they are eager for literary distinction or they are striving for wealth. And they do not know that their hearts are set on fashion at all. They are following selfishness on a larger scale. But the great mass of the community are influenced mostly by these fluctuating fashions. To this class of persons it is a great and sore stumbling block when they see professing Christians just as prompt and as eager to follow the changing of fashion as themselves. They see and say, "What does their profession amount to when they follow the fashions as much as anybody?" or "Certainly it is right to follow the fashions, for see the professing Christians do it as much as we."

Another reason why professing Christians are required not to be conformed to the world in fashion is the great influence their disregarding fashion would have on the world. If professing Christians would show their contempt for these things and not pretend to follow them or regard them, how it would shame the world and convince the world that they were living for another object, for God and for eternity! How irresistible it would be! What an overwhelming testimony in favor of our religion! Even the apparent renunciation of the world by many orders of monks has doubtless done more than anything else to put down the opposition to their religion and give it currency and influence in the world. Now suppose all this was hearty and sincere and coupled with all that is consistent and lovely in Christian character and all that is zealous and bold in labors for the conversion of the world from sin to holiness. What an influence it would have! What thunders it would pour into the ears of the world to wake them up to follow after God!

Nonconformity in Politics

In regard to politics: I will show why professing Christians are required not to be conformed to the world in politics.

Because the politics of the world are perfectly dishonest. Who does not know this? Who does not know that it is the proposed policy of every party to cover up the defects of their own candidate and the good qualities of the opposing candidate? And is not this dishonest? Every party holds up its candidate as a piece of perfection and then aims to ride himself into office by any means, fair or foul. No man can be an honest man that is committed to a party, to go with them, let them do what they may. And can a Christian do it and keep a conscience void of offense?

To conform to the world in politics is to tempt God. By falling in with the world in politics, Christians are guilty of setting up rulers over them by their own vote who do not fear nor love God and who set the law of God at defiance, break the Sabbath, and gamble and commit adultery and fight duels and swear profanely and leave the laws unexecuted at their pleasure and that care not for the weal or woe of their country, so long as they can keep their office. I say Christians do this. "For it is plain that where parties are divided, as they are in this country, there are Christians enough to turn the scale in any election. Now let Christians take the ground that they will not vote for a dishonest man or a Sabbath-breaker or gambler or whoremonger or duelist for any office, and no party could ever nominate such a character with any hope of success.["] But on the present system where men will let the laws go unexecuted and give full swing to mobs or lynch-murders or robbing the mails or anything else, so they can run in their own candidate who will give them the offices, any man is a dishonest man that will do it, be he professor or non-professor. And can a Christian do this and be blameless?

By engaging with the world in politics, Christians grieve the Spirit of God. Ask any Christian politician if he ever carried the Spirit of God with him into a political campaign. Never. I would by no means be understood to say that Christians should refuse to vote and to exercise their lawful influence in public affairs. But they ought not to follow a party.

By following the present course of politics, you are contributing your aid to undermine all government and order in the land. Who does not know that this great nation now rocks and reels because the laws are broken and trampled under foot, and the executive power refuses or dares not act? Either the magistrate does not wish to put down disorder or he temporizes and lets the devil rule. And so it is in all parts of the country and all parties. And can a Christian be consistent with his profession and vote for such men to office?

You lay a stumbling block in the way of sinners. What do sinners think when they see professing Christians acting with them in their political measures which they themselves know to be dishonest and corrupt? They say, "We understand what we are about, we are after office, we are determined to carry our party into power, we are pursuing our own interest; but these Christians profess to live for another and a higher end, and yet here they come, and join with us, as eager for the loaves and fishes as the rest of us." What greater stumbling block can they have?

You prove to the ungodly that professing Christians are actuated by the same spirit as themselves. Who can wonder that the world is incredulous as to the reality of religion? If they do not look for themselves into the Scriptures, and there learn what religion is, if they are governed by the rules of evidence from what they see in the lives of professing Christians, they ought to be incredulous. They ought to infer, so far as this evidence goes, that professors of religion do not themselves believe in it. It is the fact. I doubt, myself, whether the great mass of professors believe the Bible.

They show, so far as their evidence can go, that there is no change of heart. What is it? Is it going to the communion table once in a month or two and sometimes to prayer meeting? Is that a change of heart, when they are just as eager in the scramble for office as any other? The world must be fools to believe in a change of heart on such evidence.

Christians ought to cease from conformity to the world in politics from the influence which such a course would have on the world. Suppose Christians were to act perfectly conscientiously and consistently in this matter and to say, "We will not vote for any man to office unless he fears God and will rule the people in righteousness." Ungodly men would not set men as candidates who themselves set the laws at defiance. No. Every candidate would be obliged to show that he was prepared to act from higher motives and that he would lay himself out to make the country prosperous and to promote virtue and to put down vice and oppression and disorder and to do all he can to make the people happy and *holy!* It would shame the dishonest politicians to show that the love of God and man is the motive that Christians have in view. And a blessed influence would go over the land like a wave.

Responses to Certain Objections

I am to answer some objections that are made against the principles here advanced.

In regard to business:

Objection: "If we do not transact business on the same principles on which ungodly men do it, we cannot compete with them and all the business of the world will fall into the hands of the ungodly. If .we pursue our business for the good of others, if we buy and sell on the principle of not seeking our own wealth but the wealth of those we do business with, we cannot sustain a competition with worldly men and they will get all the business."

[Response:] Let them have it, then. You can support yourself by your industry in some humbler calling and let worldly men do all the business.

Objection: "But then, how should we get money to spread the gospel?"

[Response:] A holy church that would act on the principles of the gospel would spread the gospel faster than all the money that ever was in New York or that ever will be. Give me a holy church that would live above the world and the work of salvation would roll on faster than with all the money in Christendom.

Objection: "But we must spend a great deal of money to bring forward an educated ministry."

[Response:] Ah! if we had a *holy* ministry, it would be far more important than an educated ministry. If the ministry were holy enough, they would do without so much education. God forbid that I should undervalue an educated ministry. Let ministers be educated as well as they can, the more the better, if they are only holy enough. But it is all a farce to suppose that a literary ministry can convert the world. Let the ministry have the spirit of prayer, let the baptism of the Holy Ghost be upon them, and they will spread the gospel. Only let Christians live as they ought and the church would shake the world. If Christians in New York would do it, the report would soon fill every ship that leaves the port and waft the news on every wind till the earth was full of excitement and inquiry, and conversions would multiply like the drops of morning dew.

Suppose you were to give up your business and devote yourselves entirely to the work of extending the gospel. The church once did so and you know what followed. When that little band in Jerusalem gave up their business and spent their time in the work of God, salvation spread like a wave. And I believe, if the whole Christian church were to turn right out and convert the world, it would be done in a very short time.

And further, the fact is that you would not be required to give up your business. If Christians would do business in the spirit of the gospel, they would soon engross the business of the world. Only let the world see that if they go to a Christian to do business, he will not only deal honestly, but benevolently, that he will actually consult the interest of the person he deals with as if it were his own interest, and who would deal with anybody else? What merchant would to an ungodly man to trade, who he knew would try to get the advantage of him and cheat him, while he knew that there were Christian merchants to deal with that would consult his interests as much as they do their own? Indeed, it is a known fact that there are now Christian merchants in this city who regulate the prices of the articles they deal in. Merchants come in from the country and inquire around to see how they can buy goods, and they go to these men to know exactly what articles are worth at a fair price and govern themselves accordingly.

The advantage, then, is all on one side. The church can make it for the interest of the ungodly to do business on right principles. The church can regulate the business of the world and woe to them if they do not.

In regard to fashion:

Objection: "Is it best for Christians to be singular?"

[Response:] The reason of it is this, so few do it that it is a novelty and everybody stares when they see a professing Christian so strict as to disregard the fashions. Let them all do it and the only thing you show by it is that you are a Christian and do not wish to be confounded with the ungodly. Would it not tell on the pride of the world if all the Christians in it were united in bearing a practical testimony against its vain show.

Objection: "But in this way you carry religion too far away from the multitude. It is better not to set up an artificial distinction between the church and the world."

[Response:] True, but will not a change of heart produce a change of life?

Objection: "You will throw obstacles in the way of persons becoming Christians. Many respectable people will become disgusted with religion, and if they cannot be allowed to dress and be Christians, they will take to the world altogether."

[Response:] This is just about as reasonable as it would be for a temperance man to think he must get drunk now and then to avoid disgusting the intemperate and to retain his influence over them. The truth is that persons ought to know and ought to see in the lives of professing Christians that if they embrace religion they must be weaned from the world and must give up the love of the world and its pride and show and folly and live a holy life in watchfulness and self-denial and active benevolence.

Objection: "Is it not better for us to disregard this altogether and not pay any attention to such little things and let them take their course; let the milliner and mantua-maker do as they please and follow the usages of society in which we live and the circle in which we move?"

[Response:] Is this the way to show contempt for the fashions of the world? Do people ordinarily take this course of showing contempt for a thing, to practice it? Why, the way to show your abhorrence of the world is to follow along in the customs and the fashions of the world! Precious reasoning this.

Objection: "No matter how we dress, if our hearts are right?"

[Response:] Your heart right! Then your heart may be right when your conduct is all wrong. Just as well might the profane swearer say, "No matter what words I speak, if my heart is right." No, your heart is not right unless your conduct is right. What is outward conduct but the acting out of the heart? If your heart were right, you would not wish to follow the fashions of the world.

Objection: "What is the standard of dress? I do not see the use of all your preaching and laying down rules about plain dress unless you give us a standard."

[Response:] This is a mighty stumbling block with many. But to my mind the matter is extremely simple. The whole can be comprised in two simple rules. One is: Be sure, in all your equipage and dress and furniture, to show that you have no fellowship with the designs and principles of those who are aiming to set off themselves and to gain the applause of men. The other is: Let economy be first consulted and then convenience. Follow Christian economy; that is, save all you can for Christ's service; and then, let things be as convenient as Christian economy will admit.

Objection: "Would you have us all to turn Quakers and put on their plain dress?"

[Response:] Who does not know that the plain dress of the Quakers has won for them the respect of all the thinking part of the ungodly in the community? Now, if they had coupled with this the zeal for God and the weanedness from the world and the contempt for riches and the self-denying labor for the conversion of sinners to Christ which the gospel enjoins and the clear views of the plan of salvation which the gospel inculcates, they would long since have converted the world. And if all Christians would imitate them in their plain dress, (I do not mean the precise cut and fashion of their dress, but in a *plain* dress, throwing contempt upon the fashions of the world) who can doubt that the conversion of the world would hasten on apace?

Objection: "Would you make us all into Methodists?"

[Response:] Who does not know that the Methodists, when they were noted for their plain dress and for renouncing the fashions and show of the world, used to have power with God in prayer—

and that they have the universal respect of the world as sincere Christians. And who does not know that since they have laid aside this peculiarity and conformed to the world in dress and other things and seemed to be trying to lift themselves up as a denomination and gain influence with the world, they are losing the power of prayer? Would to God they had never thrown down this wall. It was one of the leading excellences of Wesley's system, to have his followers distinguished from others by a plain dress.

Objection: "We may be proud of a plain dress as well as of a fashionable dress. The Quakers are as proud as we are."

[Response:] So may any good thing be abused. But that is no reason why it should not be used, if it can be shown to be good. I put it back to the objector—Is that any reason why a Christian female who fears God and loves the souls of men should neglect the means which may make an impression that she is separated from the world and pour contempt on the fashions of the ungodly, in which they are dancing their way to hell?

Objection: "This is a small thing and ought not to take up so much of a minister's time in the pulpit."

[Response:] This is an objection often heard from worldly professors. But the minister that fears God will not be deterred by it. He will pursue the subject until such professing Christians are cut off from their conformity to the world or cut off from the church. It is not merely the dress, as dress, but it is the conformity to the world in dress and fashion that is the great stumbling block in the way of sinners. How can the world be converted while professing Christians are conformed to the world? What good will it do to give money to send the gospel to the heathen when Christians live so at home? Well might the heathen ask, "What profit will it be to become Christians when those who are Christians are pursuing the world with all the hot haste of the ungodly?" The great thing necessary for the church is to break off from conformity to the world and then they will have power with God in prayer, and the Holy Ghost will descend and bless their efforts and the world will be converted.

Objection: "But if we dress so, we shall be called fanatics."

[Response:] Whatever the ungodly may call you, fanatics, Methodists, or anything, you will be known as Christians and in the secret consciences of men will be acknowledged as such. It is not in the power of unbelievers to pour contempt on a holy church that are separated from the world. How was it with the early Christians? They lived separate from the world, and it made such an impression that even infidel writers say of them, "These men win the hearts of the mass of the people because they give themselves up to deeds of charity and pour contempt on the world." Depend upon it, if Christians would live so now, the last effort of hell would soon be expended in vain to defeat the spared of the gospel. Wave after wave would flow abroad till the highest mountaintops were covered with the waters of life.

In regard to politics:

Objection: "In this way, by acting on these principles and refusing to unite with the world in politics, we could have no influence in government and national affairs."

[Response:] I answer, first, it is so now. Christians, as such, have no influence. There is not a Christian principle adopted because it is Christian or because it is according to the law of God.

I answer, secondly, if there is no other way for Christians to have an influence in the government but by becoming conformed to the world in their habitual principles and parties, then let the ungodly take the government and manage it in their own way, and do you go and serve God.

I answer, thirdly, no such result will follow. Directly the reverse of this would be the fact. Only let it be known that Christian citizens will on no account assist bad men into office; only let it be known that the church will go only for men that will aim at the public good, and both parties will be sure to set up such men. And in this way, the church could legitimately exert an influence by compelling all parties to bring forward only men who are worthy of an honest man's support.

Objection: "In this way the church and the world will be arrayed against each other."

[Response:] The world is too selfish for this. You cannot make parties so. Such a line can never be a permanent division. For one year the ungodly might unite against the church and leave Christians in a small minority. But in the end, the others would form two parties, each courting the suffrages of Christians by offering candidates such as Christians can conscientiously vote for.

REMARKS

By non-conformity to the world, you may save much money for doing good. In one year a greater fund might be saved by the church than has ever been raised for the spread of the gospel.

By non-conformity to the world, a great deal of time may be saved for doing good that is now consumed and wasted in following the fashions and obeying the maxims and joining in the pursuits of the world.

At the same time, Christians in this way would preserve their peace of conscience, would enjoy communion with God, would have the spirit of prayer, and would possess far greater usefulness.

Is it not time something was done? Is it not time that some church struck out a path that should not be conformed to the world but should be according to the example and Spirit of Christ?

You profess that you want to have sinners converted. But what avails it if they sink right back again into conformity with the world? Brethren, I confess, I am filled with pain in view of the conduct of the church. Where are the proper results of the glorious revivals we have had? I believe they were genuine revivals of religion and outpourings of the Holy Ghost that the church has enjoyed the last ten years. I believe the converts of the last ten years are among the best Christians in the land. Yet after all, the great body of them are a disgrace to religion. Of what use would it be to have a thousand members added to the church to be just such as are now in it? Would religion be any more honored by it, in the estimation of ungodly men? One holy church that are really crucified to the world and the world to them would do more to recommend Christianity than all the churches in the country living as they now do. O if I had strength of body to go through the churches again instead of preaching to convert sinners, I would preach to bring up the churches to the gospel standard of holy living. Of what use is it to convert sinners and make them such Christians as these? Of what use is it to try to convert sinners and make them feel there is something in religion and when they go to trade with you or meet you

in the street, have you contradict it all and tell them, by your conformity to the world, that there is nothing in it?

Where shall I look, where shall the Lord look, for a church like the first church that will come out from the world and be separate and give themselves up to serve God? Oh, if this church would do so. But it is of little use to make Christians if they are not better. Do not understand me as saying that the converts made in our revivals are spurious. But they live so as to be a disgrace to religion. They are so stumbled by old professors that many of them do more hurt than good. The more there are of them, the more occasion infidelity seems to find for her jeers and scoffs.

Now, do you believe that God commands you not to be conformed to the world? Do you believe it? And dare you obey it, let people say what they will about you? Dare you now separate yourselves from the world and never again be controlled by its maxims and never again copy its practices and never again will be whiffled here and there by its fashions? I know a man that lives so, I could mention his name; he pays no attention to the customs of the world in this respect and what is the result? Wherever that man goes, he leaves the impression behind that he is a Christian. O if one church would do so and would engage in it with all the energy that men of the world engage in their business, they would turn the world upside down. Will you do so? Will you break off from the world now and enter into covenant with God and declare that you will dare to be singular enough to be separate from the world and from this time set your faces as a flint to obey God, let the world say what they will? Dare you do it? Will you do it?

Revivals are great events in the history of mankind. Since the time of Christ the world has witnessed many great revival movements that have come about as a result of dedicated men dealing carefully with men, preaching the gospel faithfully. Yet the work of revival is not easy. With the glory of success come great hindrances that must be pinpointed and dealt with. The most evident source of trouble is the devil. He is the true antagonist who seeks to thwart any sign of revival. Yet all too often the devil is not the source of revival failure. Men are equally capable of quenching the work of the Spirit in bringing conversions. If Christians seek to end a revival, believe it is about to end, become mechanical, proselyte, refuse the Lord credit for revival, or exercise pride, revival will falter. Many other weaknesses of Christians and churches can hinder revivals.

CHAPTER FOUR

Hindrances to Revival

I am doing a great work, so that I cannot come down. Why should the work cease, whilst I leave it, and come down to you? (Neh. 6:3).

This servant of God had come down from Babylon to rebuild the temple and reestablish the worship of God at Jerusalem, the city of his fathers' sepulchers. When it was discovered by Sanballat and certain individuals, his allies who had long enjoyed the desolations of Zion, that now the temple and the holy city were about to be rebuilt, they raised a great opposition. Sanballat and the other leaders tried in several ways to divert Nehemiah and his friends and prevent them from going forward in their work; at one time they threatened them. and then complained that they were going to rebel against the king. Again, they insisted that their design was not pious but political, to which Nehemiah replied by a simple and prompt denial, "There are no such things done as thou sayest, but thou feignest them out of thine own heart." Finally, Sanballat sent a message to Nehemiah requesting him to meet in the plain of Ono to discuss the whole matter amicably and have the difficulty adjusted, but designed to do him mischief. They had found that they could not frighten Nehemiah and now they wanted to come round him by artifice and fraud and draw him off from the vigorous prosecution of his work. But he replied, "I am doing a great work, so that I cannot come down: why should the work cease, whilst I come down to you?"

It has always been the case whenever any of the servants of God do anything in his cause and there appears to be a probability that they will succeed that Satan by his agents regularly attempts to divert their minds and nullify their labors. So it has been during the last ten years in which there have been such remarkable revivals through the length and breadth of the land. These revivals have been very great and powerful and extensive. It has been estimated that not less than two hundred thousand persons have been converted to God in that time.

And the devil has been busy in his devices to divert and distract the people of God and turn off their energies from pushing forward the great work of salvation. In remarking on the subject, I propose to show that a revival of religion is a great work, to mention several things which may put a stop to it, and endeavor to show what must be done for the continuance of this great revival.

I am to show that a revival of religion is a great work. It is a great work because in it are great interests involved. In a revival of religion are involved both the glory of God, so far as it respects the government of this world, and the salvation of man. Two things that are of infinite importance are involved in it. The greatness of a work is to be estimated by the greatness of the consequences depending on it. And this is the measure of its importance.

Things That Hinder Revival

I am to mention several things which may put a stop to a revival. Some have talked very foolishly on this subject, as if nothing could injure a genuine revival. They say, "If your revival is a work of God, it cannot be stopped; can any created being stop God?" Now I ask if this is common sense? Formerly it used to be the established belief that a revival could not be stopped because it was the work of God. And so they supposed it would go on whatever might be done to hinder it in the church or out of it. But the farmer might just as well reason so and think he could go and cut down his wheat and not hurt the crop because it is God that makes grain grow. A revival is the work of God and so is a crop of wheat; and God is as much dependent on the use of means in one case as the other. And therefore a revival is as liable to be injured as a wheat field.

A revival will stop whenever the church believe it is going to cease. The church are the instruments with which God carries on this work and they are to work in it voluntarily and with their hearts. Nothing is more fatal to a revival than for its friends to predict that it is going to stop. No matter what the enemies of the work may say about it, predicting that it will all run out and come to nothing and the like. They cannot stop it in this way; but the friends must labor and pray in faith to carry it on. It is a contradiction to say they are laboring and praying in faith to carry on the work and yet believe that it is going to stop. If they lose their faith, it will stop, of course. Whenever the friends of revivals begin to prophesy that the revival is going to stop, they should be instantly rebuked in the name of the Lord. If the idea once begins to prevail and if you cannot counteract it and root it out, the revival will infallibly cease; for it is in-

dispensable to the work that Christians should labor and pray in faith to promote it, and it is a contradiction to say that they can labor in faith for its continuance while they believe that it is about to cease.

A revival will cease when Christians consent that it should cease. Sometimes Christians see that the revival is in danger of ceasing and that if something effectual is not done, it will come to a stand. If this fact distresses them and drives them to prayer and to fresh efforts, the work will not cease. When Christians love the work of God and the salvation of souls so well that they are distressed at the mere apprehension of a decline, it will drive them to an agony of prayer and effort. If it does not drive them to agony and effort to prevent its ceasing, if they see the danger and do not try to avert it or to renew the work, they consent that it should stop. There are at this time many people all over the country who see revivals declining and that they are in great danger of ceasing altogether, and yet they manifest but little distress and seem to care but little about it. Whole churches see their condition and see what is coming unless there can be a waking up, and yet they are at ease and do not groan and agonize in prayer that God would revive his work. Some are even predicting that there is now going to be a great reaction and a great dearth come over the church as there did after Whitefield's and Edwards' day. And yet they are not startled at their own forebodings; they are cool about it and turn directly off to other things. They consent to it. It seems as if they were the devil's trumpters, sent out to scatter dismay throughout the ranks of God's elect.

A revival will cease whenever Christians become mechanical in their attempts to promote it. When their faith is strong and their hearts are warm and mellow and their prayers full of holy emotion and their words with power, then the work goes on. But when their prayers begin to be cold and without emotion and their deep-toned feeling is gone and they begin to labor mechanically and to use words without feeling, then the revival will cease.

The revival will cease whenever Christians get the idea that the work will go on without their aid. The church are co-workers with God in promoting a revival, and the work can be carried on just as far as the church will carry it on and no farther. God has been for one thousand eight hundred years trying to get the church into the work. He has been calling and urging, commanding, entreating, pressing and encouraging, to get them to take hold. He has stood all the while ready to make bare his arm to carry on the work with them. But the church have been unwilling to do their part. They seem determined to leave it to God alone to convert the world and say, "If he wants the world converted, let him do it." They ought to know that this is impossible. So far as we know neither God nor man can convert the world without the cooperation of the church. Sinners cannot be converted without their own agency, for conversion consists in their voluntary turning to God. No more can sinners be converted without the appropriate moral influences to turn them; that is, without truth and the reality of things brought full before their minds either by direct revelation or by men. God cannot convert the world by physical omnipotence, but he is dependent on the moral influence of the church.

The work will cease when the church prefer to attend to their own concerns rather than God's business. I do not admit that men have any business which is properly their own, but they think so, and in fact prefer what they consider as

their own, rather than to work for God. They begin to think they cannot afford sufficient time from their worldly employments to carry on a revival. And they pretend they are obliged to give up attending to religion and let their hearts go out again after the world. And the work must cease, of course.

When Christians get proud of their great revival, it will cease. I mean those Christians who have before been instrumental in promoting it. It is almost always the case in a revival that a part of the church are too proud or too worldly to take any part in the work. They are determined to stand aloof and wait and see what it will come to and see how it will come out. The pride of this part of the church cannot stop the revival, for the revival never rested on them. It began without them and it can go on without them. They may fold their arms and do nothing but look on and find fault; and still the work may go on. But when that part of the church who work, begin to think what a great revival they have had and how they have labored and prayed and how bold and how zealous they have been and how much good they have done, then the work will be likely to decline. Perhaps it has been published in the papers what a revival there has been in that church and how much engaged the members have been and they think how high they shall stand in the estimation of other churches all over the land because they have had such a great revival. And so they get puffed up and vain and then they can no longer enjoy the presence of God, and the Spirit withdraws from them, and the revival ceases.

The revival will stop when the church gets exhausted by labor. Multitudes of Christians commit a great mistake here in time of revival. They are so thoughtless and have so little judgment that they will break up all their habits of living, neglect to eat and sleep at the proper hours, and let the excitement run away with them so that they overdo their bodies and are so imprudent that they soon become exhausted and it is impossible for them to continue in the work. Revivals often cease and declension follows from negligence and imprudence in this respect on the part of those engaged in carrying them on.

A revival will cease when the church begins to speculate about abstract doctrines which have nothing to do with practice. If the church turn off their attention from the things of salvation and go to studying or disputing about abstract points, then revival will cease, of course.

When the Baptists are so opposed to the Presbyterians or the Presbyterians to the Baptists or both against the Methodists or Episcopalians against the rest, that they begin to make efforts to get the converts to join their church, you soon see the last of the revival. Perhaps a revival will go on for a time and all sectarian difficulties are banished till somebody circulates a book, privately, to gain proselytes. Perhaps some overzealous deacon or some mischief-making woman or some proselyting minister cannot keep still any longer and begins the work of the devil by attempting to gain proselytes and so stirs up bitterness and [by] raising a selfish strife, grieves away the Spirit and drives Christians all into parties. No more revival there.

When Christians refuse to render to the Lord according to the benefits received; this is a fruitful source of religious declensions. God has opened the windows of heaven to a church and poured them out a blessing, and then he reasonably expects them to bring in the tithes into his storehouse and devise and execute liberal things for Zion; and lo! they have refused; they have not laid

themselves out accordingly to promote the cause of Christ; and so the Spirit has been grieved and the blessing withdrawn, and in some instances a great reaction has taken place because the church would not be liberal when God has been so bountiful. I have known churches who were evidently cursed with barrenness for such a course. They had a glorious revival and afterward perhaps their meeting-house needed repairing or something else was needed which would cost a little money and they refused to do it, and so for their niggardly spirit God gave them up.

When the church in any way grieve the Holy Spirit, when they do not feel their dependence on the Spirit, whenever Christians get strong in their own strength, God curses their blessings. In many instances Christians sin against their own mercies because they get lifted up with their success and take the credit to themselves and do not give to God all the glory. As he says, "If ye will not hear and if ye will not lay it to heart to give glory unto my name, saith the Lord of hosts, I will even send a curse upon you and I will curse your blessings: yea, I have cursed them already because ye do not lay it to heart." There has been a great deal of this in this country, undoubtedly. I have seen many things that looked like it in the papers where there seemed a disposition in men to take credit for success in promoting revivals. There is doubtless a great temptation to this and it requires the utmost watchfulness on the part of ministers and churches to guard against it and not grieve the Spirit away by vaingelorying in men.

The Spirit may be grieved by a spirit of boasting of the revival. Sometimes, as soon as a revival commences, you will see it blazed out in the newspapers. And most commonly this will kill the revival. There was a case in a neighboring state where a revival commenced and instantly there came out a letter from the pastor telling that he had a revival. I saw the létter and said to myself, "That is the last we shall hear of this revival." And so it was. In a few days, the work totally ceased. And such things are not uncommon. I could mention cases and places where persons have published such things as to puff up the church and make them so proud that little or nothing more could be done for the revival.

Some, under pretense of publishing things to the praise and glory of God, have published things that savored so strongly of a disposition to exalt themselves, have made their own agency to stand out so conspicuously, as was evidently calculated to make an unhappy impression. At the protracted meeting held in this church a year ago last fall, there were five hundred hopefully converted whose names and places of residence we knew. A considerable number of them joined this church. Many of them united with other churches. Nothing was said of this in the papers. I have several times been asked why we were so silent upon the subject. I could only reply that there was such a tendency to self-exaltation in the churches that I was afraid to publish anything on the subject. Perhaps I erred. But I have so often seen mischief done by premature publications that I thought it best to say nothing about it. In the revival in this city four years ago, so much was said in the papers that appeared like self-exaltation that I was afraid to publish. I am not speaking against the practice itself of publishing accounts of revivals. But the manner of doing it is of vast importance. If it is done so as to excite vanity, it is always fatal to the revival.

So the Spirit is grieved by saying or publishing things that are calculated to undervalue the work of God. When a blessed work of God is spoken lightly of,

not rendering to God the glory due to his name, the Spirit is grieved. If anything is said about a revival, give only the plain and naked *facts* just as they are and let them pass for what they are worth.

A revival may be expected to cease when Christians lose the spirit of brotherly love. Jesus Christ will not continue with people in a revival any longer than they continue in the exercise of brotherly love. When Christians are in the spirit of a revival, they feel this love, and then you will hear them call each other brother and sister, very affectionately. But when they begin to get cold, they lose this warmth and glow of action for one another, and then this calling brother and sister will seem silly and contemptible and they will leave it off. In some churches they never call each other so, but where there is a revival, Christians naturally do it. I never saw a revival and probably there never was one in which they do not do it. But as soon as this begins to cease, the Spirit of God is grieved and departs from among them.

A revival will decline and cease unless Christians are frequently reconverted. By this I mean that Christians, in order to keep in the spirit of a revival, commonly need to be frequently convicted and humbled and broken down before God and reconverted. This is something which many do not understand when we talk about a Christian's being reconverted. But the fact is that in a revival, the Christian's heart is liable to get crusted over and lose its exquisite relish for divine things; his unction and prevalence in prayer abates, and then he must be converted over again. It is impossible to keep him in such a state as not to do injury to the work unless he pass through such a process every few days. I have never labored in revivals in company with anyone who would keep in the work and be fit to manage a revival continually who did not pass through this process of breaking down as often as once in two or three weeks. Revivals decline, commonly, because it is found impossible to make the church feel their guilt and their dependence so as to break down before God. It is important that ministers should understand this and learn how to break down the church and break down themselves when they need it, or else Christians will soon become mechanical in their work and lose their fervor and their power of prevailing with God. This was the process through which Peter passed when he had denied the Savior and by which breaking down, the Lord prepared him for the great work on the day of Pentecost. I was surprised a few years since to find that the phrase "breaking down" was a stumbling block to certain ministers and professors of religion. They laid themselves open to the rebuke administered to Nicodemus, "Art thou a master in Israel and knowest not these things?" I am confident that until some of them know what it is to be "broken down," they will never do much more for the cause of revivals.

A revival cannot continue when Christians will not practice self-denial. When the church have enjoyed a revival and begin to grow fat upon it and run into self-indulgence, the revival will soon cease. Unless they sympathize with the Son of God, who gave up all to save sinners; unless they are willing to give up their luxuries and their ease and lay themselves out in the work, they need not expect the Spirit of God will be poured out upon them. This is undoubtedly one of the principal causes of personal declension. Let Christians in a revival BEWARE when they first find an inclination creeping upon them to shrink from self-denial and to give in to one form of self-indulgence after another. It is the device of Satan to abate them off from the work of God and make them dull and gross and lazy and fearful and useless and sensual and drive away the Spirit and destroy the revival.

A revival will be stopped by controversies about new measures. Nothing is more certain to overthrow a revival than this. But as my last lecture was on the subject of new measures, I need not dwell longer on the subject now.

Revivals can be put down by the continued opposition of the Old School combined with a bad spirit in the New School. If those who do nothing to promote revivals continue their opposition and if those who are laboring to promote them allow themselves to get impatient and get into a bad spirit, the revival will cease. When the Old School write their letters in the newspapers against revivals or revival men, and the New School write letters back again against them in an angry, contentious, bitter spirit and get into a jangling controversy, revivals will cease. Let them keep about their work and not talk about the opposition nor preach nor print about it. If others choose to publish their slang and stuff, let the Lord's servants keep to their work, and all the writing and slander will not stop the revival while those who are engaged in [it] mind their business and keep to their work. It is astonishing how far this holds true in fact.

In one place where there was a revival, certain ministers formed a combination against the pastor of the church and a plan was set on foot to ruin him, and they actually got him prosecuted before his presbytery and had a trial that lasted six weeks, right in the midst of the revival; and the work still went on. The praying members of the church laid themselves out so in the work that it continued triumphantly throughout the whole scene. The pastor was called off to attend his trial, but there was another minister that labored among the people, and the members did not even go to the trial, generally, but kept praying and laboring for souls, and the revival rode out the storm. In many other places, opposition has risen up in the church, but a few humble souls have kept at their work, and a gracious God has stretched out his naked arm and made the revival go forward in spite of all opposition.

But whenever those who are actively engaged in promoting a revival get excited at the unreasonableness and pertinacity of the opposition and feel as if they could not have it so and they lose their patience and feel as if they must answer their cavils and refute their slanders, then they get down into the plains of Ono and the work must cease.

Any diversion of the public mind will hinder a revival. Anything that succeeds in diverting public attention will put a stop to a revival. In the case I have specified where the minister was put on trial before his presbytery, the reason why it did not ruin the revival was that the praying members of the church would not suffer themselves to be diverted. They did not even attend the trial, but kept praying and laboring for souls, and so public attention was kept to the subject in spite of all the efforts of the devil.

But whenever he succeeds in absorbing public attention on any other subject, he will put an end to the revival, no matter what the subject is. If an angel from heaven were to come down and preach or pass about the streets, it might be the worst thing in the world for a revival, for it would turn sinners all off from their own sins and turn the church off from praying for souls to follow this glorious being and gaze upon him, and the revival would cease.

Resistance to the temperance reformation will put a stop to revivals in church.

The time has come that it can no longer be innocent in a church to stand aloof from this glorious reformation. The time was when this could be done ignorantly. The time has been when ministers and Christians could enjoy revivals notwithstanding ardent spirit was used among them. But since light has been thrown upon the subject and it has been found that the use is only injurious, no church member or minister can be innocent and stand neutral in the cause. They must speak out and take sides. And if they do not take ground on one side, their influence is on the other. Show me a minister that has taken ground against the temperance reformation who has had a revival. Show me one who now stands aloof from it who has a revival. Show me one who now temporizes upon this point who does not come out and take a stand in favor of temperance who has a revival. It did not use to be so. But now the subject has come up and has been discussed and is understood, no man can shut his eyes upon the truth. The man's hands are red with blood who stands aloof from the temperance cause. And can he have a revival?

Revivals are hindered when ministers and churches take wrong ground in regard to any question involving human rights. Take the subject of slavery, for instance. The time was when their subject was not before the public mind. John Newton continued in the slave trade after his conversion. And so had his mind been perverted and so completely was his conscience seared in regard to this most nefarious traffic, that the sinfulness of it never occurred to his thoughts until some time after he became a child of God. Had light been poured upon his mind previously to his conversion, he never could have been converted without previously abandoning this sin. And after his conversion, when convinced of its iniquity, he could no longer enjoy the presence of God without abandoning the sin forever. So, doubtless, many slave dealers and slaveholders in our own country have been converted, notwithstanding their participation in this abomination, because the sinfulness of it was not apparent to their minds. So ministers and churches to a great extent throughout the land have held their peace and borne no testimony against this abominable abomination existing in the church and in the nation. But recently the subject has come up for discussion, and the providence of God has brought it distinctly before the eyes of all men. Light is now shed upon this subject as it has been upon the cause of temperance. Facts are exhibited and principles established and light thrown in upon the minds of men, and this monster is dragged from his horrid den and exhibited before the church, and it is demanded of them, "Is this sin?" Their testimony must be given on this subject. They are God's witnesses. They are sworn to tell "the truth, the whole truth, and nothing but the truth." It is impossible that their testimony should not be given on one side or the other. Their silence can no longer be accounted for upon the principle of ignorance and that they have never had their attention turned to the subject. Consequently, the silence of Christians upon the subject is virtually saying that they do not consider slavery as a sin. The truth is it is a subject upon which they cannot be silent without guilt. The time has come, in the providence of God, when every southern breeze is loaded down with the cries of lamentation, mourning, and woe. Two millions of degraded heathen in our own land stretch their hands, all shackled and bleeding, and send forth to the church of God the agonizing cry for help. And shall the church in her efforts to reclaim and save the world

deafen her ears to this voice of agony and despair? God forbid. The church cannot turn away from this question. It is a question for the church and for the nation to decide, and God will push it to a decision.

It is in vain for the churches to resist it for fear of distraction, contention, and strife. It is in vain to account it an act of piety to turn away the ear from hearing this cry of distress.

The church must testify and testify "the truth, the whole truth, and nothing but the truth" on this subject or she is perjured, and the Spirit of God departs from her. She is under oath to testify, and ministers and churches who do not pronounce it sin bear false testimony for God. It is doubtless true that one of the reasons for the low state of religion at the present time is that many churches have taken the wrong side of the subject of slavery, have suffered prejudice to prevail over principle, and have feared to call this abomination by its true name.

Another thing that hinders revivals is neglecting the claims of missions. If Christians do not feel for the heathen, neglect the monthly concert, and confine their attention to their own church, do not even read the Missionary Herald or use any other means to inform themselves on the subject of the claims of the world, and reject the light which God is throwing before them, and will not do what God calls them to do in this cause, the Spirit of God will depart from them.

When a church reject the calls of God upon them for educating young men for the ministry, they will hinder and destroy a revival. Look at the Presbyterian church, look at the two hundred thousand souls converted within ten years and means enough to fill the world with ministers, and yet the ministry is not increasing so fast as the population of our own country, and unless something more can be done to provide ministers, we shall become heathen ourselves. The churches do not press upon young men the duty of going into the ministry. God pours his Spirit on the churches and converts hundreds of thousands of souls, and if then the laborers do not come forth into the harvest, what can be expected but that the curses of God will come upon the churches and his Spirit will be withdrawn and revivals will cease. Upon this subject no minister, no church should be silent or inactive.

Slandering revivals will often put them down. The great revival in the days of President Edwards suffered greatly by the conduct of the church in this respect. It is to be expected that the enemies of God will revile, misrepresent, and slander revivals. But when the church herself engages in this work and many of her most influential members are abiding and abetting in calumniating and misrepresenting a glorious work of God, it is reasonable that the Spirit should be grieved away. It cannot be denied that this has been done to a grievous and God-dishonoring extent. It has been estimated that in one year since this revival commenced, one hundred thousand souls were converted to God in the United States. This was undoubtedly the greatest number that were ever converted in one year since the world began.[1] It could not be expected that, in an excitement of this extent among human beings, there should be nothing to deplore. To expect perfection in such a work as this, of such extent, and carried on by human instrumentality, is utterly unreasonable and absurd. Evils doubtless did exist and have existed. They were to be expected, of course, and guarded against, as far

as possible. And I do not believe the world's history can furnish one instance in which a revival, approaching to this in extent and influence, has been attended with so few evils and so little that is honestly to be deplored.

But how has this blessed work of God been treated? Admitting all the evils complained of to be real which is far from being true, they would only be like spots upon the disc of the glorious sun; things hardly to be thought of in comparison of the infinite greatness and excellence of the work. And yet how have a great portion of the Presbyterian church received and treated this blessed work of God? At the General Assembly, that grave body of men that represent the Presbyterian Church, in the midst of this great work, instead of appointing a day of thanksgiving, instead of praising and glorifying God for the greatness of this work, we hear from them the voice of rebuke. From the reports that were given of the speeches made there, it appears that the house was filled with complainings. Instead of devising measures to forward the work, their attention seemed to be taken up with the comparatively trifling evils that were incidental to it. And after much complaining, they absolutely appointed a committee and sent forth a "Pastoral Letter" to the churches, calculated to excite suspicions, quench the zeal of God's people, and turn them off from giving glory to God for the greatness of the blessing to finding fault and carping about the evils. When I heard what was done at that General Assembly, when I read their speeches, when I saw their pastoral letter, my soul was sick, an unutterable feeling of distress came over my mind, and I felt that God would

---

1. This was in 1831. There have been more extensive revivals since. In 1857–58, it was estimated that 50,000 conversions per week occurred for six or eight weeks in succession in the northern part of the United States.

"visit" the Presbyterian church for conduct like this. And ever since, the glory has been departing and revivals have been becoming less and less frequent—less and less powerful.[2]

And now I wish it could be known whether those ministers who poured out those complainings on the floor of the General Assembly and who were instrumental in getting up that pastoral letter have since been blessed in promoting revivals of religion—whether the Spirit of God has been upon them, and whether their churches can witness that they have an unaction from the Holy One.

Ecclesiastical difficulties are calculated to grieve away the Spirit and destroy revivals. It has always been the policy of the devil to turn off the attention of ministers from the work of the Lord to disputes and ecclesiastical litigations. President Edwards was obliged to be taken up for a long time in disputes before ecclesiastical councils; and in our days, and in the midst of these great revivals of religion, these difficulties have been alarmingly and shamefully multiplied. Some of the most efficient ministers in the church have been called off from their direct efforts to win souls to Christ to attend day after day, and in some instances week after week, to charges preferred against them or their fellow-laborers in the ministry which could never be sustained.

Look at Philadelphia: what endless and disgraceful janglings have distracted and disgraced the church of God in that city and through the length and breadth of the land. And in the Presbyterian church at large these ecclesiastical difficulties have produced evils enough to make creation weep. Brother Beman was shamefully and wickedly called off from promoting revivals to attend a trial before his own presbytery upon charges which, if true, were most of them ridiculous, but which could never be sustained. And since that time a great portion of his time has, it would seem necessarily, been taken up with the adjustment of ecclesiastical difficulties. Brother Duffield of Carlisle, Brother Barnes of Philadelphia, and others of God's most successful ministers have been hindered a considerable part of their time for years by these difficulties. Oh, tell it not in Gath! When will those ministers and professors of religion who do little or nothing themselves, let others alone, and let them work for God?

Another thing by which revivals may be hindered is censoriousness on either side and especially in those who have been engaged in carrying forward a revival. It is to be expected that the opposers of the work will watch for the halting of its friends and be sure to censure them for all that is wrong and not infrequently for that which is right in their conduct. Especially is it to be expected that many censorious and unchristian remarks will be made about those that are the most prominent instruments in promoting the work. This censoriousness on the part of the opposers of the work, whether in or out of the church, will not, however, of itself put a stop to the revival. While its promoters keep humble and in a prayerful spirit, while they do not retaliate but possess their souls in patience, while they do not suffer themselves to be diverted, to recriminate, and grieve away the Spirit of prayer, the work will go

2. The strange opposition of such men as Dr. Lyman Beecher and Mr. Nettleton had much to do with provoking and sustaining this opposition.

forward; as in the case referred to where a minister was on trial for six weeks in the midst of a revival. There the people kept in the dust and prayed, not so much for their minister for they had left him with God, but with strong crying and tears pleading with God for sinners. And God heard and blessed them and the work went on. Censoriousness in those who are opposed to the work is but little to be dreaded for they have not the Spirit and nothing depends on them, and they can hinder the work only just so far as they themselves have influence personally. But the others have the power of the Holy Spirit and the work depends on their keeping in a right temper. If they get wrong and grieve away the Spirit, there is no help; the work must cease. Whatever provocation, therefore, the promoters of this blessed work may have had, if it ceases, the responsibility will be theirs. And one of the most alarming facts in regard to this matter is that in many instances, those who have been engaged in carrying forward the work appear to have lost the Spirit. They are becoming diverted, are beginning to think that the opposition is no longer to be tolerated, and that they must come out and reply in the newspapers to what they say. It should be known and universally understood that whenever the friends and promoters of this greatest of revivals suffer themselves to be called off to newspaper janglings, to attempt to defend themselves, and reply to those who write against them, the Spirit of prayer will be entirely grieved away, and the work will cease. Nothing is more detrimental to revivals of religion, and so it has always been found, than for the promoters of them to listen to the opposition and begin to reply. This was found to be true in the days of President Edwards as you who are acquainted with his book on revivals are well aware.

Things that Encourage Revivals

I proceed to mention some things which ought to be done to continue this great and glorious revival of religion which has been in progress for the last ten years.

There should be great and deep repentings on the part of ministers. We, my brethren, must humble ourselves before God. It will not do for us to suppose that it is enough to call on the *people* to repent. We must repent, we must take the lead in repentance and then call on the churches to follow.

Especially must those repent who have taken the lead in producing the feelings of opposition and distrust in regard to revivals. Some ministers have confined their opposition against revivals and revival measures to their own congregations and created such suspicions among their own people as to prevent the work from spreading and prevailing among them. Such ministers would do well to consider the remarks of President Edwards on this subject.

"If ministers preach never so good doctrine and are never so painful and laborious in their work, yet if at such a day as this, they show to their people that they are not well-affected to this work but are very doubtful and suspicious of it, they will be very likely to do their people a great deal more hurt than good; for the very fame of such a great and extraordinary work of God, if their people were suffered to believe it to be his work, and the example of other towns together with what preaching they might hear occasionally, would be likely to have a much greater influence upon the minds of their people to awaken and animate them in religion than all their labors with them; and besides their minister's opinion would not only beget in them a suspicion of the work they hear of abroad whereby the mighty hand of God that appears in it loses its influence upon their minds, but it will also tend to create a suspicion of everything of the like nature that shall appear among themselves as being something of the same distemper that is to become so epidemical in the land, and that is, in effect, to create a suspicion of all vital religion and to put the people upon talking against it and discouraging it wherever it appears, and knocking it in the head as fast as it rises. And we that are ministers, by looking on this work from year to year, with a displeased countenance shall effectually keep the sheep from their pasture instead of doing the part of shepherds to them by feeding them; and our people had a great deal better be without any settled minister at all at such a day as this."

Others have been more public and aimed at exerting a wider influence. Some have written pieces for the public papers. Some men in high standing in the church have circulated letters which never were printed. Others have had their letters printed and circulated. There seems to have been a system of letter-writing about the country calculated to create distrust. In the days of President Edwards substantially the same course was pursued in view of which he says in his work on revivals:

"Great care should be taken that the press should be improved to no purpose contrary to the interests of this work. We read that when God fought against Sisera for the deliverance of his oppressed church, they that handle the pen of the writer came to the help of the Lord in that affair (Judg. 5:14). Whatever sort of men in Israel they were that were intended, yet as the words were indited by a Spirit that had a perfect view of all events to the end of the world and had a special eye in this song to that great event of the deliverance of God's church

in the latter days of which this deliverance of Israel was a type, it is not unlikely that they have respect to authors, those that should fight against the kingdom of Satan with their pens. Those therefore that publish pamphlets to the disadvantage of this work and tending either directly or indirectly to bring it under suspicion and to discourage or hinder it would do well thoroughly to consider whether this be not indeed the work of God and whether if it be, it is not likely that God will go forth as fire to consume all that stand in his way and so burn up those pamphlets; and whether there be not danger that the fire that is kindled in them will scorch the authors."

All these must repent. God never will forgive them nor will they ever enjoy his blessing on their preaching or be honored to labor in revivals till they repent. This duty President Edwards pressed upon ministers in his day in the most forcible terms. There doubtless have been now, as there were then, faults on both sides. And there must be deep repentance and mutual confessions of faults on both sides.

"There must be a great deal done at confessing of faults on both sides; for undoubtedly many and great are the faults that have been committed in the jangling and confusions and mixtures of light and darkness that have been of late. There is hardly any duty more contrary to our corrupt dispositions and mortifying to the pride of man; but it must be done. Repentance of faults is, in a peculiar manner, a proper duty when the kingdom of heaven is at hand or when we especially expect or desire that it would come as appears by John the Baptist's preaching. And if God does now loudly call upon us to repent, then he also calls upon us to make proper manifestations of our repentance. I am persuaded that those that have openly opposed this work or have from time to time spoken lightly of it cannot be excused in the sight of God without openly confessing their fault therein, especially if they be ministers. If they have any way, either directly or indirectly, opposed the work or have so behaved in their public performances or private conversation as has prejudiced the minds of their people against the work, if hereafter they shall be convinced of the goodness and divinity of what they have opposed, they ought by no means to palliate the matter and excuse themselves and pretend that they always thought so, and that it was only such and such imprudences that they objected against, but they ought openly to declare their conviction and condemn themselves for what they have done; for it is Christ that they have spoken against in speaking lightly of and prejudicing others against this work; yea, worse than that, it is the Holy Ghost. And though they have done it ignorantly and in unbelief, yet when they find out who it is that they have opposed, undoubtedly God will hold them bound publicly to confess it.

"And on the other side, if those that have been zealous to promote the work have in any of the forementioned instances openly gone much out of the way and done that which is contrary to Christian rules, whereby they have openly injured others or greatly violated good order and so done that which has wounded religion, they must publicly confess it and humble themselves as they would gather out the stones and prepare the way of God's people. They who have laid great stumbling blocks in others' way by their open transgression are bound to remove them by their open repentance."

There are ministers in our day, I say not in unkindness but in faithfulness and I would that I had them all here before me while I say it, who seem to have been engaged much of their time for years in doing little else than acting and talking and writing in such a way as to create suspicion in regard to revivals. And I cannot doubt that their churches would, as President Edwards says, be better with no minister at all unless they will repent and regain his [God's] blessing.

Those churches which have opposed revivals must humble themselves and repent. Churches which have stood aloof or hindered the work must repent of their sin, or God will not go with them. Look at those churches now who have been throwing suspicion upon revivals. Do they enjoy revivals? Does the Holy Ghost descend upon them to enlarge them and build them up? There is one of the churches in this city where the session have been publishing in the newspapers what they call their "Act and Testimony," calculated to excite an unreasonable and groundless suspicion against many ministers who are laboring sucessfully to promote revivals. And what is the state of that church? Have they had a revival? Why it appears from the official report to the General Assembly that it has dwindled in one year twenty-seven percent. And all such churches will continue to dwindle, in spite of everything else that can be done, unless they repent and have a revival. They may pretend to be mighty pious and jealous for the honor of God, but God will not believe they are sincere. And he will manifest his displeasure by not pouring out his Spirit. If I had a voice loud enough, I should like to make every one of those churches and ministers that have slandered revivals hear me when I say that I believe they have helped to bring the pall of death over the church and that the curse of God is on them already and will remain unless they repent. God has already sent leanness into their souls, and many of them know it.

Those who have been engaged in promoting the work must also repent. Whatever they have done that was wrong must be repented of or revivals will not return as in days past. Whenever a wrong spirit has been manifested or they have got irritated and provoked at the opposition and lost their temper or mistaken Christian faithfulness for hard words and a wrong spirit, they must repent. Those who are opposed could never stop a revival alone unless those who promote it get wrong. So we must repent if we have said things that were censorious or proud or arrogant or severe. Such a time as this is no time to stand justifying ourselves. Our first call is to repent. Let each one repent of his own sins and not fall out and quarrel about who is most to blame.

The church must take right ground in regard to politics. Do not suppose now, that I am going to preach a political sermon or that I wish to have you join and get up a Christian party in politics. No, I do not believe in that. But the time has come that Christians must vote for honest men and take consistent ground in politics, or the Lord will curse them. They must be honest men themselves and instead of voting for a man because he belongs to their party, Bank or Anti-Bank, Jackson or Anti-Jackson, they must find out whether he is honest and upright and fit to be trusted. They must let the world see that the church will uphold no man in office who is known to be a knave or an adulterer or a Sabbath-breaker or a gambler or a drunkard. Such is the spread of intelligence and the facility of communication in our country that every man can know for whom he gives his vote. And if he will give his vote only for honest men, the country will be obliged to have upright rulers. All parties will be com-

pelled to put up honest men as candidates. Christians have been exceedingly guilty in this matter. But the time has come when they must act differently, or God will curse the nation and withdraw his Spirit. As on the subject of slavery and temperance, so on this subject the church must act right or the country will be ruined. God cannot sustain this free and blessed country, which we love and pray for, unless the church will take right ground. Politics are a part of religion in such a country as this, and Christians must do their duty to the country as a part of their duty to God. It seems sometimes as if the foundations of the nation were becoming rotten, and Christians seem to act as if they thought God did not see what they do in politics. But I tell you, he does see it, and he will bless or curse this nation according to the course they take.

The churches must take right grounds on the subject of slavery. And here the question arises, what is right ground? And first I will state some things that should be avoided:

First of all, a bad spirit should be avoided. Nothing is more calculated to injure religion and to injure the slaves themselves than for Christians to get into an angry controversy on the subject. It is a subject upon which there need be no angry controversy among Christians. Slave-holding professors, like rum-selling professors, may endeavor to justify themselves and may be angry with those who press their consciences and call upon them to give up their sins. Those proud professors of religion who think a man to blame or think it is a shame to have a black skin, may allow their prejudices so far to prevail as to shut their ears and be disposed to quarrel with those who urge the subject upon them. But I repeat it, the subject of slavery is a subject upon which

Christians, praying men, *need not* and *must not* differ.

Another thing to be avoided is an attempt to take neutral ground on this subject. Christians can no more take neutral ground on this subject since it has come up for discussion than they can take neutral ground on the subject of the sanctification of the Sabbath. It is a great national sin. It is a sin of the church. The churches by their silence and by permitting slaveholders to belong to their communion have been consenting to it. All denominations have been more or less guilty, although the Quakers have of late years washed their hands of it. It is in vain for the churches to pretend it is merely a political sin. I repeat it, it is the sin of the church to which all denominations have consented. They have virtually declared that it is lawful. The very fact of suffering slaveholders quietly to remain in good standing in their churches is the strongest and most public expression of their views that it is not sin. For the church, therefore, to pretend to take neutral ground on the subject is perfectly absurd. The fact is that she is not on neutral ground at all. While she tolerates slaveholders in her communion, she justifies the practice. And as well might an enemy of God pretend that he was neither saint nor sinner, that he was going to take neutral ground and pray "good Lord and good devil," because he did not know which side would be most popular.

Great care should be taken to avoid a censorious spirit on both sides. It is a subject on which there has been, and probably will be for some time to come, a difference of opinion among Christians as to the best method of disposing of the question. And it ought to be treated with great forbearance on both sides. A denunciatory spirit, impeaching each other's motives, is un-christian, calculated to grieve the Spirit of God and to put down revivals, and is alike injurious to the church and to the slaves themselves.

In the second place I will mention several things that in my judgment the church are imperatively called upon to do on this subject:

Christians of all denominations should lay aside prejudice and inform themselves on this subject without any delay. Vast multitudes of professors of religion have indulged prejudice to such a degree as to be unwilling to read and hear and come to a right understanding of the subject. But Christians cannot pray in this state of mind. I defy anyone to possess the spirit of prayer while he is too prejudiced to examine this or any other question of duty. If the light did not shine, Christians might remain in the dark upon this point and still possess the spirit of prayer. But if they refuse to come to the light, they cannot pray. Now I call upon all you who are here present and who have not examined this subject because you were indisposed to examine it to say whether you have the spirit of prayer. Where ministers, individual Christians, or whole churches resist truth upon this point now when it is so extensively diffused and before the public mind, I do not believe they will or can enjoy a revival or religion.

Writings containing temperate and judicious discussions on this subject and such developments of facts as are before the public should be quietly and extensively circulated and should be carefully and prayerfully examined by the whole church. I do not mean by this that the attention of the church should be so absorbed by this as to neglect the main question of saving souls in the midst of them. I do not mean that such premature movements on this subject should be made as to astound the Christian community and involve them in a broil; but that praying men should act judiciously and that, as soon as sufficient information can be diffused through the community, the churches should meekly, but firmly take decided ground on the subject and express before the whole nation and the world their abhorrence of this sin.

The anti-masonic excitement which prevailed a few years since made such desolations in the churches and produced for a time so much alienation of feeling and ill will among ministers and people and the first introduction of this subject has been attended with such commotions that many good ministers who are themselves entirely opposed to slavery, dread to introduce the subject among their people through fear that their churches have not religion enough to take it up and consider it calmly and decide upon it in the spirit of the gospel. I know there is danger of this. But still the subject must be presented to the churches. And if introduced with discretion and with great prayer, there are very few churches that have enjoyed revivals and that are at the present time anywhere near a revival spirit which may not be brought to receive the truth on this subject. Let there be no mistake here. William Morgan's exposé of freemasonry was published in 1826. The consequent excitement and discussion continued until 1830. In the meantime the churches had very generally borne their testimony against freemasonry and resolved that they could not fellowship adhering masons. As a consequence the Masonic Lodges generally disbanded and gave up their charters. There was a general stampede of professed Christians from the lodges. This prepared the way and in 1830, the greatest revival the world had then ever seen commenced in the center of the anti-masonic region and spread over the whole field where the church action had been taken until its converts numbered one hundred thousand souls.

Perhaps no church in this country has had a more severe trial upon this subject than this. They were a church of young and, for the most part, inexperienced Christians. And many circumstances conspired, in my absence, to produce confusion and wrong feeling among them. But so far as I am now acquainted with the state of feeling in this church, I know of no ill will among them on this subject. The Lord has blessed us, the Spirit has been distilled upon us, and considerable numbers added to our communion every month since my return. There are doubtless in this church those who feel on this subject in very different degrees. And yet I can honestly say that I am not aware of the least difference in sentiment among them. We have from the beginning, previous to my going on my foreign tour, taken the same ground on the subject of slavery that we have on temperance. We have excluded slaveholders and all concerned in the traffic from our communion. By some out of this church this course has been censured as unwarrantable and uncharitable, and I would by no means make my own judgment or the example of this church a rule for the government of other ministers and churches. Still, I conscientiously believe that the time is not far distant when the churches will be united in this expression of abhorrence against this sin. If I do not baptize slavery by some soft and Christian name, if I call it sin, both consistency and conscience conduct to the inevitable conclusion that while this sin is persevered in, its perpetrators cannot be fit subjects for Christian communion and fellowship.

To this it is objected that there are many ministers in the Presbyterian church who are slaveholders. And it is said to be very inconsistent that we should refuse to suffer a slaveholder to come to our communion and yet belong to the same church with them, sit with them in ecclesiastical bodies, and acknowledge them as ministers. To this I answer that I have not the power to deal with those ministers and certainly I am not to withdraw from the church because some of its ministers or members are slaveholders. My duty is to belong to the church even if the devil belong to it. Where I have authority, I exclude slaveholders from the communion and I always will as long as I live. But where I have no authority, if the table of Christ is spread, I will sit down to it in obedience to his commandment, whoever else may sit down or stay away.

I do not mean, by any means, to denounce all those slaveholding ministers and professors as hypocrites and to say that they are not Christians. But this I say, that while they continue in that attitude, the cause of Christ and of humanity demands that they should not be recognized as such unless we mean to be partakers of other men's sins. It is no more inconsistent to exclude slaveholders because they belong to the Presbyterian church than it is to exclude persons who drink or sell ardent spirits. For there are a great many rum-sellers belonging to the Presbyterian church.

I believe the time has come, and although I am no prophet, I believe it will be found to have come, that the revival in the United States will continue and prevail no farther and faster than the church take right ground upon this subject. The church are God's witnesses. The fact is that slavery is, preeminently, the sin of the church. It is the very fact that ministers and professors of religion of different denominations hold slaves which sanctifies the whole abomination in the eyes of ungodly men. Who does not know that on the subject of temper-

ance every drunkard in the land will skulk behind some rum-selling deacon or wine-drinking minister? It is the most common objection and refuge of the intemperate and of moderate drinkers that is practiced by professors of religion. It is this that creates the imperious necessity for excluding traffickers in ardent spirit and rum-drinkers from the communion. Let the churches of all denominations speak out on the subject of temperance; let them close their doors against all who have anything to do with the death-dealing abomination, and the cause of temperance is triumphant. A few years would annihilate the traffic. Just so with slavery.

It is the church that mainly supports this sin. Her united testimony upon this subject would settle the question. Let Christians of all denominations meekly but firmly come forth and pronounce their verdict; let them clear their communions and wash their hands of this thing; let them give forth and write on the head and front of his great abomination, *sin!* and in three years a public sentiment would be formed that would carry all before it, and there would not be a shackled slave nor a bristling, cruel slave-driver in this land.

Still it may be said that in many churches this subject *cannot be* introduced without creating confusion and ill will. This may be. It has been so upon the subject of temperance and upon the subject of revivals too. In some churches, neither temperance nor revivals can be introduced without producing dissension. Sabbath schools and missionary operations and everything of the kind have been opposed and have produced dissensions in many churches. But is this a sufficient reason for excluding these subjects? And where churches have excluded these subjects for fear of contention, have they been blessed with revivals? Everybody knows that they have not. But where churches have taken firm ground on these subjects, although individuals and sometimes numbers have opposed, still they have been blessed with revivals. Where any of these subjects are carefully and prayerfully introduced; where they are brought forward with a right spirit and the true relative importance is attached to each one of them; if in such cases there are those who will make disturbance and resist, let the blame fall where it ought. There are some individuals who are themselves disposed to quarrel with this subject, who are always ready to exclaim, "Do not introduce these things into the church, they will create opposition." And if the minister and praying people feel it their duty to bring the matter forward, they will themselves create a disturbance and then say, "There I told you so; now see what your introducing this subject has done; it will tear the church all to pieces." And while they are themselves doing all they can to create division, they are charging the division upon the subject and not upon themselves. There are some such people in many of our churches. And neither Sabbath schools nor missions, nor revivals, nor antislavery, nor anything else that honors God or benefits the souls of men will be carried in the churches without these careful souls being offended by it.

These things, however, have been introduced and carried one by one in some churches with more and others with less opposition and perhaps in some churches with no opposition at all. And as true as God is the God of the church, as certain as that the world must be converted, this subject must be considered and pronounced sin by the church. There might, infinitely better, be no church in the world than that she should attempt to remain neutral or give a false testimony on a subject of such importance as slavery, especially since the subject has come up and it is impossible from the nature of the case that her testimony should not be in the scale on the one side or the other.

Do you ask, "What shall be done—shall we make it the all-absorbing topic of conversation and divert attention from the all-important subject of the salvation of souls in the midst of us?" I answer, "No." Let a church express her opinion upon the subject and be at peace. So far as I know, *we* are entirely at peace upon this subject. We have expressed our opinion; we have closed our communion against slaveholders and are attending to other things. I am not aware of the least unhealthy excitement among us on this subject. And where it has become an absorbing topic of conversation in a place, in most instances I believe it has been owing to the pertinacious and unreasonable opposition of a few individuals against even granting the subject a hearing.

If the church wishes to promote revivals, she must sanctify the Sabbath. There is a vast deal of Sabbath breaking in the land. Merchants break it, travelers break it, the government breaks it. A few years ago an attempt was made in the western part of this state to establish and sustain a Sabbath-keeping line of boats and stages. But it was found that the church would not sustain the enterprise. Many professors of religion would not travel in these stages and would not have their goods forwarded in canal-boats that would be detained from traveling on the Sabbath. At one time, Christians were much engaged in petitioning Congress to suspend the Sabbath mails and now they seem to be ashamed of it. But one thing is most certain, that unless something is done and done speedily and done effectually to promote the sanctification of the Sabbath by the church, the Sabbath will go by the board, and we shall not only have our mails running on the Sabbath and post offices open, but by and by, our courts of justice and halls of legislation will be kept open on the Sabbath. And what can the church do, what will this nation do, without any Sabbath?

The church must take right ground on the subject of temperance and moral reform and all the subjects of practical morality which come up for decision from time to time. There are those in the churches who are standing aloof from the subject of moral reform and who are afraid to have anything said in the pulpit against lewdness. On this subject the church need not expect to be permitted to take neutral ground. In the providence of God, it is up for discussion. The evils have been exhibited, the call has been made for reform. And what is to reform mankind but the truth? And who shall present the truth if not the church and the ministry? Away with the idea that Christians can remain neutral and keep still and yet enjoy the approbation and blessing of God.

In all such cases, the minister who holds his peace is counted among those on the other side. Everybody knows that it is so in a revival. It is not necessary for a person to rail out against the work. If he only keeps still and takes neutral ground, the enemies of the revival will all consider him as on their side. So on the subject of temperance. It is not needful that a person should rail at the cold-water society in order to be on the best terms with drunkards and moderate drinkers. Only let him plead for the moderate use of wine, only let him continue to drink it as a luxury, and all the drunkards account him on their side. If he refuses to give his influence to the temperance cause, he is claimed of course by the other side as a friend. On all these subjects when they come up,

the churches and ministers must take the right ground and take it openly and stand to it and carry it through, if they expect to enjoy the blessing of God in revivals. They must cast out from their communions such members, as in contempt of the light that is shed upon them, continue to drink or traffic in ardent spirits.

There must be more done for all the great objects of Christian benevolence. There must be much greater efforts for the cause of missions and education and the Bible and all the other branches of religious enterprise, or the church will displease God. Look at it. Think of the mercies we have received, of the wealth, numbers, and prosperity of the church. Have we rendered unto God according to the benefits we have received so as to show that the church is bountiful and willing to give their money and to work for God? No. Far from it. Have we multiplied our means and enlarged our plans in proportion as the church has increased? Is God satisfied with what has been done or has he reason to be? Such a revival as has been enjoyed by the churches of America for the last ten years! We ought to have done ten times as much as we have for missions, Bibles, education, tracts, free churches, and in all the ways designed to promote religion and save souls. If the churches do not wake up on this subject and lay themselves out on a larger scale, they may expect the revival in the United States will cease.

If Christians in the United States expect revivals to spread and prevail till the world is converted, they must give up writing letters and publishing pieces calculated to excite suspicion and jealousy in regard to revivals and must take hold of the work themselves. If the whole church as a body had gone to work ten years ago and continued it as a few individuals, whom I could name, have done, there would not now have been an impenitent sinner in the land. The millennium would have fully come in the United States before this day. Instead of standing still and writing letters from Berkshire, let ministers who think we are going wrong just buckle on the harness and go forward and show us a more excellent way. Let them teach us by their example how to do better. I do not deny that some may have made mistakes and committed errors. I do not deny that there are many things which are wrong done in revivals by some person. But is that the way to correct them, brethren? So did not Paul. He corrected his brethren by telling them kindly that he would show them a more excellent way. Let our brethren take hold and go forward. Let us hear the cry from all their pulpits. To the work. Let them lead on where the Lord will go with them and make bare his arm, and I, for one, will follow. Only let them GO ON and let us have the United States converted to God and let all minor questions cease.

If not, and if revivals do cease in this land, the ministers and churches will be guilty of all the blood of all the souls that shall go to hell in consequence of it. There is no need that the work should cease. If the church will do all her duty, the millennium may come in this country in three years. But if this writing letters is to be kept up, filling the country with suspicions and jealousies, if it is to be always so that two-thirds of the church will hang back and do nothing but find fault in time of revival, the curse of God will be on this nation, and that before long.

REMARKS

It is high time there should be great searchings of heart among Christians and ministers. Brethren, this is no time to resist the truth or to cavil and find fault because the truth is spoken out plainly. It is no time to recriminate or to strive, but we must search our own hearts and humble ourselves before God.

We must repent and forsake our sins and amend our ways and our doings or the revival will cease. Our ecclesiastical difficulties *must cease,* and all minor differences must be laid aside and given up to unite in promoting the great interests of religion. If not, revivals will cease from among us and the blood of lost millions will be found in our skirts.

If the church would do all her duty, she would soon complete the triumph of religion in the world. But if this Act and Testimony warfare is to be kept up and this system of espionage and insinuation and denunciation, not only will revivals cease but the blood of millions, who will go to hell before the church will get over the shock, will be found in the skirts of the men who have got up and carried on this dreadful contention.

Those who have circulated slanderous reports in regard to revivals must repent. A great deal has been said about heresy and about some men's denying the Spirit's influence, which is wholly groundless and has been made up out of nothing. And those who have made up the reports and those who have circulated them against their brethren must repent and pray to God that they may receive his forgiveness.

We see the constant tendency there is in Christians to declension and backsliding. This is true in all converts of all revivals. Look at the revival in President Edwards' day. The work went on till thirty thousand souls had been converted and by this time so many ministers and Christians got in such a state by writing books and pamphlets on one side and the other that they carried all by the board, and the revival ceased.

Those who had opposed the work grew obstinate and violent, and those who promoted it lost their meekness and got ill-tempered and were then driven into the very evils that had been falsely charged upon them.

And now, what shall we do? This great and glorious work of God seems to be indicating a decline. The revival is not dead—blessed be God for that—it is not dead! No, we hear from all parts of the land that Christians are reading on the subject and inquiring about the revival. In some places there are now powerful revivals. And what shall we do to lift up the standard, to move this entire nation and turn all this great people to the Lord? We must DO RIGHT. We must all have a better spirit, we must get down in the dust, we must act unitedly, we must take hold of this great work with all our hearts, and then God will bless us and the work will go on.

What is the condition of this nation? No doubt God is holding the rod of WAR over the heads of this nation. He is waiting before he lets loose his judgments to see whether the church will do right. The nation is under his displeasure because the church has conducted in such a manner with respect to revivals. And now suppose war should come, where would be our revivals? How quickly would war swallow up the revival spirit. The spirit of war is anything but the spirit of revivals. Who will attend to by claims of religion when the public mind is engrossed by the all-absorbing topic of war. See now, how this nation is *all at once* brought upon the brink of war. God brandishes his blazing sword over our heads. Will the church repent? It is THE CHURCH that God chiefly has in view. How shall we avoid the curse of war? Only by a reformation in the church. It is in vain to look to politicians to avert war. Perhaps they would generally be in favor of war. Very likely the things they

would do to avert it would run us right into it. If the church will not feel, will not awake, will not act, where shall we look for help? If the church absolutely will not move, will not tremble in view of the just judgments of God hanging over our heads, we are certainly nigh unto cursing as a nation.

Whatever is done must be done quickly. The scale is on a poise. If we do not go forward, we must go back. Things cannot remain as they are. If the church do not come up, if we do not have a more powerful revival than we have had, very soon we shall have none at all. We have had such a great revival that now small revivals do not interest the public mind. You must act as individuals. Do your own duty. You have a responsibility. Repent quickly. Do not wait till another year. Who but God knows what will be the state of these churches if things go on another year without a great and general revival of religion?

It is common when things get all wrong in the church for each individual to find fault with the church and with his brethren and overlook his own share of the blame. Do not let any one spend his time in finding fault with that abstract thing, "The Church." But as individual members of the church of Christ, let each one act and act right and get down in the dust and never speak proudly or censoriously. Go forward. Who would leave such a work and go to writing letters and go down into the plain of Ono and see if all these petty disputes cannot be adjusted and let the work cease. Let us mind our work and let the Lord take care of the rest. Do our duty and leave the issue to God.

Since these lectures were delivered great progress has been made in all benevolent enterprises in this country. Time has settled the question of the purity and inestimable value of those revivals against which so much mistaken opposition existed in the Presbyterian church. It is now known that the great and disastrous reaction predicted by opposers has not been witnessed. It must now be admitted that the converts of those revivals have composed the strength of the churches and that their Christian influence has been felt throughout the land. No revivals have ever existed the power and purity of which have been more thoroughly established by time and experience than that great and blessed work of God against which such a storm of opposition was raised. The opposition was evidently a great mistake. Let it not be said that the opposition was demanded by the great evils attending that work and that those evils and errors were arrested and corrected by that opposition. The fact is that the supposed errors and evils that were made the jusification of the opposition never existed to any such extent as to justify alarm or opposition. I have written a narrative of those revivals in which I have considered this question more fully. The churches did take hold of temperance and other branches of reform to such an extent as to avoid those evils against which they were warned. Upon the question of slavery the church was too late in her testimony to avoid the war. But the slaveholders were much alarmed and exasperated by the constantly growing oppostion to their institution throughout all that region of the north where revival influences had been felt. They took up arms to defend and perpetuate the abomination, and by so doing abolished it.

Simply put, sanctification means that an object or person is set apart for use by God. It is a consecration to God for the purpose of holy service. Complete, or entire, sanctification may be defined in several ways. A person must be fully obedient, or entirely consecrated, to God. Also, a person must be in a continued, abiding consecration to God. The contention is that if God demands obedience to his laws, then man is able to do so without flaw.

The state of entire sanctification is not accomplished by man's indifferent waiting upon God's time. Nor is it achieved in man's strength apart from the grace of God, nor is it a feeling of being right. Sanctification is a supernatural event that must be accomplished by God. The process begins at conversion and continues by the working of the Holy Spirit.

CHAPTER FIVE

Sanctification

I will remind you of some points that have been settled in this course of study.

The true intent and meaning of the law of God has been, as I trust, ascertained in the lectures on moral government. Let this point, if need be, be examined by reference to those lectures.

We have also seen in those lectures what is not and what is implied in entire obedience to the moral law.

In those lectures and also in the lectures on justification and repentance, it has been shown that nothing is acceptable to God as a condition of justification and of consequent salvation but a repentence that implies a return to full obedience to the moral law.

It has also been shown that nothing is holiness short of full obedience, for the time being, to the moral law.

It has also been shown that regeneration and repentance consist in the heart's return to full obedience, for the time being, to this law.

We have also examined the doctrine of depravity and seen that moral depravity, or sin, consists in selfishness and not at all in the constitution of men; that selfishness does not consist in the involuntary appetites, passions, and propensities but that it consists alone in the committal of the will to the gratification of the propensities.

We have seen that holiness consists not at all in the constitution of body or mind but that it belongs, strictly, only to the will or heart and consists in obedience of will to the law of God as it lies revealed in the intellect; that it is expressed in one word, love; that this love is identical with the entire consecration of the whole being to the glory of God and to the highest well-being of the universe; or in other words, that it consists in disinterested benevolence.

We have seen that all true saints, while in a state of acceptance with God, do actually render for the time being full obedience to all the known requirements of God; that is, that they do for the time being their whole duty—all that God, at this time, requires of them.

We have seen that this obedience is not rendered independent of the grace of God but is induced by the indwelling spirit of Christ received by faith and reigning in the heart. This fact will be more fully elucidated in this discussion than it has been in former lectures. A former lecture was devoted to it, but a fuller consideration of it remains to be entered upon hereafter.

The Principal Terms to be Used in This Discussion

Here let me remark that a definition of terms in all discussions is of prime importance. Especially is this true of this subject. I have observed that almost without an exception those who have written on this subject dissenting from the views entertained here do so upon the ground that they understand and define the terms sanctification and Christian perfection differently from what we do. Every one gives his own definition varying materially from others and from what we understand by the terms, and then he goes on professedly opposing the doctrine as inculcated here. Now this is not only utterly unfair but palpably absurd. If I oppose a doctrine inculcated by another man, I am bound to oppose what he really holds. If I misrepresent his sentiments, "I fight as one that beateth the air." I have been amazed at the diversity of definitions that have been given to the terms Christian perfection, sanctification, etc., and to witness the diversity of opinion as to what is and what is not implied in these terms. One objects wholly to the use of the term Christian perfection because in his estimation it implies this and that and the other thing, which I do not suppose are at all implied in it. Another objects to our using the term sanctification because that implies according to his understanding of it certain things that render its use improper. Now it is no part of my design to dispute about the use of words. I must however use some terms, and I ought to be allowed to use Bible language in its Scriptural sense as I understand it. And if I should sufficiently explain my meaning and define the sense in which I use the terms and the sense in which the Bible manifestly uses them, this ought to suffice. And I beg that nothing more or less may be understood by the language I use than I profess to mean by it. Others may, if they please, use the same terms and give a different definition of them. But I have a right to hope and expect, if they feel called upon to oppose what I say, that they will bear in mind my definition of the terms and not pretend as some have done to oppose my views while they have only differed from me in their definition of the terms used, giving their own definition varying materially and, I might say, infinitely from the sense in which I use the same terms and then arraying their arguments to prove that according to their definition of it,

sanctification is not really attainable in this life, when no one here or anywhere else that I ever heard of pretended that in their sense of the term it ever was or ever will be attainable in this life and, I might add, or in that which is to come.

Sanctification is a term of frequent use in the Bible. Its simple and primary meaning is a state of consecration to God. To sanctify is to set apart to a holy use—to consecrate a thing to the service of God. This is plainly both the Old and the New Testaments use of the term. The Greek word *hagiazo* means to sanctify, to consecrate, or devote a person or thing to a particular, especially to a sacred, use. This word is synonymous with the Hebrew *kaudash*. This last word is used in the Old Testament to express the same thing that is intended by the Greek *hagiazo*, namely, to consecrate, devote, set apart, sanctify, purify, make clean or pure. *Hagiasmos*, a substantive from *hagiazo*, means sanctification, devotion, consecration, purity, holiness.

From the Bible use of these terms it is most manifest that sanctification does not imply any constitutional change, either of soul or body. It consists in the consecration or devotion of the constitutional powers of body and soul to God and not in any change wrought in the constitution itself.

It is also evident from the Scriptural use of the term that sanctification is not a phenomenon or state of the intellect. It belongs neither to the reason, conscience, nor understanding. In short, it cannot consist in any state of the intellect whatever. All the states of this faculty are purely passive states of mind and of course, as we have abundantly seen, holiness is not properly predicable of them.

It is just as evident that sanctification in the Scriptural and proper sense of the term is not a mere feeling of any kind. It is not a desire, an appetite, a passion, a propensity, an emotion, nor indeed any kind or degree of feeling. It is not a state or phenomenon of the sensibility. The states of the sensibility are, like those of the intellect, purely passive states of mind as has been repeatedly shown. They, of course, can have no moral character in themselves.

The Bible use of the term when applied to persons forbids the understanding of it as consisting in any involuntary state or attitude of mind whatever.

The inspired writers evidently used the terms which are translated by the English word *sanctify* to designate a phenomenon of the will or a voluntary state of mind. They used the term *hagiazo* in Greek and *kaudash* in Hebrew to represent the act of consecrating oneself or anything else to the service of God and to the highest well-being of the universe. The term manifestly not only represents an act of the will, but an ultimate act or choice as distinguished from a mere volition or executive act of the will. Thus the terms rendered *sanctified* are used as synonymous with loving God with all the heart and our neighbor as ourselves. The Greek *hagiasmos,* translated by the word sanctification, is evidently intended to express a state or attitude of voluntary consecration to God, a continued act of consecration, or a state of choice as distinct from a mere act of choice, an abiding act or state of choice, a standing and controlling preference of mind, a continuous committal of the will to the highest well-being of God and of the universe. Sanctification as a state differing from a holy act is a standing, ultimate intention and exactly synonymous or identical with a state of obedience or conformity to the law of God. We have repeatedly seen that the will is the executive or controlling faculty of the mind. Sanctification consists in the will's devoting or consecrating it-

self and the whole being, all we are and have so far as powers, susceptibilities, possessions are under the control of the will, to the service of God, or which is the same thing, to the highest interests of God and of being. Sanctification then is nothing more nor less than entire obedience, for the time being, to the moral law.

Sanctification may be entire in two senses: (1) in the sense of present, full obedience, or entire consecration to God; and (2) in the sense of continued, abiding consecration or obedience to God. Entire sanctification when the terms are used in this sense consists in being established, confirmed, preserved, continued in a state of sanctification or of entire consecration to God.

In this discussion then I shall use the term entire sanctification to designate a state of confirmed and entire consecration of body, soul, and spirit, or of the whole being to God—confirmed, not in the sense (1) that a soul entirely sanctified cannot sin, but that as a matter of fact, he does not and will not sin. (2) Nor do I use the term entire sanctification as implying that the entirely sanctified soul is in no such danger of sinning as to need the thorough use and application of all the means of grace to prevent him from sinning, and to secure his continued sanctification; (3) Nor do I mean by entire sanctification a state in which there will be no further struggle or warfare with temptation or in which the Christian warfare will cease. This certainly did not cease in Christ to the end of his life nor will it with any being in the flesh; (4) Nor do I use the term as implying a state in which no further progress in holiness is possible. No such state is or ever will be possible to any creature for the plain reason that all creatures must increase in knowledge, and increase of knowledge implies increase of holiness in a holy being. The saints will doubtless grow in grace or holiness to all eternity; (5) Nor do I mean by the term entire sanctification that the entirely sanctified soul will no longer need the continual grace and indwelling Spirit of Christ to preserve it from sin and to secure its continuance in a state of consecration to God. It is amazing that such men as Dr. Beecher and others should suppose that a state of entire consecration implies that the entirely sanctified soul no longer needs the grace of Christ to preserve it. Entire sanctification, instead of implying no further dependence on the grace of Christ, implies the constant appropriation of Christ by faith as the sanctification of the soul.

But since entire sanctification as I understand the term is identical with entire and continued obedience to the law of God and since I have in lectures on moral government fully shown what is not and what is implied in full obedience to the law of God, to avoid much repetition in this place I must refer you to what I have there said upon the topics just named.

The Real Question Now at Issue

It is not whether a state of present full obedience to the Divine law is attainable in this life. For this has, I trust, been clearly established in former lectures. It is not whether a state of permanent, full obedience has been attained by all or by any of the saints on earth. But the true question at issue is, Is a state of entire, in the sense of permanent, sanctification attainable in this life?

If in this discussion I shall insist upon the fact that this state has been attained, let it be distinctly understood that the fact that the attainment has been made is only adduced in proof of the attainability of this state, that it is only one of the arguments by which the attainability of this state is proved. Let it also be distinctly borne in mind that if there should be in the estimation of anyone a defect in the proof that this state has been attained, still the integrity and conclusiveness of the other arguments in support of the attainability will not thereby be shaken. It is no doubt true that the attainability of this state in this life may be abundantly established entirely irrespective of the question whether this state has ever been attained.

The true question is, Is a state of entire, established, abiding consecration to God attainable in this life in such a sense that we may rationally expect or hope to become thus established in this life? Are the conditions of attaining this established state in the grace and love of God such that we may rationally expect or hope to fulfill them and thus become established or entirely sanctified in this life? This is undoubtedly the true and the greatly important question to be settled.

Entire Sanctification Is Attainable in This Life

It is self-evident that entire obedience to God's law is possible on the ground of natural ability. To deny this is to deny that a man is able to do as well as he can. The very language of the law is such as to level its claims to the capacity of the subject, however great or small that capacity may be. "Thou shalt love the Lord thy God with all thy heart, with all thy soul, with all thy mind, and with all thy strength." Here then it is plain that all the law demands is the exercise of whatever strength we have in the service of God. Now as entire sanctification consists in perfect obedience to the law of God and as the law requires nothing more than the right use of whatever strength we have, it is, of course, forever settled that a state of entire sanctification is attainable in this life on the ground of natural ability.

This is generally admitted by those who are called moderate Calvinists. Or perhaps I should say it generally has been admitted by them, though at present some of them seem inclined to give up the doctrine of natural ability and to take refuge in constitutional depravity rather than admit the attainableness of a state of entire sanctification in this life. But let men take refuge where they will, they can never escape from the plain letter and spirit and meaning of the law of God. Mark with what solemn emphasis it says, "Thou shalt love the Lord thy God with all thy heart, with all thy soul, with all thy mind, and with all thy strength." This is its solemn injunction whether it be given to an angel, a man, or a child. An angel is bound to exercise an angel's strength; a man, the strength of a man; and a child, the strength of a child. It comes to every moral being in the universe just as he is, where he is, and requires not that he should create new powers or possess other powers than he has, but that such as his powers are, they should all be used with the utmost perfection and constancy for God.

The provisions of grace are such as to render its actual attainment in this life the object of reasonable pursuit. It is admitted that the entire sanctification of the church is to be accomplished. It is also admitted that this work is to be accomplished, "through the sanctification of the Spirit and the belief of the truth." It is also universally agreed that this work must be begun here and also that it must be completed before the soul can enter heaven. This then is the inquiry: Is this state attainable as a matter of fact before death?

Bible Argument

I come now to consider the question directly and wholly as a Bible question, whether entire sanctification is in such a sense attainable in this life as to make its attainment an object of rational pursuit.

It is evident from the fact expressly stated that abundant means are provided for the accomplishment of this end. Ephesians 4:10–16:

> He that descended is the same also that ascended up far above all heavens, that he might fill all things. And he gave some, apostles; and some, prophets; and some, evangelists; and some, pastors and teachers; for the perfecting of the saints, for the work of the ministry, for the edifying of the body of Christ; till we all come in the unity of the faith, and of the knowledge of the Son of God, unto a perfect man, unto the measure of the stature of the fullness of Christ; that we henceforth be no more children tossed to and fro, and carried about with every wind of doctrine, by the sleight of men, and cunning craftiness, whereby they lie in wait to deceive; but speaking the truth in love, may grow up into him in all things, which is the head, even Christ; from whom the whole body fitly joined together and compacted by that which every joint supplieth, according to the effectual working in the measure of every part, maketh increase of the body, unto the edifying of itself in love.

Upon this passage I remark:
(1) That what is here spoken of is plainly applicable only to this life. It is in this life that the apostles, evangelists, prophets, and teachers exercise their ministry. These means therefore are applicable, and so far as we know, only applicable to this life.

(2) The apostle here manifestly teaches that these means are designed and adequate to perfecting the whole church as the body of Christ, "till we all come in the unity of the faith and of the knowledge of the Son of God, unto the measure of the stature of the fullness of Christ."

(3) Now observe—these means are for the perfecting of the saints till the whole church as a perfect man, "has come to the measure of the stature of the fullness of Christ." If this is not entire sanctification, what is? That this is to take place in this world is evident from what follows. For the apostle adds, "that we henceforth be no more tossed to and fro, and carried about with every wind of doctrine, by the sleight of men, and cunning craftiness, whereby they lie in wait to deceive."

(4) It should be observed that this is a very strong passage in support of the doctrine, inasmuch as it asserts that abundant means are provided for the sanctification of the church in this life. And as they whole includes all its parts, there must be sufficient provision for the sanctification of each individual.

(5) If the work is ever to be affected, it is by these means. But these means are used only in this life. Entire sanctification then must take place in this life.

(6) If this passage does not teach a state of entire sanctification, such a state is nowhere mentioned in the Bible. And if believers are not here said to be wholly sanctified by these means and of course in this life, I know not that it is anywhere taught that they shall be sanctified at all.

(7) But suppose this passage to be put into the language of a command, how should we understand it? Suppose the saints commanded to be perfect and to "grow up to the measure of the stature of the fullness of Christ," could anything less than entire sanctification be understood by such requisitions? Then by what rule of sober criticism, I would inquire, can this language used in this connection mean anything less than I have supposed it to mean?

But let us look into some of the promises. It is not my design to examine a great number of Scripture promises, but rather to show that those which I do examine fully sustain the positions I have taken. One is sufficient, if it be full and its application just, to settle this question forever. I might occupy many pages in the examination of the promises for they are exceedingly numerous and full and in point. But my design is at present to examine somewhat critically a few only out of the many. This will enable you to apply the same principles to the examination of the Scripture promises generally.

I begin by referring you to the law of God as given in Deuteronomy 10:12.

> And now, Israel, what doth the Lord thy God require of thee, but to fear the Lord thy God, to walk in all his ways, and to love him, and to serve the Lord thy God with all thy heart, and with all thy soul?

Upon this passage I remark: It professedly sums up the whole duty of man to God—to fear and love him with all the heart and all the soul. Although this is said of Israel, yet it is equally true of all men. It is equally binding upon all and is all that God requires of any man in regard to himself. Continued obedience to this requirement is entire sanctification in the sense in which I use those terms.

See Deuteronomy 30:6:

> And the Lord thy God will circumcise thine heart, and the heart of thy seed, to love the Lord thy God with all thine hearts, and with all thy soul, that thou mayest live.

Here we have a promise couched in the same language as the command just quoted.

Upon this passage I remark: It promises just what the law requires. If the law requires a state of entire sanctification or if that which the law requires is a state of entire sanctification, then this is a promise of entire sanctification. As the command is universally binding upon all and applicable to all so this promise is universally applicable to all who will lay hold upon it. Faith is an indispensable condition of the fulfillment of this promise. It is entirely impossible that we should love God with all the heart without confidence in him. God begets love in man in no other way than by so revealing himself as to inspire confidence, that confidence which works by love.

Now here there is no perceivable reason why we should not understand the language of the promise as meaning as much as the language of the command. This promise appears to have been designed to cover the whole ground of the requirement. Suppose the language in this promise to be used in a command or suppose that the form of this promise were changed into that of a command; suppose God should say as he does elsewhere, "Thou shalt love the Lord thy God with all thy heart and with all thy soul." Who would doubt that God designed to require a state of entire sanctification or consecration to himself? How then are we to understand it when used in the form of a promise? If his bountifulness equals his justice, his promises of grace must be understood to mean as much as the requirements of his justice. If he delights in giving as much as in receiving, his promises must mean as much as the language of his requirements.

This promise is designed to be fulfilled in this life. The language and connection imply this: "I will circumcise thy heart and the heart of thy seed to love the Lord thy God with all thy heart, and with all thy soul." This in some sense takes place in regeneration, but more than simple regeneration seems here to be promised. It is plain, I think, that this promise relates to a state of mind and not merely to an exercise.

This promise as it respects the church at some day must be absolute and certain. So that God will undoubtedly at some period beget this state of mind in the church. But to what particular individuals and generation this promise will be fulfilled must depend upon their faith in the promise.

See Jeremiah 31:31–34:

Behold, the days come, saith the Lord, that I will make a new covenant with the house of Israel, and with the house of Judah; not according to the covenant that I made with their fathers, in the day that I took them by the hand, to bring them out of the land of Egypt, (which my covenant they brake, although I was a husband unto them, saith the Lord;) but this shall be the covenant that I will make with the house of Israel: After these days, saith the Lord, I will put my law in their inward parts, and write it in their hearts; and I will be their God, and they shall be my people. And they shall teach no more every man his neighbor, and every man his brother, saying, Know the Lord; for they shall all know me, from the least of them unto the greatest of this, saith the Lord; for I will forgive their iniquity, and I will remember their sin no more.

Upon this passage, I remark: It was to become due or the time when its fulfillment might be claimed and expected was at the advent of Christ. This is unequivocally settled in Hebrews 8:8–12, where this passage is quoted at length as being applicable to the gospel day.

This is undeniably a promise of entire sanctification. It is a promise that the "law shall be written in the heart." It means that the very temper and spirit required by the law shall be begotten in the soul. Now if the law requires entire sanctification or perfect holiness, this is certainly a promise of it, for it is a promise of all that the law requires. To say that this is not a promise of entire sanctification is the same absurdity as to say that perfect obedience to the law is not entire sanctification, and this last is the same absurdity as to say that something more is our duty than what the law requires, and this again is to say that the law is imperfect and unjust.

A permanent state, or entire sanctification, is plainly implied in this promise. The reason for setting aside the first covenant was that it was broken: "Which my covenant they brake." One grand design of the new covenant is that it shall not be broken, for then it would be no better than the first. Permanency is implied in the fact that it is to be engraven in the heart. Permanency is plainly implied in the assertion that God will remember their sin no more. In Jeremiah 32:39–40, where the same promise is in substance repeated, you will find it expressly stated that the covenant is to be "everlasting" and that he will so "put his fear in their hearts that they shall not depart from him." Here permanency is as expressly promised as it can be.

Suppose the language of this promise to be thrown into the form of a command. Suppose God to say, "Let my law be within your hearts and let it be in your inward parts and let my fear be so within your hearts, that you shall not depart from me. Let your covenant with me be everlasting." If this language were found in a command, would any man in his senses doubt that it meant to require perfect and permanent sanctification? If not, by what rule of sober interpretation does he make it mean anything else when found in a promise? It appears to be profane trifling when such language is found in a promise to make it mean less than it does when found in a command.

This promise as it respects the church at some period of its history is unconditional and its fulfillment certain. But in respect to any particular individuals or generation of the church, its fulfillment is necessarily conditioned upon their faith. The church as a body have certainly never received this new covenant. Yet doubtless multitudes in every age of the Christian dispensation have received it. And God will hasten the time when it shall be so fully accomplished that there shall be no need for one man to say to his brother, "Know the Lord, for all shall know him from the least to the greatest."

It should be understood that this promise was made to the Christian church and not at all to the Jewish church. The saints under the old dispensation had no reason to expect the fulfillment of this and kindred promises to themselves because their fulfillment was expressly deferred until the commencement of the Christian dispensation.

It has been said that nothing more is here promised than regeneration. But were not the Old Testament saints regenerated? Yet it is expressly said that they received not the promises. Hebrews 11:13, 39–40:

> These all died in faith, not having received the promises, but having seen them afar off, and were persuaded of them, and embraced them, and confessed that they were strangers and pilgrims on the earth. And these all, having ob-

tained a good report through faith, received not the promise; God having provided some better thing for us, that they without us should not be made perfect.

Here we see that these promises were not received by the Old Testament saints. Yet they were regenerated.

It has also been said that the promise implies no more than the final perseverance of the saints. But I would inquire, did not the Old Testament saints persevere? And yet we have just seen that the Old Testament saints did not receive these promises in their fulfillment.

I will next examine the promise in Ezekiel 36:25–27:

> Then will I sprinkle clean water upon you, and ye shall be clean; from all your filthiness, and from all your idols, will I cleanse you. A new heart also will be given you, and a new spirit will I put within you; and I will take away the stony heart out of your flesh, and I will give you an heart of flesh. And I will put my Spirit within you, and cause you to walk in my statutes, and ye shall keep my judgments and do them.

Upon this I remark: It was written within nineteen years after that which we have just examined in Jeremiah. It plainly refers to the same time and is a promise of the same blessing. It seems to be admitted, nor can it be denied, that this is a promise of entire sanctification. The language is very definite and full. "Then,"—referring to some future time, when it should become due, "will I sprinkle clean water upon you, and ye shall be clean." Mark the first promise, "ye shall be clean." If to be "clean" does not mean entire sanctification, what does it mean?

The second promise is, "From all your filthiness and from all your idols will I cleanse you." If to be cleansed "from all filthiness and all idols" be not a state of entire sanctification, what is?

The third promise is, "A new heart also will I give you, and a new spirit will I put within you; I will take away the stony heart out of your flesh, and will give you an heart of flesh." If to have a "clean heart," a "new heart," a "heart of flesh," in opposition to a "heart of stone," be not entire sanctification, what is?

The fourth promise is, "I will put my Spirit within you and cause you to walk in my statutes and ye shall keep my judgments, and do them."

Let us turn the language of these promises into that of command and understand God as saying, "Make you a clean heart, a new heart, and a new spirit; put away all your iniquities, all your filthiness, and all your idols; walk in my statutes, and keep my judgments, and do them." Now what man in the sober exercise of his reason would doubt whether God meant to require a state of entire sanctification in such commands as these? The rules of legitimate interpretation would demand that we should so understand him.

If this is so, what is the fair and proper construction of this language when found in a promise? I do not hesitate to say that to me it is amazing that any doubt should be left on the mind of any man whether in these promises God means as much as in his commands couched in the same language. For example, see Ezekiel 18:30, 31:

> Repent, and turn yourselves from all your transgressions; so iniquity shall not be your ruin. Cast away from you all your transgressions, whereby ye have transgressed and make you a new heart and a new spirit; for why will ye die, O house of Israel?

Now that the language in the promise under consideration should mean as much as the language of this command is demanded by every sober rule of interpretation. And who ever dreamed that when God required his people to put away all their iniquities, he only meant that they should put away a part of them.

This promise respects the church and it cannot be pretended that it has ever been fulfilled, according to its proper import, in any past age of the church.

As it regards the church at a future period of its history, this promise is absolute in the sense that it certainly will be fulfilled.

It was manifestly designed to apply to Christians under the new dispensation rather than to the Jews under the old dispensation. The sprinkling of clean water and the outpouring of the Spirit seem plainly to indicate that the promise belonged more particularly to the Christian dispensation. It undeniably belongs to the same class of promises with that in Jeremiah 26:31–34, Joel 2:28, and many others that manifestly look forward to the gospel day as the time when they shall become due. As these promises have never been fulfilled in their extent and meaning, their complete fulfillment remains to be realized by the church as a body. And those individuals and that generation will take possession of the blessing who understand and believe and appropriate them to their own case.

I will next examine the promise in 1 Thessalonians 5:23–24:

And the very God of peace sanctify you wholly; and I pray God your whole spirit, and soul, and body, be preserved blameless unto the coming of our Lord Jesus Christ. Faithful is he that calleth you, who also will do it.

Upon this I remark: It is admitted that this is a prayer for and a promise of entire sanctification. The very language shows that both the prayer and the promise refer to this life as it is a prayer for the sanctification of the body as well as the soul; also that they might be preserved, not after, but unto the coming of our Lord Jesus Christ. This is a prayer of inspiration to which is annexed an express promise that God will do it. Its fulfillment is, from the nature of the case, conditioned upon our faith, as sanctification without faith is naturally impossible. Now if this promise, with those that have already been examined, does not honestly interpreted, fully settle the question of the attainability of entire sanctification in this life, it is difficult to understand how anything can be settled by an appeal to Scripture.

There are great multitudes of promises of the same import to which I might refer you and which, if examined in the light of the foregoing rules of interpretation, would be seen to heap up demonstration upon demonstration that this is a doctrine of the Bible. Only examine them in the light of these plain, self-evident principles and it seems to me that they cannot fail to produce conviction.

The apostles evidently expected Christians to attain this state in this life. See Colossians 3:12:

Epaphras, who is one of you, a servant of Christ, saluteth you, always laboring fervently for you in prayers, that ye may stand perfect and complete in all the will of God.

Upon this passage I remark: It was the object of the efforts of Epaphras and a thing which he expected to effect to be instrumental in causing those Christians to be "perfect and complete in all the will of God." If this language does not describe a state of entire, in the sense of permanent, sanctification, I know of none that would. If "to be perfect and complete in all the will of God" be not Christian perfection, what is? Paul knew that Epaphras was laboring to this end and with this expectation and he informed the church of it in a manner that evidently showed his approbation of the views and conduct of Epaphras.

That the apostles expected Christians to attain this state is further manifest from 2 Corinthians 7:1:

> Having therefore these promises, dearly beloved, let us cleanse ourselves from all filthiness of the flesh and spirit, perfecting holiness in the fear of God.

Now, does not the apostle speak in this passage as if he really expected those to whom he wrote, "to perfect holiness in the fear of God"? Observe how strong and full the language is: "let us cleanse ourselves from all filthiness of the flesh and spirit." If "to cleanse ourselves from all filthiness of the flesh, and all filthiness of the spirit, and to perfect holiness," be not entire sanctification, what is? That he expected this to take place in this life is evident from the fact that he requires them to be cleansed from all filthiness of the flesh as well as of the spirit. This passage plainly contemplates a state as distinguished from an act of consecration or sanctification, that is, it evidently expresses the idea of entire, in the sense of continued, sanctification.

All the intermediate steps can be taken; therefore the end can be reached. There is certainly no point in our progress toward entire sanctification where it can be said we can go no further. To this it has been objected that though all the intermediate steps can be taken, yet the goal can never be reached in this life, just as five may be divided by three *ad infinitum* without exhausting the fraction. Now this illustration deceives the mind that uses it as it may the minds of those who listen to it. It is true that you can never exhaust the fraction in dividing five by three for the plain reason that the division may be carried on *ad infinitum*. There is no end. You cannot in this case take all the intermediate steps because they are infinite. But in the case of entire sanctification, all the intermediate steps can be taken for there is an end or state of entire sanctification and that too at a point infinitely short of infinite.

That this state may be attained in this life I argue from the fact that provision is made against all the occasions of sin. Men sin only when they are tempted either by the world, the flesh, or the devil. And it is expressly asserted that in every temptation provision is made for our escape. Certainly if it is possible for us to escape without sin under every temptation, then a state of entire and permanent sanctification is attainable.

Full provision is made for overcoming the three great enemies of our souls, the world, the flesh, and the devil: (1) the world—"This is the victory that overcometh the world, even your faith." "Who is he that overcometh the world, but he that believeth that Jesus is the Christ"; (2) the flesh—"If ye walk in the Spirit, ye shall not fulfill the lusts of the flesh"; (3) Satan—"The shield of faith shall quench all the fiery darts of the wicked." And, "God shall bruise Satan under your feet shortly."

God is able to perform this work in and for us. See Ephesians 3:14–19:

> For this cause I bow my knees unto the Father of our Lord Jesus Christ, of whom the whole family in heaven and earth is named, that

he would grant you according to the riches of his glory, to be strengthened with might by his Spirit in the inner man; that Christ may dwell in your hearts by faith; that ye, being rooted and grounded in love may be able to comprehend with all saints what is the breadth and length and depth and height; and to know the love of Christ which passeth knowledge, that ye might be filled with all the fullness of God.

Upon this passage I remark: Paul evidently prays here for the entire sanctification of believers in this life. It is implied in our being "rooted and grounded in love" and being "filled with all the fullness of God" that we be as perfect in our measure and according to our capacity as he is. If to be filled with the fullness of God does not imply a state of entire sanctification, what does? That Paul did not see any difficulty in the way of God's accomplishing this work is manifest from what he says in the twentieth verse: "Now unto him that is able to do exceeding abundantly above all that we ask or think, according to the power that worketh in us."

Death Is Not a Means of Sanctification

The Bible nowhere represents death as the termination of sin in the saints, which it could not fail to do were it true that they cease not to sin until death. It has been the custom of the church for a long time to console individuals in view of death by the consideration that it would be the termination of all their sin. And how almost universal has been the custom in consoling the friends of deceased saints to mention this as a most important fact that now they had ceased from sin! Now if death is the termination of sin in the saints and if they never cease to sin until they pass into eternity,

too much stress never has been or can be laid upon that circumstance, and it seems utterly incredible that no inspired writer should ever have noticed the fact. The representations of Scripture are all directly opposed to this idea. It is said, "Blessed are the dead who die in the Lord for they rest from their labors and their works do follow them." Here it is not intimated that they rest from their sins but from their good works in this life, such works as shall follow not to curse but to bless them. The representations of Scripture are that death is the termination of the saint's sufferings and labors of love in this world for the good of men and the glory of God. But nowhere in the Bible is it intimated that the death of a saint is the termination of his serving the devil.

The Bible representations of death are utterly inconsistent with its being an indispensable means of sanctification. Death is represented in the Bible as an enemy. But if death is the only condition upon which men are brought into a state of entire sanctification, its agency is as important and as indispensable as the influence of the Holy Ghost. When death is represented in the Bible as any thing else than an enemy, it is because it cuts short the sufferings of the saints and introduces them into a state of eternal glory—not because it breaks them off from communion with the devil! How striking is the contrast between the language of the church and that of inspiration on this subject! The church is consoling the Christian in view of death that it will be the termination of his sins—that he will then cease to serve the devil and his own lusts. The language of inspiration, on the other hand, is that he will cease not from wicked but from good works and labors and sufferings for God in this world. The language of the church is that then he will enter upon a life of unalterable holiness—that he shall then and not till then be entirely sanctified. The language of inspiration is that because he is sanctified, death shall be an entrance into a state of eternal glory.

Ministers are certainly bound to set up some definite standard to which as the ministers of God they are to insist upon complete conformity. And now I would ask, what other standard can they and dare they set up than this? To insist upon anything less than this is to turn Pope and grant an indulgence to sin. But to set up this standard and then inculcate that conformity to it is not as a matter of fact attainable in this life is as absolutely to take the part of sin against God as it would be to insist upon repentance in theory and then avow that in practice it is not attainable. And here let me ask Christians what they expect ministers to preach? Do you think they have a right to connive at any sin in you or to insist upon anything else as a practicable fact than that you should abandon every iniquity? I ask by what authority can a minister preach anything less? And how shall any minister dare to inculcate the duty as a theory and yet not insist upon it as a practical matter, as something to be expected of every subject of God's kingdom?

The Expectation of Sin Begets Apathy

A denial of this doctrine has the natural tendency to beget the very apathy witnessed in the church. Professors of religion go on in sin without much conviction of its wickedness. Sin unblushingly stalks abroad even in the church of God and does not fill Christians with horror because they expect its existence as a thing of course. Tell a young convert that he must expect to backslide and he will do so of course, and with comparatively little remorse, because he looks upon it as a kind of necessity. And being led to expect it, you find him in a few months after his conversion away from God and not at all horrified with his state. Just so, inculcate the idea among Christians that they are not expected to abandon all sin, and they will of course go on in sin with comparative indifference. Reprove them for their sin and they will say, "Oh, we are imperfect creatures; we do not pretend to be perfect nor do we expect we ever shall be in this world." Many such answers as these will show you at once the God-dishonoring and soul-ruining tendency of a denial of this doctrine.

A denial of this doctrine prepares the minds of ministers to temporize and wink at great iniquity in their churches. Feeling as they certainly must if they disbelieve this doctrine that a great amount of sin in all believers is to be expected as a thing of course, their whole preaching and spirit and demeanor will be such as to beget a great degree of apathy among Christians in regard to their abominable sins.

If this doctrine is not true, how profane and blasphemous is the covenant of every church of every evangelical denomination. Every church requires its members to make a solemn covenant with God and with the church in the presence of God and angels and with their hands upon the emblems of the broken body and shed blood of the blessed Jesus "to abstain from all ungodliness and every worldly lust, to live soberly, righteously, and godly, in this present world." Now if the doctrine of the attainability of entire sanctification in this life is not true, what profane mockery is this covenant! It is a covenant to live in a state of entire sanctification, made under the most solemn circumstances, enforced by the most awful sanctions, and insisted upon by the minister of God distributing the bread and wine. Now what right has any minister on earth to require this unless it is a practicable thing and unless it is expected of him who makes the vow?

Suppose when this covenant was proposed to a convert about to unite with the church, he should take it to his closet and spread it before the Lord and inquire whether it would be right for him to make such a covenant and whether the grace of the gospel can enable him to fulfill it? Do you suppose the Lord Jesus would reply that if he made that covenant, he certainly would and must, as a matter of course, live in the habitual violation of it as long as he lives and that his grace was not sufficient to enable him to keep it? Would he, in such a case, have any right to take upon himself this covenant? No, no more than he would have a right to lie to the Holy Ghost.

A Christian Must Aim at the Attainable

It has long been maintained by orthodox divines that a person is not a Christian who does not aim at living without sin—that unless he aims at perfection he manifestly consents to live in sin and is therefore impenitent. It has been said, and I think truly, that if a man does not in the fixed purpose of his heart aim at total abstinence from sin and at being wholly conformed to the will of God, he is not yet regenerated and does not so much as mean to cease from abusing God. In *Barnes' Notes* upon 2 Corinthians 8:1, we have the following:

> The unceasing and steady aim of every Christian should be perfection—perfection in all things—in the love of God, of Christ, of man; perfection of heart and feeling and emotion; perfection in his words and plans and dealings with men; perfection in his prayers and in his

submission to the will of God. No man can be a Christian who does not sincerely desire it and who does not constantly aim at it. No man is a friend of God who can acquiesce in a state of sin and who is satisfied and contented that he is not as holy as God is holy. And any man who has no desire to be perfect as God is and who does not make it his daily and constant aim to be as perfect as God may set it down as demonstrably certain that he has no true religion.

Now if this is so, I would ask how a person can aim at and intend to do what he knows to be impossible. Is it not a contradiction to say that a man can intend to do what he knows he cannot do? To this it has been objected that if true, it proves too much—that it would prove that no man ever was a Christian who did not believe in this doctrine.

To this I reply: A man may believe in what is really a state of entire sanctification and aim at attaining it, although he may not call it by that name. This I believe to be the real fact with Christians; and they would much more frequently attain what they aim at did they know how to appropriate the grace of Christ to their own circumstances. Mrs. President Edwards, for example, firmly believed that she could attain a state of entire consecration. She aimed at and manifestly attained it and yet such were her views of constitutional depravity that she did not call her state one of entire sanctification. It has been common for Christians to suppose that a state of entire consecration is attainable, but while they believe in the sinfulness of their natures, they would not of course call even entire consecration, entire sanctification. Mrs. Edwards believed in, aimed at, and attained entire consecration. She aimed at what she believed to be attainable and she could aim at nothing more. She called it by the same name with her husband who was opposed to the doctrine of Christian perfection, as held by the Wesleyan Methodists, manifestly on the ground of his notions of physical depravity. I care not what this state is called if the thing be fully explained and insisted upon together with the conditions of attaining it. Call it what you please, Christian perfection, heavenly mindedness, the full assurance of faith or hope, or a state of entire consecration; by all these I understand the same thing. And it is certain that by whatever name it is called, the thing must be aimed at to be attained. The practicability of its attainment must be admitted or it cannot be aimed at. And now I would humbly inquire whether to preach anything short of this is not to give countenance to sin?

The Gospel Has Overcome Sin

Another argument in favor of this doctrine is that the gospel, as a matter of fact, has often not only temporarily but permanently and perfectly overcome every form of sin in different individuals. Who has not seen the most beastly lusts, drunkenness, lasciviousness, and every kind of abomination long indulged and fully ripe, entirely and forever slain by the power of the grace of God? Now how was this done? Only by bringing this sin fully into the light of the gospel and showing the individual the relation which the death of Christ sustained to that sin.

Nothing is wanting to slay any and every form of sin but for the mind to be fully baptized into the death of Christ and to see the bearings of one's own sins upon the sufferings and agonies and death of the blessed Jesus. Let me state a fact to illustrate my meaning. An habitual and most inveterate smoker of tobacco of my acquaintance after having

been plied with almost every argument to induce him to break the power of the habit and relinquish its use in vain, on a certain occasion lighted his pipe and was about to put it to his mouth, when the inquiry was started. Did Christ die to purchase this vile indulgence for me? The perceived relation of the death of Christ to this sin instantly broke the power of the habit and from that day he has been free. I could relate many other facts more striking than this where a similar view of the relation of a particular sin to the atonement of Christ has, in a moment, not only broken the power of the habit but destroyed entirely and forever the appetite for similar indulgences. And in multitudes of cases when the appetite has not been entirely slain, the will has been endowed with abundant and abiding efficiency effectually to control it. If the most inveterate habits of sin and even those that involve physical consequences and have deeply debased the physical constitution and rendered it a source of overpowering temptation to the mind can be and often have been utterly broken up and forever slain by the grace of God, why should it be doubted that by the same grace a man can triumph over all sin and that forever?

If this doctrine is not true, what is true upon the subject? It is certainly of great importance that ministers should be definite in their instructions; and if Christians are not expected to be wholly conformed to the will of God in this life, how much is expected of them? Who can say, Hitherto canst thou, must thou come, but no further? It is certainly absurd, not to say ridiculous, for ministers to be forever pressing Christians up to higher and higher attainments, saying at every step you can and must go higher, and yet all along informing them that they are expected to fall short of their whole duty that they can as a matter of fact be better than they are, far better, infinitely better; but still it is not expected that they will do their whole duty.

I have often been pained to hear men preach who were afraid to commit themselves in favor of the whole truth and who were yet evidently afraid of falling short in their instructions of insisting that men should stand "perfect and complete in all the will of God." To be consistent they are evidently perplexed and well they may be for in truth there is no consistency in their views and teaching. If they do not inculcate as a matter of fact that men ought to do and are expected to do their whole duty, they are sadly at a loss to know what to inculcate. They have evidently many misgivings about insisting upon less than this and still they fear to go to the full extent of apostolic teaching on this subject. And in their attempts to throw in qualifying terms and caveats, to avoid the impression that they believe in the doctrine of entire sanctification, they place themselves in a truly awkward position. Cases have occurred in which ministers have been asked how far we may go, must go, and are expected to go in dependence upon the grace of Christ and how holy men may be and are expected to be, and must be, in this life. They could give no other answer to this than that they can be a great deal better than they are. Now this indefiniteness is a great stumbling block to the church. It cannot be according to the teachings of the Holy Ghost.

The tendency of a denial of this doctrine is, to my mind, conclusive proof that the doctrine itself must be true. Many developments in the recent history of the church throw light upon this subject. Who does not sense that the facts developed in the temperance reformation have a direct and powerful bearing upon this question? It has been

ascertained that there is no possibility of completing the temperance reformation except by adopting the principle of total abstinence from all intoxicating drinks. Let a temperance lecturer go forth as an evangelist to promote revivals on the subject of temperance—let him inveigh against drunkenness while he admits and defends the moderate use of alcohol or insinuates, at least, that total abstinence is not expected or practicable. In this stage of the temperance reformation, everyone can see that such a man can make no progress, that he would be employed like a child in building dams of sand to obstruct the rushing of mighty waters. It is as certain as that causes produce their effects that no permanent reformation could be effected without adopting and insisting on the total abstinence principle.

And now if this is true as it respects the temperance reformation, how much more so when applied to the subjects of holiness and sin. A man might by some possibility even in his own strength overcome his habits of drunkenness and retain what might be called the temperate use of alcohol. But no such thing is possible in a reformation from sin. There is no temperate indulgence in sin. Sin as a matter of fact is never overcome by any man in his own strength. If he admits into his creed the necessity of any degree of sin or if he allows in practice any degree of sin, he becomes impenitent, consents to live in sin, and of course grieves the Holy Spirit; the certain result of which is a relapsing into a state of legal bondage to sin. And this is probably a true history of many professed Christians in the church. It is just what might be expected from the views and practice of the church upon this subject.

The secret of backsliding is that reformations are not carried deep enough. Christians are not set with all their hearts to aim at a speedy deliverance from all sin, but on the contrary are left and in many instances taught to indulge the expectation that they shall sin as long as they live. I probably never shall forget the effect produced on my mind by reading when a young convert in the diary of David Brainerd that he never expected to make any considerable attainments in holiness in this life. I can now easily see that this was a natural inference from the theory of physical sinfulness which he held. But not perceiving this at the time, I doubt not that this expression of his views had a very injurious effect upon me for many years. It led me to reason thus: if such a man as David Brainerd did not expect to make much advancement in holiness in this life, it is vain for me to expect such a thing.

Adopt the Principle of Total Abstinence

The fact is if there be anything that is important to high attainments in holiness and to the progress of the work of sanctification in this life, it is the adoption of the principle of total abstinence from sin. Total abstinence from sin must be every man's motto, or sin will certainly sweep him away as with a flood. That cannot possibly be a true principle in temperance that leaves the causes which produce drunkenness to operate in their full strength. Nor can that be true in regard to holiness which leaves the root unextracted and the certain causes of spiritual decline and backsliding at work in the very heart of the church. And I am fully convinced that until evangelists and pastors adopt and carry out in practice the principle of total abstinence from all sin, they will as certainly find themselves every few months called to do their work over again, as a temperance lecturer would

who should admit the moderate use of alcohol.

Again, who does not know that to call upon sinners to repent and at the same time to inform them that they will not and cannot and are not expected to repent, would for ever prevent their repentance? Suppose you say to a sinner, "You are naturally able to repent; but it is certain that you never will repent in this life, either with or without the Holy Spirit." Who does not see that such teaching would prevent his repentance as surely as he believed it? To say to a professor of religion, "You are naturally able to be wholly conformed to the will of God; but it is certain that you never will be, in this life, either in your own strength or by the grace of God"; if this teaching be believed, it will just as certainly prevent his sanctification as the other teaching would the repentance of the sinner. I can speak from my experience on this subject. While I inculcated the common views, I was often instrumental in bringing Christians under great conviction and into a state of temporary repentance and faith. But falling short of urging them up to a point where they would become so acquainted with Christ as to abide in him, they would of course soon relapse again into their former state. I seldom saw, and can now understand that I had no reason to expect to see, under the instructions which I then gave such a state of religious principle, such steady and confirmed walking with God among Christians, as I have seen since the change in my views and instructions.

The Conditions of This Attainment

A state of entire sanctification can never be attained by an indifferent waiting of God's time nor by any works of law or works of any kind performed in your own strength irrespective of the grace of God. By this I do not mean that were you disposed to exert your natural powers aright, you could not at once obey the law in the exercise of your natural strength and continue to do so. But I do mean that as you are wholly indisposed to use your natural powers aright without the grace of God, no efforts that you will actually make in your own strength or independent of his grace will ever result in your entire sanctification.

Not by any direct efforts to feel right. Many spend their time in vain efforts to force themselves into a right state of feeling. Now it should be forever understood that religion does not consist in mere feeling, emotion, or involuntary affection of any kind. Feelings do not result from a direct effort to feel. But, on the contrary, they are the spontaneous actings of the mind when it has under its direct and deep consideration the objects, truths, facts, or realities that are correlated to these involuntary emotions. They are the most easy and natural state of mind possible under such circumstances. So far from its requiring an effort to put them forth, it would rather require an effort to prevent them when the mind is intensely considering those objects and considerations which have a natural tendency to produce them. This is so true that when persons are in the exercise of such affections, they feel no difficulty at all in their exercise, but wonder how anyone can help feeling as they do. It seems to them so natural, so easy, and, I may say, so almost unavoidable that they often feel and express astonishment that anyone should find it difficult to exercise the feelings of which they are conscious.

The course that many persons take on the subject of religion has often appeared wonderful to me. They make themselves their own state and their interests the central point around which their own minds are continually evolv-ing. Their selfishness is so great that their own interests, happiness, and salvation fill their whole field of vision. And with their thoughts and anxieties and whole souls clustering around their own salvation, they complain of a hard heart that they cannot love God, that they do not repent and cannot believe. They manifestly regard love to God, repentence, faith, and all religion as consisting in mere feelings. Being conscious that they do not feel right as they express it, they are the more concerned about themselves, which concern but increases their embarrassment and the difficulty of exercising what they call right affections. The less they feel, the more they try to feel—the greater efforts they make to feel right without success, the more are they confirmed in their selfishness and the more are their thoughts glued to their own interests; and they are, of course, at a greater and greater distance from any right state of mind. And thus their selfish anxieties beget ineffectual efforts and these efforts but deepen their anxieties. And if in this state death should appear in a visible form before them or the last trumpet sound and they should be summoned to the solemn judgment, it would but increase their distraction, confirm and almost give omnipotence to their selfishness and render their sanctification morally impossible. It should never be forgotten that all true religion consists in voluntary states of mind and that the true and only way to attain to true religion is to look at and understand the exact thing to be done and then to put forth at once the voluntary exercise required.

Not by any efforts to obtain grace by works of law. Should the question be proposed to a Jew, "What shall I do that I may work the work of God?" he would answer, Keep the law, both moral and ceremonial; that is, keep the commandments.

To the same inquiry an Armenian would answer, Improve common grace and you will obtain converting grace; that is, use the means of grace according to the best light you have and you will obtain the grace of salvation. In this answer it is not supposed that the inquirer already has faith, but that he is in a state of unbelief and is inquiring after converting grace. The answer, therefore, amounts to this: you must become holy by your hypocrisy; you must work out sanctification by sin.

To this question most professed Calvinists would make in substance the same reply. They would reject the language while they retained the idea. Their direction would imply either that the inquirer already has faith or that he must perform some works to obtain it; that is, that he must obtain grace by works of law.

A late Calvinistic writer admits that entire and permanent sanctification is attainable, although he rejects the idea of the actual attainment of such a state in this life. He supposes the condition of attaining this state or the way to attain it is by a diligent use of the means of grace and that the saints are sanctified just so far as they make a diligent use of the means of sanctification. But as he denies that any saints ever did or will use all the means with suitable diligence, he denies also, of course, that entire sanctification ever is attained in this life. The way of attaining it, according to his teaching, is by the diligent use of means. If then this writer were asked, "What shall I do that I may work the works of God?"—or in other words what shall I do to obtain entire and permanent sanctification? His answer, it seems, would be: "Use diligently all the means of grace"; that is, you must get grace by works, or with the Armenian, improve

common grace and you will secure sanctifying grace. Neither an Armenian nor a Calvinist would formally direct the inquirer to the law as the ground of justification. But nearly the whole church would give directions that would amount to the same thing. Their answer would be a legal and not a gospel answer. For whatever answer is given to this question that does not distinctly recognize faith as the condition of abiding holiness in Christians is legal. Unless the inquirer is made to understand that this is the first, grand, fundamental duty without the performance of which all virtue, all giving up of sin, all acceptable obedience is impossible, he is misdirected. He is led to believe that it is possible to please God without faith and to obtain grace by works of law. There are but two kinds of works—works of law and works of faith. Now if the inquirer has not the "faith that works by love," to set him upon any course of works to get it is certainly to set him to get faith by works of law. Whatever is said to him that does not clearly convey the truth that both justification and sanctification are by faith without works of law is law and not gospel. Nothing before or without faith can possibly be done by anyone but works of law. His first duty, therefore, is faith; and every attempt to obtain faith by unbelieving works is to lay works at the foundation and make grace a result. It is the direct opposite of gospel truth.

"What Must I DO?"

Take facts as they arise in every day's experience to show that what I have stated is true of almost all professors and nonprofessors [of faith]. Whenever a sinner begins in good earnest to agitate the question, "What shall I do to be saved?" he resolves as a first duty to break off from his sins, that is, in unbelief. Of course his reformation is only outward. He determines to do better—to reform in this, that, and the other thing, and thus prepare himself to be converted. He does not expect to be saved without grace and faith, but he attempts to get grace by works of law. The same is true of multitudes of anxious Christians who are inquiring what they shall do to overcome the world, the flesh, and the devil. They overlook the fact that "this is the victory that overcometh the world, even our faith," that it is with "the shield of faith" they are "to quench all the fiery darts of the wicked." They ask, Why am I overcome by sin? Why can I not get above its power? Why am I thus the slave of my appetites and passions and the sport of the devil? They cast about for the cause of all this spiritual wretchedness and death. At one time they think they have discovered it in the neglect of one duty and at another time in the neglect of another. Sometimes they imagine they have found the cause to lie in yielding to one temptation and sometimes in yielding to another. They put forth efforts in this direction and in that direction and patch up their righteousness on one side while they make a rent in the other side. Thus they spend years in running round in a circle and making dams of sand across the current of their own habitudes and tendencies. Instead of at once purifying their hearts by faith, they are engaged in trying to arrest the overflowing of the bitter waters of their own propensities. Why do I sin? they inquire; and casting about for the cause, they come to the sage conclusion, It is because I neglect such a duty, that is, because I do sin. But how shall I get rid of sin? Answer: By doing my duty, that is, by ceasing from sin. Now the real inquiry is, Why do they neglect their duty? Why do they commit sin at all? Where is the foundation of all this

mischief? Will it be replied, the foundation of all this wickedness is the force of temptation—in the weakness of our hearts—in the strength of our evil propensities and habits? But all this only brings us back to the real inquiry again, How are these things to be overcome? I answer, by faith alone. No works of law have the least tendency to overcome our sins, but rather to confirm the soul in self-righteousness and unbelief.

Without Faith, All Else Is Vain

The great and fundamental sin which is at the foundation of all other sin is unbelief. The first thing is to give up that—to believe the Word of God. There is no breaking off from one sin without this. "Whatsoever is not of faith is sin." "Without faith it is impossible to please God." Thus we see that the backslider and convicted sinner when agonizing to overcome sin will almost always betake themselves to works of law to obtain faith. They will fast and pray and read and struggle and outwardly reform and thus endeavor to obtain grace. Now all this is vain and wrong. Do you ask, shall we not fast and pray and read and struggle? Shall we do nothing but sit down in antinomian security and inaction? I answer, you must do all that God commands you to do, but begin where he tells you to begin and do it in the manner in which he commands you to do it, that is, in the exercise of that faith that works by love. Purify your hearts by faith. Believe in the Son of God. And say not in your heart, "Who shall ascend into heaven that is to bring Christ down from above or who shall descend into the deep, that is, to bring up Christ again from the dead. But what saith it? The word is nigh thee, even in thy mouth and in thy heart that is, the word of faith which we preach." Now these facts show that even under the gospel almost all professors of religion, while they reject the Jewish notion of justification by works of law, have after all adopted a ruinous substitute for it and suppose that in some way they are to obtain grace by their works.

A state of entire sanctification cannot be attained by attempting to copy the experience of others. It is very common for convicted sinners or for Christians inquiring after entire sanctification in their blindness to ask others to relate their experience, to mark minutely the detail of all their exercises, and then set themselves to pray for and make direct efforts to attain the same class of exercises, not seeming to understand that they can no more exercise feelings in the detail like others than they can look like others. Human experiences differ as human countenances differ. The whole history of a man's former state of mind comes in, of course, to modify his present and future experience, so that the precise train of feelings which may be requisite in your case and which will actually occur, if you are ever sanctified, will not in all its details coincide with the exercises of any other human being. It is of vast importance for you to understand that you can be no copyist in any true religious experience and that you are in great danger of being deceived by Satan whenever you attempt to copy the experience of others. I beseech you, therefore, to cease from praying for or trying to obtain the precise experience of any person whatever. All truly Christian experiences are, like human countenances, in their outline so much alike as to be readily known as the lineaments of the religion of Jesus Christ. But no further than this are they alike, any more than human countenances are alike.

But here let it be remembered that sanctification does not consist in the various affections or emotions of which Christians speak and which are often mistaken for or confounded with true religion, but that sanctification consists in entire consecration and consequently it is all out of place for anyone to attempt to copy the feelings of another, inasmuch as feelings do not constitute religion. The feelings of which Christians speak do not constitute true religion but often result from a state of heart. These feelings may properly enough be spoken of as Christian experience for although involuntary states of mind, they are experienced by true Christians. The only way to secure them is to set the will right and the emotions will be a natural result.

Not Depending Upon Any Instrumentality

Not by waiting to make preparations before you come into this state. Observe that the thing about which you are inquiring is a state of entire consecration to God. Now do not imagine that this state of mind must be prefaced by a long introduction of preparatory exercises. It is common for persons when inquiring upon this subject with earnestness to think themselves hindered in this progress by a want of this or that or the other exercise or state of mind. They look everywhere else but at the real difficulty. They assign any other and every other but the true reason for their not being already in a state of sanctification. The true difficulty is voluntary selfishness or voluntary consecration to self-interest and self-gratification. This is the difficulty and the only difficulty to be overcome.

Not by attending meetings, asking the prayers of other Christians, or depending in any way upon the means of getting into this state. By this I do not intend to say that means are unnecessary or that it is not through the instrumentality of truth that this state of mind is induced. But I do mean that while you are depending upon any instrumentality whatever your mind is diverted from the real point before you and you are never likely to make this attainment.

Not by waiting for any particular views of Christ. When persons in the state of mind of which I have been speaking hear those who live in faith describe their views of Christ, they say, Oh, if I had such views I could believe; I must have these before I can believe. Now you should understand that these views are the result and effect of faith in the promise of the Spirit to take of the things of Christ and show them to you. Lay hold of this class of promises and the Holy Spirit will reveal Christ to you in the relations in which you need him from time to time. Take hold, then, on the simple promise of God. Take God at his word. Believe that he means just what he says and this will at once bring you into the state of mind after which you inquire.

Not in any way which you may mark out for yourself. Persons in an inquiring state are very pat, without seeming to be aware of it, to send imagination on before them to stake out the way and set up a flag where they intend to come out. They expect to be thus and thus exercised—to have such and such peculiar views and feelings when they have attained their object. Now there probably never was a person who did not find himself disappointed in these respects. God says, "I will bring the blind by a way that they know not. I will lead them in paths that they have not known: I will make darkness light before them and crooked things straight. These things will I do unto them and not forsake them." This suffering your imagination to mark out your path is a great hindrance to you as it sets you upon making many fruitless and worse than

fruitless attempts to attain this imaginary state of mind, wastes much of your time, and greatly wearies the patience and grieves the Spirit of God. While he is trying to lead you right to the point, you are hauling off from the course and insisting that this which your imagination has marked out is the way instead of that in which he is trying to lead you. And thus in your pride and ignorance you are causing much delay and abusing the long-suffering of God. He says, "This is the way, walk ye in it." But you say, no—this is the way. And thus you stand and parley and banter while you are every moment in danger of grieving the Spirit of God away from you and of losing your soul.

If there is anything in your imagination that has fixed definitely upon any particular manner, time, or place, or circumstance, you will in all probability either be deceived by the devil or be entirely disappointed in the result. You will find in all these particular items on which you had laid any stress that the wisdom of man is foolishness with God—that your ways are not his ways, nor your thoughts his thoughts. "For as the heavens are higher than the earth, so are his ways higher than your ways and his thoughts higher than your thoughts."

But this state is to be attained by faith alone. Let it be forever remembered that "without faith it is impossible to please God," and "whatsoever is not of faith, is sin." Both justification and sanctification are by faith alone. Romans 3:30: "Seeing it is one God who shall justify the circumcision by faith and the uncircumcision through faith"; and chapter 5:1: "Therefore, being justified by faith, we have peace with God, through our Lord Jesus Christ." Also, chapter 9:30–31: "What shall we say then? that the Gentiles, who followed not after righteousness, have attained to righteousness, even the righteousness which is of faith. But Israel, who followed after the law of righteousness, hath not attained to the law of righteousness. Wherefore? Because they sought it not by faith, but, as it were, by the works of the law."

But let me by no means be understood as teaching sanctification by faith as distinct from and opposed to sanctification by the Holy Spirit, or Spirit of Christ or which is the same thing, by Christ our sanctification, living and reigning in the heart. Faith is rather the instrument or condition than the efficient agent that induces a state of present and permanent sanctification. Faith simply receives Christ as king, to live and reign in the soul. It is Christ, in the exercise of his different offices and appropriated in his different relations to the wants of the soul, by faith who secures our sanctification. This he does by Divine discoveries to the soul of his Divine perfections and fullness. The condition of these discoveries is faith and obedience. He says, John 14:21–23:

> He that hath my commandments and keepeth them, he it is that loveth me; and he that loveth me shall be loved of my Father, and I will love him, and will manifest myself to him. Judas saith unto him, (not Iscariot), Lord, how is it that thou wilt manifest thyself unto us, and not unto the world? Jesus answered and said unto him, If a man love me, he will keep my words: and my Father will love him, and we will come unto him, and make our abode with him.

To ascertain the conditions of entire sanctification in this life we must consider what the temptations are that overcome us. When first converted, we have seen that the heart or will consecrates itself and the whole being to God. We have also seen that this is a state of disinterested benevolence or a commit-

tal of the whole being to the promotion of the highest good. We have also seen that all sin is selfishness or that all sin consists in the will's seeking the indulgence or gratification of self, that it consists in the will's yielding obedience to the propensities instead of obeying God as his law is revealed in the reason. Now who cannot see what needs to be done to break the power of temptation and let the soul go free? The fact is that the department of our sensibility that is related to objects of time and sense has received an enormous development and is tremblingly alive to all its correlated objects, while by reason of the blindness of the mind to spiritual objects it is scarcely developed at all in its relations to them. Those objects are seldom thought of by the carnal mind and when they are, they are only thought of. They are not clearly seen and of course they are not felt.

The thought of God, of Christ, of sin, of holiness, of heaven, and hell, excites little or no emotion in the carnal mind. The carnal mind is alive and awake to earthly and sensible objects but dead to spiritual realities. The spiritual world needs to be revealed to the soul. That soul needs to see and clearly apprehend its own spiritual condition, relations, wants. It needs to become acquainted with God and Christ, to have spiritual and eternal realities made plain and present and all-absorbing realities to the soul. It needs such discoveries of the eternal world, of the nature and guilt of sin, and of Christ; the remedy of the soul as to kill or greatly mortify lust or the appetites and passions in their relations to objects of time and sense; and thoroughly to develop the sensibility in its relations to sin and to God and to the whole circle of spiritual realities. This will greatly abate the frequency and power of temptation to self-gratification and break up the voluntary slavery of the will. The developments of the sensibility need to be thoroughly corrected. This can only be done by the revelation to the inward man, by the Holy Spirit, of those great and solemn and overpowering realities of the "spirit land" that lie concealed from the eye of flesh.

We often see those around us whose sensibility is so developed in some one direction that they are led captive by appetite and passion in that direction in spite of reason and of God. The inebriate is an example of this. The glutton, the licentious, the avaricious man are examples of this kind. We sometimes, on the other hand, see by some striking providence such a counterdevelopment of the sensibility produced as to slay and put down these particular tendencies, and the whole direction of the man's life seems to be changed; and outwardly, at least, it is so. From being a perfect slave to his appetite for strong drink, he cannot without the utmost loathing and disgust so much as hear the name of his once-loved beverage mentioned. From being a most avaricious man, he becomes deeply disgusted with wealth and spurns and despises it. Now this has been effected by a counterdevelopment of the sensibility, for in the case supposed, religion has nothing to do with it. Religion does not consist in the states of the sensibility nor in the will's being influenced by the sensibility; but sin consists in the will's being thus influenced. One great thing that needs to be done to confirm and settle the will in the attitude of entire consecration to God is to bring about a counterdevelopment of the sensibility so that it will not draw the will away from God. It needs to be mortified or crucified to the world, to objects of time and sense, by so deep and clear and powerful a revelation of self to self and of Christ to the soul as to awaken and develop all its susceptibilities in their relations to him

and to spiritual and Divine realities. This can easily be done through and by the Holy Spirit who takes of the things of Christ and shows them to us. He so reveals Christ that the soul receives him to the throne of the heart to reign throughout the whole being. When the will, the intellect, and the sensibility are yielded to him, he develops the intelligence and the sensibility by clear revelations of himself in all his offices and relations to the soul, confirms the will, mellows and chastens the sensibility by these divine revelations to the intelligence.

The Spirit Teaches of Christ

We need the light of the Holy Spirit to teach us the character of God, the nature of his government, the purity of his law, the necessity and fact of atonement—to teach us our need of Christ in all his offices and relations, governmental, spiritual, and mixed. We need the revelation of Christ to our souls in such power as to induce in us that appropriating faith, without which Christ is not and cannot be our salvation. We need to know Christ, for example, in such relations as the following:

As King, to set up his government and write his law in our hearts, to establish his kingdom within us, to sway his scepter over our whole being. As King he must be spiritually revealed and received.

As our Mediator, to stand between the offended justice of God and our guilty souls, to bring about a reconciliation between our souls and God. As Mediator he must be known and received.

As our Advocate or *Paracletos*, our next or best friend, to plead our cause with the Father, our righteous and all-prevailing advocate to secure the triumph of our cause at the bar of God. In this relation he must be apprehended and embraced.

As our Redeemer, to redeem us from the curse of the law and from the power and dominion of sin, to pay the price demanded by public justice for our release, and to overcome and break up forever our spiritual bondage. In this relation also we must know and appreciate him by faith.

As the propitation for our sins, to offer himself as a propitiatory or offering for our sins. The apprehension of Christ as making an atonement for our sins seems to be indispensable to the entertaining of a healthy hope of eternal life. It certainly is not healthy for the soul to apprehend the mercy of God without regarding the conditions of its exercise. It does not sufficiently impress the soul with a sense of the justice and holiness of God, with the guilt and desert of sin. It does not sufficiently awe the soul and humble it in the deepest dust to regard God as extending pardon without regard to the sternness of his justice as evinced in requiring that sin should be recognized in the universe, as worthy of the wrath and curse of God, as a condition of its forgiveness. It is remarkable and well worthy of all consideration that those who deny the atonement make sin a comparative trifle and seem to regard God's benevolence or love as good nature, rather than as it is, "a consuming fire" to all the workers of iniquity. Nothing does or can produce that awe of God, that fear and holy dread of sin, that self-abasing, God-justifying spirit that a thorough apprehension of the atonement of Christ will do. Nothing like this can beget that spirit of self-renunciation, of cleaving to Christ, of taking refuge in his blood. In these relations, Christ must be revealed to us and apprehended and embraced by us as the condition of our entire sanctification.

It is the work of the Holy Spirit thus to reveal his death in its relations to our individual sins and as related to our sins as individuals. The soul needs to apprehend Christ as crucified for us. It is one thing for the soul to regard the death of Christ merely as the death of a martyr, and an infinitely different thing, as every one knows who has had the experience, to apprehend his death as a real and veritable vicarious sacrifice for our sins as being truly a substitute for our death. The soul needs to apprehend Christ as suffering on the cross for it or as its substitute so that it can say, That sacrifice is for me, that suffering and that death are for my sins; that blessed Lamb is slain for my sins. If thus fully to apprehend and to appropriate Christ cannot kill sin in us, what can?

We also need to know Christ as risen for our justification. He arose and lives to procure our certain acquittal or our complete pardon and acceptance with God. That he lives and is our justification we need to know to break the bondage of legal motives and to slay all selfish fear, to break and destroy the power of temptation from this source. The clearly convinced soul is often tempted to despondency and unbelief, to despair of its own acceptance with God, and it would surely fall into the bondage of fear were it not for the faith of Christ as a risen, living, justifying Savior. In this relation, the soul needs clearly to apprehend and fully to appropriate Christ in his completeness as a condition of abiding in a state of disinterested consecration to God.

We need also to have Christ revealed to us as bearing our griefs and as carrying our sorrows. The clear apprehension of Christ as being made sorrowful for us and as bending under sorrows and griefs which in justice belonged to us tends at once to render sin unspeakably odious and Christ infinitely precious to our souls. The idea of Christ our substitute needs to be thoroughly developed in our minds. And this relation of Christ needs to be so clearly revealed to us as to become an everywhere present reality to us. We need to have Christ so revealed as to so completely ravish and engross our affections that we would sooner die at once than sin against him. Is such a thing impossible? Indeed it is not. Is not the Holy Spirit able and willing and ready thus to reveal him upon condition of our asking it in faith? Surely he is.

We need to apprehend Christ as the one by whose stripes we are healed. We need to know him as relieving our pains and sufferings by his own, as preventing our death by his own, as sorrowing that we might eternally rejoice, as grieving that we might be unspeakably and eternally glad, as dying in unspeakable agony that we might die in deep peace and in unspeakable triumph.

"As being made sin for us." We need to apprehend him as being treated as a sinner and. even as the chief of sinners on our account or for us. This is the representation of Scripture, that Christ on our account was treated as if he were a sinner. He was made sin for us, that is, he was treated as a sinner or rather as being the representative or as it were the embodiment of sin for us. O! this the soul needs to apprehend—the holy Jesus treated as a sinner and as if all sin were concentrated in him on our account! We procured this treatment of him. He consented to take our place in such a sense as to endure the cross and the curse of the law for us. When the soul apprehends this, it is ready to die with grief and love. Oh, how infinitely it loathes self under such an apprehension as this! In this relation he must not only be apprehended but appropriated by faith.

We also need to apprehend the fact that "he was made sin for us, that we

might be made the righteousness of God in him"; that Christ was treated as a sinner that we might be treated as righteous; that we might also be made personally righteous by faith in him; that we might inherit and be made partakers of God's righteousness, as that righteousness exists and is revealed in Christ; that we might in and by him be made righteous as God is righteous. It needs to embrace and lay hold by faith upon that righteousness of God which is brought home to saints in Christ through the atonement and indwelling Spirit.

We also need Christ revealed to the inward being as "head over all things to the church." All these relations are of no avail to our sanctification only in so far forth as they are directly and inwardly and personally revealed to the soul by the Holy Spirit. It is one thing to have thoughts and ideas and opinions concerning Christ and an entirely different thing to know Christ as he is revealed by the Holy Spirit. All the relations of Christ imply corresponding necessities in us. When the Holy Spirit has revealed to us the necessity and Christ as exactly suited to fully meet that necessity and urged his acceptance in that relation until we have appropriated him by faith, a great work is done. But until we are thus revealed to ourselves and Christ is thus revealed to us and accepted by us, nothing is done more than to store our heads with notions or opinions and theories while our hearts are becoming more and more at every moment like an adamant stone.

I have often feared that many professed Christians knew Christ only after the flesh; that is, they have no other knowledge of Christ than what they obtain by reading and hearing about him without any special revelation of him to the inward being by the Holy Spirit. I do not wonder that such professors and ministers should be totally in the dark upon the subject of entire sanctification in this life. They regard sanctification as brought about by the formation of holy habits, instead of resulting from the revelation of Christ to the soul in all his fullness and relations and the soul's renunciation of self and appropriation of Christ in these relations.

Christ is represented in the Bible as the head of the church. The church is represented as his body. He is to the church what the head is to the body. The head is the seat of the intellect, the will, and in short, of the living soul. Consider what the body would be without the head and you may understand what the church would be without Christ. But as the church would be without Christ, so each believer would be without Christ. But we need to have our necessities in this respect clearly revealed to us by the Holy Spirit and this relation of Christ made plain to our apprehension. The utter darkness of the human mind in regard to its own spiritual state and wants and in regard to the relations and fullness of Christ is truly wonderful. His relations, as mentioned in the Bible, are overlooked almost entirely until our wants are discovered. When these are made known and the soul begins in earnest to inquire after a remedy, it needs not inquire in vain. "Say not in thine heart, who shall ascend up to heaven? that is, to bring Christ down from above; or who shall descend into the deep? that is, to bring Christ again from the dead. But what saith it? The word is nigh thee, even in thy mouth, and in thy heart."

Oh, how infinitely blind he is to the fullness and glory of Christ who does not know himself and Christ as both are revealed by the Holy Spirit. When we are led by the Holy Spirit to look down into the abyss of our own emptiness—to behold the horrible pit and miry clay of our own habits and fleshly and worldly and infernal entanglements, when we see in the light of God that our emptiness and necessities are infinite, then, and not till then, are we prepared wholly to cast off self and to put on Christ. The glory and fullness of Christ are not discovered to the soul until it discovers its need of him. But when self in all its loathsomeness and helplessness is fully revealed, until hope is utterly extinct as it respects every kind and degree of helping ourselves, and when Christ, the all and in all, is revealed to the soul as its all-sufficient portion and salvation, then, and not until then, does the soul know its salvation. This knowledge is the indispensable condition of appropriating faith or of that act of receiving Christ or that committal of all to him that takes Christ home to dwell in the heart by faith and to preside over all its states and actions. Oh, such a knowledge and such a reception and putting on of Christ is blessed. Happy is he who knows it by his own experience.

It is indispensable to a steady and implicit faith that the soul should have a spiritual apprehension of what is implied in the saying of Christ that all power was delivered unto him. The ability of Christ to do all and even exceeding abundantly above all that we ask or think is what the soul needs clearly to apprehend in a spiritual sense, that is to apprehend it not merely as a theory or as a proposition but to see the true spiritual import of this saying. This is also equally true of all that is said in the Bible about Christ, of all his offices and relations. It is one thing to theorize and speculate and opine about Christ and an infinitely different thing to know him as he is revealed by the Holy Spirit. When Christ is fully revealed to the soul by the Comforter, it will never again doubt the attainability and reality of entire sanctification in this life.

When we sin, it is because of our ignorance of Christ. That is whenever temptation overcomes us, it is because we do not know and avail ourselves of the relation of Christ that would meet our necessities. One great thing that needs to be done is to correct the developments of our sensibility. The appetites and passions are enormously developed in their relations to earthly objects. In relation to things of time and sense, our propensities are greatly developed and are alive; but in relation to spiritual truths and objects and eternal realities, we are naturally as dead as stones. When first converted if we knew enough of ourselves and of Christ thoroughly to develop and correct the action of the sensibility and confirm our wills in a state of entire consecration, we should not fall. In proportion as the law-work preceding conversion has been thorough and the revelation of Christ at or immediately subsequent to conversion full and clear, just in that proportion do we witness stability in converts. In most if not all instances however, the convert is too ignorant of himself and of course knows too little about Christ to be established in permanent obedience. He needs renewed conviction of sin, to be revealed to himself and to have Christ revealed to him and be formed in him the hope of glory before he will be steadfast, always abounding in the work of the Lord.

It must not be inferred that the knowledge of Christ in all these relations is a condition of our coming into a state of entire consecration to God or of present sanctification. The thing insisted on is that the soul will abide in this state in the hour of temptation only so far forth as it betakes itself to Christ in such circumstances of trial and apprehends and appropriates him by faith from time to time in those relations that meet the present and pressing necessit-

ites of the soul. The temptation is the occasion of revealing the necessity, and the Holy Spirit is always ready to reveal Christ in the particular relation suited to the newly developed necessity. The perception and appropriation of him in this relation under these circumstances of trial is the *sine qua non* of our remaining in the state of entire consecration.

Christ Sustains Our Sanctification

The foregoing are some of the relations which Christ sustains to us as to our salvation. I could have enlarged greatly, as you perceive, upon each of these and easily have swelled this part of our course of study to a large volume. I have only touched upon these relations as specimens of the manner in which he is presented for our acceptance in the Bible and by the Holy Spirit. Do not understand me as teaching that we must first know Christ in all these relations before we can be sanctified. The thing intended is that coming to know Christ in these relations is a condition or is the indispensable means of our steadfastness or perseverance in holiness under temptation—that when we are tempted from time to time, nothing can secure us against a fall but the revelation of Christ to the soul in these relations one after another and our appropriation of him to ourselves by faith. The gospel has directly promised in every temptation to open a way of escape so that we shall be able to bear it. The spirit of this promise pledges to us such a revelation of Christ as to secure our standing if we will lay hold upon him by faith as revealed. Our circumstances of temptation render it necessary that at one time we should apprehend Christ in one relation and at another time in another. For example, at one time we are tempted to despair by Satan's accusing us of sin and suggesting that our sins are too great to be forgiven. In this case we need a revelation and an appropriation of Christ as having been made sin for us; that is, as having atoned for our sins—as being our justification or righteousness. This will sustain the soul's confidence and preserve its peace.

At another time we are tempted to despair of ever overcoming our tendencies to sin and to give up our sanctification as a hopeless thing. Now we need a revelation of Christ as our sanctification, etc.

At another time the soul is harassed with the view of the great sublety and sagacity of its spiritual enemies and greatly tempted to despair on that account. Now it needs to know Christ as its wisdom.

Again, it is tempted to discouragement on account of the great number and strength of its adversaries. On such occasions it needs Christ revealed as the Mighty God, as its strong tower, its hiding place, its munition of rocks.

Again, the soul is oppressed with a sense of the infinite holiness of God and the infinite distance there is between us and God on account of our sinfulness and his infinite holiness and on account of his infinite abhorrence of sin and sinners. Now the soul needs to know Christ as its righteousness and as a mediator between God and man.

Again, the Christian's mouth is closed with a sense of guilt so that he cannot look up nor speak to God of pardon and acceptance. He trembles and is confounded before God. He lies along on his face and despairing thoughts roll a tide of agony through his soul. He is speechless and can only groan out his self-accusations before the Lord. Now as a condition of rising above this temptation to despair, he needs a revelation of Christ as his advocate, as his high priest, as ever living to make interces-

sion for him. This view of Christ will enable the soul to commit all to him in this relation and maintain its peace and hold on to its steadfastness.

Again, the soul is led to tremble in view of its constant exposedness to besetments on every side, oppressed with such a sense of its own utter helplessness in the presence of its enemies as almost to despair. Now it needs to know Christ as the good shepherd, who keeps a constant watch over the sheep and carries the lambs in his bosom. He needs to know him as a watchman and a keeper.

Again, it is oppressed with the sense of its own utter emptiness and is forced to exclaim, I know that in me, that is, in my flesh, dwelleth no good thing. It sees that it has no life or unction or power or spirituality in itself. Now it needs to know Christ as the true vine from which it may receive constant and abundant spiritual nourishment. It needs to know him as the fountain of the water of life and in those relations that will meet its necessities in this direction. Let these suffice as specimens to illustrate what is intended by entire or permanent sanctification being conditioned on the revelation and appropriation of Christ in all the fullness of his official relations.

Objections Answered

I will consider those passages of Scripture which are by some supposed to contradict the doctrine we have been considering. First Kings 8:46: "If they sin against thee (for there is no man that sinneth not), and thou be angry with them, and deliver them to the enemy, so that they carry them away captives unto the land of the enemy, far or near," etc.

On this passage, I remark: That this sentiment in nearly the same language is repeated in 2 Chronicles 6:36 and in Ecclesiastes 7:20 where the same original word in the same form is used. These are the strongest passages I know of in the Old Testament and the same remarks are applicable to the three. I will quote, for the satisfaction of the reader, the note of Dr. Adam Clarke upon this passage and also that of Barclay, the celebrated and highly spiritual author of *An Apology for the True Christian Divinity,* and let me say that they appear to me to be satisfactory answers to the objection founded upon these passages:

Clarke: "'If they sin against thee.'— This must refer to some general defection from truth; to some species of false worship, idolatry, or corruption of the truth and ordinances of the Most High; as for it, they are here stated to be delivered into the hands of their enemies, and carried away captive, which was the general punishment of idolatry, and what is called, [verse 47,] acting perversely and committing wickedness.

"'If they sin against thee, for there is no man that sinneth not.' The second clause, as it is here translated, renders the supposition in the first clause, entirely nugatory; for, if there be no man that sinneth not, it is useless to say, if they sin; but this contradiction is taken away, by reference to the original *ki yechetau lak,* which should be translated, if they shall sin against thee; or should they sin against thee, *ki ein adam asher lo yecheta;* 'for there is no man that may not sin'; that is, there is no man *impeccable,* none *infallible;* none that is not liable to transgress. This is the true meaning of the phrase in various parts of the Bible, and so our translators have understood the original, for even in the thirty-first verse of this chapter, they have translated *yecheta,* if a man trespass; which certainly implies he *might* or *might not* do it; and in this way they have translated the same word, if a soul sin, in Lev. 5:1 and 6:2; 1 Sam. 2:25;

2 Chron. 4:22; and in several other places. The truth is, the Hebrew has no mood to express words in the *permissive* or *optative* way, but to express this sense it uses the *future* tense of the conjugation *kal.*

"This text has been a wonderful strong-hold for all who believe that there is no redemption from sin in this life; that no man can live without committing sin; and that we cannot be entirely freed from it till we die.

"1. The text speaks no such doctrine; it only speaks of the *possibility* of every man's sinning; and this must be true of a state of *probation.*

"2. There is not another text in the divine records that is more to the purpose than this.

"3. The doctrine is flatly in opposition to the design of the gospel; for Jesus came to save his people from their sins, and to destroy the works of the devil.

"4. It is a dangerous and destructive doctrine, and should be blotted out of every Christian's creed. There are too many who are seeking to excuse their crimes by all means in their power; and we need not embody their excuses in a creed, to complete their deception, by stating that their sins are unavoidable."

Barclay: "Secondly,—Another objection is from two passages of scripture, much of one signification. The one is 1 Kings 8:46: 'For there is no man that sinneth not.' The other is Eccl. 7:20: 'For there is not a just man upon earth, that doeth good and sinneth not.'

"I answer,—

"1. These affirm nothing of a daily and continual sinning, so as never to be redeemed from it; but only that all have sinned, that there is none that doth not sin, though not always so as never to cease to sin; and in this lies the question. Yea, in that place of the Kings he speaks within two verses of the returning of such with all their souls and hearts, which implies a possibility of leaving off sin.

"2. There is a respect to be had to the seasons and dispensations; for if it should be granted that in Solomon's time there were none that sinned not, it will not follow that there are none such now, or that it is a thing not now attainable by the grace of God under the gospel.

"3. And lastly, this whole objection hangs upon a false interpretation; for the original Hebrew word may be read in the potential mood, thus,—There is no man who may not sin, as well as in the indicative; so both the old Latin, Junius, and Tremellius, and Vatablus have it, and the same word is so used, Ps. 119:11: 'Thy word have I hid in my heart, that I might not sin against thee'—in the potential mood, and not in the indicative: which being more answerable to the universal scope of the scriptures, the testimony of the truth, and the sense of almost all interpreters, doubtless ought to be so understood, and the other interpretation rejected as spurious."

Whatever may be thought of the views of these authors, to me it is a plain and satisfactory answer to the objection founded upon these passages that the objection might be strictly true under the Old Testament dispensation and prove nothing in regard to the attainability of a state of entire sanctification under the New. What! does the New Testament dispensation differ nothing from the Old in its advantages for the acquisition of holiness? If it be true that no one under the comparatively dark dispensation of Judaism attained a state of permanent sanctification, does that prove such a state is not attainable under the gospel? It is expressly stated in the Epistle to the Hebrews that "the old covenant made nothing perfect but the bringing in of a better hope did." Under the old covenant, God expressly prom-

ised that he would make a new one with the house of Israel in "writing the law in their hearts," and in "engraving it in their inward parts." And this new covenant was to be made with the house of Israel under the Christian dispensation. What then do all such passages in the Old Testament prove in relation to the privileges and holiness of Christians under the new dispensation?

Whether any of the Old Testament saints did so far receive the new covenant by way of anticipation as to enter upon a state of permanent sanctification, it is not my present purpose to inquire. Nor will I inquire whether admitting that Solomon said in his day that there was not a just man upon the earth that liveth and sinneth not, the same could with equal truth have been asserted of every generation under the Jewish dispensation. It is expressly asserted of Abraham and multitudes of the Old Testament saints that they "died in faith, not having received the promises." Now what can this mean? It cannot be that they did not know the promises, for to them the promises were made. It cannot mean that they did not receive Christ, for the Bible expressly asserts that they did, that "Abraham rejoiced to see Christ's day"—that Moses, and indeed all the Old Testament saints, had so much knowledge of Christ as a Savior to be revealed as to bring them into a state of salvation. But still they did not receive the promise of the Spirit as it is poured out under the Christian dispensation.

This was the great thing all along promised, first to Abraham or to his seed which is Christ. Galatians 3:14, 16:

"That the blessing of Abraham might come on the Gentiles through Jesus Christ; that we might receive the promise of the Spirit through faith." "Now to Abraham and his seed were the promises made. He saith not, And to seeds, as of man; but as of one, and to thy seed, which is Christ.

And afterward to the Christian church by all the prophets. Acts 2:16–21:

But this is that which was spoken by the prophet Joel; And it shall come to pass in the last days (saith God), I will pour out of my Spirit upon all flesh, and your sons and your daughters shall prophesy, and your young men shall see visions, and your old men shall dream dreams; and on my servants, and on my handmaidens, I will pour out in those days of my Spirit; and they shall prophesy; and I will show wonders in heaven above and signs in the earth beneath; blood, and fire and vapor of smoke; the sun shall be turned into darkness, and the moon into blood, before the great and notable day of the Lord come; and it shall come to pass, that whosoever shall call on the name of the Lord shall be saved.

Acts 2:38–39:

Then Peter said unto them, Repent, and be baptized every one of you in the name of Jesus Christ for the remission of sins, and ye shall receive the gift of the Holy Ghost. For the promise is unto you, and to your children, and to all that are afar off, even as many as the Lord our God shall call.

Acts 3:24, 26:

Yea, and all the prophets from Samuel, and those that follow after, as many as have spoken, have likewise foretold of these days." "Unto you first, God having raised up his Son Jesus, sent him to bless you, in turning away every one of you from his iniquities.

And lastly, by Christ himself, which he expressly styles "the promise" of the Father. Acts 1:4–5:

And being assembled together with them, commanded them that they should not depart from Jerusalem, but wait for the promise of the Father, which, saith he, ye have heard of me. For John truly baptized with water; but ye shall be baptized with the Holy Ghost not many days hence.

They did not receive the light and the glory of the Christian dispensation nor the fullness of the Holy Spirit. And it is asserted in the Bible, "they without us," that is, without our privileges, "could not be made perfect."

The next objection is founded upon the Lord's Prayer. In this Christ has taught us to pray, "Forgive us our trespasses as we forgive those who trespass against us." Here it is objected that if a person should become entirely sanctified, he could no longer use this clause of this prayer, which, it is said, was manifestly designed to be used by the church to the end of time.

Upon this prayer I remark: Christ has taught us to pray for entire, in the sense of perpetual, sanctification. "Thy will be done on earth, as it is done in heaven." He designed that we should expect this prayer to be answered or that we should mock him by asking what we do not believe is agreeable to his will and that too which we know could not consistently be granted and that we are to repeat this insult to God as often as we pray. The petition for forgiveness of our trespasses, it is plain, must apply to past sins and not to sins we are committing at the time we make the prayer, for it would be absurd and abominable to pray for the forgiveness of a sin which we are then in the act of committing.

This prayer cannot properly be made in respect to any sin of which we have not repented, for it would be highly abominable in the sight of God to pray for the forgiveness of a sin of which we did not repent.

If there be any hour or day in which a man has committed no actual sin, he could not consistently make this prayer in reference to that hour or that day. But at the very time it would be highly proper for him to make this prayer in relation to all his past sins, and that too although he may have repented of and confessed them and prayed for their forgiveness a thousand times before. This does not imply a doubt whether God has forgiven the sins of which we have repented, but it is only a renewal of our grief and humiliation for our sins and a fresh acknowledgment of and casting ourselves upon his mercy. God may forgive when we repent, before we ask him, and while we abhor ourselves so much as to have no heart to ask for forgiveness. But his having forgiven us does not render the petition improper.

And although his sins may be forgiven, he ought still to confess them, to repent of them, both in this world and in the world to come. And it is perfectly suitable so long as he lives in the world to say the least to continue to repent and repeat the request for forgiveness. For myself, I am unable to see why this passage should be made a stumbling block; for if it be improper to pray for the forgiveness of sins of which we have repented, then it is improper to pray for forgiveness at all. And if this prayer cannot be used with propriety in reference to past sins of which we have already repented, it cannot properly be used at all except upon the absurd supposition that we are to pray for the forgiveness of sins which we are now committing and of which we have not repented. And if it be improper to use this form of prayer in reference to all past sins of which we have repented, it is just as improper to use it in reference to sins committed today or yesterday of which we have repented.

Another objection is founded on James 3:1–2:

> My brethren, be not many masters, knowing that we shall receive the greater condemnation. For in many things we offend all. If any man offend not in word, the same is a perfect man and able also to bridle the whole body."

Upon this passage I remark: The term rendered masters here may be rendered teachers, critics, or censors and be understood either in a good or bad sense. The apostle exhorts the brethren not to be many masters because if they are so, they will incur the great condemnation; "for," says he, "in many things we offend all." The fact that we all offend is here urged as a reason why we should not be many masters, which shows that the term masters is here used in a bad sense. "Be not many masters," for if we are masters "we shall receive the greater condemnation" because we are all great offenders. Now I understand this to be the simple meaning of this passage; do not many (or any) of you become censors or critics and set yourselves up to judge and condemn others. For inasmuch as you have all sinned yourselves and we are all great offenders, we shall receive the greater condemnation if we set ourselves up as censors. "For with what judgment ye judge, ye shall be judged and with what measure ye mete, it shall be measured to you again."

It does not appear to me that the apostle designs to affirm anything at all of the present character of himself or of those to whom he wrote, nor to have had the remotest allusion to the doctrine of entire sanctification, but simply to affirm a well-established truth in its application to a particular sin: that if they became censors and injuriously condemned others, inasmuch as they had all committed many sins, they should receive the greater condemnation.

That the apostle did not design to deny the doctrine of Christian perfection or entire sanctification as maintained in these lectures seems evident from the fact that he immediately subjoins, "If any man offend not in word, the same is a perfect man and able also to bridle the whole body."

Another objection is founded in 1 John 1:8: "If we say we have no sin, we deceive ourselves, and the truth is not in us."

Upon this I remark: Those who make this passage an objection to the doctrine of entire sanctification in this life assume that the apostle is here speaking of sanctification instead of justification; whereas an honest examination of the passage, if I mistake not, will render it evident that the apostle makes no allusion here to sanctification but is speaking solely of justification. A little attention to the connection in which this verse stands will, I think, render this evident. But before I proceed to state what I understand to be the meaning of this passage, let us consider it in the connection in which it stands, in the sense in which they understand it who quote it for the purpose of opposing the sentiment advocated in these lectures. They understand the apostle as affirming, that, if we say we are in a state of entire sanctification and do not sin, we deceive ourselves and the truth is not in us. Now if this were the apostle's meaning, he involves himself in this connection in two flat contradictions.

This verse is immediately preceded by the assertion that the "blood of Jesus Christ cleanseth us from all sin." Now it would be very remarkable if immediately after this assertion the apostle should mean to say that it does not cleanse us from all sin and if we say it does, we deceive ourselves, for he had just asserted that the blood of Jesus Christ does cleanse us from all sin. If this were his meaning, it involves him in as palpable a contradiction as could be expressed.

This view of the subject then represents the apostle in the conclusion of the seventh verse as saying the blood of Jesus Christ his Son cleanseth us from all sin and in the eighth verse as saying that if we suppose ourselves to be cleansed from all sin, we deceive ourselves, thus flatly contradicting what he had just said. And in the ninth verse he goes on to say that "He is faithful and just to forgive us our sins and to cleanse us from all unrighteousness," that is, the blood of Jesus cleanseth us from all sin; but if we say it does, we deceive ourselves. "But if we confess our sins, he is faithful and just to forgive us our sins, and to cleanse us from all unrighteousness." Now all unrighteousness is sin. If we are cleansed from all unrighteousness, we are cleansed from sin. And now suppose a man should confess his sin and God should in faithfulness and justice forgive his sin and cleanse him from all unrighteousness and then he should confess and profess that God had done this; are we to understand that the apostle would then affirm that he deceives himself in supposing that the blood of Jesus Christ cleanseth from all sin? But as I have already said, I do not understand the apostle as affirming anything in respect to the present moral character of anyone but as speaking of the doctrine of justification.

This then appears to me to be the meaning of the whole passage. If we say that we are not sinners, that is, have no sin to need the blood of Christ, that we have never sinned and consequently need no Savior, we deceive ourselves. For we have sinned and nothing but the blood of Christ cleanseth from sin or procures our pardon and justification. And now, if we will not deny but confess that we have sinned, "He is faithful and just to forgive us our sins and to cleanse us from all unrighteousness." "But if we say we have not sinned, we make Him a liar and his word is not in us."

These are the principal passages that occur to my mind and those I believe upon which the principal stress has been laid by the opposers of this doctrine. And as I do not wish to protract the discussion, I shall omit the examination of other passages.

There are many objections to the doctrine of entire sanctification besides those derived from the passages of Scripture which I have considered. Some of these objections are doubtless honestly felt and deserve to be considered. I will therefore proceed to notice such of them as now occur to my mind.

It is objected that the doctrine of entire and permanent sanctification in this life tends to the errors of modern perfectionism. This objection has been urged by some good men and I doubt not, honestly urged. But still I cannot believe that they have duly considered the matter. It seems to me that one fact will set aside this objection. It is well known that the Wesleyan Methodists have, as a denomination, from the earliest period of their history maintained this doctrine in all its length and breadth. Now if such is the tendency of the doctrine, it is passing strange that this tendency has never developed itself in that denomination. So far as I can learn the Methodists have been in a great measure, if not entirely, exempt from the errors held by modern perfec-

tionists. Perfectionists, as a body, and I believe with very few exceptions, have arisen out of those denominations that deny the doctrine of entire sanctification in this life.

Now the reason of this is obvious to my mind. When professors of religion who have been all their life subject to bondage begin to inquire earnestly for deliverance from their sins, they have found neither sympathy nor instruction in regard to the prospect of getting rid of them in this life. Then they have gone to the Bible and there found in almost every part of it Christ represented as a Savior from their sins. But when they proclaim this truth, they are at once treated as heretics and fanatics by their brethren until being overcome of evil, they fall into censoriousness; and finding the church so decidedly and utterly wrong in her opposition to this one great important truth, they lose confidence in their ministers and the church, and being influenced by a wrong spirit, Satan takes the advantage of them and drives them to the extreme of error and delusion. This I believe to be the true history of many of the most pious members of the Calvinistic churches. On the contrary, the Methodists are very much secured against these errors. They are taught that Jesus Christ is a Savior from all sin in this world. And when they inquire for deliverance, they are pointed to Jesus Christ as a present and all-sufficient Redeemer. Finding sympathy and instruction on this great and agonizing point, their confidence in their ministers and their brethren remains and they walk quietly with them.

It seems to me impossible that the tendency of this doctrine should be to the peculiar errors of the modern perfectionists and yet not an instance occur among all the Methodist ministers or the thousands of their members for one hundred years.

And here let me say it is my full conviction that there are but two ways in which ministers of the present day can prevent members of their churches from becoming perfectionists. One is to suffer them to live so far from God that they will not inquire after holiness of heart and the other is most fully to inculcate the glorious doctrine of entire consecration, and that it is the high privilege as well as the duty of Christians to live in a state of entire consecration to God. I have many additional things to say upon the tendency of this doctrine but at present this must suffice.

By some it is said to be identical with perfectionism and attempts are made to show in what particulars antinomian perfectionism and our views are the same.

On this I remark: It seems to have been a favorite policy of certain controversial writers for a long time, instead of meeting a proposition in the open field of fair and Christian argument, to give it a bad name and attempt to put it down, not by force of argument, but by showing that it is identical with or sustains a new relation to Pelagianism, Antinomianism, Calvinism, or some other *ism*, against which certain classes of minds are deeply prejudiced. In the recent controversy between what are called old and new school divines, who has not witnessed with pain the frequent attempts that have been made to put down the new school divinity, as it is called, by calling it Pelagianism and quoting certain passages from Pelagius and other writers to show the identity of sentiment that exists between them.

This is a very unsatisfactory method of attacking or defending any doctrine. There are no doubt many points of agreement between Pelagius and all truly orthodox divines and so there are many points of disagreement between

them. There are also many points of agreement between modern perfectionists and all evangelical Christians and so there are many points of disagreement between them and the Christian church in general. That there are some points of agreement between their views and my own is no doubt true. And that we totally disagree in regard to those points that constitute their great peculiarities is, if I understand them, also true. But did I really agree in all points with Augustine or Edwards or Pelagius or the modern perfectionists, neither the good nor the ill name of any of these would prove my sentiments to be either right or wrong. It would remain, after all, to show that those with whom I agreed were either right or wrong in order on the one hand, to establish that for which I contend or on the other, to overthrow that which I maintain. It is often more convenient to give a doctrine or an argument a bad name than it is soberly and satisfactorily to reply to it.

It is not a little curious that we should be charged with holding the same sentiments with the perfectionists, while yet they seem to be more violently opposed to our views since they have come to understand them than almost any other persons whatever. I have been informed by one of their leaders that he regards me as one of the master-builders of Babylon.

With respect to the modern perfectionists, those who have been acquainted with their writings know that some of them have gone much farther from the truth than others. Some of their leading men who commenced with them and adopted their name stopped far short of adopting some of their most abominable errors, still maintaining the authority and perpetual obligation of the moral law, and thus have been saved from going into many of the most objectionable and destructive notions of the sect. There are many more points of agreement between that class of perfectionists and the orthodox church than between the church and any other class of them. And there are still a number of important points of difference as everyone knows who is possessed of correct information upon this subject.

I abhor the practice of denouncing whole classes of men for the errors of some of that name. I am well aware that there are many of those who are termed perfectionists who as truly abhor the extremes of error into which many of that name have fallen as perhaps do any persons living.

Another objection is that persons could not live in this world if they were entirely sanctified. Strange! Does holiness injure a man? Does perfect conformity to all the laws of life and health, both physical and moral, render it impossible for a man to live? If a man break off from rebellion against God, will it kill him? Does there appear to have been anything in Christ's holiness inconsistent with life and health? The fact is that this objection is founded in a gross mistake in regard to what constitutes entire sanctification. It is supposed by those who hold this objection that this state implies a continual and most intense degree of excitement and many things which are not at all implied in it. I have thought that it is rather a glorified than a sanctified state that most men have before their minds whenever they consider this subject. When Christ was upon earth, he was in a sanctified but not in a glorified state. "It is enough for the disciple that he be as his Master." Now what is there in the moral character of Jesus Christ as represented in this history that may not and ought not to be fully copied into the life of every Christian? I speak not of his knowledge but of his spirit and temper.

Ponder well every circumstance of his life that has come down to us and say, beloved what is there in it that may not, by the grace of God, be copied into your own? And think you that a full imitation of him in all that relates to his moral character would render it impossible for you to live in the world?

Again, it is objected that should we become entirely in the sense of permanently, sanctified, we could not know it and should not be able intelligently to profess it. I answer: All that a sanctified soul needs to know or profess is that the grace of God in Christ Jesus is sufficient for him so that he finds it to be true, as Paul did, that he can do all things through Christ who strengthened him; that he does not expect to sin, but that on the contrary, he is enabled through grace "to reckon himself dead indeed unto sin, and alive unto God through Jesus Christ our Lord." A saint may not know that he shall never sin again; he may expect to sin no more because of his confidence not in his own resolutions or strength or attainments, but simply in the infinite grace and faithfulness of Christ. He may come to look upon, to regard, account, reckon himself as being dead in deed and in fact unto sin and as having down with it and as being alive unto God and to expect henceforth to live wholly to God as much as he expects to live at all; and it may be true that he will thus live without his being able to say that he knows that he is entirely in the sense of permanently, sanctified. This he need not know but this he may believe upon the strength of such promises as 1 Thessalonians 5:23–24: "And the very God of peace sanctify you wholly: and I pray God your whole spirit and soul and body be preserved blameless unto the coming of our Lord Jesus Christ. Faithful is he that calleth you who also will do it." It is also true that a Christian may attain a state in which he will really fall no more into sin, as a matter of fact, while at the same time he may not be able to express even a thorough persuasion that he shall never fall again. All he may be able intelligently to say is: "God knoweth I hope to sin no more, but the event will show. May the Lord keep me; I trust that he will."

Another objection is that the doctrine tends to spiritual pride. And is it true, indeed, that to become perfectly humble tends to pride? But entire humility is implied in entire sanctification. Is it true that you must remain in sin and of course cherish pride in order to avoid pride? Is your humility more safe in your own hands and are you more secure against spiritual pride in refusing to receive Christ as your helper than you would be in at once embracing him as a full Savior?

I have seen several remarks in the papers of late and have heard several suggestions from various quarters which have but increased the fear which I have for some time entertained that multitudes of Christians, and indeed many ministers, have radically defective views of salvation by faith in Jesus Christ. To the doctrine of entire sanctification in this life as believed and taught by some of us, it has been frequently of late objected that prayers offered in accordance with this belief and by a sanctified soul would savor strongly of spiritual pride and self-righteousness. I have seen this objection stated in its full force of late in a religious periodical in the form of a supposed prayer of a sanctified soul, the object of which was manifestly to expose the shocking absurdity, self-righteousness, and spiritual pride of a prayer or rather thanksgiving made in accordance with a belief that one is

entirely sanctified. Now, I must confess that prayer, together with objections and remarks which suggest the same idea, have created in my mind no small degree of alarm. I fear much that many of our divines, in contending for the doctrines of grace, have entirely lost sight of the meaning of the language they use and have in reality but very little practical understanding of what is intended by salvation by grace in opposition to salvation by works. If this is not the case I know not how to account for their feeling and for their stating such an objection as this to the doctrine of entire sanctification.

Now if I understand the doctrine of salvation by grace, both sanctification and justification are wrought by the grace of God and not by any works or merits of our own irrespective of the grace of Christ through faith. If this is the real doctrine of the Bible, what earthly objection can there be to our confessing, professing, and thanking God for our sanctification any more than for our justification? It is true, indeed, that in our justification our own agency is not concerned while in our sanctification it is. Yet I understand the doctrine of the Bible to be that both are brought about by grace through faith and that we should no sooner be sanctified without the grace of Christ than we should be justified without it. Now, who pretends to deny this? And yet if it is true, of what weight is that class of objections to which I have alluded? These objections manifestly turn upon the idea, no doubt latent and deep seated in the mind, that the real holiness of Christians in whatever degree it exists is in some way to be ascribed to some goodness originating in themselves and not in the grace of Christ. But do let me ask how it is possible that men who entertain really and practically right views upon this subject can by any possibility feel, as if it must be proof conclusive of self-righteousness and Pharisaism, to profess and thank God for sanctification? Is it not understood on all hands that sanctification is by grace and that the gospel has made abundant provision for the sanctification of all men? This certainly is admitted by those who have stated this objection. Now if this is so, which is the most honorable to God, to confess and complain that our sins triumph and gain dominion over us or to be able truly and honestly to thank him for having given us the victory over our sins? God has said, "Sin shall not have dominion over you for ye are not under the law, but under grace."

Now, in view of this and multitudes of kindred promises, suppose we come to God and say: "O Lord, thou hast made these great and precious promises, but as a matter of fact, they do not accord with our own experience. For sin does continually have dominion over us. Thy grace is not sufficient for us. We are continually overcome by temptation, notwithstanding thy promise that in every temptation thou wilt make a way for us to escape. Thou hast said the truth shall make us free, but we are not free. We are still the slaves of our appetites and lusts."

Now which, I inquire, is the most honorable to God, to go on with a string of confessions and self-accusations that are in flat contradiction to the promises of God and almost, to say the least, a burlesque upon the grace of the gospel or to be able through grace to confess that we have found it true in our own experience that his grace is sufficient for us, that as our day is so our strength is, and that sin does not have dominion over us because we are not under the law but under grace?

To this I know it will be answered that in this confessing of our sins we do not impeach the grace or faithfulness of God, inasmuch as all these promises are conditioned upon faith and consequently that the reason of our remaining in sin is to be ascribed to our unbelief and is therefore no disparagement to the grace of Christ. But I beg that it may be duly considered that faith itself is of the operation of God—is itself produced by grace, and therefore the fact of our being obliged to confess our unbelief is a dishonor to the grace of Christ. Is it honorable or dishonorable to God that we should be able to confess that even our unbelief is overcome and that we are able to testify from our own experience that the grace of the gospel is sufficient for our present salvation and sanctification? There is no doubt a vast amount of self-righteousness in the church, which, while it talks of grace, really means nothing by it. For a man to go any farther than to hope that he is converted seems to many minds to savor of self-righteousness. Now why is this, unless they themselves entertain self-righteous notions in regard to conversion? Many persons would feel shocked to hear a man in prayer unqualifiedly thank God that he had been converted and justified. And they might just as well feel shocked at this and upon precisely the same principle as to feel shocked if he should unqualifiedly thank God that he had been sanctified by his grace.

But again, I say that the very fact that a man feels shocked to hear a converted or a sanctified soul unqualifiedly thank God for the grace received shows that down deep in his heart lies concealed a self-righteous view of the way of salvation and that in his mind all holiness in Christians is a ground of boasting, and that if persons have become truly and fully sanctified, they really have a ground of boasting before God. I know not how else to account for this wonderful prejudice. For my own part, I do not conceive it to be the least evidence of self-righteousness when I hear a man sincerely and heartily thank God for converting and justifying him by his grace. Nor should I feel either shocked, horrified, or disgusted to hear a man thank God that he had sanctified him wholly by his grace. If in either or both cases I had the corroborative evidence of an apparently holy life, I should bless God, take courage, and feel like calling on all around to glorify God for such an instance of his glorious and excellent grace.

The feeling seems to be very general that such a prayer or thanksgiving is similar in fact and in the principle upon which it rests with that of the Pharisee noticed by our Savior. But what reason is there for this assumption? We are expressly informed that that was the prayer of a Pharisee. But the Pharisees were self-righteous and expressly and openly rejected the grace of Christ. The Pharisee then boasted of his own righteousness, originated in and consummated by his own goodness and not in the grace of Christ. Hence he did not thank God that the grace of Christ had made him unlike other men. Now, this prayer was designed to teach us the abominable folly of any man's putting in a claim to righteousness and true holiness, irrespective of the grace of God by Jesus Christ. But certainly this is an infinitely different thing from the thanksgiving of a soul who fully recognizes the grace of Christ and attributes his sanctification entirely to that grace. And I cannot see how a man who has entirely divested himself of Pharisaical notions in respect to the doctrine of sanctification can suppose these two prayers to be analogous in their principle and spirit.

Again it is objected that many who have embraced this doctrine really are spiritually proud.

To this I answer: So have many who believed the doctrine of regeneration been deceived and amazingly puffed up with the idea that they have been regenerated when they have not been. But is this a good reason for abandoning the doctrine of regeneration or any reason why the doctrine should not be preached? Let me inquire whether a simple declaration of what God has done for their souls has not been assumed as of itself sufficient evidence of spiritual pride on the part of those who embrace this doctrine while there was in reality no spiritual pride at all? It seems next to impossible, with the present views of the church, that an individual should really attain this state and profess to live without known sin in a manner so humble as not, of course, to be suspected of enormous spiritual pride. This consideration has been a snare to some who have hesitated and even neglected to declare what God had done for their souls lest they should be accused of spiritual pride. And this has been a serious injury to their piety.

But again it is objected that this doctrine tends to censoriousness.

To this I reply: It is not denied that some who have professed to believe this doctrine have become censorious. But this no more condemns this doctrine than it condemns that of regeneration. And that it tends to censoriousness might just as well be urged against every acknowledged doctrine of the Bible as against this doctrine.

Let any Christian do his whole duty to the church and the world in their present state; let him speak to them and of them as they really are, and he would of course incur the charge of censoriousness. It is therefore the most unreasonable thing in the world to suppose that the church in its present state would not accuse any perfect Christian of censoriousness. Entire sanctification implies the doing of all our duty. But to do all our duty we must rebuke sin in high places and in low places. Can this be done with all needed severity without in many cases giving offense and incurring the charge of censoriousness? No, it is impossible; and to maintain the contrary would be to impeach the wisdom and holiness of Jesus Christ himself.

It is objected that the believers in this doctrine lower the standard of holiness to a level with their own experience. To this I reply that it has been common to set up a false standard and to overlook the true spirit and meaning of the law and to represent it as requiring something else than what it does require, but this notion is not confined to those who believe in this doctrine. The moral law requires one and the same thing of all moral agents, namely that they shall be universally and disinterestedly benevolent; in other words, that they shall love the Lord their God with all their heart and their neighbor as themselves. This is all that it does require of any. Whoever has understood the law as requiring less or more than this has misunderstood it. Love is the fulfilling of the law. But I must refer the reader to what I have said upon this subject when treating of moral government.

The law, as we have seen on a former occasion, levels its claims to us as we are and a just exposition of it, as I have already said, must take into consideration all the present circumstances of our being. This is indispensable to a right apprehension of what constitutes entire sanctification. There may be, as facts show, danger of misapprehension in regard to the true spirit and meaning of the law in the sense that by theorizing and adopting a false philosophy, one may lose sight of the deepest affirmations of his reason in regard to the true spirit and meaning of the law; and I would humbly inquire whether the error has not been in giving such an interpretation of the law as naturally to beget the idea so prevalent that if a man should become holy, he could not live in this world? In a letter lately received from a beloved and useful and venerated minister of the gospel, while the writer expressed the greatest attachment to the doctrine of entire consecration to God and said that he preached the same doctrine which we hold to his people every Sabbath but by another name, still he added that it was revolting to his feelings to hear any mere man set up the claim of obedience to the law of God. Now let me inquire why should this be revolting to the feelings of piety? Must it not be because the law of God is supposed to require something of human beings in our state which it does not and cannot require? Why should such a claim be thought extravagant unless the claims of the living God be thought extravagant? If the law of God really requires no more of men than what is reasonable and possible, why should it be revolting to any mind to hear an individual profess to have attained to entire obedience? I know that the brother to whom I allude would be almost the last man deliberately and knowingly to give any strained interpretation to the law of God, and yet I cannot but feel that much of the difficulty that good men have upon this subject has arisen out of a comparison of the lives of saints with a standard entirely above that which the law of God does or can demand of persons in all respects in our circumstances, or, indeed, of any moral agent whatever.

Another objection is that as a matter of fact the grace of God is not sufficient to secure the entire sanctification of saints in this life. It is maintained that the question of the attainability of entire sanctification in this life resolves itself after all into the question whether Christians are sanctified in this life. The objectors say that nothing is sufficient grace that does not, as a matter of fact, secure the faith and obedience and perfection of the saints; and therefore, that the provisions of the gospel are to be measured by the results and that the experience of the church decides both the meaning of the promises and the extent of the provisions of grace.

Now to this I answer: If this objection be good for anything in regard to entire sanctification, it is equally true in regard to the spiritual state of every person in the world. If the fact that men are not perfect proves that no provision is made for their perfection, their being no better than they are proves that there is no provision for their being any better than they are or that they might not have aimed at being any better with any rational hope of success. But who except a fatalist will admit any such conclusion as this? And yet I do not see but this conclusion is inevitable from such premises. As well might an impenitent sinner urge that the grace of the gospel is not, as a matter of fact, sufficient for him because it does not convert him; as well might he resolve everything into the sovereignty of God and say, the sovereignty of God must convert me or I shall not be converted, and since I am not converted, it is because the grace of God has not proved itself sufficient to convert me. But who will excuse the sinner and admit his plea that the grace and

provisions of the gospel are not sufficient for him?

Let ministers urge upon both saints and sinners the claims of God. Let them insist that sinners may and can and ought immediately to become Christians and that Christians can and may and ought to live wholly to God. Let them urge Christians to live without sin and hold out the same urgency of command and the same encouragement that the new school holds out to sinners, and we shall soon find that Christians are entering into the liberty of perfect love, as sinners have found pardon and acceptance. Let ministers hold forth the same gospel to all and insist that the grace of the gospel is as sufficient to save from all sin as from a part of it, and we shall soon see whether the difficulty has not been that the gospel has been hid and denied until the churches have been kept weak through unbelief. The church has been taught not to expect the fulfillment of the promises to them, that it is dangerous error to expect the fulfillment to them, for example, of the promise in 1 Thessalonians 5:23–24: "And the very God of peace sanctify you wholly; and I pray God your whole spirit and soul and body be preserved blameless unto the coming of our Lord Jesus Christ. Faithful is he that calleth you who also will do it." When God says he will sanctify us wholly and preserve us blameless unto the coming of the Lord, masters in Israel tell us that to expect this is dangerous error.

Another objection to this doctrine is that it is contrary to the views of some of the greatest and best men in the church, that such men as Augustine, Calvin, Doddridge, [and] Edwards were of a different opinion.

To this I answer: Suppose they were; we are to call no man father in such a sense as to yield up to him the determination of our views of Christian doctrine. This objection comes with a very ill grace from those who wholly reject the opinions of these divines on some of the most important points of Christian doctrine. Those men all held the doctrine of physical moral depravity which was manifestly the ground of their rejecting the doctrine of entire sanctification in this life. Maintaining, as they seem to have done, that the constitutional susceptibilities of body and mind were sinfully depraved, consistency of course led them to reject the idea that persons could be entirely sanctified while in the body. Now, I would ask what consistency is there in quoting them as rejecting the doctrine of entire sanctification in this life while the reason of this rejection in their minds was founded in the doctrine of physical moral depravity which notion is entirely denied by those who quote their authority?

But again, it is objected that if we should attain this state of continual consecration or sanctification, we could not know it until the day of judgment and that to maintain its attainability is vain, inasmuch as no one can know whether he has attained it or not.

To this I reply: A man's consciousness is the highest and best evidence of the present state of his own mind. I understand consciousness to be the mind's recognition of its own existence and exercises and that it is the highest possible evidence to our own minds of what passes within us. Consciousness can of course testify only to our present sanctification; but with the law of God before us as our standard, the testimony of consciousness in regard to whether the mind is conformed to that standard or not is the highest evidence which the mind can have of a present state of conformity to that rule.

It is a testimony which we cannot doubt anymore than we can doubt our existence. How do we know that we exist? I answer, by our consciousness. How do I know that I breathe or love or hate or sit or stand or lie down or rise up, that I am joyful or sorrowful? In short, that I exercise any emotion or volition or affection of mind? How do I know that I sin or repent or believe? I answer, by my own consciousness. No testimony can be "so direct and convincing as this."

Now, in order to know that my repentance is genuine, I must know what genuine repentance is. So if I would know whether my love to God and man or obedience to the law is genuine, I must have clearly before my mind the real spirit and meaning and bearing of the law of God. Having the rule before my mind, my own consciousness affords "the most direct and convincing evidence possible" whether my present state of mind is conformed to the rule. The Spirit of God is never employed in testifying to what my consciousness teaches but in setting in a strong light before my mind the rule to which I am to conform my life. It is his province to make me understand, to induce me to love and obey the truth; and it is the province of consciousness to testify to my own mind whether I do or do not obey the truth when I apprehend it. When God so presents the truth as to give the mind assurance that it understands his mind and will upon any subject, the mind's consciousness of its own state in view of that truth is "the highest and most direct possible" evidence of whether it obeys or disobeys.

If a man cannot be conscious of the character of his own supreme or ultimate choice in which choice his moral character consists, how can he know when and of what he is to repent? If he has committed sin of which he is not conscious, how is he to repent of it? And if he has a holiness of which he is not conscious, how could he feel that he has peace with God?

But it is said that a man may violate the law not knowing it and consequently have no consciousness that he sinned but that afterward, a knowledge of the law may convict him of sin. To this I reply that if there was absolutely no knowledge that the thing in question was wrong, the doing of that thing was not sin, inasmuch as some degree of knowledge of what is right or wrong is indispensable to the moral character of any act. In such a case, there may be a sinful ignorance which may involve all the guilt of those actions that were done in consequence of it, but that blameworthiness lies in that state of heart that has induced this and not at all in the violation of the rule of which the mind was at the time entirely ignorant.

The Bible everywhere assumes that we are able to know and unqualifiedly requires us to know what the moral state of our mind is. It commands us to examine ourselves, to know and to prove our own selves. Now, how can this be done but by bringing our hearts into the light of the law of God and then taking the testimony of our own consciousness whether we are or are not in a state of conformity to the law? But if we are not to receive the testimony of our own consciousness in regard to our present sanctification, are we to receive it in respect to our repentance or any other exercise of our mind whatever? The fact is that we may deceive ourselves by neglecting to compare ourselves with the right standard. But when our views of the standard are right and our consciousness bears witness of a felt, decided, unequivocal state of mind, we cannot be deceived any more than we can be deceived in regard to our own existence.

But it is said our consciousness does not teach us what the power and capacities of our minds are and that, therefore, if consciousness could teach us in respect to the kind of our exercises, it cannot teach us in regard to their degree, whether they are equal to the present capacity of our mind. To this I reply:

Consciousness does as unequivocally testify whether we do or do not love God with all our heart as it does whether we love him at all. How does a man know that he lifts as much as he can or runs or walks as fast as he is able? I answer, by his own consciousness. How does he know that he repents or loves with all his heart? I answer, by his own consciousness. This is the only possible way in which he can know it.

The objection implies that God has put within our reach no possible means of knowing whether we obey him or not. The Bible does not directly reveal the fact to any man whether he obeys God or not. It reveals his duty but does not reveal the fact whether he obeys. It refers for this testimony to his own consciousness. The Spirit of God sets our duty before us but does not directly reveal to us whether we do it or not for this would imply that every man is under constant inspiration.

But it is said the Bible directs our attention to the fact, whether we outwardly obey or disobey as evidence whether we are in a right state of mind or not. But I would inquire, How do we know whether we obey or disobey? How do we know anything of our conduct but by our consciousness? Our conduct as observed by others is to them evidence of the state of our hearts. But, I repeat it, our consciousness of obedience to God is to us the highest and indeed the only evidence of our true character.

If a man's own consciousness is not to be a witness either for or against him, other testimony can never satisfy him of the propriety of God's dealing with him in the final judgment. There are cases of common occurrence where the witnesses testify to the guilt or innocence of a man contrary to the testimony of his own consciousness. In all such cases, from the very laws of his being he rejects all other testimony; and let me add that he would reject the testimony of God, and from the very laws of his being must reject it, if it contradicted his own consciousness. When God convicts a man of sin, it is not by contradicting his consciousness but by placing the consciousness which he had at the time in the clear strong light of his memory, causing him to discover clearly and to remember distinctly what light he had, what thoughts, what convictions, what intention or design, in other words, what consciousness he had at the time. And this, let me add, is the way and the only way in which the Spirit of God can convict a man of sin, thus bringing him to condemn himself. Now, suppose that God should bear testimony against a man that at such a time he did such a thing, that such and such were all the circumstances of the case; and suppose that at the same time the individual's consciousness unequivocally contradicts him. The testimony of God in this case could not satisfy the man's mind nor lead him into a state of self-condemnation. The only possible way in which this state of mind could be induced would be to annihilate his opposing consciousness and to convict him simply upon the testimony of God.

Men may overlook what consciousness is. They may mistake the rule of duty, they may confound consciousness with a mere negative state of mind or that in which a man is not conscious of a state of opposition to the truth. Yet it must forever remain true that to our own minds, "consciousness must be the highest possible evidence" of what passes within us. And if a man does not by his own consciousness know whether he does the best that he can under the circumstances—whether he has a single eye to the glory of God—and whether he is in a state of entire consecration to God—he cannot know it in any way whatever. And no testimony whatever, either of God or man, could, according to the laws of his being, satisfy him either as to conviction of guilt on the one hand or self-approbation on the other.

Let me ask how those who make this objection know that they are not in a sanctified state? Has God revealed it to them? Has he revealed it in the Bible? Does the Bible say to A. B. by name, You are not in a sanctified state? Or does it lay down a rule in the light of which his own consciousness bears this testimony against him? Has God revealed directly by his Spirit that he is not in a sanctified state, or does he hold the rule of duty strongly before the mind and thus awaken the testimony of consciousness that he is not in this state? Now just in the same way consciousness testifies of those that are sanctified that they are in this state. Neither the Bible nor the Spirit of God makes any new or particular revelation to them by name. But the Spirit of God bears witness to their spirits by setting the rule in a strong light before them. He induces that state of mind which conscience pronounces to be conformity to the rule. This is as far as possible from setting aside the judgment of God in the case, for conscience, under these circumstances, is the testimony of God and the way in which he convinces of sin on the one hand and of entire consecration on the other; and the decision of conscience is given to us in consciousness.

By some it is still objected that consciousness alone is not evidence even to ourselves of our being or not being in a state of entire sanctification; that the judgment of the mind is also employed in deciding the true intent and meaning of the law and is therefore as absolutely a witness in the case as consciousness is. "Consciousness," it is said, "gives us the exercise of our own mind and the judgment decides whether these exercises are in accordance with the law of God." So then it is the judgment rather than the consciousness that decides whether we are or are not in a state of entire sanctification; and therefore, in our judgment of the law we happen to be mistaken, than which nothing is more common in such case we are utterly deceived if we think ourselves in a state of entire sanctification.

To this I answer: It is, indeed, our judgment that decides upon the intent and meaning of the law. We may be mistaken in regard to its true application in certain cases as it respects outward conduct, but let it be remembered that neither sin nor holiness is to be found in the outward act. They both belong only to the ultimate intention. No man, as was formerly shown, can mistake his real duty. Everyone knows and cannot but know that disinterested benevolence is his duty. This is and nothing else is his duty. This he can know and about this he need not be mistaken. And sure it is that if man can be certain of anything, he can be certain in respect to the end of which he lives or in respect to his supreme, ultimate intention.

I deny that it is the judgment which is to us the witness in respect to the state of our own minds. There are several powers of the mind called into exercise in deciding upon the meaning of and in obeying the law of God, but it is consciousness alone that gives us these exercises. Nothing but consciousness can possibly give us any exercise of our own minds; that is, we have no knowledge of any exercise but by our own con-

sciousness. Suppose then the judgment is exercised, the will is exercised, and all the involuntary powers are exercised. These exercises are revealed to us only and simply by consciousness, so that it remains an invariable truth that consciousness is to us the only possible witness of what our exercises are and consequently of the state of our own minds. When therefore I say that by consciousness a man may know whether he is in a state of sanctification, I mean that consciousness is the real and only evidence that we can have of being in this state.

This objection is based upon a misapprehension of that which constitutes entire or continued sanctification. It consists, as has been shown, in abiding consecration to God and not as the objection assumes, in involuntary affections and feelings. When it is considered that entire sanctification consists in an abiding good will to God and to being in general, in living to one end, what real impossibility can there be in knowing whether we are supremely devoted to this end or supremely devoted to our own interest?

Again, it is objected that if this state were attained in this life, it would be the end of our probation. To this I reply that probation since the fall of Adam or those points on which we are in a state of probation or trial are (1) whether we will repent and believe the gospel and (2) whether we will persevere in holiness to the end of life.

Some suppose that the doctrine of the perseverance of the saints sets aside the idea of being at all in a state of probation after conversion. They reason thus: If it is certain that the saints will persevere, then their probation is ended because the question is already settled not only that they are converted, but that they will persevere to the end; and the contingency in regard to the event is indispensable to the idea of probation. To this I reply that a thing may be contingent with man that is not at all so with God. With God there is not and never was any contingency in the sense of uncertainty with regard to the final destiny of any being. But with men almost all things are contingent. God knows with absolute certainty whether a man will be converted and whether he will persevere. A man may know that he is converted and may believe that by the grace of God he shall persevere. He may have an assurance of this in proportion to the strength of his faith. But the knowledge of this fact is not at all inconsistent with his idea of his continuance in a state of trial till the day of his death, inasmuch as his perseverance depends upon the exercise of his own voluntary agency and also because his perseverance is the condition of his final salvation.

In the same way some say that if we have attained a state of entire or permanent sanctification, we can no longer be in a state of probation. I answer that perseverance in this depends upon the promises and grace of God just as the final perseverance of the saints does. In neither case can we have any other assurance of our perseverance than that of faith in the promise and grace of God, nor any other knowledge that we shall continue in this state than that which arises out of a belief in the testimony of God that he will preserve us blameless until the coming of our Lord Jesus Christ. If this be inconsistent with our probation, I see not why the doctrine of the saint's perseverance is not equally inconsistent with it. If any one is disposed to maintain that for us to have any judgment or belief grounded on the promises of God in regard to our final perseverance is inconsistent with a state of probation, all I can say is that his views of probation are very different from my own and so far as I understand from those of the church of God.

Again, there is a very high and important sense in which every moral being will remain on probation to all eternity. While under the moral government of God, obedience must forever remain a condition of the favor of God. And continued obedience will forever depend on the faithfulness and grace of God; and the only confidence we can ever have, either in heaven or on earth, that we shall continue to obey must be founded upon the faithfulness and truth of God.

Again, if it were true that entering upon a state of permanent sanctification in this life were in some sense an end of our probation, that would be no objection to the doctrine for there is a sense in which probation often ends long before the termination of this life. Where, for example, for any cause God has left sinners to fill up the measure of their iniquity, withdrawing forever his Holy Spirit from them and sealing them over to eternal death; this in a very important sense is the end of their probation, and they are as sure of hell as if they were already there. So on the other hand when a person has received after believing the sealing of the Spirit unto the day of redemption as an earnest of his inheritance, he may regard and is bound to regard this as a solemn pledge on the part of God of his final perseverance and salvation and as no longer leaving the final question of his destiny in doubt.

Now it should be remembered that in both these cases the result depends upon the exercise of the agency of the creature. In the case of the sinner given up of God, it is certain that he will not repent, though his impenitence is voluntary and by no means a thing naturally necessary. So, on the other hand, the perseverance of the saints is certain, though not necessary. If in either case there should be a radical change of character, the result would differ accordingly.

Again, while it is admitted by some that entire sanctification in this life is attainable, yet it is denied that there is any certainty that it will be attained by anyone before death; for it is said that as all the promises of entire sanctification are conditioned upon faith, they therefore secure the entire sanctification of no one.

To this I reply that all the promises of salvation in the Bible are conditioned upon faith and repentance; and therefore it does not follow on this principle that any person ever will be saved. What does all this arguing prove? The fact is that while the promises of both salvation and sanctification are conditioned upon faith, yet the promises that God will convert and sanctify the elect, spirit, soul and body, and preserve and save them must be fulfilled and will be fulfilled by free grace drawing and securing the concurrence of free will. With respect to the salvation of sinners, it is promised that Christ shall have a seed to serve him, and the Bible abounds with promises to Christ that secure the salvation of great multitudes of sinners. So the promises that the church as a body at some period of her earthly history shall be entirely sanctified are as it regards the church unconditional in the sense that they will assuredly be accomplished. But, as I have already shown, as it respects individuals the fulfillment of these promises must depend upon the exercise of faith. Both in respect to the salvation of

sinners and the sanctification of Christians, God is abundantly pledged to bring about the salvation of the one and the sanctification of the other to the extent of his promise to Christ.

It is also objected that the sanctification of the saints depends upon the sovereignty of God. To this I reply that both the sanctification of the saints and the conversion of sinners is in some sense dependent upon the sovereign grace of God. But who except an antinomian would for this reason hesitate to urge it upon sinners to repent immediately and believe the gospel? Would anyone think of objecting to the doctrine or the fact of repentance, that repentance and the conversion of sinners were dependent upon the sovereignty of God? And yet if the sovereignty of God can be justly urged as a bar to the doctrine of entire sanctification, it may, for aught I see, with equal propriety be urged as a bar to the doctrine and fact of repentance. We have no controversy with anyone upon the subject of entire sanctification who will as fully and as firmly hold out the duty and the possibility and the practical attainability of entire sanctification as of repentance and salvation. Let them both be put where the Bible puts them, upon the same ground so far as the duty and the practicability of both are concerned. Suppose anyone should assert that it were irrational and dangerous for sinners to hope or expect to be converted and sanctified and saved because all this depends upon the sovereignty of God and they do not know what God will do. Who would say this? But why not as well say it as make the objection to sanctification which we are now considering?

Love is the fundamental expression of Christians and is essential to biblical Christianity. God himself is love. All his moral attributes are merely attributes of love. This means that benevolence wills the best possible end for its object(s). Love is also a trait that all men are capable of expressing. Such demonstrations of love are evident every day and reflect the basic need of all men to love and be loved. Love can be expressed toward others and God.

In this lecture on love, Finney will set forth many expressions of love such as virtue, intelligence, universality, and liberty, to name a few. The reader will find that the expression of love involves many facets of human endeavor.

CHAPTER SIX

Attributes of Love

It has been shown that the sum and spirit of the whole law is properly expressed in one word—love. It has also been shown that this love is benevolence or good willing; that it consists in choosing the highest good of God and of universal being for its own intrinsic value in a spirit of entire consecration to this as the ultimate end of existence. Although the whole law is fulfilled in one word—love, yet there are many things implied in the state of mind expressed by this term. It is, therefore, indispensable to a right understanding of this subject that we inquire into the characteristics or attributes of this love. We must keep steadily in mind certain truths of mental philosophy. I will, therefore, call attention to certain facts in mental philosophy as they are revealed in consciousness.

Moral agents possess intellect or the faculty of knowledge. They also possess sensibility and sensitivity or in other words, the faculty or susceptibility of feeling. They also possess will or the power of choosing or refusing in every case of moral obligation.

These primary faculties are so correlated to each other that the intellect or the sensibility may control the will or the will may, in a certain sense, control them. That is, the mind is free to choose in accordance with the demands of the intellect which is the law-giving faculty or with the desires and impulses of the sensibility or to control and direct them both. The will can directly control the attention of the intellect and consequently its perceptions, thoughts, etc. It can indirectly control the states of the sensibility or feeling faculty by controlling the perceptions and thoughts of the intellect. We also know from consciousness, as was shown in a former lecture, that the voluntary muscles of the body are directly controlled by the will and that the law which obliges the attention, the feelings, and the actions is controlled directly and the feelings indirectly by the decisions of the will. The will can either command or obey. It can suffer itself to be enslaved by the impulses of the sensibility or it can assert its sovereignty and control them. The will is not influenced by either the intellect or the sensibility, by the law of necessity or force, so that the will can always resist either the demands of the intelligence or the impulses of the sensibility. But while they cannot lord it over the will through the agency of any law of force, the will has the aid of the law of necessity or force by which to control them.

Again: We are conscious of affirming to ourselves our obligation to obey the law of the intellect rather than the impulses of the sensibility, that to act virtuously we must act rationally or intelligently and not give ourselves up to the blind impulses of our feelings.

Now, inasmuch as the love required by the moral law consists in choice, willing, intention, as before repeatedly shown, and inasmuch as choice, willing, intending controls the states of the intellect and the outward actions directly by a law of necessity and by the same law controls the feelings or states of the sensibility indirectly, it follows that certain states of the intellect and of the sensibility and also certain outward actions must be implied in the existence of the love which the law of God requires. I say implied in it not as making a part of it but as necessarily resulting from it. The thoughts, opinions, judgments, feelings, and outward actions must be molded and modified by the state of the heart or will.

Here it is important to remark that in common language the same word is often used to express either an action or attitude of the will or a state of the sensibility or both. This is true of all the terms that represent what are called the Christian graces or virtues or those various modifications of virtue of which Christians are conscious and which appear in their life and temper. Of this truth we shall be constantly reminded as we proceed in our investigations for we shall find illustrations of it at every step of our progress.

Moral Attributes and Benevolence

Before I proceed to point out the attributes of benevolence, it is important to remark that all the moral attributes of God and of all holy beings are only attributes of benevolence. Benevolence is a term that comprehensively expresses them all. God is love. This term expresses comprehensively God's whole moral character. This love, as we have repeatedly seen, is benevolence. Benevolence is good-willing or the choice of the highest good of God and the universe as an end. But from this comprehensive statement, accurate though it be, we are apt to receive very inadequate conceptions of what really belongs to, as implied, in benevolence. To say that love is the fulfilling of the whole law, that benevolence is the whole of true religion; that the whole duty of man to God and his neighbor is expressed in one word, love—these statements, though true, are so comprehensive as to need with all minds much amplification and explanation.

Many things are implied in love or benevolence. By this is intended that benevolence needs to be viewed under various aspects and in various relations and its nature considered in the various relations in which it is called to act. Benevolence is an ultimate intention or the choice of an ultimate end. But if we suppose that this is all that is implied in benevolence, we shall egregiously err. Unless we inquire into the nature of the end which benevolence chooses and the means by which it seeks to accomplish that end, we shall understand but little of the import of the word benevolence. Benevolence has many attributes or characteristics. These must all harmonize in the selection of its end and in its efforts to realize it. By this is intended that benevolence is not a blind, but the most intelligent choice. It is the choice of the best possible end in obedience to the demand of the reason and of God and implies the choice of the best possible means to secure this end. Both the end and the means are chosen in obedience to the law of God and of reason.

An attribute is a permanent quality of a thing. The attributes of benevolence are those permanent qualities which belong to its very nature. Benevolence is not blind but intelligent choice. It is the choice of the highest well-being of moral agents. It seeks this end by means suited to the nature of moral agents. Hence wisdom, justice, mercy, truth, holiness, and many other attributes, as we shall see, are essential elements or attributes of benevolence.

To understand what true benevolence is, we must inquire into its attributes. Not everything that is called love has at all the nature of benevolence. Nor has all that is called benevolence any title to that appellation. There are various kinds of love. Natural affection is called love. Our preference of certain kinds of diet is called love. Hence we say we love fruit, vegetables, meat, milk, etc. Benevolence is also called love and is the kind of love, beyond all question, required by the law of God. But there is more than one state of mind that is called benevolence. There is a constitutional or phrenological benevolence which is often mistaken for and confounded with the benevolence which constitutes virtue. This so called benevolence is in truth only an imposing form of selfishness; nevertheless it is called benevolence. Many of its manifestations are like those of true benevolence. Care, therefore, should be taken in giving religious instruction to distinguish accurately between them.

Benevolence, let it be remembered, is the obedience of the will to the law of reason and of God. It is willing good as an end for its own sake and not to gratify self. Selfishness consists in the obedience of the will to the impulses of the sensibility. It is a spirit of self-gratification. The will seeks to gratify the desires and propensities for the pleasure of the gratification. Self-gratification is sought as an end and as the supreme end. It is preferred to the claims of God and the good of being. Phrenological or constitutional benevolence is only obedience to the impulse of the sensibility—a yielding to a feeling of compassion. It is only an effort to gratify a desire. It is, therefore, as really selfishness as is an effort to gratify any constitutional desire whatever.

It is impossible to get a just idea of what constitutes obedience to the Divine law and what is implied in it without considering attentively the various attributes or aspects of benevolence, properly so called. Upon this discussion we are about to enter. But before I commence the enumeration and definition of these attributes, it is important further to remark that the moral attributes of God as revealed in his works, providence, and word throw much light upon the subject before us. Also, the many precepts of the Bible and the developments of benevolence therein revealed will assist us much as we proceed in our inquiries upon this important subject.

As the Bible expressly affirms that love comprehends the whole character of God—that it is the whole that the law requires of man, that the end of the commandment is charity or love—we may be assured that every form of true virtue is only a modification of love or benevolence; that is, that every state of mind required by the Bible and recognized as virtue is, in its last analysis, resolvable into love or benevolence. In other words, every virtue is only benevolence viewed under certain aspects or in certain relations. In other words still, it is only one of the elements, peculiarities, characteristics, or attributes of benevolence. This is true of God's moral attributes. They are, as has been said, only attributes of benevolence. They are only the essential qualities that belong to the very nature of benevolence which are manifested and brought into activity wherever benevolence is brought into certain circumstances and relations. Benevolence is just, merciful, etc. Such is its nature that in appropriate circumstances these qualities, together with many others, will manifest themselves in executive acts.[1] This is and must be true of every holy being. I will now proceed to point out the attributes of that love which constitutes obedience to the law of God.

As I proceed I will call attention to the states of the intellect and of the sensibility and also to the course of outward conduct implied in the existence of this love in any mind—implied in its existence as necessarily resulting from it by the law of cause and effect. These attributes are:

Voluntariness

That is to say, it is a phenomenon of the will. There is a state of the sensibility often expressed by the term love. Love may and often does exist, as everyone knows, in the form of a mere feeling or emotion. The term is often used to express the emotion of fondness or attachment as distinct from a voluntary state of mind or a choice of the will. This emotion or feeling, as we are all aware, is purely an involuntary state of mind. Because it is a phenomenon of the sensibility and of course a passive state of mind, it has in itself no moral character. The law of God requires voluntary love or good-will as has been repeatedly shown. This love consists in choice, intention. It is choosing the highest well-being of God and the universe of sentient beings as an end. Of course, voluntariness must be one of its character-

istics. The word benevolence expresses this idea.

If it consists in choice, if it be a phenomenon of the will, it must control the thoughts and states of the sensibility as well as the outward action. This love, then, not only consists in a state of consecration to God and the universe but also implies deep emotions of love to God and man. Though a phenomenon of the will, it implies the existence of all those feelings of love and affection to God and man that necessarily result from the consecration of the heart or will to their highest well-being. It also implies all that outward course of life that necessarily flows from a state of will consecrated to this end. Let it be borne in mind that where these feelings do not arise in the sensibility and where this course of life is not, there the true love or voluntary consecration to God and the universe required by the law is not. Those follow from this by a law of necessity. Those, that is, feelings or emotions of love and a correct outward life may exist without this voluntary love as I shall have occasion to show in its proper place, but this love cannot exist without those as they follow from it by a law of necessity. These emotions will vary in their strength, as constitution and circumstances vary, but exist they must in some sensible degree whenever the will is in a benevolent attitude.

---

1. A recent writer has spoken contemptuously of "being," as he calls it, "sophisticated into believing or rather saying that faith is love, justice is love, humility is love." I would earnestly recommend to that and kindred writers the study of the thirteenth chapter of the First Corinthians. They will there find a specimen of what they please to call sophistry. If it is "sophistry," or "excessive generalization," as other writers seem to regard it, to represent love as possessing the attributes which comprise the various forms of virtue, it surely is the "generalization" and "sophistry" of inspiration. Generalization was the great peculiarity of Christ's preaching. His epitomizing all the commandments of God, and resolving the whole of obedience into love is an illustration of this, and in no other way could he have exposed the delusion of those who obeyed the letter but overlooked and outraged the spirit of the divine commandments. The same was true of the apostles and so it is of every preacher of the gospel. Every outward act is only the express of an inward voluntary state of mind. To understand ourselves or others, we must conceive clearly of the true spirit of moral law and of heart-obedience to it.

Liberty

Liberty is an attribute of this love. The mind is free and spontaneous in its exercise. It makes this choice when it has the power at every moment to choose self-gratification as an end. Of this every moral agent is conscious. It is a free, and therefore responsible, choice.

Intelligence

That is, the mind makes choice of this end intelligently. It not only knows what it chooses and why it chooses, but also that it chooses in accordance with the dictates of the intellect and the law of God; that the end is worthy of being chosen and that for this reason the intellect demands that it should be chosen, and also, that for its own intrinsic value it is chosen.

Because voluntariness, liberty, and intelligence are *natural* attributes of this love, therefore, the following are its *moral* attributes.

Virtue

Virtue is an attribute of it. Virtue is a term that expresses the moral character of benevolence; it is moral rightness. Moral rightness is moral perfection, righteousness, or uprightness. The term marks or designates its relation to moral law and expresses its conformity to it.

In the exercise of this love or choice, the mind is conscious of uprightness or of being conformed to moral law or moral obligation. In other words, it is conscious of being virtuous or holy, of being like God, of loving what ought to be loved, and of consecration to the right end.

Because this choice is in accordance with the demands of the intellect, there-fore the mind in its exercise is conscious of the approbation of that power of the intellect which we call conscience. The conscience must approve this love, choice, or intention.

Again: Because the conscience approves of this choice, therefore there is and must be in the sensibility a feeling of happiness or satisfaction, a feeling of complacency or delight in the love that is in the heart or will. This love, then, always produces self-approbation in the conscience and a felt satisfaction in the sensibility; and these feelings are often very acute and joyous, insomuch that the soul, in the exercise of this love of the heart, is sometimes led to rejoice with joy unspeakable and full of glory. This state of mind does not always and necessarily amount to joy. Much depends in this respect on the clearness of the intellectual views, upon the state of sensibility, and upon the manifestation of Divine approbation to the soul. But where peace or approbation of conscience and consequently a peaceful state of the sensibility are not, this love is not. They are connected with it by a law of necessity and must of course appear on the field of consciousness where this love exists. These, then, are implied in the love that constitutes obedience to the law of God. Conscious peace of mind and conscious joy in God must be where the true love to God exists.

Disinterestedness

Disinterestedness is another attribute of this love. By disinterestedness, it is not intended that the mind takes no interest in the object loved, for it does take a supreme interest in it. But this term expresses the mind's choice of an end for its own sake and not merely upon condition that the good belongs to self. This love is disinterested in the sense that the highest well-being of God and the universe is chosen not upon condition of its relation to self, but for its own intrinsic and infinite value. It is this attribute particularly that distinguishes this love from selfish love. Selfish love makes the relation of good to self the condition of choosing it. The good of God and of the universe, if chosen at all, is only chosen as a means or condition of prompting the highest good of self. But this love does not make good to self its end, but good to God and being in general is its end.

As disinterestedness is an attribute of this love, it does not seek its own, but the good of others. "Charity (love) seeketh not her own." It grasps in its comprehensive embrace the good of being in general and of course of necessity, secures a corresponding outward life and inward feeling. The intellect will be employed in devising ways and means for the promotion of its end. The sensibility will be tremblingly alive to the good of all and of each, will rejoice in the good of others as in its own, and will grieve at the misery of others as in its own. It "will rejoice with them that do rejoice, and weep with them that weep." There will not, cannot be envy at the prosperity of others but unfeigned joy, joy as real and often as exquisite as in its own prosperity. Benevolence enjoys everybody's good things, while selfishness is too envious at the good things of others even to enjoy its own. There is a Divine economy in benevolence. Each benevolent soul not only enjoys his own good things, but also enjoys the good things of all others so far as he knows their happiness. He drinks at the river of God's pleasure.

He not only rejoices in doing good to others, but also in beholding their enjoyment of good things. He joys in God's joy and in the joy of angels and of saints. He also rejoices in the good things of

all sentient existences. He is happy in beholding the pleasure of the beasts of the field, the fowls of the air, and the fishes of the sea. He sympathizes with all joy and all suffering known to him, nor is his sympathy with the sufferings of others a feeling of unmingled pain. It is a real luxury to sympathize in the woes of others. He would not be without this sympathy. It so accords with his sense of propriety and fitness that mingled with the painful emotion there is a sweet feeling of self-approbation, so that a benevolent sympathy with the woes of others is by no means inconsistent with happiness and with perfect happiness. God has this sympathy. He often expresses and otherwise manifests it. There is, indeed, a mysterious and an exquisite luxury in sharing the woes of others. God and angels and all holy beings know what it is. Where this result of love is not manifested, there love itself is not. Envy at the prosperity, influence, or good of others, the absence of sensible joy in view of the good enjoyed by others and of sympathy with the sufferings of others prove conclusively that this love does not exist. There is an expansiveness, an ampleness of embrace, a universality, and a divine disinterestedness in this love that necessarily manifests itself in the liberal devising of liberal things for Zion and in the copious outpourings of the floods of sympathetic feeling, both in joys and sorrows, when suitable occasions present themselves before the mind.

Impartiality

Impartiality is another attribute of this love. By this term is not intended that the mind is indifferent to the character of him who is happy or miserable, that it would be as well-pleased to see the wicked as the righteous eternally and perfectly blessed. But it is intended that other things being equal, it is the intrinsic value of their well-being which is alone regarded by the mind. Other things being equal, it matters not to whom the good belongs. It is no respecter of persons. The good of being is its end and it seeks to promote every interest according to its relative value.

Selfish love is partial. It seeks to promote self-interest first and secondarily those interests that sustain such a relation to self as will at least indirectly promote the gratification of self. Selfish love has its favorites, its prejudices, unreasonable and ridiculous. Color, family, nation, and many other things of like nature modify it. But benevolence knows neither Jew nor Greek, neither bond nor free, white nor black, Barbarian, Scythian, European, Asiatic, African, nor American, but accounts all men as men, and by virtue of their common manhood, calls every man a brother and seeks the interests of all and of each.

Impartiality, being an attribute of this love will of course manifest itself in the outward life and in the temper and spirit of its subject. This love can have no fellowship with those absurd and ridiculous prejudices that are so often rife among nominal Christians. Nor will it cherish them for a moment in the sensibility of him who exercises it. Benevolence recognizes no privileged classes on the one hand nor proscribed classes on the other. It secures in the sensibility an utter loathing of those discriminations so odiously manifested and boasted of and which are founded exclusively in a selfish state of the will. The fact that a man is a man and not that he is of our party, of our complexion, or of our town, state, or nation—that he is a creature of God, that he is capable of virtue and happiness, these are the considerations that are seized upon by this divinely impartial love. It is the intrinsic

value of his interests and not that they are the interests of one connected with self that the benevolent mind regards.

But here it is important to repeat the remark that the economy of benevolence demands that where two interests are in themselves considered of equal value in order to secure the greatest amount of good, each one should bestow his efforts where they can be bestowed to the greatest advantage. For example, every man sustains such relations that he can accomplish more good by seeking to promote the interest and happiness of certain persons rather than of others; his family, his kindred, his companions, his immediate neighbors, and those to whom in the providence of God, he sustains such relations as to give him access to them and influence over them. It is not unreasonable, it is not partial, but reasonable and impartial to bestow our efforts more directly upon them. Therefore, while benevolence regards every interest according to its relative value, it reasonably puts forth its efforts in the direction where there is a prospect of accomplishing the most good. This, I say, is not partiality, but impartiality; for be it understood it is not the particular persons to whom good can be done but the amount of good that can be accomplished that directs the efforts of benevolence. It is not because my family is my own nor because their well-being is, of course, more valuable in itself than that of my neighbor's families, but because my relations afford me higher facilities for doing them good, I am under particular obligation to aim first at promoting their good. Hence the apostle says: "If any man provide not for his own, especially for those of his own household, he hath denied the faith and is worse than an infidel."

Strictly speaking, benevolence esteems every known good according to its intrinsic and relative value but practically treats every interest according to the perceived probability of securing on the whole the highest amount of good. This is a truth of great practical importance. It is developed in the experience and observation of every day and hour. It is manifest in the conduct of God and of Christ, of apostles and martyrs. It is everywhere assumed in the precepts of the Bible and everywhere manifested in the history of benevolent effort. Let it be understood, then, that impartiality as an attribute of benevolence does not imply that its effort to do good will be modified by relations and circumstances. But on the contrary, this attribute implies that the efforts to secure the great end of benevolence, to wit, the greatest amount of good to God and the universe, will be modified by those relations and circumstances that afford the highest advantages for doing good.

The impartiality of benevolence causes it always to lay supreme stress upon God's interests, because his well-being is of infinite value and of course benevolence must be supreme to him. Benevolence, being impartial love, of course accounts God's interests and well-being as of infinitely greater value than the aggregate of all other interests. Benevolence regards our neighbor's interests as our own simply because they are in their intrinsic value as our own. Benevolence, therefore, is always supreme to God and equal to man.

Universality

Universality is another attribute of this love. Benevolence chooses the highest good of being in general. It excludes none from its regard but on the contrary embosoms all in its ample embrace. But by this it is not intended that it practically seeks to promote the good of every individual. It would if it could, but it seeks the highest practicable amount of good. The interest of every individual is estimated according to its intrinsic value, whatever the circumstances or character of each may be. But character and relations may and must modify the manifestation of benevolence or its efforts in seeking to promote this end. A wicked character and governmental relations and considerations may forbid benevolence to seek the good of some. Nay, they may demand that positive misery shall be inflicted on some as a warning to others to beware of their destructive ways.

By universality as an attribute of benevolence, it is intended that good-will is truly exercised toward all sentient beings whatever their character and relations may be and that when the higher good of the greater number does not forbid it, the happiness of all and of each will be pursued with a degree of stress equal to their relative value and the prospect of securing each interest. Enemies as well as friends, strangers and foreigners as well as relations and immediate neighbors will be enfolded in its sweet embrace. It is the state of mind required by Christ in the truly Divine precept, "I say unto you, Love your enemies, pray for them that hate you, and do good unto them that despitefully use and persecute you."

This attribute of benevolence is gloriously conspicuous in the character of God. His love to sinners alone accounts for their being today out of perdition. His aiming to secure the highest good of the greatest number is illustrated by the display of his glorious justice in the punishment of the wicked. His universal care for all ranks and conditions of sentient beings, manifested in his works and providence, beautifully and gloriously illustrates the truth that "his tender mercies are over all his works."

It is easy to see that universality must be a modification or attribute of true benevolence. It consists in good-willing, that is, in choosing the highest good of being as such and for its own sake. Of course it must, to be consistent with itself, seek the good of all and of each so far as the good of each is consistent with the greatest good upon the whole. Benevolence not only wills and seeks the good of moral beings but also the good of every sentient existence from the minutest animalcule to the highest order of beings. It, of course, produces a state of the sensibility tremblingly alive to all happiness and to all pain. It is pained at the agony of an insect and rejoices in its joy. God does this and all holy beings do this. Where this sympathy with the joys and sorrows of universal being is not, there benevolence is not. Observe, good is its end; where this is promoted by the proper means, the feelings are gratified. Where evil is witnessed, the benevolent spirit deeply and necessarily sympathizes.

Efficiency

Efficiency is another attribute or characteristic of benevolence. Benevolence consists in choice, intention. Now we know from consciousness that choice or intention constitutes the mind's deepest source or power of action. If I honestly intend a thing, I cannot but make efforts to accomplish that which I intend, provided that I believe the thing possible. If I choose an end, this choice must and will energize to secure its end. When benevolence is the supreme choice, preference, or intention of the soul, it is plainly impossible that it should not produce efforts to secure its end. It must cease to exist or manifest itself in exertions to secure its end as soon as and whenever the intelligence deems it wise to do so. If the will has

yielded to the intelligence in the choice of an end, it will certainly obey the intelligence in pursuit of that end. Choice, or intention, is the cause of all the outward activity of moral agents. They have all chosen some end, either their own gratification or the highest good of being, and all the busy bustle of this world's teeming population is nothing else than choice or intention seeking to compass its end.

Efficiency, therefore, is an attribute of benevolent intention. It must, it will, it does energize in God, in angels, in saints on earth and in heaven. It was this attribute of benevolence that led God to give his only begotten Son and that led the Son to give himself, "that whosoever believeth in him should not perish, but have everlasting life."

If love is efficient in producing outward action and efficient in producing inward feelings, it is efficient to wake up the intellect and set the world of thought in action to devise ways and means for realizing its end. It wields all the infinite natural attributes of God. It is the mainspring that moves all heaven. It is the mighty power that is heaving the mass of mind and rocking the world like a smothered volcano.

Look to the heavens above. It was benevolence that hung them out. It is benevolence that sustains those mighty rolling orbs in their courses. It was good-will endeavoring to realize its end that at first put forth creative power. The same power, for the same reason, still energizes and will continue to energize for the realization of its end so long as God is benevolent. And oh! what a glorious thought that infinite benevolence is wielding and will forever wield infinite natural attributes for the promotion of good! No mind but an infinite one can begin to conceive of the amount of good that Jehovah will secure. O blessed, glorious thought! But it is, it must be a reality as surely as God and the universe exist. It is no vain imagination; it is one of the most certain as well as the most glorious truths in the universe. Mountains of granite are but vapor in comparison with it. But the truly benevolent on earth and in heaven will sympathize with God. The power that energizes in him energizes in them. One principle animates and moves them all, and that principle is love, good-will to universal being. Well may our souls cry out, Amen, go on, God-speed the work; let this mighty power heave and wield universal mind until all the ills of earth shall be put away and until all that can be made holy are clothed in the garments of everlasting gladness.

Since benevolence is necessarily from its very nature active and efficient in putting forth efforts to secure its end and since its end is the highest good of being, it follows that all who are truly religious will and must from the very nature of true religion be active in endeavoring to promote the good of being. While effort is possible to a Christian, it is as natural to him as his breath. He has within him the very mainspring of activity, a heart set on the promotion of the highest good of universal being. While he has life and activity at all, it will and it must be directed to this end. Let this never be forgotten. An idle, an inactive, inefficient Christian is a misnomer. Religion is an essentially active principle, and when and while it exists, it must exercise and manifest itself. It is not merely good desire but it is good-willing. Men may have desires and hope and live on them without making efforts to realize their desires. They may desire without action. If their will is active, their life must be. If they really choose an ultimate end, this choice must manifest itself. The sinner does and must manifest his selfish choice and so likewise must the saint manifest his benevolence.

Complacency

Complacency is holiness, or moral excellence is another attribute of benevolence. This consists in benevolence contemplated in its relations to holy things.

This term also expresses both a state of the intelligence and of the sensibility. Moral agents are so constituted that they necessarily approve of moral worth or excellence; and when even sinners behold right character or moral goodness, they are compelled to respect and approve it by a law of their intelligence. This they not unfrequently regard as evidence of goodness in themselves. But this is doubtless just as common in hell as it is on earth. The veriest sinners on earth or in hell have by that unalterable constitution of their nature the necessity imposed upon them of paying intellectual homage to moral excellence. When a moral agent is intensely contemplating moral excellence and his intellectual approbation is emphatically pronounced, the natural and often the necessary result is a corresponding feeling of complacency or delight in the sensibility. But this being altogether an involuntary state of mind has no moral character. Complacency, as a phenomenon of will, consists in willing the highest actual blessedness of the holy being in particular as a good in itself and upon condition of his moral excellence.

This attribute of benevolence is the cause of a complacent state of the sensibility. It is true that feelings of complacency may exist when complacency of will does not exist. But complacency of feeling surely will exist when complacency of will exists. Complacency of will implies complacency of conscience or the approbation of the intelligence.

When there is a complacency of intelligence and of will, there must follow, of course, complacency of the sensibility.

It is highly worthy of observation here that this complacency of feeling is that which is generally termed love to God and to the saints in the common language of Christians and often in the popular language of the Bible. It is a vivid and pleasant state of the sensibility and very noticeable by consciousness, of course. Indeed, it is perhaps the general usage now to call this phenomenon of the sensibility, love; and for want of just discrimination, to speak of it as constituting religion.

Many seem to suppose that this feeling of delight in and fondness for God is the love required by the moral law. They are conscious of not being voluntary in it as well they may be. They judge of their religious state not by the end for which they live, that is by their choice or intention, but by their emotions. If they find themselves strongly exercised with emotions of love to God, they look upon themselves as in a state well-pleasing to God. But if their feelings or emotions of love are not active, they of course judge themselves to have little or no religion. It is remarkable to what extent religion is regarded as a phenomenon of the sensibility and as consisting in mere feelings. So common is it, indeed, that almost uniformly when professed Christians speak of their religion, they speak of their feelings or the state of their sensibility instead of speaking of their conscious consecration to God and the good of being.

It is also somewhat common for them to speak of their views of Christ and of truth in a manner that shows that they regard the states of the intellect as constituting a part, at least, of their religion. It is of great importance that just views should prevail among Christians upon this momentous subject. Virtue,

or religion, as has been repeatedly said, must be a phenomenon of the will. The attribute of benevolence which we are considering, that is complacency of will in God, is the most common light in which the Scriptures present it and also the most common form in which it lies revealed on the field of consciousness. The Scriptures often assign the goodness of God as a reason for loving him, and Christians are conscious of having much regard to his goodness in their love to him; I mean in their good will to him. They will good to him and ascribe all praise and glory to him upon the condition that he deserves it. Of this they are conscious.

Now, as was shown in a former lecture, in their love or good will to God, they do not regard his goodness as the fundamental reason for willing good to him. Although his goodness is that which at the time most strongly impresses their minds, yet it must be that the intrinsic value of his well-being is assumed and had in view by them, or they would no sooner will good than evil to him. In willing his good they must assume its intrinsic value to him as the fundamental reason for willing it and his goodness as a secondary reason or condition, but they are conscious of being much influenced in willing his good in particular by a regard to his goodness. Should you ask the Christian why he loved God or why he exercised good-will to him, he would probably reply it is because God is good. But suppose he should be further asked why he willed good rather than evil to God, he would say because good is good or valuable to him. Or if he returned the same answer as before, to wit, because God is good, he would give this answer only because he would think it impossible for anyone not to assume and to know that good is willed instead of evil because of its intrinsic value. The fact is the intrinsic value of well-being is necessarily taken along with the mind and always assumed by it as a first truth. When a virtuous being is perceived, this first truth being spontaneously and necessarily assumed, the mind thinks only of the secondary reason or condition or the virtue of the being in willing good to him.

Before I dismiss this subject, I must advert again to the subject of complacent love as a phenomenon of the sensibility and also as a phenomenon of the intellect. If I mistake not, there are sad mistakes and gross and ruinous delusions entertained by many upon this subject. The intellect, of necessity, perfectly approves of the character of God where it is apprehended. The intellect is so correlated to the sensibility that where it perceives in a strong light the divine excellence or the excellence of the divine law, the sensibility is affected by the perception of the intellect as a thing of course and of necessity; so that emotions of complacency and delight in the law and in the divine character may and often do glow and burn in the sensibility, while the intellect and the sensibility are strongly impressed with the perception of the Divine excellence. This state of the intellect and the sensibility is no doubt often mistaken for true religion. We have undoubted illustrations of this in the Bible and similar cases of it in common life. "Yet they seek me daily and delight to know my ways, as a nation that did righteousness, and forsook not the ordinance of their God: they ask of me the ordinances of justice, they take delight in approaching to God" (Isa. 58:2). "And, lo, thou art unto them as a very lovely song of one that hath a pleasant voice and can play well on an instrument: for they hear thy words, but they do them not" (Ezek. 33:32).

Nothing is of greater importance than forever to understand that religion is always and necessarily a phenomenon of the will; that it always and necessarily produces outward action and inward feeling; that on account of the correlation of the intellect and sensibility, almost any and every variety of feeling may exist in the mind as produced by the perceptions of the intellect whatever the state of the will may be; that unless we are conscious of good-will or of consecration to God and the good of being—unless we are conscious of living for this end, it avails us nothing, whatever our views and feelings may be.

And also it behooves us to consider that although these views and feelings may exist while the heart is wrong, they will certainly exist when the heart is right; that there may be feeling, and deep feeling, when the heart is in a selfish attitude; that there will and must be deep emotion and strenuous action when the heart is right. Let it be remembered that complacency as a phenomenon of the will is always a striking characteristic of true love to God; that the mind is affected and consciously influenced in willing the actual and infinite blessedness of God by a regard to his goodness. The goodness of God is not, as has been repeatedly shown, the fundamental reason for the good will, but it is one reason or a condition both of the possibility of willing and of the obligation to will his blessedness in particular. It assigns to itself and to others his goodness as the reason for willing his good, rather than the intrinsic value of good; because this last is so universally and so necessarily assumed that it thinks not of mentioning it, taking it always for granted that this will and must be understood.

Opposition to Sin

Opposition to sin is another attribute or characteristic of true love to God. This attribute certainly is implied in the very essence and nature of benevolence. Benevolence is good-willing or willing the highest good of being as an end. Now there is nothing in the universe more destructive of this good than sin. Benevolence cannot do otherwise than be forever opposed to sin as that abominable thing which it necessarily hates. It is absurd and a contradiction to affirm that benevolence is not opposed to sin. God is love or benevolence. He must, therefore, be the unalterable opponent of sin—of all sin in every form and degree.

But there is a state both of the intellect and of the sensibility that is often mistaken for the opposition of the will to sin. Opposition to all sin is and must be a phenomenon of the will, and on that ground alone it becomes virtue. But it often exists also as a phenomenon of the intellect and likewise of the sensibility. The intellect cannot contemplate sin without disapprobation. This disapprobation is often mistaken for opposition of heart or of will. When the intellect strongly disapproves of and denounces sin, there is naturally and necessarily a corresponding feeling of opposition to it in the sensibility, an emotion of loathing, or hatred, of abhorrence. This is often mistaken for opposition of the will or heart. This is manifest from the fact that often the most notorious sinners manifest strong indignation in view of oppression, injustice, falsehood, and many other forms of sin. This phenomenon of the sensibility and of the intellect, as I said, is often mistaken for a virtuous opposition to sin which it cannot be unless it involve an act of the will.

But let it be remembered that virtuous opposition to sin is a characteristic of love to God and man or of benevolence. This opposition to sin cannot possibly coexist with any degree of sin in the heart. That is this opposition cannot coexist with a sinful choice. The will cannot at the same time be opposed to sin and commit sin. This is impossible and the supposition involves a contradiction. Opposition to sin as a phenomenon of the intellect or of the sensibility may exist; in other words, the intellect may strongly disapprove of sin and the sensibility may feel strongly opposed to certain forms of it, while at the same time the will may cleave to self-indulgence in other forms. This fact no doubt accounts for the common mistake that we can at the same time exercise a virtuous opposition to sin and still continue to commit it.

Many are no doubt laboring under this fatal delusion. They are conscious not only of an intellectual disapprobation of sin in certain forms, but also at times of strong feelings of opposition to it. And yet they are also conscious of continuing to commit it. They therefore conclude that they have a principle of holiness in them and also a principle of sin, that they are partly holy and partly sinful at the same time. Their opposition of intellect and of feeling they suppose to be a holy opposition, when no doubt it is just as common in hell and even more so than it is on earth for the reason that sin is more naked there than it generally is here.

But now the inquiry may arise, how is it that both the intellect and the sensibility are opposed to it and yet that it is persevered in? What reason can the mind have for a sinful choice when urged to it neither by the intellect nor the sensibility? The philosophy of this phenomenon needs explanation. Let us attend to it.

I am a moral agent. My intellect necessarily disapproves of sin. My sensibility is so correlated to my intellect that it sympathizes with it or is affected by its perceptions and its judgment. I contemplate sin. I necessarily disapprove of it and condemn it. This affects my sensibility. I loathe and abhor it. I nevertheless commit it. Now how is this to be accounted for? The usual method is by ascribing it to a depravity in the will itself, a lapsed or corrupted state of the faculty so that it perversely chooses sin for its own sake. Although disapproved by the intellect and loathed by the sensibility, yet such it is said is the inherent depravity of the will that it pertinaciously cleaves to sin notwithstanding and will continue to do so until that faculty is renewed by the Holy Spirit and a holy bias or inclination is impressed upon the will itself.

But here is a gross mistake. In order to see the truth upon this subject, it is of indispensable importance to inquire what sin is.

It is admitted on all hands that selfishness is sin. Comparatively few seem to understand that selfishness is the whole of sin and that every form of sin may be resolved into selfishness just as every form of virtue may be resolved into benevolence. It is not my purpose now to show that selfishness is the whole of sin. It is sufficient for the present to take the admission that selfishness is sin. But what is selfishness? It is the choice of self-gratification as an end. It is the preference of our own gratification to the highest good of universal being. Self-gratification is the supreme end of selfishness. This choice is sinful. That is the moral of this selfish choice is sin. Now in no case is or can sin be chosen for its own sake or as an end. Whenever anything is chosen to gratify self, it is not chosen because the choice is sinful, but notwithstanding it is sinful. It is not the sinfulness of the choice upon which the choice fixes as an end or for its own sake, but it is the gratification to be afforded by the thing chosen.

For example, theft is sinful. But the will in an act of theft does not aim at and terminate on the sinfulness of theft but upon the gain or gratification expected from the stolen object. Drunkenness is sinful but the inebriate does not intend or choose the sinfulness for its own sake or as an end. He does not choose strong drink because the choice is sinful but notwithstanding it is so. We choose the gratification but not the sin as an end. To choose the gratification as an end is sinful but it is not the sin that is the object of choice. Our mother Eve ate the forbidden fruit. This eating was sinful. But the thing that she chose or intended was not the sinfulness of eating but the gratification expected from the fruit. It is not, it cannot in any case be true that sin is chosen as an end or for its own sake. Sin is only the quality of selfishness. Selfishness is the choice not of sin as an end or for its own sake, but of self-gratification; and this choice of self-gratification as an end is sinful. That is the moral quality of the choice is sin. To say that sin is or can be chosen for its own sake is untrue and absurd. It is the same as saying that a choice can terminate on an element, quality, or attribute of itself; that the thing chosen is really an element of the choice itself.

But it is said that sinners are sometimes conscious of choosing sin for its own sake or because it is sin; that they possess such a malicious state of mind that they love sin for its own sake; that they "roll sin as a sweet morsel under their tongue"; that "they eat up the sins of God's people as they eat bread"; that is, that they love their own sins and the sins of others as they do their necessary food and choose it for that reason or just as they do their food; that they not only sin themselves with greediness but also have pleasure in them that do the same.

Now all this may be true yet it does not at all disprove the position which I have taken, namely, that sin never is and never can be chosen as an end or for its own sake. Sin may be sought and loved as a means but never as an end. The choice of food will illustrate this. Food is never chosen as an ultimate end; it never can be so chosen. It is always as a means. It is the gratification or the utility of it in some point of view that constitutes the reason for choosing it. Gratification is always the end for which a selfish man eats. It may not be merely the present pleasure of eating which he alone or principally seeks. But nevertheless, if a selfish man, he has his own gratification in view as an end. It may be that it is not so much a present as a remote gratification he has in view. Thus he may choose food to give him health and strength to pursue some distant gratification, the acquisition of wealth or something else that will gratify him.

It may happen that a sinner may get into a state of rebellion against God and the universe of so frightful a character that he shall take pleasure in willing and in doing and saying things that are sinful just because they are sinful and displeasing to God and to holy beings. But even in this case sin is not chosen as an end but as a means of gratifying this malicious feeling. It is after all self-gratification that is chosen as an end and not sin. Sin is the means and self-gratification is the end.

Now we are prepared to understand how it is that both the intellect and sensibility can often be opposed to sin and yet the will cleave to the indulgence. An inebriate is contemplating the moral character of drunkenness. He instantly and necessarily condemns the abomination. His sensibility sympathizes with the intellect. He loathes the sinfulness of risking strong drink and himself on account of it. He is ashamed and were it possible he would spit in his own face. Now in this state it would surely be absurd to suppose that he could choose sin, the sin of drinking, as an end or for its own sake. This would be choosing it for an impossible reason and not for no reason. But still he may choose to continue his drink not because it is sinful, but notwithstanding it is so. For while the intellect condemns the sin of drinking strong drink and the sensibility loathes the sinfulness of the indulgence, nevertheless there still exists so strong an appetite, not for the sin but for the liquor, that the will seeks the gratification notwithstanding the sinfulness of it.

So it is and so it must be in every case where sin is committed in the face of the remonstrances of the intellect and the loathing of the sensibility. The sensibility loathes the sinfulness but more strongly desires the thing the choice of which is sinful. The will in a selfish being yields to the strongest impulse of the sensibility and the end chosen is in no case the sinfulness of the act but the self-gratification. Those who suppose this opposition of the intellect or of the sensibility to be a holy principle are fatally deluded. It is this kind of opposition to sin that often manifests itself among wicked men and that leads them to take credit for goodness or virtue, not an atom of which do they possess. They will not believe themselves to be morally and totally depraved while they are conscious of so much hostility to sin within them. But they should understand that this opposition is not of the will or they could not go on in sin, that it is purely an involuntary state of mind and has no moral character whatever. Let it be ever remembered, then, that a virtuous opposition to sin is always and necessarily an attribute of benevolence, a phenomenon of the will, and that it is naturally impossible that this opposition of will should coexist with the commission of sin.

As this opposition to sin is plainly implied in and is an essential attribute of benevolence or true love to God, it follows that obedience to the law of God cannot be partial in the sense that we both love God and sin at the same time.

Compassion for the Miserable

Compassion for the miserable is also an attribute of benevolence or of pure love to God and man. This is benevolence viewed in its relations to misery and to guilt.

There is a compassion also which is a phenomenon of the sensibility. It may and does often exist in the form of an emotion. But this emotion being involuntary has no moral character in itself. The compassion which is a virtue and which is required of us as a duty is a phenomenon of the will and is of course an attribute of benevolence. Benevolence, as has been often said, is good-willing or willing the highest happiness and well-being of God and the universe for its own sake or as an end. It is impossible, therefore, from its own nature that compassion for the miserable should not be one of its attributes. Compassion of will to misery is the choice or wish that it might not exist. Benevolence wills that happiness should exist for its own sake. It must, therefore, wish that misery might not exist. This attribute or peculiarity of benevolence consists in wishing the happiness of the miserable. Benevolence simply considered, is willing the good or happiness of being in general. Compassion of will is a willing particularly that the miserable should be happy.

Compassion of sensibility is simply a feeling of pity in view of misery. As has been said, it is not a virtue. It is only a

desire but not willing and consequently does not benefit its object. It is the state of mind of which James speaks—James 2:15–16: "If a brother or sister be naked, and destitute of daily food, and one of you say unto them, Depart in peace, be ye warmed and filled; notwithstanding ye give them not those things which are needful to the body, what doth it profit?" This kind of compassion may evidently coexist with selfishness. But compassion of heart or will cannot for it consists in willing the happiness of the miserable for its own sake and of course impartially. It will and from its very nature must deny self to promote its end whenever it wisely can, that is, when it is seen to be demanded by the highest general good. Circumstances may exist that render it unwise to express this compassion by actually extending relief to the miserable. Such circumstances forbid that God should extend relief to the lost in hell. But for their character and governmental relations, God's compassion would no doubt make immediate efforts for their relief.

Many circumstances may exist in which, although compassion would hasten to the relief of its object, yet on the whole the misery that exists is regarded as the less of two evils and therefore, the wisdom of benevolence forbids it to put forth exertions to save its object.

But it is of the last importance to distinguish carefully between compassion as a phenomenon of the sensibility or as a mere feeling and compassion considered as a phenomenon of the will. This, be it remembered, is the only form of virtuous compassion. Many who from the laws of their mental constitution feel quickly and deeply often take credit to themselves for being compassionate while they seldom do much for the downtrodden and the miserable. Their compassion is a mere feeling. It says, "Be ye warmed and filled," but does not that for them which is needful. It is this particular attribute of benevolence that was so conspicuous in the life of Howard Wilberforce and many other Christian philanthropists.

It should be said before I leave the consideration of this attribute that the will is often influenced by the feeling of compassion. In this case the mind is no less selfish in seeking to promote the relief and happiness of its object than it is in any other form of selfishness. In such cases self-gratification is the end sought and the relief of the suffering is only a means. Pity is stirred and the sensibility is deeply pained and excited by the contemplation of misery. The will is influenced by this feeling and makes efforts to relieve the painful emotion on the one hand and to gratify the desire to see the sufferer happy on the other. This is only an imposing form of selfishness.

We no doubt often witness displays of this kind of self-gratification. The happiness of the miserable is not in this case sought as an end or for its own sake but as a means of gratifying our own feelings. This is not obedience of will to the law of the intellect but obedience to the impulse of the sensibility. It is not a natural and intelligent compassion but just such compassion as we often see mere animals exercise. They will risk and even lay down their lives to give relief to one of their number or to a man who is in misery. In them this has no moral character. Having no reason, it is not sin for them to obey their sensibility; nay, this is a law of their being. This they cannot but do. For them then to seek their own gratification as an end is not sin. But man has reason; he is bound to obey it. He should will and seek the relief and the happiness of the miserable for its own sake or for its intrinsic value. When he seeks it for no higher reason than to gratify his feelings, he denies his

humanity. He seeks it not out of regard to the sufferer but in self-defense or to relieve his own pain and to gratify his own desires. This in him is sin.

Many, therefore, who take to themselves much credit for benevolence are after all only in the exercise of this imposing form of selfishness. They take credit for holiness when their holiness is only sin. What is especially worthy of notice here is that this class of persons appear to themselves and others to be all the more virtuous by how much more manifestly and exclusively they are led on by the impulse of feeling. They are conscious of feeling deeply, of being more sincere and earnest, in obeying their feelings. Everybody who knows them can also see that they feel deeply and are influenced by the strength of their feelings rather than by their intellect. Now so gross is the darkness of most persons upon this subject that they award praise to themselves and to others just in proportion as they are sure that they are actuated by the depth of their feelings rather than by their sober judgment.

But I must not leave this subject without observing that when compassion exists as a phenomenon of the will, it will certainly also exist as a feeling of the sensibility. A man of a compassionate heart will also be a man of compassionate sensibility. He will feel and he will act. Nevertheless, his actions will not be the effect of his feelings but will be the result of his sober judgment.

Three classes of persons suppose themselves and are generally supposed by others to be truly compassionate. The one class exhibit much feeling of compassion; but their compassion does not influence their will, hence they do not act for the relief of suffering. These content themselves with mere desires and tears. They say be ye warmed and clothed but give not the needed relief.

Another class feel deeply and give up to their feelings. Of course they are active and energetic in the relief of suffering. But being governed by feeling instead of being influenced by their intellect, they are not virtuous but selfish. Their compassion is only an imposing form of selfishness. A third class feel deeply but are not governed by blind impulses of feeling. They take a rational view of the subject, act wisely and energetically. They obey their reason. Their feelings do not lead them, neither do they seek to gratify their feelings. But these last are truly virtuous and altogether the most happy of the three. Their feelings are all the more gratified by how much less they aim at the gratification. They obey their intellect and therefore have the double satisfaction of the applause of conscience, while their feelings are also fully gratified by seeing their compassionate desire accomplished.

Mercy

Mercy is also an attribute of benevolence. This term expresses a state of feeling and represents a phenomenon of the sensibility. Mercy is often understood to be synonymous with compassion, but then it is not rightly understood.

Mercy, considered as a phenomenon of the will, is a disposition to pardon crime. Such is the nature of benevolence that it will seek the good even of those who deserve evil when this can be wisely done. It is "ready to forgive," to seek the good of the evil and unthankful and to pardon when there is repentance. It is good-will viewed in relation to one who deserves punishment. Mercy considered as a feeling or phenomenon of the sensibility is a *desire* for the pardon or good of one who deserves punishment. It is only a feeling, a desire; of course it is involuntary and has in itself no moral character.

Mercy will, of course, manifest itself in action and in effort to pardon or to procure a pardon unless the attribute of wisdom prevent. It may be unwise to pardon or to seek the pardon of a guilty one. In such cases as all the attributes of benevolence must necessarily harmonize, no effort will be made to realize its end. It was this attribute of benevolence modified and limited in its exercise by wisdom and justice that energized in providing the means and in opening the way for the pardon of our guilty race.

As wisdom and justice are also attributes of benevolence, mercy can never manifest itself by efforts to secure its end except in a manner and upon conditions that do not set aside justice and wisdom. No one attribute of benevolence is or can be exercised at the expense of another or in opposition to it. The moral attributes of God, as has been said, are only attributes of benevolence, for benevolence comprehends and expresses the whole of them.

From the term benevolence we learn that the end upon which it fixes is good. And we must infer, too, from the term itself that the means are unobjectionable, because it is absurd to suppose that good would be chosen because it is good and yet that the mind that makes this choice should not hesitate to use objectionable and injurious means to obtain its end. This would be a contradiction to will good for its own sake or out of regard to its intrinsic value and then choose injurious means to accomplish this end. This cannot be. The mind that can fix upon the highest well-being of God and the universe as an end can never consent to use efforts for the accomplishment of this end that are seen to be inconsistent with it, that is, that tend to prevent the highest good of being.

Mercy, I have said, is the readiness of benevolence to pardon the guilty. But this attribute cannot go out in exercise but upon conditions that consist with the other attributes of benevolence. Mercy as a mere feeling would pardon without repentance, or condition would pardon without reference to public justice. But viewed in connection with the other attributes of benevolence, we learn that although a real attribute of benevolence, yet it is not and cannot be exercised without the fulfillment of those conditions that will secure the consent of all the other attributes of benevolence. This truth is beautifully taught and illustrated in the doctrine and fact of atonement as we shall see. Indeed, without consideration of the various attributes of benevolence, we are necessarily all in the dark and in confusion in respect to the character and government of God, the spirit and meaning of his law, the spirit and meaning of the gospel, our own spiritual state, and the developments of character around us. Without an acquaintance with the attributes of love or benevolence, we shall not fail to be perplexed—to find apparent discrepancies in the Bible and in the divine administration—and in the manifestation of Christian character, both as revealed in the Bible and as exhibited in common life.

For example, how universalists have stumbled for want of consideration upon this subject! God is love! Well, without considering the attributes of this love, they infer that if God is love, he cannot hate sin and sinners. If he is merciful, he cannot punish sinners in hell.

Unitarians have stumbled in the same way; God is merciful, that is, disposed to pardon sin. Well, then, what need of an atonement? If merciful, he can and will pardon upon repentance without atonement.

But we may inquire, if he is merciful, why not pardon without repentance? If

his mercy alone is to be taken into view, that is, simply a disposition to pardon, that by itself would not wait for repentance. But if repentance is and must be a condition of the exercise of mercy, may there not be, nay, must there not be other conditions of its exercise? If wisdom and public justice are also attributes of benevolence and condition the exercise of mercy and forbid that is should be exercised but upon condition of repentance, why may they not, nay, why must they not equally condition its exercise upon such a satisfaction of public justice as would secure as full and as deep a respect for the law as the execution of its penalty would do? In other words, if wisdom and justice be attributes of benevolence and condition the exercise of mercy upon repentance, why may and must they not also condition its exercise upon the fact of an atonement?

As mercy is an attribute of benevolence, it will naturally and inevitably direct the attention of the intellect to devising ways and means to render the exercise of mercy consistent with the other attributes of benevolence. It will employ the intelligence in devising means to secure the repentance of the sinner and to remove all the obstacles out of the way of its free and full exercise. It will also secure the state of feeling which is also called mercy or compassion. Hence it is certain that mercy will secure efforts to procure the repentance and pardon of sinners. It will secure a deep yearning in the sensibility over them and energetic action to accomplish its end, that is to secure their repentance and pardon. This attribute of benevolence led the Father to give his only-begotten and well-beloved Son, and led the Son to give himself to die to secure the repentance and pardon of sinners. It is this attribute of benevolence that leads the Holy Spirit to make such mighty and protracted efforts to secure the repentance of sinners. It is also this attribute that energized in prophets and apostles and martyrs and saints of every age to secure the conversion of the lost in sin. It is an amiable attribute. All its sympathies are sweet and tender and kind as heaven.

Justice

Justice is an attribute of benevolence. This term also expresses a state or phenomenon of the sensibility. As an attribute of benevolence, it is the opposite of mercy when viewed in its relations to crime. It consists in a disposition to treat every moral agent according to his intrinsic desert or merit. In its relations to crime, the criminal, and the public, it consists in a tendency to punish according to law. Mercy would pardon; justice would punish for the public good.

Justice as a feeling or phenomenon of the sensibility is a feeling that the guilty deserves punishment and a desire that he may be punished. This is an involuntary feeling and has no moral character. It is often strongly excited and is frequently the cause of mobs and popular commotions. When it takes the control of the will, as it often does with sinners, it leads to what is popularly called lynching and a resort to those summary methods of executing vengeance which are so appalling.

I have said that the mere desire has no moral character. But when the will is governed by this desire and yields itself up to seek its gratification, this state of will is selfishness under one of its most odious and frightful forms. Under the providence of God, however, this form of selfishness, like every other in its turn, is overruled for good, like earthquakes, tornadoes, pestilence, and war, to purify the moral elements of society and scourge away those moral nuisances with which communities are sometimes infested. Even war itself is often but an instance and an illustration of this.

Justice, as an attribute of benevolence, is virtue and exhibits itself in the execution of the penalties of the law and in support of public order and in various other ways for the well-being of mankind. There are several modifications of this attribute. That is, it may and must be viewed under various aspects and in various relations. One of these is public justice. This is a regard to the public interests and secures a due administration of law for the public good. It will in no case suffer the execution of the penalty to be set aside, unless something be done to support the authority of the law and of the lawgiver. It also secures the due administration of rewards and looks narrowly after the public interests, always insisting that the greater interest shall prevail over the lesser, that private interest shall never set aside or prejudice a public one of greater value. Public justice is modified in its exercise by the attribute of mercy. It conditions the exercise of mercy and mercy conditions its exercise. Mercy cannot consistently with this attribute extend a pardon but upon conditions of repentance and an equivalent being rendered to the government. So on the other hand, justice is conditioned by mercy and cannot consistently with that attribute proceed to take vengeance when the highest good does not require it, when punishment can be dispensed with without public loss. Thus these attributes mutually limit each other's exercise and render the whole character of benevolence perfect, symmetrical, and heavenly.

Justice is reckoned among the sterner attributes of benevolence, but it is indispensable to the filling up of the entire circle of moral perfections. Although solemn and awful and sometimes inexpressibly terrific in its exercise, it is nevertheless one of the glorious modifications and manifestations of benevolence. Benevolence without justice would be anything but morally lovely and perfect. Nay, it could not be benevolence. This attribute of benevolence appears conspicuous in the character of God as revealed in his law, in his gospel, and sometimes as indicated most impressively by his providence.

It is also conspicuous in the history of inspired men. The Psalms abound with expressions of this attribute. We find many prayers for the punishment of the wicked. Samuel hewed Agag in pieces, and David's writings abound in expressions that show that this attribute was strongly developed in his mind, and the circumstances under which he was placed often rendered it proper to express and manifest in various ways the spirit of this attribute.

Many have stumbled at such prayers, expressions, and manifestations as are here alluded to. But this is for want of due consideration. They have supposed that such exhibitions were inconsistent with a right spirit. Oh, they say, how unevangelical! How un-Christ-like! How inconsistent with the sweet and heavenly spirit of Christ and of the gospel! But this is all a mistake. These prayers were dictated by the Spirit of Christ. Such exhibitions are only the manifestations of one of the essential attributes of benevolence. Those sinners deserved to die. It was for the greatest good that they should be made a public example. This the Spirit of inspiration knew, and such prayers under such circumstances are only an expression of the mind and will of God. They are truly the spirit of justice pronouncing sentence upon them. These prayers and suchlike things found in the Bible are no vindication of

the spirit of fanaticism and denunciation that so often have taken shelter under them. As well might fanatics burn cities and lay waste countries and seek to justify themselves by an appeal to the destruction of the old world by flood and the destruction of the cities of the plain by fire and brimstone.

Retributive justice is another modification of this attribute. This consists in a disposition to visit the offender with that punishment which he deserves because it is fit and proper that a moral agent should be dealt with according to his deeds. In a future lecture I shall enlarge upon this modification of justice.

Another modification of this attribute is commercial justice. This consists in willing exact equivalents and uprightness in business and all secular transactions. There are some other modifications of this attribute, but the foregoing may suffice to illustrate sufficiently the various departments over which this attribute presides.

This attribute, though stern in its spirit and manifestations, is nevertheless one of prime importance in all governments by moral agents whether human or divine. Indeed, without it government could not exist. It is vain for certain philosophers to think to disparage this attribute and to dispense with it altogether in the administration of government. They will if they try the experiment find to their cost and confusion that no one attribute of benevolence can say to another, "I have no need of thee." In short, let any one attribute of benevolence be destroyed or overlooked and you have destroyed its perfection, its beauty, its harmony, its propriety, its glory. You have, in fact, destroyed benevolence; it is no longer benevolence, but a sickly and inefficient and limping sentimentalism that has no God, no virtue, no beauty, no form, no comeliness in it that when we see it we should desire it.

This attribute stands by, nay, it executes law. It aims to secure commercial honesty. It aims to secure public and private integrity and tranquility. It says to violence, disorder, and injustice, Peace, be still, and there must be a great calm. We see the evidences and the illustrations of this attribute in the thunderings of Sinai and in the agony of Calvary. We hear it in the wail of a world when the foundations of the great deep were broken up, and when the windows of heaven were opened, and the floods descended, and the population of a globe was swallowed up. We see its manifestations in the descending torrent that swept over the cities of the plain, and lastly, we shall forever see its bright but awful and glorious displays in the dark and curling folds of that pillar of smoke of the torment of the damned that ascends up before God forever and ever.

Many seem to be afraid to contemplate justice as an attribute of benevolence. Any manifestation of it among men causes them to recoil and shudder as if they saw a demon. But let it have its place in the glorious circle of moral attributes; it must have—it will have—it cannot be otherwise. Whenever any policy of government is adopted in family or state that excludes the exercise of this attribute, all must be failure, defeat, and ruin.

Again: Justice being an attribute of benevolence will prevent the punishment of the finally impenitent from diminishing the happiness of God and of holy beings. They will never delight in misery for its own sake, but they will take pleasure in the administration of justice. So that when the smoke of the torment of the damned comes up in the sight of heaven, they will as they are represented, shout "Alleluia! the Lord God Omnipotent reigneth"; "Just and righteous are thy ways, thou King of saints!"

Before I pass from the consideration of this topic, I must not omit to insist that where true benevolence is there must be exact commercial justice or business honesty and integrity. This is as certain as that benevolence exists. The rendering of exact equivalents or the intention to do so much be a characteristic of a truly benevolent mind. Impulsive benevolence may exist; that is, phrenological or constitutional benevolence, falsely called, may exist to any extent and yet justice not exist. The mind may be much and very often carried away by the impulse of feeling so that a man may at times have the appearance of true benevolence while the same individual is selfish in business and overreaching in all his commercial relations. This has been a wonder and an enigma to many, but the case is a plain one. The difficulty is the man is not just, that is, not truly benevolent. His benevolence is only an imposing species of selfishness. "He that hath an ear to hear, let him hear." His benevolence results from feeling and is not true benevolence.

Again: Where benevolence is, the golden rule will surely be observed: "Whatsoever ye would that men should do to you, do ye even so to them." The justice of benevolence cannot fail to secure conformity to this rule. Benevolence is a just state of the will. It is a willing justly. It must then by a law of necessity secure just conduct. If the heart is just, the life must be.

The attribute of benevolence must secure its possessor against every species and degree of injustice; he cannot be unjust to his neighbor's reputation, his person, his property, his soul, his body, nor indeed be unjust in any respect to man or God. It will and must secure confession and restitution in every case of remembering wrong so far as this is practicable. It should be distinctly understood that a benevolent or a truly religious man cannot be unjust. He may indeed appear to be so to others, but he cannot be truly religious or benevolent and unjust at the same time. If he appears to be so in any instance, he is not and cannot be really so if he is at the time in a benevolent state of mind.

The attributes of selfishness, as we shall see in the proper place, are the direct opposite of those of benevolence. The two states of mind are as contrary as heaven and hell and can no more co-exist in the same mind than a thing can be and not be at the same time. I said that if a man truly in the exercise of benevolence appears to be unjust in any thing, he is only so in appearance and not in fact. Observe I am speaking of one who is really at the time in a benevolent state of mind. He may mistake and do that which would be unjust, did he see it differently and intend differently. Justice and injustice belong to the intention. No outward act can in itself be either just or unjust. To say that a man, in the exercise of a truly benevolent intention, can at the same time be unjust is the same absurdity as to say that he can intend justly and unjustly at the same time and in regard to the same thing, which is a contradiction. It must all along be borne in mind that benevolence is one identical thing, to wit, good-will, willing for its own sake the highest good of being and every known good according to its relative value. Consequently, it is impossible that justice should not be an attribute of such a choice. Justice consists in regarding and treating or rather in willing everything just agreeably to its nature or intrinsic and relative value and relations. To say, therefore, that present benevolence admits of any degree of present injustice is to affirm a palpable contradiction. A just man is a sanctified man, is a perfect man in the sense that he is at present in an upright state.

Veracity

Veracity is another attribute of benevolence. Veracity as an attribute of benevolence is that quality that adheres to truth. In the very act of becoming benevolent, the mind embraces truth or the reality of things. Then veracity must be one of the qualities of benevolence. Veracity is truthfulness. It is the conformity of the will to the reality of things. Truth in statement is conformity of statement to the reality of things. Truth in action is action conformed to the nature and relations of things. Truthfulness is a disposition to conform to the reality of things. It is willing in accordance with the reality of things. It is willing the right end by the right means. It is willing the intrinsically valuable as an end and the relatively valuable as a means. In short, it is the willing of everything according to the reality or facts in the case.

Veracity, then, must be an attribute of benevolence. It is, like all the attributes, only benevolence viewed in a certain aspect or relation. It cannot be distinguished from benevolence for it is not distinct from it but only a phase or form of benevolence. The universe is so constituted that if everything proceeded and were conducted and willed according to its nature and relations, the highest possible good must result. Veracity seeks the good as an end and truth as a means to secure this end. It wills the good and that it shall be secured only by means of truth. It wills truth in the end and truth in the means. The end is truly valuable and chosen for that reason. The means are truth and truth is the only appropriate or possible means.

Truthfulness of heart begets, of course, a state of the sensibility which we call the love of truth. It is a feeling of pleasure that spontaneously arises in the sensibility of one whose heart is truthful in contemplating truth; this feeling is not virtue; it is rather a part of the reward of truthfulness of heart.

Veracity as a phenomenon of the will is also often and properly called a love of the truth. It is a willing in accordance with objective truth. This is virtue and is an attribute of benevolence. Veracity as an attribute of the Divine benevolence is the condition of confidence in God as a moral governor. Both the physical and moral laws of the universe evince and are instances and illustrations of the truthfulness of God.

Falsehood in the sense of lying is naturally regarded by a moral agent with disapprobation, disgust, and abhorrence. Veracity is as necessarily regarded by him with approbation and if the will be benevolent, with pleasure.

We necessarily take pleasure in contemplating objective truth as it lies in idea on the field of consciousness. We also take pleasure in the perception and contemplation of truthfulness in the concrete realization of the idea of truth. Veracity is morally beautiful. We are pleased with it just as we are with natural beauty, by a law of necessity when the necessary conditions are fulfilled. This attribute of benevolence secures it against every attempt to promote the ultimate good of being by means of falsehood. True benevolence will no more, can no more resort to falsehood as a means of promoting good than it can contradict or deny itself. The intelligence affirms that the highest ultimate good can be secured only by a strict adherence to truth. The mind cannot be satisfied with anything else. Indeed, to suppose the contrary is to suppose a contradiction. It is the same absurdity as to suppose that the highest good could be secured only by the violation

and setting aside of the nature and relations of things. Since the intellect affirms this unalterable relation of truth to the highest ultimate good, benevolence or that attribute of benevolence which we denominate veracity or love of the truth can no more consent to falsehood than it can consent to relinquish the highest good of being as an end. Therefore, every resort to falsehood, every pious fraud falsely so called presents only a specious but real instance of selfishness.

A moral agent cannot lie for God; that is, he cannot tell a sinful falsehood thinking and intending thereby to please God. He knows, by intuition, that God cannot be pleased or truly served by a resort to lying. There is a great difference between concealing or withholding the truth for benevolent purposes and telling a willful falsehood. An innocent, persecuted, and pursued man has taken shelter under my roof from one who pursued him to shed his blood. His pursuer comes and inquires after him. I am not under obligation to declare to him the fact that he is in my house. I may and indeed ought to withhold the truth in this instance, for the wretch has no right to know it. The public and highest good demands that he should not know it. He only desires to know it for selfish and bloody purposes. But in this case I should not feel or judge myself at liberty to state a known falsehood. I could not think that this would ultimately conduce to the highest good. The person might go away deceived or under the impression that his victim was not there. But he could not accuse me of telling him a lie. He might have drawn his own inference from my refusing to give the desired information. But even to secure my own life or the life of my friend, I am not at liberty to tell a lie.

If it be said that lying implies telling a falsehood for selfish purposes and that therefore, it is not lying to tell a falsehood for benevolent purposes, I reply that our nature is such that we can no more state a willful falsehood with a benevolent intention than we can commit a sin with a benevolent intention. We necessarily regard falsehood as inconsistent with the highest good of being, just as we regard holiness and truthfulness as the indispensable condition of the highest good of being. The correlation of the will and the intellect forbids the mistake that willful falsehood is or can be the means or condition of the highest good. Universal veracity, then, will always characterize a truly benevolent man. While he is truly benevolent, he is, he must be faithful, truthful. So far as his knowledge goes, his statements may be depended upon with as much safety as the statements of an angel. Veracity is necessarily an attribute of benevolence in all beings. No liar has or can have a particle of true virtue or benevolence in him.

Patience

Patience is another attribute of benevolence. This term is frequently used to express a phenomenon of the sensibility. When thus used, it designates a calm and unruffled state of the sensibility or feelings under circumstances that tend to excite anger or impatience of feeling. The calmness of the sensibility or patience as a phenomenon of the sensibility is purely an involuntary state of mind, and although it is a pleasing and amiable manifestation, yet it is not properly virtue. It may be and often is an effect of patience as a phenomenon of the will and therefore an effect of virtue. But it is not itself virtue. This amiable temper may and often does proceed from constitutional temperament and from circumstances and habits.

Patience as a virtue must be a voluntary state of mind. It must be an attribute of love or benevolence; for all virtue, as we have seen and as the Bible teaches, is resolvable into love or benevolence. The Greek term *upon one,* so often rendered patience in the New Testament, means perseverance under trials, continuance, bearing up under affliction or privations, steadfastness of purpose despite obstacles. The word may be used in a good or in a bad sense. Thus a selfish man may patiently, that is perseveringly, pursue his end and may bear up under much opposition to his course. This is patience as an attribute of selfishness, and patience in a bad sense of the term. Patience in the good sense or in the sense in which I am considering it is an attribute of benevolence. It is the quality of constancy, a fixedness, a bearing up under trials, afflictions, crosses, persecutions, or discouragements. This must be an attribute of benevolence. Whenever patience ceases, when it hold out no longer, when discouragement prevails and the will relinquishes its end, benevolence ceases as a matter of course.

Patience as a phenomenon of the will tends to patience as a phenomenon of the sensibility. That is the quality of fixedness and steadfastness in the intention naturally tends to keep down and allay impatience of temper. As however the states of the sensibility are not directly under the control of the will, there may be irritable or impatient feelings when the heart remains steadfast. Facts or falsehoods may be suggested to the mind which may, despite the will, produce a ruffling of the sensibility even when the heart remains patient. The only way in which a temptation, for it is only a temptation while the will abides firm to its purpose, I say the only way in which a temptation of this kind can be disposed of is by diverting the attention from that view of the subject that creates the disturbance in the sensibility.

I should have said before that although the will controls the feelings by a law of necessity, yet as it does not do so directly but indirectly, it may and does often happen that feelings corresponding to the state of the will do not exist in the sensibility. Nay, for a time a state of the sensibility may exist which is the opposite of the state of the will. From this source arise many and indeed most of our temptations.

We could never be properly tried or tempted at all if the feelings must always by a law of necessity correspond with the state of the will. Sin consists in willing to gratify our feelings or constitutional impulses in opposition to the law of our reason. But if these desires and impulses could never exist in opposition to the law of the reason and consequently in opposition to a present holy choice, then a holy being could not be tempted. He could have no motive or occasion to sin. If our mother Eve could have had no feelings of desire in opposition to the state of her will, she never could have desired the forbidden fruit and of course would not have sinned.

I wish now to state distinctly what I should have said before that the state or choice of the will does not necessarily so control the feelings, desires, or emotions that these may never be strongly excited by Satan or by circumstances in opposition to the will, and thus become powerful temptations to seek their gratification instead of seeking the highest good of being. Feelings, the gratification of which would be opposed to every attribute of benevolence, may at times coexist with benevolence and be a temptation to selfishness, but opposing acts of will cannot coexist with benevolence.

All that can be truly said is that as the will has an indirect control of the feelings, desires, appetites, passions, etc., it can suppress any class of feelings when they arise by diverting the attention from their causes or by taking into consideration such views and facts as will calm or change the state of the sensibility. Irritable feelings or what is commonly called impatience may be directly caused by ill health, irritable nerves, and by many things over which the will has no direct control. But this is not impatience in the sense of sin. If these feelings are not suffered to influence the will, if the will abides in patience, if such feelings are not cherished and are not suffered to shake the integrity of the will, they are not sin. That is the will does not consent to them but the contrary. They are only temptations. If they are allowed to control the will, to break forth in words and actions, then there is sin; but the sin does not consist in the feelings but in the consent of the will to gratify them. Thus the apostle says, "Be ye angry, and sin not: let not the sun go down upon your wrath." That is, if anger arise in the feelings and sensibility, do not sin by suffering it to control your will. Do not cherish the feeling and let not the sun go down upon it. For this cherishing is sin. When it is cherished, the will consents and broods over the cause of it; this is sin. But if it be not cherished, it is not sin.

That the outward actions will correspond with the states and actions of the will, provided no physical obstacle be opposed to them, is a universal truth. But that feelings and desires cannot exist contrary to the states or decisions of the will is not true. If this were a universal truth, temptation as I have said could not exist. The outward actions will be as the will is, always; the feelings, generally. Feelings corresponding to the choice of the will will be the rule and opposing feelings the exception. But these exceptions may and do exist in perfectly holy beings. They existed in

Eve before she consented to sin, and had she resisted them, she had not sinned. They doubtless existed in Christ, or he could not have been tempted in all points like as we are.

If there be no desires or impulses of the sensibility contrary to the state of the will, there is not properly any temptation. The desire or impulse must appear on the field of consciousness before it is a motive to action and of course before it is a temptation to self-indulgence. Just as certainly then as a holy being may be tempted and not sin, just so certain it is that emotions of any kind or of any strength may exist in the sensibility without sin. If they are not indulged, if the will does not consent to them and to their indulgence or gratification, the soul is not the less virtuous for their presence.

Patience as a phenomenon of the will must strengthen and gird itself under such circumstances so that patience of will may be and, if it exist at all, must be in exact proportion to the impatience of the sensibility. The more impatience of sensibility there is, the more patience of will there must be or virtue will cease altogether. So that it is not always true that virtue is strongest when the sensibility is most calm, placid, and patient. When Christ passed through his greatest conflicts, his virtue as a man was undoubtedly most intense. When in his agony in the garden, so great was the anguish of his sensibility that he sweat as it were great drops of blood. This, he says, was the hour of the prince of darkness. This was his great trial. But did he sin? No, indeed. But why? Was he calm and placid as a summer's evening? As far from it as possible.

Patience, then, as an attribute of benevolence consists not in placid feeling but in perseverance under trials and states of the sensibility that tend to selfishness. This is only benevolence viewed in a certain aspect. It is benevolence under circumstances of discouragement, of trial, or temptation. "This is the patience of the saints."

Before dismissing the subject of patience as an emotion, I would observe that the steadfastness of the heart tends so strongly to secure patience that if an opposite state of the sensibility is more than of momentary duration, there is strong presumption that the heart is not steadfast in love. The first risings of it will produce an immediate effort to suppress it. If it continues, this is evidence that the attention is allowed to dwell upon the cause of it. This shows that the will is in some sense indulging it.

Meekness

Another attribute of benevolence is meekness. Meekness considered as a virtue is a phenomenon of the will. This term also expresses a state of the sensibility. When used to designate a phenomenon of the sensibility, it is nearly synonymous with patience. It designates a sweet and forbearing temper under provocation. Meekness as a phenomenon of the will and as an attribute of benevolence is the opposite both of resistance to injury and retaliation. It is properly and strictly forbearance under injurious treatment. This certainly is an attribute of God as our existence and our being out of hell plainly demonstrate. Christ said of himself that he was "meek and lowly in heart"; and this surely was no vain boast. How admirably and how incessantly did this attribute of his love manifest itself! The fifty-third chapter of Isaiah is a prophecy exhibiting this attribute in a most affecting light. Indeed, scarcely any feature of the character of God and of Christ is more strikingly exhibited than this. It must evidently be an attribute of benevolence.

Benevolence is good-will to all beings. We are naturally forbearing toward those whose good we honestly and diligently seek. If our hearts are set upon doing them good, we shall naturally exercise great forbearance toward them. God has greatly commended his forbearance to us in that while we were yet his enemies, he forbore to punish us and gave his Son to die for us. Forbearance is a sweet and amiable attribute. How affectingly it displayed itself in the hall of Pilate and on the cross. "He is led as a lamb to the slaughter, and as a sheep before its shearers is dumb, so he opened not his mouth."

This attribute has in this world abundant opportunity to develop and display itself in the saints. There are daily occasions for the exercise of this form of virtue. Indeed, all the attributes of benevolence are called into frequent exercise in this school of discipline. This is indeed a suitable world in which to train God's children, to develop and strengthen every modification of holiness. This attribute must always appear where benevolence exists and wherever there is an occasion for its exercise.

It is delightful to contemplate the perfection and glory of that love which constitutes obedience to the law of God. As occasions arise, we behold it developing one attribute after another, and there may be many of its attributes and modifications of which we have as yet no idea whatever. Circumstances will call them into exercise. It is probable, if not certain, that the attributes of benevolence were very imperfectly known in heaven previous to the existence of sin in the universe and that but for sin many of these attributes would never have been manifested in exercise. But the existence of sin, great as the evil is, has afforded an opportunity for benevolence to manifest its beautiful phases and to develop its sweet attributes in a most

enchanting manner. Thus the divine economy of benevolence brings good out of so great an evil.

A hasty and unforbearing spirit is always demonstrative evidence of a want of benevolence or of true religion. Meekness is and must be a peculiar characteristic of the saints in this world where there is so much provocation. Christ frequently and strongly enforced the obligation to forbearance. "But I say unto you that ye resist not evil; but whosoever shall smite thee on thy right cheek, turn to him the other also. And if any man will sue thee at the law, and take away thy coat, let him have thy cloak also. And whosoever shall compel thee to go a mile, go with him twain." How beautiful!

Humility

Humility is another modification or attribute of love. This term seems often to be used to express a sense of unworthiness, of guilt, of ignorance, and of nothingness, to express a feeling of ill-desert. It seems to be used in common language to express sometimes a state of the intelligence when it seems to indicate a clear perception of our guilt. When used to designate a state of the sensibility, it represents those feelings of shame and unworthiness, of ignorance, and of nothingness of which those are most deeply conscious who have been enlightened by the Holy Spirit in respect to their true character.

But as a phenomenon of the will and as an attribute of love, it consists in a willingness to be known and appreciated according to our real character. Humility as a phenomenon either of the sensibility or of the intelligence may coexist with great pride of heart. Pride is a disposition to exalt self, to get above others, to hide our defects, and to pass for more than we are. Deep conviction of sin and deep feelings of shame, of ignorance, and of desert of hell may coexist with a great unwillingness to confess and be known just as we are and to be appreciated just according to what our real character has been and is. There is no virtue in such humility. But humility considered as a virtue consists in the consent of the will to be known, to confess, and to take our proper place in the scale of being. It is that peculiarity of love that wills the good of being so disinterestedly as to will to pass for no other than we really are. This is an honest, a sweet, and amiable feature of love. It must perhaps be peculiar to those who have sinned. It is only love acting under or in a certain relation or in reference to a peculiar set of circumstances. It would under the same circumstances develop and manifest itself in all truly benevolent minds. This attribute will render confession of sin to God and man natural and even make it a luxury.

It is easy to see that but for this attribute the saints could not be happy in heaven. God has promised to bring into judgment every work and every secret thing whether it be good or whether it be evil. Now while pride exists, it would greatly pain the soul to have all the character known so that unless this attribute really belongs to the saints, they would be ashamed at the judgment and filled with confusion even in heaven itself. But this sweet attribute will secure them against that shame and confusion of face that would otherwise render heaven itself a hell to them. They will be perfectly willing and happy to be known and estimated according to their characters. This attribute will secure in all the saints on earth that confession of faults one to another which is so often enjoined in the Bible. By this it is not intended that Christians always think it wise and necessary to make confession of all their secret sins to man. But it is intended that they will confess to those whom they have injured and to all to whom benevolence demands that they should confess. This attribute secures its possessor against spiritual pride, against ambition to get above others. It is a modest and unassuming state of mind.

Self-Denial

Self-denial is another attribute of love. If we love any being better than ourselves, we of course deny ourselves when our own interests come in competition with his. Love is good-will. If I will good to others more than to myself, it is absurd to say that I shall not deny myself when my own inclinations conflict with their good. Now the love required by the law of God we have repeatedly seen to be good will or willing the highest good of being for its own sake or as an end. As the interests of self are not at all regarded because they belong to self but only according to their relative value, it must be certain that self-denial for the sake of promoting the higher interest of God and of the universe is and must be a peculiarity or attribute of love.

But again: The very idea of disinterested benevolence, and there is no other true benevolence, implies the abandonment of the spirit of self-seeking or of selfishness. It is impossible to become benevolent without ceasing to be selfish. In other words, perfect self-denial is implied in beginning to be benevolent. Self-indulgence ceases where benevolence begins. This must be. Benevolence is the consecration of our powers to the highest good of being in general as an end. This is utterly inconsistent with consecrations to self-interest or self-gratification. Selfishness makes good to self the end of every choice. Benevolence makes good to being in general the end of every choice. Benevolence, then, implies complete self-denial. That is it implies that nothing is chosen merely because it belongs to self but only because of its relative value and in proportion to it.

I said there was no true benevolence but disinterested benevolence; no true love but disinterested love. There is such a thing as interested love or benevolence. That is the good of others is willed, though not as an end or for its intrinsic value to them, but as a means of our own happiness or because of its relative value to us. Thus a man might will the good of his family or of his neighborhood or country or of anybody or anything that sustained such relations to self as to involve his own interests. When the ultimate reason of his willing good to others is that his own may be promoted, this is selfishness. It is making good to self his end. This a sinner may do toward God, toward the church, and toward the interests of religion in general. This is what I call interested benevolence. It is willing good as an end only to self and to all others only as a means of promoting our own good.

But again: When the will is governed by mere feeling in willing the good of others, this is only the spirit of self-indulgence and is only interested benevolence. For example, the feeling of compassion is strongly excited by the presence of misery. The feeling is intense and constitutes like all the feelings a strong impulse or motive to the will to consent to its gratification. For the time being this impulse is stronger than the feeling of avarice or any other feeling. I yield to it and then give all the money I have to relieve the sufferer. I even take my clothes from my back and give them to him. Now in this case, I am just as selfish as if I had sold my clothes to gratify my appetite for strong drink. The gratification of my feelings was my end. This is one of the most specious and most delusive forms of selfishness.

Again: When one makes his own salvation the end of prayer, of almsgiving, and of all his religious duties, this is only selfishness and not true religion, however much he may abound in them. This is only interested benevolence or benevolence to self.

Again: From the very nature of true benevolence, it is impossible that every interest should not be regarded according to its relative value. When another interest is seen by me to be more valuable in itself or of more value to God and the universe than my own, and when I see that by denying myself I can promote it, it is certain if I am benevolent that I shall do it. I cannot fail to do it without failing to be benevolent. Benevolence is an honest and disinterested consecration of the whole being to the highest good of God and of the universe. The benevolent man will, therefore, and must honestly weigh each interest as it is perceived in the balance of his own best judgment and will always give the preference to the higher interest, provided he believes that he can by endeavor and by self-denial secure it.

That self-denial is an attribute of the divine love is manifested most gloriously and affectingly in God's gift of his Son to die for men. This attribute was also most conspicuously manifested by Christ in denying himself and taking up his cross and suffering for his enemies. Observe it was not for friends that Christ gave himself. It was not unfortunate nor innocent sufferers for whom God gave his Son or for whom he gave himself. It was for enemies. It was not that he might make slaves of them that he gave his Son nor from any selfish consideration whatever but because he foresaw that by making this sacrifice himself he could secure to the universe a greater good than he should sacrifice.

It was this attribute of benevolence that caused him to give his Son to suffer so much. It was disinterested benevolence alone that led him to deny himself for the sake of a greater good to the universe. Now observe this sacrifice would not have been made unless it had been regarded by God as the lesser of two natural evils. That is, the sufferings of Christ, great and overwhelming as they were, were considered as an evil of less magnitude than the eternal sufferings of sinners. This induced him to make the sacrifice although for his enemies. It mattered not whether for friends or for enemies, if so be he could by making a less sacrifice secure a greater good to them.

Let it be understood that a self-indulgent spirit is never and can never be consistent with benevolence. No form of self-indulgence, properly so called, can exist where true benevolence exists. The fact is self-denial must be and universally is wherever benevolence reigns. Christ has expressly made whole-hearted self-denial a condition of discipleship, which is the same thing as to affirm that it is an essential attribute of holiness or love, that there cannot be the beginning of true virtue without it.

Again: Much that passes for self-denial is only a specious form of self-indulgence. The penances and self-mortifications as they are falsely called of the superstitious, what are they after all but a self-indulgent spirit? A popish priest abstains from marriage to obtain the honor and emoluments and the influence of the priestly office here and eternal glory hereafter. A nun takes the veil and a monk immures himself in a monastery; a hermit forsakes human society and shuts himself up in a cave; a devotee makes a pilgrimage to Mecca, and a martyr goes to the stake. Now if these things are done with an ultimate reference to their own glory and happiness although apparently instances of great self-denial, yet they are in fact only a spirit of self-indulgence and self-seeking. They are only following the strongest desires of good to self.

There are many mistakes upon this subject. For example, it is common for persons to deny self in one form for the sake of gratifying self in another form. In one man avarice is the ruling passion. He will labor hard, rise early, and sit up late, eat the bread of carefulness, and deny himself even the necessaries of life for the sake of accumulating wealth. Everyone can see that this is denying self in one form merely for the sake of gratifying self in another form. Yet this man will complain bitterly of the self-indulgent spirit manifested by others, their extravagance, and want of piety. One man will deny all his bodily appetites and passions for the sake of a reputation with men. This is also an instance of the same kind. Another will give the fruit of his body for the sin of his soul, will sacrifice everything else to obtain an eternal inheritance and be just as selfish as the man who sacrifices to the things of time, his soul, and all the riches of eternity.

But it should be remarked that this attribute of benevolences does and must secure the subjugation of all the propensities. It must either suddenly or gradually so far subdue and quiet them that their imperious clamor must cease. The will, as it were, be slain either suddenly or gradually so that the sensibility will become in a great measure dead to those objects that so often and so easily excited it. It is a law of the sensibility— of all the desires and passions that their indulgence develops and strengthens them, and their denial suppresses them. Benevolence consists in a refusal to gratify the sensibility and in obeying the reason. Therefore it must be true that this denial of the propensities will greatly suppress them, while the indulgence of the intellect and of the conscience will greatly develop them. Thus selfishness tends to stultify while benevolence tends greatly to strengthen the intellect.

Condescension

Condescension is another attribute of love. This attribute consists in a tendency to descend to the poor, the ignorant, or the vile for the purpose of securing their good. It is a tendency to seek the good of those whom Providence has placed in any respect below us by stooping, descending, coming down to them for this purpose. It is a peculiar form of self-denial.

God the Father, the Son, and the Holy Spirit manifest infinite condescension in efforts to secure the well-being of sinners, even the most vile and degraded. This attribute is called by Christ lowliness of heart. God is said to humble himself, that is to condescend, when he beholds the things that are done in heaven. This is true, for every creature is and must forever be infinitely below Him in every respect. But how much greater must that condescension be that comes down to earth and even to the lowest and most degraded of earth's inhabitants for purposes of benevolence! This is a lovely modification of benevolence. It seems to be entirely above the gross conceptions of infidelity.

Condescension seems to be regarded by most people and especially by infidels as rather a weakness than a virtue. Skeptics clothe their imaginary God with attributes in many respects the opposite of true virtue. They think it entirely beneath the dignity of God to come down even to notice and much more to interfere with the concerns of men. But hear the word of the Lord:

"Thus saith the High and Lofty One, who inhabiteth eternity, whose name is Holy: I dwell in the high and holy place; with him also that is of a contrite and humble spirit, to revive the spirit of the humble, and to revive the heart of the contrite ones." And again, "Thus saith the Lord, the heaven is my throne and the earth is my foot stool, where is the house that ye build unto me? and where is the place of my rest? For all those things hath my hand made and all those things have been, saith the Lord. But to this man will I look, even to him that is poor and of a contrite spirit, and that trembleth at my word." Thus the Bible represents God as clothed with condescension as with a cloak.

This is manifestly an attribute both of benevolence and of true greatness. The natural perfections of God appear all the more wonderful when we consider that he can and does know and contemplate and control not only the highest, but the lowest of all his creatures, that he is just as able to attend to every want and every creature as if this were the sole object of attention with him. So his moral attributes appear all the more lovely and engaging when we consider that his "tender mercies are over all his works," "that not a sparrow falleth to the ground without him," that he condescends to number the very hairs of the heads of his servants, and that not one of them can fall without him. When we consider that no creature is too low, too filthy, or too degraded for him to condescend to—this places his character in a most ravishing light. Benevolence is good-will to all beings. Of course one of its characteristics must be condescension to those who are below us. This in God is manifestly infinite. He is infinitely above all creatures. For him to hold communion with them is infinite condescension.

This is an attribute essentially belonging to benevolence or love in all benevolent beings. With the lowest of moral beings it may have no other development than in its relations to sentient existences below the rank of moral agents for the reason that there are no moral agents below them to whom they can stoop. God's condescension stoops to all ranks of sentient existences. This is also true with every benevolent mind as to all inferiors. It seeks the good of being in general and never thinks any being too low to have his interests attended to and cared for according to their relative value.

Benevolence cannot possibly retain its own essential nature and yet be above any degree of condescension that can effect the greatest good. Benevolence does not, cannot know anything of that loftiness of spirit that considers it too degrading to stoop anywhere or to any being whose interests need to be and can be promoted by such condescension. Benevolence has its end, and it cannot but seek this, and it does not, cannot think anything below it that is demanded to secure that end. Oh, the shame, the infinite folly and madness of pride and every form of selfishness! How infinitely unlike God it is! Christ could condescend to be born in a manger; to be brought up in humble life; to be poorer than the fox of the desert or the fowls of heaven; to associate with fishermen; to mingle with and seek the good of all classes; to be despised in life and die between two thieves on the cross. His benevolence "endured the cross and despised the shame." He was "meek and lowly in heart." The Lord of heaven and earth is as much more lowly in heart than any of his creatures as he is above them in his infinity. He can stoop to anything but to commit sin. He can stoop infinitely low.

Stability

Stability is another attribute of benevolence. This love is not a mere feeling or emotion that effervesces for a moment and then cools down and disappears. But it is choice, not a mere volition which accomplishes its object and then rests. It is the choice of an end's supreme end. It is an intelligent choice—the most intelligent choice that can be made. It is considerate choice—none so much so; a deliberate choice, a reasonable choice which will always commend itself to the highest perceptions and intuitions of the intellect. It is intelligent and impartial and universal consecration to an end, above all others the most important and captivating in its influence. Now, stability must be a characteristic of such a choice as this.

By stability it is not intended that the choice may not be changed. Nor that it never is changed but that when the attributes of the choice are considered, it appears as if stability, as opposed to instability, must be an attribute of this choice. It is a new birth, a new nature, a new creature, a new heart, a new life. These and such like are the representations of scripture. Are these representations of an evanescent state? The beginning of benevolence in the soul—this choice is represented as the death of sin, as a burial, a being planted, a crucifixion of the old man, and many such like things. Are these representations of what we so often see among professed Christians? Nay, verily. The nature of the change itself would seem to be a guarantee of its stability. We might reasonably suppose that any other choice would be relinquished sooner than this, that any other state of mind would fail sooner than benevolence. It is vain to reply to this that facts prove the contrary to be true. I answer, what facts? Who can prove them to be facts? Shall we appeal to the apparent facts in the instability of many professors of religion; or shall we appeal to the very nature of the choice and to the Scriptures? To these doubtless. So far as philosophy can go, we might defy the world to produce an instance of choice which has so many chances for stability. The representations of Scripture are such as I have mentioned above.

What then shall we conclude of those effervescing professors of religion who are soon hot and soon cold; whose religion is a spasm; "whose goodness is as the morning cloud and the early dew, which goeth away"? Why, we must conclude that they never had the root of the matter in them. That they are not dead to sin and to the world, we see. That they are not new creatures that they have not the spirit of Christ, that they do not keep his commandments, we see. What then shall we conclude but this, that they are stony-ground hearers?

Holiness

Holiness is another attribute of benevolence. This term is used in the Bible as synonymous with moral purity. In a ceremonial sense it is applied to both persons and things; to make holy and to sanctify are the same thing. To sanctify and to consecrate or set apart to a sacred use are identical. Many things were in this sense sanctified or made holy under the Jewish economy. The term holiness may in a general sense be applied to anything whatever which is set apart to a sacred use. It may be applied to the whole being of a moral agent who is set apart to the service of God.

As an attribute of benevolence, it denotes that quality which leads it to seek to promote the happiness of moral agents by means of conformity to moral law.

As a moral attribute of God, it is that

peculiarity of his benevolence which secures it against all efforts to obtain its end by other means than those that are morally and perfectly pure. His benevolence aims to secure the happiness of the universe of moral agents by means of moral law and moral government and of conformity to his own subjective idea of right. In other words, holiness in God is that quality of his love that secures its universal conformity in all its efforts and manifestations to the Divine idea of right as it lies in eternal development in the Infinite Reason. This idea is moral law. It is sometimes used to express the moral quality or character of his benevolence generally or to express the moral character of the Godhead. It sometimes seems to designate an attribute and sometimes a quality of his moral attributes. Holiness is doubtless a characteristic or quality of each and all of his moral attributes. They will harmonize in this that no one of them can consent to do otherwise than conform to the law of moral purity as developed and revealed in the Divine Reason.

That holiness is an attribute of God is everywhere assumed and frequently asserted in the Bible. If an attribute of God, it must be an attribute of love, for God is love. This attribute is celebrated in heaven as one of those aspects of the divine character that give ineffable delight. Isaiah saw the seraphim standing around the throne of Jehovah and crying one to another, "Holy! holy! holy!" John also had a vision of the worship of heaven, and says, "They rest not day nor night, saying, Holy! holy! holy! Lord God Almighty." When Isaiah beheld the holiness of Jehovah, he cried out, "Woe is me! I am undone. I am a man of unclean lips and I dwell in the midst of a people of unclean lips; for mine eyes have seen the King, the Lord of hosts!" God's holiness is infinite, and it is no wonder that a perception of it should thus affect the prophet.

Finite holiness must forever feel itself awed in the presence of infinite holiness. Job says, "I have heard of thee by the hearing of the ear, but now mine eye seeth thee: wherefore I abhor myself, and repent in dust and ashes." There is no comparing finite with infinite. The time will never come when creatures can with open face contemplate the infinite holiness of Jehovah without being like persons overcome with a harmony too intensely delightful to be calmly borne. Heaven seems not able to endure it without breaking forth into strains of inexpressible rapture.

The expressions of Isaiah and Job do not necessarily imply that at the time they were in a sinful state but their expressions no doubt related to whatever of sin they had at any time been guilty of. In the light of Jehovah's holiness they saw the comparative pollution of their character taken as a whole. This view will always, doubtless, much affect the saints. This must be; and yet in another sense they may be and are as holy in their measure as he is. They may be as perfectly conformed to what light or truth they have, as he is. This is doubtless what Christ intended when he said, "Be ye perfect, even as your Father which is in heaven is perfect." The meaning is that they should live to the same end and be as entirely consecrated to it as he is. This they must be to be truly virtuous or holy in any degree. But when they are so, a full view of the holiness of God would confound and overwhelm them.

If any one doubts this, he has not considered the matter in a proper light. He has not lifted up his thoughts, as he needs to do, to the contemplation of infinite holiness. No creature however benevolent can witness the divine benevolence without being overwhelmed with a clear vision of it. This is no doubt true of every attribute of the Divine love. However perfect creature-virtue may be, it is finite and brought into the light of the attributes of infinite virtue, it will appear like the dimmest star in the presence of the sun, lost in the blaze of his glory. Let the most just man on earth or in heaven witness and have a clear apprehension of the infinite justice of Jehovah and it would no doubt fill him with unutterable awe. So could the most merciful saint on earth or in heaven have a clear perception of the divine mercy in its fullness, it would swallow up all thought and imagination and no doubt overwhelm him. And so also of every attribute of God. Oh! when we speak of the attributes of Jehovah, we often do no know what we say. Should God unveil himself to us, our bodies would instantly perish. "No man," says he, "can see my face and live." When Moses prayed, "Show me thy glory," God condescendingly hid him in the cleft of a rock and covering him with his hand, he passed by and let Moses see only his back parts, informing him that he could not behold his face, that is his unveiled glories, and live.

Holiness or moral harmony of character is then an essential attribute of disinterested love. It must be so from the laws of our being and from the very nature of benevolence. In man it manifests itself in great purity of conversation and deportment, in a great loathing of all impurity of flesh and spirit. Let no man profess piety who has not this attribute developed. The love required by the law of God is pure love. It seeks to make its object happy only by making him holy. It manifests the greatest abhorrence of sin and all uncleanness. In creatures it pants, and doubtless ever will pant and struggle, toward infinite purity or holiness. It will never find a resting place in such a sense as to desire to ascend no higher. As it perceives more and more of the fullness and infinity of God's holiness, it will no doubt pant and struggle to ascend the eternal heights where God sits in light too intense for the strongest vision of the highest cherub.

Holiness of heart or of will produces a desire or feeling of purity in the sensibility. The feelings become exceedingly alive to the beauty of holiness and to the hatefulness and deformity of all spiritual and even physical impurity. This is called the love of holiness. The sensibility becomes ravished with the great loveliness of holiness and unutterably disgusted with the opposite. The least impurity of conversation or of action exceedingly shocks one who is holy. Impure thoughts, if suggested to the mind of a holy being, are instantly felt to be exceedingly offensive and painful. The soul heaves and struggles to cast them out as the most loathsome abominations.

Again: If I will the good of any number of beings, I must do it in obedience to the law either of my intelligence and of God or of my sensibility. But if I will in obedience to the law of my intelligence, it must be the choice of the highest good of universal being. But if I will in obedience to the law or impulse of my sensibility, it must be to gratify my feelings or desires. This is selfishness.

Again: As the will must either follow the law of the reason and of God or the impulses of the sensibility, it follows that moral agents are shut up to the necessity of being selfish or benevolent and that there is no third way because there is no third medium through which any object of choice can be presented. The mind can absolutely know nothing as an object of choice that is not recommended by one of these faculties. Selfishness, then, and benevolence are the only two alternatives.

Let it be remembered then that sin is a unit and always and necessarily consists in selfish ultimate intention and in nothing else. This intention is sin; and thus we see that every phase of sin resolves itself into selfishness. This will appear more and more as we proceed to unfold the subject of moral depravity.

The natural state of man is that of selfishness. He has not genuine, consistent concern for the welfare of others. When conversion takes place, the natural state changes from selfishness to love. The regenerated person has a real concern for the welfare of others and a true interest in the things of God. Evidences of conversion will be moral living, prayerfulness, religious works, a love for what is right, a desire to serve and glorify God, and obedience to God. If a person does not have such traits active in his or her life, then a close examination is necessary to determine whether that person is truly a convert. While it is true that both regenerate and unregenerate people will have similar feelings, the truly regenerate will live with the desire to serve and glorify God. The object of the affections is the true test of conversion.

CHAPTER SEVEN

True and False Conversion

Behold all ye that kindle a fire, that compass yourselves about with sparks; walk in the light of your fire, and in the sparks that ye have kindled. This shall ye have of my hand; ye shall lie down in sorrow (Isa. 50:11).

It is evident from the connection of these words in the chapter that the prophet was addressing those who professed to be religious and who flattered themselves that they were in a state of salvation but in fact their hope was a fire of their own kindling and sparks created by themselves. Before I proceed to discuss the subject, let me say that as I have given notice that it was my intention to discuss the nature of true and false conversion, it will be of no use but to those who will be honest in applying it to themselves. If you mean to profit by the discourse, you must resolve to make a faithful application of it to yourselves—just as honest as if you thought you were now going to the solemn judgment. If you will do this, I may hope to be able to lead you to discover your true state and if you are now deceived, direct you in the true path to salvation. If you will not do this, I shall preach in vain and you will hear in vain.

I design to show the difference between true and false conversion and shall take up the subject in the following order: (1) show that the natural state of man is a state of pure selfishness; (2) show that the character of the converted is that of benevolence; (3) that the new birth consists in a change from selfishness to benevolence; (4) point out some things wherein saints and sinners or true and spurious converts may agree and some things in which they dif-

fer; and (5) answer some objections that may be offered against the view I have taken and conclude with some remarks.

The Natural State of Man

I am to show that the natural state of man or that in which all men are found before conversion is pure unmingled selfishness. By which I mean that they have no gospel benevolence. Selfishness is regarding one's own happiness supremely and seeking one's own good because it is his own. He who is selfish places his own happiness above other interests of greater value, such as the glory of God and the good of the universe. That mankind before conversion are in this state is evident from many considerations.

Every man knows that all other men are selfish. All the dealings of mankind are conducted on this principle. If any man overlooks this and undertakes to deal with mankind as if they were not selfish but were distinterested, he will be thought deranged.

The Converted State of Man

In a converted state, the character is that of benevolence. An individual who is converted is benevolent and not supremely selfish. Benevolence is loving the happiness of others or rather choosing the happiness of others. Benevolence is a compound word that properly signifies good willing or choosing the happiness of others. This is God's state of mind. We are told that God is love; that is, he is benevolent. Benevolence comprises his whole character. All his moral attributes are only so many modifications of benevolence. An individual who is converted is in this respect like God. I do not mean to be understood that no one is converted unless he is purely and perfectly benevolent as God is, but that the balance of his mind, his prevailing choice is benevolent. He sincerely seeks the good of others for its own sake. And by disinterested benevolence I do not mean that a person who is disinterested feels no interest in his object of pursuit, but that he seeks the happiness of others for its own sake and not for the sake of its reaction on himself in promoting his own happiness. He chooses to do good because he rejoices in the happiness of others and desires their happiness for its own sake. God is purely and disinterestedly benevolent. He does not make his creatures happy for the sake of thereby promoting his own happiness but because he loves their happiness and chooses it for its own sake. Not that he does not feel happy in promoting the happiness of his creatures but that he does not do it for the sake of his own gratification. The man who is disinterested feels happy in doing good. Otherwise doing good itself would not be virtue in him. In other words, if he did not love to do good and enjoy doing good, it would not be virtue in him.

Benevolence is holiness. It is what the law of God requires: "Thou shalt love the Lord thy God, with all thy heart and soul and strength, and thy neighbor as thyself." Just as certainly as the converted man yields obedience to the law of God and just as certainly as he is like God, he is benevolent. It is the leading feature of his character that he is seeking the happiness of others and not his own happiness as his supreme end.

From Selfishness to Benevolence

True conversion is a change from a state of supreme selfishness to benevolence. It is a change in the end of pursuit and not a mere change in the means of attaining the end. It is not true that the converted and the unconverted differ only in the means they use while both are aiming at the same end. It is not true that Gabriel and Satan are pursuing the same end and both alike aiming at their own happiness only pursuing a different way. Gabriel does not obey God for the sake of promoting his own happiness. A man may change his means and yet have the same end, his own happiness. He may do good for the sake of the temporal benefit. He may not believe in religion or in any eternity and yet may see that doing good will be for his advantage in this world. Suppose then that his eyes are opened and he sees the reality of eternity, and then he may take up religion as a means of happiness in eternity. Now everyone can see that there is no virtue in this. It is the design that gives character to the act, not the means employed to effect the design. The true and the false convert differ in this. The true convert chooses as the end of his pursuit the glory of God and the good of his kingdom. This end he chooses for its own sake because he views this as the greatest good, as a greater good than his own individual happiness. Not that he is indifferent to his own happiness but he prefers God's glory because it is a greater good. He looks on the happiness of every individual according to its real importance as far as he is capable of valuing it and he chooses the greatest good as his supreme object.

Contrasting Saints and Sinners

Now I am to show some things in which true saints and deceived persons may agree and some things in which they differ.

They may agree in *leading a strictly moral life*. The difference is in their motives. The true saint leads a moral life from love of holiness; the deceived person from selfish considerations. He uses morality as a means to an end to effect his own happiness. The true saint loves it as an end.

They may be equally *prayerful* so far as the form of praying is concerned. The difference is in their motives. The true saint loves to pray; the other prays because he hopes to derive some benefit to himself from praying. The true saint expects a benefit from praying but that is not his leading motive. The other prays from no other motive.

They may be equally *zealous in religion*. One may have great zeal because his zeal is according to knowledge and he sincerely desires and loves to promote religion for its own sake. The other may show equal zeal for the sake of having his own salvation more assured and because he is afraid of going to hell if he does not work for the Lord or to quiet his conscience and not because he loves religion for its own sake.

They may be equally *conscientious in the discharge of duty;* the true convert because he loves to do duty and the other because he dare not neglect it.

Both may pay equal *regard to what is right;* the true convert because he loves what is right and the other because he knows he cannot be saved unless he does right. He is honest in his common business transactions because it is the only way to secure his own interest. Verily, they have their reward. They get the reputation of being honest among men, but if they have no higher motive, they will have no reward from God.

They may agree in their desires in many respects. They may agree in their desires to serve God; the true convert because he loves the service of God and the deceived person for the reward as the hired servant serves his master.

They may agree in their *desires to be useful;* the true convert desiring usefulness for its own sake, the deceived person because he knows that is the way to obtain the favor of God. And then in proportion as he is awakened to the importance of having God's favor will be the intensity of his desires to be useful.

In *desires for the conversion of souls,* the true saint because it will glorify God, the deceived person to gain the favor of God. He will be actuated in this just as he is in giving money. Who ever doubted that a person might give his money to the Bible Society or the Missionary Society from selfish motives alone to procure happiness or applause or obtain the favor of God? He may just as well desire the conversion of souls and labor to promote it from motives purely selfish.

To *glorify God,* the true saint because he loves to see God glorified and the deceived person because he knows that is the way to be saved. The true convert has his heart set on the glory of God as his great end and he desires to glorify God as an end for its own sake. The other desires it as a means to *his* great end, the benefit of himself.

To *repent.* The true convert abhors sin on account of its hateful nature, because it dishonors God, and therefore he desires to repent of it. The other desires to repent because he knows that unless he does repent he will be damned.

To *believe in Jesus Christ.* The true saint desires it to glorify God and because he loves the truth for its own sake.

The other desires to believe that he may have a stronger hope of going to heaven.

To *obey God.* The true saint that he may increase in holiness, the false professor because he desires the rewards of obedience.

They may agree not only in their desires, but in their *resolutions.* They may both resolve to give up sin and to obey God and to lay themselves out in promoting religion and building up the kingdom of Christ, and they may both resolve it with great strength of purpose but with different motives.

They may also agree in their *designs.* They may both really design to glorify God and to convert men and to extend the kingdom of Christ and to have the world converted; the true saint from love to God and holiness and the other for the sake of securing his own happiness. One chooses it as an end, the other as a means to promote a selfish end.

They may both *design to be truly holy;* the true saint because he loves holiness and the deceived person because he knows that he can be happy in no other way.

They may agree not only in their desires and resolutions and designs but also in their affection toward many objects.

They may both *love the Bible;* the true saint because it is God's truth and he delights in it and feasts his soul on it, the other because he thinks it is in his own favor and is the charter of his own hopes.

They may both *love God;* the one because he sees God's character to be supremely excellent and lovely in itself and he loves it for its own sake, the other because he thinks God is his particular friend that is going to make him happy forever and he connects the idea of God with his own interest.

They may both *love Christ.* The true convert loves his character; the deceived person thinks he will save *him* from hell and give him eternal life—and why should he not love him?

They may both *love Christians;* the true convert because he sees in them the image of Christ, and the deceived person because they belong to his own denomination or because they are on his side and he feels the same interest and hopes with them.

They may also agree in hating the same things. They may both hate infidelity and oppose it strenuously—the true saint because it is opposed to God and holiness, and the deceived person because it injures an interest in which he is deeply concerned and if true, destroys all his own hopes for eternity. So they may hate error; one because it is detestable in itself and contrary to God—and the other because it is contrary to his views and opinions.

I recollect seeing in writing some time ago an attack on a minister for publishing certain opinions "because," said the writer, "these sentiments would destroy all my hopes for eternity." A very good reason indeed! as good as a selfish being needs for opposing an opinion.

They may both *hate sin;* the true convert because it is odious to God and the deceived person because it is injurious to himself. Cases have occurred where an individual has hated his own sins and yet not forsaken them. How often the drunkard, as he looks back at what he once was and contrasts his present degradation with what he might have been, abhors his drink, not for its own sake but because it has ruined him. And he still loves his cups and continues to drink, though, when he looks at their effects, he feels indignation.

They may be both *opposed to sinners.* The opposition of true saints is a benevolent opposition, viewing and abhorring their character and conduct as calculated to subvert the kingdom of God.

The other is opposed to sinners because they are opposed to the religion he has espoused and because they are not on his side.

So they may both rejoice in the same things. Both may rejoice in the prosperity of Zion and the conversion of souls; the true convert because he has his heart set on it and loves it for its own sake as the greatest good, and the deceived person because that particular thing in which he thinks he has such a great interest is advancing.

Both may mourn and feel *distressed at the low state of religion in the church;* the true convert because God is dishonored, and the deceived person because his own soul is not happy or because religion is not in favor.

Both may love *the society of the saints;* the true convert because his soul enjoys their spiritual conversation, the other because he hopes to derive some advantage from their company. The first enjoys it because out of the abundance of the heart the mouth speaketh; the other because he loves to talk about the great interest he feels in religion and the hope he has of going to heaven.

Both may love *to attend religious meetings;* the true saint because his heart delights in acts of worship, in prayer and praise, in hearing the word of God, and in communion with God and his saints, and the other because he thinks a religious meeting a good place to prop up his hope. He may have a hundred reasons for loving them and yet not at all for their own sake or because he loves in itself the worship and the service of God.

Both may *find pleasure in the duties of the closet.* The true saint loves his closet because he draws near to God and finds delight in communion with God where there are no embarrassments to keep him from going right to God and conversing. The deceived person finds a kind of satisfaction in it because it is his duty to pray in secret and he feels a self-righteous satisfaction in doing it. Nay, he may feel a certain pleasure in it from a kind of excitement of the mind which he mistakes for communion with God.

They may both *love the doctrines of grace;* the true saint because they are so glorious to God, the other because he thinks them a guarantee of his own salvation.

They may both *love the precept of God's law;* the true saint because it is so excellent, so holy, and just, and good; the other because he thinks it will make him happy if he loves it and he does it as a means of happiness.

Both may *consent to the penalty of the law.* The true saint consents to it in his own case because he feels it to be just in itself for God to send him to hell. The deceived person because he thinks *he* is in no danger from it. He feels a respect for it because he knows that it is right and his conscience approves it but he has never consented to it in his own case.

They may be equally *liberal in giving* to benevolent societies. None of you doubt that two men may give equal sums to a benevolent object but from totally different motives. One gives to do good and would be just as willing to give as not if he knew that no other living person would give. The other gives for the credit of it or to quiet his conscience or because he hopes to purchase the favor of God.

They may be equally *self-denying* in many things. Self-denial is not confined to true saints. Look at the sacrifices and self-denials of the Mohammedans going on their pilgrimage to Mecca. Look at the heathen throwing themselves under the car of Juggernaut. Look at the poor ignorant papists going up and down over the sharp stones on their bare knees till they stream with blood. A Protestant congregation will not contend that there is any religion in that. But is there not self-denial? The true saint denies himself for the sake of doing more good to others. He is more set on this than on his own indulgence or his own interest. The deceived person may go equal lengths but from purely selfish motives.

They may both be *willing to suffer* martyrdom. Read the lives of the martyrs and you will have no doubt that some were willing to suffer from a wrong idea of the rewards of martyrdom and would rush upon their own destruction because they were persuaded it was the sure road to eternal life.

The Test of Motive

In all these cases, the motives of one class are directly over against the other. The difference lies in the choice of different *ends*. One chooses his own interest, the other chooses God's interest as his chief end. For a person to pretend that both these classes are aiming at the same end is to say that an impenitent sinner is just as benevolent as a real Christian or that a Christian is not benevolent like God but is only seeking his own happiness and seeking it in religion rather than in the world.

And here is the proper place to answer an inquiry which is often made: "If these two classes of persons may be alike in so many particulars, how are we to know our own real character or to tell to which class we belong? We know that the heart is deceitful above all things and desperately wicked, and how are we to know whether we love God and holiness for their own sake or whether we are seeking the favor of God and aiming at heaven for our own benefit?" I answer:

The Test of Conduct

If we are truly benevolent, it will appear in our daily transactions. This character, if real, will show itself in our business if anywhere. If selfishness rules our conduct there, as sure as God reigns we are truly selfish. If in our dealings with men we are selfish, we are so in our dealings with God. "For who so loveth not his brother, whom he hath seen, how can he love God, whom he hath not seen?" Religion is not merely love to God but love to man also. And if our daily transactions show us to be selfish, we are unconverted, or else benevolence is not essential to religion and a man can be religious without loving his neighbor as himself.

The Test of Attitude

If you are disinterested in religion, religious duties will not be a task to you. You will not go about religion as the laboring man goes to his toil for the sake of a living. The laboring man takes pleasure in his labor but it is not for its own sake. He would not do it if he could help it. In its own nature it is a task and if he takes any pleasure in it, it is for its anticipated results, the support and comfort of his family or the increase of his property.

Precisely such is the state of some persons in regard to religion. They go to it as the sick man takes his medicine because they desire its effects and they know they must have it or perish. It is a task that they never would do for its own sake. Suppose men love labor as a child loves play. They would do it all day long and never be tired of doing it without any other inducement than the pleasure in doing it. So it is in religion; where it is loved for its own sake, there is no weariness in it.

If selfishness is the prevailing character of your religion, it will take sometimes one form and sometimes another. For instance: If it is a time of general coldness in the church, real converts will still enjoy their own secret communion with God, although there may not be so much doing to attract notice in public. But the deceived person will then invariably be found driving after the world. Now let the true saints rise up and make a noise and speak their joys aloud so that religion begins to be talked of again, and perhaps the deceived professor will soon begin to bustle about and appear to be even more zealous than the true saint. He is impelled by his convictions and not affections. When there is no public interest, he feels no conviction; but when the church awakes, he is convicted and compelled to stir about to keep his conscience quiet. It is only selfishness in another form.

The Test of Motivation

If you are selfish, your enjoyment in religion will depend mainly on the strength of your hopes of heaven and not on the exercise of your affections. Your enjoyments are not in the employments of religion themselves but of a vastly different kind from those of the true saint. They are mostly from anticipating. When your evidences are renewed and you feel very certain of going to heaven, then you enjoy religion a good deal. It depends on your hope and not on your love for the things for which you hope. You hear persons tell of their having no enjoyment in religion when they lose their hopes. The reason is plain. If they loved religion for its own sake, their enjoyment would not depend on their hope. A person who loves his employment is happy anywhere. And if you loved the employments of religion,

you would be happy if God should put you in hell, provided he would only let you employ yourself in religion. If you might pray and praise God, you would feel that you could be happy anywhere in the universe, for you would still be doing the things in which your happiness mainly consists. If the duties of religion are not the things in which you feel enjoyment and if all your enjoyment depends on your hope, you have no true religion; it is all selfishness.

I do not say that true saints do not enjoy their hope. But that is not the great thing with them. They think very little about their own hopes. Their thoughts are employed about something else. The deceived person, on the contrary, is sensible that he does not enjoy the duties of religion but only that the more he does, the more confident he is of heaven. He takes only such kind of enjoyment in it as a man does who thinks that by great labor he shall have great wealth.

If you are selfish in religion, your enjoyments will be chiefly from anticipation. The true saint already enjoys the peace of God and has heaven begun in his soul. He has not merely the prospect of it, but eternal life actually begun in him. He has that faith which is the very substance of things hoped for. Nay, he has the very feelings of heaven in him. He anticipates joys higher in degree but the same in kind. He knows that he has heaven begun in him and is not obliged to wait till he dies to taste the joys of eternal life. His enjoyment is in proportion to his holiness and not in proportion to his hope.

Another difference by which it may be known whether you are selfish in religion is this—that the deceived person has only a purpose of obedience, and the other has a preference of obedience. This is an important distinction and I fear few persons make it. Multitudes have a purpose of obedience who have no true preference of obedience. Preference is actual choice or obedience of heart. You often hear individuals speak of their having had a purpose to do their or that act of obedience but failed to do it. And they will tell you how difficult it is to execute their purpose. The true saint, on the other hand, really prefers and in his heart chooses obedience, and therefore he finds it easy to obey. The one has a purpose to obey like that which Paul had before he was converted, as he tells us in the seventh chapter of Romans. He had a strong purpose of obedience but did not obey because his heart was not in it. The true convert prefers obedience for its own sake; he actually chooses it and does it. The other purposes to be holy because he knows that is the only way to be happy. The true saint chooses holiness for its own sake, and he is holy.

The Test of Confidence

The true convert and the deceived person also differ in their faith. The true saint has a confidence in the general character of God that leads him to unqualified submission to God. A great deal is said about the kinds of faith but without much meaning. True confidence in the Lord's special promises depends on confidence in God's general character. There are only two principles on which any government, human or Divine, is obeyed: fear and confidence. No matter whether it is the government of a family or a ship or a nation or a universe. All obedience springs from one of these two principles. In the one case, individuals obey from hope of reward and fear of the penalty; in the other, from that confidence in the character of the government which works by love. One child obeys his parent from confidence in his parent. He has faith which

works by love. The other yields an outward obedience from hope and fear. The true convert has this faith or confidence in God that leads him to obey God because he loves God. This is the obedience of faith. He has that confidence in God that he submits himself wholly into the hands of God.

The other has only a partial faith and only a partial submission. The devil has a partial faith. He believes and trembles. A person may believe that Christ came to save sinners and on that ground may submit to him to be saved, while he does not submit wholly to him to be governed and disposed of. His submission is only on condition that he shall be saved. It is never with that unreserved confidence in God's whole character that leads him to say, "Thy will be done." He only submits to be saved. His religion is the religion of law. The other is gospel religion. One is selfish, the other benevolent. Here lies the true difference between the two classes. The religion of one is outward and hypocritical. The other is that of the heart, holy and acceptable to God.

I will only mention one difference more. If your religion is selfish, you will rejoice particularly in the conversion of sinners where your own agency is concerned in it but will have very little satisfaction in it where it is through the agency of others. The selfish person rejoices when he is active and successful in converting sinners because he thinks he shall have a great reward. But instead of delighting in it when done by others, he will be even envious. The true saint sincerely delights to have others useful and rejoices when sinners are converted by the instrumentality of others as much as if it [were] his own. There are some who will take interest in a revival only so far as themselves are connected with it, while it would seem they had rather sinners should remain unconverted than that they should be saved by the instrumentality of an evangelist or a minister of another denomination. The true spirit of a child of God is to say, "Send, Lord, by whom thou wilt send—only let souls be saved, and thy name glorified!"

I am to answer some objections which are made against this view of the subject.

Objection 1.

"Am I not to have any regard to my own happiness?"

Answer.

It is right to regard your own happiness according to its relative value. Put it in this scale by the side of the glory of God and the good of the universe and then decide and give it the value which belongs to it. This is precisely what God does. And this is what he means when he commands you to love your neighbor as yourself.

And again: You will in fact promote your own happiness precisely in proportion as you leave it out of view. Your happiness will be in proportion to your disinterestedness. True happiness consists mainly in the gratification of virtuous desires. There may be pleasure in gratifying desires that are selfish, but it is not real happiness. But to be virtuous, your desires must be disinterested. Suppose a man sees a beggar in the street; there he sits on the curbstone, cold and hungry, without friends and ready to perish. The man's feelings are touched and he steps into a grocery close by and buys him a loaf of bread. At once the countenance of the beggar lights up and he looks unutterable gratitude. Now it is plain to be seen that the gratification of the man in the act is precisely in proportion to the singleness of his motive. If he did it purely and solely out of benevolence, his gratification is complete

in the act itself. But if he did it partly to make it known that he is a charitable and humane person, then his happiness is not complete until the deed is published to others. Suppose here is a sinner in his sins; he is truly wicked and truly wretched. Your compassion is excited and you convert and save him. If your motives were to obtain honor among men and to secure the favor of God, you are not completely happy until the deed is told and perhaps put in the newspaper. But if you wished purely to save a soul from death, then as soon as you see that done, your gratification is complete and your joy unmingled. So it is in all religious duties; your happiness is precisely in proportion as you are disinterested.

If you aim at doing good for its own sake then you will be happy in proportion as you do good. But if you aim directly at your own happiness and if you do good simply as a means of securing your own happiness, you will fail. You will be like the child pursuing his own shadow; he can never overtake it because it always keeps just so far before him. Suppose in the case I have mentioned, you have no desire to relieve the beggar but regard simply the applause of a certain individual. They you will feel no pleasure at all in the relief of the beggar; but when that individual hears of it and commends it, then you are gratified. But you are not gratified in the thing itself. Or suppose you aim at the conversion of sinners; but if it is not love to sinners that leads you to do it, how can the conversion of sinners make you happy? It has no tendency to gratify the desire that prompted the effort. The truth is God has so constituted the mind of man that it must seek the happiness of others as its end or it cannot be happy. Here is the true reason why all the world, seeking their own happiness and not the happiness of others, fail of their end. It is always just so far before them. If they would leave off seeking their own happiness and lay themselves out to do good, they would be happy.

Objection 2.

"Did not Christ regard the joy set before him? And did not Moses also have respect unto the recompense of reward? And does not the Bible say we love God because he first loved us?"

Answer 1.

It is true that Christ despised the shame and endured the cross and had regard to the joy set before him. But what was the joy set before him? Not his own salvation, not his own happiness, but the great good he would do in the salvation of the world. He was perfectly happy in himself. But the happiness of others was what he aimed at. This was the joy set before him. And that he obtained.

Answer 2.

Moses had respect to the recompense of reward. But was that his own comfort? Far from it. The recompense of reward was the salvation of the people of Israel. What did he say? When God proposed to destroy the nation and make of him a great nation, had Moses been selfish he would have said, "That is right, Lord; be it unto thy servant according to thy word." But what does he say? Why, his heart was so set on the salvation of his people and the glory of God that he would not think of it for a moment, but said, "If thou wilt, forgive their sin; and if not, blot me I pray thee out of thy book, which thou hast written." And in another case when God said he would destroy them and make of Moses a greater and mightier nation, Moses thought of God's glory and said, "Then the Egyptians shall hear of it, and all the nations will say, Because the Lord

was not able to bring this people into the land." He could not bear to think of having his own interest exalted at the expense of God's glory. It was really a greater reward to his benevolent mind to have God glorified and the children of Israel saved than any personal advantage whatever to himself could be.

Answer 3.

Where it is said, "We love him because he first loved us" the language plainly bears two interpretations; either that his love to us has provided the way for our return and the influence that brought us to love him or that we love him for his favor shown to ourselves. That the latter is not the meaning is evident because Jesus Christ has so expressly reprobated the principle in his sermon on the mount: "If ye love them which love you, what thank have ye? Do not the publicans the same?" If we love God not for his character but for his favors to us, Jesus Christ has written us reprobate.

Objection 3.

"Does not the Bible offer happiness as the reward of virtue?"

Answer.

The Bible speaks of happiness as the result of virtue but no where declares virtue to consist in the pursuit of one's own happiness. The Bible is everywhere inconsistent with this and represents virtue to consist in doing good to others. We can see by the philosophy of the mind that it must be so. If a person desires the good of others, he will be happy in proportion as he gratifies that desire. Happiness is the result of virtue, but virtue does not consist in the direct pursuit of one's own happiness but is wholly inconsistent with it.

Objection 4.

"God aims at our happiness and shall we be more benevolent than God? Should we not be like God? May we not aim at the same thing that God aims at? Should we not be seeking the same end that God seeks?"

Answer.

This objection is specious but futile and rotten. God is benevolent to others. He aims at the happiness of others and at our happiness. And to be like him, we must aim at, that is, delight in his happiness and glory and the honor and glory of the universe according to their real value.

Objection 5.

"Why does the Bible appeal continually to the hopes and fears of men, if a regard to our own happiness is not a proper motive to action?"

Answer 1.

The Bible appeals to the constitutional susceptibilities of men not to their selfishness. Man dreads harm and it is not wrong to avoid it. We may have a due regard to our own happiness according to its value.

Answer 2.

And again: mankind are so besotted with sin that God cannot get their attention to consider his true character and the reasons for loving him unless he appeals to their hopes and fears. But when they are awakened, then he presents the gospel to them. When a minister has preached the terrors of the Lord til he has got his hearers alarmed and aroused so that they will give attention, he has gone far enough in that line, and then he ought to spread out all the character of God before them to engage their hearts to love him for his own excellence.

Objection 6.

"Do not the inspired writers say, Repent, and believe the gospel, and you shall be saved?"

Answer.

Yes; but they require "true" repentance, that is to forsake sin because it is hateful in itself. It is not true repentance to forsake sin on condition of pardon or to say, "I will be sorry for my sins if you will forgive me." So they require true faith and true submission, not conditional faith or partial submission. This is what the Bible insists on. It says he shall be saved but it must be disinterested repentance and disinterested submission.

Objection 7.

"Does not the gospel hold out pardon as a motive to submission?"

Answer.

This depends on the sense in which you use the term *motive*. If you mean that God spreads out before men his whole character and the whole truth of the case as reasons to engage the sinner's love and repentance, I say, Yes; his compassion and willingness to pardon are reasons for loving God because they are a part of his glorious excellence which we are bound to love. But if you mean by "motive" a condition and that the sinner is to repent on condition he shall be pardoned, then I say that the Bible nowhere holds out any such view of the matter. It never authorizes a sinner to say, "I will repent *if* you will forgive," and no where offers pardon as a motive to repentance in such a sense as this.

With two short remarks I will close.

We see from this subject why it is that

professors of religion have such different views of the nature of the gospel. Some view it as a mere matter of accommodation to mankind by which God is rendered less strict than he was under the law, so that they may be fashionable or worldly and the gospel will come in and make up the deficiencies and save them. The other class view the gospel as a provision of divine benevolence, having for its main design to destroy sin and promote holiness and that therefore so far from making it proper for them to be less holy than they ought to be under the law, its whole value consists in its power to make them holy.

We see why some people are so much more anxious to convert sinners than to see the church sanctified and God glorified by the good works of his people. Many feel a natural sympathy for sinners and wish to have them saved from hell; and if that is gained, they have no further concern. But true saints are most affected by sin as dishonoring God. And they are most distressed to see Christians sin because it dishonors God more. Some people seem to care but little how the church live if they can only see the work of conversion go forward. They are not anxious to have God honored. It shows that they are not actuated by the love of holiness but by a mere compassion for sinners.

Salvation consists of sanctification, justification, eternal life, and glory. It is achieved by faith and not works, thereby making it totally dependent upon God as the agent and man as the receiver.

The need for salvation springs from the fact that Adam, being the natural head of the human race, fell into sin, bringing upon his posterity the curse of sin. The remedy that God has provided for mankind is his son, Jesus Christ. The death of Christ on the cross secures eternal life for all who accept him by faith. Christ's righteousness is provided for us so that we also are declared righteous by God.

CHAPTER EIGHT

The Way of Salvation

Sirs, what must I do to be saved? And they said, Believe on the Lord Jesus Christ. Who of God is made unto us wisdom, and righteousness, and sanctification, and redemption (Acts 16:30–31, with 1 Cor. 1:30).

There can be no objection to putting these texts together in this manner as only a clause in the first of them is omitted which is not essential to the sense and which is irrelevant to my present purpose.

In the passage first quoted, the apostle tells the inquiring jailer who wished to know what he must do to be saved, "Believe on the Lord Jesus Christ and thou shalt be saved." And in the other he adds the explanatory remark telling what a Savior Jesus Christ is, "Who of God is made unto us wisdom, and righteousness, and sanctification, and redemption." The following is the order in which I design to discuss the subject tonight: (1) show what salvation is and (2) show the way of salvation.

What is salvation? Salvation includes several things—sanctification, justification, and eternal life and glory. The two prime ideas are sanctification and justification. Sanctification is the purifying of the mind or making it holy. Justification relates to the manner in which we are accepted and treated by God.

The way of salvation: it is by faith, in opposition to works. Here I design to take a brief view of the gospel plan of salvation and exhibit it especially in contrast with the original plan on which it was proposed to save mankind.

A Covenant of Works?

Originally the human race was put on the foundation of law for salvation, so that if saved at all, they were to be saved on the ground of perfect and eternal obedience to the law of God. Adam was the natural head of the race. It has been supposed by many that there was a covenant made with Adam such as this, that if he continued to obey the law for a limited period all his posterity should be confirmed in holiness and happiness forever. What the reason is for this belief I am unable to ascertain; I am not aware that the doctrine is taught in the Bible. And if it is true, the condition of mankind now does not differ materially from what it was at first. If the salvation of the race originally turned wholly on the obedience of one man, I do not see how it could be called a covenant of works so far as the race is concerned. For if their weal or woe was suspended on the conduct of one head, it was a covenant of grace to them in the same manner that the present system is a covenant of grace. For according to that view, all that related to works depended on one man just as it does under the gospel; and the rest of the race had no more to do with works than they have now but all that related to works was done by the representative. Now I have supposed, and there is nothing in the Bible to the contrary, that if Adam had continued in obedience forever, his posterity would have stood forever on the same ground and must have obeyed the law themselves forever in order to be saved. It may have been that if he had obeyed always, the natural influence of his example would have brought about such a state of things that as a matter of fact all his posterity would have continued in holiness. But the salvation of each individual would still have depended on his own works. But if the works of the first father were to be so set to the account of the race that on account of his obedience they were to be secured in holiness and happiness forever, I do not see wherein it differs materially from the covenant of grace or the gospel.

As a matter of fact, Adam was the natural head of the human race and his sin has involved them in its consequences but not on the principle that his sin is literally accounted their sin. The truth is simply this, that from the relation in which he stood as their natural head, as a matter of fact his sin has resulted in the sin and ruin of his posterity. I suppose that mankind were originally all under a covenant of works and that Adam was not so their head or representative that his obedience or disobedience involved them irresistibly in sin and condemnation, irrespective of their own acts. As a fact it resulted so that "by one man's disobedience many were made sinners," as the apostle tells us in the fifth [chapter] of Romans. So that when Adam had fallen, there was not the least hope by the law of saving any of mankind. Then was revealed *the plan*, which had been provided in the counsels of eternity on foresight of this event for saving mankind by a proceeding of mere grace. Salvation was now placed on an entire new foundation by a covenant of redemption. You will find this covenant in the eighty-ninth Psalm and other places in the Old Testament. This,

you will observe, is a covenant between the Father and the Son regarding the salvation of mankind and is the foundation of another covenant, the covenant of grace. In the covenant of redemption, man is no party at all but merely the subject of the covenant, the parties being God the Father and the Son. In this covenant, the Son is made the head or representative of his people. Adam was the natural head of the human family and Christ is the covenant head of his church.

The Covenant of Grace

On this covenant of redemption was founded the covenant of grace. In the covenant of redemption, the Son stipulated with the Father to work out an atonement; and the Father stipulated that he should have a seed or nature; whatever he has done, either as God or man, is given to us by covenant or promise and is absolutely ours. I desire you should understand this. The church as a body has never yet understood the fullness and richness of this covenant and that all there is in Christ is made over to us in the covenant of grace.

And here let me say that we receive this grace by faith. It is not by works, by anything we do more or less, previous to the exercise of faith that we become interested in this righteousness. But as soon as we exercise faith, all that Christ has done, all there is of Christ, all that is contained in the covenant of grace, becomes ours by faith. Hence it is that the inspired writers make so much of faith. Faith is the voluntary compliance on our part with the condition of the covenant. It is the eye that discerns, the hand that takes hold, the medium by which we possess the blessings of the covenant. By the act of faith, the soul becomes actually possessed of all that is embraced in that act of faith. If there is not enough received to break the bonds of sin and set the soul at once at liberty, it is because the act has not embraced enough of what Christ is and what he has done.

Christ Our Wisdom

I have read the verse from Corinthians for the purpose of remarking on some of the fundamental things contained in this covenant of grace. "Of him are ye in Christ Jesus, who of God is made unto us wisdom and righteousness and sanctification and redemption." When Christ is received and believed on, he is made to us what is meant by these several particulars. But what is meant? How and in what sense is Christ our wisdom and righteousness and sanctification and redemption? I will dwell a few moments on each.

This is a very peculiar verse, and my mind has long dwelt on it with great anxiety to know its exact and full meaning. I have prayed over it as much as over any passage in the Bible that I might be enlightened to understand its real import. I have long been in the habit when my mind fastened on any passage that I did not understand, to pray over it till I felt satisfied. I have never dared to preach on this verse because I never felt fully satisfied that I understood it. I think I understand it now. At all events, I am willing to give my opinion on it. And if I have any right knowledge respecting its meaning, I am sure I have received it from the Spirit of God.

In what sense is Christ our wisdom? He is often called "the Wisdom of God." And in the Book of Proverbs he is called Wisdom. But how is he made to us wisdom?

One idea contained in it is that we have absolutely all the benefits of his wisdom; and if we exercise the faith we ought, we are just as certain to be directed by it, and it is in all respects just as well for us as if we had the same wisdom originally of our own. Else it cannot be true that he is made unto us wisdom. As he is the infinite source of wisdom, how can it be said that he is made unto us wisdom unless we are partakers of his wisdom and have it guaranteed to us; so that at any time if we trust in him, we may have it as certainly and in any degree we need to guide us infallibly as if we had it originally ourselves? That is what we need from the gospel and what the gospel must furnish to be suited to our necessities. And the man who has not learned this has not known anything as he ought. If he thinks his own theorizing and speculating are going to bring him to any right knowledge on the subject of religion, he knows nothing at all as yet. His carnal, earthly heart can no more study out the realities of religion so as to get any available knowledge of them than the heart of a beast. "What man knoweth the things of a man, save the spirit of a man which is in him? Even so the things of God knoweth no man but the Spirit of God." What can we know without experience of the character or Spirit of God? Do you say, "We can reason about God." What if we do reason? What can reason do here? Suppose here was a mind that was all pure intellect and had no other powers, and I should undertake to teach that pure intellect what it was to love. I could lecture on it and instruct that pure intellect in the words so that it could reason and philosophize about love, and yet anybody can see that it is impossible to put that pure intellect in possession of the idea of what love is unless it not only has power to exercise love but has actually exercised it! It is just as if I should talk about colors to a man born blind. He hears the word, but what idea can he attach to it unless he has seen? It is impossible to get the idea home to his mind of the difference of colors. The term is a mere word.

Just so it is in religion. One whose mind has not experienced it may reason upon it. He may demonstrate the perfections of God as he would demonstrate a proposition in Euclid. But that which is the spirit and life of the gospel can no more be carried to the mind by mere words without experience than love to a pure intellect or colors to a man born blind. You may so far give him the letter as to crush him down to hell with conviction, but to give the spiritual meaning of things without the Spirit of God is as absurd as to lecture a blind man about colors.

These two things, then, are contained in the idea of wisdom. As Christ is our representative, we are interested in all his wisdom and all the wisdom he has is exercised for us. His infinite wisdom is actually employed for our benefit. And that his wisdom, just as much as is needed, is guaranteed to be always ready to be imparted to us whenever we exercise faith in him for wisdom. From his infinite fullness, in this respect, we may receive all we need. And if we do not receive from him the wisdom which we need in any and every case, it is because we do not exercise faith.

Righteousness and Sanctification

He is made unto us righteousness. What is the meaning of this? Here my mind has long labored to understand the distinction which the apostle intended to make between righteousness and sanctification. Righteousness means holiness or obedience to law and sanctification means the same.

My present view of the distinction aimed at is that by his being made unto us righteousness, the apostle meant to be understood that Christ is our *outward* righteousness; or that his obedience is, under the covenant of grace, accounted to us. Not in the sense that on the footing of justice he obeyed "for us," and God accounts us just because our substitute has obeyed; but that we are so interested in his obedience that as a matter of grace, we are treated as if we had ourselves obeyed.

You are aware there is a view of this subject which is maintained by some different from this; that the righteousness of Christ is so imputed to us that we are considered as having been always holy. It was at one time extensively maintained that righteousness was so imputed to us that we had a right to demand salvation on the score of justice. My view of the matter is entirely different. It is that Christ's righteousness becomes ours by gift. God has so united us to Christ as on his account to treat us with favor. It is just like a case where a father had done some signal service to his country and the government thinks it proper to reward such signal service with signal reward; and not only is the individual himself rewarded, but all his family receive favors on his account because they are the children of a father who had greatly benefited his country. Human governments do this and the ground of it is very plain. It is just so in the divine government. Christ's disciples are in such a sense considered one with him, and God is so highly delighted with the signal service he has done the kingdom, from the circumstances under which he became a Savior, that God accounts his righteousness to them as if it were their own; or in other words, treats them just as he would treat Christ himself. As the government of the country under certain circumstances treats the son of a father who had greatly benefited the country just as they would treat the father and bestow on him the same favors. You will bear in mind that I am now speaking of what I called the outward righteousness; I mean the reason out of the individual why God accepts and saves them that believe in Christ. And this reason includes both the obedience of Christ to the law and his obedience unto death or suffering upon the cross to make atonement.

In what sense is Christ made unto us sanctification? Sanctification is inward purity. And the meaning is that he is our inward purity. The control which Christ himself exercises over us, his Spirit working in us to will and to do, his shedding his love abroad in our hearts, so controlling us that we are ourselves through the faith which is of the operation of God made actually holy.

I wish you to get the exact here. When it is said that Christ is our sanctification or our holiness, it is meant that he is the author of our holiness. He is not only the procuring cause by his atonement and intercession, but by his direct intercourse with the soul he himself produces holiness. He is not the remote but the immediate cause of our being sanctified. He works our works in us, not by suspending our own agency, but he so controls our minds by the influences of his Spirit in us in a way perfectly consistent with our freedom as to sanctify us. And this also is received by faith. It is by faith that Christ is received and enthroned as *king* in our hearts; when the mind, from confidence in Christ, just yields itself up to him to be led by his Spirit and guided and controlled by his hand. The act of the mind that thus throws the soul into the hand of Christ for sanctification is faith. Nothing is wanting but for the mind to break off from any confidence in itself and to give itself up to him, to be led and controlled by him absolutely, just as the child puts out its little hand to its

father to have him lead it anywhere he pleases. If the child is distrustful or not willing to be led or if it has confidence in its own wisdom and strength, it will break away and try to run alone. But if all that self-confidence fails, it will cease from its own efforts and come and give itself up to its father again to be led entirely at his will. I suppose this is similar to the act of faith by which an individual gives his mind up to be led and controlled by Christ. He ceases from his own efforts to guide and control and sanctify himself and just gives himself up as yielding as air and leaves himself in the hands of Christ as his sanctification.

It is said Christ is made of God unto us redemption. What are we to understand by that? Here the apostle plainly refers to the Jewish practice of redeeming estates or redeeming relatives that had been sold for debt. When an estate had been sold out of the family or an individual had been deprived of liberty for debt, they could be redeemed by paying the price of redemption. There are very frequent allusions in the Bible to this practice of redemption. And where Christ is spoken of as our redemption, I suppose it means just what it says. While we are in our sins under the law, we are sold as slaves in the hand of public justice, bound over to death, and have no possible way to redeem ourselves from the curse of the law. Now Christ makes himself the price of our redemption. In other words, he is our redemption money; he buys us out from under the law by paying himself as a ransom. Christ hath redeemed us from the curse of the law, being made a curse for us and thus, also, redeems us from the power of sin. But I must leave this train of thought and return to a consideration of the plan of salvation.

Under this covenant of grace, our own works or anything that we do or can do as works of law have no more to do with our salvation than if we had never existed. I wish your minds to separate entirely between salvation by works and salvation by grace. Our salvation by grace is founded on a reason entirely separate from and out of ourselves. Before it depended on ourselves. Now we receive salvation as a free gift solely on account of Jesus Christ. He is the sole author, ground, and reason of our salvation. Whether we love God or do not love God so far as it is a ground of our salvation is of no account. The whole is entirely a matter of grace through Jesus Christ. You will not understand me as saying that there is no necessity for love to God or good works. I know that "without holiness no man shall see the Lord." But the necessity of holiness is not at all on this ground. Our own holiness does not enter at all into the ground or reason for our acceptance and salvation. We are not going to be indebted to Christ for a while until we are sanctified and all the rest of the time stand in our own righteousness. But however perfect and holy we may become in this life or to all eternity, Jesus Christ will forever be the sole reason in the universe why we are not in hell. Because however holy we may become, it will be forever true that we have sinned and in the eye of justice nothing in us short of our eternal damnation can satisfy the law. But now Jesus Christ has undertaken to help, and he forever remains the sole ground of our salvation.

According to this plan, we have the benefit of his obedience to the law just as if he had obeyed for us. Not that he did obey for us in the distinction from himself, but we have the benefits of his obedience, by the gift of grace, the same as if he had done so.

I meant to dwell on the idea of Christ as our "light" and our "life" and our "strength." But I perceive there is not time tonight. I wish to touch a little on this question, "How does faith put us in possession of Christ in all these relations?"

Possessing Christ

Faith in Christ puts us in possession of Christ as the sum and substance of the blessings of the gospel. Christ was the very blessing promised in the Abrahamic covenant. And throughout the Scriptures he is held forth as the sum and substance of all God's favors to man. He is "the Bread of Life," "the Water of Life," "our Strength," "our All." The gospel has taxed all the powers of language to describe the vast variety of his relations and to show that faith is to put believers in possession of Jesus Christ in all these relations.

The manner in which faith puts the mind in possession of all these blessings is this: it annihilates all those things that stand in the way of our intercourse with Christ. He says, "Behold, I stand at the door and knock, if any man hears my voice and open the door, I will come in to him and will sup with him, and he with me." Here is a door, an obstacle to our intercourse with Christ, something that stands in the way. Take the particular of wisdom. Why do we not receive Christ as our wisdom? Because we depend on our own wisdom and think we have ourselves some available knowledge of the things of God, and as long as we depend on this we keep the door shut. That is the door. Now let us just throw this all away and give up all wisdom of our own and see how infinitely empty we are of any available knowledge as much so as a beast that perisheth as to the way of salvation until Christ shall teach us. Until we feel this, there is a door between us and Christ. We have something of our own instead of coming and throwing ourselves perfectly into the hands of Christ; we just come to him to help out our own wisdom.

How does faith put us in possession of the righteousness of Christ? This is the way. Until our mind takes hold of the righteousness of Christ, we are alive to our own righteousness. We are naturally engaged in working out a righteousness of our own, and until we cease entirely from our own works by absolutely throwing ourselves on Christ for righteousness, we do not come to Christ. Christ will not patch up our own righteousness to make it answer the purpose. If we depend on our prayers, our tears, our charities, or anything we have done or expect to do, he will not receive us. We must have none of this. But the moment an individual takes hold on Christ, he receives and appropriates all Christ's righteousness as his own as a perfect and unchangeable reason for his acceptance with God by grace.

It is just so with regard to sanctification and redemption. I cannot dwell on them so particularly as I wished. Until an individual receives Christ, he does not cease from his own works. The moment he does that by this very act he throws the entire responsibility upon Christ. The moment the mind does fairly yield itself up to Christ, the responsibility comes upon him just as the person who undertakes to conduct a blind man is responsible for his safe conduct. The believer by the act of faith pledges Christ for his obedience and sanctification. By giving himself up to Christ, all the veracity of the Godhead is put at stake that he shall be led right and made holy.

And with regard to redemption, as long as the sinner supposes that his own sufferings, his prayers, or tears, or mental agony are of any avail, he will never receive Christ. But as soon as he receives Christ, he sinks down as lost and condemned—as in fact a dead person, unless redeemed by Christ.

REMARKS

There is no such thing as spiritual life in us or anything acceptable to God until we actually believe in Christ. The very act of believing receives Christ as just that influence which alone can wake up the mind to spiritual life.

We are nothing as Christians any farther than we believe in Christ.

Many seem to be waiting to do something first before they receive Christ. Some wait to become more dead to the world. Some to get a broken heart. Some to get their doubts cleared up before they come to Christ. *This is a grand mistake.* It is expecting to do that first before faith which is only the result of faith. Your heart will not be broken, your doubts will not be cleared up, you will never die to the world until you believe. The moment you grasp the things of Christ, your mind will see as in the light of eternity the emptiness of the world, of reputation, riches, honor, and pleasure. To expect this first, preparatory to the exercise of faith, is beginning at the wrong end. It is seeking that as a preparation for faith which is always the result of faith.

Perfect faith will produce perfect love. When the mind duly recognizes Christ and receives him in his various relations, when the faith is unwavering and the views clear, there will be nothing left in the mind contrary to the law of God.

Abiding faith would produce abiding love. Faith increasing would produce increasing love. And here you ought to observe that love may be perfect at all times and yet be in different degrees at different times. An individual may love God perfectly and eternally and yet his love may increase in vigor to all eternity as I suppose it will. As the saints in glory see more and more of God's excellences, they will love him more and more and yet will have perfect love all the time. That is there will be nothing inconsistent with love in the mind while the degrees of love will be different as their views of the character of God unfold. As God opens to their view the wonders of his glorious benevolence, they will have their souls thrilled with new love to God. In this life the exercises of love vary greatly in degree. Sometimes God unfolds to his saints the wonders of his government and gives them such views as well-nigh prostrate the body, and then love is greatly raised in degree. And yet the love may have been perfect before, that is the love of God was supreme and single without any mixture of inconsistent affections. And it is not unreasonable to suppose that it will be so to all eternity, that occasions will occur in which the love of the saints will be brought into more lively exercise by new unfoldings of God's glory. As God develops to them wonder after wonder, their love will be increased indefinitely and they will have continually enlarged accessions of its strength and fervor to all eternity.

I designed to mention some things on the subject of instantaneous and pro-gressive sanctification. But there is not time tonight and they must be postponed.

You see, beloved, from this subject the way in which you can be made holy and when you can be sanctified. Whenever you come to Christ and receive him for all that he is and accept a whole salvation by grace, you will have all that Christ is to you, wisdom, and righteousness, and sanctification, and redemption. There is nothing but unbelief to hinder you from now enjoying it all. You need not wait for any preparation. There is no preparation that is of any avail. You must *receive* a whole salvation as a *free gift*. When will you thus lay hold on Christ? When will you believe? Faith, true faith, always works by love and purifies the heart and overcomes the world. Whenever you find any difficulty in your way, you may know what is the matter. It is a want of faith. No matter what may befall you outwardly, if you find yourself thrown back in religion or your mind thrown all into confusion, unbelief is the cause and faith the remedy. If you lay hold on Christ and keep hold, all the devils in hell can never drive you away from God or put out your light. But if you let unbelief prevail, you may go on in this miserable, halting way, talking about sanctification, using words without knowledge, and dishonoring God till you die.

FOR ADDITIONAL INFORMATION

Beardsley, Frank G. *A History of American Revivals*. New York, American Tract Society, 1912.

Belt, R. A. *Charles Finney, A Great Evangelist*. Des Moines, Iowa, Boone, 1944.

Day, Richard E. *Man of Like Passions: A Dramatic Biography of Charles Grandison Finney*. Grand Rapids, Michigan, Zondervan, 1942.

Drummond, Lewis A. *Charles Grandison Finney and the Birth of Modern Evangelism*. London, Hodder and Stoughton, 1983.

———. *The Life and Ministry of Charles Finney*. Minneapolis, Bethany House, 1985.

Edman, V. Raymond. *Finney Lives On*, Minneapolis, Bethany House, 1971.

Fairchild, James H. *Oberlin: The Colony and the College, 1833–1883*. Oberlin, Ohio, Goodrich, 1883.

Finney, Charles G. *The Character, Claims and Practical Workings of Freemasonry*. Cincinnati: Western Tract and Book Society, 1869.

———. *Charles G. Finney, An Autobiography*. Old Tappan, New Jersey, Fleming H. Revell, 1908. (Originally titled *Memoirs of Charles G. Finney*, Oberlin, Ohio, 1876.)

———. *Finney's Systematic Theology: The Complete 1878 Edition from One of America's Greatest Evangelists*, Minneapolis, Bethany House, 1994.

———. *Guide to the Savior, or Conditions of Attaining to and Abiding in Entire Holiness of Heart and Life*. Oberlin, Ohio, Fitch, 1848.

———. *Lectures to Professing Christians*. London, Milner, 1837.

———. *Lectures on Revivals of Religion*. William G. McLoughlin, Ed., Boston, Harvard University, Belknap Press, 1960.

———. *Lectures on Systematic Theology*. London, Tegg, 1851; Oberlin, Ohio, Fitch, Vol. 2, 1846; Vol. 3, 1847.

———. *Sermons on Gospel Themes*. Oberlin, Ohio, Goodrich, 1876.

———. *Sermons of Important Subjects*. New York, Taylor, 1836.

———. *Sermons on Various Subjects*. New York, Taylor, 1834.

———. *Skeletons on a Course of Theological Lectures*. Oberlin, Ohio, Steele, 1840.

———. *Views of Sanctification*. Oberlin, Ohio, Steele, 1840.

Fletcher, Robert S. *A History of Oberlin College from its Foundation through the Civil War*. Oberlin, Ohio, Oberlin College, 2 vols., 1943.

Hardin, William H. *Finney's Life and Lectures*. London, Oliphant, 1943.

Hardesty, Nancy A. *Your Daughters Shall Prophesy: Revivalism & Feminism in the Age of Finney*. New York, Carlson Pub., 1991.

Hardman, Keith J. *Charles Grandison Finney, 1792–1875, Revivalist and Reformer*. Syracuse, New York, Syracuse University Press, 1987.

Hewitt, Glenn A. & Jerald C. Brauer. *Regeneration and Morality: a Study of Charles Finney, Charles Hodge, John W. Nevin and Horace Bushnell*. New York, Carlson Pub., 1991.

McLoughlin, William G. *Modern Revivalism: Charles Grandison Finney to Billy Graham*. New York, Ronald Press, 1959.

Miller, Basil W. *Charles Grandison Finney*. Minneapolis, Bethany House, 1969.

Nichols, Nelson L. *History of the Broadway Tabernacle of New York City*. New York, Tuttle, Morehouse, and Taylor, 1940.

Sweet, Leonard I. *The Minister's Wife: Her Role in Nineteenth-Century American Evangelicalism*. Philadelphia, Temple University Press, 1983.

Wright, George Frederick. *Charles Grandison Finney*. Boston, Houghton, Mifflin, 1891.

GEORGE MacDONALD

George MacDonald

Edited by Charles Erlandson

Contents

GEORGE MacDONALD 1824–1905

1824–1853

HIS LIFE		WORLD EVENTS
Born December 10, Huntly, Aberdeenshire, Scotland.	**1824**	Sequoya invents Cherokee alphabet.
Mother, Helen MacKay MacDonald dies; aunt Christina MacKay raises children until 1839.	**1832**	Chopin holds first concert in Paris.
Father, George, marries Margaret McColl.	**1839**	The Opium Wars begin.
Student at King's College, Aberdeen.	**1840**	First successful photograph taken of the moon.
Left college to catalog a private library.	**1842–1843**	Riots and strikes in northern England.
Returned to school in Aberdeen.	**1843–1844**	Dumas publishes *The Three Musketeers,* 1844.
Receives M.A. degree; moves to London and tutors until 1847.	**1845**	Texas and Florida become states.
First poem, "David" published anonymously.	**1846**	*Daily News* begins with Charles Dickens as editor.
Entered Highbury Theological College; engaged to Louisa Powell, 1848; preached in Cork, Ireland for three months, 1849.	**1848–1849**	New York hosts first women's rights convention, 1848.
Served only pastorate, Arundel at Sussex; wrote "Within and Without."	**1850**	Dickens' *David Copperfield* and Hawthorne's *The Scarlet Letter* published.
Married Louisa March 8; ordained, June; translated *Twelve of the Spiritual Songs of Novalis.*	**1851**	The Crystal Palace opens London's Great Exhibition, May 1.
Daughter, Lilia Scott, born January 4.	**1852**	Harriette Beecher Stowe publishes anti-slavery novel, *Uncle Tom's Cabin.*
Resigned from Arundel church, May; daughter, Mary Josephine, born July 23.	**1853**	First potato chips made in Sarasota Springs, New York; Levi Strauss makes first pair of jeans.

1854–1865

HIS LIFE		WORLD EVENTS
Journalist with *The Christian Spectator;* began to preach on Renshaw Street; daughter, Caroline Grace, born September 16; taught at Manchester Ladies' College.	**1854**	Working Men's College, London, founded by F. D. Maurice; elevators demonstrated at New York World's Fair.
Within and Without first work to be published; sister Bella dies.	**1855**	Florence Nightingale begins work in English hospitals.
Son, Greville Matheson, born January 20; Lady Byron finances winter in Algiers.	**1856**	Crimean War ends.
Daughter, Irene born August 31; dedicated poem, "A Hidden Life" to his father.	**1857**	Transatlantic cable laid.
Father, George, died August 26; daughter, Winifred Louisa born November 6; *Phantastes* published.	**1858**	In Lourdes, St. Bernadette sees vision of the Virgin Mary.
Lectured at the London Institute; professor of English Literature at Bedford College, London.	**1859**	John Brown is hanged; Darwin publishes *On the Origin of the Species.*
Son, Ronald, born October 27; son, lectured at Hastings.	**1860**	Pony Express begins; South Carolina is first state to secede from the Union.
Son, Robert Falconer, born July 15; meets Charles Dodgson (Lewis Carroll).	**1862**	Civil War continues; Julia Warde Howe's, "Battle Hymn of the Republic" published.
Publishes *David Elginbrod,* modeled after Christian Socialist Frederick Dennison Maurice.	**1863**	In July, the Battle of Gettysburg kills more than 50,000 men.
Son, Maurice, born February 7; *Adela Cathcart* and *The Portent* published.	**1864**	Red Cross is established in Switzerland.
Son, Bernard Powell, born September 18; visited Switzerland for first time.	**1865**	William Booth's Christian Revival Association became the Salvation Army.

HIS LIFE	Year	WORLD EVENTS
Son, George MacKay, born January 23; *Unspoken Sermons* published.	1867	Purchase of Alaska from Russia dubbed Seward's Folly.
Robert Falconer published; received L.L.D. degree from Aberdeen University.	1868	Alcott's *Little Women* becomes an immediate bestseller.
Editor of *Good Words for the Young.*	1869–1872	Ulysses S. Grant becomes president, 1869.
The Miracles of Our Lord, dedicated to F. D. Maurice; Louisa's *Chamber Dramas for Children* is published.	1870	John D. Rockefeller and others begin the Standard Oil Company of Ohio.
At the Back of the North Wind and *Ranald Bannerman's Boyhood* published.	1871	National Association of Professional Baseball Players is formed in New York.
The Princess and the Goblin and *Wilfrid Cumbermede* published; lectured in America for eight months.	1872–1873	First Negro delegates participate in the Republican Party's convention, 1872.
Malcolm published.	1875	The first Kentucky Derby runs at Churchill Downs.
Received a civil pension of 100 pounds a year from Queen Victoria.	1877	Queen Victoria proclaimed Empress of India.
Mary Josephine dies, April 28.	1878	Thomas Edison receives a patent for the phonograph.
Paul Faber, Surgeon and *Sir Gibbie* published.	1879	First performance in U.S. of a Gilbert & Sullivan play, "H.M.S. Pinafore."
Diary of an Old Soul published; the family moved into Casai Coraggio at Bordighera.	1880	Thomas Edison gets patent for his electric lamp.
Louisa raised funds with performances of *The Pilgrim's Progress*; Caroline Grace marries.	1881	The gunfight at the OK Corral occurs in Tombstone, Arizona.
The Princess and Curdie and *Castle Warlock* published.	1883	Competitive examinations begin for civil service jobs in U.S.
Caroline Grace dies, May 5.	1884	Twain's *The Adventures of Huckleberry Finn* is published.

HIS LIFE	Year	WORLD EVENTS
The *Tragedie of Hamlet* and *Unspoken Sermons*, second series, published.	1885	U.S. Post Office begins special delivery service for first-class mail.
What's Mine's Mine published.	1886	The Statue of Liberty is dedicated.
Home Again published.	1887	Major earthquake in Italy, February 23.
Ronald married and moved to America; wife died in 1890; *The Elect Lady* published.	1888	The "Blizzard of '88" kills 400 people in the Eastern United States.
Unspoken Sermons, third series, published.	1889	Benjamin Harrison is inaugurated as 23rd president.
A Rough Shaking is published, the only book with an Italian background.	1890	West Point hosts the first Army-Navy football game.
Last lecture tour; Lilia dies, November 22; *Then and Back* published.	1891	The International Copyright Act is passed.
George and Louisa go to Switzerland; *The Hope of the Gospel* published.	1892	Lincoln's birthday becomes a federal holiday.
Heather and Snow and *Scotch Songs and Ballads* published.	1893	Shredded wheat and ferris wheels are invented.
Lilith published.	1895	X-rays and the first safety razor are produced.
Last novel published, *Salted with Fire*.	1897	The National Congress of Mothers is founded, becomes PTA in 1924.
The Sketch, his last published work; suffers a stroke.	1898	Spanish-American War ends.
Celebrate their golden wedding anniversary.	1901	President William McKinley is assassinated.
Louisa died, January 13 in Bordighera.	1902	The first Rose Bowl, postseason college football game, is played.
Died at Ashstead in Surrey September 18, funeral September 21, ashes placed in Louisa's grave in Bordighera, January 1, 1906.	1905	Einstein formulates Special Theory of Relativity.

GEORGE MacDONALD

Introduction

George MacDonald was born December 10, 1824, at Huntly, Aberdeenshire. He studied at King's College and took his M.A. there in 1845. In 1850 he became a minister in a Congregationalist church in Arundel, but he soon ran into trouble for preaching that unbelievers who died were given a second chance for salvation. MacDonald's congregation reduced his salary, and in 1853 the situation became so intolerable that he resigned from his position.

In the 1850s MacDonald began his career as a writer for which he is most famous. His first success came with an extended dramatic poem, "Within and Without," while he found his true literary genius with the publication of *Phantastes*, an adult fantasy, in 1858. MacDonald devoted the remainder of his life to his literary endeavors, publishing fantasies, fairy tales, poetry, novels, translations, and criticism. MacDonald eschewed external success, and although he found a sizable audience, he was perpetually dependent on benefactors, including Lady Byron, for income until his death on September 18, 1905.

MacDonald's career as a writer led to his acquaintanceships with many prominent authors of his day, including Tennyson, Carlyle, Arnold, Ruskin, and Lewis Carroll, who was close enough to the MacDonald family to be called "Uncle Dodgson" by MacDonald's children. In America MacDonald was acquainted with Whittier, Emerson, and Twain. MacDonald's influence continues to extend into the twentieth century, and he has influenced such prominent twentieth-century authors as G. K. Chesterton, W. H. Auden, Charles Williams, and C. S. Lewis.

George MacDonald is known today for his works of fiction. In particular, it is his fantasies and fairy tales that continue to capture the imaginations of his readers. MacDonald turned to novel writing in the 1860s in an effort to support himself by his writing, but his novels are often too ponderous and weighted with preaching. Even C. S. Lewis found that the "texture of his writing as a whole is undistinguished, at times fumbling."

MacDonald's fantasies and fairy tales, however, succeed in awakening a sense of wonder in the reader. In these works MacDonald uses his created worlds to show how reality is full of a meaning and unity that God has given it. As MacDonald himself wrote: "The very outside of a book had a charm to me. It was a kind of sacrament—an outward sign of an inward and spiritual grace; as, indeed, what on God's earth is not?"

Even after MacDonald turned to his literary career he continued to lecture and deliver sermons. Several volumes of his "unspoken sermons" exist, and the themes that are pronounced in his fictional work, for example that God is the source of all life, is echoed in his sermons. One can even find examples of his sermons imbedded in some of his novels.

Rejecting the Calvinism of his parents, MacDonald saw any creedal formulations as too restricting and as ultimately only opinion. As a result

MacDonald sometimes presents anomalous interpretations, and occasionally he wanders into heterodoxy, for example regarding the atonement. Nevertheless, MacDonald's sermons often evoke the same sense of wonder in God's creation and its sacramentalism as does his fiction.

"The Light Princess" originally appeared in MacDonald's 1864 novel Adela Cathcart. *In this novel a number of symbolic tales are told within the framework of a realistic narrative. In both* Adela Cathcart *and "The Light Princess" MacDonald demonstrates his theory of the healthy effect fairy tales (and all imaginative literature that proceeds from the Christian imagination) have on men.*

Ostensibly "The Light Princess" is the story of a princess whose gravity is taken away from her through the curse of a wicked fairy and the princess's attempts to overcome the effects of this curse. But there is a spiritual meaning here, as in all of MacDonald's fairy tales. In the end, the wicked fairy's curse has a good effect on the princess as she is forced to accept a sacrifice of love. True love, we see, is a giving of one's self, and to live one must die to one's self. Often considered MacDonald's best story, "The Light Princess" was successful from the beginning and has even been made into an animated film.

CHAPTER ONE

The Light Princess

I
What! No Children?

Once upon a time, so long ago that I have quite forgotten the date, there lived a king and queen who had no children.

And the king said to himself, "All the queens of my acquaintance have children, some three, some seven, and some as many as twelve; and my queen has not one. I feel ill-used." So he made up his mind to be cross with his wife about it. But she bore it all like a good patient queen as she was. Then the king grew very cross indeed. But the queen pretended to take it all as a joke, and a very good one too.

"Why don't you have any daughters, at least?" said he. "I don't say *sons;* that might be too much to expect."

"I am sure, dear king, I am very sorry," said the queen.

"So you ought to be," retorted the king; "you are not going to make a virtue of *that,* surely."

But he was not an ill-tempered king, and in any matter of less moment would have let the queen have her own way with all his heart. This, however, was an affair of state.

The queen smiled.

"You must have patience with a lady, you know, dear king," said she.

She was, indeed, a very nice queen, and heartily sorry that she could not oblige the king immediately.

The king tried to have patience, but he succeeded very badly. It was more than he deserved, therefore, when, at last, the queen gave him a daughter—as lovely a little princess as ever cried.

II
Won't I, Just?

The day grew near when the infant must be christened. The king wrote all the invitations with his own hand. Of course somebody was forgotten.

Now it does not generally matter if somebody *is* forgotten, only you must mind who. Unfortunately, the king forgot without intending to forget; and so the chance fell upon the Princess Makemnoit, which was awkward. For the princess was the king's own sister; and he ought not to have forgotten her. But she had made herself so disagreeable to the old king, their father, that he had forgotten her in making his will; and so it was no wonder that her brother forgot her in writing his invitations. But poor relations don't do anything to keep you in mind of them. Why don't they? The king could not see into the garret she lived in, could he?

She was a sour, spiteful creature. The wrinkles of contempt crossed the wrinkles of peevishness, and made her face as full of wrinkles as a pat of butter. If ever a king could be justified in forgetting anybody, this king was justified in forgetting his sister, even at a christening. She looked very odd, too. Her forehead was as large as all the rest of her face, and projected over it like a precipice. When she was angry, her little eyes flashed blue. When she hated anybody, they shone yellow and green. What they looked like when she loved anybody, I do not know; for I never heard of her loving anybody but herself, and I do not think she could have managed that if she had not somehow got used to herself.

But what made it highly imprudent in the king to forget her was—that she was awfully clever. In fact, she was a witch; and when she bewitched anybody, he very soon had enough of it; for she beat all the wicked fairies in wickedness, and all the clever ones in cleverness. She despised all the modes we read of in history, in which offended fairies and witches have taken their revenges; and therefore, after waiting and waiting in vain for an invitation, she made up her mind at last to go without one, and make the whole family miserable, like a princess as she was.

So she put on her best gown, went to the palace, was kindly received by the happy monarch, who forgot that he had forgotten her, and took her place in the procession to the royal chapel. When they were all gathered about the font, she contrived to get next to it, and throw something into the water; after which she maintained a very respectful demeanour till the water was applied to the child's face. But at that moment she turned round in her place three times, and muttered the following words loud enough for those beside her to hear:—

> "Light of spirit, by my charms,
>   Light of body, every part,
> Never weary human arms—
>   Only crush thy parents' heart!"

They all thought she had lost her wits, and was repeating some foolish nursery rhyme; but a shudder went through the whole of them notwithstanding. The baby, on the contrary, began to laugh and crow; while the nurse gave a start and a smothered cry, for she thought she was struck with paralysis: she could not feel the baby in her arms. But she clasped it and said nothing.

The mischief was done.

III
She Can't Be Ours

Her atrocious aunt had deprived the child of all her gravity. If you ask me how this was effected, I answer, "In the easiest way in the world. She had only to destroy gravitation." For the princess was a philosopher, and knew all the *ins* and *outs* of the laws of gravitation as well as the *ins* and *outs* of her boot-lace. And being a witch as well, she could abrogate those laws in a moment; or at least so clog their wheels and rust their bearings, that they would not work at all. But we have more to do with what followed than with how it was done.

The first awkwardness that resulted from this unhappy privation was, that the moment the nurse began to float the baby up and down, she flew from her arms towards the ceiling. Happily, the resistance of the air brought her ascending career to a close within a foot of it. There she remained, horizontal as when she left her nurse's arms, kicking and laughing amazingly. The nurse in terror flew to the bell, and begged the footman, who answered it, to bring up the house-steps directly. Trembling in every limb, she climbed upon the steps, and had to stand upon the very top, and reach up, before she could catch the floating tail of the baby's long clothes.

When the strange fact came to be known, there was a terrible commotion in the palace. The occasion of its discovery by the king was naturally a repetition of the nurse's experience. Astonished that he felt no weight when the child was laid in his arms, he began to wave her up and—not down; for she slowly ascended to the ceiling as before, and there remained floating in perfect comfort and satisfaction, as was testified by her peals of tiny laughter. The king stood staring up in speechless amazement, and trembled so that his beard shook like grass in the wind. At last, turning to the queen, who was just as horror-struck as himself, he said, gasping, staring, and stammering,—

"She *can't* be ours, queen!"

Now the queen was much cleverer than the king, and had begun already to suspect that "this effect defective came by cause."

"I am sure she is ours," answered she. "But we ought to have taken better care of her at the christening. People who were never invited ought not to have been present."

"Oh, ho!" said the king, tapping his forehead with his forefinger, "I have it all. I've found her out. Don't you see it, queen? Princess Makemnoit has bewitched her."

"That's just what I say," answered the queen.

"I beg your pardon, my love; I did not hear you.—John! bring the steps I get on my throne with."

For he was a little king with a great throne, like many other kings.

The throne-steps were brought, and set upon the dining-table, and John got upon the top of them. But he could not reach the little princess, who lay like a baby laughter-cloud in the air, exploding continuously.

"Take the tongs, John," said his Majesty; and getting up on the table, he handed them to him.

John could reach the baby now, and the little princess was handed down by the tongs.

IV
Where Is She?

One fine summer day, a month after these her first adventures, during which time she had been very carefully watched, the princess was lying on the bed in the queen's own chamber, fast asleep. One of the windows was open, for it was noon, and the day was so sultry that the little girl was wrapped in nothing less ethereal than slumber itself. The queen came into the room, and not observing that the baby was on the bed, opened another window. A frolicsome fairy wind, which had been watching for a chance of mischief, rushed in at the one window, and taking its way over the bed where the child was lying, caught her up, and rolling and floating her along like a piece of flue, or a dandelion seed, carried her with it through the opposite window, and away. The queen went down-stairs, quite ignorant of the loss she had herself occasioned.

When the nurse returned, she supposed that her Majesty had carried her off, and, dreading a scolding, delayed making inquiry about her. But hearing nothing, she grew uneasy, and went at length to the queen's boudoir, where she found her Majesty.

"Please, your Majesty, shall I take the baby?" said she.

"Where is she?" asked the queen.

"Please forgive me. I know it was wrong."

"What do you mean?" said the queen, looking grave.

"Oh! don't frighten me, your Majesty!" exclaimed the nurse, clasping her hands.

The queen saw that something was amiss, and fell down in a faint. The nurse rushed about the palace screaming, "My baby! my baby!"

Every one ran to the queen's room. But the queen could give no orders. They soon found out, however, that the princess was missing, and in a moment the palace was like a beehive in a garden; and in one minute more the queen was brought to herself by a great shout and a clapping of hands. They had found the princess fast asleep under a rose-bush, to which the elvish little windpuff had carried her, finishing its mischief by shaking a shower of red rose-leaves all over the little white sleeper. Startled by the noise the servants made, she woke, and, furious with glee, scattered the rose-leaves in all directions, like a shower of spray in the sunset.

She was watched more carefully after this, no doubt; yet it would be endless to relate all the odd incidents resulting from this peculiarity of the young princess. But there never was a baby in a house, not to say a palace, that kept the household in such constant good humour, at least below-stairs. If it was not easy for her nurses to hold her, at least she made neither their arms nor their hearts ache. And she was so nice to play at ball with! There was positively no danger of letting her fall. They might throw her down, or knock her down, or push her down, but couldn't *let* her down. It is true, they might let her fly into the fire or the coal-hole, or through the window, but none of these accidents had happened as yet.

If you heard peals of laughter resounding from some unknown region, you might be sure enough of the cause. Going down into the kitchen, or *the room*, you would find Jane and Thomas, and Robert and Susan, all and sum, playing at ball with the little princess. She was the ball herself, and did not enjoy it the less for that. Away she went, flying from one to another, screeching with laughter. And the servants loved the ball itself better even than the game. But they had to take some care how they threw her, for if she received an upward direction, she would never come down again without being fetched.

V
What Is to Be Done?

But above-stairs it was different. One day, for instance, after breakfast, the king went into his counting-house, and counted out his money.

The operation gave him no pleasure. "To think," said he to himself, "that every one of these gold sovereigns weighs a quarter of an ounce, and my real, live, flesh-and-blood princess weighs nothing at all!"

And he hated his gold sovereigns, as they lay with a broad smile of self-satisfaction all over their yellow faces.

The queen was in the parlour, eating bread and honey. But at the second mouthful she burst out crying, and could not swallow it. The king heard her sobbing. Glad of anybody, but especially of his queen, to quarrel with, he clashed his gold sovereigns into his money-box, clapped his crown on his head, and rushed into the parlour.

"What is all this about?" exclaimed he. "What are you crying for, queen?"

"I can't eat it," said the queen, looking ruefully at the honey-pot.

"No wonder!" retorted the king. "You've just eaten your breakfast—two turkey eggs, and three anchovies."

"Oh, that's not it!" sobbed her Majesty. "It's my child, my child!"

"Well, what's the matter with your child? She's neither up the chimney nor down the draw-well. Just hear her laughing."

Yet the king could not help a sigh, which he tried to turn into a cough, saying,—

"It is a good thing to be light-hearted, I am sure, whether she be ours or not."

"It is a bad thing to be light-headed," answered the queen, looking with prophetic soul far into the future.

"'T is a good thing to light-handed," said the king.

" 'T is a bad thing to be light-fingered," answered the queen.

" 'T is a good thing to be light-footed," said the king.

" 'T is a bad thing—" began the queen; but the king interrupted her.

"In fact," said he, with the tone of one who concludes an argument in which he has had only imaginary opponents, and in which, therefore, he has come off triumphant—"in fact, it is a good thing altogether to be light-bodied."

"But it is a bad thing altogether to be light-minded," retorted the queen, who was beginning to lose her temper.

This last answer quite discomfited his Majesty, who turned on his heel, and betook himself to his counting-house again. But he was not half-way towards it, when the voice of his queen overtook him.

"And it's a bad thing to be light-haired," screamed she, determined to have more last words, now that her spirit was roused.

The queen's hair was black as night; and the king's had been, and his daughter's was, golden as morning. But it was not this reflection on his hair that arrested him; it was the double use of the word *light*. For the king hated all witticisms, and punning especially. And besides, he could not tell whether the queen meant light-*haired* or light-*heired*; for why might she not aspirate her vowels when she was exasperated herself?

He turned upon his other heel, and rejoined her. She looked angry still, because she knew that she was guilty, or, what was much the same, knew that he thought so.

"My dear queen," said he, "duplicity of any sort is exceedingly objectionable between married people of any rank, not to say kings and queens, and the most objectionable form duplicity can assume is that of punning."

"There!" said the queen, "I never made a jest, but I broke it in the making. I am the most unfortunate woman in the world!"

She looked so rueful that the king took her in his arms; and they sat down to consult.

"Can you bear this?" said the king.

"No, I can't," said the queen.

"Well, what's to be done?" said the king.

"I'm sure I don't know," said the queen. "But might you not try an apology?"

"To my old sister, I suppose you mean?" said the king.

"Yes," said the queen.

"Well, I don't mind," said the king.

So he went the next morning to the house of the princess, and, making a very humble apology, begged her to undo the spell. But the princess declared, with a grave face, that she knew nothing at all about it. Her eyes, however, shone pink, which was a sign that she was happy. She advised the king and queen to have patience, and to mend their ways. The king returned disconsolate. The queen tried to comfort him.

"We will wait till she is older. She may then be able to suggest something herself. She will know at least how she feels, and explain things to us."

"But what if she should marry?" exclaimed the king, in sudden consternation at the idea.

"Well, what of that?" rejoined the queen.

"Just think! If she were to have children! In the course of a hundred years the air might be as full of floating children as of gossamers in autumn."

"That is no business of ours," replied the queen. "Besides, by that time they will have learned to take care of themselves."

A sigh was the king's only answer.

He would have consulted the court

physicians; but he was afraid they would try experiments upon her.

VI
She Laughs Too Much

Meantime, notwithstanding awkward occurrences, and griefs that she brought upon her parents, the little princess laughed and grew—not fat, but plump and tall. She reached the age of seventeen, without having fallen into any worse scrape than a chimney; by rescuing her from which, a little bird-nesting urchin got fame and a black face. Nor, thoughtless as she was, had she committed anything worse than laughter at everybody and everything that came in her way. When she was told, for the sake of experiment, that General Clanrunfort was cut to pieces with all his troops, she laughed; when she heard the enemy was on his way to besiege her papa's capital, she laughed hugely; but when she was told that the city would certainly be abandoned to the mercy of the enemy's soldiery—why, then she laughed immoderately. She never could be brought to see the serious side of anything. When her mother cried, she said,—

"What queer faces mamma makes! And she squeezes water out of her cheeks! Funny mamma!"

And when her papa stormed at her, she laughed, and danced round and round him, clapping her hands, and crying—

"Do it again, papa. Do it again! It's such fun! Dear, funny papa!"

And if he tried to catch her, she glided from him in an instant, not in the least afraid of him, but thinking it part of the game not to be caught. With one push of her foot, she would be floating in the air above his head, or she would go dancing backwards and forwards and sideways, like a great butterfly. It hap-

pened several times, when her father and mother were holding a consultation about her in private, that they were interrupted by vainly repressed outbursts of laughter over their heads, and looking up with indignation, saw her floating at full length in the air above them, whence she regarded them with the most comical appreciation of the position.

One day an awkward accident happened. The princess had come out upon the lawn with one of her attendants who held her by the hand. Spying her father at the other side of the lawn, she snatched her hand from the maid's, and sped across to him. Now when she wanted to run alone, her custom was to catch up a stone in each hand, so that she might come down again after a bound. Whatever she wore as part of her attire had no effect in this way: even gold, when it thus became as it were a part of herself, lost all its weight for the time. But whatever she only held in her hands retained its downward tendency.

On this occasion she could see nothing to catch up but a huge toad, that was walking across the lawn as if he had a hundred years to do it in. Not knowing what disgust meant, for this was one of her peculiarities, she snatched up the toad and bounded away. She had almost reached her father, and he was holding out his arms to receive her, and take from her lips the kiss which hovered on them like a butterfly on a rosebud, when a puff of wind blew her aside into the arms of a young page, who had just been receiving a message from his Majesty.

Now it was no great peculiarity in the princess that, once she was set agoing, it always cost her time and trouble to check herself. On this occasion there was no time. She *must* kiss—and she kissed the page. She did not mind it much; for she had no shyness in her composition; and she knew, besides, that she could not help it. So she only laughed, like a musical box. The poor page fared the worst. For the princess, trying to correct the unfortunate tendency of the kiss, put out her hands to keep her off the page; so that, along with the kiss, he received, on the other cheek, a slap with the huge black toad, which she poked right into his eye. He tried to laugh, too, but the attempt resulted in such an odd contortion of countenance, as showed that there was no danger of his pluming himself on the kiss. As for the king, his dignity was greatly hurt, and he did not speak to the page for a whole month.

I may here remark that it was very amusing to see her run, if her mode of progression could properly be called running. For first she would make a bound; then, having alighted, she would run a few steps, and make another bound. Sometimes she would fancy she had reached the ground before she actually had, and her feet would go backwards and forwards, running upon nothing at all, like those of a chicken on its back. Then she would laugh like the very spirit of fun; only in her laugh there was something missing. What it was, I find myself unable to describe. I think it was a certain tone, depending upon the possibility of sorrow—*morbidezza*, perhaps. She never smiled.

VII
Try Metaphysics

After a long avoidance of the painful subject, the king and queen resolved to hold a council of three upon it; and so they sent for the princess. In she came, sliding and flitting and gliding from one piece of furniture to another, and put herself at last in an arm-chair, in a sitting posture. Whether she could be said *to sit*, seeing she received no support

from the seat of the chair, I do not pretend to determine.

"My dear child," said the king, "you must be aware by this time that you are not exactly like other people."

"Oh, you dear funny papa! I have got a nose, and two eyes, and all the rest. So have you. So has mamma."

"Now be serious, my dear, for once," said the queen.

"No, thank you, mamma; I had rather not."

"Would you not like to be able to walk like other people?" said the king.

"No indeed, I should think not. You only crawl. You are such slow coaches!"

"How do you feel, my child?" he resumed, after a pause of discomfiture.

"Quite well, thank you."

"I mean, what do you feel like?"

"Like nothing at all, that I know of."

"You must feel like something."

"I feel like a princess with such a funny papa, and such a dear pet of a queen-mamma!"

"Now really!" began the queen; but the princess interrupted her.

"Oh, yes," she added, "I remember. I have a curious feeling sometimes, as if I were the only person that had any sense in the whole world."

She had been trying to behave herself with dignity; but now she burst into a violent fit of laughter, threw herself backwards over the chair, and went rolling about the floor in an ecstasy of enjoyment. The king picked her up easier than one does a down quilt, and replaced her in her former relation to the chair. The exact preposition expressing this relation I do not happen to know.

"Is there nothing you wish for?" resumed the king, who had learned by this time that it was useless to be angry with her.

"Oh, you dear papa!—yes," answered she.

"What is it, my darling?"

"I have been longing for it—oh, such a time!—ever since last night."

"Tell me what it is."

"Will you promise to let me have it?"

The king was on the point of saying *Yes*, but the wiser queen checked him with a single motion of her head.

"Tell me what it is first," said he.

"No no. Promise first."

"I dare not. What is it?"

"Mind, I hold you to your promise.— It is—to be tied to the end of a string— a very long string indeed, and be flown like a kite. Oh, such fun! I would rain rose-water, and hail sugar-plums, and snow whipped-cream, and— and— and—"

A fit of laughing checked her; and she would have been off again over the floor, had not the king started up and caught her just in time. Seeing that nothing but talk could be got out of her, he rang the bell, and sent her away with two of her ladies-in-waiting.

"Now, queen," he said, turning to her Majesty, "what *is* to be done?"

"There is but one thing left," answered she. "Let us consult the college of Metaphysicians."

"Bravo!" cried the king; "we will."

Now at the head of this college were two very wise Chinese philosophers—by name Hum-Drum and Kopy-Keck. For them the king sent; and straightway they came. In a long speech he communicated to them what they knew very well already—as who did not?—namely, the peculiar condition of his daughter in relation to the globe on which she dwelt; and requested them to consult together as to what might be the cause and probable cure of her *infirmity*. The king laid stress upon the word, but failed to discover his own pun. The queen laughed; but Hum-Drum and Kopy-Keck heard with humility and retired in silence.

Their consultation consisted chiefly in propounding and supporting, for the thousandth time, each his favourite theories. For the condition of the princess afforded delightful scope for the discussion of every question arising from the division of thought—in fact, of all the Metaphysics of the Chinese Empire. But it is only justice to say that they did not altogether neglect the discussion of the practical question, *what was to be done*.

Hum-Drum was a Materialist, and Kopy-Keck was a Spiritualist. The former was slow and sententious; the latter was quick and flighty: the latter had generally the first word; the former the last.

"I reassert my former assertion," began Kopy-Keck, with a plunge. "There is not a fault in the princess, body or soul; only they are wrong put together. Listen to me now, Hum-Drum, and I will tell you in brief what I think. Don't speak. Don't answer me. I *won't* hear you till I have done.—At that decisive moment, when souls seek their appointed habitations, two eager souls met, struck, rebounded, lost their way, and arrived each at the wrong place. The soul of the princess was one of those, and she went far astray. She does not belong by rights to this world at all, but to some other planet, probably Mercury. Her proclivity to her true sphere destroys all the natural influence which this orb would otherwise possess over her corporeal frame. She cares for nothing here. There is no relation between her and this world.

"She must therefore be taught, by the sternest compulsion, to take an interest in the earth as the earth. She must study every department of its history—its animal history; its vegetable history; its mineral history; its social history; its moral history; its political history; its scientific history; its literary history; its musical history; its artistical history; above all, its metaphysical history. She must begin with the Chinese dynasty and end with Japan. But first of all she must study geology, and especially the history of the extinct races of animals—their natures, their habits, their loves, their hates, their revenges. She must."

"Hold, h-o-o-old!" roared Hum-Drum. "It is certainly my turn now. My rooted and insubvertible conviction is that the causes of the anomalies evident in the princess's condition are strictly and solely physical. But that is only tantamount to acknowledging that they exist. Hear my opinion.—From some cause or other, of no importance to our inquiry, the motion of her heart has been reversed. That remarkable combination of the suction and the force-pump works the wrong way—I mean in the case of the unfortunate princess, it draws in where it should force out, and forces out where it should draw in. The offices of the auricles and the ventricles are subverted. The blood is sent forth by the veins, and returns by the arteries. Consequently it is running the wrong way through all her corporeal organism—lungs and all. Is it then at all mysterious, seeing that such is the case, that on the other particular of gravitation as well, she should differ from normal humanity? My proposal for the cure is this:—

"Phlebotomize until she is reduced to the last point of safety. Let it be effected, if necessary, in a warm bath. When she is reduced to a state of perfect asphyxy, apply a ligature to the left ankle, drawing it as tight as the bone will bear. Apply, at the same moment, another of equal tension around the right wrist. By means of plates constructed for the purpose, place the other foot and hand under the receivers of two air-pumps. Exhaust the receivers. Exhibit a pint of French brandy, and await the result."

"Which would presently arrive in the form of grim Death," said Kopy-Keck.

"If it should, she would yet die in doing our duty," retorted Hum-Drum.

But their Majesties had too much tenderness for their volatile offspring to subject her to either of the schemes of the equally unscrupulous philosophers. Indeed, the most complete knowledge of the laws of nature would have been unserviceable in her case; for it was impossible to classify her. She was a fifth imponderable body, sharing all the other properties of the ponderable.

VIII
Try a Drop of Water

Perhaps the best thing for the princess would have been to fall in love. But how a princess who had no gravity could fall into anything is a difficulty—perhaps *the* difficulty. As for her own feelings on the subject, she did not even know that there was such a beehive of honey and stings to be fallen into. But now I come to mention another curious fact about her.

The palace was built on the shores of the loveliest lake in the world; and the princess loved this lake more than father or mother. The root of this preference no doubt, although the princess did not recognize it as such, was, that the moment she got into it, she recovered the natural right of which she had been so wickedly deprived—namely, gravity. Whether this was owing to the fact that water had been employed as the means of conveying the injury, I do not know. But it is certain that she could swim and dive like the duck that her old nurse said she was. The manner in which this alleviation of her misfortune was discovered was as follows.

One summer evening, during the carnival of the country, she had been taken upon the lake by the king and queen in the royal barge. They were accompanied by many of the courtiers in a fleet of little boats. In the middle of the lake she wanted to get into the lord chancellor's barge, for his daughter, who was a great favourite with her, was in it with her father.

Now though the old king rarely condescended to make light of his misfortune, yet, happening on this occasion to be in a particularly good humour, as the barges approached each other, he caught up the princess to throw her into the chancellor's barge. He lost his balance, however, and, dropping into the bottom of the barge lost his hold of his daughter; not, however, before imparting to her the downward tendency of his own person, though in a somewhat different direction; for, as the king fell into the boat, she fell into the water. With a burst of delighted laughter she disappeared into the lake. A cry of horror ascended from the boats. They had never seen the princess go down before. Half the men were under water in a moment; but they had all, one after another come up to the surface again for breath, when—tinkle, tinkle, babble, and gush! came the princess's laugh over the water from far away. There she was, swimming like a swan. Nor would she come out for king or queen, chancellor or daughter. She was perfectly obstinate.

But at the same time she seemed more sedate than usual. Perhaps that was because a great pleasure spoils laughing. At all events, after this, the passion of her life was to get into the water, and she was always the better behaved and the more beautiful the more she had of it. Summer and winter it was quite the same; only she could not stay so long in the water when they had to break the ice to let her in. Any day, from morning to evening in summer, she might be descried—a streak of white in the blue water—lying as still as the shadow of a cloud, or shooting along like a dolphin; disappearing, and coming up again far off, just where one did not expect her.

She would have been in the lake of a night too, if she could have had her way; for the balcony of her window overhung a deep pool in it; and through a shallow reedy passage she could have swum out into the wide wet water, and no one would have been any the wiser. Indeed, when she happened to wake in the moonlight she could hardly resist the temptation. But there was the sad difficulty of getting into it. She had as great a dread of the air as some children have of the water. For the slightest gust of wind would blow her away; and a gust might arise in the stillest moment. And if she gave herself a push towards the water and just failed of reaching it, her situation would be dreadfully awkward, irrespective of the wind; for at best there she would have to remain, suspended in her night-gown, till she was seen and angled for by somebody from the window.

"Oh! if I had my gravity," thought she, contemplating the water, "I would flash off this balcony like a long white seabird, headlong into the darling wetness. Heigh-ho!"

This was the only consideration that made her wish to be like other people.

Another reason for her being fond of the water was that in it alone she enjoyed any freedom. For she could not walk out without a *cortége*, consisting in part of a troop of light-horse, for fear of the liberties which the wind might take with her. And the king grew more apprehensive with increasing years, till at last he would not allow her to walk abroad at all without some twenty silken cords fastened to as many parts of her dress, and held by twenty noblemen. Of course horseback was out of the question. But she bade good-bye to all this ceremony when she got into the water.

And so remarkable were its effects upon her, especially in restoring her for the time to the ordinary human gravity, that Hum-Drum and Kopy-Keck agreed in recommending the king to bury her alive for three years; in the hope that, as the water did her so much good, the earth would do her yet more. But the king had some vulgar prejudices against the experiment, and would not give his consent. Foiled in this, they yet agreed in another recommendation; which, seeing that one imported his opinions from China and the other from Tibet, was very remarkable indeed. They argued that, if water of external origin and application could be so efficacious, water from a deeper source might work a perfect cure; in short, that if the poor afflicted princess could by any means be made to cry, she might recover her lost gravity.

But how was this to be brought about? Therein lay all the difficulty—to meet which the philosophers were not wise enough. To make the princess cry was as impossible as to make her weigh. They sent for a professional beggar; commanded him to prepare his most touching oracle of woe; helped him out of the court charade box, to whatever he wanted for dressing up, and promised great rewards in the event of his success. But it was all in vain. She listened to the mendicant artist's story, and gazed at his marvellous make up, till she could contain herself no longer, and went into the most undignified contortions for relief, shrieking, positively screeching with laughter.

When she had a little recovered herself, she ordered her attendants to drive him away, and not give him a single copper; whereupon his look of mortified discomfiture wrought her punishment and his revenge, for it sent her into violent hysterics, from which she was with difficulty recovered.

But so anxious was the king that the suggestion should have a fair trial, that he put himself in a rage one day, and, rushing up to her room, gave her an awful whipping. Yet not a tear would flow. She looked grave, and her laughing sounded uncommonly like screaming— that was all. The good old tyrant, though he put on his best gold spectacles to look, could not discover the smallest cloud in the serene blue of her eyes.

IX
Put Me in Again

It must have been about this time that the son of a king, who lived a thousand miles from Lagobel, set out to look for the daughter of a queen. He travelled far and wide, but as sure as he found a princess, he found some fault in her. Of course he could not marry a mere woman, however beautiful; and there was no princess to be found worthy of him. Whether the prince was so near perfection that he had a right to demand perfection itself, I cannot pretend to say. All I know is, that he was a fine, handsome, brave, generous, well-bred, and well-behaved youth, as all princes are.

In his wanderings he had come across some reports about our princess; but as everybody said she was bewitched, he never dreamed that she could bewitch him. For what indeed could a prince do with a princess that had lost her gravity? Who could tell what she might not lose next? She might lose her visibility, or her tangibility; or, in short, the power of making impressions upon the radical sensorium; so that he should never be able to tell whether she was dead or alive. Of course, he made no further inquiries about her.

One day he lost sight of his retinue in a great forest. These forests are very useful in delivering princes from their courtiers, like a sieve that keeps back the bran. Then the princes get away to follow their fortunes. In this they have the advantage of the princesses, who are forced to marry before they have had a bit of fun. I wish our princesses got lost in a forest sometimes.

One lovely evening, after wandering about for many days, he found that he was approaching the outskirts of this forest; for the trees had got so thin that he could see the sunset through them; and he soon came upon a kind of heath. Next he came upon signs of human neighbourhood; but by this time it was getting late, and there was nobody in the fields to direct him.

After travelling for another hour, his horse, quite worn out with long labour and lack of food, fell, and was unable to rise again. So he continued his journey on foot. At length he entered another wood—not a wild forest, but a civilized wood, through which a footpath led him to the side of a lake. Along this path the prince pursued his way through the gathering darkness. Suddenly he paused, and listened. Strange sounds came across the water. It was, in fact, the princess laughing. Now there was something odd in her laugh, as I have already hinted; for the hatching of a real hearty laugh requires the incubation of gravity; and perhaps this was how the prince mistook the laughter for screaming. Looking over the lake, he saw something white in the water; and, in an instant, he had torn off his tunic, kicked off his sandals, and plunged in. He soon reached the white object, and found that it was a woman. There was not light enough to show that she was a princess, but quite enough to show that she was

a lady, for it does not want much light to see that.

Now I cannot tell how it came about,—whether she pretended to be drowning, or whether he frightened her, or caught her so as to embarrass her,—but certainly he brought her to shore in a fashion ignominious to a swimmer, and more nearly drowned than she had ever expected to be; for the water had got into her throat as often as she had tried to speak.

At the place to which he bore her, the bank was only a foot or two above the water; so he gave her a strong lift out of the water, to lay her on the bank. But, her gravitation ceasing the moment she left the water, away she went up into the air, scolding and screaming.

"You naughty, *naughty*, NAUGHTY, NAUGHTY man!" she cried.

No one had ever succeeded in putting her into a passion before. When the prince saw her ascend, he thought he must have been bewitched, and have mistaken a great swan for a lady. But the princess caught hold of the topmost cone upon a lofty fir. This came off; but she caught at another; and, in fact, stopped herself by gathering cones, dropping them as the stalks gave way. The prince, meantime, stood in the water, staring, and forgetting to get out. But the princess disappearing, he scrambled on shore, and went in the direction of the tree. There he found her climbing down one of the branches towards the stem. But in the darkness of the wood, the prince continued in some bewilderment as to what the phenomenon could be; until reaching the ground, and seeing him standing there, she caught hold of him, and said,—

"I'll tell papa."

"Oh no, you won't!" returned the prince.

"Yes, I will," she persisted. "What business had you to pull me down out of the water, and throw me to the bottom of the air? I never did you any harm."

"Pardon me. I did not mean to hurt you."

"I don't believe you have any brains; and that is a worse loss than your wretched gravity. I pity you."

The prince now saw that he had come upon the bewitched princess, and had already offended her. But before he could think what to say next, she burst out angrily, giving a stamp with her foot that would have sent her aloft again but for the hold she had of his arm,—

"Put me up directly."

"Put you up where, you beauty?" asked the prince.

He had fallen in love with her almost, already; for her anger made her more charming than any one else had ever beheld her; and, as far as he could see, which certainly was not far, she had not a single fault about her, except, of course, that she had not any gravity. No prince, however, would judge of a princess by weight. The loveliness of her foot he would hardly estimate by the depth of the impression it could make in mud.

"Put you up where, you beauty?" asked the prince.

"In the water, you stupid!" answered the princess.

"Come, then," said the prince.

The condition of her dress, increasing her usual difficulty in walking, compelled her to cling to him; and he could hardly persuade himself that he was not in a delightful dream, notwithstanding the torrent of musical abuse with which she overwhelmed him. The prince being therefore in no hurry, they came upon the lake at quite another part, where the bank was twenty-five feet high at least; and when they had reached the edge, he turned towards the princess, and said,—

"How am I to put you in?"

"That is your business," she an-swered, quite snappishly. "You took me out—put me in again."

"Very well," said the prince; and, catching her up in his arms, he sprang with her from the rock. The princess had just time to give one delighted shriek of laughter before the water closed over them. When they came to the surface, she found that, for a moment or two, she could not even laugh, for she had gone down with such a rush, that it was with difficulty she recovered her breath. The instant they reached the surface—

"How do you like falling in?" said the prince.

After some effort the princess panted out,—

"Is that what you call *falling in?*"

"Yes," answered the prince, "I should think it a very tolerable specimen."

"It seemed to me like going up," rejoined she.

"My feeling was certainly one of elevation too," the prince conceded.

The princess did not appear to understand him, for she retorted his question:—

"How do you like falling in?" said the princess.

"Beyond everything," answered he; "for I have fallen in with the only perfect creature I ever saw."

"No more of that: I am tired of it," said the princess.

Perhaps she shared her father's aversion to punning.

"Don't you like falling in, then?" said the prince.

"It is the most delightful fun I ever had in my life," answered she. "I never fell before. I wish I could learn. To think I am the only person in my father's kingdom that can't fall!"

Here the poor princess looked almost sad.

"I shall be most happy to fall in with

you any time you like," said the prince, devotedly.

"Thank you. I don't know. Perhaps it would not be proper. But I don't care. At all events, as we have fallen in, let us have a swim together."

"With all my heart," responded the prince.

And away they went, swimming, and diving, and floating, until at last they heard cries along the shore, and saw lights glancing in all directions. It was now quite late, and there was no moon.

"I must go home," said the princess. "I am very sorry, for this is delightful."

"So am I," returned the prince. "But I am glad I haven't a home to go to—at least, I don't exactly know where it is."

"I wish I hadn't one either," rejoined the princess; "it is so stupid! I have a great mind," she continued, "to play them all a trick. Why couldn't they leave me alone? They won't trust me in the lake for a single night!—You see where that green light is burning? That is the window of my room. Now if you would just swim there with me very quietly, and when we are all but under the balcony, give me such a push—up you call it—as you did a little while ago, I should be able to catch hold of the balcony, and get in at the window; and then they may look for me till to-morrow morning!"

"With more obedience than pleasure," said the prince, gallantly; and away they swam, very gently.

"Will you be in the lake to-morrow night?" the prince ventured to ask.

"To be sure I will. I don't think so. Perhaps," was the princess's somewhat strange answer.

But the prince was intelligent enough not to press her further; and merely whispered, as he gave her the parting lift, "Don't tell." The only answer the princess returned was a roguish look. She was already a yard above his head.

The look seemed to say, "Never fear. It is too good fun to spoil that way."

So perfectly like other people had she been in the water, that even yet the prince could scarcely believe his eyes when he saw her ascend slowly, grasp the balcony, and disappear through the window. He turned, almost expecting to see her still by his side. But he was alone in the water. So he swam away quietly, and watched the lights roving about the shore for hours after the princess was safe in her chamber. As soon as they disappeared, he landed in search of his tunic and sword, and, after some trouble, found them again. Then he made the best of his way round the lake to the other side. There the wood was wilder, and the shore steeper—rising more immediately towards the mountains which surrounded the lake on all sides, and kept sending it messages of silvery streams from morning to night, and all night long. He soon found a spot where he could see the green light in the princess's room, and where, even in the broad daylight, he would be in no danger of being discovered from the opposite shore. It was a sort of cave in the rock, where he provided himself a bed of withered leaves, and lay down too tired for hunger to keep him awake. All night long he dreamed that he was swimming with the princess.

X
Look at the Moon

Early the next morning the prince set out to look for something to eat, which he soon found at a forester's hut, where for many following days he was supplied with all that a brave prince could consider necessary. And having plenty to keep him alive for the present, he would not think of wants not yet in existence. Whenever Care intruded, this prince always bowed him out in the most princely manner.

When he returned from his breakfast to his watch cave, he saw the princess already floating about in the lake, attended by the king and queen—whom he knew by their crowns—and a great company in lovely little boats, with canopies of all the colours of the rainbow, and flags and streamers of a great many more. It was a very bright day, and soon the prince, burned up with the heat, began to long for the cold water and the cool princess. But he had to endure till twilight; for the boats had provisions on board, and it was not till the sun went down that the gay party began to vanish. Boat after boat drew away to the shore, following that of the king and queen, till only one, apparently the princess's own boat, remained. But she did not want to go home even yet, and the prince thought he saw her order the boat to the shore without her. At all events, it rowed away; and now, of all the radiant company, only one white speck remained. Then the prince began to sing. And this is what he sung:—

"Lady fair,
Swan-white,
Lift thine eyes,
Banish night
By the might
Of thine eyes.

"Snowy arms,
Oars of snow
Oar her hither,
Plashing low.
Soft and slow,
Oar her hither.

"Stream behind her
O'er the lake,
Radiant whiteness!
In her wake
Following, following for her sake,
Radiant whiteness!

"Cling about her,
Waters blue;

Part not from her,
But renew
Cold and true
Kisses round her.

"Lap me round,
Waters sad
That have left her
Make me glad,
For ye had
Kissed her ere ye left her."

Before he had finished his song, the princess was just under the place where he sat, and looking up to find him. Her ears had led her truly.

"Would you like a fall, princess?" said the prince, looking down.

"Ah! there you are! Yes, if you please, prince," said the princess, looking up.

"How do you know I am a prince, princess?" said the prince.

"Because you are a very nice young man, prince," said the princess.

"Come up then, princess."

"Fetch me, prince."

The prince took off his scarf, then his swordbelt, then his tunic, and tied them all together, and let them down. But the line was far too short. He unwound his turban, and added it to the rest, when it was all but long enough; and his purse completed it. The princess just managed to lay hold of the knot of money, and was beside him in a moment. This rock was much higher than the other, and the splash and the dive were tremendous. The princess was in ecstasies of delight, and their swim was delicious.

Night after night they met, and swam about in the dark clear lake; where such was the prince's gladness, that (whether the princess's way of looking at things infected him, or he was actually getting light-headed) he often fancied that he was swimming in the sky instead of the lake. But when he talked about being in heaven, the princess laughed at him dreadfully.

When the moon came, she brought them fresh pleasure. Everything looked strange and new in her light, with an old, withered, yet unfading newness. When the moon was nearly full, one of their great delights was to dive deep in the water, and then, turning round, look up through it at the great blot of light close above them, shimmering and trembling and wavering, spreading and contracting, seeming to melt away, and again grow solid. Then they would shoot up through the blot; and lo! there was the moon, far off, clear and steady and cold, and very lovely, at the bottom of a deeper and bluer lake than theirs, as the princess said.

The prince soon found out that while in the water the princess was very like other people. And besides this, she was not so forward in her questions or pert in her replies at sea as on shore. Neither did she laugh so much; and when she did laugh, it was more gently. She seemed altogether more modest and maidenly in the water than out of it. But when the prince, who had really fallen in love when he fell in the lake, began to talk to her about love, she always turned her head towards him and laughed. After a while she began to look puzzled, as if she were trying to understand what he meant, but could not—revealing a notion that he meant something. But as soon as ever she left the lake, she was so altered, that the prince said to himself, "If I marry her, I see no help for it: we must turn merman and mermaid, and go out to sea at once."

XI
Hiss!

The princess's pleasure in the lake had grown to a passion, and she could scarcely bear to be out of it for an hour. Imagine then her consternation, when, diving with the prince one night, a sudden suspicion seized her that the lake was not so deep as it used to be. The prince could not imagine what had happened. She shot to the surface, and, without a word, swam at full speed towards the higher side of the lake. He followed, begging to know if she was ill, or what was the matter. She never turned her head, or took the smallest notice of his question. Arrived at the shore, she coasted the rocks with minute inspection. But she was not able to come to a conclusion, for the moon was very small, and so she could not see well. She turned therefore and swam home, without saying a word to explain her conduct to the prince, of whose presence she seemed no longer conscious. He withdrew to his cave, in great perplexity and distress.

Next day she made many observations, which, alas! strengthened her fears. She saw that the banks were too dry; and that the grass on the shore, and the trailing plants on the rocks, were withering away. She caused marks to be made along the borders, and examined them, day after day, in all directions of the wind; till at last the horrible idea became a certain fact—that the surface of the lake was slowly sinking.

The poor princess nearly went out of the little mind she had. It was awful to her to see the lake, which she loved more than any living thing, lie dying before her eyes. It sank away, slowly vanishing. The tops of rocks that had never been seen till now, began to appear far down in the clear water. Before long they were dry in the sun. It was fearful to think of the mud that would soon lie there baking and festering full of lovely creatures dying, and ugly creatures coming to life, like the unmaking of a world. And how hot the sun would be without any lake! She could not bear to swim in it any more, and began to pine away. Her life seemed bound up with it; and ever as the lake sank, she pined. People said she would not live an hour after the lake was gone.

But she never cried.

Proclamation was made to all the kingdom, that whosoever should discover the cause of the lake's decrease, would be rewarded after a princely fashion. Hum-Drum and Kopy-Keck applied themselves to their physics and metaphysics; but in vain. Not even they could suggest a cause.

Now the fact was that the old princess was at the root of the mischief. When she heard that her niece found more pleasure in the water than any one else had out of it, she went into a rage, and cursed herself for her want of foresight.

"But," said she, "I will soon set all right. The king and the people shall die of thirst; their brains shall boil and frizzle in their skulls before I will lose my revenge."

And she laughed a ferocious laugh, that made the hairs on the back of her black cat stand erect with terror.

Then she went to an old chest in the room, and opening it, took out what looked like a piece of dried seaweed. This she threw into a tub of water. Then she threw some powder into the water, and stirred it with her bare arm, muttering over it words of hideous sound, and yet more hideous import. Then she set the tub aside, and took from the chest a huge bunch of a hundred rusty keys, that clattered in her shaking hands. Then she sat down and proceeded to oil them all.

Before she had finished, out from the tub, the water of which had kept on a slow motion ever since she had ceased stirring it, came the head and half the body of a huge gray snake. But the witch did not look round. It grew out of the tub, waving itself backwards and forwards with a slow horizontal motion,

till it reached the princess, when it laid its head upon her shoulder, and gave a low hiss in her ear. She started—but with joy; and seeing the head resting on her shoulder, drew it towards her and kissed it. Then she drew it all out of the tub, and wound it round her body. It was one of those dreadful creatures which few have ever beheld—the White Snakes of Darkness.

Then she took the keys and went down to her cellar; and as she unlocked the door she said to herself,—

"This *is* worth living for!"

Locking the door behind her, she descended a few steps into the cellar, and crossing it, unlocked another door into a dark, narrow passage. She locked this also behind her, and descended a few more steps. If any one had followed the witch-princess, he would have heard her unlock exactly one hundred doors, and descend a few steps after unlocking each. When she had unlocked the last, she entered a vast cave, the roof of which was supported by huge natural pillars of rock. Now this roof was the under side of the bottom of the lake.

She then untwined the snake from her body, and held it by the tail high above her. The hideous creature stretched up its head towards the roof of the cavern, which it was just able to reach. It then began to move its head backwards and forwards, with a slow oscillating motion, as if looking for something. At the same moment the witch began to walk round and round the cavern, coming nearer to the centre every circuit; while the head of the snake described the same path over the roof that she did over the floor, for she kept holding it up. And still it kept slowly oscillating. Round and round the cavern they went, ever lessening the circuit, till at last the snake made a sudden dart, and clung to the roof with its mouth.

"That's right, my beauty!" cried the princess; "drain it dry."

She let it go, left it hanging, and sat down on a great stone, with her black cat, which had followed her all round the cave, by her side. Then she began to knit and mutter awful words. The snake hung like a huge leech, sucking at the stone; the cat stood with his back arched, and his tail like a piece of cable, looking up at the snake; and the old woman sat and knitted and muttered.

Seven days and seven nights they remained thus; when suddenly the serpent dropped from the roof as if exhausted and shrivelled up till it was again like a piece of dried seaweed. The witch started to her feet, picked it up, put it in her pocket, and looked up at the roof. One drop of water was trembling on the spot where the snake had been sucking. As soon as she saw that, she turned and fled, followed by her cat. Shutting the door in a terrible hurry, she locked it, and having muttered some frightful words, sped to the next, which also she locked and muttered over; and so with all the hundred doors, till she arrived in her own cellar. Then she sat down on the floor ready to faint, but listening with malicious delight to the rushing of the water, which she could hear distinctly through all the hundred doors.

But this was not enough. Now that she had tasted revenge, she lost her patience. Without further measures, the lake would be too long in disappearing. So the next night, with the last shred of the dying old moon rising, she took some of the water in which she had revived the snake, put it in a bottle, and set out, accompanied by her cat. Before morning she had made the entire circuit of the lake, muttering fearful words as she crossed every stream, and casting into it some of the water out of her bottle.

When she had finished the circuit she muttered yet again, and flung a handful of water towards the moon. Thereupon every spring in the country ceased to throb and bubble, dying away like the pulse of a dying man. The next day there was no sound of falling water to be heard along the borders of the lake. The very courses were dry; and the mountains showed no silvery streaks down their dark sides. And not alone had the fountains of mother Earth ceased to flow; for all the babies throughout the country were crying dreadfully—only without tears.

XII
Where Is the Prince?

Never since the night when the princess left him so abruptly had the prince had a single interview with her. He had seen her once or twice in the lake; but as far as he could discover, she had not been in it any more at night. He had sat and sung, and looked in vain for his Nereid; while she, like a true Nereid, was wasting away with her lake, sinking as it sank, withering as it dried. When at length he discovered the change that was taking place in the level of the water, he was in great alarm and perplexity. He could not tell whether the lake was dying because the lady had forsaken it; or whether the lady would not come because the lake had begun to sink. But he resolved to know so much at least.

He disguised himself, and, going to the palace, requested to see the lord chamberlain. His appearance at once gained his request; and the lord chamberlain, being a man of some insight, perceived that there was more in the prince's solicitation than met the ear. He felt likewise that no one could tell whence a solution of the present difficulties might arise. So he granted the prince's prayer to be made shoeblack to the princess. It was rather cunning in the prince to request such an easy post, for the princess could not possibly soil as many shoes as other princesses.

He soon learned all that could be told about the princess. He went nearly distracted; but after roaming about the lake for days, and diving in every depth that remained, all that he could do was to put an extra polish on the dainty pair of boots that was never called for.

For the princess kept her room, with the curtains drawn to shut out the dying lake. But could not shut it out of her mind for a moment. It haunted her imagination so that she felt as if the lake were her soul, drying up within her, first to mud, then to madness and death. She thus brooded over the change, with all its dreadful accompaniments, till she was nearly distracted. As for the prince, she had forgotten him. However much she had enjoyed his company in the water, she did not care for him without it. But she seemed to have forgotten her father and mother too.

The lake went on sinking. Small slimy spots began to appear, which glittered steadily amidst the changeful shine of the water. These grew to broad patches of mud, which widened and spread, with rocks here and there, and floundering fishes and crawling eels swarming. The people went everywhere catching these, and looking for anything that might have dropped from the royal boats.

At length the lake was all but gone, only a few of the deepest pools remaining unexhausted.

It happened one day that a party of youngsters found themselves on the brink of one of these pools in the very centre of the lake. It was a rocky basin of considerable depth. Looking in, they saw at the bottom something that shone yellow in the sun. A little boy jumped in and dived for it. It was a plate of gold covered with writing. They carried it to the king.

On one side of it stood these words:—

"Death alone from death can save.
Love is death, and so is brave
Love can fill the deepest grave.
Love loves on beneath the wave."

Now this was enigmatical enough to the king and courtiers. But the reverse of the plate explained it a little. Its writing amounted to this:—

"If the lake should disappear, they must find the hole through which the water ran. But it would be useless to try to stop it by any ordinary means. There was but one effectual mode. The body of a living man could alone stanch the flow. The man must give himself of his own will; and the lake must take his life as it filled. Otherwise the offering would be of no avail. If the nation could not provide one hero, it was time it should perish."

XIII
Here I Am

This was a very disheartening revelation to the king—not that he was unwilling to sacrifice a subject, but that he was hopeless of finding a man willing to sacrifice himself. No time was to be lost, however, for the princess was lying motionless on her bed, and taking no nourishment but lake-water, which was now none of the best. Therefore the king caused the contents of the wonderful plate of gold to be published throughout the country.

No one, however, came forward.

The prince, having gone several days' journey into the forest, to consult a hermit whom he had met there on his way to Lagobel, knew nothing of the oracle till his return.

When he had acquainted himself

with all the particulars, he sat down and thought,—

"She will die if I don't do it, and life would be nothing to me without her; so I shall lose nothing by doing it. And life will be as pleasant to her as ever, for she will soon forget me. And there will be so much more beauty and happiness in the world!—To be sure, I shall not see it." (Here the poor prince gave a sigh.) "How lovely the lake will be in the moonlight, with that glorious creature sporting in it like a wild goddess!—It is rather hard to be drowned by inches, though. Let me see—that will be seventy inches of me to drown." (Here he tried to laugh, but could not.) "The longer the better, however," he resumed; "for can I not bargain that the princess shall be beside me all the time? So I shall see her once more, kiss her perhaps,—who knows? and die looking in her eyes. It will be no death. At least, I shall not feel it. And to see the lake filling for the beauty again!—All right! I am ready."

He kissed the princess's boot, laid it down, and hurried to the king's apartment. But feeling, as he went, that anything sentimental would be disagreeable, he resolved to carry off the whole affair with nonchalance. So he knocked at the door of the king's counting-house, where it was all but a capital crime to disturb him.

When the king heard the knock he started up, and opened the door in a rage. Seeing only the shoeblack, he drew his sword. This, I am sorry to say, was his usual mode of asserting his regality when he thought his dignity was in danger. But the prince was not in the least alarmed.

"Please your majesty, I'm your butler," said he.

"My butler! you lying rascal! What do you mean."

"I mean, I will cork your big bottle."

"Is the fellow mad?" bawled the king, raising the point of his sword.

"I will put the stopper—plug—what you call it, in your leaky lake, grand monarch," said the prince.

The king was in such a rage that before he could speak he had time to cool, and to reflect that it would be great waste to kill the only man who was willing to be useful in the present emergency, seeing that in the end the insolent fellow would be as dead as if he had died by his majesty's own hand.

"Oh!" said he at last, putting up his sword with difficulty, it was so long; "I am obliged to you, you young fool! Take a glass of wine?"

"No, thank you," replied the prince.

"Very well," said the king. "Would you like to run and see your parents before you make your experiment?"

"No, thank you," said the prince.

"Then we will go and look for the hole at once," said his majesty, and proceeded to call some attendants.

"Stop, please your majesty; I have a condition to make," interposed the prince.

"What!" exclaimed the king, "a condition! and with me! How dare you?"

"As you please," returned the prince, coolly. "I wish your majesty a good morning."

"You wretch! I will have you put in a sack, and stuck in the hole."

"Very well, your majesty," replied the prince, becoming a little more respectful, lest the wrath of the king should deprive him of the pleasure of dying for the princess. "But what good will that do your majesty? Please to remember that the oracle says the victim must offer himself."

"Well, you *have* offered yourself," retorted the king.

"Yes, upon one condition."

"Condition again!" roared the king, once more drawing his sword. "Begone!

Somebody else will be glad enough to take the honor off your shoulders."

"Your majesty knows it will not be easy to get another to take my place."

"Well, what is your condition?" growled the king, feeling that the prince was right.

"Only this," replied the prince; "that, as I must on no account die before I am fairly drowned, and the waiting will be rather wearisome, the princess, your daughter, shall go with me, feed me with her own hands, and look at me now and then to comfort me; for you must confess it *is* rather hard. As soon as the water is up to my eyes, she may go and be happy, and forget her poor shoeblack."

Here the prince's voice faltered, and he very nearly grew sentimental, in spite of his resolution.

"Why didn't you tell me before what your condition was? Such a fuss about nothing!" exclaimed the king.

"Do you grant it?" persisted the prince.

"Of course I do," replied the king.

"Very well. I am ready."

"Go and have some dinner, then, while I set my people to find the place."

The king ordered out his guards, and gave directions to the officers to find the hole in the lake at once. So the bed of the lake was marked out in divisions and thoroughly examined, and in an hour or so the hole was discovered. It was in the middle of a stone, near the centre of the lake, in the very pool where the golden plate had been found. It was a three-cornered hole of no great size. There was water all round the stone, but very little was flowing through the hole.

XIV
This Is Very Kind of You

The prince went to dress for the occasion, for he was resolved to die like a prince.

When the princess heard that a man had offered to die for her, she was so transported that she jumped off the bed, feeble as she was, and danced about the room for joy. She did not care who the man was; that was nothing to her. The hole wanted stopping; and if only a man would do, why, take one. In an hour or two more everything was ready. Her maid dressed her in haste, and they carried her to the side of the lake. When she saw it she shrieked, and covered her face with her hands. They bore her across to the stone, where they had already placed a little boat for her. The water was not deep enough to float it, but they hoped it would be, before long. They laid her on cushions, placed in the boat wines and fruits and other nice things, and stretched a canopy over all.

In a few minutes the prince appeared. The princess recognized him at once, but did not think it worth while to acknowledge him.

"Here I am," said the prince. "Put me in."

"They told me it was a shoeblack," said the princess.

"So I am," said the prince. "I blacked your little boots three times a day, because they were all I could get of you. Put me in."

The courtiers did not resent his bluntness, except by saying to each other that he was taking it out in impudence.

But how was he to be put in? The golden plate contained no instructions on this point. The prince looked at the hole, and saw but one way. He put both his legs into it, sitting on the stone, and, stooping forward, covered the corner that remained open with his two hands. In this uncomfortable position he resolved to abide his fate, and turning to the people, said,—

"Now you can go."

The king had already gone home to dinner.

"Now you can go," repeated the princess after him, like a parrot.

The people obeyed her and went.

Presently a little wave flowed over the stone, and wetted one of the prince's knees. But he did not mind it much. He began to sing, and the song he sang was this:—

"As a world that has no well,
Darkly bright in forest dell;
As a world without the gleam
Of the downward-going stream;
As a world without the glance
Of the ocean's fair expanse;
As a world where never rain
Glittered on the sunny plain;—
Such, my heart, thy world would be,
If no love did flow in thee.

"As a world without the sound
Of the rivulets underground;
Or the bubbling of the spring
Out of darkness wandering;
Or the mighty rush and flowing
Of the river's downward going;
Or the music-showers that drop
On the outspread beech's top;
Or the ocean's mighty voice,
When his lifted waves rejoice;—
Such, my soul, thy world would be
If no love did sing in thee.

"Lady, keep thy world's delight
Keep the waters in thy sight.
Love hath made me strong to go,
For thy sake, to realms below
Where the water's shine and hum
Through the darkness never come:
Let, I pray, one thought of me
Spring, a little well, in thee;
Lest thy loveless soul be found
Like a dry and thirsty ground."

"Sing again, prince. It makes it less tedious," said the princess.

But the prince was too much overcome to sing any more, and a long pause followed.

"This is very kind of you, prince," said the princess at last, quite coolly, as she lay in the boat with her eyes shut.

"I am sorry I can't return the compliment," thought the prince; "but you are worth dying for, after all."

Again a wavelet, and another, and another flowed over the stone, and wetted both the prince's knees; but he did not speak or move. Two—three—four hours passed in this way, the princess apparently asleep, and the prince very patient. But he was much disappointed in his position, for he had none of the consolation he had hoped for.

At last he could bear it no longer.

"Princess!" said he.

But at the moment up started the princess, crying,—

"I'm afloat! I'm afloat!"

And the little boat bumped against the stone.

"Princess!" repeated the prince, encouraged by seeing her wide awake and looking eagerly at the water.

"Well?" said she, without looking round.

"Your papa promised that you should look at me, and you haven't looked at me once."

"Did he? Then I suppose I must. But I am so sleepy!"

"Sleep then, darling, and don't mind me," said the poor prince.

"Really, you are very good," replied the princess. "I think I will go to sleep again."

"Just give me a glass of wine and a biscuit first," said the prince, very humbly.

"With all my heart," said the princess, and gaped as she said it.

She got the wine and the biscuit, however, and leaning over the side of the boat towards him, was compelled to look at him.

"Why, prince," she said, "you don't look well! Are you sure you don't mind it?"

"Not a bit," answered he, feeling very faint indeed. "Only I shall die before it is of any use to you, unless I have something to eat."

"There then," said she, holding out the wine to him.

"Ah! you must feed me. I dare not move my hands. The water would run away directly."

"Good gracious!" said the princess; and she began at once to feed him with bits of biscuit and sips of wine.

As she fed him, he contrived to kiss the tips of her fingers now and then. She did not seem to mind it, one way or the other. But the prince felt better.

"Now, for your own sake, princess," said he, "I cannot let you go to sleep. You must sit and look at me, else I shall not be able to keep up."

"Well, I will do anything to oblige you," answered she, with condescension; and, sitting down, she did look at him, and kept looking at him with wonderful steadiness, considering all things.

The sun went down, and the moon rose, and, gush after gush, the waters were rising up the prince's body. They were up to his waist now.

"Why can't we go and have a swim?" said the princess. "There seems to be water enough just about here."

"I shall never swim more," said the prince.

"Oh, I forgot," said the princess, and was silent.

So the water grew and grew, and rose up and up on the prince. And the princess sat and looked at him. She fed him now and then. The night wore on. The waters rose and rose. The moon rose likewise higher and higher, and shone full on the face of the dying prince. The water was up to his neck.

"Will you kiss me, princess?" said he, feebly. The nonchalance was all gone now.

"Yes, I will," answered the princess, and kissed him with a long, sweet, cold kiss.

"Now," said he, with a sigh of content, "I die happy."

He did not speak again. The princess gave him some wine for the last time: he was past eating. Then she sat down again, and looked at him. The water rose and rose. It touched his chin. It touched his lower lip. It touched between his lips. He shut them hard to keep it out. The princess began to feel strange. It touched his upper lip. He breathed through his nostrils. The princess looked wild. It covered his nostrils. Her eyes looked scared, and shone strange in the moonlight. His head fell back; the water closed over it, and the bubbles of his last breath bubbled up through the water. The princess gave a shriek and sprang into the lake.

She laid hold first of one leg, and then of the other, and pulled and tugged, but she could not move either. She stopped to take breath, and that made her think that he could not get any breath. She was frantic. She got hold of him, and held his head above the water, which was possible now his hands were no longer on the hole. But it was of no use, for he was past breathing.

Love and water brought back all her strength. She got under the water, and pulled and pulled with her whole might, till at last she got one leg out. The other easily followed. How she got him into the boat she never could tell; but when she did, she fainted away. Coming to herself, she seized the oars, kept herself steady as best she could, and rowed and rowed, though she had never rowed before. Round rocks, and over shallows, and through mud she rowed, till she got to the landing-stairs of the palace. By this time her people were on the shore for they had heard her shriek. She made them carry the prince to her own room, and lay him in her bed, and light a fire, and send for the doctors.

"But the lake, your highness!" said the chamberlain, who, roused by the noise, came in, in his nightcap.

"Go and drown yourself in it!" she said.

This was the last rudeness of which the princess was ever guilty; and one must allow that she had good cause to feel provoked with the lord chamberlain.

Had it been the king himself, he would have fared no better. But both he and the queen were fast asleep. And the chamberlain went back to his bed. Somehow, the doctors never came. So the princess and her old nurse were left with the prince. But the old nurse was a wise woman, and knew what to do.

They tried everything for a long time without success. The princess was nearly distracted between hope and fear, but she tried on and on, one thing after another, and everything over and over again.

At last, when they had all but given it up, just as the sun rose, the prince opened his eyes.

XV
Look at the Rain!

The princess burst into a passion of tears and *fell* on the floor. There she lay for an hour, and her tears never ceased. All the pent-up crying of her life was spent now. And a rain came on, such as had never been seen in that country. The sun shone all the time, and the great drops, which fell straight to the earth, shone likewise. The palace was in the heart of a rainbow. It was a rain of rubies, and sapphires, and emeralds, and topazes. The torrents poured from the mountains like molten gold; and if it had not been for its subterraneous outlet, the lake would have overflowed and in-undated the country. It was full from shore to shore.

But the princess did not heed the lake. She lay on the floor and wept. And this rain within doors was far more wonderful than the rain out of doors. For when it abated a little, and she proceeded to rise, she found, to her astonishment, that she could not. At length, after many efforts, she succeeded in getting upon her feet. But she tumbled down again directly. Hearing her fall, her old nurse uttered a yell of delight, and ran to her, screaming,—

"My darling child! she's found her gravity!"

"Oh, that's it! is it?" said the princess, rubbing her shoulder and her knee alternately. "I consider it very unpleasant. I feel as if I should be crushed to pieces."

"Hurrah!" cried the prince from the bed. "If you've come round, princess, so have I. How's the lake?"

"Brimful," answered the nurse.

"Then we're all happy."

"That we are indeed!" answered the princess, sobbing.

And there was rejoicing all over the country that rainy day. Even the babies forgot their past troubles, and danced and crowed amazingly. And the king told stories, and the queen listened to them. And he divided the money in his box, and she the honey in her pot, among all the children. And there was such jubilation as was never heard of before.

Of course the prince and princess were betrothed at once. But the princess had to learn to walk, before they could be married with any propriety. And this was not so easy at her time of life, for she could walk no more than a baby. She was always falling down and hurting herself.

"Is this the gravity you used to make so much of?" said she one day to the prince, as he raised her from the floor.

"For my part, I was a great deal more comfortable without it."

"No, no, that's not it. This is it," replied the prince, as he took her up, and carried her about like a baby, kissing her all the time. "This is gravity."

"That's better," said she. "I don't mind that so much."

And she smiled the sweetest, loveliest smile in the prince's face. And she gave him one little kiss in return for all his; and he thought them overpaid, for he was beside himself with delight. I fear she complained of her gravity more than once after this, notwithstanding.

It was a long time before she got reconciled to walking. But the pain of learning it was quite counterbalanced by two things, either of which would have been sufficient consolation. The first was, that the prince himself was her teacher; and the second, that she could tumble into the lake as often as she pleased. Still, she preferred to have the prince jump in with her; and the splash they made before was nothing to the splash they made now.

The lake never sank again. In process of time, it wore the roof of the cavern quite through, and was twice as deep as before.

The only revenge the princess took upon her aunt was to tread pretty hard on her gouty toe the next time she saw her. But she was sorry for it the very next day, when she heard that the water had undermined her house, and that it had fallen in the night, burying her in its ruins; whence no one ever ventured to dig up her body. There she lies to this day.

So the prince and princess lived and were happy; and had crowns of gold, and clothes of cloth, and shoes of leather, and children of boys and girls, not one of whom was ever known, on the most critical occasion, to lose the smallest atom of his or her due proportion of gravity.

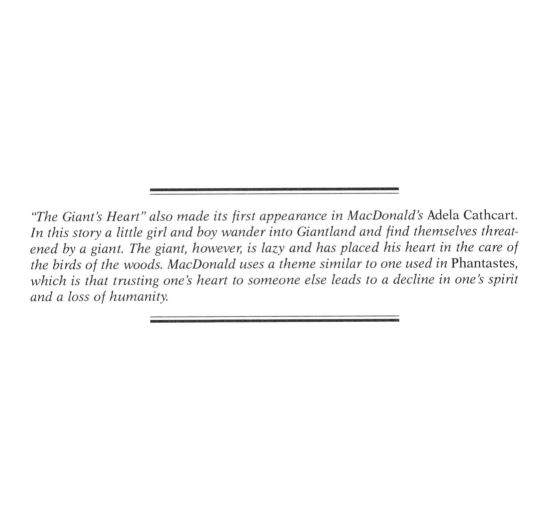

"The Giant's Heart" also made its first appearance in MacDonald's Adela Cathcart. *In this story a little girl and boy wander into Giantland and find themselves threatened by a giant. The giant, however, is lazy and has placed his heart in the care of the birds of the woods. MacDonald uses a theme similar to one used in* Phantastes, *which is that trusting one's heart to someone else leads to a decline in one's spirit and a loss of humanity.*

CHAPTER TWO

The Giant's Heart

There once was a giant who lived on the borders of Giantland where it touched on the country of common people.

Everything in Giantland was so big that the common people saw only a mass of awful mountains and clouds; and no living man had ever come from it, as far as anybody knew, to tell what he had seen in it.

Somewhere near the borders, on the other side, by the edge of a great forest, lived a labourer with his wife and a great many children. One day Tricksey-Wee, as they called her, teased her brother Buffy-Bob, till he could not bear it any longer, and gave her a box on the ear. Tricksey-Wee cried; and Buffy-Bob was so sorry and so ashamed of himself that he cried too, and ran off into the wood. He was so long gone that Tricksey-Wee began to be frightened, for she was very fond of her brother; and she was so distressed that she had first teased him and then cried, that at last she ran into the wood to look for him, though there was more chance of losing herself than of finding him.

And, indeed, so it seemed likely to turn out; for, running on without looking, she at length found herself in a valley she knew nothing about. And no wonder; for what she thought was a valley with round, rocky sides, was no other than the space between two of the roots of a great tree that grew on the borders of Giantland. She climbed over the side of it, and went towards what she took for a black, round-topped mountain, far away; but which she soon

discovered to be close to her, and to be a hollow place so great that she could not tell what it was hollowed out of. Staring at it, she found that it was a doorway; and going nearer and staring harder, she saw the door, far in, with a knocker of iron upon it, a great many yards above her head, and as large as the anchor of a big ship.

Now nobody had ever been unkind to Tricksey-Wee and therefore she was not afraid of anybody. For Buffy-Bob's box on the ear she did not think worth considering. So spying a little hole at the bottom of the door which had been nibbled by some giant mouse, she crept through it, and found herself in an enormous hall. She could not have seen the other end of it at all, except for the great fire that was burning there, diminished to a spark in the distance. Towards this fire she ran as fast as she could, and was not far from it when something fell before her with a great clatter, over which she tumbled, and went rolling on the floor.

She was not much hurt, however, and got up in a moment. Then she saw that what she had fallen over was not unlike a great iron bucket. When she examined it more closely, she discovered that it was a thimble; and looking up to see who had dropped it, beheld a huge face, with spectacles as big as the round windows in a church, bending over her, and looking everywhere for the thimble. Tricksey-Wee immediately laid hold of it in both her arms, and lifted it about an inch nearer to the nose of the peering giantess. This movement made the old lady see where it was, and, her finger popping into it, it vanished from the eyes of Tricksey-Wee, buried in the folds of a white stocking like a cloud in the sky, which Mrs. Giant was busy darning. For it was Saturday night, and her husband would wear nothing but white stockings on Sunday. To be sure, he did eat little children, but only *very* little ones; and if ever it crossed his mind that it was wrong to do so, he always said to himself that he wore whiter stockings on Sunday than any other giant in all Giantland.

At the same instant Tricksey-Wee heard a sound like the wind in a tree full of leaves, and could not think what it could be; till, looking up, she found that it was the giantess whispering to her; and when she tried very hard she could hear what she said well enough.

"Run away, dear little girl," she said, "as fast as you can; for my husband will be home in a few minutes."

"But I've never been naughty to your husband," said Tricksey-Wee, looking up in the giantess's face.

"That doesn't matter. You had better go. He is fond of little children, particularly little girls."

"Oh, then he won't hurt me."

"I am not sure of that. He is so fond of them that he eats them up; and I am afraid he couldn't help hurting you a little. He's a very good man, though."

"Oh! then—" began Tricksey-Wee, feeling rather frightened; but before she could finish her sentence she heard the sound of footsteps very far apart and very heavy. The next moment, who should come running towards her, full speed, and as pale as death, but Buffy-Bob. She held out her arms, and he ran into them. But when she tried to kiss him, she only kissed the back of his head; for his white face and round eyes were turned to the door.

"Run, children; run and hide," said the giantess.

"Come, Buffy," said Tricksey; "yonder's a great brake; we'll hide in it."

The brake was a big broom; and they had just got into the bristles of it when they heard the door open with a sound of thunder, and in stalked the giant. You would have thought you saw the whole earth through the door when he opened it, so wide was it; and when he closed it, it was like nightfall.

"Where is that little boy?" he cried, with a voice like the bellowing of a cannon. "He looked a very nice boy indeed. I am almost sure he crept through the mousehole at the bottom of the door. Where is he, my dear?"

"I don't know," answered the giantess.

"But you know it is wicked to tell lies; don't you, my dear?" retorted the giant.

"Now, you ridiculous old Thunderthump!" said his wife, with a smile as broad as the sea in the sun, "how can I mend your white stockings and look after little boys? You have got plenty to last you over Sunday, I am sure. Just look what good little boys they are!"

Tricksey-Wee and Buffy-Bob peered through the bristles, and discovered a row of little boys, about a dozen, with very fat faces and goggle eyes, sitting before the fire, and looking stupidly into it. Thunderthump intended the most of these for pickling, and was feeding them well before salting them. Now and then, however, he could not keep his teeth off them, and would eat one, by the bye, without salt.

He strode up to the wretched children. Now what made them very wretched indeed was, that they knew if they could only keep from eating, and grow thin, the giant would dislike them, and turn them out to find their way home; but notwithstanding this, so greedy were they, that they ate as much as ever they could hold. The giantess, who fed them, comforted herself with thinking that they were not real boys and girls, but only little pigs pretending to be boys and girls.

"Now tell me the truth," cried the giant, bending his face down over them. They shook with terror, and every one hoped it was somebody else the giant liked best. "Where is the little boy that ran into the hall just now? Whoever tells me a lie shall be instantly boiled."

"He's in the broom," cried one dough-faced boy. "He's in there, and a little girl with him."

"The naughty children," cried the giant, "to hide from me!" And he made a stride towards the broom.

"Catch hold of the bristles, Bobby. Get right into a tuft, and hold on," cried Tricksey-Wee, just in time.

The giant caught up the broom, and seeing nothing under it, set it down again with a force that threw them both on the floor. He then made two strides to the boys, caught the dough-faced one by the neck, took the lid off a great pot that was boiling on the fire, popped him in as if he had been a trussed chicken, put the lid on again, and saying, "There, boys! See what comes of lying!" asked no more questions; for, as he always kept his word, he was afraid he might have to do the same to them all; and he did not like boiled boys. He liked to eat them crisp, as radishes, whether forked or not, ought to be eaten. He then sat down, and asked his wife if his supper was ready. She looked into the pot, and throwing the boy out with the ladle, as if he had been a black beetle that had tumbled in and had had the worst of it, answered that she thought it was. Whereupon he rose to help her; and taking the pot from the fire, poured the whole contents, bubbling and splashing, into a dish like a vat. Then they sat down to supper. The children in the broom could not see what they had; but it

seemed to agree with them; for the giant talked like thunder, and the giantess answered like the sea, and they grew chattier and chattier.

At length the giant said, "I don't feel quite comfortable about that heart of mine." And as he spoke, instead of laying his hand on his bosom, he waved it away towards the corner where the children were peeping from the broom bristles, like frightened little mice.

"Well, you know, my darling Thunderthump," answered his wife, "I always thought it ought to be nearer home. But you know best, of course."

"Ha! ha! You don't know where it is, wife. I moved it a month ago."

"What a man you are, Thunderthump! You trust any creature alive rather than your own wife."

Here the giantess gave a sob which sounded exactly like a wave going flop into the mouth of a cave up to the roof.

"Where have you got it now?" she resumed, checking her emotion.

"Well, Doodlem, I don't mind telling *you*," answered the giant, soothingly. "The great she-eagle has got it for a nest egg. She sits on it night and day, and thinks she will bring the greatest eagle out of it that ever sharpened his beak on the rocks of Mount Skycrack. I can warrant no one else will touch it while she has got it. But she is rather capricious, and I confess I am not easy about it; for the least scratch of one of her claws would do for me at once. And she *has* claws."

I refer any one who doubts this part of my story to certain chronicles of Giantland preserved among the Celtic nations. It was quite a common thing for a giant to put his heart out to nurse, because he did not like the trouble and responsibility of doing it himself; although I must confess it was a dangerous sort of plan to take, especially with such a delicate viscus as the heart.

All this time Buffy-Bob and Tricksey-Wee were listening with long ears.

"Oh!" thought Tricksey-Wee, "if I could but find the giant's cruel heart, wouldn't I give it a squeeze!"

The giant and giantess went on talking for a long time. The giantess kept advising the giant to hide his heart somewhere in the house; but he seemed afraid of the advantage it would give her over him.

"You could hide it at the bottom of the flour-barrel," said she.

"That would make me feel chokey," answered he.

"Well, in the coal-cellar. Or in the dust-hole—that's the place! No one would think of looking for your heart in the dust-hole."

"Worse and worse!" cried the giant.

"Well, the water-butt," suggested she.

"No, no; it would grow spongy there," said he.

"Well, what *will* you do with it?"

"I will leave it a month longer where it is, and then I will give it to the Queen of the Kangaroos, and she will carry it in her pouch for me. It is best to change its place, you know, lest my enemies should scent it out. But, dear Doodlem, it's a fretting care to have a heart of one's own to look after. The responsibility is too much for me. If it were not for a bite of a radish now and then, I never could bear it."

Here the giant looked lovingly towards the row of little boys by the fire, all of whom were nodding, or asleep on the floor.

"Why don't you trust it to me, dear Thunderthump?" said his wife. "I would take the best possible care of it."

"I don't doubt it, my love. But the responsibility would be too much for *you*. You would no longer be my darling, light-hearted, airy, laughing Doodlem. It

would transform you into a heavy, oppressed woman, weary of life—as I am."

The giant closed his eyes and pretended to go to sleep. His wife got his stockings, and went on with her darning. Soon the giant's presence became reality, and the giantess began to nod over her work.

"Now, Buffy," whispered Tricksey-Wee, "now's our time. I think it's moonlight, and we had better be off. There's a door with a hole for the cat just behind us."

"All right," said Bob; "I'm ready."

So they got out of the broom-brake and crept to the door. But to their great disappointment, when they got through it, they found themselves in a sort of shed. It was full of tubs and things, and, though it was built of wood only, they could not find a crack.

"Let us try this hole," said Tricksey; for the giant and giantess were sleeping behind them, and they dared not go back.

"All right," said Bob.

He seldom said anything else than *All right*.

Now this hole was in a mound that came in through the wall of the shed, and went along the floor for some distance. They crawled into it, and found it very dark. But groping their way along, they soon came to a small crack, through which they saw grass, pale in the moonshine. As they crept on, they found the hole began to get wider and lead upwards.

"What is that noise of rushing?" said Buffy-Bob.

"I can't tell," replied Tricksey; "for, you see, I don't know what we are in."

The fact was, they were creeping along a channel in the heart of a giant tree; and the noise they heard was the noise of the sap rushing along in its wooden pipes. When they laid their ears to the wall, they heard it gurgling along with a pleasant noise.

"It sounds kind and good," said Tricksey. "It is water running. Now it must be running from somewhere to somewhere. I think we had better go on, and we shall come somewhere."

It was now rather difficult to go on, for they had to climb as if they were climbing a hill; and now the passage was wide. Nearly worn out, they saw light overhead at last, and creeping through a crack into the open air, found themselves on the fork of a huge tree. A great, broad, uneven space lay around them, out of which spread boughs in every direction, the smallest of them as big as the biggest tree in the country of common people. Overhead were leaves enough to supply all the trees they had ever seen. Not much moonlight could come through, but the leaves would glimmer white in the wind at times. The tree was full of giant birds. Every now and then, one would sweep through, with a great noise. But, except an occasional chirp, sounding like a shrill pipe in a great organ, they made no noise. All at once an owl began to hoot. He thought he was singing. As soon as he began, other birds replied, making rare game of him. To their astonishment, the children found they could understand every word they sang. And what they sang was something like this:

"I will sing a song.
　I'm the owl."
"Sing a song, you sing-song
　Ugly fowl!
What will you sing about,
Night in and Day out?"

"Sing about the night;
　I'm the owl."
"You could not see for the light,
　Stupid fowl!"
"Oh! the moon! and the dew!
And the shadows!—tu-whoo!"

The owl spread out his silent, soft, sly wings, and lighting between Tricksey-Wee and Buffy-Bob, nearly smothered them, closing up one under each wing. It was like being buried in a down bed. But the owl did not like anything between his sides and his wings, so he opened his wings again, and the children made haste to get out. Tricksey-Wee immediately went in front of the bird, and looking up into his huge face, which was as round as the eyes of the giantess's spectacles, and much bigger, dropped a pretty courtesy, and said,—

"Please, Mr. Owl, I want to whisper to you."

"Very well, small child," answered the owl, looking important, and stooping his ear towards her. "What is it?"

"Please tell me where the eagle lives that sits on the giant's heart."

"Oh, you naughty child! That's a secret. For shame!"

And with a great hiss that terrified them, the owl flew into the tree. All birds are fond of secrets; but not many of them can keep them so well as the owl.

So the children went on because they did not know what else to do. They found the way very rough and difficult, the tree was so full of humps and hollows. Now and then they plashed into a pool of rain; now and then they came upon twigs growing out of the trunk where they had no business, and they were as large as full-grown poplars. Sometimes they came upon great cushions of soft moss, and on one of them they lay down and rested. But they had not lain long before they spied a large nightingale sitting on a branch, with its bright eyes looking up at the moon. In a moment more he began to sing, and the birds about him began to reply, but in a very different tone from that in which they had replied to the owl. Oh, the birds did call the nightingale such pretty names! The nightingale sang, and the birds replied like this:—

> "I will sing a song.
>   I'm the nightingale."
> "Sing a song, long, long,
>   Little Neverfail!
> What will you sing about,
> Light in or light out?"

> "Sing about the light
>   Gone away;
> Down, away, and out of sight—
>   Poor lost day!
> Mourning for the day dead,
> O'er his dim bed."

The nightingale sang so sweetly, that the children would have fallen asleep but for fear of losing any of the song. When the nightingale stopped they got up and wandered on. They did not know where they were going, but they thought it best to keep going on, because then they might come upon something or other. They were very sorry they had forgotten to ask the nightingale about the eagle's nest, but his music had put everything else out of their heads. They resolved, however, not to forget the next time they had a chance. So they went on and on, till they were both tired, and Tricksey-Wee said at last, trying to laugh,—

"I declare my legs feel like a Dutch doll's."

"Then here's the place to go to bed in," said Buffy-Bob.

They stood at the edge of a last year's nest, and looked down with delight into the round, mossy cave. Then they crept gently in, and, lying down in each other's arms, found it so deep, and warm, and comfortable, and soft, that they were soon fast asleep.

Now close beside them, in a hollow, was another nest, in which lay a lark and his wife; and the children were awakened, very early in the morning, by a dispute between Mr. and Mrs. Lark.

"Let me up," said the lark.

"It is not time," said the lark's wife.

"It is," said the lark, rather rudely. "The darkness is quite thin. I can almost see my own beak."

"Nonsense!" said the lark's wife. "You know you came home yesterday morning quite worn out—you had to fly so very high before you saw him. I am sure he would not mind if you took it a little easier. Do be quiet and go to sleep again."

"That's not it at all," said the lark. "He doesn't want me. I want him. Let me up, I say."

He began to sing; and Tricksey-Wee and Buffy-Bob having now learned the way, answered him:—

> "I will sing a song
>   I'm the Lark."
> "Sing, sing, Throat-song
>   Little Kill-the-dark.
> What will you sing about,
>   Now the night is out?"

> "I can only call;
>   I can't think.
> Let me up—that's all.
>   Let me drink!
> Thirsting all the long night
>   For a drink of light."

By this time the lark was standing on the edge of his nest and looking at the children.

"Poor little things! You can't fly," said the lark.

"No; but we can look up," said Tricksey.

"Ah, you don't know what it is to see the very first of the sun."

"But we know what it is to wait till he comes. He's no worse for your seeing him first, is he?"

"Oh no, certainly not," answered the lark, with condescension; and then, bursting into his *Jubilate*, he sprang aloft, clapping his wings like a clock running down.

"Tell us where—" began Buffy-Bob.

But the lark was out of sight. His song was all that was left of him. That was everywhere, and he was nowhere.

"Selfish bird!" said Buffy. "It's all very well for larks to go hunting the sun, but they have no business to despise their neighbours, for all that."

"Can I be of any service to you?" said a sweet bird-voice out of the nest.

This was the lark's wife, who stayed at home with the young larks while her husband went to church.

"Oh! thank you. If you please," answered Tricksey-Wee.

And up popped a pretty brown head; and then up came a brown feathery body; and last of all came the slender legs on to the edge of the nest. There she turned, and, looking down into the nest, from which came a whole litany of chirpings for breakfast, said, "Lie still, little ones." Then she turned to the children.

"My husband is King of the Larks," she said.

Buffy-Bob took off his cap, and Tricksey-Wee courtesied very low.

"Oh, it's not me," said the bird, looking very shy. "I am only his wife. It's my husband."

And she looked up after him into the sky, whence his song was still falling like a shower of musical hailstones. Perhaps *she* could see him.

"He's a splendid bird," said Buffy-Bob; "only you know he *will* get up a little too early."

"Oh, no! he doesn't. It's only his way, you know. But tell me what I can do for you."

"Tell us, please, Lady Lark, where the she-eagle lives that sits on Giant Thunderthump's heart."

"Oh! that is a secret."

"Did you promise not to tell?"

"No; but larks ought to be discreet. They see more than other birds."

"But you don't fly up high like your husband, do you?"

"Not often. But it's no matter. I come to know things for all that."

"Do tell me, and I will sing you a song," said Tricksey-Wee.

"Can you sing too?—You have got no wings!"

"Yes. And I will sing you a song I learned the other day about a lark and his wife."

"Please do," said the lark's wife. "Be quiet, children, and listen."

Tricksey-Wee was very glad she happened to know a song which would please the lark's wife, at least, whatever the lark himself might have thought of it if he had heard it. So she sang:—

"Good-morrow, my lord!" in the
  sky alone,
Sang the lark, as the sun ascended
  his throne.
"Shine on me, my lord; I only am
  come,
Of all your servants, to welcome
  you home.
I have flown a whole hour, right
  up, I swear,
To catch the first shine of your
  golden hair!"

"Must I thank you, then," said the
  king, "Sir Lark,
For flying so high, and hating the
  dark?
You ask a full cup for half a thirst:
Half is love of me, and half love to
  be first.
There's many a bird that makes no
  haste,
But waits till I come. That's as
  much to my taste."

And the king hid his head in a
  turban of cloud;
And the lark stopped singing, quite
  vexed and cowed

But he flew up higher and thought,
  "Anon,
The wrath of the king will be over
  and gone;
And his crown, shining out of its
  cloudy fold,
Will change my brown feathers to
  a glory of gold."

So he flew, with the strength of a
  lark he flew,
But as he rose the cloud rose too;
And not a gleam of the golden hair
Came through the depth of the
  misty air;
Till, weary with flying, with
  sighing sore,
The strong sun-seeker could do no
  more.

His wings had no chrism of gold,
And his feathers felt withered and
  worn and old;
So he quivered and sank, and
  dropped like a stone
And there on his nest, where he
  left her, alone
Sat his little wife on her little eggs,
Keeping them warm with wings
  and legs.

Did I say alone? Ah, no such thing!
Full in her face was shining the
  king.
"Welcome, Sir Lark! You look
  tired," said he:
"*Up* is not always the best way to
  me.
While you have been singing so
  high and away,
I've been shining to your little wife
  all day."

He had set his crown all about the
  nest,
And out of the midst shone her
  little brown breast;
And so glorious was she in russet
  gold,
That for wonder and awe Sir Lark
  grew cold.
He popped his head under her
  wing, and lay
As still as a stone, till the king was
  away.

As soon as Tricksey-Wee had finished her song, the lark's wife began a low, sweet, modest little song of her own; and after she had piped away for two or three minutes, she said,—

"You dear children, what can I do for you?"

"Tell us where the she-eagle lives, please," said Tricksey-Wee.

"Well, I don't think there can be much harm in telling such wise, good children," said Lady Lark; "I am sure you don't want to do any mischief."

"Oh, no; quite the contrary," said Buffy-Bob.

"Then I'll tell you. She lives on the very topmost peak of Mount Skycrack; and the only way to get up is to climb on the spider's webs that cover it from top to bottom."

"That's rather serious," said Tricksey-Wee.

"But you don't want to go up, you foolish little thing! You can't go. And what do you want to go up for?"

"That is a secret," said Tricksey-Wee.

"Well, it's no business of mine," rejoined Lady Lark, a little offended, and quite vexed that she had told them. So she flew away to find some breakfast for her little ones, who by this time were chirping very impatiently. The children looked at each other, joined hands, and walked off.

In a minute more the sun was up, and they soon reached the outside of the tree. The bark was so knobby and rough, and full of twigs, that they managed to get down, though not without great difficulty. Then, far away to the north they saw a huge peak, like the spire of a church, going right up into the sky. They thought this must be Mount Skycrack, and turned their faces towards it. As they went on, they saw a giant or two, now and then, striding about the fields or through the woods, but they kept out of their way. Nor were they in much danger; for it was only one or two of the border giants that were so very fond of children.

At last they came to the foot of Mount Skycrack. It stood in a plain alone, and shot right up, I don't know how many thousand feet, into the air, a long, narrow, spear-like mountain. The whole face of it, from top to bottom, was covered with a network of spiders' webs, the threads of various sizes, from that of silk to that of whipcord. The webs shook, and quivered, and waved in the sun, glittering like silver. All about ran huge greedy spiders, catching huge silly flies, and devouring them.

Here they sat down to consider what could be done. The spiders did not heed them, but ate away at the flies.—Now at the foot of the mountain, and all around it, was a ring of water, not very broad, but very deep. As they sat watching them, one of the spiders, whose web was woven across this water, somehow or other lost his hold, and fell in on his back. Tricksey-Wee and Buffy-Bob ran to his assistance, and laying hold each of one of his legs, succeeded, with the help of the other legs, which struggled spiderfully, in getting him out upon dry land. As soon as he had shaken himself, and dried himself a little, the spider turned to the children, saying,—

"And now, what can I do for you?"

"Tell us, please," said they, "how we can get up the mountain to the she-eagle's nest."

"Nothing is easier," answered the spider. "Just run up there, and tell them all I sent you, and nobody will mind you."

"But we haven't got claws like you, Mr. Spider," said Buffy.

"Ah! no more you have, poor unprovided creatures! Still, I think we can manage it. Come home with me."

"You won't eat us, will you?" said Buffy.

"My dear child," answered the spider, in a tone of injured dignity, "I eat nothing but what is mischievous or useless. You have helped me, and now I will help you."

The children rose at once, and climbing as well as they could, reached the spider's nest in the centre of the web. Nor did they find it very difficult; for whenever too great a gap came, the spider spinning a strong cord stretched it just where they would have chosen to put their feet next. He left them in his nest, after bringing them two enormous honey-bags, taken from bees that he had caught; but presently about six of the wisest of the spiders came back with him. It was rather horrible to look up and see them all around the mouth of the nest, looking down on them in contemplation, as if wondering whether they would be nice eating. At length one of them said,—"Tell us truly what you want with the eagle, and we will try to help you."

Then Tricksey-Wee told them that there was a giant on the borders who treated little children no better than radishes, and that they had narrowly escaped being eaten by him; that they had found out that the great she-eagle of Mount Skycrack was at present sitting on his heart; and that, if they could only get hold of the heart, they would soon teach the giant better behaviour."

"But," said their host, "if you get at the heart of the giant, you will find it as large as one of your elephants. What can you do with it?"

"The least scratch will kill," replied Buffy-Bob.

"Ah! but you might do better than that," said the spider. "Now we have resolved to help you. Here is a little bag of spider-juice. The giants cannot bear spiders, and this juice is dreadful poison to them. We are all ready to go up with you, and drive the eagle away. Then you must put the heart into this other bag, and bring it down with you; for then the giant will be in your power."

"But how can we do that?" said Buffy. "The bag is not much bigger than a pudding-bag."

"But it is as large as you will be able to carry."

"Yes; but what are we to do with the heart?"

"Put it into the bag, to be sure. Only, first, you must squeeze a drop out of the other bag upon it. You will see what will happen."

"Very well; we will do as you tell us," said Tricksey-Wee. "And now, if you please, how shall we go?"

"Oh, that's our business," said the first spider. "You come with me, and my grandfather will take your brother. Get up."

So Tricksey-Wee mounted on the narrow part of the spider's back, and held fast. And Buffy-Bob got on the grandfather's back. And up they scrambled, over one web after another, up and up—so fast! And every spider followed; so that when Tricksey-Wee looked back, she saw a whole army of spiders scrambling after them.

"What can we want with so many?" she thought; but she said nothing.

The moon was now up, and it was a splendid sight below and around them. All Giantland was spread out under them, with its great hills, lakes, trees, and animals. And all above them was the clear heaven, and Mount Skycrack rising into it, with its endless ladders of spiderwebs, glittering like cords made of moonbeams. And up the moonbeams went, crawling and scrambling, and racing, a huge army of huge spiders.

At length they reached all but the very summit, where they stopped. Tricksey-Wee and Buffy-Bob could see above them a great globe of feathers,

that finished off the mountain like an ornamental knob.

"But how shall we drive her off?" said Buffy.

"We'll soon manage that," answered the grandfather-spider. "Come on, you down there."

Up rushed the whole army, past the children, over the edge of the nest, on to the she-eagle, and buried themselves in her feathers. In a moment she became very restless, and went pecking about with her beak. All at once she spread out her wings, with a sound like a whirlwind, and flew off to bathe in the sea; and then the spiders began to drop from her in all directions on their gossamer wings. The children had to hold fast to keep the wind of the eagle's flight from blowing them off. As soon as it was over, they looked into the nest, and there lay the giant's heart—an awful and ugly thing.

"Make haste, child!" said Tricksey's spider.

So Tricksey took her bag, and squeezed a drop out of it upon the heart. She thought she heard the giant give a far-off roar of pain, and she nearly fell from her seat with terror. The heart instantly began to shrink. It shrunk and shrivelled till it was nearly gone; and Buffy-Bob caught it up and put it into his bag. Then the two spiders turned and went down again as fast as they could. Before they got to the bottom, they heard the shrieks of the she-eagle over the loss of her egg; but the spiders told them not to be alarmed, for her eyes were too big to see them. By the time they reached the foot of the mountain, all the spiders had got home, and were busy again catching flies, as if nothing had happened.

After renewed thanks to their friends, the children set off, carrying the giant's heart with them.

"If you should find it at all troublesome, just give it a little more spider-juice directly," said the grandfather, as they took their leave.

Now the giant had given an awful roar of pain the moment they anointed his heart, and had fallen down in a fit, in which he lay so long that all the boys might have escaped if they had not been so fat. One did, and got home in safety. For days the giant was unable to speak. The first words he uttered were,—

"Oh, my heart! my heart!"

"Your heart is safe enough, dear Thunderthump," said his wife. "Really, a man of your size ought not to be so nervous and apprehensive. I am ashamed of you."

"You have no heart, Doodlem," answered he. "I assure you at this moment mine is in the greatest danger. It has fallen into the hands of foes, though who they are I cannot tell."

Here he fainted again; for Tricksey-Wee, finding the heart beginning to swell a little, had given the least touch of spider-juice.

Again he recovered, and said,—

"Dear Doodlem, my heart is coming back to me. It is coming nearer and nearer."

After lying silent for hours, he exclaimed,—

"It is in the house, I know!"

And he jumped up and walked about, looking in every corner.

As he arose, Tricksey-Wee and Buffy-Bob came out of the hole in the tree-root, and through the cat-hole in the door, and walked boldly towards the giant. Both kept their eyes busy watching him. Led by the love of his own heart, the giant soon spied them, and staggered furiously towards them.

"I will eat you, you vermin!" he cried. "Here with my heart!"

Tricksey gave the heart a sharp pinch. Down fell the giant on his knees, blubbering, and crying, and begging for his heart.

"You shall have it, if you behave yourself properly," said Tricksey.

"How shall I behave myself properly?" asked he, whimpering.

"Take all those boys and girls, and carry them home at once."

"I'm not able; I'm too ill. I shall fall down."

"Take them up directly."

"I can't, till you give me my heart."

"Very well!" said Tricksey; and she gave the heart another pinch.

The giant jumped to his feet, and catching up all the children, thrust some into his waistcoat-pockets, some into his breast-pocket, put two or three into his hat, and took a bundle of them under each arm. Then he staggered to the door.

All this time poor Doodlem was sitting in her armchair, crying, and mending a white stocking.

The giant led the way to the borders. He could not go so fast but that Buffy and Tricksey managed to keep up with him. When they reached the borders, they thought it would be safer to let the children find their own way home. So they told him to set them down. He obeyed.

"Have you put them all down, Mr. Thunderthump?" asked Tricksey-Wee.

"Yes," said the giant.

"That's a lie!" squeaked a little voice; and out came a head from his waistcoat pocket.

Tricksey-Wee pinched the heart till the giant roared with pain.

"You're not a gentleman. You tell stories," she said.

"He was the thinnest of the lot," said Thunderthump, crying.

"Are you all there now, children?" asked Tricksey.

"Yes, ma'am," returned they, after counting themselves very carefully, and with some difficulty; for they were all stupid children.

"Now," said Tricksey-Wee to the giant, "will you promise to carry off no more children, and never to eat a child again all your life?"

"Yes, yes! I promise," answered Thunderthump, sobbing.

"And you will never cross the borders of Giantland?"

"Never."

"And you will never again wear white stockings on a Sunday, all your life long. Do you promise?"

The giant hesitated at this, and began to expostulate; but Tricksey-Wee, believing it would be good for his morals, insisted; and the giant promised.

Then she required of him, that, when she gave him back his heart, he should give it to his wife to take care of for him forever after. The poor giant fell on his knees, and began again to beg. But Tricksey-Wee giving the heart a slight pinch, he bawled out,—

"Yes, yes! Doodlem shall have it, I swear. Only she must not put it in the flour-barrel, or in the dust-hole."

"Certainly not. Make your own bar-gain with her. And you promise not to interfere with my brother and me, or to take any revenge for what we have done?"

"Yes, yes, my dear children; I promise everything. Do pray, make haste and give me back my poor heart."

"Wait there, then, till I bring it to you."

"Yes, yes. Only make haste, for I feel very faint."

Tricksey-Wee began to undo the mouth of the bag. But Buffy-Bob, who had got very knowing on his travels, took out his knife with the presence of cutting the string; but, in reality, to be prepared for any emergency.

No sooner was the heart out of the bag, than it expanded to the size of a bullock; and the giant, with a yell of rage and vengeance, rushed on the two children, who had stepped sideways from the terrible heart. But Buffy-Bob was too quick for Thunderthump. He sprang to the heart, and buried his knife in it, up to the hilt. A fountain of blood spouted from it; and with a dreadful groan the giant fell dead at the feet of little Tricksey-Wee, who could not help being sorry for him, after all.

"The Shadows" is another story that originally appeared in Adela Cathcart. *This time the story is about a sick old man who, being between life and death, has a vision of fairies carrying him away to the Land of Shadows. While there he is taught about how shadows often help men grow spiritually. Shadows frighten men when they are doing wrong, and so shadows, being part of God's creation, have a positive moral effect upon men.*

CHAPTER THREE

The Shadows

Old Ralph Rinkelmann made his living by comic sketches, and all but lost it again by tragic poems. So he was just the man to be chosen king of the fairies, for in Fairyland the sovereignty is elective.

It is no doubt very strange that fairies should desire to have a mortal king; but the fact is, that with all their knowledge and power, they cannot get rid of the feeling that some men are greater than they are, though they can neither fly nor play tricks. So at such times as there happens to be twice the usual number of sensible electors, such a man as Ralph Rinkelmann gets to be chosen.

They did not mean to insist on his residence; for they needed his presence only on special occasions. But they must get hold of him somehow, first of all, in order to make him king. Once he was crowned, they could get him as often as they pleased; but before this ceremony, there was a difficulty. For it is only between life and death that the fairies have power over grown-up mortals, and can carry them off to their country. So they had to watch for an opportunity.

Nor had they to wait long. For old Ralph was taken dreadfully ill; and while hovering between life and death, they carried him off, and crowned him King of Fairyland. But after he was crowned, it was no wonder, considering the state of his health, that he should not be able to sit quite upright on the throne of Fairyland; or that, in consequence, all the gnomes and goblins, and ugly, cruel things that live in the holes and corners of the kingdom, should take advantage of his condition, and run quite wild, playing him, king as he was, all sorts of tricks; crowding about his throne, climbing up the steps, and actually scrambling and quarrelling like mice about his ears and eyes, so that he could see and think of nothing else. But I am not going to tell anything more about this part of his adventures just at present. By strong and sustained efforts he succeeded, after much trouble and suffering, in reducing his rebellious subjects to order. They all vanished to their respective holes and corners; and King Ralph, coming to himself, found himself in his bed half propped up with pillows.

But the room was full of dark creatures, which gambolled about in the firelight in such a strange, huge, though noiseless fashion, that he thought at first that some of his rebellious goblins had not been subdued with the rest, but had followed him beyond the bounds of Fairyland into his own private house in London. How else could these mad, grotesque hippopotamus-calves make their ugly appearance in Ralph Rinkelmann's bedroom?

But he soon found out that although they were like the underground goblins, they were very different as well, and would require quite different treatment. He felt convinced that they were his subjects too, but that he must have overlooked them somehow at his late coronation—if indeed they had been present; for he could not recollect that he had seen anything just like them before.

He resolved, therefore, to pay particular attention to their habits, ways, and characters; else he saw plainly that they would soon be too much for him; as indeed this intrusion into his chamber, where Mrs. Rinkelmann, who must be queen if he was king, sat taking some tea by the fireside, evidently foreshadowed. But she, perceiving that he was looking about him with a more composed expression than his face had worn for many days, started up, and came quickly and quietly to his side, and her face was bright with gladness. Whereupon the fire burned up more cheerily; and the figures became more composed and respectful in their behaviour, retreating towards the wall like well-trained attendants. Then the king of Fairyland had some tea and dry toast, and leaning back on his pillows, nearly fell asleep; but not quite, for he still watched the intruders.

Presently the queen left the room to give some of the young princes and princesses their tea; and the fire burned lower, and behold, the figures grew as black and as mad in their gambols as ever! Their favourite games seemed to be *Hide and Seek; Touch and Go; Grin and Vanish:* and many other such; and all in the king's bedchamber, too; so that it was quite alarming. It was almost as bad as if the house had been haunted by certain creatures which shall be nameless in a fairy story, because with them Fairyland will not willingly have much to do.

"But it is a mercy that they have their slippers on!" said the king to himself; for his head ached.

As he lay back, with his eyes half shut and half open, too tired to pay longer attention to their games, but, on the whole, considerably more amused than offended with the liberties they took, for they seemed good-natured creatures, and more frolicsome than positively ill-mannered, he became suddenly aware that two of them had stepped forward from the walls, upon which, after the manner of great spiders, most of them preferred sprawling, and now stood in the middle of the floor at the foot of his majesty's bed, becking and bowing and ducking in the most grotesquely obsequious manner; while every now and then they turned solemnly round upon one heel, evidently considering that motion the highest token of homage they could show.

"What do you want?" said the king.

"That it may please your majesty to be better acquainted with us," answered they. "We are your majesty's subjects."

"I know you are. I shall be most happy," answered the king.

"We are not what your majesty takes us for, though. We are not so foolish as your majesty thinks us."

"It is impossible to take you for anything that I know of," rejoined the king, who wished to make them talk, and said whatever came uppermost;—"for soldiers, sailors, or anything: you will not stand still long enough. I suppose you really belong to the fire brigade; at least, you keep putting its light out."

"Don't jest, please your majesty." And as they said the words—for they both spoke at once throughout the interview—they performed a grave somerset towards the king.

"Not jest!" retorted he; "and with you? Why, you do nothing but jest. What are you?"

"The Shadows, sire. And when we do jest, sire, we always jest in earnest. But perhaps your majesty does not see us distinctly."

"I see you perfectly well," returned the king.

"Permit me, however," rejoined one of the Shadows; and as he spoke he approached the king; and lifting a dark forefinger, he drew it lightly but carefully across the ridge of his forehead, from temple to temple. The king felt the soft gliding touch go, like water, into every hollow, and over the top of every height of that mountain-chain of thought. He had involuntarily closed his eyes during the operation, and when he unclosed them again, as soon as the finger was withdrawn, he found that they were opened in more senses than one. The room appeared to have extended itself on all sides, till he could not exactly see where the walls were, and all about it stood the Shadows, motionless. They were tall and solemn; rather awful, indeed, in their appearance, notwithstanding many remarkable traits of grotesqueness, for they looked just like the pictures of Puritans drawn by Cavaliers, with long arms, and very long, thin legs, from which hung large loose feet, while in their countenances length of chin and nose predominated. The solemnity of their mien, however, overcame all the oddity of their form, so that they were very *eerie* indeed to look at, dressed as they all were in funeral black.

But a single glance was all that the king was allowed to have; for the former operator waved his dusky palm across his vision, and once more the king saw only the fire-lighted walls, and dark shapes flickering about upon them. The two who had spoken for the rest seemed likewise to have vanished. But at last the king discovered them, standing one on each side of the fireplace. They kept close to the chimney-wall, and talked to each other across the length of the chimney-piece; thus avoiding the direct rays of the fire, which, though light is necessary to their appearing to human eyes, do not agree with them at all—much less give birth to them, as the king

was soon to learn. After a few minutes they again approached the bed, and spoke thus:

"It is now getting dark, please your majesty. We mean, out of doors in the snow. Your majesty may see, from where he is lying, the cold light of its great winding-sheet—a famous carpet for the Shadows to dance upon, your majesty. All our brothers and sisters will be at church now, before going to their night's work."

"Do they always go to church before they go to work?"

"They always go to church first."

"Where is the church?"

"In Iceland. Would your majesty like to see it?"

"How can I go and see it, when, as you know very well I am ill in bed? Besides, I should be sure to take cold in a frosty night like this, even if I put on the blankets, and took the feather-bed for a muff."

A sort of quivering passed over their faces, which seemed to be their mode of laughing. The whole shape of the face shook and fluctuated as if it had been some dark fluid; till, by slow degrees of gathering calm, it settled into its former rest. Then one of them drew aside the curtains of the bed, and the window-curtains not having been yet drawn, the king beheld the white glimmering night outside, struggling with the heaps of darkness that tried to quench it; and the heavens full of stars, flashing and sparkling like live jewels. The other Shadows went towards the fire and vanished in it.

Scores of Shadows immediately began an insane dance all about the room; disappearing, one after the other, through the uncovered window, and gliding darkly away over the face of the white snow; for the window looked at once on a field of snow. In a few moments the room was quite cleared of them; but instead of being relieved by their absence, the king felt immediately as if he were in a dead-house, and could hardly breathe for the sense of emptiness and desolation that fell upon him. But as he lay looking out on the snow, which stretched blank and wide before him, he spied in the distance a long dark line which drew nearer and nearer, and showed itself at last to be all the Shadows, walking in a double row, and carrying in the midst of them something like a bier. They vanished under the window, but soon reappeared, having somehow climbed up the wall of the house; for they entered in perfect order by the window, as if melting through the transparency of the glass.

They still carried the bier or litter. It was covered with richest furs, and skins of gorgeous wild beasts, whose eyes were replaced by sapphires and emeralds, that glittered and gleamed in the fire and snow light. The outermost skin sparkled with frost, but the inside ones were soft and warm and dry as the down under a swan's wing. The Shadows approached the bed, and set the litter upon it. Then a number of them brought a huge fur robe, and wrapping it round the king, laid him on the litter in the midst of the furs. Nothing could be more gentle and respectful than the way in which they moved him; and he never thought of refusing to go. Then they put something on his head, and, lifting the litter, carried him once round the room, to fall into order.

As he passed the mirror he saw that he was covered with royal ermine, and that his head wore a wonderful crown of gold, set with none but red stones: rubies and carbuncles and garnets, and others whose names he could not tell, glowed gloriously around his head, like the salamandrine essence of all the Christmas fires over the world. A sceptre lay beside him—a rod of ebony, sur-

mounted by a cone-shaped diamond, which, cut in a hundred facets, flashed all the hues of the rainbow, and threw coloured gleams on every side, that looked like Shadows too, but more ethereal than those that bore him.

Then the Shadows rose gently to the window, passed through it, and sinking slowly upon the field of outstretched snow, commenced an orderly gliding rather than march along the frozen surface. They took it by turns to bear the king, as they sped with the swiftness of thought, in a straight line towards the north.

The polestar rose above their heads with visible rapidity; for indeed they moved quite as fast as sad thoughts, though not with all the speed of happy desires. England and Scotland slid past the litter of the king of the Shadows. Over rivers and lakes they skimmed and glided. They climbed the high mountains, and crossed the valleys with a fearless bound; till they came to John-o'-Groat's house and the Northern Sea. The sea was not frozen; for all the stars shone as clear out of the deeps below as they shone out of the deeps above; and as the bearers slid along the blue-gray surface, with never a furrow in their track, so pure was the water beneath, that the king saw neither surface, bottom, nor substance to it, and seemed to be gliding only through the blue sphere of heaven, with the stars above him, and the stars below him, and between the stars and him nothing but an emptiness, where, for the first time in his life, his soul felt that it had room enough.

At length they reached the rocky shores of Iceland. There they landed, still pursuing their journey. All this time the king felt no cold; for the red stones in his crown kept him warm, and the emerald and sapphire eyes of the wild beasts kept the frosts from settling upon his litter.

Oftentimes upon their way they had to pass through forests, caverns, and rock-shadowed paths, where it was so dark that at first the king feared he should lose his Shadows altogether. But as soon as they entered such places, the diamond in his sceptre began to shine, and glow, and flash, sending out streams of light of all the colours that the painter's soul could dream of; in which light the Shadows grew livelier and stronger than ever, speeding through the dark ways with an all but blinding swiftness. In the light of the diamond, too, some of their forms became more simple and human, while others seemed only to break out into a yet more untamable absurdity.

Once, as they passed through a cave, the king actually saw some of their eyes—strange shadow-eyes: he had never seen any of their eyes before. But at the same moment when he saw their eyes, he knew their faces too, for they turned them full upon him for an instant; and the other Shadows, catching sight of these, shrank and shivered, and nearly vanished. Lovely faces they were; but the king was very thoughtful after he saw them, and continued rather troubled all the rest of the journey. He could not account for those faces being there, and the faces of Shadows, too, with living eyes.

But he soon found that amongst the Shadows a man must learn never to be surprised at anything; for if he does not, he will soon grow quite stupid, in consequence of the endless recurrence of surprises.

At last they climbed up the bed of a little stream, and then, passing through a narrow rocky defile, came out suddenly upon the side of a mountain, overlooking a blue frozen lake in the very heart of mighty hills. Overhead, the *aurora borealis* was shivering and flashing like a battle of ten thousand spears. Underneath, its beams passed faintly over the blue ice and the sides of the snow-clad mountains, whose tops shot up like huge icicles all about, with here and there a star sparkling on the very tip of one. But as the northern lights in the sky above, so wavered and quivered, and shot hither and thither, the Shadows on the surface of the lake below; now gathering in groups, and now shivering asunder; now covering the whole surface of the lake, and anon condensed into one dark knot in the centre. Every here and there on the white mountains might be seen two or three shooting away towards the tops, to vanish beyond them, so that their number was gradually, though not visibly, diminishing.

"Please your majesty," said the Shadows, "this is our church—the Church of the Shadows."

And so saying, the king's body-guard set down the litter upon a rock, and plunged into the multitudes below. They soon returned, however, and bore the king down into the middle of the lake. All the Shadows came crowding round him, respectfully but fearlessly; and sure never such a grotesque assembly revealed itself before to mortal eyes. The king had seen all kinds of gnomes, goblins, and kobolds at his coronation; but they were quite rectilinear figures compared with the insane lawlessness of form in which the Shadows rejoiced, and the wildest gambols of the former were orderly dances of ceremony beside the apparently aimless and wilful contortions of figure, and metamorphoses of shape, in which the latter indulged. They retained, however, all the time, to the surprise of the king, an identity, each of his own type, inexplicably perceptible through every change. Indeed, this preservation of the primary idea of each form was more wonderful than the bewildering and ridiculous alterations to which the form itself was every moment subjected.

"What are you?" said the king, leaning on his elbow, and looking around him.

"The Shadows, your majesty," answered several voices at once.

"What Shadows?"

"The human Shadows. The Shadows of men, and women, and their children."

"Are you not the shadows of chairs and tables, and pokers and tongs, just as well?"

At this question a strange jarring commotion went through the assembly with a shock. Several of the figures shot up as high as the aurora, but instantly settled down again to human size, as if overmastering their feelings, out of respect to him who had roused them. One who had bounded to the highest visible icy peak, and as suddenly returned, now elbowed his way through the rest, and made himself spokesman for them during the remaining part of the dialogue.

"Excuse our agitation, your majesty," said he. "I see your majesty has not yet thought proper to make himself acquainted with our nature and habits."

"I wish to do so now," replied the king.

"We are the Shadows," repeated the Shadow, solemnly.

"Well?" said the king.

"We do not often appear to men."

"Ha!" said the king.

"We do not belong to the sunshine at all. We go through it unseen, and only by a passing chill do men recognise an unknown presence."

"Ha!" said the king again.

"It is only in the twilight of the fire, or when one man or woman is alone with a single candle, or when any number of people are all feeling the same thing at once, making them one, that we

show ourselves, and the truth of things."

"Can that be true that loves the night?" said the king.

"The darkness is the nurse of light," answered the Shadow.

"Can that be true which mocks at forms?" said the king.

"Truth rides abroad in shapeless storms," answered the Shadow.

"Ha! ha!" thought Ralph Rinkelmann, "it rhymes. The Shadow caps my questions with his answers. Very strange!" And he grew thoughtful again.

The Shadow was the first to resume.

"Please your majesty, may we present our petition?"

"By all means," replied the king. "I am not well enough to receive it in proper state."

"Never mind, your majesty. We do not care for much ceremony; and indeed none of us are quite well at present. The subject of our petition weighs upon us."

"Go on," said the king.

"Sire," began the Shadow, "our very existence is in danger. The various sorts of artificial light, both in houses and in men, women, and children, threaten to end our being. The use and the disposition of gaslights, especially high in the centres, blind the eyes by which alone we can be perceived. We are all but banished from towns. We are driven into villages and lonely houses chiefly old farm-houses, out of which even our friends the fairies are fast disappearing. We therefore petition our king, by the power of his art to restore us to our rights in the house itself, and in the hearts of its inhabitants."

"But," said the king, "you frighten the children."

"Very seldom, your majesty; and then only for their good. We seldom seek to frighten anybody. We mostly want to make people silent and thoughtful; to awe them a little, your majesty."

"You are much more likely to make them laugh," said the king.

"Are we?" said the Shadow.

And approaching the king one step, he stood quite still for a moment. The diamond of the king's sceptre shot out a vivid flame of violet light, and the king stared at the Shadow in silence, and his lip quivered. He never told what he saw then; but he would say:

"Just fancy what it might be if *some* flitting thoughts were to persist in staying to be looked at."

"It is only," resumed the Shadow, "when our thoughts are not fixed upon any particular object, that our bodies are subject to all the vagaries of elemental influences. Generally, amongst worldly men and frivolous women, we only attach ourselves to some article of furniture or of dress; and they never doubt that we are mere foolish and vague results of the dashing of the waves of the light against the solid forms of which their houses are full. We do not care to tell them the truth, for they would never see it. But let the worldly man—or the frivolous woman—and then—"

At each of the pauses indicated, the mass of Shadows throbbed and heaved with emotion; but they soon settled again into comparative stillness. Once more the Shadow addressed himself to speak. But suddenly they all looked up, and the king, following their gaze, saw that the aurora had begun to pale.

"The moon is rising," said the Shadow. "As soon as she looks over the mountains into the valley, we must be gone, for we have plenty to do by the moon: we are powerful in her light. But if your majesty will come here tomorrow night, your majesty may learn a great deal more about us, and judge for himself whether it be fit to accord our petition; for then will be our grand annual assembly, in which we report to

our chiefs the things we have attempted, and the good or bad success we had."

"If you send for me," returned the king, "I will come."

Ere the Shadow could reply, the tip of the moon's crescent horn peeped up from behind an icy pinnacle, and one slender ray fell on the lake. It shone upon no Shadows. Ere the eye of the king could again seek the earth after beholding the first brightness of the moon's resurrection, they had vanished; and the surface of the lake glittered cold and blue in the pale moonlight.

There the king lay, alone in the midst of the frozen lake, with the moon staring at him. But at length he heard from somewhere a voice that he knew.

"Will you take another cup of tea, dear?" said Mrs. Rinkelmann.

And Ralph, coming slowly to himself, found that he was lying in his own bed.

"Yes, I will," he answered; "and rather a large piece of toast, if you please; for I have been a long journey since I saw you last."

"He has not come to himself quite," said Mrs. Rinkelmann, between her and herself.

"You would be rather surprised," continued Ralph "if I told you where I had been."

"I dare say I should," responded his wife.

"Then I will tell you," rejoined Ralph.

But at that moment, a great Shadow bounced out of the fire with a single huge leap, and covered the whole room. Then it settled in one corner, and Ralph saw it shaking its fist at him from the end of a preposterous arm. So he took the hint, and held his peace. And it was as well for him. For I happen to know something about the Shadows too; and I know that if he had told his wife all about it just then, they would not have sent for him the following evening.

But as the king, after finishing his tea and toast, lay and looked about him, the shadows dancing in his room seemed to him odder and more inexplicable than ever. The whole chamber was full of mystery. So it generally was, but now it was more mysterious than ever. After all that he had seen in the Shadow-church, his own room and its shadows were yet more wonderful and unintelligible than those.

This made it the more likely that he had seen a true vision; for instead of making common things look common-place, as a false vision would have done, it had made common things disclose the wonderful that was in them.

"The same applies to all art as well," thought Ralph Rinkelmann.

The next afternoon, as the twilight was growing dusky, the king lay wondering whether or not the Shadows would fetch him again. He wanted very much to go, for he had enjoyed the journey exceedingly, and he longed, besides, to hear some of the Shadows tell their stories. But the darkness grew deeper and deeper, and the Shadows did not come. The cause was, that Mrs. Rinkelmann sat by the fire in the gloaming; and they could not carry off the king while she was there. Some of them tried to frighten her away by playing the oddest pranks on the walls, the floor, and ceiling; but altogether without effect: the queen only smiled, for she had a good conscience. Suddenly, however, a dreadful scream was heard from the nursery, and Mrs. Rinkelmann rushed up-stairs to see what was the matter. No sooner had she gone than the two warders of the chimney-corners stepped out into the middle of the room, and said, in a low voice,

"Is your majesty ready?"

"Have you no hearts?" said the king; "or are they as black as your faces? Did you not hear the child scream? I must know what is the matter with her before I go."

"Your majesty may keep his mind easy on that point," replied the warders. "We had tried everything we could think of to get rid of her majesty the queen, but without effect. So a young madcap Shadow, half against the will of the older ones of us, slipped up-stairs into the nursery; and has, no doubt, succeeded in appalling the baby, for he is very lithe and long-legged.—Now, your majesty."

"I will have no such tricks played in my nursery," said the king, rather angrily. "You might put the child beside itself."

"Then there would be twins, your majesty. And we rather like twins."

"None of your miserable jesting! You might put the child out of her wits."

"Impossible, sire; for she has not got into them yet."

"Go away," said the king.

"Forgive us, your majesty. Really, it will do the child good; for that Shadow will, all her life, be to her a symbol of what is ugly and bad. When she feels in danger of hating or envying any one, that Shadow will come back to her mind and make her shudder."

"Very well," said the king. "I like that. Let us go."

The Shadows went through the same ceremonies and preparations as before; during which, the young Shadow before-mentioned contrived to make such grimaces as kept the baby in terror, and the queen in the nursery, till all was ready. Then with a bound that doubled him up against the ceiling, and a kick of his legs six feet out behind him, he vanished through the nursery door, and reached the king's bed-chamber just in time to take his place with the last who were melting through the window in the rear of the litter, and settling down upon the snow beneath. Away they went as before, a gliding blackness over the white carpet. And it was Christmas-eve.

When they came in sight of the mountain-lake, the king saw that it was crowded over its whole surface with a changeful intermingling of Shadows. They were all talking and listening alternately, in pairs, trios, and groups of every size. Here and there, large companies were absorbed in attention to one elevated above the rest, not in a pulpit, or on a platform, but on the stilts of his own legs, elongated for the nonce. The aurora, right overhead, lighted up the lake and the sides of the mountains, by sending down from the zenith, nearly to the surface of the lake, great folded vapours, luminous with all the colours of a faint rainbow.

Many, however, as the words were that passed on all sides, not a shadow of a sound reached the ears of the king: the shadow-speech could not enter his corporeal organs. One of his guides, however, seeing that the king wanted to hear and could not, went through a strange manipulation of his head and ears; after which he could hear perfectly, though still only the voice to which, for the time, he directed his attention. This, however, was a great advantage, and one which the king longed to carry back with him to the world of men.

The king now discovered that this was not merely the church of the Shadows, but their news-exchange at the same time. For, as the Shadows have no writing or printing, the only way in which they can make each other acquainted with their doings and thinkings, is to meet and talk at this word-mart and parliament of shades. And as, in the world, people read their favourite authors, and listen to their favourite speakers, so here the Shadows seek their favourite Shadows, listen to their adventures, and hear generally what they have to say.

Feeling quite strong, the king rose and walked about amongst them, wrapped in his ermine robe, with his red crown on his head, and his diamond sceptre in his hand. Every group of Shadows to which he drew near, ceased talking as soon as they saw him approach: but at a nod they went on again directly, conversing and relating and commenting, as if no one was there of other kind or of higher rank than themselves. So the king heard a good many stories. At some of them he laughed, and at some of them he cried. But if the stories that the Shadows told were printed, they would make a book that no publisher could produce fast enough to satisfy the buyers. I will record some of the things that the king heard, for he told them to me soon after. In fact, I was for some time his private secretary.

"I made him confess before a week was over," said a gloomy old Shadow.

"But what was the good of that?" rejoined a pert young one. "That could not undo what was done."

"Yes, it could."

"What! bring the dead back to life?"

"No; but comfort the murderer. I could not bear to see the pitiable misery he was in. He was far happier with the rope round his neck, than he was with the purse in his pocket. I saved him from killing himself too."

"How did you make him confess?"

"Only by wallowing on the wall a little."

"How could that make him tell?"

"*He* knows."

The Shadow was silent; and the king turned to another, who was preparing to speak.

"I made a fashionable mother repent."

"How?" broke from several voices, in

whose sound was mingled a touch of incredulity.

"Only by making a little coffin on the wall," was the reply.

"Did the fashionable mother confess too?"

"She had nothing more to confess than everybody knew."

"What did everybody know then?"

"That she might have been kissing a living child, when she followed a dead one to the grave.—The next will fare better."

"I put a stop to a wedding," said another.

"Horrid shade!" remarked a poetic imp.

"How?" said others. "Tell us how."

"Only by throwing a darkness, as if from the branch of a sconce, over the forehead of a fair girl. They are not married yet, and I do not think they will be. But I loved the youth who loved her. How he started! It was a revelation to him."

"But did it not deceive him?"

"Quite the contrary."

"But it was only a shadow from the outside, not a shadow coming through from the soul of the girl."

"Yes. You may say so. But it was all that was wanted to make the meaning of her forehead manifest—yes, of her whole face, which had now and then, in the pauses of his passion, perplexed the youth. All of it, curled nostrils, pouting lips, projecting chin, instantly fell into harmony with that darkness between her eyebrows. The youth understood it in a moment, and went home miserable. And they're not married *yet.*"

"I caught a toper alone, over his magnum of port," said a very dark Shadow; "and didn't I give it to him! I made *delirium tremens* first; and then I settled into a funeral, passing slowly along the length of the opposite wall. I gave him plenty of plumes and mourning coaches. And then I gave him a funeral service, but I could not manage to make the surplice white, which was all the better for such a sinner. The wretch stared till his face passed from purple to grey, and actually left his fifth glass only, unfinished and took refuge with his wife and children in the drawing-room, much to their surprise. I believe he actually drank a cup of tea; and although I have often looked in since, I have never caught him again, drinking alone at least."

"But does he drink less? Have you done him any good?"

"I hope so; but I am sorry to say I can't feel sure about it."

"Humph! Humph! Humph!" grunted various shadow throats.

"I had such fun once!" cried another. "I made such game of a young clergyman!"

"You have no right to make game of any one."

"Oh, yes, I have—when it is for his good. He used to study his sermons—where do you think?"

"In his study, of course. Where else should it be?"

"Yes and no. Guess again."

"Out amongst the faces in the streets?"

"Guess again."

"In still green places in the country?"

"Guess again."

"In old books?"

"Guess again."

"No, no. Tell us."

"In the looking-glass. Ha! ha! ha!"

"He was fair game; fair shadow game."

"I thought so. And I made such fun of him one night on the wall! He had sense enough to see that it was himself, and very like an ape. So he got ashamed, turned the mirror with its face to the wall, and thought a little more about his people, and a little less about himself. I was very glad; for, please your majesty,"—and here the speaker turned towards the king—"we don't like the creatures that live in the mirrors. You call them ghosts, don't you?"

Before the king could reply, another had commenced. But the story about the clergyman had made the king wish to hear one of the shadow-sermons. So he turned him towards a long Shadow, who was preaching to a very quiet and listening crowd. He was just concluding his sermon.

"Therefore, dear Shadows, it is the more needful that we love one another as much as we can, because that is not much. We have no such excuse for not loving as mortals have, for we do not die like them. I suppose it is the thought of that death that makes them hate so much. Then again, we go to sleep all day, most of us, and not in the night, as men do. And you know that we forget everything that happened the night before; therefore, we ought to love well, for the love is short. Ah! dear Shadow, whom I love now with all my shadowy soul, I shall not love thee to-morrow eve, I shall not know thee; I shall pass thee in the crowd and never dream that the Shadow whom I now love is near me then. Happy Shades! for we only remember our tales until we have told them here, and then they vanish in the shadow-churchyard, where we bury only our dead selves. Ah! brethren, who would be a man and remember? Who would be a man and weep? We ought indeed to love one another, for we alone inherit oblivion; we alone are renewed with eternal birth; we alone have no gathered weight of years.

"I will tell you the awful fate of one Shadow who rebelled against his nature, and sought to remember the past. He said, 'I *will* remember this eve.' He fought with the genial influences of kindly sleep when the sun rose on the awful dead day of light; and although he could not keep quite awake, he dreamed of the foregone eve, and he never forgot his dream. Then he tried again the next night, and the next, and the next; and he tempted another Shadow to try it with him. But at last their awful fate overtook them; for, instead of continuing to be Shadows, they began to cast shadows, as foolish men say; and so they thickened and thickened till they vanished out of our world. They are now condemned to walk the earth a man and a woman, with death behind them, and memories within them. Ah, brother Shades! let us love one another, for we shall soon forget. We are not men, but Shadows."

The king turned away, and pitied the poor Shadows far more than they pitied men.

"Oh! how we played with a musician one night," exclaimed a Shadow in another group, to which the king had first directed a passing thought, and then had stopped to listen. "Up and down we went, like the hammers and dampers on his piano. But he took his revenge on us. For after he had watched us for half an hour in the twilight, he rose and went to his instrument and played a shadow-dance that fixed us all in sound for ever. Each could tell the very notes meant for him; and as long as he played we could not stop, but went on dancing and dancing after the music, just as the magician—I mean the musician—pleased.

"And he punished us well; for he nearly danced us all off our legs and out of shape into tired heaps of collapsed and palpitating darkness. We won't go near him for some time again, if we can only remember it. He had been very miserable all day, he was so poor; and we could not think of any way of comforting him except making him laugh.

We did not succeed, with our wildest efforts; but it turned out better than we had expected, after all; for his shadow-dance got him into notice, and he is quite popular now, making money fast. If he does not take care, we shall have other work to do with him by-and-by, poor fellow!"

"I and some others did the same for a poor playwriter once. He had a Christmas piece to write, and being an original genius, it was not so easy for him to find a subject as it is for most of his class. I saw the trouble he was in, and collecting a few stray Shadows, we acted, in dumb show of course, the funniest bit of nonsense we could think of; and it was quite successful. The poor fellow watched every motion, roaring with laughter at us, and delight at the ideas we put into his head. He turned it all into words, and scenes, and actions; and the piece came off with a splendid success."

"But how long we have to look for a chance of doing anything worth doing!" said a long, thin, especially lugubrious Shadow. "I have only done one thing worth telling ever since we met last. But I am proud of that."

"What was it? What was it?" rose from twenty voices.

"I crept into a dining-room, one twilight, soon after Christmas-day. I had been drawn thither by the glow of a bright fire shining through red window-curtains. At first I thought there was no one there, and was on the point of leaving the room and going out again into the snowy street, when I suddenly caught the sparkle of eyes. I found that they belonged to a little boy who lay very still on a sofa. I crept into a dark corner by the sideboard, and watched him. He seemed very sad, and did nothing but stare into the fire.

"At last he sighed out, 'I wish mamma would come home.' 'Poor boy!'

thought I, 'there is no help for that but mamma.' Yet I would try to while away the time for him. So out of my corner I stretched a long shadow arm, reaching all across the ceiling, and pretended to make a grab at him. He was rather frightened at first; but he was a brave boy, and soon saw that it was all a joke. So when I did it again, he made a clutch at me; and then we had such fun! For though he often sighed and wished mamma would come home, he always began again with me; and on we went with the wildest game.

"At last his mother's knock came to the door, and, starting up in delight, he rushed into the hall to meet her, and forgot all about poor black me. But I did not mind that in the least; for when I glided out after him into the hall, I was well repaid for my trouble by hearing his mother say to him, 'Why, Charlie, my dear, you look ever so much better since I left you!' At that moment I slipped through the closing door, and as I ran across the snow, I heard the mother say, 'What Shadow can that be passing so quickly?' And Charlie answered with a merry laugh, 'Oh! mamma, I suppose it must be the funny Shadow that has been playing such games with me all the time you were out.' As soon as the door was shut, I crept along the wall and looked in at the dining-room window. And I heard his mamma say, as she led him into the room, 'What an imagination the boy has!' Ha! ha! ha! Then she looked at him, and the tears came in her eyes; and she stooped down over him, and I heard the sounds of a mingling kiss and sob."

"I always look for nurseries full of children," said another; "and this winter I have been very fortunate. I am sure children belong especially to us. One evening, looking about in a great city, I saw through the window into a large nursery, where the odious gas had not yet been lighted. Round the fire sat a company of the most delightful children I have ever seen. They were waiting patiently for their tea. It was too good an opportunity to be lost. I hurried away, and gathering together twenty of the best Shadows I could find, returned in a few moments; and entering the nursery, we danced on the walls one of our best dances. To be sure it was mostly extemporized; but I managed to keep it in harmony by singing this song which I made as we went on. Of course the children could not hear it: they only saw the motions that answered to it, but with them they seemed to be very much delighted indeed, as I shall presently prove to you. This was the song:—

Swing, swang, swingle, swuff!
Flicker, flacker, fling, fluff!
  Thus we go,
  To and fro;
  Here and there,
  Everywhere,
  Born and bred;
  Never dead,
    Only gone.
    On! Come on.
  Looming, glooming,
  Spreading, fuming,
  Shattering, scattering,
  Parting, darting,
  Settling, starting,
  All our life
  Is a strife,
And a wearying for rest
On the darkness' friendly breast
  Joining, splitting,
  Rising, sitting,
  Laughing, shaking,
  Sides all aching,
Grumbling, grim, and gruff.
Swingle, swangle, swuff!
  Now a knot of darkness;
    Now dissolved gloom;
  Now a pall of blackness
    Hiding all the room.
Flicker, flacker, fluff!
Black, and black enough!

Dancing now like demons;
  Lying like the dead;
Gladly would we stop it,
  And go down to bed!
But our work we still must do,
Shadow men, as well as you.

Rooting, rising, shooting,
  Heaving, sinking, creeping;
Hid in corners crooning;
  Splitting, poking, leaping,
Gathering, towering, swooning.
  When we're lurking,
  Yet we're working,
For our labour we must do,
Shadow men, as well as you.
  Flicker, flacker, fling, fluff!
  Swing, swang, swingle, swuff!

" 'How thick the Shadows are!' said one of the children—a thoughtful little girl.

" 'I wonder where they come from,' said a dreamy little boy.

" 'I think they grow out of the wall,' answered the little girl; 'for I have been watching them come; first one, and then another, and then a whole lot of them. I am sure they grow out of the walls.'

" 'Perhaps they have papas and mammas,' said an older boy, with a smile.

" 'Yes, yes; and the doctor brings them in his pocket,' said another, a consequential little maiden.

" 'No; I'll tell you,' said the older boy; 'they're ghosts.'

" 'But ghosts are white.'

" 'Oh! but these have got black coming down the chimney.'

" 'No,' said a curious-looking, white-faced boy of fourteen, who had been reading by the firelight, and had stopped to hear the little ones talk; 'they're body ghosts; they're not soul ghosts.'

"A silence followed, broken by the first, the dreamy-eyed boy, who said,

" 'I hope they didn't make me;' at which they all burst out laughing.

"Just then the nurse brought in their

tea, and when she proceeded to light the gas we vanished."

"I stopped a murder," cried another. "How? How? How?"

"I will tell you. I had been lurking about a sick room for some time, where a miser lay, apparently dying. I did not like the place at all, but I felt as if I should be wanted there. There were plenty of lurking-places about, for the room was full of all sorts of old furniture, especially cabinets, chests, and presses. I believe he had in that room every bit of the property he had spent a long life in gathering. I found that he had gold and gold in those places; for one night, when his nurse was away, he crept out of bed, mumbling and shaking, and managed to open one of the chests, though he nearly fell down with the effort. I was peeping over his shoulder, and such a gleam of gold fell upon me, that it nearly killed me. But hearing his nurse coming, he slammed the lid down, and I recovered.

"I tried very hard, but I could not do him any good. For although I made all sorts of shapes on the walls and ceilings, representing evil deeds that he had done, of which there were plenty to choose from, I could make no shapes on his brain or conscience. He had no eyes for anything but gold. And it so happened that his nurse had neither eyes nor heart for anything else either.

"One day, as she was seated beside his bed, but where he could not see her, stirring some gruel in a basin, to cool it for him, I saw her take a little phial from her bosom, and I knew by the expression of her face both what it was and what she was going to do with it. Fortunately the cork was a little hard to get out, and this gave me one moment to think.

"The room was so crowded with all sorts of things, that although there were no curtains on the four-post bed to hide from the miser the sight of his precious treasures, there was yet but one small part of the ceiling suitable for casting myself upon in the shape I wished to assume. And this spot was hard to reach. But having discovered that upon this very place lay a dull gleam of fire-light thrown from a strange old dusty mirror that stood away in some corner, I got in front of the fire, spied where the mirror was, threw myself upon it, and bounded from its face upon the oval pool of dim light on the ceiling, assuming, as I passed, the shape of an old stooping hag, who poured something from a phial into a basin. I made the handle of the spoon with my own nose, ha! ha!"

And the shadow-hand caressed the shadow-tip of the shadow-nose, before the shadow-tongue resumed.

"The old miser saw me: he would not taste the gruel that night, although his nurse coaxed and scolded till they were both weary. She pretended to taste it herself, and to think it very good; but at last retired into a corner, and after making as if she were eating it, took good care to pour it all out into the ashes."

"But she must either succeed, or starve him, at last," interposed a Shadow.

"I will tell you."

"And," interposed another, "he was not worth saving."

"He might repent," suggested a third, who was more benevolent.

"No chance of that," returned the former. "Misers never do. The love of money has less in it to cure itself than any other wickedness into which wretched men can fall. What a mercy it is to be born a Shadow! Wickedness does not stick to us. What do we care for gold!— Rubbish!"

"Amen! Amen! Amen!" came from a hundred shadow-voices.

"You should have let her murder him, and so you would have been quit of him."

"And besides how was he to escape at last? He could never get rid of her, you know."

"I was going to tell you," resumed the narrator, "only you had so many shadow-remarks to make, that you would not let me."

"Go on; go on."

"There was a little grandchild who used to come and see him sometimes— the only creature the miser cared for. Her mother was his daughter; but the old man would never see her, because she had married against his will. Her husband was now dead, but he had not forgiven her yet. After the shadow he had seen, however, he said to himself, as he lay awake that night—I saw the words on his face—'How shall I get rid of that old devil? If I don't eat I shall die; and if I do eat I shall be poisoned. I wish little Mary would come. Ah! her mother would never have served me so.' He lay awake, thinking such things over and over again, all night long, and I stood watching him from a dark corner, till the day-spring came and shook me out. When I came back the next night, the room was tidy and clean. His own daughter, a sad-faced but beautiful woman, sat by his bedside; and little Mary was curled up on the floor by the fire, imitating us, by making queer shadows on the ceiling with her twisted hands. But she could not think however they got there. And no wonder, for I helped her to some very unaccountable ones."

"I have a story about a grand-daughter, too," said another, the moment that speaker ceased.

"Tell it. Tell it."

"Last Christmas-day," he began, "I and a troop of us set out in the twilight to find some house where we could all have something to do; for we had made up our minds to act together. We tried several, but found objections to them all. At last we espied a large lonely country-house, and hastening to it, we found great preparations making for the Christmas dinner. We rushed into it, scampered all over it, and made up our minds in a moment that it would do. We amused ourselves in the nursery first, where there were several children being dressed for dinner. We generally do go to the nursery first, your majesty. This time we were especially charmed with a little girl about five years old, who clapped her hands and danced about with delight at the antics we performed; and we said we would do something for her if we had a chance.

"The company began to arrive; and at every arrival, we rushed to the hall, and cut wonderful capers of welcome. Between times, we scudded away to see how the dressing went on. One girl about eighteen was delightful. She dressed herself as if she did not care much about it, but could not help doing it prettily. When she took her last look at the phantom in the glass, she half smiled to it.—But *we* do not like those creatures that come into the mirrors at all, your majesty. We don't understand them. They are dreadful to us.—She looked rather sad and pale, but very sweet and hopeful. So we wanted to know all about her, and soon found out that she was a distant relation and a great favourite of the gentleman of the house, an old man, in whose face benevolence was mingled with obstinacy and a deep shade of the tyrannical. We could not admire him much; but we would not make up our minds all at once: Shadows never do.

"The dinner-bell rang, and down we hurried. The children all looked happy, and we were merry. But there was one cross fellow among the servants, and didn't we plague him! and didn't we get fun out of him! When he was bringing up dishes, we lay in wait for him at every corner, and sprang upon him from the floor, and from over the banisters, and down from the cornices. He started and stumbled and blundered so in consequence, that his fellow-servants thought he was tipsy. Once he dropped a plate, and had to pick up the pieces, and hurry away with them; and didn't we pursue him as he went! It was lucky for him his master did not see how he went on but we took care not to let him get into any real scrape though he was quite dazed with the dodging of the unaccountable shadows. Sometimes he thought the walls were coming down upon him, sometimes that the floor was gaping to swallow him; sometimes that he would be knocked to pieces by the hurrying to and fro, or be smothered in the black crowd.

"When the blazing plum-pudding was carried in, we made a perfect shadow-carnival about it, dancing and mumming in the blue flames, like mad demons. And how the children screamed with delight!

"The old gentleman, who was very fond of children, was laughing his heartiest laugh, when a loud knock came to the hall-door. The fair maiden started, turned paler, and then red as the Christmas fire. I saw it, and flung my hands across her face. She was very glad, and I know she said in her heart, 'You kind Shadow!' which paid me well. Then I followed the rest into the hall, and found there a jolly, handsome, brown-faced sailor, evidently a son of the house. The old man received him with tears in his eyes, and the children with shouts of joy.

The maiden escaped in the confusion, just in time to save herself from fainting. We crowded about the lamp to hide her retreat, and nearly put it out; and the butler could not get it to burn up before she had glided into her place again, relieved to find the room so dark. The sailor only had seen her go, and now he sat down beside her, and, without a word, got hold of her hand in the gloom. When we all scattered to the walls and the corners, and the lamp blazed up again, he let her hand go.

"During the rest of the dinner the old man watched the two, and saw that there was something between them, and was very angry. For he was an important man in his own estimation, and they had never consulted him. The fact was, they had never known their own minds till the sailor had gone upon his last voyage, and had learned each other's only this moment.—We found out all this by watching them, and then talking together about it afterwards.—The old gentleman saw, too, that his favourite, who was under such obligation to him for loving her so much, loved his son better than him; and he grew by degrees so jealous that he overshadowed the whole table with his morose looks and short answers. That kind of shadowing is very different from ours; and the Christmas dessert grew so gloomy that we Shadows could not bear it, and were delighted when the ladies rose to go to the drawing-room. The gentlemen would not stay behind the ladies, even for the sake of the well-known wine.

"So the moody host, notwithstanding his hospitality, was left alone at the table in the great silent room. We followed the company up-stairs to the drawing-room, and thence to the nursery for snap-dragon; but while they were busy with this most shadowy of games, nearly all the Shadows crept downstairs again to the dining-room, where the old man still sat, gnawing the bone of his own selfishness. They crowded into the room, and by using every kind of expansion—blowing themselves out like soap bubbles—they succeeded in heaping up the whole room with shade upon shade. They clustered thickest about the fire and the lamp, till at last they almost drowned them in hills of darkness.

"Before they had accomplished so much, the children tired with fun and frolic, had been put to bed. But the little girl of five years old, with whom we had been so pleased when first we arrived, could not go to sleep. She had a little room of her own; and I had watched her to bed, and now kept her awake by gambolling in the rays of the night-light. When her eyes were once fixed upon me, I took the shape of her grandfather, representing him on the wall as he sat in his chair, with his head bent down and his arms hanging listlessly by his sides. And the child remembered that that was just as she had seen him last; for she had happened to peep in at the dining-room door after all the rest had gone upstairs. 'What if he should be sitting there still,' thought she, 'all alone in the dark!' She scrambled out of bed and crept down.

"Meantime the others had made the room below so dark, that only the face and white hair of the old man could be dimly discerned in the shadowy crowd. For he had filled his own mind with shadows, which we Shadows wanted to draw out of him. Those shadows are very different from us, your majesty knows. He was thinking of all the disappointments he had had in life, and of all the ingratitude he had met with. And he thought far more of the good he had done, than the good others had

got. 'After all I have done for them,' said he, with a sigh of bitterness, 'not one of them cares a straw for me. My own children will be glad when I am gone!'

"At that instant he lifted up his eyes and saw, standing close by the door, a tiny figure in a long nightgown. The door behind her was shut. It was my little friend, who had crept in noiselessly. A pang of icy fear shot to the old man's heart, but it melted away as fast, for we made a lane through us for a single ray from the fire to fall on the face of the little sprite; and he thought it was a child of his own that had died when just the age of her child-niece, who now stood looking for her grandfather among the Shadows. He thought she had come out of her grave in the cold darkness to ask why her father was sitting alone on Christmas-day. And he felt he had no answer to give his little ghost, but one he would be ashamed for her to hear. But his grandchild saw him now, and walked up to him with a childish stateliness, stumbling once or twice on what seemed her long shroud. Pushing through the crowded shadows, she reached him, climbed upon his knee, laid her little long-haired head on his shoulders, and said,—'Ganpa! you goomy? Isn't it your Kissy-Day too, ganpa?'

"A new fount of love seemed to burst from the clay of the old man's heart. He clasped the child to his bosom, and wept. Then, without a word, he rose with her in his arms, carried her up to her room, and laying her down in her bed, covered her up, kissed her sweet little mouth unconscious of reproof, and then went to the drawing-room.

"As soon as he entered, he saw the culprits in a quiet corner alone. He went up to them, took a hand of each, and joining them in both his, said, 'God bless you!' Then he turned to the rest of the company, and 'Now,' said he, 'let's have a Christmas carol.'—And well we might; for though I have paid many visits to the house, I have never seen him cross since; and I am sure that must cost him a good deal of trouble."

"We have just come from a great palace," said another, "where we knew there were many children, and where we thought to hear glad voices, and see royally merry looks. But as soon as we entered, we became aware that one mighty Shadow shrouded the whole; and that Shadow deepened and deepened, till it gathered in darkness about the reposing form of a wise prince. When we saw him, we could move no more, but clung heavily to the walls, and by our stillness added to the sorrow of the hour. And when we saw the mother of her people weeping with bowed head for the loss of him in whom she had trusted, we were seized with such a longing to be Shadows no more, but winged angels, which are the white shadows cast in heaven from the Light of Light, so as to gather around her, and hover over her with comforting, that we vanished from the walls, and found ourselves floating high above the towers of the palace, where we met the angels on their way, and knew that our service was not needed."

By this time there was a glimmer of approaching moonlight, and the king began to see several of those stranger Shadows, with human faces and eyes, moving about amongst the crowd. He knew at once that they did not belong to his dominion. They looked at him, and came near him, and passed slowly, but they never made any obeisance, or gave sign of homage. And what their eyes said to him, the king only could tell. And he did not tell.

"What are those other Shadows that move through the crowd?" said he to one of his subjects near him.

The Shadow started, looked around, shivered slightly, and laid his finger on his lips. Then leading the king a little aside, and looking carefully about him once more,—

"I do not know," said he, in a low tone, "what they are. I have heard of them often, but only once did I ever see any of them before. That was when some of us one night paid a visit to a man who sat much alone, and was said to think a great deal. We saw two of those sitting in the room with him, and he was as pale as they were. We could not cross the threshold, but shivered and shook, and felt ready to melt away. Is not your majesty afraid of them too!"

But the king made no answer; and before he could speak again, the moon had climbed above the mighty pillars of the church of the Shadows, and looked in at the great window of the sky.

The shapes had all vanished; and the king, again lifting up his eyes, saw but the walls of his own chamber, on which flickered the Shadow of a Little Child. He looked down, and there, sitting on a stool by the fire, he saw one of his own little ones, waiting to say good night to his father, and go to bed early, that he might rise early too, and be very good and happy all Christmas-day.

And Ralph Rinkelmann rejoiced that he was a man, and not a Shadow.

But as the Shadows vanished they left the sense of song in the king's brain. And the words of their song must have been something like these:—

Shadows, Shadows, Shadows all!
Shadow birth and funeral!
Shadow moons gleam overhead;
Over shadow graves we tread.
Shadow-hope lives, grows, and
   dies
Shadow-love from Shadow-eyes

Shadow-ward entices on
To shadow-words on shadow-stone,
Closing up the shadow-tale
With a shadow-shadow-wail.

Shadow-man, thou art a gloom
Cast upon a shadow-tomb
Through the endless shadow-air,
From the Shadow sitting there,
On a moveless shadow-throne,
Glooming through the ages gone
North and south, in and out,
East and west, and all about,

Flinging Shadows everywhere
On the Shadow-painted air.
Shadow-man, thou hast no story,
Nothing but a shadow-glory.

But Ralph Rinkelmann said to himself,—

"They are but Shadows that sing
thus, for a Shadow can see but Shadows. A man sees a man where a Shadow
sees only a Shadow."

And he was comforted in himself.

"The Golden Key" appeared in Dealings with the Fairies, which was published in 1867, and is also considered one of MacDonald's finest fairy tales. The story involves a boy who finds a golden key at the bottom of a rainbow and sets out in search of the one lock it will open. What he discovers is Fairyland, a place that lies above earth and is intermediate between our present dwelling place and our ultimate home. Fairyland is a higher world, one of glory and wonder, and MacDonald uses it to express his belief that as creation grows in spiritual wisdom it also becomes freer and more beautiful.

CHAPTER FOUR

The Golden Key

There was a boy who used to sit in the twilight and listen to his great-aunt's stories.

She told him that if he could reach the place where the end of the rainbow stands he would find there a golden key.

"And what is the key for?" the boy would ask. "What is it the key of? What will it open?"

"That nobody knows," his aunt would reply. "He has to find that out."

"I suppose, being gold," the boy once said, thoughtfully, "that I could get a good deal of money for it if I sold it."

"Better never find it than sell it," returned his aunt.

And then the boy went to bed and dreamed about the golden key.

Now all that his great-aunt told the boy about the golden key would have been nonsense, had it not been that their little house stood on the borders of Fairyland. For it is perfectly well known that out of Fairyland nobody ever can find where the rainbow stands. The creature takes such good care of its golden key, always flitting from place to place, lest any one should find it! But in Fairyland it is quite different. Things that look real in this country look very thin indeed in Fairyland, while some of the things that here cannot stand still for a moment, will not move there. So it was not in the least absurd of the old lady to tell her nephew such things about the golden key.

"Did you ever know anybody to find it?" he asked, one evening.

"Yes. Your father, I believe, found it."

"And what did he do with it, can you tell me?"

"He never told me."

"What was it like?"

"He never showed it to me."

"How does a new key come there always?"

"I don't know. There it is."

"Perhaps it is the rainbow's egg."

"Perhaps it is. You will be a happy boy if you find the nest."

"Perhaps it comes tumbling down the rainbow from the sky."

"Perhaps it does."

One evening, in summer, he went into his own room and stood at the lattice-window, and gazed into the forest which fringed the outskirts of Fairyland. It came close up to his great-aunt's garden, and, indeed, sent some straggling trees into it. The forest lay to the east, and the sun, which was setting behind the cottage, looked straight into the dark wood with his level red eye. The trees were all old, and had few branches below, so that the sun could see a great way into the forest; and the boy, being keen-sighted, could see almost as far as the sun. The trunks stood like rows of red columns in the shine of the red sun, and he could see down aisle after aisle in the vanishing distance. And as he gazed into the forest he began to feel as if the trees were all waiting for him, and had something they could not go on with till he came to them. But he was hungry, and wanted his supper. So he lingered.

Suddenly, far among the trees, as far

as the sun could shine, he saw a glorious thing. It was the end of a rainbow, large and brilliant. He could count all the seven colours, and could see shade after shade beyond the violet; while before the red stood a colour more gorgeous and mysterious still. It was a colour he had never seen before. Only the spring of the rainbow-arch was visible. He could see nothing of it above the trees.

"The golden key!" he said to himself, and darted out of the house, and into the wood.

He had not gone far before the sun set. But the rainbow only glowed the brighter. For the rainbow of Fairyland is not dependent upon the sun as ours is. The trees welcomed him. The bushes made way for him. The rainbow grew larger and brighter; and at length he found himself within two trees of it.

It was a grand sight, burning away there in silence, with its gorgeous, its lovely, its delicate colours, each distinct, all combining. He could now see a great deal more of it. It rose high into the blue heavens, but bent so little that he could not tell how high the crown of the arch must reach. It was still only a small portion of a huge bow.

He stood gazing at it till he forgot himself with delight—even forgot the key which he had come to seek. And as he stood it grew more wonderful still. For in each of the colours, which was as large as the column of a church, he could faintly see beautiful forms slowly ascending as if by the steps of a winding stair. The forms appeared irregularly—now one, now many, now several, now none—men and women and children—all different, all beautiful.

He drew nearer to the rainbow. It vanished. He started back a step in dismay. It was there again, as beautiful as ever. So he contented himself with standing as near it as he might, and watching the forms that ascended the glorious colours towards the unknown height of the arch, which did not end abruptly, but faded away in the blue air, so gradually that he could not say where it ceased.

When the thought of the golden key returned, the boy very wisely proceeded to mark out in his mind the space covered by the foundation of the rainbow, in order that he might know where to search, should the rainbow disappear. It was based chiefly upon a bed of moss.

Meantime it had grown quite dark in the wood. The rainbow alone was visible by its own light. But the moment the moon rose the rainbow vanished. Nor could any change of place restore the vision to the boy's eyes. So he threw himself down on the mossy bed, to wait till the sunlight would give him a chance of finding the key. There he fell fast asleep.

When he awoke in the morning the sun was looking straight into his eyes. He turned away from it, and the same moment saw a brilliant little thing lying on the moss within a foot of his face. It was the golden key. The pipe of it was of plain gold, as bright as gold could be. The handle was curiously wrought and set with sapphires. In a terror of delight he put out his hand and took it, and had it.

He lay for a while, turning it over and over, and feeding his eyes upon its beauty. Then he jumped to his feet, remembering that the pretty thing was of no use to him yet. Where was the lock to which the key belonged? It must be somewhere, for how could anybody be so silly as make a key for which there was no lock? Where should he go to look for it? He gazed about him, up into the air, down to the earth, but saw no keyhole in the clouds, in the grass, or in the trees.

Just as he began to grow disconsolate, however, he saw something glimmering in the wood. It was a mere glimmer that he saw, but he took it for a glimmer of rainbow, and went towards it.—And now I will go back to the borders of the forest.

Not far from the house where the boy had lived, there was another house, the owner of which was a merchant, who was much away from home. He had lost his wife some years before, and had only one child, a little girl, whom he left to the charge of two servants, who were very idle and careless. So she was neglected and left untidy, and was sometimes ill-used besides.

Now it is well known that the little creatures commonly called fairies, though there are many different kinds of fairies in Fairyland, have an exceeding dislike to untidiness. Indeed, they are quite spiteful to slovenly people. Being used to all the lovely ways of the trees and flowers, and to the neatness of the birds and all woodland creatures, it makes them feel miserable, even in their deep woods and on their grassy carpets to think that within the same moonlight lies a dirty, uncomfortable, slovenly house. And this makes them angry with the people that live in it, and they would gladly drive them out of the world if they could. They want the whole earth nice and clean. So they pinch the maids black and blue, and play them all manner of uncomfortable tricks.

But this house was quite a shame, and the fairies in the forest could not endure it. They tried everything on the maids without effect, and at last resolved upon making a clean riddance, beginning with the child. They ought to have known that it was not her fault, but they have little principle and much mischief in them, and they thought that if they got rid of her the maids would be sure to be turned away.

So one evening, the poor little girl having been put to bed early, before the sun was down, the servants went off to the village, locking the door behind them. The child did not know she was alone, and lay contentedly looking out of her window towards the forest, of which, however, she could not see much, because of the ivy and other creeping plants which had straggled across her window. All at once she saw an ape making faces at her out of the mirror, and the heads carved upon a great old wardrobe grinning fearfully. Then two old spider-legged chairs came forward into the middle of the room, and began to dance a queer, old-fashioned dance. This set her laughing, and she forgot the ape and the grinning heads.

So the fairies saw they had made a mistake, and sent the chairs back to their places. But they knew that she had been reading the story of Silverhair all day. So the next moment she heard the voices of the three bears upon the stair, big voice, middle voice, and little voice, and she heard their soft, heavy tread, as if they had had stockings over their boots, coming nearer and nearer to the door of her room, till she could bear it no longer. She did just as Silverhair did and as the fairies wanted her to do: she darted to the window, pulled it open, got upon the ivy, and so scrambled to the ground. She then fled to the forest as fast as she could run.

Now, although she did not know it, this was the very best way she could have gone; for nothing is ever so mischievous in its own place as it is out of it; and, besides, these mischievous creatures were only the children of Fairyland, as it were, and there are many other beings there as well; and if a wanderer gets in among them, the good ones will always help him more than the evil ones will be able to hurt him.

The sun was now set, and the darkness coming on, but the child thought of no danger but the bears behind her.

If she had looked round, however, she would have seen that she was followed by a very different creature from a bear. It was a curious creature, made like a fish, but covered, instead of scales, with feathers of all colours, sparkling like those of a humming-bird. It had fins, not wings, and swam through the air as a fish does through the water. Its head was like the head of a small owl.

After running a long way, and as the last of the light was disappearing, she passed under a tree with drooping branches. It propped its branches to the ground all about her, and caught her as in a trap. She struggled to get out, but the branches pressed her closer and closer to the trunk. She was in great terror and distress, when the air-fish, swimming into the thicket of branches, began tearing them with its beak. They loosened their hold at once, and the creature went on attacking them, till at length they let the child go. Then the air-fish came from behind her, and swam on in front, glittering and sparkling all lovely colours; and she followed.

It led her gently along till all at once it swam in at a cottage-door. The child followed still. There was a bright fire in the middle of the floor, upon which stood a pot without a lid, full of water that boiled and bubbled furiously. The air-fish swam straight to the pot and into the boiling water, where it lay quiet. A beautiful woman rose from the opposite side of the fire and came to meet the girl. She took her up in her arms, and said,—

"Ah, you are come at last! I have been looking for you a long time."

She sat down with her on her lap, and there the girl sat staring at her. She had never seen anything so beautiful. She was tall and strong, with white arms and neck, and a delicate flush on her face. The child could not tell what was

the colour of her hair, but could not help thinking it had a tinge of dark green. She had not one ornament upon her, but she looked as if she had just put off quantities of diamonds and emeralds. Yet here she was in the simplest, poorest little cottage, where she was evidently at home. She was dressed in shining green.

The girl looked at the lady, and the lady looked at the girl.

"What is your name?" asked the lady.

"The servants always called me Tangle."

"Ah, that was because your hair was so untidy. But that was their fault, the naughty women! Still it is a pretty name, and I will call you Tangle too. You must not mind my asking you questions, for you may ask me the same questions, every one of them, and any others that you like. How old are you?"

"Ten," answered Tangle.

"You don't look like it," said the lady.

"How old are you, please?" returned Tangle.

"Thousands of years old," answered the lady.

"You don't look like it," said Tangle.

"Don't I? I think I do. Don't you see how beautiful I am?"

And her great blue eyes looked down on the little Tangle, as if all the stars in the sky were melted in them to make their brightness.

"Ah! but," said Tangle, "when people live long they grow old. At least I always thought so."

"I have no time to grow old," said the lady. "I am too busy for that. It is very idle to grow old. But I cannot have my little girl so untidy. Do you know I can't find a clean spot on your face to kiss?"

"Perhaps," suggested Tangle, feeling ashamed, but not too much so to say a word for herself, "perhaps that is because the tree made me cry so."

"My poor darling!" said the lady, looking now as if the moon were melted in her eyes, and kissing her little face, dirty as it was, "the naughty tree must suffer for making a girl cry."

"And what is your name, please?" asked Tangle.

"Grandmother," answered the lady.

"Is it, really?"

"Yes, indeed. I never tell stories, even in fun."

"How good of you!"

"I couldn't if I tried. It would come true if I said it, and then I should be punished enough."

And she smiled like the sun through a summer-shower. "But now," she went on, "I must get you washed and dressed, and then we shall have some supper."

"Oh! I had supper long ago," said Tangle.

"Yes, indeed you had," answered the lady, "three years ago. You don't know that it is three years since you ran away from the bears. You are thirteen and more now."

Tangle could only stare. She felt quite sure it was true.

"You will not be afraid of anything I do with you—will you?" said the lady.

"I will try very hard not to be; but I can't be certain, you know," replied Tangle.

"I like your saying so, and I shall be quite satisfied," answered the lady.

She took off the girl's night-gown, rose with her in her arms, and going to the wall of the cottage, opened a door. Then Tangle saw a deep tank, the sides of which were filled with green plants, which had flowers of all colours. There was a roof over it like the roof of the cottage. It was filled with beautiful clear water, in which swam a multitude of such fishes as the one that had led her to the cottage. It was the light their colours gave that showed the place in which they were.

The lady spoke some words Tangle could not understand, and threw her into the tank.

The fishes came crowding about her. Two or three of them got under her head and kept it up. The rest of them rubbed themselves all over her, and with their wet feathers washed her quite clean. Then the lady, who had been looking on all the time, spoke again; whereupon some thirty or forty of the fishes rose out of the water underneath Tangle, and so bore her up to the arms the lady held out to take her. She carried her back to the fire, and, having dried her well, opened a chest, and taking out the finest linen garments, smelling of grass and lavender, put them upon her, and over all a green dress, just like her own, shining like hers, and soft like hers, and going into just such lovely folds from the waist, where it was tied with a brown cord, to her bare feet.

"Won't you give me a pair of shoes too, grandmother?" said Tangle.

"No, my dear, no shoes. Look here. I wear no shoes."

So saying, she lifted her dress a little, and there were the loveliest white feet, but no shoes. Then Tangle was content to go without shoes too. And the lady sat down with her again, and combed her hair, and brushed it, and then left it to dry while she got the supper.

First she got bread out of one hole in the wall; then milk out of another; then several kinds of fruit out of a third; and then she went to the pot on the fire, and took out the fish now nicely cooked, and, as soon as she had pulled off its feathered skin, ready to be eaten.

"But," exclaimed Tangle. And she stared at the fish, and could say no more.

"I know what you mean," returned the lady. "You do not like to eat the messenger that brought you home. But it is the kindest return you can make. The creature was afraid to go until it saw me put the pot on, and heard me promise it should be boiled the moment it returned with you. Then it darted out of the door at once. You saw it go into the pot of itself the moment it entered, did you not?"

"I did," answered Tangle, "and I thought it very strange; but then I saw you, and forgot all about the fish."

"In Fairyland," resumed the lady, as they sat down to the table, "the ambition of the animals is to be eaten by the people; for that is their highest end in that condition. But they are not therefore destroyed. Out of that pot comes something more than the dead fish, you will see."

Tangle now remarked that the lid was on the pot. But the lady took no further notice of it till they had eaten the fish, which Tangle found nicer than any fish she had ever tasted before. It was as white as snow, and as delicate as cream. And the moment she had swallowed a mouthful of it, a change she could not describe began to take place in her. She heard a murmuring all about her, which became more and more articulate, and at length, as she went on eating, grew intelligible. By the time she had finished her share, the sounds of all the animals in the forest came crowding through the door to her ears; for the door still stood wide open, though it was pitch dark outside; and they were no longer sounds only; they were speech, and speech that she could understand. She could tell what the insects in the cottage were saying to each other too. She had even a suspicion that the trees and flowers all about the cottage were holding midnight communications with each other; but what they said she could not hear.

As soon as the fish was eaten, the lady went to the fire and took the lid off the pot. A lovely little creature in human shape, with large white wings, rose out

of it, and flew round and round the roof of the cottage; then dropped, fluttering, and nestled in the lap of the lady. She spoke to it some strange words, carried it to the door, and threw it out into the darkness. Tangle heard the flapping of its wings die away in the distance.

"Now have we done the fish any harm?" she said, returning.

"No," answered Tangle, "I do not think we have. I should not mind eating one every day."

"They must wait their time, like you and me too, my little Tangle."

And she smiled a smile which the sadness in it made more lovely.

"But," she continued, "I think we may have one for supper to-morrow."

So saying she went to the door of the tank, and spoke; and now Tangle understood her perfectly.

"I want one of you," she said,—"the wisest."

Thereupon the fishes got together in the middle of the tank, with their heads forming a circle above the water, and their tails a larger circle beneath it. They were holding a council, in which their relative wisdom should be determined. At length one of them flew up into the lady's hand, looking lively and ready.

"You know where the rainbow stands?" she asked.

"Yes, mother, quite well," answered the fish.

"Bring home a young man you will find there, who does not know where to go."

The fish was out of the door in a moment. Then the lady told Tangle it was time to go to bed; and, opening another door in the side of the cottage, showed her a little arbour, cool and green, with a bed of purple heath growing in it, upon which she threw a large wrapper made of the feathered skins of the wise fishes, shining gorgeous in the firelight.

Tangle was soon lost in the strangest, loveliest dreams. And the beautiful lady was in every one of her dreams.

In the morning she woke to the rustling of leaves over her head, and the sound of running water. But, to her surprise, she could find no door—nothing but the moss-grown wall of the cottage. So she crept through an opening in the arbour, and stood in the forest. Then she bathed in a stream that ran merrily through the trees and felt happier; for having once been in her grandmother's pond, she must be clean and tidy ever after; and, having put on her green dress, felt like a lady.

She spent that day in the wood, listening to the birds and beasts and creeping things. She understood all that they said, though she could not repeat a word of it; and every kind had a different language, while there was a common though more limited understanding between all the inhabitants of the forest. She saw nothing of the beautiful lady, but she felt that she was near her all the time; and she took care not to go out of sight of the cottage. It was round, like a snow-hut or a wigwam, and she could see neither door nor window in it. The fact was, it had no windows; and though it was full of doors, they all opened from the inside, and could not even be seen from the outside.

She was standing at the foot of a tree in the twilight, listening to a quarrel between a mole and a squirrel, in which the mole told the squirrel that the tail was the best of him, and the squirrel called the mole Spade-fists, when, the darkness having deepened around her, she became aware of something shining in her face, and looking round, saw that the door of the cottage was open, and the red light of the fire flowing from it like a river through the darkness. She left Mole and Squirrel to settle matters as they might, and darted off to the cottage. Entering, she found the pot boiling on the fire, and the grand, lovely lady sitting on the other side of it.

"I've been watching you all day," said the lady. "You shall have something to eat by-and-by, but we must wait till our supper comes home."

She took Tangle on her knee, and began to sing to her—such songs as made her wish she could listen to them for ever. But at length in rushed the shining fish, and snuggled down in the pot. It was followed by a youth who had outgrown his worn garments. His face was ruddy with health, and in his hand he carried a little jewel, which sparkled in the firelight.

The first words the lady said were, "What is that in your hand, Mossy?"

Now Mossy was the name his companions had given him, because he had a favourite stone covered with moss, on which he used to sit whole days reading; and they said the moss had begun to grow upon him too.

Mossy held out his hand. The moment the lady saw that it was the golden key, she rose from her chair, kissed Mossy on the forehead, made him sit down on her seat, and stood before him like a servant. Mossy could not bear this, and rose at once. But the lady begged him with tears in her beautiful eyes, to sit, and let her wait on him.

"But you are a great, splendid, beautiful lady," said Mossy.

"Yes, I am. But I work all day long— that is my pleasure; and you will have to leave me so soon!"

"How do you know that, if you please, madam?" asked Mossy.

"Because you have got the golden key."

"But I don't know what it is for. I can't find the keyhole. Will you tell me what to do?"

"You must look for the keyhole. That

is your work. I cannot help you. I can only tell you that if you look for it you will find it."

"What kind of a box will it open? What is there inside?"

"I do not know. I dream about it, but I know nothing."

"Must I go at once?"

"You may stop here to-night, and have some of my supper. But you must go in the morning. All I can do for you is to give you clothes. Here is a girl called Tangle, whom you must take with you."

"That *will* be nice," said Mossy.

"No, no!" said Tangle. "I don't want to leave you, please, grandmother."

"You must go with him, Tangle. I am sorry to lose you, but it will be the best thing for you. Even the fishes, you see, have to go into the pot, and then out into the dark. If you fall in with the Old Man of the Sea, mind you ask him whether he has not got some more fishes ready for me. My tank is getting thin."

So saying, she took the fish from the pot, and put the lid on as before. They sat down and ate the fish and then the winged creature rose from the pot, circled the roof, and settled on the lady's lap. She talked to it, carried it to the door, and threw it out into the dark. They heard the flap of its wings die away in the distance.

The lady then showed Mossy into just such another chamber as that of Tangle; and in the morning he found a suit of clothes laid beside him. He looked very handsome in them. But the wearer of Grandmother's clothes never thinks about how he or she looks, but thinks always how handsome other people are.

Tangle was very unwilling to go.

"Why should I leave you? I don't know the young man," she said to the lady.

"I am never allowed to keep my children long. You need not go with him except you please, but you must go some

day; and I should like you to go with him, for he has found the golden key. No girl need be afraid to go with a youth that has the golden key. You will take care of her, Mossy, will you not?"

"That I will," said Mossy.

And Tangle cast a glance at him, and thought she should like to go with him.

"And," said the lady, "if you should lose each other as you go through the—the—I never can remember the name of that country,—do not be afraid, but go on and on.

She kissed Tangle on the mouth and Mossy on the forehead, led them to the door, and waved her hand eastward. Mossy and Tangle took each other's hand and walked away into the depth of the forest. In his right hand Mossy held the golden key.

They wandered thus a long way, with endless amusement from the talk of the animals. They soon learned enough of their language to ask them necessary questions. The squirrels were always friendly, and gave them nuts out of their own hoards; but the bees were selfish and rude, justifying themselves on the ground that Tangle and Mossy were not subjects of their queen, and charity must begin at home, though indeed they had not one drone in their poorhouse at the time. Even the blinking moles would fetch them an earth-nut or a truffle now and then, talking as if their mouths, as well as their eyes and ears, were full of cotton wool, or their own velvety fur. By the time they got out of the forest they were very fond of each other, and Tangle was not in the least sorry that her grandmother had sent her away with Mossy.

At length the trees grew smaller, and stood farther apart, and the ground began to rise, and it got more and more steep, till the trees were all left behind, and the two were climbing a narrow path with rocks on each side. Suddenly they came upon a rude doorway, by which they entered a narrow gallery cut in the rock. It grew darker and darker, till it was pitch-dark, and they had to feel their way. At length the light began to return, and at last they came out upon a narrow path on the face of a lofty precipice. This path went winding down the rock to a wide plain, circular in shape, and surrounded on all sides by mountains. Those opposite to them were a great way off, and towered to an awful height, shooting up sharp, blue, ice-enamelled pinnacles. An utter silence reigned where they stood. Not even the sound of water reached them.

Looking down, they could not tell whether the valley below was a grassy plain or a great still lake. They had never seen any space look like it. The way to it was difficult and dangerous, but down the narrow path they went, and reached the bottom in safety. They found it composed of smooth, light-coloured sandstone, undulating in parts, but mostly level. It was no wonder to them now that they had not been able to tell what it was, for this surface was everywhere crowded with shadows. It was a sea of shadows. The mass was chiefly made up of the shadows of leaves innumerable, of all lovely and imaginative forms, waving to and fro, floating and quivering in the breath of a breeze whose motion was unfelt, whose sound was unheard. No forests clothed the mountain-sides, no trees were anywhere to be seen, and yet the shadows of the leaves, branches, and stems of all various trees covered the valley as far as their eyes could reach.

They soon spied the shadows of flowers mingled with those of the leaves, and now and then the shadow of a bird with open beak, and throat distended with song. At times would appear the forms of strange, graceful creatures, running up and down the shadow-boles and along the branches, to disappear in the wind-tossed foliage. As they walked they waded knee-deep in the lovely lake. For the shadows were not merely lying on the surface of the ground, but heaped up above it like substantial forms of darkness, as if they had been cast upon a thousand different planes of air. Tangle and Mossy often lifted their heads and gazed upwards to descry whence the shadows came; but they could see nothing more than a bright mist spread above them, higher than the tops of the mountains, which stood clear against it. No forests, no leaves, no birds were visible.

After a while, they reached more open spaces, where the shadows were thinner; and came-even to portions over which shadows only flitted, leaving them clear for such as might follow. Now a wonderful form, half bird-like, half human, would float across on outspread sailing pinions. Anon an exquisite shadow group of gambolling children would be followed by the loveliest female form, and that again by the grand stride of a Titanic shape, each disappearing in the surrounding press of shadowy foliage. Sometimes a profile of unspeakable beauty or grandeur would appear for a moment and vanish. Sometimes they seemed lovers that passed linked arm in arm, sometimes father and son, sometimes brothers in loving contest, sometimes sisters entwined in gracefullest community of complex form. Sometimes wild horses would tear across, free, or bestrode by noble shadows of ruling men. But some of the things which pleased them most they never knew how to describe.

About the middle of the plain they sat down to rest in the heart of a heap of shadows. After sitting for a while, each, looking up, saw the other in tears: they were each longing after the country whence the shadows fell.

"We *must* find the country from which the shadows come," said Mossy.

"We must, dear Mossy," responded Tangle. "What if your golden key should be the key to *it?*"

"Ah! that would be grand," returned Mossy. "But we must rest here for a little, and then we shall be able to cross the plain before night."

So he lay down on the ground, and about him on every side, and over his head, was the constant play of the wonderful shadows. He could look through them, and see the one behind the other, till they mixed in a mass of darkness. Tangle, too, lay admiring, and wondering, and longing after the country whence the shadows came. When they were rested they rose and pursued their journey.

How long they were in crossing this plain I cannot tell; but before night Mossy's hair was streaked with gray, and Tangle had got wrinkles on her forehead.

As evening drew on, the shadows fell deeper and rose higher. At length they reached a place where they rose above their heads, and made all dark around them. Then they took hold of each other's hand, and walked on in silence and in some dismay. They felt the gathering darkness, and something strangely solemn besides, and the beauty of the shadows ceased to delight them. All at once Tangle found that she had not a hold of Mossy's hand, though when she lost it she could not tell.

"Mossy, Mossy!" she cried aloud in terror.

But no Mossy replied.

A moment after, the shadows sank to her feet, and down under her feet, and the mountains rose before her. She turned towards the gloomy region she had left, and called once more upon

Mossy. There the gloom lay tossing and heaving, a dark, stormy, foaming sea of shadows, but no Mossy rose out of it, or came climbing up the hill on which she stood. She threw herself down and wept in despair.

Suddenly she remembered that the beautiful lady had told them, if they lost each other in a country of which she could not remember the name, they were not to be afraid, but to go straight on.

"And besides," she said to herself, "Mossy has the golden key, and so no harm will come to him, I do believe."

She rose from the ground, and went on.

Before long she arrived at a precipice, in the face of which a stair was cut. When she had ascended halfway, the stair ceased, and the path led straight into the mountain. She was afraid to enter, and turning again towards the stair, grew giddy at sight of the depth beneath her, and was forced to throw herself down in the mouth of the cave.

When she opened her eyes, she saw a beautiful little creature with wings standing beside her, waiting.

"I know you," said Tangle. "You are my fish."

"Yes. But I am a fish no longer. I am an aëranth now."

"What is that?" asked Tangle.

"What you see I am," answered the shape. "And I am come to lead you through the mountain."

"Oh! thank you, dear fish—aëranth, I mean," returned Tangle, rising.

Thereupon the aëranth took to his wings, and flew on through the long, narrow passage, reminding Tangle very much of the way he had swum on before when he was a fish. And the moment his white wings moved, they began to throw off a continuous shower of sparks of all colours, which lighted up the passage before them. All at once he vanished, and Tangle heard a low, sweet sound, quite different from the rush and crackle of his wings. Before her was an open arch, and through it came light, mixed with the sound of sea-waves.

She hurried out, and fell, tired and happy, upon the yellow sand of the shore. There she lay, half asleep with weariness and rest, listening to the low plash and retreat of the tiny waves, which seemed ever enticing the land to leave off being land, and become sea. And as she lay, her eyes were fixed upon the foot of a great rainbow standing far away against the sky on the other side of the sea. At length she fell fast asleep.

When she awoke, she saw an old man with long white hair down to his shoulders, leaning upon a stick covered with green buds, and so bending over her.

"What do you want here, beautiful woman?" he said.

"Am I beautiful? I am so glad!" answered Tangle, rising. "My grandmother is beautiful."

"Yes. But what do you want?" he repeated, kindly.

"I think I want you. Are not you the Old Man of the Sea?"

"I am."

"Then grandmother says, have you any more fishes ready for her?"

"We will go and see, my dear," answered the Old Man, speaking yet more kindly than before. "And I can do something for you, can I not?"

"Yes—show me the way up to the country from which the shadows fall," said Tangle.

For there she hoped to find Mossy again.

"Ah! indeed, that would be worth doing," said the Old Man. "But I cannot, for I do not know the way myself. But I will send you to the Old Man of the Earth. Perhaps he can tell you. He is much older than I am."

Leaning on his staff, he conducted her along the shore to a steep rock, that looked like a petrified ship turned upside down. The door of it was the rudder of a great vessel, ages ago at the bottom of the sea. Immediately within the door was a stair in the rock, down which the Old Man went, and Tangle followed. At the bottom the Old Man had his house, and there he lived.

As soon as she entered it, Tangle heard a strange noise, unlike anything she had ever heard before. She soon found that it was the fishes talking. She tried to understand what they said; but their speech was so old-fashioned, and rude, and undefined, that she could not make much of it.

"I will go and see about those fishes for my daughter," said the Old Man of the Sea.

And moving a slide in the wall of his house, he first looked out, and then tapped upon a thick piece of crystal that filled the round opening. Tangle came up behind him, and peeping through the window into the heart of the great deep green ocean, saw the most curious creatures, some very ugly, all very odd, and with especially queer mouths, swimming about everywhere, above and below, but all coming towards the window in answer to the tap of the Old Man of the Sea. Only a few could get their mouths against the glass; but those who were floating miles away yet turned their heads towards it. The Old Man looked through the whole flock carefully for some minutes, and then turning to Tangle, said, "I am sorry I have not got one ready yet. I want more time than she does. But I will send some as soon as I can."

He then shut the slide.

Presently a great noise arose in the sea. The Old Man opened the slide again, and tapped on the glass, whereupon the fishes were all as still as sleep.

"They were only talking about you," he said. "And they do speak such non-sense!—To-morrow," he continued, "I must show you the way to the Old Man of the Earth. He lives a long way from here."

"Do let me go at once," said Tangle.

"No. That is not possible. You must come this way first."

He led her to a hole in the wall, which she had not observed before. It was covered with the green leaves and white blossoms of a creeping plant.

"Only white-blossoming plants can grow under the sea," said the Old Man. "In there you will find a bath, in which you must lie till I call you."

Tangle went in, and found a smaller room or cave, in the further corner of which was a great basin hollowed out of a rock, and half-full of the clearest sea-water. Little streams were constantly running into it from cracks in the wall of the cavern. It was polished quite smooth inside, and had a carpet of yellow sand in the bottom of it. Large green leaves and white flowers of various plants crowded up over it, draping and covering it almost entirely.

No sooner was she undressed and lying in the bath, than she began to feel as if the water were sinking into her, and she were receiving all the good of sleep without undergoing its forgetfulness. She felt the good coming all the time. And she grew happier and more hopeful than she had been since she lost Mossy. But she could not help thinking how very sad it was for a poor old man to live there all alone, and have to take care of a whole seaful of stupid and riotous fishes.

After about an hour, as she thought, she heard his voice calling her, and rose out of the bath. All the fatigue and aching of her long journey had vanished.

She was as whole, and strong, and well as if she had slept for seven days.

Returning to the opening that led into the other part of the house, she started back with amazement, for through it she saw the form of a grand man, with a majestic and beautiful face, waiting for her.

"Come," he said; "I see you are ready."

She entered with reverence.

"Where is the Old Man of the Sea?" she asked, humbly.

"There is no one here but me," he answered, smiling. "Some people call me the Old Man of the Sea. Others have another name for me, and are terribly frightened when they meet me taking a walk by the shore. Therefore I avoid being seen by them, for they are so afraid, that they never see what I really am. You see me now.—But I must show you the way to the Old Man of the Earth."

He led her into the cave where the bath was, and there she saw, in the opposite corner, a second opening in the rock.

"Go down that stair, and it will bring you to him," said the Old Man of the Sea.

With humble thanks Tangle took her leave. She went down the winding-stair, till she began to fear there was no end to it. Still down and down it went, rough and broken, with springs of water bursting out of the rocks and running down the steps beside her. It was quite dark about her, and yet she could see. For after being in that bath, people's eyes always give out a light they can see by. There were no creeping things in the way. All was safe and pleasant, though so dark and damp and deep.

At last there was not one step more, and she found herself in a glimmering cave. On a stone in the middle of it sat a figure with its back towards her—the figure of an old man bent double with age. From behind she could see his white beard spread out on the rocky floor in front of him. He did not move as she entered, so she passed round that she might stand before him and speak to him. The moment she looked in his face, she saw that he was a youth of marvellous beauty. He sat entranced with the delight of what he beheld in a mirror of something like silver, which lay on the floor at his feet, and which from behind she had taken for his white beard. He sat on, heedless of her presence, pale with the joy of his vision. She stood and watched him. At length, all trembling, she spoke. But her voice made no sound. Yet the youth lifted up his head. He showed no surprise, however, at seeing her—only smiled a welcome.

"Are you the Old Man of the Earth?" Tangle had said.

And the youth answered, and Tangle heard him, though not with her ears: "I am. What can I do for you?"

"Tell me the way to the country whence the shadows fall."

"Ah! that I do not know. I only dream about it myself. I see its shadows sometimes in my mirror: the way to it I do not know. But I think the Old Man of the Fire must know. He is much older than I am. He is the oldest man of all."

"Where does he live?"

"I will show you the way to his place. I never saw him myself."

So saying, the young man rose, and then stood a while gazing at Tangle.

"I wish I could see that country too," he said. "But I must mind my work."

He led her to the side of the cave, and told her to lay her ear against the wall.

"What do you hear?" he asked.

"I hear," answered Tangle, "the sound of a great water running inside the rock."

"That river runs down to the dwelling of the oldest man of all—the Old Man of the Fire. I wish I could go to see him. But I must mind my work. That river is the only way to him."

Then the Old Man of the Earth stooped over the floor of the cave, raised a huge stone from it, and left it leaning. It disclosed a great hole that went plumb-down.

"That is the way," he said.

"But there are no stairs."

"You must throw yourself in. There is no other way."

She turned and looked him full in the face—stood so for a whole minute, as she thought: it was a whole year—then threw herself headlong into the hole.

When she came to herself, she found herself gliding down fast and deep. Her head was under water, but that did not signify, for, when she thought about it she could not remember that she had breathed once since her bath in the cave of the Old Man of the Sea. When she lifted up her head a sudden and fierce heat struck her, and she dropped it again instantly, and went sweeping on.

Gradually the stream grew shallower. At length she could hardly keep her head under. Then the water could carry her no farther. She rose from the channel, and went step for step down the burning descent. The water ceased altogether. The heat was terrible. She felt scorched to the bone, but it did not touch her strength. It grew hotter and hotter. She said, "I can bear it no longer." Yet she went on.

At the long last, the stair ended at a rude archway in an all but glowing rock. Through this archway Tangle fell exhausted into a cool mossy cave. The floor and walls were covered with moss—green, soft, and damp. A little stream spouted from a rent in the rock and fell into a basin of moss. She plunged her face into it and drank. Then she lifted her head and looked around. Then she rose and looked again. She saw no one in the cave. But the moment she stood upright she had a marvellous sense that she was in the secret of the earth and all its ways. Everything she had seen, or learned from books; all that her grandmother had said or sung to her, all the talk of the beasts, birds, and fishes, all that had happened to her on her journey with Mossy, and since then in the heart of the earth with the Old Man and the Older Man—all was plain: she understood it all, and saw that everything meant the same thing, though she could not have put it into words again.

The next moment she descried, in a corner of the cave, a little naked child, sitting on the moss. He was playing with balls of various colours and sizes, which he disposed in strange figures upon the floor beside him. And now Tangle felt that there was something in her knowledge which was not in her understanding. For she knew there must be an infinite meaning in the change and sequence and individual forms of the figures into which the child arranged the balls, as well as in the varied harmonies of their colours, but what it all meant she could not tell.

He went on busily, tirelessly, playing his solitary game, without looking up, or seeming to know that there was a stranger in his deep-withdrawn cell. Diligently as a lace-maker shifts her bobbins, he shifted and arranged his balls. Flashes of meaning would now pass from them to Tangle, and now again all would be not merely obscure, but utterly dark. She stood looking for a long time, for there was fascination in the sight; and the longer she looked the more an indescribable vague intelligence went on rousing itself in her mind. For seven years she had stood there watching the naked Child with his coloured balls, and it seemed to her like seven hours, when all at once the shape the balls took, she knew not why, reminded her of the Valley of Shadows,

and she spoke: "Where is the Old Man of the Fire?" she said.

"Here I am," answered the Child, rising and leaving his balls on the moss. "What can I do for you?"

There was such an awfulness of absolute repose on the face of the Child that Tangle stood dumb before him. He had no smile, but the love in his large gray eyes was deep as the centre. And with the repose there lay on his face a shimmer as of moonlight, which seemed as if any moment it might break into such a ravishing smile as would cause the beholder to weep himself to death. But the smile never came, and the moonlight lay there unbroken. For the heart of the child was too deep for any smile to reach from it to his face.

"Are you the oldest man of all?" Tangle at length, although filled with awe, ventured to ask.

"Yes, I am. I am very, very old. I am able to help you, I know. I can help everybody."

And the Child drew near and looked up in her face so that she burst into tears.

"Can you tell me the way to the country the shadows fall from?" she sobbed.

"Yes. I know the way quite well. I go there myself sometimes. But you could not go my way; you are not old enough. I will show you how you can go."

"Do not send me out into the great heat again," prayed Tangle.

"I will not," answered the Child.

And he reached up, and put his little cool hand on her heart.

"Now," he said, "you can go. The fire will not burn you. Come."

He led her from the cave, and following him through another archway, she found herself in a vast desert of sand and rock. The sky of it was of rock, lowering over them like solid thunderclouds; and the whole place was so hot that she saw, in bright rivulets, the yellow gold and white silver and red copper trickling molten from the rocks. But the heat never came near her.

When they had gone some distance, the Child turned up a great stone, and took something like an egg from under it. He next drew a long curved line in the sand with his finger, and laid the egg in it. He then spoke something Tangle could not understand. The egg broke, a small snake came out, and, lying in the line in the sand, grew and grew till he filled it. The moment he was thus full-grown, he began to glide away, undulating like a sea-wave.

"Follow that serpent," said the Child. "He will lead you the right way."

Tangle followed the serpent. But she could not go far without looking back at the marvellous Child. He stood alone in the midst of the glowing desert, beside a fountain of red flame that had burst forth at his feet, his naked whiteness glimmering a pale rosy red in the torrid fire. There he stood, looking after her, till, from the lengthening distance, she could see him no more. The serpent went straight on, turning neither to the right nor left.

Meantime Mossy had got out of the lake of shadows, and, following his mournful, lonely way, had reached the sea-shore. It was a dark, stormy evening. The sun had set. The wind was blowing from the sea. The waves had surrounded the rock within which lay the Old Man's house. A deep water rolled between it and the shore upon which a majestic figure was walking alone.

Mossy went up to him and said,—

"Will you tell me where to find the Old Man of the Sea?"

"I am the Old Man of the Sea," the figure answered. "I see a strong kingly man of middle age," returned Mossy.

Then the Old Man looked at him more intently, and said, "Your sight, young man, is better than that of most who take this way. The night is stormy: come to my house and tell me what I can do for you."

Mossy followed him. The waves flew from before the footsteps of the Old Man of the Sea, and Mossy followed upon dry sand.

When they had reached the cave, they sat down and gazed at each other.

Now Mossy was an old man by this time. He looked much older than the Old Man of the Sea, and his feet were very weary.

After looking at him for a moment, the Old Man took him by the hand and led him into his inner cave. There he helped him to undress, and laid him in the bath. And he saw that one of his hands Mossy did not open.

"What have you in that hand?" he asked.

Mossy opened his hand, and there lay the golden key.

"Ah!" said the Old Man, "that accounts for your knowing me. And I know the way you have to go."

"I want to find the country whence the shadows fall," said Mossy.

"I dare say you do. So do I. But meantime, one thing is certain.—What is that key for, do you think?"

"For a keyhole somewhere. But I don't know why I keep it. I never could find the keyhole. And I have lived a good while, I believe," said Mossy, sadly. "I'm not sure that I'm not old. I know my feet ache."

"Do they?" said the Old Man, as if he really meant to ask the question; and Mossy, who was still lying in the bath, watched his feet for a moment before he replied.

"No, they do not," he answered. "Perhaps I am not old either."

"Get up and look at yourself in the water."

He rose and looked at himself in the

water, and there was not a gray hair on his head or a wrinkle on his skin.

"You have tasted of death now," said the Old Man. "Is it good?"

"It is good," said Mossy. "It is better than life."

"No," said the Old Man: "it is only more life.—Your feet will make no holes in the water now."

"What do you mean?"

"I will show you that presently."

They turned to the outer cave, and sat and talked together for a long time. At length the Old Man of the Sea arose and said to Mossy, "Follow me."

He led him up the stair again, and opened another door. They stood on the level of the raging sea, looking towards the east. Across the waste of waters, against the bosom of a fierce black cloud, stood the foot of a rainbow, glowing in the dark.

"This indeed is my way," said Mossy, as soon as he saw the rainbow, and stepped out upon the sea. His feet made no holes in the water. He fought the wind, and clomb the waves, and went on towards the rainbow.

The storm died away. A lovely day and a lovelier night followed. A cool wind blew over the wide plain of the quiet ocean. And still Mossy journeyed eastward. But the rainbow had vanished with the storm.

Day after day he held on, and he thought he had no guide. He did not see how a shining fish under the waters directed his steps. He crossed the sea, and came to a great precipice of rock, up which he could discover but one path. Nor did this lead him farther than half-way up the rock, where it ended on a platform. Here he stood and pondered.—It could not be that the way stopped here, else what was the path for? It was a rough path, not very plain, yet certainly a path.—He examined the face of the rock. It was smooth as glass.

But as his eyes kept roving hopelessly over it, something glittered, and he caught sight of a row of small sapphires. They bordered a little hole in the rock.

"The keyhole!" he cried.

He tried the key. It fitted. It turned. A great clang and clash, as of iron bolts on huge brazen caldrons echoed thunderously within. He drew out the key. The rock in front of him began to fall. He retreated from it as far as the breadth of the platform would allow. A great slab fell at his feet. In front was still the solid rock, with this one slab fallen forward out of it.

But the moment he stepped upon it, a second fell, just short of the edge of the first, making the next step of a stair, which thus kept dropping itself before him as he ascended into the heart of the precipice. It led him into a hall fit for such an approach—irregular and rude in formation, but floor, sides, pillars, and vaulted roof, all one mass of shining stones of every colour that light can show. In the centre stood seven columns, ranged from red to violet. And on the pedestal of one of them sat a woman, motionless, with her face bowed upon her knees. Seven years had she sat there waiting. She lifted her head as Mossy drew near. It was Tangle. Her hair had grown to her feet, and was rippled like the windless sea on broad sands. Her face was beautiful, like her grandmother's, and as still and peaceful as that of the Old Man of the Fire. Her form was tall and noble. Yet Mossy knew her at once.

"How beautiful you are, Tangle!" he said, in delight and astonishment.

"Am I?" she returned. "Oh, I have waited for you so long! But you, you are like the Old Man of the Sea. No. You are like the Old Man of the Earth. No, no. You are like the oldest man of all. You are like them all. And yet you are my own old Mossy! How did you come here? What did you do after I lost you? Did you find the keyhole? Have you got the key still?"

She had a hundred questions to ask him, and he a hundred more to ask her. They told each other all their adventures, and were as happy as man and woman could be. For they were younger and better, and stronger and wiser, than they had ever been before.

It began to grow dark. And they wanted more than ever to reach the country whence the shadows fall. So they looked about them for a way out of the cave. The door by which Mossy entered had closed again, and there was half a mile of rock between them and the sea. Neither could Tangle find the opening in the floor by which the serpent had led her thither. They searched till it grew so dark that they could see nothing, and gave it up.

After a while, however, the cave began to glimmer again. The light came from the moon, but it did not look like moonlight, for it gleamed through those seven pillars in the middle, and filled the place with all colours. And now Mossy saw that there was a pillar beside the red one, which he had not observed before. And it was of the same new colour that he had seen in the rainbow when he saw it first in the fairy forest. And on it he saw a sparkle of blue. It was the sapphires round the keyhole.

He took the key. It turned in the lock to the sounds of Æolian music. A door opened upon slow hinges, and disclosed a winding stair within. The key vanished from his fingers. Tangle went up. Mossy followed. The door closed behind them. They climbed out of the earth; and, still climbing, rose above it. They were in the rainbow. Far abroad, over ocean and land, they could see through its transparent walls the earth beneath their feet. Stairs beside stairs wound up together, and beautiful beings of all ages climbed along with them.

They knew that they were going up to the country whence the shadows fell.

And by this time I think they must have got there.

MacDonald's sermons appear primarily in three series titled Unspoken Sermons. *The first of these series was published in 1867. "The Cry, 'Eloi, Eloi'" is taken from this first volume and deals with Christ's sufferings. MacDonald finds that although Christ endured the most intense suffering and most severe trial that men can face when He was on the cross, His will was triumphant. His cry on the cross was a cry of desolation, but it was also a cry of faith. In the same way, even when we cannot feel God's presence or feel like doing good, we must nevertheless continue to hold fast to God.*

Though the law cannot fulfill love, love can fulfill the law is a theme MacDonald uses in "Love Thy Neighbour," which is also from the first volume of sermons. MacDonald sets out to answer the question of how we may love our neighbors and arrives at the conclusion that we must begin by obedience. Once a man has united himself with God by obedient action, the truth of love is made known to him. Human society is built upon two loves: love for God and love for man. It is only in loving our neighbor that we can truly show love for God.

"The God of the Living" starts with Christ's answer to the Sadducees concerning the resurrection of the dead, a theme MacDonald was fond of discussing. MacDonald's sacramental theology is revealed here when he discusses the nature of our present bodies and states that they are "the means of revelation to us, the camera in which God's eternal shows are set forth." Our resurrection bodies will fulfill the same function as our present ones, only more gloriously.

CHAPTER FIVE

The Cry, "Eloi, Eloi"

"My God, my God, why hast thou forsaken me?" (Matt. 27:46).

I do not know that I should dare to approach this of all utterances into which human breath has ever been moulded, most awful in import, did I not feel that, containing both germ and blossom of the final devotion it contains therefore the deepest practical lesson the human heart has to learn. The Lord, the Revealer, hides nothing that can be revealed, and will not warn away the foot that treads in naked humility even upon the ground of that terrible conflict between him and evil, when the smoke of the battle, that was fought not only with garments rolled in blood but with burning and fuel of fire rose up between him and his Father, and for the one terrible moment ere he broke the bonds of life, and walked weary and triumphant into his arms, hid God from the eyes of his Son. He will give us even to meditate the one thought that slew him at last, when he could bear no more, and fled to the Father to know that he loved him, and was well pleased with him.

For Satan had come at length yet again, to urge him with his last temptation; to tell him that although he had done his part, God had forgotten his; that although he had lived by the word of his mouth, that mouth had no word more to speak to him; that although he had refused to tempt him, God had left him to be tempted more than he could bear, that although he had worshiped none other, for that worship God did not care. The Lord hides not his sacred sufferings, for truth is light, and would be light in the minds of men. The Holy Child, the Son of the Father, has nothing to conceal, but all the Godhead to reveal. Let us then put off our shoes, and draw near, and bow the head, and kiss those feet that bear forever the scars of our victory. In those feet we clasp the safety of our suffering, our sinning brotherhood.

Christ's Perfect Will

It is with the holiest fear that we should approach the terrible fact of the sufferings of our Lord. Let no one think that those were less because he was more. The more delicate the nature, the more alive to all that is lovely and true, lawful and right, the more does it feel the antagonism of pain, the inroad of death upon life; the more dreadful is that breach of the harmony of things whose sound is torture. He felt more than man could feel, because he had a larger feeling. He was even therefore worn out sooner than another man would have been.

These sufferings were awful indeed when they began to invade the region about the will; when the struggle to keep consciously trusting in God began to sink in darkness; when the will of The Man put forth its last determined effort in that cry after the vanishing vision of the Father: *My God, my God, why hast thou forsaken me?* Never had it been so with him before. Never before had he been unable to see God beside him. Yet never was God nearer him than now. For never was Jesus more divine. He could not see, could not feel him near; and yet it is "*My* God" that he cries.

Thus the will of Jesus, in the very moment when his faith seems about to yield, is finally triumphant. It has no *feeling* now to support it, no beatific vision to absorb it. It stands naked in his soul and tortured, as he stood naked and scourged before Pilate. Pure and simple and surrounded by fire, it declares for God. The sacrifice ascends in the cry, *My God*. The cry comes not out of happiness, out of peace, out of hope. Not even out of suffering comes that cry. It was a cry *in* desolation, but it came out of faith. It is the last voice of truth, speaking when it can but cry. The divine horror of that moment is unfathomable by human soul. It was blackness of darkness. And yet he would believe. Yet he would hold fast. God was his God yet. *My God*—and in the cry came forth the victory, and all was over soon. Of the peace that followed that cry, the peace of a perfect soul, large as the universe, pure as light, ardent as life, victorious for God and his brethren, he himself alone can ever know the breadth and length, and depth and height.

Without this last trial of all, the temptations of our Master had not been so full as the human cup could hold; there would have been one region through which we had to pass wherein we might call aloud upon our Captain-Brother, and there would be no voice or hearing: he had avoided the fatal spot! The temptations of the desert came to the young, strong man with his road before him, and the presence of his God around him, nay gathered their very force from the exuberance of his conscious faith. "Dare and do, for God is with thee," said the devil. "I know it, and therefore I will wait," returned the king of his brothers.

And now, after three years of divine action, when his course is run, when the old age of finished work is come, when the whole frame is tortured until the regnant brain falls whirling down the blue gulf of fainting, and the giving up of the ghost is at hand, when the friends have forsaken him and fled, comes the voice of the enemy again at his ear: "Despair and die, for God is not with thee. All is in vain. Death, not life, is thy refuge. Make haste to Hades, where thy torture will be over. Thou hast deceived thyself. He never was with thee. He was the God of Abraham. Abraham is dead. Whom makest thou thyself?"

"My God, my God, why hast thou forsaken me?" the Master cries. For God was his God still, although he had forsaken him—forsaken *his vision* that his faith might glow out triumphant; forsaken *himself?* no; come nearer to him than ever: come nearer, even as—but with a yet deeper, more awful pregnancy of import—even as the Lord himself withdrew from the bodily eyes of his friends, that he might dwell in their profoundest being.

I do not think it was our Lord's deepest trial when in the garden he prayed that the cup might pass from him, and prayed yet again that the will of the Father might be done. For that will was then present with him. He was living and acting in that will. But now the foreseen horror has come. He is drinking the dread cup, and The Will has vanished from his eyes. Were that Will visible in his suffering, his will could bow with tearful gladness under the shelter of its grandeur. But now his will is left alone to drink the cup of The Will in torture. In the sickness of this agony, the will of Jesus arises perfect at last; and of itself, unsupported now, declares—a naked consciousness of misery hung in the waste darkness of the universe—declares for God, in defiance of pain, of death, of apathy, of self, of negation, of the blackness within and around it; calls aloud upon the vanished God.

This is the Faith of the Son of God. God withdrew, as it were, that the perfect will of the Son might arise and go forth to find the will of the Father.

Is it possible that even then he thought of the lost sheep who could not believe that God was their Father and for them, too, in all their loss and blindness and unlove, cried, saying the word they might say, knowing for them that *God* means *Father* and more, and knowing now, as he had never known till now, what a fearful thing it is to be without God and without hope? I dare not answer the question I put.

Creeping about in the Valleys

But wherein or what can this Alpine apex of faith have to do with the creatures who call themselves Christians creeping about in the valleys, hardly knowing that there are mountains above them, save that they take offence at, and stumble over, the pebbles washed across their path by the glacier streams? I will tell you. We are and remain such creeping Christians, because we look at ourselves and not at Christ; because we gaze at the marks of our own soiled feet, and the trail of our own defiled garments, instead of up at the snows of purity, whither the soul of Christ clomb.

Each, putting his foot in the footprint of the Master, and so defacing it, turns to examine how far his neighbor's footprint corresponds with that which he still calls the Master's, although it is but his own. Or, having committed a petty fault, I mean a fault such as only a petty creature could commit, we mourn over the defilement to ourselves, and the shame of it before our friends, children, or servants, instead of hastening to make the due confession and amends to our fellow, and then, forgetting our pal-

try self, with its well-earned disgrace, lift up our eyes to the glory which alone will quicken the true man in us, and kill the peddling creature we so wrongly call our *self*. The true self is that which can look Jesus in the face, and say, *My Lord*.

When the inward sun is shining, and the wind of thought, blowing where it lists amid the flowers and leaves of fancy and imagination, rouses glad forms and feelings, it is easy to look upwards, and say, *My God*. It is easy when the frosts of external failure have braced the mental nerves to healthy endurance and fresh effort after labor, it is easy then to turn to God and trust in him, in whom all honest exertion gives an ability as well as a right to trust. It is easy in pain, so long as it does not pass certain undefinable bounds, to hope in God for deliverance, or pray for strength to endure.

But what is to be done when all feeling is gone? when a man does not know whether he believes or not, whether he loves or not? when art, poetry, religion are nothing to him, so swallowed up is he in pain, or mental depression, or disappointment, or temptation, or he knows not what? It seems to him then that God does not care for him, and certainly he does not care for God. If he is still humble, he thinks that he is so bad that God cannot care for him. And he then believes for the time that God loves us only because and when and while we love him; instead of believing that God loves us always because he is our God, and that we live only by his love. Or he does not believe in a God at all, which is better.

So long as we have nothing to say to God, nothing to do with him, save in the sunshine of the mind when we feel him near us, we are poor creatures, willed upon, not willing; reeds, flowering reeds, it may be, and pleasant to behold, but only reeds blown about of the wind; not bad, but poor creatures.

And how, in such a condition, do we generally act? Do we not sit mourning over the loss of our feelings? or worse, make frantic efforts to rouse them? or ten times worse, relapse into a state of temporary atheism, and yield to the pressing temptation? or, being heartless, consent to remain careless, conscious of evil thoughts and low feelings alone, but too lazy, too content to rouse ourselves against them? We know we must get rid of them some day, but meantime—never mind; we do not *feel* them bad, we do not feel anything else good; we are asleep and we know it, and we cannot be troubled to wake. No impulse comes to arouse us, and so we remain as we are.

God does not, by the instant gift of his Spirit, make us always feel right, desire good, love purity, aspire after him and his will. Therefore either he will not, or he cannot. If he will not, it must be because it would not be well to do so. If he cannot, then he would not if he could; else a better condition than God is conceivable to the mind of God—a condition in which he could save the creatures whom he has made, better than he can save them. The truth is this: He wants to make us in his own image, *choosing* the good, *refusing* the evil. How should he effect this if he were *always* moving us from within, as he does at divine intervals, towards the beauty of holiness? God gives us room *to be;* does not oppress us with his will; "stands away from us," that we may act from ourselves, that we may exercise the pure will for good.

Do not, therefore, imagine me to mean that we can do anything of ourselves without God. If we choose the right at last, it is all God's doing, and only the more his that it is ours, only in a far more marvelous way his than if he

had kept us filled with all holy impulses precluding the need of choice. For up to this very point, for this very point, he has been educating us, leading us, pushing us, driving us, enticing us, that we may choose him and his will, and so be tenfold more his children, of his own best making, in the freedom of the will found our own first in its loving sacrifice to him, for which in his grand fatherhood he has been thus working from the foundations of the earth, than we could be in the most ecstatic worship flowing from the divinest impulse, without this *willing* sacrifice.

For God made our individuality as well as, and a greater marvel than, our dependence; made our *apartness* from himself, that freedom should bind us divinely dearer to himself, with a new and inscrutable marvel of love; for the Godhead is still at the root, is the making root of our individuality, and the freer the man, the stronger the bond that binds him to him who made his freedom. He made our wills, and is striving to make them free; for only in the perfection of our individuality and the freedom of our wills can we be altogether his children. This is full of mystery, but can we not see enough in it to make us very glad and very peaceful?

Not in any other act than one which, in spite of impulse or of weakness, declares for the truth, for God, does the will spring into absolute freedom, into true life.

Making Our Wills One with God's

See, then, what lies within our reach every time that we are thus lapped in the folds of night. The highest condition of the human will is in sight, is attainable. I say not the highest condition of the human being, that surely lies in the beatific vision, in the sight of God. But the highest condition of the human will, as distinct, not as separated from God, is when, not seeing God, not seeming to itself to grasp him at all, it yet holds him fast. It cannot continue in this condition, for, not finding, not seeing God, the man would die; but the will thus asserting itself, the man has passed from death into life, and the vision is nigh at hand.

Then first, thus free, in thus asserting its freedom, is the individual will one with the will of God; the child is finally restored to the father; the childhood and the fatherhood meet in one, the brotherhood of the race arises from the dust; and the prayer of our Lord is answered, "I in them and thou in me, that they may be made perfect in one." Let us then arise in God-born strength every time that we feel the darkness closing, or become aware that it has closed around us, and say, "I am of the light and not of the darkness."

Troubled soul, thou art not bound to feel, but thou art bound to arise. God loves thee whether thou feelest or not. Thou canst not love when thou wilt, but thou art bound to fight the hatred in thee to the last. Try not to feel good when thou art not good, but cry to him who is good. He changes not because thou changest. Nay, he has an especial tenderness of love towards thee for that thou art in the dark, and hast no light, and his heart is glad when thou dost arise and say, "I will go to my Father." For he sees thee through all the gloom through which thou canst not see him.

Will thou his will. Say unto him: "My God, I am very dull and low and hard; but thou art wise and high and tender, and thou art my God. I am thy child. Forsake me not." Then fold the arms of thy faith, and wait in quietness until light goes up in thy darkness. Fold the arms of thy faith I say, but not of thy action: bethink thee of something that thou oughtest to do, and go and do it, if it be but the sweeping of a room, or the preparing of a meal, or a visit to a friend. Heed not thy feelings: Do thy work.

As God lives by his own will, and we live in him, so has he given to us power to will in ourselves. How much better should we not fare if, finding that we are standing with our heads bowed away from the good, finding that we have no feeble inclination to seek the source of our life, we should yet *will* upwards toward God, rousing that essence of life in us, which he has given us from his own heart, to call again upon him who is our life, who can fill the emptiest heart, rouse the deadest conscience, quicken the dullest feeling, and strengthen the feeblest will!

Then, if ever the time should come, as perhaps it must come to each of us, when all consciousness of well-being shall have vanished, when the earth shall be but a sterile promontory, and the heavens a dull and pestilent congregation of vapors, when man nor woman shall delight us more, nay, when God himself shall be but a name, and Jesus an old story, then, even then, when a death far worse than "that phantom of grisly bone" is griping at our hearts, and having slain love, hope, faith, forces existence upon us only in agony, then, even then, we shall be able to cry out with our Lord, "My God, my God, why hast thou forsaken me?" Nor shall we die then, I think, without being able to take up his last words as well, and say, *"Father, into thy hands I commend my spirit."*

CHAPTER SIX

Love Thy Neighbour

Thou shalt love thy neighbour as thyself (Matt. 23:39).

The original here quoted by our Lord is to be found in the words of God to Moses *(Lev. 19:18) "Thou shalt not avenge, nor bear any grudge against the children of thy people, but thou shalt love thy neighbour as thyself: I am the Lord."* Our Lord never thought of being original. The older the saying the better, if it utters the truth he wants to utter. In him it becomes fact: The *Word* was made *flesh.* And so, in the wondrous meeting of extremes, the words he spoke were no more words, but spirit and life.

Love and the Law

The same words are twice quoted by St. Paul, and once by St. James, always in a similar mode: Love they represent as the fulfilling of the law.

Is the converse true then? Is the fulfilling of the law love? The apostle Paul says: "Love worketh no ill to his neighbour, therefore love is the fulfilling of the law." Does it follow that *working no ill* is love? Love will fulfil the law: will the law fulfil love? No, verily. If a man keeps the law, I know he is a lover of his neighbour. But he is not a lover because he keeps the law: he keeps the law because he is a lover. No heart will be content with the law for love. The law cannot fulfil love.

"But, at least, the law will be able to fulfil itself, though it reaches not to love."

I do not believe it. I am certain that it is impossible to keep the law towards one's neighbour except one loves him. The law itself is infinite, reaching to such delicacies of action, that the man who tries most will be the man most aware of defeat. We are not made for law, but for love. Love is law, because it is infinitely more than law. It is of an altogether higher region than law—is, in fact, the creator of law. Had it not been for love, not one of the *shalt-nots* of the law would have been uttered. True, once uttered, they shew themselves in the form of justice, yea, even in the inferior and worldly forms of prudence and self-preservation; but it was love that spoke them first.

Were there no love in us, what sense of justice could we have? Would not each be filled with the sense of his own wants, and be for ever tearing to himself? I do not say it is *conscious* love that breeds justice, but I do say that without love in our nature justice would never be born. For I do not call that justice which consists only in a sense of *our own* rights. True, there are poor and withered forms of love which are immeasurably below justice now; but even now they are of speechless worth, for they will grow into that which will supersede, because it will necessitate, justice.

Fulfilling the Law

Of what use then is the law? To lead us to Christ, the Truth,—to waken in our minds a sense of what our deepest nature, the presence, namely, of God *in us,* requires of us,—to let us know, in part by failure, that the purest effort of will of which we are capable cannot lift us up even to the abstaining from wrong to our neighbour. What man, for instance, who loves not his neighbour and yet wishes to keep the law, will dare be confident that never by word, look, tone, gesture, silence, will he bear false witness against that neighbour? What man can judge his neighbour aright save him whose love makes him refuse to judge him? Therefore are we told to love and not judge. It is the sole justice of which we are capable, and that perfected will comprise all justice. Nay more, to refuse our neighbour love, is to do him the greatest wrong.

But of this afterwards. In order to fulfil the commonest law, I repeat, we must rise into a loftier region altogether, a region that is above law, because it is spirit and life and makes the law: in order to keep the law towards our neighbour, we must love our neighbour. We are not made for law, but for grace—or for faith, to use another word so much misused. We are made on too large a scale altogether to have any pure relation to mere justice, if indeed we can say there is such a thing. It is but an abstract idea which, in reality, will not be abstracted. The law comes to make us long for the needful grace,—that is, for the divine condition, in which love is all, for God is Love.

Though the fulfilling of the law is the practical form love will take, and the neglect of it is the conviction of lovelessness; though it is the mode in which a man's *will* must begin at once to be love to his neighbour, yet, that our Lord meant by the love of our neighbour, not the fulfilling of the law towards him, but that condition of being which results in the fulfilling of the law and more, is sufficiently clear from his story of the good

Samaritan. "Who is my neighbour?" said the lawyer. And the Lord taught him that every one to whom he could be or for whom he could do anything was his neighbour; therefore, that each of the race, as he comes within the touch of one tentacle of our nature, is our neighbour. Which of the inhibitions of the law is illustrated in the tale? Not one. The love that is more than law, and renders its breach impossible, lives in the endless story, coming out in active kindness, that is, the recognition of kin, of *kind* of nighness, of *neighbourhood;* yea, in tenderness and lovingkindness—the Samaritan-heart akin to the Jew-heart, the Samaritan hands neighbours to the Jewish wounds.

Thou shalt love thy neighbour as thyself.

So direct and complete is this parable of our Lord, that one becomes almost ashamed of further talk about it. Suppose a man of the company had put the same question to our Lord that we have been considering had said, "But I may keep the law and yet not love my neighbour," would he not have returned: "Keep thou the law thus, not in the letter, but in the spirit, that is, in the truth of action, and thou wilt soon find, O Jew, that thou lovest thy Samaritan"? And yet, when thoughts and questions arise in our minds, he desires that we should follow them. He will not check us with a word of heavenly wisdom scornfully uttered. He knows that not even *his* words will apply to every question of the willing soul; and we know that his spirit will reply. When we want to know more, that more will be there for us. Not every man, for instance, finds his neighbour in need of help, and he would gladly hasten the slow results of opportunity by true thinking. Thus would we be ready for further teaching from that Spirit who is the Lord.

Learning to Love Thy Neighbour

"But how," says a man, who is willing to recognize the universal neighbour-head, but finds himself unable to fulfil the bare law towards the woman even whom he loves best,—"How am I then to rise into that higher region, that empyrean of love?" And, beginning straightway to try to love his neighbour, he finds that the empyrean of which he spoke is no more to be reached in itself than the law was to be reached in itself. As he cannot keep the law without first rising into the love of his neighbour, so he cannot love his neighbour without first rising higher still.

The whole system of the universe works upon this law—the driving of things upward towards the centre. The man who will love his neighbour can do so by no immediately operative exercise of the will. It is the man fulfilled of God from whom he came and by whom he is, who alone can as himself love his neighbour who came from God too and is by God too.

The mystery of individuality and consequent relation is deep as the beginnings of humanity, and the questions thence arising can be solved only by him who has, practically, at least, solved the holy necessities resulting from his origin. In God alone can man meet man. In him alone the converging lines of existence touch and cross not. When the mind of Christ, the life of the Head, courses through that atom which the man is of the slowly revivifying body, when he is alive too, then the love of the brothers is there as conscious life. From Christ through the neighbours comes the life that makes him a part of the body.

It *is* possible to love our neighbour as ourselves. Our Lord *never spoke* hyperbolically, although, indeed, that is the supposition on which many unconsciously interpret his words, in order to be able to persuade themselves that they believe them. We may see that it is possible before we attain to it; for our perceptions of truth are always in advance of our condition.

True, no man can see it perfectly until he is it; but we must see it, that we may be it. A man who knows that he does not yet love his neighbour as himself may believe in such a condition, may even see that there is no other goal of human perfection, nothing else to which the universe is speeding, propelled by the Father's will. Let him labour on, and not faint at the thought that God's day is a thousand years: millennium is likewise one day—yea, this day, for we have him, The Love, in us, working even now the far end.

Steps to Loving Thy Neighbour

But while it is true that only when a man loves God with all his heart, will he love his neighbour as himself, yet there are mingled processes in the attainment of this final result. Let us try to aid such operation of truth by looking farther. Let us suppose that the man who believes our Lord both meant what he said, and knew the truth of the matter, proceeds to endeavour obedience in this of loving his neighbour as himself. He begins to think about his neighbours generally, and he tries to feel love towards them.

He finds at once that they begin to classify themselves. With some he feels no difficulty, for he loves them already, not indeed because they *are*, but because they have, by friendly qualities, by showing themselves lovable, that is loving, already, moved his feelings as the wind moves the waters, that is without any self-generated action on his part. And he feels that this is nothing much to the point; though, of course, he would be farther from the desired end if he had none such to love, and farther still if he loved none such.

He recalls the words of our Lord, "If ye love them which love you, what reward have ye?" and his mind fixes upon—let us say—one of a second class, and he tries to love him. The man is no enemy—we have not come to that class of neighbours yet—but he is dull, uninteresting—in a negative way, he thinks, unlovable. What is he to do with him? With all his effort, he finds the goal as far off as ever.

Naturally, in his failure, the question arises, "Is it my duty to love him who is unlovable?"

Certainly not, if he is unlovable. But that is a begging of the question.

Thereupon the man falls back on the primary foundation of things, and asks—

"How, then, is the man to be loved by me? Why should I love my neighbour as myself?"

We must not answer "Because the Lord says so." It is because the Lord says so that the man is inquiring after some help to obey. No man can love his neighbour *merely* because the Lord says so. The Lord says so because it is right and necessary and natural, and the man wants to feel it thus right and necessary and natural. Although the Lord would be pleased with any man for doing a thing because he said it, he would show his pleasure by making the man more and more dissatisfied until he knew why the Lord had said it. He would make him see that he could not in the deepest sense—in the way the Lord loves—obey any command until he saw the reasonableness of it.

Observe I do not say the man ought to put off obeying the command until he see its reasonableness: that is another thing quite, and does not lie in the scope of my present supposition. It is a beautiful thing to obey the rightful source of a command: it is a more beautiful thing to worship the radiant source of our light, and it is for the sake of obedient vision that our Lord commands us. For then our heart meets his: we see God.

Why Should I Love My Neighbour?

Let me represent in the form of a conversation what might pass in the man's mind on the opposing sides of the question.—"Why should I love my neighbour?"

"He is the same as I, and therefore I ought to love him."

"Why? I am I. He is he."

"He has the same thoughts, feelings, hopes, sorrows, joys, as I."

"Yes; but why should I love him for that? He must mind his, I can only do with mine."

"He has the same consciousness as I have. As things look to me, so things look to him."

"Yes; but I cannot get into his consciousness, nor he into mine. I feel myself; I do not feel him. My life flows through my veins, not through his. The world shines into my consciousness, and I am not conscious of his consciousness. I wish I could love him, but I do not see why. I am an individual; he is an individual. My self must be closer to me than he can be. Two bodies keep me apart from his self. I am isolated with myself."

Love in Action

Now, here lies the mistake at last. While the thinker supposes a duality in himself which does not exist, he falsely judges the individuality a separation. On the contrary, it is the sole possibility and very bond of love. *Otherness* is the essential ground of affection. But in spiritual things, such a unity is presupposed in the very contemplation of them by the spirit of man, that wherever anything does not exist that ought to be there, the space it ought to occupy, even if but a blank, assumes the appearance of a separating gulf. The negative looks a positive.

Where a man does not love, the not-loving must seem rational. For no one loves because he sees why, but because he loves. No human reason can be given for the highest necessity of divinely created existence. For reasons are always from above downwards. A man must just feel this necessity, and then questioning is over. It justifies itself. But he who has not felt has it not to argue about. He has but its phantom, which he created himself in a vain effort to understand, and which he supposes to be it.

Love cannot be argued about in its absence, for there is no reflex, no symbol of it near enough to the fact of it, to admit of just treatment by the algebra of the reason or imagination. Indeed, the very talking about it raises a mist between the mind and the vision of it. But let a man once love, and all those difficulties which appeared opposed to love, will just be so many arguments for loving.

Let a man once find another who has fallen among thieves; let him be a neighbour to him, pouring oil and wine into his wounds, and binding them up, and setting him on his own beast, and paying for him at the inn; let him do all this merely from a sense of duty; let him even, in the pride of his fancied, and the ignorance of his true calling, bate no jot of his Jewish superiority; let him condescend to the very baseness of his own lowest nature; yet such will be the virtue of obeying an eternal truth even to his poor measure, of putting in actuality what he has not even seen in theory, of doing the truth even without believing

it, that even if the truth does not after the deed give the faintest glimmer as truth in the man, he will yet be ages nearer the truth than before, for he will go on his way loving that Samaritan neighbour a little more than his Jewish dignity will justify.

Nor will he question the reasonableness of so doing, although he may not care to spend any logic upon its support. How much more if he be a man who would love his neighbour if he could, will the higher condition unsought have been found in the action! For man is a whole; and so soon as he *unites himself* by obedient action, the truth that is in him makes itself known to him, shining from the new whole. For his action is his response to his maker's design, his individual part in the creation of himself, his yielding to the All in all, to the tides of whose harmonious cosmoplastic life all his being thenceforward lies open for interpenetration and assimilation. When will once begins to aspire, it will soon find that action must precede feeling, that the man may know the foundation itself of feeling.

With those who recognize no authority as the ground of tentative action, a doubt, a suspicion of truth, ought to be ground enough for putting it to the test.

The End of the Divine Education

The whole system of divine education as regards the relation of man and man, has for its end that a man should love his neighbour as himself. It is not a lesson that he can learn by itself, or a duty the obligation of which can be shown by argument, any more than the difference between right and wrong can be defined in other terms than their own.

"But that difference," it may be objected, "manifests itself of itself to every mind: it is self-evident; whereas the loving of one's neighbour is *not* seen to be a primary truth; so far from it, that far the greater number of those who hope for an eternity of blessedness through him who taught it, do not really believe it to be a truth; believe, on the contrary, that the paramount obligation is to take care of one's self at much risk of forgetting one's neighbour."

But the human race generally has got as far as the recognition of right and wrong; and therefore most men are born capable of making the distinction. The race has not yet lived long enough for its latest offspring to be born with the perception of the truth of love to the neighbour. It is to be seen by the present individual only after a long reception of and submission to the education of life. And once seen, it is believed.

Love for God and Love for Man

The whole constitution of human society exists for the express end, I say, of teaching the two truths by which man lives, love to God and love to man. I will say nothing more of the mysteries of the parental relation, because they belong to the teaching of the former truth, than that we come into the world as we do, to look up to the love over us, and see in it a symbol, poor and weak, yet the best we can have or receive of the divine love.[1] And thousands more would find it easy to love God if they had not such miserable types of him in the self-seeking, impulse-driven, purposeless, faithless beings who are all they have for father and mother, and to whom their children are no dearer than her litter is to the unthinking dam.

What I want to speak of now, with regard to the second great command-

ment, is the relation of brotherhood and sisterhood. Why does my brother come of the same father and mother? Why do I behold the helplessness and confidence of his infancy? Why is the infant laid on the knee of the child? Why do we grow up with the same nurture? Why do we behold the wonder of the sunset and the mystery of the growing moon together? Why do we share one bed, join in the same games, and attempt the same exploits? Why do we quarrel, vow revenge and silence and endless enmity, and, unable to resist the brotherhood within us, wind arm in arm and forget all within the hour?

Is it not that love may grow lord of all between him and me? Is it not that I may feel towards him what there are no words or forms of words to express— a love namely, in which the divine self rushes forth in utter self-forgetfulness to live in the contemplation of the brother—a love that is stronger than death,—glad and proud and satisfied?

But if love stop there, what will be the result? Ruin to itself; loss of the brotherhood. He who loves not his brother for deeper reasons than those of a common parentage will cease to love him at all. The love that enlarges not its borders, that is not ever spreading and including, and deepening, will contract, shrivel, decay, die. I have had the sons of my mother that I may learn the universal brotherhood. For there is a bond between me and the most wretched liar that ever died for the murder he would not even confess, closer infinitely than that which springs only from having one father and mother. That we are the sons and the daughters of God born from his heart, the outcoming

---

1. It might be expressed after a deeper and truer fashion by saying that, God making human affairs after his own thoughts, they are therefore such as to be the best teachers of love to him and love to our neighbour. This is an immeasurably nobler and truer manner of regarding them than as a scheme or plan invented by the divine intellect.

offspring of his love, is a bond closer than all other bonds in one. No man ever loved his own child aright who did not love him for his humanity, for his divinity, to the utter forgetting of his origin from himself. The son of my mother is indeed my brother by this greater and closer bond as well; but if I recognize that bond between him and me at all, I recognize it for my race.

True, and thank God! the greater excludes not the less it makes all the weaker bonds stronger and truer, nor forbids that where all are brothers, some should be those of our bosom. Still my brother according to the flesh is my first neighbour, that we may be very nigh to each other, whether we will or no, while our hearts are tender, and so may learn *brotherhood*. For our love to each other is but the throbbing of the heart of the great brotherhood, and could come only from the eternal Father, not from our parents.

Then my second neighbour appears, and who is he? Whom I come in contact with soever. He with whom I have any transactions, any human dealings whatever. Not the man only with whom I dine; not the friend only with whom I share my thoughts; not the man only whom my compassion would lift from some slough; but the man who makes my clothes; the man who prints my book; the man who drives me in his cab: the man who begs from me in the street, to whom, it may be, for brotherhood's sake, I must not give; yea, even the man who condescends to me.

With all and each there is a chance of doing the part of a neighbour, if in no other way yet by speaking truly, acting justly, and thinking kindly. Even these deeds will help to that love which is born of righteousness. All true action clears the springs of right feeling, and lets their waters rise and flow. A man must not choose his neighbour; he must take the neighbour that God sends him. In him, whoever he be, lies, hidden or revealed, a beautiful brother. The neighbour is just the man who is next to you at the moment, the man with whom any business has brought you in contact.

Loving the Other

Thus will love spread and spread in wider and stronger pulses till the whole human race will be to the man sacredly lovely. Drink-debased, vice-defeatured, pride-puffed, wealth-bollen, vanity-smeared, they will yet be brothers, yet be sisters, yet be God-born neighbours. Any rough-hewn semblance of humanity will at length be enough to move the man to reverence and affection. It is harder for some to learn thus than for others. There are those whose first impulse is ever to repel and not to receive. But learn they may, and learn they must. Even these may grow in this grace until a countenance unknown will awake in them a yearning of (affection rising to pain), because there is for it no expression, and they can only give the man to God and be still.

And now will come in all the arguments out of which the man tried in vain before to build a stair up to the sunny heights of love. "Ah brother! thou hast a soul like mine," he will say. "Out of shine eyes thou lookest, and sights and sounds and odours visit thy soul as mine, with wonder and tender comforting. Thou too lovest the faces of thy neighbours. Thou art oppressed with thy sorrows, uplifted with thy joys. Perhaps thou knowest not so well as I, that a region of gladness surrounds all thy grief, of light all thy darkness, of peace all thy tumult. Oh, my brother! I will love thee. I cannot come very near thee: I will love thee the more. It may be thou dost not love thy neighbour; it may be thou thinkest only how to get from him, how to gain by him. How lonely then must thou be! how shut up in thy poverty-stricken room, with the bare walls of thy selfishness, and the hard couch of thy unsatisfaction! I will love thee the more. Thou shalt not be alone with thyself. Thou art not me, thou art another life—a second self; therefore I can, may, and will love thee."

When once to a man the human face is the human face divine, and the hand of his neighbour is the hand of a brother, then will he understand what St. Paul meant when he said, "I could wish that myself were accursed from Christ for my brethren." But he will no longer understand those who, so far from feeling the love of their neighbour an essential of their being, expect to be set free from its law in the world to come. There, at least, for the glory of God, they may limit its expansive tendencies to the narrow circle of their heaven. On its battlements of safety, they will regard hell from afar, and say to each other, "Hark! Listen to their moans. But do not weep, for they are our neighbours no more."

St. Paul would be wretched before the throne of God, if he thought there was one man beyond the pale of his mercy, and that as much for God's glory as for the man's sake. And what shall we say of the man Christ Jesus? Who, that loves his brother, would not, upheld by the love of Christ, and with a dim hope that in the far-off time there might be some help for him, arise from the company of the blessed, and walk down into the dismal regions of despair, to sit with the last, the only unredeemed, the Judas of his race, and be himself more blessed in the pains of hell, than in the glories of heaven?

Who, in the midst of the golden harps and the white wings, knowing that one of his kind, one miserable brother in the old-world-time when men were taught to love their neighbour as themselves, was howling unheeded far below in the vaults of the creation, who, I say, would not feel that he must arise, that he had no choice, that, awful as it was, he must gird his loins, and go down into the smoke and the darkness and the fire, travelling the weary and fearful road into the far country to find his brother?—who, I mean, that had the mind of Christ, that had the love of the Father?

But it is a wild question. God is, and shall be, all in all. Father of our brothers and sisters! thou wilt not be less glorious than we, taught of Christ, are able to think thee. When thou goest into the wilderness to seek, thou wilt not come home until thou hast found. It is because we hope not for them in thee, not knowing thee, not knowing thy love, that we are so hard and so heartless to the brothers and sisters whom thou hast given us.

Life Is in Loving

One word more: This love of our neighbour is the only door out of the dungeon of self, where we mope and mow, striking sparks, and rubbing phosphorescences out of the walls, and blowing our own breath in our own nostrils, instead of issuing to the fair sunlight of God, the sweet winds of the universe. The man thinks his consciousness is himself; whereas his life consisteth in the inbreathing of God, and the consciousness of the universe of truth. To have himself, to know himself, to enjoy himself, he calls life; whereas, if he would forget himself, tenfold would be his life in God and his neighbours.

The region of man's life is a spiritual region. God, his friends, his neighbours, his brothers all, is the wide world in which alone his spirit can find room.

Himself is his dungeon. If he feels it not now, he will yet feel it one day—feel it as a loving soul would feel being prisoned in a dead body, wrapped in sevenfold cerements, and buried in a stone-ribbed vault within the last ripple of the sound of the chanting people in the church above.

His life is not in knowing that he lives, but in loving all forms of life. He is made for the All, for God, who is the All, is his life. And the essential joy of his life lies abroad in the liberty of the All. His delights, like those of the Ideal Wisdom, are with the sons of men. His health is in the body of which the Son of man is the head. The whole region of life is open to him—nay, he must live in it or perish.

Nor thus shall a man lose the con-sciousness of wellbeing. Far deeper and more complete, God and his neighbour will flash it back upon him—pure as life. No more will he agonize "with sick assay" to generate it in the light of his own decadence. For he shall know the glory of his own being in the light of God and of his brother.

But he may have begun to love his neighbour, with the hope of ere long loving him as himself, and notwithstanding start back affrighted at yet another word of our Lord, seeming to be another law yet harder than the first, although in truth it is not another, for without obedience to it the former cannot be attained unto. He has not yet learned to love his neighbour as himself whose heart sinks within him at the word, *I say unto you, Love Your enemies.*

CHAPTER SEVEN

The God of the Living

He is not a God of the dead, but of the living; for all live unto him (Luke 20:38).

Christ and the Sadducees

It is a recurring cause of perplexity in our Lord's teaching, that he is too simple for us; that while we are questioning with ourselves about the design of Solomon's carving upon some gold-plated door of the temple, he is speaking about the foundations of Mount Zion, yea, of the earth itself, upon which it stands. If the reader of the Gospel supposes that our Lord was here using a verbal argument with the Sadducees, namely, "I *am* the God of Abraham, Isaac, and Jacob; therefore they *are*," he will be astonished that no Sadducee was found with courage enough to reply: "All that God meant was to introduce himself to Moses as the same God who had aided and protected his fathers while they were alive, saying, I am he that was the God of thy fathers. They found me faithful. Thou, therefore, listen to me, and thou too shalt find me faithful *unto* the death."

But no such reply suggested itself even to the Sadducees of that day, for their eastern nature could see argument beyond logic. Shall God call himself the God of the dead, of those who were alive once, but whom he either could not or would not keep alive? Is that the Godhood, and its relation to those who worship it? The changeless God of an ever-born and ever-perishing torrent of life; of which each atom cries with burning heart, *My God!* and straightway passes into the Godless cold! "Trust in me, for I took care of your fathers once upon a time, though they are gone now. Worship and obey me, for I will be good to you for threescore years and ten, or thereabouts; and after that, when you are not, and the world goes on all the same without you, I will call myself your God still." God changes not. Once God he is always God. If he has once said to a man, "I am thy God, and that man has died the death of the Sadducee's creed," then we have a right to say that God is the God of the dead.

"And wherefore should he not be so far the God of the dead, if during the time allotted to them here, he was the faithful God of the living?" What Godlike relation can the ever-living, life-giving, changeless God hold to creatures who partake not of his life, who have death at the very core of their being, are not worth their Maker's keeping alive? To let his creatures die would be to change, to abjure his Godhood, to cease to be that which he had made himself. If they are not worth keeping alive, then his creating is a poor thing, and he is not so great, nor so divine as even the poor thoughts of those his dying creatures have been able to imagine him.

But our Lord says, "All live unto him." With Him death is not. Thy life sees our life, O Lord. All of whom *all* can be said, are present to thee. Thou thinkest about us, eternally more than we think about thee. The little life that burns within the body of this death, glows unquenchable in thy true-seeing eyes. If thou didst forget us for a moment then indeed death would be. But unto thee we live. The beloved pass from our sight, but they pass not from shine. This that we call death, is but a form in the eyes of men. It looks something final, an awful cessation, an utter change. It seems not probable that there is anything beyond. But if God could see us before we were, and make us after his ideal, that we shall have passed from the eyes of our friends can be no argument that he beholds us no longer.

"All live unto Him." Let the change be ever so great, ever so imposing; let the unseen life be ever so vague to our conception, it is not against reason to hope that God could see Abraham, after his Isaac had ceased to see him; saw Isaac after Jacob ceased to see him, saw Jacob after some of the Sadducees had begun to doubt whether there ever had been a Jacob at all. He remembers them; that is, he carries them in his mind: he of whom God thinks, lives. He takes to himself the name of *Their God*. The Living One cannot name himself after the dead; when the very Godhead lies in the giving of life. Therefore they must be alive. If he speaks of them, remembers his own loving thoughts of them, would he not have kept them alive if he could; and if he could not, how could he create them? Can it be an easier thing to call into life than to keep alive?

"But if they live to God, they are aware of God. And if they are aware of God, they are conscious of their own being: Whence then the necessity of a resurrection?"

The Resurrection of the Body

For their relation to others of God's children in mutual revelation; and for fresh revelation of God to all.—But let us inquire what is meant by the resurrection of the body. "With what body do they come?"

Surely we are not required to believe that the same body is raised again. That is against science, common sense, Scripture. St. Paul represents the matter quite otherwise. One feels ashamed of arguing such a puerile point. Who could wish his material body which has indeed died over and over again since he was born, never remaining for one hour composed of the same matter, its endless activity depending upon its endless change, to be fixed as his changeless possession, such as it may then be, at the moment of death, and secured to him in worthless identity for the ages to come?

A man's material body will be to his consciousness at death no more than the old garment he throws aside at night, intending to put on a new and a better in the morning. To desire to keep the old body seems to me to argue a degree of sensual materialism excusable only in those pagans who in their Elysian fields could hope to possess only such a thin, fleeting, dreamy, and altogether funebrial existence, that they might well long for the thicker more tangible bodily being in which they had experienced the pleasures of a tumultuous life on the upper world. As well might a Christian desire that the hair which has been shorn from him through all his past life should be restored to his risen and glorified head.

Yet not the less is the doctrine of the Resurrection gladdening as the sound of the silver trumpet of its visions, needful as the very breath of life to our longing souls. Let us know what it means, and we shall see that it is thus precious.

The Camera of God's Revelation

Let us first ask what is the use of this body of ours. It is the means of revelation to us, the *camera* in which God's eternal shows are set forth. It is by the body that we come into contact with nature, with our fellow-men with all their revelations of God to us. It is through the body that we receive all the lessons of passion, of suffering, of love, of beauty, of science. It is through the body that we are both trained outwards from ourselves, and driven inwards into our deepest selves to find God. There is glory and might in this vital evanescence, this slow glacier-like flow of clothing and revealing matter, this ever uptossed rainbow of tangible humanity. It is no less of God's making than the spirit that is clothed therein.

We cannot yet have learned all that we are meant to learn through the body. How much of the teaching even of this world can the most diligent and most favoured man have exhausted before he is called to leave it! Is all that remains to be lost? Who that has loved this earth can but believe that the spiritual body of which St. Paul speaks will be a yet higher channel of such revelation?

The meek who have found that their Lord spake true, and have indeed inherited the earth, who have seen that all matter is radiant of spiritual meaning, who would not cast a sigh after the loss of mere animal pleasure, would I think, be the least willing to be without a body, to be unclothed without being again clothed upon. Who, after centuries of glory in heaven, would not rejoice to behold once more that patient-headed child of winter and spring, the meek snowdrop? In whom, amidst the golden choirs, would not the vision of an old sunset wake such a song as the ancient dwellers of the earth would with gently flattened palm hush their throbbing harps to hear?

All this revelation, however, would render only a body necessary, not this body. The fulness of the word *resurrec-* *tion* would be ill met if this were all. We need not only a body to convey revelation to us, but a body to reveal us to others. The thoughts, feelings, imaginations which arise in us, must have their garments of revelation whereby shall be made manifest the unseen world within us to our brothers and sisters around us; else is each left in human loneliness.

Now, if this be one of the uses my body served on earth before, the new body must be like the old. Nay, it must be the same body, glorified as we are glorified, with all that was distinctive of each from his fellows more visible than ever before. The accidental, the nonessential, the unrevealing, the incomplete will have vanished. That which made the body what it was in the eyes of those who loved us will be tenfold there. Will not this be the resurrection of the body? of the same body though not of the same dead matter?

Every eye shall see the beloved; every heart will cry, "My own again!—more mine because more himself than ever I beheld him!" For do we not say on earth, "He is not himself to-day," or "She looks her own self" or "She is more like herself than I have seen her for long"? And is not this when the heart is glad and the face is radiant? For we carry a better likeness of our friends in our hearts than their countenances, save at precious seasons, manifest to us.

The Resurrection and the Restoration of Fellowship

Who will dare to call anything less than this a resurrection? Oh, how the letter killeth! There are those who can believe that the dirt of their bodies will rise the same as it went down to the friendly grave, who yet doubt if they will know their friends when they rise again. And they call *that* believing in the resurrection!

What! shall a man love his neighbour as himself, and must he be content not to know him in heaven? Better be content to lose our consciousness, and know ourselves no longer. What! shall God be the God of the families of the earth, and shall the love that he has thus created towards father and mother, brother and sister, wife and child, go moaning and longing to all eternity; or worse, far worse, die out of our bosoms? Shall God be God, and shall this be the end?

Ah, my friends! what will resurrection or life be to me, how shall I continue to love God as I have learned to love him through you, if I find he cares so little for this human heart of mine, as to take from me the gracious visitings of your faces and forms? True, I might have a gaze at Jesus, now and then; but he would not be so good as I had thought him. And how should I see him if I could not see you? God will not take you, has not taken you from me to bury you out of my sight in the abyss of his own unfathomable being; where I cannot follow and find you, myself lost in the same awful gulf. No, our God is an unveiling, a revealing God. He will raise you from the dead, that I may behold you, that that which vanished from the earth may again stand forth, looking out of the same eyes of eternal love and truth, holding out the same mighty hand of brotherhood, the same delicate and gentle, yet strong hand of sisterhood, to me, this me that knew you and loved you in the days gone by.

I shall not care that the matter of the forms I loved a thousand years ago has returned to mingle with the sacred goings on of God's science, upon that far-off world wheeling its nursery of growing loves and wisdoms through space; I shall not care that the muscle which now sends the ichor through your veins is not formed of the very particles which once sent the blood to the pondering brain, the flashing eye, or the nervous right arm; I shall not care, I say, so long as it is yourselves that are before me, beloved; so long as through these forms I know that I look on my own, on my loving souls of the ancient time; so long as my spirits have got garments of revealing after their own old lovely fashion, garments to reveal themselves to me.

The new shall then be dear as the old, and for the same reason, that it reveals the old love. And in the changes which, thank God, must take place when the mortal puts on immortality, shall we not feel that the nobler our friends are, the more they are themselves; that the more the idea of each is carried out in the perfection of beauty, the more like they are to what we thought them in our most exalted moods, to that which we saw in them in the rarest moments of profoundest communion, to that which we beheld through the veil of all their imperfections when we loved them the truest?

Lord, evermore give us this resurrection, like thine own in the body of thy Transfiguration. Let us see, and hear, and know, and be seen, and heard, and known, as thou seest, hearest, and knowest. Give us glorified bodies through which to reveal the glorified thoughts which shall then inhabit us, when not only shalt thou reveal God, but each of us shall reveal thee.

And for this, Lord Jesus, come thou, the child, the obedient God, that we may be one with thee, and with every man and woman whom thou hast made, in the Father.

"Life" is taken from the second series of MacDonald's Unspoken Sermons, *published in 1886. " 'More life!' is the unconscious prayer of all creation. . . ." This is MacDonald's message, and when men say they are tired of life or are discontented what they really mean is that they do not have enough of life. This life that we long for is nothing less than God Himself. Only by uniting our will with God's, by being conformed to the Being of our origins, can we truly have life.*

CHAPTER EIGHT

Life

"I came that they may have life, and may have it abundantly" (John 10:10).

More Life

In a word, He came to supply all our lack—from the root outward; for what is it we need but more life? What does the infant need but more life? What does the bosom of his mother give him but life in abundance? What does the old man need, whose limbs are weak and whose pulse is low, but more of the life which seems ebbing from him? Weary with feebleness, he calls upon death, but in reality it is life he wants. It is but the encroaching death in him that desires death. He longs for rest, but death cannot rest; death would be as much an end to rest as to weariness: even weakness cannot rest; it takes strength as well as weariness to rest.

How different is the weariness of the strong man after labour unduly prolonged, from the weariness of the sick man who in the morning cries out, "Would God it were evening!" and in the evening, "Would God it were morning!" Low-sunk life imagines itself weary of life, but it is death, not life, it is weary of. Never a cry went out after the opposite of life from any soul that knew what life is. Why does the poor, worn, out-worn suicide seek death? Is it not in reality to escape from death?—from the death of homelessness and hunger and cold; the death of failure disappointment, and distraction; the death of the exhaustion of passion; the death of madness—of a household he cannot rule; the death of crime and fear of discovery?

He seeks the darkness because it seems a refuge from the death which possesses him. He is a creature possessed by death; what he calls his life is but a dream full of horrible phantasms.

"More life!" is the unconscious prayer of all creation, groaning and travailing for the redemption of its lord, the son who is not yet a son. Is not the dumb cry to be read in the faces of some of the animals, in the look of some of the flowers, and in many an aspect of what we call Nature?

The Difficulty of God's Creation

All things are possible with God, but all things are not easy. It is easy for him to *be*, for there he has to do with his own perfect will: it is not easy for him to create—that is, after the grand fashion which alone will satisfy his glorious heart and will, the fashion in which he is now creating us. In the very nature of being—that is, God—it must be hard—and divine history shows how hard—to create that which shall be not himself, yet like himself. The problem is, so far to separate from himself that which must yet on him be ever and always and utterly dependent, that it shall have the existence of an individual, and be able to turn and regard him—choose him and say, "I will arise and go to my Father," and so develop in itself the highest *divine* of which it is capable—the will for the good against the evil—the will to be one with the life whence it has come, and in which it still is—the will to close the round of its procession in its return, so working the perfection of reunion—to shape in its own life the ring of eternity—to live immediately, consciously, and active-willingly from its source, from its own very life—to restore to the beginning the end that comes of that beginning—to be the thing the maker thought of when he willed, ere he began to work its being.

I imagine the difficulty of doing this thing, of effecting this creation, this separation from himself such that will in the creature shall be possible—I imagine, I say, the difficulty of such creation so great, that for it God must begin inconceivably far back in the infinitesimal regions of beginnings—not to say before anything in the least resembling man, but eternal miles beyond the last farthest-pushed discovery in *protoplasm*—to set in motion that division from himself which in its grand result should be individuality, consciousness, choice, and conscious choice—choice at last pure, being the choice of the right, the true, the divinely harmonious. Hence the final end of the separation is not individuality; that is but a means to it; the final end is oneness—an impossibility without it. For there can be no unity, no delight of love, no harmony, no good in being, where there is but one. Two at least are needed for oneness; and the greater the number of individuals, the greater, the lovelier, the richer, the diviner is the possible unity.

God's Sacrificial Creation

God is life, and the will-source of life. In the outflowing of that life, I know him; and when I am told that he is love, I see that if he were not love he would not, could not create. I know nothing deeper in him than love, nor believe there is in him anything deeper than love—nay, that there can be anything deeper than love. The being of God is love, therefore creation. I imagine that from all eternity he has been creating. As he saw it was not good for man to be alone, so has he never been alone himself;—from all eternity the Father has had the Son, and the never-begun existence of that Son I imagine an easy outgoing of the Father's nature; while to make other beings—beings like us, I imagine the labour of a God, an eternal labour.

Speaking after our poor human fashions of thought—the only fashions possible to us—I imagine that God has never been contented to be alone even with the Son of his love, the prime and perfect idea of humanity, but that he has from the first willed and laboured to give existence to other creatures who should be blessed with his blessedness—creatures whom he is now and always has been developing into likeness with that Son—a likeness for long to be distant and small, but a likeness to be for ever growing: perhaps never one of them yet, though unspeakably blessed, has had even an approximate idea of the blessedness in store for him.

Let no soul think that to say God undertook a hard labour in willing that many sons and daughters should be sharers of the divine nature, is to abate his glory! The greater the difficulty, the greater is the glory of him who does the thing he has undertaken—without shadow of compromise, with no half-success, but with a triumph of absolute satisfaction to innumerable radiant souls! He knew what it would cost!—not energy of will alone, or merely that utterance and separation from himself which is but the first of creation, though that may well itself be pain—but sore suffering such as we cannot imagine, and could only be God's, in the bringing out, call it birth or development, of the

God-life in the individual soul—a suffering still renewed, a labour thwarted ever by that soul itself, compelling him to take, still at the cost of suffering, the not absolutely best, only the best possible means left him by the resistance of his creature.

Man finds it hard to get what he wants, because he does not want the best; God finds it hard to give, because he would give the best, and man will not take it. What Jesus did, was what the Father is always doing; the suffering he endured was that of the Father from the foundation of the world, reaching its climax in the person of his Son. God provides the sacrifice; the sacrifice is himself. He is always, and has ever been, sacrificing himself to and for his creatures. It lies in the very essence of his creation of them.

The worst heresy, next to that of dividing religion and righteousness, is to divide the Father from the Son—in thought or feeling or action or intent; to represent the Son as doing that which the Father does not himself do. Jesus did nothing but what the Father did and does. If Jesus suffered for men, it was because his Father suffers for men; only he came close to men through his body and their senses, that he might bring their spirits close to his Father and their Father, so giving them life, and losing what could be lost of his own. He is God our Savior: it is because God is our Savior that Jesus is our Savior. The God and Father of Jesus Christ could never possibly be satisfied with less than giving himself to his own!

The unbeliever may easily imagine a better God than the common theology of the country offers him; but not the lovingest heart that ever beat can even reflect the length and breadth and depth and height of that love of God which shows itself in his Son—one, and of one mind, with himself. The whole history

is a divine agony to give divine life to creatures. The outcome of that agony, the victory of that creative and again creative energy, will be radiant life, whereof joy unspeakable is the flower. Every child will look in the eyes of the Father, and the eyes of the Father will receive the child with an infinite embrace.

The Only Reality Is Life

The life the Lord came to give us is a life exceeding that of the highest undivine man, by far more than the life of that man exceeds the life of the animal the least human. More and more of it is for each who will receive it, and to eternity. The Father has given to the Son to have life in himself; that life is our light. We know life only as light; it is the life in us that makes us see. All the growth of the Christian is the more and more life he is receiving. At first his religion may hardly be distinguishable from the mere prudent desire to save his soul; but at last he loses that very soul in the glory of love, and so saves it; self becomes but the cloud on which the white light of God divides into harmonious unspeakable.

"In the midst of life we are in death," said one; it is more true that in the midst of death we are in life. Life is the only reality; what men call death is but a shadow—a word for that which cannot be—a negation, owing the very idea of itself to that which it would deny. But for life there could be no death. If God were not, there would not even be nothing. Not even nothingness preceded life. Nothingness owes its very idea to existence.

One form of the question between matter and spirit is, which was first, and caused the other—things or thoughts; whether things without thought caused thought, or thought without things caused things. To those who cannot doubt that thought was first, causally preceding the earliest material show, it is easily plain that death can be the cure for nothing, that the cure for everything must be life—that the ills which come with existence, are from its imperfection, not of itself—that what we need is more of it. We who *are,* have nothing to do with death; our relations are alone with life. The thing that can mourn can mourn only from lack; it cannot mourn because of being, but because of not enough being. We are vessels of life, not yet full of the wine of life; where the wine does not reach, there the clay cracks, and aches, and is distressed. Who would therefore pour out the wine that is there, instead of filling to the brim with more wine!

All the being must partake of essential being; life must be assisted, upheld, comforted, every part, with life. Life is the law, the food, the necessity of life. Life is everything. Many doubtless mistake the joy of life for life itself; and, longing after the joy, languish with a thirst at once poor and inextinguishable; but even that thirst points to the one spring. These love self, not life, and self is but the shadow of life. When it is taken for life itself, and set as the man's centre, it becomes a live death in the man, a devil he worships as his god; the worm of the death eternal he clasps to his bosom as his one joy!

The soul compact of harmonies has more life, a larger being, than the soul consumed of cares; the sage is a larger life than the clown; the poet is more alive than the man whose life flows out that money may come in; the man who loves his fellow is infinitely more alive than he whose endeavour is to exalt himself above him; the man who strives to be better, than he who longs for the praise of the many; but the man to whom God is all in all, who feels his

life-roots hid with Christ in God, who knows himself the inheritor of all wealth and worlds and ages, yea, of power essential and in itself, that man has begun to be alive indeed.

Our One Lack Is Life

Let us in all the troubles of life remember—that our one lack is life—that what we need is more life—more of the life-making presence in us making us more, and more largely, alive. When most oppressed, when most weary of life, as our unbelief would phrase it, let us bethink ourselves that it is in truth the inroad and presence of death we are weary of. When most inclined to sleep let us rouse ourselves to live. Of all things let us avoid the false refuge of a weary collapse, a hopeless yielding to things as they are. It is the life in us that is discontented; we need more of what is discontented, not more of the cause of its discontent.

Discontent, I repeat, is the life in us that has not enough of itself, is not enough to itself, so calls for more. He has the victory who, in the midst of pain and weakness, cries out, not for death, not for the repose of forgetfulness, but for strength to fight; for more power, more consciousness of being, more God in him; who, when sorest wounded, says with Sir Andrew Barton in the old ballad:—

> Fight on my men, says Sir Andrew
> Barton,
> I am hurt, but I am not slain;
> I'll lay me down and bleed awhile,
> And then I'll rise and fight
> again;

—and that with no silly notion of playing the hero—what have creatures like us to do with heroism who are not yet barely honest!—but because so to fight is the truth, and the only way.

If, in the extreme of our exhaustion, there should come to us, as to Elijah when he slept in the desert, an angel to rouse us, and show us the waiting bread and water, how would we carry ourselves? Would we, in faint unwillingness to rise and eat, answer, "Lo I am weary unto death! The battle is gone from me! It is lost, or unworth gaining! The world is too much for me! Its forces will not heed me! They have worn me out! I have wrought no salvation even for my own, and never should work any, were I to live for ever! It is enough; let me now return whence I came; let me be gathered to my fathers and be at rest!"? I should be loth to think that, if the enemy, in recognizable shape, came roaring upon us, we would not, like the red-cross knight, stagger, heavy sword in nerveless arm, to meet him; but, in the feebleness of foiled effort, it wants yet more faith to rise and partake of the food that shall bring back more effort, more travail, more weariness.

The true man trusts in a strength which is not his, and which he does not feel, does not even always desire; believes in a power that seems far from him, which is yet at the root of his fatigue itself and his need of rest—rest as far from death as is labour. To trust in the strength of God in our weakness; to say, "I am weak: so let me be: God is strong;" to seek from him who is our life, as the natural, simple cure of all that is amiss with us, power to do, and be, and live, even when we are weary,—this is the victory that overcometh the world.

To believe in God our strength in the face of all seeming denial, to believe in him out of the heart of weakness and unbelief, in spite of numbness and weariness and lethargy; to believe in the wide-awake real, through all the stupefying, enervating, distorting dream; to will to wake, when the very being seems athirst for a godless repose;—these are the broken steps up to the high fields where repose is but a form of strength, strength but a form of joy, joy but a form of love. "I am weak," says the true soul, "but not so weak that I would not be strong; not so sleepy that I would not see the sun rise; not so lame but that I would walk! Thanks be to him who perfects strength in weakness, and gives to his beloved while they sleep!"

If we will but let our God and Father work his will with us, there can be no limit to his enlargement of our existence, to the flood of life with which he will overflow our consciousness. We have no conception of what life might be, of how vast the consciousness of which we could be made capable. Many can recall some moment in which life seemed richer and fuller than ever before; to some, such moments arrive mostly in dreams: shall soul, awake or asleep, infold a bliss greater than its Life, the living God, can seal, perpetuate, enlarge? Can the human twilight of a dream be capable of generating or holding a fuller life than the morning of divine activity?

Surely God could at any moment give to a soul, by a word to that soul, by breathing afresh into the secret caves of its being, a sense of life before which the most exultant ecstasy of earthly triumph would pale to ashes! If ever sunlit, sail-crowded sea, under blue heaven flecked with wind-chased white, filled your soul as with a new gift of life, think what sense of existence must be yours, if he whose thought has but fringed its garment with the outburst of such a show, take his abode with you, and while thinking the gladness of a God inside your being, let you know and feel that he is carrying you as a father in his bosom!

God Is Life

I have been speaking as if life and the consciousness of it were one; but the consciousness of life is not life, it is only the outcome of life. The real life is that which is of and by itself—is life because it wills itself—which *is,* in the active, not the passive sense: this can only be God. But in us there ought to be a life correspondent to the life that is God's; in us also must be the life that wills itself—a life in so far resembling the self-existent life and partaking of its image, that it has a share in its own being. There is an original act possible to the man, which must initiate the reality of his existence. He must live in and by willing to live.

A tree lives; I hardly doubt it has some vague consciousness, known by but not to itself, only to the God who made it; I trust that life in its lowest forms is on the way to thought and blessedness, is in the process of that separation, so to speak, from God, in which consists the creation of living souls; but the life of these lower forms is not life in the high sense—in the sense in which the word is used in the Bible: true life knows and rules itself; the eternal life is life come awake. The life of the most exalted of the animals is not such whatever it may become, and however I may refuse to believe their fate and being fixed as we see them.

But as little as any man or woman would be inclined to call the existence of the dog, looking strange lack out of his wistful eyes, an existence to be satisfied with—his life an end sufficient in itself, as little could I, looking on the human pleasure, the human refinement, the common human endeavour around me, consent to regard them as worthy the name of life. What in them is true dwells amidst an unchallenged corruption, demanding repentance and labour and prayer for its destruction. The condition of most men and women seems to me a life in death, an abode in unwhited sepulchres, a possession of withering forms by spirits that slumber, and babble in their dreams.

That they do not feel it so is nothing. The sow wallowing in the mire may rightly assert it her way of being clean, but theirs is not the life of the God-born. The day must come when they will hide their faces with such shame as the good man yet feels at the memory of the time when he lived like them.

There is nothing for man worthy to be called life, but the life eternal—God's life, that is, after his degree shared by the man made to be eternal also. For he is in the image of God, intended to partake of the life of the most high, to be alive as he is alive. Of this life the outcome and the light is righteousness, love, grace, truth; but the life itself is a thing that will not be defined, even as God will not be defined: it is a power, the formless cause of form. It has no limits whereby to be defined. It shows itself to the soul that is hungering and thirsting after righteousness, but that soul cannot show it to another, save in the shining of its own light.

The ignorant soul understands by this life eternal only an endless elongation of consciousness; what God means by it is a being like his own, a being beyond the attack of decay or death, a being so essential that it has no relation whatever to nothingness; a something which is, and can never go to that which is not, for with that it never had to do, but came out of the heart of life, the heart of God, the fountain of being; an existence partaking of the divine nature, and having nothing in common, any more than the Eternal himself, with what can pass or cease: God owes his being to no one, and his child has no lord but his Father.

Oneness with God

This life, this eternal life, consists for man in absolute oneness with God and all divine modes of being, oneness with every phase of right and harmony. It consists in a love as deep as it is universal, as conscious as it is unspeakable; a love that can no more be reasoned about than life itself—a love whose presence is its all-sufficing proof and justification, whose absence is an annihilating defect: he who has it not cannot believe in it: how should death believe in life, though all the birds of God are singing jubilant over the empty tomb! The delight of such a being, the splendour of a consciousness rushing from the wide open doors of the fountain of existence, the ecstasy of the spiritual sense into which the surge of life essential, immortal, increase, flows in silent fulness from the heart of hearts—what may it, what must it not be, in the great day of God and the individual soul!

What then is our practical relation to the life original? What have we to do towards the attaining to the resurrection from the dead? If we did not make, could not have made ourselves, how can we, now we are made, do anything at the unknown roots of our being? What relation of conscious unity can be betwixt the self-existent God and beings who live at the will of another, beings who could not refuse to be—cannot even cease to be, but must, at the will of that other, go on living, weary of what is not life, able to assert their relation to life only by refusing to be content with what is not life?

The self-existent God is that other by whose will we live; so the links of the unity must already exist, and can but require to be brought together. For the link in our being wherewith to close the circle of immortal oneness with the Father, we must of course search the deepest of man's nature: there only, in all assurance, can it be found. And there we do find it. For the *will* is the deepest, the strongest, the divinest thing in man; so, I presume, is it in God, for such we find it in Jesus Christ.

Here, and here only, in the relation of the two wills, God's and his own, can a man come into vital contact—on the eternal idea, in no one-sided unity of completest dependence, but in willed harmony of dual oneness—with the All-in-all. When a man can and does entirely say, "Not my will, but thine be done"— when he so wills the will of God as to do it, then is he one with God—one, as a true son with a true father. When a man wills that his being be conformed to the being of his origin, which is the life in his life, causing and bearing his life, therefore absolutely and only of its kind, one with it more and deeper than words or figures can say—to the life which is itself, only more of itself, and more than itself, causing itself—when the man thus accepts his own causing life, *and sets himself to live the will of that causing life*, humbly eager after the privileges of his origin,—thus receiving God, he becomes, in the act, a partaker of the divine nature, a true son of the living God, and an heir of all he possesses: by the obedience of a son, he receives into himself the very life of the Father. Obedience is the joining of the links of the eternal round. Obedience is but the other side of the creative will. Will is God's will, obedience is man's will; the two make one.

The root-life, knowing well the thousand troubles it would bring upon him, has created, and goes on creating other lives, that, though incapable of self-being, they may, by willed obedience, share in the bliss of his essential self-ordained being. If we do the will of God, eternal life is ours—no mere continuity of existence, for that in itself is worthless as hell, but a being that is one with the essential Life, and so within his reach to fill with the abundant and endless outgoings of his love. Our souls shall be vessels ever growing, and ever as they grow, filled with the more and more life proceeding from the Father and the Son, from God the ordaining, and God the obedient.

What the delight of the being, what the abundance of the life he came that we might have, we can never know until we have it. But even now to the holy fancy it may sometimes seem too glorious to support—as if we must die of very life—of more being than we could bear—to awake to a yet higher life, and be filled with a wine which our souls were heretofore too weak to hold! To be for one moment aware of such pure simple love towards but one of my fellows as I trust I shall one day have towards each, must of itself bring a sense of life such as the utmost effort of my imagination can but feebly shadow now—a mighty glory of consciousness!—not to be always present, indeed, for my love, and not my glory in that love, is my life.

There would be, even in that one love, in the simple purity of a single affection such as we were created to generate, and intended to cherish, towards all, an expansion of life inexpressible, unutterable. For we are made for love, not for self. Our neighbour is our refuge; *self* is our demon-foe. Every man is the image of God to every man, and in proportion as we love him, we shall know the sacred fact. The precious thing to human soul is, and one day shall be known to be, every human soul. And if it be so between man and man, how will it not be betwixt the man and his Maker, between the child and his eternal Father, between the created and the creating Life? Must not the glory of existence be endlessly redoubled in the infinite love of the creature—for all love is infinite—to the infinite God, the great one life, than whom is no other—only shadows, lovely shadows of him!

Reader to whom my words seem those of inflation and foolish excitement, it can be nothing to thee to be told that I seem to myself to speak only the words of truth and soberness; but what if the cause why they seem other to thy mind be—not merely that thou art not whole, but that thy being nowise thirsts after harmony, that thou art not of the truth, that thou hast not yet begun to live? How should the reveller, issuing worn and wasted from the haunts where the violent seize joy by force to find her perish in their arms—how should such reveller, I say, break forth and sing with the sons of the morning, when the ocean of light bursts from the fountain of the east? As little canst thou, with thy mind full of petty cares, or still more petty ambitions, understand the groaning and travailing of the creation. It may indeed be that thou art honestly desirous of saving thy own wretched soul, but as yet thou canst know but little of thy need of him who is *the first and the last and the living one.*

In 1870 MacDonald published a volume titled The Miracles of Our Lord. *In the "Introduction" MacDonald briefly outlines why he does not find miracles difficult to accept. Christ's miracles are simply a natural outcome of His being united to God the Father through obedience.*

One of the classes that MacDonald divides Christ's miracles into is those of "The Government of Nature." These miracles are easy for MacDonald to accept because if God visited men in the form of man "he would naturally show himself Lord over their circumstances." To the objection that some might pose that the laws of God should not change, MacDonald answers that what we perceive to be a breach of God's laws is not so to God. In all of these miracles Christ showed that nature and all of creation was subject to the Father.

CHAPTER NINE

The Miracles of Our Lord: Introduction

I have been requested to write some papers on our Lord's miracles. I venture the attempt in the belief that, seeing they are one of the modes in which his unseen life found expression, we are bound through them to arrive at some knowledge of that life. For he has come, The Word of God, that we may know God: every word of his then, as needful to the knowing of himself, is needful to the knowing of God, and we must understand, as far as we may, every one of his words and every one of his actions, which, with him, were only another form of word. I believe this the immediate end of our creation. And I believe that this will at length result in the unravelling for us of what must now, more or less, appear to every man the knotted and twisted coil of the universe.

Belief in the Miracles

It seems to me that it needs no great power of faith to believe in the miracles—for true faith is a power, not a mere yielding. There are far harder things to believe than the miracles. For a man is not required to believe in them save as believing in Jesus. If a man can believe that there is a God, he may well believe that, having made creatures capable of hungering and thirsting for him, he must be capable of speaking a word to guide them in their feeling after him. And if he is a grand God, a God worthy of being God, yea (his metaphysics even may show the seeker), if he is a

God capable of being God, he will speak the clearest grandest word of guidance which he can utter intelligible to his creatures.

For us, that word must simply be the gathering of all the expressions of his visible works into an infinite human face, lighted up by an infinite human soul behind it, namely, that potential essence of man, if I may use a word of my own, which was in the beginning with God. If God should *thus* hear the cry of the noblest of his creatures, for such are all they who do cry after him, and in very deed show them his face, it is but natural to expect that the deeds of the great messenger should be just the works of the Father done in little. If he came to reveal his Father in miniature, as it were (for in these unspeakable things we can but use figures, and the homeliest may be the holiest), to tone down his great voice, which, too loud for men to hear it aright, could but sound to them as an inarticulate thundering, into such a still small voice as might enter their human ears in welcome human speech, then the words that his Father does so widely, so grandly that they transcend the vision of men, the Son must do briefly and sharply before their very eyes.

This, I think, is the true nature of the miracles, an epitome of God's processes in nature beheld in immediate connection with their source—a source as yet lost to the eyes and too often to the hearts of men in the far-receding gradations of continuous law. That men might see the will of God at work, Jesus did the works of his Father thus.

Objections to the Miracles

Here I will suppose some honest, and therefore honourable, reader objecting: But do you not thus place the miracles in dignity below the ordinary processes of nature? I answer: The miracles are mightier far than any goings on of nature as beheld by common eyes, dissociating them from a living will; but the miracles are surely less than those mighty goings on of nature with God beheld at their heart. In the name of him who delighted to say "My Father is greater than I," I will say that his miracles in bread and in wine were far less grand and less beautiful than the works of the Father they represented, in making the corn to grow in the valleys, and the grapes to drink the sunlight on the hill-sides of the world, with all their infinitudes of tender gradation and delicate mystery of birth. But the Son of the Father be praised, who, as it were, condensed these mysteries before us, and let us see the precious gifts coming at once from gracious hands—hands that love could kiss and nails could wound.

There are some, I think, who would perhaps find it more possible to accept the New Testament story if the miracles did not stand in the way. But perhaps, again, it would be easier for them to accept both if they could once look into the true heart of these miracles. So long as they regard only the surface of them, they will, most likely, see in them only a violation of the laws of nature: when they behold the heart of them, they will recognize there at least a possible fulfilment of her deepest laws.

With such, however, is not my main business now, any more than with those who cannot believe in a God at all, and therefore to whom a miracle is an absurdity. I may, however, just make this one remark with respect to the latter—that perhaps it is better they should believe in no God than believe in such a God as they have yet been able to imagine. Perhaps thus they are nearer to a true faith—except indeed they prefer the notion of the unconscious generating the conscious, to that of a self-existent love, creative in virtue of its being love. Such have never loved woman or child save after a fashion which has left them content that death should seize on the beloved and bear them back to the maternal dust. But I doubt if there can be any who thus would choose a sleep-walking Pan before a wakeful Father. At least, they cannot know the Father and choose the Pan.

The Works of the Son Are the Works of the Father

Let us then recognize the works of the Father as epitomized in the miracles of the Son. What in the hands of the Father are the mighty motions and progresses and conquests of life, in the hands of the Son are miracles. I do not myself believe that he valued the working of these miracles as he valued the utterance of the truth in words; but all that he did had the one root, *obedience*, in which alone can any son be free. And what is the highest obedience? Simply a following of the Father—a doing of what the Father does. Every true father wills that his child should be as he is in his deepest love, in his highest hope. All that Jesus does is of his Father. What we see in the Son is of the Father. What his works mean concerning him, they mean concerning the Father.

Much as I shrink from the notion of a formal shaping out of design in any great life, so unlike the endless freedom and spontaneity of nature (and He is the Nature of nature), I cannot help observing that his first miracle was one of creation—at least, is to our eyes more like creation than almost any other—for who can say that it was creation, not knowing in the least what creation is, or what was the process in this miracle?

CHAPTER TEN

The Government of Nature

The miracles I include in this class are the following:

1. The turning of water into wine, already treated of, given by St. John.
2. The draught of fishes, given by St. Luke.
3. The draught of fishes, given by St. John.
4. The feeding of the four thousand, given by St. Matthew and St. Mark.
5. The feeding of the five thousand, recorded by all the Evangelists.
6. The walking on the sea, given by St. Matthew, St. Mark, and St. John.
7. The stilling of the storm, given by St. Matthew, St. Mark, and St. Luke.
8. The fish bringing the piece of money, told by St. Matthew alone.

The Nature of These Miracles

These miracles, in common with those already considered, have for their end the help or deliverance of man. They differ from those, however, in operating mediately, through a change upon external things, and not at once on their human objects.

But besides the fact that they have to do with what we call nature, they would form a class on another ground. In those cases of disease, the miracles are for the setting right of what has gone wrong, the restoration of the order of things,—namely, of the original condition of hu-manity. No doubt it is a law of nature that where there is sin there should be suffering; but even its cure helps to restore that righteousness which is high-est nature, for the cure of suffering must not be confounded with the absence of suffering.

But the miracles of which I have now to speak, show themselves as interfering with what we may call the righteous laws of nature. Water should wet the foot, should ingulf him who would tread its surface. Bread should come from the oven last, from the field first. Fishes should be now here now there, accord-ing to laws ill understood of men—nay, possibly according to a piscine choice quite unknown of men. Wine should take ripening in the grape and in the bottle. In all these cases it is otherwise.

Yet even in these, I think, the restora-tion of an original law—the supremacy of righteous man, is foreshown. While a man cannot order his own house as he would, something is wrong in him, and therefore in his house. I think a true man should be able to rule winds and waters and loaves and fishes, for he comes of the Father who made the house for him. Had Jesus not been capa-ble of these things, he might have been the best of men, but either he could not have been a perfect man, or the perfect God, if such there were, was not in har-mony with the perfect man. Man is not master in his own house because he is not master in himself, because he is not a law unto himself—is not himself obe-dient to the law by which he exists. Har-mony, that is law, alone is power.

Discord is weakness. God alone is perfect, living, self-existent law.

A Defense of These Miracles

I will try, in a few words, to give the ground on which I find it possible to accept these miracles. I cannot lay it down as for any other man. I do not wonder at most of those to whom the miracles are a stumbling-block. I do a little wonder at those who can believe in Christ and yet find them a stumbling-block.

How God creates, no man can tell. But as man is made in God's image, he may think about God's work, and dim analogies may arise out of the depth of his nature which have some resemblance to the way in which God works. I say then, that, as we are the offspring of God—the children of his will, like as the thoughts move in a man's mind, we live in God's mind. When God thinks anything, then that thing *is*. His thought of it is its life. Everything is because God thinks it into being. Can it then be very hard to believe that he should alter by a thought any form or appearance of things about us?

"It is inconsistent to work otherwise than by law."

True; but we know so little of this law that we cannot say what is essential in it, and what only the so far irregular consequence of the unnatural condition of those for whom it was made, but who have not yet willed God's harmony. We know so little of law that we cannot certainly say what would be an infringement of this or that law. That which at first sight appears as such, may be but the operating of a higher law which rightly dominates the other. It is the law, as we call it, that a stone should fall to the ground. A man may place his hand beneath the stone, and then *if his hand be strong enough*, it is the law that the

stone shall not fall to the ground. The law has been lawfully prevented from working its full end.

In similar ways, God might stop the working of one law by the intervention of another. Such intervention, if not understood by us, would be what we call a miracle. Possibly a different condition of the earth, producible according to law, might cause everything to fly off from its surface instead of seeking it. The question is whether or not we can believe that the usual laws might be set aside by laws including higher principles and wider operations. All I have to answer is—Give me good reason, and I can. A man may say—"What seems good reason to you, does not to me." I answer, "We are both accountable to that being, if such there be, who has lighted in us the candle of judgment. To him alone we stand or fall. But there must be a final way of right, towards which every willing heart is led,—and which no one can find who does not seek it."

All I want to show here, is a conceivable region in which a miracle might take place without any violence done to the order of things. Our power of belief depends greatly on our power of imagining a region in which the things might be. I do not see how some people *could* believe what to others may offer small difficulty. Let us beware lest what we call faith be but the mere assent of a mind which has cared and thought so little about the objects of its so-called faith, that it has never seen the difficulties they involve. Some such believers are the worst antagonists of true faith— the children of the Pharisees of old.

Harmony with a Higher Law

If any one say we ought to receive nothing of which we have no experience, I answer, there is in me a necessity, a desire before which all my experience shrivels into a mockery. Its complement must lie beyond. We ought, I grant, to accept nothing for which we cannot see the probability of some sufficient reason, but I thank God that this sufficient reason is not for me limited to the realm of experience. To suppose that it was, would change the hope of a life that might be an ever-burning sacrifice of thanksgiving, into a poor struggle with events and things and chances—to doom the Psyche to perpetual imprisonment in the worm. I desire the higher; I care not to live for the lower. The one would make me despise my fellows and recoil with disgust from a self I cannot annihilate; the other fills me with humility, hope, and love. Is the preference for the one over the other foolish then—even to the meanest judgment?

A higher condition of harmony with law, may one day enable us to do things which must now *appear* an interruption of law. I believe it is in virtue of the absolute harmony in him, his perfect righteousness, that God can create at all. If man were in harmony with this, if he too were righteous, he would inherit of his Father a something in his degree correspondent to the creative power in Him; and the world he inhabits, which is but an extension of his body, would, I think, be subject to him in a way surpassing his wildest dreams of dominion, for it would be the perfect dominion of holy law—a virtue flowing to and from him through the channel of a perfect obedience.

I suspect that our Lord in all his dominion over nature, set forth only the complete man—man as God means him one day to be. Why should he not know where the fishes were? or even make them come at his will? Why should not that will be potent as impulse in them? If we admit what I hail as the only fundamental idea upon which I can speculate harmoniously with facts, and as

alone disclosing regions wherein contradictions are soluble, and doubts previsions of loftier truth—I mean the doctrine of the Incarnation; or if even we admit that Jesus was good beyond any other goodness we know, why should it not seem possible that the whole region of inferior things might be more subject to him than to us? And if more, why not altogether? I believe that some of these miracles were the natural result of a physical nature perfect from the indwelling of a perfect soul, whose unity with the Life of all things and in all things was absolute—in a word, whose sonship was perfect.

These Miracles Reveal the Father

If in the human form God thus visited his people, he would naturally show himself Lord over their circumstances. He will not lord it over their minds, for such lordship is to him abhorrent: they themselves must see and rejoice in acknowledging the lordship which makes them free. There was no grand display, only the simple doing of what at the time was needful. Some say it is a higher thing to believe of him that he took things just as they were, and led the revealing life without the aid of wonders. On any theory this is just what he did as far as his own life was concerned. But he had no ambition to show himself the best of men. He comes to reveal the Father. He will work even wonders to that end, for the sake of those who could not believe as he did and had to be taught it.

No miracle was needful for himself: he saw the root of the matter—the care of God. But he revealed this root in a few rare and hastened flowers to the eyes that could not see to the root. There is perfect submission to lower law for himself, but revelation of the Father to them by the introduction of higher laws operating in the upper regions bordering upon ours, not separated from ours by an impassable gulf—rather connected by gently ascending stairs, many of whose gradations he could blend in one descent. He revealed the Father as being *under* no law, but as law itself and the cause of the laws we know—the cause of all harmony because himself *the* harmony.

Men had to be delivered not only from the fear of suffering and death, but from the fear, which is a kind of worship, of nature. Nature herself must be shown subject to the Father and to him whom the Father had sent. Men must believe in the great works of the Father through the little works of the Son: all that he showed was little to what God was doing. They had to be helped to see that it was God who did such things as often as they were done. He it is who causes the corn to grow for man. He gives every fish that a man eats. Even if things are terrible yet they are God's, and the Lord will still the storm for their faith in Him—tame a storm, as a man might tame a wild beast—for his Father measures the waters in the hollow of his hand, and men are miserable not to know it. For himself, I repeat, his faith is enough; he sleeps on his pillow nor dreams of perishing.

The Government of the Animal Kingdom

On the individual miracles of this class, I have not much to say. The first of them was wrought in the animal kingdom.

He was teaching on the shore of the lake, and the people crowded him. That he might speak with more freedom, he stepped into an empty boat, and having prayed Simon the owner of it, who was washing his nets near by, to thrust it a little from the shore, sat down, and no longer incommoded by the eagerness of his audience, taught them from the boat. When he had ended he told Simon to launch out into the deep, and let down his nets for a draught. Simon had little hope of success, for there had been no fish there all night; but he obeyed, and caught such a multitude of fishes that the net broke. They had to call another boat to their aid, and both began to sink from the overload of fishes.

But the great marvel of it wrought on the mind of Simon as every wonder tends to operate on the mind of an honest man: it brought his sinfulness before him. In self-abasement he fell down at Jesus' knees. Whether he thought of any individual sins at the moment, we cannot tell; but he was painfully dissatisfied with himself. He knew he was not what he ought to be. I am unwilling however to believe that such a man desired, save, it may be, as a passing involuntary result of distress, to be rid of the holy presence. I judge rather that his feeling was like that of the centurion—that he felt himself unworthy to have the Lord in his boat. He may have feared that the Lord took him for a good man, and his honesty could not endure such a mistake: "Depart from me, for I am a sinful man, O Lord."

The Lord accepted the spirit, therefore *not* the word of his prayer.

"Fear not; from henceforth thou shalt catch men."

His sense of sinfulness, so far from driving the Lord from him, should draw other men to him. As soon as that cry broke from his lips, he had become fit to be a fisher of men. He had begun to abjure that which separated man from man.

After his resurrection, St. John tells us the Lord appeared one morning, on the shore of the lake, to some of his disciples, who had again been toiling all night in vain. He told them once more how to cast their net, and they were not able to draw it for the multitude of fishes.

"It is the Lord," said St. John, purer-hearted, perhaps therefore keener-eyed, than the rest.

Since the same thing had occurred before, Simon had become the fisher of men, but had sinned grievously against his Lord. He knew that Lord so much better now, however, that when he heard it was he, instead of crying *Depart from me*, he cast himself into the sea to go to him.

The Miraculous Feedings

I take next the feeding of the four thousand with the seven loaves and the few little fishes, and the feeding of the five thousand with the five loaves and the two fishes.

Concerning these miracles, I think I have already said almost all I have to say. If he was the Son of God, the bread might as well grow in his hands as the corn in the fields. It is, I repeat, only a doing in condensed form, hence one more easily associated with its real source, of that which God is for ever doing more widely, more slowly, and with more detail both of fundamental wonder and of circumstantial loveliness. Whence more fittingly might food come than from other hands of such an elder brother?

No doubt there will always be men who cannot believe it:—happy are they who demand a good reason, and yet can believe a wonder! Associated with words which appeared to me foolish, untrue, or even poor in their content, I should not believe it. Associated with such things as he spoke, I can receive it with ease, and I cherish it with rejoicing.

It must be noted in respect of the feeding of the five thousand, that while the other evangelists merely relate the deed as done for the necessities of the multitude, St. John records also the use our Lord made of the miracle. It was the outcome of his essential relation to humanity. Of humanity he was ever the sustaining food. To humanity he was about to give himself in an act of such utter devotion as could only be shadowed—not in the spoken, afterwards in the acted symbol of the eucharist.

The miracle was a type of his life as the life of the world, a sign that from him flows all the weal of his creatures. The bread we eat is but its outer husk: the true bread is the Lord himself, to have whom in us is eternal life. "Except ye eat the flesh of the Son of man and drink his blood ye have no life in you." He knew that the grand figure would disclose to the meditation of the loving heart infinitely more of the truth of the matter than any possible amount of definition and explanation, and yet must ever remain far short of setting forth the holy fact to the boldest and humblest mind.

But lest they should start upon a wrong track for the interpretation of it, he says to his disciples afterwards, that this body of his should return to God; that what he had said concerning the eating of it had a spiritual sense: "It is the spirit that giveth life; the flesh profiteth nothing"—for that. In words he contradicts what he said before, that they might see the words to have meant infinitely more than as words they were able to express; that not their bodies on his body, but their souls must live on his soul, by a union and communion of which the eating of his flesh and the drinking of his blood was, after all, but a poor and faint figure.

In this miracle, for the souls as for the bodies of men, he did and revealed the work of the Father. He who has once understood the meaning of Christ's words in connection with this miracle, can never be content they should be less than true concerning his Father in heaven. Whoever would have a perfect Father, must believe that he bestows his very being for the daily food of his creatures. He who loves the glory of God will be very jealous of any word that would enhance his greatness by representing him incapable of suffering. Verily God has taken and will ever take and endure his share, his largest share of that suffering in and through which the whole creation groans for the sonship.

Christ's Walking on the Water

Follows at once the equally wonderful story of his walking on the sea to the help of his disciples. After the former miracle, the multitude would have taken him by force to make him their king. Any kind of honour they would readily give him except that obedience for the truth's sake which was all he cared for. He left them and went away into a mountain alone to pray to his Father. Likely he was weary in body, and also worn in spirit for lack of that finer sympathy which his disciples could not give him being very earthly yet. He who loves his fellows and labours among those who can ill understand him will best know what this weariness of our Lord must have been like. He had to endure the world-pressure of surrounding humanity in all its ungodlike phases.

Hence even he, the everlasting Son of the Father, found it needful to retire for silence and room and comfort into solitary places. There his senses would be free, and his soul could the better commune with the Father. The mountain-top was his chamber, the solitude around him its closed door, the evening sky over his head its open window. There he gathered strength from the will of the Father for what yet remained to be done for the world's redemption. How little could the men below, who would have taken him by force and made him a king, understand of such communion! Yet every one of them must go hungering and thirsting and grasping in vain, until the door of that communion was opened for him. They would have made him a king: he would make them poor in spirit, mighty in aspiration, all kings and priests unto God.

But amidst his prayer, amidst the eternal calm of his rapturous communion, he saw his disciples thwarted by a wind stronger than all their rowing: he descended the hill and walked forth on the water to their help.

If ignorant yet devout speculation may be borne with here, I venture to say that I think the change of some kind that was necessary somehow before the body of the Son of Man could, like the Spirit of old, move upon the face of the waters, passed, not upon the water, but, by the will of the Son of Man himself, upon his own body. I shall have more to say concerning this in a following chapter—now I merely add that we know nothing yet, or next to nothing, of the relation between a right soul and a healthy body.

To some no doubt the notion of a healthy body implies chiefly a perfection of all the animal functions, which is, on the supposition, a matter of course; but what I should mean by an absolutely healthy body is, one entirely under the indwelling spirit, and responsive immediately to all the laws of its supremacy, whatever those laws may be in the divine ideal of a man. As we are now, we find the diseased body tyrannizing over the almost helpless mind: the healthy body would be the absolutely obedient body. What power over his own dwelling a Savior coming fresh from the closest speech with him who made that body for holy subjection, might have, who can tell!

If I hear of any reasonable wonder resulting therefrom, I shall not find it hard to believe, and shall be willing to wait until I, pure, inhabit an obedient house, to understand the plain thing which is now a mystery. Meantime I can honour the laws I do know, and which honest men tell me they have discovered, no less than those honest men who—without my impulse, it may be, to speculate in this direction—think such as I foolish in employing the constructive faculty with regard to these things.

But where, I pray them, lies any field so absolutely its region as the unknown which yet the heart yearns to know? Such cannot be the unknowable. It is endless comfort to think of something that *might* be true. And the essence of whatever seems to a human heart to be true, I expect to find true—in greater forms, and without the degrading accidents which so often accompany it in the brain of the purest thinker. Why should I not speculate in the only direction in which things to me worthy of speculation appear likely to lie?

There is a wide *may be* around us; and every true speculation widens the probability of changing the *may be* into the *is*. The laws that are known and the laws that shall be known are all lights from the Father of lights: he who reverently searches for such will not long mistake a flash in his own brain for the candle of the Lord. But if he should mistake, he will be little the worse, so long as he is humble, and ready to acknowledge error; while, if he should be right, he will be none the worse for having seen the glimmer of the truth from afar—may, indeed, come to gather a little honour from those who, in the experimental verification of an idea, do not altogether forget that, without some foregone speculation, the very idea on which they have initiated their experiment, and are now expending their most

valued labour would never have appeared in their firmament to guide them to new facts and realities.

Nor would it be impossible to imagine how St. Peter might come within the sphere of the holy influence, so that he, too, for a moment should walk on the water. Faith will yet prove itself as mighty a power as it is represented by certain words of the Lord which are at present a stumbling-block even to devout Christians, who are able to accept them only by putting explanations upon them which render them unworthy of his utterance. When I say *a power,* I do not mean in itself, but as connecting the helpless with the helpful, as uniting the empty need with the full supply, as being the conduit through which it is right and possible for the power of the creating God to flow to the created necessity.

When the Lord got into the boat, the wind ceased, "and immediately," says St. John, "the ship was at the land whither they went." As to whether the ceasing of the wind was by the ordinary laws of nature, or some higher law first setting such in operation, no one who has followed the spirit of my remarks will wonder that I do not care to inquire: they are all of one. Nor, in regard to their finding themselves so quickly at the end of their voyage, will they wonder if I think that we may have just one instance of space being subject to the obedient God, and that his wearied disciples, having toiled and rowed hard for so long, might well find themselves at their desired haven as soon as they received him into their boat.

Either God is all in all, or he is nothing. Either Jesus is the Son of the Father, or he did no miracle. Either the miracles are fact, or I lose—not my faith in this man—but certain outward signs of truths which these very signs have aided me to discover and understand and see in themselves.

The Stilling of the Storm

The miracle of the stilling of the storm naturally follows here.

Why should not he, who taught his disciples that God numbered the very hairs of their heads, do what his Father is constantly doing—still storms—bring peace out of uproar? Of course, if the storm was stilled, it came about by natural causes—that is, by such as could still a storm. That anything should be done by unnatural causes, that is, causes not of the nature of the things concerned, is absurd.

The sole question is whether nature works alone, as some speculators think, or whether there is a soul in her, namely, an intent;—whether these things are the result of thought, or whether they spring from a dead heart; unconscious, yet productive of conscious beings, to think, yea, speculate eagerly concerning a conscious harmony hinted at in their broken music and conscious discord; beings who, although thus born of unthinking matter, invent the notion of an all lovely, perfect, self-denying being, whose thought gives form to matter, life to nature, and thought to man—subjecting himself for their sakes to the troubles their waywardness has brought upon them, that they too may at length behold a final good—may see the Holy face to face—think his thoughts and will his wisdom!

That things should go by a law which does not recognize the loftiest in him, a man feels to be a mockery of him. There lies little more satisfaction in such a condition of things than if the whole were the fortuitous result of ever conflicting, never combining forces. Wherever individual and various necessity, choice, and prayer, come in, there must be the present God, able and ready to fit circumstances to the varying need of the thinking, willing being he has created.

Machinery will not do here—perfect as it may be. That God might make a world to go on with absolute physical perfection to all eternity, I could easily believe; but where the gain?—nay, where the fitness, if he would train thinking beings to his own freedom? For such he must be ever present, ever have room to order things for their growth and change and discipline and enlightenment. The present living idea informing the cosmos, is nobler than all forsaken perfection—nobler, as a living man is nobler than an automaton.

If one should say: "The laws of God ought to admit of no change," I answer: The same working of unalterable laws might under new circumstances *look* a breach of those laws. That God will never alter his laws, I fully admit and uphold, for they are the outcome of his truth and fact; but that he might not act in ways unrecognizable by us as consistent with those laws, I have yet to see reason ere I believe. Why should his perfect will be limited by our understanding of that will? Should he be paralyzed because we are blind? That he should ever require us to believe of him what we think wrong, I do not believe; that he should present to our vision what may be inconsistent with our half-digested and constantly changing theories, I can well believe. Why not—if only to keep us from petrifying an imperfect notion, and calling it an *Idea?*

What I would believe is, that a present God manages the direction of those laws, even as a man, in his inferior way, works out his own will in the midst and by means of those laws. Shall God create that which shall fetter and limit and enslave himself? What should his laws, as known to us, be but the active mode in which he embodies certain truths—that mode also the outcome of his own nature? If so, they must be always capable of falling in with any, if not of effecting every, expression of his will.

The Fish with Money in Its Mouth

There remains but one miracle of this class to consider—one to some minds involving greater difficulties than all the rest. They say the story of the fish with a piece of money in its mouth is more like one of the tales of eastern fiction than a sober narrative of the quiet-toned gospel. I acknowledge a likeness: why might there not be some likeness between what God does and what man invents?

But there is one noticeable difference: there is nothing of colour in the style of the story. No great roe, no valley of diamonds, no earthly grandeur whatever is hinted at in the poor bare tale.

Peter had to do with fishes every day of his life: an ordinary fish, taken with the hook, was here the servant of the Lord—and why should not the poor fish have its share in the service of the Master? Why should it not show for itself and its kind that they were utterly his? that along with the waters in which they dwelt, and the wind which lifteth up the waves thereof, they were his creatures, and gladly under his dominion?

What the scaly minister brought was no ring, no rich jewel, but a simple piece of money, just enough, I presume, to meet the demand of those whom, although they had no legal claim, our Lord would not offend by a refusal; for he never cared to stand upon his rights, or treat that as a principle which might be waived without loss of righteousness. I take for granted that there was no other way at hand for those poor men to supply the sum required of them.

God's Words to His Children *(1887) is a collection of MacDonald's sermons from diverse sources. In "The Only Freedom," which was originally published in* The English Pulpit To-Day, *MacDonald speaks of a slavery that is liberty. Freedom lies in obedience, for Christ Himself was free because of His complete devotion to the will of the Father. Freedom means acting like God out of the essence of our nature and choosing good with our whole hearts.*

"The Resurrection Harvest," which also appears in God's Words to His Children, *originally appeared in MacDonald's 1868 novel* The Seaboard Parish. *MacDonald sees that this world is full of resurrections. The sun enacts a resurrection every night and day, and we ourselves "die" every night to rise every morning. In the seasons of the earth and in the animal world there are also resurrections. All of these are dim shadows of the resurrection into life that we shall have, a resurrection out of evil and into good that begins even in this life.*

CHAPTER ELEVEN

The Only Freedom

"Paul, a servant of Jesus Christ" (Rom. 1:1).

The Meaning of "Servant"

St. Paul, in addressing the Romans, begins thus: "Paul, a servant of Jesus Christ." Well, you all know that it is more than that that he says. I do not know why they put the word "bondservant" in the margin. For my part, I should translate it just as it stands, "Paul, a slave of Jesus Christ." And again—for he does not want to be exclusive even in this humility—when he is writing to the Philippians, he joins another with him, namely, Timothy, his young friend, and he says, "Paul and Timothy, slaves of Jesus Christ." But the word does mean just that. It is not what we call a servant in our day, for they could not come and go as they pleased. They were not even servants who were slaves taken in war, but it means even more than the bondslave. It means a born slave, and there we have it—"a born slave of Jesus Christ."

It is a figure, you know; but the plague of it is that most people, who deal with the figures in the New Testament, make them to mean less because they are figures. That is the way in which the commonplace devil that possesses many men and women makes them treat all the high and holy things. Where there is a figure used in the New Testament, it means more than it can say; and more than any word that man can utter did St. Paul mean when he said that he was a born slave of Jesus Christ.

No doubt there is in the word an element which St. Paul did not mean—did not feel. You know how a mother will sometimes, just out of tenderness to her child, call it bad names. So St. Paul here, just in the despair of faith, takes delight in belonging to Christ utterly, altogether, inconceivably, saved by Christ himself, for he could not tell or feel—he knew that he could not even feel—how much he belonged to Christ; and he used a word that indicates in it something which is not real, not true. He says, "I am the slave of Jesus Christ," and yet, if any man in this world was free besides the Lord himself, that man was St. Paul.

As for us, as soon as we begin to say high things in our human speech, we immediately begin to say them wrong. There is no help for it. Whatever of high things can be put into words is not right; it is not correct. We are only trying after what language is unequal to. It cannot do all, and therefore sometimes we just go wrong the other way, and use, as it were, the wrong word in a kind of agony of outreaching after the true.

Paul the Enthusiast

"But St. Paul was an enthusiast." Yes, I believe that he was an enthusiast; and, if he had not been an enthusiast about such a thing as this, he would not have been worthy to be a slave to the lowest of Christ's people. There is no reality in the relation of things that are high, if we be not enthusiastic about them, if they do not possess us hold us, fill us, lead us, drive us, teach us, feed us, live in us, and make us live in them. No good can be done without enthusiasm. There is no reality of love without enthusiasm.

What! shall I know anything at all that is genuine about Jesus Christ? Am I a fool capable of believing that that man came from the bosom of the Father to be to me my loving Brother and my Savior; to take me, at his own torture, out of my misery, out of myself, which is my torture, into the life of his Father in heaven? Shall I believe that—shall I even believe that he had not a selfish thought in him, and not be enthusiastic about him? Have I the faculty of enthusiasm in me? Is it possible for me to give myself away—to do anything that is not urged and suggested by the lower self? Am I capable of these things at all?

Then, if I am not enthusiastic about Jesus Christ, this whole faculty of my nature lies useless, rotting in me, for there is nothing else in the universe to call it out, or capable of calling it out. The poor enthusiasms that one sees in the world for things that are less than the truth, or that are small passing facts of our condition here—look how they last when a man is vigorous, and how they wither when he grows older! But you will find that St. Paul, at the very last of his life, was more a slave of Jesus Christ than ever before—far more his slave than when he lay struck blind and helpless by the light of his appearing.

For my part, it seems to me a grand proof—and we can have no external proof better, though we may have better proof in ourselves, for the least feeling of these things in ourselves is a higher and better proof than anything brought from the outside—I say that the fact that a man like St. Paul, (brought up as he was, with such a brain and such a heart, and turned the wrong way at

first,) should be capable of burning with such enthusiasm for a man of whose history he knew very little that was real or true until he saw him in heavenly glory—that after that he should live to be the rejoicing slave of Jesus Christ— is it a wonder that such a fact should weigh with me ten times more than the denial of the highest intellect of this world who gives me by the very terms that he uses, concerning what he thinks my faith, the conviction that he knows nothing about what I believe? He talks as if he did, but he knows nothing about it. St. Paul knew the Lord Christ; and, therefore, heart and soul, mind, body, and brain, he belonged to Jesus Christ, even as his born slave.

Slavery that Is a Liberty

But let us try to understand a little what is meant by a slavery which is a liberty. One of the first feelings of the noble-minded youth is a love of liberty. In our history he has been taught it from his earliest thought, and he feels that the grand thing is that he shall be free and the slave of no man. As a rule he has a very low notion of what liberty is, and in most cases it does not grow very much better as he gets older; but still there is, at the root of it, a something genuine and real, which is capable of being interpreted into a high and holy thing.

But is it, as the boy thinks about it? Well, it is just to do as he likes; or, if he carries it a little higher, and thinks of political liberty, it is that nobody may meddle with him, that he is to stand without any weight, or bond, or command upon him. And for the sake of this kind of liberty, too often, he will bind his soul in chains of misery. Sometimes, for instance, he will run away from school; he will run away from home; he will shirk doing the things that his parents tell him; and, in order that his feet may be free to wander where they will, he ties up his inner man in a sense of wrath, in garments of pain, in a feeling of bondage; and because he would be free he makes himself a slave far deeper than any outward law could make him.

Suppose, however, that there was no law of parent, or teacher, or magistrate, or ruler of any kind whatever, laid upon us, and suppose that the man has plenty of money and all kinds of what he calls freedom to go and do what he pleases. Suppose that, outside, he is aware of no bondage whatever. That cannot last long. As soon as there comes a touch of pain, the least sense of weakness—as soon as the first white begins to come on the hair—well, perhaps not quite so soon as that, but when he has the first feeling, "I am not quite capable of what I used to do,"—as soon as any of these merest touches come on the consciousness of a man, the sense of freedom begins to go.

But suppose that in the heyday of a man's strength, in the heartiness of ripe youth, before middle age has begun to come, he can move as he pleases and do as he wills, and suppose that there is no one to say nay to him, is he free? Young man, would you think that that was all right? Would you think that this was your calling? Would you say, "For this end came I into the world, that I might do whatever I liked"? And would you feel that you were grand and free? If you do feel so, you will not believe me, but I tell you—and one day you will believe me if you remember it, which is not likely—I tell you that, to me and to every man who has had the experience of any effort of true liberty, you are a most wretched slave, for your very ideal is slavery; your very high notion is mean and despicable.

You cannot see it; I know that, but you do not see everything yet; and the time is coming when you will be compelled to see it, and can no more help seeing it than now you can help—or, rather, I should say, will help not seeing it. For what is it that drives you on? There is a devil who has whispered to you—affected, perhaps, a certain convolution of your brain, touched you at some certain spot; and you say that you are free, and all the time you are the real sport of temptation. You call it liberty. You stay till the point of the arrow that directs you turns against you and pierces you to the centre. You stay till the devil that tempted you mocks you, and you gaze at him and get no help; for there is no such thing in the world as liberty, except under the law of liberty; that is, the acting according to the essential laws of our own being—not our feelings which go and come.

The man that will rage one hour and be cold the next—what a fool he is if he supposes that he is to walk either by his rage or by his coldness! It is a law that he is to obey. He is to follow the lines upon which this being of his is constructed, this central, original, heart-emotion of his existence. Why, as soon might a man attempt to drive some great engine backward—as soon might he lay hold of its centre pinion and try to stop it, as you can think to make it go well with your being if you live contrary to the very essence of your being; for, let me tell you, you are not bad, or, if you are bad, you are damnably bad.

You are not made bad. God forbid; for God made us, and he made nothing bad, and if you will be bad that is fearful indeed. The lines of our being are laid, I will not even say by the hand of the living God, they were laid in his heart. The idea of every one of us was known and thought over in that heart; and, out of his heart we have gone. He has set before us a way that we may turn, and, of our own free will, run back to him, embrace the Father's knees, and be lifted to the Father's heart.

Liberty Lies in Obedience

There is no liberty but in doing right. There is no freedom but in living out of the deeps of our nature—not out of the surface. Why, look at you. You lose your temper. You think that you are free when you go into a rage. Half-an-hour after you are ashamed. God grant that you may be sorry. That is something more. But you are ashamed of yourself; and yet you think that you are a free man. You acted out the mere surface of your nature—a something which it needed but half-an-hour to make you ashamed of.

That is not liberty. That is acting out of your poor, mean, despicable self, which we have all got, and not out of the divine self, the deepest in us, for the deepest in us is God. We did not come into this world because we willed it. We did not say what we should be. It is God in every man that enables that man even to stretch out his hand. The moment may come when he can lift it no more. Let him will, and will to do it with an agony of willing; yet he cannot raise his hand any more. He cannot do it. It is God; none else.

But I am talking about liberty, and what I want to impress upon those who will be impressed is this—that the one only liberty lies in obedience. Can you lay hold of it? Do you think that Jesus Christ—and he will let me put it so because it is for the sake of the truth—do you think that Jesus Christ would have felt free one moment if he had not been absolutely devoted to the will of his Father in heaven? Suppose it had been possible, which, thank the Lord Christ and his Father, it was not, else we were now in the darkness of helplessness—suppose it had been possible that Jesus

Christ should have been less devoted to his Father, for he might have said in the same high, figurative sense that he was the slave of his Father; for, look you, he cares for nothing but his Father's will. There is nothing else that he has anything to do with. The very reason for which he came into the world was "that the world may know that I am of the Father." "As the Father has given me commandment," he says, "so I do;" and then he says, "Arise, let us go hence"—away to the death, because the Father willed it.

Oh, if Jesus had been less the slave of his Father, do you think that he would have felt that he was a free man? Do you not think that that was what made the devil? He had a notion of being free. "Here I am. I will be the slave of no man—not even of the God that made me." And so all goes wrong, and he is the devil—no archangel any longer—and a mean devil, too, who tries to pull all down into the same abyss with himself well knowing that he cannot even give them his pride to uphold them. If, friends, it should be slavery to obey the very source of our being, think what mean creatures we are that, having come from that source, to follow the law of our life is a slavery.

Slaves of Christ

Well, then, we are the born slaves— ah, thank God, we are the born slaves of Christ! But then he is liberty himself, and all his desire is that we should be such noble, true, right creatures that we never can possibly do or think a thing that shall bind a thread round our spirits and make us feel as if we were bound anywhere. He wants us to be free—not as the winds—not to be free as the man who owns no law, but to be free by being law, by being right, by being truth. When you know that the law goes in one way, is it freedom to bring your will against that law, or to avoid it, and go another way, when the very essence of your existence means that you do not oppose, but yield to the conditions—I do not mean arbitrary conditions, but the essential conditions—of your being, those conditions that make your being divine, for God has made us after his own fashion, and when we do as God would do, as God delights to do—when we act according to the divine mind and nature, we are acting according to our own deepest self, which is the law and will of God. Jesus Christ might have said, "I am the slave of my Father in heaven." He has nowhere used the phrase, but it was in that sense that St. Paul said, "I am the slave of Jesus Christ."

Oh, I appeal to you women—I mean those of you that love Jesus Christ— what would you not do to show him that you love him? Then when I say the words there comes a painful thought, whether some of you may not be like children who indulge in all kinds of tender caresses, but who, when told to do something, begin to pout and refuse to obey. Oh, to think that you should love with all your feeling—that you should love the Lord so much, and yet take so little trouble to know from the story left behind what he really now at this moment wants you to do! That is the way to show your love to him.

But, I put it to you again, what would you not do to show that you love him? There were two women who seem to have gone as far as women could go to show their love to him. You know the story—something that one cannot speak. You know the story. Some of you would do that, oh, how rejoicingly! And when you say "Master," you would like to say with St. Paul, just because you have no other word strong enough, "Lord, I am thy bondslave." That was St.

Paul's feeling when he used the word. But then St. Paul spent his whole life, all his thoughts, all his energies, simply to obey this Lord and Master; and so he was the one free man—not the only free man; there were some more amongst the apostles, and, by his preaching, here and there and everywhere, there started up free men, or, at least, men who were beginning to grow free by beginning to be the slaves of Jesus Christ.

Willing to Love

But let me show you a little more. I do not say that the moment you begin to obey the Lord Jesus Christ, and to be his slave, then you are free. I do not say that then you know what is meant by liberty. I will show you. There are many things that we know are right, and we are not inclined to do them. There are many things that we know are wrong, and we are inclined to do them. But when the law of liberty comes, the will of Jesus Christ, we begin to try to do the things we do not like to do, and not to do the things that we do like to do.

But do you not see that here is a strife? So long as we are in this condition, so long as we know that we have to do the things that we do not like, and that we must not do the things we would like, we are not free. We are only fighting for freedom, but we are not free. We do not know liberty yet; and yet, on the other hand (try to follow me), if we liked the good things, and did not like the bad thing, and without any thought or effort of our own, just went to the good thing and not to the bad thing, we should not be free either, because we should be going just by the impulse in us.

So there comes a contradiction which it is not easy to explain or understand. But, you know, God could not be satisfied to make us like the animals. A good dog does not bite, because he is not inclined to bite. He loves you, but you do not say that he is high morally because he is not inclined to do anything bad. But if we, choosing, against our liking, to do the right, go on so until we are enabled by doing it to see into the very loveliness and essence of the right, and know it to be altogether beautiful, and then at last never think of doing evil, but delight with our whole souls in doing the will of God, why then, do you not see, we combine the two, and we are free indeed, because we are acting like God out of the essence of our nature, knowing good and evil, and choosing the good with our whole hearts and delighting in it?

It is not enough to love because we cannot help it. We must love, too, because we will it with our whole nature, and then, do you not see, when we come to love one another perfectly, we do not need to be told, "Thou shalt not steal; thou shalt not kill; thou shalt not bear false witness," because the thing is absolutely abhorrent to us, if the thought would come up at all? But, when we have learned to love our neighbor as ourselves the thought of killing and stealing never comes out, or of defrauding or of doing ignoble things and calling them "business." Nothing of that kind. We positively love our neighbor, and to hurt him would be to hurt ourselves worse. That is liberty, but we can come to that only by willing it, the root of our being is that will. We must fall in with it. We must will it ourselves, and then, at last, the lovely will of God will possess us from head to feet and fingers, and we shall live in the very breath of God and act like God himself, free like the Living One, because we are one with the source of our life and our being.

So, friends, you see how all through, as far as the words go, we have got to deal with something like contradictions, but in the meaning of the thing your own hearts tell you—the hearts of many of you, at least, tell you—what it is, and you will see that there is no contradiction in it at all. Though it might be exceedingly difficult to lay it out all plain in logical language, your hearts can understand it. Nay, they witness to it because they have grown hungry. You want to be such children of God as this. You want to be free from the oppression of evil in every way. Nay, the time will come when you will lay down the arms of your battle, fighting for the truth. You will have to lay them down even because you have conquered.

How conquered? Because you are perfectly satisfied with God, one with his will, rejoicing in his joy, living in his life, having no fear, no ambition, no anxiety, but a constant strength of life that death and hell cannot touch. You would not be afraid then if you were cast into the middle of hell fire. The flames could not touch you. If you had a body that they could scorch and burn, yet the soul within you would rise superior even to that torture, because, being of the very nature of God, partakers of the divine nature, you would be able to bear pain in triumph, and with a sense of freedom in the midst of it, and slavery would be far from you.

Free Men of Christ

But I have just a word to say now to those specially who think that they have belonged to Christ for many years. Are you in any sense, can you say it out of your heart and meaning it, "I am a slave of Christ?" Object to the term, and I say, are you the free man of Christ? for they mean the same thing. His slave is his free brother. Is there anything that you do now? And we cannot divide our lives, we cannot say that the private gentleman will be saved when the man of business will be condemned; we are either all Christ's, or not at all, for he has told us that no man can serve two masters.

Are you doing anything now that is not just all that you would like, suppose the thing were to come to be laid open to the purest eyes of those who know you? If there is such a thing as you would not like seen, does the Master see it, or does he not? If he does not, he is no Master; we want a greater. If you think he will let it slip, God forbid that I should serve that Master! I want a Master that will not pass over a farthing, a Master who will not let me go from his cleansing hand even if that hand be washing me with fire so long as there is any spot of defilement on my spirit; and the least shadow of dishonesty is the deepest defilement.

Are you not sometimes content with saying, "I do as my neighbor would do to me"? You cannot say, "I do as I would like my neighbor to do to me," perhaps. I wonder whether you could say, then, what the Lord said; for remember he never said, "Thou shalt love thy neighbor as thyself." That was not what he taught. That was taught long before. The spirit of God taught it, but not by Jesus Christ. What Christ taught was, "Love one another as I have loved you." Do we behave to our fellow-men as Christ has behaved to us? If we do not, we are not his slaves. We may be even following in the track of his triumph—I do not say that we shall not get in, but I am clear upon this—that we never shall enter until we have passed through what ordeal is needful to make us clean as God himself. We have got to be good, and if we will not willingly of ourselves, he will make us. It is what he made us for, and it ought to be the business of our lives.

O Lord, raise up, we pray thee, thy power, and come among us, and with great might succor us; that whereas, through our sins and wickedness, we are sore let and hindered in running the race that is set before us, thy bountiful grace and mercy may speedily help and deliver us through the satisfaction of thy Son our Lord, to whom, with thee, and the HOLY GHOST, be honor and glory, world without end. *Amen.*

CHAPTER TWELVE

The Resurrection Harvest

"If by any means I might attain unto the resurrection of the dead, not as though I had already attained, either were already perfect" (Phil. 3:11–12).

The Resurrection of the Sun

The world, my friends, is full of resurrections, and it is not always of the same resurrection that St. Paul speaks. Every night that folds us up in darkness is a death; and those of you that have been out early and have seen the first of the dawn, will know it—the day rises out of the night like a being that has burst its tomb and escaped into life. That you may feel that the sunrise is a resurrection—the word resurrection just means a rising again—I will read you a little description of it from a sermon by a great writer and great preacher called Jeremy Taylor. Listen:

"But as when the sun approaching towards the gates of the morning, he first opens a little eye of heaven and sends away the spirits of darkness, and gives light to a cock, and calls up the lark to matins, and by and by gilds the fringes of a cloud, and peeps over the eastern hills, thrusting out his golden horns like those which decked the brows of Moses, when he was forced to wear a veil, because himself had seen the face of God; and still while a man tells the story, the sun gets up higher, till he shows a fair face and a full light, and then he shines one whole day, under a cloud often, and sometimes weeping great and little showers, and sets quickly; so is a man's reason and his life."

Is not this a resurrection of the day out of the night? Or hear how Milton makes his Adam and Eve praise God in the morning:—

> Ye mists and exhalations, that
>   now rise
> From hill or steaming lake,
>   dusky or gray,
> Till the sun paint your fleecy
>   skirts with gold,
> In honor to the world's great
>   Author rise;
> Whether to deck with clouds the
>   uncolored sky,
> Or wet the thirsty earth with
>   falling showers,
> Rising or falling, still advance
>   his praise.

The Resurrection from Sleep

But it is yet more of a resurrection to you. Think of your own condition through the night and in the morning. You die, as it were, every night. The death of darkness comes down over the earth; but a deeper death, the death of sleep, descends on you. A power overshadows you; your eyelids close, you cannot keep them open if you would; your limbs lie moveless; the day is gone; your whole life is gone; you have forgotten everything; an evil man might come and do with your goods as he pleased; you are helpless.

But the God of the resurrection is awake all the time, watching his sleeping men and women, even as a mother who watches her sleeping baby, only with larger eyes and more full of love than hers; and so, you know not how, all at once you know that you are what you are; that there is a world that wants you outside of you, and a God that wants you inside of you; you rise from the death of sleep, not by your own power, for you know nothing about it; God put his hand over your eyes, and you were dead; he lifted his hand and breathed light on you, and you rose from the dead, thanked the God that raised you up, and went forth to do your work. From darkness to light; from blindness to seeing; from knowing nothing to looking abroad on the mighty world; from helpless submission to willing obedience—is not this a resurrection indeed?

That St. Paul saw it to be such may be shown from his using the two things with the same meaning when he says, "Awake, thou that sleepest, and arise from the dead, and Christ shall give thee light." No doubt he meant a great deal more. No man who understands what he is speaking about can well mean only one thing at a time.

Resurrections in Nature

But to return to the resurrections we see around us in nature. Look at the death that falls upon the world in winter. And look how it revives when the sun draws near enough in the spring to wile the life in it once more out of its grave. See how the pale, meek snow-drops come up with their bowed heads, as if full of the memory of the fierce winds they encountered last spring, and yet ready in the strength of their weakness to encounter them again. Up comes the crocus, bringing its gold safe from the dark of its colorless grave into the light of its parent gold. Primroses, and anemones, and blue-bells, and a thousand other children of the spring, hear the resurrection-trumpet of the wind from the west and south, obey, and leave their graves behind to breathe the air of the sweet heavens. Up and up they come till the year is glorious with the rose and lily, till the trees are not only clothed upon with new garments of loveliest green, but the fruit-tree bringeth forth its fruit, and the little children of men are made glad with apples, and cherries, and hazelnuts.

The earth laughs out in green and gold. The sky shares in the grand resurrection. The garments of its mourning, wherewith it made men sad, its clouds of snow and hail and stormy vapors, are swept away, have sunk indeed to the earth, and are now humbly feeding the roots of the flowers whose dead stalks they beat upon all the winter long. Instead, the sky has put on the garments of praise. Her blue, colored after the sapphire-floor on which stands the throne of him who is the Resurrection and the Life, is dashed and glorified with the pure white of sailing clouds, and at morning and evening prayer, puts on colors in which the human heart drowns itself with delight—green and gold and purple and rose. Even the icebergs, floating about in the lonely summer seas of the north, are flashing all the glories of the rainbow. But, indeed, is not this whole world itself a monument of the resurrection? The earth was without form and void. The wind of God moved on the face of the waters, and up arose this fair world. Darkness was on the face of the deep: God said, "Let there be light," and there was light.

Resurrection in the Animal World

In the animal world, as well, you behold the goings of the resurrection. Plainest of all, look at the story of the butterfly—so plain that the pagan Greeks called it and the soul by one name—Psyche. Psyche meant with them a butterfly or the soul, either. Look how the creeping thing, ugly to our eyes, so that we can hardly handle it without a shudder, finding itself growing sick with age, straightway falls a-spinning and weaving at its own shroud, coffin, and grave, all in one—to prepare, in fact, for its resurrection; for it is for the sake of the resurrection that death exists. Patiently it spins its strength, but not its life, away, folds itself up decently, that its body may rest in quiet till the new body is formed within it; and at length when the appointed hour has arrived, out of the body of this crawling thing breaks forth the winged splendor of the butterfly—not the same body—a new built out of the ruins of the old—even as St. Paul tells us that it is not the same body we have in the resurrection, but a nobler body like ourselves, with all the imperfect and evil thing taken away.

No more creeping for the butterfly; wings of splendor now. Neither yet has it lost the feet wherewith to alight on all that is lovely and sweet. Think of it—up from the toilsome journey over the low ground, exposed to the foot of every passer-by destroying the lovely leaves upon which it fed, and the fruit which they should shelter, up to the path at will through the air, and a gathering of food which hurts not the source of it, a food which is but as a tribute from the loveliness of the flowers to the yet higher loveliness of the flower-angel; is not this a resurrection? Its children too shall pass through the same process, to wing the air of a summer noon, and rejoice in the ethereal and the pure.

The Resurrection of the Body

I come now naturally to speak of what we commonly call the resurrection. Some say: "How can the same dust be raised again, when it may be scattered to the winds of heaven?" It is a question I hardly care to answer. The mere difficulty can in reason stand for nothing with God; but the apparent worthlessness of the supposition renders the question uninteresting to me. What is of import is, that I should stand clothed upon, with a body which is *my* body because it serves my ends, justifies my consciousness of identity by being, in all that was good in it, like that which I had before, while now it is tenfold capable of expressing the thoughts and feelings that move within me. How can I care whether the atoms that form a certain inch of bone should be the same as those which formed that bone when I died? All my lifetime I never felt or thought of the existence of such a bone! On the other hand, I object to having the same worn muscles, the same shriveled skin, with which I may happen to die. Why give me the same body as that? Why not rather my youthful body, which was strong, and facile, and capable? The matter in the muscle of my arm at death would not serve to make half the muscle I had when young.

But I thank God St. Paul says it will *not* be the same body. That body dies—up springs another body. I suspect myself that those are right who say that this body being the seed, the moment it dies in the soil of this world, that moment is the resurrection of the new body. The life in it rises out of it in a new body. This is not after it is put in the mere earth; for it is dead then, and the germ of life gone out of it. If a seed rots, no new body comes of it. The seed dies into a new life, and so does man. Dying and rotting are two very different things.

But I am not sure by any means. As I say, the whole question is rather uninteresting to me. What do I care about my old clothes after I have done with them? What is it to me to know what becomes of an old coat or an old pulpit-gown? I have no such clinging to the flesh. It seems to me that people believe their bodies to be themselves, and are therefore very anxious about them— and no wonder then. Enough for me that I shall have eyes to see my friends, a face that they shall know me by, and a mouth to praise God withal. I leave the matter with one remark, that I am well content to rise as Jesus rose, however that was. For me the will of God is so good that I would rather have his will done than my own choice given me.

The Resurrection Unto Life

But I now come to the last, because infinitely the most important, part of my subject—the resurrection for the sake of which all the other resurrections exist—the resurrection unto life. This is the one of which St. Paul speaks in my text. This is the one I am most anxious— indeed, the only one I am anxious to set forth, and impress upon you.

Think, then, of all the deaths you know; the death of the night, when the sun is gone, when friend says not a word to friend, but both lie drowned and parted in the sea of sleep; the death of the year, when winter lies heavy on the graves of the children of summer, when the leafless trees moan in the blasts from the ocean, when the beasts even look dull and oppressed, when the children go about shivering with cold, when the poor and improvident are miserable with suffering; or think of such a death of disease as befalls us at times, when the man who says, "Would God it were morning!" changes but his word, and not his tune, when the morning comes, crying, "Would God it were evening!" when what life is left is known to us only by suffering, and hope is among the things which were once and are no more—think of all these, think of them all together, and you will have but the dimmest, faintest picture of the death,

from which the resurrection, of which I have now to speak, is the rising.

I shrink from the attempt, knowing how weak words are to set forth *the* death, set forth *the* resurrection. Were I to sit down to yonder organ, and crash out the most horrible dissonances that ever took shape in sound, I should give you but a weak figure of this death; were I capable of drawing from many a row of pipes an exhalation of dulcet symphonies and voices sweet, such as Milton himself could have invaded our ears withal, I could give you but a faint figure of this resurrection. Nevertheless, I must try what I can do in my own way.

If into the face of the dead body, lying on the bed, waiting for its burial, the soul of the man should begin to dawn again, drawing near from afar to look out once more at those eyes, to smile once again through those lips, the change on that face would be indeed great and wondrous, but nothing for marvel or greatness to that which passes on the countenance, the very outward bodily face of the man who wakes from his sleep, arises from the dead, and receives light from Christ.

Too often indeed, the reposeful look on the face of the dead body would be troubled, would vanish away at the revisiting of the restless ghost; but when a man's own right true mind, which God made in him, is restored to him again, and he wakes from the death of sin, then comes the repose without the death.

It may take long for the new spirit to complete the visible change, but it begins at once, and will be perfected. The bloated look of self-indulgence passes away like the leprosy of Naaman, the cheek grows pure, the lips return to the smile of hope instead of the grin of greed, and the eyes that made innocence shrink and shudder with their yellow leer grow childlike and sweet and faithful. The mammon-eyes, hitherto fixed on the earth, are lifted to meet their kind; the lips that mumbled over figures and sums of gold learn to say words of grace and tenderness. The truculent, repellent, self-satisfied face begins to look thoughtful and wistful, as if searching for some treasure of whose whereabouts it had no certain sign. The face, anxious, wrinkled, peering, troubled, on whose line you read the dread of hunger, poverty and nakedness, thaws into a smile; the eyes reflect in courage the light of the Father's care; the back grows erect under its burden with the assurance that the hairs of its head are all numbered.

From Selfishness to Love

But the face can with all its changes set but dimly forth the rising from the dead which passes within. The heart, which cared but for itself, becomes aware of surrounding thousands like itself, in the love and care of which it feels a drawing blessedness undreamt of before. From selfishness to love—is not this a rising from the dead? The man whose ambition declares that his way in this world would be to subject everything to his desires, to bring every human care, affection, power, and aspiration to his feet—(such a world it would be, and such a king it would have, if individual ambition might work its will, if a man's opinion of himself could be made out in the world, degrading, compelling, oppressing, doing everything for his own glory, and such a glory)—but a pang of light strikes this man to the heart an arrow of truth, feathered with suffering and loss and dismay, finds out—the open joint in his armor, I was going to say—no, finds out the joint in the coffin where his heart lies festering in a death so dead that itself calls it life. He trembles, he awakes, he rises from the dead. No more he

seeks the slavery of all: where can he find whom to serve? how can he become if but a threshold in the temple of Christ, where all serve all, and no man thinks first of himself?

He, to whom the mass of his fellows, as he massed them, was common and unclean, bows before every human sign of the presence of the creating God. The sun which was to him but a candle with which to search after his own ends, wealth, power, place, praise—the world which was but the cavern where he thus searched—are now full of the mystery of the loveliness, full of the truth of which sun and wind and land and sea are symbols and signs. From a withered old age of unbelief, the dim eyes of which refuse the glory of things a passage to the heart, he is raised up a child full of admiration, surprise, and gladness. Everything is glorious to him; he can believe, and therefore he sees. It is from the grave into the sunshine, from the night into the morning, from death into life.

To come out of the ugly into the beautiful; out of the mean and selfish into the noble and loving; out of the paltry into the great; out of the false into the true; out of the filthy into the clean; out of the commonplace into the glorious; out of the corruption of disease into the fine vigor and gracious movements of health; in a word, out of evil into good— is not this a resurrection indeed—*the resurrection of all, the resurrection of life?* God grant that with St. Paul we may attain to this resurrection of the dead!

This rising from the dead is often a long and a painful process. Even after he had preached the gospel to the Gentiles, and suffered much for the sake of his Master, Paul sees the resurrection of the dead towering grandly before him, not yet climbed, not yet attained unto— a mountainous splendor and marvel still shining aloft in the air of existence, still, thank God, to be attained, but ever growing in height and beauty as, forgetting those things that are behind, he presses towards the mark, if by any means he may attain to the resurrection of the dead.

Blessed Resurrections

Every blessed moment, in which a man bethinks himself that he has been forgetting his high calling, and sends up to the Father a prayer for aid; every time a man resolves that what he has been doing he will do no more; every time that the love of God, or the feeling of the truth, rouses a man to look first up at the light, then down at the skirts of his own garments—that moment a divine resurrection is wrought in the earth. Yea, every time that a man passes from resentment to forgiveness, from cruelty to compassion, from harshness to tenderness, from indifference to carefulness, from selfishness to honesty, from honesty to generosity, from generosity to love,—a resurrection, the bursting of a fresh bud of life out of the grave of evil, gladdens the eye of the Father watching his children.

Awake, then, thou that sleepest, and arise from the dead, and Christ will give the light! As the harvest rises from the wintry earth, so rise thou up from the trials of this world, a full ear in the harvest of him who sowed thee in the soil that thou mightest rise above it. As the summer rises from the winter, so rise thou from the cares of eating, and drinking, and clothing into the fearless sunshine of confidence in the Father. As the morning rises out of the night, so rise thou from the darkness of ignorance to do the will of God in the daylight; and as a man feels that he is himself when he wakes from the troubled and grotesque visions of the night into the glory of the sunrise, even so wilt thou feel that then first thou knowest what thy life, the gladness of thy being, is. As from painful tossing in disease, rise into the health of well-being. As from the awful embrace of thy own dead body, burst forth in thy spiritual body. Arise thou, responsive to the indwelling will of the Father, even as thy body will resound to the indwelling soul.

White wings are crossing: glad waves
    are tossing;
The earth flames out in crimson and
    green:
Spring is appearing, summer is
    nearing—
        Where hast thou been?

Down in some cavern, death's sleepy
    tavern,
Housing, carousing with spectres of
    night?
The trumpet is pealing sunshine and
    healing—
        Spring to the light!

"Divine and Human Relationship" originally appeared in The Christian World Pulpit. *MacDonald stresses in this sermon, as he does elsewhere, that it is obedience, and not just comprehension or theorization, that matters. We become the sons and daughters of God by being obedient to His will, and we learn obedience to God through our human relationships.*

CHAPTER THIRTEEN

Divine and Human Relationship

*"For whosoever shall do the will of my Father which is in heaven,
the same is my brother, and sister, and mother"* (Matt. 12:50).

A little sad, was it not, that his mother and his brethren were not sitting about him? For, as another evangelist says, "he looked round on those that were about him." His disciples, who were learning of him, were nearest to him naturally, and his mother and his brethren were outside. They did not know him yet.

It takes a long time, and, what is more, a true heart, to know anybody. There are people that belong to the same family through the whole of a long life, and yet do not know each other to the very end. Do you remember they had set out to stop him? That is why they were outside; but for their stopping him they would have been at home. That lovely mother of his was not the first to understand him aright. Of course she understood him a good deal, and when the sword should have gone through her soul, she would understand him well. But there were other women, and they not so lovely as she, far less lovely in some ways, who understood him better, because the sword had passed through their souls, and they knew the evil thing which brought them to his feet. These were outside desiring to speak to him, because they said, "He is beside himself." He was going too far, and they must stop him.

It was the necessity of his relations to see that he did not play the part of a madman. There are tens of thousands of so-called Christian people who are quite capable of doing the same thing at the present day, simply because they have little more of Christ in or about them than the common name that is given freely enough now, and is easy enough to carry. Nay, more, there are tens of thousands of those who are honest towards Christ, but yet know so little of what was in him or what he meant to do, that they would stop him.

It is a sad thing, friends, for any of us to be called by his name, and not know him. It is the business of our human being to know Christ, and nothing else is our business. If it is true that we are made into the image of God, the sole, paramount, all-including and absorbing business of existence is to know that image of God in which we are made, to know it in the living Son of God—the one only ideal man. The nearer I come to the change, the more absolutely I am convinced of this, and I have no words strong enough to put the statement in. But alas, for most of us, we like to pare away the words of Christ instead of looking at them until they fill heaven and earth.

Christ's Mother and Brothers

Let us see what he meant in these lovely, awful, precious words. For the love of Christ is an awful thing. There is nothing in that which goes half way, or which makes exception. The Son of God loves so utterly that he will have his children clean, and if hurt and sorrow, pain and torture, will do to deliver any one of them from the horrible thing, from the death that he cherishes at the very root of his soul, the loving Christ, though it hurts him all the time, and though he feels every sting himself, will do it.

"Who are my mother and my brethren?" So he asks; and then he answers: "Whosoever does the will of my Father in heaven." You observe he is always talking about his Father in heaven. You would think he knew nothing else. He has but one word, as it seems, over and over again. It has been said that he was possessed with love for humanity, and that is true; but he was possessed before that, and as the beginning of that, with love to his Father in heaven. That was the root, the power, the energy of all that was manifest even in the eternal Son of God himself. It could not be otherwise. He was not to be misled with any outside shows of power and beauty. He knew the heart of them all, and that it was the living will of God, by which all things arose, subsisted, and went on growing and growing. The Father—the Father—the Father was all in all in the heart of the Son, and because the Father, therefore the children of the Father, all the men and women, savage and refined, throughout the universe.

And does it make us at all sorrowful that he said the words to his disciples, that he does not seem to include the rest of the company, and seems to exclude his mother and brethren? Is it a hard word, do you think? Oh, friends, the power of God himself can give you nothing worth having, but this that he would give, which the few about him had already taken, and which some of us have begun to take. Life is the only thing—life, that is the essential of well-being. It is because we are but half-alive now, half-created, you may say, and not

nearly that, that we are not blessed. We so often choose death, the thing that separates and kills, for everything that parts us from our fellow, and everything that parts us from God, is a killing of us.

Whosoever is wide and free, and will do the will of God—not understand it, not care about it, not theorize about it, but do it—is a son of God. It is in the act that man stands up as a son of God. He may be ever such a philosopher, ever such a theologian, ever such a patriot or benevolent man; but it is only he who, in the act, in the doing of the thing, stands up before God, that is a son of God. That is the divine dignity: "My Father worketh hitherto, and I work." It is he who works that is the son of God.

Do I mean outside works or inside works? I mean whatever a man does, whether it be the giving up all that he has to go and preach the gospel, or whether it be putting down the smallest rising thought of injustice, of anger and wrong, of selfishness in his soul. The act is where the will of man stands up against liking, against temptation, and leads him simply to do that which God would have him to do, easy or difficult; it may be to mount a throne, it may be to be sawn asunder. The man who does what God would have him do, what is he? "My brother," says Christ. The woman who does that? "My sister," says Christ. And as if he would go to the very depth of tenderness, he is not satisfied with saying "brother" or "sister." Woman, that has longed to have children and has none, did you ever think you might have a Son of God for your son? If you would be the "mother" of the Son of God, do the will of his Father, and yours and you will not mourn long.

Our Relationship to the Father

But was he putting away his mother? Was it an unkind, an unfilial thing to say? Did he, in saying, "Who is my mother, who is my brother?" repudiate the earthly mother and the earthly brother and sister? No, verily. But, friends, it is a profound, absolute fact that our relation to God is infinitely nearer than any relation by nature. Our mother does not make us; we come forth of her, but forth also of the very soul of God. We are nearer, unspeakably nearer, infinitely and unintelligibly (to our very poor intellects) nearer to God than to the best, loveliest, dearest mother on the face of the earth.

The Lord, first of all, only spake an absolute fact; but then he goes deeper and deeper still. This cannot be until the thing is known and acknowledged. But look: if a mother has two children, one of whom is as bad as a boy can be, and the other as good; the one is her child and the other is not her child; they are both born of her body, but the one that loves her and obeys her is born of her soul; yea, of her very spirit, and she says "This is my child," and she says to the other, with groans, "You are none of mine." And his being no child is the misery of the thing; she would die for the one who is no child, but for the one who is her child she would live forever.

And so when we become the sons and daughters of God indeed by saying, "Oh, my Father, I care for nothing but what thou carest for; I will not lament for this thing; because I see thou cost not care about it, I will not care either;" when you say, "This is sore to bear, but it is thy will, and therefore I thank thee for it, so sure am I of thy will, O my Father in heaven:" when we come to be able to talk like that, then we are in the same mind as Jesus Christ, whose delight, and whose only delight, was to do the will of his Father in heaven. But for God's sake, do not cling to your own poor will. It is not worth having. It is a poor, miserable, degrading thing to fall

down and worship the inclination of your own heart, which may have come from any devil, or from any accident of your birth, or from the weather, or from anything. Take the will of God, eternal, pure, strong, living, and true, the only good thing; take that, and Christ will be your brother. If we knew the glory of that, I believe we could even delight in going against the poor small things that we should like in ourselves, delight even in thwarting ourselves.

Our Relationship to Our Parents

To return to my subject. Was Christ refusing his mother? Was he saying, "I come of another breed, and I have nothing to do with you?" Was that the spirit of it? The Son of God forbid! Never, never! But I must show here a deeper and a better thing. It is of the wisdom and tenderness of God that we come into the world as we do, that we form families, little centres, and groups of spiritual nerves and power in the world. I do not see how in any other way we come to understand God.

And, oh! you parents, who make it impossible for your children to understand God, what shall be said of or for you? If we had not fathers and mothers to love, I do not know how our hearts would understand God at all. I know not how I ever should. Then, again, if we had no brothers and sisters to love, how ever should we begin to learn this essential thing, that we should love our neighbor—that is, every man who comes near us to be affected with look or word—as ourselves?

It were an impossibility. God begins with us graciously and easily. He brings us near, first, to mother, then to father, then to sister, then to brother—brings us so near to them that we cannot escape them. The months of infancy and the years of childhood are unspeakably precious from this fact, that we cannot escape the holy influences of family. So many are our needs, so quiescent are our needs, that love is, as it were, heaped upon us and forced into us: and we are taught—as we cannot help learning—to love.

Our Relationship with Others

But woe to the man or woman who stops there, and can only love because the child, or the sister, or the brother is his or hers! The same human soul, the same hungry human affection, the same aspiring, although blotted and spoiled, human spirit, is within every head, dwelling in every heart, and we are brothers and sisters wherever God has made man or woman; and until we have learned that, we are only going on, it may be a little, to learn Christ, but we have not yet learned him. What! Shall Christ love a man, and I not love him? Shall Christ say to a woman, "My sister," and I not bow before her! It is preposterous. But then my own mother, my own father, my own brothers and sisters—if they be his too, they come first, they come nearer.

But I do assert that there is a closer, infinitely closer, relation between any one that loves God and any other that loves God, than there is between any child and any mother where they do not both love him. The one has its root, the other has its leaves and flowers as well. We cannot love anybody too much; but we do not, we can never, love our own child aright until we have learned to love—not the mildness of the child—but the humanity of the child, the goodness, the thing that God meant, that came out of his will. That is the thing we have to love even in our children, or else the love is a poor dying thing, because we ourselves are dying. I am supposing that we do not possess the love of God, which is

the only eternal thing. But if we love God, dearer and dearer grow the faces of father and mother, wife and child, until there is no end to it. It goes on, not only eternally in time, but eternally in growth, expanding. We do not understand it, because we are no farther on.

Every bit we get farther, we understand more, and perceive more, and feel more; and the child of God is infinite, because he is a child of God. The child is like the Father. We have our share in God's infinitude, and therefore the Lord Christ himself called us "gods" when he quoted from the Psalms. Whoever can, let him understand the words, "I say, ye are gods." The children of God must be gods in some sense. Little gods, indeed, but what is their completion and salvation? "Ye shall sit down with me in my throne, even as I am set down with my Father in his throne." And brothers and sisters, I cannot conceive any other sufficing redemption than this, that we should be set down on the throne of the King of kings, with the Lord our Master, as he said. Do you call this presumption? I appeal to Christ, for he has spoken. I believe in nothing but Christ; and so I trust to believe everything that is true, to know it when I see it.

Claiming Christ

Are you lonely? Has lover or friend forsaken you? Has death taken father or mother, husband or wife, sister or brother from you? If you could see aright, that is a trifle; a profound trifle, though, for God's trifles are precious and great. Dear in the sight of God is the death of his saints. But it is a trifle. I will tell you what would be the terrible thing. Have you been false to them? Have you wronged them? Have you been such that there has been a separation, a tearing of your souls asunder? That is death, and the devil, and damnation.

Why is it death that we fear? He hath abolished death. He died and he was not dead; up he rose again radiant with light and victory. So are they all who believe in him; for he said, "He that liveth and believeth in me shall never die." You may defy death. Only have the "patience of Christ;" there is given us that phrase; wait in his name and you shall have all you want. For when Christ has had his way with you, you would as soon ask for anything that he did not like as you would beg of God to destroy the universe he had created. There would be nothing to you desirable that is not desirable in his eyes.

Think of this: that you can have One who is more than brother or sister, father or mother, husband or wife, or child,—One from whose heart all these flowed out—One from whom came the love that analyzed itself into these forms because of its infinitude. You can have him for your own friend, for brother, sister, mother, son. Whatever relation is possible in humanity, that relation does the heart of Christ feel to every one that can take it.

Do you want, therefore, to forget, and take Christ as a make-up for the others that are gone? Never! never! That is not his way. For how constantly does he tell you to love one another? That is the glory of Christ's teaching; that is his gospel; there is not an atom of selfishness in God or in Christ, for he delights to see us loving one another. He cannot be satisfied except by seeing us love each other perfectly—that is his delight. Nay, more than this, I repeat, we cannot love one of our own aright unless Christ is

in us making us love that person to the idea of that relationship. Never father loved child, never child loved father, to the idea of fatherhood and childhood, unless Christ was not only born in him but had grown up in him; and in none has he grown to that degree that he understands thoroughly, feels thoroughly, believes thoroughly—or anything like thoroughly—any relation in life, so far as I know.

Do not take from the glory of the words of Christ; do not be afraid to claim from him what he gives you, and would have you take. Claim him, man, woman, boy, girl, claim him as your own; for without him you are as nothing. Claim him, by taking the will of God for your one care, your one object, your one desire; and Christ will be yours altogether. "Behold I stand at the door, and knock: if any man hear my voice, and open the door I will come in to him, and will sup with him, and he with me."

Partaking of the same food together—that food being the very will of God: "it is my meat and drink to do thy will:" that is the very food concerning which our Lord says: "man shall not live by bread alone, but by every word that proceedeth out of the mouth of God." That is the will of God; it is the very food and drink of the true heart; and when Jesus and the man who has opened to him the door sit down together, it is to share together in the understanding of the will of the Father of both—that Father to whom he went when he said: "Go to my brethren, and say unto them, I ascend unto my Father, and your Father; and to my God and your God."

FOR ADDITIONAL INFORMATION

Docherty, John. *Literary Products of the Lewis Carroll—George MacDonald Friendship, The*. Lewiston, New York, E. Mellen Pub., 1995.

Reid, Gordon, ed. *The Wind from the Stars by George MacDonald*. London, Harper Collins, 1992.

Hein, Rolland. *George MacDonald: Victorian Mythmaker*. Mountain View, California, Starsong, 1993.

MacDonald, George. *Alec Forbes of Howglen*. New York, Garland Pub., 1975.

———. *At the Back of the North Wind*. London: Blackie & Son, 1920.

———. *Creation in Christ*. Wheaton, Illinois, H. Shaw, 1976.

———. *David Elginbrod*. New York, Garland Pub., 1975

———. *Expression of Characters, An—the Letters of George MacDonald*. Grand Rapids, W. B. Eerdmans, Pub., 1994.

———. *Heart of George MacDonald, A One-Volume Collection of His Most Important Fiction, Essays, Sermons, Drama, Poetry, and Letters, The*. Wheaton Library Services, Shaw Publishers, 1994.

Raeper, William. *George MacDonald*. Batavia, Illinois, Lion Publishing, 1987.

Sadler, Glenn Edward, ed. *An Expression of Character: The Letters of George MacDonald*. Grand Rapids, Michigan, Eerdmans Publishing Co., 1994.

Saintsbury, Elizabeth. *George MacDonald, A Short Life*. Edinburgh, Scotland, Canongate, 1987.

ANDREW MURRAY

Andrew Murray

Edited by Charles Erlandson

Contents

ANDREW MURRAY 1828–1917

HIS LIFE	1828–1855	WORLD EVENTS
Born in Graaff Reinet, South Africa, where father was pastor.	1828	Authors Tolstoi, Ibsen, and Jules Verne born.
Andrew and brother, John, sent to school in Scotland; 1840 letter home talks about revivals.	1838	Great Spiritual Awakening in Scotland.
Both brothers graduate from Aberdeen University with M.A. degrees.	1845	First Monday in November established as the day for Presidential elections.
Continued education in Utrecht, Holland; Andrew "born again," November 14, 1845; established Netherlands Christian Students' Association; brothers ordained 1848 at the Hague; returned to South Africa.	1845–1848	First known baseball game is played in Hoboken, New Jersey in 1846; Mexican-American War continues.
Andrew appointed to Bloemfontein in New Orange River Sovereignty.	1848	Gold discovered in California at Sutter's sawmill.
Preached during vacations in Transvaal, contracted Yellow Fever, near death for six weeks, 1849.	1849–1852	Longest suspension bridge in the world opens across the Ohio River, 1849.
Traveled to London to appeal to Privy Council regarding Britain withdrawing from the Sovereignty; sought medical help and doctor's report resulted in a year's stay in Europe; recruited ministers, teachers and professors for South Africa.	1853–1854	The Coinage Act allows minting of $3 gold pieces, 1853; after two years in isolation, Thoreau publishes Walden, 1854.
Married Miss Rutherford of Cape Town; returned to Bloemfontein.	1855	Livingstone discovers Victoria Falls of Zambezi River.

WORLD EVENTS	1857–1872	HIS LIFE
The slavery issue divides the Presbyterian Church.	1857	Attended Synod in Cape Town; first-born daughter introduced to grandparents.
Phillip Schaff begins publishing *History of the Christian Church*.	1858–1859	Opened Grey College as rector; publishes *Jesus the Children's Friend*.
Pony Express begins operation—from Missouri to California in 10 days.	1860	Pastor at Worcester; Dutch Reformed Conference held at Worcester.
Dunant proposes an international relief organization, the Red Cross.	1862	Elected Moderator of the Synod.
Tolstoi's *War and Peace* published 1864–1869.	1864	Wrote *What Manner of Child Shall This Be?* Called to church in Cape Town as assistant pastor; established Young Men's Christian Association.
Reconstruction of the Union begins; senate overrides Civil Rights bill veto by President Johnson; the National Labor Union is organized, seeking an "Eight Hour System."	1866	Addresses at Bath Conference published in *Evangelical Christendom*; preached to 200 thieves before Christmas dinner; father, Andrew, Sr., died; brother, Charles, becomes pastor at Graaff Reinet.
Russia sells Alaska to the U.S. for $7,200,000.	1867	Returned to Cape Town; published thirteen lectures, *Modern Unbelief*.
Rockefeller founds Standard Oil Company.	1870	Published *Have Mercy on Me*, dedicated to Cape Town congregation.
P. T. Barnum opens "Great Travelling Museum, Menagerie, Caravan and Hippodrome," 1871.	1871–1906	Accepted call to church in Wellington, village of 4,000.
Yellowstone National Park is established.	1872	Youngest child, daughter, died at 2½ years of age.

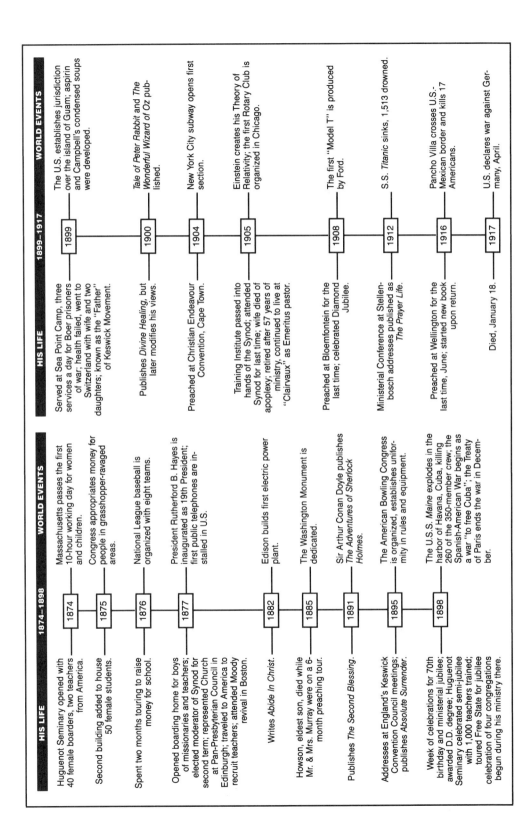

1874–1898

Year	HIS LIFE	WORLD EVENTS
1874	Huguenot Seminary opened with 40 female boarders, two teachers from America.	Massachusetts passes the first 10-hour working day for women and children.
1875	Second building added to house 50 female students.	Congress appropriates money for people in grasshopper-ravaged areas.
1876	Spent two months touring to raise money for school.	National League baseball is organized with eight teams.
1877	Opened boarding home for boys of missionaries and teachers; elected moderator of Synod for second term; represented Church at Pan-Presbyterian Council in Edinburgh; traveled to America to recruit teachers; attended Moody revival in Boston.	President Rutherford B. Hayes is inaugurated as 19th President; first public telephones are installed in U.S.
1882	Writes *Abide In Christ*.	Edison builds first electric power plant.
1885	Howson, eldest son, died while Mr. & Mrs. Murray were on a 6-month preaching tour.	The Washington Monument is dedicated.
1891	Publishes *The Second Blessing*.	Sir Arthur Conan Doyle publishes *The Adventures of Sherlock Holmes.*
1895	Addresses at England's Keswick Convention Council meetings; publishes *Absolute Surrender*.	The American Bowling Congress is organized, establishes uniformity in rules and equipment.
1898	Week of celebrations for 70th birthday and ministerial jubilee; awarded D.D. degree; Huguenot Seminary celebrated semi-jubilee with 1,000 teachers trained; toured Free State for jubilee celebration of four congregations begun during his ministry there.	The U.S.S. *Maine* explodes in the harbor of Havana, Cuba, killing 260 of the 350-member crew; the Spanish-American War begins as a war "to free Cuba"; the Treaty of Paris ends the war in December.

1899–1917

Year	HIS LIFE	WORLD EVENTS
1899	Served at Sea Point Camp, three services a day for Boer prisoners of war; health failed, went to Switzerland with wife and two daughters; known as the "Father" of Keswick Movement.	The U.S. establishes jurisdiction over the island of Guam; aspirin and Campbell's condensed soups were developed.
1900	Publishes *Divine Healing*, but later modifies his views.	*Tale of Peter Rabbit* and *The Wonderful Wizard of Oz* published.
1904	Preached at Christian Endeavour Convention, Cape Town.	New York City subway opens first section.
1905	Training Institute passed into hands of the Synod; attended Synod for last time; wife died of apoplexy; retired after 57 years of ministry, continued to live at "Clairvaux" as Emeritus pastor.	Einstein creates his Theory of Relativity; the first Rotary Club is organized in Chicago.
1908	Preached at Bloemfontein for the last time; celebrated Diamond Jubilee.	The first "Model T" is produced by Ford.
1912	Ministerial Conference at Stellenbosch addresses published as *The Prayer Life.*	S.S. *Titanic* sinks, 1,513 drowned.
1916	Preached at Wellington for the last time, June; started new book upon return.	Pancho Villa crosses U.S.-Mexican border and kills 17 Americans.
1917	Died, January 18.	U.S. declares war against Germany, April.

ANDREW MURRAY

Introduction

Andrew Murray, the son of a minister, was born May 9, 1828, at Graaff Reinet in South Africa. He was sent to Scotland early in his life to study theology and received his degree at the age of seventeen. Ordained in 1848, he served in the ministry from 1850 until 1906. For a time he was the only minister in what later became the Orange Free State.

Murray was very concerned with the work of the Holy Spirit and placed a great emphasis on personal piety, particularly prayer. He was a leader in the holiness movement in South Africa and is often considered a precursor of the Pentecostal movement. Although Murray had mystical inclinations, he never allowed his mystical, pietistic spirit to become a pretext for inactivity.

On the contrary, Murray was led to initiate many organizations and movements. A partial list of the movements he organized includes the Mission Institute (1877), the Bible and Prayer Union (1883), the Minister's Missionary Union (1886), and the Prayer Union (1904). Murray also helped establish the Huguenot Seminary, undertook seven evangelization tours, co-founded a series of holiness conventions, and was the moving force behind the Student Volunteer Movement in South Africa.

Murray's opposition to the liberal tendencies of some leaders in the Dutch Reformed Church led him to write a series of works which launched his long and prolific vocation as an author. Before his death on January 18, 1917, 250 of his works had been published and had found enthusiastic audiences in the United States and England. *Abide in Christ,* Murray's most popular work, was published in many languages and continues to sell well today.

Although Andrew Murray's 250 written works deal with a variety of topics, there are several interrelated themes which he loved to discuss. Many of his works, for example *The Spirit of Christ,* deal with the work of the Holy Spirit. This emphasis on the Holy Spirit led Murray to be extremely concerned about the personal holiness and piety of the individual believer. Works such as *Like Christ* and *Abide in Christ,* Murray's most popular work, reflect this emphasis. Such a concern for piety can sometimes lead to an exaggerated account of man's abilities and his role in sanctification. But Murray, a member of the Calvinistic Dutch Reformed Church, also loved the theme of "absolute surrender," which is the title of one of his volumes.

Murray's concern for personal piety is also found in his great belief in the power of prayer. In books like *With Christ in the School of Prayer* and *The Prayer Life,* prayer is Murray's exclusive focus, but in nearly all of his works there is a presentation of the necessity of prayer and a plea for more of it. Murray insisted, for example, that it is only through prayer that the call to evangelize the nations could be effectively answered, a theme found in works such as *The Key to the Missionary Problem* and *The State of the Church.*

Andrew Murray never acquired an attractive prose style. His work does not rely on elegant diction to convey his point; he was more concerned with the content of his writing. He acknowledged this but wrote in the hopes that "the call to repentance and prayer and a new consecration" may "reach many hearts."

"Abide in me" was Christ's command when about to leave for heaven. From these words comes the title of Murray's most famous work, *Abide in Christ*, first published in 1882 and reprinted many times since then.

"Abide in Christ," Murray exhorts, "All You Who Have Come to Him," which is the title of the first chapter in *Abide in Christ*. In this selection Murray reminds believers that Christ not only calls us by saying "Come to me," but also by saying *"Abide* in me."

We are to abide in Christ because "God Himself Has United You to Him." A true understanding of how we are united to Christ as a branch is united to the vine gives us a great assurance as we trust in Christ who is working through us.

Christ also asks us to abide in Him "Day by Day." By using the example of God's provision of manna for the Israelites, Murray conveys his message in this chapter that "faithfully to fill the present is your only security for the future."

"In Affliction and Trial" we are also to abide in Christ, for this is the Father's object in sending trials. In affliction and trial, as Murray says, "we shall learn to choose abiding in Him as our only portion."

When we abide in Christ we should abide in Him "As Christ in the Father." The origin, mode, and glory of Christ's abiding in the Father, characterized by unity in love and life, should also be ours in our abiding in Christ.

Abiding in Christ means that the believer lives in Christ "And Not in Self." To abide in Christ means, ultimately, that our old selves must die and that it is no longer we who live but Christ in us.

CHAPTER ONE

All You Who Have Come to Him

"Come unto me" (Matt. 11:28).
"Abide in me" (John 15:4).

Come Unto Me

It is to you who have heard and hearkened to the call, *"Come unto me,"* that this new invitation comes, "Abide in me." The message comes from the same loving Savior. You doubtless have never repented having come at His call. You experienced that His word was truth; all His promises He fulfilled; He made you partakers of the blessings and the joy of His love. Was not His welcome most hearty, His pardon full and free, His love most sweet and precious? You more than once, at your first coming to Him, had reason to say, "The half was not told me."

And yet you have had to complain of disappointment: as time went on, your expectations were not realized. The blessings you once enjoyed were lost; the love and joy of your first meeting with your Savior, instead of deepening, have become faint and feeble. And often you have wondered what the reason could be, that with such a Savior, so mighty and so loving, your experience of salvation should not have been a fuller one.

The answer is very simple. You wandered from Him. The blessings He bestows are all connected with His "Come to ME," and are only to be enjoyed in close fellowship with Himself. You either did not fully understand, or did not rightly remember, that the call meant, "Come *to me* to stay with *me*." And yet this was in very deed His object and purpose when first He called you to Himself. It was not to refresh you for a few short hours after your conversion with the joy of His love and deliverance, and then to send you forth to wander in sadness and sin. He had destined you to something better than a short-lived blessedness, to be enjoyed only in times of special earnestness and prayer, and then to pass away, as you had to return to those duties in which far the greater part of life has to be spent.

No, indeed; He had prepared for you an abiding dwelling with Himself, where your whole life and every moment of it might be spent, where the work of your daily life might be done, and where all the while you might be enjoying unbroken communion with Himself. It was even this He meant when to that first word, *"Come to me,"* He added this, *"Abide in me."* As earnest and faithful, as loving and tender, as the compassion that breathed in that blessed *"Come,"* was the grace that added this no less blessed *"Abide."* As mighty as the attraction with which that first word drew you, were the bonds with which this second, had you but listened to it, would have kept you. And as great as were the blessings with which that coming was rewarded, so large, yea, and much greater, were the treasures to which that abiding would have given you access.

Abide in Me

And observe especially, it was not that He said, "Come to me and abide with me," but, "*Abide in me.*" The intercourse was not only to be unbroken, but most intimate and complete. He opened His arms, to press you to His bosom; He opened His heart, to welcome you there; He opened up all His divine fullness of life and love, and offered to take you up into its fellowship, to make you wholly one with Himself. There was a depth of meaning you cannot yet realize in His words: "Abide IN ME."

And with no less earnestness than He had cried, "Come to me," did He plead, had you but noticed it, "*Abide in me.*" By every motive that had induced you to come, did He beseech you to abide. Was it the fear of sin and its curse that first drew you? the pardon you received on first coming could, with all the blessings flowing from it, only be confirmed and fully enjoyed on abiding in Him. Was it the longing to know and enjoy the infinite love that was calling you? the first coming gave but single drops to taste—'tis only the abiding that can really satisfy the thirsty soul, and give to drink of the rivers of pleasure that are at His right hand. Was it the weary longing to be made free from the bondage of sin, to become pure and holy, and so to find rest, the rest of God for the soul? this too can only be realized as you abide in Him—only abiding in Jesus gives rest in Him. Or if it was the hope of an inheritance in glory, and an everlasting home in the presence of the Infinite One: the true preparation for this, as well as its blessed foretaste in this life, are granted only to those who abide in Him.

In very truth, there is nothing that moved you to come, that does not plead with thousandfold greater force: "Abide in Him." You did well to come; you do

better to abide. Who would, after seeking the King's palace, be content to stand in the door, when he is invited in to dwell in the King's presence, and share with Him in all the glory of His royal life? Oh, let us enter in and abide, and enjoy to the full all the rich supply His wondrous love hath prepared for us!

And yet I fear that there are many who have indeed come to Jesus, and who yet have mournfully to confess that they know but little of this blessed abiding in Him. With some the reason is, that they never fully understood that this was the meaning of the Savior's call. With others, that though they heard the word, they did not know that such a life of abiding fellowship was possible, and indeed within their reach. Others will say that, though they did believe that such a life was possible, and seek after it, they have never yet succeeded in discovering the secret of its attainment. And others, again, alas! will confess that it is their own unfaithfulness that has kept them from the enjoyment of the blessing. When the Savior would have kept them, they were not found ready to stay; they were not prepared to give up everything, and always, only, wholly to abide in Jesus.

To all such I come now in the name of Jesus, their Redeemer and mine, with the blessed message: "*Abide in me.*" In His name I invite them to come, and for a season meditate with me daily on its meaning, its lessons, its claims, and its promises. I know how many, and, to the young believer, how difficult, the questions are which suggest themselves in connection with it. There is especially the question, with its various aspects, as to the possibility, in the midst of wearying work and continual distraction, of keeping up, or rather being kept in, the abiding communion.

I do not undertake to remove all difficulties; this Jesus Christ Himself alone must do by His Holy Spirit. But what I would fain by the grace of God be permitted to do is, to repeat day by day the Master's blessed command, "Abide in me," until it enter the heart and find a place there, no more to be forgotten or neglected. I would fain that in the light of Holy Scripture we should meditate on its meaning, until the understanding, that gate to the heart, opens to apprehend something of what it offers and expects. So we shall discover the means of its attainment, and learn to know what keeps us from it, and what can help us to it. So we shall feel its claims, and be compelled to acknowledge that there can be no true allegiance to our King without simply and heartily accepting this one, too, of His commands. So we shall gaze on its blessedness, until desire be inflamed, and the will with all its energies be roused to claim and possess the unspeakable blessing.

Come, my brethren, and let us day by day set ourselves at His feet, and meditate on this word of His, with an eye fixed on Him alone. Let us set ourselves in quiet trust before Him, waiting to hear His holy voice—the still small voice that is mightier than the storm that rends the rocks—breathing its quickening spirit within us, as He speaks: "Abide in me." The soul that truly hears *Jesus Himself speak the word,* receives with the word the power to accept and to hold the blessing He offers.

And it may please Thee, blessed Savior, indeed, to speak to us; let each of us hear Thy blessed voice. May the feeling of our deep need, and the faith of Thy wondrous love, combined with the sight of the wonderfully blessed life Thou art waiting to bestow upon us, constrain us to listen and to obey, as often as Thou speakest: "Abide in me." Let day by day the answer from our heart be clearer and fuller: "Blessed Savior, I do abide in Thee."

CHAPTER TWO

God Himself Has United You to Him

Of God are ye in Christ Jesus, who was made unto us wisdom from God, both righteousness and sanctification, and redemption (1 Cor. 1:30 RV *marg.*).
"My Father is the husbandman" (John 15:1).

"Ye are in Christ Jesus." The believers at Corinth were still feeble and carnal, only babes in Christ. And yet Paul wants them, at the outset of his teaching, to know distinctly that they are in Christ Jesus. The whole Christian life depends on the clear consciousness of our position in Christ. Most essential to the abiding in Christ is the daily renewal of our faith's assurance, "I am in Christ Jesus." All fruitful preaching to believers must take this as its starting-point: "Ye are in Christ Jesus."

Of God in Christ

But the apostle has an additional thought, of almost greater importance: "OF GOD are ye in Christ Jesus." He would have us not only remember our union to Christ, but specially that it is not our own doing, but the work of God Himself. As the Holy Spirit teaches us to realize this, we shall see what a source of assurance and strength it must become to us. If it is of God alone that I am in Christ, then God Himself, the Infinite One, becomes my security from all I can need or wish in seeking to abide in Christ.

Let me try to understand what it means, this wonderful, "OF GOD in Christ." In becoming partakers of the union with Christ, there is a work God does and a work we have to do. God does His work by moving us to do our work.

The work of God is hidden and silent; what we do is something distinct and tangible. Conversion and faith, prayer and obedience, are conscious acts of which we can give a clear account; while the spiritual quickening and strengthening that come from above are secret and beyond the reach of human sight. And so it comes that when the believer tries to say, "I am in Christ Jesus," he looks more to the work he did, than to that wondrous secret work of God by which he was united to Christ. Nor can it well be otherwise at the commencement of the Christian course. "I know that I have believed," is a valid testimony.

But it is of great consequence that the mind should be led to see that at the back of our turning, and believing, and accepting of Christ, there was God's almighty power doing its work—inspiring our will, taking possession of us, and carrying out its own purpose of love in planting us into Christ Jesus. As the believer enters into this, the divine side of the work of salvation, he will learn to praise and to worship with new exultation, and to rejoice more than ever in the divineness of that salvation he has been made partaker of. At each step he reviews, the song will come, "This is the Lord's doing"—divine omnipotence working out what eternal love had devised. "OF GOD I am in Christ Jesus."

The words will lead him even further and higher, even to the depths of eternity. "Whom He hath predestinated, *them* He also called." The calling in time is the manifestation of the purpose in eternity. Ere the world was, God had fixed the eye of His sovereign love on you in the election of grace, and chosen you in Christ. That you know yourself to be in Christ, is the stepping-stone by which you rise to understand in its full meaning the word, "OF GOD I am in Christ Jesus." With the prophet, your language will be, "The Lord hath appeared of old unto me: yea, I have loved thee with an everlasting love, therefore with loving-kindness have I drawn thee."

And you will recognize your own salvation as a part of that "mystery of His will, according to the good pleasure of His will which He purposed in Himself," and join with the whole body of believers in Christ as these say, "In whom we also have obtained an inheritance, being predestinated according to the purpose of Him who worketh all things after the counsel of His own will." Nothing will more exalt free grace, and make man bow very low before it, than this knowledge of the mystery "OF GOD in Christ."

Knowledge of God in Christ Produces Faith

It is easy to see what a mighty influence it must exert on the believer who seeks to abide in Christ. What a sure standing-ground it gives him, as he rests his right to Christ and all His fullness on nothing less than the Father's own purpose and work! We have thought of Christ as the Vine, and the believer as the branch; let us not forget that other precious word, "My Father is the husbandman." The Savior said, "Every plant which my heavenly Father hath not planted, shall be rooted up"; but every branch grafted by Him in the True Vine, shall never be plucked out of His hand. As it was the Father to whom

Christ owed all He was, and in whom He had all His strength and His life as the Vine, so to the Father the believer owes his place and his security in Christ. The same love and delight with which the Father watched over the beloved Son Himself, watch over every member of His body, every one who is in Christ Jesus.

What confident trust this faith inspires—not only as to the being kept in safety to the end, but specially as to the being able to fulfil in every point the object for which I have been united to Christ. The branch is as much in the charge and keeping of the husbandman as the vine; his honor as much concerned in the well-being and growth of the branch as of the vine. The God who chose Christ to be Vine fitted Him thoroughly for the work He had as Vine to perform; The God who has chosen me and planted me in Christ, has thereby engaged to secure, if I will but let Him, by yielding myself to Him, that I in every way be worthy of Jesus Christ.

Oh that I did but fully realize this! What confidence and urgency it would give to my prayer to the God and Father of Jesus Christ! How it would quicken the sense of dependence, and make me see that praying without ceasing is indeed the one need of my life—an unceasing waiting, moment by moment, on the God who has united me to Christ, to perfect His own divine work, to work in me both to will and to do of His good pleasure.

And what a motive this would be for the highest activity in the maintenance of a fruitful branch-life! Motives are mighty powers; it is of infinite importance to have them high and clear. Here surely is the highest: "You are God's workmanship, created in Christ Jesus unto good works": grafted by Him into Christ, unto the bringing forth of much fruit. Whatever God creates is exquisitely suited to its end. He created the sun to give light: how perfectly it does its work! He created the eye to see: how beautifully it fulfils its object! He created the new man unto good works: how admirably it is fitted for its purpose.

OF GOD I am in Christ: created anew, made a branch of the Vine, fitted for fruit-bearing. Would to God that believers would cease looking most at their old nature, and complaining of their weakness, as if God called them to what they were unfitted for! Would that they would believingly and joyfully accept the wondrous revelation of how God, in uniting them to Christ, has made Himself chargeable for their spiritual growth and fruitfulness! How all sickly hesitancy and sloth would disappear, and under the influence of this mighty motive—the faith in the faithfulness of Him of whom they are in Christ—their whole nature would rise to accept and fulfil their glorious destiny!

O my soul! yield yourself to the mighty influence of this word: "OF GOD ye are in Christ Jesus." It is the same GOD OF WHOM Christ is made all that He is for us, OF WHOM we also are in Christ, and will most surely be made what we must be to Him. Take time to meditate and to worship, until the light that comes from the throne of God has shone into you, and you have seen your union to Christ as indeed the work of His almighty Father. Take time, day after day, and let, in your whole religious life, with all it has of claims and duties, of needs and wishes, God be everything.

See Jesus, as He speaks to you, "Abide in me," pointing upward and saying, "MY FATHER IS THE HUSBANDMAN. *Of Him* you are in me, *through Him* you abide in me, and *to Him* and to His glory shall be the fruit you bear." And let your answer be, Amen, Lord! So be it. From eternity Christ and I were ordained for each other; inseparably we belong to each other: it is God's will; I shall abide in Christ. It is of God I am in Christ Jesus.

CHAPTER THREE

Day by Day

And the people shall go out and gather the portion of a day in his day (Ex. 16:4 *marg.*).

The Day's Portion in its Day

Such was the rule for God's giving and man's working in the ingathering of the manna. It is still the law in all the dealings of God's grace with His children. A clear insight into the beauty and application of this arrangement is a wonderful help in understanding how one, who feels himself utterly weak, can have the confidence and the perseverance to hold on brightly through all the years of his earthly course. A doctor was once asked by a patient who had met with a serious accident: "Doctor, how long shall I have to lie here?" The answer, "Only a day at a time," taught the patient a precious lesson. It was the same lesson God had recorded for His people of all ages long before: The day's portion in its day.

It was, without doubt, with a view to this and to meet man's weakness, that God graciously appointed the change of day and night. If time had been given to man in the form of one long unbroken day, it would have exhausted and overwhelmed him; the change of day and night continually recruits and recreates his powers. As a child, who easily makes himself master of a book, when each day only the lesson for the day is given him, would be utterly hopeless if the whole book were given him at once; so it would be with man, if there were no divisions in time. Broken small and divided into fragments, he can bear them; only the care and the work of each day have to be undertaken—the day's portion in its day. The rest of the night fits him for making a fresh start with each new morning; the mistakes of the past can be avoided, its lessons improved. And he has only each day to be faithful for the one short day, and long years and a long life take care of themselves, without the sense of their length or their weight ever being a burden.

Most sweet is the encouragement to be derived from this truth in the life of grace. Many a soul is disquieted with the thought as to how it will be able to gather and to keep the manna needed for all its years of travel through such a barren wilderness. It has never learnt what unspeakable comfort there is in the word: The day's portion for its day. That word takes away all care for the morrow most completely. Only today is yours; tomorrow is the Father's.

The question: What security have you that during all the years in which you have to contend with the coldness, or temptations, or trials of the world, you will always abide in Jesus? is one you need, yea, you may not ask. Manna, as your food and strength, is given only by the day; faithfully to fill the present is your only security for the future. Accept, and enjoy, and fulfil with your whole heart the part you have this day to perform. His presence and grace enjoyed today will remove all doubt whether you can entrust the morrow to Him too.

How great the value which this truth teaches us to attach to each single day! We are so easily led to look at life as a great whole, and to neglect the little today, to forget that the single days do indeed make up the whole, and that the value of each single day depends on its influence on the whole. One day lost is a link broken in the chain, which it often takes more than another day to mend. One day lost influences the next, and makes its keeping more difficult. Yea, one day lost may be the loss of what months or years of careful labour had secured. This experience of many a believer could confirm this.

Abiding Day by Day

Believer! would you abide in Jesus, let it be day by day. You have already heard the message: Moment by moment; the lesson of day by day has something more to teach. Of the moments there are many where there is no direct exercise of the mind on your part; the abiding is in the deeper recesses of the heart, kept by the Father, to whom you entrusted yourself. But just this is the work that with each new day has to be renewed for the day—the distinct renewal of surrender and trust for the life of moment by moment.

God has gathered up the moments and bound them up into a bundle, for the very purpose that we might take measure of them. As we look forward in the morning, or look back in the evening, and weigh the moments, we learn how to value and how to use them rightly. And even as the Father, with each new morning, meets you with the promise of just sufficient manna for the day for yourself and those who have to partake with you, meet Him with the bright and loving renewal of your accep-

tance of the position He has given you in His beloved Son.

Accustom yourself to look upon this as one of the reasons for the appointment of day and night. God thought of our weakness, and sought to provide for it. Let each day have its value from your calling to abide in Christ. As its light opens on your waking eyes, accept it on these terms: A day, just one day only, but still a day, given to abide and grow up in Jesus Christ. Whether it be a day of health or sickness, joy or sorrow, rest or work, of struggle or victory, let the chief thought with which you receive it in the morning thanksgiving be this: "A day that the Father gave; in it I may, I must become more closely united to Jesus." As the Father asks, "Can you trust me just for this one day to keep you abiding in Jesus, and Jesus to keep you fruitful?" you cannot but give the joyful response: "I will trust and not be afraid."

The day's portion for its day was given to Israel in the morning very early. The portion was for use and nourishment during the whole day, but the giving and the getting of it was the morning's work. This suggests how greatly the power to spend a day aright, to abide all the day in Jesus, depends on the morning hour. If the firstfruits be holy, the lump is holy. During the day there come hours of intense occupation in the rush of business or the throng of men, when only the Father's keeping can maintain the connection with Jesus unbroken. The morning manna fed all the day; it is only when the believer in the morning secures his quiet time in secret to renew distinctly and effectually loving fellowship with his Savior, that the abiding can be kept up all the day.

But what cause for thanksgiving that it may be done! In the morning, with its freshness and quiet, the believer can look out upon the day. He can consider its duties and its temptations, and pass them through beforehand, as it were, with his Savior, throwing all upon Him who has undertaken to be everything to him. Christ is his manna, his nourishment, his strength, his life: he can take the day's portion for the day, Christ as his for all the needs the day may bring, and go on in the assurance that the day will be one of blessing and of growth.

And then, as the lesson of the value and the work of the single day is being taken to heart, the learner is all unconsciously being led on to get the secret of "day by day continually" (Ex. 29:38). The blessed abiding grasped by faith for each day apart is an unceasing and ever-increasing growth. Each day of faithfulness brings a blessing for the next; makes both the trust and the surrender easier and more blessed.

And so the Christian life grows: as we give our whole heart to the work of each day, it becomes all the day, and from that every day. And so each day separately, all the day continually, day by day successively, we abide in Jesus. And the days make up the life: what once appeared too high and too great to attain, is given to the soul that was content to take and use "every day his portion" (Ezra 3:4), "as the duty of every day required." Even here on earth the voice is heard: "Well done, good and faithful servant, thou hast been faithful over few, I will make thee ruler over many: enter thou into the joy of thy Lord."

Our daily life becomes a wonderful interchange of God's daily grace and our daily praise: "Daily He loadeth us with His benefits"; "that I may daily perform my vows." We learn to understand God's reason for daily giving, as He most certainly gives, only enough, but also fully enough, for each day. And we get into His way, the way of daily asking and expecting only enough, but most certainly fully enough, for the day. We begin to number our days not from the sun's rising over the world, or by the work we do or the food we eat, but the daily renewal of the miracle of the manna—the blessedness of daily fellowship with Him who is the Life and the Light of the world. The heavenly life is as unbroken and continuous as the earthly; the abiding in Christ each day has for that day brought its blessing; we abide in Him every day, and all the day. Lord, make this the portion of each one of us.

CHAPTER FOUR

In Affliction and Trial

"Every branch that beareth fruit, he purgeth it, that it may bring forth more fruit" (John 15:2).

In the whole plant world there is not a tree to be found so specially suited to the image of man in his relation to God, as the vine. There is none of which the fruit and its juice are so full of spirit, so quickening and stimulating. But there is also none of which the natural tendency is so entirely evil—none where the growth is so ready to run into wood that is utterly worthless except for the fire. Of all plants, not one needs the pruning knife so unsparingly and so unceasingly. None is so dependent on cultivation and training, but with this none yields a richer reward to the husbandman.

In His wonderful parable, the Savior, with a single word, refers to this need of pruning in the vine, and the blessing it brings. But from that single word what streams of light pour in upon this dark world, so full of suffering and of sorrow to believers! What treasures of teaching and comfort to the bleeding branch in its hour of trial: "Every branch that beareth fruit, *He purgeth it*, that it may bring forth more fruit." And so He has prepared His people, who are so ready when trial comes to be shaken in their confidence, and to be moved from their abiding in Christ, to hear in each affliction the voice of a messenger that comes to call them to abide still more closely. Yes, believer, most specially in times of trial, abide in Christ.

God's Object in Sending Trials

Abide in Christ! This is indeed *the Father's object* in sending the trial. In the storm the tree strikes deeper roots in the soil; in the hurricane the inhabitants of the house abide within, and rejoice in its shelter. So by suffering the Father would lead us to enter more deeply into the love of Christ. Our hearts are continually prone to wander from Him; prosperity and enjoyment all too easily satisfy us, dull our spiritual perception, and unfit us for full communion with Himself.

It is an unspeakable mercy that the Father comes with His chastisement, makes the world round us all dark and unattractive, leads us to feel more deeply our sinfulness, and for a time lose our joy in what was becoming so dangerous. He does it in the hope that, when we have found our rest in Christ in time of trouble, we shall learn to choose abiding in Him as our only portion; and when the affliction is removed, have so grown more firmly into Him, that in prosperity He still shall be our only joy. So much has He set His heart on this, that though He has indeed no pleasure in afflicting us, He will not keep back even the most painful chastisement if He can but thereby guide His beloved child to come home and abide in the beloved Son. Christian! pray for grace to see in every trouble, small or great, the Father's finger pointing to Jesus, and saying, Abide in Him.

Partakers in God's Blessings

Abide in Christ: so will you become *partaker of all the rich blessings God designed for you* in the affliction. The purposes of God's wisdom will become clear to you, your assurance of the unchangeable love become stronger, and the power of His Spirit fulfil you the promise: "He chasteneth us for our profit, that we might be partakers of His holiness."

Abide in Christ: and your cross becomes the means of fellowship with His cross, and access into its mysteries—the mystery of the curse which He bore for you, of the death to sin in which you partake with Him, of the love in which, as sympathizing High Priest, He descended into all your sorrows.

Abide in Christ: growing in conformity to your blessed Lord in His sufferings, deeper experience of the reality and the tenderness of His love will be yours.

Abide in Christ: in the fiery oven, one like the Son of Man will be seen as never before; the purging away of the dross and the refining of the gold will be accomplished, and Christ's own likeness reflected in you.

O abide in Christ: the power of the flesh will be mortified, the impatience and self-will of the old nature be humbled, to make place for the meekness and gentleness of Christ. A believer may pass through much affliction, and yet secure but little blessing from it all. Abiding in Christ is the secret of securing all that the Father meant the chastisement to bring us.

Consolation in Christ

Abide in Christ: in Him you shall find *sure and abundant consolation*. With the afflicted comfort is often first, and the profit of the affliction second. The Father loves us so, that with Him our real and abiding profit is His first object, but He does not forget to comfort too. When He comforts it is that He may turn the bleeding heart to Himself to receive the blessing in fellowship with Him; when He refuses comfort, His object is still the same. It is in making us partakers of His holiness that true comfort comes. The Holy Spirit is the Comforter, not only because He can suggest comforting thoughts of God's love, but far more, because He makes us holy, and brings us into close union with Christ and with God. He teaches us to abide in Christ; and because God is found there, the truest comfort will come there too.

In Christ the heart of the Father is revealed, and higher comfort there cannot be than to rest in the Father's bosom. *In Him* the fullness of the divine love is revealed, combined with the tenderness of a mother's compassion—and what can comfort like this? *In Him* you see a thousand times more given you than you have lost; see how God only took from you that you might have room to take from Him what is so much better. *In Him* suffering is consecrated, and becomes the foretaste of eternal glory; in suffering it is that the Spirit of God and of glory rests on us. Believer! would you have comfort in affliction?—Abide in Christ.

Bearing Fruit in Christ

Abide in Christ: so will you *bear much fruit*. Not a vine is planted but the owner thinks of the fruit, and the fruit only. Other trees may be planted for ornament, for the shade, for the wood— the vine *only for the fruit*. And of each vine the husbandman is continually asking how it can bring forth more fruit, much fruit.

Believer! abide in Christ in times of affliction, and you shall bring forth more fruit. The deeper experience of Christ's tenderness and the Father's love will urge you to live to His glory. The surrender of self and selfwill in suffering will prepare you to sympathize with the misery of others, while the softening that comes of chastisement will fit you for becoming, as Jesus was, the servant of all. The thought of the Father's desire for fruit in the pruning will lead you to yield yourself afresh, and more than ever, to Him, and to say that now you have but one object in life—making known and conveying His wonderful love to fellow-men. You shall learn the blessed art of forgetting self, and, even in affliction, availing yourself to your separation from ordinary life to plead for the welfare of others.

Dear Christian, in affliction abide in Christ. When you see it coming, meet it in Christ; when it is come, feel that you are more in Christ than in it, for He is nearer you than affliction ever can be; when it is passing, still abide in Him. And let the one thought of the Savior, as He speaks of the pruning, and the one desire of the Father, as He does the pruning, be yours too: "Every branch that beareth fruit, He purgeth, that it may bring forth *more fruit.*"

So shall your times of affliction become your times of choicest blessing— preparation for richest fruitfulness. Led into closer fellowship with the Son of God, and deeper experience of His love and grace—established in the blessed confidence that He and you entirely belong to each other—more completely satisfied with Him and more wholly given up to Him than ever before—with your own will crucified afresh, and the heart brought into deeper harmony with God's will—you shall be a vessel cleansed, meet for the Master's use, prepared for every good work.

True believer! O try and learn the blessed truth, that in affliction your first, your only, your blessed calling is to abide in Christ. Be much with Him alone. Beware of the comfort and the distractions that friends so often bring. Let Jesus Christ Himself be your chief companion and comforter. Delight yourself in the assurance that closer union with Him, and more abundant fruit through Him, are sure to be the results of trial, because it is the Husbandman Himself who is pruning, and will ensure the fulfillment of the desire of the soul that yields itself lovingly to His work.

CHAPTER FIVE

As Christ in the Father

"As the Father hath loved me, so I have loved you. Abide in my love, even as I abide in my Father's love" (John 15:9, 10).

Christ had taught His disciples that to abide in Him was to abide in His love. The hour of His suffering is nigh, and He cannot speak much more to them. They doubtless have many questions to ask as to what that abiding in Him and His love is. He anticipates and meets their wishes, and gives them HIS OWN LIFE as the best exposition of His command. As example and rule for their abiding in His love, they have to look to His abiding in the Father's love. In the light of His union with the Father, their union with Him will become clear. *His life in the Father is the law of their life in Him.*

The thought is so high that we can hardly take it in, and is yet so clearly revealed, that we dare not neglect it. Do we not read in John 6:57, *"As* I live by the Father, *even so* he that eateth me, he shall live by me"? And the Savior prays so distinctly (John 17:22), "that they may be one *even as* we are one: I in them, and Thou in me." The blessed union of Christ with the Father and His life in Him is the only rule of our thoughts and expectations in regard to our living and abiding in Him.

The Origin of Christ's Abiding

Think first of *the origin* of that life of Christ in the Father. They were ONE— one in life and one in love. In this His abiding in the Father had its root. Though dwelling here on earth, He knew that He was one with the Father; that the Father's life was in Him, and His love on Him. Without this knowledge, abiding in the Father and His love would have been utterly impossible. And it is thus only that you can abide in Christ and His love. Know that you are one with Him—one in the unity of nature. By His birth He became man, and took your nature that He might be one with you. By your new birth you become one with Him, and are made partaker of His divine nature. The link that binds you to Him is as real and close as bound Him to the Father—the link of a divine life. Your claim on Him is as sure and always availing as was His on the Father. Your union with Him is as close.

And as it is the union of a divine life, it is one of an infinite love. In His life of humiliation on earth He tasted the blessedness and strength of knowing Himself the object of an infinite love, and of dwelling in it all the day; from His own example He invites you to learn that herein lies the secret of rest and joy. You are one with Him: yield yourself now to be loved by Him; let your eyes and heart open to the love that shines and presses in on you on every side. Abide in His love.

The Mode of Christ's Abiding

Think then too of *the mode* of that abiding in the Father and His love which is to be the law of your life. "I kept my

Father's commandments and abide in His love." His was a life of subjection and dependence, and yet most blessed. To our proud self-seeking nature the thought of dependence and subjection suggests the idea of humiliation and servitude; in the life of love which the Son of God lived, and to which He invites us, they are the secret of blessedness. The Son is not afraid of losing aught by giving up all to the Father, for He knows that the Father loves Him, and can have no interest apart from that of the beloved Son. He knows that as complete as is the dependence on His part is the communication on the part of the Father of all He possesses. Hence when He had said, "The Son can do nothing of Himself, except He sees the Father do it," He adds at once, "Whatsoever things the Father doeth, them also doeth the Son likewise: for the Father loveth the Son, and showeth Him all things that Himself doeth."

The believer who studies this life of Christ as the pattern and the promise of what his may be, learns to understand how the "Without me ye can do nothing," is but the forerunner of "I can do all things through Christ who strengtheneth me." We learn to glory in infirmities, to take pleasure in necessities and distresses for Christ's sake; for "when I am weak, then am I strong." He rises above the ordinary tone in which so many Christians speak of their weakness, while they are content to abide there, because he has learnt from Christ that in the life of divine love the emptying of self and the sacrifice of our will is the surest way to have all we can wish or will. Dependence, subjection, self-sacrifice, are for the Christian as for Christ the blessed path of life. Like as Christ lived through and in the Father, even so the believer lives through and in Christ.

The Glory of Christ's Abiding

Think of the *glory* of this life of Christ in the Fathers' love. Because He gave Himself wholly to the Father's will and glory, the Father crowned Him with glory and honor. He acknowledged Him as His only representative; He made Him partaker of His power and authority; He exalted Him to share His throne as God.

And even so will it be with him who abides in Christ's love. If Christ finds us willing to trust ourselves and our interests to His love, if in that trust we give up all care for our own will and honor, if we make it our glory to exercise and confess absolute dependence on Him in all things, if we are content to have no life but in Him, *He will do for us what the Father did for Him.* He will lay of His glory on us: As the name of our Lord Jesus is glorified in us, we are glorified in Him (2 Thess. 1:12). He acknowledges us as His true and worthy representatives; He entrusts us with His power; He admits us to His counsels, as He allows our intercession to influence His rule of His church and the world; He makes us the vehicles of His authority and His influence over men. His Spirit knows no other dwelling than such, and seeks no other instruments for His divine work. Blessed life of love for the soul that abides in Christ's love, even as He in the Father's!

Abiding in Christ's Love

Believer! abide in the love of Christ. Take and study His relation to the Father as pledge of what thine own can become. As blessed, as mighty, as glorious as was His life in the Father, can yours be in Him. Let this truth, accepted under the teaching of the Spirit in faith, remove every vestige of fear, as if abiding in Christ were a burden and a work.

In the light of His life in the Father, let it henceforth be to you a blessed rest in the union with Him, an overflowing fountain of joy and strength.

To abide in His love, His mighty, saving, keeping, satisfying love, even as He abode in the Father's love—surely the very greatness of our calling teaches us that it never can be a work we have to perform; it must be with us as with Him, the result of the spontaneous outflowing of a life from within, and the mighty inworking of the love from above. What we only need is this: to take time and study the divine image of this life of love set before us in Christ. We need to have our souls still unto God, gazing upon that life of Christ in the Father until the light from heaven falls on it, and we hear the living voice of our Beloved whispering gently to us personally the teaching He gave to the disciples.

Soul, be still and listen; let every thought be hushed until the word has entered your heart too: "Child! I love thee, even as the Father loved me. Abide in my love, even as I abide in the Father's love. Thy life on earth in me is to be the perfect counterpart of mine in the Father."

And if the thought will sometimes come: Surely this is too high for us; can it be really true? only remember that the greatness of the privilege is justified by the greatness of the object He has in view. *Christ was the revelation of the Father on earth*. He could not be this if there were not the most perfect unity, the most complete communication of all the Father had to the Son. He could be it because the Father loved Him, and He abode in that love. *Believers are the revelation of Christ on earth*. They cannot be this unless there be perfect unity, so that the world can know that He loves them and has sent them. But they can be it if Christ loves them with the infinite love that gives itself and all it has, and if they abide in that love.

Lord, show us Thy love. Make us with all the saints to know the love that passeth knowledge. Lord, show us in Thine own blessed life what it is to abide in Thy love. And the sight shall so win us, that it will be impossible for us one single hour to seek any other life than the life of abiding in Thy love.

CHAPTER SIX

And Not in Self

In me, that is, in my flesh, dwelleth no good thing (Rom. 7:18).

Dead to Self

To have life in Himself is the prerogative of God alone, and of the Son, to whom the Father hath also given it. To seek life, not in itself, but in God, is the highest honor of the creature. To live in and to himself is the folly and guilt of sinful man; to live to God in Christ, the blessedness of the believer. To deny, to hate, to forsake, to lose his own life, such is the secret of the life of faith. "I live, yet NOT I, but Christ liveth in me"; "NOT I, but the grace of God which is with me": this is the testimony of each one who has found out what it is to give up his own life, and to receive instead the blessed life of Christ within us. There is no other path to true life, to abiding in Christ, than that which our Lord went before us—through death.

At the first commencement of the Christian life, but few see this. In the joy of pardon, they feel constrained to live for Christ, and trust with the help of God to be enabled to do so. They are as yet ignorant of the terrible enmity of the flesh against God, and its absolute refusal in the believer to be subject to the law of God. They know not yet that nothing but death, the absolute surrender to death of all that is of nature, will suffice, if the life of God is to be manifested in them with power.

But bitter experience of failure soon teaches them the insufficiency of what they have yet known of Christ's power to save, and deep heart-longings are awakened to know Him better. He lovingly points them to His cross. He tells them that as there, in the faith of His death as their substitute, they found their title to life, so there they shall enter into its fuller experience too. He asks them if they are indeed willing to drink of the cup of which He drank—to be crucified and to die with Him. He teaches them that in Him they are indeed already crucified and dead—all unknowing, at conversion they became partakers of His death. But what they need now is to give a full and intelligent consent to what they received ere they understood it, by an act of their own choice to will to die with Christ.

This demand of Christ's is one of unspeakable solemnity. Many a believer shrinks back from it. He can hardly understand it. He has become so accustomed to a low life of continual stumbling, that he hardly desires, and still less expects, deliverance. Holiness, perfect conformity to Jesus, unbroken fellowship with His love, can scarcely be counted distinct articles of his creed. Where there is not intense longing to be kept to the utmost from sinning, and to be brought into the closest possible union with the Savior, the thought of being crucified with Him can find no entrance. The only impression it makes is that of suffering and shame: such a one is content that Jesus bore the cross, and so won for him the crown he hopes to wear.

How different the light in which the

believer who is really seeking to abide fully in Christ looks upon it. Bitter experience has taught him how, both in the matter of entire surrender and simple trust, his greatest enemy in the abiding life, is SELF. Now it refuses to give up its will; then again, by its working, it hinders God's work. Unless this life of self, with its willing and working, be displaced by the life of Christ, with *His* willing and working, to abide in Him will be impossible.

And then comes the solemn question from Him who died on the cross: "Are you ready to give up self to the death?" You yourself, the living person born of God, are already in me dead to sin and alive to God; but are you ready now, in the power of this death, to mortify your members, to give up self entirely to its death of the cross, to be kept there until it be wholly destroyed? The question is a heart-searching one. Am I prepared to say that the old self shall no longer have a word to say; that it shall not be allowed to have a single thought, however natural—not a single feeling, however gratifying—not a single wish or work, however right?

Putting the Self to Death

Is this in very deed what He requires? Is not our nature God's handiwork, and may not our natural powers be sanctified to His service? They may and must indeed. But perhaps you have not yet seen how the only way they can be sanctified is that they be taken from under the power of self, and brought under the power of the life of Christ. Think not that this is a work that you can do, because you earnestly desire it, and are indeed one of His redeemed ones.

No, there is no way to the altar of consecration but through death. As you yielded yourself a sacrifice on God's altar as one alive from the dead (Rom. 6:13; 12:1), so each power of your nature—each talent, gift, possession, that is really to be holiness to the Lord—must be separated from the power of sin and self, and laid on the altar to be consumed by the fire that is ever burning there. It is in the mortifying, the slaying of self, that the wonderful powers with which God has fitted you to serve Him, can be set free for a complete surrender to God, and offered to Him to be accepted, and sanctified, and used. And though, as long as you are in the flesh, there is no thought of being able to say that self is dead, yet when the life of Christ is allowed to take full possession, self can be so kept in its crucifixion place, and under its sentence of death, that it shall have no dominion over you, not for a single moment. Jesus Christ becomes your second self.

Believer! would you truly and fully abide in Christ, prepare yourself to part for ever from self, and not to allow it, even for a single moment, to have aught to say in your inner life. If you are willing to come entirely away out of self, and to allow Jesus Christ to become your life within you, inspiring all your thinking, feeling, acting, in things temporal and spiritual, He is ready to undertake the charge. In the fullest and widest sense the word life ever can have, He will be *your life*, extending His interest and influence to each one, even the minutest, of the thousand things that make up your daily life. To do this He asks but one thing: Come away out of self and its life, abide in Christ and the Christ life, and Christ will be your life. The power of His holy presence will cast out the old life.

To this end give up self at once and for ever. If you have never yet dared to do it, for fear you might fail of your engagement, do it now, in view of the promise Christ gives you that His life will take the place of the old life. Try and realize that though self is not dead, you are indeed dead to self. Self is still strong and living, but it has *no power over you*. You, your renewed nature—you, your new self, begotten again in Jesus Christ from the dead—are indeed dead to sin and alive to God. Your death in Christ has freed you completely from the control of self: it has no power over you, except as you, in ignorance, or unwatchfulness, or unbelief, consent to yield to its usurped authority.

Come and accept by faith simply and heartily the glorious position you have in Christ. As one who in Christ has a life dead to self, as one who is freed from the dominion of self, and has received His divine life to take the place of self, to be the animating and inspiring principle of your life, venture boldly to plant the foot upon the neck of this enemy of yours and your Lord's. Be of good courage, only believe; fear not to take the irrevocable step, and to say that you have once for all given up self to the death for which it has been crucified in Christ (Rom. 6:6). And trust Jesus the Crucified One to hold self to the cross, and to fill its place in you with His own blessed resurrection life.

In this faith, abide in Christ! Cling to Him; rest on Him; hope on Him. Daily renew your consecration; daily accept afresh your position as ransomed from your tyrant, and now in turn made a conqueror. Daily look with holy fear on the enemy, self, struggling to get free from the cross, seeking to allure you into giving it some little liberty, or else ready to deceive you by its profession of willingness now to do service to Christ. Remember, self seeking to serve God is more dangerous than self refusing obedience. Look upon it with holy fear, and hide yourself in Christ: in Him alone is your safety.

Abide thus in Him; He has promised to abide in you. He will teach you to be humble and watchful. He will teach you to be happy and trustful. Bring every interest of your life, every power of your nature, all the unceasing flow of thought, and will, and feeling, that makes up life, and trust Him to take the place that self once filled so easily and so naturally. Jesus Christ will indeed take possession of you and dwell in you; and in the restfulness and peace and grace of the new life you shall have unceasing joy at the wondrous exchange that has been made—the coming out of self to abide in Christ alone.

In addition to Abide in Christ, *Murray authored several works whose emphasis is directly on Christ. One such work is his 1884* Like Christ. *The subtitle of this work,* Thoughts on the Blessed Life of Conformity to the Son of God, *serves as a guide to Murray's central theme in the book. An interesting and helpful feature of* Like Christ *is the prayers which Murray provides at the conclusion of each chapter and which are related to the preceding chapter.*

We are like Christ, Murray states, because we are "Crucified With Him." While it is not our work to crucify ourselves, God has given us a work to do in recognizing that our old nature has already been crucified. Our work is also to maintain our fellowship with the Crucified One.

Like Christ, we are "Not of the World." Murray finds that the secret of Christ's work as Savior is found in an understanding that though He was "in the world," he was "not of the world."

We should seek to be like Christ "In His Use of Scripture." Christ's life and reliance on Scripture show us that "the life of God in human flesh and the word of God in human speech are inseparably connected." Also like Christ, we should see in Scripture an image and likeness of ourselves and of what God means for us to be.

CHAPTER SEVEN

Crucified with Him

I am crucified with Christ: nevertheless I live; yet not I, but Christ liveth in me. God forbid that I should glory save in the cross of our Lord Jesus Christ, by whom the world is crucified unto me, and I unto the world (Gal. 2:20, 6:14).

Crucified with Christ

Taking up the cross was always spoken of by Christ as the test of discipleship. On three different occasions (Matt. 10:38, 16:24; Luke 14:27) we find the words repeated, "If any man will come after me, let him take up his cross and follow me." While the Lord was still on His way to the cross, this expression—taking up the cross—was the most appropriate to indicate that conformity to Him to which the disciple is called.[1]

But now that He has been crucified, the Holy Spirit gives another expression, in which our entire conformity to Christ is still more powerfully set forth—the believing disciple is himself crucified with Christ. The cross is the chief mark of the Christian as of Christ; the crucified Christ and the crucified Christian belong to each other. One of the chief elements of likeness to Christ consists in being crucified with Him. Whoever wishes to be like Him must seek to understand the secret of fellowship with His cross.

At first sight the Christian who seeks conformity to Jesus is afraid of this truth; he shrinks from the painful suffering and death with which the thought of the cross is connected. As his spiritual discernment becomes clearer, however, this word becomes all his hope and joy, and he glories in the cross, because it makes him a partner in a death and victory that has already been accomplished, and in which the deliverance from the powers of the flesh and of the world has been secured to him. To understand this we must notice carefully the language of Scripture.

"I am crucified with Christ," Paul says; "nevertheless I live; yet not I, but Christ liveth in me." Through faith in Christ we become partakers of Christ's life. That life is a life that has passed through the death of the cross, and *in which the power of that death is always working.* When I receive that life, I receive at the same time the full power of the death on the cross working in me in its never-ceasing energy. "I have been crucified with Christ; yet I live; and yet no longer I, but Christ liveth in me" (RV); the life I now live is not my own life, but the life of the Crucified One, is the life of the cross.

The being crucified is a thing past and done: "Knowing this, that our old man *was* (RV) crucified with Him;" "They that are Christ's *have* crucified

---

1. Christians entirely miss the point of the Lord's command when they refer the taking up of the cross only to the crosses or trials of life. It means much more. The cross means death. Taking up the cross means going out to die. It is just in the time of prosperity that we most need to bear the cross. Taking up the cross and following Him is nothing less than living every day with our own life and will given up to death.

the flesh;" "I glory in the cross of our Lord Jesus Christ, by whom the world *hath been* (RV) crucified unto me, and I unto the world." These texts all speak of something that has been done in Christ, and into which I am admitted by faith.

Maintaining the Position of the Crucifixion

It is of great consequence to understand this, and to give bold utterance to the truth; I have been crucified with Christ; I have crucified the flesh. I thus learn how perfectly I share in the finished work of Christ. If I am crucified and dead with Him, then I am a partner in His life and victory. I learn to understand the position I must take to allow the power of that cross and that death to manifest itself in mortifying or (RV) making dead the old man and the flesh, in destroying the body of sin (Rom. 6:6).

For there is still a great work for me to do. But that work is not to crucify myself: I have been crucified; the old man was crucified, so the Scripture speaks. But what I have to do is always to regard and treat it as crucified, and not to suffer it to come down from the cross. I must maintain my crucifixion position. I must keep the flesh in the place of crucifixion.

To realize the force of this I must notice an important distinction. I have been crucified and am dead: the old Adam was crucified, but is not yet dead. When I gave myself to my crucified Savior, sin and flesh and all, He took me wholly; I with my evil nature was taken up with Him in His crucifixion. But here a separation took place. In fellowship with Him I was freed from the life of the flesh; I myself died with Him; in the inmost center of my being I received new life: Christ lives in *me*. But the flesh, in which I yet am, the old man that was crucified with Him, remained

condemned to an accursed death, but is not yet dead.

And now it is my calling, in fellowship with and in the strength of my Lord, to see that the old nature be kept nailed to the cross, until the time comes that it is entirely destroyed. All its desires and affections cry out, "Come down from the cross, save thyself and us." It is my duty to glory in the cross, and with my whole heart to maintain the dominion of the cross, and to set my seal to the sentence that has been pronounced, to make dead every uprising of sin, as already crucified, and so not to suffer it to have dominion. This is what Scripture means when it says, "If ye through the spirit do make to die (R.V.) the deeds of the body, ye shall live" (Rom. 8:13). "Make dead therefore your members which are upon the earth."

Thus I continually and voluntarily acknowledge that in my flesh dwells no good thing; that my Lord is Christ the Crucified One; that I have been crucified and *am dead* in Him; that the flesh has been crucified and, though not yet dead, has been forever given over to the death of the cross. And so I live like Christ, in very deed crucified with Him.

Two Things Necessary to Understand the Crucifixion

In order to enter fully into the meaning and the power of this fellowship of the crucifixion of our Lord, two things are specially necessary to those who are Christ's followers. The first is the clear consciousness of this their fellowship with the Crucified One through faith. At conversion they became partakers of it without fully understanding it. Many remain in ignorance all their life long through a want of spiritual knowledge. Brother, pray that the Holy Spirit may reveal to you your union to the Crucified One. "I have been crucified with Christ";

"I glory in the cross of Christ, through which I have been crucified to the world." Take such words of Holy Scripture, and by prayer and meditation make them your own, with a heart that expects and asks the Holy Spirit to make them living and effectual within you. Look upon yourself in the light of God as what you really are, "crucified with Christ."

Then you will find the grace for a second thing you need to enable you to live as a crucified one, in whom Christ lives. You will be able always to look upon and to treat the flesh and the world as nailed to the cross. The old nature seeks continually to assert itself, and to make you feel as if it is expecting too much that you should always live this crucifixion life. Your only safety is in fellowship with Christ. "Through Him and His cross," says Paul, "I have been crucified to the world." In Him the crucifixion is an accomplished reality; in Him you have died, but also have been made alive: Christ lives in you.

With this fellowship of His cross let it be with you, the deeper the better: it brings you into deeper communion with His life and His love. To be crucified with Christ means freed from the power of sin: a redeemed one, a conqueror. Remember that the Holy Spirit has been specially provided to glorify Christ in you, to reveal within you, and make your very own, all that is in Christ for you. Do not be satisfied, with so many others, only to know the cross in its power to atone: the glory of the cross is, that it was not only to Jesus, but is to us too, the path to life, but that each moment it can become to us the power that destroys sin and death, and keeps us in the power of the eternal life. Learn from your Savior the holy art of using it for this.

Faith in the power of the cross and its victory will day by day make dead the deeds of the body, the lusts of the flesh. This faith will teach you to count the cross, with its continual death to self, all your glory. Because you regard the cross, not as one who is still on the way to crucifixion, with the prospect of a painful death, but as one to whom the crucifixion is past, who already lives in Christ, and now only bears the cross as the blessed instrument through which the body of sin is done away (Rom. 6:6, RV). The banner under which complete victory over sin and the world is to be won is the cross.

Above all, remember what still remains the chief thing. It is Jesus, the living, loving Savior, who Himself enables you to be like Him in all things. His sweet fellowship, His tender love, His heavenly power, make it a blessedness and joy to be like Him, the Crucified One, make the crucifixion life a life of resurrection-joy and power. IN HIM the two are inseparably connected. In Him you have the strength to be always singing the triumphant song: God forbid that I should glory, save in the cross of our Lord Jesus Christ, through which the world hath been crucified unto me, and I unto the world.

A Prayer to Understand the Cross

Precious Savior, I humbly ask Thee to show me the hidden glory of the fellowship of Thy cross. The cross was my place, the place of death and curse. Thou didst become like us, and hast been crucified with us. And now the cross is Thy place, the place of blessing and life. And Thou callest me to become like Thee, and as one who is crucified with Thee, to experience how entirely the cross has made me free from sin.

Lord, give me to know its full power. It is long since I knew the power of the cross to redeem from the curse. But how long I strove in vain as a redeemed one to overcome the power of sin, and to obey the Father as Thou hast done! I could not break the power of sin. But now I see, this comes only when Thy disciple yields himself entirely to be led by Thy Holy Spirit into the fellowship of Thy cross. There Thou dost give him to see how the cross *has broken for ever* the power of sin, and has made him free. There Thou, the Crucified One, dost live in him and impart to him Thine own Spirit of whole-hearted self-sacrifice, in casting out and conquering sin.

Oh, my Lord, teach me to understand this better. In this faith I say, "I have been crucified with Christ." Oh, Thou who lovedst me to the death, not Thy cross, but Thyself the Crucified One, Thou art He whom I seek, and in whom I hope. Take me, Thou Crucified One, and hold me fast, and teach me from moment to moment to look upon all that is of self as condemned, and only worthy to be crucified. Take me, and hold me, and teach me, from moment to moment, that in Thee I have all I need for a life of holiness and blessing. Amen.

CHAPTER EIGHT

Not of the World

"These are in the world." "The world hath hated them, because they are not of the world, even as I *am not of the world." "They are not of the world,* even as I *am not of the world"* (John 17:11, 14, 16).
"Even as *He is, so are we in this world"* (1 John 4:17).

If Jesus was not of the world, why was He in the world? If there was no sympathy between Him and the world, why was it that He lived in it, and did not remain in that high and holy and blessed world to which He belonged? The answer is, the Father had sent Him into the world. In these two expressions, "In the world," "Not of the world," we find the whole secret of His work as Savior, of His glory as the God-man.

"In the world"; in human nature, because God would show that this nature belonged to Him, and not the god of this world, that it was most fit to receive the divine life, and in this divine life to reach its highest glory.

"In the world"; in fellowship with men, to enter into loving relationship with them, to be seen and known of them, and thus to win them back to the Father.

"In the world"; in the struggle with the powers which rule the world, to learn obedience, and so to perfect and sanctify human nature.

"Not of the world," but of heaven, to manifest and bring nigh the life that is in God, and which man had lost, that men might see and long for it.

"Not of the world"; witnessing against its sin and departure from God, its impotence to know and please God.

"Not of the world"; founding a kingdom entirely heavenly in origin and na-

ture, entirely independent of all that the world holds desirable or necessary, with principles and laws the very opposite of those that rule in the world.

"Not of the world"; in order to redeem all who belong to Him, and bring them into that new and heavenly kingdom which He had revealed.

"In the world," "Not of the world." In these two expressions we have revealed to us the great mystery of the person and work of the Savior. "Not *of* the world," in the power of His divine holiness judging and overcoming it; still *in* the world, and through His humanity and love seeking and saving all that can be saved. The most entire separation from the world, with the closest fellowship with those in the world; these two extremes meet in Jesus, in His own person He has reconciled them. And it is the calling of the Christian in his life to prove that these two dispositions, however much they may seem at variance, can in our life too be united in perfect harmony. In each believer there must be seen a heavenly life shining out through earthly forms.

Errors of Extremities

To take one of these two truths and exclusively cultivate it, is not so difficult. So you have those who have taken "Not of the world," as their motto. From the earliest ages, when people thought they must fly to cloisters and deserts to serve God, to our own days, when some seek to show the earnestness of their piety by severity in judging all that is in the world, there have been those who counted this the only true religion. There was separation from sin, but then there was also no fellowship with sinners. The sinner could not feel that he was surrounded with the atmosphere of a tender heavenly love. It was a one-sided and therefore a defective religion.

Then there are those who, on the other side, lay stress on "In the world," and very specially appeal to the words of the apostle, "For then must ye needs go out of the world." They think that, by showing that religion does not make us unfriendly or unfit to enjoy all that there is to enjoy, they will induce the world to serve God. It has often happened that they have indeed succeeded in making the world very religious, but at too high a price—religion became very worldly.

In the World but Not of It

The true follower of Jesus must combine both. If he does not clearly show that he is not of the world, and prove the greater blessedness of a heavenly life, how will he convince the world of sin, or prove to her that there is a higher life, or teach her to desire what she does not yet possess? Earnestness, and holiness, and separation from the spirit of the world must characterize him. His heavenly spirit must manifest that he belongs to a kingdom not of this world. An unworldly, an other-worldly, a heavenly spirit must breathe in him.

And still he must live as one who is "in the world." Expressly placed here of God, among those who are of the world, to win their hearts, to acquire influence over them, and to communicate to them of the Spirit which is in him, it must be the great study of his life how he can fulfil this his mission. Not, as the wisdom of the world would teach, by yielding, and complying, and softening down the solemn realities of religion, will he succeed. No, but only by walking in the footsteps of Him who alone can teach how to be in the world and yet not of it. Only by a life of serving and suffering love, in which the Christian distinctly confesses that the glory of God is the aim of his existence, and in which, full of the Holy Spirit, he brings men into direct contact with the warmth and love of the heavenly life, can he be a blessing to the world.

Imitating Christ

Oh, who will teach us the heavenly secret, of uniting every day in our lives what is so difficult to unite—to be in the world, and not of the world? He can do it who has said: "They are not of the world, EVEN AS I am not of the world." That "EVEN AS" has a deeper meaning and power than we know. If we suffer the Holy Spirit to unfold that word to us, we shall understand what it is to be in the world as He was in the world. That "EVEN AS" has its root and strength in a life union. In it we shall discover the divine secret, that *the more entirely one is not of the world, the more fit he is to be in the world*. The freer the Church is of the spirit and principles of the world, the more influence she will exert in it.

The life of the world is self-pleasing and self-exaltation. The life of heaven is holy, self-denying love. The weakness of the life of many Christians who seek to separate themselves from the world, is that they have too much of the spirit of the world. They seek their own happiness and perfection more than aught else.

Jesus Christ was not of the world, and had nothing of its spirit; this is why He could love sinners, could win them and save them. The believer is as little of the world as Christ. The Lord says: "Not of the world, EVEN AS I am not of the world." In this new nature he is born from heaven, has the life and love of heaven in him; his supernatural heavenly life gives him power to be in the world without being of it.

The disciple who believes fully in the Christ-likeness of his inner life, will experience the truth of it. He cultivates and gives utterance to the assurance: "EVEN AS Christ, so am I not of the world, because I am in Christ." He understands that alone in close union with Christ can his separation from the world be maintained; in as far as Christ lives in him can he lead a heavenly life. He sees that the only way to answer to his calling is, on the one side, as crucified to the world to withdraw himself from its power; and, on the other, as living in Christ to go into it and bless it. He lives in heaven and walks on earth.

Christians! see here the true imitation of Jesus Christ. "Wherefore come out from among them, and be ye separate, saith the Lord." Then the promise is fulfilled, "I will dwell in them and walk in them." Then Christ sends you, as the Father sent Him, to be in the world as the place ordained of your Father to glorify Him, and to make known His love. Not so much in the desire to leave earth for heaven, as in the willingness to live the life of heaven here on earth, does a truly unworldly, a heavenly spirit, manifest itself.

"Not of the world" is not only separation from and testimony against the world, but is the living manifestation of the spirit, and the love, and the power of the other world, of the heaven to which we belong, in its divine work of making this world partaker of its blessedness.

A Prayer to Be in the World but Not of It

O Thou great High Priest! who in Thy high-priestly power didst pray for us to the Father, as those who, no more than Thyself, belong to the world, and still must remain in it, let Thy all-prevailing intercession now be effectual in our behalf.

The world has still entrance to our hearts, its selfish spirit is still too much within us. Through unbelief the new nature has not always full power. Lord, we beseech of Thee, as fruit of Thy all-powerful intercession, let that word be fully realized in us: "Not of the world, EVEN AS I am not of the world." In our likeness to Thee is our only power against the world.

Lord, we can only be like Thee when we are one with Thee. We can only walk like Thee when we abide in Thee. Blessed Lord, we surrender ourselves to abide in Thee alone. A life entirely given to Thee Thou dost take entire possession of. Let Thy Holy Spirit, who dwells in us, unite us so closely with Thyself that we may always live as not of the world. And let Thy Spirit so make known to us Thy work in the world, that it may be our joy in deep humility and fervent love to exhibit to all what a blessed life there is in the world for those who are not of the world. May the proof that we are not of the world be the tenderness and fervency with which, like Thee, we sacrifice ourselves for those who are in the world. Amen.

CHAPTER NINE

In His Use of Scripture

"That all things must be fulfilled which were written in the law of Moses, and the Prophets, and in the Psalms, concerning me" (Luke 24:44).

What the Lord Jesus accomplished here on earth as man He owed greatly to His use of the Scriptures. He found in them the way marked in which He had to walk, the food and the strength on which He could work, the weapon by which He could overcome every enemy. The Scriptures were indeed indispensable to Him through all His life and passion: from beginning to end His life was the fulfilment of what had been written of Him in the volume of the Book.

It is scarcely necessary to adduce proofs of this. In the temptation in the wilderness it was by His *"It is written"* that He conquered Satan. In His conflicts with the Pharisees He continually appealed to the Word: *"What saith the Scripture?" "Have ye not read?" "Is it not written?"* In His intercourse with His disciples it was always from the Scriptures that He proved the certainty and necessity of His sufferings and resurrection: *"How otherwise can the Scriptures be fulfilled?"* And in His intercourse with His Father in His last sufferings, it is in the words of Scripture that He pours out the complaint of being forsaken, and then again commends His spirit into the Father's hands.

All this has a very deep meaning. He was Himself the living Word. He had the Spirit without measure. If ever any one, He could have done without the written Word. And yet we see that it is every-thing to Him. More than any one else He thus shows us that *the life of God in human flesh and the word of God in human speech* are inseparably connected. Jesus would not have been what He was, could not have done what He did, had He not yielded Himself step by step to be led and sustained by the Word of God.

The Divine Seed of Scripture

Let us try and understand what this teaches us. The Word of God is more than once called Seed, it is the seed of the divine life. We know what seed is. It is that wonderful organism in which the life, the invisible essence of a plant or tree, is so concentrated and embodied that it can be taken away and made available to impart the life of the tree elsewhere. This use may be twofold. As fruit we eat it, for instance, in the corn that gives us bread; and the life of the plant becomes our nourishment and our life. Or we sow it, and the life of the plant reproduces and multiplies itself. In both aspects the Word of God is seed.

True life is found only in God. But that life cannot be imparted to us unless set before us in some shape in which we know and apprehend it. It is in the Word of God that the invisible divine life takes shape, and brings itself within our reach, and becomes communicable. The life, the thoughts, the sentiments, the power of God are embodied in His words. And it is only through His Word that the life of God can really enter into us. His Word is the seed of the heavenly life.

As the bread of life we eat it, we feed upon it. In eating our daily bread, the body takes in the nourishment which visible nature, the sun and the earth, prepared for us in the seed-corn. We assimilate it, and it becomes our very own, part of ourselves, it is our life. In feeding upon the Word of God, the powers of the heavenly life enter into us, and become our very own; we assimilate them, they become a part of ourselves, the life of our life.

Or we use the seed to plant. The words of God are sown in our heart. They have a divine power of reproduction and multiplication. The very life that is in them, the divine thought, or disposition, or power that each of them contains, takes roots in the believing heart and grows up; and the very thing of which the word was the expression, is produced within us. The words of God are the seeds of the fullness of the divine life.

When the Lord Jesus was made man, He became entirely dependent upon the Word of God, He submitted Himself wholly to it. His mother taught it Him. The teachers of Nazareth instructed Him in it. In meditation and prayer, in the exercise of obedience and faith, He was led, during His silent years of preparation, to understand and appropriate it. The Word of the Father was to the Son the life of His soul. What He said in the wilderness was spoken from His inmost personal experience: "Man shall not live by bread alone, but by every word that proceedeth out of the mouth of God."

He felt He could not live but as the Word brought Him the life of the Father. His whole life was a life of faith, a de-

pending on the Word of the Father. The Word was to Him not instead of the Father, but the vehicle for the living fellowship with the living God. And He had His whole mind and heart so filled with it, that the Holy Spirit could at each moment find within Him, all ready for use, the right word to suggest just as He needed it.

Child of God! would you become a man of God, strong in faith, full of blessing, rich in fruit to the glory of God, be full of the Word of God. Like Christ, make the Word your bread. Let it dwell richly in you. Have your heart full of it. Feed on it. Believe it. Obey it. It is only by believing and obeying that the Word can enter into our inward parts, into our very being.

Take it day by day as the Word that proceedeth, not has proceeded, but proceedeth, is proceeding out of the mouth of God, as the Word of the living God, who in it holds living fellowship with His children, and speaks to them in living power. Take your thoughts of God's will, and God's work, and God's purpose with you, and the world, not from the church, not from Christians around you, but from the Word taught you by the Father, and like Christ, you will be able to fulfil all that is written in the Scripture concerning you.

The Image of Christ in Scripture

In Christ's use of Scripture the most remarkable thing is this: *He found Himself there; He saw there His own image and likeness.* And He gave Himself to the fulfilment of what He found written there. It was this that encouraged Him under the bitterest sufferings, and strengthened Him for the most difficult work. Everywhere He saw traced by God's own hand the divine waymark: *through suffering to glory.* He had but one thought: to be what the Father had said He should be, to have His life correspond exactly to the image of what He should be as He found it in the Word of God.

Disciple of Jesus, in the Scriptures *thy likeness too is to be found,* a picture of what the Father means thee to be. Seek to have a deep and clear impression of what the Father says in His word that thou shouldest be. If this is once fully understood, it is inconceivable what courage it will give to conquer every difficulty. To know: it is ordained of God; I have seen what has been written concerning me in God's book; I have seen the image of what I am called in God's counsel to be: this thought inspires the soul with a faith that conquers the world.

The Lord Jesus found His own image not only in the institutions, but specially in the believers of the Old Testament. Moses and Aaron, Joshua, David, and the prophets, were types. And so He is Himself again, the image of believers in the New Testament. It is especially in *Him and His example* that we must find our own image in the Scriptures. "To be changed into the same image, from glory to glory, by the Spirit of the Lord," we must in the Scripture-glass gaze on that image as our own. In order to accomplish His work in us, the Spirit teaches us to take Christ as in very deed our Example, and to gaze on every feature as the promise of what we can be.

Blessed the Christian who has truly done this; who has not only found Jesus in the Scriptures, but also in His image the promise and example of what he is to become. Blessed the Christian who yields himself to be taught by the Holy Spirit not to indulge in human thoughts as to the Scriptures and what it says of believers, but in simplicity to accept what it reveals of God's thoughts about His children.

Living According to Scripture

Child of God! it was "according to the Scriptures" that Jesus Christ lived and died; it was "according to the Scriptures" that He was raised again: all that the Scriptures said He must do or suffer He was able to accomplish, because He knew and obeyed them. All that the Scriptures had promised that the Father should do for Him, the Father did.

O give thyself up with an undivided heart to learn in the Scriptures what God says and seeks of thee. Let the Scriptures in which Jesus found every day the food of His life, be thy daily food and meditation. Go to God's Word each day with the joyful and confident expectation, that through the blessed Spirit, who dwells in us, the Word will indeed accomplish its divine purpose in thee.

Every word of God is full of a divine life and power. Be assured that when thou dost seek to use the Scriptures as Christ used them, they will do for thee what they did for Him. God has marked out the plan of thy life in His Word; each day thou wilt find some portion of it there. Nothing makes a man more strong and courageous than the assurance that he is just living out the will of God. God Himself, who had thy image portrayed in the Scriptures, will see to it that the Scriptures are fulfilled in thee, if like His Son thou wilt but surrender thyself to this as the highest object of thy life.

A Prayer for Blessings from God's Word

O Lord, my God! I thank Thee for Thy precious Word, the divine glass of all unseen and eternal realities. I thank Thee that I have in it the image of Thy Son, who is Thy image, and also, O wonderful grace! my image. I thank Thee that as I gaze on Him I may also see what I can be.

O my Father! teach me rightly to understand what a blessing Thy Word can bring me. To Thy Son, when here on earth, it was the manifestation of Thy will, the communication of Thy life and strength, the fellowship with Thyself. In the acceptance and the surrender to Thy Word He was able to fulfil all Thy counsel. May Thy Word be all this to me too.

Make it to me, each day afresh through the unction of the Holy Spirit, the Word proceeding from the mouth of God, the voice of Thy living presence speaking to me. May I feel with each word of Thine that it is God coming to impart to me somewhat of His own life.

Teach me to keep it hidden in my heart as a divine seed, which in its own time will spring up and reproduce in me in divine reality the very life that was hid in it, the very thing which I at first only saw in it as a thought. Teach me above all, O my God, to find in it Him who is its center and substance, Himself the Eternal Word. Finding Him, and myself in Him, as my Head and Exemplar, I shall learn like Him to count Thy Word my food and my life.

I ask this, O my God, in the name of our blessed Christ Jesus. Amen.

A third volume that concentrates on Christ is Jesus Himself. *Published in 1893,* Jesus Himself *consists of a revision of two addresses that Murray gave. The second address is presented here.*

In this address, which also has the title "Jesus Himself," Murray suggests that the secret of the Christian's strength and joy is the presence of Jesus. We have Christ's sure promise that He will be with us to the end of the world, and the secret of holiness is that He now indwells us instead of sin. To secure the enjoyment of Christ's abiding in us we need to have close intercourse with Him every day.

CHAPTER TEN

Jesus Himself

"Lo, I am with you always" (Matt. 28:20).

When I think of all the struggles and difficulties and failures of which many complain, and know that many are trying to make a new effort to begin a holy life, their hearts fearing all the time that they would fail again, owing to so many difficulties and temptations and the natural weakness of their character, my heart longs to be able to tell them in words so simple that a little child could understand, what the secret is of the Christian life.

And then the thought comes to me, Can I venture to hope that it will be given to me to take that glorious, heavenly, divine Lord Jesus and to show Him to these souls, so that they can see Him in His glory? And can it be given to me to open their eyes to see that there is a divine, almighty Christ, who does actually come into the heart and who faithfully promises, "I will come and dwell with you, and I will never leave you"?

No; my words cannot do that. But then I thought, my Lord Jesus can use me as a simple servant to take such feeble ones by the hand and encourage and help them; to say, Oh, come, come, come, into the presence of Jesus and wait on Him, and He will reveal Himself to thee. I pray God that He may use His precious Word.

The Presence of the Lord Jesus

The presence of the Lord Jesus Christ is the secret of the Christian's strength and joy. You know that when He was upon earth, He was present in bodily form with His disciples. They walked about together all day, and at night they went into the same house, and sometimes slept together and ate and drank together. They were continually together. It was the presence of Jesus that was the training school of His disciples. They were bound to Him by that wonderful intercourse of love during three long years, and in that intercourse they learned to know Christ, and Christ instructed and corrected them, and prepared them for what they were afterward to receive. And now when He is going away, He says to them: "Lo, behold, I am with you always—all the days—even unto the end of the world."

What a promise! And just as really as Christ was with Peter in the boat, just as Christ sat with John at the table, as really can I have Christ with me. And more really, for they had their Christ in the body and He was to them a man, an individual separate from them, but I may have glorified Christ in the power of the throne of God, the omnipotent Christ, the omnipresent Christ.

What a promise! You ask me, How can that be? And my answer is, Because Christ is God, and because Christ after having been made man, went up into the throne and the life of God. And now that blessed Christ Jesus, with His loving, pierced heart; that blessed Jesus Christ, who lived upon earth; that same Christ glorified into the glory of God, can be in me and can be with me all the days.

You say, Is it really possible for a man in business, for a woman in the midst of a large and difficult household, for a poor man full of care; is it possible? Can I always be thinking of Jesus? Thank God, you need not always be thinking of Him. You may be the manager of a bank, and your whole attention may be required to carry out the business that you have to do. But thank God, while I have to think of my business, Jesus will think of me, and He will come in and will take charge of me. That little child, three months old, as it sleeps in its mother's arms, lies helplessly there; it hardly knows its mother, it does not think of her, but the mother thinks of the child.

And this is the blessed mystery of love, that Jesus the God-man waits to come in to me in the greatness of His love; and as He gets possession of my heart, He embraces me in those divine arms and tells me, "My child, I the Faithful One, I the Mighty One will abide with thee, will watch over thee and keep thee all the days." He tells me He will come into my heart, so that I can be a happy Christian, a holy Christian, and a useful Christian. You say, Oh! if I could only believe that, if I could think that it is possible to have Christ always, every hour, every moment with me.

Taking and Keeping Charge of Me

My brother, my sister, it is just literally this that is my message to you. When Jesus said to His disciples, "Lo, I am with you always," He meant it in the fullness of the divine omnipresence, in the fullness of the divine love, and he longs tonight to reveal Himself to you and to me as we have never seen Him before.

And now just think a moment what a blessed life that must be—the presence of Jesus always abiding. Is not that the secret of peace and happiness? If I could just attain (that is what each heart says) to that blessed state in which every day and all the day I felt Jesus to be watching and ever keeping me, oh, what peace I would have in the thought, "I have no care if He cares for me, and I have no fear if He provides for me." Your heart says that this is too good to be true, and that it is too glorious to be for you. Still you acknowledge it must be most blessed. Fearful one, erring one, anxious one, I bring you God's promise, it is for me and for you. Jesus will do it; as God, He is able, and Jesus is willing and longing as the Crucified One to keep you in perfect peace. This is a wonderful fact, and it is the secret of joy unspeakable.

The Secret of Holiness

Instead of indwelling sin, an indwelling Christ conquering it; instead of indwelling sin, the indwelling life and light and love of the blessed Son of God. He is the secret of holiness. "Christ is made unto us sanctification." Remember that it is Christ Himself who is made unto us sanctification. Christ coming into me, taking charge of my whole being; my nature and my thoughts and my affections and my will; ruling all things. It is this that will make me holy. We talk about holiness, but do you know what holiness is? You have as much holiness as you have of Christ, for it is written, "Both he that sanctifieth and they who are sanctified are all of one;" and Christ sanctifies by bringing God's life into me.

We read in Judges, "The Spirit of the Lord clothed Gideon." But you know that there is in the New Testament an equally wonderful text, where we read, "Put on the Lord Jesus Christ," that is, clothe yourself with Christ Jesus. And what does this mean? It does not only mean, by imputation of righteousness outside of me, but to clothe myself with the living character of the living Christ, with the living love of the living Christ.

Put on the Lord Jesus

Oh! what a work. I cannot do it unless I believe and understand that He whom I have to put on is as a garment covering my whole being. I have to put on a living Christ who has said, "Lo, I am with you all the days." Just draw the folds closer round you, of that robe of light with which Christ would array you. Just come and acknowledge that Christ is with you, on you, in you. Oh, put Him on!

And when you look at one characteristic of His after another; and you hear God's word, "Let this mind be in you which was also in Jesus Christ," and it tells you He was obedient unto the death; and then you answer, Christ the obedient one, Christ whose whole life was obedience, it is that Christ whom I have received and put on. He becomes my life and His obedience rests upon me, until I learn to whisper as Jesus did, "My Father, Thy will be done; lo, I come to do Thy will."

This, too, is the secret of influence in witness and work.

Difficult to Be Obedient

How comes it that it is so difficult to be obedient and how comes it that I so often sin? People sing, "Oh, to be wholly Thine," and sing it from their hearts. How comes it then that they are disobedient again? Where does the disobedience come from? And the answer comes, It is because I am trying to obey a distant Christ, and thus His commands do not come with power.

Look what I find in God's Word.

When God wanted to send any man upon His service, He first met him and talked with him and cheered him time after time. God appeared to Abraham seven or eight times, and gave to him one command after another; and so Abraham learned to obey Him perfectly. God appeared to Joshua and to Gideon, and they obeyed. And why are we not obedient? Because we have so little of this near intercourse with Jesus. But, oh, if we knew this blessed, heavenly secret of having the presence of Christ with us every day, every hour, every minute, what a joy it would be to obey! We could not walk in this consciousness—My Lord Jesus is with me and around me—and not obey Him! Oh, do you not begin to long and say, This is what I must have, the ever-abiding presence of Jesus! There are some Christians who try not to be disobedient, who come to their Sunday and week-day duties most faithfully, and pray for grace and a blessing, and they complain of so little blessing and power, so little power! And why? Because there is not enough of the living Jesus in their hearts.

I sometimes think of this as a most solemn truth. There is a great diversity of gifts amongst ministers and others who speak; but I am sure of this, that a man's gifts are not the measure of his real power. I am sure of this, that God can see what neither you nor I can see. Sometimes people feel something of it; but in proportion as a man has in reality, not as a sentiment or an aspiration, or a thought, but in reality, the very spirit and presence of Jesus upon him, there comes out from him an unseen silent influence. That secret influence is the holy presence of Jesus.

Holy Presence of Jesus

"Lo, I am with you always." And now, if what I have said has sufficed just to indicate what a desirable thing it is, what a blessed thing it is to live for, then let me now give you an answer to the question that arises in more than one heart. I can hear some one say, "Tell me how I can get this blessed abiding presence of Jesus, and when I have got it, how I can ever keep it. I think if I have this, I have all. The Lord Jesus has come very near to me. I have tried to turn away from everything that can hinder, and have had my Lord very near. But how can I know that He will be with me always?" If you were to ask the Lord, "Oh, my blessed Lord Christ, what must I do, how can I enjoy Thy never-failing presence?" His first answer would be, "Only believe. I have said it often, and you only partly understood it, but I will say it again—My child, only believe."

It is by faith. We sometimes speak of faith as trust, and it is a very helpful thing to tell men that faith is trust: but when people say, as they sometimes do, that it is nothing else but trust, that is not the case. It is a far wider word than trust. It is by faith that I learn to know the invisible One, the invisible God, and that I see Him. Faith is my spiritual eyesight for the unseen and heavenly. You often try hard to trust God, and you fail. Why? Because you have not taken time first to see God. How can you trust God fully until you have met Him and known Him?

You ask, "Where ought I to begin?" You ought to begin with first believing; with presenting yourself before this God in the attitude of silent worship, and asking Him to let a sense of His greatness and His presence come upon you. You must ask Him to let your heart be covered over with His holy presence. You must seek to realize in your heart the presence of an almighty and all-loving God, an unspeakably loving God. Take time to worship Him as the omnipotent God, to feel that the very power

that created the world, the very power that raised Jesus from the dead, is at this moment working in your heart. We do not experience it because we do not believe. We must take time to believe. Jesus says, "Oh, my child, shut your eyes to the world, and shut out of your heart all these thoughts about religion, and begin to believe in God Himself." That is the first article of the Creed—"I believe in God."

By Believing I Open My Heart

By believing I open my heart to receive this glorious God, and I bow and worship. And then as I believe this, I look up and I see the Lamb upon the Throne, and I believe that the almighty power of God is in Jesus for the very purpose of revealing His presence to my heart. Why are there two upon the Throne? Is not God enough? The Lamb of God is upon the Throne in your interest and in mine; the Lamb upon the Throne is Christ Himself, with power as God to take possession of me. Oh, do not think you cannot get that realization. And do not think of it as now only within your reach; but cultivate the habit of faith. "Jesus, I believe in Thy glory; I believe in Thine omnipotence; I believe in Thy power working within me. I believe in Thy living, loving presence with me, revealing itself in divine power."

Do not be occupied with feelings or experiences. You will find it far simpler and easier just to trust and say, "I am sure He is all for me." Get rid of yourself for the time; don't think or speak about yourself; but think what Jesus is. And then remember it is believe always. I sometimes feel that I cannot find words to tell how God wants His people to believe from morning till night. Every breath ought to be just believing. Yes, it is indeed true; the Lord Jesus loves us to be just believing from morning to evening, and you must begin to make that the chief thing in life. In the morning when you wake, let your heart go forth with a large faith in this; and in the watches of the night let this thought be present with you—my Saviour Jesus is round me and near me, and you can look up and say, "I want to trust Thee always." You know what trust is. It is so sweet to trust. And now cannot you trust Jesus; this presence, this keeping presence? He lives for you in heaven. You are marked with His blood, and He loves you; and cannot you say, "My King, my King, He is with me all the days?" Oh, trust Jesus to fulfill His own promises.

There is a second answer that I think Christ would give if we come to Him believing, and say, "Is there anything more, my blessed Master?" I think I can hear His answer.

"My Child, Always Obey"

Do not fail to understand the lesson contained in this one word. You must distinctly and definitely take that word OBEY and obedience, and learn to say for yourselves: "Now I have to obey, and by the grace of God I am going to obey in everything." At our recent exhibition at the Cape, Mr. Rhodes, our Prime Minister, went to the gate, thinking he had got the fee in his pocket. When he got to the gate, however, he found he had not enough money, and said to the door-keeper, "I am Mr. Rhodes; let me in and I will take care you do not suffer." But the man said, "I cannot help that, sir, I have my orders," and he refused to let Mr. Rhodes in. He had to borrow from a friend, and pay before he could pass the gate. At a dinner afterward Mr. Rhodes spoke about it, and said it was a real joy to see a man stick to his order like that. That is it. The man had his orders, and that was enough to him, and

whoever came to the gate had to pay his fee before he could enter. God's children ought to be like soldiers, and be ready to say, "I must obey."

Oh! to have that thought in our hearts—"Jesus, I love to obey Thee." There must be personal intercourse with the Savior, and then comes the joy of personal service and allegiance. Are you ready to obey in all feebleness and weakness and fear? Can you say, "Yes, Lord Jesus, I will obey"? If so, then give yourself up absolutely. Then your feeling will be, "I am not going to speak one word if I think that Jesus would not like to hear it. I am not going to have an opinion of my own, but my whole life is to be covered with the purity of His obedience to the Father and His self-sacrificing love to me. I want Christ to have my whole life, my whole heart, my whole character. I want to be like Christ and to obey." Give yourself up to this loving obedience.

The third thought is this: If I say, "My Master, blessed Savior, tell me all, I will believe, I do obey, and I will obey. Is there anything more I need to secure the enjoyment of Thine abiding presence?" And I catch this answer.

"My Child, Close Intercourse with Me Every Day"

Ah, there is the fault of many who try to obey and try to believe; they do it in their own strength, and they do not know that if the Lord Jesus is to reign in their hearts, they must have close communion with Him every day. You cannot do all He desires, but Jesus will do it for you. There are many Christians who fail here, and on that account do not understand what it is to have fellowship with Jesus.

Do let me try and impress this upon you: God has given you a loving, living Savior, and how can He bless if you do not meet Him? The joy of friendship is found in intercourse; and Jesus asks for this every day, that He may have time to influence me, to tell me of Himself, to teach me, to breathe His Spirit unto me, to give me new life and joy and strength. And remember, intercourse with Jesus does not mean half-an-hour or an hour in your closet. A man may study his Bible or his commentary carefully; he may look up all the parallel passages in the chapter; when he comes out of his closet he may be able to tell you all about it, and yet he has never met Jesus that morning at all. You have prayed for five or ten minutes, and you have never met Jesus.

And so we must remember that though the Bible is most precious, and the reading of it most blessed and needful; yet prayer and Bible reading are not fellowship with Jesus. What we need every morning is to meet Jesus, and to say, "Lord, here is the day again, and I am just as weak in myself as ever I was; do Thou come and feed me this morning with Thyself and speak to my soul." Oh, friends, it is not your faith that will keep you standing, but it is a living Jesus, met every day in fellowship and worship and love. Wait in His presence, however cold and faithless you feel. Wait before Him and say: "Lord, helpless as I am, I believe and rest in the blessed assurance that what Thou hast promised Thou wilt do for me."

I ask my Master once again, "Lord Jesus, is that all?" And His answer is: "No, my child; I have one thing more." "And what is that? Thou hast told me to believe, and to obey, and to abide near to Thee: what wouldst Thou have more?"

"Work for Me, My Child"

"Remember, I have redeemed thee for My service; I have redeemed thee to have a witness to go out into the world confessing Me before men." Oh, do not hide your treasure, or think that if Jesus is with you, you can hide it. One of two things will happen—either you must give all up, or it must come out.

You have perhaps heard of the little girl, who, after one of Mr. Moody's meetings, was found to be singing some of the hymns we all know. The child's parents were in a good position in society, and while singing those hymns in the drawing-room her mother forbade her. One day she was singing the hymn "Oh, I'm so glad that Jesus loves me," when her mother said, "My child, how is it that you sing this when I have forbidden it?" She replied, "Oh, mother, I cannot help it; it comes out of itself."

If Jesus Christ be in the heart, He must come out. Remember, it is not only our duty to confess Him; it is that, but it is something more. If you do not do it, it is just an indication that you have not given yourself up to Jesus; your character, your reputation, your all. You are holding back from Him. You must confess Jesus in the world, in your home; and in fact everywhere.

You know the Lord's command, "Go ye into all the world, and preach the Gospel to every creature;" "and, lo, I am with you," meaning, "Any one may work for Me, and I will be with him." It is true of the minister, the missionary, and every believer who works for Jesus. The presence of Jesus is intimately connected with work for Him. You say, "I have never thought of that before. I have my Sunday work, but during the week I am not doing work for Him." You cannot have the presence of Jesus, and let this continue to be the case. I do not believe you could have the presence of Jesus all the week and yet do nothing for Him; therefore my advice is, work for Him who is worthy, His blessing and His presence will be found in the work.

A Blessed Privilege to Work for Christ

It is a blessed privilege to work for Christ in this perishing world. Oh, why is it that our hearts often feel so cold and closed up, and so many of us say, "I do not feel called to Christ's work"? Be willing to yield yourself for the Lord's service, and He will reveal Himself to you.

Christ comes with His wondrous promise, and what He says, He says to all believers: "Lo, I am with you always; that is My promise; this is what I in My power can do; this is what I faithfully engage to perform; will you have it?"

"I Give Myself to Thee, O Soul"

To each of those who have come to Him, Christ says, "I give Myself to thee, to be absolutely and wholly thine every hour of every day; to be with thee and in thee every moment, to bless thee and sustain thee, and to give thee each moment the consciousness of My presence; I will be wholly, wholly, wholly thine."

And now, what is the other side? He wants me to be wholly His. Are you ready to take this as your motto now, "Wholly for God"?

O God, breathe Thou Thy presence in my heart that Thou mayest shine forth from my life. "Wholly for God," let this be our motto. Come let us cast ourselves on our faces before His feet. Our missionary from Nyassaland says he has often been touched by seeing how the native Christians, when they are brought to Jesus, do not stand in prayer; they do not kneel; but they cast themselves upon the earth with their foreheads to the ground, and there they lie, and with loud voices cry unto God. I sometimes feel that I wish we could do that ourselves; but we need not do it literally. Let us do it in spirit, for the everlasting Son of God has come into our hearts. Are you going to take Him and to keep Him there, to give Him glory and let Him have His way?

Come now and say, "I will seek Thee with my whole heart; I am wholly Thine." Yield yourself entirely to Him to have complete possession. He will take and keep possession. Come now. Jesus delights in the worship of His saints. Our whole life can become one continuous act of worship and work of love and joy, if we only remember and value this, that Jesus has said, "Lo, I am with you all the days, even unto the end of the world."

All of Murray's works deal not only with "Jesus Himself" but also with the Holy Spirit. An example of a work which deals primarily with the nature and work of the Spirit is Murray's 1888 work The Spirit of Christ. *As in* Like Christ, *each chapter in* The Spirit of Christ *concludes with a prayer related to the theme of the chapter.*

In "Worship in the Spirit," Murray interprets the Scripture that "the true worshippers shall worship the Father in spirit and in truth." For Murray, to worship in spirit is to worship God not by man's own strength but by God's Spirit. To worship in truth does not mean to worship sincerely or uprightly but to worship God in all that true worship implies, both in its demands and its promises.

The Spirit of Christ is also "The Spirit of Truth." The word of this Spirit in the lives of believers is to reveal the fullness of grace and truth which are in Christ and to make Christ to be the Truth in us.

Murray takes the meaning of our bodies as "The Temple of the Holy Spirit" very seriously. The three divisions of the temple in Jerusalem—the outer court, the Holy Place, and the Most Holy Place—correspond to regions within man. We must discern God not only in the outer court of our external life and the Holy Place of our souls but ultimately in the Most Holy Place of our spirits.

Living by the Spirit must be accompanied by "Walking in the Spirit." Those who walk by the Spirit do so by crucifying the flesh and accepting the power of the cross.

CHAPTER ELEVEN

Worship in the Spirit

"The hour cometh, and now is, when the true worshippers shall worship the Father in spirit *and in truth, for such doth the Father seek to be His worshippers. God is* a spirit, *and they that worship Him must worship Him* in spirit *and in truth"* (John 4:23, 24).

We are the circumcision, who worship by the Spirit of God and glory in Christ Jesus, and have no confidence in the flesh (Phil. 3:3).

To worship is man's highest glory. He was created for fellowship with God: of that fellowship worship is the sublimest expression. All the exercises of the religious life—meditation and prayer, love and faith, surrender and obedience, all culminate in worship. Recognizing what God is in His holiness, His glory, and His love, realizing what I am as a sinful creature, and as the Father's redeemed child, in worship I gather up my whole being and present myself to my God, to offer Him the adoration and the glory which is His due. The truest and fullest and nearest approach to God is worship. Every sentiment and every service of the religious life is included in it: to worship is man's highest destiny, because in it God is all.

Jesus tells us that with His coming a new worship would commence. All that heathen or Samaritans had called worship, all even that the Jews had known of worship in accordance with the provisional revelation of God's law, would make way for something entirely and distinctively new—the worship in spirit and in truth. This is the worship He was to inaugurate by the giving of the Holy Spirit. This is the worship which now alone is well pleasing to the Father. It is for this worship specially that we have received the Holy Spirit. Let us, at the very commencement of our study of the work of the Spirit, take in the blessed thought that the great object for which the Holy Spirit is within us is, that we worship in spirit and in truth. "Such doth the Father seek to be His worshippers"—for this He sent forth His Son and His Spirit.

Worship in Spirit

When God created man a living soul, that soul, as the seat and organ of his personality and consciousness, was linked, on the one side, through the body, with the outer visible world, on the other side, through the spirit, with the unseen and the divine. The soul had to decide whether it would yield itself to the spirit, by it to be linked with God and His will, or to the body and the solicitations of the visible. In the fall, the soul refused the rule of the spirit, and became the slave of the body with its appetites. Man became flesh; the spirit lost its destined place of rule, and became little more than a dormant power; it was now no longer the ruling principle, but a struggling captive. And the spirit now stands in opposition to the flesh, the name for the life of soul and body together, in their subjection to sin.

When speaking of the unregenerate man in contrast with the spiritual (1 Cor. 2:14), Paul calls him psychical, soullish, or animal, having only the natural life. The life of the soul comprehends all our moral and intellectual faculties, as they may even be directed towards the things of God, apart from the renewal of the divine Spirit. Because the soul is under the power of the flesh, man is spoken of as having become flesh, as being flesh. As the body consists of flesh and bone, and the flesh is that part of it which is specially endowed with sensitiveness, and through which we receive our sensations from the outer world, the flesh denotes human nature, as it has become subject to the world of sense.

And because the whole soul has thus come under the power of the flesh, the Scripture speaks of all the attributes of the soul as belonging to the flesh, and being under its power. So it contrasts, in reference to religion and worship, the two principles from which they may proceed. There is a fleshly wisdom and a spiritual wisdom (1 Cor. 2:12; Col. 1:9). There is a service of God trusting in the flesh and glorying in the flesh, and a service of God by the spirit (Phil. 3:3, 4; Gal. 6:13). There is a fleshly mind and a spiritual mind (Col. 2:18, 19). There is a will of the flesh, and a will which is of God working by His Spirit (John 1:13; Phil. 2:13). There is a worship which is a satisfying of the flesh, because it is in the power of what flesh can do (Col. 3:18, 23), and a worship of God which is in the Spirit. It is this worship Jesus came to make possible, and to realize in us, by giving a new spirit in our inmost part, and then, within that, God's Holy Spirit.

Worship in Spirit and in Truth

Such a worship in spirit is worship in truth. Just as the words *in Spirit* do not mean internal as contrasted with external observances, but Spiritual, inwrought by God's Spirit, as opposed to what man's natural power can effect, so the words *in truth* do not mean hearty, sincere, upright. In all the worship of the Old Testament saints, they knew that God sought truth in the inward parts; they sought Him with their whole hearts, and most uprightly—and yet they attained not to that worship in spirit and truth, which Jesus brought us when He rent the veil of the flesh.

Truth here means the substance, the reality, the actual possession of all that the worship of God implies, both in what it demands and what it promises. John speaks of Jesus as "the Only Begotten of the Father, full of grace and truth." And he adds, "For the Law was given by Moses; grace and truth came by Jesus Christ." If we take truth as opposed to falsehood, the law of Moses was just as true as the Gospel of Jesus; they both came from God. But if we understand what it means that the law gave only a shadow of "good things to come," and that Christ brought us the things themselves, their very substance, we see how He was full of truth, because He was Himself *the Truth*, the reality, the very life and love and power of God imparting itself to us. We then also see how it is only a worship *in spirit* that can be a worship *in truth*, in the actual enjoyment of that divine power, which is Christ's own life and fellowship with the Father, revealed and maintained within us by the Holy Spirit.

"The true worshippers worship the Father in spirit and in truth." All worshippers are not true worshippers. There may be a great deal of earnest, honest worship without its being worship in spirit and in truth. The mind may be intensely occupied, the feelings may be deeply moved, the will may be mightily roused, while yet there is but little of the spiritual worship which stands in the truth of God. There may be great attachment to Bible truth, and yet through the predominating activity of that which cometh not from God's working, but from man's effort, it may not be the Christ-given, Spirit-breathed worship which God seeks.

There must be accordance, harmony, unity between God, who is a spirit, and the worshippers drawing near in the Spirit. Such doth the Father seek to worship Him. The infinite, perfect, Holy Spirit, which God the Father is, must have some reflection in the spirit which is in the child. And this can only be as the Spirit of God dwells in us.

If we would strive to become such worshippers in spirit and in truth—true worshippers—the first thing we need is a sense of the danger in which we are from the flesh and its worship. As believers we have in us a double nature—flesh and spirit. The one is the natural part which is ever ready to intrude itself, and to undertake the doing of what is needed in the worship of God. The other is the spiritual part, which may still be very weak, and which possibly we do not yet know how to give its full sway. Our mind may delight in the study of God's Word, our feelings may be moved by the wonderful thoughts there revealed, our will may—we see this in Romans 7:22—delight in the law of God after the inward man, and we may yet be impotent to do that law, to render the obedience and worship we see and approve.

We need the Holy Spirit's indwelling for life and worship alike. And to receive this we need first of all to have the flesh silenced. "Be silent, all flesh, before the Lord." "Let no flesh glory in His presence." To Peter had already been revealed by the Father that Jesus was the Christ, and yet in his thoughts of the cross he savoured not, his mind was not according to, the things of God, but the things of men. Our own thoughts of divine things, our own efforts to waken or

work the right feelings must be given up, our own power to worship must be brought down and laid low, and every approach to God must take place under a very distinct and very quiet surrender to the Holy Spirit. And as we learn how impossible it is at our will any moment to ensure the Spirit's working, we shall learn that if we would worship in the Spirit we must walk in the Spirit. *"Ye are* not in the flesh but *in the Spirit, if so be* the Spirit of God dwelleth in you." As the Spirit dwells and rules in me, I am in the Spirit, and can worship in the Spirit.

"The hour cometh, and now is, when the true worshippers shall worship the Father in spirit and in truth. For such doth the Father seek to be His worshippers." Yes, the Father seeks such worshippers, and what He seeks He finds, because He Himself works it. That we might be such worshippers, He sent His own Son to seek and to save the lost; to save us with this salvation, that we should become His true worshippers, who enter in through the rent veil of the flesh, and worship Him in the Spirit.

And then He sent the Spirit of His Son, the Spirit of Christ, to be in us the truth and reality of what Christ had been, His actual presence, to communicate within us the very life that Christ had lived. Blessed be God! the hour has come, and is now, we are living in it this very moment, that the true worshippers shall worship the Father in spirit and in truth. Let us believe it, the Spirit has been given, and dwells within us, for this one reason, because the Father seeks such worshippers. Let us rejoice in the confidence that we can attain to it, we can be true worshippers, because the Holy Spirit has been given.

Let us realize in holy fear and awe that He dwells within us. Let us humbly, in the silence of the flesh, yield ourselves to His leading and teaching. Let us wait in faith before God for His workings. And let us practice this worship. Let every new insight into what the work of the Spirit means, every exercise of faith in His indwelling or experience of His working, terminate in this as its highest glory: the adoring worship of the Father, the giving Him the praise, the thanks, the honor, and love which are His alone.

A Prayer for Worship in the Spirit

O God! Thou art a Spirit, and they that worship Thee must worship Thee in spirit and in truth. Blessed be Thy name! Thou didst send forth Thine own Son to redeem and prepare us for the worship in the Spirit; and Thou didst send forth Thy Spirit to dwell in us and fit us for it. And now we have access to the Father, as through the Son, so in the Spirit.

Most Holy God! we confess with shame how much our worship has been in the power and the will of the flesh. By this we have dishonored Thee, and grieved Thy Spirit, and brought infinite loss to our own souls. O God! forgive and save us from this sin. Teach us, we pray Thee, never, never to attempt to worship Thee but in spirit and in truth.

Our Father! Thy Holy Spirit dwells in us. We beseech Thee, according to the riches of Thy glory, to strengthen us with might by Him, that our inner man may indeed be a spiritual temple, where spiritual sacrifices are unceasingly offered. And teach us the blessed art, as often as we enter Thy presence, of yielding self and the flesh to the death, and waiting for and trusting the Spirit who is in us, to work in us a worship, a faith and love, acceptable to Thee through Christ Jesus. And, oh! that throughout the universal church, a worship in spirit and in truth may be sought after, and attained, and rendered to Thee day by day. We ask it in the name of Jesus. Amen.

CHAPTER TWELVE

The Spirit of Truth

"But when the Comforter is come, whom I will send unto you from the Father, even the Spirit of Truth, *which proceedeth from the Father, He shall bear witness to me"* (John 15:26).

"When He, the Spirit of Truth, *is come, He shall guide you into all the Truth; for He shall not speak from Himself; but whatsoever things He shall hear, these shall He speak"* (John 16:13).

God created man in His image; to become like Himself, capable of holding fellowship with Him in His glory. In Paradise two ways were set before man for attaining to this likeness to God. These were typified by the two trees—that of life, and that of knowledge. God's way was the former—through life would come the knowledge and likeness of God; in abiding in God's will, and partaking of God's life, man would be perfected. In recommending the other, Satan assured man that knowledge was the one thing to be desired to make us like God. And when man chose the light of knowledge above the life in obedience, he entered upon the terrible path that leads to death.[1] The desire to know became his greatest temptation; his whole nature was corrupted, and knowledge was to him more than obedience and more than life.

Under the power of this deceit, that promises happiness in knowledge, the human race is still led astray. And nowhere does it show its power more terribly than in connection with the true religion and God's own revelation of

Himself. Even when the word of God is accepted, the wisdom of the world and of the flesh ever enters in; even spiritual truth is robbed of its power when held, not in the life of the Spirit, but in the wisdom of man. Where truth enters into the inward parts, as God desires, there it becomes the life of the spirit. But it may also only reach the outer parts of the soul, the intellect and reason, and while it occupies and pleases there, and satisfies us with the imagination that it will thence exercise its influence, its power is nothing more than that of human argument and wisdom, that never reaches to the true life of the spirit.

For there is a truth of the understanding and feelings, which is only natural, the human image or form, the shadow of divine truth. There is a truth which is substance and reality, communicating to him who holds it the actual possession, the life of the things of which others only think and speak. The truth in shadow, in form, in thought, was all the law could give; and in that the religion of the Jews consisted. The truth of substance, the truth as a divine life, was

---

1. After I had found the illustration of the two trees elsewhere, and written the above, I noticed the following in Godet on John 1:4: "Is it not natural in such a context to see in the two words *Life* and *Light*, and in the relations which John establishes between them, an allusion to the tree of life and to that of knowledge? After having eaten of the former, man would have been called to feed on the second. John initiates us into the real essence of these primordial and mysterious facts, and gives us in this verse, as it were, the philosophy of Paradise."

what Jesus brought as the Only-begotten, full of grace and truth. He is Himself "the Truth."[2]

The Spirit of Truth

In promising the Holy Spirit to His disciples, our Lord speaks of Him as the Spirit of Truth. That truth, which He Himself is, that truth and grace and life which He brought from heaven as a substantial spiritual reality to communicate to us, that truth has its existence in the Spirit of God: He is the Spirit, the inner life of that divine truth. And when we receive Him, and just as far as we receive Him, and give up to Him, He makes Christ, and the life of God, to be truth in us divinely real; He gives it to be in us of a truth.

In His teaching and guiding into the truth, He does not give us only words and thoughts and images and impressions, coming to us from without, from a book or a teacher outside of us. He enters the secret roots of our life, and plants the truth of God there as a seed, and dwells in it as a divine life. And when, in faith, and expectation, and surrender, this hidden life is cherished and nourished there, He quickens and strengthens it, so that it grows stronger and spreads its branches through the whole being. And so, not from without but from within, not in word but in power, in life and truth, the Spirit reveals Christ and all He has for us. He makes the Christ, who has been to us so much only an image, a thought, a Saviour outside and above us, to be truth within us. The Spirit brings with His incoming the truth into us; and then, having possessed us from within, guides us, as we can bear it, into all the truth.

In His promise to send the Spirit of Truth from the Father, our Lord very definitely tells us what His principal work would be. "He shall bear witness of ME." He had just before said, "I am the Truth;" the Spirit of Truth can have no work but just to reveal and impart the fulness of grace and truth that there are in Christ Jesus. He came down from the glorified Lord in heaven to bear witness within us, and so through us, of the reality and the power of the redemption which Christ has accomplished there.

There are Christians who are afraid that to think much of the Spirit's presence within us will lead us away from the Savior above us. A looking within to ourselves may do this; we may be sure that the silent, believing, adoring recognition of the Spirit within us will only lead to a fuller, a more true and spiritual apprehension that Christ alone is indeed all in all. "He shall bear witness of me." "He shall glorify me." It is He will make our knowledge of Christ life and truth, an experience of the power with which He works and saves.

Receiving the Spirit of Truth

To know what the disposition or state of mind is in which we can fully receive this guiding into all truth, note the remarkable words our Lord uses concerning the Spirit: "He shall guide you into all the truth, *for* He shall not speak from Himself; but whatsoever things He shall hear, these shall He speak." The mark of this Spirit of Truth is a wondrous divine teachableness.

In the mystery of the Holy Trinity there is nothing more beautiful than this, that with a divine equality on the part of the Son and the Spirit, there is

---

2. "The word *true* in John, as in classical writers, signifies not the *true* in opposition to the *false*, but the *veritable*, the perfect realization of the idea in opposition to all its imperfect manifestations." Godet, John 1:9.

also a perfect subordination. The Son could claim that men should honor Him even as they honored the Father, and yet counted it no derogation from that honor to say, The Son can do nothing of Himself; as I hear, so I speak. And even so the Spirit of Truth never speaks from Himself. We should think He surely could speak from Himself; but no, only what He hears, that He speaks. The Spirit that fears to speak out of its own, that listens for God to speak, and only speaks when God speaks, this is the Spirit of Truth.

And this is the disposition He works, the life He breathes, in those who truly receive Him—that gentle teachableness which marks the poor in spirit, the broken in heart, who have become conscious that as worthless as their righteousness, is their wisdom, or power of apprehending spiritual truth; that they need Christ as much for the one as the other, and that the Spirit within them alone can be the Spirit of Truth. He shows us how, even with the word of God in our hands and on our tongues, we may be utterly wanting in that waiting, docile, submissive spirit to which alone its spiritual meaning can be revealed. He opens our eyes to the reason why so much Bible reading, and Bible knowledge, and Bible preaching has so little fruit unto true holiness; because it is studied and held with a wisdom that is not from above, that was not asked for and waited for from God. The mark of the Spirit of Truth was wanting. He speaketh not, He thinketh not from Himself; what He hears, that He speaks. The Spirit of Truth receives everything day by day, step by step, from God in heaven. He is silent, and does not speak, except and until He hears.

Waiting on the Spirit of Truth

These thoughts suggest to us the great danger of the Christian life—seek-
ing to know the truth of God in His word without the distinct waiting on the Spirit of Truth in the heart. The tempter of Paradise still moves about among men. Knowledge is still his great temptation. How many Christians there are who could confess that their knowledge of divine truth does but little for them: it leaves them powerless against the world and sin; they know little of the light and the liberty, the strength and the joy the truth was meant to bring. It is because they take to themselves God's truth in the power of human wisdom and human thought, and wait not for the Spirit of Truth to lead them into it. Most earnest efforts to abide in Christ, to walk like Christ, have failed because their faith stood more in the wisdom of man than in the power of God. Most blessed experiences have been short-lived, because they knew not that the Spirit of Truth was within them to make Christ and His holy presence an abiding reality.

These thoughts suggest the great need of the Christian life. Jesus said, "If any man will come after me, let him deny himself, and follow me." Many a one follows Jesus without denying himself. And there is nothing that more needs denying than our own wisdom, the energy of the fleshly mind, as it exerts itself in the things of God.

Let us learn that in all our intercourse with God, in His word or prayer, in every act of worship, the first step ought to be a solemn act of abnegation, in which we deny our power to understand God's word, or to speak our words to Him, without the special divine leading of the Holy Spirit. Christians need to deny even more than their own righteousness, their own wisdom; this is often the most difficult part of the denial of self.

In all worship we need to realize the alone sufficiency and the absolute indispensableness, not only of the blood, but as much of the Spirit of Jesus. This is the meaning of the call to be silent unto God, and in quiet to wait on Him; to hush the rush of thoughts and words in God's presence, and in deep humility and stillness to wait, and listen, and hear what God will say. The Spirit of Truth never speaks from Himself: what He hears, that He speaks. A lowly, listening, teachable spirit is the mark of the presence of the Spirit of Truth.

And then, when we do wait, let us remember that even then the Spirit of Truth does not at once or first speak in thoughts that we can at once apprehend and express. These are but on the surface. To be true they must be rooted deep. They must have hidden depth in themselves. The Holy Spirit is the Spirit of Truth because He is the Spirit of Life: the Life is the Light. Not to thought or feeling does He speak in the first place, but in the hidden man of the heart, in the spirit of a man which is within him, in his inmost parts. It is only to faith that it is revealed what His teaching means, and what His guidance into the truth.

Let our first work therefore today again be to believe; that is, to recognize the living God in the work He undertakes to do. Let us believe in the Holy Spirit as the Divine Quickener and Sanctifier, who is already within us, and yield up all to Him. He will prove Himself the Divine Enlightener: the Life is the Light. Let the confession that we have no life or goodness of our own be accompanied by the confession that we have no wisdom either; the deeper our sense of this, the more precious will the promise of the Spirit's guidance become. And the deep assurance of having the Spirit of Truth within us will work in us the holy teacher's likeness, and the quiet hearkening to which the secrets of the Lord shall be revealed.

A Prayer for the Spirit of Truth

O Lord God of Truth! who seekest truth in the inward parts in them that worship Thee, I do bless Thee again that Thou hast given me too the Spirit of Truth, and that He now dwells in me. I bow before Thee in lowly fear to ask that I may know Him aright, and walk before Thee in the living consciousness that the Spirit of Truth, the Spirit of Christ, who is the Truth, is indeed within me, the inmost self of my new life. May every thought and word, every disposition and habit, be the proof that the Spirit of Christ, who is the Truth, dwells and rules within me.

Especially do I ask Thee that He may witness to me of Christ Jesus. May the truth of His atonement and blood as it works with living efficacy in the upper sanctuary, dwell in me and I in it. May His life and glory no less be truth in me, a living experience of His presence and power. O my Father! may the Spirit of Thy Son, the Spirit of Truth, indeed be my life. May each word of Thy Son through Him be made true in me.

I do thank Thee once again, O my Father, that He dwelleth within me. I bow my knees that Thou wouldest grant that, according to the riches of Thy glory, He may work mightily in me and all Thy saints. Oh, that all Thy people may know this their privilege and rejoice in it: the Holy Spirit within them to reveal Christ, full of grace and truth, as truth in them. Amen.

CHAPTER THIRTEEN

The Temple of the Holy Spirit

Know ye not that ye are the temple of God, and that the Spirit of God *dwelleth in you?* (1 Cor. 3:16).

In using the illustration of the temple as the type of God's dwelling in us by the Holy Spirit, Scripture invites us to study the analogy. The temple was made in all things according to a pattern seen by Moses on the Mount, a shadow cast by the eternal spiritual realities which it was to symbolize. One of these realities—for divine truth is exceeding rich and full and has many and very diverse applications. One of these realities shadowed forth by the temple, is man's threefold nature. Because man was created in the image of God, the temple is not only the setting forth of the mystery of man's approach into the presence of God, but equally of God's way of entering into man, to take up His abode with him.

We are familiar with the division of the temple into three parts. There was its exterior, seen by all men, with the outer court, into which every Israelite might enter, and where all the external religious service was performed. There was the Holy Place, into which alone the priests might enter, to present to God the blood or the incense, the bread or the oil, they had brought from without. But though near, they were still not within the veil; into the immediate presence of God they might not come. God dwelt in the Holiest of all, in a light inaccessible, where none might venture nigh. The momentary entering of the High Priest once a year was but to bring into full consciousness the truth that there was no place for man there, until the veil should have been rent and taken away.

God's Indwelling in His Temple

Man is God's temple. In him, too, there are the three parts. In the body you have the outer court, the external visible life, where all the conduct has to be regulated by God's law, and where all the service consists in looking to that which is done without us and for us to bring us nigh to God. Then there is the soul, with its inner life, its power of mind and feeling and will. In the regenerate man this is the Holy Place, where thoughts and affections and desires move to and fro as the priests of the sanctuary, rendering God their service in the full light of consciousness. And then comes within the veil, hidden from all human sight and light, the hidden inmost sanctuary, "the secret place of the Most High," where God dwells, and where man may not enter, until the veil is rent at God's own bidding.

Man has not only body and soul, but also spirit. Deeper down than where the soul with its consciousness can enter, there is a spirit-nature linking man with God. So fearful is sin's power, that in some this power is given up to death: they are sensual, not having the Spirit. In others, it is nothing more than a dormant power, a possibility waiting for the quickening of the Holy Spirit. In the believer it is the inner chamber of the heart, of which the Spirit has taken possession, and from out of which He waits to do His glorious work, making soul and body holy to the Lord.

And yet this indwelling, unless where it is recognized, and yielded to, and humbly maintained in adoration and love, often brings comparatively little blessing. And the one great lesson which the truth that we are God's temple, because His Spirit dwells in us, must teach us, is this, to acknowledge the holy presence that dwells within us. This alone will enable us to regard the whole temple, even to the outmost court, as sacred to His service, and to yield every power of our nature to His leading and will.

The most sacred part of the temple, that for which all the rest existed and on which all depended, was the Holiest of all. Even though the priests might never enter there, and might never see the glory that dwelt there, *all their conduct was regulated, and all their faith animated, by the thought of the unseen presence there*. It was this that gave the sprinkling of the blood and the burning of the incense their value. It was this made it a privilege to draw nigh, and give confidence to go out and bless. It was the Most Holy, the Holiest of all, that made the place of their serving to them a Holy Place. Their whole life was controlled and inspired by the faith of the unseen indwelling glory within the veil.

It is not otherwise with the believer. Until he learns by faith to tremble in presence of the wondrous mystery that he is God's temple, because God's Spirit dwelleth in him, he never will yield himself to his high vocation with the holy reverence or the joyful confidence that becomes him. As long as he looks only into the Holy Place, into the heart, as far as man can see and know what

passes there, he will often search in vain for the Holy Spirit, or only find cause for bitter shame that his workings are so few and feeble. Each of us must learn to know that there is a Holiest of all in that temple which he himself is; the secret place of the Most High within us must become the central truth in our temple worship. This must be to us the meaning of our confession: "I believe in the Holy Ghost."

Faith in God's Indwelling

And how is this deep faith in the hidden indwelling to become ours? Taking our stand upon God's blessed Word, we must accept and appropriate its teaching. We must take trouble to believe that God means what it says. I am a temple; just such a temple as God commanded to be built of old; He meant me to see in it what I am to be. There the Holiest of all was the central point, the essential thing. It was all dark, secret, hidden till the time of unveiling came. It demanded and received the faith of priest and people.

The Holiest of all within me, too, is unseen and hidden, a thing for faith alone to know and deal with. Let me, as I approach to the Holy One, bow before Him in deep and lowly reverence. Let me there say that I believe what He says, that His Holy Spirit, God, one with the Father and the Son, even now has His abode within me. I will meditate, and be still, until something of the overwhelming glory of the truth fall upon me, and faith begin to realize it: I am His temple, and in the secret place He sits upon His throne. As I yield myself in silent meditation and worship day by day, surrendering and setting open my whole being to Him, He will in His divine, loving, living power, shine into my consciousness the light of His presence.

As this thought fills the heart, the

faith of the indwelling though hidden presence will influence; the Holy Place will be ruled from the Most Holy. The world of consciousness in the soul, with all its thoughts and feelings, its affections and purposes, will come and surrender themselves to the holy power that sits within on the throne. Amid the terrible experience of failure and sin a new hope will dawn. Though long I most earnestly strove, I could not keep the Holy Place for God, because I knew not that He kept the Most Holy for Himself. If I give Him there the glory due to His name, in the holy worship of the inner temple, He will send forth His light and His truth through my whole being, and through mind and will reveal His power to sanctify and to bless.

And through the soul, thus coming ever more mightily under His rule, His power will work out even into the body. With passions and appetites within, yea, with every thought brought into subjection, the hidden Holy Spirit will through the soul penetrate ever deeper into the body. Through the Spirit the deeds of the body will be made dead, and the river of water, that flows from under the throne of God and the Lamb, will go through all the outer nature, with its cleansing and quickening power.

O Brother, do believe that you are the temple of the living God, and that the Spirit of God dwelleth in you! You have been sealed with the Holy Spirit; He is the mark, the living assurance of your sonship and your Father's love. If this have hitherto been a thought that has brought you but little comfort, see if the reason is not here. You sought for Him in the Holy Place, amid the powers and services of your inner life which come within your vision. And you could hardly discern Him there. And so you could not appropriate the comfort and strength the Comforter was meant to bring.

No, my brother, not there, not there. Deeper down, in the secret place of the Most High, there you will find Him. There faith will find Him. And as faith worships in holy reverence before the Father, and the heart trembles at the thought of what it has found, wait in holy stillness on God to grant you the mighty working of His Spirit, wait in holy stillness for the Spirit, and be assured He will, as God, arise and fill His temple with His glory.

And then remember, the veil was but for a time. When the preparation was complete, the veil of the flesh was rent. As you yield your soul's inner life to the inmost life of the Spirit, as the traffic between the Most Holy and the Holy becomes more true and unbroken, the fulness of the time will come in your soul. In the power of Him, in whom the veil was rent that the Spirit might stream forth from His glorified body, there will come to you, too, an experience in which the veil shall be taken away, and the Most Holy and the Holy be thrown into one. The hidden glory of the Secret Place will stream into your conscious daily life: the service of the Holy Place will all be in the power of the eternal Spirit.

Brother, let us fall down and worship! "Be silent, all flesh, before the Lord; for He is waked up out of His holy habitation."

A Prayer to Know God's Indwelling

Most Holy God! in adoring wonder I bow before Thee in presence of this wondrous mystery of grace: my spirit, soul, and body Thy temple.

In deep silence and worship I accept the blessed revelation, that in me too there is a Holiest of all, and that there Thy hidden glory has its abode.

O my God, forgive me that I have so little known it.

I do now tremblingly accept the blessed truth: God the Spirit, the Holy Spirit, who is God Almighty, dwells in me.

O my Father, reveal within what it means, lest I sin against Thee by saying it and not living it.

Blessed Jesus! to Thee, who sittest upon the throne, I yield my whole being. In Thee I trust to rise up in power and have dominion within me.

In Thee I believe for the full streaming forth of the living waters.

Blessed Spirit! Holy Teacher! Mighty Sanctifier! Thou art within me. On Thee do I wait all the day. I belong to Thee. Take entire possession of me for the Father and the Son. Amen.

CHAPTER FOURTEEN

Walking by the Spirit

Walk by the Spirit, and ye shall not fulfil the lust of the flesh. They that are of Christ Jesus have crucified the flesh, with the passions and lusts thereof. If we live by the Spirit, by the Spirit let us also walk (Gal. 5:16, 24–25).

"If we live by the Spirit, by the Spirit let us walk." These words suggest to us very clearly the difference between the sickly and the healthy Christian life. In the former the Christian is content to "live by the Spirit;" he is satisfied with knowing that he has the new life; but he does not walk by the Spirit. The true believer, on the contrary, is not content without having his whole walk and conversation in the power of the Spirit. He walks by the Spirit, and so does not fulfil the lusts of the flesh.

Failure to Walk in the Spirit

As the Christian strives thus to walk worthy of God and well-pleasing to Him in all things, he is often sorely troubled at the power of sin, and asks what the cause may be that he so often fails in conquering it. The answer to this question he ordinarily finds in his want of faith or faithfulness, in his natural feebleness or the mighty power of Satan. Alas! if he rests content with this solution. It is well for him if he press on to find the deeper reason why all these things, from which Christ secured deliverance for him, still can overcome. One of the deepest secrets of the Christian life is the knowledge that the one great power that keeps the Spirit of God from ruling, that the last enemy that must yield to Him, is the flesh. He that knows what *the flesh* is, how it works and how it must be dealt with, will be conqueror.

We know how it was on account of their ignorance of this that the Galatians so sadly failed. It was this led them to attempt to perfect in the flesh what was begun in the Spirit (3:3). It was this made them a prey to those who desired "to make a fair show in the flesh" that they might "glory in the flesh" (6:12, 13). They knew not how incorrigibly corrupt the flesh was. They knew not that, as sinful as our nature is when fulfilling its own lusts, as sinful is it when making "a fair show in the flesh;" it apparently yields itself to the service of God, and undertakes to perfect what the Spirit had begun.

Because they knew not this, they were unable to check the flesh in its passions and lusts; these obtained the victory over them, so that they did what they did not wish. They knew not that, as long as the flesh, self-effort, and self-will had any influence in serving God, it would remain strong to serve sin, and that the only way to render it impotent to do evil was to render it impotent in its attempts to do good.

It is to discover the truth of God concerning the flesh, both in its service of God and of sin, that this epistle was written. Paul wants to teach them how the Spirit, and the Spirit alone, is the power of the Christian life, and how this cannot be except as the flesh, with all that it means, is utterly and entirely set aside. And in answer to the question how this can be, he gives the wonderful answer which is one of the central thoughts of God's revelation. The crucifixion and death of Christ is the revelation not only of an atonement for sin, but of a power which frees from the actual dominion of sin, as it is rooted in the flesh.

When Paul in the midst of his teaching about the walk in the Spirit (16–26) tells us, "They that are Christ's have *crucified* the flesh with its passions and lusts," he tells us what the only way is in which deliverance from the flesh is to be found. To understand this word, "crucified the flesh," and abide it, is the secret of walking not after the flesh but after the Spirit. Let each one who longs to walk by the Spirit try to enter into its meaning.

"The Flesh"

In Scripture this expression means the whole of our human nature in its present condition under the power of sin. It includes our whole being, spirit, soul, and body. After the fall, God said, "man is flesh" (Gen. 6:3). All his powers, intellect, emotions, will—all are under the power of the flesh. Scripture speaks of the will of the flesh, of the mind of the flesh (fleshly mind), of the passions and lusts of the flesh. It tells us that in our flesh dwelleth no good: the mind of the flesh is at enmity against God.

On this ground it teaches that nothing that is of the flesh, that the fleshly mind or will thinks or does, however fair the show it makes, and however much men may glory in it, can have any value in the sight of God. It warns us that our greatest danger in religion, the cause of our feebleness and failure, is our having confidence in the flesh, its wisdom and its work. It tells us that, to be pleasing to God, this flesh, with its self-will and self-effort, must entirely be dispossessed, to make way for the willing and the working of Another, even the Spirit of God. And that the only way to be made free from the power of the flesh, and have it put out of the way, is to have it crucified and given over to the death.

Crucifying the Flesh

"They that are of Christ Jesus *have crucified* the flesh." Men often speak of crucifying the flesh as a thing that has to be done. Scripture always speaks of it as a thing that has been done, an accomplished fact. "Knowing this, that our old man *was crucified* with Him." "*I have been crucified* with Christ." "They that are of Christ Jesus *have crucified* the flesh." "The cross of our Lord Jesus Christ, through which the world *hath been crucified* unto me, and I unto the world."

What Christ, through the eternal Spirit, did on the cross, He did not as an individual, but in the name of that human nature which, as its Head, He had taken upon Himself. Every one who accepts Christ receives Him as the Crucified One, receives not only the merit but the power of His crucifixion, is united and identified with Him, and is called on intelligently and voluntarily to realize and maintain that identification. "They that are of Christ Jesus" have, in virtue of their accepting the crucified Christ as their life, given up their flesh to that cross which is of the very essence of the person and character of Christ as He now lives in heaven; they "have crucified the flesh with its passions and lusts."[1]

---

1. In *The Law of Liberty in the Spiritual Life,* by Rev. E. H. Hopkins, will be found a singularly clear and scriptural exposition of the Life of Faith. The chapters on Conformity to the Death of Christ and on Conflict will be found most helpful to the right understanding of the relation of the believer to the Flesh and the Spirit.

But what does this mean: "They have *crucified* the flesh"? Some are content with the general truth: the cross takes away the curse which there was on the flesh. Others think of causing the flesh pain and suffering, of the duty of denying and mortifying it. Others, again, of the moral influence the thought of the cross will exercise.

In each of these views there is an element of truth. But if they are to be realized in power, we must go to the root-thought: to crucify the flesh is, to give it over to the curse. The cross and the curse are inseparable (Deut. 21:23; Gal. 3:13). To say, "Our old man has been crucified with Him," "I have been crucified with Christ," means something very solemn and awful. It means this: I have seen that my old nature, myself, deserves the curse; that there is no way of getting rid of it but by death: I voluntarily give it to the death. I have accepted as my life the Christ who came to give Himself, His flesh, to the cursed death of the cross; who received His new life alone owing to that death and in virtue of it: I give my old man, my flesh, self, with its will and work, as a sinful, accursed thing, to the cross. It is nailed there: in Christ I am dead to it, and free from it. It is not yet dead; but day by day in union with Christ will I keep it there, making dead, as they still seek to rise up, every one of its members and deeds in the power of the Holy Spirit.

Accepting the Power of the Cross

The power of this truth depends upon its being known, accepted, and acted on. If I only know the cross in its substitution, but not, as Paul gloried in it, in its fellowship (Gal. 6:14), I never can experience its power to sanctify. As the blessed truth of its fellowship dawns upon me, I see how by faith I enter into and live in spiritual communion with that Jesus who, as my head and leader, made and proved the cross the only ladder to the Throne. This spiritual union, maintained by faith, becomes a moral one. I have the same mind or disposition that was in Christ Jesus. I regard the flesh as sinful, and only fit for the curse. I accept the cross, with its death to what is flesh, secured to me in Jesus, as the only way to become free from the power of self, and to walk in the new life by the Spirit of Christ.

The way in which this faith in the power of the cross, as at once the revelation and the removal of the curse and the power of the flesh, is very simple, and yet very solemn. I begin to understand that my one danger in living by the Spirit is yielding to the flesh or self in its attempt to serve God. I see that it renders the cross of Christ of none effect (1 Cor. 1:17; Gal. 3:3, 5:12, 13; Phil. 3:3, 4; Col. 2:18–23).

I see how all that was of man and nature, of law and human effort, was for ever judged of God on Calvary. There flesh proved that, with all its wisdom and all its religion, it hated and rejected the Son of God. There God proved how the only way to deliver from the flesh was to give it to death as an accursed thing. I begin to understand that the one thing I need is: to look upon the flesh as God does; to accept of the death-warrant the cross brings to everything in me that is of the flesh, to look upon it, and all that comes from it, as an accursed thing.

As this habit of soul grows on me, I learn to fear nothing so much as myself. I tremble at the thought of allowing the flesh, my natural mind and will, to usurp the place of the Holy Spirit. My whole posture towards Christ is that of lowly fear, in the consciousness of having within me that accursed thing that is ever ready, as an angel of light, to intrude itself in the Holiest of all, and lead me astray to serve God, not in the Spirit of Christ, but in the power that is of nature. It is in such a lowly fear that the believer is taught to believe fully the need, but also the provision, of the Holy Spirit to take entirely the place which the flesh once had, and day by day to glory in the cross, of which he can say, "By it I have been crucified to the world."

We often seek for the cause of failure in the Christian life. We often think that because we are sound on what the Galatians did not understand—justification by faith alone—their danger was not ours. Oh that we knew to what an extent we have allowed the flesh to work in our religion!

Let us pray God for grace to know it as our bitterest enemy, and the enemy of Christ. Free grace does not only mean the pardon of sin; it means the power of the new life through the Holy Spirit. Let us consent to what God says of the flesh, and all that comes of it: that it is sinful, condemned, accursed. Let us fear nothing so much as the secret workings of our flesh. Let us accept the teaching of God's word: "In my flesh dwelleth no good thing;" "The carnal mind is enmity against God."

Let us ask God to show us how entirely the Spirit must possess us, if we are to be pleasing to Him in all things. Let us believe that as we daily glory in the cross, and, in prayer and obedience, yield the flesh to the death on the cross, Christ will accept our surrender, and will, by His divine power, maintain mightily in us the life of the Spirit. And we shall learn not only to live by the Spirit, but, as those who are made free from the power of the flesh, by its crucifixion, maintained by faith, in very deed to walk by the Spirit.

A Prayer to Walk by the Spirit

Blessed God! I beseech Thee to reveal to me the full meaning of what Thy word has been teaching me, that it is as one who has crucified the flesh with its passions and lusts, that I can walk by the Spirit.

O my Father! teach me to see that all that is of nature and of self is of the flesh; that the flesh has been tested by Thee, and found wanting, worthy of nothing but the curse and death. Teach me that my Lord Jesus led the way, and acknowledged the justice of Thy curse, that I too might be willing and have the power to give it up to the cross as an accursed thing. Oh, give me grace day by day greatly to fear before Thee, lest I allow the flesh to intrude into the work of the Spirit, and to grieve Him. And teach me that the Holy Spirit has indeed been given to be the life of my life, and to fill my whole being with the power of the death and the life of my blessed Lord living in me.

Blessed Lord Jesus! who didst send Thy Holy Spirit, to secure the uninterrupted enjoyment of Thy presence, and Thy saving power within us, I yield myself to be entirely Thine, to live wholly and only under His leading. I do with my whole heart desire to regard the flesh as crucified and accursed. I solemnly consent to live as a crucified one. Saviour! Thou dost accept my surrender; I trust in Thee to keep me this day walking through the Spirit. Amen.

The work of the Holy Spirit is also a prominent theme in Murray's 1895 work Humility, *the subtitle of which is* The Beauty of Holiness.

In "Humility: The Glory of the Creature," Murray discusses how it was God's plan from the beginning to allow His creatures to share in His glory by being vessels for His glory. Pride separates us from this dependence on God, but humility restores us to our proper position before God.

While it is easy to believe we are humble before God, the true test of our humility is our "Humility in Daily Life." The only humility which we truly possess is the humility we show in our ordinary conduct.

"Humility and Exaltation" describes God's command to humble ourselves and His promise to exalt us when we have humbled ourselves. God's dealings with men are always characterized by two steps. The first is a time of preparation, and the second is a time of fulfillment. These correspond to humility and exaltation.

CHAPTER FIFTEEN

Humility: The Glory of the Creature

They shall cast their crowns before the throne, saying: Worthy art Thou, our Lord and our God, to receive the glory and the honor and the power: for Thou didst create all things, and because of Thy will they were, and were created (Rev. 4:11).

When God created the universe, it was with the one object of making the creature partaker of His perfection and blessedness, and so showing forth in it the glory of His love and wisdom and power. God wished to reveal Himself in and through created beings by communicating to them as much of His own goodness and glory as they were capable of receiving. But this communication was not a giving to the creature something which it could possess in itself, a certain life or goodness, of which it had the charge and disposal. By no means.

But as God is the ever-living, ever-present, ever-acting One, who upholdeth all things by the word of His power, and in whom all things exist, the relation of the creature to God could only be one of unceasing, absolute, universal dependence. As truly as God by His power once created, so truly by that same power must God every moment maintain. The creature has not only to look back to the origin and first beginning of existence, and acknowledge that it there owes everything to God; its chief care, its highest virtue, its only happiness, now and through all eternity, is to present itself an empty vessel, in which God can dwell and manifest His power and goodness.

The life God bestows is imparted not once for all, but each moment continu-

ously, by the unceasing operation of His mighty power. Humility, the place of entire dependence on God, is, from the very nature of things, the first duty and the highest virtue of the creature, and the root of every virtue.

And so pride, or the loss of this humility, is the root of every sin and evil. It was when the now fallen angels began to look upon themselves with self-complacency that they were led to disobedience, and were cast down from the light of heaven into outer darkness. Even so it was, when the serpent breathed the poison of his pride, the desire to be as God, into the hearts of our first parents, that they, too, fell from their high estate into all the wretchedness in which man is now sunk. In heaven and earth, pride, self-exaltation, is the gate and the birth, and the curse, of hell.

The Restoration of Humility

Hence, it follows that nothing can be our redemption, but the restoration of the lost humility, the original and only true relation of the creature to its God. And so Jesus came to bring humility back to earth, to make us partakers of it, and by it to save us. In heaven He humbled Himself to become man. The humility we see in Him possessed Him in heaven; it brought Him, he brought it, from there. Here on earth "He humbled Himself, and became obedient unto death"; His humility gave His death its value, and so became our redemption.

And now the salvation He imparts is nothing less and nothing else than a communication of His own life and death, His own disposition and spirit, His own humility, as the ground and root of His relation to God and His redeeming work. Jesus Christ took the place and fulfilled the destiny of man, as a creature, by His life of perfect humility. His humility is our salvation. His salvation is our humility.

And so the life of the saved ones, of the saints, must needs bear this stamp of deliverance from sin, and full restoration to their original state; their whole relation to God and man marked by an all-pervading humility. Without this there can be no true abiding in God's presence, or experience of His favor and the power of His spirit; without this no abiding faith, or love or joy or strength. Humility is the only soil in which the graces root; the lack of humility is the sufficient explanation of every defect and failure. Humility is not so much a grace or virtue along with others; it is the root of all, because it alone takes the right attitude before God, and allows Him as God to do all.

The Call to Humility

God has so constituted us as reasonable beings, that the truer the insight into the real nature or the absolute need of a command, the readier and fuller will be our obedience to it. The call to humility has been too little regarded in the church, because its true nature and importance has been too little apprehended. It is not a something which we bring to God, or He bestows; it is simply *the sense of entire nothingness, which comes when we see how truly God is all,*

and in which we make way for God to be all. When the creature realizes that this is the true nobility, and consents to be with his will, his mind and his affections, the form, the vessel in which the life and glory of God are to work and manifest themselves, he sees that humility is simply acknowledging the truth of his position as creature, and yielding to God his place.

In the life of earnest Christians, of those who pursue and profess holiness, humility ought to be the chief mark of their uprightness. It is often said that it is not so. May not one reason be that in the teaching and example of the church, it has never had that place of supreme importance which belongs to it? And that this, again, is owing to the neglect of this truth, that strong as sin is as a motive to humility, there is one of still wider and mightier influence, that which makes the angels, that which made Jesus, that which makes the holiest of saints in heaven, so humble; that the first and chief mark of the relation of the creature, the secret of his blessedness, is the humility and nothingness which leaves God free to be all?

I am sure there are many Christians who will confess that their experience has been very much like my own in this, that we had long known the Lord without realizing that meekness and lowliness of heart are to be the distinguishing feature of the disciple as they were of the Master. And further, that this humility is not a thing that will come of itself, but that it must be made the object of special desire and prayer and faith and practice. As we study the word, we shall see what very distinct and oft-repeated instructions Jesus gave His disciples on this point, and how slow they were in understanding Him.

Let us, at the very commencement of our meditations, admit that there is nothing so natural to man, nothing so insidious and hidden from our sight, nothing so difficult and dangerous, as pride. Let us feel that nothing but a very determined and persevering waiting on God and Christ will discover how lacking we are in the grace of humility, and how impotent to obtain what we seek. Let us study the character of Christ until our souls are filled with the love and admiration of His lowliness. And let us believe that, when we are broken down under a sense of our pride, and our impotence to cast it out, Jesus Christ Himself will come in to impart this grace, too, as a part of His wondrous life within us.

CHAPTER SIXTEEN

Humility in Daily Life

He that loveth not his brother whom he hath seen, how can he love God whom he hath not seen? (John 4:20).

Humility in Relationships

What a solemn thought, that our love to God will be measured by our everyday intercourse with men and the love it displays; and that our love to God will be found to be a delusion, except as its truth is proved in standing the test of daily life with our fellow-men. It is even so with our humility. It is easy to think we humble ourselves before God: humility towards men will be the only sufficient proof that our humility before God is real; that humility has taken up its abode in us, and become our very nature; that we actually, like Christ, have made ourselves of no reputation. When in the presence of God lowliness of heart has become, not a posture we assume for a time, when we think of Him, or pray to Him, but the very spirit of our life, it will manifest itself in all our bearing towards our brethren.

The lesson is one of deep import: the only humility that is really ours is not that which we try to show before God in prayer, but that which we carry with us, and carry out, in our ordinary conduct; the insignificances of daily life are the importances and the tests of eternity, because they prove what really is the spirit that possesses us. It is in our most unguarded moments that we really show and see what we are. To know the humble man, to know how the humble man behaves, you must follow him in the common course of daily life.

Is not this what Jesus taught? It was when the disciples disputed who should be greatest; when He saw how the Pharisees loved the chief place at feasts and the chief seats in the synagogues; when He had given them the example of washing their feet—that He taught His lessons of humility. Humility before God is nothing if not proved in humility before men.

It is even so in the teaching of Paul. To the Romans he writes: "In honor preferring *one another*"; "Set not your mind on high things, but condescend to *those that are lowly*"; "Be not wise in your own conceit." To the Corinthians: "Love," and there is no love without humility as its root, "vaunteth not itself, is not puffed up, seeketh not its own, is not provoked." To the Galatians: "Through love be servants *one of another*. Let us not be desirous of vainglory, provoking *one another*, envying *one another*." To the Ephesians, immediately after the three wonderful chapters on the heavenly life: "Therefore, walk with all lowliness and meekness, with long-suffering, forbearing *one another* in love"; "Giving thanks always, subjecting yourselves *one to another* in the fear of Christ." To the Philippians: "Doing nothing through faction or vainglory, but in lowliness of mind, each counting *others* better than himself. Have the mind in you which was also in Christ Jesus, who emptied Himself, taking the form of a servant, and humbled Himself." And to the Colossians: "Put on a heart of compassion, kindness, humility, meekness, long-suffering, forbearing *one another*, and forgiving *each other*, even as the Lord forgave you."

It is in our relation to one another, in our treatment of one another, that the true lowliness of mind and the heart of humility are to be seen. Our humility before God has no value, but as it prepares us to reveal the humility of Jesus to our fellow-men. Let us study humility in daily life in the light of these words.

The humble man seeks at all times to act up to the rule, *"In honor preferring one another; Servants one of another; Each counting others better than himself; Subjecting yourselves one to another."* The question is often asked, how we can count others better than ourselves, when we see that they are far below us in wisdom and in holiness, in natural gifts, or in grace received. The question proves at once how little we understand what real lowliness of mind is. True humility comes when, in the light of God, we have seen ourselves to be nothing, have consented to part with and cast away self, to let God be all.

The soul that has done this, and can say, So have I lost myself in finding Thee, no longer compares itself with others. It has given up forever every thought of self in God's presence; it meets its fellow-men as one who is nothing, and seeks nothing for itself; who is a servant of God, and for His sake a servant of all. A faithful servant may be wiser than the master, and yet retain the true spirit and posture of the servant. The humble man looks upon every, the feeblest and unworthiest, child of God, and honors him and prefers him in honor as the son of a king. The spirit of Him who washed the disciples' feet, makes it a joy to us to be indeed the least, to be servants one of another.

Humility in Temptations

The humble man feels no jealousy or envy. He can praise God when others are preferred and blessed before him. He can bear to hear others praised and himself forgotten, because in God's presence he has learned to say with Paul, "I am nothing." He has received the spirit of Jesus, who pleased not Himself, and sought not His own honor, as the spirit of his life.

Amid what are considered the temptations to impatience and touchiness, to hard thoughts and sharp words, which come from the failings and sins of fellow-Christians, the humble man carries the oft-repeated injunction in his heart, and shows it in his life, *"Forbearing one another, and forgiving one another, even as the Lord forgave you."* He has learned that in putting on the Lord Jesus he *has put on the heart of compassion, kindness, humility, meekness, and long-suffering.* Jesus has taken the place of self, and it is not an impossibility to forgive as Jesus forgave. His humility does not consist merely in thoughts or words of self-depreciation, but, as Paul puts it, in "a heart of humility," encompassed by compassion and kindness, meekness and long-suffering—the sweet and lowly gentleness recognized as the mark of the Lamb of God.

In striving after the higher experiences of the Christian life, the believer is often in danger of aiming at and rejoicing in what one might call the more human, the manly, virtues, such as boldness, joy, contempt of the world, zeal, self-sacrifice—even the old Stoics taught and practiced these—while the deeper and gentler, the diviner and more heavenly graces, those which Jesus first taught upon earth, because He brought them from heaven; those which are more distinctly connected with His cross and the death of self—

poverty of spirit, meekness, humility, lowliness—are scarcely thought of or valued. Therefore, let us put on a heart of compassion, kindness, humility, meekness, long-suffering; and let us prove our Christ-likeness, not only in our zeal for saving the lost, but before all in our intercourse with the brethren, forbearing and forgiving one another, *even as the Lord forgave us.*

Shortcomings in Humility

Fellow-Christians, do let us study the Bible portrait of the humble man. And let us ask our brethren, and ask the world, whether they recognize in us the likeness to the original. Let us be content with nothing less than taking each of these texts as the promise of what God will work in us, as the revelation in words of what the Spirit of Jesus will give as a birth within us. And let each failure and shortcoming simply urge us to turn humbly and meekly to the meek and lowly lamb of God, in the assurance that where He is enthroned in the heart, His humility and gentleness will be one of the streams of living water that flow from within us.[1]

Once again I repeat what I have said before. I feel deeply that we have very little conception of what the church suffers from the lack of this divine humility—the nothingness that makes room for God to prove His power. It is not long since a Christian, of an humble, loving spirit, acquainted with not a few mission stations of various societies, expressed his deep sorrow that in some cases the spirit of love and forbearance

was sadly lacking. Men and women, who in Europe could each choose their own circle of friends, brought close together with others of uncongenial minds, find it hard to bear, and to love, and to keep the unity of the Spirit in the bond of peace. And those who should have been fellow-helpers of each other's joy, became a hindrance and a weariness. And all for the one reason, the lack of the humility which counts itself nothing, which rejoices in becoming and being counted the least, and only seeks, like Jesus, to be the servant, the helper and comforter of others, even the lowest and unworthiest.

And whence comes it that men who have joyfully given up themselves for Christ, find it so hard to give up themselves for their brethren? Is not the blame with the church? It has so little taught its sons that the humility of Christ is the first of the virtues, the best of all the graces and powers of the Spirit. It has so little proved that a Christlike humility is what it, like Christ, places and preaches first, as what is in very deed needed, and possible too.

But let us not be discouraged. Let the discovery of the lack of this grace stir us to larger expectation from God. Let us look upon every brother who tries or vexes us, as God's means of grace, God's instrument for our purification, for our exercise of the humility Jesus our Life breathes within us. And let us have such faith in the all of God, and the nothing of self, that, as nothing in our own eyes, we may, in God's power, only seek to serve one another in love.

---

1. "I knew Jesus, and He was very precious to my soul: but I found something in me that would not keep sweet and patient and kind. I did what I could to keep it down, but it was there. I besought Jesus to do something for me, and when I gave Him my will, He came to my heart, and took out all that would not be sweet, all that would not be kind, all that would not be patient, and then He shut the door." George Foxe.

CHAPTER SEVENTEEN

Humility and Exaltation

"He that humbleth himself shall be exalted" (Luke 14:11, 18:13).
God giveth grace to the humble. Humble yourself in the sight of the Lord, and He shall exalt you (James 4:10).
Humble yourselves therefore under the mighty hand of God, that He may exalt you in due time (1 Pet. 5:6).

Humble Yourself

Just yesterday I was asked the question, How am I to conquer this pride? The answer was simple. Two things are needed. Do what God says is your work: humble yourself. Trust Him to do what He says is His work: He will exalt you.

The command is clear: humble yourself. That does not mean that it is your work to conquer and cast out the pride of your nature, and to form within yourself the lowliness of the holy Jesus. No, this is God's work; the very essence of that exaltation, wherein He lifts you up into the real likeness of the beloved Son.

What the command does mean is this: take every opportunity of humbling yourself before God and man. In the faith of the grace that is already working in you; in the assurance of the more grace for victory that is coming; up to the light that conscience each time flashes upon the pride of the heart and its workings; notwithstanding all there may be of failure and falling, stand persistently as under the unchanging command: humble yourself. Accept with gratitude everything that God allows from within or without, from friend or enemy, in nature or in grace, to remind you of your need of humbling, and to help you to it. Reckon humility to be indeed the mother-virtue, your very first

duty before God, the one perpetual safeguard of the soul, and set your heart upon it as the source of all blessing.

The promise is divine and sure: He that humbleth himself shall be exalted. See that you do the one thing God asks: humble yourself. God will see that He does the one thing He has promised. He will give more grace; He will exalt you in due time.

The Two Stages of Humility

All God's dealings with man are characterized by two stages. There is the time of preparation, when command and promise, with the mingled experience of effort and impotence, of failure and partial success, with the holy expectancy of something better which these waken, train and discipline men for a higher stage. Then comes the time of fulfillment, when faith inherits the promise, and enjoys what it had so often struggled for in vain.

This law holds good in every part of the Christian life, and in the pursuit of every separate virtue. And that because it is grounded in the very nature of things. In all that concerns our redemption, God must needs take the initiative. When that has been done, man's turn comes. In the effort after obedience and attainment, he must learn to know his impotence, in self-despair to die to himself, and so be fitted voluntarily and intelligently to receive from God the end, the completion of that of which he had accepted the beginning in ignorance. So, God who had been the Beginning, ere man rightly knew Him, or fully understood what His purpose was, is longed for and welcomed as the End, as the All in All.

It is even thus, too, in the pursuit of humility. To every Christian the command comes from the throne of God Himself: humble yourself. The earnest attempt to listen and obey will be rewarded—yes, rewarded—with the painful discovery of two things. The one, what depth of pride, that is of unwillingness to count oneself and to be counted nothing, to submit absolutely to God, there was, that one never knew. The other, what utter impotence there is in all our efforts, and in all our prayers too for God's help, to destroy the hideous monster.

Blessed the man who now learns to put his hope in God, and to persevere, notwithstanding all the power of pride within him, in acts of humiliation before God and men. We know the law of human nature: acts produce habits, habits breed dispositions, dispositions form the will, and the rightly-formed will is character. It is not otherwise in the work of grace. As acts, persistently repeated, beget habits and dispositions, and these strengthen the will, He who works both to will and to do comes with His mighty power and Spirit; and the humbling of the proud heart with which the penitent saint cast himself so often before God, is rewarded with the "more grace" of the humble heart, in which the Spirit of Jesus has conquered, and brought the new nature to its maturity, and He the meek and lowly One now dwells for ever.

Humility and Exaltation

Humble yourselves in the sight of the Lord, and He will exalt you. And wherein does the exaltation consist? The highest glory of the creature is in being only a vessel, to receive and enjoy and show forth the glory of God. It can do this only as it is willing to be nothing in itself, that God may be all. Water always fills first the lowest places. The lower, the emptier a man lies before God, the speedier and the fuller will be the inflow of the divine glory.

The exaltation God promises is not, cannot be, any eternal thing apart from Himself: all that He has to give or can give is only more of Himself, Himself to take more complete possession. The exaltation is not, like an earthly prize, something arbitrary, in no necessary connection with the conduct to be rewarded. No, but it is in its very nature the effect and result of the humbling of ourselves. It is nothing but the gift of such a divine indwelling humility, such a conformity to and possession of the humility of the Lamb of God, as fits us for receiving fully the indwelling of God.

He that humbleth himself shall be exalted. Of the truth of these words Jesus Himself is the proof; of the certainty of their fulfillment to us He is the pledge. Let us take His yoke upon us and learn of Him, for He is meek and lowly of heart. If we are but willing to stoop to IIim, as He has stooped to us, He will yet stoop to each one of us again, and we shall find ourselves not unequally yoked with Him. As we enter deeper into the fellowship of His humiliation, and either humble ourselves or bear the humbling of men, we can count upon it that the Spirit of His exaltation, "the Spirit of God and of glory," will rest upon us. The presence and the power of the glorified Christ will come to them that are of an humble spirit. When God can again have His rightful place in us, He will lift us up.

Make His glory thy care in humbling thyself; He will make thy glory His care in perfecting thy humility, and breathing into thee, as thy abiding life, the very Spirit of His Son. As the all-pervading life of God possesses thee, there will be nothing so natural, and nothing so sweet, as to be nothing, with not a thought or wish for self, because all is occupied with Him who filleth all. "Most gladly will I glory in my weakness, that the strength of Christ may rest upon me."

Brother, have we not here the reason that our consecration and our faith have availed so little in the pursuit of holiness? It was by self and its strength that the work was done under the name of faith; it was for self and its happiness that God was called in; it was, unconsciously, but still truly, in self and its holiness that the soul rejoiced. We never knew that humility, absolute, abiding, Christlike humility and self-effacement, pervading and marking our whole life with God and man, was the most essential element of the life of the holiness we sought for.

It is only in the possession of God that I lose myself. As it is in the height and breadth and glory of the sunshine that the littleness of the mote playing in its beams is seen, even so humility is the taking our place in God's presence to be nothing but a mote dwelling in the sunlight of His love.

How great is God! how small am I!
Lost, swallowed up in Love's
    immensity!
        God only there, not I.

May God teach us to believe that to be humble, to be nothing in His presence, is the highest attainment, and the fullest blessing, of the Christian life. He speaks to us: "I dwell in the high and holy place, and with him that is of a contrite and humble spirit." Be this our portion!

Oh, to be emptier, lowlier,
    Mean, unnoticed, and unknown,
And to God a vessel holier,
    Filled with Christ, and Christ alone!

Murray's emphasis on the Holy Spirit and a life of holiness can also be seen in Absolute Surrender, *an 1895 collection of addresses. The title address, "Absolute Surrender," was the theme for a series of holiness conventions Murray organized and is a theme that is common in Murray's writings. Absolute surrender is the one thing that the church needs. God not only claims absolute surrender from us as our Creator but also works it in us, maintains it in us, and blesses us by it.*

"The Fruit of the Spirit is Love," Murray tells us, because God Himself is love. This love, which can only come from the Spirit, is the only power by which we can really do our daily work as believers.

In "Peter's Repentance" Murray comments on Peter's denial of Christ and his repentance afterwards. Though Peter was a devoted disciple who was a man of absolute surrender, he was still living to himself. Peter's repentance, however, allowed him to be delivered from himself.

"Ye Are the Branches" is another common theme in Murray's writings and is similar to his understanding of what it means to abide in Christ and to practice absolute surrender. We are entirely dependent upon Christ, our true Vine, for life. Our work is to abide in Him and to have a life of absolute surrender because it is only in close communion with the Vine that we can bear fruit.

CHAPTER EIGHTEEN

Absolute Surrender

And Ben-hadad the king of Syria gathered all his host together: and there were thirty and two kings with him, and horses, and chariots: and he went up and besieged Samaria, and warred against it. And he sent messengers to Ahab king of Israel into the city, and said unto him, thus saith Ben-hadad, Thy silver and thy gold is mine; thy wives also and thy children, even the goodliest, are mine. And the king of Israel answered and said, My lord, O king, according to thy saying, I am thine and all that I have (1 Kings 20:1–4).

What Ben-hadad asked was *absolute surrender;* and what Ahab gave was what was asked of him—*absolute surrender.* I want to use these words: "My lord, O king, according to thy saying, I am thine, and all that I have," as the words of absolute surrender with which every child of God ought to yield himself to his Father. We have heard it before, but we need to hear it very definitely— the condition of God's blessing is absolute surrender of all into His hands. Praise God! if our hearts are willing for that, there is no end to what God will do for us, and to the blessing God will bestow.

Absolute surrender—let me tell you where I got those words. I used them myself often, and you have heard them numberless times. But in Scotland once I was in a company where we were talking about the condition of Christ's church, and what the great need of the church and of believers is; and there was in our company a godly worker who has much to do in training workers, and I asked him what he would say was the great need of the church, and the message that ought to be preached. He answered very quietly and simply and determinedly: *"Absolute surrender to God is the one thing."*

The words struck me as never before.

And that man began to tell how, in the workers with whom he had to deal, he finds that if they are sound on that point, even though they be backward, they are willing to be taught and helped, and they always improve; whereas others who are not sound there very often go back and leave the work. The condition for obtaining God's full blessing is *absolute surrender* to Him.

And now, I desire by God's grace to give to you this message—that your God in Heaven answers the prayers which you have offered for blessing on yourselves and for blessing on those around you by this one demand: *Are you willing to surrender yourselves absolutely into His hands?* What is our answer to be? God knows there are hundreds of hearts who have said it, and there are hundreds more who long to say it but hardly dare to do so. And there are hearts who have said it, but who have yet miserably failed, and who feel themselves condemned because they did not find the secret of the power to live that life. May God have a word for all!

God Claims It from Us

Yes, it has its foundation in the very nature of God. God cannot do otherwise. Who is God? He is the Fountain of life, the only Source of existence and power and goodness, and throughout the universe there is nothing good but what God works. God has created the sun, and the moon, and the stars, and the flowers, and the trees, and the grass; and are they not all absolutely surrendered to God? Do they not allow God to work in them just what He pleases? When God clothes the lily with its beauty, is it not yielded up, surrendered, given over to God as He works in it its beauty? And God's redeemed children, oh, can you think that God can work His work if there is only half or a part of them surrendered? God cannot do it. God is life, and love, and blessing, and power, and infinite beauty, and God delights to communicate Himself to every child who is prepared to receive Him; but ah! this one lack of absolute surrender is just the thing that hinders God. And now He comes, and as God, He claims it.

You know in daily life what absolute surrender is. You know that everything has to be given up to its special, definite object and service. I have a pen in my pocket, and that pen is absolutely surrendered to the one work of writing, and that pen must be absolutely surrendered to my hand if I am to write properly with it. If another holds it partly, I cannot write properly. This coat is absolutely given up to me to cover my body. This building is entirely given up to religious services.

And now, do you expect that in your immortal being, in the divine nature that you have received by regeneration, God can work His work, every day and every hour, unless you are entirely given up to Him? God cannot. The temple of Solomon was absolutely surrendered to God when it was dedicated to Him. And every one of us is a temple of God, in which God will dwell and work mightily on one condition—absolute surrender to Him. God claims it, God is worthy of it, and without it God cannot work His blessed work in us.

God Will Work It Himself

I am sure there is many a heart that says: "Ah, but that absolute surrender implies so much!" Someone says: "Oh, I have passed through so much trial and suffering, and there is so much of the self-life still remaining, and I dare not face the entire giving of it up, because I know it will cause so much trouble and agony."

Alas! alas! that God's children have such thoughts of Him, such cruel thoughts. Oh, I come to you with a message, fearful and anxious one. God does not ask you to give the perfect surrender in your strength, or by the power of your will; God is willing to work it in you. Do we not read: "It is God that worketh in us, both to will and to do of his good pleasure"? And that is what we should seek for—to go on our faces before God, until our hearts learn to believe that the everlasting God Himself will come in to turn out what is wrong, to conquer what is evil, and to work what is well-pleasing in His blessed sight. God Himself will work it in you.

Look at the men in the Old Testament, like Abraham. Do you think it was by accident that God found that man, the father of the faithful and the friend of God, and that it was Abraham himself, apart from God, who had such faith and such obedience and such devotion? You know it is not so. God raised him up and prepared him as an instrument for His glory.

Did not God say to Pharaoh: "For this cause have I raised thee up, for to show in thee my power"?

And if God said that of him, will not

God say it far more of every child of His?

Oh, I want to encourage you, and I want you to cast away every fear. Come with that feeble desire; and if there is the fear which says: "Oh, my desire is not strong enough, I am not willing for everything that may come, I do not feel bold enough to say I can conquer everything"—I pray you, learn to know and trust your God now. Say: "My God, I am willing that Thou shouldst make me willing." If there is anything holding you back, or any sacrifice you are afraid of making, come to God now, and prove how gracious your God is, and be not afraid that He will command from you what He will not bestow.

God comes and offers to work this absolute surrender in you. All these searchings and hungerings and longings that are in your heart, I tell you they are the drawings of the divine magnet, Christ Jesus. He lived a life of absolute surrender, He has possession of you; He is living in your heart by His Holy Spirit. You have hindered and hindered Him terribly, but He desires to help you to get hold of Him entirely. And He comes and draws you now by His message and words. Will you not come and trust God to work in you that absolute surrender to Himself? Yes, blessed be God, He can do it, and He will do it.

God Accepts It
When We Bring It to Him

God works it in the secret of our heart, God urges us by the hidden power of His Holy Spirit to come and speak it out, and we have to bring and to yield to Him that absolute surrender. But remember, when you come and bring God that absolute surrender, it may, as far as your feelings or your consciousness go, be a thing of great imperfection, and you may doubt and hesitate and say:

"Is it absolute?"

But, oh, remember there was once a man to whom Christ had said:

"If thou canst believe, all things are possible to him that believeth."

And his heart was afraid, and he cried out:

"Lord, I believe, help thou mine unbelief."

That was a faith that triumphed over the devil, and the evil spirit was cast out. And if you come and say: "Lord, I yield myself in absolute surrender to my God," even though it be with a trembling heart and with the consciousness: "I do not feel the power, I do not feel the determination, I do not feel the assurance," it will succeed. Be not afraid, but come just as you are, and even in the midst of your trembling the power of the Holy Ghost will work.

Have you never yet learned the lesson that the Holy Ghost works with mighty power, while on the human side everything appears feeble? Look at the Lord Jesus Christ in Gethsemane. We read that He, "through the eternal Spirit," offered Himself a sacrifice unto God. The almighty Spirit of God was enabling Him to do it. And yet what agony and fear and exceeding sorrow came over Him, and how He prayed! Externally, you can see no sign of the mighty power of the Spirit, but the Spirit of God was there. And even so, while you are feeble and fighting and trembling, in faith in the hidden work of God's Spirit do not fear, but yield yourself.

And when you do yield yourself in absolute surrender, let it be in the faith that God does now accept of it. That is the great point, and that is what we so often miss—that believers should be thus occupied with God in this matter of surrender. I pray you, be occupied with God. We want to get help, every one of us, so that in our daily life God shall be clearer to us, God shall have the right place, and be "all in all." And if we are to have that through life, let us begin now and look away from ourselves, and look up to God.

Let each believe—while I, a poor worm on earth and a trembling child of God, full of failure and sin and fear, bow here, and no one knows what passes through my heart, and while I in simplicity say, O God, I accept Thy terms; I have pleaded for blessing on myself and others, I have accepted Thy terms of absolute surrender—while your heart says that in deep silence, remember there is a God present that takes note of it, and writes it down in His book, and there is a God present who at that very moment takes possession of you. You may not feel it, you may not realize it, but God takes possession if you will trust Him.

God Maintains It

That is the great difficulty with many. People say: "I have often been stirred at a meeting, or at a convention, and I have consecrated myself to God, but it has passed away. I know it may last for a week or for a month, but away it fades, and after a time it is all gone."

But listen! It is because you do not believe what I am now going to tell you and remind you of. When God has begun the work of absolute surrender in you, and when God has accepted your surrender, then God holds Himself bound to care for it and to keep it. Will you believe that?

In this matter of surrender there are two: God and I—I a worm, God the everlasting and omnipotent Jehovah. Worm, will you be afraid to trust yourself to this mighty God now? God is willing. Do you not believe that He can keep you continually, day by day, and moment by moment?

Moment by moment I'm *kept*
   in His love;
Moment by moment I've life
   from above.

If God allows the sun to shine upon you moment by moment, without intermission, will not God let His life shine upon you every moment? And why have you not experienced it? Because you have not trusted God for it, and you do not surrender yourself absolutely to God in that trust.

A life of absolute surrender has its difficulties. I do not deny that. Yea, it has something far more than difficulties: it is a life that with men is absolutely impossible. But by the grace of God, by the power of God, by the power of the Holy Spirit dwelling in us, it is a life to which we are destined, and a life that is possible for us, praise God! Let us believe that God will maintain it.

Some of you have read the words of that aged saint who, on his ninetieth birthday, told of all God's goodness to him—I mean George Muller. What did he say he believed to be the secret of his happiness, and of all the blessing with which God had visited him? He said he believed there were two reasons. The one was that he had been enabled by grace to maintain a good conscience before God day by day; the other was, that he was a lover of God's Word. Ah, yes, a good conscience is unfeigned obedience to God day by day, and fellowship with God every day in His Word, and prayer—that is a life of absolute surrender.

Such a life has two sides—on the one side, *absolute surrender to work what God wants you to do;* on the other side, to let God work what He wants to do.

First, *to do what God wants you to do.*

Give up yourselves absolutely to the will of God. You know something of that will; not enough, far from all. But say absolutely to the Lord God: "By Thy grace I desire to do Thy will in everything, every moment of every day." Say: "Lord God, not a word upon my tongue but for Thy glory, not a movement of my temper but for Thy glory, not an affection of love or hate in my heart but for Thy glory, and according to Thy blessed will."

Someone says: "Do you think that possible?"

I ask, What has God promised you, and what can God do to fill a vessel absolutely surrendered to Him? Oh, God wants to bless you in a way beyond what you expect. From the beginning ear hath not heard, neither hath the eye seen, what God hath prepared for them that wait for Him. God has prepared unheard-of things you never can think of; blessings much more wonderful than you can imagine, more mighty than you can conceive. They are divine blessings. Oh, say now:

"I give myself absolutely to God, to His will, to do only what God wants."

It is God who will enable you to carry out the surrender.

And, on the other side, come and say: "I give myself absolutely to God, *to let Him work in me to will and to do of His good pleasure,* as He has promised to do."

Yes, the living God wants to work in His children in a way that we cannot understand, but that God's Word has revealed, and He wants to work in us every moment of the day. God is willing to maintain our life. Only let our absolute surrender be one of simple, childlike, and unbounded trust.

Absolute Surrender to God Will Wonderfully Bless Us

What Ahab said to his enemy, King Ben-hadad—"My lord, O king, according to thy word I am thine, and all that

I have"—shall we not say to our God and loving Father? If we do say it, God's blessing will come upon us. God wants us to be separate from the world; we are called to come out from the world that hates God. Come out for God, and say: "Lord, anything for Thee." If you say that with prayer, and speak that into God's ear, He will accept it, and He will teach you what it means.

I say again, God will bless you. You have been praying for blessing. But do remember, there must be absolute surrender. At every tea-table you see it. Why is tea poured into that cup? Because it is empty, and given up for the tea. But put ink, or vinegar, or wine into it, and will they pour the tea into the vessel? And can God fill you, can God bless you if you are not absolutely surrendered to Him? He cannot. Let us believe God has wonderful blessings for us, if we will but stand up for God, and say, be it with a trembling will, yet with a believing heart:

"O God, I accept Thy demands. I am thine and all that I have. Absolute surrender is what my soul yields to Thee by divine grace."

You may not have such strong and clear feelings of deliverances as you would desire to have, but humble yourselves in His sight, and acknowledge that you have grieved the Holy Spirit by your self-will, self-confidence, and self-effort. Bow humbly before Him in the confession of that, and ask Him to break the heart and to bring you into the dust before Him. Then, as you bow before Him, just accept God's teaching that in your flesh "there dwelleth no good thing," and that nothing will help you except another life which must come in. You must deny self once for all. Denying self must every moment be the power of your life, and then Christ will come in and take possession of you.

When was Peter delivered? When was

the change accomplished? The change began with Peter weeping, and the Holy Ghost came down and filled his heart.

God the Father loves to give us the power of the Spirit. We have the Spirit of God dwelling within us. We come to God confessing that, and praising God for it, and yet confessing how we have grieved the Spirit. And then we bow our knees to the Father to ask that He would strengthen us with all might by the Spirit in the inner man, and that He would fill us with His mighty power. And as the Spirit reveals Christ to us, Christ comes to live in our hearts forever, and the self-life is cast out.

Let us bow before God in humiliation, and in that humiliation confess before Him the state of the whole church. No words can tell the sad state of the church of Christ on earth. I wish I had words to speak what I sometimes feel about it. Just think of the Christians around you. I do not speak of nominal Christians, or of professing Christians, but I speak of hundreds and thousands of honest, earnest Christians who are not living a life in the power of God or to His glory. So little power, so little devotion or consecration to God, so little conception of the truth that a Christian is a man utterly surrendered to God's will! Oh, we want to confess the sins of God's people around us, and to humble ourselves. We are members of that sickly body, and the sickliness of the body will hinder us, and break us down, unless we come to God, and in confession separate ourselves from partnership with worldliness, with coldness toward each other, unless we give up ourselves to be entirely and wholly for God.

How much Christian work is being done in the spirit of the flesh and in the power of self! How much work, day by day, in which human energy—our will and our thoughts about the work—is continually manifested, and in which there is but little of waiting upon God, and upon the power of the Holy Ghost! Let us make confession. But as we confess the state of the church and the feebleness and sinfulness of work for God among us, let us come back to ourselves. Who is there who truly longs to be delivered from the power of the self-life, who truly acknowledges that it *is* the power of self and the flesh, and who is willing to cast all at the feet of Christ? There is deliverance.

I heard of one who had been an earnest Christian, and who spoke about the "cruel" thought of separation and death. But you do not think that, do you? What are we to think of separation and death? This: death was the path to glory for Christ. For the joy set before Him He endured the cross. The cross was the birthplace of His everlasting glory. Do you love Christ? Do you long to be *in* Christ, and not *like* Him? Let death be to you the most desirable thing on earth—death to self, and fellowship with Christ. Separation—do you think it a hard thing to be called to be entirely free from the world, and by that separation to be united to God and His love, by separation to become prepared for living and walking with God every day? Surely one ought to say:

"Anything to bring me to separation, to death, for a life of full fellowship with God and Christ."

Oh! come and cast this self-life and flesh-life at the feet of Jesus. Then trust Him. Do not worry yourselves with trying to understand all about it, but come in the living faith that Christ will come into you with the power of His death and the power of His life; and then the Holy Spirit will bring the whole Christ—Christ crucified and risen and living in glory—into your heart.

CHAPTER NINETEEN

The Fruit of the Spirit Is Love

I want to look at the fact of a life filled with the Holy Spirit more from the practical side, and to show how this life will show itself in our daily walk and conduct.

Under the Old Testament you know the Holy Spirit often came upon men as a divine spirit of revelation to reveal the mysteries of God, or for power to do the work of God. But He did not then dwell in them. Now, many just want the Old Testament gift of power for work, but know very little of the New Testament gift of the indwelling Spirit, animating and renewing the whole life. When God gives the Holy Spirit, His great object is the formation of a holy character. It is a gift of a holy mind and spiritual disposition, and what we need above everything else, is to say:

"I must have the Holy Spirit sanctifying my whole inner life if I am really to live for God's glory."

You might say that when Christ promised the Spirit to the disciples He did so that they might have power to be witnesses. True, but then they received the Holy Ghost in such heavenly power and reality that He took possession of their whole being at once and so fitted them as holy men for doing the work with power as they had to do it. Christ spoke of power to the disciples, but it was the Spirit filling their whole being that worked the power.

I wish now to dwell upon the passage found in Galatians 5:22:

"The fruit of the Spirit is love."

We read that "Love is the fulfilling of the law," and my desire is to speak on love as a fruit of the Spirit with a two-fold object. One is that this word may be a searchlight in our hearts, and give us a test by which to try all our thoughts about the Holy Spirit and all our experience of the holy life. Let us try ourselves by this word. Has this been our daily habit, to seek the being filled with the Holy Spirit as the Spirit of love? "The fruit of the Spirit is love." Has it been our experience that the more we have of the Holy Spirit the more loving we become? In claiming the Holy Spirit we should make this the first object of our expectation. The Holy Spirit comes as a Spirit of love.

Oh, if this were true in the church of Christ how different her state would be! May God help us to get hold of this simple, heavenly truth that the fruit of the Spirit is a love which appears in the life, and that just as the Holy Spirit gets real possession of the life, the heart will be filled with real, divine, universal love.

One of the great causes why God cannot bless His Church is *the want of love*. When the body is divided, there cannot be strength. In the time of their great religious wars, when Holland stood out so nobly against Spain, one of their mottoes was: "Unity gives strength." It is only when God's people stand as one body, one before God in the fellowship of love, one toward another in deep affection, one before the world in a love that the world can see—it is only then that they will have power to secure the blessing which they ask of God.

Remember that if a vessel that ought to be one whole is cracked into many pieces, it cannot be filled. You can take a potsherd, one part of a vessel, and dip out a little water into that, but if you want the vessel full, the vessel must be whole. That is literally true of Christ's church, and if there is one thing we must pray for still, it is this: Lord, melt us together into one by the power of the Holy Spirit; let the Holy Spirit, who at Pentecost made them all of one heart and one soul, do His blessed work among us. Praise God, we can love each other in a divine love, for "the fruit of the Spirit is love." Give yourselves up to love, and the Holy Spirit will come; receive the Spirit, and He will teach you to love more.

God Is Love

Now, why is it that the fruit of the Spirit is love? *Because God is love.*

And what does that mean?

It is the very nature and being of God to delight in communicating Himself. God has no selfishness, God keeps nothing to Himself. God's nature is to be always giving. In the sun and the moon and the stars, in every flower you see it, in every bird in the air, in every fish in the sea. God communicates life to His creatures. And the angels around His throne, the seraphim and cherubim who are flames of fire—whence have they their glory? It is because God is love, and He imparts to them of His brightness and His blessedness. And we, His redeemed children—God delights to pour His love into us. And why? Because, as I said, God keeps nothing for Himself. From eternity God had His only begotten Son, and the Father gave Him all things, and nothing that God had was kept back. "God is love."

One of the old church fathers said that we cannot better understand the Trinity than as a revelation of divine love—the Father, the loving One, the Fountain of love; the Son, the beloved one, the Reservoir of love, in whom the love was poured out; and the Spirit, the living love that united both and then overflowed into this world. The Spirit of Pentecost, the Spirit of the Father, and the Spirit of the Son is love. And when the Holy Spirit comes to us and to other men, will He be less a Spirit of love than He is in God? It cannot be; He cannot change His nature. The Spirit of God is love, and "the fruit of the Spirit is love."

The Restoration of Love

Why is that so? That was the one great need of mankind, that was the thing which Christ's redemption came to accomplish: *to restore love to this world.*

When man sinned, why was it that he sinned? Selfishness triumphed—he sought self instead of God. And just look! Adam at once begins to accuse the woman of having led him astray. Love to God had gone, love to man was lost. Look again: of the first two children of Adam the one becomes a murderer of his brother.

Does not that teach us that sin had robbed the world of love? Ah! what a proof the history of the world has been of love having been lost! There may have been beautiful examples of love even among the heathen, but only as a little remnant of what was lost. One of the worst things sin did for man was to make him selfish, for selfishness cannot love.

The Lord Jesus Christ came down from heaven as the Son of God's love. "God so loved the world that He gave His only begotten Son." God's Son came to show what love is, and He lived a life of love here upon earth in fellowship with His disciples, in compassion over the poor and miserable, in love even to His enemies, and He died the death of love. And when He went to heaven, whom did He send down? The Spirit of love, to come and banish selfishness and envy and pride, and bring the love of God into the hearts of men. "The fruit of the Spirit is love."

And what was the preparation for the promise of the Holy Spirit? You know that promise as found in the fourteenth chapter of John's gospel. But remember what precedes in the thirteenth chapter. Before Christ promised the Holy Spirit, He gave a new commandment, and about that new commandment He said wonderful things. One thing was: "Even as I have loved you, so love ye one another." To them His dying love was to be the only law of their conduct and intercourse with each other. What a message to those fishermen, to those men full of pride and selfishness! "Learn to love each other," said Christ, "as I have loved you." And by the grace of God they did it. When Pentecost came, they were of one heart and one soul. Christ did it for them.

And now He calls us to dwell and to walk in love. He demands that though a man hate you, still you love him. True love cannot be conquered by anything in heaven or upon the earth. The more hatred there is, the more love triumphs through it all and shows its true nature. This is the love that Christ commanded His disciples to exercise.

What more did He say? "By this shall all men know that ye are my disciples, if ye have love one to another."

You all know what it is to wear a badge. And Christ said to His disciples in effect:

"I give you a badge, and that badge is LOVE. That is to be your mark. It is the only thing in heaven or on earth by which men can know me."

Oh! do not we begin to fear that love has fled from the earth? That if we were to ask the world: "Have you seen us wear the badge of love?" the world would say: "No; what we have heard of the church of Christ is that there is not a place where there is no quarreling and separation." Let us ask God with one heart that we may wear the badge of Jesus' love. God is able to give it.

Love Expels and Conquers Selfishness

"The fruit of the Spirit is love." Why? Because *nothing but love can expel and conquer our selfishness.*

Self is the great curse, whether in its relation to God, or to our fellow-men in general, or to fellow-Christians, thinking of ourselves and seeking our own. Self is our greatest curse. But, praise God, Christ came to redeem us from self. We sometimes talk about deliverance from the self-life—and thank God for every word that can be said about it to help us—but I am afraid some people think deliverance from the self-life means that now they are going to have no longer any trouble in serving God; and they forget that deliverance from self-life means to be a vessel overflowing with love to everybody all the day.

And there you have the reason why many people pray for the power of the Holy Ghost, and they get something, but oh, so little! because they prayed for power for work, and power for blessing, but they have not prayed for power for full deliverance from self. That means not only the righteous self in intercourse with God, but the unloving self in intercourse with men. And there *is* deliverance. "The fruit of the Spirit is love." I bring you the glorious promise of Christ that He is able to fill our hearts with love.

A great many of us try hard at times to love. We try to force ourselves to love, and I do not say that is wrong; it is better than nothing. But the end of it is always very sad. "I fail continually," such an one must confess. And what is the reason? The reason is simply this: Because they have never learned to believe and accept the truth that the Holy Spirit can pour God's love into their heart. That blessed text; often it has been limited!—"The love of God is shed abroad in our hearts." It has often been understood in this sense: It means the love of God *to me*. Oh, what a limitation! That is only the beginning. The love of God is always the love of God in its entirety, in its fullness as an indwelling power, a love of God to me that leaps back to Him in love, and overflows to my fellowmen in love—God's love to me, and my love to God, and my love to my fellow-men. The three are one; you cannot separate them.

Do believe that the love of God can be shed abroad in your heart and mine so that we can love all the day.

"Ah!" you say, "how little I have understood that!"

Why is a lamb always gentle? Because that is its nature. Does it cost the lamb any trouble to be gentle? No. Why not? It *is* so beautiful and gentle. Has a lamb to study to be gentle? No. Why does that come so easy? It is its nature. And a wolf—why does it cost a wolf no trouble to be cruel, and to put its fangs into the poor lamb or sheep? Because that is its nature. It has not to summon up its courage; the wolf-nature is there.

And how can I learn to love? Never until the Spirit of God fills my heart with God's love, and I begin to long for God's love in a very different sense from which I have sought it so selfishly, as a comfort and a joy and a happiness and a pleasure to myself; never until I begin to learn that "God is love," and to claim it, and receive it as an indwelling power for self-sacrifice; never until I begin to see that my glory, my blessedness, is to be like God and like Christ, in giving up

everything in myself for my fellow-men. May God teach us that! Oh, the divine blessedness of the love with which the Holy Spirit can fill our hearts! "The fruit of the Spirit is love."

Living the Daily Life of Love

Once again I ask, Why must this be so? And my answer is: *Without this we cannot live the daily life of love.*

How often, when we speak about the consecrated life, we have to speak about *temper,* and some people have sometimes said:

"You make too much of temper."

I do not think we can make too much of it. Do you see yonder clock? You know what those hands mean. The hands tell me what is within the clock, and if I see that the hands stand still, or that the hands point wrong, or that the clock is slow or fast, I say that there is something inside the clock that is wrong. And temper is just like the revelation that the clock gives of what is within. Temper is a proof whether the love of Christ is filling the heart, or not. How many there are who find it easier in church, or in prayer-meeting, or in work for the Lord—diligent, earnest work—to be holy and happy than in the daily life with wife and children and servant; easier to be holy and happy outside the home than in it! Where is the love of God? In Christ. God has prepared for us a wonderful redemption in Christ, and He longs to make something supernatural of us. Have we learned to long for it, and ask for it, and expect it in its fullness?

Then there is the *tongue!* We sometimes speak of the tongue when we talk of the better life, and the restful life, but just think what liberty many Christians give to their tongues. They say:

"I have a right to think what I like."

When they speak about each other,

when they speak about their neighbors, when they speak about other Christians, how often there are sharp remarks! God keep me from saying anything that would be unloving; God shut my mouth if I am not to speak in tender love. But what I am saying is a fact. How often there are found among Christians who are banded together in work, sharp criticism, sharp judgment, hasty opinion, unloving words, secret contempt of each other, secret condemnation of each other! Oh, just as a mother's love covers her children and delights in them and has the tenderest compassion with their foibles or failures, so there ought to be in the heart of every believer a motherly love toward every brother and sister in Christ. Have you aimed at that? Have you sought it? Have you ever pleaded for it? Jesus Christ said: "As I have loved you . . . love one another." And He did not put that among the other commandments, but He said in effect:

"That is a NEW commandment, the one commandment: Love one another as I have loved you."

It is in our daily life and conduct that the fruit of the Spirit is love. From that there comes all the graces and virtues in which love is manifested: joy, peace, longsuffering, gentleness, goodness; no sharpness or hardness in your tone, no unkindness or selfishness; meekness before God and man. You see that all these are the gentler virtues. I have often thought as I read those words in Colossians, "Put on therefore as the elect of God, holy and beloved, bowels of mercies, kindness, humbleness of mind, meekness, long-suffering," that if we had written, we should have put in the foreground the manly virtues, such as zeal, courage and diligence; but we need to see how the gentler, the most womanly virtues are specially connected with dependence upon the Holy Spirit. These are indeed heavenly graces. They never

were found in the heathen world. Christ was needed to come from heaven to teach us. Your blessedness is longsuffering, meekness, kindness; your glory is humility before God. The fruit of the Spirit that He brought from heaven out of the heart of the crucified Christ, and that He gives in our heart, is first and foremost—love.

You know what John says: "No man hath seen God at any time. If we love one another, God dwelleth in us." That is, I cannot see God, but as a compensation I can see my brother, and if I love him, God dwells in me. Is that really true? That I cannot see God, but I must love my brother, and God will dwell in me? Loving my brother is the way to real fellowship with God. You know what John further says in that most solemn test, "If a man say, I love God, and hateth his brother, he is a liar; for he that loveth not his brother whom he hath seen, how can he love God whom he hath not seen?" (1 John 4:20). There is a brother, a most unlovable man. He worries you every time you meet him. He is the very opposite disposition to yours. You are a careful businessman, and you have to do with him in your business. He is most untidy, unbusiness-like. You say: "I cannot love him."

Oh, friend, you have not learned the lesson that Christ wanted to teach above everything. Let a man be what he will, you are to love him. Love is to be the fruit of the Spirit all the day and every day. Yes, listen! if a man loves not his brother whom he hath seen—if you don't love that unlovable man whom you have seen, how can you love God whom you have not seen? You can deceive yourself with beautiful thoughts about loving God. You must prove your love to God by your love to your brother; that is the one standard by which God will judge your love to Him. If the love of

God is in your heart you will love your brother. "The fruit of the Spirit is love."

And what is the reason that God's Holy Spirit cannot come in power? Is it not possible?

You remember the comparison I used in speaking of the vessel. I can dip a little water into a potsherd, a bit of a vessel; but if a vessel is to be full, it must be unbroken. And the children of God, wherever they come together, to whatever church or mission or society they belong, must love each other intensely, or the Spirit of God cannot do His work. We talk about grieving the Spirit of God by worldliness and ritualism and formality and error and indifference, but, I tell you, the one thing above everything that grieves God's Spirit is this want of love. Let every heart search itself, and ask that God may search it.

Divine Power in Daily Life

Why are we taught that "the fruit of the Spirit is love"? *Because the Spirit of God has come to make our daily life an exhibition of divine power and a revelation of what God can do for His children.*

In the second and the fourth chapters of Acts we read that the disciples were of one heart and of one soul. During the three years they had walked with Christ they never had been in that spirit. All Christ's teaching could not make them of one heart and one soul. But the Holy Spirit came from heaven and shed the love of God in their hearts, and they were of one heart and one soul. The same Holy Spirit that brought the love of heaven into their hearts must fill us too. Nothing less will do. Even as Christ did, one might preach love for three years with the tongue of an angel, but that would not teach any man to love unless the power of the Holy Spirit should come upon him to bring the love of heaven into his heart.

Think of the church at large. What divisions! Think of the different bodies. Take the question of holiness, take the question of the cleansing blood, take the question of the baptism of the Spirit— what differences are caused among dear believers by such questions! That there should be differences of opinion does not trouble me. We have not all got the same constitution and temperament and mind. But how often hate, bitterness, contempt, separation, unlovingness are caused by the holiest truths of God's Word! Our doctrines, our creeds, have been more important than love. We often think we are valiant for the truth, and we forget God's command to speak the truth *in love*. And it was so in the time of the Reformation between the Lutheran and Calvinistic churches. What bitterness there was then in regard to the Holy Supper, which was meant to be the bond of union between all believers! And so, down the ages, the very dearest truths of God have become mountains that have separated us.

If we want to pray in power, and if we want to expect the Holy Spirit to come down in power, and if we want indeed that God shall pour out His Spirit, we must enter into a covenant with God that we love one another with a heavenly love.

Are you ready for that? Only that is true love that is large enough to take in all God's children, the most unloving and unlovable, and unworthy, and unbearable, and trying. If my vow—absolute surrender to God—was true, then it must mean absolute surrender to the divine love to fill me; to be a servant of love to love every child of God around me. "The fruit of the Spirit is love."

Oh, God did something wonderful when He gave Christ, at His right hand, the Holy Spirit to come down out of the heart of the Father and His everlasting love. And how we have degraded the

Holy Spirit into a mere power by which we have to do our work! God forgive us! Oh, that the Holy Spirit might be held in honor as a power to fill us with the very life and nature of God and of Christ!

The Power of Love

"The fruit of the Spirit is love." I ask once again, Why is it so? And the answer comes: *That is the only power in which Christians really can do their work.*

Yes, it is that we need. We want not only love that is to bind us to each other, but we want a divine love in our work for the lost around us. Oh, do we not often undertake a great deal of work, just as men undertake work of philanthropy, from a natural spirit of compassion for our fellow-men? Do we not often undertake Christian work because our minister or friend calls us to it? and do we not often perform Christian work with a certain zeal but without having had a baptism of love?

People often ask: "What is the baptism of fire?"

I have answered more than once: I know no fire like the fire of God, the fire of everlasting love that consumed the sacrifice on Calvary. The baptism of love is what the church needs, and to get that we must begin at once to get down upon our faces before God in confession, and plead:

"Lord, let love from heaven flow down into my heart. I am giving up my life to pray and live as one who has given himself up for the everlasting love to dwell in and fill him."

Ah, yes, if the love of God were in our hearts, what a difference it would make! There are hundreds of believers who say:

"I work for Christ, and I feel I could work much harder, but I have not the gift. I do not know how or where to begin. I do not know what I can do."

Brother, sister, ask God to baptize you with the Spirit of love, and love will find its way. Love is a fire that will burn through every difficulty. You may be a shy, hesitating man, who cannot speak well, but love can burn through everything. God fill us with love! We need it for our work.

You have read many a touching story of love expressed, and you have said, How beautiful! I heard one not long ago. A lady had been asked to speak at a rescue home where there were a number of poor women. As she arrived there and got to the window with the matron, she saw outside a wretched object sitting, and asked:

"Who is that?"

The matron answered: "She has been into the house thirty or forty times, and she has always gone away again. Nothing can be done with her, she is so low and hard."

But the lady said: "She must come in."

The matron then said: "We have been waiting for you, and the company is assembled, and you have only an hour for the address."

The lady replied: "No, this is of more importance"; and she went outside where the woman was sitting and said:

"My sister, what is the matter?"

"I am not your sister," was the reply.

Then the lady laid her hand on her, and said: "Yes, I am your sister, and I love you"; and so she spoke until the heart of the poor woman was touched.

The conversation lasted some time, and the company were waiting patiently. Ultimately the lady brought the woman into the room. There was the poor, wretched, degraded creature, full of shame. She would not sit on a chair, but sat down on a stool beside the speaker's seat, and she let her lean against her, with her arms around the poor woman's neck, while she spoke to the assembled people. And that love touched the woman's heart; she had found one who really loved her, and that love gave access to the love of Jesus.

Praise God! there is love upon earth in the hearts of God's children; but oh, that there were more!

O God, baptize our ministers with a tender love, and our missionaries, and our colporters, and our Bible-readers, and our workers, and our young men's and young women's associations. Oh, that God would begin with us now, and baptize us with heavenly love!

The Work of Intercession

Once again. *It is only love that can fit us for the work of intercession.*

I have said that love must fit us for our work. Do you know what the hardest and the most important work is that has to be done for this sinful world? It is the work of intercession, the work of going to God and taking time to lay hold on Him.

A man may be an earnest Christian, an earnest minister, and a man may do good, but alas! how often he has to confess that he knows but little of what it is to tarry with God! May God give us the great gift of an intercessory spirit, a spirit of prayer and supplication! Let me ask you in the name of Jesus not to let a day pass without praying for all saints, and for all God's people.

I find there are Christians who think little of that. I find there are prayer unions where they pray for the members, and not for all believers. I pray you, take time to pray for the church of Christ. It is right to pray for the heathen,

as I have already said. God help us to pray more for them. It is right to pray for missionaries and for evangelistic work, and for the unconverted. But Paul did not tell people to pray for the heathen or the unconverted. Paul told them to pray for believers. Do make this your first prayer every day: "LORD, bless thy saints everywhere."

The state of Christ's church is indescribably low. Plead for God's people that He would visit them, plead for each other, plead for all believers who are trying to work for God. Let love fill your heart. Ask Christ to pour it out afresh into you every day. Try to get it into you by the Holy Spirit of God: I am separated unto the Holy Spirit, and the fruit of the Spirit is love. God help us to understand it.

May God grant that we learn day by day to wait more quietly upon Him. Do not wait upon God only for ourselves, or the power to do so will soon be lost; but give ourselves up to the ministry and the love of intercession, and pray more for God's people, for God's people round about us, for the Spirit of love in ourselves and in them, and for the work of God we are connected with; and the answer will surely come, and our waiting upon God will be a source of untold blessing and power. "The fruit of the Spirit is love."

Have you a lack of love to confess before God? Then make confession and say before Him, "O Lord, my want of heart, my want to love—I confess it." And then, as you cast that want at His feet, believe that the blood cleanses you, that Jesus comes in His mighty, cleansing, saving power to deliver you, and that He will give His Holy Spirit.

"The fruit of the Spirit is love."

Peter's Repentance

And the Lord turned, and looked upon Peter. And Peter remembered the word of the Lord, how he had said unto him, Before the cock crow, thou shalt deny me thrice. And Peter went out, and wept bitterly (Luke 22:61, 62).

That was the turning-point in the history of Peter. Christ had said to him: "Thou canst not follow me now." Peter was not in a fit state to follow Christ, because he had not been brought to an end of himself; he did not know himself, and he therefore could not follow Christ. But when he went out and wept bitterly, then came the great change. Christ previously said to him: "When thou art converted, strengthen thy brethren." Here is the point where Peter was converted from self to Christ.

I thank God for the story of Peter. I do not know a man in the Bible which gives us greater comfort. When we look at his character, so full of failures, and at what Christ made him by the power of the Holy Ghost, there is hope for every one of us. But remember, before Christ could fill Peter with the Holy Spirit and make a new man of him, he had to go out and weep bitterly; he had to be humbled. If we want to understand this, I think there are four points that we must look at. First, let us look at *Peter the devoted disciple of Jesus;* next, at *Peter as he lived the life of self;* then at *Peter in his repentance;* and last, at *what Christ made of Peter by the Holy Spirit.*

Peter the Devoted Disciple of Christ

Christ called Peter to forsake his nets, and follow Him. Peter did it at once, and he afterward could say rightly to the Lord:

"We have forsaken all and followed thee."

Peter was a man of *absolute surrender;* he gave up all to follow Jesus. Peter was also a man of *ready obedience.* You remember Christ said to him, "Launch out into the deep, and let down the net." Peter the fisherman knew there were no fish there, for they had been toiling all night and had caught nothing; but he said: "At thy word I will let down the net." He submitted to the word of Jesus. Further, he was a man of *great faith.* When he saw Christ walking on the sea, he said: "Lord, if it be thou, bid me come unto thee"; and at the voice of Christ he stepped out of the boat and walked upon the water.

And Peter was a man of *spiritual insight.* When Christ asked the disciples: "Whom do ye say that I am?" Peter was able to answer: "Thou art the Christ, the Son of the living God." And Christ said: "Blessed art thou, Simon Barjona; for flesh and blood hath not revealed it unto thee, but my Father which is in heaven." And Christ spoke of him as the *rock* man, and of his having the keys of the kingdom. Peter was a splendid man, a devoted disciple of Jesus, and if he were living nowadays, everyone would say that he was an advanced Christian. And yet how much there was wanting in Peter!

Peter Living the Life of Self

You recollect that just after Christ had said to him: "Flesh and blood hath not revealed it unto thee, but my Father which is in heaven," Christ began to speak about His sufferings, and Peter dared to say: "Be it far from thee, Lord; this shall not be unto thee." Then Christ had to say:

"Get thee behind me, Satan; for thou savorest not the things that be of God, but those that be of men."

There was Peter in his self-will, trusting his own wisdom, and actually forbidding Christ to go and die. Whence did that come? Peter trusted in himself and his own thoughts about divine things. We see later on, more than once, that among the disciples there was a questioning who should be the greatest, and Peter was one of them, and he thought he had a right to the very first place. He sought his own honor even above the others. It was the life of self strong in Peter. He had left his boats and his nets, but not his old self.

When Christ had spoken to him about His sufferings, and said: "Get thee behind me, Satan," He followed it up by saying: "If any man will come after me, let him deny himself, and take up his cross, and follow me." No man can follow Him unless he do that. Self must be utterly denied. What does that mean? When Peter denied Christ, we read that he said three times: "I do not know the man"; in other words: "I have nothing to do with Him; He and I are not friends; I deny having any connection with Him." Christ told Peter that he must deny self. Self must be ignored, and its every claim rejected. That is THE ROOT OF TRUE DISCIPLESHIP; but Peter did not understand it, and could not obey it. And what happened? When the last night came, Christ said to him: "Before the cock crow twice thou shalt deny me thrice."

But with what self-confidence Peter said: "Though all should forsake thee, yet will not I. I am ready to go with thee, to prison and to death."

Peter meant it honestly, and Peter really intended to do it; but Peter did not know himself. He did not believe he was so bad as Jesus said he was.

We perhaps think of individual sins that come between us and God, but what are we to do with that self-life which is all unclean, our very nature? What are we to do with that flesh that is entirely under the power of sin? Deliverance from that is what we need. Peter knew it not, and therefore it was that in his self-confidence he went forth and denied his Lord.

Notice how Christ uses the word *deny* twice. He said to Peter the first time, *"Deny self"*; He said to Peter the second time, *"Thou wilt deny me."* It is either of the two. There is no choice for us; we must either deny self or deny Christ. There are two great powers fighting each other—the self-nature in the power of sin, and Christ in the power of God. Either of these must rule within us.

It was self that made the devil. He was an angel of God, but he wanted to exalt self. He became a devil in hell. Self was the cause of the fall of man. Eve wanted something for herself, and so our first parents fell into all the wretchedness of sin. We their children have inherited an awful nature of sin.

Peter's Repentance

Peter denied his Lord thrice, and then the Lord looked upon him; and that look of Jesus broke the heart of Peter, and all at once there opened up before him the terrible sin that he had committed, the terrible failure that had come, and the depth into which he had fallen, and "Peter went out and wept bitterly."

Oh! who can tell what that repentance must have been? During the following hours of that night, and the next day, when he saw Christ crucified and buried, and the next day, the Sabbath—oh, in what hopeless despair and shame he must have spent that day!

"My Lord is gone, my hope is gone, and I denied my Lord. After that life of love, after that blessed fellowship of three years, I denied my Lord. God have mercy on me!"

I do not think we can realize into what a depth of humiliation Peter sank then. But that was the turning point and the change; and on the first day of the week Christ was seen of Peter, and in the evening He met him with the others. Later on at the Lake of Galilee He asked him: "Lovest thou me?" until Peter was made sad by the thought that the Lord reminded him of having denied Him thrice; and said in sorrow, but in uprightness:

"Lord, thou knowest all things; thou knowest that I love thee."

The Deliverance from Self

You know Christ took him with others to the footstool of the throne, and bade them wait there; and then on the day of Pentecost the Holy Spirit came, and Peter was a changed man. I do not want you to think only of the change in Peter, in that boldness, and that power, and that insight into the Scriptures, and that blessing with which he preached that day. Thank God for that. But there was something for Peter deeper and better. Peter's whole nature was changed. The work that Christ began in Peter when He looked upon him, was perfected when he was filled with the Holy Ghost.

If you want to see that, read the first epistle of Peter. You know wherein Peter's failings lay. When he said to Christ, in effect: "Thou never canst suffer; it

cannot be"—it showed he had not a conception of what it was to pass through death into life. Christ said: "Deny *thyself*," and in spite of that he denied his Lord. When Christ warned him: "Thou shalt deny me," and he insisted that he never would, Peter showed how little he understood what there was in himself. But when I read his epistle and hear him say: "If ye be reproached for the name of Christ, happy are ye, for the Spirit of God and of glory resteth upon you," then I say that is not the old Peter, but that is the very Spirit of Christ breathing and speaking within him.

I read again how he says: "Hereunto ye are called, to suffer, even as Christ suffered." I understand what a change had come over Peter. Instead of denying Christ, he found joy and pleasure in having self denied and crucified and given up to the death. And therefore it is in the Acts we read that, when he was called before the Council, he could boldly say: "We must obey God rather than men," and that he could return with the other disciples and rejoice that they were counted worthy to suffer for Christ's name.

You remember his self-exaltation; but now he has found out that "the ornament of a meek and quiet spirit is in the sight of God of great price." Again he tells us to be "subject one to another, and be clothed with humility."

Dear friend, I beseech you, look at Peter utterly changed—the self-pleasing, the self-trusting, the self-seeking Peter, full of sin, continually getting into trouble, foolish and impetuous, but now filled with the Spirit and the life of Jesus. Christ had done it for him by the Holy Ghost.

And now, what is my object in having thus very briefly pointed to the story of Peter? That story must be the history of every believer who is really to be made a blessing by God. That story is a prophecy of what everyone can receive from God in heaven.

Now let us just glance hurriedly at what these lessons teach us.

The *first lesson* is this—You may be a very earnest, godly, devoted believer, in whom the power of the flesh is yet very strong.

That is a very solemn truth. Peter, before he denied Christ, had cast out devils and had healed the sick; and yet the flesh had power, and the flesh had room in him. Oh, beloved, we want to realize that it is just on account of there being so much of that self-life in us that the power of God cannot work in us as mightily as God is willing that it should work. Do you realize that the great God is longing to double His blessing, to give tenfold blessing through us? But there is something hindering Him, and that something is a proof of nothing but the self-life. We talk about the pride of Peter, and the impetuosity of Peter, and the self-confidence of Peter. It is all rooted in that one word, *self*. Christ had said, "Deny self," and Peter had never understood, and never obeyed; and every failing came out of that.

What a solemn thought, and what an urgent plea for us to cry: O God, do discover this to us, that none of us may be living the self-life! It has happened to many a one who had been a Christian for years, who had perhaps occupied a prominent position, that God found him out and taught him to find himself out, and he became utterly ashamed, falling down broken before God. Oh, the bitter shame and sorrow and pain and agony that came to him, until at last he found that there was deliverance! Peter went out and wept bitterly, and there may be many a godly one in whom the power of the flesh still rules.

And then my *second lesson* is—It is the work of our blessed Lord Jesus to discover the power of self.

How was it that Peter, the carnal Peter, self-willed Peter, Peter with the strong self-love, ever became a man of Pentecost and the writer of his epistle? It was because Christ had him in charge, and Christ watched over him, and Christ taught and blessed him. The warnings that Christ had given him were part of the training; and last of all there came that look of love. In His suffering Christ did not forget him, but turned round and looked upon him, and "Peter went out and wept bitterly." And the Christ who led Peter to Pentecost is waiting today to take charge of every heart that is willing to surrender itself to Him.

Are there not some saying: "Ah! that is the mischief with me; it is always the self-life, and self-comfort, and self-consciousness, and self-pleasing, and self-will; how am I to get rid of it?"

My answer is: It is Christ Jesus who can rid you of it; none else but Christ Jesus can give deliverance from the power of self. And what does he ask you to do? He asks that you should humble yourself before Him.

CHAPTER TWENTY-ONE

Ye Are the Branches

Everything depends on our being right ourselves in Christ. If I want good apples, I must have a good apple tree; and if I care for the health of the apple tree, the apple tree will give me good apples. And it is just so with our Christian life and work. *If our life with Christ be right,* all will come right. There may be the need of instruction and suggestion and help and training in the different departments of the work; all that has value. But in the long run, the greatest essential is to have the full life in Christ—in other words, to have Christ in us, working through us. I know how much there is often to disturb us, or to cause anxious questionings; but the Master has such a blessing for every one of us, and such perfect peace and rest, and such joy and strength, if we can only come into, and be kept in, the right attitude toward Him.

I will take my text from the parable of the Vine and the Branches, in John 15:5: "I am the vine, ye are the branches." Especially these words: "Ye are the branches."

What a simple thing it is to be a branch, the branch of a tree, or the branch of a vine! The branch grows out of the vine, or out of the tree, and there it lives and grows, and in due time, bears fruit. It has no responsibility except just to receive from the root and stem sap and nourishment. And if we only by the Holy Spirit knew our relationship to Jesus Christ, our work would be changed into the brightest and most heavenly thing upon earth. Instead of there ever being soul weariness or exhaustion, our work would be like a new experience, linking us to Jesus as nothing else can. For, alas! is it not often true that our work comes between us and Jesus? What folly! The very work that He has to do in me, and I for Him, I take up in such a way that it separates me from Christ. Many a laborer in the vineyard has complained that he has too much work, and not time for close communion with Jesus, and that his usual work weakens his inclination for prayer, and that his too much intercourse with men darkens the spiritual life. Sad thought, that the bearing of fruit should separate the branch from the vine! That must be because we have looked upon our work as something other than the branch bearing fruit. May God deliver us from every false thought about the Christian life.

Now just a few thoughts about THIS BLESSED BRANCH-LIFE.

A Life of Absolute Dependence

The branch has nothing; it just depends upon the vine for everything. *Absolute dependence* is one of the most solemn and precious of thoughts. A great German theologian wrote two large volumes some years ago to show that the whole of Calvin's theology is summed up in that one principle of *absolute dependence upon God;* and he was right. Another great writer has said that *absolute, unalterable dependence upon God alone* is the essence of the religion of angels, and should be that of men also. God is everything to the angels, and He is willing to be everything to the Christian. If I can learn every moment of the day to depend upon God, everything will come right. You will get the higher life if you depend absolutely upon God.

Now, here we find it with the vine and the branches. Every vine you ever see, or every bunch of grapes that comes upon your table, let it remind you that the branch is absolutely dependent on the vine. The vine has to do the work, and the branch enjoys the fruit of it.

What has the vine to do? It has to do a great work. It has to send its roots out into the soil and hunt under the ground—the roots often extend a long way out—for nourishment, and to drink in the moisture. Put certain elements of manure in certain directions, and the vine sends its roots there, and then in its roots or stems it turns the moisture and manure into that special sap which is to make the fruit that is borne. The vine does the work, and the branch has just to receive from the vine the sap, which is changed into grapes.

I have been told that at Hampton Court, London, there is a vine that sometimes bore a couple of thousand bunches of grapes, and people were astonished at its large growth and rich fruitage. Afterward it was discovered what was the cause of it. Not so very far away runs the River Thames, and the vine had stretched its roots away hundreds of yards under the ground, until it had come to the riverside, and there in all the rich slime of the riverbed it had found rich nourishment, and obtained moisture, and the roots had drawn the sap all that distance up and up into the vine, and as a result there was the abundant, rich harvest. The vine had the work to do, and the branches had just to depend upon the vine, and receive what it gave.

Is that literally true of my Lord Jesus? Must I understand that when I have to work, when I have to preach a sermon, or address a Bible class, or to go out and visit the poor, neglected ones, that all the responsibility of the work is on Christ?

That is exactly what Christ wants you to understand. Christ wants that in all your work, the very foundation should be the simple, blessed consciousness: Christ must care for all.

And how does He fulfil the trust of that dependence? He does it by sending down the Holy Spirit—not now and then only as a special gift, for remember the relationship between the vine and the branches is such that hourly, daily, unceasingly there is the living connection maintained. The sap does not flow for a time, and then stop, and then flow again, but from moment to moment the sap flows from the vine to the branches. And just so, my Lord Jesus wants me to take that blessed position as a worker, and morning by morning and day by day and hour by hour and step by step, in every work I have to go out to just to abide before Him in the simple utter helplessness of one who knows nothing, and is nothing, and can do nothing. Oh, beloved workers, study that word *nothing*. You sometimes sing: "Oh, to be nothing, nothing"; but have you really studied that word and prayed every day, and worshiped God, in the light of it? Do you know the blessedness of that word nothing?

If I am something, then God is not everything; but when I become *nothing*, God can become *all*, and the everlasting God in Christ can reveal Himself fully. That is the higher life. We need to become nothing. Someone has well said that the seraphim and cherubim are flames of fire because they know they are nothing, and they allow God to put His fullness and His glory and brightness into them. They are nothing, and

God is all in them and around them. Oh, become nothing in deep reality, and, as a worker, study only one thing—to become poorer and lower and more helpless, that Christ may work all in you.

Workers, here is your first lesson: learn to be nothing, learn to be helpless. The man who has got something is not absolutely dependent; but the man who has got nothing is absolutely dependent. Absolute dependence upon God is the secret of all power in work. The branch has nothing but what it gets from the vine, and you and I can have nothing but what we get from Jesus.

A Life of Deep Restfulness

Oh, that little branch, if it could think, and if it could feel, and if it could speak—that branch away in Hampton Court vine, or on some of the million vines that we have in South Africa, in our sunny land—if we could have a little branch here today to talk to us, and if we could say: "Come, branch of the vine, I want to learn from thee how I can be a true branch of the living Vine," what would it answer? The little branch would whisper:

"Man, I hear that you are wise, and I know that you can do a great many wonderful things. I know you have much strength and wisdom given to you but I have one lesson for you. With all your hurry and effort in Christ's work you never prosper. The first thing you need is to come and rest in your Lord Jesus. That is what I do. Since I grew out of that vine I have spent years and years, and all I have done is just to rest in the vine. When the time of spring came I had no anxious thought or care. The vine began to pour its sap into me, and to give the bud and leaf. And when the time of summer came I had no care, and in the great heat I trusted the vine to bring moisture to keep me fresh. And

in the time of harvest, when the owner came to pluck the grapes, I had no care. If there was anything in the grapes not good, the owner never blamed the branch, the blame was always on the vine. And if you would be a true branch of Christ, the living Vine, just rest on Him. Let Christ bear the responsibility."

You say: "Won't that make me slothful?"

I tell you it will not. No one who learns to rest upon the living Christ can become slothful, for the closer your contact with Christ the more of the Spirit of His zeal and love will be borne in upon you. But, oh, begin to work in the midst of your entire dependence by adding to that *deep restfulness*. A man sometimes tries and tries to be dependent upon Christ, but he worries himself about this absolute dependence; he tries and he cannot get it. But let him sink down into entire restfulness every day.

In Thy strong hand I lay me down.
  So shall the work be done;
For who can work so wondrously
  As the Almighty One?

Worker, take your place every day at the feet of Jesus, in the blessed peace and rest that come from the knowledge—

I have no care, my cares are His;
I have no fear, He cares for all
  my fears.

Come, children of God, and understand that it is the Lord Jesus who wants to work through you. You complain of the want of fervent love. It will come from Jesus. He will give the divine love in your heart with which you can love people. That is the meaning of the assurance: "The love of God is shed abroad in our hearts by the Holy Spirit"; and of that other word: "The love of Christ constraineth us." Christ can give you a fountain of love, so that you cannot help loving the most wretched and the most ungrateful, or those who have wearied you hitherto.

Rest in Christ, who can give wisdom and strength, and you do not know how that restfulness will often prove to be the very best part of your message. You plead with people and you argue, and they get the idea: "There is a man arguing and striving with me." They only feel: "Here are two men dealing with each other." But if you will let the deep rest of God come over you, the rest in Christ Jesus, the peace and rest and holiness of heaven, that restfulness will bring a blessing to the heart, even more than the words you speak.

A Life of Much Fruitfulness

You know the Lord Jesus repeated that word *fruit* often in that parable. He spoke, first, of *fruit*, and then of *more fruit*, and then of *much fruit*. Yes, you are ordained not only to bear fruit, but to bear *much fruit*. "Herein is my Father glorified, *that ye bear much fruit*." In the first place, Christ said: "I am the Vine, and my Father is the Husbandman. My Father is the Husbandman who has charge of me and you." He who will watch over the connection between Christ and the branches of God; and it is in the power of God through Christ we are to bear fruit.

Oh, Christians, you know this world is perishing for the want of workers. And it wants not only more workers, the workers are saying, some more earnestly than others: "We need not only more workers, but we need our workers to have a new power, a different life; that we workers should be able to bring more blessing."

Children of God, I appeal to you. You know what trouble you take, say, in a case of sickness. You have a beloved friend apparently in danger of death, and nothing can refresh that friend so much as a few grapes, and they are out of season; but what trouble you will take to get the grapes that are to be the nourishment of this dying friend! And, oh, there are around you people who never go to church, and so many who go to church, but do not know Christ. And yet the heavenly grapes, the grapes of Eshcol, the grapes of the heavenly Vine are not to be had at any price, except as the child of God bears them out of his inner life in fellowship with Christ. Except the children of God are filled with the sap of the heavenly Vine, except they are filled with the Holy Spirit and the love of Jesus, they cannot bear much of the real heavenly grape. We all confess there is a great deal of work, a great deal of preaching and teaching and visiting, a great deal of machinery, a great deal of earnest effort of every kind; but there is not much manifestation of the power of God.

What is wanting? There is wanting the close connection between the worker and the heavenly Vine. Christ, the heavenly Vine, has blessings that He could pour on tens of thousands who are perishing. Christ, the heavenly Vine, has power to provide the heavenly grapes. But "Ye are the branches," and you cannot bear heavenly fruit unless you are in close connection with Jesus Christ.

Do not confound *work* and *fruit*. There may be a good deal of work for Christ that is not the fruit of the heavenly Vine. Do not seek for work only. Oh! study this question of fruit-bearing. It means the very life and the very power and the very spirit and the very love within the heart of the Son of God—it means the heavenly Vine Himself coming into your heart and mine.

You know there are different sorts of grapes, each with a different name, and every vine provides exactly that peculiar aroma and juice which gives the grape its particular flavor and taste. Just so, there is in the heart of Christ Jesus a life, and a love, and a Spirit, and a blessing, and a power for men, that are entirely heavenly and divine, and that will come down into our hearts. Stand in close connection with the heavenly Vine and say:

"Lord Jesus, nothing less than the sap that flows through Thyself, nothing less than the Spirit of Thy divine life is what we ask. Lord Jesus, I pray Thee let Thy Spirit flow through me in all my work for Thee."

I tell you again that the sap of the heavenly Vine is nothing but the Holy Spirit. The Holy Spirit is the life of the heavenly Vine, and what you must get from Christ is nothing less than a strong inflow of the Holy Spirit. You need it exceedingly, and you want nothing more than that. Remember that. Do not expect Christ to give a bit of strength here, and a bit of blessing yonder, and a bit of help over there. As the vine does its work in giving its own peculiar sap to the branch, so expect Christ to give His own Holy Spirit into your heart, and then you will bear much fruit. And if you have only begun to bear fruit, and are listening to the word of Christ in the parable, "more fruit," "much fruit," remember that in order that you should bear more fruit you just require more of Jesus in your life and heart.

We ministers of the gospel, how we are in danger of getting into a condition of *work, work, work!* And we pray over it, but the freshness and buoyancy and joy of the heavenly life are not always present. Let us seek to understand that the life of the branch is a life of much fruit, because it is a life rooted in Christ, the living, heavenly Vine.

A Life of Close Communion

Let us again ask: What has the branch to do? You know that precious inexhaustible word that Christ used: *Abide.* Your life is to be an abiding life. And how is the abiding to be? It is to be just like the branch in the vine, abiding every minute of the day. There are the branches, in close communion, in unbroken communion, with the vine, from January to December. And cannot I live every day—it is to me an almost terrible thing that we should ask the question—cannot I live in abiding communion with the heavenly Vine?

You say: "But I am so much occupied with other things."

You may have ten hours' hard work daily, during which your brain has to be occupied with temporal things; God orders it so. But the abiding work is the work of the *heart,* not of the brain, the work of the heart clinging to and resting in Jesus, a work in which the Holy Spirit links us to Christ Jesus. Oh, do believe that deeper down than the brain, deep down in the inner life, you can abide in Christ, so that every moment you are free the consciousness will come:

"Blessed Jesus, I am still in Thee."

If you will learn for a time to put aside other work and to get into this abiding contact with the heavenly Vine, you will find that fruit will come.

What is the application to our life of this abiding communion? What does it mean?

It means *close friendship with Christ in secret prayer.* I am sure there are Christians who do long for the higher life, and who sometimes have got a great blessing, and have at times found a great inflow of heavenly joy and a great outflow of heavenly gladness; and yet after a time it has passed away. They have not understood that close personal actual communion with Christ is an absolute necessity for daily life. Take time to be alone with Christ. Nothing in heaven or earth can free you from the necessity for that, if you are to be happy and holy Christians.

Oh! how many Christians look upon it as a burden and a tax, and a duty, and a difficulty to get much alone with God! That is the great hindrance to our Christian life everywhere. We want more quiet fellowship with God, and I tell you in the name of the heavenly Vine that you cannot be healthy branches, branches into which the heavenly sap can flow, unless you take plenty of time for communion with God. If you are not willing to sacrifice time to get alone with Him, and to give Him time every day to work in you, and to keep up the link of connection between you and Himself, He cannot give you that blessing of His unbroken fellowship. Jesus Christ asks you to live in close communion with Him. Let every heart say: "O, Christ, it is this I long for, it is this I choose." And He will gladly give it you.

A Life of Absolute Surrender

This word, absolute surrender, is a great and solemn word, and I believe we do not understand its meaning. But yet the little branch preaches it.

"Have you anything to do, little branch, besides bearing grapes?"

"No, *nothing.*"

"Are you fit for nothing?"

Fit for nothing! The Bible says that a bit of vine cannot even be used as a pen; it is fit for nothing but to be burned.

"And now, what do you understand, little branch, about your relationship to the vine?"

"My relationship is just this: I am utterly given up to the vine, and the vine can give me as much or as little sap as it chooses. Here I am at its disposal and the vine can do with me what it likes."

Oh, friends, we want this absolute surrender to the Lord Jesus Christ. The more I speak the more I feel that this is one of the most difficult points to make clear, and one of the most important and needful points to explain—what this absolute surrender is. It is often an easy thing for a man or a number of men to come out and offer themselves up to God for entire consecration, and to say: "Lord, it is my desire to give up myself entirely to Thee." That is of great value, and often brings very rich blessing. But the one question I ought to study quietly is: What Is Meant by Absolute Surrender?

It means that just as literally as Christ was given up entirely to God, I am giving up entirely to Christ. Is that too strong? Some think so. Some think that never can be; that just as entirely and absolutely as Christ gave up His life to do nothing but seek the Father's pleasure, and depend on the Father absolutely and entirely, I am to do nothing but to seek the pleasure of Christ. But that is actually true. Christ Jesus came to breathe His own Spirit into us, to make us find our very highest happiness in living entirely for God, just as He did. Oh, beloved brethren, if that is the case, then I ought to say:

"Yes, as true as it is of that little branch of the vine, so true, by God's grace, I would have it to be of me. I would live day by day that Christ may be able to do with me what He will."

Ah! here comes the terrible mistake that lies at the bottom of so much of our own religion. A man thinks:

"I have my business and family duties, and my relationships as a citizen, and all this I cannot change. And now alongside all this I am to take in religion and the service of God, as something that will keep me from sin. God help me to perform my duties properly!"

This is not right. When Christ came,

He came and bought the sinner with His blood. If there was a slave market here and I were to buy a slave, I should take that slave away to my own house from his old surroundings, and he would live at my house as my personal property, and I could order him about all the day. And if he were a faithful slave, he would live as having no will and no interests of his own, his one care being to promote the well-being and honor of his master. And in like manner I, who have been bought with the blood of Christ, have been bought to live every day with the one thought—How can I please my Master?

Oh, we find the Christian life so difficult because we seek for God's blessing while we live in our own will. We should be glad to live the Christian life according to our own liking. We make our own plans and choose our own work, and then we ask the Lord Jesus to come in and take care that sin shall not conquer us too much, and that we shall not go too far wrong; we ask Him to come in and give us so much of His blessing. But our relationship to Jesus ought to be such that we are entirely at His disposal, and every day come to Him humbly and straightforwardly and say:

"Lord, is there anything in me that is not according to Thy will, that has not been ordered by Thee, or that is not entirely given up to Thee?"

Oh, if we would wait and wait patiently, I tell you what the result would be. There would spring up a relationship between us and Christ so close and so tender that we should afterward be amazed at how we formerly could have lived with the idea: "I am surrendered to Christ." We should feel how far distant our intercourse with Him had previously been, and that He can, and does indeed, come and take actual possession of us, and gives unbroken fellowship all the day. The branch calls us to absolute surrender.

I do not speak now so much about the giving up of sins. There are people who need that, people who have got violent tempers, bad habits, and actual sins which they from time to time commit, and which they have never given up into the very bosom of the Lamb of God. I pray you, if you are branches of the living Vine, do not keep one sin back. I know there are a great many difficulties about this question of holiness, I know that all do not think exactly the same with regard to it. That would be to me a matter of comparative indifference if I could see that all are honestly longing to be free from every sin. But I am afraid that unconsciously there are in hearts often compromises with the idea that we cannot be without sin, we must sin a little every day; we cannot help it. Oh, that people would actually cry to God: "Lord, do keep me from sin!" Give yourself utterly to Jesus, and ask Him to do His very utmost for you in keeping you from sin.

There is a great deal in our work, in our church and our surroundings that we found in the world when we were born into it, and it has grown all round us, and we think that it is all right, it cannot be changed. We do not come to the Lord Jesus and ask Him about it. Oh! I advise you, Christians, *bring everything into relationship with Jesus* and say:

"Lord, everything in my life has to be in most complete harmony with my position as a branch of Thee, the blessed Vine."

Let your surrender to Christ be absolute. I do not understand that word *surrender* fully; it gets new meanings every now and then; it enlarges immensely from time to time. But I advise you to speak it out: "Absolute surrender to Thee, O Christ, is what I have chosen." And Christ will show you what is not according to His mind, and lead you on to deeper and higher blessedness.

In conclusion, let me gather up all in one sentence. Christ Jesus said: "I am the Vine, ye are the branches." In other words: "I, the living One who have so completely given myself to you, am the Vine. You cannot trust me too much. I am the Almighty Worker, full of a divine life and power."

You are the branches of the Lord Jesus Christ. If there is in your heart the consciousness that you are not a strong, healthy, fruit-bearing branch, not closely linked with Jesus, not living in Him as you should be—then listen to Him say: "I am the Vine, I will receive you, I will draw you to myself, I will bless you, I will strengthen you, I will fill you with my Spirit. I, the Vine, have taken you to be my branches, I have given myself utterly to you; children, give yourselves utterly to me. I have surrendered myself as God absolutely to you, I became man and died for you that I might be entirely yours. Come and surrender yourselves entirely to be mine."

What shall our answer be? Oh, let it be a prayer from the depths of our heart, that the living Christ may take each one of us and link us close to Himself. Let our prayer be that He, the living Vine, shall so link each of us to Himself that we shall go away with our hearts singing: "He is my Vine, and I am His branch—I want nothing more—now I have the everlasting Vine." Then, when you get alone with Him, worship and adore Him, praise and trust Him, love Him and wait for His love. "Thou art my Vine, and I am Thy branch. It is enough, my soul is satisfied."

Glory to His blessed name!

Murray's concern for the holiness of the believer is often expressed in his numerous writings on prayer. With Christ in the School of Prayer, *written in 1885, is one work that deals exclusively with our ministry of prayer. Appropriately enough, a prayer concludes each chapter in this volume.*

Murray presents some practical advice in "Prayer Must Be Definite." Being definite in our prayers enables us to know ourselves better. Definite prayer also indicates that we not only wish to have something but also will it.

Murray is concerned not only with private prayer but also with "The Power of United Prayer." For Murray corporate prayer is important because, "The bond that unites a man to his fellowmen is no less real than that which unites them to God: he is one with them." Truly united, corporate prayer must have agreement, must be in Christ's name, and should be for a special purpose.

"Obedience: The Path to Power in Prayer" explores the relationship between faith and works. In it Murray finds that obedience and faith are two aspects of the same act and that they strengthen each other.

In "The All-Prevailing Plea" Murray describes the power of Christ's name and suggests that we may use a name in such a way only if we are united with its owner. Our union with Christ's name entitles us to the promises associated with it.

"The Ministry of Intercession" examines our calling as priests before God. A priest, Murray states, is one who does not live for himself but with God and for God. Murray exhorts us to fulfill our priestly task of intercession through Christ's blood and His Spirit.

CHAPTER TWENTY-TWO

Prayer Must Be Definite

And Jesus answered him, and said, "What wilt thou that I should do unto thee?" (Mark 10:51; Luke 18:41).

Definite Prayer

The blind man had been crying out aloud, and that a great deal, "Thou Son of David, have mercy on me." The cry had reached the ear of the Lord; He knew what he wanted, and was ready to grant it him. But ere He does it, He asks him: *"What wilt thou* that I should do unto thee?" He wants to hear from his own lips, not only the general petition for mercy, but the distinct expression of what his desire was. Until he speaks it out, he is not healed.

There is now still many a suppliant to whom the Lord puts the same question, and who cannot, until it has been answered, get the aid he asks. Our prayers must not be a vague appeal to His mercy, an indefinite cry for blessing, but the distinct expression of definite need. Not that His loving heart does not understand our cry, or is not ready to hear. But He desires it for our own sakes. Such definite prayer teaches us to know our own needs better. It demands time, and thought, and self-scrutiny to find out what really is our greatest need. It searches us and puts us to the test as to whether our desires are honest and real, such as we are ready to persevere in. It leads us to judge whether our desires are according to God's Word, and whether we really believe that we shall receive the things we ask. It helps us to wait for the special answer, and to mark it when it comes.

And yet how much of our prayer is vague and pointless. Some cry for mercy, but take not the trouble to know what mercy must do for them. Others ask, perhaps, to be delivered from sin, but do not begin by bringing any sin by name from which the deliverance may be claimed. Still others pray for God's blessing on those around them, for the outpouring of God's Spirit on their land or the world, and yet have no special field where they wait and expect to see the answer.

To all the Lord says: And what is it now you really want and expect Me to do? Every Christian has but limited powers, and as he must have his own special field of labor in which he works, so with his prayers too. Each believer has his own circle, his family, his friends, his neighbors. If he were to take one or more of these by name, he would find that this really brings him into the training-school of faith, and leads to personal and pointed dealing with his God. It is when in such distinct matters we have in faith claimed and received answers, that our more general prayers will be believing and effectual.

We all know with what surprise the whole civilised world heard of the way in which trained troops were repulsed by the Transvaal Boers at Majuba. And to what did they owe their success? In the armies of Europe the soldier fires upon the enemy standing in large masses, and never thinks of seeking an aim for every bullet. In hunting game the Boer had learnt a different lesson: his practiced eye knew to send every bullet on its special message, to seek and find its man.

Such aiming must gain the day in the spiritual world too. As long as in prayer we just pour out our hearts in a multitude of petitions, without taking time to see whether every petition is sent with the purpose and expectation of getting an answer, not many will reach the mark. But if, as in silence of soul we bow before the Lord, we were to ask such questions as these: What is now really my desire? Do I desire it in faith, expecting to receive? Am I now ready to place and leave it in the Father's bosom? Is it a settled thing between God and me that I am to have the answer? We should learn so to pray that God would see and we would know what we really expect.

It is for this, among other reasons, that the Lord warns us against the vain repetitions of the Gentiles, who think to be heard for their much praying. We often hear prayers of great earnestness and fervor, in which a multitude of petitions are poured forth, but to which the Savior would undoubtedly answer, "What wilt thou that I should do unto thee?"

If I am in a strange land, in the interests of the business which my father owns, I would certainly write two different sorts of letters. There will be family letters giving expression to all the intercourse to which affection prompts; and there will be business letters, containing orders for what I need. And there may be letters in which both are found. The answers will correspond to the letters. To each sentence of the letters containing the family news I do not expect a special answer. But for each order I send I am confident of an answer whether the desired article has been forwarded. In our dealings with God the business element must not be wanting. With our expression of need and sin, of love and faith and consecration, there must be the pointed statement of what we ask and expect to receive; it is in the answer that the Father loves to give us the token of His approval and acceptance.

The Use of the Will in Prayer

But the word of the Master teaches us more. He does not say, What dost thou *wish?* but, What dost thou *will?* One often wishes for a thing without willing it. I wish to have a certain article, but I find the price too high; I resolve not to take it; I *wish,* but do not *will* to have it. The sluggard wishes to be rich, but does not will it. Many a one wishes to be saved, but perishes because he does not will it.

The will rules the whole heart and life; if I really will to have anything that is within my reach, I do not rest till I have it. And so, when Jesus says to us, "What wilt thou?" He asks whether it is indeed our purpose to have what we ask at any price, however great the sacrifice. Dost thou indeed so will to have it that, though He delay it long, thou dost not hold thy peace till He hear thee? Alas! how many prayers are wishes, sent up for a short time and then forgotten, or sent up year after year as matter of duty, while we rest content with the prayer without the answer.

But, it may be asked, is it not best to make our wishes known to God, and then to leave it to Him to decide what is best, without seeking to assert our will? By no means. This is the very essence of the prayer of faith, to which Jesus sought to train His disciples, that it does not only make known its desire and then the decision to God. That would be the prayer of submission, for cases in which we cannot know God's will.

But the prayer of faith, finding God's will in some promise of the Word, pleads for that till it come. In Matthew 8:28 we read Jesus said to the blind man: *"Believe ye* that I can do this?" Here, in Mark, He says: *"What wilt thou* that I should do?" In both cases He said that faith had saved them. And so He said to the Syrophenician woman, too: "Great is thy *faith:* be it unto thee even as thou *wilt."* Faith is nothing but the purpose of the will resting on God's Word, and saying: I must have it. To believe truly is to will firmly.

But is not such a will at variance with our dependence on God and our submission to Him? By no means; it is much rather the true submission that honors God. It is only when the child has yielded his own will in entire surrender to the Father, that he receives from the Father liberty and power to will what he would have. But, when once the believer has accepted the will of God, as revealed through the Word and Spirit, as his will, too, then it is the will of God that His child should use this renewed will in His service.

The will is the highest power in the soul; grace wants above everything to sanctify and restore this will, one of the chief traits of God's image, to full and free exercise. As a son, who only lives for his father's interests, who seeks not his own but his father's will, is trusted by the father with his business, so God speaks to His child in all truth, "What wilt thou?" It is often spiritual sloth that, under the appearance of humility, professes to have no will, because it fears the trouble of searching out the will of God, or, when found, the struggle of claiming it in faith. True humility is ever in company with strong faith, which only seeks to know what is according to the will of God, and then boldly claims the fulfilment of the promise: "Ye shall ask *what ye will,* and it shall be done unto you."

"Lord, Teach Us to Pray"

Lord Jesus! teach me to pray with all my heart and strength, that there may be no doubt with Thee or with me as to what I have asked. May I so know what I desire that, even as my petitions are recorded in heaven, I can record them on earth too, and note each answer as it comes. And may my faith in what Thy Word has promised be so clear that the Spirit may indeed work in me the liberty to will that it shall come. Lord! renew, strengthen, sanctify wholly my will for the work of effectual prayer.

Blessed Savior! I do beseech Thee to reveal to me the wonderful condescension Thou showest us, thus asking us to say what we will that Thou shouldest do, and promising to do whatever we will. Son of God! I cannot understand it; I can only believe that Thou hast indeed redeemed us wholly for Thyself, and dost seek to make the will, as our noblest part, Thy most efficient servant. Lord! I do most unreservedly yield my will to Thee, as the power through which Thy Spirit is to rule my whole being. Let Him take possession of it, lead it into the truth of Thy promises, and make it so strong in prayer that I may ever hear Thy voice saying: "Great is thy faith: be it unto thee even as thou wilt." Amen.

CHAPTER TWENTY-THREE

The Power of United Prayer

"Again I say unto you, That if two of you shall agree on earth as touching any thing that they shall ask, it shall be done for them of my Father which is in heaven. For where two or three are gathered together in my name, there am I in the midst of them" (Matt. 18:19, 20).

United Prayer

One of the first lessons of our Lord in His school of prayer was: Not to be seen of men. Enter thy inner chamber; be alone with the Father. When He has thus taught us that the meaning of prayer is personal individual contact with God, He comes with a second lesson: You have need not only of secret solitary, but also of public united prayer. And He gives us a very special promise for the united prayer of two or three who agree in what they ask. As a tree has its root hidden in the ground and its stem growing up into the sunlight, so prayer needs equally for its full development the hidden secrecy in which the soul meets God alone, and the public fellowship with those who find in the name of Jesus their common meeting-place.

The reason why this must be so is plain. The bond that unites a man to his fellow-men is no less real and close than that which unites him to God: he is one with them. Grace renews not alone our relation to God but to man too. We not only learn to say "My Father," but "Our Father." Nothing would be more unnatural than that the children of a family should always meet their father separately, but never in the united expression of their desires or their love.

Believers are not only members of one family, but even of one body. Just as each member of the body depends on the other, and the full action of the spirit dwelling in the body depends on the union and co-operation of all, so Christians cannot reach the full blessing God is ready to bestow through His Spirit, but as they seek and receive it in fellowship with each other. It is in the union and fellowship of believers that the Spirit can manifest His full power. It was to the hundred and twenty continuing in one place together, and praying with one accord, that the Spirit came from the throne of the glorified Lord.

The Marks of True United Prayer

The marks of true united prayer are given us in these words of our Lord. The first is *agreement* as to the thing asked. There must not only be generally the consent to agree with anything another may ask: there must be some special thing, matter of distinct united desire; the agreement must be, as all prayer, in spirit and in truth. In such agreement it will become very clear to us what exactly we are asking, whether we may confidently ask according to God's will, and whether we are ready to believe that we have received what we ask.

The second mark is the gathering in, or into, the name of Jesus. We shall afterwards have much more to learn of the need and the power of the name of

Jesus in prayer here our Lord teaches us that the Name must be the center of union to which believers gather, the bond of union that makes them one, just as a home contains and unites all who are in it. "The name of the Lord is a strong tower; the righteous runneth into it and escape." That Name is such a reality to those who understand and believe it, that to meet within it is to have Himself present. The love and unity of His disciples have to Jesus infinite attraction: "Where two or three are gathered in my name, *there am I in the midst of them*." It is the living presence of Jesus, in the fellowship of His loving praying disciples, that gives united prayer its power.

The third mark is, the sure answer: "It shall be done for them of my Father." A prayer meeting for maintaining religious fellowship, or seeking our own edification, may have its use; this was not the Savior's view in its appointment. He meant it as a means of securing *special answer to prayer*. A prayer meeting without recognised answer to prayer ought to be an anomaly. When any of us have distinct desires in regard to which we feel too weak to exercise and needful faith, we ought to seek strength in the help of others. In the unity of faith and of love and of the Spirit, the power of the name and the presence of Jesus acts more freely and the answer comes more surely. The mark that there has been true united prayer is the fruit, the answer, the receiving of the thing we have asked: "I say unto you, *It shall be done* for them of my Father which is in heaven."

Power in United Prayer

What an unspeakable privilege this of united prayer is, and what a power it might be. If the believing husband and wife knew that they were joined together in the name of Jesus to experience His presence and power in united prayer (see 1 Peter); if friends believed what mighty help two or three praying in concert could give each other; if in every prayer meeting the coming together in the Name, the faith in the Presence, and the expectation of the answer, stood in the foreground; if in every church united effectual prayer were regarded as one of the chief purposes for which they are banded together, the highest exercise of their power as a church; if in the church universal the coming of the kingdom, the coming of the King Himself, first in the mighty outpouring of His Holy Spirit, then in His own glorious person, were really matter of unceasing united crying to God—O who can say what blessing might come to, and through, those who thus agreed to prove God in the fulfilment of His promise.

In the Apostle Paul we see very distinctly what a reality his faith in the power of united prayer was. To the Romans he writes (15:30): "I beseech you, brethren, by the love of the Spirit, that ye *strive together with me* in your prayer to God for me." He expects in answer to be delivered from his enemies, and to be prospered in his work. To the Corinthians (2 Cor. 1:11), "God will still deliver us, ye also helping together on our behalf by your supplications;" their prayer is to have a real share in his deliverance. To the Ephesians he writes: "With all prayer and supplication praying at all seasons in the Spirit for all the saints and on my behalf, that utterance may be given unto me." His power and success in his ministry he makes to depend on their prayers.

With the Philippians (1:19) he expects that his trials will turn to his salvation and the progress of the gospel "*through your supplications and* the supply of the Spirit of Jesus Christ." To the Colossians

(4:3) he adds to the injunction to continue steadfast in prayer: "Withal praying for us too, that God may open unto us a door for the word." And to the Thessalonians (2 Thess. 3:1) he writes: "Finally, brethren, pray for us, that the word of the Lord may run and be glorified, and that we may be delivered from unreasonable men." It is everywhere evident that Paul felt himself the member of a body, on the sympathy and co-operation of which he was dependent, and that he counted on the prayers of these churches to gain for him, what otherwise might not be given. The prayers of the church were to him as real a factor in the work of the kingdom, as the power of God.

Who can say what power a church could develop and exercise, if it gave itself to the work of prayer day and night for the coming of the kingdom, for God's power on His servants and His word, for the glorifying of God in the salvation of souls? Most churches think their members are gathered into one simply to take care of and build up each other. They know not that God rules the world by the prayers of His saints; that prayer is the power by which Satan is conquered; that by prayer the church on earth has disposal of the powers of the heavenly world. They do not remember that Jesus has, by His promise, consecrated every assembly in His name to be a gate of heaven, where His presence is to be felt, and His power experienced in the Father fulfilling their desires.

We cannot sufficiently thank God for the blessed week of united prayer, with which Christendom in our days opens every year. As proof of our unity and our faith in the power of united prayer, as a training-school for the enlargement of our hearts to take in all the needs of the church universal, as a help to united persevering prayer, it is of unspeakable value. But very specially as a stimulus to continued union in prayer in the smaller circles, its blessing has been great. And it will become even greater, as God's people recognise what it is, all to meet as one in the name of Jesus, to have His Presence in the midst of a body all united in the Holy Spirit, and boldly to claim the promise that it shall be done of the Father what they agree to ask.

"Lord, Teach Us to Pray"

Blessed Lord! who didst in Thy high-priestly prayer ask so earnestly for the unity of Thy people, teach us how Thou dost invite and urge us to this unity by Thy precious promise given to united prayer. It is when we are one in love and desire that our faith has Thy presence and the Father's answer.

O Father! we pray for Thy people, and for every smaller circle of those who meet together, that they may be one. Remove, we pray, all selfishness and self-interest, all narrowness of heart and estrangement, by which that unity is hindered. Cast out the spirit of the world and the flesh, through which Thy promise loses all its power. O let the thought of Thy presence and the Father's favor draw us all nearer to each other.

Grant especially, Blessed Lord, that Thy church may believe that it is by the power of united prayer that she can bind and loose in heaven; that Satan can be cast out; that souls can be saved; that mountains can be removed; that the kingdom can be hastened. And grant, good Lord! that in the circle with which I pray, the prayer of the church may indeed be the power through which Thy name and Word are glorified. Amen.

CHAPTER TWENTY-FOUR

Obedience: The Path to Power in Prayer

"Ye did not choose me, but I chose you, and appointed you, that ye should go and bear fruit, and that your fruit should abide: that whatsoever ye shall ask *the Father in my name, He may give it you"* (John 15:16).
The fervent effectual prayer of a righteous *man availeth much* (James 5:16).

Consecration and Prayer

The promise of the Father's giving whatsoever we ask is here once again renewed, in such a connection as to show us to whom it is that such wonderful influence in the council chamber of the Most High is to be granted. "I chose you," the Master says, "and appointed you that ye should go and bear fruit, and that your fruit should abide;" and then He adds, *to the end "that* whatsoever ye," the fruit-bearing ones, "shall ask of the Father in my name, He may give it you."

This is nothing but the fuller expression of what He had spoken in the words, "If ye abide in me." He had spoken of the object of this abiding as the bearing "fruit," "more fruit," "much fruit": in this was God to be glorified, and the mark of discipleship seen. No wonder that He now adds, that where the reality of the abiding is seen in fruit abounding and abiding, this would be the qualification for praying so as to obtain what we ask. Entire consecration to the fulfillment of our calling is the condition of effectual prayer, is the key to the unlimited blessings of Christ's wonderful prayer-promises.

There are Christians who fear that such a statement is at variance with the doctrine of free grace. But surely not of free grace rightly understood, nor with so many express statements of God's blessed word. Take the words of St. John (1 John 3:22): "Let us love in deed and truth: *hereby* shall we assure our heart before Him. And whatsoever we ask, we receive of Him, *because* we keep His commandments, and do the things that are pleasing in His sight." Or take the oft-quoted words of James: "The fervent effectual prayer of a *righteous* man availeth much"; that is, of a man of whom, according to the definition of the Holy Spirit, it can be said, "He that doeth righteousness, is righteous even as He is righteous."

Mark the spirit of so many of the Psalms, with their confident appeal to the integrity and righteousness of the supplicant. In Psalm 18 David says: "The Lord rewarded me according to my righteousness; according to the cleanness of my hands hath He recompensed me. . . . I was upright before Him, and I kept myself from mine iniquity: therefore hath the Lord recompensed me according to my righteousness." (Ps. 18:20–26. See also Ps. 7:3–5; 15:1, 2; 17:3, 6; 26:1–6; 119:121, 153.)

If we carefully consider such utterances in the light of the New Testament, we shall find them in perfect harmony with the explicit teaching of the Savior's parting words: *"If ye keep* my commandments, ye shall abide in my love"; "Ye are my friends *if ye do* what I command you." The word is indeed meant literally: "I appointed you that ye should go and bear fruit, *that*," then, "whatsoever ye shall ask of the Father in my name, He may give it you."

Let us seek to enter into the spirit of what the Savior here teaches us. There is a danger in our evangelical religion of looking too much at what it offers from one side, as a certain experience to be obtained in prayer and faith. There is another side which God's word puts very strongly, that of obedience as the only path to blessing. What we need is to realize that in our relationship to the infinite being whom we call God, who has created and redeemed us, the first sentiment that ought to animate us is that of subjection: the surrender to His supremacy, His glory, His will, His pleasure, ought to be the first and uppermost thought of our life.

The question is not, how we are to obtain and enjoy His favor, for in this the main thing may still be self. But what this Being in the very nature of things rightfully claims, and is infinitely and unspeakably worthy of, is that His glory and pleasure should be my one object. Surrender to His perfect and blessed will, a life of service and obedience, is the beauty and the charm of heaven. Service and obedience, these were the thoughts that were uppermost in the mind of the Son, when He dwelt upon earth. Service and obedience, these must become with us the chief objects of desire and aim, more so than rest or light, or joy or strength: in them we shall find the path to all the higher blessedness that awaits us.

Just note what a prominent place the Master gives it, not only in this 15th chapter, in connection with the abiding, but in the 14th, where He speaks of the indwelling of the Three-One God. In

verse 15 we have it: "*If ye* love me, *keep my commandments*," and the Spirit will be given you of the Father. Then verse 21: "He that hath *my commandments and keepeth them*, he it is that loveth me"; and he shall have the special love of my Father resting on him, and the special manifestation of myself. And then again, verse 23, one of the highest of all the exceeding great and precious promises: "If a man love me *he will keep my words*, and the Father and I will come and take up our abode with him." Could words put it more clearly that obedience is the way to the indwelling of the Spirit, to His revealing the Son within us, and to His again preparing us to be the abode, the home of the Father?

The indwelling of the Three-One God is the heritage of them that obey. Obedience and faith are but two aspects of one act—surrender to God and His will. As faith strengthens for obedience, it is in turn strengthened by it: faith is made perfect by works. It is to be feared that often our efforts to believe have been unavailing because we have not taken up the only position in which a large faith is legitimate or possible—that of entire surrender to the honor and the will of God. It is the man who is entirely consecrated to God and His will who will find the power come to claim everything that his God has promised to be for him.

Obedience Yields Fruitfulness

The application of this in the school of prayer is very simple, but very solemn. "I chose you," the Master says, "and appointed you that ye should go and bear fruit," much fruit (vv. 5, 8), "and that your fruit should abide," that your life might be one of abiding fruit and abiding fruitfulness, *"that"* thus, as fruitful branches abiding in me, "whatsoever ye shall ask of the Father in my name, He may give it you."

O how often we have sought to be able to pray the effectual prayer for much grace to bear fruit, and have wondered that the answer came not. It was because we were reversing the Master's order. We wanted to have the comfort and the joy and the strength first, that we might do the work easily and without any feeling of difficulty or self-sacrifice. And He wanted us in faith, without asking whether we felt weak or strong, whether the work was hard or easy, in the obedience of faith to do what He said: the path of fruit-bearing would have led us to the place and the power of prevailing prayer.

Obedience is the only path that leads to the glory of God. Not obedience instead of faith, nor obedience to supply the shortcomings of faith; no, but faith's obedience gives access to all the blessings our God has for us. The baptism of the Spirit (14:16), the manifestation of the Son (14:21), the indwelling of the Father (14:23), the abiding in Christ's love (15:10), the privilege of His holy friendship (15:14), and the power of all-prevailing prayer (15:16)—all wait for the obedient.

Let us take home the lessons. Now we know the great reason why we have not had power in faith to pray prevailingly. Our life was not as it should have been: simple downright obedience, abiding fruitfulness, was not its chief mark. And with our whole heart we approve of the divine appointment: men to whom God is to give such influence in the rule of the world, as at their request to do what otherwise would not have taken place, men whose will is to guide the path in which God's will is to work, must be men who have themselves learned obedience, whose loyalty and submission to authority must be above all suspicion. Our whole soul approves the law: obedience and fruit-bearing, the path to prevailing prayer. And with shame we acknowledge how little our lives have yet borne this stamp.

Let us yield ourselves to take up the appointment the Savior gives us. Let us study His relation to us as Master. Let us seek no more with each new day to think in the first place of comfort, or joy, or blessing. Let the first thought be: I belong to the Master. Every moment and every movement I must act as His property, as a part of Himself, as one who only seeks to know and do His will. A servant, a slave of Jesus Christ—let this be the spirit that animates me. If He says, "No longer do I call you servants, but I have called you friends," let us accept the place of friends: "Ye are my friends if ye do the things which I command you."

The one thing He commands us as His branches is to bear fruit. Let us live to bless others, to testify of the life and the love there is in Jesus. Let us in faith and obedience give our whole life to that which Jesus chose us for and appointed us to—fruit-bearing. As we think of His electing us to this, and take up our appointment as coming from Him who always gives all He demands, we shall grow strong in the confidence that a life of fruit-bearing, abounding and abiding, is within our reach. And we shall understand why this fruit-bearing alone can be the path to the place of all prevailing prayer. It is the man who, in obedience to the Christ of God, is proving that he is doing what his Lord wills, for whom the Father will do whatsoever he will: "Whatsoever we ask we receive, because we keep His commandments, and do the things that are pleasing in His sight."

"Lord, Teach Us to Pray"

Blessed Master! teach me to apprehend fully what I only partly realize, that it is only through the will of God, accepted and acted out in obedience to His commands, that we obtain the power to grasp His will in His promises and fully to appropriate them in our prayers. And teach me that it is in the path of fruit-bearing that the deeper growth of the branch into the Vine can be perfected, and we attain to that perfect oneness with Thyself in which we ask whatsoever we will.

O Lord! reveal to us, we pray Thee, how with all the hosts of heaven, and with Thyself the Son on earth, and with all the men of faith who have glorified Thee on earth, *obedience to God is our highest privilege, because it gives access to oneness with Himself in that which is His highest glory—His all-perfect will.* And reveal to us, we pray Thee, how, in keeping Thy commandments and bearing fruit according to Thy will, our spiritual nature will grow up to the full stature of the perfect man, with power to ask and to receive whatsoever we will.

O Lord Jesus! reveal Thyself to us, and the reality of Thy purpose and Thy power to make these Thy wonderful promises the daily experience of all who utterly yield themselves to Thee and Thy words. Amen.

CHAPTER TWENTY-FIVE

The All-Prevailing Plea

"Whatsoever ye shall ask in my Name, that will I do. If ye shall ask me any thing in my Name, that will I do. That whatsoever ye shall ask the Father in my Name, He may give it you. Verily, verily, I say unto you, If ye shall ask anything of the Father, He will give it you in my Name. Hitherto ye have asked nothing in my Name: ask, and ye shall receive. In that day ye shall ask in my Name" (John 14:13, 14; 15:16; 16:23, 24, 26).

Hitherto the disciples had not asked in the Name of Christ, nor had He Himself ever used the expression. The nearest approach is, "met together in my Name." Here in His parting words, He repeats the word unceasingly in connection with those promises of unlimited meaning, *"Whatsoever," "Anything," "What ye will,"* to teach them and us that His Name is our only, but also our all-sufficient plea. The power of prayer and the answer depend on the right use of the Name.

The Power of Christ's Name

What is a person's name? That word or expression in which the person is called up or represented to us. When I mention or hear a name, it calls up before me the whole man, what I know of him, and also the impression he has made on me. The name of a king includes his honor, his power, his kingdom. His name is the symbol of his power. And so each name of God embodies and represents some part of the glory of the Unseen One. And the Name of Christ is the expression of all He has done and all He is and lives to do as our mediator.

And what is it to do a thing in the name of another? It is to come with the power and authority of that other, as his representative and substitute. We know how such a use of another's name always supposes a community of interest. No one would give another the free use of his name without first being assured that his honor and interest were as safe with that other as with himself.

And what is it when Jesus gives us power over His Name, the free use of it, with the assurance that whatever we ask in it will be given to us? The ordinary comparison of one person giving another, on some special occasion, the liberty to ask something in his name, comes altogether short here—Jesus solemnly gives to *all* His disciples a general and unlimited power of the free use of His Name at *all* times for *all* they desire. He could not do this if He did not know that He could trust us with His interests, that His honor would be safe in our hands.

The free use of the name of another is always the token of great confidence, of close union. He who gives his name to another stands aside, to let that other act for him; he who takes the name of another, gives up his own as of no value. When I go in the name of another, I deny myself, I take not only his name, but himself and what he is, instead of myself and what I am.

Union with Christ's Name

Such a use of the name of a person may be in virtue of *a legal union*. A merchant leaving his home and business, gives his chief clerk a general power, by which he can draw thousands of pounds in the merchant's name. The clerk does this, not for himself, but only in the interests of the business. It is because the merchant knows and trusts him as wholly devoted to his interests and business, that he dares put his name and property at his command.

When the Lord Jesus went to heaven, He left His work, the management of His kingdom on earth, in the hands of His servants. He could not do otherwise than also give them His Name to draw all the supplies they needed for the due conduct of His business. And they have the spiritual power to avail themselves of the Name of Jesus just to the extent to which they yield themselves to live only for the interests and the work of the Master. The use of the Name always supposes the surrender of our interests to Him whom we represent.

Or such a use of the name may be in virtue of a *life union*. In the case of the merchant and his clerk, the union is temporary. But we know how oneness of life on earth gives oneness of name: a child has the father's name because he has his life. And often the child of a good father has been honored or helped by others for the sake of the name he bore. But this would not last long if it were found that it was only a name, and that the father's character was wanting. The name and the character or spirit must be in harmony. When such is the case, the child will have a double claim on the father's friends: the character secures and increases the love and esteem rendered first for the name's sake.

So it is with Jesus and the believer: we are one, we have one life, one Spirit with Him; for this reason we may come in His Name. Our power in using that Name, whether with God, or men, or devils, *depends on the measure of our spiritual life-union*. The use of the name rests on the unity of life; the Name and the Spirit of Jesus are one.

Or the union that empowers to the use of the Name may be *the union of love*. When a bride whose life has been one of poverty, becomes united to the bridegroom, she gives up her own name, to be called by his, and has now the full right to use it. She purchases in his name, and that name is not refused. And this is done because the bridegroom has chosen her for himself, counting on her to care for his interests: they are now one.

And so the Heavenly Bridegroom could do nothing less; having loved us and made us one with Himself, what could He do but give those who bear His Name the right to present it before the Father, or to come with it to Himself for all they need. And there is no one who gives himself really to live in the Name of Jesus, who does not receive in ever-increasing measure the spiritual capacity to ask and receive in that Name what he will. The bearing of the name of another supposes my having given up my own, and with it my own independent life; but then, as surely, my possession of all there is in the name I have taken instead of my own.

The Promise of Christ's Name

Such illustrations show us how defective the common view is of a messenger sent to ask in the name of another, or a guilty one appealing to the name of a surety. No, Jesus Himself is with the Father; it is not an absent one in whose name we come. Even when we pray to Jesus Himself, it must be in His Name. The name represents the person; to ask in the Name is to ask in full union of interest and life and love with Himself, as one who lives in and for Him. Let the Name of Jesus only have undivided supremacy in my heart and life, my faith will grow to the assurance that what I ask in that Name cannot be refused. The name and the power of asking go together: when the Name of Jesus has become the power that rules my life, its power in prayer with God will be seen too.

We see thus that everything depends on our own relation to the Name: the power it has on my life is the power it will have in my prayers. There is more than one expression in Scripture which can make this clear to us. When it says, *"Do all* in the Name of the Lord Jesus," we see how this is the counterpart of the other, *"Ask all."* To do all and to ask all in His Name, these go together.

When we read, "We shall walk in the Name of our God," we see how the power of the Name must rule in the whole life; only then will it have power in prayer. It is not to the lips but to the life God looks to see what the Name is to us. When Scripture speaks of "men who have given their lives for the Name of the Lord Jesus," or of one "ready to die for the Name of the Lord Jesus," we see what our relation to the Name must be: when it is everything to me, it will obtain everything for me. If I let it have all I have, it will let me have all it has.

"WHATSOEVER ye shall ask in my Name, that will I do." Jesus means the promise literally. Christians have sought to limit it: it looked too free; it was hardly safe to trust man so unconditionally. We did not understand that the word "in my Name" is its own safeguard. It is a spiritual power which no one can use further than he obtains the capacity for, by his living and acting in that Name. As we bear that Name before men, we have power to use it before God.

O let us plead for God's Holy Spirit to show us what the Name means, and what the right use of it is. It is through the Spirit that the Name, which is above every name in heaven, will take the place of supremacy in our heart and life too.

Disciples of Jesus! let the lessons of this day enter deep into your hearts. The Master says: Only pray in my Name; whatsoever ye ask will be given. Heaven is set open to you; the treasures and powers of the world of spirit are placed at your disposal on behalf of men around you. O come, and let us learn to pray in the Name of Jesus. As to the disciples, He says to us, "Hitherto ye have not asked in my Name: ask, and ye shall receive."

Let each disciple of Jesus seek to avail himself of the rights of his royal priesthood, and use the power placed at his disposal for his circle and his work. Let Christians awake and hear the message: your prayer can obtain what otherwise will be withheld, can accomplish what otherwise remains undone. O awake, and use the name of Jesus to open the treasures of heaven for this perishing world. Learn as the servants of the King to use His Name: "WHATSOEVER ye shall ask in my Name, THAT WILL I DO."

"Lord, Teach Us to Pray"

Blessed Lord! it is as if each lesson Thou givest me has such fullness and depths of meaning, that if I can only learn that one, I shall know how to pray aright. This day I feel again as if I needed but one prayer every day: Lord! teach me what it is to pray in Thy Name. Teach me so to live and act, to walk and speak, so to do all in the Name of Jesus, that my prayer cannot be anything else but in that blessed Name too.

And teach me, Lord! to hold fast the precious promise that WHATSOEVER we ask in Thy Name, Thou wilt do, the Father will give. Though I do not yet fully understand, and still less have fully attained, the wondrous union Thou meanest when Thou sayest, IN MY NAME, I would yet hold fast the promise until it fills my heart with the undoubting assurance: Anything in the Name of Jesus.

O my Lord! let Thy Holy Spirit teach me this. Thou didst say of Him, "The Comforter, whom the Father shall send IN MY NAME." He knows what it is to be sent from heaven in Thy Name, to reveal and to honor the power of that Name in Thy servants, to use that Name alone, and so to glorify Thee. Lord Jesus! let Thy Spirit dwell in me, and fill me. I would, I do yield my whole being to His rule and leading. Thy Name and Thy Spirit are one; through Him Thy Name will be the strength of my life and my prayer. Then I shall be able for Thy Name's sake to forsake all, in Thy Name to speak to men and to God, and to prove that this is indeed the Name above every name.

Lord Jesus! O teach me by Thy Holy Spirit to pray in Thy Name. Amen.

The Ministry of Intercession

An holy priesthood, to offer up spiritual sacrifices acceptable to God by Jesus Christ (1 Pet. 2:5).
Ye shall be named the Priests of the Lord (Isa. 61:6).

"The Spirit of the Lord God is upon me: because the Lord hath anointed me." These are the words of Jesus in Isaiah. As the fruit of His work all redeemed ones are priests, fellow-partakers with Him of His anointing with the Spirit as High Priest. "Like the precious ointment upon the beard of Aaron, that went down to the skirts of his garments." As every son of Aaron, so every member of Jesus' body has a right to the priesthood. But not every one exercises it: many are still entirely ignorant of it. And yet it is the highest privilege of a child of God, the mark of greatest nearness and likeness to Him, "who ever liveth to pray." Do you doubt if this really be so? Think of what constitutes priesthood.

The Work of the Priesthood

This has two sides, one Godward, the other manward. "Every priest is *ordained for men* in things *pertaining to God*" (Heb. 5:1); or, as it is said by Moses (Deut. 10:8, see also 21:5, 33:10; Mal. 2:6): "The Lord separated the tribe of Levi, *to stand before the Lord* to minister unto Him, and *to bless His Name*." On the one hand, the priest had the power to draw nigh to God, to dwell with Him in His house, and to present before Him the blood of the sacrifice or the burning incense. This work he did not do, however, on his own behalf, but for the sake

of the people whose representative he was. This is the other side of his work. He received from the people their sacrifices, presented them before God, and then came out to bless in His name, to give the assurance of His favor and to teach them His law.

A priest is thus a man who does not at all live for himself. *He lives with God and for God.* His work is as God's servant to care for His house, His honor, and His worship, to make known to men His love and His will. *He lives with men and for men* (Heb. 5:2). His work is to find out their sin and need, and to bring it before God, to offer sacrifice and incense in their name, to obtain forgiveness and blessing for them, and then to come out and bless them in His name. This is the high calling of every believer. "Such honor have all His saints." They have been redeemed with the one purpose to be in the midst of the perishing millions around them God's priests, who in conformity to Jesus, the Great High Priest, are to be the ministers and stewards of the grace of God to all around them.

The Walk of the Priesthood

As God is holy, so the priest was to be especially holy. This means not only separated from everything unclean, but *holy unto God*, being set apart and given up to God for His disposal. The separation from the world and setting apart unto God was indicated in many ways.

It was seen in the clothing: the holy garments, made after God's own order, marked them as His (Ex. 27). It was seen in the command as to their special purity and freedom from all contact from death and defilement (Lev. 21:22). Much that was allowed to an ordinary Israelite was forbidden to them. It was seen in the injunction that the priest must have no bodily defect or blemish; bodily perfection was to be the type of wholeness and holiness in God's service. And it was seen in the arrangement by which the priestly tribes were to have no inheritance with the other tribes; God was to be their inheritance. Their life was to be one of faith: set apart unto God, they were to live on Him as well as for Him.

All this is the emblem of what the character of the New Testament priest is to be. Our priestly power with God depends on our personal life and walk. We must be of them of whose walk on earth Jesus says, "They have not defiled their garments."

In the surrender of what may appear lawful to others in our separation from the world, we must prove that our consecration to be holy to the Lord is whole-hearted and entire. The bodily perfection of the priest must have its counterpart in our too being "without spot or blemish"; "the man of God perfect, thoroughly furnished unto all good works," "perfect and entire, wanting nothing" (Lev. 21:17–21; Eph. 5:27; 2 Tim. 2:7; James 1:4). And above all, we consent to give up all inheritance on earth; to forsake all, and like Christ to have only God as our portion: to possess as not possessing, and hold all for God alone; it is this marks the true priest, the man who only lives for God and his fellow-men.

The Way to the Priesthood

In Aaron God had chosen all his sons to be priests: each of them was a priest by birth. And yet he could not enter upon his work without a special act of ordinance—his consecration. Every child of God is priest in right of his birth, his blood relationship to the Great High Priest; but this is not enough: he will exercise his power only as he accepts and realizes his consecration.

With Aaron and his sons it took place thus (Ex. 29): After being washed and clothed, they were anointed with the holy oil. Sacrifices were then offered, and with the blood the right ear, the right hand, and the right foot were touched. And then they and their garments were once again sprinkled with the blood and the oil together. And so it is as the child of God enters more fully into what THE BLOOD and THE SPIRIT of which he already is partaker, are to him, that the power of the holy priesthood will work in him. The blood will take away all sense of unworthiness; the Spirit, all sense of unfitness.

Let us notice what there was new in the application of the blood to the priest. If ever he had as a penitent brought a sacrifice for his sin, seeking forgiveness, the blood was sprinkled on the altar, but not on his person. But now, for priestly consecration, there was to be closer contact with the blood; ear and hand and foot were by a special act brought under its power, and the whole being taken possession of and sanctified for God. And so, when the believer, who had been content to think chiefly of the blood sprinkled on the mercy-seat as what he needs for pardon, is led to seek full priestly access to God, he feels the need of a fuller and more abiding experience of the power of the blood, as really sprinkling and cleansing the heart from an evil conscience so that he has "no more conscience of sin" (Heb. 10:2), as cleansing from all sin. And it is as he gets to enjoy this, that the consciousness is awakened of his wonderful right of most intimate access to God, and of the full assurance that his intercessions are acceptable.

And as the blood gives the right, the Spirit gives the power, and fits for believing intercession. He breathes into us the priestly spirit—burning love for God's honor and the saving of souls. He makes us so one with Jesus that prayer in His Name is a reality. He strengthens us to believing, importunate prayer. The more the Christian is truly filled with the Spirit of Christ, the more spontaneous will be his giving himself up to the life of priestly intercession. Beloved fellow-Christians! God needs, greatly needs, priests who can draw near to Him, who live in His presence, and by their intercession draw down the blessings of His grace on others. And the world needs, greatly needs, priests who will bear the burden of the perishing ones, and intercede on their behalf.

Are you willing to offer yourself for this holy work? You know the surrender it demands—nothing less than the Christ-like giving up of all, that the saving purposes of God's love may be accomplished among men. Oh, be no longer of those who are content if they have salvation, and just do work enough to keep themselves warm and lively. O let nothing keep you back from giving yourselves to be wholly and only priests—nothing else, nothing less than the priests of the Most High God. The thought of unworthiness, of unfitness, need not keep you back.

In *the Blood*, the objective power of the perfect redemption works in you: in *the Spirit*, its full subjective personal experience as a divine life is secured. *The Blood* provides an infinite worthiness to make your prayers most acceptable: *The Spirit* provides a divine fitness, teaching you to pray just according to the will of God. *Every priest knew that when he presented a sacrifice according to the law of the sanctuary, it was accepted:* under the covering of the Blood and Spirit you have the assurance that all the wonderful promises to prayer in the name of Jesus will be fulfilled in you.

Abiding in union with the Great High Priest, "you shall ask what you will, and it shall be done unto you." You will have power to pray the effectual prayer of the righteous man that availeth much. You will not only join in the general prayer of the church for the world, but be able in your own sphere to take up your special work in prayer—as priests, to transact it with God, to receive and know the answer, and so to bless in His name. Come, brother, come, and be a priest, *only* priest, *all* priest. Seek now to walk before the Lord in the full consciousness that you have been set apart for the holy ministry of intercession. This is the true blessedness of conformity to the image of God's Son.

"Lord, Teach Us to Pray"

O Thou my blessed High Priest, accept the consecration in which my soul now would respond to Thy message.

I believe in the HOLY PRIESTHOOD OF THY SAINTS, and that I too am a priest, with power to appear before the Father, and in the prayer that avails much bring down blessing on the perishing around me.

I believe in the POWER OF THY PRECIOUS BLOOD to cleanse from all sin, to give me perfect confidence toward God, and bring me near in the full assurance of faith that my intercession will be heard.

I believe in the ANOINTING OF THE SPIRIT, coming down daily from Thee, my Great High Priest, to sanctify me, to fill me with the consciousness of my priestly calling, and with love to souls, to teach me what is according to God's will, and how to pray the prayer of faith.

I believe that, as Thou my Lord Jesus art Thyself in all things my life, so Thou, too, art THE SURETY FOR MY PRAYER-LIFE, and wilt Thyself draw me up into the fellowship of Thy wondrous work of intercession.

In this faith I yield myself this day to my God, as one of His anointed priests, to stand before His face to intercede in behalf of sinners, and to come out and bless in His name.

Holy Lord Jesus! accept and seal my consecration. Yea, Lord, do Thou lay Thy hands on me, and Thyself conse-crate me to this Thy holy work. And let me walk among men with the con-sciousness and the character of a priest of the Most High God.

Unto Him that loved us, and washed us from our sins IN HIS OWN BLOOD, AND HATH MADE US kings and priests unto God and His Father; TO HIM be glory and dominion for ever and ever. Amen.

Another one of Murray's volumes on prayer, The Prayer-Life, *was the outcome of a conference of ministers held in 1912, which was held in response to the low spiritual state of the church.*

Murray finds it a reproach to God, in "The Sin of Prayerlessness," that we do not accept God's invitation to converse with Him and that we cannot make time for Him as we would for a friend. He finds that prayerlessness is a sin that causes a deficient spiritual life and reduces the power of the church.

The prayer life and the spiritual life are inseparable, as seen in "The Example of Our Lord." At every critical moment in His life Christ was found in prayer, and through prayer God's will on earth was accomplished by Christ.

Murray gives us "Hints for the Inner Chamber." Here Murray gives practical advice and emphasizes the connection between God's Word and prayer and between the inner chamber and the outer world.

The Sin of Prayerlessness

If conscience is to do its work, and the contrite heart is to feel its misery, it is necessary that each individual should mention his sin by name. The confession must be severely personal. In a meeting of ministers there is probably no single sin which each one of us ought to acknowledge with deeper shame—"Guilty, verily guilty"—than the sin of prayerlessness.

What is it, then, that makes prayerlessness such a great sin? At first it is looked upon merely as a weakness. There is so much talk about lack of time, and all sorts of distractions, that the deep guilt of the situation is not recognized. Let it be our honest desire that, for the future, the sin of prayerlessness may be to us truly sinful.

A Reproach to God

There is the holy and most glorious God who invites us to come to Him, to hold converse with Him, to ask from Him such things as we need, and to experience what a blessing there is in fellowship with Him. He has created us in His own image, and has redeemed us by His own Son, so that in converse with Him we might find our highest glory and salvation.

What use do we make of this heavenly privilege? How many there are who take only five minutes for prayer! They say that they have no time, and that the heart desire for prayer is lacking; they do not know how to spend half an hour with God! It is not that they absolutely do not pray; they pray every day—but they have no joy in prayer, as a token of communion with God which shows that God is everything to them.

If a friend comes to visit them, they have time, they make time, even at the cost of sacrifice, for the sake of enjoying converse with him. Yes, they have time for everything that really interests them, but not time to practice fellowship with God, and delight themselves in Him! They find time for a creature who can be of service to them; but day after day, month after month passes, and there is no time to spend one hour with God.

Do not our hearts begin to acknowledge what a dishonor, what a despite of God this is, that I dare to say I cannot find time for fellowship with Him? If this sin begins to appear plain to us, shall we not with deep shame cry out: "Woe is me, for I am undone, O God; be merciful to me, and forgive this awful sin of prayerlessness."

The Cause of a Deficient Spiritual Life

It is a proof that, for the most part, our life is still under the power of "the flesh." Prayer is the pulse of life; by it the doctor can tell what is the condition of the heart. The sin of prayerlessness is a proof for the ordinary Christian or minister, that the life of God in the soul is in deadly sickness and weakness.

Much is said, and many complaints are made, about the feebleness of the church to fulfil her calling, to exercise an influence over her members, to deliver them from the power of the world, and to bring them to a life of holy consecration to God. Much is also spoken about her indifference to the millions of heathen whom Christ entrusted to her, that she might make known to them His love and salvation.

What is the reason why many thousands of Christian workers in the world have not a greater influence? Nothing save this—the prayerlessness of their service. In the midst of all their zeal in the study and in the work of the church, of all their faithfulness in preaching and conversation with the people, they lack that ceaseless prayer which has attached to it the sure promise of the Spirit, and the power from on high. It is nothing but the sin of prayerlessness which is the cause of the lack of a powerful spiritual life!

The Loss the Church Suffers

It is the business of a minister to train believers up to a life of prayer; but how can a leader do this, if he himself understands little the art of conversing with God, and of receiving from the Holy Spirit, every day, out of heaven, abundant grace for himself and for his work? A minister cannot lead a congregation higher than he is himself. He cannot with enthusiasm point out a way, or explain a work, in which he is not himself walking or living.

How many thousands of Christians there are who know next to nothing of the blessedness of prayer fellowship with God! How many there are who know something of it, and long for a further increase of this knowledge, but in the preaching of the Word they are not persistently urged to keep on till they obtain the blessing. The reason is simply and only that the minister under-stands so little about the secret of powerful prayer, and does not give prayer the place in his service which, in the nature of the case, and in the will of God, is indispensably necessary. Oh, what a difference we should notice in our congregations, if ministers could be brought to see in its right light the sin of prayerlessness, and were delivered from it!

The Impossibility of Preaching the Gospel to All Men

Many feel that the great need of missions is the obtaining of men and women who will give themselves to the Lord to strive in prayer for the salvation of souls. It has also been said that God is eager and able to deliver and bless the world He has redeemed, if His people were but willing, if they were but ready, to cry to Him day and night. But how can congregations be brought to that, unless there comes, first, an entire change in ministers, and that they begin to see that the indispensable thing is not preaching, not pastoral visitation, not church work, but fellowship with God in prayer till they are clothed with power from on High?

Oh, that all thought and work and expectation concerning the kingdom might drive us to the acknowledgment of the sin of prayerlessness! God help us to root it out! God deliver us from it through the blood and power of Christ Jesus! God teach every minister of the Word to see what a glorious place he may occupy, if he first of all is delivered from this root of evils; so that with courage and joy, in faith and perseverance, he can go on with his God!

The sin of prayerlessness! The Lord lay the burden of it so heavy on our hearts, that we may not rest till it is taken far from us through the name and power of Jesus. He will make this possible for us.

A Witness from America

In 1898, there were two members of the Presbytery, New York, who attended the Northfield Conference for the deepening of the spiritual life. They returned to their work with the fire of a new enthusiasm. They endeavored to bring about a revival in the entire Presbytery. In a meeting which they held, the chairman was guided to ask the brethren a question concerning their prayer-life: "Brethren," said he, "let us today make confession before God and each other. It will do us good. Will every one who spends half an hour every day with God in connection with his work, hold up a hand?" One hand was held up. He made a further request: "All who thus spend fifteen minutes, hold up a hand." Not half of the hands were held up. Then he said: "Prayer, the working power of the church of Christ, and half of the workers make hardly any use of it! All who spend five minutes hold up hands." All hands went up. But one man came later with the confession that he was not quite sure if he spent five minutes in prayer every day. "It is," said he, "a terrible revelation of how little time I spend with God."

CHAPTER TWENTY-EIGHT

The Example of Our Lord

The connection between the prayer-life and the Spirit-life is close and indissoluble. It is not merely that we receive the Spirit through prayer, but the Spirit-life requires, as an indispensable thing, a continuous prayer-life. I can be led continually by the Spirit, only as I continually give myself to prayer.

Christ's Prayers

This was very evident in the life of our Lord. A study of His life will give us a wonderful view of the power and holiness of prayer.

Consider His baptism. It was when He was baptized and prayed, that heaven was opened and the Holy Spirit came down upon Him. God desired to crown Christ's surrender of Himself to the sinner's baptism in Jordan (which was also a surrender of Himself to the sinner's death), with the gift of the Spirit for the work that He must accomplish.

But this could not have taken place, had He not prayed. In the fellowship of worship the Spirit was bestowed on Him to lead Him out into the desert to spend forty days there in prayer and fasting. Turn to Mark 1:32–35: "And at even, when the sun did set, they brought unto Him all that were diseased, and them that were possessed with devils. And all the city was gathered together at the door. . . . And in the morning rising up a great while before day, He went out, and departed into a solitary place, and there prayed."

The work of the day and evening had exhausted Him. In His healing of the sick and casting out devils, power had gone out of Him. While others still slept, He went away to pray and to renew His strength in communion with His Father. He had need of this, otherwise He would not have been ready for the new day. The holy work of delivering souls demands constant renewal through fellowship with God.

Think again of the calling of the apostles as given in Luke 6:12, 13: "And it came to pass in those days, that He went out into a mountain to pray, and continued all night in prayer to God. And when it was day, He called unto Him His disciples; and of them He chose twelve, whom also He named apostles." Is it not clear that if any one wishes to do God's work, he must take time for fellowship with Him, to receive His wisdom and power? The dependence and helplessness of which this is an evidence, open the way, and give God the opportunity of revealing His power. How great was the importance of the choosing of the apostles for Christ's own work, for the early church, and for all time! It had God's blessing and seal; the stamp of prayer was on it.

Christ's Prayers with the Disciples

Read Luke 9:18, 20: "And it came to pass, as He was alone praying, His disciples were with Him: and He asked them saying, Whom say the people that I am? . . . Peter answering said, The Christ of God." The Lord had prayed that the Father might reveal to them who He was. It was in answer to that prayer that

Peter said: "The Christ of God"; and the Lord then said: "Flesh and blood hath not revealed it unto thee, but My Father which is in heaven" (Matt. 16:17). This great confession was the fruit of prayer.

Read further Luke 9:28–36: "He took Peter and John and James, and went up into a mountain to pray. And as He prayed, the fashion of His countenance was altered . . . and there came a voice out of the cloud, saying, This is My beloved Son, hear Him." Christ had desired that, for the strengthening of their faith, God might give them an assurance from heaven that He was the Son of God. Prayer obtained for our Lord Jesus Himself, as well as for His disciples, what happened on the Mount of Transfiguration.

Does it not become still more clear that what God wills to accomplish on earth needs prayer as its indispensable condition? And there is but one way for Christ and believers. A heart and mouth open towards heaven in believing prayer, will certainly not be put to shame.

Read Luke 11:1–13: "As He was praying in a certain place, when He ceased, one of His disciples said unto Him, Lord teach us to pray." And then He gave them that inexhaustible prayer: "Our Father who art in heaven." In this He showed what was going on in His heart, when He prayed that God's name might be hallowed, and His kingdom come, and His will be done, and all of this "on earth as it is in heaven." How will this ever come to pass? Through prayer. This prayer has been uttered through the ages by countless millions, to their unspeakable comfort. But forget not this—it was born out of the prayer of our Lord Jesus. He had been praying, and therefore was able to give that glorious answer.

Read John 14:16: "I will pray the Father, and He shall give you another Comforter." The entire dispensation of the New Testament, with the wonderful outpouring of the Holy Spirit, is the outcome of the prayer of the Lord Jesus. It is as though God had impressed on the gift of the Holy Spirit this seal—in answer to the prayer of the Lord Jesus, and later of His disciples, the Holy Spirit will surely come. But it will be in answer to prayer like that of our Lord, in which He took time to be alone with God and in that prayer offered Himself wholly to God.

Christ's Final Prayers

Read John 17, the high-priestly, most holy prayer! Here the Son prays first for Himself, that the Father will glorify Him, by giving Him power for the Cross, by raising Him from the dead, by setting Him at His right hand. These great things could not take place save through prayer. Prayer had power to obtain them.

Afterwards He prayed for His disciples, that the Father might preserve them from the evil one, might keep them from the world, and might sanctify them. And then, further, He prayed for all those who through their word might believe on Him, that all might be one in love, even as the Father and the Son were one. This prayer gives us a glimpse into the wonderful relationship between the Father and the Son, and teaches us that all the blessings of heaven come continually through the prayer of Him who is at God's right hand and ever prays for us. But it teaches us, also, that all these blessings must in the same manner be desired and asked for by us. The whole nature and glory of God's blessings consist in this—they must be obtained in answer to prayer, by hearts entirely surrendered to Him, and hearts that believe in the power of prayer.

Now we come to the most remarkable

instance of all. In Gethsemane we see that our Lord, according to His constant habit, consulted and arranged with the Father the work He had to do on earth. First He besought Him in agony and bloody sweat to let the cup pass from Him—when He understood that this could not be, then He prayed for strength to drink it, and surrendered Himself with the words: "Thy will be done." He was able to meet the enemy full of courage, and in the power of God gave Himself over to the death of the Cross. He had prayed.

Oh, why is it that God's children have so little faith in the glory of prayer, as the great power for subjecting our own wills to that of God, as well as for the confident carrying out of the work of God in spite of our great weakness? Would that we might learn from our Lord Jesus how impossible it is to walk with God, to obtain God's blessing or leading, or to do His work joyously and fruitfully, apart from close unbroken fellowship with Him who is ever a living fountain of spiritual life and power.

Let every Christian think over this simple study of the prayer-life of our Lord Jesus, and endeavor from God's Word, with prayer for the leading of the Holy Spirit, to learn what the life is which the Lord Jesus Christ bestows upon him and supports in him. It is nothing else than a life of daily prayer. Let each minister especially recognize how entirely vain it is to attempt to do the work of our Lord in any other way than that in which He did it. Let us, as workers, begin to believe that we are set free from the ordinary business of the world, that we may, above everything, have time, in our Savior's name, and with His Spirit, and in oneness with Him, to ask for and obtain blessing for the world.

Hints for the Inner Chamber

At the conference, a brother who had earnestly confessed his neglect of prayer, but who was able, later, to declare that his eyes had been opened to see that the Lord really supplied grace, for all that He required from us, asked if some hints could not be given as to the best way of spending time profitably in the inner chamber. There was no opportunity then for giving an answer. Perhaps the following thoughts may help.

Begin with Thanksgiving

(1) As you enter the inner chamber let your first work be to thank God for the unspeakable love which invites you to come to Him, and to converse freely with Him. If your heart is cold and dead, remember that religion is not a matter of feeling, but has to do first with the will. Raise your heart to God, and thank Him for the assurance you have that He looks down on you and will bless you. Through such an act of faith you honor God, and draw your soul away from being occupied with itself. Think also of the glorious grace of the Lord Jesus, who is willing to teach you to pray, and to give you the disposition to do so. Think, too, of the Holy Spirit who was purposely given to cry "Abba Father" in your heart, and to help your weakness in prayer. Five minutes spent thus will strengthen your faith, for your work in the inner chamber. Once more I say—Begin with an act of thanksgiving, and praise God for the inner chamber and the promise of blessing there.

Scripture and Prayer

(2) You must prepare yourself for prayer by prayerful Bible study. The great reason why the inner chamber is not attractive is that people do not know how to pray. Their stock of words is soon exhausted, and they do not know what further to say, because they forget that prayer is not a soliloquy, where everything comes from one side; but it is a dialogue, where God's child listens to what the Father says, and replies to it, and then asks for the things he needs.

Read a few verses from the Bible. Do not concern yourself with the difficulties contained in them. You can consider these later; but take what you understand, apply it to yourself, and ask the Father to make His Word light and power in your heart. Thus you will have material enough for prayer from the Word which the Father speaks to you; you will also have the liberty to ask for things you need. Keep on in this way, and the inner chamber will become at length, not a place where you sigh and struggle only, but one of living fellowship with the Father in heaven. Prayerful study of the Bible is indispensable for powerful prayer.

Prayer Follows the Word

(3) When you have thus received the Word into your heart, turn to prayer. But do not attempt it hastily or thoughtlessly, as though you knew well enough how to pray. Prayer in our own strength brings no blessing. Take time to present

yourself reverently and in quietness before God. Remember His greatness and holiness and love. Think over what you wish to ask from Him. Do not be satisfied with going over the same things every day. No child goes on saying the same thing day after day to his earthly father.

Converse with the Father is colored by the needs of the day. Let your prayer be something definite, arising either out of the Word which you have read, or out of the real soul-needs which you long to have satisfied. Let your prayer be so definite that you can say as you go out, "I know what I have asked from my Father, and I expect an answer." It is a good plan sometimes to take a piece of paper, and write down what you wish to pray for. You might keep such a paper for a week or more, and repeat the prayers till some new need arise.

Prayer for Others

(4) What has been said is in reference to your own needs. But you know that we are allowed to pray that we may help also in the needs of others. One great reason why prayer in the inner chamber does not bring more joy and blessing is that it is too selfish, and selfishness is the death of prayer.

Remember your family; your congregation, with its interests; your own neighborhood; and the church to which you belong. Let your heart be enlarged, and take up the interests of missions, and of the church through the whole world. Become an intercessor, and you will experience for the first time the blessedness of prayer, as you find out that God will make use of you to share His blessing with others through prayer. You will begin to feel that there is something worth living for, as you find that you have something to say to God, and that He from heaven will do things in

answer to your prayers which otherwise would not have been done.

A child can ask his father for bread. A full-grown son converses with him about all the interests of his business, and about his further purposes. A weak child of God prays only for himself, a full-grown man in Christ understands how to consult with God over what must take place in the kingdom. Let your prayer-list bear the names of those for whom you pray—your minister, and all other ministers, and the different missionary affairs with which you are connected.

Thus the inner chamber will really become a wonder of God's goodness, and a fountain of great joy. It will become the most blessed place on earth. It is a great thing to say, but it is the simple truth, that God will make it a Bethel, where His angels shall ascend and descend, and where you will cry out: "The Lord shall be my God." He will make it also Peniel, where you will see the face of God, as a prince of God, as one who wrestled with the angel, and overcame him.

Prayer and Life

(5) Do not forget the close bond between the inner chamber and the outer world. The attitude of the inner chamber must remain with us all the day. The object of the inner chamber is so to unite us to God that we may have Him always abiding with us. Sin, thoughtlessness, yielding to the flesh, or the world, unfit us for the inner chamber, and bring a cloud over the soul. If you have stumbled, or fallen, return to the inner chamber, let your first work be to invoke the blood of Jesus, and to claim cleansing by it. Rest not till by confession you have repented of and put away

your sin. Let the precious blood really give you a fresh freedom of approach to God.

Remember that the roots of your life in the inner chamber strike far out in body and soul, so as to manifest themselves in business life. Let "the obedience of faith," in which you pray in secret, rule you constantly. The inner chamber is intended to bind man to God, to supply him with power from God, to enable him to live for God alone. God be thanked for the inner chamber, and for the blessed life which He will enable us there to experience and nourish.

Murray saw prayer as the power behind the actions of the church. This was particularly true for missions, and Murray wrote several volumes relating to missions. His 1911 The State of the Church *was an outcome of a missionary conference and focuses on the state of the home church.*

"The State of the Home Church" summarizes the verdict of the World Missionary Conference, which is that the home church was unfit for the work that God had put before it.

In "A Plea for More Prayer" Murray states that prayer "is the highest proof of the image of God in which we have been created, and of the exercise of our kinglike privilege of ruling the world." He relates this to the verdicts of the conference.

A final section of The State of the Church *is devoted to "Hints on Intercession." For Murray prayer is the answer to the weakness of the church. This prayer must be intelligent, definite, believing, and persevering.*

The State of the Home Church

The State of the Home Church—these words have through the World Missionary Conference received a new meaning. One of the outstanding and abiding results of that remarkable gathering has been the new and vivid picture presented to the church of the world-wide need of the Gospel message, and the world-wide opening there was for the bringing of that gospel to every creature; and then at once the question arose, Will the church be able to enter these open doors? It was clearly seen that the state of the home church was an all-important factor in the possible solution of the great questions which were raised by the Conference.

The Need to Vitalize the Home Church

Indeed, before the Conference itself assembled, in the very first papers that were issued calling for prayer on behalf of the Conference, it was pointed out that everything would depend on the home base for foreign missions: that is, on the fitness and readiness of the church to respond to God's call. It is well worth our while to read again some of the sentences from that first call to prayer.

"As we contemplate the work to be done, we are conscious that the fundamental difficulty is not one of men or money, but of spiritual power. The Christian experience of the church is not deep, intense, and living enough, to meet the world's need. The end of the Conference will be attained only if it lead to the more perfect manifestation by the church of the Spirit of the Incarnation, and of the Cross. The only hope of the church being able to meet the opportunity is, that there should be a new vitalizing of the whole of the church. . . . This quickening of the whole life of the church is indeed a great thing—an impossible thing, we are tempted to think. But does it seem so impossible when we get the conviction that God, being what He is, wills it? It does not seem so impossible when we saturate ourselves in the thought of the Gospels, with their repeated teaching, 'Ask and ye shall receive.'"

In the *Reports of the Conference* we find the same thoughts expressed in different words. Thus in Vol. I, "Carrying the Gospel," we read under 3A, "The missionary problem of the church today is not primarily a financial problem, but it is how to ensure a vitality equal to the imperial expansion of the missionary program. The only hope of this is for Christians to avail themselves of the more abundant life through Christ, bestowed in the pathway of obedience to Him."

Again, "A crucial factor in the evangelization of the non-Christian world is the state of the church in Christian lands. Until there is a more general consecration on the part of the members of the home church, there can be no hope of such an expansion of the missionary enterprise, as to result in making the knowledge of Jesus Christ readily accessible to every human being."

Once more: "The most direct and effective way to promote the evangelization of the world is to influence the workers, and indeed the whole membership of the church, to yield themselves completely to the sway of Christ as Lord, and to establish and preserve at all costs those habits of spiritual culture which ensure lives of a Christlike witnessing and spiritual power."

The Introduction to the Report on "The Home Base of Missions" (Vol. VI), on its very first page speaks of securing, above all else, "such a spiritual atmosphere throughout the church, that the very temper and spirit of Jesus Christ shall live anew in the hearts of all His followers, and that through them His life may flow forth to the world lying in darkness."

This is further emphasized in the first chapter, which opens thus: "The subject which had been entrusted to the Commission drives us back at every turn to the question of the spiritual condition of the home church. Has that church sufficient vitality for the tremendous task to which it is called? We realize that the fundamental problem is that of the deepened sincerity of the religious experience of the church, the quality of its obedience, the intensity and daring of its faith."

At the close we read: "There can be no forward movement in missions, no great offering of life, except as these are attained through a deepening and broadening of the spiritual life of the leaders of the church, and a real spiritual revival among the members. New methods can accomplish nothing unless begun, continued, and completed in prayer, and permeated from first to last with the Holy Spirit of God. Back to divine wisdom, to the living power of Jesus Christ, back through prayer to the source of all power, must be the watchword of all missionary societies, of all the leaders of the church, and ulti-

mately of the entire membership, if the great commission of our Lord Jesus Christ is to be carried out.

"We therefore recommend that every endeavor be made to propagate the spirit and habit of prayer among all Christian workers, old and young, confident that when the entire church shall devoutly pray for the coming of the kingdom, the triumph will already have been achieved. We must make men understand that it is only their lack of faith and half-hearted consecration that hinders the rapid advance of the work, only their own coldness that keeps back His redemption. We must ever bear in mind that He is eager and able to save the world already redeemed by Him, if only we, His professed followers on earth, were willing that He should. We are frank to confess that it is futile to talk about making Christ known to the world unless there be a great expansion of vitality in the members of the churches of Christendom. That this is the will of God, that the most remote human soul shall have the opportunity to know Jesus Christ as his personal Redeemer, there can be no doubt; that the opportunity and means are sufficient we are all aware; the work halts only because the entire church is not yet in full submission to His will."

The Need for a Supernatural Revival

Other commissions see and speak of the same great need in the use of words such as these. Cooperation, if it is to lead to unity, necessitates a spiritual revival, which must be in its very nature supernatural; the reinforcements needed depend on the spiritual state of the churches which are to supply them; the very religions which Christianity is to replace teach her that her own life must first be lived on the supernatural plane, the power of a living faith in a living God.

"If our missionaries are to be fitly and fully prepared 'to convince the world,' they must go forth from a church in which the Spirit of Christ is evidently at work, in whose whole policy and character and life the gospel is continuously and irrefutably proved to be in very truth the power of God unto salvation." Let me beg every reader, be he minister or member, to look back and take in the thoughts which have been expressed in reference to the state of the church, until he comes to realize the intense solemnity of what that state implies, of the place which God calls her to take, and what is needed if God and the world are to find her ready for the work that awaits her.

Here, spread out before us, lies a world dying in its need of the very message which the church of Christ alone can bring. This world in its need is accessible and open for this message as it never has been in the ages past. The Lord Jesus Christ, having laid down His life to redeem this world, waits still for that message of His redeeming love to be brought to those for whom He died, and His church has not the power, nor vitality, nor consecration, which would make it possible for her to fulfil her blessed task.

If the plea for more prayer for that revival which is so much needed is to be attended to by God's people, if that prayer is to be effectual and much availing, the state of the church as it has been described must become an unbearable burden, and we must learn to give ourselves no rest, and to give God no rest until He make His church a joy in the earth.

A Plea for More Prayer

What a difference between the first mountain springs where a great river has its rise, and the vast expanse of water where it reaches the sea and carries fleets on its bosom. Such, and even much greater, is the difference between prayer in the simplicity of its first beginnings, and the incomprehensible mystery of what it becomes when it makes man a partner with God in the rule of the world. Instead of its being the simple channel through which a child or a newly converted heathen obtains his request from God, it becomes the heavenly power that can dispose of all the riches of God and bring down the blessings of the Spirit on countless souls.

What a study prayer is! I know not whether to thank God most for prayer in its blessed simplicity, as it is the comfort of those who hardly ever go beyond their personal needs, or in the profound depths in which it reveals to us how close and wonderful the union is between God and man.

I feel as if I cannot end this book without once again attempting to point the reader to this latter aspect of it. I do so with fear and trembling; the thoughts are so wonderful and beyond our reach that one hardly ventures to hope that he can make them plain. And yet with God's help we must make the attempt.

Rulers in God's Image

When God undertook the stupendous work of creating man in His own image and after His likeness, His great object was to have a being in whom He could perfectly reveal all the glory of His divine power. Man was to be here on earth what God is in heaven, the king and ruler. He was made in the image of God in this specially, that just as God is self-determined, and is what He is by His own blessed will, so man also, as far as a creature dependent on God could become so, was to have the fashioning of his own character and being, and so fitting himself for the power of ruling others. As we have it in the New Testament, we are made kings and priests unto God. As priests we turn our face Godward to worship and receive His blessing. As kings, we turn manward to dispense that blessing in ruling and guiding them.

The great thought of God was thus to train man for the place that he is to have with Christ upon the throne. God's purpose was that man should so rule that God would do nothing but through him, and that man should understand that he would do nothing but through God. It is in this wonderful relationship that prayer has its mystery and its glory. God promises to dispense His Spirit and to exercise His power according to the wish of man. If man will avail himself of his high prerogative, and fully yield himself to the Holy Spirit's teaching in regard to the will of God, God will make literally true, what Christ promised, "If ye abide in Me, and My words abide in you, YE SHALL ASK WHAT YE WILL AND IT SHALL BE DONE UNTO YOU." The prayer of faith will remove mountains.

We are told that in nature every spirit

seeks to clothe itself in a suitable body. The life in a tree creates for itself in the fruit the embodiment of its inmost nature. And so with God, who is Spirit. The creation of man was not an afterthought but part of His eternal purpose to reveal Himself completely throughout all creation. The first step in that path was the creation of man out of the dust, in His image and likeness. The next was the coming of the eternal Son to unite and forever to identify Himself with human nature. Then followed the resurrection from the dead, and ascension to heaven of Christ in His glorified humanity. And last of all came the outpouring of the Holy Spirit by which the church became His body, the fullness of Him that filleth all in all. In that body Christ is to be revealed when He comes in glory, and in that body the Father will dwell in the Son. Through all eternity man is to be the revelation of what God is, and through man Christ will rule the world.

And it is in prayer that even now man takes his part in the rule of the world. As a preparation for his future glory he even now, in the holy priesthood of intercession, begins to understand what the inconceivable power of prayer can be, because it is the highest proof of the image of God in which we have been created, and of the exercise of our kinglike privilege of ruling the world.

Our Hindrance of God's Work

The point at which it becomes difficult for us to believe all this is when we are told that God is longing to pour out blessing, but is prevented by His people. They are the hindrance in the way. God allows His work to suffer loss, terrible loss, because He will not break the law He Himself made. He respects the liberty He Himself gave man; in infinite long-suffering He bides His time till man becomes willing to pray and receive His blessing.

In Vol. VI the Report says, "We must make men understand that it is only their lack of faith and halfhearted consecration that hinders the rapid advance of the work, only their own coldness that keeps back His redemption from a lost world. We must ever bear in mind that He is eager and able to save the world already redeemed by Him, if only we, His professed followers on earth, were willing that He should."

One would think that men on hearing this would say: It is impossible; it cannot be true that millions are perishing, because God's people are not praying. But it is true. But a truth which the natural mind cannot grasp. It is only the Holy Spirit that can enlighten the heart to apprehend the spiritual reality of this wonderful partnership into which God has taken up His people in the salvation of the world.

One would say, How can the church be so infatuated as to spend all her strength in doing a work that is comparatively a failure, that ends in a decline of membership, when she has the divine promise that in answer to prayer the power of the Holy Spirit can make the dry bones to live? There is no explanation but this: People hear it with the hearing of the ear, but the truth has no power over them, simply because they do not yield themselves, in holy fellowship with God, to receive the Spirit and the Spirit-born conviction that prayer can bring down into the heart the life that there is in Christ Jesus.

How often the complaint is heard that it is so hard to pray aright, to pray enough, to pray in power. The reason is simple. We think very much of prayer as a means of getting blessing for ourselves. We enter so little into the thought of yielding ourselves entirely to the holy fellowship with God, and the self-denying sacrifice needed in bearing the needs of our fellow-men. We are so little conscious of our being kings; no wonder that the confidence of our priestly access to God for the work of bringing down blessing on the world, is but feeble. A man's thought rules his actions; the ideas he fosters make his character.

Oh that God's children might take hold of the wonderful promises that whatsoever they ask in the name of Jesus it shall be done unto them, and learn to look upon themselves as God's chosen intercessors, the channels without whom His love cannot do its work. They may be sure that prayer will begin to have a new attraction, and fellowship with God will become their highest privilege.

Five Things to Remember

I fear of wearying my reader by the repetition of the chief thoughts that occupy us in this book as a plea for more prayer. And yet I will risk once again summing up what it is that I think God wants us to consider.

The verdict of the World Missionary Conference that the church is unwilling and unfit for doing the work God puts before her.

The confession of the churches that they are impotent to keep hold of their members; the world spirit is too strong.

The sad truth that both these things are owing to a lack of that spiritual life and power without which our work must be in vain.

The conviction that nothing but the power of God's Holy Spirit in our heart and life can cure the evil.

The faith that God longs with all His heart to give His Spirit to the fervent prayer of the righteous man that availeth much, and so to lift His church to the life that there is for her in Christ Jesus.

As we study and pray over these thoughts, step by step, in God's presence, the mystery of prayer will open out to us. We shall see that God has actually made us "partners in the business," made us kings and priests to dispense His blessings to a feeble church and a perishing world. We shall hear a call to forsake that half-hearted, selfish, prayerless life in which we have lived, and to begin as intercessors to take our place before God, in the assurance that He has put the quickening of the church in our hands, and will give to persevering, believing intercession the high honor of restoring His children to the life which He has meant for them.

Let each of us take a prayer-card, and write upon it the five points we have just mentioned. Let us think and pray over them until we realize that there is really something that needs praying for, and our hearts get so interested in it that prayer shall become the spontaneous expression of our strong desire for God's blessing on His church.

Hints on Intercession

Intercession to be effectual must be intelligent, definite, believing, and persevering. First of all, intelligent. That means that I am not to be content with what others think or write, but to set myself with all my heart to realize what it is that I am asking for. "Thou shalt love the Lord thy God with all thy mind and with all thy strength." That applies to prayer too. Let us apply it to the great unsolved problem that has been occupying us, and now calls for our prayers: How can the church be lifted up out of her low spiritual state, into the abundant life that there is in Christ Jesus?

If one is really to pray with effect, he must prove to God that he feels grieved at that low spiritual condition of the church, and that he has set his heart upon the blessing of that abundant life that there is in Christ.

Just think a moment of the proofs we have had of that feeble life.

1. We have the verdict of the Conference that the church as a whole is indifferent to the call to the work for which she was placed in the world, and so is spiritually unfit for taking part in it.

2. We have the confession in the churches of their decline in membership as a proof that they are not able to drive back the spirit of the world.

3. Both these symptoms indicate a lack of spiritual life and power.

4. And with this there is the absolute impossibility of doing anything to bring about a change.

Take time and think out these thoughts. Pray to God to give you a vi-sion of their terrible reality, the grief and dishonor they are to Him, the terrible loss of souls that they imply, and the part that you have in it all. Begin to admit what a great work it is that you are undertaking, to pray for that great revolution which is needed if a change is to come. Pray for your ministers, pray for your congregation, pray for the believers with whom you have fellowship in prayer, pray for your whole church, that God may show us all what really the true state of the church is. Unless we are willing to take time, to turn aside from the world, to give ourselves to the holy exercise of laboring and striving in prayer, we have no right to hope for deliverance.

It is a hard work, a difficult work, a solemn work. But let us not try to serve God with what costs us nothing. It cost Christ everything, His blood and His life, to conquer death, and win for us a share in His abundant life. God's intercessors must learn in deep humility and contrition really to give their whole life and strength to bear the burden of the state of their fellow-Christians, if they are to have power to prevail.

Faith and Hope in Prayer

And now, let us look on the other side, the abundant life that is waiting for the church, and see what ground there is for faith and hope in prayer.

1. What is impossible with men is possible with God. God has given to His church the promise of the Holy Spirit, as the divine power which will fit her

for the work she has to do. The more we study carefully the state of the church, the unspiritual worldly life of the majority of her members, the lack of power in her ministers, even many of those who long for better times, the tremendous difficulty of rousing even a single congregation to a higher spiritual life, the deeper shall we feel how hopeless the prospect is of a true deep revival in which Christians shall really yield themselves wholly to a new life in Christ Jesus. But just let this impossibility be what drives us into the arms of God, and into a new faith of what He can do.

2. Think of how Christ has promised that the Father should give the Holy Spirit to them that ask it. Think of that, until your whole heart is filled with the assurance, God will, God can, God must, we say it with reverence, give His Spirit where His believing people unite in whole-hearted prayer and consecration.

3. With this, think of the very special power that has been given to prayer, and the boundless possibilities to which it gives us the key. Take time, if you want to exercise yourself in prayer, and learn the art—take time, and let all the promises of answer to prayer fill you with the confident assurance of what is going to come. This is one of the great privileges of prayer, that it throws you upon God, and opens the heart for God to make His promises a personal gift to yourself.

4. Begin then and take time, and just as you studied the state of the church in its feebleness and sin, begin to study God's Word as if for the first time you were trying to find out what God really has promised to do for His church here upon earth. Take Christ's teaching in John 14—16, and believe that the power of the Holy Spirit is meant to make the promise, "If ye love Me, My Father will love you, and I will love you, and we will come and make our abode with you," a literal reality. Take the experience of Paul in all that Christ did for him, and regard that as a pattern of what God is willing to do now. And set yourself steadfastly to ask God definitely to work in you, and those around you, and in His church in its low estate, what He has promised. Do not rest until the vision of what God is willing to do fills your heart so that you can think of nothing else. You have given your whole life to be occupied with this as its chief aim; rest not until your heart is fully possessed with it.

Then you will be prepared to take your place as an intercessor in power. Your prayers will become more intelligent, but also more fervent, more believing, more persevering. You will begin to understand something of what prayer means in its fullness—a taking hold of God, a giving Him no rest, a going on to be importunate in prayer, until your faith receives the quiet assurance that God will give what you are asking.

Pray, above all, for the gift of the Holy Spirit to have entire possession of you, and of all God's children who are pleading with you for the new life. Pray fervently, determinedly, for the ministers who are willing to yield themselves to God's work. Pray for all ministers as the leaders of the flock of God. Give yourself as a whole sacrifice to God for the great work of seeking the revival of His church, and through her the evangelization of the world.

God seeks intercessors. God has need of intercessors. God wonders at the lack of intercessors. Rest not till God sees that you are one.

The Key to the Missionary Problem, *published in 1902, is another work of Murray's whose focus is missions. It too was a result of a conference, the Ecumenical Mission-ary Conference held in New York in 1900. Like* The State of the Church, *it is intrinsi-cally valuable and is also interesting from a historical point of view.*

"A Call to Prayer and Humiliation" touches upon not only some of the more important themes of the conference, but also upon two themes that were among the most important to Murray: prayer and humility. In it Murray explores the connection between success in the mission field and our faithfulness in prayer and humility.

CHAPTER THIRTY-THREE

A Call to Prayer and Humiliation

In the previous pages I have more than once had occasion to speak of prayer. As I come to the closing chapters of the book, and review the argument, I feel that all that has been said will profit little, unless it lead up to prayer. As we look at the extent of the field, and the greatness of the work that has yet to be done; at the utterly inadequate force which the church has as yet in the field, and the absence of any signs that she is ready at once to place herself and all her resources at her Lord's disposal; at our absolute impotence to give life either in the church at home or the work abroad, and our entire dependence upon the power that comes from above in answer to prayer and faith; at the love of our Lord to His people and to the perishing, and the promises He has given and waits to fulfil—we feel that our only hope is to betake ourselves to prayer. Prayer, more prayer, much prayer, very special prayer, in the first place, for the work to be done in our home churches on behalf of foreign missions, is indeed the one great need of the day. "Our help cometh from the Lord, who made heaven and earth."

If I may be allowed to say it, I was somewhat surprised at the little direct mention that was made of prayer as one of the most important factors, the chief source of power, in mission work. Chapter VIII of the Report is indeed entitled *Prayer and Beneficence,* but almost all the addresses deal chiefly with the latter subject. Mr. Eddy spoke of the unselfish prayer-life as developed by the use of prayer cycles. In a short but suggestive address Mrs. J. H. Randall said:

> One great and imperative need today of foreign mission work is the almost forgotten secret of prevailing prayer. Missions have progressed so slowly abroad because piety and prayer have been so shallow at home. Only get people praying for mission work, and they must give. Nothing but continuous prayer will solve the missionary problems of today. God must be inquired of to do these things for them. Ye have not because ye ask not. God has promised great things to His Son and His church concerning the heathen. God has promised great things to His children in the work of extending and hastening His kingdom. But notice—these promises are conditioned. His Son, His church, His children, are to intercede and to sacrifice. The consequence of habitual intercession will be a new outpouring of the Holy Spirit upon the individual, the church, and upon all the missionary work of the world. Whoever prays most, helps most.

If these words are true—and they are the very truth of God—surely the first care of the leaders of mission work in our churches and societies, to whom the spiritual training of their members is entrusted by God, should be to seek for grace and wisdom from on high to give prayer the place in all their appeals and exhortations which it has in the will and purpose of God.

Rev. W. Perkins said:

The Foreign Mission Movement was born in prayer, and prayer is the vital breath by which it lives. . . . Great as the results are of foreign missions, they would have been a hundredfold greater if the church of Christ had been what she ought to be in the two great matters of prayer beneficence. . . . What is needed is that the spiritual life of every Christian, and that of the whole church, should be so deepened, instructed, and inspired by the Holy Ghost, that it shall become as natural and easy to pray daily for foreign missions as to pray for daily bread. . . . There must be wrought in the heart of the church the conviction that the law of sacrifice is the law of life, and that we must find time for prayer, even though it may mean the withdrawal of time from pleasure and business. Sacrifice alone is fruitful.

There must be wrought into the heart of the church by the Spirit of God a penetrating and abiding sense of the world's dire need, its misery and darkness and despair. A power must come that shall make the need so real, so terrible, that our first feeling shall be one of helplessness in presence of it; our next feeling, "I must go and pray about it"; and the next, "I will give up and sacrifice some things that almost are like necessities, in presence of woes like these which Christ died to remove, and for the removal of which He waits, and has waited long."

Call of the Church to Prayer

If these words are to be taken seriously, and are to do any good, the great question is surely, How are the leaders of our mission work to waken and to train the churches to the life of prayer they speak of? If it be true—the results of foreign missions would have been a hundredfold greater, if the church had been what she ought to have been in the matter of prayer—there can be no more urgent duty resting upon the church than to give itself to prayer, first of all, that its members at home may be roused and sanctified to take their part in the struggle with the hosts of darkness, "praying with all prayer and supplication in the Spirit."

And if it be found that there are multitudes who give but do not pray, or give little and pray little, those who know what prayer is must only pray and labor the more earnestly that the life of Christians may be so deepened by the Holy Ghost, that it shall become "as natural and easy to pray daily for foreign missions as to pray for daily bread." God can do it. Let it be our definite aim and prayer—God will do it.

I trust that what I have said in regard to the Conference, and the place it gave to the discussion of prayer, will not be misunderstood. In all nature so much depends upon the law of proportion. It is so in the spiritual life too. One finds nowhere evangelical teaching in which the work of the Holy Spirit, and the power of prayer to secure His working, are not acknowledged. These truths have a place in the articles of our Creed.

And yet it is only where they have a first place, and everything else is made subordinate to them, that the Christian life will be truly healthy. And it is only when, in the discussion of how our mission work is to attain greater success, and how the world can best be won for Christ, the power of the Holy Spirit, and the power of believing prayer, indeed get the attention and the prominence that they have in the mind of God, that the supernatural character of our work and its results can be fully apprehended.

Of all the questions claiming the care and guidance of the leaders of our mission work at home, there is not one that demands more urgent consideration, that is more difficult of decision, and that will bring a richer reward, than this: "How can the churches be educated to more persistent, fervent, believing prayer? Prayer will at once be the means and the proof of a stronger Christian life, of more devotion to Christ's service, and of the blessing of heaven descending on our work. Much prayer would be the token that we had found again the path by which the Pentecostal church entered on its triumphant course.

We cannot teach people to pray by telling them to do so. Prayer is the pulse of the life. The call to more prayer must be connected with the deepening of the spiritual life. The two great conditions of true prayer are ever: an urgent sense of need, and a full assurance of a supply for that need. We must bring God's children to see and feel the need. The work entrusted to them, the obligation to do it, the consequence to ourselves, to Christ, to the perishing, of neglecting it, our absolute impotence to do it in our own strength—these great truths must get the mastery, and urge us.

And then, on the other side, the love of Christ to us and to the world, our access to God in Him as intercessor, the certainty of persevering prayer being heard, the blessedness of a life of prayer, and the blessings to the world it can bring—these, too, must live in us and encourage us. We must learn to pray in secret, and wait on God, and take hold on His strength. We must teach Christians to pray in little companies, with the joy and the love and the faith that fellowship brings. We must gather the church at times in special seasons of prayer, when the consciousness can be quickened and wrought deep into her life that, as her only and supreme aim is the bringing joy and glory to her Lord in the salvation of souls, so her only and sufficient trust is in Him who, in answer to her prayer, gives His divine power, and works above what she can ask or think.

Confession of Sin

In the heading of this chapter I have spoken of Prayer and Humiliation. I confess that I somewhat missed this note in the Conference. Incidental mention was frequently made of shortcoming in pastors and laymen, in interest and prayer and beneficence, of the failure of the church as a whole to do its duty. And yet the solemnity, the awfulness of the neglect of our Lord's commission, of the terrible sin of disobedience to His last command, of the entire lack of sympathy with the desire for gratifying His love or seeking His glory, on the part of the great majority of Christians, was not pressed as some think it should be, and must be, ere a return to the true state can come. There is an optimism that loves to speak of what is bright and hopeful. It thinks that thus thanks are brought to God and courage to His servants. It is above everything afraid of pessimism.

And yet optimism and pessimism are errors equally to be avoided. They are equally one-sided; they are both extremes. The divine wisdom has taught us, "I lead (walk) in the midst of the paths of judgment." Experience teaches us that, when we have to deal with two apparently conflicting truths, there is but one way to see the true relation, and to be kept from giving either undue prominence. That way is to look first to the one as if it were all, and thoroughly master all it means. Turn then to the other, and grasp as fully all it implies. When we know both, we are in a position to walk "in the midst" of the path of truth.

Apply this to missions. On the one

side there is, oh! so much to rejoice in, to thank God for, and to take courage from. In the Conference Report this note was often struck. And we never can give God too much praise for what He has wrought during the past century, and specially during the past twenty years.

On the other hand, as compared with the work that has been done, there is so much work that has not been done that could have been done, that has not been done for no other reason than that the church was not what she ought to be. When once we are brought face to face with this truth: Millions are perishing today without the knowledge of Christ, and will go on perishing, simply because the church is not doing the work for which she was redeemed and endowed with God's Spirit, our hearts will spontaneously cry out in humiliation and shame, and make confession of our sin. The sin of blood-guiltiness; the sin of disobedience; the sin of unbelief; the sin of selfishness and worldliness, grieving the Holy Spirit and quenching Christ's love in our hearts; the sin of not living wholly for Christ, for His love and His kingdom—these sins will become a burden greater than we can bear, until we have laid them at our Lord's feet and had them removed by Him.

Let no one say that these are the sins of those who take no, or very little, interest in missions; at a Conference you speak to those whose whole heart and life are given up to them. In Scripture we find that the men who were most jealous for the honor of God, most diligent in His service, and least guilty of the sin, were the first to confess it and mourn over it. Moses and David, Ezra, Nehemiah, and Daniel—the godliest men of their times—were the men to take up the sin and bring it before God. Is not the sin of the members, the vast majority of them, to be counted as the sin of the whole body? Are not the most

devoted friends of Christ and of missions—the men who in church or society, as committee members, or workers, are the leaders—the very men who, in virtue of their spiritual insight, ought to feel the sin most, to carry it to God, and then to appeal to the erring ones to come and join them in humiliation and confession?

Humiliation Precedes Restoration and Renewal

We speak of the need of a Pentecostal era: it will have to be preceded by a great putting away of and turning from sin. It is frequently said, Any very deep spiritual revival in the church will have to be preceded by a deeper sense of sin. And that cannot be until the men, to whom the Lord gives the deepest sense of the sin of His people, have gathered them with a call to repentance and surrender to full obedience. The Missionary Appeal gives one of the grandest opportunities for convicting Christians of sin, as it points to and brings home the lack of true devotion and entire surrender to God's service, the lack of love and prayer and self-denial and obedience, and uncovers the worldliness and selfishness that lies at the root of all.

This has at all times been God's way. Humiliation precedes restoration and renewal. On the day of Pentecost it was the preaching of "this same Jesus, whom ye have crucified," that broke the hearts, and prepared for the receiving of the Holy Spirit. We still need the same preaching to God's people. "This same Jesus," whose command ye have disobeyed and neglected, whose love ye have despised and grieved, God hath made Him both Lord and Christ. If we are to summon Christians to a life of higher devotion in God's service, the wrong, the shame, the guilt of our present state must be set before them.

We never shall win them from the low level of a selfish salvation, to live wholly and only for the love and honor of Christ, unless the evil of the one be known and forsaken as the entrance to the other.

It is when the sin is felt and confessed, that Christ's pardoning love will afresh be felt, and that a new experience of His power and love will become the incentive to make that love known to others. It is the contrite heart God makes alive. It is to the humbled soul He gives more grace. An essential element in a true missionary revival will be the broken heart and the contrite spirit in view of past neglect and sin.

This preaching of humiliation on account of our lack of obedience to Christ's great command will be no easy thing. It will need men who take time to wait before God for the vision of what this sin of the church really implies. Hudson Taylor spent five years in China, and felt for its heathen darkness, without realizing what it is. He spent five years more in England working and praying for China, and still he did not know how great its awful need was. It was only when he began to prepare a statement on China's needs, for publication, that he so felt the full horror of the thick darkness that he could find no rest till God gave him the twenty-four workers he had prayed for, and that he was willing to accept the responsibility to lead them out.

We shall need men who will give themselves, in study and prayer and love, to take in all the terrible meaning of the words we utter so easily—that the church is disobedient to her Lord's last and great command. As they yield themselves to the awful truth of thirty millions a year dying in hopeless darkness, because God's people do not care; of Christ's love seeking in vain to find a channel through us to save the perishing ones, because we refuse to place ourselves at His disposal; of our resting perfectly content with a selfish religion that hopes for heaven with a Christ whose cross it refuses to bear upon earth—these men will begin to feel that they are dealing with a power of darkness in God's children which nothing can penetrate or remove but God's almighty power. They will feel that nothing less than the power of the Spirit who convicts of sin can convict or arouse the church.

Role of Spiritual Leaders

In such humiliation the pastors will feel that they must take the lead. The preaching of humiliation cannot be in power, if the pastor has no experience of it. The missionary problem is a personal one—to the pastor too. Both on their own behalf and as representatives of the people, they must take the lead. "Let the priests, the ministers of the Lord, weep between the porch and the altar and say, Spare thy people, O Lord, and give not thine heritage to reproach, that the heathen should rule over them."

Is there any one church or parish of which it can in truth be said that the extension of Christ's kingdom is the one end for which it lives, and that its chief concern is that every man on earth should have the gospel without delay? Is it not admitted on every hand that the church is not what it should be?[1] And is it not plain that if this continues so, the evangelization of the world in this generation will be an impossibility?

---

1. Of the Free Church of Scotland Dr. Smith, in his *Short History*, says—"Only one-third of the communicants give for Foreign Missions. This is still the day of small things with the prayer of faith and labor of love." And of the church as a whole—"The most hopeful estimate cannot go farther

With the Church as a whole so guilty before God, does there not appear to be a call for every minister to take some part of the blame to himself for this state of things, and to seek with his people to come under the deep conviction that they have not given themselves to Christ with that entire devotion which His love and His work in the world claim? That they have not sufficiently renounced their own interest and ease, and the spirit of the world, with all their strength to carry out the great command of their Lord? And all because their heart and life have not been wholly yielded to the transforming power of Christ's Spirit and love.

In whatever respect we regard the lamentable state of unfaithfulness in which the greater part of the church lives, and in which we all in some degree share, there is no possible way for the ministry to remove the evil and promote a better state of things, but by every one of us confessing in the presence of God our lack of that enthusiastic love to Christ, of that whole-hearted surrender to the leading of His Spirit, which would have enabled us to be true witnesses to Him and to His will—that the one work of the church and the believer is to have every creature know of Him and His love. Nothing can be more reasonable than that every minister, who sees and mourns the worldliness and selfishness of the majority of Christians, and the feebleness in work and prayer of so many who are not indifferent, should suspect himself to some extent to be responsible for this. The ministry has been instituted to secure knowledge of and obedience to Christ's commands in the church: there is a manifest failure in this: then surely our one need is to confess our shortcoming, and cry to God for a holy, devoted, spiritual ministry, able to lead the church to fulfil her destiny to bring the gospel to every creature.

When once the spirit of humiliation takes hold upon the ministry, there will be hope for the people. If in the public preaching and praying the tone of contrition and confession be clear and deep, there will assuredly be a response in the hearts and the inner chambers of all earnest souls; and those who are now our best contributors will feel how much more God asks—and is willing to give, through His Holy Spirit—of fervent love and prevailing prayer, and the full consecration of all to His service. And it will be proved in our mission work: "He that humbleth himself shall be exalted." Repentance is ever the gate of larger blessing.

Listen for a moment to what He that holdeth the seven stars in His right hand said to the church of Ephesus. "I know thy works, and thy labor, and thy patience, and how thou canst not bear them that are evil: and thou hast tried them which say they are apostles, and are not, and hast found them liars: and hast borne, and hast patience, and for My name's sake hast labored, and hast not fainted." It would be difficult to draw a picture more nearly that of a model church. What diligence and zeal in good works; what patience in suffering; what purity in discipline; what zeal for orthodoxy; and what unwearied perseverance in it all! And what is best—all for His name's sake.

And yet the Lord was not satisfied. "Nevertheless I have somewhat against thee, because thou hast left thy first love. Remember therefore from whence

than this, that in the most evangelical churches not more than a third, and in the least active not more than a tenth, of the communicants pray, give, or in any way energise for the nations whom the Lord charged every one of His members to disciple."

thou art fallen, and repent, and do the first works; or else I will come unto thee quickly, and remove thy candlestick out of her place, except thou repent."

Restoration of First Love

The church had lost its first love. The tenderness and fervor of the first love, of the personal attachment to the Lord Jesus, was now lacking. The works were still being done, and that in His name, with the acknowledgment of Him as their Lord, but they were no longer the first works, in the spirit of the first love. He calls them to look back, and remember whence they were fallen, and repent, and do the first works. It is possible to work much and earnestly for Christ and His cause in a way which leaves nothing to be desired, as far as man can judge; but there may be lacking that without which the works are as nothing in His sight—that which He counts the greatest of all—love, the love of a personal attachment to Christ.

God is Love. Christ loved us and gave Himself. His love was a tender, holy giving of Himself, a personal friendship and fellowship. That love of His, cherished in the heart in daily close intercourse, responded to by a love that clings to Him, proved by His love pervading all our labor for others—it is this makes our work acceptable. It was this first love and enthusiastic attachment to Christ gave the Pentecostal church its power. It was this Pentecostal love out of which Christ calls them to remember that they were fallen, and to which, in repentance, they were to return. Noth-

ing less can satisfy the heart of Him who loved us. Shall we not give it Him?

It is this Pentecostal love to which we must return in our mission work. We saw how God made the Moravian Church the first church of the Reformation to take the Pentecostal stand, and give itself wholly to bringing the gospel to every creature. And we saw that it was love—a passionate, adoring contemplation of Christ's dying love, a passionate desire to make that love known, and, still more, to gratify that love by bringing to it the souls it had died to save—that made that least of the churches in this respect the greatest of all.

As we mourn over the state of the church, with all its unfaithfulness to Christ and to the perishing souls of heathendom, let us, above all, penitently make confession of this sin—the loss of the first love. Let us remember how even Peter, after his fall out of his first love, could not be restored till the searching question, "Lovest thou Me?" had deeply wounded him, and he penitently, but confidently, had answered, "Thou knowest that I love Thee." And as we repent and mourn the past, let us wait before our Lord with the one prayer: Love, Lord! it is Thy love we need.

We know about it; we have preached of it; we have sought to find it; but now we wait in humility and reverence and wonder for Thee, the Loving One, to shed it abroad in our hearts by the Holy Spirit. We look to Thee, at length, to enable us in its power to take the world so into our hearts that, like Thee, we only live and die that love may triumph over every human soul.

FOR ADDITIONAL INFORMATION

Douglas, William. *Andrew Murray and His Message: One of God's Choice Saints*. Fort Washington, Pennsylvania, Christian Literature Crusade, 1957.

Du Plessis, J. *Life of Andrew Murray of South Africa, The*. London, Marshall Brothers Ltd., 1919.

Erlandson, Charles, ed. *Andrew Murray, the Best from all His Works*. Nashville, Thomas Nelson, 1988.

Lindner, William. *Andrew Murray and William Law*. Men of Faith Series, Minneapolis, Bethany House Publishers, 1996.

McPherson, Anna Talbott. *They Dared to be Different: The Shepherd Heart*. Chicago, Moody Press, 1967.

Murray, Andrew. *Absolute Surrender and Other Addresses*. New York, Revell, 1897.

———. *Andrew Murray Collection No. 2*. New York, Barbour and Company, 1995.

———. *Believer's New Life, The*. Minneapolis, Bethany Press, 1984.

———. *Believer's Secret of the Master's Indwelling, The*. Minneapolis, Bethany Press, 1977.

———. *Be Perfect, A Message from the Father in Heaven to His Children on Earth*. Chicago, Revell, 1893.

———. *Children for Christ: Thoughts for Christian Parents on the Consecration of the Home Life, The*. London, James Nisbet & Co., 1887.

———. *Holy in Christ: Thoughts on the Calling of God's Children to be Holy as He Is Holy*. New York, Revell, 1887.

———. *Inner Chamber and the Inner Life, The*. Grand Rapids, Michigan, Zondervan, 1958.

———. *Ministry of Intercession, A Plea for More Prayer*. New York, Revell, 1898.

———. *Money: Thoughts for God's Stewards*. New York, Revell, 1897.

———. *School of Obedience, The*. Chicago, Illinois, Bible Institute, Colportage Association, 1899.

———. *Two Covenants and the Second Blessing*. New York, Revell, 1899.

———. *Waiting on God! Daily Messages for a Month*. New York, Revell, 1896.

———. *With Christ in the School of Prayer on Our Training for the Ministry of Intercession*. Westwood, New Jersey, Revell, 1965.

———. *Working for God: A Sequel to Waiting on God*. New York, Revell, 1901.

CHARLES H. SPURGEON

Charles H. Spurgeon

Abridged and edited by Charles Erlandson

Contents

CHARLES H. SPURGEON 1834–1892

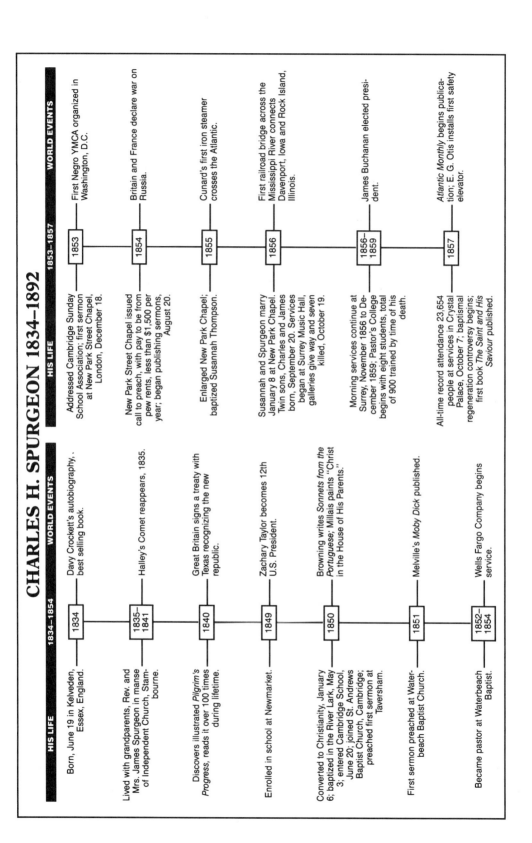

1834–1854

HIS LIFE

Born, June 19 in Kelveden, Essex, England.

Lived with grandparents, Rev. and Mrs. James Spurgeon in manse of Independent Church, Stambourne.

Discovers illustrated *Pilgrim's Progress*, reads it over 100 times during lifetime.

Enrolled in school at Newmarket.

Converted to Christianity, January 6; baptized in the River Lark, May 3; entered Cambridge School, June 20; joined St. Andrews Baptist Church, Cambridge; preached first sermon at Taversham.

First sermon preached at Waterbeach Baptist Church.

Became pastor at Waterbeach Baptist.

WORLD EVENTS

Davy Crockett's autobiography, best selling book.

Halley's Comet reappears, 1835.

Great Britain signs a treaty with Texas recognizing the new republic.

Zachary Taylor becomes 12th U.S. President.

Browning writes *Sonnets from the Portuguese*; Millais paints "Christ in the House of His Parents."

Melville's *Moby Dick* published.

Wells Fargo Company begins service.

| 1834 | 1835–1841 | 1840 | 1849 | 1850 | 1851 | 1852–1854 |

1853–1857

HIS LIFE

Addressed Cambridge Sunday School Association; first sermon at New Park Street Chapel, London, December 18.

New Park Street Chapel issued call to preach, with pay to be from pew rents, less than $1,500 per year; began publishing sermons, August 20.

Enlarged New Park Chapel; baptized Susannah Thompson.

Susannah and Spurgeon marry January 8 at New Park Chapel. Twin sons, Charles and James born, September 20. Services began at Surrey Music Hall, galleries give way and seven killed, October 19.

Morning services continue at Surrey, November 1856 to December 1859; Pastor's College begins with eight students, total of 900 trained by time of his death.

All-time record attendance 23,654 people at services in Crystal Palace, October 7; baptismal regeneration controversy begins; first book *The Saint and His Saviour* published.

WORLD EVENTS

First Negro YMCA organized in Washington, D.C.

Britain and France declare war on Russia.

Cunard's first iron steamer crosses the Atlantic.

First railroad bridge across the Mississippi River connects Davenport, Iowa and Rock Island, Illinois.

James Buchanan elected president.

Atlantic Monthly begins publication; E. G. Otis installs first safety elevator.

| 1853 | 1854 | 1855 | 1856 | 1856–1859 | 1857 |

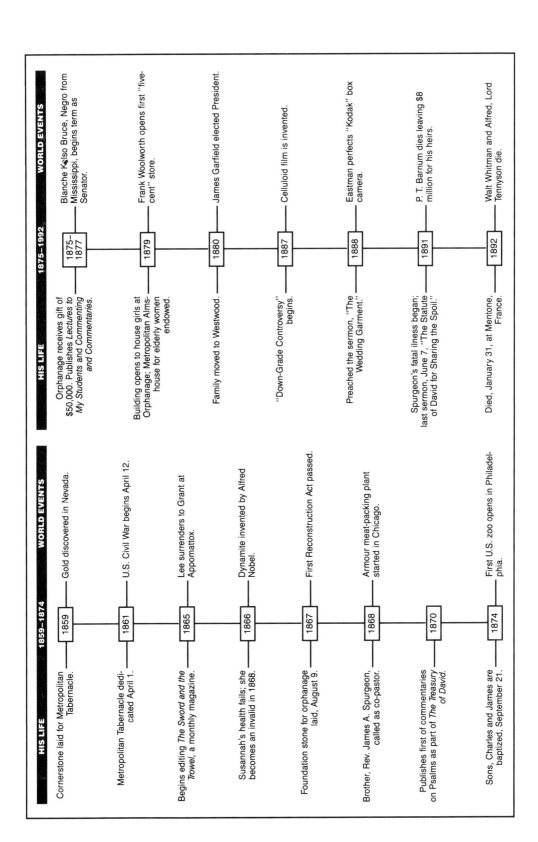

HIS LIFE	1859–1874	WORLD EVENTS
Cornerstone laid for Metropolitan Tabernacle.	1859	Gold discovered in Nevada.
Metropolitan Tabernacle dedicated April 1.	1861	U.S. Civil War begins April 12.
Begins editing *The Sword and the Trowel*, a monthly magazine.	1865	Lee surrenders to Grant at Appomattox.
Susannah's health fails; she becomes an invalid in 1868.	1866	Dynamite invented by Alfred Nobel.
Foundation stone for orphanage laid, August 9.	1867	First Reconstruction Act passed.
Brother, Rev. James A. Spurgeon, called as co-pastor.	1868	Armour meat-packing plant started in Chicago.
Publishes first of commentaries on Psalms as part of *The Treasury of David*.	1870	
Sons, Charles and James are baptized, September 21.	1874	First U.S. zoo opens in Philadelphia.

HIS LIFE	1875–1992	WORLD EVENTS
Orphanage receives gift of $50,000. Publishes *Lectures to My Students and Commenting and Commentaries*.	1875–1877	Blanche Kelso Bruce, Negro from Mississippi, begins term as Senator.
Building opens to house girls at Orphanage; Metropolitan Almshouse for elderly women endowed.	1879	Frank Woolworth opens first "five-cent" store.
Family moved to Westwood.	1880	James Garfield elected President.
"Down-Grade Controversy" begins.	1887	Celluloid film is invented.
Preached the sermon, "The Wedding Garment."	1888	Eastman perfects "Kodak" box camera.
Spurgeon's fatal illness began; last sermon, June 7. "The Statue of David for Sharing the Spoil."	1891	P. T. Barnum dies leaving $8 million for his heirs.
Died, January 31, at Mentone, France.	1892	Walt Whitman and Alfred, Lord Tennyson die.

CHARLES H. SPURGEON

Introduction

Charles Haddon Spurgeon was born on June 19, 1834, in Kelvedon in Essex County, England. Raised in a Christian home, he nevertheless experienced a season of doubt which ended in a dramatic conversion in 1849. In 1851 the seventeen-year-old Spurgeon obtained his first regular pastorate. Everywhere he preached throughout his life, enthusiastic crowds thronged to hear him, and on one occasion he preached to a gathering of 23,654. His dynamic, theological, and mellifluous sermons led those who heard him to call him "The Prince of Preachers."

On March 31, 1861, the first Sunday service was held in Spurgeon's Metropolitan Tabernacle. Built to accommodate up to six thousand of Spurgeon's crowds, it was still never large enough to contain those who wanted to hear him. Spurgeon's ministry in the Metropolitan Tabernacle was known not only for his electrifying sermons but also for its Christian service. As great as his influence was through his preaching, it may have been even greater through the many young pastors he trained in his Pastor's College. He was also responsible for establishing an almshouse and an orphanage. Altogether, there were sixty-six Spurgeonic institutions. In addition to his sermons, which he revised and published weekly and which sold extremely well, he also began publishing a monthly magazine, *The Sword and Trowel*, in 1865.

Spurgeon suffered from gout for most of his life and was in chronically poor health after 1867. He died January 31, 1892, leaving a legacy of written material that continues to exert a tremendous influence on believers throughout the world.

It is virtually impossible to winnow the best of Spurgeon's written work down to the size of one volume. His output was simply enormous. He was interested in books from a very early age, and even at the age of fifteen he was prolific, writing a two hundred ninety-five-page essay titled *Popery Unmasked*. His printed sermons occupy sixty-two volumes of four hundred eighty small-print pages each, and in addition to his sermons he published one hundred forty works during his lifetime.

When the name Spurgeon is mentioned, his sermons immediately come to mind. Many reasons have been given for the greatness of those works. For example, Spurgeon was always theologically oriented, and the most profound truths of the Christian doctrine are illuminated in his sermons. In particular, he strongly defended Calvinistic theology in all of its splendor.

But Spurgeon's sermons are far from dry: Their simplicity is refreshing and reaches all men. Spurgeon's sermons also strike one as being vital and earnest. They are close to life and Spurgeon's faith genuinely touched to the depths of his soul. Finally, Spurgeon always had the welfare of his audience in mind, and there is a persistent evangelistic tone in his sermons.

Spurgeon's other works are also worthy of mention. His *Treasury of David* is widely regarded as one of the best commentaries ever written on the Psalms.

Lectures to My Students is read by pastors today, and his works on grace are considered classics on that topic. Perhaps it is presumptuous to call any collection "The Best of Spurgeon," but after reading a volume of Spurgeon's works one might be convinced that that is exactly what he has just read.

The first sermon selected for this volume, "Grace Abounding over Abounding Sin," was delivered on March 4, 1888, at the Metropolitan Tabernacle. In it, Spurgeon expounds one of his favorite themes throughout his sermons and his other works: grace. Spurgeon finds that if we want to see where God's grace abounds we need only look at where men have sinned most. Like many of Spurgeon's sermons, "Grace Abounding over Abounding Sin" concludes with an appeal to sinners to accept this grace.

Eighteen eighty-eight, the year "Grace Abounding over Abounding Sin" was given, found Spurgeon engaged in the Down-Grade Controversy, the most bitter controversy of his life. Keenly aware of the apostasy of the times and the increasing strength of those in the church who denied the full authority of Scripture, Spurgeon published several articles in The Sword and the Trowel *urging those of faith to dissociate themselves from such men. It was from the title of the first of these that the controversy received its name. Eventually, as a result of the controversy this provoked and the feelings that ran contrary to his own, Spurgeon left the Baptist Union. Many of Spurgeon's sermons of 1887 and 1888 reflect the Down-Grade Controversy, and the pain it brought to him.*

CHAPTER ONE

Grace Abounding over Abounding Sin

Moreover the law entered, that the offense might abound. But where sin abounded, grace did much more abound (Rom. 5:20).

The first sentence will serve as a preface; the second sentence will be the actual text.

The Law and Abounding Offense

"Moreover the law entered, that the offense might abound." Man was a sinner before the law of Ten Commandments had been given. He was a sinner through the offense of his first father, Adam; and he was, also, practically a sinner by his own personal offense; for he rebelled against the light of nature, and the inner light of conscience. Men, from Adam downward, transgressed against that memory of better days which had been handed down from father to son, and had never been quite forgotten. Man everywhere, whether he knew anything about the law of Moses or not, was alienated from his God. The Word of God contains this truthful estimate of our race: "They are all gone out of the way, they are together become unprofitable; there is none that doeth good, no, not one."

The law was given, however, according to the text, "that the offense might abound." Such was the effect of the law. It did not hinder sin, nor provide a remedy for it; but its actual effect was that the offense abounded. How so?

It was so, first, because it revealed the offense. Man did not in every instance clearly discern what was sin; but when the law came, it pointed out to man that this evil, which he thought little of, was an abomination in the sight of God. Man's nature and character was like a dark dungeon which knew no ray of light. Yonder prisoner does not perceive the horrible filthiness and corruption of the place wherein he is immured, so long as he is in darkness. When a lamp is brought, or a window is opened and the light of day comes in, he finds out to his dismay the hideous condition of his den. He spies loathsome creatures upon the walls, and marks how others burrow out of sight because the light annoys them. He may, perhaps, have guessed that all was not as it should be, but he had not imagined the abundance of the evils. The light has entered, and the offense abounds.

Law does not make us sinful, but it displays our sinfulness. In the presence of the perfect standard we see our shortcomings. The law of God is the looking-glass in which a man sees the spots upon his face. It does not wash you— you cannot wash in a looking-glass; but it prompts you to seek the cleansing water. The design of the law is the revealing of our many offenses, that, thereby, we may be driven out of self-righteousness to the Lord Jesus, in whom we have redemption through his blood, the forgiveness of sin.

The law causes the offense to abound by making an offender to stand without excuse. Before he knew the law perfectly, his sin was not so willful. While he did but faintly know the commands, he could, as it were, but faintly break them; but as soon as he distinctly knows what is right, and what is wrong, then every cloak is taken away from him. Sin becomes exceeding sinful when it is committed against light and knowledge. Is it not so with some of you? Are you not forced to admit that you commit many sins in one, now that you have been made to know the law, and yet willfully offend against it, by omission or commission? He who knows his Master's will and does it not, will be beaten with many stripes, because he is guilty of abounding offenses. The law enters to strip us of every cloak of justification, and so to drive us to seek the robe of Christ's righteousness.

Next, I think the law makes the offense to abound by causing sin to be, more evidently, a presumptuous rebellion against the great Lawgiver. To sin in the front of Sinai, with its wonderful display of divine majesty, is to sin indeed. To rebel against a law promulgated with sound of trumpet, and thunders, and pomp of God, is to sin with a high hand and a defiant heart. When thou hast heard the Ten Commands, when thou knowest the law of the kingdom, when thy Maker's will is plainly set before thee, then to transgress is to transgress with an insolence of pride which will admit of no excuse.

Once more: the entrance of the law makes the offense to abound in this sense, that the rebellious will of man rises up in opposition to it. Because God commands, man refuses; and because he forbids, man desires. There are some men who might not have sinned in a particular direction if the commandment had not forbidden it. The light of the law, instead of being a warning to them to avoid evil, seems to point out to them the way in which they can most offend. Oh, how deep is the depravity of hu-

man nature! The law itself provokes it to rebel. Men long to enter, because trespassers are warned to keep away. Their minds are so at enmity against God, that they delight in that which is forbidden, not so much because they find any particular pleasure in the thing itself, but because it shows their independence and their freedom from the restraints of God. This vicious self-will is in all of us by nature; for the carnal mind is enmity against God; and therefore the law, though in itself holy and just and good, provokes us to do evil. We are like lime, and the law is as cold water, which is in itself of a cooling nature; yet, no sooner does the water of the law get at the lime of our nature, than a heat of sin is generated: "thus, the law entered, that the offense might abound."

The Use of the Law

Why, then, did God send the law? Is it not an evil thing that the offense should abound? In itself it may seem so to be; but God dealeth with us as physicians sometimes deal with their patients. A disease, which will be fatal if it spends itself within the patient, must be brought to the surface: the physician therefore prescribes a medicine which displays the evil. The evil was all within, but it did not abound as to its visible effects; it is needful that it should do so, that it may be cured.

The law is the medicine which throws out the depravity of man, makes him see it in his actions, and even provokes him to display it. The evil is in man, like rabbits in yonder brushwood: the law sets alight to the cover, and the hidden creatures are seen. The law stirs the mud at the bottom of the pool, and proves how foul the waters are. The law compels the man to see that sin dwelleth in him, and that it is a powerful tyrant over his nature. All this is with a view to his cure.

God be thanked when the law so works as to take off the sinner from all confidence in himself! To make the leper confess that he is incurable is going a great way towards compelling him to go to that Divine Savior, who alone is able to heal him. This is the object and end of the law towards men whom God will save.

Consider for a moment. You may take it as an axiom, a thing self-evident, that there can be no grace where there is no guilt: there can be no mercy where there is no sin. There can be justice, there can be benevolence; but there cannot be mercy unless there is criminality. If you are not a sinner God cannot have mercy upon you. If you have never sinned God cannot display pardoning grace towards you, for there is nothing to pardon. It were a misuse of words to talk of forgiving a man who has done no wrong, or to speak of bestowing undeserved favor upon a person who deserves reward. It would be an insult to innocence to offer it mercy. You must, therefore, have sin or you cannot have grace—that is clear.

Next, consider that there will be no seeking after grace where there is no sense of sin. We may preach till we are hoarse, but you good people, who have never broken the law, and are not guilty of anything wrong, will never care for our message of mercy. You are such kind people that, out of compliment to religion, you say, "Yes, we are sinners. We are all sinners." But you know in your heart of hearts you do not mean it. You will never ask for grace; for you have no sense of shame or guilt. None of you will seek mercy, till first you have pleaded guilty to the indictment which the law of God presents against you. Oh, that you felt your sins! Oh, that you knew your need of forgiveness! for then you would see yourselves to be in such a condition that only the free, rich, sovereign grace of God can save you.

Furthermore, I am sure that there will be no reception and acceptance of grace by any man, till there is a full confession of sin and a burdensome sense of its weight. Why should you receive grace when you do not want it? What is the use of it to you? Why should you bow your knee to God, and receive, as the free gift of his charity, that which you feel you deserve? Have you not already earned eternal life? Are you not as good as other people? Have you not some considerable claim upon God? Do I startle you with these plain questions? Have I not heard you say much the same?

The other day when we preached the electing love of God, you grumbled and muttered that God was unjust to choose one rather than another. What did this mean? Did it not mean that you felt you had some claim upon God? O sir, if this is your spirit, I must deal plainly with you! If you have any claim upon your Maker, plead it, and be you sure that he will not deny you your just rights. But I would advise you to change your method of dealing with your Judge: you will never prevail in this fashion. In truth, you have no claim upon him; but must appeal to his pure mercy. You are not in a position for him to display free grace to you till your mouth is shut, and you sit down in dust and ashes, silently owning that you deserve nothing at his hands but infinite displeasure. Confess that whatever he gives you that is good and gracious must be given freely to one who deserves nothing. Hell gapes at your feet: cease from pride, and humbly sue out a pardon.

You see, then, the use of the law: it is to bring you where grace can be fitly shown you. It shuts you up that you may cry to Jesus to set you free. It is a storm which wrecks your hopes of self-salvation, but washes you upon the Rock of Ages. The condemning sentence of the law is meant to prepare you for the absolution of the gospel. If you condemn yourself and plead guilty before God, the royal pardon can then be extended towards you. The self-condemned shall be forgiven through the precious blood of Jesus, and the sovereign grace of God.

Oh, my hearer, you must sit down there in the dust, or else God will not look at you! You must yield yourself to him, owning his justice, honoring his law: this is the first condition of his mercy, and to this his grace brings all who feel its power. The Lord will have you bow before him in self-abhorrence, and confess his right to punish you. Remember, "He will have mercy on whom he will have mercy, and he will have compassion on whom he will have compassion," and he will have you know this, and agree to it. His grace must reign triumphantly, and you must kiss its silver scepter.

Thus has the first sentence served us for a preface: God bless it to us!

Grace over Sin

The doctrine of the text itself is this, that "where sin abounded, grace did much more abound"; and I shall try to bring out that truth, first, by saying that THIS IS SEEN IN THE WHOLE WORK OF GRACE, from beginning to end.

I would direct your attention to the context. The safest way to preach upon a text, is to follow out the idea which the inspired writer was endeavoring to convey. Paul has, in this place, been speaking of the abounding result for evil of one sin in the case of Adam, the federal head of the race. That one sin of Adam's abounded terribly. Look at the multitudinous generations of our race which have gone down to death. Who slew all these? Sin is the wolf which has devoured the flocks of men. Sin has poisoned the streams of manhood at their fountain-head, and everywhere they run with poisoned waters. Concerning this, Paul says, "Where sin abounded, grace did much more abound."

First, then, *sin abounded in its effect upon the whole human race:* one sin overthrew all humanity; one fatal fault, the breach of a plain and easy law, made sinners of us all. "By one man's disobedience many were made sinners." Simple as was the command which Adam broke, it involved obedience or disobedience to the sovereignty of God. All the trees of the garden were generously given to happy Adam in Paradise: "Of every tree of the garden thou mayest freely eat." There was but one tree reserved for God by the prohibition, "Thou shalt not eat of it: for in the day that thou eatest thereof thou shalt surely die." Adam had no need to touch that fruit, there were all the other trees for him. Nothing was denied him which was really for his good; he was only forbidden that which would ruin him. We all look back to that Paradisaical state and wish we could have been put in some such a position as he: yet he dared to trespass on God's reserves, and thus to set himself up above his Maker. He judged it wise to do what God forbade: he ran the risk of death in the foolish hope of rising into a still higher state.

See the consequences of that sin on all sides, the world is full of them. Yet, saith Paul, "Where sin abounded, grace did much more abound," and he gives us this as a proof of it: "And not as it was by one that sinned, so is the gift: for the judgment was by one to condemnation, but the free gift is of many offenses unto justification" (Rom. 5:16). The Lord Jesus came into the world, not alone to put away Adam's sin, but all the sins which have followed upon it. The second Adam has repaired the desperate ruin of the first, and much more. By his death upon the cross, our Divine Substitute has put away those myriads of sins, which have been committed by men since the first offense in Eden.

Think of this! Take the whole aggregate of believers, and let each one disburden his conscience of its load of sin. What a mountain! Pile it up! Pile it up! It rises huge as high Olympus! Age after age believers come and lay their enormous loads in this place. "The Lord hath made to meet on him the iniquities of us all." What Alps! What Himalayas of sin! If there were only mine and yours, my brother, what mountains of division would our sins make! But the great Christ, the free gift of God to us, when he bare our sins in his own body on the tree, took all those countless sins away. "Behold the Lamb of God, which taketh away the sin of the world!" Here is infinite grace to pardon immeasurable sin! Truly the "one man's offense" abounded horribly; but the "one man's obedience," the obedience of the Son of God, hath superabounded. As the arch of heaven far exceedeth in its span the whole round globe of the earth, so doth grace much more abound over human sin.

Follow me further, when I notice, secondly, that *sin abounded in its ruinous effects.* It utterly destroyed humanity. In the third chapter of the Romans you see how, in every part of his nature, man is depraved by sin. Think of the havoc which the tyrant, sin, has made of our natural estate and heritage. Eden is withered—its very site is forgotten. Our restfulness among the trees of the field, freely yielding their fruit, is gone, and God hath said, "In the sweat of thy face shalt thou eat bread." The field we till has lost its spontaneous yield of corn: "Thorns also and thistles shall it bring forth to thee." Our life has lost its glory and immortality; for "Dust thou art, and unto dust shalt thou return." Every woman in her pangs of travail, every

man in his weariness of labor, and all of us together in the griefs of death, see what sin has done for us as to our mortal bodies.

Alas, it has gone deeper: it has ruined our souls. Sin has unmanned man. The crown and glory of his manhood it has thrown to the ground. All our faculties are out of gear; all our tendencies are perverted. Beloved, let us rejoice that the Lord Jesus Christ has come to redeem us from the curse of sin, and he will undo the evil of evil. Even this poor world he will deliver from the bondage of corruption; and he will create new heavens and a new earth, wherein dwelleth righteousness. The groans and painful travail of the whole creation shall result in a full deliverance, through the grace of our Lord Jesus Christ, and somewhat more.

As for ourselves, we are lifted up to a position far higher than that which we should have occupied had the race continued in its innocence. The Lord Jesus Christ found us in a horrible pit and in the miry clay, and he not only lifted us up out of it, but he set our feet upon a rock, and established our goings. Raised from hell, we are lifted not to the bowers of Eden, but to the throne of God. Redeemed human nature has greater capacities than unfallen human nature. To Adam the Lord did not say, "Thou art a son of God, joint heir with the Only Begotten"; but he has said that to each believer redeemed by the precious blood of Jesus. Beloved, such a thing as fellowship with Christ in his sufferings could not have been known to Adam in Paradise. He could not have known what it is to be dead, and to have his life hid with Christ in God.

Blessed be his name, our Lord Jesus Christ can say, "I restored that which I took away"! He restored more than ever was taken away from us; for he hath made us to be partakers of the divine nature, and in his own person he hath placed us at God's right hand in the heavenly places. Inasmuch as the dominion of the Lord Jesus is more glorious than that of unfallen Adam, manhood is now more great and glorious than before the Fall. Grace has so much more abounded, that in Jesus we have gained more than in Adam we lost. Our Paradise Regained is far more glorious than our Paradise Lost.

Again, *sin abounded to the dishonor of God.* I was trying the other day to put myself into the position of Satan at the gates of Eden, that I might understand his diabolical policy. He had become the archenemy of God, and when he saw this newly-made world, and perceived two perfectly pure and happy creatures placed in it, he looked on with envy, and plotted mischief. He heard the Creator say, "In the day that thou eatest thereof thou shalt surely die," and he hoped here to find an opportunity for an assault upon God. If he could induce those new-made creatures to eat of the forbidden fruit, he would place their Maker upon the horns of a dilemma: either he must destroy the creatures which he had made, or else he must be untrue. The Lord had said, "Ye shall surely die," and he must thus undo his own work, and destroy a creature which he had made in his own image, after his own likeness.

Satan, probably, perceived that man was an extraordinary being, with a wonderful mystery of glory hanging about his destiny; and, if he could make him sin, he would cause God to destroy him, and so far defeat the eternal purpose. On the other hand, if the Lord did not execute the sentence, then he would not be truthful, and throughout all his great universe it would be reported that the Lord's word had been broken. Either he had changed his mind, or he had spoken in jest, or he had been proven to have threatened too severe a penalty. In either case, the evil spirit hoped to triumph. It was a deep, far-reaching scheme to dim the splendor of the King of kings.

Beloved, did it not seem as if sin had abounded beyond measure, when first the woman and then the man had been deceived, and had done despite to God? Behold how grace, through our Lord Jesus Christ, did much more abound! God is more honored in the redemption of man than if there had never been a Fall. The Lord has displayed the majesty of his justice, and the glory of his grace, in the great sacrifice of his dear Son, in such a manner that angels, and principalities, and powers will wonder throughout all ages. More of God is to be seen in the great work of redeeming love than could have been reflected in the creation of myriads of worlds, had each one of them been replete with marvels of divine skill, and goodness, and power. In Jesus crucified Jehovah is glorified as never before. Where sin abounded to the apparent dishonor of God, grace doth much more abound to the infinite glory of his ever-blessed name.

Again, *sin abounded by degrading human character.* What a wretched being man is, as a sinner against God! Unchecked by law, and allowed to do as he pleases, what will not man become? See how Paul describes men in these progressive times—in these enlightened centuries: "This know also, that in the last days perilous times shall come. For men shall be lovers of their own selves, covetous, boasters, proud, blasphemers, disobedient to parents, unthankful, unholy, without natural affection, trucebreakers, false accusers, incontinent, fierce, despisers of those that are good, traitors, heady, highminded, lovers of pleasures more than lovers of God; having a form of godliness, but denying the power thereof."

Human nature was not at all slandered by Whitefield when he said that, "left to himself, man is half beast and half devil." I do not mean merely men in savage countries, I am thinking of men in London. Only the other day a certain newspaper gave us plenty of proof of the sin of this city: I will say no more—could brutes or demons be worse? Read human history, Assyrian, Roman, Greek, Saracenic, Spanish, English; and if you are a lover of holiness, you will be sick of man. Has any other creature, except the fallen angels, ever become so cruel, so mean, so false? Behold what villains, what tyrants, what monsters sin has made!

But now look on the other side, and see what the grace of God has done. Under the molding hand of the Holy Spirit a gracious man becomes the noblest work of God. Man, born again and rescued from the Fall, is now capable of virtues, to which he never could have reached before he sinned. An unfallen being could not hate sin with the intensity of abhorrence which is found in the renewed heart. We now know by personal experience the horror of sin, and there is now within us an instinctive shuddering at it. An unfallen being could not exhibit patience, for it could not suffer, and patience has its perfect work to do. When I have read the stories of the martyrs in the first ages of the Christian church, and during the Marian persecution in England, I have adored the Lord, who could enable poor feeble men and women thus to prove their love to their God and Savior. What great things they suffered out of love to God; and how grandly did they thus honor him!

O God, what a noble being thy grace has made man to be! I have felt great reverence for sanctified humanity, when I have seen how men could sing God's praises in the fires. What noble deeds men have been capable of, when the love of God has been shed abroad in their hearts! I do not think angels, or archangels, have ever been able to exhibit so admirable an all-round character as the grace of God hath wrought in once fallen men whom he has, by his grace, inspired with the divine life. In human character, "where sin abounded, grace did much more abound." I believe God looks out of heaven today, and sees in many of his poor, hidden people such beauties of virtue, such charms of holiness, that he himself is delighted with them. "The Lord taketh pleasure in them that fear him." These are such true jewels that the Lord has a high estimate of them, and sets them apart for himself: "They shall be mine, saith the Lord of hosts, in that day when I make up my jewels."

Again, dear friends, *sin abounded to the causing of great sorrow*. It brought with it a long train of woes. The children of sin are many, and each one causeth lamentation. We cannot attempt to fathom the dark abysses of sorrow which have opened in this world since the advent of sin. Is it not a place of tears—yea, a field of blood? Yet by a wonderful alchemy, through the existence of sin, grace has produced a new joy, yea, more than one new joy. The calm, deep joy of repentance must have been unknown to perfect innocence. This right orient pearl is not found in the rivers of Eden. Yea, and that joy which is in heaven in the presence of the angels of God over sinners that repent is a new thing, whose birth is since the Fall.

God himself knows a joy which he could not have known had there been no sin. Behold, with tearful wonder, the great Father as he receives his returning prodigal, and cries to all about him, "Let us eat, and be merry: for this my son was dead, and is alive again; he was lost, and is found." O brethren, how could almighty love have been victorious in grace had there been no sin to battle with? Heaven is the more heaven for us, since there we shall sing of robes washed white in the blood of the Lamb. God hath greater joy in man, and man hath greater joy in God, because grace abounded over sin. We are getting into deep waters now! How true our text is!

Once more, *sin abounded to hinder the reign of Christ*. I believe that Satan's design in leading men into sin at the first, was to prevent the supremacy of the Lord Jesus Christ as man and God in one person. I do not lay it down as a doctrine, specifically taught in Scripture, but still it seems to me a probable truth, that Satan foresaw that the gap which was made in heaven by the fall of the angels was to be filled up by human beings, whom God would place near his throne. Satan thought that he saw before him the beings who would take the places of the fallen spirits, and he envied them. He knew that they were made in the image of the Only-Begotten, the Christ of God, and he hated him because he saw united in his person God whom he abhorred, and man whom he envied.

Satan shot at the second Adam through the breast of the first Adam. He meant to overthrow the Coming One; but, fool that he was, the Lord Jesus Christ, by the grace of God, is now exalted higher than ever we could conceive him to have been, had there been no sin to bear, no redemption to work out. Jesus, wounded and slain, has about him higher splendor than before. O Kings of kings and Lord of lords, Man of Sorrows, we sing hallelujahs unto thee! All our hearts beat true to thee! We love thee beyond all else! Thou art he whom we will praise for ever and ever!

Jesus sits on no precarious throne in the empire of love. We would each one maintain his right with the last pulse of our hearts. King of kings and Lord of lords! Hallelujah! Where sin abounded, grace hath much more abounded to the glory of the Only-Begotten Son of God.

Grace over Sin in Special Cases

I find time always flies fastest when our subject is most precious. I have a second head, which deserves a lengthened consideration; but we must be content with mere hints. This great fact, that where sin abounded, grace did much more abound, crops up everywhere. THIS IS TO BE SEEN IN SPECIAL CASES.

The first special case is *the introduction of the law*. When the law of Ten Commands was given, through man's sin, it ministered to the abounding of the offense; but it also ministered to the aboundings of grace. It is true there were ten commands; but there was more than tenfold grace. With the law there came forward a High Priest. The world had never seen a High Priest before, arrayed in jewelled breastplate, and garments of glory and beauty. There was the law; but at the same time there was the holy place of the Tabernacle of the Most High with its altar, its laver, its candlestick, and its table of shew-bread. There was, also, the secret shrine where the majesty of God dwelt. God had, by those symbols and types, come to dwell among men.

It is true, sin abounded through the law; but, then, sacrifices for sin also abounded. Heretofore, there had been no morning and evening lambs; there had been no day of atonement; no sprinkling of blood; no benediction from the Lord's High Priest. For every sin that the law revealed, a sacrifice was provided. Sins of ignorance, sins of their holy things, sins of all sorts were met by special sacrifices; so that the sins uncovered to the conscience, were also covered by the sacrifice.

The story of Israel is another case in point. How often the nation rebelled; but how often did mercy rejoice over judgment! Truly the history of the chosen people shows how sin abounded, and grace did much more abound.

Run your eye down history and pause at *the crucifixion of our Lord Jesus.* This is the highest peak of the mountains of sin. They crucified the Lord of glory. Here sin abounded. But do I need to tell you that grace did here much more abound? You can look at the death of Christ till Pilate vanishes, and Caiaphas fades away, and all the clamor of the priests and Jews is hushed, and you see nothing and hear nothing but free grace and dying love.

There followed upon the crucifixion of our Lord, *the casting away of the Jewish people for a while.* Sin abounded when the Lord thus came to his own and his own received him not. Yes; but the casting away of them was the saving of the nations. "We turn to the Gentiles," said the apostle; and that was a blessed turning for you and for me. Was it not? They that were bidden to the feast were not worthy, and the master of the house, being angry, invited other guests. Mark, "being angry"! What did he do when he was angry? Why, he did the most gracious thing of all; he said, "Go ye out into the highways and hedges, and as many as ye shall find bid to the supper." Sin abounded, for Israel would not enter the feast of love; but grace did much more abound, for the heathen entered the kingdom.

The heathen world at that time was sunk in the blackest darkness, and sin abounded. You have only to study ancient history and you will fetch a heavy sigh to think that men could be so vile.

A poor and unlettered people were chosen of God to receive the gospel of Jesus, and they went about telling of an atoning Savior, in their own simple way, until the Roman empire was entirely changed. Light and peace and truth came into the world, and drove away slavery and tyranny and bestial lust. Where sin abounded, grace did much more abound. What wonderful characters were produced in the terrible reign of Diocletian! What consecration to God was seen in the confessors! What fearlessness in common Christians! What invincible loyalty to Christ in the martyrs! Out of barbarians the Lord made saints, and the degraded rose to holiness sublime.

If I were to ask you, now, to give the best illustrations of grace abounding in individuals, I think your impulse would be to choose *men in whom sin once abounded.* What characters do we preach of most, when we would magnify the grace of God? We talk of David, and Manasseh, and swearing Peter, and the dying thief, and Saul of Tarsus, and the woman that was a sinner. If we want to show where grace abounded, we naturally turn our eyes to the place where sin abounded. Is it not so? Therefore, I need not give you any more cases—it is proven that where sin abounded, grace did much more abound.

Grace over Sin in Our Lives

Lastly; and this is what I want to hold you to, dear friends, at this time: THIS HOLDS TRUE TO EACH ONE OF US.

Let me take the case of the *open sinner.* What have you been? Have you grossly sinned? Have you defiled your body with unhallowed passions? Have you been dishonest to your fellow-men? Does some scarlet sin stain your conscience, even as you sit in the pew? Have you grown hardened in sin by long perseverance in it? Are you conscious that you have frequently, willfully, and resolutely sinned? Are you getting old, and have you been soaking these seventy years in the crimson dye of sin till you are saturated through and through with its color? Have you even been an implacable opponent of the gospel? Have you persecuted the saints of God? Have you tried by argument to batter down the gospel, or by ridicule to put it to reproach?

Then hear this text: "Where sin abounded, grace did much more abound"; and as it was in the beginning, it is now and ever shall be, till this world shall end. The grace of God, if thou believe in the Lord Jesus Christ, will triumph over the greatness of thy wickedness. "All manner of sin and blasphemy shall be forgiven unto men." Throw down your weapons of rebellion; surrender at discretion; kiss the pierced hand of Jesus which is now held out to you, and this very moment you shall be forgiven, and you shall go your way a pardoned man, to begin a new life, and to bear witness that "where sin abounded, grace did much more abound."

Perhaps this does not touch you, my friend. Listen to my next word which is addressed to *the instructed sinner.* You are a person whose religious education has made you aware of the guilt of sin; you have read your Bible, and you have heard truthful preaching; and although you have never been a gross open sinner, yet you know that your life teems with sins of omission and commission. You know that you have sinned against light and knowledge. You have done despite to a tender conscience very often; and therefore you rightly judge that you are even a greater sinner than the more openly profane.

Be it so; I take you at that. Do not run back from it. Let it be so; for "where sin

abounded, grace did much more abound." Oh, that you may be as much instructed in the remedy, as you are instructed in the disease! Oh, that you may have as clear a view of the righteousness of Christ, as you have of your own unrighteousness! Christ's work is a divine work, broad enough to cover all your iniquity, and to conquer all your sin. Believe this! Give glory to God by believing it; and according to your faith, so be it unto you.

I address another, who does not answer either of these two descriptions exactly; but he has lately begun to seek mercy, and the more he prays the more he is *tempted.* Horrible suggestions rush into his mind; damnable thoughts beset and bewilder him. Ah, my friend, I know what this means: the nearer you are to mercy, the nearer you seem to get to hell-gate! When you most solemnly mean to do good, you feel another law in your members bringing you into captivity. You grow worse where you hoped you would have grown better.

Very well, then; grip my text firmly as for your life: "Where sin abounded, grace did much more abound." If a whole legion of devils should be let loose upon you, Christ will glorify himself by mastering them all. If now you cannot repent, nor pray, nor do anything, remember that text, "When we were yet without strength, in due time Christ died for the ungodly." Look over the heads of all these doubts, and devils, and inabilities, and see Jesus lifted on the cross, like the brazen serpent upon the pole; and look thou to him, and the fiery serpents shall flee away from thee, and thou shalt live. Believe this text to be true, for true it is: "Where sin abounded, grace did much more abound."

"Ah!" saith another, "my case is still worse, sir; I am of a *despondent* turn of mind; I always look upon the black side of everything, and now if I read a promise I am sure it is not for me. If I see a threatening in God's Word, I am sure it is for me. I have no hope. I do not seem as if I should ever have any. I am in a dungeon into which no light can enter: it is dark, dark, dark, and worse darkness is coming. While you are trying to comfort me, I put the comfort away." I know you. You are like the poor creature in the Psalm, of whom we read—"His soul abhorreth all manner of meat." Even the gospel itself he cannot relish. Yes; I know you; you are writing bitter things against yourself: this morning you have been newly dipping your pen in gall; but your writing is that of a poor bewildered creature; it is not to be taken notice of. I see your writing, in text hand, great black words of condemnation; but there is nothing in them all.

Verily, verily I say unto thee, thine handwriting shall be blotted out, and the curse, causeless, shall not come. Thus saith the Lord, "Your covenant with death shall be disannulled, and your agreement with hell shall not stand, for the Lord Jesus Christ has redeemed you, and where sin abounded, grace shall much more abound." Broken in pieces, all asunder, ground between the millstones, reduced to nothing, yet believe this revelation of God, that where sin abounded, grace did much more abound. Notice that *"much more"*—"much more abound." If thou canst grip it, and know it to be of a certainty the great principle upon which God acts, that grace shall outstrip sin, then there is hope of thee; nay, more than hope, there is salvation for thee on the spot. If thou believest in Jesus, whom God has set forth to be a propitiation for sin, thou art forgiven.

Oh, my hearers, do not despise this grace! Come, and partake of it. Does any one say, as Paul foresaw that some would say, "Let us sin, that grace may abound"? Ah, then, such an infamous inference is the mark of the reprobate, and your damnation is just. He that turns God's mercy into a reason for sin, has within him something worse than a heart of stone: surely his conscience is seared with a hot iron. Beloved, I hope better things of you, for I trust that on the contrary, the sound of the silver bells of infinite love, free pardon, abounding grace, will make you hasten to the hospital of mercy, that you may receive healing for your sinfulness, strength for your feebleness, and joy for your sorrow. Lord, grant that in this house, in every case wherein sin has abounded, grace may yet more abound, for Jesus' sake! Amen.

Early in Spurgeon's ministry, before the Metropolitan Tabernacle had been built, he preached at the Surrey Gardens Music Hall in order to accommodate his large audiences. His first sermon there, which he delivered on October 19, 1856, quickly became a debacle. Denied the use of Exeter Hall, his attempt to preach in an indoor place with a total seating capacity of ten thousand seemed impossible to many. At first, everything proceeded normally, but just after he began to pray someone perversely shouted "Fire!" and within minutes a panic had erupted that left seven people dead and twenty-eight others injured. Spurgeon was blamed by many for the catastrophe, and his burden was made even greater by the fact that only a month earlier his wife had given birth to twins. Only twenty-two at the time, this incident was to haunt him for the rest of his life.

"Compel Them to Come In," delivered on December 5, 1858, at the Surrey Gardens Music Hall, is representative of Spurgeon's evangelistic sermons that were aimed directly at sinners. Some consider it his "sermon with the greatest soul-saving testimony," and of it Spurgeon himself wrote "The sermon entitled 'Compel them to come in' has been so signally owned of God, that scarcely a week occurs without some case of its usefulness coming to light."

CHAPTER TWO

Compel Them to Come In

Compel them to come in (Luke 14:23).

I feel in such a haste to go out and obey this commandment this morning, by compelling those to come in who are now tarrying in the highways and hedges, that I cannot wait for an introduction, but must at once set about my business.

Hear then, O ye that are strangers to the truth as it is in Jesus—hear then the message that I have to bring you. Ye have fallen, fallen in your father Adam; ye have fallen also in yourselves, by your daily sin and your constant iniquity; you have provoked the anger of the Most High; and as assuredly as you have sinned, so certainly must God punish you if you persevere in your iniquity, for the Lord is a God of justice, and will by no means spare the guilty. But have you not heard, hath it not long been spoken in your ears, that God, in his infinite mercy, has devised a way whereby, without any infringement upon his honor, he can have mercy upon you, the guilty and the undeserving?

To you I speak; and my voice is unto you, O sons of men; Jesus Christ, very God of very God, hath descended from heaven, and was made in the likeness of sinful flesh. Begotten of the Holy Ghost, he was born of the Virgin Mary; he lived in this world a life of exemplary holiness, and of the deepest suffering, till at last he gave himself up to die for our sins, "the just for the unjust, to bring us to God." And now the plan of salvation is simply declared unto you—"Whosoever believeth in the Lord Jesus Christ shall be saved." For you who have violated all the precepts of God, and have disdained his mercy and dared his vengeance, there is yet mercy proclaimed, for "whosoever calleth upon the name of the Lord shall be saved." "For this is a faithful saying and worthy of all acceptation, that Christ Jesus came into the world to save sinners, of whom I am chief"; "whosoever cometh unto him he will in no wise cast out, for he is able also to save unto the uttermost them that come unto God by him, seeing he ever liveth to make intercession for us."

Now all that God asks of you—and this he gives you—is that you will simply look at his bleeding, dying son, and trust your souls in the hands of him whose name alone can save from death and hell. Is it not a marvellous thing, that the proclamation of this gospel does not receive the unanimous consent of men? One would think that as soon as ever this was preached, "That whosoever believeth shall have eternal life," every one of you, "casting away every man his sins and his iniquities," would lay hold on Jesus Christ, and look alone to his cross. But alas! such is the desperate evil of our nature, such the pernicious depravity of our character, that this message is despised, the invitation to the gospel feast is rejected, and there are many of you who are this day enemies of God by wicked works, enemies to the God who preaches Christ to you today, enemies to him who sent his Son to give his life a ransom for many. Strange I say it is that it should be so, yet nevertheless it is the fact, and hence the necessity for the command of the text,—"Compel them to come in."

Children of God, ye who have believed, I shall have little or nothing to say to you this morning; I am going straight to my business—I am going after those that will not come—those that are in the byways and hedges, and God going with me, it is my duty now to fulfill this command, "Compel them to come in."

First, I must *find you out;* secondly, I will go to work to *compel you to come in.*

I Must Find You Out

If you read the verses that precede the text, you will find an amplification of this command: "Go out quickly into the streets and lanes of the city, and bring in .hither the poor, the maimed, the halt, and the blind;" and then, afterwards, "Go out into the highways," bring in the vagrants, the highwaymen, "and into the hedges," bring in those that have no resting-place for their heads, and are lying under the hedges to rest, bring them in also, and "compel them to come in." Yes, I see you this morning, you that are *poor.* I am to compel *you* to come in. You are poor in circumstances, but this is no barrier to the kingdom of heaven, for God hath not exempted from his grace the man that shivers in rags, and who is destitute of bread. In fact, if there be any distinction made, the distinction is on your side, and for your benefit—"Unto you is the word of salvation sent;" "For the poor have the gospel preached unto them."

But especially I must speak to you who are *poor, spiritually.* You have no faith, you have no virtue, you have no good work, you have no grace, and what is poverty worse still, you have no hope. Ah, my Master has sent you a gracious invitation. Come and welcome to the marriage feast of his love. "Whosoever will, let him come and take of the waters of life freely." Come, I must lay hold upon you, though you be defiled with foulest filth, and though you have nought but rags upon your back, though your own righteousness has become as filthy clouts, yet must I lay hold upon you, and invite you first, and even compel you to come in.

And now I see you again. You are not only poor, but you are *maimed.* There was a time when you thought you could work out your own salvation without God's help, when you could perform good works, attend to ceremonies, and get to heaven by yourselves; but now you are maimed, the sword of the law has cut off your hands, and now you can work no longer; you say, with bitter sorrow—

The best performance of my hands,
Dares not appear before thy throne.

You have lost all power now to obey the law; you feel that when you would do good, evil is present with you. You are maimed; you have given up, as a forlorn hope, all attempt to save yourself, because you are maimed and your arms are gone. But you are worse off than that, for if you could not work your way to heaven, yet you could walk your way there along the road by faith; but you are maimed in the feet as well as in the hands; you feel that you cannot believe, that you cannot repent, that you cannot obey the stipulations of the gospel. You feel that you are utterly undone, powerless in every respect to do anything that can be pleasing to God. In fact, you are crying out—

Oh, could I but believe,
   Then all would easy be,
I would, but cannot, Lord relieve,
   My help must come from thee.

To you am I sent also. Before *you* am I to lift up the bloodstained banner of the cross, to you am I to preach this gospel, "Whoso calleth upon the name of the Lord shall be saved;" and unto you am I to cry "Whosoever will, let him come and take of the water of life freely."

There is yet another class. You are *halt.* You are halting between two opinions. You are sometimes seriously inclined, and at another time worldly gaiety calls you away. What little progress you do make in religion is but a limp. You have a little strength, but that is so little that you make but painful progress. Ah, limping brother, to you also is the word of this salvation sent. Though you halt between two opinions, the master sends me to you with this message: "How long halt ye between two opinions? if God be God, serve him; if Baal be God, serve him." Consider thy ways; set thine house in order, for thou shalt die and not live. Because I will do this, prepare to meet thy God, O Israel! Halt no longer, but decide for God and his truth.

And yet I see another class—*the blind.* Yes, you that cannot see yourselves, that think yourselves good when you are full of evil, that put bitter for sweet and sweet for bitter, darkness for light and light for darkness; to you am I sent. You, blind souls that cannot see your lost estate, that do not believe that sin is so exceedingly sinful as it is, and who will not be persuaded to think that God is a just and righteous God, to you am I sent. To you too that cannot see the Savior, that see no beauty in him that

you should desire him; who see no excellence in virtue, no glories in religion, no happiness in serving God, no delight in being his children; to you, also, am I sent.

Ay, to whom am I not sent if I take my text? For it goes further than this—it not only gives a particular description, so that each individual case may be met, but afterwards it makes a general sweep, and says, "Go into the highways and hedges." Here we bring in all ranks and conditions of men—my lord upon his horse in the highway, and the woman trudging about her business, the thief waylaying the traveller—all these are in the highway, and they are all to be compelled to come in, and there away in the hedges there lie some poor souls whose refuges of lies are swept away, and who are seeking now to find some little shelter for their weary heads, to you, also, are we sent this morning. This is the universal command—compel them to come in.

Now, I pause after having described the character, I pause to look at the herculean labor that lies before me. Well did Melanchthon say, "Old Adam was too strong for young Melanchthon." As well might a little child seek to compel a Samson, as I seek to lead a sinner to the cross of Christ. And yet my Master sends me about the errand. Lo, I see the great mountain before me of human depravity and stolid indifference, but by faith I cry, "Who art thou, O great mountain? before Zerubbabel thou shalt become a plain." Does my Master say, compel them to come in? Then, though the sinner be like Samson and I a child, I shall lead him with a thread. If God saith *do* it, if I attempt it in faith *it shall be done;* and if with a groaning, struggling, and weeping heart, I so seek this day to compel sinners to come to Christ, the sweet compulsions of the Holy Spirit shall go with every word, and some indeed shall be compelled to come in.

I Compel You to Come In

And now to the work—directly to the work. Unconverted, unreconciled, unregenerate men and women, I am to COMPEL YOU TO COME IN. Permit me first of all to accost you in the highways of sin and tell you over again my errand. The King of heaven this morning sends a gracious invitation to you. He says, "As I live, saith the Lord, I have no pleasure in the death of him that dieth, but had rather that he should turn unto me and live." "Come now and let us reason together saith the Lord, though your sins be as scarlet they shall be as wool; though they be red like crimson they shall be whiter than snow." Dear brother, it makes my heart rejoice to think that I should have such good news to tell you, and yet I confess my soul is heavy because I see you do not think it good news, but turn away from it, and do not give it due regard. Permit me to tell you what the King has done for you. He knew your guilt, he foresaw that you would ruin yourself. He knew that his justice would demand your blood, and in order that this difficulty might be escaped, that his justice might have its full due, and that you might yet be saved, *Jesus Christ hath died.*

Will you just for a moment glance at this picture? You see that man there on his knees in the garden of Gethsemane, sweating drops of blood. You see this next; you see that miserable sufferer tied to a pillar and lashed with terrible scourges, till the shoulder bones are seen like white islands in the midst of a sea of blood. Again you see this third picture; it is the same man hanging on the cross with hands extended, and with feet nailed fast, dying, groaning, bleeding; methought the picture spoke and

said, "It is finished." Now all this hath Jesus Christ of Nazareth done, in order that God might consistently with his justice pardon sin; and the message to you this morning is this—"Believe on the Lord Jesus Christ and thou shalt be saved." That is trust him, renounce thy works, and thy ways, and set thine heart alone on this man, who gave himself for sinners.

Well brother, I have told you the message, what sayest thou unto it? Do you turn away? You tell me it is nothing to you; you cannot listen to it; that you will hear me by-and-by; but you will go your ways this day and attend to your farm and merchandise. Stop brother, I was not told merely to tell you and then go about my business. No; I am told to compel you to come in; and permit me to observe to you before I further go, that there is one thing I can say—and to which God is my witness this morning, that I am in earnest with you in my desire that you should comply with this command of God. You may despise your own salvation, but I do not despise it; you may go away and forget what you shall hear, but you will please to remember that the things I now say cost me many a groan ere I came here to utter them. My inmost soul is speaking out to you, my poor brother, when I beseech you by him that liveth and was dead, and is alive for evermore, consider my master's message which he bids me now address to you.

I Command You to Come In

But do you spurn it? Do you still refuse it? Then I must change my tone a minute. I will not merely tell you the message, and invite you as I do with all earnestness, and sincere affection—I will go further. Sinner, in God's name I *command* you to repent and believe. Do you ask me whence my authority? I am an ambassador of heaven. My credentials, some of them secret, and in my own heart; and others of them open before you this day in the seals of my ministry, sitting and standing in this hall, where God has given me many souls for my hire. As God the everlasting one hath given me a commission to preach his gospel, I command you to believe in the Lord Jesus Christ; not on my own authority, but on the authority of him who said, "Go ye into all the world and preach the gospel to every creature;" and then annexed this solemn sanction, "He that believeth and is baptized shall be saved, but he that believeth not shall be damned."

Reject my message, and remember, "He that despised Moses's law, died without mercy under two or three witnesses: of how much sorer punishment, suppose ye, shall he be thought worthy, who hath trodden under foot the Son of God." An ambassador is not to stand below the man with whom he deals, for we stand higher. If the minister chooses to take his proper rank, girded with the omnipotence of God, and anointed with his holy unction, he is to command men, and speak with all authority compelling them to come in: "command, exhort, rebuke with all longsuffering."

I Exhort You to Flee to Christ

But do you turn away and say you will not be commanded? Then again will I change my note. If that avails not, all other means shall be tried. My brother, I come to you simple of speech, and I *exhort* you to flee to Christ. O my brother, dost thou know what a loving Christ he is? Let me tell thee from my own soul what I know of him. I, too once despised him. He knocked at the door of my heart and I refused to open it. He came to me, times without number, morning by morning, and night by night; he checked me in my conscience and spoke to me by his Spirit, and when, at last, the thunders of the law prevailed in my conscience, I thought that Christ was cruel and unkind. O I can never forgive myself that I should have thought so ill of him.

But what a loving reception did I have when I went to him. I thought he would smite me, but his hand was not clenched in anger but opened wide in mercy. I thought full sure that his eyes would dart lightning-flashes of wrath upon me; but, instead thereof, they were full of tears. He fell upon my neck and kissed me; he took off my rags and did clothe me with his righteousness, and caused my soul to sing aloud for joy; while in the house of my heart and in the house of his church there was music and dancing, because his son that he had lost was found, and he that was dead was made alive.

I exhort you, then, to look to Jesus Christ and to be lightened. Sinner, you will never regret,—I will be bondsman for my Master that you will never regret it,—you will have no sigh to go back to your state of condemnation; you shall go out of Egypt and shall go into the promised land and shall find it flowing with milk and honey. The trials of Christian life you shall find heavy, but you will find grace will make them light. And as for the joys and delights of being a child of God, if I lie this day you shall charge me with it in days to come. If you will taste and see that the Lord is good, I am not afraid but that you shall find that he is not only good, but better than human lips ever can describe.

I Appeal to Your Own Self-Interests

I know not what arguments to use with you. I appeal to your own self-interests. Oh my poor friend, would it not be better for you to be reconciled to the God of heaven, than to be his enemy? What are you getting by opposing God? Are you the happier for being his enemy? Answer, pleasure-seeker: hast thou found delights in that cup? Answer me, self-righteous man: hast thou found rest for the sole of thy foot in all thy works? Oh thou that goest about to establish thine own righteousness, I charge thee let conscience speak. Hast thou found it to be a happy path? Ah, my friend, "Wherefore dost thou spend thy money for that which is not bread, and thy labor for that which satisfieth not; hearken diligently unto me, and eat ye that which is good, and let your soul delight itself in fatness." I exhort you by everything that is sacred and solemn, everything that is important and eternal, flee for your lives, look not behind you, stay not in all the plain, stay not until you have proved, and found an interest in the blood of Jesus Christ, that blood which cleanseth us from all sin.

Are you still cold and indifferent? Will not the blind man permit me to lead him to the feast? Will not my maimed brother put his hand upon my shoulder and permit me to assist him to the banquet? Will not the poor man allow me to walk side-by-side with him? Must I use some stronger words? Must I use some other compulsion to compel you to come in? Sinners, this one thing I am resolved upon this morning, if you be not saved ye shall be without excuse. Ye, from the grey-headed down to the tender age of childhood, if ye this day lay not hold on Christ, your blood shall be on your own head. If there be power in man to bring his fellow, (as there is when man is helped by the Holy Spirit) that power shall be exercised this morning, God helping me.

Come, I am not to be put off by your rebuffs: if my exhortation fails, I must come to something else. My brother I ENTREAT you, I entreat you stop and consider. Do you know what it is you are rejecting this morning? You are rejecting Christ, your only Savior. "Other foundation can no man lay;" "there is none other name given among men whereby we must be saved." My brother, I cannot bear that ye should do this, for I remember what you are forgetting: the day is coming when you will want a Savior. It is not long ere weary months shall have ended, and your strength begin to decline; your pulse shall fail you, your strength shall depart, and you and the grim monster—death, must face each other. What will you do in the swellings of Jordan without a Savior? Death-beds are stony things without the Lord Jesus Christ. It is an awful thing to die anyhow; he that hath the best hope, and the most triumphant faith, finds that death is not a thing to laugh at. It is a terrible thing to pass from the seen to the unseen, from the mortal to the immortal, from time to eternity, and you will find it hard to go through the iron gates of death without the sweet wings of angels to conduct you to the portals of the skies. It will be a hard thing to die without Christ.

I cannot help thinking of you. I see you acting the suicide this morning, and I picture myself standing at your bedside and hearing your cries, and knowing that you are dying without hope. I cannot bear that. I think I am standing by your coffin now, and looking into your clay-cold face, and saying, "This man despised Christ and neglected the great salvation." I think what bitter tears I shall weep then, if I think that I have been unfaithful to you, and how those eyes fast closed in death, shall seem to chide me and say, "Minister, I attended the music hall, but you were not in earnest with me; you amused me, you preached to me, but you did not plead with me. You did not know what Paul meant when he said, 'As though

God did beseech you by us we pray you in Christ's stead, be ye reconciled to God.'"

I Entreat You Because I Must

I entreat you let this message enter your heart for another reason. I picture myself standing at the bar of God. As the Lord liveth, the day of judgment is coming. You believe that? You are not an infidel; your conscience would not permit you to doubt the Scripture. Perhaps you may have pretended to do so, but you cannot. You feel there must be a day when God shall judge the world in righteousness. I see you standing in the midst of that throng, and the eye of God is fixed on you. It seems to you that he is not looking anywhere else, but only upon you, and he summons you before him; and he reads your sins, and he cries, "Depart ye cursed into everlasting fire in hell!"

My hearer, I cannot bear to think of you in that position; it seems as if every hair on my head must stand on end to think of any hearer of mine being damned. Will you picture yourselves in that position? The word has gone forth, "Depart, ye cursed." Do you see the pit as it opens to swallow you up? Do you listen to the shrieks and the yells of those who have preceded you to that eternal lake of torment? Instead of picturing the scene, I turn to you with the words of the inspired prophet, and I say, "Who among us shall dwell with the devouring fire? Who among us shall dwell with everlasting burnings?" Oh! my brother, I cannot let you put away religion thus; no, I think of what is to come after death. I should be destitute of all humanity if I should see a person about to poison himself, and did not dash away the cup; or if I saw another about to plunge from London Bridge, if I did not assist in preventing him from doing

so; and I should be worse than a fiend if I did not now, with all love, and kindness, and earnestness, beseech you to "lay hold on eternal life," "to labour not for the meat that perisheth, but for the meat that endureth unto everlasting life."

Some hyper-Calvinist would tell me I am wrong in so doing. I cannot help it. I must do it. As I must stand before my Judge at last, I feel that I shall not make full proof of my ministry unless I entreat with many tears that ye would be saved, that ye would look unto Jesus Christ and receive his glorious salvation.

But does not this avail? are all our entreaties lost upon you; do you turn a deaf ear? Then again I change my note. Sinner, I have pleaded with you as a man pleadeth with his friend, and were it for my *own* life I could not speak more earnestly this morning than I do speak concerning *yours*. I did feel earnest about my own soul, but not a whit more than I do about the souls of my congregation this morning; and therefore, if ye put away these entreaties I have something else;—I must *threaten* you. You shall not always have such warnings as these. A day is coming, when hushed shall be the voice of every gospel minister, at least for you; for your ear shall be cold in death. It shall not be any more threatening; it shall be the fulfilment of the threatening. There shall be no promise, no proclamations of pardon and of mercy; no peace-speaking blood, but you shall be in the land where the Sabbath is all swallowed up in everlasting nights of misery, and where the preachings of the gospel are forbidden because they would be unavailing. I charge you then, listen to this voice that now addresses your conscience; for if not, God shall speak to you in his wrath, and say unto you in his hot displeasure, "I called and ye refused; I stretched out my hand

and no man regarded; therefore will I mock at your calamity; I will laugh when your fear cometh."

Sinner, I threaten you again. Remember, it is but a short time you may have to hear these warnings. You imagine that your life will be long, but do you know how short it is? Have you ever tried to think how frail you are? Did you ever see a body when it has been cut in pieces by the anatomist? Did you ever see such a marvellous thing as the human frame?

> Strange, a harp of a thousand
> strings,
> Should keep in tune so long.

Let but one of those cords be twisted, let but a mouthful of food go in the wrong direction, and you may die. The slightest chance, as we have it, may send you swift to death, when God wills it. Strong men have been killed by the smallest and slightest accident, and so may you. In the chapel, in the house of God, men have dropped down dead. How often do we hear of men falling in our streets—rolling out of time into eternity, by some sudden stroke. And are you sure that heart of yours is quite sound? Is the blood circulating with all accuracy? Are you quite sure of that? And if it be so, how long shall it be?

O, perhaps there are some of you here that shall never see Christmas-day; it may be the mandate has gone forth already, "Set thine house in order, for thou shalt die and not live." Out of this vast congregation, I might with accuracy tell how many will be dead in a year; but certain it is that the whole of us shall never meet together again in any one assembly. Some out of this vast crowd, perhaps some two or three, shall depart ere the new year shall be ushered in. I remind you, then, my brother, that either the gate of salvation may be shut, or else you may be out of the place where the gate of mercy stands. Come, then, let the threatening have power with you. I do not threaten because I would alarm without cause, but in hopes that a brother's threatening may drive you to the place where God hath prepared the feast of the gospel.

What Is It that Keeps You from Christ?

And now, *must I turn hopelessly away?* Have I exhausted all that I can say? No, I will come to you again. Tell me what it is, my brother, that keeps you from Christ. I hear one say, "Oh, sir, it is because I feel myself too guilty." That cannot be, my friend, that cannot be. "But, sir, I am the chief of sinners." Friend, you are not. The chief of sinners died and went to heaven many years ago; his name was Saul of Tarsus, afterwards called Paul the apostle. He was the chief of sinners, I know he spoke the truth. "No," but you say still, "I am too vile." You cannot be viler than the *chief* of sinners. You must, at least, be second worst. Even supposing you are the worst now alive, you are second worst, for he was chief.

But suppose you are the worst, is not that the very reason why you should come to Christ? The worse a man is, the more reason he should go to the hospital or physician. The more poor you are, the more reason you should accept the charity of another. Now, Christ does not want any merits of yours. He gives freely. The worse you are, the more welcome you are. But let me ask you a question: Do you think you will ever get better by stopping away from Christ? If so, you know very little as yet of the way of salvation at all. No, sir, the longer you stay the worse you will grow; your hope will grow weaker, your despair will become stronger; the nail with which

Satan has fastened you down will be more firmly clenched, and you will be less hopeful than ever. Come, I beseech you, recollect there is nothing to be gained by delay, but by delay everything may be lost.

"But," cries another, "I feel I cannot believe." No, my friend, and you never will believe if you look first at your believing. Remember, I am not come to invite you to faith, but am come to invite you to Christ. But you say, "What is the difference?" Why, just this. If you first of all say, "I want to believe a thing," you never do it. But your first inquiry must be, "What is this thing that I am to believe?" Then will faith come as the consequence of that search. Our first business has not to do with faith, but with Christ.

Come, I beseech you, on Calvary's mount, and see the cross. Behold the Son of God, he who made the heavens and the earth, dying for your sins. Look to him, is there not power in him to save? Look at his face so full of pity. Is there not love in his heart to prove him *willing* to save? Sure sinner, the sight of Christ will help thee to believe. Do not believe first, and then go to Christ, or else thy faith will be a worthless thing; go to Christ without any faith, and cast thyself upon him, sink or swim.

But I hear another cry, "Oh sir, you do not know how often I have been invited, how long I have rejected the Lord." I do not know, and I do not want to know; all I know is that my Master has sent me, to compel you to come in; so come along with you now. You may have rejected a thousand invitations; don't make this the thousandth-and-one. You have been up to the house of God, and you have only been gospel hardened. But do I not see a tear in your eye? Come my brother don't be hardened by this morning's sermon. O, Spirit of the living God come and melt this heart for it has

never been melted, and compel him to come in! I cannot let you go on such idle excuses as that; if you have lived so many years slighting Christ, there are so many reasons why now you should not slight him.

But did I hear you whisper that this was not a convenient time? Then what must I say to you? When will that convenient time come? Shall it come when you are in hell? Will that time be convenient? Shall it come when you are on your dying bed, and the death throttle is in your throat—shall it come then? Or when the burning sweat is scalding your brow; and then again, when the cold clammy sweat is there, shall those be convenient times? When pains are racking you, and you are on the borders of the tomb?

No, sir, this morning is the convenient time. May God make it so. Remember, I have no authority to ask you to come to Christ *tomorrow*. The Master has given you no invitation to come to him next Tuesday. The invitation is, "*Today* if ye will hear his voice, harden not your hearts as in the provocation," for the Spirit saith "today." "Come *now* and let us reason together;" why should you put it off? It may be the last warning you shall ever have. Put it off, and you may never weep again in chapel. You may never have so earnest a discourse addressed to you. You may not be pleaded with as I would plead with you now. You may go away, and God may say, "He is given unto idols, let him alone." He shall throw the reins upon your neck; and then, mark—your course is sure, but it is sure damnation and swift destruction.

I Pray and Weep for You

And now again, is it all in vain? Will you not now come to Christ? Then what more can I do? I have but one more resort, and that shall be tried. I can be permitted to weep for you; I can be allowed to pray for you. You shall scorn the address if you like; you shall laugh at the preacher; you shall call him fanatic if you will; he will not chide you, he will bring no accusation against you to the great Judge. Your offense, so far as he is concerned, is forgiven before it is committed; but you will remember that the message that you are rejecting this morning is a message from one who loves you, and it is given to you also by the lips of one who loves you. You will recollect that you may play your soul away with the devil, that you may listlessly think it a matter of no importance; but there lives at least one who is in earnest about your soul, and one who before he came here wrestled with his God for strength to preach to you, and who when he has gone from this place will not forget his hearers of this morning.

I say again, when words fail us we can give tears—for words and tears are the arms with which gospel ministers compel men to come in. You do not know, and I suppose could not believe, how anxious a man whom God has called to the ministry feels about his congregation, and especially about some of them. I heard but the other day of a young man who attended here a long time, and his father's hope was that he would be brought to Christ. He became acquainted, however, with an infidel; and now he neglects his business, and lives in a daily course of sin. I saw his father's poor wan face; I did not ask him to tell me the story himself, for I felt it was raking up a trouble and opening a sore; I fear, sometimes, that good man's grey hairs may be brought with sorrow to the grave.

Young men, you do not pray for yourselves, but your mothers wrestle for you. You will not think of your own

souls, but your father's anxiety is exercised for you. I have been at prayer meetings, when I have heard children of God pray there, and they could not have prayed with more earnestness and more intensity of anguish if they had been each of them seeking their own soul's salvation. And is it not strange that we should be ready to move heaven and earth for your salvation, and that still you should have no thought for *yourselves*, no regard to eternal things?

Now I turn for one moment to some here. There are some of you here members of Christian churches, who make a profession of religion, but unless I be mistaken in you—and I shall be happy if I am—your profession is a lie. You do not live up to it, you dishonor it; you can live in the perpetual practice of absenting yourselves from God's house, if not in sins worse than that. Now I ask such of you who do not adorn the doctrine of God your Savior, do you imagine that you can call me your pastor, and yet that my soul cannot tremble over you and in secret weep for you? Again, I say it may be but little concern to you how you defile the garments of your Christianity, but it is a great concern to God's hidden ones, who sigh and cry, and groan for the iniquities of the professors of Zion.

Now does anything else remain to the minister besides weeping and prayer? Yes, there is one thing else. God has given to his servants not the power of regeneration, but he has given them something akin to it. It is impossible for any man to regenerate his neighbor; and yet how are men born to God? Does not the apostle say of such an one that he was begotten by him in his bonds? Now the minister has a power given him of God, to be considered both the father and the mother of those born to God, for the apostle said he travailed in birth for souls till Christ was formed in them.

What can we do then? We can now appeal to the Spirit. I know I have preached the gospel, that I have preached it earnestly. I challenge my Master to honor his own promise. He has said it shall not return unto me void, and it shall not. It is in his hands, not mine. I cannot compel you, but thou O Spirit of God who hast the key of the heart, thou canst compel. Did you ever notice in that chapter of the Revelation, where it says, "Behold I stand at the door and knock," a few verses before, the same person is described, as he who hath the key of David. So that if knocking will not avail, he has the key and can and will come in. Now if the knocking of an earnest minister prevail not with you this morning, there remains still that secret opening of the heart by the Spirit, so that you shall be compelled.

I thought it my duty to labor with you as though I must do it; now I throw it into my Master's hands. It cannot be his will that we should travail in birth, and yet not bring forth spiritual children. It is with *him;* he is master of the heart, and the day shall declare it, that some of you constrained by sovereign grace have become the willing captives of the all-conquering Jesus, and have bowed your hearts to him through the sermon of this morning.

A great advocate of open-air preaching, Spurgeon delivered "Heaven and Hell" on September 4, 1855, in a field beside King Edward's Road in Hackney. He had not originally intended it for publication and apologized for any faults it might have in composition, noting that this sermon "was watered by many prayers of the faithful in Zion." In "Heaven and Hell" Spurgeon contrasts the glory of heaven with the terrors of hell to reach a diverse audience composed of the saved and the unsaved and people of all different ages. "Heaven and Hell" is uniquely intriguing because it concludes with a description of Spurgeon's famous conversion six years earlier.

CHAPTER THREE

Heaven and Hell

And I say unto you, That many shall come from the east and west, and shall sit down with Abraham, and Isaac, and Jacob, in the kingdom of heaven. But the children of the kingdom shall be cast out into outer darkness: there shall be weeping and gnashing of teeth (Matt. 8:11, 12).

This is a land where plain speaking is allowed, and where the people are willing to afford a fair hearing to any one who can tell them that which is worth their attention. Tonight I am quite certain of an attentive audience, for I know you too well to suppose otherwise. This field, as you are all aware, is private property. And I would just give a suggestion to those who go out in the open air to preach—that it is far better to get into a field or a plot of unoccupied building ground, than to block up the roads and stop business; it is moreover far better to be somewhere under protection, so that we can at once prevent disturbance.

Tonight, I shall, I hope, encourage you to seek the road to heaven. I shall also have to utter some very sharp things concerning the end of the lost in the pit of hell. Upon both these subjects I will try and speak, as God helps me. But I beseech you, as you love your souls, weigh right and wrong this night; see whether what I say be the truth of God. If it be not, reject it utterly, and cast it away; but if it is, at your peril disregard it; for as you shall answer before God, the great Judge of heaven and earth, it will go ill with you if the words of his servant and of his Scripture be despised.

My text has two parts. The first is very agreeable to my mind, and gives

me pleasure; the second is terrible in the extreme; but since they are both the truth, they must be preached. The first part of my text is, "I say unto you, that many shall come from the east and west, and shall sit down with Abraham, and Isaac, and Jacob, in the kingdom of heaven." The sentence which I call the black, dark, and threatening part is this: "But the children of the kingdom shall be cast out into outer darkness: there shall be weeping and gnashing of teeth."

The Promise

Let us take the first part. Here is a MOST GLORIOUS PROMISE. I will read it again—"Many shall come from the east and west, and shall sit down with Abraham, and Isaac, and Jacob, in the kingdom of heaven." I like that text, because it tells me what heaven is, and gives me a beautiful picture of it. It says, it is a place where I shall sit down with Abraham, and Isaac, and Jacob. O what a sweet thought that is for the working-man. He often wipes the hot sweat from his face, and he wonders whether there is a land where he shall have to toil no longer. He scarcely ever eats a mouthful of bread that is not moistened with the sweat of his brow. Often he comes home weary, and flings himself upon his couch, perhaps too tired to sleep. He says, "Oh! is there no land where I can rest? Is there no place where I can sit, and for once let these weary limbs be still? Is there no land where I can be quiet?" Yes, thou son of toil and labor,

There is a happy land
Far, far, away—

where toil and labor are unknown. Beyond yon blue welkin there a city fair and bright, its walls are jasper, and its light is brighter than the sun. There "the weary are at rest, and the wicked cease from troubling." Immortal spirits are yonder, who never wipe sweat from their brow, for "they sow not, neither do they reap;" they have not to toil and labor.

There on a green and flow'ry mount
    Their wearied souls shall sit:
And with transporting joys recount
    The labors of their feet.

To my mind, one of the best views of heaven is that *it is a land of rest*— especially to the working-man. Those who have not to work hard, think they will love heaven as a place of service. That is very true. But to the working-man, to the man who toils with his brain or with his hands, it must ever be a sweet thought that there is a land where we shall rest. Soon, this voice will never be strained again: soon, these lungs will never have to exert themselves beyond their power; soon, this brain shall not be racked for thought; but I shall sit at the banquet-table of God; yea, I shall recline on the bosom of Abraham, and be at ease for ever. Oh! weary sons and daughters of Adam, you will not have to drive the ploughshare into the unthankful soil in heaven, you will not need to rise to daily toils before the sun has risen, and labor still when the sun hath long ago gone to his rest; but ye shall be still, ye shall be quiet, ye shall rest yourselves, for all are rich in heaven, all

are happy there, all are peaceful. Toil, trouble, travail, and labor are words that cannot be spelled in heaven; they have no such things there, for they always rest.

The Heavenly Company

And mark the *good company they sit with*. They are to "sit down with Abraham, and Isaac, and Jacob." Some people think that in heaven we shall know nobody. But our text declares here, that we "shall sit down with Abraham, and Isaac, and Jacob." Then I am sure that we shall be aware that they are Abraham, and Isaac, and Jacob. I have heard of a good woman, who asked her husband, when she was dying, "My dear, do you think you will know me when you and I get to heaven?" "Shall I know you?" he said, "why, I have always known you while I have been here, and do you think I shall be a greater fool when I get to heaven?" I think it was a very good answer. If we have known one another here, we shall know one another there. I have dear departed friends up there, and it is always a sweet thought to me, that when I shall put my foot, as I hope I may, upon the threshold of heaven, there will come my sisters and brothers to clasp me by the hand, and say, "Yes, thou lovedst one, and thou art here."

Dear relatives that have been separated, you will meet again in heaven. One of you has lost a mother—she is gone above; and if you follow the track of Jesus, you shall meet her there. Methinks I see yet another coming to meet you at the door of paradise; and though the ties of natural affection may be in a measure forgotten—I may be allowed to use a figure—how blessed would she be as she turned to God, and said, "Here I am, and the children that thou hast given me." We shall recognize our friends—husband, you will know your wife again. Mother, you will know those dear babes of yours—you marked their features when they lay panting and gasping for breath. You know how ye hung over their graves when the cold sod was sprinkled over them, and it was said, "Earth to earth, dust to dust, and ashes to ashes." But ye shall hear those loved voices again; ye shall hear those sweet voices once more; ye shall yet know that those whom ye loved have been loved by God.

Would not that be a dreary heaven for us to inhabit, where we should be alike unknowing and unknown? I would not care to go to such a heaven as that. I believe that heaven is a fellowship of the saints, and that we shall know one another there. I have often thought I should love to see Isaiah; and, as soon as I get to heaven, methinks, I would ask for him, because he spoke more of Jesus Christ than all the rest. I am sure I should want to find out George Whitefield—he who so continually preached to the people, and wore himself out with a more than seraphic zeal. O yes! we shall have choice company in heaven when we get there. There will be no distinction of learned and unlearned, clergy and laity, but we shall walk freely one among another; we shall feel that we are brethren; we shall "sit down with Abraham, and Isaac, and Jacob."

I have heard of a lady who was visited by a minister on her deathbed, and she said to him, "I want to ask you one question, now I am about to die." "Well," said the minister, "what is it?" "Oh!" said she, in a very affected way, "I want to know if there are two places in heaven, because I could not bear that Betsy in the kitchen should be in heaven along with me, she is so unrefined." The minister turned round and said, "O, don't trouble yourself about that, madam. There is no fear of that; for until you get rid of your accursed pride, you will never enter heaven at all." We must all get rid of our pride. We must come down and stand on an equality in the sight of God, and see in every man a brother, before we can hope to be found in glory. Ay, we bless God, we thank him that will set down no separate table for one and for another. The Jew and the Gentile will sit down together. The great and the small shall feed in the same pasture, and we shall "sit down with Abraham, and Isaac, and Jacob, in the kingdom of heaven."

But my text hath a yet greater depth of sweetness, for it says, that "*many* shall come and shall sit down." Some narrow-minded bigots think that heaven will be a very small place, where there will be a very few people, who went to their chapel or their church. I confess, I have no wish for a very small heaven, and love to read in the Scriptures that there are many mansions in my Father's house. How often do I hear people say, "Ah! strait is the gate and narrow is the way, and few there be that find it. There will be very few in heaven; there will be most lost." My friend I differ from you. Do you think that Christ will let the devil beat him? that he will let the devil have more in hell than there will be in heaven? No: it is impossible. For then Satan would laugh at Christ. There will be more in heaven than there are among the lost. God says, that "there will be a number that no man can number who will be saved;" but he never says that there will be a number that no man can number that will be lost. There will be a host beyond all count who will get into heaven.

What glad tidings for you and for me! for if there are so many to be saved why should not I be saved? why should not you? why should not yon man, over there in the crowd, say, "Cannot I be one among the multitude?" And may not that poor woman there take heart, and say, "Well, if there were but half-a-dozen saved, I might fear that I should not be one; but since many are to come, why should not I also be saved?" Cheer up, disconsolate! Cheer up, son of mourning, child of sorrow, there is hope for thee still! I can never know that any man is past God's grace. There be a few that have sinned that sin that is unto death and God gives them up; but the vast host of mankind are yet within the reach of sovereign mercy—"And many of them shall come from the east, and from the west, and shall sit down in the kingdom of heaven."

Look at my text again, and you will see where these people come from. They are to "come from the east and west." The Jews said that they would all come from Palestine, every one of them, every man, woman, and child; that there would not be one in heaven that was not a Jew. And the Pharisees thought that if they were not all Pharisees they could not be saved. But Jesus Christ said there will be many that will come from the east and from the west. There will be a multitude from that far off land of China, for God is doing a great work there, and we hope that the gospel will yet be victorious in that land. There will be a multitude from this western land of England; from the western country beyond the sea, in America; and from the south, in Australia; and from the north, in Canada, Siberia, and Russia. From the uttermost parts of the earth there shall come many to sit down in the kingdom of God.

But I do not think this text is to be understood so much geographically as spiritually. When it says that they "shall come from the east and west," I think it does not refer to nations particularly, but to different kinds of people. Now, "the east and the west" signify those who are the very furthest off from reli-

gion; yet many of them will be saved and get to heaven. There is a class of persons who will always be looked upon as hopeless. Many a time have I heard a man or woman say of such a one, "He cannot be saved: he is too abandoned. What is *he* good for? Ask *him* to go to a place of worship—he was drunk on Saturday night. What would be the use of reasoning with *him?* There is no hope for him. He is a hardened fellow. See what he has done these many years. What good will it be to speak to him?"

Now, hear this, ye who think your fellows worse than yourselves—ye who condemn others, whereas ye are often just as guilty: Jesus Christ says "many shall come from the east and west." There will be many in heaven that were drunkards once. I believe, among that blood-bought throng, there are many who reeled in and out the tavern half their lifetime. But by the power of divine grace they were able to dash the liquor cup to the ground. They renounced the riot of intoxication—fled away from it—and served God. Yes! There will be many in heaven who were drunkards on earth. There will be many harlots: some of the most abandoned will be found there.

You remember the story of Whitefield's once saying that there would be some in heaven who were "the devil's castaways"; some that the devil would hardly think good enough for him, and yet whom Christ would save. Lady Huntingdon once gently hinted that such language was not quite proper. But just at the time there happened to be heard come a ring at the bell and Whitefield went down stairs. Afterwards he came up and said, "Your ladyship, what do you think a poor woman had to say to me just now? She was a sad profligate and she said, 'O, Mr. Whitefield, when you were preaching you told us that Christ would take in the devil's castaways and I am one of them,'" and that was the means of her salvation.

Shall anybody ever check us from preaching to the lowest of the low? I have been accused of getting all the rabble of London around me. God bless the rabble! God save the rabble! then, say I. But suppose they are "the rabble"! Who need the gospel more than they do? Who require to have Christ preached to them more than they do? We have lots of those who preach to ladies and gentlemen and we want someone to preach to the rabble in these degenerate days. Oh! here is comfort for me, for many of the rabble are to come from the east and from the west.

Oh! what would you think if you were to see the difference between some that are in heaven and some that shall be there! there might be found one whose hair hangs across his eyes, his locks are matted, he looks horrible, his bloated eyes start from his face, he grins almost like an idiot, he has drunk away his very brain until life seems to have departed so far as sense and being are concerned; yet I would tell you, "that man is capable of salvation"—and in a few years I might say "look up yonder;" see you that bright star? discern you that man with a crown of pure gold upon his head? do you notice that being clad in robes of sapphire and in garments of light? That is the selfsame man who sat there a poor benighted, almost idiotic being; yet sovereign grace and mercy have saved him! There are none, except those as I have said before, who have sinned the unpardonable sin, who are beyond God's mercy—fetch me out the worst, and still I would preach the gospel to them; fetch me out the vilest, still I would preach to them, because I recollect my master said, "Go ye out into the highways and hedges and compel them to come in that my house may be filled."

"Many shall come from the east and west, and shall sit down with Abraham, and Isaac, and Jacob, in the kingdom of heaven."

They Shall Come

There is one more word I must notice before I have done with this sweet portion—that is the word "shall." Oh! I love God's "shalls" and "wills." There is nothing comparable to them. Let a man say "shall," what is it good for? "I will," says man, and he never performs; "I shall," says he, and he breaks his promise. But it is never so with God's "shalls." If he says, "shall," it shall be; when he says, "will," it will be. Now he has said here, "many shall come." The devil says, "they shall not come;" but "they shall come." Their sins say, "you can't come;" God says, you "shall come." You, yourselves, say, "we won't come;" God says, "you shall come."

Yes! there are some here who are laughing at salvation, who can scoff at Christ, and mock at the gospel; but I tell you some of you shall come yet. "What!" you say, "can God make me become a Christian?" I tell you yes, for herein rests the power of the gospel. It does not ask your consent; but it gets it. It does not say, will you have it, but it makes you willing in the day of God's power. Not against your will, but it makes you willing. It shows you its value, and then you fall in love with it, and straightway you run after it and have it. Many people have said, "we will not have anything to do with religion," yet they have been converted.

I have heard of a man who once went to chapel to hear the singing, and as soon as the minister began to preach, he put his fingers in his ears and would not listen. But by-and-by some tiny insect settled on his face, so that he was obliged to take one finger out of his ear to brush it away. Just then the minister said, "he that hath ears to hear, let him hear." The man listened; and God met with him at that moment to his soul's conversion. He went out a new man, a changed character. He who came in to laugh retired to pray; he who came in to mock went out to bend his knee in penitence: he who entered to spend an idle hour went home to spend an hour in devotion with his God. The sinner became a saint; the profligate became a penitent.

Who knows that there may not be some like that here? The gospel wants not your consent, it gets it. It knocks the enmity out of your heart. You say "I do not want to be saved;" Christ says you shall be. He makes your will turn round, and then you cry, "Lord, save, or I perish." Ah, might heaven exclaim, "I knew I would make you say that;" and then he rejoices over you because he has changed your will and made you willing in the day of his power. If Jesus Christ were to stand on this platform tonight, what would many people do with him? "O!" say some, "we would make him a king." I do not believe it. They would crucify him again if they had the opportunity. If he were to come and say, "Here I am, I love you, will you be saved by me?" Not one of you would consent if you were left to your will. If he should look upon you with those eyes, before whose power the lion would have crouched, if he spoke with that voice which poured forth a cataract of eloquence like a stream of nectar rolling down from the cliffs above, not a single person would come to be his disciple; no, it wants the power of the Spirit to make men come to Jesus Christ.

He himself said, "No man can come to me except the Father who hath sent me draw him." Ah! we want that; and here we have it. They shall come! They shall come! ye may laugh, ye may despise us; but Jesus Christ shall not die for nothing. If some of you reject him there are some that will not. If there are some that are not saved, others *shall* be. Christ *shall* see his seed, he *shall* prolong his days, and the pleasure of the Lord *shall* prosper in his hands. Some think that Christ died and yet that some for whom he died will be lost. I never could understand that doctrine. If Jesus my surety bore my griefs and carried my sorrows, I believe myself to be as secure as the angels in heaven. God cannot ask payment twice. If Christ paid my debt shall I have to pay it again? No.

> Free from sin I walk at large,
> The Saviour's blood's my full
>   discharge;
> At his dear feet content I lay,
> A sinner saved, and homage pay.

They shall come! They shall come! And nought in heaven, nor on earth, nor in hell, can stop them from coming.

And now, thou chief of sinners, list one moment while I call thee to Jesus. There is one person here tonight who thinks himself the worst soul that ever lived. There is one who says to himself, "I do not deserve to be called to Christ I am sure!" Soul! I call thee! thou lost, most wretched outcast, this night, by authority given me of God, I call thee to come to my Savior. Some time ago, when I went into the County Court to see what they were doing, I heard a man's name called out, and immediately the man said, "Make way! make way! they call me!" And up he came. Now, I call the chief of sinners tonight, and let him say, "Make way! Make way doubts! Make way fears! Make way sins! Christ calls me! And if Christ calls me, that is enough!"

I'll to his gracious feet approach
   Whose sceptre mercy gives;
Perhaps he may command my touch!
   And then the suppliant lives.

I can but perish if I go;
   I am resolved to try;
For if I stay away, I know
   I must for ever die.

But, should I die with mercy sought,
   When I the King have tried,
That were to die, (delightful thought!)
   As sinner never died.

Go and try my Savior! Go and try my Savior! If he casts you away after you have sought him, tell it in the pit that Christ would not hear you. But *that* you shall never be allowed to do. It would dishonor the mercy of the covenant, for God to cast away one penitent sinner; and it never shall be while it is written "many shall come from the east and west, and shall sit down with Abraham, and Isaac, and Jacob, in the kingdom of heaven."

The second part of my text is heart-breaking. I could preach with great delight to myself from the first part; but here is a dreary task to my soul, because there are gloomy words here. But, as I have told you, what is written in the Bible must be preached whether it be gloomy or cheerful. There are some ministers who never mention anything about hell. I heard of a minister who once said to his congregation—"If you do not love the Lord Jesus Christ you will be sent to that place which it is not polite to mention." He ought not to have been allowed to preach again, I am sure, if he could not use plain words. Now, if I saw that house on fire over there, do you think I would stand and say, "I believe the operation of combustion is proceeding yonder!" No; I would call out, "Fire! Fire!" and then everybody would know what I meant.

Children of the Kingdom Cast Out

So, if the Bible says, "The children of the kingdom shall be cast out into outer darkness," am I to stand here and mince the matter at all? God forbid. We must speak the truth as it is written. It is a terrible truth, for it says, *"the children of the kingdom* shall be cast out!" Now, who are those children? I will tell you— "The children of the kingdom" are those people who are noted for the externals of piety, but who have nothing of the internals of it. People whom you will see with their Bibles and Hymn Books marching off to chapel as religiously as possible, or going to church as devoutly and demurely as they can, looking as somber and serious as parish beadles, and fancying that they are quite sure to be saved, though their heart is not in the matter, nothing but their bodies. These are the persons who are "the children of the kingdom." They have no grace, no life, no Christ, and they shall be cast into outer darkness.

Again, these people are *the children of pious fathers and mothers.* There is nothing touches a man's heart, mark you, like talking about his mother. I have heard of a swearing sailor, whom nobody could manage, not even the police, who was always making some disturbance wherever he went. Once he went into a place of worship, and no one could keep him still; but a gentleman went up and said to him, "Jack, you had a mother once." With that the tears ran down his cheeks. He said, "Ha! bless you, sir, I had; and I brought her grey hairs with sorrow to the grave, and a pretty fellow I am to be here tonight." He then sat down, quite sobered and subdued by the very mention of his mother.

Ah! and there are some of you "children of the kingdom" who can remember your mothers. Your mother took you on her knee and taught you early to pray: your father tutored you in the ways of godliness. And yet you are here tonight without grace in your heart—without hope of heaven. You are going downwards towards hell as fast as your feet can carry you. There are some of you who have broken your poor mother's heart. Oh! if I could tell you what she has suffered for you when you have at night been indulging in your sin. Do you know what your guilt will be, ye "children of the kingdom," if ye perish after a pious mother's prayers and tears have fallen upon you? I can conceive of no one entering hell with a worse grace than the man who goes there with drops of his mother's tears on his head, and with his father's prayers following him at his heels.

Some of you will inevitably endure this doom, some of you young men and women shall wake up one day and find yourselves in outer darkness, while your parents shall be up there in heaven, looking down upon you with upbraiding eyes, seeming to say, "What! after all we did for you, all we said, are ye come to this?" "Children of the kingdom!" do not think that a pious mother can save you. Do not think because your father was a member of such-and-such a church that his godliness will save you. I can suppose some one standing at heaven's gate and demanding, "Let me in! Let me in!" What for? "Because my mother is in there." Your mother had nothing to do with you. If she was holy, she was holy for herself; if she was evil, she was evil for herself. "But my grandfather prayed for me." That is no use: Did you pray for yourself? "No; I did not." Then grandfathers' prayers and grandmothers' prayers, and fathers' and mothers' prayers, may be piled on the top of one another till they reach the stars, but they never can make a ladder for you to go to heaven by. You must seek

God for yourself; or rather God must seek you. You must have vital experience of godliness in your heart, or else you are lost, even though all your friends were in heaven.

That was a dreadful dream which a pious mother once had, and told to her children. She thought the judgment-day was come. The great books were opened. They all stood before God. And Jesus Christ said, "Separate the chaff from the wheat; put the goats on the left hand, and the sheep on the right." The mother dreamed that she and her children were standing just in the middle of the great assembly. And the angel came, and said, "I must take the mother: she is a sheep: she must go to the right hand. The children are goats: they must go on the left." She thought as she went her children clutched her, and said, "Mother, can we part? Must we be separated?" She then put her arms around them, and seemed to say, "My children, I would, if possible, take you with me." But in a moment the angel touched her: her cheeks were dried, and, now, overcoming natural affection, being rendered supernatural and sublime, resigned to God's will, she said, "My children, I taught you well, I trained you up, and you forsook the ways of God, and now all I have to say is, Amen to your condemnation." Thereupon they were snatched away, and she saw them in perpetual torment, while she was in heaven.

Young man, what will you think, when the last day comes, to hear Christ say, "Depart, ye cursed!" And there will be a voice just behind him, saying, Amen. And as you inquire whence came the voice, you will find it was your mother. Or, young woman, when thou art cast away into outer darkness, what will you think to hear a voice saying, Amen. And as you look, there sits your father, his lips still moving with the solemn curse. "Ah! children of the kingdom," the penitent reprobates will enter heaven, many of them; publicans and sinners will get there; repenting drunkards and swearers will be saved; but many of "the children of the kingdom" will be cast out. Oh! to think that you who have been so well trained should be lost, while many of the worse will be saved. It will be the hell of hell for you to look up and see there "poor Jack" the drunkard lying in Abraham's bosom, while you who have had a pious mother are cast into hell, simply because you would not believe on the Lord Jesus Christ, but put his gospel from you, and lived and died without it! That were the very sting of all, to see ourselves cast away, when the chief of sinners finds salvation.

They Shall Be Cast Out

Now list to me a little while—I will not detain you long—whilst I undertake the doleful task of telling you what is to become of these "children of the kingdom." Jesus Christ says, they are to be "cast into outer darkness, where there is weeping and gnashing of teeth."

First, notice, they are to be *cast out*. They are not said to go; but when they come to heaven's gates they are to be *cast* out. As soon as hypocrites arrive at the gates of heaven, Justice will say, "There he comes! there he comes! he spurned a father's prayers, and mocked a mother's tears. He has forced his way downward against all the advantages mercy has supplied. And now, there he comes. Gabriel, take the man." The angel binding you hand and foot, holds you one single moment over the mouth of the chasm. He bids you look down—down—down. There is no bottom: and you hear coming up from the abyss, "sullen moans, and hollow groans, and shrieks of tortured ghosts." You quiver,

your bones melt like wax, and your marrow quakes within you. Where is now thy might? and where thy boasting and bragging? Ye shriek and cry, ye beg for mercy; but the angel with one tremendous grasp, seizes you fast, and then hurls you down, with the cry, "Away, away!" And down you go to the pit that is bottomless, and roll for ever downward—downward—downward—ne'er to find a resting-place for the sole of your foot. Ye shall be cast out.

And *where are you to be cast to?* Ye are to be cast "into outer darkness;" ye are to be put in the place where there will be no hope. For, by "light," in Scripture, we understand "hope"; and you are to be put "into outer darkness," where there is no light—no hope. Is there a man here who has no hope? I cannot suppose such a person. One of you, perhaps, says, "I am thirty pounds in debt, and shall be sold up by-and-by; but I have a hope that I may get a loan, and so escape my difficulty." Says another, "My business is ruined, but things may take a turn yet—I have a hope." Says another, "I am in great distress, but I hope that God will provide for me." Another says, "I am fifty pounds in debt; I am sorry for it: but I will set these strong hands to work, and do my best to get out of it." One of you thinks a friend is dying; but you have a hope that perhaps the fever may take a turn—that he may yet live.

But, in hell, there is no hope. They have not even the hope of dying—the hope of being annihilated. They are for ever—for ever—for ever—lost! On every chain in hell, there is written "for ever." In the fires, there, blaze out the words, "for ever." Up above their heads, they read, "for ever." Their eyes are galled, and their hearts are pained with the thought that it is "for ever." Oh! if I could tell you tonight that hell would one day be burned out, and that those who were lost might be saved, there would be a jubilee in hell at the very thought of it. But it cannot be—it is *"for ever"* they are "cast into outer darkness."

But I want to get over this as quickly as I can, for who can bear to talk thus to his fellow creatures? What is it that the lost are doing? They are "weeping and gnashing their teeth." Do you gnash your teeth now? You would not do it except you were in pain and agony. Well, in hell there is always gnashing of teeth. And do you know why? There is one gnashing his teeth at his companion, and mutters—"I was led into hell by you; you led me astray, you taught me to drink the first time." And the other gnashes his teeth and says, "What if I did, you made me worse than I should have been in after times." There is a child who looks at her mother, and says, "Mother, you trained me up to vice." And the mother gnashes her teeth again at the child, and says, "I have no pity for you, for you excelled me in it and led me into deeper sin." Fathers gnash their teeth at their sons, and sons at their fathers.

And, methinks, if there are any who will have to gnash their teeth more than others, it will be seducers, when they see those whom they have led from the paths of virtue, and hear them saying, "Ah! we are glad you are in hell with us, you deserve it, for you led us here." Have any of you, tonight, upon your consciences the fact that you have led others to the pit? O may sovereign grace forgive you. "We have gone astray like lost sheep," said David. Now, a lost sheep never goes astray alone if it is one of a flock. I lately read of a sheep that leaped over the parapet of a bridge, and was followed by every one of the flock. So if one man goes astray he leads others with him. Some of you will have to account for others' sins when you get to hell, as well as your own. Oh, what

"weeping and gnashing of teeth" there will be in that pit!

A Final Warning and Plea

Now shut the black book. Who wants to say any more about it? I have warned you solemnly. I have told you of the wrath to come! The evening darkens, and the sun is setting. Ah! and the evenings darken with some of you. I can see gray-headed men here. Are your gray hairs a crown of glory or a fool's cap to you? Are you on the very verge of heaven, or are you tottering on the brink of your grave, and sinking down to perdition?

Let me warn you, gray-headed men; your evening is coming. O poor tottering gray-head, wilt thou take the last step into the pit? Let a young child step before thee and beg thee to consider. There is thy staff—it has nothing of earth to rest upon; and now, ere thou diest, bethink thyself this night; let seventy years of sin start up; let the ghosts of thy forgotten transgressions march before thine eyes. What wilt thou do with seventy wasted years to answer for, with seventy years of criminality to bring before God? God give thee grace this night to repent and to put thy trust in Jesus.

And you middle-aged men are not safe: the evening lowers with you too; you may soon die. A few mornings ago, I was roused early from my bed, by the request that I would hasten to see a dying man. I hurried off with all speed to see the poor creature; but when I reached the house he was dead—a corpse. As I stood in the room, I thought, "Ah! that man little thought he should die so soon." There were his wife and children and friends—they little thought he should die, for he was hale, strong, and hearty but a few days before. None of you have a lease of your lives. If you have, where is it? Go and see if you have it anywhere in your chests at home. No! ye may die tomorrow. Let me therefore warn you by the mercy of God; let me speak to you as a brother may speak; for I love you, you know I do, and would press the matter home to your hearts. Oh to be amongst the many who shall be accepted in Christ—how blessed that will be! And God has said that whosoever shall call on his name shall be saved: he casts out none that come unto him through Christ.

And now, ye youths and maidens, one word with you. Perhaps ye think that religion is not for you. "Let us be happy," say you: "let us be merry and joyous." How long, young man, how long? "Till I am twenty-one." Are you sure that you will live till then? Let me tell you one thing. If you do live till that time, if you have no heart for God now, you will have none then. Men do not get better if left alone. It is with them as with a garden: if you let it alone, and permit weeds to grow, you will not expect to find it better in six months—but worse. Ah! men talk as if they could repent when they like. It is the work of God to give us repentance. Some even say, "I shall turn to God on such-and-such a day." Ah! If you felt aright, you would say, "I must run to God, and ask him to give me repentance now; lest I should die before I have found Jesus Christ my Savior."

Now one word in conclusion. I have told you of heaven and hell; what is the way, then, to escape from hell and to be found in heaven? I will not tell you my old tale again to-night. I recollect when I told it you before, a good friend in the crowd said, "Tell us something fresh old fellow." Now really in preaching ten times a week, we cannot always say things fresh. You have heard John Gough, and you know he tells his tales over again. I have nothing but the old gospel. "He that believeth and is baptized shall be saved." There is nothing here of works. It does not say "He who is a good man shall be saved," but "he who believes and is baptized."

Well, what is it to believe? It is to put your trust entirely upon Jesus. Poor Peter once believed, and Jesus Christ said to him, "Come on, Peter, walk to me on the water." Peter went stepping along on the tops of the waves without sinking; but when he looked at the waves, he began to tremble, and down he went. Now, poor sinner, Christ says, "Come on; walk on in your sins; come to me;" and if you do, he will give you power. If you believe on Christ, you will be able to walk over your sins—to tread upon them, and overcome them.

I can remember the time when my sins first stared me in the face. I thought myself the most accursed of all men. I had not committed any very great open transgressions against God; but I recollected that I had been well trained and tutored, and I thought my sins were thus greater than other people's. I cried to God to have mercy, but I feared that he would not pardon me. Month after month I cried to God, but he did not hear me, and I knew not what it was to be saved. Sometimes I was so weary of the world that I desired to die: but then I recollected that there was a worse world after this, and that it would be an ill matter to rush before my Maker unprepared. At times I wickedly thought God a most heartless tyrant, because he did not answer my prayer; and then, at others, I thought, "I deserve his displeasure; if he sends me to hell, he will be just."

But I remember the hour when I stepped into a place of worship, and saw a tall thin man step into the pulpit: I have never seen him from that day, and probably never shall, till we meet in heaven. He opened the Bible, and read, with a feeble voice, "Look unto me and be ye saved, all the ends of the earth; for

I am God, and beside him there is none else." Ah! thought I, I am one of the ends of the earth; and then, turning round, and fixing his gaze on me, as if he knew me, the minister said, "Look, look, look." Why, I thought I had a great deal to *do*, but I found it was only to *look*. I thought I had a garment to spin out for myself: but I found that if I looked, Christ would give me a garment.

Look, sinner, that is to be saved. Look unto him all ye ends of the earth, and be saved. This is what the Jews did, when Moses held up the brazen serpent. He said, "Look!" and they looked. The serpents might be twisting round them, and they might be nearly dead; but they simply looked, and the moment they looked, the serpents dropped off, and they were healed. Look to Jesus, sinner. "None but Jesus can do helpless sinners good." There is a hymn we often sing, but which I do not think is quite right, it says,

> Venture on him, venture wholly;
> Let no other trust intrude.

Now, it is no venture to trust in Christ, not in the least. He who trusts in Christ is quite secure. I recollect that when dear John Hyatt was dying, Matthew Wilks said to him, in his usual tone, "Well, John, could you trust your soul in the hands of Jesus Christ now?" "Yes," said he, "a million! a million souls!" I am sure that every Christian that has ever trusted in Christ can say, "Amen" to that. Trust in him; he will never deceive you. My blessed Master will never cast you away.

I cannot speak much longer, and I have only to thank you for your kindness. I never saw so large a number so still and quiet. I really think, after all the hard things that have been said, that the English people know who loves them, and that they will stand by the man who stands by them. I thank every one of you, and above all, I beg you, if there be reason or sense in what I have said, bethink yourselves of what you are, and may the blessed Spirit reveal to you your state! May he show you that you are dead, that you are lost, ruined. May he make you feel what a dreadful thing it would be to sink into hell! May he point you to heaven! May he take you as the angel did of old, and put his hand upon you, and say, "Flee! flee! flee! Look to the mountain; look not behind thee; stay not in all the plain." And may we all meet in heaven at last; and there we shall be happy for ever.

One of Spurgeon's most reprinted sermons is "Songs in the Night," which was delivered early in his career at the New Park Street Baptist Church. "Any man can sing in the day," Spurgeon says. But the one who has faith in God can sing songs in the night because God Himself is the author and subject of his songs. Spurgeon finds that such songs, impossible for natural man, are "one of the best arguments in all the world in favor of your religion." Throughout most of the sermon Spurgeon addresses the children of God, but he turns to sinners in his conclusion, as was his custom, and concludes by warning that there is a night coming in which there will be no songs of joy.

CHAPTER FOUR

Songs in the Night

But none saith, Where is God my Maker, who giveth songs in the night?
(Job 35:10).

Elihu was a wise man, exceedingly wise, though not as wise as the all-wise Jehovah, who sees light in the clouds, and finds order in confusion; hence Elihu, being much puzzled at beholding Job so afflicted, cast about him to find the cause of it, and he very wisely hit upon one of the most likely reasons, although it did not happen to be the right one in Job's case. He said within himself, "Surely, if men are sorely tried and troubled, it is because, while they think about their troubles, and distress themselves about their fears, they do not say, 'Where is God my Maker, who giveth songs in the night?'" Elihu's reason is right in the majority of cases. The great cause of a Christian's distress, the reason of the depths of sorrow into which many believers are plunged, is simply this—that while they are looking about, on the right hand and on the left, to see how they may escape their troubles, they forget to look to the hills whence all real help cometh; they do not say, "Where is God my Maker, who giveth songs in the night?"

We shall, however, leave that enquiry, and dwell upon those sweet words, "God my Maker, who giveth songs in the night." The world hath its night. It seemeth necessary that it should have one. The sun shineth by day, and men go forth to their labors; but they grow weary, and nightfall cometh on, like a sweet boon from heaven. The darkness draweth the curtains, and shutteth out the light, which might prevent our eyes from slumber; while the sweet, calm stillness of the night permits us to rest upon the bed of ease, and there forget awhile our cares, until the morning sun appeareth, and an angel puts his hand upon the curtain, undraws it once again, touches our eyelids, and bids us rise, and proceed to the labors of the day. Night is one of the greatest blessings men enjoy; we have many reasons to thank God for it.

Yet night is to many a gloomy season. There is "the pestilence that walketh in darkness;" there is "the terror by night"; there is the dread of robbers and of fell disease, with all those fears that the timorous know, when they have no light wherewith they can discern different objects. It is then they fancy that spiritual creatures walk the earth; though, if they knew rightly, they would find it to be true that—

Millions of spiritual creatures walk
    the earth
Unseen, both when we wake, and
    when we sleep—

and that at all times they are round about us, not more by night than by day.

Night is the season of terror and alarm to most men; yet even night hath its songs. Have you never stood by the seaside at night, and heard the pebbles sing, and the waves chant God's praises? Or have you never risen from your couch, and thrown up the window of your chamber, and listened there? Listened to what? Silence—save now and then a murmuring sound, which seems sweet music then. And have you not fancied that you have heard the harps of gold playing in heaven? Did you not conceive that yon stars—those eyes of God, looking down on you, were also mouths of song, that every star was singing God's glory, singing as it shone its mighty Maker's well-deserved praise? Night hath its songs; we need not much poetry in our spirit to catch the song of night, and hear the spheres as they chant praises which are loud to the heart, though they be silent to the ear— the praises of the mighty God, who bears up the unpillared arch of heaven, and moves the stars in their courses.

Man, too, like the great world in which he lives, must have his night. For it is true that man is like the world around him; he is himself a little world; he resembles the world in almost everything; and if the world hath its night, so hath man. And many a night do we have—nights of sorrow, nights of persecution, nights of doubt, nights of bewilderment, nights of affliction, nights of anxiety, nights of ignorance, nights of all kinds, which press upon our spirits, and terrify our souls. But blessed be God, the Christian man can say, "My God giveth me songs in the night."

It is not necessary, I take it, to prove to you that Christian men have nights; for if you are Christians, you will find that *you* have them, and you will not want any proof, for nights will come quite often enough. I will, therefore, proceed at once to the subject; and notice, with regard to songs in the night, first, *their source*, God giveth them; secondly, *their matter*,—what do we sing about in the night? Thirdly, *their excellence*— they are hearty songs, and they are sweet ones; and fourthly, *their uses*, their benefits to ourselves and others.

The Author of Our Songs in the Night

I. First, songs in the night—WHO IS THE AUTHOR OF THEM? *"God,"* says the text, our "Maker, giveth songs in the night."

Any man can sing in the day. When the cup is full, man draws inspiration from it; when wealth rolls in abundance around him, any man can sing to the praise of a God who gives a plenteous harvest, or sends home a loaded argosy. It is easy enough for an Aeolian harp to whisper music when the winds blow; the difficulty is for music to come when no wind bloweth. It is easy to sing when we can read the notes by daylight; but he is the skillful singer who can sing when there is not a ray of light by which to read—who sings from his heart, and not from a book that he can see, because he has no means of reading, save from that inward book of his own living spirit, whence notes of gratitude pour forth in songs of praise.

No man can make a song in the night himself; he may attempt it, but he will find how difficult it is. It is not natural to sing in trouble, "Bless the Lord, O my soul, and all that is within me bless his holy name," for that is a daylight song. But it was a divine song which Habakkuk sang when in the night he said, "Although the fig-tree shall not blossom," and so on, "yet I will rejoice in the Lord, I will joy in the God of my salvation." Methinks, on the margin of the Red Sea, any man could have made a song like that of Moses, "The horse and his rider hath he thrown into the sea;" the difficulty would have been to compose a song before the Red Sea had been divided, and to sing it before Pharaoh's hosts had been drowned, while yet the darkness of doubt and fear was resting on Israel's hosts. Songs in the night come only from God; they are not in the power of man.

But what does the text mean, when it asserts that God giveth songs in the night? We think we find two answers to the question. The first is, that usually in the night of a Christian's experience, *God is his only song*. If it be daylight in my heart, I can sing songs touching my graces, songs touching my sweet experiences, songs touching my duties, songs touching my labors; but let the night come, my graces appear to have withered; my evidences, though they are there, are hidden; now I have nothing left to sing of but my God. It is strange that, when God gives his children mercies, they generally set their hearts more on the mercies than on the Giver of them; but when the night comes, and he sweeps all the mercies away, then at once they each say, "Now, my God, I have nothing to sing of but thee; I must come to thee, and to thee only. I had cisterns once; they were full of water; I drank from them then; but now the created streams are dry, sweet Lord, I quaff no stream but thine own self, I drink from no fount but from thee."

Ay, child of God, thou knowest what I say; or if thou dost not understand it yet, thou wilt do so by-and-by! It is in the night we sing of God, and of God alone. Every string is tuned, and every power hath its tribute of song, while we praise God, and nothing else. We can sacrifice to ourselves in daylight; we only sacrifice to God by night. We can sing high praises to ourselves when all is joyful; but we cannot sing praise to any save our God when circumstances are untoward, and providences appear adverse. God alone can furnish us with songs in the night.

And yet again, not only does God give the song in the night, because he is the only subject upon which we can sing then, but because *he is the only One who inspires songs in the night*. Bring me a poor, melancholy, distressed child of God; I seek to tell him precious promises, and whisper to him sweet words of comfort; he listeneth not to me, he is like the deaf adder, he heeds not the voice of the charmer, charm he never so wisely. Send him round to all the comforting divines, and all the holy Barnabases who ever preached, and they will do very little with him; they will not be able to squeeze a song out of him, do what they may. He is drinking the gall and wormwood; he says, "O Lord, I have eaten ashes like bread, and mingled my drink with weeping;" and comfort him as you may, it will be only a woeful note or two of mournful resignation that you will get from him; you will evoke no psalms of praise, no hallelujahs, no joyful sonnets.

But let God come to his child in the night, let him whisper in his ear as he lies on his bed, and now you can see his eyes glisten in the night season. Do you not hear him say—

'Tis Paradise, if thou art here;
If thou depart, 'tis hell?

I could not have cheered him: it is God that has done it; for God "giveth songs in the night." It is marvellous, brethren, how one sweet word of God will make many songs for Christians. One word of God is like a piece of gold, and the Christian is the gold-beater, and he can hammer that promise out for whole weeks. I can say myself, I have lived on one promise for weeks, and wanted no other. I had just simply to hammer the promise out into gold-leaf, and plate my whole existence with joy from it. The Christian gets his songs from God; God gives him inspiration, and teaches him how to sing: "God my Maker, who giveth songs in the night." So, then, poor Christian, thou needest not go pumping up thy poor heart to make it glad. Go to thy Maker, and ask him to give thee a song in the night; for thou art a poor dry well. You have heard it said that, when a pump is dry, you must pour water down it first of all, and then you will get some up. So, Christian, when thou art dry, go to thy God, ask him to pour some joy down thee, and then thou wilt get more joy up from thine own heart. Do not go to this comforter or that, for you will find them "Job's comforters" after all; but go thou first and foremost to thy Maker, for he is the great Composer of songs and Teacher of music, he it is who can teach thee how to sing.

The Subject of Our Songs in the Night

II. Thus we have dwelt upon the first point; now turn to the second. WHAT IS GENERALLY THE MATTER CONTAINED IN A SONG IN THE NIGHT? What do we sing about?

Why, I think, when we sing by night, there are three things we sing about. Either we sing about the day that is over, or about the night itself, or else about the morrow that is to come. Those are all sweet themes, when God our Maker gives us songs in the night. In the midst of the night, the most usual method is for Christians to sing about *the day that is over.* The man says, "It is night now, but I can remember when it was daylight. Neither moon nor stars appear at present; but I recollect when I saw the sun. I have no evidences just now; but there was a time when I could say, 'I know that my Redeemer liveth.' I have my doubts and fears at this present moment; but it is not long since I could say with full assurance, 'I know that he shed his blood for me.' It may be darkness now; but I know the promises *were sweet;* I know I had blessed seasons in his house. I am quite sure of this, I used

to enjoy myself in the ways of the Lord; and though now my path is strewn with thorns, I know it is the King's highway. It was a way of pleasantness once, it will be a way of pleasantness again. 'I will remember the years of the right hand of the Most High.'"

Christian, perhaps the best song thou canst sing, to cheer thee in the night, is the song of yestermorn. Remember, it was not always night with thee; night is a new thing to thee. Once thou hadst a glad heart and a buoyant spirit; once thine eye was full of fire; once thy foot was light; once thou couldst sing for very joy and ecstasy of heart. Well, then, remember that God who made thee sing yesterday has not left thee in the night. He is not a daylight God who cannot know his children in darkness, but he loves thee now as much as ever; though he has left thee for a little while, it is to prove thee, to make thee trust him better, and love and serve him more. Let me tell you some of the sweet things of which a Christian may make a song when it is night with him.

If we are going to sing of the things of yesterday, let us begin with what God did for us in past times. My beloved brethren, you will find it a sweet subject for song at times to begin to sing of electing love and covenant mercies. When thou thyself art low, it is well to sing of the Fountain-head of mercy, of that blessed decree wherein thou wast ordained unto eternal life, and of that glorious Man who undertook thy redemption; of that solemn covenant signed, and sealed, and ratified, in all things ordered well; of that everlasting love which, ere the hoary mountains were begotten, or ere the aged hills were children, chose thee, loved thee firmly, loved thee fast, loved thee well, loved thee eternally.

I tell thee, believer, if thou canst go back to the years of eternity,—if thou canst in thy mind run back to that period before the everlasting hills were fashioned, or the fountains of the great deep were scooped out, and if thou canst see thy God inscribing thy name in his eternal Book—if thou canst read in his loving heart eternal thoughts of love to thee, thou wilt find this a charming means of giving thee songs in the night. There are no songs like those which come from electing love, no sonnets like those that are dictated by meditations on discriminating mercy.

Think, Christian, of the eternal covenant, and thou wilt get a song in the night. But if thou hast not a voice tuned to so high a key as that, let me suggest some other mercies thou mayest sing of; they are the mercies thou hast experienced. What, man! canst thou not sing a little of that blessed hour when Jesus met thee, when a blind slave thou wast sporting with death, and he saw thee, and said, "Come, poor slave, come with me"? Canst thou not sing of that rapturous moment when he snapped thy fetters, dashed thy chains to the earth, and said, "I am the Breaker; I am come to break thy chains, and set thee free"? Though thou art ever so gloomy now, canst thou forget that happy morning when, in the house of God, thy voice was loud, almost as a seraph's voice, in praise, for thou couldst sing, "I am forgiven! I am forgiven; a monument of grace, a sinner saved by blood"? Go back, man; sing of that moment, and then thou wilt have a song in the night.

Or, if thou hast almost forgotten that, then surely thou hast some precious milestone along the road of life that is not quite overgrown with moss, on which thou canst read some happy inscription of God's mercy towards thee. What! didst thou never have a sickness like that which thou art suffering now, and did he not raise thee up from it? Wast thou never poor before, and did he

not supply thy wants? Wast thou never in straits before, and did he not deliver thee? Come, man! I beseech thee, go to the river of thine experience, and pull up a few bulrushes, and weave them into an ark, wherein thine infant faith may float safely on the stream. I bid thee not forget what God hath done for thee. What! hast thou buried thy diary? I beseech thee, man, turn over the book of thy remembrance. Canst thou not see some sweet hill Mizar? Canst thou not think of some blessed hour when the Lord met with thee at Hermon? Hast thou never been on the Delectable Mountains? Hast thou never been fetched from the den of lions? Hast thou never escaped the jaw of the lion, and the paw of the bear? Nay, O man, I know thou hast! Go back, then, a little way, to the mercies of the past; and though it is dark now, light up the lamps of yesterday, and they shall glitter through the darkness, and thou shalt find that God hath given thee a song in the night.

"Ay!" says one, "but you know that, when we are in the dark, we cannot see the mercies that God has given us. It is all very well for you to talk to us thus, but we cannot get hold of them." I remember an old experimental Christian speaking about the great pillars of our faith; he was a sailor, and we were then on board ship, and there were sundry huge posts on the shore, to which the vessels were usually fastened by throwing a cable over them. After I had told him a great many promises, he said, "I know they are good promises, but I cannot get near enough to shore to throw my cable around them; that is the difficulty." Now, it often happens that God's past mercies and lovingkindnesses would be good sure posts to hold on to, but we have not faith enough to throw our cable around them, so we go slipping down the stream of unbelief, because we cannot stay ourselves by our former mercies.

I will, however, give you something over which I think you can throw your cable. If God has never been kind to you, one thing you surely know, and that is, he has been kind to others. Come, now; if thou art in ever so great straits, surely there have been others in greater straits. What! art thou lower down than poor Jonah was when he went to the bottom of the mountains? Art thou worse off than thy Master when he had not where to lay his head? What! conceivest thou thyself to be the worst of the worst? Look at Job there, scraping himself with a potsherd, and sitting on a dunghill. Art thou as low as he? Yet Job rose up, and was richer than before; and out of the depths Jonah came, and preached the Word; and our Savior Jesus hath mounted to his throne.

O Christian, only think of what God has done for others! If thou canst not recollect that he has done anything for thee, yet remember, I beseech thee, what his usual rule is, and do not judge hardly of my God. You remember when Benhadad was overcome and fled, his servants said to him, "Behold now, we have heard that the kings of the house of Israel are merciful kings; let us, I pray thee, put on sackcloth on our loins, and ropes upon our heads, and go out to the king of Israel: peradventure he will save thy life." So they girded sackcloth on their loins, and put ropes on their heads, and said, "Thy servant Benhadad saith, 'I pray thee, let me live.'" What said the king? "Is he yet alive? he is my brother." And truly, poor soul, if thou hadst never had a merciful God, yet others have had; the King of kings is merciful; go and try him. If thou art ever so low in thy troubles, look to the hills, from whence cometh thy help. Others have had help therefrom, and so mayest thou. Up might start hundreds of God's children, and show us their hands full of comforts and mercies; and they could say, "The Lord gave us these without money and without price; and why should he not give to thee also, seeing that thou too art the King's son?"

Thus, Christian, thou mayest get a song in the night out of other people, if thou canst not get a song from thyself. Never be ashamed of taking a leaf out of another man's experience book. If thou canst find no good leaf in thine own, tear one out of someone else's; if thou hast no cause to be grateful to God in darkness, or canst not find cause in thine own experience, go to someone else, and, if thou canst, harp God's praise in the dark, and like the nightingale, sing his praise sweetly when all the world has gone to rest; sing in the night of the mercies of yesterday.

But I think, beloved, there is never so dark a night but there is something to sing about, even *concerning that night;* for there is one thing I am sure we can sing about, let the night be ever so dark, and that is, "It is of the Lord's mercies that we are not consumed, and because his compassions fail not." If we cannot sing very loudly, yet we can sing a little low tune, something like this, "He hath not dealt with us after our sins, nor rewarded us according to our iniquities." "Oh!" says one, "I do not know where I shall get my dinner tomorrow; I am a poor wretch." So you may be, my dear friend; but you are not so poor as you deserve to be. Do not be mightily offended about that; if you are, you are no child of God; for the child of God acknowledges that he has no right to the least of God's mercies, but that they come through the channel of grace alone. As long as I am out of hell, I have no right to grumble; and if I were in hell, I should have no right to complain, for I felt, when convinced of sin, that never creature deserved to go there more than

I did. We have no cause to murmur; we can lift up our hands, and say, "Night! thou art dark, but thou mightest have been darker. I am poor, but if I could not have been poorer, I might have been sick. I am poor and sick, yet I have some friends left; my lot cannot be so bad but it might have been worse."

Therefore, Christian, you will always have one thing to sing about, "Lord, I thank thee it is not all darkness!" Besides, however dark the night is, there is always a star or moon. There is scarcely a night that we have, but there are just one or two little lamps burning in the sky, and however dark it may be, I think you may find some little comfort, some little joy, some little mercy left, and some little promise to cheer thy spirit. The stars are not put out, are they? Nay, if thou canst not see them, they are there; but methinks one or two must be shining on thee, therefore give God a song in the night. If thou hast only one star, bless God for that one, and perhaps he will make it two; and if thou hast only two stars, bless God twice for the two stars, and perhaps he will make them four. Try, then, if thou canst not find a song in the night.

But, beloved, there is another thing of which we can sing yet more sweetly; and that is, we can sing of *the day that is to come*. Often do I cheer myself with the thought of the coming of the Lord. We preach now, perhaps, with little success; "the kingdoms of this world" have not yet "become the kingdoms of our God and of his Christ." We are laboring, but we do not see the fruit of our labor. Well, what then? We shall not always labor in vain, or spend our strength for nought. A day is coming when every minister of Christ shall speak with unction, when all the servants of God shall preach with power, and when colossal systems of heathenism shall tumble from their pedestals, and mighty, gigan-

tic delusions shall be scattered to the winds. The shout shall be heard, "Alleluia! Alleluia! the Lord God Omnipotent reigneth."

For that day do I look; it is to the bright horizon of Christ's second coming that I turn my eyes. My anxious expectation is, that the blessed Sun of righteousness will soon arise with healing in his wings, that the oppressed shall be righted, that despotism shall be cut down, that liberty shall be established, that peace shall be made lasting, and that the glorious liberty of the children of God shall be extended throughout the known world. Christian! if it is night with thee, think of the morrow; cheer up thy heart with the thought of the coming of thy Lord. Be patient, for you know who has said, "Behold, I come quickly; and my reward is with me, to give every man according as his work shall be."

One thought more upon that point. There is another sweet tomorrow of which we hope to sing in the night. Soon, beloved, you and I shall lie on our dying bed, and we shall not lack a song in the night then: and I do not know where we shall get that song, if we do not get it from the tomorrow. Kneeling by the bed of an apparently dying saint recently, I said, "Well, sister, the Lord has been very precious to you; you can rejoice in his covenant mercies, and his past lovingkindnesses." She put out her hand, and said, "Ah, sir! do not talk about them now; I want the sinner's Savior as much now as ever; it is not a saint's Savior I want, it is still a sinner's Savior that I need, for I am a sinner still." I found that I could not comfort her with the past; so I reminded her of the golden streets, of the gates of pearl, of the walls of jasper, of the harps of gold, of the songs of bliss, and then her eyes glistened; she said, "Yes, I shall be there soon; I shall see them by-and-by;" and then she seemed so glad.

Ah, believer, you may always cheer yourself with that thought! Thy head may be crowned with thorny troubles now, but it shall wear a starry crown presently; thy hand may be filled with cares, it shall grasp a harp soon, a harp full of music. Thy garments may be soiled with dust now; they shall be white by-and-by. Wait a little longer. Ah, beloved! how despicable our troubles and trials will seem when we look back upon them! Looking at them here in the prospect, they seem immense; but when we get to heaven, they will seem to us just nothing at all; we shall talk to one another about them in heaven, and find all the more to converse about, according as we have suffered more here below. Let us go on, therefore; and if the night be ever so dark, remember there is not a night that shall not have a morning; and that morning is to come by-and-by. When sinners are lost in darkness, *we* shall lift up our eyes in everlasting light. Surely I need not dwell longer on this thought. There is matter enough for songs in the night in the past, the present, and the future.

The Excellences of Our Songs in the Night

III. And now I want to tell you, very briefly, WHAT ARE THE EXCELLENCES OF SONGS IN THE NIGHT ABOVE ALL OTHER SONGS.

In the first place, when you hear a man singing a song in the night—I mean in the night of trouble—you may be quite sure it is *a hearty one*. Many of you sing very heartily now; I wonder whether you would sing as loudly if there were a stake or two in Smithfield for all of you who dared to do it. If you sang under pain and penalty, that would show your heart to be in your song. We can all sing very nicely indeed when everybody else sings; it is the easiest thing in the world to open our mouth, and let the words come out; but when the devil puts his hand over our mouth, can we sing then? Can you say, "Though he slay me, yet will I trust in him"? That is hearty singing, that is real song that springs up in the night.

Again, the song we sing in the night will be *lasting*. Many songs we hear our fellow-creatures singing will not do to sing by-and-by. They can sing now rollicking drinking songs; but they will not sing them when they come to die. No; but the Christian who can sing in the night, will not have to leave off his song; he may keep on singing it for ever. He may put his foot in Jordan's stream, and continue his melody; he may wade through it, and keep on singing still until he is landed safe in heaven; and when he is there, there need not be a pause in his strain, but in a nobler, sweeter song he may still continue singing the Savior's power to save.

Again, the songs we warble in the night are those that show we have *real faith in God*. Many men have just enough faith to trust God as far as providence goes as they think right; but true faith can sing when its possessors cannot see, it can take hold of God when they cannot discern him.

Songs in the night, too, prove that we have *true courage*. Many sing by day who are silent by night, they are afraid of thieves and robbers; but the Christian who sings in the night proves himself to be a courageous character. It is the bold Christian who can sing God's sonnets in the darkness.

He who can sing songs in the night, proves also that he has *true love to Christ*. It is not love to Christ merely to praise him while everybody else praises him; to walk arm in arm with him when he has the crown on his head, is no great thing to do. To walk with Christ in rags, is something more. To believe in Christ when he is shrouded in darkness, to stick hard and fast by the Savior when all men speak ill of him, and forsake him—that proves true faith and love. He who singeth a song to Christ in the night, singeth the best song in all the world, for he singeth from the heart.

The Use of Our Songs in the Night

IV. I will not dwell further on the excellences of night songs, but just, in the last place, SHOW YOU THEIR USE.

Well, beloved, it is very useful to sing in the night of our troubles, first, *because it will cheer ourselves*. When some of you were boys, living in the country, and had some distance to go alone at night, do you not remember how you whistled and sang to keep your courage up? Well, what we do in the natural world, we ought to do in the spiritual. There is nothing like singing to keep up our spirits. When we have been in trouble, we have often thought ourselves to be well-nigh overwhelmed with difficulty; so we have said, "Let us have a song." We have begun to sing; and we have proved the truth of what Martin Luther says, "The devil cannot bear singing, he does not like music."

It was so in Saul's day; an evil spirit rested on him, but when David played his harp, the evil spirit went from him. This is usually the case; and if we can begin to sing, we shall remove our fears. I like to hear servants sometimes humming a tune at their work; I love to hear a ploughman in the country singing as he goes along with his horses. Why not? You say he has no time to praise God; but if he can sing a song, surely he can sing a psalm, it will take no more time. Singing is the best thing to purge ourselves of evil thoughts. Keep your mouth full of songs, and you will often keep your heart full of praises; keep on singing as long as you can, you will find it a good method of driving away your fears.

Sing in trouble, again, *because God loves to hear his people sing in the night*. At no time does God love his children's singing so well as when he has hidden his face from them, and they are all in darkness. "Ah!" says God, "that is true faith that can make them sing praises when I do not appear to them; I know there is faith in them, that makes them lift up their hearts, even when I seem to withhold from them all my tender mercies and all my compassions." Sing then, Christian, for singing pleases God. In heaven we read that the angels are employed in singing, be you employed in the same way; for by no better means can you gratify the Almighty One of Israel, who stoops from his high throne to observe us poor, feeble creatures of a day.

Sing, again, for another reason; *because it will cheer your companions*. If any of them are in the valley and in the darkness with you, it will be a great help to comfort them. John Bunyan tells us that, as Christian was going through the valley, he found it a dreadful place; horrible demons and hobgoblins were all about him, and poor Christian thought he must perish for certain; but just when his doubts were the strongest, he heard a sweet voice; he listened to it, and he heard a man in front of him singing, "Yea, though I walk through the valley of the shadow of death, I will fear no evil." Now, that man did not know who was near him, but he was unwittingly cheering a pilgrim behind.

Christian, when you are in trouble, sing; you do not know who is near you. Sing! perhaps you will get a good companion by it. Sing! perhaps there will be another heart cheered by your song. There is some broken spirit, it may be, that will be bound up by your sonnets. Sing! there is some poor distressed brother, perhaps, shut up in the Castle of Despair, who, like King Richard, will hear your song inside the walls, and sing to you again, and you may be the means of getting him ransomed and released. Sing, Christian, wherever you go; try, if you can, to wash your face every morning in a bath of praise. When you go down from your chamber, never go to look on man till you have first looked on your God; and when you have looked on him, seek to come down with a face beaming with joy,—carry a smile, for you will cheer up many a poor, wayworn pilgrim by it. And when thou fastest, Christian, when thou hast an aching heart, do not appear to men to fast, appear cheerful and happy; anoint thy head, and wash thy face; be happy for thy brother's sake; it will tend to cheer him up, and help him through the valley.

One more reason, and I know it will be a good one for you. Try and sing in the night, Christian, *for that is one of the best arguments in all the world in favor of your religion.* Our divines nowadays spend a great deal of time in trying to prove the truth of Christianity to those who disbelieve it; I should like to have seen Paul trying that plan. Elymas the sorcerer withstood him; how did Paul treat him? He said, "O full of all subtlety and all mischief, thou child of the devil, thou enemy of all righteousness, wilt thou not cease to pervert the right ways of the Lord?" That is about all the politeness such men ought to have when they deny God's truth; we start with this assumption, that the Bible is God's Word, but we are not going to prove God's Word. If you do not believe it, we will bid you "Good-bye;" we will not argue with you. Religion is not a thing merely for your intellect to prove the greatness of your own talent; it is a thing that demands your faith. As a messenger of heaven, I demand that faith; if you do not choose to give it, on your own head be your doom.

O Christian, instead of disputing, let me tell you how to prove your religion! Live it out! Live it out! Give the external as well as the internal evidence; give the external evidence of your own life. You are sick; there is your neighbor, who laughs at religion, let him come into your house. When he was sick, he said, "Oh! send for the doctor;" and there he was fretting, and fuming, and making all manner of noises. When you are sick, send for him; tell him that you are resigned to the Lord's will, that you will kiss the chastening rod, that you will take the cup, and drink it, because your Father gives it. You need not make a boast of this, or it will lose all its power: but do it because you cannot help doing it. Your neighbor will say, "There is something in such a religion as that."

And when you come to the borders of the grave (he was there once, and you heard how he shrieked, and how frightened he was), give him your hand, and say to him, "Ah! I have a Christ who is with me now, I have a religion that will make me sing in the night." Let him hear how you can sing, "Victory, victory, victory," through him that loved you. I tell you, we may preach fifty thousand sermons to prove the gospel, but we shall not prove it half so well as you will through singing in the night. Keep a cheerful face, keep a happy heart, keep a contented spirit, keep your eye bright, and your heart aloft, and you will prove Christianity better than all the Butlers, and all the wise men who ever lived. Give them the "analogy" of a holy life, and then you will prove religion to them; give them the "evidences" of internal piety, developed externally, and you will give the best possible proof of Christianity. Try and sing songs in the night; for they are so rare that, if thou canst sing them, thou wilt honor thy God, and bless thy friends.

I have been all this while addressing the children of God, and now there is a sad turn that this subject must take; just a word or so, and then I have done. There is a night coming, in which there will be no songs of joy,—a night when a song shall be sung, of which misery shall be the subject, set to the music of wailing and gnashing of teeth; there is a night coming when woe, unutterable woe, shall be the theme of an awful, terrific *miserere*. There is a night coming for the poor soul, and unless he repent, it will be a night wherein he will have to sigh, and cry, and moan, and groan for ever.

I hope I shall never preach a sermon without speaking to the ungodly, for oh, how I love them! Swearer, your mouth is black with oaths now; and if you die, you must go on blaspheming throughout eternity, and be punished for it throughout eternity! But list to me, blasphemer! Dost thou repent? Dost thou feel thyself to have sinned against God? Dost thou feel a desire to be saved? List thee! thou mayest be saved; thou mayest be saved. There is another; she has sinned against God enormously, and she blushes even now while I mention her case; dost thou repent of thy sin? Then there is pardon for thee; remember him who said, "Go, and sin no more." Drunkard! but a little while ago thou wast reeling down the street, and now thou repentest; drunkard, there is hope for thee.

"Well," sayest thou, "what shall I do to be saved?" Let me again tell thee the old way of salvation; it is, "Believe on the Lord Jesus Christ, and thou shalt be saved." We can get no further than that, do what we will; this is the sum and substance of the gospel. "He that believeth and is baptized shall be saved." So saith the Savior himself. Dost thou ask, "What is it to believe?" Am I to tell thee again? I cannot tell thee except that it is to look to Christ. Dost thou see the Savior there? He is hanging on the cross; there are his dear hands, pierced with nails, fastened to a tree, as if they were waiting for thy tardy footsteps, because thou wouldst not come. Dost thou see his dear head there? It is hanging on his breast, as if he would lean over, and kiss thy poor soul. Dost thou see his blood, gushing from his head, his hands, his feet, his side? It is running after thee, because he well knew that thou wouldst never run after him.

Sinner, to be saved, all thou hast to do is to look at that Man! Canst thou not do it now? "No," thou sayest, "I do not believe that will save me." Ah, my poor friend, try it, I beseech thee, try it; and if thou dost not succeed, when thou hast tried it, I will be bondsman for my Lord—here, take me, bind me, and I will suffer thy doom for thee. This I will venture to say; if thou castest thyself on Christ, and he deserteth thee, I will be willing to go halves with thee in all thy misery and woe; for he will never do it, never, *never*, NEVER!

> No sinner was ever empty sent
> back,
> Who came seeking mercy for
> Jesus's sake.

I beseech thee, therefore, try him, and thou shalt not try him in vain; but thou shalt find him "able to save them to the uttermost that come unto God by him;" and thou shalt be saved now, and saved for ever.

"Everybody's Sermon," delivered July 25, 1858, is another one of Spurgeon's sermons that is often reprinted. Spurgeon is at his best here in his use of illustrations taken from everyday life. What he presents is a vision of earth in which everything in our lives—every time and every place, every animal and every kind of scenery, and especially every vocation—contains a sermon for men, if they are willing to listen. Spurgeon's title is appropriate, for he shows how God speaks to all men in their daily lives, whether they are farmers or butchers, physicians or jewelers.

CHAPTER FIVE

Everybody's Sermon

I have multiplied visions, and used similitudes (Hos. 12:10).

When the Lord would win his people Israel from their iniquities, he did not leave a stone unturned, but gave them precept upon precept, line upon line, here a little and there a little. He taught them sometimes with a rod in his hand, when he smote them with sore famine and pestilence, and invasion; at other times he sought to win them with bounties, for he multiplied their corn and their wine and their oil, and he laid no famine upon them. But all the teachings of his providence were unavailing, and whilst his hand was stretched out, still they continued to rebel against the Most High. He hewed them by the prophets. He' sent them first one, and then another; the golden-mouthed Isaiah was followed by the plaintive Jeremy; while at his heels, in quick succession, there followed many far-seeing, thunder-speaking seers. But though prophet followed prophet in quick succession, each of them uttering the burning words of the Most High, yet they would have none of his rebukes, but they hardened their hearts, and went on still in their iniquities.

Among the rest of God's agencies for striking their attention and their conscience, was the use of similitudes. The prophets were accustomed not only to preach, but to be themselves as signs and wonders to the people. For instance, Isaiah named his child, Maher-shalal-hash-baz, that they might know that the judgment of the Lord was hastening upon them; and this child was ordained to be a sign, "for before the child shall have knowledge to cry, my father and my mother, the riches of Damascus and the spoil of Samaria shall be taken away before the king of Assyria." On another occasion, the Lord said unto Isaiah, "Go and loose the sackcloth from off thy loins, and put off thy shoe from thy foot." And he did so, walking naked and barefoot. And the Lord said, "Like as my servant Isaiah hath walked naked and barefoot three years for a sign and wonder upon Egypt and upon Ethiopia; so shall the king of Assyria lead away the Egyptians prisoners, and the Ethiopians captives young and old, naked and barefoot, to the shame of Egypt."

Hosea, the prophet, himself had to teach the people by a similitude. You will notice in the first chapter a most extraordinary similitude. The Lord said to him, "Go, take unto thee a wife of whoredoms; for the land hath committed great whoredom, departing from the Lord;" and he did so, and the children begotten by this marriage were made as signs and wonders to the people. As for his first son, he was to be called Jezreel, "for yet a little while, and I will avenge the blood of Jezreel upon the house of Jehu." As for his daughter, she was to be called Lo-ruhamah, "for I will no more have mercy upon the house of Israel; but I will utterly take them away." Thus by divers significant signs, God made the people think.

He made his prophets do strange things, in order that the people might talk about what he had done, and then the meaning which God would have them learn, should come home more powerfully to their consciences, and be the better remembered.

God is every day preaching to us by similitudes. When Christ was on earth he preached in parables, and, though he is in heaven now, he is preaching in parables today. Providence is God's sermon. The things which we see about us are God's thoughts and God's words to us; and if we were but wise there is not a step that we take, which we should not find to be full of mighty instruction. O ye sons of men! God warns you every day by his own word; he speaks to you by the lips of his servants, his ministers; but, besides this, by similitudes he addresses you at every time. He leaves no stone unturned to bring his wandering children to himself, to make the lost sheep of the house of Israel return to the fold. In addressing myself to you this morning, I shall endeavor to show how every day, and every season of the year, in every place, and in every calling which you are made to exercise, God is speaking to you by similitudes.

Similitudes in Daily Life

I. EVERY DAY God speaks to you by similitudes. Let us begin with the *early morning*. This morning you awakened and you found yourselves unclothed, and you began to array yourselves in your garments. Did not God, if you would but have heard him, speak to you by a similitude? Did he not as much as say to thee, "Sinner, what will it be when thy vain dreams shall have ended, if thou shouldst wake up in eternity to find thyself naked? Wherewithal shalt thou array thyself? If in this life thou dost cast away the wedding garment, the spotless righteousness of Jesus Christ, what wilt thou do when the

trump of the archangel shall awaken thee from thy clay cold couch in the grave, when the heavens shall be blazing with lightnings, and the solid pillars of the earth shall quake with the terrors of God's thunder? How wilt thou be able to dress thyself then?" Canst thou confront thy Maker without a covering for thy nakedness? Adam dared not, and canst thou attempt it? Will he not affright thee with his terrors? Will he not cast thee to the tormentors that thou mayest be burned with unquenchable fire, because thou didst forget the clothing of thy soul while thou wast in this place of probation?

Well, you have put on your dress, and you come down to your families, and your children gather round your table for the morning meal. If you have been wise, *God has been preaching to you by a similitude then*. He seemed to say to thee—"Sinner, to whom should a child go but to his father? And where should be his resort when he is hungry but to his father's table?" And as you fed your children, if you had an ear to hear, the Lord was speaking to you and saying, "How willingly would I feed you! How would I give you of the bread of heaven and cause you to eat angels' food! But thou hast spent thy money for that which is not bread, and thy labor for that which satisfieth not. Hearken diligently unto me, and eat ye that which is good, let thy soul delight itself in fatness." Did he not stand there as a Father, and say, "Come, my child, come to my table. The precious blood of my Son has been shed to be thy drink, and he has given his body to be thy bread. Why wilt thou wander hungry and thirsty? Come to my table, O my child, for I love my children to be there and to feast upon the mercies I have provided."

You left your home and you went to your business. I know not in what calling your time was occupied—of that we will say more before we shall have gathered up the ends of your similitudes this morning—but you spend your time in your work; and surely, beloved, all the time that your fingers were occupied, God was speaking to your heart if the ears of your soul had not been closed, so that you were heavy and ready to slumber, and could not hear his voice. And when the sun was shining in high heaven, and the hour of noon was reached, mightest thou not have lifted up thine eye and remembered that if thou hadst committed thy soul to God, thy path should have been as the shining light which shineth more and more unto the perfect day? Did he not speak to thee and say, "I brought the sun from the darkness of the east; I have guided him and helped him to ascend the slippery steeps of heaven, and now he standeth in his zenith, like a giant that hath run his race, and hath attained his goal. And even so will I do with thee. Commit thy ways unto me and I will make thee full of light, and thy path shall be as brightness, and thy life shall be as the noonday; thy sun shall not go down by day, but the days of thy morning shall be ended, for the Lord God shall be thy light and thy salvation."

And the sun began to set, and the shadows of evening were drawing on, and did not the Lord then remind thee of thy death? Suns have their setting, and men have their graves. When the shadows of the evening were stretched out, and when the darkness began to gather, did he not say unto thee, "O, man, take heed of thine eventide, for the light of the sun shall not endure for ever? There are twelve hours wherein a man shall work, but when they are past there is no work nor device in the night of that grave whither we are all hastening. Work while ye have the light, for the night cometh wherein no man can work.

Therefore, whatsoever thine hand findeth to do, do it with all thy might."

Look, I say, to the sun at his setting, and observe the rainbow hues of glory with which he paints the sky, and mark how he appears to increase his orb, as he nears the horizon. O man, kneel down and learn this prayer—"Lord, let my dying be like the setting of the sun; help me, if clouds and darkness are round about me, to light them up with splendor; surround me, O my God, with a greater brightness at my death than I have shown in all my former life. If my death-bed shall be the miserable pallet, and if I expire in some lone cot, yet nevertheless, grant, O Lord, that my poverty may be gilded with the light that thou shalt give me, and that I may exhibit the grandeur of a Christian's departure at my dying hour." God speaketh to thee, O man, by similitude, from the rising to the setting of the sun.

And now, thou hast lit thy candles and thou sittest down; thy children are about thee, and the Lord sends thee a little preacher to preach thee a sermon, if thou wilt hear. It is a little gnat, and it flieth round and round about thy candle, and delighteth itself in the light thereof, till, dazzled and intoxicated, it begins to singe its wings and burn itself. Thou seekest to put it away, but it dashes into the flame, and having burned itself it can scarcely fan itself through the air again. But as soon as it has recruited its strength again, madlike it dashes to its death and destruction.

Did not the Lord say to thee, "Sinner, thou art doing this also; thou lovest the light of sin; oh, that thou wert wise enough to tremble at the fire of sin, for he who delights in the sparks thereof must be consumed in the burning"? Did not thy hand seem to be like the hand of the Almighty, who would put thee away from thine own destruction, and who rebukes and smites thee by his providence, as much as to say to thee, "Poor silly man, be not thine own destruction"? And while thou seest perhaps with a little sorrow the death of the foolish insect, might not that forewarn thee of thine awful doom, when, after having been dazzled with the giddy round of this world's joys, thou shalt at last plunge into the eternal burning and lose thy soul, so madly, for nothing but the enjoyments of an hour? Doth not God preach to thee thus?

And now it is time for thee to retire to thy rest. Thy door is bolted, and thou hast fast closed it. Did not that remind thee of that saying, "When once the master of the house is risen up, and hath shut to the door, and ye begin to stand without, and to knock at the door, saying, 'Lord, Lord, open unto us;' and he shall answer and say unto you, 'I know not whence you are'"? In vain shall be your knocking then, when the bars of immutable justice shall have fast closed the gates of mercy on mankind; when the hand of the Almighty Master shall have shut his children within the gates of paradise, and shall have left the thief and the robber in the cold chilly darkness, the outer darkness, where there shall be weeping and wailing and gnashing of teeth. Did he not preach to thee by similitude? Even then, when thy finger was on the bolt, might not his finger have been on thy heart?

And at night time thou wast startled. The watchman in the street awoke thee with the cry of the hour of the night, or his tramp along the street. O man, if thou hadst ears to hear, thou mightest have heard in the steady tramp of the policeman the cry, "Behold, the bridegroom cometh; go ye out to meet him." And every sound at midnight that did awaken thee from thy slumber and startle thee upon thy bed, might seem to forewarn thee of that dread trump of the

archangel which shall herald the coming of the Son of man, in the day he shall judge both the quick and the dead, according to my gospel. O that ye were wise, that ye understood this, for all the day long from dewy morning till the darkness of the eventide, and the thick darkness of midnight, God evermore doth preach to man—he preacheth to him by similitudes.

Similitudes Throughout the Year

II. And now we turn the current of our thoughts, and observe that ALL THE YEAR round God doth preach to man by similitudes. It was but a little while ago that we were sowing our seeds in our garden, and scattering the corn over the broad furrows. God had sent the seed time, to remind us that we too are like the ground, and that he is scattering seed in our hearts each day. And did he not say to us, "Take heed, O man, lest thou shouldst be like the highway whereon the seed was scattered, but the fowls of the air devoured it. Take heed that thou be not like the ground that had its basement on a hard and arid rock, lest this seed should spring up and by-and-by should wither away when the sun arose, because it had not much depth of earth. And be thou careful, O son of man, that thou art not like the ground where the seed did spring up, but the thorns sprang up and choked it; but be thou like the good ground whereon the seed did fall, and it brought forth fruit, some twenty, some fifty, and some a hundred fold."

We thought, when we were sowing the seed, that we expected one day to see it spring up again. Was there not a lesson for us there? Are not our actions all of them as seeds? Are not our little words like grains of mustardseed? Is not our daily conversation like a handful of the corn that we scatter over the soil? And ought we not to remember that our words shall live again, that our acts are as immortal as ourselves, that after having laid a little while in the dust to be matured, they shall certainly arise? The black deeds of sin shall bear a dismal harvest of damnation; and the right deeds which God's grace has permitted us to do, shall, through his mercy and not through our merit, bring forth a bounteous harvest in the day when they who sow in tears shall reap in joy. Doth not seed time preach to thee, O man, and say, "Take heed that thou sowest good seed in thy field."

And when the seed sprang up, and the season had changed, did God cease then to preach? Ah! no. First the blade, then the ear, and then the full corn in the ear, had each its homily. And when at last the harvest came, how loud the sermon which it preached to us! It said to us, "O Israel, I have set a harvest for thee. Whatsoever a man soweth that shall he also reap. He that soweth to the flesh shall of the flesh reap corruption, and he that soweth to the Spirit shall of the Spirit reap life everlasting."

If you have to journey in the country, you will, if your heart is rightly attuned, find a marvelous mass of wisdom couched in a corn-field. Why, I could not attempt for a moment to open the mighty mines of golden treasure which are hidden there. Think, beloved, of the joy of the harvest. How does it tell us of the joy of the redeemed, if we, being saved, shall at last be carried like shocks of corn fully ripe into the garner. Look at the ear of corn when it is fully ripe, and see how it dippeth toward the earth! It held its head erect before, but in getting ripe how humble does it become! And how does God speak to the sinner, and tell him, that if he would be fit for the great harvest he must drop his head and cry, "Lord have mercy upon me a sinner." And when we see the weeds

spring up amongst wheat, have we not our Master's parable over again of the tares among the wheat; and are we not reminded of the great day of division, when he shall say to the reaper, "Gather first the tares and bind them in bundles, to burn them; but gather the wheat into my barn."

O yellow field of corn, thou preachest well to me, for thou sayest to me, the minister, "Behold, the fields are ripe already to the harvest. Work thou thyself, and pray thou the Lord of the harvest to send forth more laborers into the harvest." And it preaches well to thee, thou man of years, it tells thee that the sickle of death is sharp, and that thou must soon fall, but it cheers and comforts thee, for it tells thee that the wheat shall be safely housed, and it bids thee hope that thou shalt be carried to thy Master's garner to be his joy and his delight for ever. Hark, then, to the rustling eloquence of the yellow harvest.

In a very little time, my beloved, you will see the birds congregated on the housetops in great multitudes, and after they have whirled round and round and round, as if they were taking their last sight at Old England, or rehearsing their supplications before they launched away, you will see them, with their leader in advance, speed across the purple sea to live in sunnier climes, while winter's cold hand shall strip their native woods. And doth not God seem to preach to you, sinners, when these birds are taking their flight? Do you not remember how he himself puts it? "Yea, the stork in the heaven knoweth her appointed times; and the turtle, and the crane, and the swallow, observe the time of their coming; but my people know not the judgment of the Lord." Doth he not tell us that there is a time of dark winter coming upon this world; a time of trouble, such as there has been none like it, neither shall be any more;

a time, when all the joys of sin shall be nipped and frost-bitten, and when the summer of man's estate shall be turned into the dark winter of his disappointment? And does he not say to you, "Sinner! fly away—away—away to the goodly land, where Jesus dwells! Away from self and sin! Away from the city of destruction! Away from the whirl of pleasures, and from the tossing to and fro of trouble! Haste thee, like a bird to its rest! Fly thou across the sea of repentance and faith, and build thy nest in the land of mercy, that when the great day of vengeance shall pass o'er this world, thou mayest be safe in the clefts of the rock."

I remember well, how once God preached to me by a similitude in the depth of winter. The earth had been black, and there was scarcely a green thing or a flower to be seen. As you looked across the field, there was nothing but blackness—bare hedges and leafless trees, and black, black earth, wherever you looked. On a sudden God spake, and unlocked the treasures of the snow, and white flakes descended until there was no blackness to be seen, and all was one sheet of dazzling whiteness. It was at that time that I was seeking the Savior, and it was then I found him; and I remember well that sermon which I saw before me; "Come now, and let us reason together; though your sins be as scarlet they shall be as snow, though they be red like crimson they shall be whiter than wool."

Sinner! thy heart is like that black ground; thy soul is like that black tree and hedgerow, without leaf or blossom; God's grace is like the white snow—it shall fall upon thee till thy doubting heart shall glitter in whiteness of pardon, and thy poor black soul shall be covered with the spotless purity of the Son of God. He seems to say to you, "Sinner, you are black, but I am ready to forgive you; I will wrap thy heart in the ermine of my Son's righteousness, and with my Son's own garments on, thou shalt be holy as the Holy One."

And the *wind* of today, as it comes howling through the trees—many of which have been swept down—reminds us of the Spirit of the Lord, which "bloweth where it listeth," and when it pleaseth; and it tells us to seek earnestly after that divine and mysterious influence which alone can speed us on our voyage to heaven; which shall cast down the trees of our pride, and tear up by the roots the goodly cedars of our self-confidence; which shall shake our refuges of lies about our ears, and make us look to him who is the only covert from the storm, the only shelter when "the blast of the terrible ones is as a storm against the wall."

Ay, and when the *heat* is coming down, and we hide ourselves beneath the shadow of the tree, an angel standeth there, and whispereth, "Look upwards, sinner, as thou hidest thyself from the burning rays of Sol beneath the tree; so there is One who is like the apple tree among the trees of the wood, and he bids thee come and take shadow beneath his branches, for he will screen thee from the eternal vengeance of God, and give thee shelter when the fierce heat of God's anger shall beat upon the heads of wicked men."

Similitudes in Every Place

III. And now again, EVERY PLACE to which you journey, every *animal* that you see, every *spot* you visit, has a sermon for you. Go into your farm-yard, and your ox and your ass shall preach to you. "The ox knoweth his owner, and the ass his master's crib; but Israel doth not know, my people doth not consider." The very dog at your heels may rebuke you. He follows his master; a stranger will he not follow, for he knows not the voice of a stranger, but ye forsake your God and turn aside unto your crooked ways. Look at the chicken by the side of yonder pond, and let it rebuke your ingratitude. It drinks, and every sip it takes it lifts its head to heaven and thanks the Giver of the rain for the drink afforded to it; while thou eatest and drinkest, and there is no blessing pronounced at thy meals, and no thanksgiving bestowed upon thy Father for his bounty. The very horse is checked by the bridle, and the whip is for the ass; but thy God hath bridled thee by his commandments, and he hath chastened by his providence, yet art thou more obstinate than the ass or the mule; still thou wilt not run in his commandments, but thou turnest aside, willfully and wickedly following out the perversity of thine own heart.

Is it not so? Are not these things true of you? If you are still without God and without Christ, must not these things strike your conscience? Would not any one of them lead you to tremble before the Most High, and beg of him that he would give you a new heart and a right spirit, and that no longer you might be as the beasts of the field, but might be a man of the divine Spirit, living in obedience to your Creator.

And in *journeying*, you have noticed how often the road is rough with stones, and you have murmured because of the way over which you have to tread; and have you not thought that those stones were helping to make the road better, and that the worst piece of road when mended with hard stones would in time become smooth and fit to travel on? And did you think how often God has mended you; how many stones of affliction he has cast upon you; how many wagon loads of warnings you have had spread out upon you, and you have been none the better, but have only grown

worse; and when he comes to look on you to see whether your life has become smooth, whether the highway of your moral conduct has become more like the king's highway of righteousness, how might he say, "Alas! I have repaired this road, but it is none the better; let it alone until it becomes a very bog and quagmire, until he who keeps it thus ill shall have perished in it himself."

And thou hast gone by the sea-side, and has not the sea talked to thee? Inconstant as the sea art thou, but thou art not one half so obedient. God keeps the sea, the mountain-waved sea, in check with a belt of sand; he spreads the sand along the sea-shore, and even the sea observes the landmark. "Fear ye not me?" saith the Lord; "will ye not tremble at my presence, which have placed the sand for the bound of the sea by a perpetual decree, that it can not pass it; and though the waves thereof toss themselves, yet can they not prevail; though they roar, yet can they not pass over it?" It is so. Let thy conscience prick thee. The sea obeys him from shore to shore, and yet thou wilt not have him to be thy God, but thou sayest, "Who is the Lord that I should fear him? Who is Jehovah that I should acknowledge his sway?"

Hear the *mountains* and the *hills*, for they have a lesson. Such is God. He abideth for ever—think not that he shall change.

And now, sinner, I entreat thee to open thine eyes as thou goest home to-day, and if nothing that I have said shall smite thee, perhaps God shall put into thy way something that shall give thee a text, from which thou mayest preach to thyself a sermon that never shall be forgotten. Oh! if I had but time, and thought, and words, I would bring the things that are in heaven above, and in the earth beneath, and in the waters under the earth, and I would set them all

give their warning before they had passed from thine inspection, and I know that their voice would be, "Consider the Lord, thy Creator, and fear and serve him, for he hath made thee, and thou hast not made thyself;" we obey him, and we find it is our beauty to be obedient, and our glory ever to move according to his will; and thou shalt find it to be the same.

Obey him while thou mayest, lest haply when this life is over all these things shall rise up against thee, and the stone in the street shall clamor for thy condemnation, and the beam out of the wall shall bear witness against thee, and the beasts of the field shall be thine accusers, and the valley and hill shall begin to curse thee. O man, the earth is made for thy warning. God would have thee be saved. He hath set hand posts everywhere in nature and in providence, pointing thee the way to the city of refuge, and if thou art but wise thou needest not miss thy way; it is but thy willful ignorance and thy neglect that shall cause thee to run on in the way of error, for God hath made the way straight before thee and given thee every encouragement to run therein.

Similitudes in Every Calling

IV. And now, lest I should weary you, I will just notice that every man in his CALLING has a sermon preached to him.

The *farmer* has a thousand sermons; I have brought them out already; let him open wide his eyes, and he shall see more. He need not go an inch without hearing the songs of angels, and the voices of spirits wooing him to righteousness, for all nature round about him has a tongue given to it, when man hath an ear to hear.

There are others, however, engaged in a business which allows them to see but very little of nature, and yet even there

God has provided them with a lesson. There is the *baker* who provides us with our bread. He thrusts his fuel into the oven, and he causeth it to glow with heat, and he puts bread therein. Well may he, if he be an ungodly man, tremble as he stands at the oven's mouth, for there is a text which he may well comprehend as he stands there: "For the day cometh that shall burn as an oven, and all the proud and they that do wickedly shall be as stubble; they shall be consumed. Men ingather them in bundles and cast them into the fire, and they are burned." Out of the oven's mouth comes a hot and burning warning, and the man's heart might melt like wax within him if he would but regard it.

Then see the *butcher*. How doth the beast speak to him? He sees the lamb almost lick his knife, and the bullock goes unconsciously to the slaughter. How might he think every time that he smites the unconscious animal (who knows nothing of death), of his own doom. Are we not, all of us who are without Christ, fattening for the slaughter? Are we not more foolish than the bullock, for doth not the wicked man follow his executioner, and walk after his own destroyer into the very chambers of hell? When we see a drunkard pursuing his drunkenness, or an unchaste man running in the way of licentiousness, is he not as an ox going to the slaughter, until a dart smite him through the liver? Hath not God sharpened his knife and made ready his ax that the fatlings of this earth may be killed, when he shall say to the fowls of the air and the beasts of the field, "Behold, I have made a feast of vengeance for you, and ye shall feast upon the blood of the slain, and make yourselves drunken with the streams thereof"? Ay, butcher, there is a lecture for you in your trade; and your business may reproach you.

And ye whose craft is to sit still all day, making shoes for our feet, the lapstone in your lap may reproach you, for your heart, perhaps, is as hard as that. Have you not been smitten as often as your lapstone, and yet your heart has never been broken or melted? And what shall the Lord say to you at last, when your stony heart being still within you, he shall condemn you and cast you away because you would have none of his rebukes and would not turn at the voice of his exhortation.

Let the *brewer* remember that as he brews he must drink. Let the *potter* tremble lest he be like a vessel marred upon the wheel. Let the *printer* take heed, that his life be set in heavenly type, and not in the black letter of sin. *Painter,* beware! for paint will not suffice, we must have unvarnished realities.

Others of you are engaged in business where you are continually using scales and measures. Might you not often put yourselves into those scales? Might you not fancy you saw the great Judge standing by with his gospel in one scale and you in the other, and solemnly looking down upon you, saying, *"Mene, mene, tekel*—thou art weighed in the balances and found wanting"*? Some of you use the measure, and when you have measured out, you cut off the portion that your customer requires. Think of your life too, it is to be of a certain length, and every year brings the measure a little further, and at last there come the scissors that shall clip off your life, and it is done. How knowest thou when thou art come to the last inch? What is that disease thou hast about thee, but the first snip of the scissors? What that trembling in thy bones, that failing in thy eyesight, that fleeing of thy memory, that departure of thy youthful vigor, but the first rent? How soon shalt thou be

rent in twain, the remnant of thy days past away, and thy years all numbered and gone, misspent and wasted for ever!

But you say you are engaged as a *servant* and your occupations are diverse. Then diverse are the lectures God preaches to you. "A servant waits for his wages and the hireling fulfilleth his day." There is a similitude for thee, when thou hast fulfilled thy day on earth, and shalt take thy wages at last. Who then is thy master? Art thou serving Satan and the lusts of the flesh, and wilt thou take out thy wages at last in the hot metal of destruction? or art thou serving the fair prince Emmanuel, and shalt thy wages be the golden crowns of heaven? Oh! happy art thou if thou servest a good master, for according to thy master shall be thy reward; as is thy labor such shall the end be.

Or art thou one that *guideth the pen,* and from hour to hour wearily thou writes? Ah! man, know that thy life is a writing. When thy hand is not on the pen, thou art a writer still; thou art always writing upon the pages of eternity; thy sins thou art writing or else thy holy confidence in him that loved thee. Happy shall it be for thee, O writer, if thy name is written in the Lamb's book of life, and if that black writing of thine, in the history of thy pilgrimage below, shall have been blotted out with the red blood of Christ, and thou shalt have written upon thee, the fair name of Jehovah, to stand legible for ever.

Or perhaps thou art a *physician* or a *chemist;* thou prescribest or preparest medicines for man's body. God stands there by the side of thy pestle and thy mortar; and by the table where thou writest thy prescriptions, and he says to thee, "Man, thou art sick; I can prescribe for thee. The blood and righteousness of Christ, laid hold of by faith, and applied by the Spirit, can cure thy soul. I can compound a medicine for thee that shall rid thee of thy ills and bring thee to the place where the inhabitants shall no more say, 'I am sick.' Wilt thou take my medicine or wilt thou reject it? Is it bitter to thee, and dost thou turn away from it? Come, drink my child, drink, for thy life lieth here; and how shalt thou escape if thou neglect so great salvation?" Do you cast iron, or melt lead, or fuse the hard metals of the mines? then pray that the Lord may melt thine heart and cast thee in the mold of the gospel! Do you make garments for men? oh, be careful that you find a garment for yourself for ever.

Are you busy in *building* all day long, laying the stone upon its fellow and the mortar in its crevice? Then remember thou art building for eternity too. Oh that thou mayest thyself be built upon a good foundation! Oh that thou mayest build thereon, not wood, hay, or stubble, but gold, and silver, and precious stones, and things that will abide the fire! Take care, man, lest thou shouldest be God's scaffold, lest thou shouldest be used on earth to be a scaffolding for building his church, and when his church is built thou shouldest be cast down and burned up with fire unquenchable. Take heed that thou art built upon a rock, and not upon the sand, and that the vermilion cement of the Savior's precious blood unites thee to the foundation of the building, and to every stone thereof.

Art thou a *jeweler*, and dost thou cut the gem and polish the diamond from day to day? Would to God thou wouldest take warning from the contrast which thou presentest to the stone on which thou dost exercise thy craft. Thou cuttest it, and it glitters the more thou dost cut it; but though thou hast been cut and ground, though thou hast had cholera and fever, and hast been at death's door many a day, thou art none the

brighter, but the duller, for alas! thou art no diamond. Thou art but the pebble-stone of the brook, and in the day when God makes up his jewels he shall not enclose thee in the casket of his treasures; for thou art not one of the precious sons of Zion, comparable unto fine gold. But be thy situation what it may, be thy calling what it may, there is a continual sermon preached to thy conscience. I would that thou wouldest now from this time forth open both eye and ear, and see and hear the things that God would teach thee.

And now, dropping the similitude while the clock shall tick but a few times more, let us put the matter thus— Sinner, thou art as yet without God and without Christ; thou art liable to death every hour. Thou canst not tell but that thou mayest be in the flames of hell before the clock shall strike ONE today. Thou art today "condemned already," because thou believest not in the Son of God. And Jesus Christ saith to thee this day, "Oh, that thou wouldest consider thy latter end!" He cries to thee this morning, "How often would I have gathered thee as a hen gathereth her chickens under her wings, but ye would not."

I entreat you, consider your ways. If it be worth while to make your bed in hell, do it. If the pleasures of this world are worth being damned to all eternity for enjoying them, if heaven be a cheat and hell a delusion, go on with your sins. But, if there be hell for sinners and heaven for repenting ones, and if thou must dwell a whole eternity in one place or the other, without similitude, I put a plain question to thee—Art thou wise in living as thou dost, without thought— careless, and godless?

Wouldst thou ask now the way of salvation? It is simply this—"Believe on the Lord Jesus Christ and thou shalt be saved." He died; he rose again; thou art to believe him to be thine; thou art to believe that he is able to save unto the uttermost them that come unto God by him. But, more than that, believing that to be a fact, thou art to cast thy soul upon that fact and trust to him, sink or swim. Spirit of God! help us each to do this; and by similitude, or by providence, or by thy prophets, bring us each to thyself and save us eternally, and unto thee shall be the glory.

Among Spurgeon's most interesting sermons were some that he delivered upon special occasions, such as "India's Ills and England's Sorrows," given on September 6, 1857. When a mutiny had occurred in India against Britain's rule, a service of national humiliation was planned, and Spurgeon was asked to speak. The day before the service he tested the acoustics of the Crystal Palace, which had not been built to house such a meeting, by repeating, "Behold the Lamb of God which taketh away the sin of the world." His words were heard by a man who had been working in the building and who came to Spurgeon several days later to tell him that the message of the verse had caused him to come to know Christ.

Twenty-three thousand six hundred fifty-four attended the service, undoubtedly the largest indoor congregation up until that time. Spurgeon called for national repentance and humiliation and reminded his countrymen that only righteousness could exalt a nation. Spurgeon also took the opportunity to condemn the nation for all of its sins and exhorted his countrymen to weep.

CHAPTER SIX

India's Ills and England's Sorrows

Oh that my head were waters, and mine eyes a fountain of tears, that I might weep day and night for the slain of the daughter of my people (Jer. 9:1).

Sometimes tears are base things; the offspring of a cowardly spirit. Some men weep when they should knit their brows, and many a woman weepeth when she should resign herself to the will of God. Many of those briny drops are but an expression of child-like weakness. It were well if we could wipe such tears away, and face a frowning world with a constant countenance. But oft times tears are the index of strength. There are periods when they are the noblest things in the world. The tears of penitents are precious: a cup of them were worth a king's ransom. It is no sign of weakness when a man weeps for sin, it shows that he hath strength of mind; nay more, that he hath strength imparted by God, which enables him to forswear his lusts and overcome his passions, and to turn unto God with full purpose of heart.

And there are other tears, too, which are the evidences not of weakness, but of might—the tears of tender sympathy are the children of strong affection, and they are strong like their parents. He that loveth much, must weep much; much love and much sorrow must go together in this vale of tears. The unfeeling heart, the unloving spirit, may pass from earth's portal to its utmost bound almost without a sigh except for itself; but he that loveth, hath digged as many wells of tears as he has chosen objects of affection; for by as many as our friends are multiplied, by so many must our griefs be multiplied too, if we have love enough to share in their griefs and to bear their burden for them. The largest-hearted man will miss many sorrows that the little man will feel, but he will have to endure many sorrows the poor narrow-minded spirit never knoweth.

It needs a mighty prophet like Jeremiah to weep as mightily as he. Jeremiah was not weak in his weeping; the strength of his mind and the strength of his love were the parents of his sorrow. "Oh that my head were waters, and mine eyes a fountain of tears, that I might weep day and night for the slain of the daughter of my people." This is no expression of weak sentimentalism; this is no utterance of mere whining presence; it is the burst of a strong soul, strong in its affection, strong in its devotion, strong in its self-sacrifice. I would to God we knew how to weep like this; and if we might not weep so frequently as Jeremy, I wish that when we did weep, we did weep as well.

It would seem as if some men had been sent into this world for the very purpose of being the world's weepers. God's great house is thoroughly furnished with everything; everything that can express the thoughts and the emotions of the inhabitant, God hath made. I find in nature, plants to be everlasting weepers. There by the lonely brook, where the maiden cast away her life, the willow weeps for ever; and there in the graveyard where men lie slumbering till the trumpet of the archangel shall awaken them, stands the dull cypress, mourning in its somber garments.

Now as it is with nature, so it is with the race of man. Mankind have bravery and boldness; they must have their heroes to express their courage. Mankind have some love to their fellow-creatures; they must have their fine philanthropists to live out mankind's philanthropy. Men have their sorrows; they must have their weepers; they must have men of sorrows who have it for their avocation, and their business, to weep, from the cradle to the grave; to be ever weeping, not so much for themselves as for the woes of others.

It may be I have some such here; I shall be happy to enlist their sympathies; and truly if I have none of that race, I shall boldly appeal to the whole mass of you, and I will bring before you causes of great grief; and when I bid you by the love you bear to man, and to his God, to begin to weep; if you have tears, these hard times will compel you to shed them now. Come, let me show you wherefore I have taken this my text, and why I have uttered this mournful language; and if your hearts be not as stolid as stone, sure there should be some tears shed this morning. For if I be not foolish in my utterances and faint in my speech, you will go home to your chambers to weep there. "Oh that *my* head were waters and *mine* eyes a fountain of tears, that I might weep day and night for the slain of the daughter of my people."

Weeping for Persons Actually Slain

I want your griefs this morning, first, *for persons actually slain*—"the slain of the daughter of our people;" and then I shall need your tears *for those morally slain*, "the slain of the daughter of our people."

I. To begin, then, with ACTUAL MURDER AND REAL BLOODSHED. My brethren, our hearts are sick nigh unto death with the terrible news brought us post after post, telegraph after telegraph; we have read many letters of the *Times*, day after day, until we have folded up that paper, and professed before God that we could read no more. Our spirits have been harrowed by the most fearful and unexpected cruelty. We, perhaps, may not have been personally interested in the bloodshed, so far as our own husbands, wives, brothers, and sisters have been concerned, but we have felt the tie of kindred very strongly when we have found our race so cruelly butchered in the land of the East.

It is for us today humbly to confess our crime. The government of India has been a cruel government; it has much for which to appear before the bar of God. Its tortures—if the best evidence is to be believed—have been of the most inhuman kind; God forgive the men who have committed such crimes in the British name. But those days are past. May God blot out the sin. We do not forget our own guilt; but an overwhelming sense of the guilt of others, who have with such cold-hearted cruelty tormented men and women, may well excuse us if we do not dilate upon the subject.

Alas! alas, for our brethren there! They have died; alas for them! They have been slain by the sword of treachery, and traitorously murdered by men who swore allegiance. Alas for them! But, O ye soldiers, we weep not for you. Even when ye were tortured, ye had not that high dishonor to bear to which the other sex has been obliged to submit. O England! weep for thy daughters with a bitter lamentation; let thine eyes run down with rivers of blood for them. Had they been crushed within the folds of the hideous boa, or had the fangs of the tiger been red with their blood, happy would their fate have been compared with the indignities they have endured! O Earth! thou hast beheld crimes which antiquity could not parallel; thou hast seen bestial lust gratified upon the purest and the best of mortals. God's fairest creatures stained; those loved ones, who could not brook the name of lust, given up to the embraces of incarnate devils!

Weep, Britain, weep; weep for thy sons and for thy daughters! If thou art cold-hearted now, if thou readest the tale of infamy now without a tear, thou art no mother to them! Sure thine heart must have failed thee, and thou hast become less loving than thine own lions, and less tender than beasts of prey, if thou dost not weep for the maiden and the wife! Brethren, I am not straining history; I am not endeavoring to be pathetic where there is no pathos. No; my subject of itself is all pathos; it is my poor way of speaking that doth spoil it. I have not today to act the orator's part, to garnish up that which was nothing before; I have not to magnify little griefs—rather I feel that all my utterances do but diminish the woe which every thoughtful man must feel. Oh, how have our hearts been harrowed, cut in pieces, molten in the fire! Agony hath seized upon us, and grief unutterable, when, day after day, our hopes have been disappointed, and we have heard that still the rebel rages in his fury, and still with despotic might doth as he pleaseth with the sons and daughters, the husbands and the wives of England.

Weep, Christians, weep! And ye ask me of what avail shall be your weeping. I have bidden you weep today, because the spirit of vengeance is gathering; Britain's wrath is stirred; a black cloud is hanging over the head of the mutinous Sepoys! Their fate shall be most dreadful, their doom most tremendous, when England shall smite the murderers, as justly she must. There must be a judicial punishment enacted upon these men, so terrible that the earth shall tremble, and both the ears of him that heareth it shall tingle!

I am inclined, if I can, to sprinkle some few cooling tears upon the fires of vengeance. No, no; we will not take vengeance upon ourselves. "Vengeance is mine, I will repay, saith the Lord." Let not Britain's soldiers push their enemies to destruction, through a spirit of vengeance, as men; let them do it as the appointed executioners of the sentence of our laws. According to the civil code of every country under heaven, these men are condemned to die. Not as soldiers should we war with them, but as malefactors we must execute the law upon them. They have committed treason against government, and for that crime alone the doom is death! But they are murderers, and rightly or wrongly, our law is, that the murderer must die the death. God must have this enormous sin punished; and though we would feel no vengeance as Britons, yet, for the sake of government, God's established government on earth, the ruler who beareth the sword must not now bear the sword in vain.

Long have I held that war is an enormous crime; long have I regarded all battles as but murder on a large scale; but this time, I, a peaceful man, a follower of the peaceful Savior, do propound war. No, it is not war that I propound, but a just and proper punishment. I will not aid and abet soldiers as *warriors*, but as *executioners* of a lawful sentence, which ought to be executed upon men, who, by the double crime of infamous debauchery, and fearful bloodshed, have brought upon themselves the ban and curse of God; so that they must be punished, or truth and innocence can never walk this earth. As a rule I do not believe in the utility of capital punishment, but the crime has been attended with all the horrid guilt of the cities of the plain, and is too bestial to be endured.

But still, I say, I would cool down the vengeance of Britons, and therefore I would bid you weep. Ye talk of vengeance, but ye know not the men with whom ye have to deal; many a post may come, and many a month run round, and many a year may pass before ye hear of victory over those fierce men. Be not too proud. England talked once of her great deeds, and she hath since been humbled. She may yet again learn that she is not omnipotent.

But ye people of God, weep, weep for this sin that hath broken loose; weep for this hell that hath found its way to earth; go to your chambers and cry out to God to stop this bloodshed. You are to be the saviors of your nation. Not on the bayonets of British soldiery, but on the prayers of British Christians, do we rest. Run to your houses, fall upon your knees; lament most bitterly, for this desperate sin; and then cry to God to save! Remember, he heareth prayer—prayer moveth the arm of the Omnipotent. Let us proclaim a fast; let us gather a solemn assembly; let us cry mightily unto him; let us ask the God of armies to avenge himself; let us pray him so to send the light of the gospel into the land, that such a crime may be impossible a second time; and this time, so to put it down, that it may never have an opportunity of breaking loose again. I know not whether our government will proclaim a national fast; but certain I am it is time that every Christian should celebrate one in his own heart. I bid all of you with whom my word has one atom of respect, if my exhortation has one word of force, I do exhort you to spend special time in prayer just now.

Oh! my friends, ye cannot hear the shrieks, ye have not seen the terror-stricken faces, ye have not beheld the flying fugitives; but you may picture them in your imagination; and he must be accursed who does not pray to God, and lift up his soul in earnest prayer, that he would be pleased now to put his shield between our fellow-subjects and their enemies. And you, especially, the representatives of divers congregations in various parts of this land, give unto God no rest until he be pleased to bestir himself. Make this your cry: "O Lord our God arise, and let thine enemies be scattered, and let all them that hate thee become as the fat of rams." So shall God, through your prayers, haply, establish peace and vindicate justice, and "God, even our own God, shall bless us, and that right early."

Weeping for the Morally Slain

II. But I have now a greater reason for your sorrow—a more disregarded, and yet more dreadful source of woe. If the first time we said it with plaintive voice, we must a second time say it yet more plaintively—"Oh that my head were waters, and mine eyes a fountain of tears, that I might weep day and night," FOR THE MORALLY SLAIN of the daughter of my people. The old adage is still true, "One-half of the world knows nothing about how the other half lives." A large proportion of you professing Christians have been respectably brought up; you have never in your lives been the visitants of the dens of infamy, you have never frequented the haunts of wickedness, and you know but very little of the sins of your fellow creatures. Perhaps it is well that you should remain as ignorant as you are; for, where to be ignorant is to be free from temptation, it would be folly to be wise.

But there are others who have been obliged to see the wickedness of their fellows; and a public teacher, especially, is bound not to speak from mere hearsay, but to know from authentic sources what is the spirit of the times. It is our business to look with eagle eye through every part of this land, and see what crime is rampant—what kind of crime, and what sort of infamy. Ah, my friends! with all the advancement of piety in this land, with all the hopeful signs of better times, with all the sunlight of glory heralding the coming morn, with all the promises and with all our hopes, we are still obliged to bid you weep because sin aboundeth and iniquity is still mighty. Oh, how many of our sons and daughters, of our friends and relatives, are slain by sin! Ye weep over battle-fields, ye shed tears on the plains of Balaklava; there are worse battlefields than there, and worse deaths than those inflicted by the sword.

Ah, weep ye for the *drunkenness* of this land! How many thousands of our race reel from our gin-palaces into perdition! Oh, if the souls of departed drunkards could be seen at this hour by the Christians of Britain, they would tremble, lift up their hands in sorrow, and begin to weep. My soul might be an everlasting Niobé, perpetually dropping showers of tears, if it might know the doom and the destruction brought on them by that one demon, and by that one demon only! I am no enthusiast, I am no total abstainer.—I do not think the cure of England's drunkenness will come from that quarter. I respect those who thus deny themselves, with a view to the good of others, and should be glad to believe that they accomplish their object. But though I am no total abstainer, I hate drunkenness as much as any man breathing, and have been the means of bringing many poor creatures to relin-

quish this bestial indulgence. We believe drunkenness to be an awful crime and a horrid sin; we look on all its dreadful effects, and we stand prepared to go to war with it, and to fight side by side with abstainers, even though we may differ from them as to the mode of warfare. Oh, England, how many thousands of thy sons are murdered every year by that accursed devil of drunkenness, that hath such sway over this land!

But there are other crimes too. Alas, for that crime of *debauchery!* What scenes hath the moon seen every night! Sweetly did she shine last evening; the meadows seemed as if they were silvered with beauty when she shone upon them. But ah! what sins were transacted beneath her pale sway! Oh, God, thou only knowest: our hearts might be sickened, and we might indeed cry for "A lodge in some vast wilderness," had we seen what God beheld when he looked down from the moon-lit sky! Ye tell me that sins of that kind are common in the lower class of society. Alas, I know it; alas, how many a girl hath dashed herself into the river to take away her life, because she could not bear the infamy that was brought upon her! But lay not this to the poor; the infamy and sin of our streets begin not with them. It beginneth with the highest ranks—with what we call the noblest classes of society. Men that have defiled themselves and others will stand in our senates, and walk among our peers; men whose characters are not reputable—it is a shame to speak even of the things that are done of them in secret—are received into the drawingrooms and into the parlors of the highest society, while the poor creature who has been the victim of their passions is hooted and cast away!

O Lord God, thou alone knowest the awful ravages that this sin hath made. Thy servant's lips can utter no more than this; he hath gone to the verge of his utterance, he feeleth that he hath no further license in his speech, still he may well cry—"Oh that my head were waters, and mine eyes a fountain of tears, that I might weep day and night for the slain of the daughter of my people!" If ye have walked the hospital, if ye have seen the refuges, if ye have talked with the inmates—and if ye know the gigantic spread of that enormous evil, ye may well sympathize with me when I say, that at the thought of it my spirit is utterly cast down. I feel that I would rather die than live whilst sin thus reigns and iniquity thus spreads.

But are these the only evils? Are these the only demons that are devouring our people? Ah, would to God it were so. Behold, throughout this land, how are men falling by every sin, disguised as it is under the shape of pleasure. Have ye never, as from some distant journey ye have returned to your houses at midnight, seen the multitudes of people who are turning out of casinos, low theaters, and other houses of sin? I do not frequent those places, nor from earliest childhood have I ever trodden those floors; but, from the company that I have seen issuing from these dens, I could only lift up my hands, and pray God to close such places; they seem to be the gates of hell, and their doors, as they very properly themselves say, "Lead to the pit."

Ah, may God be pleased to raise up many who shall warn this city, and bid Christian people cry day and night "for the slain of the daughter of our people!" Christians, never leave off weeping for men's sins and infamies. There are sins by day; God's own day, this day is defiled, is broken in pieces and trodden under foot. There are sins every morning committed, and sins each night. If ye could see them ye might be never

happy, if ye could walk in the midst of them and behold them with your eyes, if God would give you grace, ye might perpetually weep, for ye would always have cause for sorrow. "Oh that my head were waters, and mine eyes a fountain of tears, that I might weep day and night for the slain of the daughter of my people."

Weeping for Those Without Christ

But now I must just throw in something which will more particularly apply to you. Perhaps I have very few here who would indulge in open and known sin; perhaps most of you belong to the good and amiable class who have every kind of virtue, and of whom it must be said, "One thing thou lackest." My heart never feels so grieved as at the sight of you. How often have I been entertained most courteously and hospitably, as the Lord's servant, in the houses of men and of women whose characters are supremely excellent, who have every virtue that could adorn a Christian, except faith in the Lord Jesus Christ; who might be held up as the very mirrors and patterns to be imitated by others. How has my heart grieved when I have thought of these, still undecided, still godless, prayerless and Christless. I have many of you in this congregation today—I could not put my finger upon one solitary fault in your character; you are scrupulously correct in your morals—Alas, alas, alas for you, that you should still be dead in trespasses and sins, because you have not been renewed by divine grace! So lovely, and yet without faith; so beautiful, so admirable, and yet not converted.

O God, when drunkards die, when swearers perish, when harlots and seducers sink to the fate they have earned, we may well weep for such sinners; but when these who have walked in our midst and have almost been acknowledged as believers, are cast away because they lack the one thing needful, it seems enough to make angels weep. O members of churches, ye may well take up the cry of Jeremiah when ye remember what multitudes of these you have in your midst—men who have a name to live and are dead: and others, who though they profess not to be Christians, are almost persuaded to obey their Lord and Master, but are yet not partakers of the divine life of God.

But now I shall want, if I can, to press this pathetic subject a little further upon your minds. In the day when Jeremiah wept this lamentation with an exceeding loud and bitter cry, Jerusalem was in all her mirth and merriment. Jeremiah was a sad man in the midst of a multitude of merry makers; he told them that Jerusalem should be destroyed, that their temple should become a heap, and Nebuchadnezzar should lay it with the ground. They laughed him to scorn; they mocked him. Still the viol and the dance were only to be seen. Do you not picture that brave old man, for he was bravely plaintive, sitting down in the courts of the Temple? And though as yet the pillars were unfallen, and the golden roof was yet unstained, he lifted up his hands and pictured to himself this scene of Jerusalem's Temple burned with fire, her women and her children carried away captive, and her sons given to the sword. And when he pictured this, he did, as it were, in spirit set himself down upon one of the broken pillars of the Temple, and there, in the midst of desolation which was not as yet—but which faith, the evidence of things not seen, did picture to him—cry, "Oh that my head were waters, and mine eyes a fountain of tears."

And now, today, here are many of you masquers and merry makers in this ball of life; ye are here merry and glad today, and ye marvel that I should talk of you as persons for whom we ought to weep. "Weep ye for me!" you say; "I am in health, I am in riches, I am enjoying life; why weep for me? I need none of your sentimental weeping!" Ah, but we weep because we foresee the future. If you could live here always, we might not, perhaps, weep for you; but we, by the eye of faith, look forward to the time when the pillars of heaven must totter, when this earth must shake, when death must give up its prey, when the great white throne must be set in the clouds of heaven, and the thunders and lightnings of Jehovah shall be launched in armies, and the angels of God shall be marshalled in their ranks, to swell the pomp of the grand assize—we look forward to that hour, and by faith we see you standing before the Judge; we see his eye sternly fixed on you; we hear him read the book; we mark your tottering knee, whilst sentence after sentence of thundering wrath strikes on your appalled ear; we think we see your blanched countenances; we mark your terror beyond all description, when he cries, "Depart, ye cursed!" We hear your shrieks; we hear you cry, "Rocks hide us; mountains on us fall!" We see the angel with fiery brand pursuing you; we hear your last unutterable shriek of woe as you descend into the pit of hell—and we ask you if you could see this as we see it, would you wonder that at the thought of your destruction we are prepared to weep? "Oh that my head were waters, and mine eyes were a fountain of tears that I might weep" over you who will not stand in the judgment, but must be driven away like chaff into the unquenchable fire!

And by the eye of faith we look further than that; we look into the grim and awful future: our faith looks through the gate of iron bound with adamant; we see the place of the condemned; our ear, opened by faith, hears "The sullen groans, and hollow moans, and shrieks of tortured ghosts!" Our eye anointed with heavenly eye salve, sees the worm that never dieth, it beholds the fire that never can be quenched, and sees you writhing in the flame!

O professors, if ye believed not in the wrath to come, and in hell eternal, I should not wonder that ye were unmoved by such a thought as this. But if ye believe what your Savior said when he declared that he would destroy both body and soul in hell, I must wonder that ye could endure the thought without weeping for your fellow-creatures who are going there. If I saw mine enemy marching into the flames, I would rush between him and the fire and seek to preserve him; and will you see men and women marching on in a mad career of vice and sin, well aware that "the wages of sin is death," and will you not interpose so much as a tear? What! are you more brutal than the beast, more stolid than the stone! It must be so, if the thought of the unutterable torment of hell doth not draw tears from your eyes and prayer from your hearts. Oh, if today some strong archangel could unbolt the gates of hell, and for a solitary second permit the voice of wailing and weeping to come up to our ears; oh, how should we grieve! Each man would put his hand upon his loins and walk this earth in terror. That shriek might make each hair stand on an end upon our heads, and then make us roll ourselves in the dust for anguish and woe—

Oh, doleful state of dark despair,
When God has far removed,
And fixed their dreadful station where
They must not taste his love.

Oh that my head were waters, and mine eyes a fountain of tears, that I might weep for some of you that are going there this day.

Remember, again, O Christian, that those for whom we ask you to weep this day are persons who have had great privilege, and consequently, if lost, must expect greater punishment. I do not today ask your sympathies for men in foreign lands; I shall not bid you weep for Hottentots or Mahomedans though ye might weep for them, and ye have goodly cause to do so—but I ask this day your tears for the slain of the daughter of your own people. Oh! what multitudes of heathens we have in all our places of worship! what multitudes of unconverted persons in all the pews of the places where we usually assemble to worship God; and I may add, what hundreds we have here who are without God, without Christ, without hope in the world. And these are not like Hottentots who have not heard the Word: they have heard it, and they have rejected it.

Many of you, when you die, cannot plead, as an excuse that you did not know your duty; you heard it plainly preached to you, you heard it in every corner of the streets, you had the book of God in your houses. You cannot say that you did not know what you must do to be saved. You read the Bible, you understand salvation—many of you are deeply taught in the theory of salvation; when ye perish, your blood must be of your own head, and the Master may well cry over you today, "Woe unto thee, Bethsaida, woe unto thee, Chorazin! For if the mighty works that were done in thee, had been done in Tyre and Sidon, they would have repented long ago in sackcloth and ashes."

I wonder at myself this day; I hate my eyes, I feel as if I could pluck them from their sockets now, because they will not weep as I desire, over poor souls who are perishing! How many have I among you whom I love and who love me! We are no strangers to one another, we could not live at a distance from each other, our hearts have been joined together long and firmly. Ye have stood by me in the hour of tribulation; ye have listened to the Word, ye have been pleased with it; I bear you witness that if you could pluck out your eyes for me you would do it. And yet I know there are many of you true lovers of God's Word in appearance, and certainly great lovers of God's servant; but alas for you, that you should still be in the gall of bitterness and in the bonds of iniquity! Alas, my sister, I can weep for thee! Woe, woe, my brother, I can weep for thee! we have met together in God's house, we have prayed together, and yet we must be sundered. Shepherd, some of thy flock will perish! O sheep of my pasture, people of my care, must I have that horrid thought upon me, that I must lose you? Must we, at the day of judgment, say farewell for ever? Must I bear my witness against you?

I shall be honest; I have dealt faithfully with your souls. God is my witness, I have often preached in weakness; often have I had to groan before him that I have not preached as I could desire; but I have never preached insincerely. Nobody will ever dare to accuse me of dishonesty in this respect; not one of your smiles have I ever courted. I have never dreaded your frowns; I have been in weariness oftentimes, when I should have rested, preaching God's Word. But what of that? That were nothing; only this much, there is some responsibility resting upon you. And remember, that to perish under the sound of the Gospel is to perish more terribly than anywhere else.

But, my hearers, must that be your lot? And must I be witness against you

in the day of judgment? I pray God it may not be so; I beseech the Master, that he may spare us each such a fate as that.

Weeping for Our Families

And now, dear friends, I have one word to add before I leave this point. Some of you need not look round on this congregation to find cause for weeping. My pious brethren and sisters, you have cause enough to weep in your own families. Ah, mother! I know thy griefs; thou hast had cause to cry to God with weeping eyes for many a mournful hour, because of thy son; thine offspring hath turned against thee; and he that came forth of thee has despised his mother's God. Father, thou hast carefully brought up thy daughter; thou hast nourished her when she was young, and taken her fondly in thine arms; she was the delight of thy life, yet she hath sinned against thee and against God. Many of you have sons and daughters that you often mention in your prayers, but never with hope. You have often thought that God has said of your son, "Ephraim is given to idols; let him alone;" the child of your affection has become an adder stinging your heart! Oh, then weep, I beseech you. Parents, do not leave off weeping for your children; do not become hardened towards them, sinners though they be; it may be that God may yet bring them to himself.

It was but last church meeting that we received into our communion a young friend who was educated and brought up by a pious minister in Colchester. She had been there many years, and when she came away to London the minister said to her, "Now, my girl, I have prayed for you hundreds of times, and I have done all I can with you; your heart is as hard as a stone; I must leave you with God!" That broke her heart, she is now converted to Jesus. How many sons and daughters have made their parents feel the same! "There," they have said, "I must leave you; I cannot do more." But in saying that, they have not meant that they would leave them unwept for; but they have thought within themselves, that if they were damned, they would follow them weeping to the very gates of hell, if by tears they could decoy them into heaven.

How can a man be a Christian, and not love his offspring? How can a man be a believer in Jesus Christ, and yet have a cold and hard heart in the things of the kingdom, towards his children? I have heard of ministers of a certain sect, and professors of a certain class, who have despised family prayer, who have laughed at family godliness and thought nothing of it. I cannot understand how the men can know as much as they do about the gospel, and yet have so little of the spirit of it. I pray God, deliver you and deliver me from anything like that. No, it is our business to train up our children in the fear of the Lord; and though we cannot give them grace, it is ours to pray to the God who can give it; and in answer to our many supplications, he will not turn us away, but he will be pleased to take notice of our prayers and to regard our sighs.

And now, Christian mourners, I have given you work enough; may God the Holy Spirit enable you to do it. Let me exhort you, yet once again, to weep. Do you need a copy? Behold your Master; he has come to the brow of the hill; he sees Jerusalem lying on the hill opposite to him; he looks down upon it, as he sees it there—beautiful for situation, the joy of the whole earth—instead of feeling the rapture of an artist who surveys the ramparts of a strong city, and marks the position of some magnificent tower in the midst of glorious scenery, he bursts out, and he cries, "O Jerusalem, Jerusalem! how often would I have gathered thy children together as a hen gathereth her chickens under her wings, but ye would not. Behold, your house is left unto you desolate."

Go ye now your ways, and as ye stand on any of the hills around, and beheld this Behemoth city lying in the valley, say, "O London, London! how great thy guilt. Oh, that the Master would gather thee under his wing, and make thee his city, the joy of the whole earth! O London, London! full of privileges, and full of sin; exalted to heaven by the gospel, thou shalt be cast down to hell by thy rejection of it!" And then, when ye have wept over London, go and weep over the street in which you live, as you see the sabbath broken, and God's laws trampled upon, and men's bodies profaned— go ye and weep! Weep, for the court in which you live in your humble poverty; weep for the square in which you live in your magnificent wealth; weep for the humbler street in which you live in competence; weep for your neighbors and your friends, lest any of them, having lived godless, may die godless! Then go to your house, weep for your family, for your servants, for your husband, for your wife, for your children. Weep, weep; cease not weeping, till God hath renewed them by his Spirit. And if you have any friends with whom you sinned in your past life, be earnest for their salvation.

George Whitefield said there were many young men with whom he played at cards, in his lifetime, and spent hours in wasting his time when he ought to have been about other business; and when he was converted, his first thought was, "I must by God's grace have these converted too." And he never rested, till he could say, that he did not know of one of them, a companion of his guilt, who was not now a companion with him in the tribulation of the gospel.

Oh, let it be so with you! Nor let your

exertions end in tears; mere weeping will do nothing without action. Get you on your feet; ye that have voices and might, go forth and preach the gospel, preach it in every street and lane of this huge city; ye that have wealth, go forth and spend it for the poor, and sick, and needy, and dying, the uneducated, the unenlightened; ye that have time, go forth and spend it in deeds and goodness; ye that have power in prayer, go forth and pray; ye that can handle the pen, go forth and write down iniquity— every one to his post, every one of you to your gun in this day of battle; now for God and for his truth; for God and for the right; let every one of us who knows the Lord seek to fight under his banner! O God, without whom all our exertions are vain, come now and stir up thy church to greater diligence and more affectionate earnestness, that we may not have in future such cause to weep as we have this day! Sinners, believe on the Lord Jesus; he hath died; look to him and live, and God the Almighty bless you! To God the Father, Son, and Holy Ghost, be glory for ever and ever.

"The Greatest Wonder of All" is taken from Seven Wonders of Grace, *a posthumous collection of Spurgeon's works devoted to exploring the wonders of God's grace. Here Spurgeon uses a passage from Ezekiel to delineate the nature of the doom from which God's grace delivers men and describe how this grace proceeds. Spurgeon concludes with a plea to his reader to consider his own situation before God, in light of the coming judgment.*

CHAPTER SEVEN

The Greatest Wonder of All

And I was left (Ezek. 9:8).

Salvation never shines so brightly to any man's eyes as when it comes to himself. Then is grace illustrious indeed when we can see it working with divine power upon ourselves. To our apprehension, our own case is ever the most desperate, and mercy shown to us is the most extraordinary. We see others perish, and wonder that the same doom has not befallen ourselves. The horror of the ruin which we dreaded, and our intense delight at the certainty of safety in Christ unite with our personal sense of unworthiness to make us cry in amazement, "And I was left."

Ezekiel, in vision, saw the slaughtermen smiting right and left at the bidding of divine justice, and as he stood unharmed among the heaps of the slain, he exclaimed with surprise, "I was left." It may be, the day will come when we, too, shall cry with solemn joy, "And I, too, by sovereign grace, am spared while others perish." Special grace will cause us to marvel. Especially will it be so at the last dread day.

Read the story of the gross idolatry of the people of Jerusalem, as recorded in the eighth chapter of Ezekiel's prophecy, and you will not wonder at the judgment with which the Lord at length overthrew the city. Let us set our hearts to consider how the Lord dealt with the guilty people. "Six men came from the way of the higher gate, which lieth toward the north, and every man with a slaughter weapon in his hand." The destruction wrought by these executioners was swift and terrible, and it was typical of other solemn visitations. All through history the observing eye notices lines of justice, red marks upon the page where the Judge of all the earth has at last seen it needful to decree a terrible visitation upon a guilty people.

All these past displays of divine vengeance point at a coming judgment even more complete and overwhelming. The past is prophetic of the future. A day is surely coming when the Lord Jesus, who came once to save, will descend a second time to judge. Despised mercy has always been succeeded by deserved wrath, and so must it be in the end of all things. "But who may abide the day of his coming? or who shall stand when he appeareth?" When sinners are smitten, who will be left? He shall lift the balances of justice, and make bare the sword of execution. When his avenging angels shall gather the vintage of the earth, who among us shall exclaim in wondering gratitude, "And I was left"? Such an one will be a wonder of grace indeed; worthy to take rank with those marvels of grace of whom we have spoken in the former discourses of this book. Reader, will you be an instance of sparing grace, and cry, "And I was left"?

The Character of the Doom

We will use the wonderfully descriptive vision of this chapter that we may with holy fear behold *the character of the doom* from which grace delivers us, and then we will dwell upon the exclamation of our text, "I was left," considering it as the joyful utterance of *the persons who are privileged to escape the destruction.*

By the help of the Holy Spirit, let us first solemnly consider THE TERRIBLE DOOM from which the prophet in vision saw himself preserved, regarding it as a figure of the judgment which is yet to come upon all the world.

Observe, first, that it was a *just* punishment inflicted upon those who had been often warned; a punishment which they wilfully brought upon themselves. God had said that if they set up idols he would destroy them, for he would not endure such an insult to his Godhead. He had often pleaded with them, not with words only, but with severe providences, for their land had been laid desolate, their city had been besieged, and their kings had been carried away captive; but they were bent on backsliding to the worship of their idol gods. Therefore, when the sword of the Lord was drawn from its scabbard, it was no novel punishment, no freak of vengeance, no unexpected execution.

So, in the close of life, and at the end of the world, when judgment comes on men, it will be just and according to the solemn warnings of the word of God. When I read the terrible things which are written in God's book in reference to future punishment, especially the awful things which Jesus spoke concerning the place where their worm dieth not and their fire is not quenched, I am greatly pressed in spirit. Some there be who sit in judgment upon the great Judge, and condemn the punishment which he inflicts as too severe. As for myself, I cannot measure the power of God's anger, but let it burn as it may, I am sure that it will be just. No needless

pang will be inflicted upon a single one of God's creatures: even those who are doomed for ever will endure no more than justice absolutely requires, no more than they themselves would admit to be the due reward of their sins, if their consciences would judge aright.

Mark you, this is the very hell of hell that men will know that they are justly suffering. To endure a tyrant's wrath would be a small thing compared with suffering what one has brought upon himself by willful wanton choice of wrong. Sin and suffering are indissolubly bound together in the constitution of nature; it cannot be otherwise, nor ought it to be. It is right that evil should be punished. Those who were punished in Jerusalem could not turn upon the executioners and say, "We do not deserve this doom;" but every cruel wound of the Chaldean sword and every fierce crash of the Babylonian battle-axe fell on men who in their consciences knew that they were only reaping what they themselves had sown. Brethren, what wonders of grace shall we be if from a judgment which we have so richly deserved we shall be rescued at the last!

Slaughter Was Preceded by Separation

Let us notice very carefully that this slaughter was *preceded by a separation* which removed from among the people those who were distinct in character. Before the slaughtermen proceeded to their stern task a man appeared among them clothed in linen with a writer's inkhorn by his side, who marked all those who in their hearts were grieved at the evil done in the city. Until these were marked the destroyers did not commence their work. Whenever the Lord lays bare his arm for war he first gathers his saints into a place of safety. He did not destroy the world by the flood till Noah and his family were safe in the ark. He would not suffer a single firedrop to fall on Sodom till Lot had escaped to Zoar. He carefully preserves his own; nor flood nor flame, nor pestilence nor famine shall do them ill. We read in Revelation that the angel said, "Hurt not the earth, neither the sea, nor the trees, till we have sealed the servants of our God in their foreheads."

Vengeance must sheathe her sword, till love has housed its darlings. When Christ cometh to destroy the earth, he will first catch away his people. Ere the elements shall melt with fervent heat, and the pillars of the universe shall rock and reel beneath the weight of wrathful deity, he will have caught up his elect into the air so that they shall be ever with the Lord. When he cometh he shall divide the nations as a shepherd divideth his sheep from the goats; no sheep of his shall be destroyed: he shall without fail take the tares from among the wheat, but not one single ear of wheat shall be in danger.

O that we may be among the selected ones and prove his power to keep us in the day of wrath. May each one of us say amid the wreck of matter and the crash of worlds, "And I was left." Dear friend, are you marked in the forehead, think you? If at this moment my voice were drowned by the trumpet of resurrection, would you be amongst those who awake to safety and glory? Would you be able to say, "The multitude perished around me, but I was left"? It will be so if you hate the sins by which you are surrounded, and if you have received the mark of the blood of Jesus upon your souls; if not, you will not escape, for there is no other door of salvation but his saving name. God grant us grace to belong to that chosen number who wear the covenant seal, the mark of him who counteth up the people.

Judgment Was Placed in the Mediator's Hands

Next, this judgment was placed *in the Mediator's hands*. I want you to notice this. Observe that, according to the chapter, there was no slaughter done except where the man with the writer's inkhorn led the way. So again we read in the tenth chapter, that "One cherub stretched forth his hand from between the cherubims unto the fire that was between the cherubims, and took thereof and put it into the hands of him that was clothed with linen; who took it, and went out," and cast it over the city. See you this. God's glory of old shone forth between the cherubim, that is to say, over the place of propitiation and atonement, and as long as that glow of light remained no judgment fell on Jerusalem, for God in Christ condemns not. But by-and-by "The glory of the God of Israel was gone up from the cherub, whereupon he was, to the threshold of the house," and then judgment was near to come. When God no longer deals with men in Christ his wrath burns like fire, and he commissions the ambassador of mercy to be the messenger of wrath. The very man who marked with his pen the saved ones threw burning coals upon the city and led the way for the destruction of the sinful.

What does this teach but this—"The Father judgeth no man, but hath committed all judgment unto the Son"? I know of no truth more dreadful to meditate upon. Think of it, ye careless ones: the very Christ who died on Calvary is he by whom you will be sentenced. God will judge the world by this man Christ Jesus: he it is that will come in the clouds of heaven, and before him shall be gathered all nations; and when those who have despised him shall look upon his face they will be terrified beyond conception. Not the lightnings, not the thunders, not the dreadful sound of the last tremendous trump shall so alarm them as that face of injured love. Then will they cry to the mountains and hills to hide them from the face of him that sitteth upon the throne.

Why, it is the face of him that wept for sinners, the face which scoffers stained with bloody drops extracted by the thorny crown, the face of the incarnate God who, in infinite mercy, came to save mankind! But because they have despised him, because they would not be saved, because they preferred their own lusts to infinite love, and would persist in rejecting God's best proof of kindness, therefore will they say, "Hide us from the face," for the sight of that face shall be to them more accusing, and more condemning, than all else besides. How dreadful is this truth! The more you consider it, the more will it fill your soul with terror! Would to God it might drive you to fly to Jesus, for then you will behold him with joy in that day.

Destruction Began at the Sanctuary

This destruction, we are told, *began at the sanctuary.* Suppose the Lord were to visit London in his anger, where would he begin to smite? "Oh," somebody says, "of course the destroying angel would go down to the low music halls and dancing rooms, or he would sweep out the back slums and the drink palaces, the jails and places where women of ill life do congregate." Turn to the Scripture which surrounds our text. The Lord says, "Begin at my sanctuary." Begin at the churches, begin at the chapels, begin at the church members, begin at the ministers, begin at the bishops, begin at those who are teachers of the gospel. Begin at the chief and front of the religious world, begin at the high professors who are looked up to as ex-

amples. What does Peter say? "The time is come that judgment must begin at the house of God: and if it first begin at us, what shall the end be of them that obey not the gospel of God? And if the righteous scarcely be saved, where shall the ungodly and the sinner appear?"

The first thing the slaughtermen did was to slay the ancient men which were before the temple, even the seventy elders of the people, for they were secret idolaters. You may be sure that the sword which did not spare the chief men and fathers made but short work with the baser sort. Elders of our churches, ministers of Christ, judgment will begin with us; we must not expect to find more lenient treatment than others at the last great assize; nay, rather, if there shall be a specially careful testing of sincerity it will be for us who have taken upon ourselves to lead others to the Savior.

For this cause let us see well to it that we be not deceived or deceivers, for we shall surely be detected in that day. To play the hypocrite is to play the fool. Will a man deceive his Maker, or delude the Most High? It cannot be. You church members, all of you, should look well to it, for judgment will begin with you. God's fire is in Zion and his furnace in Jerusalem.

In the olden time the people fled to churches and holy places for sanctuary; but how vain will this be when the Lord's avengers shall come forth, since there the havoc will begin! How fiercely shall the sword sweep through the hosts of carnal professors, the men who called themselves servants of God, while they were slaves of the devil; who drank of the cup of the Lord but were drunken with the wine of their own lusts: who could lie and cheat and commit fornication, and yet dared to approach the sacred table of the Lord? What cutting and hewing will there be among the base-born professors of our churches! It were better for such men that they had never been born, or, being born, that their lot had fallen amid heathen ignorance, so that they might have been unable to add sin to sin by lying unto the living God. "Begin at my sanctuary." The word is terrible to all those who have a name to live and are dead. God grant that in such testing times when many fail we may survive every ordeal and through grace exclaim in the end, "And I was left."

Only Those with the Mark Were Spared

After the executioners had begun at the sanctuary it is to be observed that they *did not spare any except those upon whom was the mark*. Old and young, men and women, priests and people, all were slain who had not the sacred sign; and so in the last tremendous day all sinners who have not fled to Christ will perish. Our dear babes that died in infancy we believe to be all washed in the blood of Jesus and all saved; but for the rest of mankind who have lived to years of responsibility there will be only one of two things—they must either be saved because they had faith in Christ, or else the full weight of divine wrath must fall upon them.

Either the mark of Christ's pen or of Christ's sword must be upon every one. There will be no sparing of one man because he was rich, nor of another because he was learned, nor of a third because he was eloquent, nor of a fourth because he was held in high esteem. Those who are marked with the blood of Christ are safe! Without that mark all are lost! This is the one separating sign—do you wear it? Or will you die in your sins? Bow down at once before the feet of Jesus and beseech him to mark you as his own, that so you may be one

of those who will joyfully cry, "And I was left."

The Nature of Those Who Escaped

Now, secondly, I have to call your very particular attention to THE PERSONS WHO ESCAPED, who could each say, "And I was left." We are told that those were marked for mercy who did "sigh and cry for the abominations that were done in the midst thereof." Now we must be very particular about this. It is no word of mine, remember: it is God's word, and therefore I beg you to hear and weigh it for yourselves. We do not read that the devouring sword passed by those quiet people who never did anybody any harm: no mention is made of such an exemption. Neither does the record say that the Lord saved those professors who were judicious, and maintained a fair name and repute until death.

No; the only people that were saved were those who were exercised in heart, and that heart-work was of a painful kind: they sighed and cried because of abounding sin. They saw it, protested against it, avoided it, and last of all wept over it continually. Where testimony failed it remained for them to mourn; retiring from public labors they sat them down and sighed their hearts away because of the evils which they could not cure; and when they felt that sighing alone would do no good they took to crying in prayer to God that he would come and put an end of the dreadful ills which brooded over the land.

I would not say a hard thing, but I wonder, if I were able to read the secret lives of professors of religion whether I should find that they all sigh and cry over the sins of others? Are the tenth of them thus engaged? I am afraid that it does not cause some people much anxiety when they see sin rampant around them. They say that they are sorry, but it never frets them much, or causes them as much trouble as would come of a lost sixpence or a cut finger.

Did you ever feel as if your heart would break over an ungodly son? I do not believe that you are a Christian man if you have such a son and have not felt an agony on his behalf. Did you ever feel as if you could lay down your life to save that daughter of yours? I cannot believe that you are a Christian woman if you have not sometimes come to that. When you have gone through the street and heard an oath, has not your blood chilled in you? has not horror taken hold upon you because of the wicked? There cannot be much grace in you if that has not been the case. If you can go up and down in the world fully at ease because you are prospering in business, and things go smoothly with you, if you forget the woe of this city's sin and poverty, and the yet greater woe which cometh upon it, how dwelleth the love of God in you? The saving mark is only set on those who sigh and cry, and if you are heartless and indifferent there is no such mark on you.

"Are we to be always miserable?" asks one. Far from it. There are many other things to make us rejoice, but if the sad state of our fellow men does not cause us to sigh and cry, then we have not the grace of God in us. "Well," says one, "but every man must look to himself." That is the language of Cain—"Am I my brother's keeper?" That kind of talk is in keeping with the spirit of the wicked one and his seed, but the heir of heaven abhors such language. The genuine Christian loves his race, and therefore he longs to see it made holy and happy. He cannot bear to see men sinning, and so dishonoring God and ruining themselves. If we really love the Lord we shall sometimes lie awake at night sighing to think how his name is blasphemed, and how little progress his

gospel makes. We shall groan to think that men should despise the glorious God who made them, and who daily loads them with benefits. . . .

But it was not their mourning which saved those who escaped—it was the mark which they all received which preserved them from destruction. We must all bear the mark of Jesus Christ. What is that? It is the mark of faith in the atoning blood. That sets apart the chosen of the Lord, and that alone. If you have that mark—and you have it not unless you sigh and cry over the sins of others—then in that last day no sword of justice can come near you. Did you read that word, "But come not nigh any man upon whom is the mark." Come not even near the marked ones lest they be afraid. The grace-marked man is safe even from the near approach of ill. Christ bled for him, and therefore he cannot, must not, die. Let him alone, ye bearers of the destroying weapons. Just as the angel of death, when he flew through the land of Egypt, was forbidden to touch a house where the blood of the lamb was on the lintel and the two side posts, so is it sure that avenging justice cannot touch the man who is in Christ Jesus. Who is he that condemneth since Christ has died?

Have you, then, the blood mark? Yes or no. Do not refuse to question yourself upon this point. Do not take it for granted, lest you be deceived. Believe me, your all hangs upon it. If you are not registered by the man clothed in linen you will not be able to say, "And I was left."

Humility in Those Who Were Left

This brings me to this last point which I desire to speak of. *What were the prophet's emotions when he said, "And I was left"?* He saw men falling right and left, and *he* himself stood like a lone rock amidst a sea of blood; and he cried in wonder, "And I was left."

Let us hear what he further says—"I fell on my face." He lay prostrate with *humility*. Have you a hope that you are saved? Fall on your face, then! See the hell from which you are delivered, and bow before the Lord. Why are you to be saved more than anyone else? Certainly not because of any merit in you. It is due to the sovereign grace of God alone. Fall on your face and own your indebtedness.

Why was I made to hear thy voice,
And enter while there's room,
When thousands make a wretched
    choice,
And rather starve than come?

"And I was left."

If a man has been a drunkard, and has at length been led to flee to Christ, when he says, "And I was left," he will feel the hot tears rising to his eyes, for many other drinkers have died in delirium. One who has been a public sinner, when she is saved will not be able to think of it without astonishment. Indeed, each saved man is a marvel to himself. Nobody here wonders more at divine grace in his salvation than I do myself. Why was I chosen, and called, and saved? I cannot make it out, and I never shall; but I will always praise, and bless, and magnify my Lord for casting an eye of love upon me. Will you not do the same, beloved, if you feel that you by grace are left? Will you not fall on your face and bless the mercy which makes you to differ?

What did the prophet do next? Finding that he was left he began to pray for others. "Ah, Lord," said he, "wilt thou destroy all the residue of Israel?" Intercession is an instinct of the renewed heart. When the believer finds that he is safe he must pray for his fellow-men.

Though the prophet's prayer was too late, yet, blessed be God, ours will not be. We shall be heard. Pray, then, for perishing men. Ask God, who has spared you, to spare those who are like you.

Somebody has said, there will be three great wonders in heaven, first, to see so many there whom we never expected to meet in glory; secondly, to miss so many of whom we felt sure that they must be safe; and thirdly, the greatest wonder of all will be to find ourselves there. I am sure that everyone who has a hope of being in glory feels it to be a marvel; and he resolves, "If I am saved, I will sing the loudest of them all, for I shall owe most to the abounding mercy of God."

Who Will Be Left?

Let me ask a few questions, and I have done. The first—and let each man ask it of himself—shall I be left when the ungodly are slain? Answer it now to yourselves. Men, women, children, will you be spared in that last great day? Are you in Christ? Have you a good hope in him? Do not lie unto yourselves. You will be weighed in the balances; will you be found wanting or not? "Shall I be left?" Let that question burn into your souls.

Next, will my relatives be saved? My wife, my husband, my children, my brother, my sister, my father, my mother—will these all be saved? Happy are we who can say, "Yes, we believe they will," as some of us can joyfully hope. But if you have to say, "No, I fear that my boy is unconverted, or that my father is unsaved;" then do not rest till you have wrestled with God for their salvation. Good woman, if you are obliged to say, "I fear my husband is unconverted," join me in prayer. Bow your heads at once and cry unto your God, "Lord, save our children! Lord, save our parents! Lord, save our husbands and wives, our brothers and sisters; and let the whole of our families meet in heaven, unbroken circles, for thy name's sake!"

May God hear that prayer if it has come from the lips of sincerity! I could not endure the thought of missing one of my boys in heaven: I hope I shall see them both there, and therefore I am in deep sympathy with any of you who have not seen your households brought to Christ. O for grace to pray earnestly and labor zealously for the salvation of your whole households.

The next earnest enquiry is, if you and your relatives are saved, how about your neighbors, your fellow-workmen, your companions in business? "Oh," say you, "many of them are scoffers. A good many of them are still in the gall of bitterness." A sorrowful fact, but have you spoken to them? It is wonderful what a kind word will do. Have you tried it? Did you ever try to speak to that person who meets you every morning as you go to work? Suppose he should be lost! Oh, it will be a bitter feeling for you to think that he went down to the pit without your making an effort to bring him to God. Do not let it be so.

"But we must not be too pushing," says one. I do not know about that. If you saw poor people in a burning house nobody would blame you for being officious if you helped to save them. When a man is sinking in the river, if you jump in and pull him out nobody will say, "You were rude and intrusive, for you were never introduced to him!" This world has been lost, and it must be saved; and we must not mind manners in saving it. We must get a grip of sinking sinners somehow, even if it be by the hair of their heads, ere they sink, for if they sink they are lost for ever. They will forgive us very soon for any roughness that we use; but we shall not forgive ourselves if, for want of a little energy, we permit them to die without a knowledge of the truth.

Oh, beloved friends, if you are left while others perish, I beseech you, by the mercies of God, by the bowels of compassion which are in Christ Jesus, by the bleeding wounds of the dying Son of God, do love your fellow men, and sigh and cry about them if you cannot bring them to Christ. If you cannot save them you can weep over them. If you cannot give them a drop of cold water in hell, you can give them your heart's tears while yet they are in this body.

But are you in very deed reconciled to God yourselves? Reader, are you cured of the awful disease of sin? Are you marked with the blood-red sign of trust in the atoning blood? Do you believe in the Lord Jesus Christ? If not, the Lord have mercy upon you! May you have sense enough to have mercy upon yourself. May the Spirit of God instruct you to that end. Amen.

As a corollary of Spurgeon's fervent evangelistic message of grace, he was supremely concerned with how men may most effectively be reached with the gospel of grace. "Qualifications for Soul-Winning—Manward" is taken from Spurgeon's The Soul Winner *and immediately succeeds "Qualifications for Soul-Winning—Godward." Spurgeon's advice is always compelling and practical and is sound advice for every believer, even when not specifically engaged in "soul-winning" activities.*

CHAPTER EIGHT

Qualifications for Soul-Winning—Manward

You remember, brethren, that on the last occasion when I gave you a lecture on soul-winning, I spoke of the qualifications, Godward, that would fit a man to be a soul-winner; and I tried to describe to you the kind of man that the Lord was most likely to use in the winning of souls. This afternoon, I propose to take as my subject—

THE CHARACTERISTICS OF A SOUL-WINNER, MANWARD.

I might almost mention the very same points that I enumerated before as being those which will best tell manward, for I do think that those qualities that commend themselves to the notice of God, as being most adapted to the end He desires, are also likely to be approved by the object acted upon, that is, the soul of man.

Intelligence

There have been many men in the world who have not been at all adapted for this work; and, first, let me say that *an ignoramus is not likely to be much of a soul-winner.* A man who only knows that he is a sinner, and that Christ is a Savior, may be very useful to others in the same condition as himself, and it is his duty to do the best he can with what little knowledge he possesses; but, on the whole, I should not expect such a man to be very largely used in the service of God. If he had enjoyed a wider and deeper experience of the things of God, if he had been in the highest sense a learned man because taught of God, he could have used his knowledge for the good of others; but being to a great extent ignorant of the things of God himself, I do not see how he can make them known to other people. Truly, there must be some light in that candle which is to lighten men's darkness, and *there must be some information in that man who is to be a teacher of his fellows.* The man who is almost or altogether ignorant, whatever will he has to do good, must be left out of the race of great soul-winners; he is disqualified from even entering the lists, and therefore, let us all ask, brethren, that we may be well instructed in the truth of God, that we may be able to teach others also.

Sincerity

Granted that you are not of the ignorant class to which I have been referring, but supposing that you are well instructed in the best of all wisdom, what are the qualities that you must have towards men if you are to win them for the Lord? I should say, there must be about us *an evident sincerity;* not only sincerity, but such sincerity that it shall be manifest at once to anyone who honestly looks for it. It must be quite clear to your hearers that you have a firm belief in the truths that you are preaching; otherwise, you will never make them believe them. Unless they are convinced, beyond all question, that you do believe these truths yourselves, there will be no efficacy and no force in your preaching. No one must suspect you of proclaiming to others what you do not fully believe in yourself; if it should ever be so, your work will be of no effect. All who listen to you ought to be conscious that you are exercising one of the noblest crafts, and performing one of the most sacred functions that ever fell to the lot of man. If you have only a feeble appreciation of the gospel you profess to deliver, it is impossible for those who hear your proclamation of it to be greatly influenced by it.

I heard it asked, the other day, of a certain minister, "Did he preach a good sermon?" and the reply to the enquiry was, "What he *said* was very good." "But did you not profit by the sermon?" "No, not in the slightest degree." "Was it not a good sermon?" Again came the first answer, "What he *said* was very good." "What do you mean? Why did you not profit by the sermon if what the preacher said was very good?" This was the explanation that the listener gave, "I did not profit by the discourse because I did not believe in the man who delivered it; he was simply an actor performing a part; I did not believe that he felt what he preached, nor that he cared whether we felt or believed it or not."

Where such a state of things as that exists, the hearers cannot be expected to profit by the sermon, no matter what the preacher may say; they may try to fancy that the truths he utters are precious, they may resolve that they will feed upon the provision whoever may set the dish before them; but it is no use, they cannot do it, they cannot separate the heartless speaker from the message he delivers so carelessly. As soon as a man lets his work become a matter of mere form or routine, it sinks into a performance in which the preacher is sim-

ply an actor. He is only acting a part, as he might in a play at the theater; and not speaking from his inmost soul, as a man sent from God.

I do beseech you, brethren, speak from your hearts, or else do not speak at all. If you can be silent, be silent; but if you must speak for God, be thoroughly sincere about it. It would be better for you to go back to business, and weigh butter or sell reels of cotton, or do anything rather than pretend to be ministers of the gospel unless God has called you to the work. I believe that the most damnable thing a man can do is to preach the gospel merely as an actor, and to turn the worship of God into a kind of theatrical performance. Such a caricature is more worthy of the devil than of God. Divine truth is far too precious to be made the subject of such a mockery. You may depend upon it that, when the people once suspect that you are insincere, they will never listen to you except with disgust, and they will not be at all likely to believe your message if you give them cause to think that you do not believe it yourselves.

Earnestness

I hope I am not wrong in supposing that all of us are thoroughly sincere in our Master's service; so I will go on to what seems to me to be the next qualification, manward, for soul-winning, and that is, *evident earnestness*. The command to the man who would be a true servant of the Lord Jesus Christ is, "Thou shalt love the Lord thy God with all thy heart, and with all thy soul, and with all thy strength, and with all thy mind." If a man is to be a soul-winner, there must be in him intensity of emotion as well as sincerity of heart. You may preach the most solemn warnings, and the most dreadful threatenings, in such an indifferent or careless way that no one will be in the least affected by them; and you may repeat the most affectionate exhortations in such a half-hearted manner that no one will be moved either to love or fear.

I believe, brethren, that for soul-winning there is more in this matter of earnestness than in almost anything else. I have seen and heard some who were very poor preachers, who yet brought many souls to the Savior through the earnestness with which they delivered their message. There was positively nothing in their sermons (until the provision merchant used them to wrap round his butter), yet those feeble sermons brought many to Christ. It was not what the preachers said, so much as how they said it, that carried conviction to the hearts of their hearers. The simplest truth was so driven home by the intensity of the utterance and emotion of the man from whom it came that it told with surprising effect. If any gentleman here would present me with a cannonball, say one weighing fifty or a hundred pounds, and let me roll it across the room; and another would entrust me with a rifle-ball, and a rifle out of which I could fire it, I know which would be the more effective of the two. Let no man despise the little bullet, for very often that is the one that kills the sin, and kills the sinner, too.

So, brethren, it is not the bigness of the words you utter; it is the force with which you deliver them that decides what is to come of the utterance. I have heard of a ship that was fired at by the cannon in a fort, but no impression was made upon it until the general in command gave the order for the balls to be made red-hot, and then the vessel was sent to the bottom of the sea in three minutes. That is what you must do with your sermons, make them red-hot; never mind if men do say you are too enthusiastic, or even too fanatical, give them red-hot shot, there is nothing else half as good for the purpose you have in view. We do not go out snow-balling on Sundays, we go fire-balling; we ought to hurl grenades into the enemy's ranks.

What earnestness our theme deserves! We have to tell of an earnest Savior, an earnest heaven, and an earnest hell. How earnest we ought to be when we remember that in our work we have to deal with souls that are immortal, with sin that is eternal in its effects, with pardon that is infinite, and with terrors and joys that are to last for ever and ever! A man who is not in earnest when he has such a theme as this—can he possess a heart at all? Could one be discovered even with a microscope? If he were dissected, probably all that could be found would be a pebble, a heart of stone, or some other substance equally incapable of emotion. I trust that, when God gave us hearts of flesh for ourselves, He gave us hearts that could feel for other people also.

Love for Those Who Hear

These things being taken for granted, I should say, next, that it is necessary for a man who is to be a soul-winner, that he should have an *evident love to his hearers.* I cannot imagine a man being a winner of souls when he spends most of his time in abusing his congregation, and talking as if he hated the very sight of them. Such men seem happy only when they are emptying vials of wrath over those who have the unhappiness of listening to them. I heard of a brother preaching from the text, "A certain man went down from Jerusalem to Jericho, and fell among thieves." He began his discourse thus, "I do not say that this man came to the place where we are, but I do know another man who did come to this place, and fell among thieves." You can easily guess what would be the result of such vitriol-throwing. I know of one who preached from the passage, "And Aaron held his peace," and one who heard him said that the difference between him and Aaron was, that Aaron held his peace, and the preacher did not; but, on the contrary, he raved at the people with all his might.

You must have a real desire for the good of the people if you are to have much influence over them. Why, even dogs and cats love the people who love them, and human beings are much the same as these dumb animals. People very soon get to know when a cold man gets into the pulpit, one of those who seem to have been carved out of a block of marble. There have been one or two of our brethren of that kind, and they have never succeeded anywhere. When I have asked the cause of their failure, in each case the reply has been, "He is a good man, a very good man; he preaches well, very well, but still we do not get on with him." I have asked, "Why do you not like him?" The reply has been, "Nobody ever did like him." "Is he quarrelsome?" "Oh! dear no, I wish he would make a row." I try to fish out what the drawback is, for I am very anxious to know, and at last someone says, "Well, sir, I do not think he has any heart; at least, he does not preach and act as if he had any."

It is very sad when the failure of any ministry is caused by want of heart. You ought to have a great big heart, like the harbor at Portsmouth or Plymouth, so that all the people in your congregation could come and cast anchor in it, and feel that they were under the lee of a great rock. Do you not notice that men succeed in the ministry, and win souls for Christ, just in proportion as they are men with large hearts? Think, for instance, of Dr. Brock; there was a mass of a man, one who had bowels of compassion; and what is the good of a minis-ter who has not? I do not hold up the accumulation of flesh as an object worthy of your attainment; but I do say that you must have big hearts, if you are to win men to Jesus; you must be Greathearts if you are to lead many pilgrims to the Celestial City.

I have seen some very lean men who said that they were perfectly holy, and I could almost believe that they could not sin, for they were like old bits of leather, there did not appear to be anything in them that was capable of sinning. I met one of these "perfect" brethren once, and he was just like a piece of sea-weed, there was no humanity in him. I like to see a trace of humanity somewhere or other about a man, and people in general like it, too; they get on better with a man who has some human nature in him. Human nature, in some aspects, is an awful thing; but when the Lord Jesus Christ took it, and joined His own divine nature to it, He made a grand thing of it, and human nature is a noble thing when it is united to the Lord Jesus Christ.

Those men who keep themselves to themselves, like hermits, and live a supposed sanctified life of self-absorption, are not likely to have any influence in the world, or to do good to their fellow-creatures. You must love the people, and mix with them, if you are to be of service to them. There are some ministers who really are much better men than others, yet they do not accomplish so much good as those who are more human, those who go and sit down with the people, and make themselves as much as possible at home with them. You know, brethren, that it is possible for you to appear to be just a wee bit too good, so that people will feel that you are altogether transcendental beings, and fitter to preach to angels, and cherubim, and seraphim, than to the fallen sons of Adam.

Just be men among men; keeping yourselves clear of all their faults and vices, but mingling with them in perfect love and sympathy, and feeling that you would do anything in your power to bring them to Christ, so that you might even say with the apostle Paul, "Though I be free from all men, yet have I made myself servant unto all, that I might gain the more. And unto the Jews I became as a Jew, that I might gain the Jews; to them that are under the law, as under the law, that I might gain them that are under the law; to them that are without law, as without law (being not without law to God, but under the law to Christ), that I might gain them that are without law. To the weak became I as weak, that I might gain the weak: I am made all things to all men, that I might by all means save some."

Unselfishness

The next qualification, manward, for soul-winning is *evident unselfishness*. A man ceases to bring men to Christ as soon as he becomes known as a selfish man. Selfishness seems to be ingrained in some people; you see it at the table at home, in the house of God, everywhere. When such individuals come to deal with a church and congregation, their selfishness soon manifests itself; they mean to get all they can, although in the Baptist ministry they do not often get much.

I hope each of you, brethren, will be willing to say, "Well, let me have but food and raiment, and I will be therewith content." If you try to put the thought of money altogether away from you, the money will often come back to you doubled; but if you seek to grab and grasp all, you will very likely find that it will not come to you at all. Those who are selfish in the matter of salary, will be the same in everything else; they will

not want their people to know anybody who can preach better than themselves; and they cannot bear to hear of any good work going on anywhere except in their own chapel. If there is a revival at another place, and souls are being saved, they say, with a sneer, "Oh! yes, there are many converts, but what are they? Where will they be in a few months' time?" They think far more of their own gain of one new member per year than of their neighbor's hundreds at one time.

If your people see that kind of selfishness in you, you will soon lose power over them; if you make up your mind that you will be a great man, whoever has to be thrust on one side, you will go to the cats as sure as you are alive. What are you, my dear brother, that people should all bow down and worship you, and think that in all the world there is none beside you? I tell you what it is; the less you think of yourself, the more will people think of you; and the more you think of yourself, the less will people think of you. If any of you have any trace of selfishness about you, pray get rid of it at once, or you will never be fit instruments for the winning of souls for the Lord Jesus Christ.

Holiness

Then I am sure that another thing that is wanted in a soul-winner is *holiness of character*. It is no use talking about "the higher life" on Sundays, and then living the lower life on week days. A Christian minister must be very careful, not only to be innocent of actual wrongdoing, but not to be a cause of offense to the weak ones of the flock. All things are lawful, but all things are not expedient. We ought never to do anything that we judge to be wrong, but we ought also to be willing to abstain from things which might not be wrong in themselves, but which might be an occasion of stumbling to others. When people see that we not only preach about holiness, but that we are ourselves holy men, they will be drawn towards holy things by our character as well as by our preaching.

Seriousness

I think also that, if we are to be soul-winners, there must be about us *a seriousness of manner*. Some brethren are serious by nature. There was a gentleman in a railway carriage, some time ago, who overheard a conversation between two of the passengers. One of them said, "Well, now, I think the church of Rome has great power, and is likely to succeed with the people, because of the evident holiness of her ministers. There is, for instance, Cardinal _____, he is just like a skeleton; through his long fasting and prayers, he has reduced himself almost to skin and bone. Whenever I hear him speak, I feel at once the force of the holiness of the man. Now, look at Spurgeon, he eats and drinks like an ordinary mortal; I would not give a pin to hear him preach." His friend heard him very patiently, and then said quite quietly, "Did it ever strike you that the Cardinal's appearance was to be accounted for by the fact of his liver being out of order? I do not think it is grace that makes him as lean as he is, I believe it is his liver."

So, there are some brethren who are naturally of a melancholy disposition, they are always very serious; but in them it is not a sign of grace, it is only an indication that their livers are out of order. They never laugh, they think it would be wicked to do so; but they go about the world increasing the misery of human kind, which is dreadful enough without the addition of their unnecessary portion. Such people evidently imagine that they were predestinated to pour buckets of cold water upon all human mirth and joy. So, dear brethren, if any of you are very serious, you must not always attribute it to grace, for it may be all owing to the state of your liver.

The most of us, however, are far more inclined to that laughter which doeth good like medicine, and we shall need all our cheerfulness, if we are to comfort and lift up those who are cast down; but we shall never bring many souls to Christ, if we are full of that levity which characterizes some men. People will say, "It is all a joke; just hear how those young fellows jest about religion, it is one thing to listen to them when they are in the pulpit, but it is quite another matter to listen to them when they are sitting round the supper table."

I have heard of a man who was dying, and he sent for the minister to come and see him. When the minister came in, the dying man said to him, "Do you remember a young man walking with you one evening, some years ago, when you were going out to preach?" He said, he did not. "I recollect it very well," replied the other. "Do you not remember preaching at such-and-such a village, from such-and-such a text, and after the service a young man walked home with you?" "Oh, yes, I remember that very well!" "Well, I am the young man who walked home with you that night; I remember your sermon, I shall never forget it." "Thank God for that," said the preacher. "No," answered the dying man, "you will not thank God when you have heard all I have to say. I walked with you to the village, but you did not say much to me on the way there, for you were thinking over your sermon; you deeply impressed me while you were preaching, and I was led to think about giving my heart to Christ. I wanted to speak to you about my soul on the way home; but the moment you got out you cracked a joke, and all the way back you made such fun upon serious subjects, that I could not say anything about what I felt, and it thoroughly disgusted me with religion, and all who professed it, and now I am going to be damned, and my blood will lie at your door, as sure as you are alive," and so he passed out of the world. One would not like anything of that sort to happen to himself; therefore, take heed, brethren, that you give no occasion for it. There must be a prevailing seriousness about our whole lives, otherwise we cannot hope to lead other men to Christ.

Tenderness

Finally, if we are to be much used of God as soul-winners, there must be in our hearts *a great deal of tenderness.* I like a man to have a due amount of holy boldness, but I do not care to see him brazenfaced and impudent. A young man goes into a pulpit, apologizes for attempting to preach, and hopes the people will bear with him; he does not know that he has anything particular to say, if the Lord had sent him he might have had some message for them, but he feels himself so young and inexperienced that he cannot speak very positively about anything. Such talk as that will never save a mouse, much less an immortal soul. If the Lord has sent you to preach the gospel, why should you make any apologies? Ambassadors do not apologize when they go to a foreign court; they know that their monarch has sent them, and they deliver their message with all the authority of king and country at their back.

Nor is it worthwhile for you to call attention to your youth. You are only a trumpet of ram's horn; and it does not matter whether you were pulled off the ram's head yesterday, or five-and-twenty years ago. If God blows through you, there will be noise enough, and something more than noise; if He does not, nothing will come of the blowing. When you preach, speak out straight, but be very tender about it; and if there is an unpleasant thing to be said, take care that you put it in the kindest possible form.

Some of our brethren had a message to deliver to a certain Christian brother, and when they went to him they put it so awkwardly that he was grievously offended. When I spoke to him about the same matter, he said, "I would not have minded your speaking to me; you have a way of putting an unpleasant truth so that a man cannot be offended with you however much he may dislike the message you bring to him." "Well, but," I said, "I put the matter just as strongly as the other brethren did." "Yes, you did," he replied, "but they said it in such a nasty kind of a way that I would not stand it. Why, sir, I had rather be blown up by you than praised by those other people!"

There is a way of doing such things so that the person reproved feels positively grateful to you. One may kick a man downstairs in such a fashion that he will rather like it; while another may open a door in such an offensive way that you do not want to go through till he is out of the way. Now, if I have to tell anyone certain unpalatable truths which it is necessary that he should know if his soul is to be saved, it is a stern necessity for me to be faithful to him; yet I will try so to deliver my message that he shall not be offended at it. Then, if he does take offense, he must; the probability is that he will not, but that what I say will take effect upon his conscience.

I know some brethren who preach as if they were prize-fighters. When they are in the pulpit, they remind me of the Irishman at Donnybrook Fair; all the way through the sermon they appear to be calling upon someone to come up and fight them, and they are never happy except when they are pitching into somebody or other. There is a man who often preaches on Clapham Common, and he does it so pugnaciously that the infidels whom he assails cannot endure it, and there are frequent fights and rows. There is a way of preaching so as to set everybody by the ears; if some men were allowed to preach in heaven, I am afraid they would set the angels fighting. I know a number of ministers of this stamp.

There is one who, to my certain knowledge, has been at over a dozen places during his not very long ministerial life. You can tell where he has been by the ruin he leaves behind him. He always finds the churches in a sad state, and he straightway begins to purify them, that is, to destroy them. As a general rule, the first thing, out goes the principal deacon, and the next, away go all the leading families, and before long, the man has purified the place so effectively that the few people who are left cannot keep him. Off he goes to another place, and repeats the process of destruction. He is a kind of spiritual ship-scuttler, and he is never happy except when he is boring a hole through the planks of some good vessel. He says he believes the ship is unsound; so he bores, and bores, until just as she is going down, he slips off, and gets aboard another vessel, which very soon sinks in the same manner. He feels that he is called to the work of separating the precious from the vile, and a preciously vile mess he makes of it. I have no reason to believe it is the condition of the liver in this brother, it is more likely that there is something wrong with his heart; certainly, there is an evil disease upon him that always makes me get into a bad temper with him. It is dangerous

to entertain him above three days, for he would quarrel in that time with the most peaceably disposed man in the world. I never mean to recommend him to a pastorate again; let him find a place for himself if he can, for I believe that, wherever he goes, the place will be like the spot where the foot of the Tartar's horse is put down, the grass will never again grow there.

If any of you brethren have even a little of this nasty, bitter spirit about you, go to sea that you may get rid of it. I hope it may happen to you according to the legend which is told concerning Mahomet. "In every human being," so the story runs, "there are two black drops of sin. The great prophet himself was not free from the common lot of evil; but an angel was sent to take his heart, and squeeze out of it the two black drops of sin." Get those black drops out somehow while you are in college; if you have any malice, or ill-will, or bad temper in you, pray the Lord to take it out of you while you are here; do not go into the churches to fight as others have done. "Still," says a brother, "I am not going to let the people tread on me. I shall take the bull by the horns." You will be a great fool if you do. I never felt that I was called to do anything of the kind. Why not let the bull alone, to go where he likes? A bull is a very likely creature to project you into space if you get meddling with his horns. "Still," says another, "we must set things right." Yes, but the best way to set things right is not to make them more wrong than they are. Nobody thinks of putting a mad bull into a china shop in order to get the china cleaned, and no one can by a display of evil temper set right anything that is wrong in our churches. Take care always to speak the truth in love, and especially when you are rebuking sin.

I believe, brethren, that soul-winning is to be done by men of the character I have been describing; and most of all will this be the case when they are surrounded by people of a similar character. You want to get the very atmosphere in which you live and labor permeated with this spirit before you can rightly expect the fullest and richest blessings. Therefore, may you and all your people be all that I have pictured, for the Lord Jesus Christ's sake! Amen.

Spurgeon's 1875 work, Lectures to My Students, *continues to be a valuable aid to pastors. Though "The Preacher's Private Prayer" is intended for an audience of pastors, Spurgeon's advice is applicable to all men of prayer, such as Spurgeon himself was. He finds that constant prayer is a necessity in the lives of pastors and will incomparably assist them in their work, advice that is true for all those who pray.*

CHAPTER NINE

The Preacher's Private Prayer

Of course the preacher is above all others distinguished as a man of prayer. He prays as an ordinary Christian, else he were a hypocrite. He prays more than ordinary Christians, else he were disqualified for the office which he has undertaken. "It would be wholly monstrous," says Bernard, "for a man to be highest in office and lowest in soul; first in station and last in life." Over all his other relationships the preeminence of the pastor's responsibility casts a halo, and if true to his Master, he becomes distinguished for his prayerfulness in them all. As a citizen, his country has the advantage of his intercession; as a neighbor those under his shadow are remembered in supplication. He prays as a husband and as a father; he strives to make his family devotions a model for his flock; and if the fire on the altar of God should burn low anywhere else, it is well tended in the house of the Lord's chosen servant—for he takes care that the morning and evening sacrifice shall sanctify his dwelling. But there are some of his prayers which concern his office, and of those our plan in these lectures leads us to speak most. He offers peculiar supplications *as a minister,* and he draws near to God in this respect, over and above all his approaches in his other relationships.

Incessant Prayer

I take it that as a minister *he is always praying.* Whenever his mind turns to his work, whether he is in it or out of it, he ejaculates a petition, sending up his holy desires as well-directed arrows to the skies. He is not always in the act of prayer, but he lives in the spirit of it. If his heart be in his work, he cannot eat or drink, or take recreation, or go to his bed, or rise in the morning, without evermore feeling a fervency of desire, a weight of anxiety, and a simplicity of dependence upon God; thus, in one form or other he continues in prayer. If there be any man under heaven, who is compelled to carry out the precept—"Pray without ceasing," surely it is the Christian minister. He has peculiar temptations, special trials, singular difficulties, and remarkable duties, he has to deal with God in awful relationships, and with men in mysterious interests; he therefore needs much more grace than common men, and as he knows this, he is led constantly to cry to the strong for strength, and say, "I will lift up mine eyes unto the hills, from whence cometh my help."

Alleine once wrote to a dear friend, "Though I am apt to be unsettled and quickly set off the hinges, yet, methinks, I am like a bird out of the nest, I am never quiet till I am in my old way of communion with God; like the needle in the compass, that is restless till it be turned towards the pole. I can say, through grace, with the church, 'With my soul have I desired thee in the night, and with my spirit within me have I sought thee early.' My heart is early and late with God; 'tis the business and delight of my life to seek him." Such must be the even tenor of your way, O men of

God. If you as ministers are not very prayerful, you are much to be pitied. If, in the future, you shall be called to sustain pastorates, large or small, if you become lax in secret devotion, not only will you need to be pitied, but your people also; and, in addition to that, you shall be blamed, and the day cometh in which you shall be ashamed and confounded.

It may scarcely be needful to commend to you the sweet uses of private devotion, and yet I cannot forbear. To you, as the ambassadors of God, the mercy-seat has a virtue beyond all estimate; the more familiar you are with the court of heaven the better shall you discharge your heavenly trust. Among all the formative influences which go to make up a man honored of God in the ministry, I know of none more mighty than his own familiarity with the mercy-seat. All that a college course can do for a student is coarse and external compared with the spiritual and delicate refinement obtained by communion with God. While the unformed minister is revolving upon the wheel of preparation, prayer is the tool of the great potter by which he molds the vessel. All our libraries and studies are mere emptiness compared with our closets. We grow, we wax mighty, we prevail in private prayer.

Prayer Aids in Preparation

Your prayers will be your ablest assistants *while your discourses are yet upon the anvil*. While other men, like Esau, are hunting for their portion, you, by the aid of prayer, will find the savory meat near at home, and may say in truth what Jacob said so falsely, "The Lord brought it to me." If you can dip your pens into your hearts, appealing in earnestness to the Lord, you will write well; and if you can gather your matter on

your knees at the gate of heaven, you will not fail to speak well. Prayer, as a mental exercise, will bring many subjects before the mind, and so help in the selection of a topic, while as a high spiritual engagement it will cleanse your inner eye that you may see truth in the light of God. Texts will often refuse to reveal their treasures till you open them with the key of prayer. How wonderfully were the books opened to Daniel when he was in supplication! How much Peter learned upon the housetop!

The closet is the best study. The commentators are good instructors, but the Author himself is far better, and prayer makes a direct appeal to him and enlists him in our cause. It is a great thing to pray one's self into the spirit and marrow of a text; working into it by sacred feeding thereon, even as the worm bores its way into the kernel of the nut. Prayer supplies a leverage for the uplifting of ponderous truths. One marvels how the stones of Stonehenge could have been set in their places; it is even more to be enquired after whence some men obtained such admirable knowledge of mysterious doctrines: was not prayer the potent machinery which wrought the wonder? Waiting upon God often turns darkness into light. Persevering enquiry at the sacred oracle uplifts the veil and gives grace to look into the deep things of God. A certain Puritan divine at a debate was observed frequently to write upon the paper before him; upon others curiously seeking to read his notes, they found nothing upon the page but the words, "More light, Lord," "More light, Lord," repeated scores of times: a most suitable prayer for the student of the Word when preparing his discourse.

You will frequently find fresh streams of thought leaping up from the passage before you, as if the rock had been struck by Moses' rod; new veins of precious ore will be revealed to your astonished gaze as you quarry God's Word and use diligently the hammer of prayer. You will sometimes feel as if you were entirely shut up, and then suddenly a new road will open before you. He who hath the key of David openeth, and no man shutteth. If you have ever sailed down the Rhine, the water scenery of that majestic river will have struck you as being very like in effect to a series of lakes. Before and behind the vessel appears to be enclosed in massive walls of rock, or circles of vine-clad terraces, till on a sudden you turn a corner, and before you the rejoicing and abounding river flows onward in its strength. So the laborious student often finds it with a text; it appears to be fast closed against you, but prayer propels your vessel, and turns its prow into fresh waters, and you behold the broad and deep stream of sacred truth flowing in its fulness, and bearing you with it. Is not this a convincing reason for abiding in supplication? Use prayer as a boring rod, and wells of living water will leap up from the bowels of the Word. Who will be content to thirst when living waters are so readily to be obtained!

The best and holiest men have ever made prayer the most important part of pulpit preparation. It is said of McCheyne, "Anxious to give his people on the Sabbath what had cost him somewhat, he never, without an urgent reason, went before them without much previous meditation and prayer. His principle on this subject was embodied in a remark he made to some of us who were conversing on the matter. Being asked his view of diligent preparation for the pulpit, he reminded us of Exodus 27:20. *'Beaten oil—beaten oil for the lamps of the sanctuary.'* And yet his prayerfulness was greater still. Indeed, he could not neglect fellowship with God before entering the congregation. He needed to be bathed in the love of God. His ministry was so much a bringing out of views that had first sanctified his own soul, that the healthiness of his soul was absolutely needful to the vigor and power of his ministrations." "With him the commencement of all labor invariably consisted in the preparation of his own soul. The walls of his chamber were witnesses of his prayerfulness and of his tears, as well as of his cries."

Prayer Assists in Delivery

Prayer will singularly assist you in the delivery of your sermon; in fact, nothing can so gloriously fit you to preach as descending fresh from the mount of communion with God to speak with men. None are so able to plead with men as those who have been wrestling with God on their behalf. It is said of Alleine, "He poured out his very heart in prayer and preaching. His supplications and his exhortations were so affectionate, so full of holy zeal, life and vigor, that they quite overcame his hearers; he melted over them, so that he thawed and mollified, and sometimes dissolved the hardest hearts." There could have been none of this sacred dissolving of heart if his mind had not been previously exposed to the tropical rays of the Sun of Righteousness by private fellowship with the risen Lord. A truly pathetic delivery, in which there is no affectation, but much affection, can only be the offspring of prayer. There is no rhetoric like that of the heart, and no school for learning it but the foot of the cross. It were better that you never learned a rule of human oratory, but were full of the power of heavenborn love, than that you should master Quintilian, Cicero, and Aristotle, and remain without the apostolic anointing.

Prayer may not make you eloquent after the human mode, but it will make you truly so, for you will speak out of the heart; and is not that the meaning of the word eloquence? It will bring fire from heaven upon your sacrifice, and thus prove it to be accepted of the Lord.

As fresh springs of thought will frequently break up during preparation in answer to prayer, so will it be in the delivery of the sermon. Most preachers who depend upon God's Spirit will tell you that their freshest and best thoughts are not those which were premeditated, but ideas which come to them, flying as on the wings of angels; unexpected treasures brought on a sudden by celestial hands, seeds of the flowers of paradise, wafted from the mountains of myrrh. Often and often when I have felt hampered, both in thought and expression, my secret groaning of heart has brought me relief, and I have enjoyed more than usual liberty. But how dare we pray in the battle if we have never cried to the Lord while buckling on the harness! The remembrance of his wrestlings at home comforts the fettered preacher when in the pulpit: God will not desert us unless we have deserted him. You, brethren, will find that prayer will ensure you strength equal to your day.

As the tongues of fire came upon the apostles, when they sat watching and praying, even so will they come upon you. You will find yourselves, when you might perhaps have flagged, suddenly upborne, as by a seraph's power. Wheels of fire will be fastened to your chariot, which had begun to drag right heavily, and steeds angelic will be in a moment harnessed to your fiery car, till you climb the heavens like Elijah, in a rapture of flaming inspiration.

Prayer after the Sermon

After the sermon, how would a conscientious preacher give vent to his feelings and find solace for his soul if access to the mercy-seat were denied him? Elevated to the highest pitch of excitement, how can we relieve our souls but in importunate pleadings. Or depressed by a fear of failure, how shall we be comforted but in moaning out our complaint before our God. How often have some of us tossed to and fro upon our couch half the night because of conscious shortcomings in our testimony! How frequently have we longed to rush back to the pulpit again to say over again more vehemently, what we have uttered in so cold a manner! Where could we find rest for our spirits but in confession of sin, and passionate entreaty that our infirmity or folly might in no way hinder the Spirit of God!

It is not possible in a public assembly to pour out all our heart's love to our flock. Like Joseph, the affectionate minister will seek where to weep; his emotions, however freely he may express himself, will be pent up in the pulpit, and only in private prayer can he draw up the sluices and bid them flow forth. If we cannot prevail with men for God, we will, at least, endeavor to prevail with God for men. We cannot save them, or even persuade them to be saved, but we can at least bewail their madness and entreat the interference of the Lord. Like Jeremiah, we can make it our resolve, "If ye will not hear it, my soul shall weep in secret places for your pride, and mine eye shall weep sore and run down with tears." To such pathetic appeals the Lord's heart can never be indifferent; in due time the weeping intercessor will become the rejoicing winner of souls.

There is a distinct connection between importunate agonizing and true success, even as between the travail and the birth, the sowing in tears and the reaping in joy. "How is it that your seed comes up so soon?" said one gardener to another. "Because I steep it," was the reply. We must steep all our teachings in tears, "when none but God is nigh," and their growth will surprise and delight us. Could any one wonder at Brainerd's success, when his diary contains such notes as this: "Lord's Day, April 25th—This morning spent about two hours in sacred duties, and was enabled, more than ordinarily, to agonize for immortal souls; though it was early in the morning, and the sun scarcely shone at all, yet my body was quite wet with sweat." The secret of Luther's power lay in the same direction. Theodorus said of him: "I overheard him in prayer, but, good God, with what life and spirit did he pray! It was with so much reverence, as if he were speaking to God, yet with so much confidence as if he were speaking to his friend."

My brethren, let me beseech you to be men of prayer. Great talents you may never have, but you will do well enough without them if you abound in intercession. If you do not pray over what you have sown, God's sovereignty may possibly determine to give a blessing, but you have no right to expect it, and if it comes it will bring no comfort to your own heart. I was reading yesterday a book by Father Faber, late of the Oratory, at Brompton, a marvellous compound of truth and error. In it he relates a legend to this effect. A certain preacher, whose sermons converted men by scores, received a revelation from heaven that not one of the conversions was owing to his talents or eloquence, but all to the prayers of an illiterate lay-brother, who sat on the pulpit steps, pleading all the time for the success of the sermon. It may in the all-revealing day be so with us. We may discover, after having labored long and wearily in preaching, that all the honor belongs to another builder, whose prayers were gold, silver, and precious stones, while our sermonizings being apart from prayer, were but hay and stubble.

Prayer Throughout the Ministry

When we have done with preaching, we shall not, if we are true ministers of God, have done with praying, because the whole church, with many tongues, will be crying, in the language of the Macedonian, "Come over and help us" in prayer. If you are enabled to prevail in prayer you will have many requests to offer for others who will flock to you, and beg a share in your intercessions, and so you will find yourselves commissioned with errands to the mercy-seat for friends and hearers.

Such is always my lot, and I feel it a pleasure to have such requests to present before my Lord. Never can you be short of themes for prayer, even if no one should suggest them to you. Look at your congregation. There are always sick folk among them, and many more who are soul-sick. Some are unsaved, others are seeking and cannot find. Many are desponding, and not a few believers are backsliding or mourning. There are widows' tears and orphans' sighs to be put into our bottle, and poured out before the Lord. If you are a genuine minister of God you will stand as a priest before the Lord, spiritually wearing the ephod and the breast-plate whereon you bear the names of the children of Israel, pleading for them within the veil. I have known brethren who have kept a list of persons for whom they felt bound especially to pray, and I doubt not such a record often reminded them of what might otherwise have slipped their memory.

Nor will your people wholly engross you; the nation and the world will claim their share. The man who is mighty in prayer may be a wall of fire around his country, her guardian angel and her shield. We have all heard how the enemies of the Protestant cause dreaded the prayers of Knox more than they feared armies of ten thousand men. The famous Welch was also a great intercessor for his country; he used to say, "he wondered how a Christian could lie in his bed all night and not rise to pray." When his wife, fearing that he would take cold, followed him into the room to which he had withdrawn, she heard him pleading in broken sentences, "Lord, wilt thou not grant me Scotland?" O that we were thus wrestling at midnight, crying, "Lord, wilt thou not grant us our hearers' souls?"

The minister who does not earnestly pray over his work must surely be a vain and conceited man. He acts as if he thought himself sufficient of himself, and therefore needed not to appeal to God. Yet what a baseless pride to conceive that our preaching can ever be in itself so powerful that it can turn men from their sins, and bring them to God without the working of the Holy Ghost. If we are truly humble-minded we shall not venture down to the fight until the Lord of Hosts has clothed us with all power, and said to us, "Go in this thy might."

The preacher who neglects to pray much must be very careless about his ministry. He cannot have comprehended his calling. He cannot have computed the value of a soul, or estimated the meaning of eternity. He must be a mere official, tempted into a pulpit because the piece of bread which belongs to the priest's office is very necessary to him, or a detestable hypocrite who loves the praise of men, and cares not for the praise of God. He will surely become a mere superficial talker, best approved where grace is least valued and a vain show most admired. He cannot be one of those who plough deep and reap abundant harvests. He is a mere loiterer,

not a laborer. As a preacher he has a name to live and is dead. He limps in his life like the lame man in the Proverbs, whose legs were not equal, for his praying is shorter than his preaching.

I am afraid that, more or less, most of us need self-examination as to this matter. If any man here should venture to say that he prays as much as he ought, as a student, I should gravely question his statement; and if there be a minister, deacon, or elder present who can say that he believes he is occupied with God in prayer to the full extent to which he might be, I should be pleased to know him. I can only say, that if he can claim this excellence, he leaves me far behind, for I can make no such claim: I wish I could; and I make the confession with no small degree of shame-facedness and confusion, but I am obliged to make it. If we are not more negligent than others, this is no consolation to us; the shortcomings of others are no excuses for us.

How few of us could compare ourselves with Mr. Joseph Alleine, whose character I have mentioned before? "At the time of his health," writes his wife, "he did rise constantly at or before four of the clock, and would be much troubled if he heard smiths or other craftsmen at their trades before he was at communion with God; saying to me often, 'How this noise shames me. Does not my Master deserve more than theirs?' From four till eight he spent in prayer, holy contemplation, and singing of psalms, in which he much delighted and did daily practice alone, as well as in the family. Sometimes he would suspend the routine of parochial engagements, and devote whole days to these secret exercises, in order to which, he would contrive to be alone in some void house, or else in some sequestered spot in the open valley. Here there would be much prayer and meditation on God and heaven."

Could we read Jonathan Edwards' description of David Brainerd and not blush? "His life," says Edwards, "shows the right way to success in the words of the ministry. He sought it as a resolute soldier seeks victory in a siege or battle; or as a man that runs a race for a great prize. Animated with love to Christ and souls, how did he labor always fervently, not only in word and doctrine, in public and private, but in *prayers* day and night, 'wrestling with God' in secret, and 'travailing in birth,' with unutterable groans and agonies! 'until Christ were formed' in the hearts of the people to whom he was sent! How did he thirst for a blessing upon his ministry, 'and watch for souls as one that must give account!' How did he 'go forth in the strength of the Lord God,' seeking and depending on the special influence of the Spirit to assist and succeed him! And what was the happy fruit at last, after long waiting and many dark and discouraging appearances: like a true son of Jacob, he persevered in wrestling through all the darkness of the night, until the breaking of the day."

Might not Henry Martyn's journal shame us, where we find such entries as these; "Sept. 24th—The determination with which I went to bed last night, of devoting this day to prayer and fasting, I was enabled to put into execution. In my first prayer for deliverance from worldly thoughts, depending on the power and promises of God, for fixing my soul while I prayed, I was helped to enjoy much abstinence from the world for nearly an hour. Then read the history of Abraham, to see how familiarly God had revealed himself to mortal men of old. Afterwards, in prayer for my own sanctification, my soul breathed freely and ardently after the holiness of God, and this was the best season of the day."

We might perhaps more truly join with him in his lament after the first year of his ministry that "he judged he had dedicated too much time to public ministrations, and too little to private communion with God."

The Blessings of Private Prayer

How much of blessing we may have missed through remissness in supplication we can scarcely guess, and none of us can know how poor we are in comparison with what we might have been if we had lived habitually nearer to God in prayer. Vain regrets and surmises are useless, but an earnest determination to amend will be far more useful. We not only ought to pray more, but we *must.* The fact is, the secret of all ministerial success lies in prevalence at the mercy-seat.

One bright benison which private prayer brings down upon the ministry is an indescribable and inimitable something, better understood than named; it is a dew from the Lord, a divine presence which you will recognize at once when I say it is "an unction from the Holy One." What is it? I wonder how long we might beat our brains before we could plainly put into words what is meant by *preaching with unction;* yet he who preaches knows its presence, and he who hears soon detects its absence; Samaria, in famine, typifies a discourse without it; Jerusalem, with her feasts of fat things full of marrow, may represent a sermon enriched with it. Every one knows what the freshness of the morning is when orient pearls abound on every blade of grass, but who can describe it, much less produce it of itself?

Such is the mystery of spiritual anointing; we know, but we cannot tell to others what it is. It is as easy as it is foolish to counterfeit it, as some do who use expressions which are meant to betoken fervent love, but oftener indicate sickly sentimentalism or mere cant. "Dear Lord!" "Sweet Jesus!" "Precious Christ!" are by them poured out wholesale, till one is nauseated. These familiarities may have been not only tolerable, but even beautiful when they first fell from a saint of God, speaking, as it were, out of the excellent glory, but when repeated flippantly they are not only intolerable, but indecent, if not profane.

Some have tried to imitate unction by unnatural tones and whines; by turning up the whites of their eyes, and lifting their hands in a most ridiculous manner. McCheyne's tone and rhythm one hears from Scotchmen continually: we much prefer his spirit to his mannerism; and all mere mannerism without power is as foul carrion of all life bereft, obnoxious, mischievous. Certain brethren aim at inspiration through exertion and loud shouting; but it does not come: some we have known to stop the discourse, and exclaim, "God bless you," and others gesticulate wildly, and drive their fingernails into the palms of their hands as if they were in convulsions of celestial ardor. Bah! The whole thing smells of the green-room and the stage. The getting up of fervor in hearers by the simulation of it in the preacher is a loathsome deceit to be scorned by honest men. "To affect feeling," says Richard Cecil, "is nauseous and soon detected, but to feel is the readiest way to the hearts of others."

Unction is a thing which you cannot manufacture, and its counterfeits are worse than worthless; yet it is in itself priceless, and beyond measure needful if you would edify believers and bring sinners to Jesus. To the secret pleader with God this secret is committed; upon him rests the dew of the Lord, about him is the perfume which makes glad the heart. If the anointing which we bear come not from the Lord of hosts we are deceivers, and since only in prayer can we obtain it, let us continue instant, constant, fervent in supplication. Let your fleece lie on the threshing-floor of supplication till it is wet with the dew of heaven. Go not to minister in the temple till you have washed in the laver. Think not to be a messenger of grace to others till you have seen the God of grace for yourselves, and had the word from his mouth.

Time spent in quiet prostration of soul before the Lord is most invigorating. David "sat before the Lord;" it is a great thing to hold these sacred sittings; the mind being receptive, like an open flower drinking in the sunbeams, or the sensitive photographic plate accepting the image before it. Quietude, which some men cannot abide, because it reveals their inward poverty, is as a palace of cedar to the wise, for along its hallowed courts the King in his beauty deigns to walk.

> Sacred silence! thou that art
> Floodgate of the deeper heart,
> Offspring of a heavenly kind;
> Frost o' the mouth, and thaw
> o' the mind.

Priceless as the gift of utterance may be, the practice of silence in some aspects far excels it. Do you think me a Quaker? Well, be it so. Herein I follow George Fox most lovingly; for I am persuaded that we most of us think too much of speech, which after all is but the shell of thought. Quiet contemplation, still worship, unuttered rapture, these are mine when my best jewels are before me. Brethren, rob not your heart of the deep sea joys; miss not the far-down life, by for ever babbling among the broken shells and foaming surges of the shore.

I would seriously recommend to you, when settled in the ministry, the celebration of extraordinary seasons of devotion. If your ordinary prayers do not keep up the freshness and vigor of your souls, and you feel that you are flagging, get alone for a week, or even a month if possible. We have occasional holidays, why not frequent holy days? We hear of our richer brethren finding time for a journey to Jerusalem; could we not spare time for the less difficult and far more profitable journey to the heavenly city? Isaac Ambrose, once pastor at Preston, who wrote that famous book, "Looking unto Jesus," always set apart one month in the year for seclusion in a hut in a wood at Garstang. No wonder that he was so mighty a divine, when he could regularly spend so long a time in the mount with God.

I notice that the Romanists are accustomed to secure what they call "Retreats," where a number of priests will retire for a time into perfect quietude, to spend the whole of the time in fasting and prayer, so as to inflame their souls with ardor. We may learn from our adversaries. It would be a great thing every now and then for a band of truly spiritual brethren to spend a day or two with each other in real burning agony of prayer. Pastors alone could use much more freedom than in a mixed company. Times of humiliation and supplication for the whole church will also benefit us if we enter into them heartily. Our seasons of fasting and prayer at the Tabernacle have been high days indeed; never has heaven-gate stood wider; never have our hearts been nearer the central glory. I look forward to our

month of special devotion, as mariners reckon upon reaching land. Even if our public work were laid aside to give us space for special prayer, it might be a great gain to our churches. A voyage to the golden rivers of fellowship and meditation would be well repaid by a freight of sanctified feeling and elevated thought.

Our silence might be better than our voices if our solitude were spent with God. That was a grand action of old Jerome, when he laid all his pressing engagements aside to achieve a purpose to which he felt a call from heaven. He had a large congregation, as large a one as any of us need want; but he said to his people, "Now it is of necessity that the New Testament should be translated, you must find another preacher: the translation must be made; I am bound for the wilderness, and shall not return till my task is finished." Away he went with his manuscripts, and prayed and laboured, and produced a work—the Latin Vulgate—which will last as long as the world stands; on the whole a most wonderful translation of Holy Scripture. As learning and prayerful retirement together could thus produce an immortal work, if we were sometimes to say to our people when we felt moved to do so, "Dear friends, we really must be gone for a little while to refresh our souls in solitude," our profiting would soon be apparent, and if we did not write Latin Vulgates, yet we should do immortal work, such as would abide the fire.

Though Spurgeon did not like his prayers to be recorded, some, such as "To the King Eternal," have survived and were gathered posthumously. As powerful as his prayers, like his sermons, may be in print, there is no real way to compare them to what they must have sounded like when his own magnificent voice spoke them.

CHAPTER TEN

To the King Eternal

Our God and Father, draw us to Thyself by Thy Spirit, and may the few minutes that we spend in prayer be full of the true spirit of supplication. Grant that none of us with closed eyes may yet be looking abroad over the fields of vanity, but may our eyes be really shut to everything else now but that which is spiritual and divine. May we have communion with God in the secret of our hearts, and find Him to be to us as a little sanctuary.

O Lord, we do not find it easy to get rid of distracting thoughts, but we pray Thee help us to draw the sword against them and drive them away, and as when the birds came down upon his sacrifice Abraham drove them away, so may we chase away all cares, all thoughts of pleasure, everything else, whether it be pleasing or painful, that would keep us away from real fellowship with the Father and with His Son Jesus Christ.

Adoration

We would begin with adoration. We worship from our hearts the Three in One, the infinitely glorious Jehovah, the only living and true God. We adore the Father, the Son, and the Holy Ghost, the God of Abraham, of Isaac, and of Jacob. We are not yet ascended to the place where pure spirits behold the face of God, but we shall soon be there, perhaps much sooner than we think, and we would be there in spirit now, casting our crowns upon the glassy sea before the throne of the Infinite Majesty, and as-

cribing glory and honor, and power and praise, and dominion and might to Him that sitteth upon the throne, and unto the Lamb for ever and ever.

All the church doth worship Thee, O God, every heart renewed by grace takes a delight in adoring Thee, and we, among the rest, though least and meanest of them all, yet would bow as heartily as any worshipping, loving, praising, in our soul, being silent unto God because our joy in Him is altogether inexpressible.

Lord help us to worship Thee in life as well as lip. May our whole being be taken up with Thee. As when the fire fell down on Elijah's sacrifice of old and licked up even the water that was in the trenches, so may the consuming fire of the Divine Spirit use up all our nature, and even that which might seem to hinder, even out of that may God get glory by the removal of it. Thus could we adore.

We Remember Our Condition

But, oh! dear Savior, we come to Thee, and we remember what our state is, and the condition we are in encourages us to come to Thee now as beggars, as dependents upon Thy heavenly charity. Thou art a Savior, and as such Thou art on the outlook for those that need saving, and here we are, here we come. We are the men and women Thou art looking for, needing a Savior.

Great Physician, we bring Thee our wounds and bruises and putrifying sores, and the more diseased we are and the more conscious we are today of the depravity of our nature, of the deep-seated corruption of our hearts, the more we feel that we are the sort of beings that Thou art seeking for, for the whole have no need of a physician but they that are sick.

Glorious Benefactor, we can meet Thee on good terms, for we are full of poverty, we are just as empty as we can be. We could not be more abjectly dependent than we are. Since Thou wouldest display Thy mercy here is our sin; since Thou wouldest show Thy strength here is our weakness; since Thou wouldest manifest Thy lovingkindness here are our needs; since Thou wouldest glorify Thy grace here are we, such persons as can never have a shadow of a hope except through Thy grace, for we are undeserving, ill-deserving, hell-deserving, and if Thou do not magnify Thy grace in us we must perish for ever.

And somehow we feel it sweet to come to Thee in this way. If we had to tell Thee that we had some good thing in us which Thou didst require of us, we should be questioning whether we were not flattering ourselves and presumptuously thinking that we were better than we are. Lord Jesus, we come just as we are; this is how we came at first, and this is how we come still, with all our failures, with all our transgressions, with all and everything that is what it ought not to be we come to Thee. We do bless Thee that Thou dost receive us and our wounds, and by Thy stripes we are healed; Thou dost receive us and our sins, and by Thy sin-bearing we are set clear and free from sin. Thou dost receive us and our death, even our death, for Thou art He that liveth and was dead, and art alive for evermore.

We just come and lie at Thy feet, obedient to that call of Thine, "Come unto Me all ye that labor and I will give you rest." Let us feel sweet rest, since we do come at Thy call. May some come that have never come till this day, and may others who have been coming these many years consciously come again, coming unto Thee as unto a living stone, chosen of God and precious, to build our everlasting hopes upon.

Supplication

But, Lord, now that we are come so near Thee, and on right terms with Thee, we venture to ask Thee this, that we that love Thee may love Thee very much more. Oh! since Thou hast been precious, Thy very name has music in it to our ears, and there are times when Thy love is so inexpressibly strong upon us that we are carried away with it. We have felt that we would gladly die to increase Thine honor. We have been willing to lose our name and our repute if so be Thou mightest be glorified, and truly we often feel that if the crushing of us would lift Thee one inch the higher, we would gladly suffer it.

For oh! Thou blessed King, we would set the crown on Thy head, even if the sword should smite our arm off at the shoulder blade. Thou must be King whatever becomes of us; Thou must be glorified whatever becomes of us.

But yet we have to mourn that we cannot get always to feel as we should this rapture and ardor of love. Oh! at times Thou dost manifest Thyself to us so charmingly that heaven itself could scarce be happier than the world becomes when Thou art with us in it. But when Thou art gone and we are in the dark, oh! give us the love that loves in the dark, that loves when there is no comfortable sense of Thy presence. Let us not be dependent upon feeling, but may we ever love Thee, so that if Thou didst turn Thy back on us by the year together we would think none the less of Thee, for Thou art unspeakably to be beloved whatsoever Thou doest, and if Thou dost give us rough words, yet still we would cling to Thee, and if the rod be used till we tingle again, yet still will we love Thee, for Thou art infinitely to be beloved of all men and angels, and Thy Father loved Thee. Make our hearts to love Thee evermore the same. With all the capacity for love that there is in us, and with all the more that Thou canst give us, may we love our Lord in spirit and in truth.

Help us, Lord, to conquer sin out of love to Thee. Help some dear strugglers that have been mastered by sin sometimes, and they are struggling against it; give them the victory, Lord, and when the battle gets very sharp, and they are tempted to give way a little, help them to be very firm and very strong, never giving up hope in the Lord Jesus, and resolving that if they perish they will perish at His feet and nowhere else but there.

Lord raise up in our churches many men and women that are all on fire with love to Christ and His divine gospel. Oh! give us back again men like Antipas, Thy faithful martyr, men like Paul, Thy earnest servant who proclaimed Thy truth so boldly. Give us Johns, men to whom the Spirit may speak, who shall bid us hear what the Spirit saith unto the churches. Lord revive us! Lord revive us; revive Thy work in the midst of the years in all the churches. Return unto the Church of God in this country, return unto her. Thine adversaries think to have it all their own way, but they will not, for the Lord liveth, and blessed be our Rock.

Because of truth and righteousness, we beseech Thee lay bare Thine arm in these last days. O Shepherd of Israel,

deal a heavy blow at the wolves and keep Thy sheep in their own true pastures, free from the poisonous pastures of error. O God, we would stir Thee up. We know Thou sleepest not, and yet sometimes it seems as if Thou didst sleep awhile and leave things to go on in their own way.

We beseech Thee awake. Plead Thine own cause. We know Thine answer, "Awake! awake! put on thy strength, O Zion." This we would do, Lord, but we cannot do it unless Thou dost put forth Thy strength to turn our weakness into might.

Great God, save this nation! O God of heaven and earth, stay the floods of infidelity and of filthiness that roll over this land. Would God we might see better days! Men seem entirely indifferent now. They will not come to hear the Word as once they did. God of our fathers let Thy Spirit work again among the masses. Turn the hearts of the people to the hearing of the Word, and convert them when they hear it. May it be preached with the Holy Ghost sent down from heaven.

Our hearts are weary for Thee, Thou King, Thou King forgotten in thine own land, Thou King despised among Thine own people, when wilt Thou yet be glorious before the eyes of all mankind? Come, we beseech Thee, come quickly, or if Thou comest not personally, send forth the Holy Spirit with a greater power than ever that our hearts may leap within us as they see miracles of mercy repeated in our midst.

Father, glorify Thy Son. Somehow our prayer always comes to this before we have done. "Father, glorify Thy Son that Thy Son also may glorify Thee," and let the days come when He shall see of the travail of His soul and shall be satisfied. Bless all work done for Thee, whether it be in the barn or in the cathedral, silently and quietly at the street door, or in the Sunday-school or in the classes. O Lord, bless Thy work. Hear also prayers that have been put up by wives for their husbands, children for their parents, parents for their children. Let the holy service of prayer never cease, and let the intercession be accepted of God, for Jesus Christ's sake. Amen.

Spurgeon considered his Treasury of David *to be the masterpiece of his literary works, and many are inclined to agree with him. He spent over twenty years writing its seven volumes that amounted to some two million words and were published volume-by-volume from 1870 to 1886. It contained "an original exposition of the book, a collection of illustrative extracts from the whole range of literature, a series of homiletical hints upon almost every verse and a list of writers upon each psalm." One condenser of the work has said that it was much more than a mere commentary on the Psalms: "Truly it may be termed a theological anthology of the whole realm of Christian truth."*

His commentary on Psalm 119 was published separately and called "The Golden Alphabet." The selection presented here is the original exposition portion of his commentary on the first eight verses of Psalm 119.

CHAPTER ELEVEN

Psalm One Hundred and Nineteen—Verses 1 to 8

1 Blessed *are* the undefiled in the way, who walk in the law of the Lord.
2 Blessed *are* they that keep his testimonies, *and that* seek him with the whole heart.
3 They also do no iniquity: they walk in his ways.
4 Thou hast commanded *us* to keep thy precepts diligently.
5 O that my ways were directed to keep thy statutes!
6 Then shall I not be ashamed, when I have respect unto all thy commandments.
7 I will praise thee with uprightness of heart, when I shall have learned thy righteous judgments.
8 I will keep thy statutes: O forsake me not utterly.

These first eight verses are taken up with a contemplation of the blessedness which comes through keeping the statutes of the Lord. The subject is treated in a devout manner rather than in a didactic style. Heart-fellowship with God is enjoyed through a love of that word which is God's way of communing with the soul by his Holy Spirit. Prayer and praise and all sorts of devotional acts and feelings gleam through the verses like beams of sunlight through an olive grove. You are not only instructed, but influenced to holy emotion, and helped to express the same.

Lovers of God's holy words are blessed, because they are preserved from defilement (verse 1), because they are made practically holy (verses 2 and 3), and are led to follow after God sincerely and intensely (verse 2). It is seen that this holy walking must be desirable because God commands it (verse 4); therefore the pious soul prays for it (verse 5), and feels that its comfort and courage must depend upon obtaining it (verse 6). In the prospect of answered prayer, yea, while the prayer is being answered the heart is full of thankfulness (verse 7), and is fixed in solemn resolve not to miss the blessing if the Lord will give enabling grace (verse 8).

The changes are rung upon the words *"way"*—"undefiled in the way," "walk in his ways," "O that my ways were directed"; *"keep"*—"keep his testimonies," "keep thy precepts diligently," "directed to keep," "I will keep"; and *"walk"*—"walk in the law," "walk in his ways." Yet there is no tautology, nor is the same thought repeated, though to the careless reader it may seem so.

The change from statements about others and about the Lord to more personal dealing with God begins in the third verse, and becomes more clear as we advance, till in the later verses the communion becomes most intense and soul moving. O that every reader may feel the glow.

"Blessed"

The psalmist is so enraptured with the word of God that he regards it as his highest ideal of blessedness to be conformed to it. He has gazed on the beauties of the perfect law, and, as if this verse were the sum and outcome of all his emotions, he exclaims, "Blessed is the man whose life is the practical transcript of the will of God." True religion is not cold and dry; it has its exclamations and raptures. We not only judge the keeping of God's law to be a wise and proper thing, but we are warmly enamored of its holiness, and cry out in adoring wonder, "Blessed are the undefiled!" meaning thereby, that we eagerly desire to become such ourselves, and wish for no greater happiness than to be perfectly holy. It may be that the writer labored under a sense of his own faultiness, and therefore envied the blessedness of those whose walk had been more pure and clean; indeed, the very contemplation of the perfect law of the Lord upon which he now entered was quite enough to make him bemoan his own imperfections, and sigh for the blessedness of an undefiled walk.

True religion is always practical, for it does not permit us to delight ourselves in a perfect rule without exciting in us a longing to be conformed to it in our daily lives. A blessing belongs to those who hear and read and understand the word of the Lord; yet is it a far greater blessing to be actually obedient to it, and to carry out in our walk and conversation what we learn in our searching of the Scriptures. Purity in our way and walk is the truest blessedness.

This first verse is not only a preface to the whole psalm, but it may also be regarded as the text upon which the rest is a discourse. It is similar to the benediction of the first Psalm, which is set in the forefront of the entire book: there is a likeness between this 119th Psalm and the Psalter, and this is one point of it, that it begins with a benediction. In this, too, we see some foreshadowing of the Son of David, who began his great sermon as David began his great psalm. It is well to open our mouth with blessings. When we cannot bestow them, we can show the way of obtaining them, and even if we do not yet possess them ourselves, it may be profitable to contemplate them, that our desires may be excited, and our souls moved to seek after them. Lord, if I am not yet so blessed to be among the undefiled in thy way, yet I will think much of the happiness which these enjoy, and set it before me as my life's ambition.

As David thus begins his psalm, so should young men begin their lives, so should new converts commence their profession, so should all Christians begin every day. Settle it in your hearts as a first postulate and sure rule of practical science that holiness is happiness, and that it is our wisdom first to seek the Kingdom of God and his righteousness. Well begun is half done. To start with a true idea of blessedness is beyond measure important. Man began with being blessed in his innocence, and if our fallen race is ever to be blessed again, it must find it where it lost it at the beginning, namely, in conformity to the command of the Lord.

"The undefiled in the way." They are in the way, the right way, the way of the Lord, and they keep that way, walking with holy carefulness and washing their feet daily, lest they be found spotted by the flesh. They enjoy great blessedness in their own souls; indeed, they have a foretaste of heaven where the blessedness lieth much in being absolutely undefiled; and could they continue utterly and altogether without defilement, doubtless they would have the days of heaven upon the earth. Outward evil would little hurt us if we were entirely rid of the evil of sin, an attainment

which with the best of us lies still in the region of desire, and is not yet fully reached, though we have so clear a view of it that we see it to be blessedness itself; and therefore we eagerly press towards it.

He whose life is in a gospel sense undefiled, is blessed, because he could never have reached this point if a thousand blessings had not already been bestowed on him. By nature we are defiled and out of the way, and we must therefore have been washed in the atoning blood to remove defilement, and we must have been converted by the power of the Holy Ghost, or we should not have been turned into the way of peace, nor be undefiled in it. Nor is this all, for the continual power of grace is needed to keep a believer in the right way, and to preserve him from pollution. All the blessings of the covenant must have been in a measure poured upon those who from day to day have been enabled to perfect holiness in the fear of the Lord. Their way is the evidence of their being the blessed of the Lord.

David speaks of a high degree of blessedness; for some are in the way, and are true servants of God, but they are as yet faulty in many ways and bring defilement upon themselves. Others who walk in the light more fully, and maintain closer communion with God, are enabled to keep themselves unspotted from the world, and these enjoy far more peace and joy than their less watchful brethren. Doubtless, the more complete our sanctification the more intense our blessedness. Christ is our way, and we are not only alive in Christ, but we are to live in Christ; the sorrow is that we bespatter his holy way with our selfishness, self-exaltation, willfulness, and carnality, and so we miss a great measure of the blessedness which is in him as our way. A believer who errs is still saved, but the joy of his salvation is not experienced by him; he is rescued but not enriched, greatly borne with, but not greatly blessed.

How easily may defilement come upon us even in our holy things, yea, even *in the way*. We may even come from public or private worship with defilement upon the conscience gathered when we were on our knees. There was no floor to the tabernacle but the desert sand, and hence the priests at the altar were under frequent necessity to wash their feet, and by the kind foresight of their God, the laver stood ready for their cleansing, even as for us our Lord Jesus still stands ready to wash our feet, that we may be clean every whit. Thus our text sets forth the blessedness of the apostles in the upper room when Jesus had said of them, "Ye are clean."

What blessedness awaits those who follow the Lamb whithersoever he goeth, and are preserved from the evil which is in the world through lust. These shall be the envy of all mankind "in that day." Though now they despise them as precise fanatics and Puritans, the most prosperous of sinners shall then wish that they could change places with them. O my soul, seek thou thy blessedness in following hard after thy Lord, who was holy, harmless, undefiled; for there hast thou found peace hitherto, and there wilt thou find it for ever.

"Who walk in the law of the Lord." In them is found habitual holiness. Their walk, their common everyday life is obedience unto the Lord. They live by rule, that rule the command of the Lord God. Whether they eat or drink, or whatsoever they do, they do all in the name of their great Master and Exemplar. To them religion is nothing out of the way, it is their everyday walk: it molds their common actions as well as their special devotions. This ensures blessedness. He who walks in God's law walks in God's

company, and he must be blessed; he has God's smile, God's strength, God's secret with him, and how can he be otherwise than blessed?

The holy life is a walk, a steady progress, a quiet advance, a lasting continuance. Enoch walked with God. Good men always long to be better, and hence they go forward. Good men are never idle, and hence they do not lie down or loiter, but they are still walking onward to their desired end. They are not hurried, and worried, and flurried, and so they keep the even tenor of their way, walking steadily towards heaven; and they are not in perplexity as to how to conduct themselves, for they have a perfect rule, which they are happy to walk by. The law of the Lord is not irksome to them; its commandments are not grievous, and its restrictions are not slavish in their esteem. It does not appear to them to be an impossible law, theoretically admirable but practically absurd, but they walk by it and in it. They do not consult it now and then as a sort of rectifier of their wanderings, but they use it as a chart for their daily sailing, a map of the road for their life-journey.

Nor do they ever regret that they have entered upon the path of obedience, else they would leave it, and that without difficulty, for a thousand temptations offer them opportunity to return; their continued walk in the law of the Lord is their best testimony to the blessedness of such a condition of life. Yes, they are blessed even now. The psalmist himself bore witness to the fact: he had tried and proved it, and wrote it down, as a fact which defied all denial. Here it stands in the forefront of David's *magnum opus*, written on the topmost line of his greatest psalm—"BLESSED ARE THEY WHO WALK IN THE LAW OF THE LORD." Rough may be the way, stern the rule, hard the discipline—all these we

know and more,—but a thousand heaped-up blessednesses are still found in godly living, for which we bless the Lord.

We have in this verse blessed persons who enjoy five blessed things, a blessed way, blessed purity, a blessed law, given by a blessed Lord, and a blessed walk therein; to which we may add the blessed testimony of the Holy Ghost given in this very passage that they are in very deed the blessed of the Lord.

The blessedness which is thus set before us we must aim at, but we must not think to obtain it without earnest effort. David has a great deal to say about it; his discourse in this psalm is long and solemn, and it is a hint to us that the way of perfect obedience is not learned in a day; there must be precept upon precept, line upon line, and after efforts long enough to be compared with the 176 verses of this psalm we may still have to cry, "I have gone astray like a lost sheep; seek thy servant; for I do not forget thy commandments."

It must, however, be our plan to keep the word of the Lord much upon our minds; for this discourse upon blessedness has for its pole-star the testimony of the Lord, and only by daily communion with the Lord by his word can we hope to learn his way, to be purged from defilement, and to be made to walk in his statutes. We set out upon this exposition with blessedness before us; we see the way to it, and we know where the law of it is to be found: let us pray that as we pursue our meditation we may grow into the habit and walk of obedience, and so feel the blessedness of which we read.

"Blessed Are They That Keep His Testimonies"

What! A second blessing? Yes, they are doubly blessed whose outward life is supported by an inward zeal for God's glory. In the first verse we had an undefiled way, and it was taken for granted that the purity in the way was not mere surface work, but was attended by the inward truth and life which comes of divine grace. Here that which was implied is expressed. Blessedness is ascribed to those who treasure up the testimonies of the Lord: in which is implied that they search the Scriptures, that they come to an understanding of them, that they love them, and then that they continue in the practice of them. We must first get a thing before we can keep it. In order to keep it well we must get a firm grip of it: we cannot keep in the heart that which we have not heartily embraced by the affections. God's word is his witness or testimony to grand and important truths which concern himself and our relation to him: this we should desire to know; knowing it, we should believe it; believing it, we should love it; and loving it, we should hold it fast against all comers.

There is a doctrinal keeping of the word when we are ready to die for its defense, and a practical keeping of it when we actually live under its power. Revealed truth is precious as diamonds, and should be kept or treasured up in the memory and in the heart as jewels in a casket, or as the law was kept in the ark; this however is not enough, for it is meant for practical use, and therefore it must be kept or followed, as men keep to a path, or to a line of business. If we keep God's testimonies they will keep us; they will keep us right in opinion, comfortable in spirit, holy in conversation, and hopeful in expectation. If they were ever worth having—and no thoughtful person will question that—then they are worth keeping; their designed effect does not come through a temporary seizure of them, but by a per-

severing keeping of them: "in keeping of them there is great reward."

We are bound to keep with all care the word of God, because it is *his* testimonies. He gave them to us, but they are still his own. We are to keep them as a watchman guards his master's house, as a steward husbands his lord's goods, as a shepherd keeps his employer's flock. We shall have to give an account, for we are put in trust with the gospel, and woe to us if we be found unfaithful. We cannot fight a good fight, nor finish our course, unless we keep the faith. To this end the Lord must keep us: only those who are kept by the power of God unto salvation will ever be able to keep his testimonies.

What a blessedness is therefore evidenced and testified by a careful belief in God's word, and a continual obedience "hereunto." God has blessed them, is blessing them, and will bless them for ever. That blessedness which David saw in others he realized for himself, for in verse 168 he says, "I have kept thy precepts and thy testimonies," and in verses 54 to 56 he traces his joyful songs and happy memories to this same keeping of the law, and he confesses, "This I had because I kept thy precepts." Doctrines which we teach to others we should experience for ourselves.

"And that seek him with the whole heart." Those who keep the Lord's testimonies are sure to seek after himself. If his word is precious we may be sure that he himself is still more so. Personal dealing with a personal God is the longing of all those who have allowed the word of the Lord to have its full effect upon them. If we once really know the power of the gospel we must seek the God of the gospel. "O that I knew where I might find HIM," will be our wholehearted cry. See the growth which these sentences indicate: first, in the way, then walking in it, then finding and keeping

the treasure of truth, and to crown all, seeking after the Lord of the way himself. Note also that the further a soul advances in grace the more spiritual and divine are its longings; an outward walk does not content the gracious soul, nor even the treasured testimonies; it reaches out in due time after God himself, and when it in a measure finds him, still yearns for more of him, and seeks him still.

Seeking after God signifies a desire to commune with him more closely, to follow him more fully, to enter into more perfect union with his mind and will, to promote his glory, and to realize completely all that he is to holy hearts. The blessed man has God already, and for this reason he seeks him. This may seem a contradiction: it is only a paradox.

God is not truly sought by the cold researches of the brain: we must seek him with the heart. Love reveals itself to love: God manifests his heart to the heart of his people. It is in vain that we endeavor to comprehend him by reason; we must apprehend him by affection. But the heart must not be divided with many objects if the Lord is to be sought by us. God is one, and we shall not know him till our heart is one. A broken heart need not be distressed at this, for no heart is so whole in its seekings after God as a heart which is broken, whereof every fragment sighs and cries after the great Father's face. It is the divided heart which the doctrine of the text censures, and strange to say, in scriptural phraseology, a heart may be divided and not broken, and it may be broken but not divided; and yet again it may be broken and be whole, and it never can be whole until it is broken. When our whole heart seeks the holy God in Christ Jesus, it has come to him of whom it is written, "as many as touched him were made perfectly whole."

That which the psalmist admires in this verse he claims in the tenth, where he says, "With my whole heart have I sought thee." It is well when admiration of a virtue leads to the attainment of it. Those who do not believe in the blessedness of seeking the Lord will not be likely to arouse their hearts to the pursuit, but he who calls another blessed because of the grace which he sees in him is on the way to gaining the same grace for himself.

If those who *seek* the Lord are blessed, what shall be said of those who actually dwell with him and know that he is theirs?

> To those who fall, how kind thou
>   art!
>   How good to those who seek
> But what to those who find?
>   Ah! this
>   Nor tongue nor pen can show!
> The love of Jesus—what it is,
>   None but his loved ones know.

"They Also Do No Iniquity"

Blessed indeed would those men be of whom this could be asserted without reserve and without explanation: we shall have reached the region of pure blessedness when we altogether cease from sin. Those who follow the word of God do no iniquity, the rule is perfect, and if it be constantly followed no fault will arise. Life, to the outward observer, at any rate, lies much in doing, and he who in his doings never swerves from equity, both towards God and man, has hit upon the way of perfection, and we may be sure that his heart is right. See how a whole heart leads to the avoidance of evil, for the psalmist says, "That seek him with the whole heart. They also do no iniquity."

We fear that no man can claim to be absolutely without sin, and yet we trust there are many who do not designedly, wilfully, knowingly, and continuously do anything that is wicked, ungodly, or unjust. Grace keeps the life righteous as to act even when the Christian has to bemoan the transgressions of the heart. Judged as men should be judged by their fellows, according to such just rules as men make for men, the true people of God do no iniquity: they are honest, upright, and chaste, and touching justice and morality they are blameless. Therefore are they happy.

"They walk in his ways." They attend not only to the great main highway of the law, but to the smaller paths of the particular precepts. As they will perpetrate no sin of commission, so do they labor to be free from every sin of omission. It is not enough to them to be blameless, they wish also to be actively righteous. A hermit may escape into solitude that he may do no iniquity, but a saint lives in society that he may serve his God by walking in his ways.

We must be positively as well as negatively right: we shall not long keep the second unless we attend to the first, for men will be walking one way or another, and if they do not follow the path of God's law they will soon do iniquity. The surest way to abstain from evil is to be fully occupied in doing good. This verse describes believers as they exist among us: although they have their faults and infirmities, yet they hate evil, and will not permit themselves to do it; they love the ways of truth, right and true godliness, and habitually they walk therein. They do not claim to be absolutely perfect except in their desires, and there they are pure indeed, for they pant to be kept from all sin, and to be led into all holiness.

"Thou Hast Commanded Us to Keep Thy Precepts Diligently"

So that when we have done all we are unprofitable servants, we have done only that which it was our duty to have done, seeing we have our Lord's command for it. God's precepts require *careful* obedience: there is no keeping them by accident. Some give to God a careless service, a sort of hit or miss obedience, but the Lord has not commanded such service, nor will he accept it. His law demands the love of all our heart, soul, mind, and strength; and a careless religion has none of these.

We are also called to *zealous* obedience. We are to keep the precepts abundantly: the vessels of obedience should be filled to the brim, and the command carried out to the full of its meaning. As a man diligent in business arouses himself to do as much trade as he can, so must we be eager to serve the Lord as much as possible. Nor must we spare pains to do so, for a diligent obedience will also be *laborious and self-denying*. Those who are diligent in business rise up early and sit up late, and deny themselves much of comfort and repose. They are not soon tired, or if they are they persevere even with aching brow and weary eyes. So should we serve the Lord. Such a Master deserves diligent servants; such service he demands, and will be content with nothing less. How seldom do men render it, and hence many through their negligence miss the double blessing spoken of in this psalm.

Some are diligent in superstition and will worship; be it ours to be diligent in keeping God's precepts. It is no use travelling fast if we are not in the right road. Men have been diligent in a losing business, and the more they have traded the more they have lost: this is bad enough in commerce, we cannot afford to have it so in our religion.

God has not commanded us to be diligent in *making* precepts, but in *keeping* them. Some bind yokes upon their own necks, and make bonds and rules for others: but the wise course is to be satisfied with the rules of holy Scripture, and to strive to keep them all, in all places, towards all men, and in all respects. If we do not this, we may become eminent in our own religion, but we shall not have kept the command of God, nor shall we be accepted of him.

The psalmist began with the third person: he is now coming near home, and has already reached the first person plural, according to our version; we shall soon hear him crying out personally for himself. As the heart glows with love to holiness, we long to have a personal interest in it. The word of God is a heart-affecting book, and when we begin to sing its praises it soon comes home to us, and sets us praying to be ourselves conformed to its teachings.

"O That My Ways Were Directed to Keep Thy Statutes!"

Divine commands should direct us in the subject of our prayers. We cannot of ourselves keep God's statutes as he would have them kept, and yet we long to do so: what resort have we but prayer? We must ask the Lord to work our works in us, or we shall never work out his commandments. This verse is a sigh of regret because the psalmist feels that he has not kept the precepts diligently, it is a cry of weakness appealing for help to one who can aid, it is a request of bewilderment from one who has lost his way and would fain be directed in it, and it is a petition of faith from one who loves God and trusts in him for grace.

Our ways are by nature opposed to the way of God, and must be turned by the Lord's direction in another direction from that which they originally take or they will lead us down to destruction. God can direct the mind and will without violating our free agency, and he will do so in answer to prayer; in fact,

he has begun the work already in those who are heartily praying after the fashion of this verse. It is for present holiness that the desire arises in the heart. O that it were so now with me: but future persevering holiness is also meant, for he longs for grace to keep henceforth and for ever the statutes of the Lord.

The sigh of the text is really a prayer, though it does not exactly take that form. Desires and longings are of the essence of supplication, and it little matters what shape they take. "O that" is as acceptable a prayer as "Our Father."

One would hardly have expected a prayer for direction; rather should we have looked for a petition for enabling. Can we not direct ourselves? What if we cannot row, we can steer. The psalmist herein confesses that even for the smallest part of his duty he felt unable without grace. He longed for the Lord to influence his will, as well as to strengthen his hands. We want a rod to point out the way as much as a staff to support us in it.

The longing of the text is prompted by admiration of the blessedness of holiness, by a contemplation of the righteous man's beauty of character, and by a reverent awe of the command of God. It is a personal application to the writer's own case of the truths which he had been considering. "O that my ways," etc. It were well if all who hear and read the word would copy this example and turn all that they hear into prayer. We should have more keepers of the statutes if we had more who sighed and cried after the grace to do so.

"Then Shall I Not Be Ashamed"

He had known shame, and here he rejoices in the prospect of being freed from it. Sin brings shame, and when sin is gone, the reason for being ashamed is banished. What a deliverance this is, for to some men death is preferable to shame! *"When I have respect unto all thy commandments."* When he respects God he shall respect himself and be respected. Whenever we err we prepare ourselves for confusion of face and sinking of heart: if no one else is ashamed of me I shall be ashamed of myself if I do iniquity. Our first parents never knew shame till they made the acquaintance of the old serpent, and it never left them till their gracious God had covered them with sacrificial skins. Disobedience made them naked and ashamed. We, ourselves, will always have cause for shame till every sin is vanquished, and every duty is observed. When we pay a continual and universal respect to the will of the Lord, then we shall be able to look ourselves in the face in the looking-glass of the law, and we shall not blush at the sight of men or devils, however eager their malice may be to lay somewhat to our charge.

Many suffer from excessive diffidence, and this verse suggests a cure. An abiding sense of duty will make us bold, we shall be afraid to be afraid. No shame in the presence of man will hinder us when the fear of God has taken full possession of our minds. When we are on the king's highway by daylight, and are engaged upon royal business, we need ask no man's leave. It would be a dishonor to a king to be ashamed of his livery and his service; no such shame should ever crimson the cheek of a Christian, nor will it if he has due reverence for the Lord his God. There is nothing to be ashamed of in a holy life; a man may be ashamed of his pride, ashamed of his wealth, ashamed of his own children, but he will never be ashamed of having in all things regarded the will of the Lord his God.

It is worthy of remark that David promises himself no immunity from shame till he has carefully paid homage to all the precepts. Mind that word *"all,"* and leave not one command out of your respect. Partial obedience still leaves us liable to be called to account for those commands which we have neglected. A man may have a thousand virtues, and yet a single failing may cover him with shame.

To a poor sinner who is buried in despair, it may seem a very unlikely thing that he should ever be delivered from shame. He blushes, and is confounded, and feels that he can never lift up his face again. Let him read these words: "Then shall I not be ashamed." David is not dreaming, nor picturing an impossible case. Be assured, dear friend, that the Holy Spirit can renew in you the image of God, so that you shall yet look up without fear. O for sanctification to direct us in God's way, for then shall we have boldness both towards God and his people, and shall no more crimson with confusion.

"I Will Praise Thee"

From prayer to praise is never a long or a difficult journey. Be sure that he who prays for holiness will one day praise for happiness. Shame having vanished, silence is broken, and the formerly silent man declares, "I will praise thee." He cannot but promise praise while he seeks sanctification. Mark how well he knows upon what head to set the crown. "I will praise *thee*." He would himself be praiseworthy, but he counts God alone worthy of praise. By the sorrow and shame of sin he measures his obligations to the Lord who would teach him the art of living as that he should clean escape from his former misery.

"With uprightness of heart." His heart would be upright if the Lord would teach him, and then it should praise its teacher. There is such a thing as false and feigned praise, and this the Lord

abhors; but there is no music like that which comes from a pure soul which standeth in its integrity. Heart praise is required, uprightness in that heart, and teaching to make the heart upright. An upright heart is sure to bless the Lord, for grateful adoration is a part of its uprightness; no man can be right unless he is upright towards God, and this involves the rendering to him the praise which is his due.

"When I shall have learned thy righteous judgments." We must learn to praise, learn that we may praise, and praise when we have learned. If we are ever to learn, the Lord must teach us, and especially upon such a subject as his judgments, for they are a great deep. While these are passing before our eyes, and we are learning from them, we ought to praise God, for the original is not, "when I have learned," but, "in my learning." While yet I am a scholar I will be a chorister: my upright heart shall praise thine uprightness, my purified judgment shall admire thy judgments. God's providence is a book full of teaching, and to those whose hearts are right it is a music book, out of which they chant to Jehovah's praise. God's word is full of the record of his righteous providences, and as we read it we feel compelled to burst forth into expressions of holy delight and ardent praise. When we both read of God's judgments and become joyful partakers in them, we are doubly moved to song—song in which there is neither formality, nor hypocrisy, nor lukewarmness, for the heart is upright in the presentation of its praise.

"I Will Keep Thy Statutes"

A calm resolve. When praise calms down into solid resolution it is well with the soul. Zeal which spends itself in singing, and leaves no practical residuum of holy living, is little worth: "I will praise" should be coupled with "I will keep." This firm resolve is by no means boastful, like Peter's humble prayer for divine help, *"O forsake me not utterly."* Feeling his own incapacity he trembles lest he should be left to himself, and this fear is increased by the horror which he has of falling into sin. The "I will keep" sounds rightly enough now that the humble cry is heard with it. This is a happy amalgam: resolution and dependence.

We meet with those who to all appearance humbly pray, but there is no force of character, no decision in them, and consequently the pleading of the closet is not embodied in the life: on the other hand, we meet with abundance of resolve attended with an entire absence of dependence upon God, and this makes as poor a character as the former. The Lord grant us to have such a blending of excellences that we may be "perfect and entire, wanting nothing."

This prayer is one which is certain to be heard, for assuredly it must be highly pleasing to God to see a man set upon obeying his will, and therefore it must be most agreeable to him to be present with such a person, and to help him in his endeavors. How can he forsake one who does not forsake his law?

The peculiar dread which tinges this prayer with a somber hue is the fear of utter forsaking. Well may the soul cry out against such a calamity. To be left, that we may discover our weakness, is a sufficient trial: to be altogether forsaken would be ruin and death. Hiding the face in a little wrath for a moment brings us very low: an absolute desertion would land us ultimately in the lowest hell. But the Lord never has utterly forsaken his servants, and he never will, blessed be his name. If we long to keep his statutes he will keep us; yea, his grace will keep us keeping his law.

There is rather a descent from the

mount of benediction with which the first verse began to the almost wail of this eighth verse, yet this is spiritually a growth, for from admiration of goodness we have come to a burning longing after God and communion with him, and an intense horror lest it should not be enjoyed. The sigh of verse 5 is now supplanted by an actual prayer from the depths of a heart conscious of its undesert, and its entire dependence upon divine love. The two "I wills" needed to be seasoned with some such lowly petition, or it might have been thought that the good man's dependence was in some degree fixed upon his own determination. He presents his resolutions like a sacrifice, but he cries to heaven for the fire.

Spurgeon's theology was distinctly Calvinistic, and he labored much to defend his views. In contrast to the hyper-Calvinists, whom he often argued against, Spurgeon's Calvinistic theology led him to a vigorously evangelistic approach. "A Defense of Calvinism" is the thirteenth chapter of the second volume of his autobiography, which was compiled by his widow and published in 1897.

Elsewhere Spurgeon wrote: "We use the term 'Calvinism' for shortness. The doctrine which is called 'Calvinism' did not spring from Calvin; we believe that it sprang from the great founder of all truth." In "A Defense of Calvinism," Spurgeon eloquently presents and defends Calvinism, and, as always in Spurgeon's works, grace is one of his primary themes.

CHAPTER TWELVE

A Defense of Calvinism

It is a great thing to begin the Christian life by believing good solid doctrine. Some people have received twenty different "gospels" in as many years; how many more they will accept before they get to their journey's end, it would be difficult to predict. I thank God that He early taught me *the* gospel, and I have been so perfectly satisfied with it, that I do not want to know any other. Constant change of creed is sure loss. If a tree has to be taken up two or three times a year, you will not need to build a very large loft in which to store the apples. When people are always shifting their doctrinal principles, they are not likely to bring forth much fruit to the glory of God.

It is good for young believers to begin with a firm hold upon those great fundamental doctrines which the Lord has taught in His Word. Why, if I believed what some preach about the temporary, trumpery salvation which only lasts for a time, I would scarcely be at all grateful for it; but when I know that those whom God saves He saves with an everlasting salvation, when I know that He gives to them an everlasting righteousness, when I know that He settles them on an everlasting foundation of everlasting love, and that He will bring them to His everlasting kingdom, oh, then I do wonder, and I am astonished that such a blessing as this should ever have been given to me!

Pause, my soul! adore, and wonder!
Ask, "Oh, why such love to me?"

Grace hath put me in the number
Of the Savior's family:
Hallelujah! Thanks, eternal
thanks, to Thee!

A Personal Testimony

I suppose there are persons whose minds naturally incline towards the doctrine of free-will. I can only say that mine inclines as naturally towards the doctrines of sovereign grace. Sometimes, when I see some of the worst characters in the street, I feel as if my heart must burst forth in tears of gratitude that God has never let me act as they have done! I have thought, if God had left me alone, and had not touched me by His grace, what a great sinner I should have been! I should have run to the utmost lengths of sin, dived into the very depths of evil, nor should I have stopped at any vice or folly, if God had not restrained me. I feel that I should have been a very king of sinners, if God had let me alone. I cannot understand the reason why I am saved, except upon the ground that God would have it so. I cannot, if I look ever so earnestly, discover any kind of reason in myself why I should be a partaker of divine grace. If I am not at this moment without Christ, it is only because Christ Jesus would have His will with me, and that will was that I should be with Him where He is, and should share His glory. I can put the crown nowhere but upon the head of Him whose mighty grace has saved me from going down into the pit.

Looking back on my past life, I can see that the dawning of it all was of God; of God effectively. I took no torch with which to light the sun, but the sun enlightened me. I did not commence my spiritual life—no, I rather kicked, and struggled against the things of the Spirit: when He drew me, for a time I did not run after Him: there was a natural hatred in my soul of everything holy and good. Wooings were lost upon me—warnings were cast to the wind—thunders were despised; and as for the whispers of His love, they were rejected as being less than nothing and vanity. But, sure I am, I can say now, speaking on behalf of myself, "He only is my salvation." It was He who turned my heart, and brought me down on my knees before Him. I can in very deed, say with Doddridge and Toplady—

> Grace taught my soul to pray,
> And made my eyes o'erflow;

and coming to this moment, I can add—

> 'Tis grace has kept me to this
> day,
> And will not let me go.

Well can I remember the manner in which I learned the doctrines of grace in a single instant. Born, as all of us are by nature, an Arminian, I still believed the old things I had heard continually from the pulpit, and did not see the grace of God. When I was coming to Christ, I thought I was doing it all myself, and though I sought the Lord earnestly, I had no idea the Lord was seeking me. I do not think the young convert is at first aware of this. I can recall the very day and hour when first I received those truths in my own soul—when they were, as John Bunyan says, burnt into my heart as with a hot iron, and I can recollect how I felt that I had grown on a sudden from a babe into a man—that I had made progress in Scriptural knowledge, through having found, once for all, the clue to the truth of God.

One week-night, when I was sitting in the house of God, I was not thinking much about the preacher's sermon, for I did not believe it. The thought struck me, *"How did you come to be a Christian?"* I sought the Lord. *"But how did you come to seek the Lord?"* The truth flashed across my mind in a moment—I should not have sought Him unless there had been some previous influence in my mind to *make me* seek Him. I prayed, thought I, but then I asked myself, *How came I to pray?* I was induced to pray by reading the Scriptures. *How came I to read the Scriptures?* I did read them, but what led me to do so? Then, in a moment, I saw that God was at the bottom of it all, and that He was the Author of my faith, and so the whole doctrine of grace opened up to me, and from that doctrine I have not departed to this day, and I desire to make this my constant confession. "I ascribe my change wholly to God."

I once attended a service where the text happened to be, *"He shall choose our inheritance for us;"* and the good man who occupied the pulpit was more than a little of an Arminian. Therefore, when he commenced, he said, "This passage refers entirely to our temporal inheritance, it has nothing whatever to do with our everlasting destiny, for," said he, "we do not want Christ to choose for us in the matter of heaven or hell. It is so plain and easy, that every man who has a grain of common sense will choose heaven, and any person would know better than to choose hell. We have no need of any superior intelligence, or any greater Being, to choose heaven or hell for us. It is left to our own free-will, and we have enough wisdom given us, sufficiently correct means to judge for ourselves," and therefore, as he very logically inferred, there was no necessity for Jesus Christ, or anyone, to make a choice for us. We could choose the inheritance for ourselves without any assistance. "Ah!" I thought, "but, my good brother, it may be very true that we *could*, but I think we should want something more than common sense before we *should* choose aright."

God's Election

First, let me ask, must we not all of us admit an overruling providence, and the appointment of Jehovah's hand, as to the means whereby we came into this world? Those men who think that, afterwards, we are left to our own free-will to choose this one or the other to direct our steps, must admit that our entrance into the world was not of our own will, but that God had then to choose for us. What circumstances were those in our power which led us to elect certain persons to be our parents? Had we anything to do with it? Did not God Himself appoint our parents, native place, and friends? Could He not have caused me to be born with the skin of the Hottentot, brought forth by a filthy mother who would nurse me in her "kraal," and teach me to bow down to pagan gods, quite as easily as to have given me a pious mother, who would each morning and night bend her knee in prayer on my behalf? Or, might He not, if He had pleased, have given me some profligate to have been my parent, from whose lips I might have early heard fearful, filthy, and obscene language? Might He not have placed me where I should have had a drunken father, who would have immured me in a very dungeon of ignorance, and brought me up in the chains of crime? Was it not God's providence that I had so happy a lot, that both my parents were His children, and endeav-

ored to train me up in the fear of the Lord?

John Newton used to tell a whimsical story, and laugh at it, too, of a good woman who said, in order to prove the doctrine of election, "Ah! sir, the Lord must have loved me before I was born, or else He would not have seen anything in me to love afterwards." I am sure it is true in my case; I believe the doctrine of election, because I am quite certain that, if God had not chosen me, I should never have chosen Him; and I am sure He chose me before I was born, or else He never would have chosen me afterwards; and He must have elected me for reasons unknown to me, for I never could find any reason in myself why He should have looked upon me with special love. So I am forced to accept that great Biblical doctrine.

I recollect an Arminian brother telling me that he had read the Scriptures through a score or more times, and could never find the doctrine of election in them. He added that he was sure he would have done so if it had been there, for he read the Word on his knees. I said to him, "I think you read the Bible in a very uncomfortable posture, and if you had read it in your easy chair, you would have been more likely to understand it. Pray, by all means, and the more, the better, but it is a piece of superstition to think there is anything in the posture in which a man puts himself for reading: and as to reading through the Bible twenty times without having found anything about the doctrine of election, the wonder is that you found anything at all: you must have galloped through it at such a rate that you were not likely to have any intelligible idea of the meaning of the Scriptures."

If it would be marvellous to see one river leap up from the earth full-grown, what would it be to gaze upon a vast spring from which all the rivers of the earth should at once come bubbling up, a million of them born at a birth? What a vision would it be! Who can conceive it? And yet the love of God is that fountain, from which all the rivers of mercy, which have ever gladdened our race—all the rivers of grace in time, and of glory hereafter—take their rise. My soul, stand thou at that sacred fountainhead, and adore and magnify for ever and ever God, even our Father, who hath loved us!

In the very beginning, when this great universe lay in the mind of God, like unborn forests in the acorn cup; long ere the echoes awoke the solitudes; before the mountains were brought forth; and long ere the light flashed through the sky, God loved His chosen creatures. Before there was any created being—when the ether was not fanned by an angel's wing, when space itself had not an existence, when there was nothing save God alone—even then, in that loneliness of deity, and in that deep quiet and profundity, His bowels moved with love for His chosen. Their names were written on His heart, and then were they dear to His soul. Jesus loved His people before the foundation of the world—even from eternity! and when He called me by His grace, He said to me, "I have loved *thee* with an everlasting love: therefore with lovingkindness have I drawn thee."

Then, in the fullness of time, He purchased me with His blood; He let His heart run out in one deep gaping wound for me long ere I loved Him. Yea, when He first came to me, did I not spurn Him? When He knocked at the door, and asked for entrance, did I not drive Him away, and do despite to His grace? Ah! I can remember that I full often did so until, at last, by the power of His effectual grace, He said, "I must, I will come in;" and then He turned my heart, and made me love Him. But even till now I

should have resisted Him, had it not been for His grace.

Well, then, since He purchased me when I was dead in sins, does it not follow, as a consequence necessary and logical, that He must have loved me first? Did my Savior die for me because I believed on Him? No; I was not then in existence; I had then no being. Could the Savior, therefore, have died because I had faith, when I myself was not yet born? Could that have been possible? Could that have been the origin of the Savior's love towards me? Oh! no; my Savior died for me long before I believed.

"But," says someone, "He foresaw that you would have faith; and, therefore, He loved you." What did He foresee about my faith? Did He foresee that I should get that faith myself, and that I should believe on Him of myself? No; Christ could not foresee that, because no Christian man will ever say that faith came of itself without the gift and without the working of the Holy Spirit. I have met with a great many believers, and talked with them about this matter; but I never knew one who could put his hand on his heart, and say, "I believed in Jesus without the assistance of the Holy Spirit."

I am bound to the doctrine of the depravity of the human heart, because I find myself depraved in heart, and have daily proofs that in my flesh there dwelleth no good thing. If God enters into covenant with unfallen man, man is so insignificant a creature that it must be an act of gracious condescension on the Lord's part; but if God enters into covenant with *sinful* man, he is then so offensive a creature that it must be, on God's part, an act of pure, free, rich, sovereign grace. When the Lord entered into covenant with me, I am sure that it was all of grace, nothing else but grace. When I remember what a den of unclean beasts and birds my heart was, and how strong was my unrenewed will, how obstinate and rebellious against the sovereignty of the divine rule, I always feel inclined to take the very lowest room in my Father's house, and when I enter heaven, it will be to go among the less than the least of all saints, and with the chief of sinners.

Salvation Is of the Lord

The late lamented Mr. Denham has put, at the foot of his portrait, a most admirable text, "Salvation is of the Lord." That is just an epitome of Calvinism; it is the sum and substance of it. If anyone should ask me what I mean by a Calvinist, I should reply, "He is one who says, *Salvation is of the Lord*." I cannot find in Scripture any other doctrine than this. It is the essence of the Bible. "He *only* is my rock and my salvation." Tell me anything contrary to this truth, and it will be a heresy; tell me a heresy, and I shall find its essence here, that it has departed from this great, this fundamental, this rock-truth, "God is my rock and my salvation." What is the heresy of Rome, but the addition of something to the perfect merits of Jesus Christ—the bringing in of the works of the flesh, to assist in our justification? And what is the heresy of Arminianism but the addition of something to the work of the Redeemer? Every heresy, if brought to the touchstone, will discover itself here.

I have my own private opinion that there is no such thing as preaching Christ and Him crucified, unless we preach what nowadays is called Calvinism. It is a nickname to call it Calvinism; Calvinism is the gospel, and nothing else. I do not believe we can preach the gospel, if we do not preach justification by faith, without works; nor unless we preach the sovereignty of God in His dispensation of grace; nor unless we exalt the electing, unchangeable, eternal, immutable, conquering love of Jehovah; nor do I think we can preach the gospel, unless we base it upon the special and particular redemption of His elect and chosen people which Christ wrought out upon the cross; nor can I comprehend a gospel which lets saints fall away after they are called, and suffers the children of God to be burned in the fires of damnation after having once believed in Jesus. Such a gospel I abhor.

If ever it should come to pass,
　That sheep of Christ might fall away,
My fickle, feeble soul, alas!
　Would fall a thousand times a day.

If one dear saint of God had perished, so might all; if one of the covenant ones be lost, so may all be; and then there is no gospel promise true, but the Bible is a lie, and there is nothing in it worth my acceptance, I will be an infidel at once when I can believe that a saint of God can ever fall finally. If God hath loved me once, then He will love me for ever. God has a master-mind; He arranged everything in His gigantic intellect long before He did it; and once having settled it, He never alters it, "This shall be done," saith He, and the iron hand of destiny marks it down, and it is brought to pass. "This is My purpose," and it stands, nor can earth or hell alter it. "This is My decree," saith He, "promulgate it, ye holy angels; rend it down from the gate of heaven, ye devils, if ye can; but ye cannot alter the decree, it shall stand for ever."

God altereth not His plans; why should He? He is Almighty, and therefore can perform His pleasure. Why should He? He is the All-wise, and therefore cannot have planned wrongly. Why should He? He is the everlasting God, and therefore cannot die before His plan is accomplished. Why should He change? Ye worthless atoms of earth, ephemera of a day, ye creeping insects upon this bay-leaf of existence, ye may change *your* plans, but He shall never, never change *His*. Has He told me that His plan is to save me? If so, I am for ever safe.

My name from the palms of His hands
  Eternity will not erase;
Impress'd on His heart it remains,
  In marks of indelible grace.

I do not know how some people, who believe that a Christian can fall from grace, manage to be happy. It must be a very commendable thing in them to be able to get through a day without despair. If I did not believe the doctrine of the final perseverance of the saints, I think I should be of all men the most miserable, because I should lack any ground of comfort. I could not say, whatever state of heart I came into, that I should be like a well-spring of water, whose stream fails not; I should rather have to take the comparison of an intermittent spring, that might stop on a sudden, or a reservoir, which I had no reason to expect would always be full.

I believe that the happiest of Christians and the truest of Christians are those who never dare to doubt God, but who take His Word simply as it stands, and believe it, and ask no questions, just feeling assured that if God has said it, it will be so. I bear my willing testimony that I have no reason, nor even the shadow of a reason, to doubt my Lord, and I challenge heaven, and earth, and hell to bring any proof that God is untrue. From the depths of hell I call the fiends, and from this earth I call the tried and afflicted believers, and to heaven I appeal, and challenge the long experience of the blood-washed host, and there is not to be found in the three realms a single person who can bear

witness to one fact which can disprove the faithfulness of God, or weaken His claim to be trusted by His servants. There are many things that may or may not happen, but this I know *shall* happen—

He *shall* present my soul,
  Unblemish'd and complete,
Before the glory of His face,
  With joys divinely great.

All the purposes of man have been defeated, but not the purposes of God. The promises of man may be broken—many of them are made to be broken—but the promises of God shall all be fulfilled. He is a promise-maker, but He never was a promise-breaker; He is a promise-keeping God, and every one of His people shall prove it to be so. This is my grateful, personal confidence, "The Lord *will* perfect that which concerneth *me*"—unworthy *me*, lost and ruined *me*. He will yet save *me*; and—

I, among the blood-wash'd throng,
Shall wave the palm, and wear
  the crown,
  And shout loud victory.

I go to a land which the plough of earth hath never upturned, where it is greener than earth's best pastures, and richer than her most abundant harvests ever saw. I go to a building of more gorgeous architecture than man hath ever builded; it is not of mortal design; it is "a building of God, a house not made with hands, eternal in the heavens." All I shall know and enjoy in heaven, will be given to me by the Lord, and I shall say, when at last I appear before Him—

Grace all the work shall crown
  Through everlasting days;
It lays in Heaven the topmost stone,
  And well deserves the praise.

Christ's Sufficient Work

I know there are some who think it necessary to their system of theology to limit the merit of the blood of Jesus: if my theological system needed such a limitation, I would cast it to the winds. I cannot, I dare not allow the thought to find a lodging in my mind, it seems so near akin to blasphemy. In Christ's finished work I see an ocean of merit; my plummet finds no bottom, my eye discovers no shore. There must be sufficient efficacy in the blood of Christ, if God had so willed it, to have saved not only all in this world, but all in ten thousand worlds, had they transgressed their Maker's law. Once admit infinity into the matter, and limit is out of the question. Having a divine person for an offering, it is not consistent to conceive of limited value; bound and measure are terms inapplicable to the divine sacrifice. The intent of the divine purpose fixes the *application* of the infinite offering, but does not change it into a finite work.

Think of the numbers upon whom God has bestowed His grace already. Think of the countless hosts in Heaven: if thou wert introduced there today, thou wouldst find it as easy to tell the stars, or the sands of the sea, as to count the multitudes that are before the throne even now. They have come from the East, and from the West, from the North, and from the South, and they are sitting down with Abraham, and with Isaac, and with Jacob in the Kingdom of God; and beside those in heaven, think of the saved ones on earth. Blessed be God, His elect on earth are to be counted by millions, I believe, and the days are coming, brighter days than these, when there shall be multitudes upon multitudes brought to know the Savior, and to rejoice in Him.

The Father's love is not for a few only, but for an exceeding great company. "A great multitude, which no man could number," will be found in heaven. A man can reckon up to very high figures; set to work your Newtons, your mightiest calculators, and they can count great numbers, but God and God alone can tell the multitude of His redeemed. I believe there will be more in heaven than in hell. If anyone asks me why I think so, I answer, because Christ, in everything, is to "have the pre-eminence," and I cannot conceive how He could have the pre-eminence if there are to be more in the dominions of Satan than in paradise. Moreover, I have never read that there is to be in hell a great multitude, which no man could number. I rejoice to know that the souls of all infants, as soon as they die, speed their way to paradise. Think what a multitude there is of them! Then there are already in heaven unnumbered myriads of the spirits of just men made perfect—the redeemed of all nations, and kindreds, and people, and tongues up till now; and there are better times coming, when the religion of Christ shall be universal; when—

> He shall reign from pole to pole,
>   With illimitable sway;

when whole kingdoms shall bow down before Him, and nations shall be born in a day, and in the thousand years of the great millennial state there will be enough saved to make up all the deficiencies of the thousands of years that have gone before. Christ shall be Master everywhere, and His praise shall be sounded in every land. Christ shall have the pre-eminence at last; His train shall be far larger than that which shall attend the chariot of the grim monarch of hell.

Christ's Limited Atonement

Some persons love the doctrine of universal atonement because they say, "It is so beautiful. It is a lovely idea that Christ should have died for all men; it commends itself," they say, "to the instincts of humanity; there is something in it full of joy and beauty." I admit there is, but beauty may be often associated with falsehood. There is much which I might admire in the theory of universal redemption, but I will just show what the supposition necessarily involves. If Christ on His cross intended to save every man, then He intended to save those who were lost before He died. If the doctrine be true, that He died for all men, then He died for some who were in hell before He came into this world, for doubtless there were even then myriads there who had been cast away because of their sins.

Once again, if it was Christ's intention to save all men, how deplorably has He been disappointed, for we have His own testimony that there is a lake which burneth with fire and brimstone, and into that pit of woe have been cast some of the very persons who, according to the theory of universal redemption, were bought with His blood. That seems to me a conception a thousand times more repulsive than any of those consequences which are said to be associated with the Calvinistic and Christian doctrine of special and particular redemption. To think that my Savior died for men who were or are in hell, seems a supposition too horrible for me to entertain. To imagine for a moment that He was the Substitute for all the sons of men, and that God, having first punished the Substitute, afterwards punished the sinners themselves, seems to conflict with all my ideas of divine justice. That Christ should offer an atonement and satisfaction for the sins of all men, and that afterwards some of those very men should be punished for the sins for which Christ had already atoned, appears to me to be the most monstrous iniquity that could ever have been imputed to Saturn, to Janus, to the goddess of the Thugs, or to the most diabolical heathen deities. God forbid that we should ever think thus of Jehovah, the just and wise and good!

There is no soul living who holds more firmly to the doctrines of grace than I do, and if any man asks me whether I am ashamed to be called a Calvinist, I answer—I wish to be called nothing but a Christian; but if you ask me, do I hold the doctrinal views which were held by John Calvin, I reply, I do in the main hold them, and rejoice to avow it. But far be it from me even to imagine that Zion contains none but Calvinistic Christians within her walls, or that there are none saved who do not hold our views. Most atrocious things have been spoken about the character and spiritual condition of John Wesley, the modern prince of Arminians. I can only say concerning him that, while I detest many of the doctrines which he preached, yet for the man himself I have a reverence second to no Wesleyan; and if there were wanted two apostles to be added to the number of the twelve, I do not believe that there could be found two men more fit to be so added than George Whitefield and John Wesley. The character of John Wesley stands beyond all imputation for self-sacrifice, zeal, holiness, and communion with God; he lived far above the ordinary level of common Christians, and was one "of whom the world was not worthy." I believe there are multitudes of men who cannot see these truths, or, at least, cannot see them in the way in which we put them, who nevertheless have received Christ as their Savior, and are as dear to the heart of the God of grace as the soundest Calvinist in or out of heaven.

The Problem with Hyper-Calvinism

I do not think I differ from any of my hyper-Calvinistic brethren in what I do believe, but I differ from them in what they do not believe. I do not hold any less than they do, but I hold a little more, and, I think, a little more of the truth revealed in the Scriptures. Not only are there a few cardinal doctrines, by which we can steer our ship North, South, East, or West, but as we study the Word, we shall begin to learn something about the North-west and North-east, and all else that lies between the four cardinal points. The system of truth revealed in the Scriptures is not simply one straight line, but two; and no man will ever get a right view of the gospel until he knows how to look at the two lines at once.

For instance, I read in one book of the Bible, "The Spirit and the bride say, Come. And let him that heareth say, Come. And let him that is athirst come. And whosoever will, let him take the water of life freely." Yet I am taught, in another part of the same inspired Word, that "it is not of him that willeth, nor of him that runneth, but of God that sheweth mercy." I see, in one place, God in providence presiding over all, and yet I see, and I cannot help seeing, that man acts as he pleases, and that God has left his actions, in a great measure, to his own free-will. Now, if I were to declare that man was so free to act that there was no control of God over his actions, I should be driven very near to atheism; and if, on the other hand, I should declare that God so over-rules all things that man is not free enough to be responsible, I should be driven at once into antinomianism or fatalism.

That God predestines, and yet that man is responsible, are two facts that few can see clearly. They are believed to be inconsistent and contradictory, but they are not. The fault is in our weak judgment. Two truths cannot be contradictory to each other. If, then, I find taught in one part of the Bible that everything is fore-ordained, *that is true;* and if I find, in another Scripture, that man is responsible for all his actions, *that is true;* and it is only my folly that leads me to imagine that these two truths can ever contradict each other. I do not believe they can ever be welded into one upon any earthly anvil, but they certainly shall be one in eternity. They are two lines that are so nearly parallel, that the human mind which pursues them farthest will never discover that they converge, but they do converge, and they will meet somewhere in eternity, close to the throne of God, whence all truth doth spring.

The Doctrine of God's Grace Preserves Us from Sin

It is often said that the doctrines we believe have a tendency to lead us to sin. I have heard it asserted most positively, that those high doctrines which we love, and which we find in the Scriptures, are licentious ones. I do not know who will have the hardihood to make that assertion, when they consider that the holiest of men have been believers in them. I ask the man who dares to say that Calvinism is a licentious religion, what he thinks of the character of Augustine, or Calvin, or Whitefield, who in successive ages were the great exponents of the system of grace; or what will he say of the Puritans, whose works are full of them? Had a man been an Arminian in those days, he would have been accounted the vilest heretic breathing, but now *we* are looked upon as the heretics, and they as the orthodox. *We* have gone back to the old school; *we* can trace our descent from the apostles. It is that vein of free-grace, running through the sermonizing of Baptists, which has saved us as a denomination. Were it not for that, we should not stand where we are today. We can run a golden line up to Jesus Christ Himself, through a holy succession of mighty fathers, who all held these glorious truths; and we can ask concerning them, "Where will you find holier and better men in the world?"

No doctrine is so calculated to preserve a man from sin as the doctrine of the grace of God. Those who have called it "a licentious doctrine" did not know anything at all about it. Poor ignorant things, they little knew that their own vile stuff was the most licentious doctrine under heaven. If they knew the grace of God in truth, they would soon see that there was no preservative from lying like a knowledge that we are elect of God from the foundation of the world. There is nothing like a belief in my eternal perseverance, and the immutability of my Father's affection, which can keep me near to Him from a motive of simple gratitude. Nothing makes a man so virtuous as belief of the truth. A lying doctrine will soon beget a lying practice. A man cannot have an erroneous belief without by-and-by having an erroneous life. I believe the one thing naturally begets the other. Of all men, those have the most disinterested piety, the sublimest reverence, the most ardent devotion, who believe that they are saved by grace, without works, through faith, and that not of themselves, it is the gift of God. Christians should take heed, and see that it always is so, lest by any means Christ should be crucified afresh, and put to an open shame.

"On Religious Grumblers" shows a witty and folksy side of Spurgeon that one does not immediately associate with his name. It is taken from an 1868 work titled John Ploughman's Talk, *a work in which Spurgeon discards his usual manner of speech for "strong proverbial expressions and homely phrases" that he might reach the common man he was always most interested in. "That I have written in a semi-humorous vein needs no apology," he writes in the preface, "since thereby sound moral teaching has gained a hearing from at least 300,000 persons. There is no particular virtue in being seriously unreadable."*

Spurgeon chose the persona of John Ploughman to reach the common man but also because "Every minister has put his hand to the plough: and it is his business to break up the fallow ground." The character of John Ploughman was patterned partially after his grandfather.

CHAPTER THIRTEEN

On Religious Grumblers

When a man has a particularly empty head he generally sets up for a great judge, especially in religion. None so wise as the man who knows nothing. His ignorance is the mother of his impudence, and the nurse of his obstinacy; and though he does not know B from a bull's foot, he settles matters as if all wisdom were at his fingers' ends—the Pope himself is not more infallible. Hear him talk after he has been at meeting and heard a sermon, and you will know how to pull a good man to pieces if you never knew it before. He sees faults where there are none, and if there be a few things amiss, he makes every mouse into an elephant. Although you might put all his wit into an egg-shell, he weighs the sermon in the balances of his conceit with all the airs of a bred-and-born Solomon, and if it be up to his standard, he lays on his praise with a trowel; but if it be not to his taste, he growls and barks and snaps at it like a dog at a hedgehog.

Wise men in this world are like trees in a hedge, there is only here and there one; and when these rare men talk together upon a discourse, it is good for the ears to hear them; but the bragging wiseacres I am speaking of are vainly puffed up by their fleshly minds, and their quibbling is as senseless as the cackle of geese on a common. Nothing comes out of a sack but what was in it, and as their bag is empty they shake nothing but wind out of it. It is very likely that neither ministers nor their sermons are perfect—the best garden may have a few weeds in it, the cleanest corn may have some chaff—but cavillers cavil at anything or nothing, and find fault for the sake of showing off their deep knowledge: sooner than let their tongues have a holiday, they would complain that the grass is not a nice shade of blue, and say that the sky would have looked neater if it had been whitewashed.

Highflying Ignoramuses

One tribe of these Ishmaelites is made up of highflying ignoramuses who are very mighty about the doctrine of a sermon—here they are as decisive as sledge-hammers and as certain as death. He who knows nothing is confident in everything; hence they are bull-headed beyond measure. Every clock, and even the sundial, must be set according to their watches; and the slightest difference from their opinion proves a man to be rotten at heart. Venture to argue with them, and their little pot boils over in quick style; ask them for reason, and you might as well go to a sand-pit for sugar. They have bottled up the sea of truth, and carry it in their waistcoat pockets; they have measured heaven's line of grace, and have tied a knot in a string at the exact length of electing love; and as for the things which angels long to know, they have seen them all as boys see sights in a peepshow at our fair. Having sold their modesty and become wiser than their teachers, they ride a very high horse, and jump over all five-barred gates of

Bible-texts which teach doctrines contrary to their notions.

When this mischief happens to good men, it is a great pity for such sweet pots of ointment to be spoiled by flies, yet one learns to bear with them just as I do with old Violet, for he is a rare horse, though he does set his ears back and throw out his legs at times. But there is a black bragging lot about, who are all sting and no honey; all whip and no hay; all grunt and no bacon. These do nothing but rail from morning to night at all who cannot see through their spectacles. If they would but mix up a handful of good living with all their bushels of bounce, it would be more bearable; but no, they don't care for such legality; men so sound as they are can't be expected to be good at anything else; they are the heavenly watch-dogs to guard the house of the Lord from those thieves and robbers who don't preach sound doctrine, and if they do worry the sheep, or steal a rabbit or two by the sly, who would have the heart to blame them?

The Lord's *dear* people, as they call themselves, have enough to do to keep their doctrine sound; and if their manners are cracked, who can wonder! no man can see to everything at once. These are the moles that want catching in many of our pastures, not for their own sakes, for there is not a sweet mouthful in them, but for the sake of the meadows which they spoil. I would not find half a fault with their doctrine, if it were not for their spirit; but vinegar is sweet to it, and crabs are figs in comparison. It must be very high doctrine that is too high for me, but I must have high experience and high practice with it, or it turns my stomach. However, I have said my say, and must leave the subject, or somebody will ask me, "What have you to do with Bradshaw's windmill?"

The Poor Trade of Judging Preachers

Sometimes it is the way the preacher speaks which is hauled over the coals, and here again is a fine field for fault-hunting, for every bean has its black, and every man has his failing. I never knew a good horse which had not some odd habit or other, and I never yet saw a minister worth his salt who had not some crotchet or oddity: now, these are the bits of cheese which cavillers smell out and nibble at: this man is too slow, and another too fast; the first is too flowery, and the second is too dull. Dear me, if all God's creatures were judged in this way, we should wring the dove's neck for being too tame, shoot the robins for eating spiders, kill the cows for swinging their tails, and the hens for not giving us milk. When a man wants to beat a dog, he can soon find a stick; and at this rate any fool may have something to say against the best minister in England.

As to a preacher's manner, if there be but plain speaking, none shall cavil at it because it wants polish, for if a thing is good and earnestly spoken, it cannot sound much amiss. No man should use bad language in the pulpit—and all language is bad which common people cannot make head or tail of—but godly, sober, decent, plain words none should carp at. A countryman is as warm in fustian as a king in velvet, and a truth is as comfortable in homely words as in fine speech. As to the way of dishing up the meat, hungry men leave that to the cook, only let the meat be sweet and substantial.

If hearers were better, sermons would be better. When men say they can't hear, I recommend them to buy a horn, and remember the old saying, "There's none so deaf as those who will not hear." When young speakers get down-hearted because of hard, unkind remarks, I generally tell them of the old man and his boy and his ass, and what came of trying to please everybody. No piper ever suited all ears. Where whims and fancies sit in the seat of judgment, a man's opinion is only so much wind, therefore take no more notice of it than of the wind whistling through a keyhole.

I have heard men find fault with a discourse for what was not in it; no matter how well the subject in hand was brought out, there was another subject about which nothing was said, and so all was wrong; which is as reasonable as finding fault with my ploughing because it does not dibble the holes for the beans, or abusing a good corn-field because there are no turnips in it. Does any man look for every truth in one sermon? As well look for every dish at one meal, and rail at a joint of beef because there are neither bacon, nor veal, nor green peas, nor parsnips on the table. Suppose a sermon is not full of comfort to the saint, yet if it warn the sinner, shall we despise it? A handsaw would be a poor tool to shave with, shall we therefore throw it away? Where is the use of always trying to hunt out faults? I hate to see a man with a fine nose smelling about for things to rail at like a rat-catcher's dog sniffing at rat holes. By all means let us down with error, root and branch, but do let us save our billhooks till there are brambles to chop, and not fall foul of our own mercies.

Judging preachers is a poor trade, for it pays neither party concerned in it. At a ploughing match they do give a prize to the best of us; but these judges of preaching are precious slow to give anything even to those whom they profess to think so much of. They pay in praise, but give no pudding. They get the gospel for nothing, and if they do not grumble, think that they have made an abundant return.

Everybody thinks himself a judge of a sermon, but nine out of ten might as well pretend to weigh the moon. I believe that, at bottom, most people think it an uncommonly easy thing to preach, and that they could do it amazingly well themselves. Every donkey thinks itself worthy to stand with the king's horses; every girl thinks she could keep house better than her mother; but thoughts are not facts; for the sprat thought itself a herring, but the fisherman knew better.

I dare say those who can whistle fancy that they can plough; but there's more than whistling in a good ploughman, and so let me tell you there's more in good preaching than taking a text, and saying, firstly, secondly, and thirdly. I try my hand at preaching myself, and in my poor way I find it no very easy thing to give the folks something worth hearing; and if the fine critics, who reckon us up on their thumbs, would but try their own hands at it, they might be a little more quiet. Dogs, however, always will bark, and what is worse, some of them will bite too; but let decent people do all they can, if not to muzzle them, yet to prevent them doing any great mischief.

Fault-Finders

It is a dreadful thing to see a happy family of Christians broken up by talkative fault-finders, and all about nothing, or less than nothing. Small is the edge of the wedge, but when the devil handles the beetle, churches are soon split to pieces, and men wonder why. The fact is, the worst wheel of the cart creaks most, and one fool makes many, and thus many a congregation is set at ears with a good and faithful minister, who would have been a lasting blessing to them if they had not chased away their best friend. Those who are at the bottom of the mischief have generally no part or lot in the matter of true godliness, but, like sparrows, fight over corn which is not their own, and, like jackdaws, pull to pieces what they never helped to build. From mad dogs, and grumbling professors, may we all be delivered, and may we never take the complaint from either of them.

Fault-finding is dreadfully catching: one dog will set a whole kennel howling, and the wisest course is to keep out of the way of a man who has the complaint called the grumbles. The worst of it is, that the foot and mouth disease go together, and he who bespatters others generally rolls in the mud himself before long. "The fruit of the Spirit is love," and this is a very different apple from the sour Siberian crab which some people bring forth. Good bye, all ye sons of Grizzle, John Ploughman would sooner pick a bone in peace than fight over an ox roasted whole.

Connolly, Ken. *Biographical Sketch of C. H. Spurgeon.* Pasadena, Texas, Pilgrim Publications, 1990.

Dallimore, Arnold A. *Spurgeon: A New Biography.* Carlisle, Pennsylvania, Banner of Truth, 1985.

Day, Richard Ellsworth. *The Shadow of the Broad Rim—The Life-Story of Charles Haddon Spurgeon.* Valley Forge, Pennsylvania, Judson Press, 1934.

Drummond, Lewis A. *Spurgeon: The Prince of Preachers.* Kregel Publications, Grand Rapids, Michigan, 1992.

Fullerton, W. Y. *Charles Spurgeon.* Chicago, Moody, 1980.

Hayden, Eric W. *Highlights in the Life of C. H. Spurgeon.* Pasadena, Texas, Pilgrim Publications, 1990.

Pike, G. Holden. *The Life & Work of Charles Haddon Spurgeon.* Carlisle, Pennsylvania. Banner of Truth, 1992.

Ross, Bob L. *Pictorial Biography of C. H. Spurgeon.* Pasadena, Texas, Pilgrim Publications, 1974.

Spurgeon, C. H. *Complete Index to C. H. Spurgeon's Sermons, 1855–1917.* Pasadena, Texas, Pilgrim Publications, 1980.

———. *Imputed Righteousness.* Pasadena, Texas, Pilgrim Publications, 1990.

———. *Metropolitan Tabernacle: Its History & Work & Spurgeon's Jubilee Services.* Pasadena, Texas, Pilgrim Publications, 1990.

———. *The Two Wesleys.* Pasadena, Texas, Pilgrim Publications, 1975.

———. *Charles Haddon Spurgeon—Autobiography: the Early years, 1834–1860, Vol. 1.* Carlisle, Pennsylvania, Banner of Truth, 1976.

———. *Charles Haddon Spurgeon—Autobiography: The Full Harvest. 1861–1892. Vol. 2.* Carlisle, Pennsylvania, Banner of Truth, 1975.

Triggs, Kathy. *Charles Spurgeon.* Minneapolis, Minnesota, Bethany House, 1986.

DWIGHT L. MOODY

Dwight L. Moody

Abridged and edited by Stephen Rost

Contents

DWIGHT L. MOODY 1837–1899

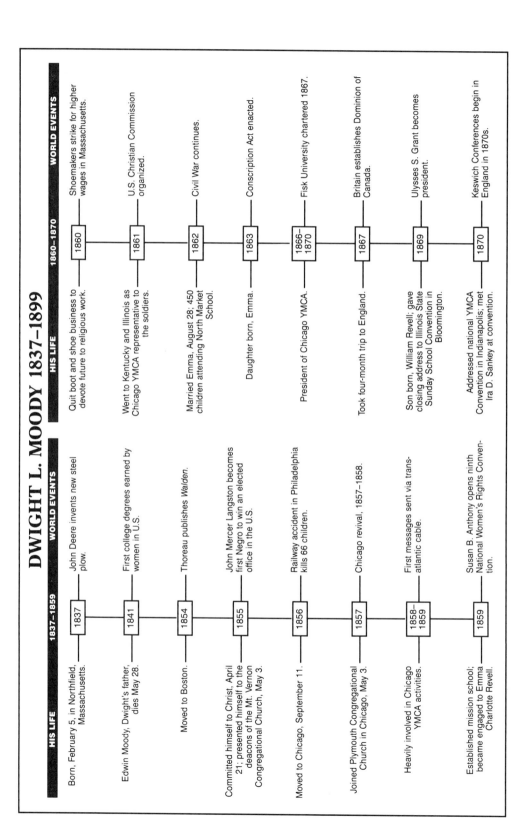

HIS LIFE | **1837–1859** | **WORLD EVENTS**

- **1837** — Born, February 5, in Northfield, Massachusetts. / John Deere invents new steel plow.
- **1841** — Edwin Moody, Dwight's father, dies May 28. / First college degrees earned by women in U.S.
- **1854** — Moved to Boston. / Thoreau publishes *Walden*.
- **1855** — Committed himself to Christ, April 21; presented himself to the deacons of the Mt. Vernon Congregational Church, May 3. / John Mercer Langston becomes first Negro to win an elected office in the U.S.
- **1856** — Moved to Chicago, September 11. / Railway accident in Philadelphia kills 66 children.
- **1857** — Joined Plymouth Congregational Church in Chicago, May 3. / Chicago revival, 1857–1858.
- **1858–1859** — Heavily involved in Chicago YMCA activities. / First messages sent via transatlantic cable.
- **1859** — Established mission school; became engaged to Emma Charlotte Revell. / Susan B. Anthony opens ninth National Women's Rights Convention.

HIS LIFE | **1860–1870** | **WORLD EVENTS**

- **1860** — Quit boot and shoe business to devote future to religious work. / Shoemakers strike for higher wages in Massachusetts.
- **1861** — Went to Kentucky and Illinois as Chicago YMCA representative to the soldiers. / U.S. Christian Commission organized.
- **1862** — Married Emma, August 28; 450 children attending North Market School. / Civil War continues.
- **1863** — Daughter born, Emma. / Conscription Act enacted.
- **1866–1870** — President of Chicago YMCA. / Fisk University chartered 1867.
- **1867** — Took four-month trip to England. / Britain establishes Dominion of Canada.
- **1869** — Son born, William Revell; gave closing address to Illinois State Sunday School Convention in Bloomington. / Ulysses S. Grant becomes president.
- **1870** — Addressed national YMCA Convention in Indianapolis; met Ira D. Sankey at convention. / Keswich Conferences begin in England in 1870s.

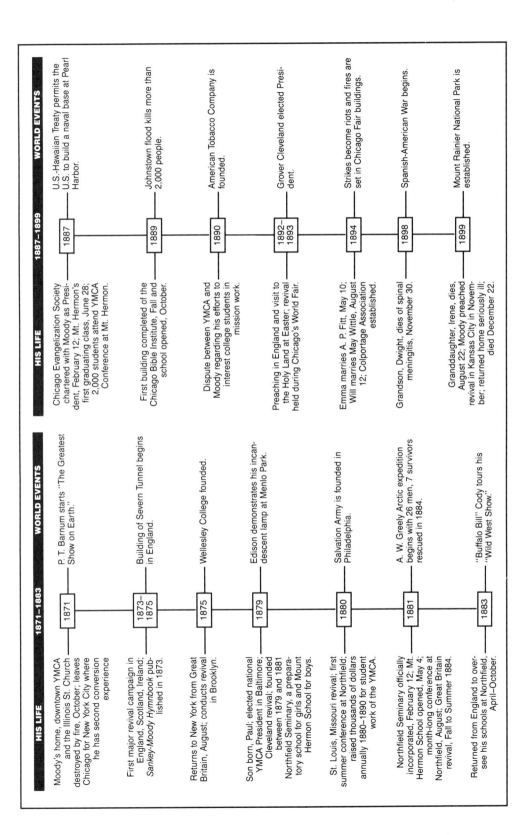

1871–1883

HIS LIFE	Year	WORLD EVENTS
Moody's home, downtown YMCA and the Illinois St. Church destroyed by fire, October; leaves Chicago for New York City where he has second conversion experience	1871	P. T. Barnum starts "The Greatest Show on Earth."
First major revival campaign in England, Scotland, Ireland; Sankey-Moody Hymnbook published in 1873.	1873–1875	Building of Severn Tunnel begins in England.
Returns to New York from Great Britain, August; conducts revival in Brooklyn.	1875	Wellesley College founded.
Son born, Paul; elected national YMCA President in Baltimore; Cleveland revival; founded between 1879 and 1881 Northfield Seminary, a preparatory school for girls and Mount Hermon School for boys.	1879	Edison demonstrates his incandescent lamp at Menlo Park.
St. Louis, Missouri revival; first summer conference at Northfield; raised thousands of dollars annually 1880–1890 for student work of the YMCA.	1880	Salvation Army is founded in Philadelphia.
Northfield Seminary officially incorporated, February 12; Mt. Hermon School opened, May 4; month-long conference at Northfield, August; Great Britain revival, Fall to Summer 1884.	1881	A. W. Greely Arctic expedition begins with 26 men, 7 survivors rescued in 1884.
Returned from England to oversee his schools at Northfield, April–October.	1883	"Buffalo Bill" Cody tours his "Wild West Show."

1887–1899

HIS LIFE	Year	WORLD EVENTS
Chicago Evangelization Society chartered with Moody as President, February 12; Mt. Hermon's first graduating class, June 28; 2,000 students attend YMCA Conference at Mt. Hermon.	1887	U.S.-Hawaiian Treaty permits the U.S. to build a naval base at Pearl Harbor.
First building completed of the Chicago Bible Institute, Fall and school opened, October.	1889	Johnstown flood kills more than 2,000 people.
Dispute between YMCA and Moody regarding his efforts to interest college students in mission work.	1890	American Tobacco Company is founded.
Preaching in England and visit to the Holy Land at Easter; revival held during Chicago's World Fair.	1892–1893	Grover Cleveland elected President.
Emma marries A. P. Fitt, May 10; Will marries May Wittle, August 12; Colportage Association established.	1894	Strikes become riots and fires are set in Chicago Fair buildings.
Grandson, Dwight, dies of spinal meningitis, November 30.	1898	Spanish-American War begins.
Granddaughter, Irene, dies, August 22; Moody preached revival in Kansas City in November; returned home seriously ill; died December 22.	1899	Mount Rainier National Park is established.

DWIGHT L. MOODY

Introduction

Dwight L. Moody (1837–99) is, along with Billy Graham, one of America's most celebrated evangelists. He was part of a rapidly growing heritage of preaching in America: the traveling evangelist. After the Wesleys, Whitefield, and Finney paved the way in earlier days, Moody came on the scene to continue the evangelist movement with outstanding success.

Moody did not have the type of childhood one would consider conducive to raising successful children. His father was an alcoholic and eventually died from his addiction. He left the large Moody family heavily in debt. Eventually creditors took most of what they had, leaving the family destitute. The kind help of a Unitarian minister enabled the family to begin recovering, but they were never far removed from poverty.

Moody did not receive a thorough education because of family problems. His religious training was even worse. Around the age of seventeen, Moody left his home in Northfield, Massachusetts, and went to Boston, hoping to find a job in his uncle's shoe store. At first the uncle was opposed to such an arrangement, but he later agreed on the condition that Moody would live where he was told, abstain from drinking and other vices, and attend church. This arrangement forced Moody to attend the Mount Vernon Congregational Church, and he was converted in 1855.

Seeking greener pastures, Moody arrived in Chicago in 1856 and became a shoe clerk. Later he worked as a salesman and debt collector. These jobs enabled him to save thousands of dollars. But his heart was in the ministry, and in 1859 he organized a Sunday school mission which became quite successful. This led him to give up secular work and become a full-time minister. He became involved with the YMCA and was a popular speaker at city-wide revival meetings and other engagements.

With his popularity soaring, Moody engaged in traveling evangelistic work. This took him to the eastern United States as well as England.

But his influence did not stop with the pulpit. His deep concern for education led him to establish several schools for girls and boys. And his greatest legacy was the Moody Bible Institute, founded in 1886 in Chicago.

Moody died in 1899, leaving behind a rich life filled with great success, not only as a winner of souls but also as an educator of minds.

Faithfulness is an important characteristic in any Christian. The Bible is full of examples of individuals who were used by God because they were found faithful. In this message Moody stresses the importance of being a faithful worker in God's vineyard.

He begins by telling about his long years in the ministry and the fact that God has been a faithful employer. The pay of the ministry is far greater than silver or gold, and the sooner one gets involved, Moody says, the better. Throughout the sermon he supports his claim with examples of people who have had fruitful ministries.

Moody believed effective ministry could be developed in groups of any size. Often he encountered people who taught small groups of boys and girls. Such people felt that their work was not important, but Moody always assured them that even the smallest numbers were valuable. In his mind, the tiniest group could contain a potential Luther or Wesley. He emphasized this over and over again to any teacher who came to him with a defeated countenance. To Moody, obedience, not size, was the standard set by God and the measure of a Christian's faith.

CHAPTER ONE

The Reward of the Faithful

I want to call your attention to the fourth chapter, gospel of Saint John and part of the thirty-sixth verse: "And he that reapeth receiveth wages and gathereth fruit unto life eternal." I want you to get the text into your hearts. We have a thousand texts to every sermon, but they slip over the hearts of men and women. If I can get this text into your hearts today, with the Spirit of God, these meetings will be the brightest and most glorious ever held in Chicago; for it is the Word of the Lord, and His Word is worth more than ten thousand sermons. "He that reapeth receiveth wages." I can speak from experience. I have been in the Lord's service for twenty-one years, and I want to testify that He is a good paymaster—that He pays promptly. Oh, I think I see faces before me light up at these words. You have been out in the harvest fields of the Lord, and you know this to be true. To go out and labor for Him is a thing to be proud of—to guide a poor, weary soul to the way of life, and turn his face towards the golden gates of Zion. The Lord's wages are better than silver and gold, because He says that the loyal soul shall receive a crown of glory.

If the mayor of Chicago gave a proclamation stating that he had work for the men, women, and children of the city, and he would give them a dollar a day, people would say this was very good of the mayor. This money, however, would fade away in a short time. But here is a proclamation coming directly from the throne of grace to every man, woman, and child in the wide world to gather into God's vineyard, where they will find treasures that will never fade, and these treasures will be crowns of everlasting life; and the laborer will find treasures laid up in his Father's house, and when, after serving faithfully here, he will be greeted by friends assembled there. Work for tens of thousands of men, women, and children! Think of it and the reward. These little children, my friends, are apt to be overlooked; but they must be led to Christ. Children have done a great deal in the vineyard. They have led parents to Jesus. It was a little girl that led Naaman to Christ. Christ can find useful work for these little ones. He can see little things, and we ought to pay great attention to them.

As I was coming along the street today I thought that if I could only impress upon you all that we have come here as to a vineyard, to reap and to gather, we shall have a glorious harvest, and we want every class to assist us. The first class we want is the ministers.

The Work of Ministers

There was one thing that pleased me this morning, and that was the eight thousand people who came to this building, and the large number of ministers who seized me by the hand, with the tears trickling down their cheeks, and who gave me a "God bless you!" It gave me a light heart. There are some ministers who get behind the posts, as if they were ashamed of being seen in our company and of our meetings. They come to criticize the sermon and pick it to pieces. No effort is required to do this. We don't want the ministers to criticize but to help us and tell us when we are wrong. There was one minister in this city who did me a great deal of good when I first started out. When I commenced to teach the Word of God I made very many blunders. I have learned that in acquiring anything a man must make many blunders. If a man is going to learn any kind of trade—carpenter's, plumber's, painter's—he will make any amount of mistakes. Well, this minister, an old man, used to take me aside and tell me my errors. So we want the ministers to come to us and tell us of our blunders, and if we get them to do this and join hands with us, a spiritual fountain will break over every church in the city.

Many ministers have said to me, "What do you want us to do?" The Lord must teach us what our work shall be. Let every child of God come up to these meetings, and say, "Teach me, O God, what I can do to help these men and women who are inquiring the way to be saved," and at the close of the meetings draw near to them and point out the way. If men and women are to be converted in great meetings, it is by personal dealings with them. What we want is personal contact with them. If a number of people were sick, and a doctor prescribed one kind of medicine for them all, you would think this was wrong. This audience is spiritually diseased, and what we want is that Christian workers will go to them and find out their trouble. Five minutes' private consultation will teach them. What we want is to get [to] the people. Everyone has his own particular burden; every family has a different story to tell. Take the gospel of the Lord to them and show its application; tell them what to do with it, so as to answer their own cases.

Let the minister come into the inquiry room.

An old man—a minister in Glasgow, Scotland—was one of the most active in our meetings. When he would be preaching elsewhere he would drive up in a cab with his Bible in his hand. It made no difference what part of Glasgow he was preaching in; he managed to attend nearly every one of our services. The old man would come in, tenderly speak to those assembled, and let one soul after another see the light. His congregation was comparatively small when we got there, but, by his painstaking efforts to minister to those in search of the Word, when we left Glasgow his church could not hold the people who sought admission. I do not know of any man who helped us like Dr. Andrew Bonair. He was always ready to give the weak counsel and point out the way to the soul seeking Christ. If we have not ministers enough, let those we have come forward, and their elders and deacons will follow them.

The Work of Teachers

The next class we want to help us to reach the people is Sunday school teachers, and I value their experience next to that of the ministers. In the cities where we have been, teachers have come to me and said, "Mr. Moody, pray for my Sunday school scholars," and I have taken them aside and pointed out their duties and shown how they themselves ought to be able to pray for their pupils. Next meeting very often they would come, and the prayer would go up from them, "God bless my scholars."

In one city we went to, a Sunday school superintendent came to his minister and said, "I am not fit to gather sinners to life eternal; I cannot be superintendent any longer." The minister asked, "What is the reason?" and the man said, "I am not right with God." Then the minister advised him that the best thing, instead of resigning, was to get right with God. So he prayed with that teacher that the truth would shine upon him; and God lit up his soul with the Word. Before I left that town, the minister told me all doubt had fled from that superintendent's mind, and he had gone earnestly to work and gathered, from the time of his conversion, over six hundred scholars into the school of his church.

The Lord can bless, of course, in spite of schools and teachers; but they are the channels of salvation. Bring your classes together, and pray to God to convert them. We have from three thousand to five thousand teachers here. Suppose they said, "I will try to bring my children to Christ," what a reformation we should have! Don't say that that boy is too small or that girl is too puny or insignificant. Everyone is valuable to the Lord. A teacher, whom I found at our services when she ought to have been attending to her class, upon my asking why she was at our meeting, said, "Well, I have a very small class—only five little boys." "What?" said I, "You have come here and neglected these little ones? Why, in that little towhead may be the seeds of a reformation. There may be a Luther, a Wheaton, a Wesley, or a Bunyan among them. You may be neglecting a chance for them, the effects of which will follow them through life." If you do not look to those things, teachers, someone will step into your vineyard and gather the riches you would have.

Look what a teacher did in southern Illinois. She had taught a little girl to love the Savior, and the teacher said to her, "Can't you get your father to come to the Sunday school?" This father was a swearing, drinking man, and the love of God was not in his heart. But under the tuition of that teacher, the little girl went to her father and told him of Jesus' love and led him to that Sunday school. What was the result? I heard, before leaving for Europe, that he had been instrumental in founding over seven hundred and eighty Sabbath schools in southern Illinois. And what a privilege a teacher has—a privilege of leading souls to Christ. Let every Sabbath school teacher say, "By the help of God I will try to lead my scholars to Christ."

The Work of Young Men

It seems to me that we have more help in our revivals from young men, except from mothers, than from any other class. The young men are pushing, energetic workers. Old men are good for counsel, and they should help, by their good words, the young men in making Christianity aggressive. These billiard halls have been open long enough. There is many a gem in those places, that only needs the way pointed out to fill their souls with love of Him. Let the young men go plead with them, bring them to the tabernacle, and don't let them go out without presenting the claims of Christ. Show them His never-dying love. Take them by the hand and say, "I want you to become a Christian." What we want is a hand-to-hand conflict with the billiard saloons and drinking halls. Do not fear, but enter them and ask the young men to come. I know that some of you say, in a scornful way, "We will never be allowed to enter; the people who go there will cast us out." This is a mistake. I know that I have gone to them and remonstrated and have never been unkindly treated. And some of the best workers have been men who have been proprietors of these places and men who have been constant frequenters. There are young men there breaking their mothers' hearts and losing themselves for all eternity. The Spirit of the

Lord Jesus Christ asks you to seek them out. If we cannot get them to come here, let the building be thrown aside, and let us go down and hunt them up and tell them of Christ and heaven. If we cannot get a multitude to preach to, let us preach, even if it be to one person. Christ preached one of His most wonderful sermons to that woman at the well; and shall we not be willing to go to one, as He did, and tell that one of salvation? And let us preach to men, even if they are under the influence of liquor.

I may relate a little experience. In Philadelphia, at one of our meetings, a drunken man rose up. Till that time I had no faith that a drunken man could be converted. When anyone approached he was generally taken out. This man got up and shouted, "I want to be prayed for!" The friends who were with him tried to draw him away, but he shouted only louder, and three times he repeated his request. His call was attended to, and he was converted. God has power to convert a man even if he is drunk.

I have still another lesson. I met a man in New York, who was an earnest worker, and I asked him to tell me his experiences. He said he had been a drunkard for over twenty years. His parents had forsaken him, and his wife had cast him off and married someone else. He went into a lawyer's office in Poughkeepsie, mad with drink. This lawyer proved a good Samaritan. He reasoned with him and told him he could be saved. The man scouted the idea. He said, "I must be pretty low when my father and mother, my wife and kindred, cast me off, and there is no hope for me here or hereafter." But this good Samaritan showed him how it was possible to secure salvation, got him on his feet, got him on his beast, like the good Samaritan of old, and guided his face toward Zion. And this man said to me, "I have not drunk a glass of liquor since." He is now leader of a young men's meeting in New York. I asked him to come up last Saturday night to Northfield, my native town, where there are a good many drunkards, thinking he might encourage them to seek salvation. He came and brought a young man with him. They held a meeting, and it seemed as if the power of God rested upon that meeting when these two men went on telling what God had done for them—how He had destroyed the works of the devil in their hearts, and brought peace and unalloyed happiness to their souls. These grog shops here are the works of the devil—they are ruining men's souls every hour. Let us fight against them, and let our prayers go up in our battle, "Lord, manifest Thy power in Chicago this coming month." It may seem a very difficult thing for us, but it is a very easy thing for God to convert rumsellers.

A young man in New York got up and thrilled the meeting with his experience. "I want to tell you," he said, "that nine months ago a Christian came to my house and said he wanted me to become a Christian. He talked to me kindly and encouragingly, pointing out the error of my ways, and I became converted. I had been a hard drinker, but since that time I have not touched a drop of liquor. If any one had asked who the most hopeless man in that town was, they would have pointed to me." Today this young man is the superintendent of a Sabbath school.

Eleven years ago, when I went to Boston, I had a cousin who wanted a little of my experience. I gave him all the help I could, and he became a Christian. He did not know how near death was to him. He wrote to his brother and said, "I am very anxious to get your soul to Jesus." The letter somehow went to another city and lay from the 28th of February to the 28th of March—just one month. [When he received it,] he saw it was in his brother's handwriting and tore it open and read the above words. It struck a chord in his heart, and was the means of converting him. And this was the Christian who led this drunken young man to Christ.

This young man had a neighbor who had drunk for forty years, and he went to that neighbor and told him what God had done for him, and the result was another conversion.

I tell you these things to encourage you to believe that the drunkards and saloon keepers can be saved. There is work for you to do, and by-and-by the harvest shall be gathered, and what a scene will be on the shore when we hear the Master on the throne shout, "Well done! Well done!"

Let me say a word to you, mothers. We depend a good deal upon you. It seems to me that there is not a father and mother in all Chicago who should not be in sympathy with this work. You have daughters and sons, and if work is done now, they will be able to steer clear of many temptations and will be able to lead better lives here. It seems to me selfishness if they sit down inactive and say, "There is no use in this. We are safe ourselves, what is the use of troubling?" If the mothers and fathers of the whole community would unite their prayers and send up appeals to God to manifest His power, in answer to them there would be mighty work.

I remember in Philadelphia we wanted to see certain results, and we called a meeting of mothers. There were from five to eight thousand mothers present, and each of them had a particular burden upon her heart. There was a mother who had a wayward daughter, another a reckless son, another a bad husband. We spoke to them confidently, and we bared our hearts to one another. They prayed for aid from the Lord and that grace might be shown to these sons and daughters and husbands, and the result was that our inquiry rooms were soon filled with anxious and earnest inquirers.

Let me tell you about a mother in Philadelphia. She had two wayward sons. They were wild, dissipated youths. They were to meet on a certain night and join in dissipation. The rendezvous was at the corner of Market and Thirteenth streets, where our meetings were held. One of the young men entered the large meeting, and when it was over went to the young men's meeting near at hand, and was quickened, and there he prayed that the Lord might save him. His mother had gone to the meeting that night, and, arriving too late, found the door closed. When that young man went home he found his mother praying for him, and the two mingled their prayers together. While they were praying together the other brother came from the other meeting, and brought tidings of being converted, and at the next meeting the three got up and told their experience. I never heard an audience so thrilled before or since.

A wayward boy in London, whose mother was very anxious for his salvation, said to her, "I am not going to be bothered with your prayers any longer. I will go to America and be rid of them." "But, my boy," she said, "God is on the sea, and in America, and He hears my prayers for you." Well, he came to this country, and as they sailed into the port of New York, some of the sailors told him that Moody and Sankey were holding meetings in the Hippodrome. The moment he landed he started for our place of meeting, and there he found Christ. He became a most earnest worker, and he wrote to his mother and told her that her prayers had been answered; that he had been saved, and that he had found his mother's God. Mothers and fathers, lift up your hearts in prayer, that there may be hundreds of thousands saved in this city.

When I was in London, there was one lady dressed in black up in the gallery. All the rest were ministers. I wondered who that lady could be. At the close of the meeting I stepped up to her, and she asked me if I did not remember her. I did not, but she told me who she was, and her story came to my mind.

When we were preaching in Dundee, Scotland, a mother came up with her two sons, sixteen and seventeen years old. She said to me, "Will you talk to my boys?" I asked her if she would talk to the inquirers, and told her there were more inquirers than workers. She said she was not a good enough Christian— was not prepared enough. I told her I could not talk to her then. Next night she came to me and asked me again, and the following night she repeated her request. Five hundred miles she journeyed to get God's blessing for her boys. Would to God we had more mothers like her. She came to London, and the first night I was there, I saw her in the Agricultural Hall. She was accompanied by only one of her boys—the other had died. Toward the close of the meeting I received this letter from her:

Dear Mr. Moody: For months I have never considered the day's work ended unless you and your work had been specially prayed for. Now it appears before us more and more. What in our little measure we have found has no doubt been the happy experience of many others in London. My husband and I have sought as our greatest privilege to take unconverted friends one by one to the Agricultural Hall, and I thank God that, with a single exception, those brought under the preaching from your lips have accepted Christ as their Savior, and are rejoicing in His love.

That lady was a lady of wealth and position. She lived a little way out of London; but she gave up her beautiful home and took lodgings near the Agricultural Hall, so as to be useful in the inquiry room. When we went down to the Opera House she was there; when we went down to the east end there she was again, and when I left London she had the names of 150 who had accepted Christ from her. Some said that our work in London was a failure. Ask her if the work was a failure, and she will tell you. If we had a thousand such mothers in Chicago we would lift it.

Go and bring your friends to the meetings here. Think of the privilege, my friends, of saving a soul. If we are going to work for good we must be up and about it. Men say, "I have not the time." Take it. Ten minutes every day for Christ will give you good wages. There is many a man who is working for you. Take them by the hand. Some of you with silver locks, I think I hear you saying, "I wish I was young, how I would rush into the battle." Well, if you cannot be a fighter, you can pray and lead on the others. There are two kinds of old people in the world. One grows chilled and sour, and there are others who light up every meeting with their genial presence, and cheer on the workers. Draw near, old age, and cheer on the others, and take them by the hand and encourage them.

There was a building on fire. The flames leaped around the staircase, and from a third-story window a little child was seen who cried for help. The only way to reach it was by a ladder. One was obtained and a fireman ascended, but when he had almost reached the child, the flames broke from the window and leaped around him. He faltered and seemed afraid to go further. Suddenly someone in the crowd shouted, "Give him a cheer," and cheer after cheer went up. The fireman was [charged] with new energy, and rescued the child. Just so with our young men. Whenever you see them wavering, cheer them on. If you cannot work yourself, give them cheers to [spur] them on in their glorious work. May the blessing of God fall upon us this afternoon, and let every man and woman be up and doing.

Charity, or love, is the heart of Christianity. It was the very thing that brought Christ to earth to save human souls. For his text Moody selected the great love chapter, 1 Corinthians 13. In it the ingredient for true success rings loud and clear: a Christian must have true love for people if he is to successfully win them to Christ. No other motive will produce the same results or incur God's blessing.

Often Christians confuse duty for love. It is possible to function for a time out of duty, but only love will enable one to work with the fullest satisfaction and contentment. To be a Christian entails loving others and being willing to help all those in need. A loving spirit brings unity, happiness, and success. God is pleased with and able to work through the lives of Christians who love others.

CHAPTER TWO

Charity

You will find the text in the first verse of the chapter I read this evening—1 Corinthians, thirteenth chapter: "Though I speak with the tongues of men and of angels, and have not charity, I am become as sounding brass, or a tinkling cymbal." You, I have no doubt, wondered how it is that you have not met with more success. I think if I have asked myself this question once, I have a thousand times, "Why is it that I have not had greater success?" But I never read this chapter without finding it out. It is a chapter that every Christian ought to read at least once a week, I think with a great deal of profit. A man may be a preacher and have all the eloquence of a Demosthenes—he may be the greatest pulpit orator that ever lived, but if love is not the motivating power, "it is as sounding brass or a tinkling cymbal." A good many churches have eloquent ministers. The people go there and listen critically and closely, but there are no converts. They have wondered why. The cause has been the lack of love. If a minister has not got love deep in his heart you may as well put a boy in the pulpit and make him beat a big drum. His talking is like the "sounding of brass."

Failures to make converts in those churches are common, and the reason so many preachers have failed is because love has not been the motivating power. The prophet may understand prophecy and interpret it in such a clear way as to astonish you. I have met men and sat down beside them, and they would dig out the most wonderful truths out of prophecy which I could

not see. I have sat at their feet and wondered at their power in this respect, and wondered also why it was that they were not blessed with more converts. I have sought the cause, and invariably found it was want of love.

A man, though he is deep in learning and in theology, if he has no love in his heart he will do no good. A man may understand all the mysteries of life, may be wonderful in seeking out truths, yet [he] may not be blessed by winning men. Paul says that though a man understand all mysteries, if he have no love his understanding goes for nothing; and he goes a step further and says that a man may give large sums to feed the poor, but if love does not accompany the gift it goes for naught in the sight of God. The only fruit on the tree of life worth having is love. Love must be the motive power. A man may give his thousands to the poor and get the gift written about in the paper, where you will see that he is a good philanthropic man, yet if love does not prompt the deed, it goes for nothing in God's sight. Many a man here is very liberal to the poor. If you ask him for a donation to a charitable purpose, he draws his purse and puts down one thousand dollars; if you come to him for a subscription for this or that theological seminary he will draw his check instantly; but God looks down into that man's heart, and if he has no love it goes for nothing. Some men would give everything they have—would give their body for what they think is a good cause—for some truth they've got hold of; yet there is no love in the act.

The Motivating Power

The main teaching of this chapter is that love must be the motivating power in all our actions. If our actions are merely performed out of a sense of duty, God will not accept us. I've heard this word "duty" in connection with Christian work till I am tired of it. I have come down to a meeting and someone has got up and asked a brother to get up and speak. After considerable persuasion he has got upon his feet and said, "Well, I did not intend to speak when I came down tonight, but I suppose it is my duty to say something." And it is the same with the Sunday school; many teachers take up classes from a sense of duty. There is no love in them, and their services go for nothing. Let us strike for a higher plane—let us throw a little love into our actions, and then our services will be accepted by God if love will be the motivating power.

I have an old mother way down in the Connecticut mountains, and I have been in the habit of going to see her every year for twenty years. Suppose I go there and say, "Mother, you were very kind to me when I was young—you were very good to me; when father died you worked hard for us all to keep us together, and so I have come to see you because it is my duty." I went then only because it was my duty. Then she should say to me, "Well, my son, if you only come to see me because it is your duty, you need not come again." And that is the way with a great many of the servants of God. They work for Him because it is their duty—not for love. Let us abolish this word duty, and feel that it is only a privilege to work for God, and let us try to remember that what is done merely from a sense of duty is not acceptable to God.

One night when I had been speaking in this way in London, a minister said to me after services, "Now, Moody, you are all wrong. If you take this word duty out from its connection with our works, you will soon have all the churches and Sunday schools empty." "Well," said I, "I will try and convince you that I am all right. You are married?" "Yes." "Well, suppose this was your wife's birthday, and you bought a present of a book for her, and you went home and said, 'Now, my wife, this is your birthday, I have felt it my duty to buy something for you— here's a book; take it.' Would your wife not be justified in refusing it?" "Well," said he, "I think you are correct; she would be right in refusing it." That wife would want a present given her through love, not duty. What Christ wants is that we will work for Him because we love Him. The first impulse of a young convert is to love, and if a young man attempts to talk to people without [having] been won to Christ by love—without [having] been converted by the true spirit of the Holy Ghost—his efforts fall short of their mark. If he has been touched to the heart with the love of Jesus, the first thing he does is to shout out that love which is waiting for all hearts. Paul, in the fifth chapter of Galatians, tells you that the fruit of the Spirit is "love, joy, peace, long-suffering." That is the fruit of the Spirit. He commences this line with love at the head of the list, and if love is not the motive we have not been born of the Spirit.

Let us ask ourselves the question, "Is love the motivating power that urges us to go out and work for God?" This is the first question that we ought to ask ourselves. Without it a great deal of work will go for naught. The work will be swept away like chaff without it. Christ looks down and examines our hearts and actions, and although our deeds may be great in the eyes of the world, they may not be in His eyes.

A Different Measure

Look at that woman in Jerusalem. All the rich people were casting in their treasures to the Lord. I can see the women and men come into the temple, some giving one hundred dollars, others giving three hundred dollars, and others putting in five hundred dollars, and if there had been newspapers in Jerusalem in those days, there would have been notices of these contributions. It would have [looked] very well in print. But by-and-by a poor widow woman comes along and puts in a humble two mites. I can see the Lord sitting at the treasury when that woman comes with her little all, and hear Him saying, "That woman hath given more than all of them." Why? Not owing to the large amount. No; but simply because it was love that prompted that woman.

The one great thing that the church lacks at the present day, and if you ask me to put it into as small space as possible I can put it into a word of four letters—and that is, "love." Show me a church in which the members love one another, and I will show you a church that is on fire in the cause of Christ. In it there is a revival every day for the twelve months of the year—the 365 days of the year are filled with continual manifestations of Christ's love. That is the lack today. There is lukewarmness—coldness one toward another. In Second Timothy Paul tells what Christians' lives should be—sound in faith, sound in love, and sound in patience. If a man is not sound in faith, we would draw his head right off; if he is not sound in faith, put him out. But let him be ever so unsound in love, he will be kept in. How many men are here in Chicago who are in churches and who are continually picking to pieces and slandering their brothers. They are continually going about finding fault with someone. They have no love.

Those who do not love in the way stated in this chapter, ponder well its meaning. Let the question go home to every heart here tonight: "Is there anyone I do not love?" If you are treasuring up in your heart any feeling of hatred toward any man or woman, God will not love you. You must be ready to forgive and love. I do not know that we could put up anything better on the platform than that motto that "God is love," and may it be burned into your heart. You say you love those who love you. Any black-hearted hypocrite can love those who love him. But what Christ wants to teach us is to love those that hate us and slight us. If you can only convince men that you love them, you can influence them. That is what we want to do in order to touch the hearts of those we come in contact with [during] the coming month. If one of us went to a bad man and said to him, "You are the worst man in Chicago," that would not touch him; it would only harden his heart the more. We want to go to him lovingly, and show him the love that Christ offers him. When the Son of man came into the world it was love that moved Him, and we will never do any good with anybody till our own hearts are touched with that same love. If we are not loving toward others they will not like us, and instead of trying to talk for Christ we had better keep away. A worker must win the hearts and affections of the people before he can do any effective work.

When in London, Dr. Arnott came down from Edinburgh to one of our meetings, and he told those people something—I don't think the Londoners understood him, but if they knew of farm life as I did, they would have known what he meant. He said, "When I was on my father's farm, when they wanted to teach a calf to drink, they would bring it to the pail and a man would dip his finger into the milk and put it into the calf's mouth, drawing his hand slowly away, and before you knew it the calf was drinking for itself. And so," he said, "if you want to win people to Christ you have to go lovingly to them and lead them gradually to Him." If you do not make people love you, you need not talk to them. Oh, that God may show you this truth tonight, that the great lever of the Christian is love! If a Sabbath school teacher does not love his scholars—if he goes to them as if it was a lesson he wished to get over, it will not be long before they find it out. They will see it in his eyes, in his face, in his actions.

And so, let us see tonight the necessity of having the love of God in our hearts, and so when we approach that drunkard or that gambler we can win him to Christ; and so that when you show him the gospel and tell him you want him to be saved, he will receive you with a welcome. If you go to him from a sense of duty you will make no progress with him, but if you go to him and talk of the love of Christ, and show kindness in your actions, he will hear you.

The Power of a Smile

A minister in London said to me one night, "Mr. Moody, I want you to pray for a lot of people who will be at the meeting tonight"; and when I went there I saw in one corner a father, mother, and four or five children. And I prayed for them. When I got home I asked the minister about the family, and he said they had been won to Jesus by a smile. He said he was passing by a house in that city one day at the window of which a little child was standing. He liked children, and smiled to [the child] and bowed. This minister was in the habit

of passing the house every day, and the second time he noticed the child again, and he smiled again. The next time there were several children there, and he smiled and bowed again. When he came again he saw the same children standing there, but he saw a lady standing with them. He thought it would not be right to bow to the lady, but he smiled at the children, and when she saw him looking so pleasant, the lady said, "That man must be a minister."

My friends, it would be a good thing if all ministers had a smile on their faces. There are more men driven away from churches by sour looks than by anything else. A minister ought to have a clear conscience, and he would wear a pleasant smile. Some of you will say, "Well, Christ was melancholy, and wept over sinners." Ah, but it was love. There is such a thing as a man weeping in his love. Well, the lady said to her little ones, "I want you to follow that gentleman, for I am sure he is a minister." And when he came round again the children went after him, shadowing him through several streets, until by-and-by he turned into an Independent church. The children followed him right in and they brought home a good report. They said they never had such a preacher, although probably they did not understand a word he said. But you know a little pat on the head and a kindly look goes a long way with children. Well, the result was that the mother came and she brought the father. They became converted, and thus, a whole family was brought to Christ by a smile.

We want to believe that the love of Christ is the best thing we can have. If a man wants to buy a horse he goes around till he finds the best horse for his money. You women, if you want to buy a dress, go from one store to another and search till you find the best dress. And it is the universal law of the world over. So if we can show the sinners, by love, that the religion of Jesus Christ is the best thing to have, we can win the world to us. If we can only show that we are full of love and not full of envy and malice and bitterness, everyone can be won to Christ. If the Spirit of love can come upon all of us, so that we can talk to everyone kindly, it will not be long before salvation shall break over us through Christ.

You go into a church that is all aglow with love and into another where there is a lack, and mark the difference. In the latter the people get as far away from the pulpit as possible; and mark the coldness, and see how quickly they get out of the church. Their hearts are cold to one another, and they have no sympathy. But when their hearts are all aglow they crowd round and are genial toward one another, and say, "God bless the sermon," however poor the minister who preaches. The reason that we have so many poor ministers is because we have so few praying people. Look at Joshua. While he was fighting for the Lord, Moses was up on the mountain praying. So we want everyone to pray for their ministers while they are fighting for the Lord. When a man comes to me and grumbles and complains about his minister, I ask him, "Do you ever pray for your minister?" He runs away. It spikes his guns. They do not work with the minister, never think of praying for him. We want to see every man red hot for the Savior, and he will wake up the church. If he had got his heart red hot, sparks will kindle in the little circle, and the whole church will be ablaze. Every soul will be filled with the glory of Christ. There is not a man in all Chicago—I do not care what he is; he may be an atheist, a pantheist, a drunkard, or a gambler—I do not believe that a man's heart is so hard but that God can break it.

Breaking Through

Mr. Warner, superintendent of probably one of the largest Sunday schools in the world, had a theory that he would never put a boy out of his school for bad conduct. He argued that if a boy misbehaved himself, it was through bad training at home, and that if he put him out of the school no one would take care of him. Well, this theory was put to the test one day. A teacher came to him and said, "I have a boy in my class that must be taken out; he breaks the rules continually; he swears and uses obscene language; and I cannot do anything with him." Mr. Warner did not care [to put] the boy out, so he sent the teacher back to his class. But the teacher came again and said that unless the boy was taken from his class, he must leave it. Well, he left, and a second teacher was appointed. The second teacher came with the same story and met with the same reply from Mr. Warner. And the teacher resigned. A third teacher was appointed, and he came with the same story as the others. Mr. Warner then thought he would be compelled to turn the boy out at last. One day a few teachers were standing about, and Mr. Warner said, "I will bring this boy up and read his name out in the school, and publicly excommunicate him." Well, a young lady came up and said to him, "I am not doing what I might for Christ; let me have the boy; I will try and save him." But Mr. Warner said, "If these young men cannot do it you will not." But she begged to have him, and Mr. Warner consented. She was a wealthy young lady, and surrounded with all the luxuries of life.

The boy went to her class, and for several Sundays he behaved himself and broke no rule. But one Sunday he broke loose, and in reply to something she said, spat in her face. She took out her pocket handkerchief and wiped her face, but said nothing. Well, she thought upon a plan, and she said to him, "John"—we will call him John—"John, come home with me." "No," said he, "I won't; I won't be seen on the streets with you." She was fearful of losing him altogether if he went out of the school that day, and she said to him, "Will you let me walk home with you?" "No, I won't," said he. "I won't be seen on the street with you." Then she thought upon another plan. She thought of the "Old Curiosity Shop," and she said, "I won't be at home tomorrow or Tuesday, but if you will come round to the front door on Wednesday morning there will be a little bundle for you." "I don't want it; you may keep your old bundle." She went home, but made up the bundle. She thought that curiosity might make him come.

Wednesday morning arrived, and he got over his mad fit, and he thought he would just like to see what was in this bundle. The little fellow knocked at the door, which was opened, and he told his story. She said, "Yes, here is the bundle." The boy opened it and found a vest, a coat, and other clothing, and a little note written by the young lady, which read something like this:

Dear Johnnie: Ever since you have been in my class I have prayed for you every morning and evening, that you might be a good boy, and I want you to stay in my class. Do not leave me.

The next morning, before she was up, the servant came to her and said there was a little boy below who wished to see her. She dressed hastily, and went downstairs, and found Johnnie on the sofa weeping. She put her arms around his neck, and he said to her, "My dear teacher, I have not had any peace since I got this note from you. I want you to forgive me." "Won't you let me pray for you to come to Jesus?" And she went down on her knees and prayed. And now, Mr. Warner said, that boy was the best boy in the Sunday school.

And so it was love that broke that boy's heart. May the Lord give us that love in abundance! May we be so full of love that everyone may see that it only prompts us to bring them to heaven!

The text, as presented by Moody, asks the age-old question, "Who is my neighbor?" This issue is a fundamental part of the great commandment to love God first, then love your neighbor as yourself. Such love clearly places a high value on others.

Yet we often misjudge the identity of our neighbor, as the parable clearly shows. Moody masterfully tells how an injured man never received basic care from the very people who were in the businesss of helping. In modern terms, the priest represents the busy pastor, and the Levite a potential deacon. Both are so consumed with the mechanics of the ministry that they completely overlook its true purpose.

Now the Samaritan is the great contradiction. In Moody's thinking he represents the undesirable person we all shun and consider unfit for contact under any circumstance. Yet this same outcast is also the hero, for he clearly demonstrates the essence of the ministry: concern for a neighbor's needs before personal interests.

Moody used this message to attack the petty fighting among various denominations and individuals of his day. Their foolish emphasis on trivial matters caused them to miss the weightier matters of the kingdom. Such a message, to love your neighbor, has never gone out of style.

CHAPTER THREE

The Good Samaritan

You will find my text in part of the twenty-ninth verse of the tenth chapter of Luke, "And who is my neighbor?" We are told that as Christ stood with His disciples, a man, a lawyer, stood up and tempted Him and said, "Master, what shall I do to inherit eternal life?" He asked what he could do to inherit eternal life, what he could do to buy salvation. And the Lord answered his question, "What is written in the Law? How readest thou?" To which the lawyer answered, "Thou shalt love the Lord God with all thy heart, and with all thy soul, and with all thy strength, and with all thy mind, and thy neighbor as thyself." "Thou hast answered right," but who is "thy neighbor"? He drew a vivid picture, which has been told for the last eighteen hundred years, and I do not know anything that brings out more truthfully the wonderful power of the gospel than this story, which we have heard read tonight—the story of the man who went down from Jerusalem to Jericho, and who fell among thieves.

Jerusalem was called the "city of peace." Jericho and the road leading to it were infested with thieves. Probably it had been taken possession of by the worst of Adam's sons. I do not know how far the man got from Jerusalem to Jericho, but the thieves had come out and fallen upon him, and had taken all his money, and stripped him of his clothes, and left him wounded—left him, I suppose, for dead. By-and-by a priest came down the road from Jerusalem. We are told that he came by chance. Perhaps he was going down to dedicate some syna-gogue, or preach a sermon on some important subject, and had the manuscript in his pocket. As he was going along on the other side he heard a groan, and he turned around and saw the poor fellow lying bleeding on the ground and pitied him. He went up close, took a look at him, and said, "Why, that man's a Jew, he belongs to the seed of Abraham. If I remember aright, I saw him in the syna-gogue last Sunday. I pity him. But I have too much business, and I cannot attend to him."

He felt a pity for him, and looked on him, and probably wondered why God allowed such men as those thieves to come into the world, and passed by. There are a good many men just like him. They stop to discuss and wonder why sin came into the world, and look upon a wounded man, but do not stop to pick up a poor sinner, forgetting the fact that sin is in the world already, and it has to be rooted out.

But another man came along, a Levite, and he heard the groans. He turned and looked on him with pity, too. He felt compassion for him. He was one of those men that, if we had him here, we should probably make him an elder or a deacon. He looked at him and said, "Poor fellow! He's all covered with blood, he has been badly hurt, he is nearly dead, and they have taken all his money and stripped him naked. Ah, well, I pity him!" He [wanted] to help him, but he, too, had pressing business, and [he] passed by on the other side.

He had scarcely got out of sight when another came along, riding on a beast.

He heard the groans of the wounded man, went over and took a good look at him. The traveler was a Samaritan. When he looked down he saw the man was a Jew. Ah, how the Jews looked down upon the Samaritans. There was a great, high partition wall between the Jews and the Samaritans. The Jews would not allow them in the temple. They would not have any dealings with them. They would not associate with them.

Beyond Pity

I can see him coming along that road, with his good, benevolent face; and as he passes he hears a groan from this poor fellow. He draws in his beast and pauses to listen. "And he came to where he was." This is the sweetest thing to my mind in the whole story. A good many people would like to help a poor man if he was on the platform, if it cost them no trouble. They want him to come to them. They are afraid to touch the wounded man; he is all bloody, and they will get their hands soiled.

And that was just the way with the priest and the Levite. This poor man, perhaps, had paid half of all his means to help the service of the temple, and might have been a constant worshipper, but they only felt pity for him.

This good Samaritan "came to where he was," and after he saw him he had compassion on him. That word "compassion"—how sweet it sounds! The first thing he did on hearing him cry for water—the hot sun had been pouring down upon his head—was to go and get it from a brook. Then he went and got a bag that he had with him—what we might call a carpetbag or a saddlebag in the west—and poured oil on his wounds. Then he thought, "The poor fellow is weak," and he went and got a little wine. He had been lying so long in the burning sun that he was nearly dead now—he was left half-dead—and the wine revived him. He looked him over, and he saw his wounds that wanted to be bound up. But he had nothing to do this with. I can see him now tearing the lining out of his coat, and with it binding up his wounds. Then he took him up and laid him on his bosom till he revived, and when the poor fellow had strength enough, the good Samaritan put him on his own beast. If the Jew had not been half-dead he would never have allowed him to put his hands on him. He would have treated him with scorn. But he was half-dead, and he could not prevent the good Samaritan treating him kindly and putting him on his beast.

Did you ever stop to think what a strong picture it would have been if the Samaritan had not been able himself to get the man on the beast—if he had had to call for any assistance? Perhaps a man would have come along, and he would have asked him to help him with the wounded man. "What are you?" he might have said. "I am a Samaritan." "You are a Samaritan, are you? I cannot help you, I am a Jew."

There is a good deal of that spirit now, just as strong as it was then. When we are trying to get a poor man on the right way, when we are tugging at him to get his face toward Zion, we ask someone to help us, and he says, "I am a Roman Catholic." "Well," you say, "I am a Protestant." So they give no assistance to one another. The same party spirit of old is present today. The Protestants will have nothing to do with the Catholics, the Jews will have nothing to do with the Gentiles. And there was a time—but, thank God, we are getting over it—when a Methodist would not touch a Baptist, or a Presbyterian a Congregationalist; and if we saw a Methodist taking a man out of the ditch, a Baptist would say,

"Well, what are you going to do with him?" "Take him to a Methodist church." "Well, I'll have nothing to do with him." A great deal of this has gone by, and the time is coming when, if we are trying to get a man out of the ditch, and they see us tugging at him, and we are so weak that we cannot get him on the beast, they will help him. And that is what Christ wants.

Well, the Samaritan gets him on his beast, and says to him, "You are very weak; my beast is sure-footed, he will take you to the inn, and I will hold you." He holds him firmly; and God is able to hold everyone He takes out of the pit. I see them going along that road, he holding [the Jew] on, and he gets him to the inn. He gets him there, and he says to the innkeeper, "Here is a wounded man; the thieves have been after him; give him the best attention you can; nothing is too good for him." And I can imagine the good Samaritan as stopping there all night, sitting up with him, and attending to his wants. And the next morning he gets up, and says to the landlord, "I must be off," leaving a little money to pay for what the man has had; "and if that is not enough, I will pay what is necessary when I return from my business in Jericho." This good Samaritan gave this landlord two pence to pay for what he had got, and promised to come again and repay whatever had been spent to take care of the man. And he had given him, besides, all his sympathy and compassion.

Not Creeds, But Compassion

Christ told this story in answer to the lawyer who came to tempt Him, and showed that the Samaritan was the neighbor. Now this story is brought out here to teach the churchgoers this thing: that it is not creeds or doctrines that we want, so much as compassion and sympathy. I have been talking about the qualifications which we require in working for Christ. First night I took "courage," then "love," and last night "faith," and now it is "compassion and sympathy."

If we have not compassion and sympathy our efforts will go for naught. There are hundreds of Christians who work here who do very little because they have not sympathy. If they go to lift up a man, they must put themselves in his place. If you place yourself in sympathy with a man you are trying to do good to, you will soon lift him up.

When at the Hippodrome in New York, a young man came up to me; he looked very sad, his face was troubled. I asked him what was the matter, and he said, "I am a fugitive from justice. In England, when I was young, my father used to take me into the public house with him, and I learned the habit of drinking, and liquor has become to me like water. A few months ago I was in England, where I was head clerk in a large firm; I was doing well. I had fifty dollars a week. Well, one night I was out, and I had some money of my employers with me, and I got to gambling and lost it. I ran away from England and left a wife and two lovely children. Here I am; I cannot get anything to do; I have no letters of recommendation; and what shall I do?" "Believe in the Lord Jesus Christ," said I. "I cannot become a Christian with that record behind me, there is no hope for me," he replied. "There is hope; seek Jesus, and leave everything behind," I told him. "Well," said he, "I cannot do that until I make restitution." But I kept him to that one thing. He wrote me a letter, and said that the sermon "Ye Must be Born Again," had made a great impression on him. He could not sleep that night, and he finally passed from darkness into light. He came to me, and he said, "I am willing to go back to England and surrender myself, and go into prison, if Christ wants it." I said to him, "Don't do that; but write to your employers and say that if Christ helps you you will make restitution. Live as economically as you can, and be industrious, and you will soon find all well." The man wrote to his employers, and I got a letter from him shortly afterward, and he told me that his wife was coming out to New York. When I was last there I made inquiry about him, and found that he was doing well. He only wanted sympathy—someone to take him by the hand and help him.

A Bit of Sympathy

I believe that there are not less than ten thousand young men in Chicago who are just waiting for someone to come to them with sympathy. You do not know how far a loving word will go. When I came to this city twenty years ago, I remember I walked up and down the streets trying to find a situation; and I recollect how, when they roughly answered me, their treatment would chill my soul. But when someone would say, "I feel for you; I would like to help you, but I can't; but you will be all right soon," I went away happy and light-hearted. That man's sympathy did me good.

When I first went away from home and to a place some thirteen miles away, it seemed as if I could never be any further away. My brother had gone to live at that town a year and a half before. I recollect, as I walked down the street with him, I was very homesick, and could hardly keep down the tears. My brother said to me, "There's a man here will give you a cent; he gives a cent to every new boy that comes here." I thought that he would be the best man I had ever met. By-and-by he came along, and I thought he was going to

pass me. My brother stopped him, thinking, I suppose, I was going to lose the cent, and the old gentleman—he was an old gentleman—looked at me and said, "Why, I have never seen you before: you must be a new boy." "Yes," said my brother, "he has just come." The old man put his trembling hand upon my head, and patted it and told me that I had a Father in heaven, although my earthly father was dead, and he gave me a new cent. I don't know where that cent went to, but the kindly touch of that old man's hand upon my head has been felt by me all these years.

What we want is sympathy from men. There are hundreds of men with hearts full of love, who, if they received but words of sympathy, their hearts would be won to a higher life. But I can imagine men saying, "How are you going to reach them? How are you going to do it? How are you going to get into sympathy with these people?" It is very easily done. Put yourself in their places. There is a young man, a great drunkard; perhaps his father was a drunkard. If you had been surrounded with influences like his, perhaps you would have been a worse drunkard than he is. Well, just put yourself in his place, and go and speak to him lovingly and kindly.

I want to tell you a lesson taught me in Chicago a few years ago. In the months of July and August a great many deaths occurred among children, you all know. I remember I attended a great many funerals; sometimes I would go to two or three funerals a day. I got so used to it that it did not trouble me to see a mother take the last kiss and the last look at her child, and see the coffin lid closed. I got accustomed to it, as in the war we got accustomed to the great battles, and to see the wounded and the dead never troubled us. When I got home one night I heard that one of my Sunday school pupils was dead, and her mother wanted me to come to the house. I went to the poor home, and saw the father drunk. Adelaide had been brought from the river. The mother told me she washed for a living, the father earned no money, and poor Adelaide's work was to get wood for the fire. She had gone to the river that day and seen a piece floating on the water, had stretched out for it, had lost her balance, and fallen in. The poor [mother] was very much distressed. "I would like you to help me, Mr. Moody," she said, "to bury my child. I have no lot; I have no money." Well, I took the measure for the coffin and came away.

I had my little girl with me, and she said, "Papa, suppose we were very, very poor, and Mamma had to work for a living, and I had to get sticks for the fire, and was to fall into the river: would you be very sorry?" This question reached my heart. "Why, my child, it would break my heart to lose you," I said, and I drew her to my bosom. "Papa, do you feel bad for that mother?" she said, and this word woke my sympathy for the woman. And I started and went back to the house and prayed that the Lord might bind up that wounded heart.

When the day came for the funeral I went to Graceland. I had always thought my time too precious to go out there, but I went. The drunken father was there and the poor mother. I bought a lot, the grave was dug, and the child was laid among strangers. There was another funeral coming up, and the corpse was laid near the grave of little Adelaide. And I thought how I would feel if it had been my little girl that I had been laying there among strangers. I went to my Sabbath school thinking this, and suggested that the children should contrib-

ute and buy a lot in which we might bury a hundred poor little children. We soon got it, and the papers had scarcely been made out when a lady came and said, "Mr. Moody, my little girl died this morning, let me bury her in the lot you have got for the Sunday school children." The request was granted, and she asked me to go to the lot and say prayers over her child. I went to the grave—it was a beautiful day in June, and I remember asking her what the name of her child was. She said Emma. That was the name of my little girl, and I thought, "What if it had been my own child?" We should put ourselves in the places of others. I could not help shedding a tear. Another woman came shortly after and wanted to put another one into the grave. I asked his name. It was Willie, and it happened to be the name of my little boy—the first two laid there were called by the same names as my two children, and I felt sympathy and compassion for those two women.

If you want to get into sympathy, put yourself into a man's place. Chicago needs Christians whose hearts are full of compassion and sympathy. If we haven't got it, pray that we may have it, so that we may be able to reach those men and women that need kindly words and kindly actions far more than sermons. The mistake is that we have been preaching too much and sympathizing too little. The gospel of Jesus Christ is a gospel of deeds and not of words. May the Spirit of the Lord come upon us this night. May we remember that Christ was moved in compassion for us, and may we, if we find some poor man going down among thieves, or lying wounded and bleeding, look upon him with sympathy, and get below him, and raise him up.

Heaven is the destiny of all who are truly born again. Yet the Bible reveals very little about such a place. The fact that little is said does not make heaven questionable or less desirable.

Moody encountered many who were skeptical about heaven. Yet his faith in the Bible supported his strong belief that such a place existed. Heaven is the place where all departed saints reside. It is the place that fulfills the promise Jesus made when He said He was going to prepare a place for His own (John 14:2).

Throughout this sermon Moody stressed the importance of working for the future and not the present. To be consumed with the treasures of this world would cost the lost person eternal bliss, and the Christian a fruitful life.

The church was never intended to be a place of rest and comfort, but work and toil, always pointing to the fact that the Christian's life is to be spent serving Christ, with heaven as the final place of rest when the work on earth is done.

CHAPTER FOUR

Heaven

PART ONE

I was on my way to a meeting one night with a friend, and he asked, as we were drawing near the church, "Mr. Moody, what are you going to preach about?" "I am going to preach about heaven," I said. I noticed a scowl passing over his face, and I said, "What makes you look so?" "Why, your subject of heaven. What's the use of talking upon a subject that's all speculation? It's only wasting time on a subject about which you can only speculate." My answer to that friend was, "If the Lord didn't want us to speak about heaven He would never have told us about such a place in the Scriptures, and, as Timothy says, 'All the Scriptures are given by inspiration, and all parts are profitable.'" There's no part of the Word of God that is not profitable, and I believe if men would read more carefully these Scriptures they would think more of heaven.

If we want to get men to fix their hearts and attention upon heaven we must get them to read more about it. Men who say that heaven is a speculation have not read their Bibles. In the blessed Bible there are allusions scattered all through it. If I were to read to you all the passages on heaven from Genesis to Revelation, it would take me all night and tomorrow to do it. When I took some of the passages lately and showed them to a lady, "Why," said she, "I didn't think there was so much about heaven in the Bible." If I were to go into a foreign land and spend my days there, I would like to know all about it; I would like to read all about it. I would want to know all about its climate, its inhabitants, their customs, their privileges, their government. I would find nothing about that land that would not interest me. Suppose you all were going away to Africa, to Germany, to China, and were going to make one of those places your home, and suppose that I had just come from some of those countries; how eagerly you would listen. I can imagine how the old gray-haired men and the young men and the deaf would crowd around and put up their hands to learn anything about it.

My friends, where are you going to spend eternity? Your life here is very brief. Life is but an inch of time; it is but a span; but a fiber, which will soon be snapped, and you will be ushered into eternity. Where are you going to spend it? If I were to ask you who were going to spend your eternity in heaven to stand up, nearly every one of you would rise. There is not a man here, not one in Chicago, who has not some hope of reaching heaven. Now, if we are going to spend our future there, it becomes us to go to work and find out all about it. I call your attention to this truth: that heaven is just as much a place as Chicago. It is a destination—it is a locality. Some people say there is no heaven. Some men will tell you this earth is all the heaven we have. Queer kind of heaven this. Look at the poverty, the disease in the city; look at the men out of employment walking around our streets, and they say this is heaven. How low a man has [become] when he comes to think in this way. There is a land where the weary are at rest; there is a land where there is peace and joy—where no sorrow dwells. And as we think of it and speak about it, how sweet it looms up before us.

I remember, soon after I got converted, a pantheist got hold of me and just tried to draw me back to the world. Those men who try to get hold of a young convert are the worst set of men. I don't know a worse man than he who tries to pull young Christians down. He is nearer the borders of hell than any man I know. When this man knew I had found Jesus he just tried to pull me down. He tried to argue with me, and I did not know the Bible very well then, and he got the best of me. The only thing to get the best of these atheists, pantheists, or infidels is to have a good knowledge of the Bible. Well, this pantheist told me God was everywhere—in the air, in the sun, in the moon, in the earth, in the stars, but really he meant nowhere. And the next time I went to pray it seemed as if I was not praying anywhere or to anyone.

We have ample evidence in the Bible that there is such a place as heaven, and we have abundant manifestation that His influence from heaven is felt among us. He is not in person among us; only in Spirit. The sun is 95 million miles from the earth, yet we feel its rays. In Second Chronicles we read, "If my people, which are called by my name, shall humble themselves, and pray, and seek my face, and turn from their wicked ways; then will I hear from heaven and forgive their sin, and will heal their land." Here is one reference, and when it is read a great many people might ask, "How far away is heaven? Can you tell us that?" I don't know how far away it is, but there is one thing I can tell you: He can hear prayer as soon as the words

are uttered. There has not been a prayer said that He has not heard; not a tear shed that He has not seen. We don't want to learn the distance. What we want to know is that God is there, and Scripture tells us that.

Turn to First Kings and we read, "And hearken thou to the supplication of Thy servant and of Thy people Israel, when they shall pray toward this place, and hear Thou in heaven, Thy dwelling place, and when Thou hearest forgive." Now, it is clearly taught in the Word of God that the Father dwells there. It is His dwelling place, and in Acts we see that Jesus is there too. "But he being full of the Holy Ghost looked up steadfastly into heaven and saw the glory of God, and Jesus standing on the right hand of God," and by the eye of faith we can see them there tonight too. And by faith we shall be brought into His presence, and we shall be satisfied when we gaze upon Him. Stephen, when he was surrounded by the howling multitude, saw the Son of man there, and when Jesus looked down upon earth and saw this first martyr in the midst of his persecution, He looked down and gave him a welcome. We'll see Him by-and-by.

The Charm of Heaven

It is not the jasper streets and golden gates that attract us to heaven. What are your golden palaces on earth—what is that that makes them so sweet? Is it the presence of some loving wife or fond children? Let them be taken away and the charm of your home is gone. And so it is Christ that is the charm of heaven to the Christian. Yes, we shall see Him there. How sweet the thought that we shall dwell with Him forever, and shall see the nails in His hands and in His feet which He received for us.

I read a little story not long since

which went to my heart. A mother was on the point of death, and the child was taken away from her in case it would annoy her. [The child] was crying continually to be taken to [her] mother and teased the neighbors. By-and-by the mother died, and the neighbors thought it was better to bury the mother without letting the child see her dead face. They thought the sight of the dead mother would not do the child any good, and so they kept her away. When the mother was buried and the child was taken back to the house, the first thing she did was to run into her mother's sitting room and look all round it, and from there to the bedroom, but no mother was there. And she went all over the house crying, "Mother, Mother!" but the child could not find her, and then said to the neighbor, "Take me back, I don't want to stay here if I cannot see my mother." It wasn't the home that made it so sweet to the child. It was the presence of the mother. And so it is not heaven that is alone attractive to us; it is the knowledge that Jesus, our leader, our brother, our Lord, is there.

And the spirits of loved ones, whose bodies we have laid in the earth, will be there. We shall be in good company there. When we reach that land we shall meet all the Christians who have gone before us. We are told in Matthew, too, that we shall meet angels there. "Take heed lest ye despise not one of these little ones, for I say unto you that in heaven their angels do always behold the face of my Father which is in heaven." Yes, the angels are there, and we shall see them when we get home.

He is there, and where He is His disciples shall be, for He has said, "I go and prepare a mansion for you, that wheresoever I am there ye may be also." I believe that when we die the spirit leaves the body and goes to the mansion above, and by-and-by the body will be resurrected and it shall see Jesus. Very often people come to me and say, "Mr. Moody, do you think we shall know each other in heaven?" Very often it is a mother who has lost a dear child, and who wishes to see it again. Sometimes it is a child who has lost a mother, a father, and who wants to recognize them in heaven. There is just one verse in Scripture in answer to this, and that is, "We shall be satisfied." It is all I want to know. My brother who went up there the other day I shall see, because I will be satisfied. We will see all those we loved on earth up there, and if we loved them here we will love them ten thousand times more when we meet them there.

Assured of a Place

Another thought. In the tenth chapter of Luke we are told our names are written there if we are Christians. Christ just called His disciples up and paired them off and sent them out to preach the gospel. Two of us—Mr. Sankey and myself—going about and preaching the gospel is nothing new. You will find them away back eighteen hundred years ago going off two by two, like brothers Bliss and Whittle, and brothers Needham and Morehouse, to different towns and villages. They had gone out, and there had been great revivals in all the cities, towns, and villages they had entered. Everywhere they had met with the greatest success. Even the very devils were subject to them. Disease had fled before them. When they met a lame man they said to him, "You don't want to be lame any longer," and he walked. When they met a blind man they but told him to open his eyes, and behold he could see. And they came to Christ and rejoiced over their great success, and

He said to them, "I will give you something to rejoice over. Rejoice that your names are written in heaven." Now, there are a great many people who do not believe in such an assurance as this: "Rejoice, because your names are written in heaven." How are you going to rejoice if your names are not written there?

While speaking about this some time ago, a man told me we were preaching a very ridiculous doctrine when we preached this doctrine of assurance. I ask you in all candor, what are you going to do with this assurance if we don't preach it? It is stated that our names are written there, blotted out of the Book of Death and transferred to the Book of Life.

I was with a friend while in Europe—she is in this hall tonight. On one occasion we were traveling from London to Liverpool, and the question was put as to where we would stop. We said we would go to the Northwestern at Lime Street, as that was the hotel where Americans generally stopped. When we got there the house was full, could not let us in. Every room was engaged. But this friend said, "I am going to stay here. I engaged a room ahead. I sent a telegram on."

My friends, that is just what the Christians are doing—sending their names in ahead. They are sending a message up saying, "Lord Jesus, I want one of those mansions you are preparing; I want to be there." That's what they're doing. And every man and woman here who wants one, if you have not already got one, had better make up [your] mind. Send your names up now. I would rather a thousand times have my name written in the Lamb's Book than have all the wealth of the world rolling at my feet.

A man may get station in this world, but it will fade away; he may get wealth, but it will prove a bubble. "What shall it profit a man if he gain the whole world and lose his own soul?" It is a solemn question, and let it go around the hall tonight: "Is my name written in the Book of Life?" I can imagine that man down there saying, "Yes; I belong to the Presbyterian church; my name's on the church's books." It may be, but God keeps His books in a different fashion than that in which the church records of this city are kept. You may belong to a good many churches; you may be an elder or a deacon and be a bright light in your church, and yet you may not have your name written in the Book of Life. Judas was one of the twelve, and yet he hadn't his name written in the Book of Life. Satan was among the elect—he dwelt among the angels, and yet he was cast from the high hallelujahs. Is your name written in the Book of Life?

A man told me while speaking upon this subject, "That is all nonsense you are speaking." And a good many men here are of the same opinion; but I would like them to turn to Daniel, twelfth chapter, "And there shall be a time of trouble, such as never was since there was a nation, even to that same time: and at that time thy people shall be delivered, every one that shall be found written in the book." Everyone shall be delivered whose names shall be found written in the book. And we find Paul, in the letters which he wrote to the Philippians, addressing them as those "dear yokefellows, whose names were written in the Book of Life." If it is not our privilege to know that our names are written in the Book of Life, here is Paul sending greeting to his yokefellows, "whose names were written in the book." Let us not be deceived in this. We see it too plainly throughout the Holy Word. In the chapter of Revelation which we have just read, we have three different passages referring to it, and in the twenty-seventh verse, almost the last words in the Scriptures, we read, "And there shall in no wise enter into it anything that defileth, neither whatsoever worketh abomination or maketh a lie: but they which are written in the Lamb's Book of Life."

My friends, you will never see the city unless your name is written in that Book of Life. It is a solemn truth. Let it go home to everyone and sink into the hearts of all here tonight. Don't build your hopes on a false foundation; don't build your hopes on an empty profession. Be sure your name is written there. And the next thing after your own names are written there is to see that the names of the children God has given you are recorded there. Let the fathers and mothers assembled tonight hear this and take it to their hearts. See that your children's names are there. Ask your conscience if the name of your John, your Willie, your Mary, your Alice—ask yourselves whether their names are recorded in the Book of Life. If not, make it the business of your life, rather than to pile up wealth for them, make it the one object of your existence to secure for them eternal life rather than to pave the way to their death and ruin.

I read some time ago of a mother in an eastern city who was stricken with consumption. At her dying hour she requested her husband to bring the children to her. The oldest one was brought first to her, and she laid her hand on his head and gave him her blessing and dying message. The next one was brought, and she gave him the same; and one after another came to her bedside until the little infant was brought in. She took it and pressed it to her bosom, and the people in the room, fearing that she was straining her strength, took

the child away from her. As this was done she turned to the husband and said, "I charge you, sir, bring all those children home with you." And so God charges us. The promise is to ourselves and to our children. We can have our names written there, and then by the grace of God we can call our children to us and know that their names are also recorded there. That great roll is being called, and those bearing the names are summoned every day—every hour; that great roll is being called tonight, and if your name were shouted could you answer with joy? You have heard of a soldier who fell in our war. While he was dying, he was heard to cry, "Here! here!" Some of his comrades went up to him thinking he wanted water, but he said, "They are calling the roll of heaven, and I am answering." And in a faint voice he whispered, "Here!" and passed away to heaven.

If that roll was called tonight would you be ready to answer: "Here"? I am afraid not. Let us wake up. May every child of God wake up tonight. There is work to do. Fathers and mothers, look to your children. If I could only speak to one class, I would preach to parents, and try to show them the great responsibility that rests upon them.

There is a man living on the bank of the Mississippi River. The world calls him rich, but if he could call back his first-born son he would give up all his wealth. The boy was brought home one day unconscious. When the doctor examined him, he turned to the father who stood at the bedside and said, "There is no hope." "What?" exclaimed the father, "Is it possible my boy has got to die?" "There is no hope," replied the doctor. "Will he not come to?" asked the father. "He may resume consciousness, but he cannot live." "Try all your skill, doctor. I don't want my boy to die." By-and-by the boy regained a glimmering of consciousness, and when he was told that his death was approaching, he said to his father, "Won't you pray for my lost soul, Father? You have never prayed for me." The old man only wept. It was true. During the seventeen years that God had given him his boy, he had never spent an hour in prayer for his soul, but the object of his life had been to accumulate wealth for that first-born. Am I speaking to a prayerless father or mother tonight? Settle the question of your soul's salvation, and pray for the son or daughter God has given you.

But I have another anecdote to tell. It was Ralph Wallace who told me of this one. A certain gentleman had been a member of the Presbyterian church. His little boy was sick. When he went home, his wife was weeping, and she said, "Our boy is dying. He has had a change for the worse. I wish you would go in and see him." The father went into the room and placed his hand on the brow of his dying boy, and [he] could feel that the cold, damp sweat was gathering there; that the cold, icy hand of death was feeling for the chords of life. "Do you know, my boy, that you are dying?" asked the father. "Am I? Is this death? Do you really think I am dying?" "Yes, my son, your end on earth is near." "And will I be with Jesus tonight, Father?" "Yes, you will be with the Savior." "Father, don't you weep, for when I get there I will go right straight to Jesus and tell Him that you have been trying all my life to lead me to Him."

God has given me two little children, and ever since I can remember I have directed them to Christ, and I would rather lead them to Jesus than give them the wealth of the world. If you have got a child, go and point the way. I challenge any man to speak of heaven without speaking of children, "for of such is the kingdom of heaven." Fathers and mothers and professed Christians

ignore this sometimes. They go along themselves and never try to get any to heaven with them. Let us see to this at once, and let us pray that there may be many names written in the Lamb's Book of Life tonight.

PART TWO

You who were here last night remember that the subject upon which I spoke was "Heaven, and Who Were There." We tried to prove from Scripture that God the Father, and Christ the Son, and angels, and redeemed saints who have gone up from earth are there, and that if we have been born of God our names are recorded there.

Now I will commence tonight right where I left off last night, and the next thought upon the subject that presents itself is: "Are we laying our treasures there?" If we are living as God would have us live, we are doing this. There are a great many people who forget that there are eleven commandments. They think there are only ten. The eleventh commandment is, "Lay up for yourselves treasures in heaven." How many of us remember—ah! How people in Chicago forget the words of the Lord now in His wonderful Sermon on the Mount: "Lay not up for yourselves treasures upon earth, where moth and rust doth corrupt, and where thieves break through and steal; but lay up for yourselves treasures in heaven, where neither moth nor rust doth corrupt, and where thieves do not break through nor steal."

How few of our people pay any heed to these words? That's why there are so many broken hearts among us; that's why so many men and women are disappointed and going through the streets with shattered hopes; it's because they have not been laying up treasures in heaven. They pile up treasures on earth, and some calamity comes upon them and sweeps all away. The Chicago fire burned up a good many of these treasures. A great number of people put their treasures in banks, which dissolve, and away they go. Some have put their treasures in railway shares which have all disappeared like a vapor; and that is why so many are brokenhearted today, and in great distress, and do not know what is before them. If they had taken heed of the words of this commandment, this thing would not have happened to them. "Lay up your treasures in heaven."

Where Your Heart Is

It doesn't take long in conversation with a man to find out where his heart is. Wherever it is, there is his treasure. Go to a political man and talk to him about Hayes and Wheeler or Tilden or Hendricks on any political question, and how his heart gets ablaze and his eye sparkles. His treasure is in politics. Go talk to a man who loves the theater about a new play, and see how his eye glistens. His heart is set upon pleasure—upon the world. And yet [there is] another class whose heart is set on business: go and talk to [a businessman] about some new speculation and show him where he can make a few thousand dollars, and you will soon tell where his treasure lies. But talk about heaven and all interest is lost. I could not help that thought coming to me last night, when I saw before me some dozing—some almost asleep, as if they thought I was talking about a myth; and others were sitting with eyes aglow, and all attention when I mentioned heaven. Ah! They expected to go there and were glad to hear about it.

Some men think it is too far away to lay up their treasures. I was talking to a businessman before the fire about laying up treasures in heaven, and he said, "I like to have my treasure where I can see it." And that is the way with a great many people—they like to have their treasures here so they can see them. It is a great mistake. People go on accumulating what they must leave behind them. How many here do not devote five minutes to anything else than money-making? It is money, money, money, and if they get it they are satisfied. You will see occasionally in the newspapers accounts of men dying who are worth so many millions. It is a great mistake. He cannot take it with him. If it is in business, it isn't his. If it is in banks, it isn't his. If in real estate, he cannot take it. It isn't his. Now, ask yourselves tonight, "Where is my treasure? Is my heart set upon things down here?" If it is set upon wealth it will by-and-by take to itself wings and fly away. Oh, think of this. If your heart is set upon pleasure, it will melt away; if your heart is set upon station or reputation, some tongue may blast it in a moment, and it is gone. If your hopes and heart are set upon some loved wife or dear children, whom you have set up in your hearts as an idol in place of your God, death may come and snatch your god from your life. It is wrong to set up anything, however dear to us, in the place of our God. And so it is wrong "to lay up treasures for yourselves upon earth."

Now, are you—are the people of Chicago heeding this commandment? Ask yourselves this as you are passing through the street tomorrow: "How many of the people of this city are obeying this commandment: 'Lay up for yourselves treasures in heaven'?"

I remember before the Chicago fire hearing of a minister coming up to see his son. He found him completely absorbed in real estate. You remember before the fire how everyone was mad about real estate. It was a mania with all of us. If we could get a corner lot, no matter whether we threw ourselves in debt, or smothered it with mortgages, we were confident that in time, when prices went up, we would make our fortune. This minister came up, and when he saw his son he tried to talk about his soul, but it was no use. Real estate was there. He talked about real estate in the morning, in the afternoon, and [at] night. No use of trying to talk of heaven to him. His only heaven was real estate. The son had a boy in his store, but he being absent the father was left to mind the business one day. When a customer came in and started upon the subject of real estate, it was not long before the minister stepped off and was speaking to the customer about his soul, and telling him he would rather have a corner lot in the New Jerusalem than all the corner lots in Chicago. And the people used to say that no real estate could be sold when the father was around. The trouble was that the son had real estate in his heart—that was his god—and his father had in his heart treasures in heaven. If we have anything in our hearts which we put up as our god, let us ask Him to come to us and take it away from us.

I remember when I went to California just to try and get a few souls saved on the Pacific coast. I went into a school there and asked, "Have you got someone who can write a plain hand?" "Yes." Well, we got up [to] the blackboard, and the lesson upon it proved to be the very text we have tonight, "Lay up for yourselves treasures in heaven." And I said, "Suppose we write upon that board some of the earthly treasures? And we will begin with 'gold.'" The teacher readily put down gold, and they all comprehended it; for all had run to that

country in the hope of finding it. "Well, we will put down 'houses' next, and then 'land.' Next we will put down 'fast horses.'" They all understood what fast horses were—they knew a good deal more about fast horses than they knew about the kingdom of God. Some of them, I think, actually made fast horses serve as gods. "Next we will put down 'tobacco.'" The teacher seemed to shrink at this. "Put it down," said I, "many a man thinks more of tobacco than he does of God. Well, then, we will put down 'rum.'" He objected to this—didn't like to put it down at all. "Down with it. Many a man will sell his reputation, will sell his home, his wife, children, everything he has. It is the god of some men." Many here in Chicago will sell their present and their eternal welfare for it.

"Now," said I, "suppose we put down some of the heavenly treasures. Put down 'Jesus' to head the list, then 'heaven,' then 'river of life,' then 'crown of glory,'" and went on till the column was filled, and just drew a line and showed the heavenly and the earthly things in contrast. My friends, they could not stand comparison. If a man just does that, he cannot but see the superiority of the heavenly over the earthly treasures.

Well, it turned out that the teacher was not a Christian. He had gone to California on the usual hunt—gold; and when he saw the two columns placed side by side, the excellence of the one over the other was irresistible, and he was the first soul God gave me on that Pacific coast. He accepted Christ, and that man came to the station when I was coming away and blessed me for coming to that place.

Those of you who do not lay your treasures up in heaven will be sure to be disappointed. You cannot find a man who has devoted his life to the treasures of this life—not one in the wide, wide world—but [he] has been disappointed. Something arises in life to sweep all away, or the amount of joy which they expect to obtain from their riches falls short of their anticipations. If men center their affections on heaven they will have no disappointment; all is joy and comfort from that source, and the whole current of their lives will be drifting toward heaven.

Someone has heard of a farmer who, when someone—an agent—called upon him to give something for the Christian Commission, promptly drew a check for ten thousand dollars. He wanted the agent to have dinner with him, and after they had dined the farmer took the man out on the veranda and pointed to the rich lands sweeping far away, laden with rich products. "Look over these lands," said the farmer. "They are all mine." He took him to the pasture and showed the agent the choice stock, the fine horses he had, and then pointed to a little town, and then to a large hall where he lived, saying, "They are all mine. I came here as a poor boy, and I have earned all that you see." When he got through my friend asked him, "Well, what have you got up yonder?" "Where?" replied the farmer, who evidently knew where my friend meant. "What have you got in heaven?" "Well," said the farmer, "I haven't anything there." "What?" replied my friend, "You, a man of your discretion, wisdom, business ability, have made no provision for your future?" He hadn't, and in a few weeks he died—a rich man here and a beggar in eternity. A man may be wise in the eyes of the world to pursue this course, but he is a fool in the sight of God. Wealth to most men proves nothing more or less than a great rock upon which his eternity is wrecked.

A great many Christians wonder how it is they don't get on better—how it is that they don't get on. It is because [they] have got [their] hearts on things down here. When they look toward heaven they don't have a love for the world. [They] are then living for another world. We are pilgrims and strangers upon the earth. It is easy to have love for God when we have our treasures there. The reason, then, why so many of us do not grow in Christianity is because we have our treasures here.

Mr. Morehouse told me he was looking down the harbor of Liverpool one day, when he saw a vessel coming up, and she was being towed up by a tug. The vessel was sunk in the water nearly to her edge, and he wondered it did not sink altogether. Upon inquiry he found that it was loaded with lumber and that it was waterlogged. Another vessel came up, her sails set, no tug assisting her, and she soon darted past the waterlogged vessel. And so it is with some Christians. They are waterlogged. They may belong to a church, and if they find anything in the church disagreeing with them they won't go back. They want the whole church to come out and look for them, and tow them in. If the church doesn't, they think they are not getting the attention due them. When men go up in balloons they take bags of sand with them, and when they want to rise higher they throw them out. There are a great many Christians who have got too many bags of sand, and to rise they [need] to throw some out. Look at the poor men here in the city—the rich Christians can relieve themselves by giving some of their bags of sand to them. A great many Christians would feel much better if they relieved themselves of their bags of sand. "He that giveth to the poor lendeth to the Lord," and if you want to be rich in eternity, just give to the poor with your heart, and the Lord will bless not only you, but all connected with you.

A Place of Rest

The next thing is our rest in heaven! A great many people have got a false idea about the church. They have got an idea that the church is a place to rest in. Instead of thinking that it is a place of work, they turn it into a resting place. To get into a nicely cushioned pew, and contribute to charities, listen to the minister, and do their share to keep the church out of bankruptcy, is all they want. The idea of work for them—actual work in the church—never enters their mind. In Hebrews we see the words, "There is a rest for the people of God." We have got all eternity to rest in. Here is the place for work; we must work till Jesus comes. This is the place of toil—eternity of repose. "Blessed are they that die in the Lord, for their works do follow them." Let us do the work that God gives us today. Don't think that you have to rest in the world where God sent His Son who was murdered.

I remember hearing a man who had worked successfully for the Lord complaining that he didn't have the success he used to, and one night he threw himself on his bed sick of life and wanting to die. While in this state of mind he dreamed that he was dead and that he had ascended to heaven. And as he was walking down the crystal pavement of paradise he saw all at once three friends in a chariot, and when the chariot came opposite to where he was one of them stepped out and came to him. He noticed that His face was illuminated with a heavenly radiance, and He came to this man and took him to the battlements of heaven. "Look down," said He; "what do you see?" "I see the dark world," replied the dreamer. "Look

down again, and tell me what you see." "I see men walking blindfolded over bridges, and below them are bottomless pits," was the dreamer's reply. "Will you prepare to stay here, or go back to earth and tell those men of their danger—tell them of the bottomless pits over which they walk?" At this the man awoke from his sleep and said he didn't want to die anymore. He just wanted to remain down here and warn his fellow men [of] the dangers which surrounded them.

When we turn a soul to Christ we do not know what will turn up—what will be the result of it. It may be the means of saving a million souls. The one man may convert another man, and those two may convert a hundred, and that hundred may convert a thousand, and the current keeps widening and widening and deepening and deepening, and as time rolls on the fruit will ripen which you have gathered for God. It is a great privilege, my friends, to work for God.

I want to call your attention to the eleventh chapter of Hebrews. After Paul mentions Jacob and Isaac and Enoch, he says, "These all died in faith, not having received the promises, but having seen them afar off, and were persuaded of them, and embraced them, and confessed that they were strangers and pilgrims on the earth." Are the Christians of Chicago living like pilgrims and strangers, and by their faith do they show "that they seek another country"; do they show by their fruits and their deeds that they are pilgrims and strangers here? When I get into a man's mind the beauties of that country beyond the grave, it looks as if his only thought was for it. We are to be pilgrims and strangers passing through this world on our way to a better land. The moment Abraham by faith got sight of that land, he declared himself a pilgrim and a stranger. This earth had no charm for him then. Lot might go down to that city of Sodom or Gomorrah, and that city might be burned up. We might fix our affections on this city. Chicago has been burned twice, and it will be burned again—this whole world shall pass away with all its boasted riches and glory, and where shall we be then? If we build our hopes here we shall be disappointed; if we build our hopes upon that foundation whose builder and maker is God, we shall not be disappointed. We are told in Matthew to set our affections on things above, and that "there shall be joy in heaven over one sinner that repenteth."

There are rumors of war in Europe, and if war were declared it would probably excite the whole civilized world. Trade would be affected, and relations of all kinds. I don't know whether it would excite heaven at all. If the President of the United States issued a proclamation, I don't know whether it would be noticed in heaven or not, but the papers would speak of it, the people would be excited, and great changes might take place over it. If Queen Victoria died, telegrams would go all over the world, newspapers would speak of it, the whole world would be excited—I don't know if it would be noticed in heaven at all. But if that girl there should repent there would be joy in heaven. Just think of it— think of a little girl, of a little girl being the cause of joy in heaven. I don't think the papers would record it—they would never notice it. There would be no headline in the morning telling the people that there had been joy in heaven over the repentance of a little girl in the tabernacle. "There is joy over one sinner that repenteth." I have been wondering who it is that rejoiced in heaven when He brought back that lost sheep. We

are told that there is joy in the presence of the angels; but who else is it that rejoices? It may be that I am going a little too far, but I think that I have a right to believe that the redeemed saints who have gone up from earth may be led to rejoice when they hear in heaven of the conversion of some living ones here.

Perhaps while I am speaking, some loving mother may be looking over the battlements of heaven on her boy in the gallery yonder, and it may be that while she was on earth she prayed earnestly and constantly, and when she got there she pleaded at the throne for mercy to her son. It may be that as she is watching some angel will carry the news to her of that boy's conversion and take his name there to be recorded in the Book of Life. Perhaps that mother and the Lord Jesus Christ will rejoice over that son, or it may be some daughter. Perhaps it is some child who is looking from that country down to her mother in this hall, and when the news of her acceptance of salvation reaches that little child she will strike her golden harp and shout, "Mother, Mother is coming!" While I was touching on this topic in Manchester I remember a man getting up and shouting, "Oh, Mother, I am coming!" The mother had been fruitless in her endeavors to convert that man while on earth, but her intercession there and the influence of her prayers here touched his heart and he decided.

I remember in the Exposition building in Dublin, while I was speaking about heaven, I said something to the effect that "perhaps at this moment a mother is looking down from heaven upon her daughter here tonight," and I pointed down to a young lady in the audience. Next morning I received this letter:

On Wednesday when you were speaking of heaven you said, "It may be this moment there is a mother looking down from heaven expecting the salvation of her child who is here." You were apparently looking at the very spot where my child was sitting. My heart said, "That is *my* child. That is *her* mother." Tears sprang to my eyes. I bowed my head and prayed, "Lord, direct that word to my darling child's heart; Lord, save my child."

I was then anxious till the close of the meeting, when I went to her. She was bathed in tears. She rose, put her arms round me, and kissed me. When walking down to you she told me it was that same remark (about the mother looking down from heaven) that found the way home to her, and asked me, "Papa, what can I do for Jesus?"

May the Spirit of God bring hundreds to the cross of Christ tonight.

The significance of the blood sacrifice began in Eden with the death of several animals to provide clothing for Adam and Eve after they disobeyed God. From that time up to the death of Christ, blood played an important role in biblical history.

The sin of Adam passed on the curse of death to all humanity. Cain and Abel were the first people to show the right and wrong approach to pleasing God in presenting offerings to Him: Abel's blood sacrifice was acceptable; Cain's produce offering was not.

The importance of blood is clearly demonstrated by the story of Abraham. The command for him to sacrifice his son was the first clear picture of what God was later going to do with His Son for the benefit of the world. The blood of Christ made it possible for all individuals to be saved. The blood washed the sinner clean, paying the debt that no one could pay to God.

As Moody described the death of Christ, he made it clear that such a payment was of the greatest value with eternal dividends. All that is required is faith in Christ for the remission of sin. By trusting Christ the sinner finds eternal life and happiness.

CHAPTER FIVE

The Precious Blood

PART ONE

The subject tonight will be "The Precious Blood." I want to call your attention first to the second chapter and sixteenth verse of Genesis, "And the LORD God commanded the man, saying, Of every tree of the garden thou mayest freely eat: But of the tree of the knowledge of good and evil, thou shalt not eat of it: for in the day that thou eatest thereof thou shalt surely die." There cannot be a law without a penalty. There is not a law in our land but has a penalty attached to it. If our legislative representatives or members of Congress were to make a law and have no penalty appended to it, it would be worthless. We might make a law forbidding men to steal, but if we had no penalty to that law I don't think we could [walk] home without having our watches stolen from us. We could not live without law, and God put Adam into the garden under a law, attached to which was a penalty. Well, we know how he disobeyed and how he fell, and so the penalty of death came upon him. Many people stumble over this. I used to wonder how it was that the penalty of death fell upon him when he lived, I think, some nine hundred and ninety-nine years after he broke the law; but when I understood my Bible better, I learned that it was death to the soul—not physical death, but spiritual death. When God came to seek him in the garden, we are told that he hid himself; he was ashamed of his iniquity—just like hundreds of his sons in Chicago; and then we find Him dealing with Adam by showing him grace. This was the very first thing He did.

A great many people think God was very severe in His treatment of Adam; but whenever the offense was committed, whenever the law was broken, He showed mercy, showed grace; and by this grace a way of escape was presented to them. Ah, that little hymn expresses it: "Grace, friend, contrived a way," by which Adam could regain the life he had forfeited. And so we read that the Lord made "coats of skin" to clothe them before He drove them out of paradise. They received grace before, as we see in the twenty-fourth verse: "He drove out the man, and He placed at the east end of the Garden of Eden cherubims and a flaming sword, which turned every way to keep the way of the tree of life." There's grace and government: and from that day till the present God has been dealing with us in that way.

He rides, we may say, in a chariot with two wheels—one grace and the other government. We can see in this world how it would be if we had no government. There would be no living in it. Adam broke the divine law, and so he had to suffer the penalty; but He gave him grace to be redeemed by. He showed Adam and Eve grace by killing the animals and then covering their nakedness with coats made from the skins. I can imagine Adam's turning to Eve and saying, "Well, in spite of what we've done, God loves us after all. He has clothed us; He has given us grace for our sin." And here we find the first glimpse of the doctrine of substitution—the substitution of the just for the unjust; the great doctrine of atonement and substitution foreshadowed in Genesis.

Then, as we go on, we find the story of Cain and Abel, and we are told that "in process of time it came to pass that Cain brought of the fruit of the ground an offering unto the Lord. And Abel, he also brought of the firstlings of his flock, and of the fat thereof; and the Lord had respect unto Abel and to his offering; but unto Cain and his offering He had not respect. And Cain was very wroth and his countenance fell." Now we find that Cain brought a bloodless sacrifice—"he brought of the fruit of the ground"—and Abel brought a bleeding lamb. Right on the morning of grace we see here that God had marked a way for men to come to Him, and that way was the way that Abel took, and Cain came to God with a sacrifice of his own, in his own way. So we find men and women in the churches of today coming to God with a sacrifice, not in God's way, but in their own—coming with their own good deeds, or their works, or their righteousness, and ignoring the Lamb altogether, ignoring the blood completely. They don't want to come that way; they want to come in their own fashion. Cain, perhaps, reasoned that he didn't see why the products of the earth, why the fruit, shouldn't be as acceptable to God as a bleeding lamb. He didn't like a bleeding lamb, and so he brought his fruit. Now we don't know how there was any difference between those two boys. Both must have been brought up in the same way; both came from the same parents, yet we find in the offering there was a difference between them. One came with the blood, and the other without the blood, and the one with the blood had the acceptable sacrifice to God.

We pass over to the second dispensation—to the eighth chapter of Genesis—where we find Noah coming out of the ark and putting blood between him and his sins. "And Noah builded an altar unto the LORD; and took of every clean beast and of every clean fowl, and offered burnt offerings on the altar." God had Noah bring those animals clear through the Flood so that he could offer them as a sacrifice when he came from the ark. He took a couple of each kind into the ark, and when he came out [he made] a blood offering the very first thing. He was a man of God; he walked in the fear of the Lord, and so he made the offering of blood. The first thing in the first dispensation we see is blood, and the first thing in the second dispensation is blood.

A Blood Sacrifice

In the twenty-second chapter of Genesis we find the story of Abraham and his only son, Isaac. Abraham was a follower of God, a man who loved and feared God, and He commanded him to make a blood sacrifice. We read in this chapter that He commanded Abraham to make the sacrifice of his only son. And we read that the next morning the old man saddled his ass and started. He didn't tell his wife anything about it. If he had she would likely have persuaded him to remain where he was. But he had heard the voice of God, and he obeyed the command; he had heard God's wish, and he was going to do it.

So, early in the morning—he didn't wait till ten or twelve o'clock but went early in the morning—he takes two of his young men with him and his son, Isaac, and you can see him starting out on the three days' journey. They have the wood and the fire, for he is going to worship his God. As he goes on he looks at his boy and says, "It is a strange commandment that God has given. I love this boy dearly. I don't understand it; but I know it's all right, for the Judge of all the earth makes no mistakes." An order from the Judge of heaven is enough for him.

The first night comes, and their little camp is made, and Isaac is asleep. But the old man doesn't sleep. He looks into his [son's] face sadly and says, "I will have no boy soon; I shall never see him on earth again; but I must obey God." I can see him marching on the next day, and you might have seen him drying his tears as he glanced upon that only son and thought upon what he had been called upon to do. The second night comes; tomorrow is the day for the sacrifice. What a night that must have been to Abraham. "Tomorrow," he says sadly, "I must take the life of that boy—my only son, dearer to me than my life— dearer to me than anything on earth."

And the third day comes, and as they go along they see the mountain in the distance; then he says to the young men, "You stay here with the beasts." He takes the wood and the fire, and along with his boy prepares to ascend Mount Moriah, from which could be seen the spot where a few hundred years later the Son of man was offered up. As they ascend the mountain Isaac says, "There's the wood and the fire, Father, but where's the sacrifice?"—thus showing that the boy knows nothing of what is in store. How the question must sink down into the old man's heart. And he answers, "The Lord will provide a sacrifice." It is not time to tell him, and they go on until they come to the place appointed by God, and build the altar, and lay the wood upon it.

Everything is ready, and I can just imagine the old man taking the boy by the hand, and, leading him to a rock, sitting down there, and telling him how God had called upon him to come out

of his native land; how God had been in communion with him for fifty years; what God had done for him. "And now," he says, "my boy, when I was in my bed three nights ago, God came to me with a strange message, in which He told me to offer my child as a sacrifice. I love you, my son, but God has told me to do this, and I must obey Him. So let us both go down on our knees and pray to Him." After they have sent up a petition to God, Abraham lays him on the altar and kisses him for the last time. He lifts the knife to drive it into his son's heart, when all at once he hears a voice: "Abraham, Abraham, spare thine only son."

Ah, there was no voice heard on Calvary to save the Son of man. God showed mercy to the son of Abraham. You fathers and mothers, just picture to yourselves how you would suffer if you had to sacrifice your only son; and think what it must have [cost] God to give up His only Son. We are told that Abraham was glad. The manifestations of Abraham's faith so pleased God that He showed him the grace of heaven, and lifted the curtain of time to let him look down into the future to see the Son of God offered, bearing the sins of the world. From the peak of this very mountain might have been seen the very spot where died the Savior of the world.

We find Abel the first man who went to heaven, and he went by way of blood, and we find it in all the worships of God from the earliest times. Mr. Sankey sings solos upon the redeeming blood. I can imagine when Abel got there how he sang the song of redemption. How the angels gathered around him and listened to that song; it was the first time they had ever heard that song; but six thousand years have gone, and there's a great chorus of the saints redeemed by the atoning blood. The first man that went to heaven went by the way of blood, and the last man who passes through those pearly gates must go the same way. We find not only Abel and Abraham and Isaac and Jacob, but all of them, went there through an atonement.

Now, we find in the twelfth chapter and second verse of Exodus—the most important chapter in the Word of God: "This month shall be unto you the beginning of months: it shall be the first month of the year to you." And then in the fourth verse, "And if the household be too little for the lamb, let him and his neighbor next unto his house take it according to the number of the souls; every man according to his eating shall make your count for the lamb." Now it doesn't say "if the lamb be too small for the household," but "if the household be too little for the lamb." You may have some pretty large households; your houses may be too small for them, but Christ has plenty of room. We don't start from the cradle to heaven, but from the cross. That's where eternal life begins—when we come to Calvary; when we come to Christ and get grace. We don't come to heaven when we are born into the natural world, but into the spiritual world. That's where we date our spiritual lives from. Before that our lives are a blank so far as grace is concerned.

A Sign of Blood

Adam dated from the time of the [Fall], and Noah when he came from the ark dated from the blood offering, and so the children of Israel when they came out of Egypt. And even today when they take up their pens and date 1876 years— when do they date from? Why, from the blood of Christ. Everything dates from blood. In this chapter we see the command to sacrifice. They slew the lamb. God didn't say, "Put a lamb to your front door, and I will spare you," but on the houses.

Some groups of people say, "Preach anything but the death; preach the life of Christ." You may preach that, and you'll never save a soul. It is not Christ's sympathy—His life—we preach, it is His sacrifice. That's what brings men out of darkness. I can imagine some proud Egyptians that day, who when they heard the bleating of the lambs—there must have been over two hundred thousand lambs—saying, "What an absurd performance. Every man has got a lamb, and they have got the best lambs out of the flock, too, and they are going to cover their houses with the blood." They looked upon this as an absurd proceeding—a flaw in their character. You may find a good many flaws in your character, but you cannot find a flaw in the Lamb of God.

When the hour came, you could see them all slaying their lambs, and not only that, but putting the blood on the doorposts. To those Egyptians or to the men of the world, how absurd it looked. They probably said, "Why are you disfiguring your houses in that way?" It was not upon the threshold. God didn't want that, but they were to put it upon the lintels and doorposts—where God could see it that night so that (thirteenth verse) He might see it as a token. This blood was to be a substitution for death, and all who hadn't that token in the land of Egypt had their first-born smitten at midnight. There was a wail from Egypt from one end to the other. But death didn't come near the homes where there was the token. It was death that kept death out of the dwelling.

Many people say, "I wish I was as good as that woman who has been ministering to the sick for the last fifty years. I would feel sure of heaven." My friends, if you have the blood behind you, you are as safe as anybody on this earth. It is not because that woman has been living a life of sacrifices in her ministrations to the poor that she will enter the kingdom of God. It is not our life of good deeds or our righteousness that will take us to heaven, but the atonement. And the question ought to come to everyone tonight, "Are we sheltered behind the blood?" If not, death will come by-and-by and you will be separated from God for eternity. If you have not a substitute you will die. Death is passed upon all of us. Why? Because of our sin. If we have not a substitute we have no hope.

Not only were they to have a token, but they were to do something else. We read in the eleventh verse, "And thus shall ye eat it; with your loins girded, your shoes on your feet, and your staff in your hand; and ye shall eat it in haste; it is the Lord's passover." Now a great many people wonder why they haven't got more spiritual power and have not the joy of the Lord with them all the time. It is because they haven't got the blood of the Lamb with them. These pilgrims had a long journey before them, and the Lord told them to eat the lamb. If we feed upon the Lamb we will get strength in proportion. My friends, be sure before you commence on your pilgrimage that you are sheltered behind the blood, for when He sees the blood, death will pass over you. And let me ask this assemblage tonight if every one of you have the token.

I was speaking to a man some time ago, who, when I asked him if he had the token said, "I have a prayer," and when he got to heaven he would pray, and he thought that would admit him. I said to him, "You won't get in that way. You must be cleansed by the blood of Christ. That is the only power that will open the gates of heaven—the only countersign."

When I went east the other night, the conductor came around and called for the tickets. I pulled out my ticket and he punched it. He didn't know whether it was a white or a black man who presented it, I believe. He didn't care who it was; all he wanted was the token. So all that God wants is the token of our salvation. It doesn't depend upon our deeds, our righteousness, or upon our lives; it depends upon whether or not we are sheltered behind the blood. That is the question. It didn't matter in that land of Goshen whether the child was six months or years old if it was behind the blood. It was not their moral character, nor their connections, but the blood that saved them. It is the atonement that saves, and that is the teaching all through your Bible.

There is another verse in the twenty-ninth chapter of Exodus I want to call your attention to: "And thou shalt slay the ram, and thou shalt take his blood, and sprinkle it round about upon the altar." Now we see that Aaron the high priest could not come to God with his prayers alone. He had to sprinkle the blood upon the altar. There was a time when I didn't believe in the substitution and in the blood, and my prayers went no higher than my head; but when I came to God by Jesus Christ—by the way of blood—it was different. I never knew a man who came to God really but who came this way. That great high priest had to come this way, too.

Then, again in the thirtieth chapter, tenth verse, we see, "And Aaron shall make an atonement upon the horns of it once in a year with the blood of the sin offering of atonements: once in the year shall he make atonement upon it throughout your generations: it is most holy unto the LORD." Now, an atonement is the only thing that makes a sinner and God one—is the only thing that will bring God and the sinner together. I would like, if I had time, to give you all the passages touching upon atonement in the Old Testament, but it would take too long.

Anointed with Blood

Turn again to the eighth chapter of Leviticus. This book of Leviticus is one of the most valuable, because it relates all about the worship of God. I remember when I used to read this book I used to wonder what it was all about—a verse like this, for instance: "And he slew it; and Moses took of the blood of it, and put it upon the tip of Aaron's right ear, and upon the thumb of his right hand, and upon the great toe of his right foot." I would say, "What does this mean? 'Put it upon the tip of Aaron's right ear.'" What for? I think I have got a little light upon the subject since those days. "Blood upon the ear?" So that a man could hear the voice of God, of course. And so a man who has accepted the atonement can hear the Word rightly. Blood upon the hand of a man, so that he who works for God can work rightly. Hundreds of men think they are working out their salvation, and they are only deceiving themselves. Bear in mind then that a man cannot do anything until he is sheltered behind the blood. When a man is in this position then he can go and be acceptable to God. Then blood upon the feet, so that a man can walk with God. You know when God came to Adam he hid himself. He hadn't the blood, and he couldn't walk with God. He put those people in question behind the blood, and He walked among them. When they came to the Red Sea the mighty waters opened, and God walked with them. In the wilderness they wanted water, and a rod struck the rock, and a crystal stream gushed forth. Why? Because they had had the substitution.

Many people say this is a very mysterious thing. We don't understand why God wants blood as an atonement. A man said to me, "I detest your religion; I hate your God." "Why?" I asked. "I detest a God who demands blood," he replied. Now, God is not an unjust God. He doesn't demand it without giving us a reason. He tells us in His Word that "the life of the flesh is in the blood." Take the blood out of me and I am a dead man. Life has been forfeited, the law has been broken, and the penalty must come upon us, and His blood He gives us is life; it is the life of our flesh. Three times we see "blood" mentioned in the twenty-third and twenty-fourth verses, and the reason is that it is life. You and I have lost life by the Fall, and what we want is to get back that life we lost, and we have it offered to us by the atonement of Christ. I have often thought I would far rather be out of Eden and have the blood than be in Eden without it. Adam might have been there ten years, and Satan might have been there ten years, and Satan might have come and got him. But some can't see why God permitted Adam to fall. They can't begin to discern the philosophy of it. They can't see why God ever permitted original sin to come into the world. The best answer to that was given by the Reverend Andrew Bonair, who said, "It was a great deal more wonderful that God should send His Son down to bear the brunt of it." Let us thank God we have a refuge, a substitute for the sin we are groaning under.

Turn to the fifty-third chapter of Isaiah. You hear a good many people saying, "I don't believe in the Old Testament, I believe in the New." My friends, both are inseparable. A scarlet thread runs through the two and binds them together. "We, like sheep, have gone astray," but "he was wounded for our transgressions, he was bruised for our iniquities: the chastisement of our peace was upon him; and with his stripes we are healed." My friends, in the fifty-third chapter of Isaiah we see it prophesied seven hundred years before it took place that He would die and be a substitute for you and me, that we might live. And now, my friends, let us accept Him. It seems base ingratitude not to praise God every hour of our lives that He has given such a Savior. Let us take time. Many a young man thinks it noble to scoff at this; I think it the basest ingratitude. This atonement is the only hope of my eternal life. Take the doctrine of substitution out of my Bible, and I would not take it home with me tonight. Let us praise God that He loved us so as to give us His only Son so that we might be saved.

I remember some years ago reading about a New York family. A young man, during the gold fever, went out to the Pacific, and left his wife and little boy. Just as soon as he was successful he was going to send money. A long time elapsed, but at last a letter came enclosing a draft, and telling his wife to come on. The woman took a passage in one of the fine steamers of the Pacific line, full of hope and joy at the prospect of soon being united to her husband. They had not been out many days when a voice went ringing through the ship, "Fire! Fire!" The pumps were set to work and the buckets were brought into operation, but the fire gained upon them. There was a powder magazine on board, and the captain ordered all the boats to be instantly lowered. He knew whenever the fire reached the powder they would all be lost. The people scrambled into the boats and the mother and boy were left on deck. As the last boat was being pushed off the woman begged to be taken in. The majority insisted the boat was too full, and wanted to push off, but one man put in a word for her, and they said they could allow one more on

board, but no more. What did the mother do? Did she go on board and leave her son? No. She put her boy into that lifeboat and told him if he ever lived to see his father to tell him, "I died to save you." And the boat pulled away from that ship, and left the mother standing there. The vessel went on burning. Presently an explosion was heard, and all was buried in the ocean. Suppose that young man was here tonight. Suppose you spoke to him about the act of his mother, and he turned round and scoffed at it. "Why," you would say, "that ungrateful wretch doesn't deserve to live," and this is what you are doing. He laid down His life for you. Now will you speak contemptuously about Him? Will you speak lightly of the blood laid down on Calvary for you? Let us rather all thank God we have such a Savior. Let us live for Him when He died for us.

PART TWO

You who were here last night remember that we spoke of the precious blood, and that we looked at a few passages in the Old Testament bearing upon the subject. Tonight I want to take up some passages referring to the subject in the New Testament. Soon after we came back from Europe to this country, I received a letter from a lady saying that she had looked forward to our coming back to this country with a great deal of interest, and that her interest remained after we had commenced our services until I came to the lecture on the blood when she gave up all hope of our doing any good. In closing that letter, she said, "Where did Jesus ever teach the perilous and barbarous doctrine that men were to be redeemed by the shedding of His blood? Never, never did Jesus teach that monstrous idea."

Let us turn to the fourteenth chapter of Mark, twenty-fourth verse, and we will find, "And he said unto them, This is my blood of the new testament, which is shed for many," and also in Matthew, twenty-sixth chapter and twenty-eighth verse: "For this is my blood of the new testament, which is shed for many for the remission of sins." There are a good many passages, but it is not necessary to refer to more. If Christ did not teach it, and also the apostles—if Christ did not preach it, then I have read my Bible wrong all these years. I haven't got the key to the Scriptures; it is a sealed book to me, and if I don't preach it—if I give it up, I've nothing left to preach. Take the blessed doctrine of the blood out of my Bible, and my capital is gone, and I've got to take to something else.

I remember when in the old country, a young man came to me—a minister came round to me and said he wanted to talk with me. He said to me, "Mr. Moody, you are either all right, and I am all wrong, or else I am right, and you are all wrong." "Well, sir," said I, "you have the advantage of me. You have heard me preach, and know what doctrines I hold, whereas, I have not heard you, and don't know what you preach." "Well," said he, "the difference between your preaching and mine is that you make out that salvation is got by Christ's death, and I make out that it is attained by His life." "Now, what do you do with the passages bearing upon the death?" And I quoted the passages, "Without the shedding of blood there is no remission," and "He Himself, bore our own sins by His own body on the tree," and asked him what he did with them, for instance. "I never preach on them at all." I quoted a number of passages more, and he gave me the same answer. "Well, what do you preach?" I finally asked. "Moral essays," he replied. Said I, "Did you ever know anybody to be saved by that kind of thing—did you ever convert anybody by them?" "I never aimed at that kind of conversion; I mean to get men to heaven by culture—by refinement." "Well," said I, "if I didn't preach those texts, and only preached culture, the whole thing would be a sham." "And it is a sham to me," was his reply. I tell you the moment a man breaks away from this doctrine of blood, religion becomes a sham, because the whole teaching of this book is of one story, and this is that Christ came into the world, and died for our sins.

I want to call your attention to the nineteenth chapter of John, and the thirty-fourth verse: "But one of the soldiers with a spear pierced his side, and forthwith came there out blood and water." There came out blood and water. Now, it was prophesied years before, that there should open a fountain, which should wash away sin and uncleanness, and it seems that this fountain was opened here by the spear of the soldier, and out of the fountain came blood and water. It was the breaking of the crown of hell, and the giving of the crown to heaven. When the Roman soldier drove out the blood, out came the water, and it touched that spear, and it was not long before Christ had that Roman government. It is a throne and a footstool now, and by-and-by it will sway the earth from pole to pole. This earth has been redeemed by the blessed blood of Christ. Peter says in his first Epistle, first chapter, eighteenth and nineteenth verses:

Forasmuch as ye know that ye were not redeemed with corruptible things, as silver and gold, from your vain conversation received by tradition from your fathers; But with the precious blood of Christ, as of a lamb without blemish and without spot.

You are not redeemed by such corruptible things as gold or silver, but by the precious blood of the Lamb—"the precious blood of Christ—as of a lamb without blemish."

If silver and gold could have redeemed us, it would have been the easiest thing to have made a pile of gold ten thousand times larger than the bulk of the earth. But gold couldn't do it. Why, the poorest thing in heaven is gold. As I said last night, the law had been broken, and the penalty of death had come upon us, and it required life to redeem us. Now, it says we shall be redeemed. My friends, redemption is to me one of the most precious treasures in the Word of God—to think that Christ has bought me by His blood. I am no longer my own, I am His. He has ransomed me.

A friend of mine once told me that he was going out from Dublin one day, and met a boy who had one of those English sparrows in his hand. It was frightened and just seemed to sit as if it pined for liberty, but the boy held it so tight that it could not get away. The boy's strength was too much for the bird. My friend said, "Open your hand and let the bird go. You will never tame him; he is wild." But the boy replied, "Faith an' I'll not; I've been a whole hour trying to catch him, an' now I've got him, I'm going to keep him." So the man took out his purse and asked the boy if he would sell it. A bargain was made, and the sparrow was transferred to the man's hand. He opened his hand, and at first it did not seem to realize it had liberty, but by-and-by it flew away, and as it went it chirped, as much as to say, "You have redeemed me." And so Christ has come down and offered to redeem us and give us liberty when we were bound with sin. Satan was stronger than we were. He has had six thousand years' experience. He did not come to buy us from Satan, but from the penalty of our sin.

All of One Blood

Another thought about the blood. It makes us all one. The blood brings us into one family, into the household of faith. I remember during the war Dr. Kirk, one of the most eloquent men I ever heard, was speaking in Boston. At that time, you recollect, there was a good deal said about the Irish and the black man, and what an amount of talk about the war of races. He said while preaching one night, "I saw a poor Irishman and a black man and an Englishman, and the blood of Christ came down and fell upon them and made them one." My friends, it brings nationalities together, it brings those scattered with the seeds of discord together and makes them one. Let us turn to Acts seventeen, verse twenty-six, and we read, "And hath made of one blood all nations of men for to dwell on all the face of the earth, and hath determined the times before appointed, and the bounds of their habitation." That's what the blood of Christ does. It just makes us one. I can tell [men] that [have] been redeemed by the blood. They speak all the same language. I don't require to be in [their] company ten minutes before I can tell whether or not [they have] been redeemed. They have only one language, and you can tell when they speak whether they are outside the blood or sheltered by it. The blood has two voices—one is for salvation and the other is for condemnation. The blood tonight cries out for my salvation or for my condemnation. If we are sheltered behind the blood, it cries for our salvation, for we see in Galatians, "It cries for our peace." There is no peace till a man has been sheltered by that blood.

Again, I would like to call your attention to the twenty-sixth chapter of Matthew, twenty-eighth verse, where we find Christ speaking of His blood: "For this is my blood of the new testament, which is shed for . . . the remission of sins." This blood was "shed for the remission of sins." Then in Hebrews ninth chapter and twenty-second verse, where it says, "without shedding of blood is no remission [of sins]." Men don't realize that this is God's plan of salvation. Said a man to me last night after the meeting, "Why, God has got a plan to save us." Certainly He has. You must be saved by God's plan. It was love that prompted God to send His Son to save us and shed His blood. That was the plan. And without the blood what hope have you? There is not a sin from your childhood—from your cradle—up till now that can be forgiven, unless by the blood. Let us take God at His word: "Without the shedding of blood there is no remission [of sins]." Without the blood, [there is] no remission whatever. I don't see how a man can fail to comprehend this. That's what Christ died for; that's what Christ died on Calvary for. If a man makes light of that blood what hope has he? How are you going to get into the kingdom of God? You cannot join in the song of the saints if you don't go into heaven that way. You cannot sing the song of redemption. If you did I suppose you would be off in some corner with a harp of your own and singing, "I saved myself; I saved myself." You can't get in that way. You must accept the plan of redemption and come in through it. "He that climbeth up some other way, the same is a thief and a robber."

Then, in the tenth chapter of Hebrews, we find Paul, if he wrote this, just taking up the very thought, "He that despised Moses' law died without mercy under two or three witnesses." You know when a man made light of the Law under the Mosaic dispensation, whenever two witnesses came into court and swore that he hadn't kept the Law, they just took him out and stoned him to death. Take up the next verse: "Of how much surer punishment suppose ye shall be thought worthy who hath trodden under foot the Son of God and hath counted the blood of the covenant wherewith He was sanctified an unholy thing, and hath done despite unto the spirit of grace."

My friends, what hope is there if a man tramples the blood of Christ under his foot, if he says, "I will have nothing to do with that blood"? I ask in all candor, what mercy is there? What hope has he if he "hath trodden underfoot the Son of God and hath counted the blood of the covenant wherewith He was sanctified an unholy thing"? This is the only way to get to heaven—no other way. Turn again to the twelfth verse of the same chapter and we see, "But this man, after he had offered one sacrifice for sins"—mark that, He had settled the question of sin—"forever, sat down on the right hand of God."

The high priests could never sit down. Their work was never done; but our High Priest hath put sin away by one sacrifice and then ascended to God. And in this same chapter of Hebrews we see again, "Having therefore, brethren, boldness to enter into the holiest by the blood of Jesus, by a new and living way, which He hath consecrated for us through the vail, that is to say, his flesh, and having an High Priest over the house of God, let us draw near with a true heart, in full assurance of faith, having our hearts sprinkled from an evil conscience, and our bodies washed with pure water. Let us hold fast the profession of our faith without wavering, for He is faithful that promised." I want to call your attention to the twentieth verse more particularly—"By a new and living way." Now Christ has opened a new and living way. We cannot get to heaven by our own deeds now. He has opened "a new and a living way."

We don't need a high priest to go once a year and pray to God. Thank God we are all kings and all priests. We can go straight to the Father in the name of the Lord Jesus Christ. When Christ died the temple veil was rent from the top to the bottom—not from the bottom to the top—and every poor son of Adam can walk right in and worship—right into the presence of God, if he only comes by the way of the blood. Yes, thank God, He has opened a new and a living way whereby we can come to Him. Let us thank God for the new and the living way. We don't need any bishop, we don't need any pope, we don't need any priest or prophet now; but everyone can be made king and priest, and we can come through this living way to His presence and ask Him to take away our sins. There's not a man in this assembly but can come to Him tonight.

There's a good deal about the blood in Hebrews that I would like to bring up; time passes, and I have just to fly through the subject. Now I don't know any doctrine I have preached that has been talked about more than the doctrine of blood. Why, the moment Satan gets a man to leave out this doctrine of blood, he has gained all he wants. It is the most pernicious idea to leave it out. A man may be a brilliant preacher, may have a brilliant intellect, and he may have large crowds of people, but if he leaves this out, no one will be blessed under his ministry, no one will be born into God's kingdom. If a man leaves out this blood he may as well go and whistle in the streets and try to convert people that way, for all the good he will do in saving souls.

It is said that old Dr. Alexander of Princeton College, when a young student used to start out to preach, always gave him a piece of advice. The old man would stand with his gray locks and his venerable face and say, "Young man,

make much of the blood in your ministry." Now, I have traveled considerably during the past few years, and never met a minister who made much of the blood and much of the atonement but God had blessed his ministry, and souls were born into the light by it. But a man who leaves it out, the moment he goes, his church falls to pieces like a rope of sand, and his preaching has been barren of good result.

And so if you find a man preaching who has covered up this doctrine of blood, don't sit under his ministry; I don't care what denomination he belongs to, get out of it. Fly from it as those who flew from Sodom. Never mind how you get out of it—leave it. It is a whitened sepulcher. There is no life if they don't preach the blood. It is the only way we've got to conquer Satan, the only way we can enter heaven, and we cannot get there unless we have washed our robes in the blood of the Lamb. If we expect to conquer we must be first washed by that blood. A man who has not realized what the blood has done for him has not the token of salvation.

It is told of Julian the apostate, that while he was fighting he received an arrow in his side. He pulled it out, and taking a handful of blood threw it into the air, and cried, "Galilean, Galilean, thou hast conquered!" Yes, the Galilean is going to conquer, and you must bear in mind if you don't accept the blood—don't submit to it and let it cleanse you—the rocks will fall on you, because the decree of heaven is that every knee will bow to the will of heaven. The blood is a call of mercy now. He wants you to come—He beseeches you to accept and be saved.

I heard of an old minister who had preached the gospel for fifty years faithfully. "Ah!" many here will say, "I wish I was as safe to go to heaven as he."

When he was reaching his end he asked that his Bible should be brought to him. His eyes were growing dim in death, and he said to one of those about him, "I wish you would turn to the first epistle of John, chapter one, verse seven," and when it was found, the old man put his dying finger on the passage where it says, "But if we walk in the light as he is in light, we have fellowship one with another, and the blood of Jesus Christ his Son cleanseth us from all sin." And he said, "I die in the hope of that." It was the blood in his ministry that cleansed him. And so it is the only way by which our sins can be washed away. Why, there was a question once asked in heaven when a great crowd were gathering there, "Who are those?" And the answer was, "They are those who have come by great tribulation and have been washed by the blood of the Lamb."

Disposition of the Blood

Now, the question here tonight is, what are you going to do with that blood? We have had it for two nights, and before I close I would like to ask you, what are you going to do about it? You must do either of two things—take it or reject it. Trample it underfoot or cleanse your sins by it. I heard of a lady who told a servant to cook a lamb. She told him how to do it up and all about it, but she didn't tell him what to do with the blood. So he went to her and asked, "What are you going to do with the blood of the lamb?" She had been under conviction for some time, and such a question went like an arrow to her soul. She went to her room and felt uneasy, and the question kept continually coming to her, "What are you going to do with the blood of the lamb," and before morning she was on her knees asking for the mercy of the blood of the Lamb.

Now the most solemn truth in the gospel is that the only thing He left down here is His blood. His body and bones He took away, but He left His blood on Calvary. There is either of two things we must do. One is to send back the message to heaven that we don't want the blood of Christ to cleanse us of our sin, or else accept it. Why, when we come to our dying hour the blood will be worth more than all the kingdoms of the world to us. Can you afford to turn your back upon it and make light of it?

Dr. King, when the war was going on, went down to the field with the Christian Commission. He used to go among the soldiers, and during one of his visits he heard a man cry, "Blood! Blood! Blood!" He thought that, as the man had just been taken off the battlefield, the scene of carnage and blood was still upon his mind. The doctor went to him, and tried to talk to the man about Christ, and to divert his mind from the scenes of the field. "Ah, Doctor," said the man, feebly, "I was not thinking of the battlefield, but of the blood of Christ"; and he whispered the word "blood" once more and was gone.

Dear friends, do you want all your sins washed away from you? [The blood] was shed for the remission of sins, and without the shedding of blood there would be no remission. There is blood on the mercy seat tonight. "I am not looking to your sins now," God says, "but come and press in, press in, and receive remission." Thank God, the blood is still on the mercy seat. It is there, and He beseeches you to accept it. What more can He do for your salvation? Now, my friends, don't go out of this tabernacle laughing and scoffing at the precious offering made to you, but just bow your head now and lift up your voice, "O God of heaven, may the blood of Thy Son cleanse me from all sin." The blood is sufficient.

Some years ago I was journeying to the Pacific coast, and nearly every stage-driver I met was talking about a prominent stagedriver who had just died. You know that in driving over these rocky roads they depend a good deal upon the brake. This poor man, when he was dying, was heard to say, "I am on the down grade and cannot keep the brake." Just about that time one of the most faithful men of God, Alfred Cookman, passed away. His wife and friends gathered around his deathbed, and when his last moments arrived, it seemed as if heaven had opened before him, as with a shout he cried, "I am sweeping through the gates washed by the blood of the Lamb." What a comfort this must have been to his friends. What a comfort it must have been to him, the blood of the atonement in his last hours.

My friends, if you want a glorious end like the end of that sainted man you must come to the blood of Christ.

Moody sought to address the many excuses used by individuals to avoid any commitment to Christ.

One of the more popular excuses focused on the integrity of the Bible. Moody recognized the fact that belief in the Bible was paramount. To him, the problem was not the book but those who attacked it—for, in his mind, they never read the Bible carefully.

Other excuses abounded: God is a hard master; Christianity makes one gloomy; if I'm one of the elect I'll make it no matter what; too many hypocrites in the Church; I have plenty of time; I am too bad; I cannot believe. Moody stipulated that no excuse was adequate. No excuse could ever prevail over the need to come to Christ.

CHAPTER SIX

Excuses

PART ONE

Mr. Moody then said the text he would take was to be found in [Luke chapter fourteen] the nineteenth verse: "I pray thee have me excused." Christ had been invited to dine with a rich Pharisee, and it seemed as though this man had gathered his friends together in a kind of conspiracy to catch Christ. They watched Him. A man who had dropsy was placed before Jesus, as though they wanted to see what He would do. Christ read their hearts, and so before them He healed the man. He asked them if it was lawful to heal on the Sabbath day. But they didn't want to answer for fear they'd betray themselves, and so they held their peace. Then Christ put the question to them in another way and asked them if any of them had an ox or an ass fall into the pit, should he not straightway pull it out on the Sabbath day? And then He healed the man, as the Pharisees and lawyers weren't able to answer Him.

Then He told them about the feast, and told them to be humble. When a man prepares a feast, men rush in, but when God prepares one they all begin to make excuses, and don't want to go. The first excuse was that made by Adam, "The woman Thou gavest me, she gave me to eat." These men that excused themselves made manufactured excuses; they didn't really have any. The drunkard, the libertine, the businessman, the citizen, the harlot, all had their excuses. If God were to take men at their word about these excuses, and swept every one into his grave who had an excuse, there would be a very small congregation in the tabernacle next Sunday; there would be little business in Chicago, and in a few weeks the grass would be growing on these busy streets. Every man who was nursing a sin had an excuse, as though God had asked them to go into a plague-stricken city, or a hospital, or to hear a dry lecture, or something repelling and objectionable, something that wasn't for their greatest good.

Take the excuses. There wasn't one that wasn't a lie. The devil made them all; and if the sinner hadn't one already, the devil was there at his elbow to suggest one about the truth of the Bible, or something of that sort. One of the excuses mentioned was that the man invited had bought a piece of ground, and had to look at it. Real estate and corner lots were keeping a good many men out of God's kingdom. It was a lie to say that he had to go and see it then, for he ought to have looked at it before he bought it. Then the next man said he'd bought some oxen and must prove them. That was another lie; for if he hadn't proved them before he bought them as he ought to have done, he could have done it after the supper just as well as before it. But the third man had the silliest, the worst, excuse of all; he said he had married a wife, and couldn't come. Why didn't he bring her with him? She'd have liked the supper just as well as he would and would have enjoyed a supper, as almost any young bride would.

No Valid Excuse

These seemed to be foolish excuses, but they were not any more so than the excuses of today. Indeed, the excuses of men are getting worse and worse all the time. They say they can't believe the Bible; it's so mysterious. Well, what of it? Infidels, skeptics, pantheists, deists, said they didn't believe the Bible. Had they ever used it? Did they read it as carefully as they read any other book? This was their excuse. If everybody could understand everything the Bible said it wouldn't be God's Book. If Christians, if theologians had studied it for forty, fifty, sixty years, and only then began to understand it, how could a man expect to understand it by one reading? A child the first day at school couldn't even know the alphabet, and yet it wasn't a sign that it was a poor school because he didn't learn the first day all about grammar, arithmetic, and geometry. Another said God was a hard master. No; that was one of Satan's lies. The devil's the hard master. In the Tombs in New York there is over the door the remark, "The way of the transgressor is hard." God's yoke is easy, His burden light. Ask prisoners, ask gamblers, ask sinners, if Satan's yoke is easy. It's the hardest of all . . . Is God a hard master, Christians? . . . God's service a hard one? How will that sound in the Judgment? Many said it wasn't that, but there is such a struggle. Wasn't all life a struggle? Some said they were wicked. Those are just the kind Jesus came to save. They weren't too wicked to be saved. They were so worldly minded, so hard-hearted; that was another falsehood.

Look at what God did for Bunyan and John Newton, and many others who were the [most] wicked, and even the thief on the cross. God is already reconciled; He doesn't need the sinner to be reconciled to Him. The Lord prepares the sinner.

A touching story was told of an English father and son, who had become estranged, but who were united over the deathbed of the wife and mother. The father was stern, but he was reconciled by the prayers of the dying parent. And this was so with God: the sinner had left Him, God was removed from him, but God and the sinner were brought near by the death of our Lord Jesus Christ.

This afternoon I chose for my text the fourteenth verse of the fourteenth chapter of Luke, and you will remember I took up certain of the excuses of the present day in regard to accepting Christ. One of these excuses I said was that Christ was a hard master; it was a very difficult thing to become a Christian, and the other was that Christ would not receive them. Now, I just want to take up where I left off, and notice the excuses we hear in the inquiry room, in the streets of Chicago—everywhere. I said this afternoon you were not invited, when asked to come to Christ, to a dry lecture on a disagreeable subject but to a marriage feast. The Lord has said, "Blessed is he who shall be at the marriage supper of the Lord." I have missed a good many appointments in my life, but there is one I will not miss. I would rather be at the marriage feast than have the whole world rolled at my feet. I want to be there and sit down with Isaac and Jacob and Abraham at that supper. It is an invitation for joy and gladness that comes from the King of kings, from the Lord of Glory, to every man and woman in this assembly—the invitation to be at the marriage supper of the Lamb. It is not a personal invitation, but a universal one—"Go out into the highways and hedges and compel them to come in, that my house may be filled." Bid them come, "the poor and the maimed and the halt and the blind," to the marriage feast, prepared at great expense by our blessed Redeemer.

I said in the afternoon that people began to make excuses very early in the history of Christianity, and they are still at it. Nineteen hundred years have rolled away and still there are excuses. One of the excuses that we very often hear people giving is that they don't want to become Christians because it will make them gloomy—they will have to put on long faces, button their coats up, cut off all joy, and walk through the world till they get to heaven, where they will have pleasure forevermore. We look forward to that happy future, but thank God, we have some pleasure here. Indeed, no man in the world should be so happy as a man of God. It is one continual source of gladness. He can look up and say, "God is my Father," "Christ is my Savior, and the church is my mother." All who think otherwise than that a Christian's life is one of unceasing joy are deceiving themselves.

I was going by a saloon the other day and saw a sign, "Drink and be merry." Poor, blind, deluded fellows, if they think this will make them merry. If you want to be merry you must come to the living fountain that bursts from the throne of God; then you will have true pleasure. A man away from God cannot have true pleasure. He is continually thirsting for something he cannot get— thirsting for something that can quench his thirst, and he cannot get it until he comes to the living fountain. My friends, that is just another wile of the devil to keep men from grace. It is false. The more a man is lifted up to heaven the more joy and peace and gladness he has. He is lifted away from gloom.

Look at a man on his way to execution. Suppose I run up to him, holding out my hand, and say, "There is a pardon that has been signed by the Gover-

nor," and I give it him. Would he be gloomy and joyless? That is Christ. He comes down with a pardon to us poor men and women on our way to execution. Yonder is a man starving. I go to him and give him bread. Is that going to make him gloomy? A poor man comes along crying with thirst, and I give him a glass of ice water; would that make him gloomy? That is what Christ is doing for us. He has a well of living water, and He asks every thirsty soul to drink freely. Don't you believe for a moment that Christianity is going to make you gloomy.

I remember when I was a boy I thought I would wait till I [was about to] die and then become a Christian. I thought if I had consumption, or some lingering disease, I would have plenty of time to become one, and in the meantime, I would enjoy the best of the pleasures of the world. My friends, I was at that time under the power of the devil. The idea that a man has more pleasure away from church is one of the devil's lies. Do not believe it, but accept of this universal invitation to the marriage feast.

PART TWO

I can imagine some men saying, "Mr. Moody has not touched my case at all. That is not the reason why I won't accept Christ. I don't know if I am one of the elect." How often am I met with this excuse—how often do I hear it in the inquiry room! How many men fold their arms and say, "If I am one of the elect I will be saved, and if I am not I won't. No use in your bothering about it." Why don't some of those [businessmen] say, "If God is going to make me a successful [businessman] in Chicago I will be one whether I like it or not, and if he hasn't I won't."

If you are sick and a doctor prescribes for you, don't take the medicine; throw it out of the door; it doesn't matter, for if God has decreed you are going to die you will, and if He hasn't you will get better. If you use that argument you may as well not walk home from this tabernacle. If God has said you'll get home, you'll get [there]—you'll fly through the air if you have been elected to go home. These illustrations are just the same as the excuse. You cannot go up there and give that excuse. The water of life is offered freely to everyone.

No unconverted man in the wide, wide world has anything to do with the doctrine of election any more than I have to do with the government of China. The epistle of Paul was written to godly men. Suppose I pick up a letter and open it, and it tells me about the death of my wife. Dear me—my wife, dead. But I look on the other side of the letter and find that it is directed to another man. And so a great many people take Paul's letter to the churches and take it as a personal letter. This is what you have to take up: "Whosoever will, let him drink of the water of life freely." He came down sixty years after His resurrection and said to John—put it so broadly that no one will mistake it; put it so broadly that no one in Chicago can be stumbling over it, so that all men may see it plainly—"Whosoever will, let him drink of the water of life freely." If you will, you will; if you won't, you won't.

Do you think that God will come down here to give you salvation, without giving you the power to take it, and then condemn you to eternity for not taking it? With the gift comes the power, and you can take it and live if you will. Don't stumble over election anymore. You have to deal with that broad proclamation: "Whosoever will, let him drink of the waters of life freely."

I can imagine someone in the gallery clear up there saying, "I never have bothered my head about election, I don't believe men are gloomy when they become Christians. If I was alone I would tell you my reason, but I do not like to get up in this large assembly and talk here. The fact is there are hypocrites in the churches. I know a man, a prominent man in the church, who cheated me out of twenty-five dollars. I won't accept this invitation because of those hypocrites in the churches." My friend, you will find very few there if you get to heaven. There won't be a hypocrite in the next world, and if you don't want to be associated with hypocrites in the next world, you will take this invitation. Why, you will find hypocrites everywhere. One of the apostles was himself the very prince of hypocrites, but he didn't get to heaven. You will find plenty of hypocrites in the church. They have been there for the last eighteen hundred years and will probably remain there. But what is that to you? This is an individual matter between you and your God. Is it because there are hypocrites that you are not going to accept the invitation?

"Ah, well, Mr. Moody, that is not my case. I am a businessman, and I have no time. Since the Chicago fire I have had as much as I could attend to in recovering what I lost." I believe if I stood at the door and asked anyone who went out to accept the invitation, I believe hundreds of you would say, "Mr. Moody, you will have to excuse me tonight; time is very precious with me, and you'll have to excuse me." What have you been doing the last twenty, thirty, forty, fifty years that you haven't had a moment to devote to the acceptance of the invitation? That is the cry of the world today: "Time is precious; business must be attended to, and we have no time to spare."

Some of you will say, "I cannot wait; I have to go home and put the children to bed; this is more important." My friends, to accept this invitation is more important than anything else in the world. There is nothing in the world that is so important as the question of accepting the invitation. How many mechanics in this building have spent five years learning their trade, in order to support their families and support themselves a few years—forty or fifty years at the longest? How many professional men have toiled and worked hard for years to get such an education that they might go out to the world and cope with it, and during all these years have not had a minute to seek their salvation? Is that a legitimate excuse? Tell Him tonight that you haven't time or let this be the night—the hour—cost you what it will, when you shall say, "By the grace of God, I will accept the invitation and press up to the marriage supper of the Lamb."

"Oh, but that is not my case," says another, "I have time. If I thought I could become a Christian I would sit here all night and let business and everything else go, and I would press into the kingdom of God. I am not fit to become a Christian, that's the trouble with me." He says, "Go into the highways and hedges," and "bring in hither the poor, and the maimed, and the halt and the blind,"—just invite them all, without distinction of sect or creed, station or nationality; never mind whether they are rich or poor. If the Lord doesn't complain about your fitness, you shouldn't look to see if you have the right kind of clothes.

God Overcomes Excuses

I had to notice during the war, when enlisting was going on, sometimes a man would come up with a nice silk hat on, patent leather boots, nice kid gloves, and a fine suit of clothes, which probably cost him one hundred dollars; perhaps the next man who came along would be a hodcarrier, dressed in the poorest kind of clothes. Both had to strip alike and put on the regimental uniform. So when you come and say you are not fit, haven't got good clothes, haven't got righteousness enough, remember that He will furnish you with the uniform of heaven, and you will be set down at the marriage feast of the Lamb.

I don't care how black and vile your heart may be, only accept the invitation of Jesus Christ, and He will make you fit to sit down with the rest at that feast. How many are continually crying out, "I am too bad; no use [in my] trying to become a Christian." This is the way the devil works. Sometimes he will say to a man, "You don't want to be saved; you're good enough already," and he will point to some black-hearted hypocrite and say, "Look at him and see how you appear in comparison; you are far better than he is." But by-and-by the man gets a glimpse of the blackness of his own heart, and his conscience troubles him. Then says the devil, "You are too bad to be saved; the Lord won't save such as you; you are too vile; you must get better before you try to get God to save you." And so men try to make themselves better and instead get worse all the time. The gospel bids you come as you are. Seek first the kingdom of heaven—make no delay; come just as you are.

I heard of an artist who wanted to get a man to sit for a painting of the prodigal son. He went down to the almshouses and the prisons but couldn't get one. Going through the streets one day he found a poor wretched man, a beggar, coming along, and he asked him if he would sit for the study. He said he would. A bargain was made, and the artist gave him his address. The time for the appointment arrived, and the beggar duly appeared and said to the artist, "I have come to keep that appointment which I made with you." "An appointment with me?" replied the artist; "You are mistaken; I have an appointment with a beggar today." "Well," said the man, "I am that beggar, but I thought I would put on a new suit of clothes before I came to see you." "I don't want you," was the artist's reply, "I want a beggar." And so a great many people come to God with their self-righteousness, instead of coming in their raggedness. Why, someone has said, "It is only the ragged sinners that open God's wardrobe. If you want to start out to get a pair of shoes from a passer-by, you would start out barefooted, wouldn't you?"

I remember a boy to whom I gave a pair of boots, and I found him shortly after in his bare feet again. I asked him what he had done with them, and he replied that when he was dressed up it spoiled his business. When he was dressed up no one would give him anything. By keeping his feet naked he got as many as five pairs of boots a day. So if you want to come to God, don't dress yourself up. It is the naked sinners God wants to save. Come to Him after you have cast off your self-righteousness, and the Son of God will receive you.

I remember some years ago a man who had gone to sea. He led a wild, reckless life. When his mother was alive she was a praying mother. (Ah, how many men have been saved by their mothers after they have gone up to heaven.) And perhaps her influence made him think sometimes. When at sea a desire [to] lead a better life came over him, and when he got on shore he thought he

would join the Free Masons. He made application, but, upon investigation, his character proved he was only a drunken sailor, and he was blackballed. He next thought of joining the Odd Fellows, and applied, but his application met with a like result. While he was walking up Fulton Street one day a little tract was given him—an invitation to the prayer meeting. He came, and Christ received him. I remember him getting up in the meeting, and telling how the Free Masons had blackballed him, how the Odd Fellows had blackballed him, and how Christ had received him as he was. A great many orders and societies will not receive you, but I tell you, He will receive you, vile as you are—He, the Savior of sinners—He, the Redeemer of the lost world—He bids you come just as you are.

Ah, but there is another voice coming down from the gallery yonder: "I have intellectual difficulties; I cannot believe." A man came to me some time ago, and said, "I cannot." "Cannot what?" "Well," said he, "I cannot believe." "Who?" "Well," he repeated, "I cannot believe." "Who?" I asked. "Well, I can't believe myself." "Well, you don't want to." Make yourself out false every time, but believe in the truth of Christ. If a man says to me, "Mr. Moody, you have lied to me; you have dealt falsely with me," it may be so, but no man on the face of the earth can ever say that God ever dealt unfairly, or that He lied to him. If God says a thing, it is true. We don't ask you to believe in any man on the face of the earth, but we ask you to believe in Jesus Christ, who never lied—who never deceived anyone. If a man says he cannot believe Him, he says what is untrue.

"Ah, well, all those excuses don't apply to me," says another; "I can't feel." That is the very last excuse. When a man comes with [that] excuse, he is getting pretty near to the Lord.

We are having a body of men in England giving a new translation of the Scriptures. I think we should get them to put in a passage relating to feeling. With some people it is feel, feel, feel all the time. What kind of feeling have you got? Have you got a desire to be saved—have you got a desire to be present at the marriage supper? Suppose a gentleman asked me to dinner. I say, "I will see how I feel." "Sick?" he might ask. "No; it depends on how I feel." That is not the question—it is whether I will accept the invitation or not. The question with us is, will we accept salvation—will [we] believe? There is not a word about feelings in the Scriptures. When you come to your end, and you know that in a few days you will be in the presence of the Judge of all the earth, you will remember this excuse about feelings. You will be saying, "I went up to the tabernacle, I remember, and I felt very good, and before the meeting was over I felt very bad, and I didn't feel I had the right kind of feeling to accept the invitation." Satan will then say, "I made you feel so." Suppose you build your hopes and fix yourself upon the Rock of Ages, the devil cannot come to you. Stand upon the Word of God, and the waves of unbelief cannot touch you; the waves of persecution cannot assail you; the devil and all the fiends of hell cannot approach you if you only build your hopes upon God's Word. Say, "I will trust Him, though He slay me—I will take God at His word."

Satan's Lies

I haven't exhausted all the excuses. If I had you would make more before tomorrow morning. What has to be done with all the excuses is to bundle them all up and label them "Satan's lies." There is not an excuse but it is a lie. When you stand at the throne of God no man can give an excuse. If you have got a good excuse, don't give it up for anything I have said; don't give it up for anything your friend may have said. Take it up to the bar of God, and state it to Him; but if you have not got a good excuse—an excuse that will stand eternity—let it go tonight, and flee to the arms of a loving Savior.

It is easy enough to excuse yourself to hell, but you cannot excuse yourself to heaven. If you want an excuse, Satan will always find one ready for you. Accept the invitation now, my friends. Let your stores be closed till you accept this invitation; let your households go till you accept this invitation. Do not let the light come, do not eat, do not drink, till you accept the most important thing to you in this wide world. Will you stay tonight and accept this invitation? Don't make light of it. I can imagine some of you saying, "I never get so low as to make light of religion."

Suppose I get an invitation to dinner from a citizen of Chicago for tomorrow, and I don't answer it—I tear the invitation up. Would not that be making light of it? Suppose you pay no attention to the invitation tonight—is not that making light of it? Would anyone here be willing to write out an excuse something like this: "The tabernacle, October 29. To the King of heaven: While sitting in the tabernacle today, I received a very pressing invitation from one of your servants to sit at the marriage ceremony of the Son of God. I pray you have me excused." Is there a man or woman in this assembly would take their pen and write their name at the bottom of it? Is there a man or woman whose right hand would not forget its cunning, and whose tongue would not cleave to their mouth, if they were trying to do it? Well, you are doing this if you get up and go right out after you have heard the invitation. Who will write this: "To the Lord of lords and King of Glory: While sitting in the tabernacle this beautiful Sabbath evening, October 29, 1876, I received a pressing invitation from one of your servants to be present at the marriage supper. I hasten to accept." Will anyone sign this? Who will put their name to it? Is there not a man or woman saying, down deep in their soul, "By the grace of God I will sign it"; "I will sign it by the grace of God, and will meet that sainted mother who has gone there"; "I will sign and accept that invitation, and meet that loving wife or dear child." Are there not some here tonight who will accept that invitation?

I remember while preaching in Glasgow, an incident occurred which I will relate. I had been preaching there several weeks, and the night was my last one, and I pleaded with them as I had never pleaded there before. I urged those people to meet me in that land. It is a very solemn thing to stand before a vast audience for the last time, and think you may never have another chance of asking them to come to Christ. I told them I would not have another opportunity, and urged them to accept and just asked them to meet me at that marriage supper. At the conclusion, I soon saw a tall young lady coming into the inquiry room. She had scarcely come in when another tall young lady came in, and she went up to the first and put her arms round her and wept. Pretty soon another young lady came, and went up to the first two and just put her arms around them both. I went over to see what it was, and found that, although they had been sitting in different parts of the building, the sure arrow of conviction went down to their souls, and brought them to the inquiry room. Another young lady came

down from the gallery, and said, "Mr. Moody, I want to become a Christian." I asked a young Christian to talk to her; and when she went home that night about ten o'clock—her mother was sitting up for her—she said, "Mother, I have accepted the invitation to be present at the marriage supper of the Lamb." Her mother and father laid awake that night talking about the salvation of the child. That was Friday night, and next day (Saturday) she was unwell, and before long her sickness developed into scarlet fever, and a few days after I got this letter:

Mr. Moody—Dear Sir: It is now my painful duty to [tell] you that the dear girl concerning whom I wrote to you on Monday, has been taken away from us by death. Her departure, however, has been signally softened to us, for she told us yesterday she was "going home to be with Jesus"; and after giving messages to many, told us to let Mr. Moody and Mr. Sankey know that she died a happy Christian.

My dear sir, let us have your prayer that consolation and needed resignation and strength may be continued to us, and that our two dear remaining little ones may be kept in health if the Lord wills. I repeated a line of the hymn,

In the Christian's home in glory,
There remains a land of rest,

when she took it up at once, and tried to sing, "When the Savior's gone before to fulfill my soul's request." This was the last conscious thing she said. I should say that my dear girl also expressed a wish that the lady she conversed with on Friday evening should also know that she died a happy Christian.

When I heard this, I said to Mr. Sankey, "If we do nothing else we have been paid for coming across the Atlantic. There is one soul we have saved, whom we will meet on the resurrection morn."

Oh, my dear friends, are there not some here tonight who will decide this question? Do accept this invitation; let the sickness come, let sorrow come, you will be sure of meeting at the marriage supper of the Lamb. Blessed is he who shall be found at that marriage feast.

Daniel is one of the great Bible figures with which even the unchurched have some vague familiarity.

Moody gave few sermons dealing with biblical characters, but those characters he selected were particularly outstanding. Daniel displayed the attributes of a true man of God. Moody found in him the qualities that lent themselves to the needs of the day.

This three-part message begins with Daniel's life as a child in Babylon. His desire to remain separate from the pagan nation brings about many great opportunities for him. He is well-educated, and as a result of faithfulness to God, he is placed within the inner circle of important men in the Babylonian kingdom.

Throughout his life, Daniel remained a man of great devotion to God. This not only led to his rise in power, but he was also subjected to great persecution. Moody brings out the character and witness of Daniel and encourages the audience to see him as an example of what a Christian should be. Daniel is also used as a model of how to win souls, a common theme in Moody's preaching.

CHAPTER SEVEN

The Prophet Daniel

PART ONE

I want to talk about the life of the prophet Daniel. The word means "God [is my Judge] . . . ." Therefore, he had to report himself to God and hold himself responsible to Him. I do not know just what time Daniel went down to Babylon. I know that in the third year of King Jehoiakim, Nebuchadnezzar took ten thousand of the chief men of Jerusalem and carried them captive down to Babylon. I am glad these chief men who stirred on the war were given into the great king's hands. Unlike too many of the ringleaders in our great war, they got the punishment on their own heads. Among the captives were four young men. They had been converted doubtless under Jeremiah, the "weeping prophet" that God had sent to the children of Israel. Many had mocked at [Jeremiah] when he lifted up his voice against their sins. They had laughed at his tears and told him to his face, as many say of us, that he was getting up a false excitement. But these four young men listened, and had the backbone to [stand up] for God.

And now, after they were [brought] to Babylon, the king said a number of the children should be educated, and ordered the same kind of meat and wine set before them that were used in his own palace, and that at the end of a year they should be brought before him. Daniel and his three friends were among these.

Now no young man ever comes to the city but has great temptation cross his path as he enters it. And just at this turning point in his life, as in Daniel's, must lie the secret of his success. If you see success in statesmen, in lawyers, or men in any walk in life, you ask the secret of it, and you find it in this same time of youth. Jacob turned away from God, and David turned away from God, but only just in proportion as they had not fully and entirely given themselves up to Him when they were young men.

Sold Out to God

Yes, that was the secret of this young man Daniel's success; he took his stand with God right on his entering the gate of Babylon and cried to God to keep him steadfast. And he needed to cry hard. A law of his and his nation's God was that no man should eat meat offered to idols; but now came the king's first edict, that this young man should eat the meat he himself did. I do not think it took young Daniel long to make up his mind. The law of God forbade it, and he would not do it. "He purposed in his heart"—in his heart, mark that—that he would not defile himself. He did not do it in his head, but love in his heart prompted him.

If some Chicago Christians could have advised Daniel, they'd have said, "Don't you do it; don't set aside the meat; that would be a species of Phariseeism. The moment you take your stand and say you won't eat it, you say in effect you are better than other people." That is the kind of talk too often heard now. Oh, yes, "When you are in Rome do as the Romans do"; they would have insisted to the poor young captive that he might, and ought to, carry out the commandments of his God when he was in his own country, but not there where he was a poor slave; he could not possibly carry along his religion down there to Babylon. Thank God, this young man said he would not eat, and ordering the meat taken away, got the eunuch to bring him [vegetables]. And behold, when he came before the king, the eunuch's fears were gone, for the faces of Daniel and the rest of the dear boys were fairer and fatter than any that the king looked down upon. They hadn't noses, like too many in our streets, as red as if they were just going to blossom. It is God's truth, and Daniel tested it, that cold water, with a clear conscience, is better than wine.

And the king one day had a dream, and all the wise men were called. But they all said, "We cannot interpret it; it is too hard." The king in wrath threatened them, and, still getting no answer, made an edict that all the wise men should be put to death. And the officers came to Daniel with the rest of the wise men, but Daniel was not afraid. I can imagine he prayed to God, falling low on his knees with his face to the earth, and asked Him what to do; and then he crawled into bed and slept like a child. We would hardly sleep well under such circumstances. And in his sleep God told him the meaning of the dream. There must have been joy among the wise men that one of their number had found it and that the king would save their lives. And he is brought before the king and cries out, "O king, while thou did'st lie with thy head on thy pillow, thou did'st dream, and in thy dream thou sawest a great image." I can imagine at these opening words how the king's eyes flashed, and how he cried out with joy, "Yes, that is it, the whole

thing comes back to me now." And then Daniel, in a deathlike stillness, unfolds all the interpretation, and tells the king that the golden head of the great image represents his own government. I suppose Babylon was the biggest city ever in the world. It was sixty miles around. Some writers put the walls from sixty-five to eighty-five feet high, and twenty-five feet wide; four chariots could ride abreast on top of them. A street fifteen miles long divided the grand city, and hanging gardens in acres made the public parks. It was like Chicago—so flat that they had to resort to artificial mounds; and, again like Chicago, the products of vast regions flowed right into and through it.

This great kingdom, Daniel told the king, was his own; but he said a destroying kingdom should come, and afterward a third and fourth kingdom, when at the last, the God of heaven should set up His kingdom. And Daniel himself lived to see the first overthrown, when the Medes and Persians came in, and centuries after came Alexander, and then the Romans. I believe in the literal fulfillment, so far, of Daniel's God-given words, and in the sure fulfillment of the final prophecy of the "stone cut out of the mountains without hands," that by-and-by shall grind the kingdoms of this world into dust, and bring in the kingdom of peace. Then will be the millennium, and Christ will sway His scepter over all the earth. Well, the king was very much pleased. He gave [Daniel] a place near the throne, and he became one of the chief men of the world, and all his three friends were put in high office. God had blessed them signally, and He blessed them still more, and that was perhaps a harder thing—in keeping them true to Him in their prosperity. Their faith and fortunes waxed strong together.

Time went on, and [then there was] a

crisis indeed. "Nebuchadnezzar, the king," we read, "made an image of gold, one hundred and ten feet high and nine feet wide." It was not gilded, but solid gold. When Babylon was pillaged the second time, a single god was found in the temple that was worth between two and three million pounds sterling. The king's monstrous image was set up in the plains of Dura, near to the city. I suppose he wanted to please his kingly vanity by inaugurating a universal religion. When the time came for the dedication, I do not suppose Daniel was there. He was perhaps in Egypt or some other province, on affairs of the empire. Counselors, satraps, high secretaries, and the princes of the people were ordered to hasten to the dedication, and when they should hear the sound of the cornet, flute, and psaltery announce that the great idol was consecrated, they were to bow down and worship it.

Perhaps they called the ceremony the unveiling of the monument, as we should say, but one command is certain, that at the given signal all the people were to fall to the earth in worship. But in the law of God there is something against that: "Thou shalt have no other gods but Me." God's law went right against the king's. Oh, would all of us have Daniel's three friends to do the right thing at any hazard! Would none of us, without backbone, have advised him to just bow down a little so that no one would notice it, or to merely bow down but not worship it! The hour came, and Daniel's friends refused to bow down. They refused utterly to bend the knee to a god of gold. How many cry out in this city, "Give me gold, give me money, and I will do anything." Such may think that men in Nebuchadnezzar's time should not bow down to a golden idol, but they themselves are every day doing just that very thing.

Money is their golden image, or position, or golden ambition.

Well, the informers came to the king, and told him that Shadrach, Meshach, and Abednego had stood with unbended knee, and straightway they were hurried before him, the old king speechless with rage and gesturing his commands. I can imagine that one last chance was given them, after the king finally regained his voice, and that one of them, probably Meshach, spoke up in respectful but firm voice, that they must obey God rather than man. At once the raging king cried out, "What is your God that He can deliver you out of our hands?" And in the same breath screamed a command to bind them hand and foot and cast them into the fiery furnace, and make it seven times hotter than ever. The command was instantly executed, and the flames leaped out from the door and consumed the officers who cast them in.

But Jesus was with His servants as the flames wreathed about them, and soon word was brought to the king that four men walked about in the flames. Yes, they walked there with Jesus—they didn't run—as in a green pasture and beside still waters. And directly the king rushed up and cried, "Ye sons of the living God, come forth." And behold, even the hair of their heads was not singed. Then made the king a royal edict, that all in his realm should reverence the God of Meshach, Shadrach, and Abednego.

These glorious heroes braved even death because God was with them. Oh, friends, we want to be Christians with the same backbone; men and women who stand up for the right, and never mind what the world may say. I believe, before God, there would be ten thousand conversions in Chicago in the next twenty-four hours had we only a perfect consecration. God grant it us out of the abundance of His grace. I cannot go on now, but will finish about Daniel next Sunday morning.

PART TWO

Last Sunday morning, we got to the second dream of King Nebuchadnezzar. This morning we will just take up where we broke off. The king had a dream, and he was greatly troubled. This time the particulars of the dream had not gone from him. They stood out vivid and clear in his mind as he sent out to fetch the wise men, and [he] called to them to give him the interpretation. But they could not give it.

When [the king] had his first dream he had summoned these same sooth-sayers, but they had stood silent. And now they stood silent again as the second dream was told them; they could not interpret it.

Once again he sends for the prophet Daniel that he had named after one of his gods, Belteshazzar. And the young prophet comes before the king, and as quick as the king sees him he feels sure that he will not get the meaning. Calling out from his throne, he tells how he had dreamed a dream, wherein he saw a tree in the midst of the earth, with branches that reached to heaven and the sight thereof to the ends of the earth; the beasts of the field had shelter under it, and the fowls of the air dwelt in the boughs thereof; and the tree was very fair and had much fruit, and all flesh was fed on it. And then, lowering his voice, he tells how, as he gazed, he saw a watcher and a holy one come down from heaven, who cried aloud, "Hew down the tree."

"And now," cries the king, "can you tell me the interpretation?" And for a time Daniel stands still and motionless. Does his heart fail him? The record simply says, that "for one hour he was as-tonished." The ready words doubtless rush to his lips, but he hates to let them out; he doesn't want to tell how the king's kingdom and mind are going to depart from him, and he is to wander forth to eat grass like a beast. The king, too, hesitates; a dark foreboding for a time gets the better of curiosity. But, directly, he nerves himself to hear the worst, and speaks very kindly, "Do not be afraid to tell me, oh, Daniel; let not the dream or its interpretation trouble thee." And at last Daniel speaks, "O king, thou art the man; God has exalted thee over every king, and over all the world, but thou shalt be brought low; thou shalt be driven out from men and eat grass among the beasts of the field; but thy kingdom—as the great watcher spared the stump of the tree—shall afterwards return to thee. Wherefore, O king, break off thy sins by righteousness and thine iniquities by showing mercy to the poor, if it may be a lengthening of thy tranquility."

And straightway the king repented in sackcloth and ashes, and so God [averted] the doom. But twelve months from that time Nebuchadnezzar was walking in his palace and boasting, "Is not this my great Babylon that I have built by the might of my power and for the honor of my majesty?" And behold while he yet spake, a voice came from heaven, saying, "Thy kingdom hath departed," and undoubtedly God then touched his reason, and straightway he ran madly through the gates to eat grass.

But his kingdom had not passed from him forever, and, according to the prophet's word, at the end of seven years, or possibly seven months, his reason came back, and he returned to his palace, and all his princes and officers gathered about him. Then immediately he sent out a new proclamation, and its closing words show his repentance and how Daniel had brought this mighty king to God.

> And at the end of the days I Nebuchadnezzar lifted up mine eyes unto heaven, and mine understanding returned unto me, and I blessed the Most High, and I praised and honoured him that liveth for ever, whose dominion is an everlasting dominion, and his kingdom is from generation to generation. . . .
>
> At the same time my reason returned unto me; and for the glory of my kingdom, mine honour and brightness returned unto me; and my counsellors and my lords sought unto me; and I was established in my kingdom, and excellent majesty was added unto me.
>
> Now I, Nebuchadnezzar, praise and extol . . . the King of heaven, all whose works are truth, and his ways judgment: and those that walk in pride he is able to abase (Dan. 4:34, 36, 37).

And then he passes from the stage; This is the last record of him; and undoubtedly he and Daniel now walk the crystal pavement together. Oh, that mighty monarch was led to the God of the Hebrews by the faith of this Hebrew slave, and just because he had a religion and dared to make it known.

God's Word on the Wall

But now we lose sight of the prophet for a few years, perhaps fifteen or twenty. The next we hear is that Belshazzar was on the throne, possibly as regent. He was believed to have been a grandson of Nebuchadnezzar. One day he said he would make Daniel the third ruler of the people if he would tell him the handwriting on the wall. He was probably second himself, and Daniel would be next to him. Of this prince we have only one glimpse. The feast scene is the first and last we have of him, and it is enough.

It was a great feast, and fully a thousand of his lords sat down together. Feasts in those days sometimes lasted six months. How long this one lasted we don't know. The king caroused with his princes and satraps and all the mighty men of Babylon, drinking and rioting and praying to gods of silver and gold and brass and stubble; just what we're doing today, if we bow the knee to the gods of this world. And the revelers, waxing wanton, even went into the temple and lay sacrilegious hands on the sacred vessels brought away from Jerusalem, and drank out of them, drank toasts to idols and harlots. And undoubtedly as they [were] drinking, they scoffed at the God of Israel. I see them swearing and rioting when—the king turns pale and trembles from head to foot. Above the golden candlesticks, on a bare space on the wall, he sees the writing of the God of Zion. He distinctly sees the terrible finger. His voice shakes with terror, but manages to falter out, "Bring in the wise men; any man that can read the handwriting I will make third ruler of the kingdom." And they come trooping in, but there is no answer, none of them can read it. They are skilled in Chaldean lore, but this [stumps] them. At last the queen comes in and whispers, "O king, there is one man in the kingdom who can read that writing; when your grandfather could not interpret his dreams he sent for Daniel the Hebrew, and he knew all about them. Can we not find him?"

And they find him, and now we see the man of God again standing before a king's throne. To the king's hurried promises of gifts and honors, he replies, "You can keep your rewards," and quietly turns his eyes on the writing. And he reads it at the first glance, for it is his Father's handwriting. "Mene," he says, "thy kingdom hath departed from thee"; "*tekel:* thou art weighed in the balance and found wanting." Oh, sinner, what if God should put you in the balance, and you have not got Christ in your soul? How that word of doom must have rung through the palace that night! "*Upharsin:* thy kingdom is divided, it is given over to the hands of the enemy."

And the destruction did not tarry. The king recovered himself, banished his fears, the dream, and its interpretation as idle, and he went on drinking in his hall. He thought he was perfectly secure. He thought the great walls of Babylon perfectly safe. But Darius was besieging the city. The enemy was right upon him. Was that safe?

Oh, sinners of Chicago, death and hell are right on you! Death and hell, I say . . . are just as close, maybe, as the slayer's sword to those midnight revelers. While they reveled, the river Euphrates, that flowed under the walls, was turned into another channel; the hosts of Medes and Persians rushed through, unobstructed, and in a few minutes more battered down the king's gate and broke through the palace guard into the inmost palace chamber. And the king was slain, and his blood flowed in that banquet hall.

We are next told Darius took the throne and set over the people one hundred twenty rulers, and over these three presidents, of whom Daniel was first. And so we find him in office again. I do not know how long he was in that position. But by-and-by a conspiracy took [hold] among his fellow officers to get rid of him. They got jealous and said, "Let's see if we can't get this man removed; he's bossed us long enough, the sanctimonious old Hebrew." And then he was so impracticable, they couldn't do anything with him. There were plenty of collectors and treasurers, but he kept such a close eye on them that they only made their salaries. There was no plundering of the government with Daniel at the head. He was president of the princes, and all revenue accounts passed before him. I can overhear the plotters whispering, "If we can only put him out of the way, we can make enough in two or three years to retire from office, have a city house in Babylon, and two or three villas in the country, have enough for all our days, we can go down to Egypt and see something of the world; as things are now we can only get our exact dues, and it will take years to get anything respectable—yes, let's down with this pious Jew." Well, they worked things so as to get an investigating committee, hoping to catch him in his accounts. But they found no occasion nor fault against him. If he had put any relatives in office it would have been found out; if he had been guilty of speculation, or in any way broken the unalterable statutes of the kingdom, it would have come to light. Oh, what a bright light was that, standing alone in that great city for God and the majesty of law!

Faithful in Prayer

But at last they struck on one weak point, they called it—he would worship no one but the God of Israel. The law of his God was his only assailable side. "If we can only get Darius," the conspirators plotted, "to forbid anyone making a request for thirty days except from the king himself, we shall trap him, and then can cast him among the lions; we will take good care to have the lions hungry." And the hundred and twenty princes took long counsel together. "Take care," they said; "you must draw up the paper which is to be signed by the king with a deal of care and discretion. The king loves [Daniel], and he has influence. Don't speak of the movement outside of this meeting; it might come to the ears of the king, and we must talk to the king ourselves." When the [proposal] was all ready, the hundred and twenty princes came to the king and opened their business with flattering speech.

If people come to praise me, I know they've something else coming—they've got a purpose for telling me I am a good man. And so we naturally hear these men saying, "King Darius, live forever." They tell him how prosperous the realm is, and how much the people think of him. And then they tell him, in the most plausible manner that ever was, that if he would be remembered by children's children to all ages, just to sign this decree; it would be a memorial of his greatness and goodness forever. And the king replies graciously, "What is the decree you wish me to sign?" and, casting his eye over the paper, goes on, "I don't see any objection to that." In the pleasure of granting a request he thinks nothing of Daniel, and the princes carefully refrain from jogging his memory. And he asks for his signet ring and gives the royal stamp.

The edict has become one of the laws of the Medes and Persians, that alter not; it reads, "Any man that worships any God but me for thirty days shall be cast into the lions' den." The news spreads all through the city; it comes out perhaps in the Babylon *Inter-ocean*, and quickly gets to the ears of Daniel. I can imagine some of them going to the prophet and advising him about the edict. "If you can only get out of the way for a little time, if you can just quit Babylon for thirty days, it will advance your own and the public interest together. You are the chief secretary and treasurer, in fact you are the chief ruler in the government; you are an important man, and can do as you please. Well, now, just you get out of Babylon. Or, if you will stay in Babylon, don't let them

catch you on your knees; at all events, don't pray at the window toward Jerusalem. If you will pray, close that window and pull down the curtain, and put something in the keyhole."

How many young men there are who don't dare to pray before their roommates; they've no moral courage. How many young men say to me, "Mr. Moody, don't ask me to get down on my knees at this prayer meeting." They want moral courage. Oh, thousands of men have been lost for want of moral courage, to dare to get down on their knees and pray to God. The idea of policy coming in here is all wrong. I can imagine how that old prince, Daniel, now in his gray hair, would view such a thought, that he is going to desert his God in his old age. All the remonstrances that must have been made fell dead; he just went on praying as usual three times a day, with his face toward Jerusalem. Our businessmen, too many of them, "don't have any time to pray," business is so pressing. But this old prophet found plenty of time, though secretary and treasurer of the most important empire in the world. And, besides his own business, he had to attend, doubtless, to much belonging by right to those hundred and twenty. But he would never have been too busy or ashamed at a prayer meeting to stand up for God. He had a purpose, and he dared to make it known. He knew whom he worshipped. The idea of looking back to church records of years ago to see whether a man has professed religion is all wrong. In Babylon they knew whom Daniel believed in; these hundred and twenty knew the very day after the passing of the edict.

[Daniel] knows they are watching near his window when the hour comes for prayer. He can see two men close at his side, and knows they are spies; perhaps they may be taking down every word he says for the papers. The moment comes, and he falls on his knees, and in tones louder than ever makes his prayer to the God of Israel, Abraham, Isaac, and Jacob. He doesn't omit to pray for the king. (It is right to pray for our rulers. If we quit praying for our rulers, our country will go to pieces. The reason they are not better, oftentimes, is just because we do not pray for them.) And now the spies rush to the king and say, "O Darius, live forever; do you know there is a man in your kingdom that won't obey you?" "Won't obey me! Who is he?" "Why, that man Daniel." And the king says, "I know he won't bow down and worship me; I know that he worships the God of heaven." Then the king sets his heart to deliver him all the day from the hands of those one hundred and twenty men. But they come to him and say, "If you want to break your law your kingdom will depart, your subjects will no longer obey you; you must deliver him to the lions' den."

And Darius is compelled, and at last gives the word to have him sent away and cast into the lions' den, and these men take good care to have the den filled with the hungriest beasts in Babylon. He is thrown headlong into the den, but the angel of God flies down, and [Daniel] lights unharmed on the bottom. The lions' mouths are stopped. They are as harmless as lambs. The old prophet at the [usual] hour drops on his knees and prays with his face towards Jerusalem, as calmly as in his chamber. And when it gets late, he just lays his head on one of the lions and goes to sleep, and undoubtedly no one in all Babylon slept sweeter than Daniel in the lions' den.

In the palace the king cannot sleep. He orders his chariot, and early in the morning rattles over the pavement and jumps down at the lions' den. I see him alight from his chariot in eager haste, and hear him cry down through the mouth of the den, "Oh, Daniel, servant of the living God, is thy God whom thou reverest continually, able to deliver thee from the lions?" Hark! Why, it is a resurrection voice! It is Daniel saying, "My God is able; He hath sent one of his angels and hath shut the lions' mouths." I can see them now just embrace each other, and together they jump into the chariot and away they go back to the palace to breakfast.

PART THREE

I want to say some further things about Daniel. I want to refer to how an angel came to him, and, as we read in the twelfth chapter of Daniel, told him he was a man greatly beloved. Another angel had come to him with the same message. It is generally thought this last angel was the same one spoken of in Revelation, first chapter, thirteenth verse, as coming to John when banished at the Isle of Patmos. People thought he was sent off there alone; but no; the angel of God was with him. And so with Daniel. Here in the tenth chapter and fifth verse he says, "Then I lifted up mine eyes, and behold, a certain man clothed with fine linen, and otherwise arrayed as God's messenger, who cried, 'Oh, Daniel, a man greatly beloved, understand the words which I speak unto thee, and stand upright, for unto thee am I now sent.'" It was Daniel's need that brought him from the glory land. It was the Son of God right by his side in that strange land. And that was the second time that the word came to him that he was greatly beloved. Yes, three times a messenger came from the throne of God to tell him this.

I love to speak of that precious verse in the eleventh chapter, the thirty-second verse: "The people that do know their God shall be strong, and do exploits," and also of the twelfth chapter and second and third verses: "And many of them that sleep in the dust of the earth shall awake, some to everlasting life, and some to shame and everlasting contempt; and they that be wise shall shine as the brightness of the firmament; and they that turn many to righteousness as the stars for ever and ever."

This was the angel's comfort to Daniel, and a great comfort it was. The fact with all of us is that we like to shine. There is no doubt about that. Every mother likes her child to shine. If her boy shines at school by getting to the head of his class, the proud mother tells all the neighbors, and she has a right to. But it is not the great of this world that will shine the brightest. For a few years they may shed bright light, but they go out in darkness, without an inner light. Supplying the brightness they go out in black darkness.

Where are the great men who did not know Daniel's God? Did they shine long? Why, we know of Nebuchadnezzar and the rest of them scarcely a thing, except as they fill in the story about these humble men of God. We are not told that statesmen shall shine; they may for a few years or days, but they are soon forgotten. Look at those great ones who passed away in the days of Daniel. How wise in counsel they were, how mighty and victorious over hundreds of nations. What gods upon earth they were! Yet their names are forgotten and written in the grave. So-called philosophers—do they live? Behold men of science—scientific men they call themselves—going down into the bowels of the earth, digging away at some carcass and trying to make it talk against the voice of God. They shall go down to death by-and-by, and their names shall rot. But the man of God shines. Yes, he it is who shall shine as the stars forever and ever. This Daniel has been gone for

2,500 years, but still increasing millions read of his life and actions. And so it shall be to the end; he will only get better known and better loved; he shall only shine the brighter as the world grows older. Of a truth, they that be wise and turn many to righteousness shall shine on, like stars to eternity.

And this blessed, thrice blessed, happiness, like all the blessings of God's kingdom, is for everyone. Even without the first claim to education or refinement you can shine if you will. One of you sailors there can shine forever if you only go to work for the kingdom. The Bible doesn't say the great shall shine but they that turn many to righteousness.

A false impression has got hold of many of God's people. They have the idea that only a few can talk about God's affairs. Nine-tenths of the people say, if anything is to be done for the souls of men, "Oh, the ministers must do it." It doesn't enter into the heart of the people that they have any part in the matter. It is the devil's work to keep Christians from the blessed luxury of winning souls to God. Anyone can do this work. A little girl only eleven years old came to me in a Sunday school and said, "Won't you please pray that God will make me a winner of souls?" I felt so proud of her, and my pride was justified, for she has become one of the best winners of souls in this country. Oh, suppose she lives threescore years, and goes on winning four or five souls every year; at the end of her journey there will be three hundred souls on the way to glory. And how long will it be before that little company swells to a great army. Don't you see how that little mountain [brook] keeps swelling till it carries everything before it? Little trickling streams have run into it, till now, a mighty river, it has great cities on its banks, and the commerce of all nations floating on its waters. So when a single soul is won to Christ you cannot see the result. A single one multiplies to a thousand and that into ten thousand. Perhaps a million shall be the fruit; we cannot tell. We only know that the Christian who has turned so many to righteousness shall indeed shine forever and ever. Look at those poor fishermen, Jesus' disciples, how unlettered. They were not learned men, but great in winning souls. So [there is] not a child here but can work for God.

A Desire to Work for God

The one thing that keeps people from work is that they don't have the desire. If a man has this desire God soon qualifies him. And what we want is God's qualification; it must come from Him. I have been thinking what shall be done for the next thirty days that I continue to preach here. If I should just put it to vote, and asked all Christians who wanted prayers to rise, all of you, I know, would rise. There are at least three thousand Christians here. Now, is it too much to ask that three thousand Christians will each lead one soul to Christ this coming week? The Son of God died on the cross for you. Right here in this tabernacle you can tell those weeping over their sins about God and heaven. How many times I have watched, just to see if Christians would speak to these sorrowing ones! If we only had open-eyed watchers for souls, there wouldn't be a night but five hundred or a thousand inquirers would crowd into the inquiry rooms. These anxious inquirers are at every meeting, just waiting to have warm-hearted Christians bring them to Christ. They are timid, but will always listen to one speaking to them about Christ. Suppose each one of you now prayed, "Give me some soul this week for my hire." What

would be the result? This room would not hold the multitude sending up shouts of praise to God and making heaven glad. Where there is an anxious sinner there is the place for the Christian.

A little bed-ridden boy I knew kept mourning that he couldn't work for Jesus. The minister told him to pray, and pray he did; and the persons he prayed for one by one felt the load of their sins and professed Christ. When he heard that such a one had not given in, he just turned his face to the wall and prayed harder. Well, he died, [and] by his little memorandum it was found that he had prayed for fifty-six persons daily by name, and before he was buried all of them had given their hearts to Jesus. Tell me that little boy won't shine in the kingdom of God! These little ones can be used by God.

I remember a good many years ago I resolved I wouldn't let a day pass without talking to someone about their soul's salvation. And it was in that school God qualified me to speak the gospel. If we [are] faithful over small things God will promote us. If God says, "Speak to that young man," obey the word, and you will be given by-and-by plenty of souls. I went down past the corner of Clark and Lake streets one day, and, fulfilling my vow, on seeing a man leaning up against a lamppost, I went up to him and said, "Are you a Christian?" He damned me and cursed me and said to mind my own business. He knew me, but I didn't know him. He said to a friend of his that afternoon that he had never been so insulted in his life, and he told him to say to me that I was damning the cause I pretended to represent. Well, the friend came and delivered his message. "Maybe I am doing more hurt than good," I said; "maybe I am mistaken and God hasn't shown me the right way." That was the time I was sleeping and living in the Young Men's Christian Association rooms, where I was then president, secretary, janitor, and everything else. Well, one night after midnight I heard a knock at the door. And there on the step leading into the street stood this stranger I had made so mad at the lamppost, and he said he wanted to talk to me about his soul's salvation. He said, "Do you remember the man you met about three months ago at a lamppost, and how I cursed you? I have had no peace since that night, I couldn't sleep. Oh, tell me what to do to be saved." And we just fell down on our knees, and I prayed, and that day he went to the noon prayer meeting and openly confessed the Savior, and soon after went to the war a Christian man. I do not know but he died on some southern battlefield or in a hospital, but I expect to see him in the kingdom of God. Oh, how often have I thanked God for that word to that dying sinner that He put into my mouth!

And I have just been engaged in this personal work all my life. God's business is not to be done wholesale. Think of the Master Himself talking just to Nicodemus and then how He talked to that poor woman at the well of Samaria. Christ's greatest utterances were delivered to congregations of one or two. How many are willing to speak to tens of thousands but not to speak to a few! I knew a man who was going to get rich and do large things for God but he never did anything; he wouldn't do little things—that was the secret. Oh, be willing, Christians, to be built into the temple, as a polished capstone, or just a single brick—no matter just how, but somehow. Say to yourself in your home, in your Sunday school classes, in your daily rounds, "I'll not let this sun go down till I lead one soul to Christ." And then, having done all, shall you shine as

gems in the great white throne forever and ever.

I want to tell you how I got the first impulse to work solely for the conversion of men. For a long time after my conversion I didn't accomplish anything. I hadn't got into my right place; that was it. I hadn't thought enough of this personal work. I'd get up in prayer meeting, and I'd pray with the others, but just to go up to a man and take hold of his coat and get him down on his knees, I hadn't yet got around to that.

It was in 1860 the change came. In the Sunday school I had a pale delicate young man as one of the teachers. I knew his burning piety, and assigned him to the worst class in the school. They were all girls, and it was an awful class. They kept gadding around in the schoolroom and were laughing and carrying on all the while. And this young man had better success than anyone else. One Sunday he was absent, and I tried myself to teach the class, but [I] couldn't do anything with them; they seemed farther off than ever from any concern about their souls. Well, the day after his absence, early Monday morning, the young man came into the store where I worked, and, tottering and bloodless, [he] threw himself down on some boxes. "What's the matter?" I said. "I have been bleeding at the lungs, and they have given me up to die," he said. "But you are not afraid to die?" I questioned. "No," said he. "I am not afraid to die, but I have got to stand before God and give an account of my stewardship, and not one of my Sabbath school scholars has been brought to Jesus. I have failed to bring one, and haven't any strength to do it now." He was so weighed down that I got a carriage and took that dying man in it, and we called at the homes of every one of his scholars, and to each one he said, as best his faint voice would let him, "I have come to just ask you to come to the Savior," and then he prayed as I never heard before. And for ten days he labored in that way, sometimes walking to the nearest houses. And at the end of that ten days every one of that large class had yielded to the Savior.

Full well I remember the night before he went away (for the doctors said he must hurry to the south), how we held a true lovefeast. It was the very gate of heaven, that meeting. He prayed and prayed; he didn't ask them, he didn't think they could pray; and then we sang, "Blessed Be the Tie That Binds." It was a beautiful night in June that he left on the Michigan Southern, and I was down to the train to help him off. And every one [of] those girls gathered there again, all unknown to each other; and the depot seemed a second gate to heaven, in the joyful, yet tearful, communion and farewells between those newly re-deemed souls and him whose crown of rejoicing it will be that he led them to Jesus. At last the gong sounded, and, supported on the platform, the dying man shook hands with each one and whispered, "I will meet you yonder."

Some of the very best, most constant teachers I had before going to Europe were converted at that time, and they, in their turn, have gathered many sheaves, and I myself was led by this incident, this wonderful blessing of God on individual effort, to throw up my business and give my whole strength to God's work.

Shall not that young man have a high place, a place very near the Savior of men, in the day when He makes up His jewels? Oh, friends, if you want to shine in the kingdom of God, work for Him today. Shall we not, every one, go out of this building saying, "I will try to bring one soul to Christ today?"

Blindness comes in physical and spiritual varieties. In this message, Moody describes how spiritual blindness has been placed upon humanity by the devil for the purpose of hiding the gospel.

Moody uses the analogy of physical blindness very effectively, showing that it is very similar to spiritual blindness. However, unlike physical sightlessness, there is hope of recovery for those without spiritual vision.

Several forms of blindness exist: greed, work, ambition, pleasure, fashion, and alcohol prevent those afflicted from coming to Christ. Illustrations abound, giving the sermon extra power in touching many hearts, giving them a chance to see their dilemma and do something about it.

CHAPTER EIGHT

Spiritual Blindness

You who have been here during the week have heard me speaking on the fourth chapter of Luke and the eighteenth verse. I spoke on the first three clauses of that verse, and we have now come to the next clause, in which He tells us that He came to give sight to the blind—for the recovery of sight to the blind. Paul tells us, in his second epistle to the Corinthians, fourth chapter, third and fourth verse,

> But if our gospel be hid, it is hid to them that are lost; in whom the god of this world hath blinded the minds of them which believe not, lest the light of the glorious gospel of Christ, who is the image of God, should shine unto them.

"If the gospel be hid, . . . in whom the god of this world hath blinded." This world is just one large blind asylum—it is full of blind people. Last Wednesday night I tried to tell you that the world was full of broken hearts; last night I tried to tell you that the world was full of captives, bound hand and foot in sin, and tonight I tell you that it is full of blind people. Not only blind people, but they are bound and brokenhearted. You might say that nearly all those in the world come under [those] three headings.

Now just look at the contrast between Satan and Christ. Satan breaks men's hearts. But Christ binds them up. Satan binds the people of this earth hand and foot, but Christ breaks the fetters and sets them free; Satan makes us blind, but Christ opens our eyes. He came to do this, and just see how He was received. He went into that synagogue at Nazareth and preached this glorious gospel, and commenced by telling them that the Spirit of the Lord was upon Him. He went on to tell them that He had come to save them; and what did they do? They thrust Him out of the city and took Him to the brow of the hill, and they would have hurled Him into hell if they could. And men have been as bitter toward the gospel all along these eighteen hundred years. Why, some men would tear the preacher of it limb from limb if it wasn't for the law.

Then we find when He goes to Bethany, and raises up the brother of Martha and Mary and binds up broken hearts as He goes along and preaches mercy, that they want to kill Him. We find Him in the third chapter of Mark setting the captive free. Here we find a man possessed of demons, whom no one could cure, set at liberty by the Son of man, and because they lost a few swine in the healing, they told Him to depart from their coasts. Then we find Him just a few days before His death, almost on His way to Calvary, giving sight to that blind man. And for all this they take him to that mount and nail him to a cross. Oh what blindness!

Physical and Spiritual Blindness

We are told that there are 3,000,000 people in the world who are called blind. Everyone calls them blind because they haven't their natural sight. But do you ever think how many are spiritually blind in this world? Why, if there are 3,000,000 people in the world who have not their natural sight, how many do you suppose are spiritually blind? We sympathize with those who have lost their sight. Nothing appeals to our sympathy so readily. I believe I could raise thousands of dollars among you by telling you about some blind one who is suffering for the necessities of life through his affliction. How many of you wouldn't put your hand in your pockets and give liberally? How it moves our compassion—how it moves our hearts as we see blind men, women, or children in the streets. How your heart goes out to those poor unfortunates.

I was at a meeting in London, and I heard a man speaking with wonder, but power and earnestness. "Who is that man?" I asked, my curiosity being excited. "Why, that is Dr.———. He is blind." I felt some interest in this man, and at the close of the meeting I sought an interview, and he told me that he had been stricken blind when very young. His mother took him to a doctor and asked him about his sight. "You must give up all hope," the doctor said. "Your boy is blind, and will be forever." "What, do you think my boy will never see?" asked his mother. "Never again." The mother took her boy to her bosom and cried, "Oh, my boy, who will take care of you when I am gone—who will look [after] you!" Forgetting the faithfulness of that God she had [taught] him to love. He became a servant of the Lord, and was permitted to print the Bible in twelve different languages, printed in the raised letters, so that all blind people could read the Scriptures themselves. He had a congregation, my friends, of 3,000,000 people, and I think that blind man was one of the happiest beings in all London. He was naturally blind, but he had eyes to his soul, and could see a bright eternity in the future. He had built his foundation upon the living God.

We pity those who have not their natural sight; but how you should pity yourself if you are spiritually blind. If we could get all the spiritually blind in this city! You talk about those great political meetings, they would be nothing to the crowd you would collect. Why, just look at all the men in this city who are blind, and many of them are in the churches. This has been the trouble with men always. Christ couldn't get men to understand they were blind; He couldn't even get His disciples to open their eyes until after He went up to heaven. And then they received the spiritual truth. How many are the professed children of God we read of in the book of Revelation?

Money Blindness

I think tonight I might pick up some of the different classes who are blind. I am somewhat acquainted with the rich men of this city, and I don't think it would take long to prove that the leading men of this city are blind—blind to their own interests. Take a man just spending all his strength and energies to get money. He is money blind. He is so blind in his pursuit that he cannot see the God of heaven. Money is his god. His cry is continually "Money, money," and it is the cry of many here in Chicago. They don't care about God, don't care about salvation, don't heed their eternal condition so long as they get money, money, money. And a great many of them have got it. But how lean their souls are. God has given them the desire of their heart, but He has given them leanness of soul.

I heard of a man who had accumulated great wealth. And death came upon him suddenly, and he realized, as the saying is, that "there was no bank in the shroud," that he couldn't take anything away with him; we may have all the money on earth, but we must leave it behind us. He called a lawyer in and commenced to will away his property before he went away. His little girl couldn't understand exactly where he was going, and she said, "Father, have you got a home in that land you are going to?" The arrow went down to his soul. "Got a home there?" The rich man had hurled away God, and neglected to secure a home there for the sake of his money, and he found it was now too late. He was money mad, and he was money blind. It wouldn't be right for me to give names, but I could tell you a good many here in Chicago who are going on in this way—spending all their lives in the accumulation of what they cannot take with them. This is going on while many poor people are suffering for the necessities of life. These men don't know they are blind—money is their god.

Business Blindness

There is another class who don't care so much for money. We might call them business blind. It is business, business, business with them all the time. In the morning they haven't time to worship. They must attend to business; must get down to the store. Down they run, and haven't time to get home to dinner. They mustn't let anyone get ahead of them; and they get home late at night, and their families have gone to bed. They scarcely ever see their children. It is all business with them.

A man told me not long ago, "I must attend to my business. That is my first consideration, and see that none gets ahead of me." That is his god. I don't care if he is an elder or a deacon in the church. [Business] is his god. The god of business has blinded him. Look at the

merchant prince who died the other day. Men called him a clever, shrewd man. Call that shrewdness—to pile up wealth for a lifetime and leave no record behind so that we know he has gone to heaven? He rose above men in his business; he devoted his whole soul to it, and the world called him a power among men; the world called him great. But let the Son of God write his obituary; let Him put an epitaph on his tombstone, and it would be, "Thou fool." Man says, "I must attend to business first"; God says, "Seek first the kingdom of God." I don't care what your business may be; it may be honorable, legitimate, and all that, and you think you must attend to it first; bear in mind that God tells every man to seek His kingdom first.

Political Blindness

There is another class of people who are blind. They don't care so much about riches, they are not very ambitious to become rich, they don't spend their lives in business matters. They are politically blind. They are mad over politics; they are bound up in the subject. There will be a great many broken hearts in a week hence. They have got their favorite candidate to attend to and they cannot find time to worship God. How little prayer there has been about the election. There has been a good deal of work, but how much praying has been done? We want prayer to go up all over our land that high and honest men may rule over us. But they are so excited over this election that they have no time to pray to the God of heaven. They are politically blind.

How many men within our recollection, who have set their hearts upon the Presidential chair, have gone down to the grave with disappointment? They were poor, blind men, and the world called them great. Oh, how foolish; how blind. They didn't seek God; they only sought one thing—greatness—position and office. They were great, brilliant, clever men, but when they were summoned into the presence of their God, what a wreck. Men so brilliant might have wielded an influence for the Son of God that would have lived in the hearts of the people for generations to come, and the streams of their goodness might have flowed long after they went to heaven. But they lived for the world, and their works went to dust.

Pleasure Blindness

But a great number of people don't care for business or politics, they only want a little money so as to get pleasure. How many men have been blinded by pleasure. A lady told me in the inquiry room she would like to become a Christian, but there was a ball coming on, and she didn't want to become a Christian until after the ball. The ball was worth more then to her than the kingdom of God. For this ball she would put off the kingdom of God until it was over, forgetting that death might come to her in the meantime and usher her into the presence of God. How blind she was, and many are just like her. The kingdom of God is offered to them without money and without price, and yet for a few days of pleasure they forfeit heaven and everything dear to their eternity.

I was talking to a lady who, with the tears running down her cheeks upon my speaking to her, said, "The fact is, if I become a Christian I have to give up all pleasure. I cannot go to a theater; I cannot read any novels; I cannot play cards. I have nothing else to do." Oh, what blindness! Look at the pleasure of being taken into the Lord's vineyard, and the joy and luxury of working for Him and leading souls to Christ. And people with their eyes wide open would rather bend

down to the god of pleasure than become Christians.

Fashion Blindness

Then there is the god of fashion. How many women just devote their lives to it. They want to see the last bonnet, the last cloak, the last dress. They can't think of anything else. Said a lady to me, "I am always thinking of fashion; it doesn't matter if I get down on my knees to pray, I am always thinking of a new dress." You may laugh at this, but it's true. Pleasure in the ballroom and fashion is the god of a great many people. Oh, that we may lift our eyes to something nobler. Suppose you don't have so many dresses and give something to the poor, you will have something then which will give you joy and comfort that will last you always. I pity the man or woman who lives for the day like the butterfly—those whose minds are fixed upon fashion and pleasure, and have no time to look to their perishing souls. A good many people don't know they are [blind].

Look at that young man. You call him a fast young man. He has got a salary of one thousand dollars, and it costs him three thousand dollars to live. Where does he get the money? Where does it come from? His father cannot give it to him because he is poor. His employer begins to get suspicious. "I only give him one thousand dollars a year, and he is living at the rate of three thousand dollars. By-and-by he looks into his account book and finds it overdrawn. Thus he is ruined—character blasted. Oh, how many are of this stamp in Chicago? It is only a question of time. How many young men have we got living beyond their income—taking money out of their employer's drawer. They say, "Well, I am going to the theater tonight, and I will just take a dollar; I will put it back next week." But when next week comes, he hasn't put it back and takes another dollar. He has taken two dollars now. He keeps on draw, draw, drawing, when by-and-by it all comes out. He loses his place, doesn't get any letters of recommendation, and the poor man is ruined. My friends, this is not the description of an isolated case. This class is all over the country. I wish I could send you the letters I get about just such cases.

I got one the other day from a young mother with a family of beautiful children. She told me how happy they had lived—husband, wife, and children, and how one night her husband came home excited, his face white with terror, and said, "I've got to fly from justice. Good-bye." He has gone from her, and she said it seemed as if she could die; her husband disgraced and starving couldn't get anything to do. Her cry seemed to be "Help, help me." Is not the country full of such cases? Is it not blindness and madness for men to go on in this way? If anyone is here tonight following in the way of these men, I pray God your eyes may be opened before you are led to death and ruin.

Alcohol Blindness

You know we had a full meeting today, and the subject was "Intemperance." How many young men are there who spend their time in the saloons of the city? I am afraid many will be led astray next Tuesday. I always dread an election day—I generally see so many young men beastly drunk. They are led away, and that is another quick road down to hell. May the young men see the folly of this, and on that day stand firm. May God open your eyes. How many young men are there whose characters have been blasted by strong drink? How many brilliant men in the Chicago bar have gone down to death by

it? Some of the noblest statesmen, some of the most brilliant orators and men of all professions have been borne down to the drunkard's grave. May God open your eyes to show the folly of tampering with strong drink.

Now, many men say, "I am not going down to the grave of a drunkard." They think they have strength to stop when they like. When it gets hold, there is nothing within us by which we can save ourselves. He alone can give you power to resist the cup of temptation. He alone can give you power to overcome its influence, if you only will believe Him. The god of this world has been trying to make you believe that a man can do it himself, and Christ will have nothing to do with him. The god of this world is a liar. I come with authority to tell you—I don't care how far gone you are; don't care how blessed you may be—that the Son of God can and will save you if you only believe Him. If there is one here tonight under the power of strong drink come [to Him] tonight. We lift up our voice to warn you.

Look at that man in a boat on Niagara River. He is only about a mile from the rapids. A man on the bank shouts to him, "Young man, young man, the rapids are not far away, you'd better pull for the shore." "You attend to your own business; I will take care of myself," he replies. Like a great many people here, and ministers, too, they don't want any evangelist here—don't want any help, however great the danger ahead. On he goes, sitting coolly in his boat. Now he has got a little nearer, and a man from the bank of the river sees his danger, and shouts, "Stranger, you'd better pull for the shore; if you go further you'll be lost. You can be saved now if you pull in." "Mind your business, and you'll have enough to do; I'll take care of myself." Like a good many men, he is asleep to the danger that's hanging over him while he is in the current. And I say, drinking young man, don't you think you are standing still. You are in the current, and if you don't pull for a rock of safety you will go over the precipice.

On he goes. I can see him in the boat laughing at the danger. A man on the bank is looking at him, and he lifts up his voice and cries, "Stranger, stranger, pull for the shore; if you don't you will lose your life"; and the young man laughs at him—mocks him. That is the way with hundreds in Chicago. If you go to them and point out their danger, they will jest and joke at you.

By-and-by he says, "I think I hear the rapids—yes, I hear them roar"; and he seizes his oars and pulls with all his strength, but the current is too great, and nearer and nearer he is drawn on to that abyss, until he gives one unearthly scream, and over he goes. Ah, my friends, this is the case with hundreds in this city. They are in the current of riches, of pleasure, of drink, that will take them to the whirlpool. Satan has got them blindfolded, and they are on their road to the bottomless pit.

We hear some men say in a jesting way, "Oh, we are sowing our wild oats; we will get over this by-and-by." I have seen men reap their wild oats. It's all well enough sowing, but when it comes to the reaping it's a different thing. I remember I went home one night and found all the people in alarm. They had seen a man come running down the street, and as he approached the house he gave an unearthly roar, and in terror

they bolted the door. He came right up to my door and, instead of ringing the bell, just tried to push the door in. They asked him what he wanted, and he told them he wanted to see me. They said I was at the meeting, and away he ran, and they could hear him groan as he disappeared. I was coming along North Clark Street, and he shot past me like an arrow. But he had seen me, and [he] turned and seized me by the arm, saying eagerly, "Can I be saved tonight? The devil is coming to take me to hell at one o'clock tonight." "My friend, you are mistaken." [I] thought the man was sick. But he persisted that the devil had come and laid his hand upon him and told him that he might have till one o'clock, and he said, "Won't you go up to my room and sit with me?" I got some men up to his room to see to him. At one o'clock the devils came into that room, and all the men in that room could not hold him. He was reaping what he had sown. When the Angel of Death came and laid his cold hand on him, oh, how he cried for mercy—how he beseeched for pardon.

Ah, yes, young men, you may say in a laughing and jesting way, you are sowing your wild oats, but the reaping time is coming. May God show you tonight what folly it is—what a miserable life you are leading. May we lift our hearts here to the God of all grace, so that we may see our lost and ruined condition if we do not come to Him. Christ stands ready and willing to save—to save tonight all those who are willing to be saved.

The Bible is filled with the call for people to repent and come to God in one form or another. Moody never failed in any sermon to make the same call. No matter what the message dealt with, he always encouraged the unconverted to renounce whatever it was holding them back and accept Christ.

Repentance is more than a feeling of sorrow for sin. It consists of totally turning away from the sin or sins that are preventing a person from coming to Christ. God hates sin and demands full repentance from the sinner.

Men such as Cain, Judas, and King Saul displayed signs of sorrow for their actions, but they never gave any evidence of totally turning away from their sin.

CHAPTER NINE

Repentance

You will find my text tonight in the seventeenth chapter of Acts, part of the thirtieth verse: "but now commandeth all men everywhere to repent." I have heard a number of complaints about the preaching here in the tabernacle, that repentance has not been touched upon. The fact is, that I have never had very great success in preaching upon repentance. When I have preached it people haven't repented. I've had far more success when I've preached Christ's goodness. But tonight I will preach about repentance, so you will have no more cause of complaint. I believe in repentance just as much as I believe in the Word of God.

When John the Baptist came to preach to the Jewish nation his one cry was, "Repent! Repent!" But when Christ came he changed it to, "The blood of the Lamb taketh away the sin of the world." I would rather cry, "The blood of the Lamb taketh away the sin of the world," than talk about repentance. And when Christ came [He said,] "Repent ye," but He soon pointed them to something higher—He told them about the goodness of God. It is the goodness of God that produces repentance.

When, upon the Day of Pentecost they asked what to do to be saved, [He told] men, "Repent, every one of you." When Christ sent His disciples out to preach, two by two, we find the message He gave them to deliver was, "Repent ye, for the kingdom of heaven is at hand." It is clearly preached throughout the Scriptures. There is a good deal of trouble among people about what repentance really is. If you ask people what it is, they will tell you, "It is feeling sorry." If you ask a man if he repents, he will tell you, "Oh, yes; I generally feel sorry for my sins." That is not repentance. It is something more than feeling sorry. Repentance is turning right about and forsaking sin. I wanted to speak on Sunday about that verse in Isaiah, which says, "Let the guilty forsake his way, and the unrighteous man his thoughts." That is what it is. If a man doesn't turn from his sin he won't be accepted of God, and if righteousness doesn't produce a turning about—a turning from bad to good—it isn't true righteousness.

Sorry, But Unrepentant

Unconverted people have got an idea that God is their enemy. Now, let me impress this, and I told you the same the other night, God hates sin with a perfect hatred; He will punish sin wherever He finds it. Yet He at the same time loves the sinner and wants him to repent and turn to Him. If men will only turn they will find mercy, and find it just the moment they turn to Him. You will find men sorry for their misdeeds. Cain, no doubt, was sorry, but that was not true repentance. There is no cry recorded in the Scriptures as coming from him, "O my God, O my God, forgive me." There was no repentance in him, only feeling sorry. Look at Judas. There is no sign that he turned to God—no sign that he came to Christ asking forgiveness. Yet he probably felt sorry. He was very likely filled with remorse and despair;

but he didn't repent. Repentance is turning to Him who loved us and gave Himself for us. Look at King Saul, and see the difference between him and King David. David fell as low as Saul and a good deal lower—he fell from a higher pinnacle—but what was the difference between the two? David turned back to God and confessed his sin and was forgiven. But look at King Saul. There was no repentance there, and God couldn't save him till he repented.

You will find, all through the Scriptures, where men have repented God has forgiven them. Look at that publican when he went up to pray; he felt his sin so great that he couldn't look up to heaven—all he could do was to smite his heart and cry, "God forgive me a sinner." There was turning to God—repentance—and that man went down to his home forgiven. Look at that prodigal. His father couldn't forgive him while he was still in a foreign land and squandering his money in riotous living, but the moment he came home repentant, how soon that father forgave him—how quickly he came to meet him with the word of forgiveness. It wouldn't have done any good to forgive the boy while he was in that foreign country unrepentant. He would have despised all favors and blessings from his father. That is the position [in which] the sinner stands toward God. He cannot be forgiven and get His blessing until he comes to God repenting of all his sins and asking the blessing.

Now, we read in Scripture that God deals with us as a father deals with a son. Fathers and mothers, you who have children, let me ask by way of illustration, suppose you go home, and you find that while you have been here your boy has gone to your private drawer and stolen five dollars of your money. You go to him and say, "John, did you take that money?" "Yes, father, I took that money,"

he replies. When you hear him saying this without any apparent regret, you won't forgive him. You want to get at his conscience; you know it would do him an injury to forgive him unless he confesses his wrong. Suppose he won't do it. "Yes," he says, "I stole your money, but I don't think I've done wrong." The mother cannot, the father cannot forgive him, unless he sees he has done wrong, and wants forgiveness.

That's the trouble with the sinners in Chicago. They've turned against God, broken His commandments, trampled His law under their feet, and their sins hang upon them; until they show signs of repentance their sin will remain. But the moment they see their iniquity and come to God, forgiveness will be given them and their iniquity will be taken out of their way. Said a person to me the other day, "It is my sin that stands between me and Christ." "It isn't," I replied, "it's your own will." That's what stands between the sinner and forgiveness. Christ will take all your iniquities away if you will. Men are so proud that they won't acknowledge and confess before God. Don't you see on the face of it, if your boy won't repent you cannot forgive him, and how is God going to forgive a sinner if he doesn't repent? If He was allowing an unrepentant sinner into His kingdom, there would be war in heaven in twenty-four hours. You cannot live in a house with a boy who steals everything he can lay his hands on. You would have to banish him from your house.

A Self-willed Son

Look at King David [and] his son Absalom. After he had been sent away he got his friends to intercede for him to get him back to Jerusalem. They succeeded in getting him back to the city, but someone told the king that he hadn't repented, and his father would not see him. After he had been in Jerusalem some time, trying his best to get into favor and position again without repentance, he sent a friend, Joab, to the king, and told him to say to his father, "Examine me, and if you find no iniquity in me, take me in." He was forgiven, but the most foolish thing King David ever did was to forgive that young prince. What was the result? He drove him from the throne. That's what the sinner would do if he got into heaven unrepentant. He would just drive God from the throne—tear the crown from Him. No unrepentant sinner can get into the kingdom of heaven.

Ah, some people say, "I believe in the mercy of God; I don't believe God will allow one to perish; I believe everyone will get to heaven." Look at those antediluvians. Do you think He swept all those sinners, all those men and women who were too wicked to live on earth—do you believe He swept them all into heaven and left the only righteous man to wade through the flood? Do you think He would do this? And yet many men believe all will go into heaven. The day will come when you will wake up and know that you have been deceived by the devil. No unrepentant sinner will ever get into heaven; unless he forsakes his sin he cannot enter there. The law of God is very plain on this point: "Except a man repent." That's the language of Scripture. And when this is so plainly set down, why is it that men fold their arms and say, "God will take me into heaven anyway."

Suppose a governor elected today comes into office in a few months, and he finds a great number of criminals in prison, and he goes and says, "I feel for those prisoners. They cannot stay in jail any longer." Suppose some murders have been committed, and he says, "I am tender hearted; I can't punish those

men," and he opens the prison door and lets them all out. How long would that governor be in his position? These very men who are depending on the mercy of God would be the first to raise their voice against that governor. These men would say, "These murderers must be punished or society will be imperiled; life will not be safe." And yet they believe in the mercy of God whether they repent or not. My dear friends, don't go on under that delusion; it is a snare of the devil. I tell you the Word of God is true, and it tells us, "Except a man repent" there is not one ray of hope held out. May the Spirit of God open your eyes tonight and show you the truth—let it go into your hearts. "Let the wicked forsake his way and the unrighteous his thoughts."

Repentance and Fear

Now, my friends, repentance is not fear. A great many people say I don't preach up the terrors of religion. I don't want to—don't want to scare men into the kingdom of God. I don't believe in preaching that way. If I did get some in that way they would soon get out. If I wanted to scare men into heaven I would just hold the terror of hell over their heads and say, "Go right in." But that's not the way to win men. They don't have any slaves in heaven. They are all sons, and they must accept salvation voluntarily. Terror never brought a man in yet.

Look at a vessel tossed upon the billows, and sailors think it is going to the bottom and death is upon them. They fall down on their knees. And you would think they were all converted. They are not converted; they're only scared. There's no repentance there, and as soon as the storm is over and they get on shore, they are the same as ever. All their terror has left them—they've forgotten it, and they fall into their old habits. How many men have, while lying on a sick bed, and they thought they saw the terrors of death gathering around them, made resolutions to live a new life if they only get well again? But the moment they get better they forget all about their resolutions. It was only fear with them; that's not what we want to feel. Fear is one thing, and repentance is another. True repentance is the Holy Ghost showing sinners their sin. That's what we want. May the Holy Ghost reveal to each one out of Christ here tonight their lost condition unless they repent.

If God threw Adam out of Eden on account of one sin, how can you expect to get into the heavenly paradise with ten thousand? I can imagine someone saying, "I haven't got anything to repent of." If you are one of those Pharisees, I can tell you that this sermon will not reach your heart. I would like to find one man who could come up here and say, "I have no sin." If I was one of those who thought I had no sin to repent of, I'd never go to church; I would certainly not come up to the tabernacle. But could you find a man walking the streets of Chicago who could say this honestly? I don't believe there's a day passed over my head during the last twenty years but when night came I found I had some sin to repent of.

It is impossible for a man to live without sinning. There are so many things to draw away the heart and affections of men from God. I feel as if I ought to be repenting all the time. Is there a man here who can say honestly, "I have not got a sin that I need ask forgiveness for"? "I haven't one thing to repent of"? Some men seem to think that God has got ten different laws for each of those Ten Commandments, but if you have been guilty of breaking one you are guilty of breaking all. If a man steals

five dollars and another steals five hundred dollars, the one is as guilty of theft as the other. A man who has broken one commandment of God is as guilty as he who has broken ten. If a man doesn't feel this, and come to Him repentant and turn his face from sin toward God, there is not a ray of hope. Nowhere can you find one ray from Genesis to Revelation. Don't go out of this tabernacle saying, "I have nothing to repent."

I heard of a man who said he had been converted. A friend asked him if he had repented. "No," said he, "I never trouble my head about it." My friends, when a man becomes converted, the work has to be a little deeper than that. He has to become repentant, and try to atone for what he has done. If he is at war with anyone he has to go and be reconciled to his enemy. If he doesn't his conversion is the work of Satan. When a man turns to God he is made a new creature—a new man. His impulses all the time are guided by love. He loves his enemies and tries to repair all wrong he has done. This is a true sign of conversion. If this sign is not apparent, his conversion has never gotten from his head to his heart. We must be born of the spirit; hearts must be regenerated—born again. When a man repents and turns to the God of heaven, then the work is deep and thorough. I hope that everyone here tonight will see the necessity of true repentance when they come to God for a blessing, and may the Spirit move you to ask it tonight.

I can imagine some of you saying, "How, am I to repent tonight?" My friends, there are only two parties in the world. There has been a great political contest here today, and there have been two sides. We will not know before forty-eight hours which side has triumphed. There is great interest now to know which side has been the stronger. Now, there are two parties in this world—those for Christ and those against Him, and to change to Christ's party is only moving from the old party to the new. You know that the old party is bad, and the new one is good, and yet you don't change. Suppose I was called to New York tonight and went down to the Illinois Central Depot to catch the ten o'clock train. I go on the train, and a friend should see me and say, "You are on the wrong train for New York. You are on the Burlington train." "Oh, no," I say, "you are wrong; I asked someone, and he told me this was the right train." "Why," this friend replies, "I've been in Chicago for twenty years and know that you are on the wrong train," and the man talks, and at last convinces me, but I sit still, although I believe I am on the wrong train for New York, and I go on to Burlington. If you don't get off the wrong train and get on the right one, you will not reach heaven. If you have not repented, seize your baggage tonight and go to the other train.

A Change in Direction

If a man is not repentant his face is turned away from God, and the moment his face is turned toward God peace and joy follow. There are a great many people hunting after joy, after peace. Dear friends, if you want to find it tonight, just turn to God, and you will get it. You need not hunt for it any longer; only come and get it. When I was a little boy I remember I tried to catch my shadow. I don't know if you were ever so foolish; but I remember running after it and trying to get ahead of it. I could not see why the shadow always kept ahead of me. Once I happened to be racing with my face to the sun, and I looked over my head and saw my shadow coming back of me, and it kept behind me all the way. It is the same with the Sun of Righteous-

ness, peace and joy will go with you while you go with your face toward Him, and these people who are getting at the back of the Son are in the darkness all the time. Turn to the light of God, and the reflection will flash in your heart. Don't say that God will not forgive you. It is only your will which keeps His forgiveness from you.

My sister, I remember, told me her little boy said something naughty one morning, when his father said to him, "Sammy, go and ask your mother's forgiveness." "I won't," replied the child. "If you don't ask your mother's forgiveness I'll put you to bed." It was early in the morning—before he went to business, and the boy didn't think he would do it. He said, "I won't," again. They undressed him and put him to bed. The father came home at noon expecting to find his boy playing about the house. He didn't see him about, and asked his wife where he was. "In bed still." So he went up to the room, and sat down by the bed, and said, "Sammy, I want you to ask your mother's forgiveness." But the answer was, "No." The father coaxed and begged, but could not induce the child to ask forgiveness. The father went away, expecting certainly that when he came home at night the child would have got all over it. At night, however, when he got home he found the little fellow still in bed. He had lain there all day. He went to him and tried to get him to go to his mother, but it was no use. His mother went and was equally unsuccessful. That father and mother could not sleep any that night. They expected every moment to hear their little son knock at their door. Now, they wanted to forgive the boy. My sister told me it was just as if death had come into their home. She never passed through such a night.

In the morning she went to him and

said, "Now, Sammy, you are going to ask my forgiveness," but the boy turned his face to the wall and wouldn't speak. The father came home at noon, and the boy was as stubborn as ever. It looked as though the child was going to conquer. It was for the good of the boy that they didn't want to give him his own way. It is a great deal better for us to submit to God than to have our own way. Our own way will lead us to ruin; God's way leads to life everlasting. The father went off to his office, and that afternoon my sister went in to her son about four o'clock and began to reason with him. And, after talking for some time, she said, "Now, Sammy, say 'mother.'" "Mother," said the boy. "Now say 'for.'" "For." "Now just say 'give.'" And the boy repeated "give." "Me," said the mother. "Me," and the little fellow fairly leaped out of bed. "I have said it," he cried; "take me down to Papa, so that I can say it to him."

Oh, sinner, go to Him and ask His forgiveness. This is repentance. It is coming in with a broken heart and asking the King of heaven to forgive you. Don't say you can't. It is a lie. It is your stubborn will—it is your stubborn heart.

Now, let me say here tonight, you are in a position to be reconciled to God now. You are not in a position to deny this reconciliation a week, a day, an hour. God tells you, "Now."

Look at that beautiful steamer *Atlantic*. There she is in the bay, groping her way along a rocky coast. The captain doesn't know, as his vessel plows through that ocean, that in a few moments it will strike a rock and hundreds of those on board will perish in a watery grave. If he knew, in a minute he could strike a bell, and the steamer would be turned from that rock, and the people would be saved. The vessel has struck, but he knows now too late.

You have time now. In five minutes, for all you and I know, you may be in eternity. God hangs a mist over our eyes as to our summons. So *now* God calls—*now*, everyone repent, and all your sins will be taken from you. I have come in the name of the Master to ask you to turn to God now. May God help you to turn and live.

By the time Moody arrived on the evangelistic scene the biblical literacy rate in America had plummeted. There was a time in American history when more than ninety percent of the population read the Bible regularly. Sermons were full of illustrations taken directly from the Bible.

Unlike the other evangelists before and after him, Moody devoted several sermons to the topic of Bible study. According to him, the important tools for effective study are a large-print Bible, concordance, and a Bible dictionary.

Moody studied entire books, special biblical topics, as well as important Bible characters. Intensive Bible study contributed a lasting influence to his own life. He realized that a sermon would eventually be forgotten, but if his audience could be stimulated into the habitual study of God's Word, they would experience greater spiritual maturity.

CHAPTER TEN

How to Study the Bible

PART ONE

One thing I have noticed in studying the Word of God, and that is, when a man is filled with the Spirit, he deals largely with the Word of God; whereas, the man who is filled with his own ideas, refers rarely to the Word of God. He gets along without it, and you seldom see it mentioned in his discourses. A great many use it only as a textbook. They get their text from the Bible, and go on without any further allusion to it. They ignore it; but when a man is filled with the Word, as Stephen was, he cannot help speaking Scripture. You will find that Moses was constantly repeating the commandments. You will find too, that Joshua, when he came across Jordan with his people, there they stood, and the Law of the Lord God was read to them, and you will find all through Scripture the man of God dealing much with His Word. Why, you will find Christ constantly referring to them, and saying, "Thus saith the Scriptures." Now, as old Dr. Bonair of Glasgow said, "The Lord didn't tell Joshua how to use a sword, but He told him how he should meditate on the Lord day and night, and then he would have good success."

When we find a man meditating on the words of God, my friends, that man is full of boldness and is successful. And the reason why we have so little success in our teaching is because we know so little of the Word of God. You must know it and have it in your heart. A great many have it in their head and not in their heart. If we have the Spirit of God in our heart, then we have something to work upon. He does not use us because He is not in us. Know, as we come to this word today, as Mr. Sankey has been singing:

No word He hath spoken
Was ever yet broken.

Let us take this thought in John 10:35: "and the Scripture cannot be broken." There is a great deal of infidelity around, and it has crept into many of the churches too. These doubters take up the Bible and wonder if they can believe it all—if it is true from [front] to back, and a good many things in it they believe are not true. I have a good deal of admiration for that black man who was approached by some infidel—some skeptical man who told him, "Why, the Bible is not true; all scientific men tell us that now; it's only a bundle of fables." "The Bible isn't true?" replied the black man; "Why, I was a blasphemer and a drinker, and that book just made me stop swearing, drinking, lying and blaspheming and you say it isn't true?" My friends, the black man had the best of the argument. Do you think if the Bible was a bad book it would make men good? Do you think if it was a false book it would make men good? And so let us take our stand on the black man's platform and be convinced that it is true. When we take it into our hands, let us know that it is the Word of God and try to understand it. Many of the passages appear to us difficult to understand, but if we could understand it clearly from front to back at first, it would be as a human book, but the very fact that we cannot understand it all at once, is the highest proof that it is the Word of God.

Now, another thought is that a great many people read it, but they read it as a task. They say, "Well, I've read it through, I know all that's in it," and lay it aside. How many people prefer the morning paper in order to get news? They prefer it, but it is a false idea. This Bible is the only newspaper. It tells you all that has taken place for the last six thousand years, and it tells you all the news of the future. Why, seventeen hundred years before Christ, the people were told in it of the coming of Christ. They knew He was coming. The daily papers could not tell us of this. They may be written by learned men, brilliant editorial writers, but they couldn't have told this. If you want news, study the Bible—the blessed old Bible—and you will find it has all the news of the world.

Now we come to the question [of] how to study it. A great many read it as I used to read it, just to ease my conscience. I had a rule before I was converted to read two chapters a day. If I didn't do it before I retired, I used to jump out of bed and read them, but if you had asked me fifteen minutes after what I had read, I could not have told you. Now this is the trouble with many—they read with the head and not with the heart. A man may read his Bible, but when he has closed it you may ask him what chapter he read last, and he cannot tell you. He sometimes puts a mark in it to tell him; without the mark he doesn't know, his reading has been so careless. It is to keep him from reading it again. [That's] just as I used to do when hoeing corn. I used to put a stick in the furrow to mark the place where I had hoed last. A good many people are just like this. They pick up a chapter here, and there is no connection

in their reading, and consequently [they] don't know anything about the Word of God. If we want to understand it we've got to study it—read it on our knees, asking the Holy Ghost to give us the understanding to see what the Word of God is, and if we go about it that way, and turn our face, as Joshua did, in prayer, and set ourselves to study these blessed and heavenly truths, the Lord will not disappoint us, and we will soon know our Bible. And when we know our Bible then it is that God can use us.

Important Resources

Let me say there are three books which every Christian ought to have, and, if you [don't] have them, go and buy them before you get your tea. The first is a good Bible—a good large-printed Bible. I don't like those little-printed ones which you can scarcely see—get one in large print. A good many object to a large Bible because they can't carry it in their pocket. Well, if you can't carry it in your pocket, [you can] carry it under your arm. It is showing what you are—it is showing your flag. Now a great many of you are coming in from the country to these meetings, and when you get on the cars, you see people who are not ashamed to sit down and play cards. I don't see why the children of God should be ashamed of carrying their Bibles under their arms in the cars. "Ah!" some say, "that is the spirit of a Pharisee." It would be the pharisaical spirit if you hadn't dipped down into heavenly truths, if you haven't the Spirit of God with you. Some say, "I haven't it." Suppose you don't read so many of these daily papers, and read the Bible a little more often. Some say, "I haven't time." Take time. I don't believe there is a businessman in Chicago who couldn't find an hour a day to read his Bible if he wanted to.

Get a good Bible, then a good concordance, and then a scriptural [dictionary]. Whenever you come to something in the Word of God that you don't know, hunt for its meaning in those books. Suppose after the meeting I am looking all over the platform and Dr. Kittredge says, "What are you looking for?" and I answer, "Oh, nothing, nothing." He would leave. If he thought I hadn't dropped something he wouldn't stay. But, suppose I had lost a very valuable ring which some esteemed friend had given me, and I told him this. He would stay with me, and we would move this organ, and those chairs, and look all over, and by looking carefully, we would find it. If a man hunts for truths in the Word of God and reads it as if he was looking for nothing particular, he will get nothing.

When the men went to California in the gold excitement, they went to dig for gold, and they worked day and night with a terrible energy just to get gold. Now, my friends, if they wanted to get the pure gold they had to dig for it, and when I was there I was told that the best gold was [found] by digging deep for it. So the best truths are [found] by digging deep for them.

When I was in Boston I went into Mr. Prang's chromo establishment. I wanted to know how the work was done. He took me to a stone several feet square, where he took the first impression, but when he took the paper off the stone I could see no sign of a man's face; the paper was just tinged. I said I couldn't see any sign of a man's face there. "Wait a little," he said. He took me to another stone, but when the paper was lifted I couldn't see any impression yet. He took me up—up to eight, nine, ten stones— and then I could see just the faintest outlines of a man's face. He went on till he got up to about the twentieth stone, and I could see the impression of a face,

but he said it was not very correct yet. Well, he went on until he got up, I think, to the twenty-eighth stone, and a perfect face appeared, and it looked as if all it had to do was to speak and it would be human. If you read a chapter of the Bible and don't see anything in it, read it a second time, and if you cannot see anything in it, read it a third time. Dig deep. Read it again and again, and even if you have to read it twenty-eight times, do so, and you will see the man Christ Jesus, for He is in every page of the Word. And if you take Christ out of the Old Testament you will take the key out of the Word.

Value of the Old Testament

Many men in the churches nowadays are saying that they believe the teachings in the New Testament are to be believed, but those in the Old are not. Those who say this don't know anything about the New. There is nothing in the Old Testament that God has not put His seal upon. "Why," some people say to me, "Moody, you don't believe in the Flood! All the scientific men tell us it is absurd." Let them tell us. Jesus tells us of it, and I would rather take the word of Jesus than that of any other one. I haven't got much respect for those men who dig down for stones with shovels in order to take away the Word of God. Men don't believe in the story of Sodom and Gomorrah, but we have it sealed in the New Testament: "As it was in the days of Sodom and Gomorrah." They don't believe in Lot's wife, but He says, "Remember Lot's wife."

So there is not a thing that men today mock at but the Son of God endorses. They don't believe in the swallowing of Jonah. They say it is impossible that a whale could swallow Jonah—its throat is too small. They forgot that the whale was prepared for Jonah; as one woman said, "Why, God could prepare a man to swallow a whale, let alone prepare a whale to swallow a man." We find that He endorses all the points in the Old Testament, from Genesis to Revelation. We have only one book—we haven't two. The moment a man begins to cut and slash away, it all goes. Some don't believe in the first five books. They would do well to look into the third chapter of John, where they will see the Samaritan woman at the well looking for the coming of Christ from the first five books of Moses. I tell you, my friends, if you look for Him you will find Him all through the Old Testament. You will find Him in Genesis—in every book in the Bible. Just turn to Luke 24:27, you will find Him, after He had risen again, speaking about the Old Testament prophets: "And beginning at Moses, and all the prophets, he expounded unto them in all the scriptures the things concerning Himself." Concerning Himself. Doesn't that settle the question? I tell you I am convinced in my mind that the Old Testament is as true as the New.

And He began at Moses and all the prophets.

Mark that, "all the prophets." Then in the forty-fourth verse:

And He said unto them, These are the words which I spake unto you, while I was yet with you, that all things must be fulfilled, which were written in the law of Moses, and in the prophets and in the psalms concerning Me. Then opened He their understanding that they might understand the scriptures.

If we take Christ out of the Old Testament what are you going to do with the psalms and prophets? The book is a sealed book if we take away the New from it. Christ unlocks the Old and Jesus the New. Philip, in teaching the people, found Christ in the fifty-third chapter of Isaiah, "All we like sheep have gone astray; we have turned every one to his own way; and the LORD hath laid on him the iniquity of us all." Why, the early Christians had nothing but the Old Testament to preach the gospel from—at Pentecost they had nothing else. So if there is any man or woman in this assembly who believes in the New Testament, and not in the Old, dear friends, you are deluded by Satan, because if you read the Word of God you will find Him spoken of throughout both books. I notice if a man goes to cut up the Bible and comes to you with one truth and says, "I don't believe this, and I don't believe that," I notice when he begins to doubt portions of the Word of God, he soon doubts it all.

Some Possible Plans

Now the question is how to study the Bible. Of course, I cannot tell you how you are to study it; but I can tell you how I have studied it, and that may help you. I have found it a good plan to take up one book at a time. It is a good deal better to study one book at a time than to run through the Bible. If we study one book and get its key, it will, perhaps, open up others. Take up the book of Genesis, and you will find eight beginnings; or, in other words, you pick up the key of several books. The gospel was written that man might believe on Jesus Christ, and every chapter speaks of it. Now, take the book of Genesis; it says it is the book of beginnings. That is the key; then the book of Exodus—it is the book of redemption; that is the key word of the whole. Take up the book of Leviticus, and we find that it is the book of sacrifices. And so on through all the different books; you will find each one with a key.

Another thing: we must study it unbiased. A great many people believe certain things. They believe in certain creeds and doctrines, and they run through the book to get Scripture in accordance with them. If a man is a Calvinistic man, he wants to find something in accordance with his doctrine. But if we go to seek truth the Spirit of God will come. Don't seek it in the blue light of Presbyterianism, in the red light of Methodism, or in the light of Episcopalianism, but study it in the light of Calvary.

Another way to study it is not only to take one book at a time; but I have been wonderfully blessed by taking up one word at a time. Take up the word and go to your concordance and find out all about it. I remember I took up the word "love," and turned to the Scriptures and studied it, and got so that I felt I loved everybody. I got full of it. When I went on the street I felt as if I loved everybody I saw. It ran out of my fingers. Suppose you take up the subject of love and study it. You will get so full of it that all you have got to do is to open your lips and a flood of the love of God flows upon the meeting. If you go into a court you will find a lawyer pleading a case. He gets everything bearing upon one point, heaped up so as to carry his argument with all the force he can, in order to convince the jury. Now it seems to me a man should do the same in talking to an audience; just think that he has a jury before him, and he wants to convict a sinner. If it is love, get all you can upon the subject and talk love, love.

Take up the word "grace." I didn't know what Calvary was till I studied grace. I got so full of the wonderful grace that I had to speak. I had to run out and tell people about it. If you want to find out those heavenly truths take up the concordance, and heap up the evidence, and you cannot help but preach. Take heaven; there are people all the time wondering what it is and where it is. Take your concordance and see what the Word of God says it is. Let these men who are talking against blood look into the Word of God, and they will find if it doesn't teach that it teaches nothing else. When we preach about that, some people think we are taking our own views. But the Word says, "the life of all flesh is in the blood, and without blood there is no remission." The moment a man talks against blood he throws out the Bible. Take up Saul; study him. You will find hundreds of men in Chicago just like him. Take up Lot; study that character. Let me say right here that if we are going to have (and I firmly believe in my soul that we are going to have) a revival in the northwest—if we are going to have it, you must bring the people to the study of the Word of God. I have been out here for a good number of years, and I am tired and sick of these spasmodic meetings; tired of the bonfires which, after a little, are reduced to a bundle of shavings.

When I see men speaking to inquirers in the inquiry room without holding the Word of God up to them, I think their work will not be lasting. What we want to do is to get people to study the Word of God in order that the work may be thorough and lasting. I notice when a man is brought coolly and calmly and intelligently, that man will have a reason for being a Christian. We must do that. We must bring a man to the Word of God if we don't want this western country filled with backsliders. Let us pray that we will have a scriptural revival. And if we preach only the Word in our churches and in our Sunday schools, we will have a revival that will last to eternity.

Letting the Word Speak

Let us turn back to one of the Old Testament revivals, when the people had been brought up from Babylon. Look at the eighth chapter of Nehemiah:

And Ezra the priest brought the law before the congregation both of men and women, and all that could hear with understanding, upon the first day of the seventh month. And he read therein before the street that was before the water gate from the morning until midday, before the men and the women, and those that could understand; and the ears of all the people were attentive unto the book of the law.

No preaching there; he merely read the Word of God—that is, God's Word—not man's. A great many of us prefer man's word to that of God. We are running after eloquent preachers—after men who can get up eloquent moral essays.

They leave out the Word of God. We want to get back to the Word of God. They had an all-day meeting there, something like this, "And Ezra opened the book in the sight of all the people; (for he was above all the people;) and when he opened it all the people stood up" (Neh. 8:5). I can see the great crowd standing up to listen to the prophet, just like young robins taking in what the old robins bring them,

And Ezra blessed the LORD, the great God. And all the people answered, Amen, Amen, with lifting up their hands: and they bowed their heads, and worshiped the LORD with their faces to the ground. . . . So they read in the book in the law of God distinctly, and gave the sense, and caused them to understand the reading *(Neh. 8:6, 8)*.

Now, it strikes me it is about the height of preaching to get people that understand the reading of the Word. It would be a great deal better if a preacher would sometimes stop when he had a remark, and say, "Mr. Jones, do you understand that?" "No, I don't," and then the preacher might make it a little plainer, so that he could understand it. There would be a great difference in the preaching in some of the churches. He would talk a little less about metaphysics and science and speak about something else. "Then he said unto them, go your way, eat the fat, and drink the sweet, and send portions unto them for whom nothing is prepared: for this day is holy unto our LORD: neither be ye sorry; for the joy of the LORD is your strength" (Neh. 8:10). "For the joy of the Lord is your strength." If you will show me a Bible Christian living on the Word of God, I will show you a joyful man. He is mounting up all the time. He has got new truths that lift him up over every obstacle, and he mounts over difficulties higher and higher, like a man I once heard of who had a bag of gas fastened on either side, and if he just touched the ground with his foot, over a wall or a hedge he would go; and so these truths make us so light that we bound over every obstacle.

And when we have those truths our work will be successful. Just turn over to Jeremiah 20:9, to this blessed old prophet. There was a time when he was not going to speak about the Word of God anymore. Now, I just want to show you this, when a man is filled with the Word of God you cannot keep him still. If a man has got the Word, he must speak or die. "Then I said, I will not make mention of him, nor speak anymore in his name. But his word was in mine heart as a burning fire shut up in my bones, and I was weary with forbearing, and I could not stay." It set him on fire, and so a man filled with the Word of God is filled as with a burning fire, and it is so easy for a man to work when he is filled with the Word of God.

I heard of a man the other week who was going to preach against the blood. I was very anxious to see what he would say about it, and I got the paper next morning and I found there was nothing else there than scriptural quotations. I said that was the very best thing he could do. As we see in the twenty-third chapter of Jeremiah: "Is not my word like as a fire, saith the LORD; . . . that breaketh the rock in pieces?" Those hard, flinty rocks will be broken if we give them the Word of God. Those men in the northwest that we cannot reach by our own words, give them this, and see if they cannot be reached. Not only that, if we are full of Scripture ourselves give them what God says, you will find it easy to preach—you will say we haven't to get up so many sermons. It seems to me if we had more of the Word of God in our services and gave up more of our own thoughts, there would be a hundred times more converted than there are. A preacher, if he wants to give his people the Word, must have fed on the Word himself. A man must get water out of a well when there is water. He may dip his bucket in if it is empty, but he will get nothing.

I think the best thing I have heard in Chicago I heard the other day, and it has fastened itself upon my mind, and I must tell it to your ministers. We had for our subject in Farwell Hall the other day, the seventh chapter of John, when the Reverend Mr. Gibson said if a man was to come among a lot of thirsty men with an empty bucket they wouldn't come to him to drink. He said he believed that was the trouble with most of the ministers, as that had been the trouble with himself. He hadn't got a bucket of living water, and the people wouldn't come to him to drink. Just look at an audience of thirsty men, and you bring in a bucket of clear sparkling water, and see how they will go for it. If you go into your Sunday schools and the children look into your buckets and see them empty, there is nothing for them there. So, my friends, if we attempt to feed others we must first be fed ourselves.

Marking Your Bible

There is another thing which has wonderfully helped me. That is to mark my Bible whenever I hear anything that strikes me. If a minister has been preaching to me a good sermon, I put his name down next to the text, and then it recalls what has been said, and I can show it to others. You know we laymen have the right to take what we hear to one another. If ministers saw people doing this they would preach a good deal better sermons. Not only that, but if we understood our Bibles better, the ministers would preach better. I think if people knew more about the Word than they do, so many of them would not be carried away with false doctrine.

There is no place I have ever been where people so thoroughly understand their Bibles as in Scotland. Why, little boys could quote Scripture and take me up on a text. They have the whole nation just educated, as it were, with the Word of God. Infidelity cannot come there. A man got up in Glasgow at a corner, and began to preach universal salvation. "Oh, sir," said an old woman, "that will never save the likes of me." She had heard enough preaching to know that it would never save her. If a man comes among them with any false doctrine, these Scotchmen instantly draw their Bibles on him. I had to keep my eyes open, and be careful what I said there. They knew their Bibles a good deal better than I did. And so if the preachers would get the people to read the Word of God more carefully and note what they heard, there would not be so much infidelity among us.

I want to tell you how I was blessed a few years ago, upon hearing a discourse upon the thirtieth chapter of Proverbs. The speaker said the children of God were like four things. The first thing was, "The ants are a people not strong," and he went on to compare the children of God to the ants. He said the people of God were like ants. They pay no attention to the things of the present, but go on steadily preparing for the future. The next thing he compared them to was the conies. "The conies are but a feeble folk." It is a very weak little thing. "Well," said I, "I wouldn't like to be as a coney." But he went on to say that it built upon a rock. The children of God were very weak, but they laid their foundation upon a rock. "Well," said I, "I will be like a coney, and build my hopes upon a rock." The Irishman said he trembled himself, but the rock upon which his house was built never did.

The next thing the speaker compared them to was a locust. I didn't think much of locusts, and I thought I wouldn't care about being like one. But he went on to read, they have "no king, yet they go forth all of them by bands." There were the Congregationalist, the Presbyterian, the Methodist bands going forth without a king; but by-and-by our King will come back again, and these bands will fly to Him. "Well, I will be like a locust; my King's away," I thought. The next comparison was a spider. I didn't like this at all; but he said if we went into a gilded palace filled with luxury, we might see a spider holding on to something, oblivious to all the luxury below. It was laying hold of the things above. "Well," said I, "I would like to be a spider." I heard this a good many years ago, and I just put the speaker's name to it, and it makes the sermon.

But take your Bibles and mark them. Don't think of wearing it out. It is a rare thing to find a man wearing his Bible out nowadays—and Bibles are cheap too. You are living in a land where there are plenty. Study them and mark them, and don't be afraid of wearing them. Now don't you see how much better it would be to study it? And if you are talking to a man instead of talking about your neighbors, just talk about the Bible, and when Christian men come together just compare notes, and ask one another, "What have you found new in the Word of God since I saw you last?" Some men come to me and ask me if I have picked up anything new, and I give them what I have, and they give me what they have.

An Englishman asked me some time ago, "Do you know much about Job?" "Well, I know a little," I replied. "If you've got the key of Job you've got the key to the whole Bible," [he said.] "What!" I replied; "I thought it was a poetical book." "Well," said he, "I will just divide Job into seven headings. The first is the perfect man—untried—and that is Adam and Eve before they fell. The second heading is tried by adversity—Adam, after the fall. The third is the wisdom of the world—the three friends who came to try to help Job out of his difficulties. They had no power to help him at all. He could stand his scolding wife, but he couldn't stand them. The fourth heading takes the form of the Mediator, and in the fifth heading God speaks at last. He heard Him before by the ear, but he hears Him now by the soul, and he falls down flat upon his face. A good many men in Chicago are like Job. They think they are mighty good men, but directly they hear the voice of God they know they are sinners; they are in the dust. There isn't much talk about their goodness then. Here he was with his face down. Job learned his lesson. That was the sixth heading, and in these headings were the burdens of Adam's sin. The seventh heading was when God showed him His face. Well, I learned the key to the Bible. I cannot tell how this helped me. I told it to another man, and he asked me if I ever thought of how he got his property back and his sheep back. He gave Job double what he had, and gave him ten children besides, so that he should have ten in heaven besides his ten on earth.

PART TWO

A great many are asking the question, will this work hold out? Are these young converts going to stand? Now I am no prophet, nor the son of a prophet, but one thing I can predict that every one of these new converts that goes to studying his Bible and loves this book above every other book is sure to hold out. The world will have no charm for him; he will get the world under his feet, because in this book he will find something better than the world can give him. Now what I want to say to these young converts, and to old converts, is to love the Word of God. Set more and more store by it. Then the troubles in your Christian life will pass away like a morning cloud. You will feed and live on the Word of God, and it will become the joy of your soul.

Some Key Texts

Now, to help some of you to a right course in studying God's Word, I want to point out a number of texts that you might begin with, and then, in the same way, you can collect others. I want to call your attention first to a part of the fourth chapter of Matthew. A little boy

in the seat there, while giving his experience the other day, felt so sure about his strength that he defied Satan. I trembled. Those of us who are older, and know more about the devil's power, know that we can only meet him with the Word of God. We can't withstand him by our feelings or by our being converted; he only laughs at such weapons.

Read in this fourth chapter, from the third verse on, and see how Christ overcame Satan. Not by His feelings, not because He had been baptized of John in Jordan, but by the Word of the living God. Three times Satan advanced to the charge, but every time he was thrust through by the sword of the Spirit. And that must be your sword. Don't say, like the little boy in Scotland, "Old Nick, just you get behind me," but say, "O Lord, just put him behind me." You can't do anything against Satan of yourself; you can only overcome him through Christ and by the Word of the living God.

Then take Romans 10:15 and 17. It shows there was a work done for you on Calvary, but that there is another work quite distinct from that. "And how shall they preach, except they be sent? . . . faith cometh by hearing, and hearing by the Word of God." How many mourning Christians there are who know little about God, and the reason is just that they do not study the Word of God. You are little acquainted with this precious book.

I don't see how Christians can habitually read the newspapers on Sunday. I wouldn't advise you even to read your religious weeklies on that day. I find too many are making these take the place of the Bible. Let us have one day exclusively to study and read the Word of God. If we can't take time during the week, we will have Sunday uninterrupted.

What can botanists tell you of the lily of the valley? You must study this book for that. What can geologists tell you of the Rock of Ages, or mere astronomers about the Bright Morning Star? In these pages we find all knowledge unto salvation; there we read of the ruin of man by nature, redemption by the blood, and regeneration by the Holy Ghost. These three things run all through and through them.

But let us stick to the thought: how to study this Bible. A favorite way with me is just to take up one word or expression and run through the different places where it is. Take the "I ams" of John; "I am the bread of life"; "I am the water of life"; "I am the way, the truth, and the life"; "I am the resurrection"; "I am all, and in all." God gives to his children a blank, and on it they can write whatever they most want, and He will fill the bill.

And then the promises. A Scotchman found 31 thousand distinct promises in the Word of God. There is not a despondent soul in this tabernacle this morning but God has a promise just to suit him. They abound even in the books of Job and Jonah.

And now let us follow on the thought, "What is God able to do?" Just get all the blessed texts on that subject to heart, and you can't help speaking for God. Then you can indeed say, "God is my Father, Jesus is my Savior, and heaven is my home." There is a blessed verse in the gospel of John. There is no more fruitful subject in the Bible than is opened up there. The conversions there and through the Bible, notice, are different from each other, though all resounding to the glory of God. Think of Nicodemus, the woman at the well, and Matthew the publican. And then the conversions in the Acts, and those of the Philippian jailer and Cornelius. We make a great deal more ado about this simple act than the Bible teaches. Conversion is just to believe on Christ and

follow Him, and may be but the work of a moment.

Mr. Moody went on to say: Take up these texts of Peter having the word "precious"; "precious blood," "precious Christ," "precious faith," "precious trial of faith," "precious promises of God." Just take one word of the apostle, and trace it out.

Many persons do not believe in assurance as to salvation. Turn to the third chapter of the first epistle of John, "Beloved, now are we the sons of God, . . ." The fifth verse of that chapter says, "And ye know that he was manifested to take away our sins"; . . .and then we come to "I know that my Redeemer liveth." All the Bible puts it in that way. When it speaks of hope, it means a certain hope, not a doubtful hope. The "hope of a glorious resurrection" was a sure hope. Then the nineteenth verse, "And hereby we know that we are of the truth, . . ." and then, "We know that we have passed from death unto life . . ." and "Ye know that no murderer hath eternal life, . . ." and also, "Hereby we know that he abideth in us, by the spirit which he hath given us." (1 John 3:14, 15, 24) There is no reason, nay, there is no excuse, for Christians doubting that they are saved; it is presumptuous not to take God at His word. Again, the second verse of the third chapter of the epistle of John says, "Beloved, now are we the sons of God, and it doth not yet appear what we shall be; but we know that, when He shall appear, we shall be like Him; . . ."

So I find great comfort and advantage in just taking up the Word of God in this way and studying it with a view to some single truth. Take up in this way a single name or life or character. Thus Lazarus, in his different stages, is the type of the dead soul—the soul dead in trespasses and sins; then he is the saved soul; then the feasting, rejoicing soul; then he testifies to the goodness of God. Galatians shows how we are first called, then justified, then sanctified; all through there is a beautiful connection, and you have only to stand right with one of these thoughts and follow the trail out.

And then take up the Christian's growth in grace, Psalm twenty-three, verse two, "Lie down in green pastures"; "Sitting at the feet of Jesus"; Ephesians, chapter 6, verses 13 and 14, "He is able to make us stand"; Psalms, "Walk through the valley of the shadow of death"; Hebrews, chapter 12, verse 1, "Run with patience the race that is set before us"; Psalms 18, verse 21, and in Isaiah, chapter 40, verse 31, "They shall mount up with wings as eagles."

The Christian, these verses show, goes up higher and higher, like a balloon, till the world is lost to sight; till he becomes like Christ and possesses eyes that can gaze unblinded on the glory of the city of God.

Trust is an important part of life. But, according to Moody, the most *important act of trust is to depend on Christ for salvation. In this chapter, an onlooker gives his account of Moody's "inquiry room talk." The inquiry room was where men and women could discuss their spiritual condition with trained workers who, in turn, pointed the way to Christ.*

Moody compares trust in Christ with that of a boy's trust in a mother's promise or the leap of a child into the arms of her father. Likewise, God tells men and women to have simple, childlike trust in Him.

God never forsakes those who trust in Him, and He is always with His children just as the parent is there for his child.

Trust

Mr. Moody said in opening his regular address he would make the sermon an inquiry room talk. He was not going to have anyone in the congregation go away and say they hadn't an offer of salvation. He was going to turn the tabernacle into an inquiry room. And first he would call attention to a verse in the Psalms. Some who had counted the verses in the Bible found that the eighth and ninth verses of the one hundred and eighteenth Psalm were the middle verses of the Bible: "It is better to trust in the LORD than to put confidence in man. It is better to trust in the LORD than to put confidence in princes." And also he read the third and fourth verses of the twenty-sixth chapter of Isaiah: "Thou wilt keep him in perfect peace, whose mind is stayed on thee: because he trusteth in thee. Trust ye in the LORD forever: for in the LORD JEHOVAH is everlasting strength."

A boy whose mother promises him anything knows how to trust her. If she promises him a pair of skates at Christmas, he doesn't begin to analyze what trust is; he doesn't begin to ask what his feeling is. He simply says, "Mother said so, and that's enough." There was nothing miraculous about it; it was simply trust. This is the idea of trusting in God. They must trust God, even if they don't know what the result will be.

In the sixty-second Psalm, eighth verse it said, "Trust in him at all times; ye people, pour out your heart before him: God is a refuge for us . . . ." It was the same in the midnight darkness as in the daylight. It was the child in the light whose father was in the dark. The child leaped into [her] father's arms though [she] didn't see him. It was the simple trust that the father was there.

Trust God at all times. Trust Him as one would trust a banker whom he had tried, a doctor whom he had confidence in; or a lawyer who had been tried and had never lost a case. They had an advocate with the Father, even Jesus Christ the Righteous. How to trust Him was shown in Proverbs to be with "all the heart"; not a little but with the whole heart. Don't trust the minister with the soul's salvation, but [trust] God. God wants the whole heart; God hates half-heartedness; God detests half-heartedness.

An incident of Alexander's [reign] illustrated this, where the emperor was warned to beware of his medicine. The emperor took the note of warning in one hand and the medicine in the other, and, because he trusted in his physician, took his draft. That was perfect trust. Paul said, "I am persuaded that He is able to keep that which I have committed unto Him."

The next step was, Who will trust Him? This is answered in the ninth Psalm at the tenth verse: "And they that know thy name will put their trust in thee . . . ." He must be known to be trusted; He must be believed to be trusted. No infidel could trust God because he didn't know Him. No one could go down to hell trusting in God. Then came the trust: "Thou wilt keep them in perfect peace that trust thee."

In the sixteenth chapter of Proverbs, at the twentieth verse, was described the joy of the one who trusted God: "whoso trusteth in the LORD, happy is he." In the thirty-second Psalm, at the tenth verse again it was said, "Many sorrows shall be to the wicked: but he that trusteth in the LORD, mercy shall compass him about." The joy is thus described in the fifth Psalm, at the eleventh verse: "But let all those that put their trust in thee rejoice: let them ever shout for joy, because thou defendest them: let them also that love thy name be joyful in thee."

The inquirer asked about feeling—how should he feel? He [Moody] would say, "Let your feelings take care of themselves, you have only to come to God." They couldn't be saved by their feelings, nor by their good morals—by trying to break off their sins here and there. It was like lopping off the twigs of a tree, while Christ laid the axe to the root. In the twenty-ninth chapter of Proverbs it was said, "Whoso putteth his trust in the LORD shall be safe," or in the margin, "set on high."

The next question was: Why didn't they get this trust? Was it pride; the fear of neighbors? Why didn't they get this trust? Again in the thirty-seventh Psalm reference was [made] to this: "Fret not thyself because of evildoers, . . . Commit thy way unto the LORD, and he shall bring it to pass." He was the widows' God, the orphans' God. Let none fret for the coming winter; the Lord will provide. He will be a present help. Mr. Moody told a number of illustrative incidents and was especially practical in urging all who feared for the winter to trust in God, to rest in Him, and He would never leave, never forsake them.

Conversion is often portrayed as a long process that consists of several stages before completion. In this selection Moody addresses the issue of sudden conversion.

Using many examples from the Bible, he shows that sudden conversion is not the abhorrent teaching that it was apparently said to be in his day. It merely consists of one realizing his or her lost condition and turning to God for salvation. No lengthy process is involved, and nothing beyond turning to God for help is required. Once a sinner realizes the need for salvation and acts on that realization, conversion takes place. No special feelings are necessary because feelings can deceive.

God desires everyone to come to Him, and whenever a person makes that decision in simple faith, God is faithful to save, with or without emotional "evidence." Conversions vary from person to person. What is important is that one has forsaken sin and accepted Christ.

CHAPTER TWELVE

Sudden Conversion

I propose tonight to take a subject rather than a text, and that subject is sudden conversion—instant salvation. One reason why I am led to take up this subject is because I have received a large number of letters asking me how it is that I can teach such a pernicious doctrine that a man can be saved all at once—that salvation is instantaneous. One of the writers goes on to state that it is clearly taught in the Word of God that conversion is a gradual thing—that it is a life work—and that it is a dangerous thing to teach that a man can come into this tabernacle a sinner and go out a saved man. Now, let us see what is taught in the Word of God, and if it doesn't teach instantaneous salvation, let us give up the idea. I hold to it as I do to my life, and I would as quickly give up my life as give up this doctrine, unless it can be proved that it is not according to the Word of God.

Now, I will admit that light is one thing and birth is another. A soul must be born before it can see light. A child must be born before it can be taught; it must be born before it can walk; it must be born before it can be educated. I think the grandest mistake among ministers is that they are talking to dead men; that they are talking to men in the flesh instead of men born of God. Now, let us get them into Christ, and then educate them and build them up to the highest faith. Let us not try to teach men who are not born of God. The Scripture is very clear on this point. It gives no uncertain sound. If a man is dead in sin you may as well talk to a corpse as talk to him about spiritual things. To tell an unrenewed man—an unregenerated man—to worship, serve, and love God, is absurd; you may as well tell a man to leap over Lake Michigan as to tell a man not born of God to serve Him.

Now the first illustration I want to call your attention to is when the voice came down from heaven to Noah: "Come thou and all thy home into the ark, for thee have I seen righteous before me in this generation." Now, there was a minute when Noah was outside the ark, and another when he was inside, and by being inside he was saved. As long as he was outside of the ark he was exposed to the wrath of God just like the rest of those antediluvians. If he stayed out, and remained with those antediluvians, he would have been swept away, as they were. It was not his righteousness, it was not his faith nor his works that saved him; it was the ark. And my friends, we have not, like Noah, to be one hundred and twenty years making an ark for our safety. God has provided an ark for us, and the question is: are you inside or outside this ark? If you are inside you are safe; if you are outside you are not safe. If you are outside you are exposed to the wrath of God continually, and you cannot tell the day nor the hour nor the minute when you may be swept into eternity.

Into the Ark

When I was in Manchester in one of the inquiry meetings, I went up to the gallery to speak to some people there.

While we were standing in a little group, a man came up and stood near us. He was a respectable-looking man, and I thought by his general appearance he was skeptical. I didn't think he had come up as an inquirer, but as I stood I noticed tears trickling down his face, and I went to him and asked him if he wanted to seek Christ, and he answered, "Yes." I went on talking to him, but he could not see what I meant. I thought I would use an illustration, and after I had put it to him I asked him if he saw it. He said, "No." I gave him another illustration, and asked him, "Do you see it now?" But he again replied, "No." I used two or three more illustrations, but he could not see them. He told me, "Mr. Moody, the fact is I do not feel the evidence of God." "But," I said, "I tell you you are not to be saved by your feelings," and I gave him this illustration; "What was it that saved Noah? Was it his ark, or was it his feelings, or his life, or his prayers?" "I see it now; it's all right," and he went away. This was Thursday night, and he had to leave on a night train. On the Sunday afternoon, while preaching in the Free Trade Hall, a man came and tapped me on the shoulder, and asked me if I knew him. I said, "No," and he said, "Do you remember when you spoke to me on Thursday and used the illustration of Noah's ark to save me?" "Yes," I answered. "Well, I got in then, and have been there ever since. The ark keeps me. Thank God for that illustration of the ark." May God help you to see this illustration tonight, and may you not be trying to save yourselves by your feelings, your tears, by your wounds. God has provided an ark, and every man who is in it is saved, and everyone who is out of it is lost.

Let us take another Bible illustration. Look at those two angels coming down to Sodom. They knew that God was going to destroy it utterly, and they led Lot out. What was it that saved his life? Was it his feelings, his tears? It was by obeying the call: "Escape for your life." And now God says, "Escape for your life"—escape to Mount Calvary. Don't delay, because He is going to destroy this world as He did Sodom. While Lot was in Sodom he was liable to the wrath of God, but the moment he got outside of Sodom he was safe. As long as a man remains out of Christ he is liable to the wrath of God and the fire of heaven. Look again, look at those children of Israel when they were commanded to put the blood on the doorposts and they would be saved from the hand of death. What was it that saved them? Was it the blood, or was it their feelings? The moment the blood was there they were saved; and if a man is behind the blood he is as safe as if he were walking the crystal pavement of heaven. When the blood was there the Angel of Death passed over. One moment the blood was off the posts, and the next moment it was on. It was instantaneous salvation.

Into the City of Refuge

You know Joshua received a command from God that he should erect six cities, three on each side of the Jordan, which were to be cities of refuge. There were to be great turnpikes and highways to these cities which were to be kept in proper repair, and the gates of the cities were to be kept open day and night, and signposts were to be placed along the road to provide for the man's guidance to these cities of refuge. The moment a man got inside one of those cities he was safe. His safety was instantaneous—the moment he stepped over the boundary line.

Just look at two men out in the woods chopping wood. As one of the men brings his ax down on the tree, it splits and flies from his hand and kills his companion. He knows what the consequences will be when the killing is discovered. He knows that it will be sure death the moment the news reaches the nearest relative of the deceased. The man who will not avenge the death of his relative is not considered a true man. If a relative would not avenge the death of a kinsman it was considered very dishonorable among the Israelites. The man knows that there is a city of refuge ten miles away, and if he can but reach it he is safe. Thank God, our city of refuge is not ten miles away. That man just leaps upon the highway. He does not take time to argue or think; he just leaps upon the highway and makes for the city of refuge. The news soon spreads that a man has been killed, and the murderer is making for the city of refuge. Whenever the brother learns that his kinsman has been killed, he starts after that poor fugitive. On they go—the avenger and the fugitive flying to his haven of hope. It is a life and death struggle. Look at him! See him as he leaps ditches and speeds along the road. Some people see him flying past. "Make haste," they cry, "because the avenger is upon you. Fly for your life." Ah, sinner, you do not know how far the avenger is behind you. Tonight he may be upon you. We do not know the day, the hour, when he will overtake us. The avenger, he knows, now is after him. On he goes, bounding over every obstacle, his speed at its utmost, and his face resolutely set toward the gate wherein his safety lies. He is terribly in earnest. See him leap over the highway; see his bruises; and on he goes panting and nearly exhausted. He sees the gates of the city. The officers see him from the walls, and they shout, "Hasten on, for the avenger is drawing near! He is behind thee." One moment he is outside the walls—the next moment he is inside. He is a saved man. One moment out, the next moment

in. What are these illustrations in the Bible for unless to show us how we are to be saved? Don't you see from this that conversion is instantaneous? One minute you may be outside, and the next minute you are inside.

Into the Land of Freedom

I will give you another illustration, which I think you will be able to get hold of. You will remember when we had slavery we used to have men come up from Kentucky, Tennessee, and other slave states in order to escape from slavery. I hope if there are any southern people here they will not think in this allusion I am trying to wound their feelings. We all remember when these black men came here how they used to be afraid lest someone should come and take them back. Why, I remember in the store we had a poor fugitive, and he used to be quaking all the time. Sometimes a customer would come in, and he would be uneasy all the time. He was afraid it was someone to take him back to slavery. But somebody tells him if he was in Canada he would be perfectly safe, and he says, "If I could only get into Canada, if I could only get under the Union Jack, I would be free." There are no slaves under the Union Jack he has been told—that is the flag of freedom; the moment he gets under it he is a free man. So he starts. We'll say there are no railways, and the poor fellow has got ten miles ahead when his master comes up, and he hears that his slave has fled for Canada and sets off in pursuit. Someone tells the poor fugitive that his master is after him. What does the poor fugitive do? What does he do? He redoubles his exertions and presses on, on, on, on. He was born a slave, and he knows a slave belongs to his master. Faster he goes. He knows his master is after him, and he will be taken if he comes up with him before he reaches the line. He says, "If I can only hold out and get under the English flag, the English government will protect me. The whole English army will come to protect me if need be." On he presses. He is now nearing the boundary line. One minute he is a slave and in an instant he is a free man.

My friends, don't mistake. These men can be saved tonight if they cross the line. Your old master, Satan, may be pressing down upon you, but there is a land of liberty up there, and the banner of heaven is that flag of love, and under the flag you are protected from all danger, and if an enemy comes near you God says, "If you touch him you touch the apple of my eye." And He will hold you in His right hand and keep you for the day of redemption. Will you go out of this hall tonight and doubt sudden conversion? Will you say a man cannot be saved all at once? Look what He said to Moses. He told Him to put a brazen serpent on a pole, and whenever a man looked at that serpent he would live. If some of the preachers we have now in Chicago had lived then they would have said a man may look six thousand years at that and he wouldn't be saved. A man would die while they were discussing it.

A few days ago, I heard of a minister who said I was preaching a most pernicious doctrine when I preached sudden conversion. But point out to me one single conversion in this blessed Bible that was not a sudden conversion. Why, every conversion recorded in the Bible was instantaneous, and if preachers tell men conversion is a life work they are keeping men out of the kingdom of God. We can have instant conversion. "Now is the day of salvation." I tell you sinners, escape for your lives, fly to the haven of safety—look, look, look, at the crucified One, and you will be saved tonight. Look and live. You will become a child of God

for time and eternity. The blessing will come upon you—whenever we look we can be saved. Just go back to that camp of Israel. Everyone who looked at that brazen serpent was well. The remedy was instantaneous.

When I was in England they were at me all the time about this sudden conversion. They said it was a life work from the cradle down to the grave. I did all I could to show them it. One day I was walking down the streets of York when I saw a soldier coming down. You can tell a soldier in England in an instant by his coat. I stepped up to him and said, "My friend, I am a stranger in this country, and you will pardon me if I ask you a question. How long did it take you to become a soldier?" Well, he laughed in my face. I suppose he thought I was very green to ask him such a question. But he told me that he made up his mind to enlist in Queen Victoria's army, and he went to a recruiting sergeant, and he put an English shilling into the palm of his hand, and from that moment he was a soldier. When he had taken that shilling, from that moment he became one of the Queen's army, and if he goes back he becomes a deserter and, if caught, is put into prison.

He first made up his mind to enlist, and that is the way to become a Christian. Make up your mind. The next thing he did was to take the shilling, and from that moment he became a soldier. When you make up your mind to be a Christian, the next thing you have to do is to accept His terms—take salvation as a gift. You wonder how a man can become a Christian as that man became a soldier. He was a citizen one moment; the next moment he was a soldier. He was no longer his own master when he had accepted that shilling. He belonged to the English army. So the moment you enlist in Christ's army you belong to

Him. If you want to become a Christian take Christ's shilling as a gift. The minute you take that gift, that minute you are a child of God. See what He says: To as many as receive Him gave He power to become the sons and daughters of [God]. When you accept Him He becomes your way, your truth, your light, your all in all. You can have His gift if you will receive Him tonight.

While I was in New York an Irishman stood up in a young converts' meeting and told how he had been saved. He said in his broken Irish brogue that I used an illustration and that that illustration saved him. And I declare that is the only man I ever knew who was converted without being spoken to. He said I used an illustration of a wrecked vessel, and said that all would perish unless some assistance came. Presently a lifeboat came alongside and the captain shouted, "Leap into the lifeboat—leap for your lives, or you will perish," and when I came to the point I said, "Leap into the lifeboat; Christ is your lifeboat," and he just leaped into the lifeboat of salvation and was saved. If a man goes out of the tabernacle tonight without salvation it won't be my fault; it will be his own. It will not be because the ark is not open, but because he will not accept the invitation to enter; it will not be because the blessing is not there, but because he will not take it, for it's there. May God open your eyes to accept Him before you leave this building—to accept salvation as a gift.

Moody was raised in a poverty-stricken, spiritually dead home. Because of his own difficult childhood he was fully aware of the importance parents play in the lives of their children.

His address to parents consists of stern warnings to be active in the conversion of their children. The home is the fundamental place for the gain or loss of a child's soul, and many parents have failed in bringing their children along the right path spiritually, only to experience sorrow in later years.

Both mothers and fathers are responsible for their child's spiritual development. Often fathers do not recognize the importance of their influence in such matters. If they display a disregard for religion, it is quite possible the sons will do the same. If a mother is too busy to nurture a religious desire in her child, she may find herself losing that child to sin. While the minister can only preach the gospel on a limited basis, the home can create a warm environment for its steady growth and eventual fruition in the life of a boy or girl.

CHAPTER THIRTEEN

Address to Parents

PART ONE

I want to call your attention to Deuteronomy 5:29. "Oh that there were such an heart in them, that they would fear me, and keep all my commandments always, that it might be well with them, and with their children forever!" And also the sixth chapter and seventh verse, "And thou shalt teach them diligently unto thy children, and shalt talk of them when thou sittest in thine house, and when thou walkest by the way, and when thou liest down, and when thou risest up."

I used to think when I was superintendent on the North Side, when I was laboring among the children and trying to get the parents interested to save their children, that if I ever did become a preacher I would have but one text and one sermon, and that should be addressed to parents, because when we get them interested their interest will be apparent in the children. We used to say, if we get the lambs in, the old sheep will follow, but I didn't find that to be the case. When we got the children interested in one Sunday, the parents would be sometimes pulling the other way all the week, and, before Sunday came again, the impression that had been made would be gone. And I came to the conclusion that, unless we could get the parents interested, or could get some kind Christian to look after those children, it would almost be a sin to bring them to Christ. If there is no one to nurse them, to care for them, and just to water the seed, why they are liable to

be drawn away and, when they grow up, to be far more difficult to reach.

I wish to say tonight that I am as strong as ever upon sudden conversion, and there are a great many ministers, a great many parents, who scoff and laugh when they hear of children who have been brought unto Christ at these meetings.

Now, in many of the churches the sermons go over their heads; they don't do the young any good; they don't understand the preaching, and if they are impressed here we ought not to discourage them. My friends, the best thing we can do is to bring them early to Christ. These earliest impressions never, never leave them, and I do not know why they should not grow up in the service of Christ. I contend that those who are converted early are the best Christians. Take the man who is converted at fifty. He has continually to fight against his old habits; but take a young man or a young girl, and they get a character to form and a whole long life to give to Christ. An old man unconverted got up in an inquiry meeting recently and said he thought we were very hard-hearted down in the tabernacle; we went right by when we saw some young person. He thought, as he was old, he might be snatched away before these young people; but with us it seemed as if Christ was of more importance to the young than the old. I confess truly that I have that feeling. If a young man is converted he perhaps has a long life of fifty years to devote to Christ, but an old man is not worth much. Of course, his soul is worth much, but he is not worth much for labor.

An Object Lesson

While down at a convention in Illinois an old man got up, past seventy years; he said he remembered but one thing about his father, and that one thing followed him all through life. He could not remember his death, he had no recollection of his funeral, but he recollected his father one winter night, taking a little chip, and with his pocket knife whittling out a cross, and with the tears in his eyes he held up that cross and told how God in His infinite love sent His Son down here to redeem us, how He had died on the cross for us. The story of the cross followed him through life; and I tell you if you teach these children truths they will follow them through life. We have got so much unbelief among us, like those disciples when they rebuked the people for bringing the children to Christ, but He said, "Suffer little children to come unto me, and forbid them not, for of such is the kingdom of heaven."

I heard of a Sunday school concert at which a little child of eight was going to recite. Her mother had taught her, and when the night came the little thing was trembling so she could hardly speak. She commenced, "Jesus said," and completely broke down. Again she tried it, "Jesus said, suffer," but she stopped once more. A third attempt was made by her: "Suffer little children—and don't anybody stop them, for He wants them all to come," and that is the truth. There is not a child who has parents in the tabernacle but He wants, and if you bring them in the arms of your faith, ask the Son of God to bless them, train them in the knowledge of God, and teach them as you walk your way, as you lie down at night, as you rise up in the

morning, they will be blessed. But I can imagine some skeptic in yonder gallery saying, "That's well enough, but it's all talk. Why, I have known children of ministers and Christian people who have turned out worse than others." I've heard that all my life, but I tell you that is one of the devil's lies. I will admit I've heard of many Christian people having bad children, but they are not the worst children. That was tested once. A whole territory was taken in which fathers and mothers were Christians, and it was found that two-thirds of the children were members of churches, but they took a portion of [the] country where all the fathers and mothers were not Christians, and it was found that not one in twelve of the children attended churches. That was the proportion.

Look at a good man who has a bad son. Do you want to know the reason? In the first place children do not inherit grace. Because fathers and mothers are good that is no reason why their children should be good. Children are not born good. Men may talk of natural goodness, but I don't find it. Goodness must come down from the Father of Light. To have a good nature a man must be born of God. There is another reason—a father may be a very good man, but the mother may be pulling in another way. She may be ambitious, and may want her children to occupy a high worldly position. She has some high ambition and trains the child for the world. Again, it may be the reverse—a holy, pious mother and a worldly father, and it is pretty hard when father and mother do not pull together. Another reason is, and you will excuse me the expression, but a great many people have got very little sense about bringing up children. Now, I've known mothers who punish their children by making them read the Bible. Do not be guilty of such a thing. If you want children not to hate the

Bible, do not punish them by making them read it. It is the most attractive book in the world. But that is the way to spoil its attractiveness, and make them hate it with a perfect hate. There is another reason. A great many people are engaged in looking after other people's children and neglecting their own. No father or mother has a right to do this, whatever may be the position they hold in the world. The father may be a statesman or a great businessman, but he is responsible for his children. If they do not look after their children they will have to answer for it someday. There will be a blight in their paths, and their last days will be very bitter.

Diligent Instruction

There are a great many reasons which I might bring forward if I had time; why good people's children turn out bad; but let me say one word about bringing up these children, how to train them in Christian ways. The Word is very plain: "teach them diligently." In the street cars, as we go about our business night and morning, talk of Christ and heavenly things. It seems to me as if these things were the last things many of us think about and as if Christ was banished from our homes. A great many people have a good name as Christians. They talk about ministers and Sunday schools, and [they] will come down and give a dinner to the bootblacks and seem to be strong patrons of the cause of Christ, but when it comes to talking to children personally about Christ, that is another thing. The Word is very plain: "teach them diligently." And if we want them to grow up a blessing to the church of God and to the world, we must teach them.

I can imagine some of you saying, "It may be very well for Mr. Moody to lay down theories, but there are a great many difficulties in the way." I heard of a minister who said he had the grandest theory upon the bringing up of children. God gave him seven children, and he found that his theory was all wrong. They were all differently constituted. I will admit that this is one difficulty; but if our heart is set upon this one thing— to have our children in glory—God will give us all the light we need. He is not going to leave us in darkness. If that is not the aim of your heart, make it this very night. I would rather, if I went tonight, leave my children in the hope of Christ than leave them millions of [dollars]. It seems to me as if we were too ambitious to have them make a name, instead of to train them up for the life they are to lead forever. And another thing about [discipline]: never teach them revenge. If a baby falls down on the floor, don't give it a book with which to strike the floor. They have enough of revenge in them without being taught it. Then, don't teach them to lie. You don't like that; but how many parents have told their children to go to the door, when they did not want to see a visitor, and say, "Mother is not in." That is a lie. Children are very keen to detect. They very soon see those lies, and this lays the foundation for a good deal of trouble afterward. "Ah," some of you say, "I never do this." Well, suppose some person comes in that you don't want to see. You give them a welcome, and when he goes you entreat him to stay, but the moment he is out of the door you say, "What a bore!" The children wonder at first, but they very soon begin to imitate the father and mother. Children are very good imitators.

Positive Example

A father and mother never ought to do a thing that they don't want their children to do. If you don't want them to smoke, don't you smoke; if you don't want them to chew, don't you chew; if you don't want them to play billiards, don't you play billiards; if you don't want them to drink, don't you drink, because children are grand imitators. A lady once told me she was in her pantry on one occasion, and she was surprised by the ringing of the bell. As she whirled round to see who it was, she broke a tumbler. Her little child was standing there, and she thought her mother was doing a very correct thing, and the moment the lady left the pantry, the child commenced to break all the tumblers she could get hold of. You may laugh, but children are very good imitators. If you don't want them to break the Sabbath day, keep it holy yourself; if you want them to go to church, go to church yourself. It is very often by imitation that they utter their first oath, that they tell their first lie, and then they grow upon them. And when they try to quit the habit, it has grown so strong upon them that they cannot do it. "Ah," some say, "we do not believe in children being converted. Let them grow up to manhood and womanhood, and then talk of converting them." They forget that in the meantime their characters are formed, and perhaps [they] have commenced to enter those dens of infamy, and when they have arrived at manhood and womanhood, we find it is too late to alter their character. How unfaithful we are. "Teach them diligently."

How many parents in this vast assembly know where their sons are? Their sons may be in the halls of vice. Where does your son spend his evenings? You don't care enough for him to ascertain what kind of company he keeps, what kind of books he reads; [you] don't care whether or not he is reading those miserable, trashy novels and getting false ideas of life. You don't know till it is too late. Oh, may God wake us up and teach us the responsibility devolving upon us in training our children.

Active Concern

While in London, an officer in the Indian army, hearing of us being over there, said, "Lord, now is the time for my son to be saved." He got a furlough and left India and came to London. When he came there for that purpose, of course God was not going to let him go away without the blessing. How many men are interested in their sons who would do as this man did? How many men are sufficiently interested in them to bring them here? How many parents stand in the way of the salvation of their children? I don't know anything that discouraged me more than when I was superintendent on the North Side than when, after begging with parents to allow their children to come to Sunday school—and how few of them came— whenever spring arrived those parents would take their children from the school and lead them into those German gardens. And a great many are reaping the consequences.

I remember one mother who heard that her boy was impressed at our meeting. She said her son was a good enough boy, and he didn't need to be converted. I pleaded with that mother, but all my pleading was of no account. I tried my influence with the boy; but while I was pulling one way she was pulling the other. Her influence prevailed. Naturally it would. Well, to make a long story short, some time after, I happened to be in the county jail, and I saw him there. "How did you come here?" I asked. "Does your mother know where you are?" "No, don't tell her; I came in under an assumed name, and I am going to Joliet for four years. Do not let my mother know of this," he pleaded. "She thinks I am in the army." I used to call on that mother, but I had promised her boy I would not tell her, and for four years she mourned over that boy. She thought he had died on the battlefield or in a southern hospital. What a blessing he might have been to that mother, if she had only helped us to bring him to Christ. But that mother is only a specimen of hundreds and thousands of parents in Chicago. If we would have more family altars in our homes and train [our children] to follow Christ, why, the Son of God would lead them into "green pastures," and instead of having sons who curse the mothers who gave them birth, they would bless their fathers and mothers.

In the Indiana Penitentiary I was told of a man who had come there under an assumed name. His mother heard where he was. She was too poor to ride there, and she footed it. Upon her arrival at the prison she at first did not recognize her son in his prison suit and short hair, but when she did see who it was, that mother threw her arms about that boy and said, "I am to blame for this; if I had only taught you to obey God and keep the Sabbath you would not have been here." How many mothers, if they were honest, could attribute the ruination of their children to the early training? God has said if we don't teach them those blessed commandments He will destroy us, and the law of God never changes. It does not only apply to those callous men who make no profession of religion, but to those who stand high in the church if they make the same mistake.

Punishment for Failure

Look at that high priest Eli. He was a good man and a kind one, but one thing he neglected to do—to train his children for God. The Lord gave him warning, and at last destruction came upon his house. Look at that old man ninety-eight years old, with his white hair, like some of the men on the platform, sitting in the town of Shiloh waiting to hear the result of the battle. The people of Israel came into the town and took out the ark of God, and when it came into the camp a great shout went up to heaven, for they had the ark of their God among them. They thought they were going to succeed, but they had disobeyed God. When the battle came on they fought manfully, but no less than thirty thousand of the Israelites fell by the swords of their enemies, and a messenger came running from the field through the streets of Shiloh to where Eli was, crying, "Israel is defeated, the ark is taken, and Hophni and Phinehas have been slain in battle." And when the old priest heard it [he] fell backward by the side of the gate, and his neck broke, and he died. Oh, what a sad ending to that man, and when his daughter-in-law heard the news there was another death in that family recorded. In that house destruction was complete.

My friends, God is true, and if we do not obey Him in this respect He will punish us. It is only a question of time. Look at King David. See him waiting for the tidings of the battle. He had been driven from his throne by his own son whom he loved, but when the news came that he was slain, see how he cried, "Oh, my son Absalom, would to God I had died for thee." It was worse than death to him, but God had to punish him because he did not train his son to love the Lord.

My friends, if He punished Eli and David He will punish you and me. May God forgive us for the past, and may we commence a new record tonight. My friends, if you have not a family altar erect one tonight. Let us labor that our children may be brought to glory. Don't say children are too young. Mothers and fathers, if you hear your children have been impressed with religion, don't stand in the way of their conversion, but encourage them all you can.

While I was attending a meeting in a certain city some time ago, a lady came to me and said, "I want you to go home with me; I have something to say to you." When we reached her home, there were some friends there. After they had retired, she put her arms on the table, and tears began to come into her eyes, but with an effort she repressed her emotion. After a struggle she went on to say that she was going to tell me something which she had never told any other living person. I should not tell it now, but she has gone to another world. She said she had a son in Chicago, and she was very anxious about him. When he was young he got interested in religion at the rooms of the Young Men's Christian Association. He used to go out in the street and circulate tracts. He was her only son, and she was very ambitious he should make a name in the world, and wanted to get him into the very highest circles. Oh what a mistake people make about these highest circles. Society is false. It is a sham. She was deceived like a good many more votaries of fashion and hunters after wealth at the present time. She thought it was beneath her son to go down and associate with these young men who hadn't much money. She tried to get him away from them, but they had more influence than she had, and finally, to break his whole association, she packed him off to a boarding school. He went soon to Yale College, and she supposed he got into one of those miserable secret societies there that have ruined so many young men, and the next thing she heard was that the boy had gone astray.

She began to write letters urging him to come into the kingdom of God, but she heard that he tore up the letters without reading them. She went to him to try and regain whatever influence she possessed over him, but her efforts were useless, and she came home with a broken heart. He left New Haven, and for two years they heard nothing of him. At last they heard he was in Chicago, and his father found him and gave him thirty thousand dollars to start in business. They thought it would change him, but it didn't. They asked me when I went back to Chicago to try and use my influence with him. I got a friend to invite him to his house one night, where I intended to meet him, but he heard I was to be there and did not come near. Like a good many other young men, who seem to be afraid of me, I tried many times to reach him but could not. While I was traveling one day on the New Haven railroad, I bought a New York paper, and in it I saw a dispatch saying he had been drowned in Lake Michigan. His father came on to find his body, and, after considerable searching, he discovered it. All the clothes and his body were covered with sand. The body was taken home to that brokenhearted mother. She said, "If I thought he was in heaven I would have peace." Her disobedience of God's law came back upon her.

So, my friends, if you have a boy impressed with the gospel, help him to come to Christ. Bring him in the arms of your faith, and he will unite you closer to Him. Let us have faith in Him, and let us pray day and night that our children may be born of the Spirit.

PART TWO

I have had a little trouble to find a text for tonight. All last night and this morning I was trying to find one but could not. This morning, however, in coming out of Farwell Hall prayer meeting, a mother whom I have known for a great many years came to me with tears running down her cheeks and nearly sinking to the floor with grief. "O! Mr. Moody," she said, "have these meetings to close and not one of my children saved?" and the thought flashed on my mind, "I have got a text." And it is in the ninth chapter of Mark, [verse nineteen] which we have read: "bring him unto me."

The disciples had failed to cure this man's son. James, John, and Peter had been with the Master upon the mount, where they had seen the transfiguration, and when they came down from that scene they found a great company around His disciples asking them questions. I suppose the skeptics were laughing and ridiculing the religion of Jesus Christ and its teachers. His disciples had failed—they had not been able to cast out the dumb spirit, and the father said, when asked a question, "I have brought my son to your disciples, and they cannot heal him." And He said, "bring him unto me." When he was brought, the devil threw him down. The moment the poor deaf and dumb man came into the presence of Christ, the spirit within began to tear at him. This is often the case now. Sometimes when there is a good deal of prayer going up for people they become worse. When the Spirit begins with men, instead of getting better they sometimes become worse, and it seems as if God did not answer prayer; but this is only a sign that God is at work.

Take Him to Jesus

A mother was praying for and giving good counsel to a loved son lately, and he said [that] if ever she spoke to him about religion again he would leave the house. Whenever the Word was pre-sented to him, he became worse. That mother did not take her son to the preachers, but thank God, she took him to Christ. She didn't take him to the church, she did not take him to her friends—she knew that if he was to be saved it was only by Jesus Christ. She took him to the Master, and the result was that within forty-eight hours after saying this to his mother, that wayward boy was brought to the feet of Jesus. So if any have been praying earnestly and faithfully for their sons without success, my dear friends, get your eyes off the church, off friends, off everything else but Him, and let our prayer go up day and night, and it will be heard, because we have God's word [on] it. An answer is sure.

We are not sure whether the sun will rise tomorrow morning, but we are sure that He will answer our prayers. It is sure. If we hold on to God in prayer and find that we don't get our supplications answered in a month—in a year—we are to hold on till the blessing comes. Now, it may be that this mother, like a great many mothers, has been looking to the prayers here—looking to what has been going on in these meetings, and has been saying, "There are so many Christian people praying, and surely God will bless my boys owing to these prayers." Now, we must get our eyes off [of] multitudes, sermons, others' prayers, and let all our expectations be only from Him, and a blessing will come.

These meetings have been very profitable, and during the weeks past I have noticed that those fathers and mothers who have gone out after other people's children, have had their own wonderfully blessed. Whatever good you do to other people's children . . . will come back upon yours. It may be that that mother was very selfish, and wanted her sons blessed only; she hasn't, perhaps, been trying to bring others under the influence of the Lord Jesus Christ. Every day fathers and mothers come to me with tears in their eyes—fathers and mothers who have gone out after other people's children—testifying how their children have been blessed. A mother who has been working for Him here, told me that her five children—every one of them—had been blessed by these meetings, and I suppose that if I put it to the vote many parents here would stand up and testify as to the answers received to prayers and personal efforts for their children. I was very much surprised lately to see an old citizen coming into our meetings with a wayward son by his side night after night. Every evening he was to be seen with him, and last Monday evening he got up and told what God had done for him in answer to personal effort. That father woke up and did not rest till he was answered.

Now it seems to me, just as we are leaving this city, that a great many parents are beginning to wake up to the fact that these meetings are about to be closed, and their children have not been blessed. When we were in Great Britain, in Manchester, a father woke up to the fact that we were going away from that town. Just as we were about closing he got wonderfully interested in the meetings, and when we had gone to another town he said to his wife, "I have made a mistake: I should have taken you and the children and the servants to those meetings. Now I'm going to take my son from business, and take you and the children and the servants to the town where they are being held now and take a house and have you all attend the meetings." He came and took a house and sat down determined to remain there till all had been blessed. I remember him coming to me one night soon after arriving and saying, "Mr. Moody,

my wife has [been] converted; thank God for that. If I get nothing else I am well paid." A few nights [later] he came in and said his son had become converted, and then told me one of the servants had been brought under the influence, and so he went on until the last day we were to be in that town arrived, and he came to me and said the last one of the family had yielded himself up to Christ, and he went back to his native city rejoicing. When we were in London the father and son came up and assisted in the work, and I don't know a happier man in all Europe than that one.

How many parents living almost within sight of this building have felt no interest in these meetings; yet they know their children are hastening down to death and ruin. Business must be attended to [, and] time is very precious, and they have gone to waste, [as far as] bringing their sons and daughters under religious influences [is concerned]. And the result will be that many and many a family in this city will see dark days and bitter hours, and many a parent will go down to their graves on account of wayward children. Now, why won't you even in the closing hours of these meetings—why won't parents wake up and bring their children to Christ? Just hold them up in the arms of [your] faith and pray, "Lord, Jesus, save these children that God has given me; grant, O God, that they may be with me in glory."

Confess Your Faults

It may be that some father or mother is saying, "I have not been living right myself in God's sight; so how can I talk to my children of Him?" It seems to me the best thing to do under those circumstances is to make a confession. I knew a father who a few days ago told his children that he had not been living right. The tears rolled down his cheeks as he asked their forgiveness. "Why," said one child, "do you ask us for forgiveness? Why, father, you have always been kind to us." "I know I have, my child," he answered, "but I have not been doing my whole duty toward you: I've never had a family altar. I have paid more heed to your temporal welfare than to your spiritual, but I am going to have a family altar now." He took down his Bible and began there, and it wasn't long before his children were touched.

Suppose you haven't been living in accordance with the gospel: why not make an open confession to your wife—to your children—set up a family altar, and pray for your children? It will not be long before you will be blessed. Let us come to Him. Let us look straight away from the churches. Let us look from every influence to only the Master Himself, and let His words ring in the soul of every parent here tonight: "bring Him unto me." Have you got a wayward son? He may be in some distant state or foreign land, and by the last news you received of him was rushing headlong down to ruin. My friend, you can reach him—you can reach him by intercession at the throne.

A short time after I got here I received a letter from Scotland—I haven't time to read it. The letter was sent to a minister, and he forwarded it to me. It was the gushing of a loving father. He asked us to look out for his boy, whose name was Willie. That name touched my heart because it was the name of my own boy. I asked Mr. Sawyer to try and get on the track of that boy some weeks ago, but all his efforts were fruitless. But in Scotland that Christian father was holding that boy up to God in prayer, and last Friday, in yonder room, among those asking for prayer was that Willie, and

he told me a story there that thrilled my heart. [He] testified how the prayers of that father and mother in that far-off land had been instrumental in affecting his salvation. Don't you think the heart of that father and mother will rejoice? He said he was rushing madly to destruction, but there was a power in those prayers that saved that boy. Don't you think, my friends, that God hears and answers prayers, and shall we not lift up our voices to Him in prayer that He will bless the children He has given us?

You know how Elisha was blessed by the Shunammite woman, and she was blessed in return by a child. You know how the child died, and how she resolved to go at once to the man of God. I can imagine Elisha sitting on Mount Carmel, and seeing that woman far off, and saying to his servant, "Do you see that woman? I think I know her face—it is the Shunammite, now that I see her face. Go run and ask her [if] it is well with her." Off the servant runs, and when the servant comes to her she says, "It is well." Although her child is dead she says, "It is well." She knows that the man who gave her the child could raise it up. She runs up to the master and falls down, putting her arms about his feet; and the servant tries to put her away. But Elisha won't let him. He says to the servant, "Here, take this staff and go and lay it upon the face of the dead child," and tells the servant to go home with her; but she won't leave the man of God. She doesn't want to lean upon the staff or the servant. It wasn't the servant or the staff that she wanted, but the man of God that she wanted with her. "You come with me," she says. "You can raise him up." She would not leave him till he came to her house. He went in and closed the door and prayed to God that the child would be restored, and then lay upon the child, mouth to mouth, eyes to eyes, hands to hands, and the child began to sneeze, and there was the child of the Shunammite woman raised up. Bear in mind that it was not the servant nor the staff, but the Master Himself that saved the child. My friends, if we lean upon the Master we shall not be disappointed. The moment that child was brought to the Master the wish of that woman was granted, and if we as parents bring our children to Him, we shall not be disappointed.

But there is another thing I want to call your attention to. We don't fast enough. This fasting doesn't mean fasting from meat, as many people think necessary. It seems to me if I had a wayward boy I should put myself at the feet of Christ, and fast a little, by keeping away from amusements, [and] from theaters. I find a great many worldly Christians going off into the theaters. They say, "I only go for a little relaxation; of course, I could stop going whenever I like and needn't be influenced by them; I only go occasionally." A worldly Christian said to me, "I only go once a month." "Well," said I, "how about your boy; he may not have the will power you have, and your example in going only once a month may only be the means of his going there all the time." My friends, a man may have great will power, yet his son may have very little. Therefore, a little fasting in this regard would be good for our children.

Avoid Hurtful Influences

We should abstain from all pleasures that are liable to be hurtful to our children. If you fathers and mothers want your children to keep from evil influences you ought to keep away from them yourselves. If they see you indulging in these pleasures, they think they are on the right side by doing the same thing.

A young man says, "I don't want to be any better than my father; and he goes to the theaters." Now, there are young men who have come into the inquiry rooms one night and the next night have gone off to the theaters. I don't know if a man with the Spirit of God should go there. These men may one night be here and the next night may go off to some amusement where they hear as a waltz, "What Shall the Harvest Be" or "Almost Persuaded." How Christian men and women can go to such places as that, I cannot conceive. If it is not sacrilege, then nothing is. What can those worldly Christians expect from their children if they frequent such places? I think the time has come for a little fasting. When Christ died it was to separate His church from the world, and how can a man who has consecrated himself as a child of God, go back to the world without trampling that blood under his feet? When will the day come when a man of God shall make known by his conversation, by his actions, by his general appearance, that he has been freed from the curse of the world?

Then another thing. It seems to me that every man should have a family altar in his house. And if we cannot deliver prayers, let us take up each of our children by name; let us ask that Johnny, while playing with his schoolmates, may be kept from temptation. Why, we forget that a little child's temptations are just as much to him as ours are to us. The boy at school has just as heavy trials as we have. And then pray for Mary. If she is in trouble, bring it out and pray that God may give her power to overcome any besetting sin that she may have in her heart. I believe the day has come when we should have more religion in our families, more family altars. I believe that the want of this is doing more injury to the growth of our children than anything else. Why, long before the church was in a building, it was in the homes of the people. We can make the family altar a source of happiness. By it we can make the home the [most] pleasant place in the world. Let us, when we get up in the morning, bright and fresh, have some family devotions. If a man runs downtown immediately on getting up, doesn't get home until five o'clock, and then has family devotions, the children will be tired and [fall] sound asleep. And it seems to me that we should give a little more time to our children and call them around the altar in the morning. Or suppose we ask them to recite a verse, to recite a portion of a hymn—it must not necessarily be a long one—and, after that, have some singing, if the children can sing. Do not be in a hurry to get it out of the way, as if the service was a nuisance; take a little time. Let them sing some religious hymns. The singing need not be all psalms, but there should be a few simple religious hymns. Let the little children be free from all restraint. Then pray for each of them.

Tie Church and
Home Lessons Together

Another thing. It seems to me that we devote too little time to studying the Sunday school lesson. You know now we have a uniform lesson all over the country. That lesson should be taken up by parents and they should try to explain it to their children. But how many ever think of this—how many parents ever take the trouble to inquire even as to the kind of Sunday school teachers who instruct their children? And then we should take our children into the churches with us. It seems to me we are retrograding at the present day. A great many of our children are never seen in the churches at all. Even if the sermon doesn't touch them they are getting into

good habits. And then if the minister says a weak thing, don't take it up, don't pick it out or speak of it before the children, because you are bringing your minister into disrespect with your children. If you have a minister whom you cannot respect, you ought to get out of that church as soon as you can.

Encourage them to bring the text home; let the Word be spoken to them at all times, in season and out of season. If the great Bible truths sink down into their hearts, the fruit will be precious: wisdom will blossom upon them, and they will become useful in the church and in the world. Now, how many parents will not take the trouble to explain to the children what the minister preaches? Take your children into the pews and let them hear the Word of God, and if they do not understand it show it to them. You know the meat they require is the same as we feed on; but if the pieces are too large for them we must cut it up for them—cut it finer. If the sermon is a hard one, cut it into thin slices so that they can take it. There was a time when our little boy did not like to go to church and would get up in the morning and say to his mother, "What day is tomorrow?" "Tuesday." "Next day?" "Wednesday." "Next day?" "Thursday," and so on till he came to the answer, "Sunday." "Dear me," he would moan. I said to his mother, "We cannot have our boy grow up to hate Sunday in that way; that will never do."

That is the way I used to feel when I was a boy. I used to look upon Sunday with a certain amount of dread. Very few kind words were associated with that day. I don't know that the minister ever said a kind thing or ever even put his hand on my head. I don't know that the minister even noticed me, unless it was when I was asleep in the gallery, and he woke me up. This kind of thing won't do. We must make Sunday the most attractive day of the week; not a day to be dreaded but a day of pleasure. Well, the mother took the work up with this boy. Bless those mothers in their work with the children. Sometimes I feel as if I would rather be the mother of John Wesley or Martin Luther or John Knox than have all the glories in the world. Those mothers who are faithful with the children God has given them will not go unrewarded. My wife went to work and took those Bible stories and put those blessed truths in a light that the child could comprehend, and soon the [boy's] feeling of dread for the Sabbath was the other way. "What day's tomorrow?" he would ask. "Sunday." "I am glad." And if we make these Bible truths interesting—break them up in some shape so that these children can get at them, then they will begin to enjoy them.

Now, there's no influence like a mother's, and if the mothers will give a little time to the children in this way, and read them some Bible story, or tell it [to them] in a simple way, it will not be long before the children know the Bible from beginning to end. I know a little boy, eleven years of age, who got up last Monday in the meeting and told how he found Christ. His father began by telling him Bible stories, and now he knows them as well as I do. The little fellow of eleven years is quite a preacher. Let us pick out the stories that will interest them from Genesis to Revelation, and that is the way to bring our children to Christ. It will fill them with the gospel— fill them with Christ. They will soon be so full of Jesus that when an infidel comes to unseat their faith, he will find no room for infidelity.

Now, New Year's Day is coming on. I haven't much time to speak about that now, but let me ask what are you going to do when the young men come to your homes on that day? Are you going to

set wine before them? Are you going to tempt the sons of others to go astray? Don't offer them, I implore you, that hellish cup; don't be the instruments to lead the children of others away from the God of their fathers. I hope that in this city this infernal custom will soon be swept away. The idea of having some of our best young men reeling on the streets beastly drunk on the first day of the year is revolting, and yet there are Christians who, when young men visit them on New Year's Day, just urge the cup on them—press them to take it. They have got some new kind of wine, and they want them to taste it, and urge the young man just to take a little and the young man hasn't got will—hasn't got backbone enough to resist the temptation; [he] hasn't the power to say no. He goes to another house, and the same thing is repeated, and so on, until at night the poor fellow goes home intoxicated and breaks the heart of [his] mother. Remember when you offer the cup, if it is not to your own boy it is to somebody else's boy.

I have a great respect for that old woman who, with ribbons flying, ran into a crowded thoroughfare and rescued a child from under a wagon. Someone asked her, "Is he your child?" "No," she replied, "but he is someone's child." She had a mother's heart, and bear in mind when a young man comes to you, as you put the cup before him—remember, he is some other one's child. God has given us a charge, not only in looking to the salvation of our own children, but we have to see to the salvation of the children of others.

Do All You Can

Now, let me say a word to the unfaithful fathers. At the close of this meeting, if you have been unfaithful to the children God has given you, why not stay and then go home and make an honest confession to your children? If you have a boy who is a reckless young man—if he is a drunkard, ask yourselves, "Have I done all that I could; have I ever set before him the truth of Christ?"

Not long ago a young man went home late. He had been in the habit of going home late, and the father began to [believe] that he had gone astray. He told his wife to go to bed and dismissed the servants and said he would sit up till his son came home. The boy came home drunk, and the father in his anger gave him a push into the street and told him never to enter his house again, and [he] shut the door. He went into the parlor and sat down and began to think, "Well, I may be to blame for that boy's conduct, after all. I have never prayed with him; I have never warned him of the dangers of the world." And the result of his reflections was that he put on his overcoat and hat and started out to find his boy. The first policeman he met he asked eagerly, "Have you seen my boy?" "No." On he went till he met another. "Have you seen anything of my son?" He ran from one to another all that night, but not until the morning did he find him. He took him by the arm and led him home and kept him till he was sober. Then he said, "My dear boy, I want you to forgive me; I've never prayed for you; I've never lifted my heart to God for you; I've been the means of leading you astray, and I want your forgiveness." The boy was touched, and what was the result? Within twenty-four hours that son became a convert and gave up that cup.

It may be that some father has had a wayward son. Go to God, and on your knees confess it. Let the voice of Jesus sink down in your heart tonight. "Bring him unto me." A father whom I have known for many years said to me this afternoon, with the tears trickling down his cheeks, "I want to tell you something that I have never told in public. Forty-three years ago, when I was five years old, I was sick with scarlet fever, and my mother knelt down and prayed to God if it was His will, that her boy might be spared. My father was a drinking man, and she also prayed that I might be kept safe from the cup. My mother died early, but my mother's prayer has followed me all those years, and I have never touched one drop of liquor." Last night a young man, the son of that man, got up and told his experiences. Yes, the mother's prayer for her little boy, five years old, was answered. That prayer was answered. Why shall we not lift up our hearts in prayer for our children? Let us plead day and night till God saves them—till he brings them into the ark of safety. May the God of Israel save our children.

I remember being in the camp and a man came to me and said, "Mr. Moody, when the Mexican war began I wanted to enlist. My mother, seeing I was resolved, said if I became a Christian I might go. She pleaded and prayed that I might become a Christian, but I wouldn't. I said when the war was over I would become a Christian, but not till then. All her pleading was in vain, and at last, when I was going away, she took out a watch and said, 'My son, your father left this to me when he died. Take it, and I want you to remember that every day at twelve o'clock your mother will be praying for you.' Then she gave me her Bible and marked out passages and put a few different references in the flyleaf. When I had been gone four months, I took the watch, and it was twelve o'clock, but I remembered that my mother at that hour was praying for me. Something prompted me to ask the officer to relieve me for a little, and I stepped behind a tree out on those plains of Mexico and cried to the God of my mother to save me." My friends, God saved him, and he went through the Mexican war. "And now," he said, "I have enlisted again to see if I can do any good for my Master's cause." And the old man was down among the soldiers there preaching Christ. My friends, let us believe that God answers prayer, and let us not cease our supplication till salvation comes to our children, and all our little ones are brought into the ark of safety.

The conversion of men is very important to Moody because men are the leaders in the kingdom of God. He does not discount the importance of women, but he believes that men are harder to win to Christ. They do not see the importance of religion and are indecisive about spiritual matters.

Moody calls for a decision to be made by the men of the city: either follow God or Baal. To him there is not a third way, and the time to decide is now. The kingdom of God is at hand; enter it today.

Excuses abound, but for Moody the primary problem is a lack of moral courage to come forward. He hammers away at this issue and demands that every indecisive man hearing his voice come forward for salvation. This sermon resulted in the conversion of two thousand men.

CHAPTER FOURTEEN

Address to Young Men

I want to call your attention tonight to a text which you will find in the eighteenth chapter of First Kings, twenty-first verse: "And Elijah came unto all the people, and said, How long halt ye between two opinions? If the Lord be God, follow him: but if Baal, then follow him. And the people answered him not a word." We find in this portion of the Word of God that Elijah was calling the people of Israel back; he was calling them to a decision as to whether they were for God or Baal, and a great many were wavering, just halting between two opinions, like the people of Chicago at the present time.

During the last eight weeks a great deal has been said upon the subject of religion. Men have talked about it all over the city. A great many are talking; a great many are taking their stand for, and a great many against Him. Now, what will you do tonight? I will just divide this audience into two portions— one against and one for Him. It seems to me a practical question to ask an audience like this, "How long halt ye between two opinions? If the Lord be God follow him, but if Baal, then follow him." A man who is undecided about any question of any magnitude never has any comfort; never has any peace. Not only that, but we don't like a man who cannot decide upon a question. I like men of decision and firmly believe that more men are lost by indecision than by anything else. Am I not talking to many men tonight who intend someday to settle this question? Probably everyone here intends to make heaven his home,

but Satan is trying to get you to put off the settlement of the question till it will be too late. If he can only get men to put [it] off till tomorrow, which never comes, he has accomplished all he wants.

How many in this audience have promised some friend years ago that they would settle this question? Maybe you said you would do it when you came of age. That time has gone with some of you, and it has not been settled yet. Some have reached thirty, some forty, and others have reached fifty years; their eyes are growing dim, and they are hastening toward eternity, and this is not settled with them yet. Some of you have promised dying brothers that you would meet them in that world; some have promised dying wives that you would see them in that land of light; and again, others have given their word to dying children that you would meet them in heaven. Years have rolled away, and still you have not decided. You have kept putting it off week by week and year by year. My friends, why not decide tonight? "How long halt ye between two opinions?" If the Lord be God serve Him; if not, turn your back upon Him. It seems to me a question every man can settle if he will.

Turning Points

You like those grand old characters in the Bible who have made a decisive stand. Look at Moses! The turning point in his life was when he decided to give up the gilded court of Pharaoh and cast his lot with God's people. You will find that every man who has left a record in the Bible has been [a] man of decision. What made Daniel so great? It was because he was a man of decision. What saved the prodigal? It was not that he got into his father's arms; it was not his coming home. The turning point was when he decided the question: "I will arise and go to my father." It was the decision of the young man that saved him. Many a man has been lost because of indecision. Look at Felix, look at Agrippa. Felix said, "Go thy way for this time; when I have a convenient season I will call for thee." See what Agrippa said: "Almost thou persuadest me to be a Christian." Look at Pilate—all lost; lost because of his indecision. His mind was thoroughly convinced that Jesus was the true Christ. He said, "I find no fault in Him," but he hadn't the courage to take his stand for Him.

Thousands have gone down to the caverns of death for want of courage. My friends, let us look this question in the face. If there is anything at all in the religion of Christ, give everything for it. If there is nothing in it—if it is a myth, if our mothers who have prayed over us have been deceived, if the praying people of the last eighteen hundred years have been deluded, let us find it out. The quicker the better. If there is nothing in the religion of Christ let us throw it over, and eat, drink, and be merry, for time will soon be gone. If there is no devil to deceive us, no hell to receive us—if Christianity is a sham, let us come out like men and say so.

I hope to live to see the time when there will only be two classes in this world—Christians and infidels—those who take their stand bravely for Him, and those who take their stand against Him. This idea of men standing still and saying, "Well, I don't know, but I think there must be something in it," is absurd. If there is anything in it there is

everything in it. If the Bible of our mothers is not true, let us burn it. Is there one in this audience willing to say and do this? If it is a myth, why spend so much money in publishing it? Why send out millions of Bibles to the nations of the earth? Let us destroy it if it is false, and all those institutions giving the gospel to the world. What is the use of all this waste of money? Are we mad, are we lunatics who have been deluded? Let us burn the book and send up a shout over its ashes: "There is no God; there is no hell; there is no heaven; there is no hereafter. When men die, they die like dogs in the street!"

But my friends, if it is true—if heaven, if a hereafter in the Bible is true, let us come out boldly, like men, for Christ. Let us take our stand and not be ashamed of the gospel of Jesus Christ. Why, it seems to me a question that ought to be settled in this nineteenth century easily enough, whether you are for or against Him. Why, if Baal be God, follow him; but if the Lord be God follow Him. If there is no truth in the religion of Jesus Christ, you may as well tear down all your churches, destroy your hospitals, your blind asylums. It's a waste of money to build them. Baalites don't build blind asylums, don't build hospitals or orphan asylums. If there hadn't been any Christians in the world, there would have been no charitable institutions. If it hadn't been for Christianity you would have had no praying mothers. Is it true that their prayers have exercised a pernicious influence? Is it true that a boy who had a praying father and mother, or a good teacher, is no better off than a boy who has been brought up amid blasphemy and infamy? Is it true? It must be either one way or the other.

Did bad men write that Bible? Certainly not, or they wouldn't have consigned themselves to eternal perdition.

The very fact that the Bible has lived and grown during these eighteen hundred years is a strong proof that it came from God. Men have tried to put it out of the world; they have tried to burn it out of the world, but they have failed. It has come down to us—down these eighteen hundred years amid persecution, and now we are in a land where it is open to all, and no man need be without one. What put it into the minds of those men to give money liberally to print and circulate this book? Bad men wouldn't do this.

This is a question that, it seems to me, couldn't be decided tonight. If it is not good, then take your stand. If the Lord be God, follow Him, but if Baal be God, then follow him. Someone asked Alexander how he conquered the world, and he replied that he conquered it by not delaying. If you want to conquer the devil you must not delay—accept eternal life as a gift tonight.

A Long Dry Spell

Let us take the surroundings of this text. We are told that Elijah stood before Ahab and told him [that] because of the evil deeds of Israel and the king, no rain would come upon the land for three years and a half. After that Elijah went to the brook Cherith, where he was fed by the ravens, after which he went to Zarephath and there dwelt with a poor widow for months and months. Three years and a half rolled away, and not one drop of rain or dew had come from heaven. Probably when Elijah told the king there would be no rain, he laughed at him. The idea that he should have the key of heaven! He [scoffed at] the very idea at first. But after a little it became a very serious matter. The brooks began to dry up, the cattle could not get water, the crops failed the first year, the next year they were worse, the third year

they were even a worse failure, and the people began to flee out of his kingdom to get food, and yet they did not call upon Elijah's God. They had four hundred and fifty prophets of Baal and four hundred prophets of the groves, and yet all their prayers did not bring rain. Why did they not ask God for rain? Baal was not an answerer of prayer. The devil never answers prayer. If prayer has ever been answered, it has been answered by the God of our fathers, by the God of our mothers.

After Elijah has been gone three and a half years he returns and meets Obadiah the governor of the king's house. Ahab [has said to Obadiah,] "You go down that way, and I'll go down this way and see if we can't discover water." They haven't been separated long when Obadiah meets Elijah and asks him to come to the king. The prophet tells him to go and say to Ahab, "Elijah is here." But Obadiah doesn't want to leave him. "If I lose sight of you this time, when the king knows you have stepped through my lands it may cost me my life. Don't you know I've been a servant of the true God all the time, and I've had a hundred of the prophets of the Lord in a cave? If you don't come I will lose my life." Elijah tells him to go and bring Ahab, and instead of Elijah going to Ahab, Ahab comes to him. When the king comes he says [to Elijah], "Art thou he that troubleth Israel?"

That is the way with men. They bring down the wrath of God upon themselves, and then blame God's people. A great many people are blaming God for these hard times. Look on the millions and millions of [dollars] spent for whiskey. Why, it is about time for famine to strike the land. If men had millions of [dollars], it wouldn't be long before all the manhood would be struck out of them.

Now, the people of Israel had gone

over to Baal; they had forgotten the God that brought them out of Egypt—the God of Jacob and Abraham and of their fathers. "Now," said Elijah, "let's have this settled. Let some of your people make an offering to their God on Mount Carmel, and I will make an offering to my God, and the God that answers by fire will be the God." The king agreed, and the day arrived. You could see a great stir among the people that day. They were moving up to Mount Carmel. By-and-by Ahab came up in his royal carriage, and those four hundred and fifty prophets of Baal and four hundred prophets of the groves made a great impression. Dressed in priestly robes, they moved solemnly up that mountain. The king swept along in his chariot, and, perhaps, passed by the poor priest Elijah, who came slowly up, leaning upon his staff, his long white hair streaming about his shoulders. People don't believe in sensations. That was one of the greatest sensations of their age. What was going to happen? No doubt the whole nation had been talking about this Elijah, and when he came to that mountain, the crowd looked upon him as the man who held the key of heaven. When he came up he addressed the children of Israel. Perhaps there were hundreds of thousands. "How long halt ye between two opinions? If the Lord be God follow him: but if Baal, then follow him. And the people answered him not a word." Their eight hundred and fifty prophets had made a great impression upon them, and the king was afraid too.

In Need of Moral Courage

These people are just like a great many people now. They are afraid to go into the inquiry room for what people will say. If they do go in they get behind a post, so that they can't be seen. They are afraid the people in the store will

find it out, and make fun of them. Moral courage is wanted by them, as it was wanted by [the Israelites]. How many among us have not the moral courage to come out for the God of their mothers? They know these black-hearted hypocrites around them are not to be believed. They know these men who scoff at their religion are not their friends, while their mothers will do everything for them. The truest friends we can have are those who believe in Christ.

"And the people answered him not a word. Then said Elijah unto the people, I, even I only, remain a prophet of the LORD; but Baal's prophets are four hundred and fifty men. Let them therefore give us two bullocks; and let them choose one bullock for themselves, and cut it in pieces, and lay it on wood, and put no fire under: and I will dress the other bullock, and lay it on wood, and put no fire under: And call ye on the name of your gods, and I will call on the name of the LORD: and the God that answereth by fire, let him be God. And all the people answered and said, It is well spoken" (1 Kgs. 18:21–24).

"Yes, sir, that's right. We'll stand by that decision." They built an altar, and laid their bullock on it, and began to cry to Baal, "O Baal! O Baal! Baal! Baal!" No answer. They cry louder and louder, but no answer comes. They pray from morning till noon, but not a sound. Elijah says, "Louder; you must pray louder. He must be on a journey; he must be asleep. He must be on a journey or asleep." They cry louder and louder. Some people say it doesn't matter what a man believes, so long as he is earnest. These men were terribly in earnest. No Methodists shout as they did. They cry as loud as their voices will let them, but no answer. They take their knives and cut themselves in their earnestness.

Look at those four hundred and fifty prophets of Baal and four hundred prophets of the grove, all covered with blood, as they cry out in their agony. They have no God. Young man, who is your master? Whom do you serve? If you are serving Baal, I tell you if ever you get into trouble he will not answer you.

No answer came. Three o'clock came, the hour for the evening sacrifice, and Elijah prepared his altar. He would have nothing to do with the altar of Baal. He merely took twelve stones, representing the twelve tribes of Israel, and built his altar, and laid his bullock on. No doubt some skeptic said he had some fire concealed in his garment, for he dug a trench all around it to hold water. Then he told them to bring four barrels of water and emptied them over his sacrifice. Four more barrels were brought and thrown on the bullock, making eight, and then four barrels more were added, making twelve in all. Then, there lay that bullock, dripping with water, and Elijah came forward.

Every ear and eye was open. Those bleeding Baalites looked at him. What was going to be the end of it? He came forward, calm as a summer evening. He prayed to the God of Isaac and Abraham—when, behold, look! look! down it came—fire from the very throne of God, and consumed the wood and the stones and the sacrifice, and the people cried, "The Lord is the God!" The question was decided. The God that answereth by fire is the God of man. My friends, who is your God now? The God who answers prayer? Or have you no God?

I can imagine some of you saying, "If I had been on Mount Carmel and seen that I would have believed it." But I will tell you of a mount on which occurred another scene. That was a wonderful scene, but it does not compare with the scene on Calvary. Look there! God's own beloved Son hanging between two thieves and crying, "Father, forgive them, for they know not what they do." Talk about wonderful things. This has been the wonder of ages.

A man once gave me a book of wonderful things. I saw a good many wonders in it, but I did not see anything so wonderful in it as the story of the Cross. My friends, see His expiring look. See what happened. The very rocks were rent, the walls of the temple were rent, and all nature owned its God. The sun veiled its face and darkness fell over the earth when the Son of man expired on Mount Calvary. Where can you find a more wonderful sight than this? Those Israelites lived on the other side of the Cross; we live on this side of it.

If a man wants proof of His gospel look around this assembly. See men who thirty days ago were slaves, bound hand and foot to some hellish passion which was drawing them to hell. What a transformation there is. All things seem changed to them. They have got a new nature. "Is not this the power of God?" said a young convert to me today, "It seems as if we were living in the days of miracles, and the Son of God is coming down and giving men complete victory over lusts and passions." That is what the Son of God does for men, and yet, with all the proofs before their eyes, men are undecided.

What is it that keeps you from your decision? I wish I had time to tell you many of the reasons. Hundreds of thousands of men are thoroughly convinced, but they lack moral courage to come out and confess their sins. Others are being led captive by some sin. They have got some [particular] sin, and as long as they hold on to it there is no hope. A man the other day said he would like to become a Christian, but he had a bet upon the election, and he wanted that settled first. He did not think that he might die before that was decided. Eternity is drawing on. Suppose we die without God, without hope, without everlasting life: it seems to me it would have been better never to have been born.

My friends, I ask you tonight, why not come out like men? Say, "Cost what it will, I will accept Jesus tonight." Now, have moral courage. Come. How many of you are thoroughly convinced in your minds that you ought to be Christians tonight? Now just ask yourselves the question: "What hinders me, what stands in my way?" I can imagine some of you looking behind you to see how the one sitting there looks. If he seems serious, you look serious; if he laughs, you will laugh and come to the conclusion that you'll not accept Him tonight. You think of your companions, and you say you cannot stand their jeers. Is not that so? Come. Trample the world under your feet and take the Lord tonight, cost what it will. Say, "By the grace of God I will serve Him from this hour." Turn your backs upon hell, and set your faces toward heaven, and it will be the best night of your lives.

Have you ever seen a man who accepted Christ regret it? You cannot find a man who has changed masters and gone over to Christ who has regretted it. This is one of the strongest proofs of Christianity. Those who have never followed Him only regret it. I have seen hundreds dying when in the army and when a missionary, and I never saw a man who died conscious but who regretted that he had not lived a Christian life.

My friends, if you accept Him tonight it will be the best hour of your life. Let this night be the best night of your lives. Let me bring this to your mind: if you are lost it will be because you do not decide. "How long halt ye between two opinions? if the LORD be God, follow him: but, if Baal, then follow him." How many men in this assembly want to be on the Lord's side? Those who want to take their stand on the side of the true God rise. (Upon this request by Mr. Moody nearly two thousand men instantly arose.)

The ministry of Christ was to call sinners to repentance and provide a means for their salvation, as Moody points out early in this sermon. Jesus attracted large crowds, and people of many backgrounds were confronted with the gospel message: every person is a sick sinner, and Jesus Christ is the great Physician who has come to heal our sickness. It doesn't matter who or what you are; the need is the same.

The remainder of the sermon focuses on the spiritual needs of prostitutes. Moody apparently has a unique concern for them. He makes it clear in his sermon that Jesus spent time with sinful women and they accepted Him as Savior. Moody points out that the prostitutes of his day need help from Christians, and if Jesus was willing to interact with them, so should Christian women be willing to go into the brothels to share their faith with prostitutes and point them to a better life. Moody's concern was evident to many prostitutes, and many were converted.

The sermon ends with the reading of a letter from a woman who confirms the idea that she and others like her wanted release from their lifestyle, but they needed the help of Christians to show them the way.

Though Moody preached the need for spiritual restoration, he never forgot the importance of social involvement. In his mind the two worked together as tools for improving the plight of individuals here on earth. Throughout his life he devoted much time and money to causes that would bring peace and comfort to those in great need, both spiritually and physically.

CHAPTER FIFTEEN

Sinners Called to Repentance

I want to call your attention tonight to a text which you will find in the fifth chapter of Luke and thirty-second verse. The text is also recorded in Matthew and in Mark, and whenever you find a passage recorded by all three of the evangelists you may know that it is one of those important truths which He wants to impress upon people. "I came not to call the righteous, but sinners to repentance." It was when He first came down to Capernaum that He uttered these words. He had been cast out of Nazareth; they didn't want Him; they wouldn't have salvation. And He came down to Capernaum, and there He found Levi sitting at the receipt of customs, and He called him to become one of His disciples. Levi was so full of joy when he found Christ—as all young converts are—that he got up a great feast, and he invited all the publicans and sinners to it. I suppose he wanted to get them all converted—that was the reason he prepared a sumptuous feast. It was not to hear Jesus, but just to partake of the feast that Levi had prepared for them. And Jesus was there too among these publicans and sinners. The Pharisees were there too, and they began to murmur against His disciples, saying, "Why do these men eat with publicans and sinners?" and it was on this occasion that Christ uttered this wonderful text: "I came not to call the righteous, but the sinners to repentance." That is what He came into this world for; He came into the world just for the very purpose of saving sinners.

Now a good many men come to Chi-

cago to do a certain work. Some come to practice law; that's their profession. Others come to practice medicine, because that's their business; some are businessmen and some are mechanics. And when Christ came into this world He came for a purpose; He had a profession, if you will allow me the expression—He came to call sinners to repentance.

You know when He was going down to the Samaritan town His disciples went down to see whether they would let Him come there. We find Him on His way from Galilee to Jerusalem. You know there was such a hatred between the Jews and the Samaritans that they would have no dealings with each other, and He sent His disciples on to see if He would be allowed to enter. The Samaritans would not allow Him there, and His disciples were so incensed that James and John asked Jesus to "command fire to come down from heaven and consume them, even as Elias did." "Why," said the Son of man, "I didn't come to destroy men's lives, but to save them." That's what He came for. He came to bless men; He came to do men good, and there is not a sinner here tonight who cannot be saved and will be saved tonight if they wish.

You may call this world a great hospital, and all the people are born sick. A great many people imagine their souls are never diseased, who think they don't need a physician; but when people wake up to the fact that their souls are diseased, then they find the need of a physician. But there is no need for the physician unless you feel you are sick. You know you could not send a physician to a man who was well. Suppose I go [to] the West Side and ask a celebrated physician to come over and see Mr. White. Suppose he comes round and finds Mr. White sitting in his drawing room perfectly well. "Why, how is this? Mr. Moody told me you were sick, and bade me make a professional call." Not only is the physician disgusted but the patient is too. The world doesn't send for a physician till sickness comes. When it feels sick then it sends for a doctor, and the doctor comes. And whenever a man feels his need of Christ and calls, that moment He comes and is healed. There is a Physician here tonight for every sinner; I don't care what your sins may be, or how long you have been living in sin; I don't care if your life has been as black as hell, the great Physician is here. What for? Just to heal every man and woman that wants to be healed.

Accepting Sickness and the Remedy

Now, the great trouble is to make people believe they are sick; but the moment you believe that you are, then it is that you are willing to take the remedy. I remember some years ago a patent medicine came out, and the whole of Chicago was placarded about it. I could not turn my head but I saw "Paine's Painkiller." On the walls, on the curbstones, everywhere was "painkiller," "painkiller." I felt disgusted at the sight of these bills constantly telling me about this patent medicine. But one day I had a terrible headache, so bad that I could hardly see, and was walking down the streets and saw the bills again and went and bought some. When I was well I didn't care for it, but when I got sick I found it was the very thing I wanted. If there is one here who feels the need

of a Savior, remember the greater the sin the greater the need of a Savior.

I remember when I was coming back from Europe on the steamer there was a young officer; I felt greatly drawn toward him because I could see he was dying. It didn't seem to him as if he was dying, but you know death is very deceitful. He seemed to be joyous and lighthearted. He would talk about his plans, and take out his guns, and tell how he intended to go hunting when he arrived; but it seemed to me that he would not live to see this country. By-and-by he was taken down on his bed, and then the truth came to him that death was upon him. He got a friend to write out a telegram, which this friend was to send to his mother when they arrived. It read: "Mother, I am real sick.—Charlie." As soon as the boat touched the shore he was to send it. "But," said someone, "why not tell her in the telegram to come?" "Ah," he replied, "she will come." He knew whenever she read it and saw that he wanted help, she would come. It was the knowledge of his need that would bring her.

So Christ is waiting to hear our need, and man's need brings out the help of God. As I said before, the real trouble is that men don't think they need Him. You know that in one place—in the fifteenth chapter of Luke—they brought this charge against Him: "This man receiveth sinners, and eateth with them." This charge was brought against Him again and again. I am told by Hebrew scholars that instead of "receiveth" it should be rendered, "He is looking out for them." And that's what He was doing. He was looking out for them. He didn't care how black in sin they might be, He was ready to take them.

Now, a great many say, "I am too great a sinner to be saved." That is like a hungry man saying he is too hungry to eat, or a sick man saying he is too

---

sick to send for a doctor, or a beggar saying, "I am too poor to beg; I'll wait till I get some money first." If a man is hungry and perishing, you must relieve him.

No One Beyond Help

Now there is not a sinner in Chicago but has his representative in the Bible. Take, for instance, the publicans. You know the Jews thought this class about the lowest in the world. They put them lower than any other kind of sinner. They placed them along with the sinners—"publicans and sinners." The publicans were the tax collectors, and they defrauded the people at every turn. For instance, a man in South Chicago will pay [more than], perhaps, a hundred thousand dollars for the privilege of just collecting the taxes, and then he goes to work and screws the people out of a hundred and fifty thousand dollars. He doesn't care a straw for justice or appearances. He comes into the cottage of the widow and taxes half [of all] she has. At every house the tax collector puts the blocks to his victims, and famine often comes in when he goes out. The people detest him; they hate him with a perfect hatred. They always find him a drag on them, and [they] feel he hasn't a bit of sympathy for them. Their money, they find, is taken without warrant; their homes are broken up, and trouble and starvation come on them. And so the [Jewish] publican was hated wherever he turned. He was the agent of the Roman tyrant, and the people were brought up to shun him. He deserved it all, and even more, by his heartless exactions; and yet Christ forgave even him.

And just so rum-sellers can be saved. And another class that Christ had mercy on was the thieves when, on the cross, he saved a thief. There may be some

thief here tonight. I tell you, my friend, you may be saved if you only will. There may be someone here who is persecuting a good wife, and making her home a perfect hell on earth. But you, too, may be saved. There may be some here persecuting the church, but there's salvation for you. When Saul was persecuting the Christians from city to city, he was stopped short by the voice of God; he was converted. And those high-headed Pharisees, so well versed in the law of Moses, even they were converted—Joseph of Arimathea was a Pharisee, and so was Nicodemus.

But tonight I want to talk about another class that Jesus dealt with and led to a higher life. I want to talk about fallen women. There are some people who believe that these have fallen so low that Christ will pass them by. But my friends, that thought comes from the evil one. In all this blessed Book there is not one, not a solitary one of this class mentioned that ever came to Him but that He received them. Yes, He even went out of His way and sought [them] out.

At a Pharisee's Feast

Now I want to take three representative cases where these women had to do with Christ. One is the case of an awakened one. The Spirit of God has dealt with her anxious, awakened soul. The Lord was one day at Jerusalem and a banquet was given [for] Him by Simeon. There was a banquet table in the house, arranged according to the fashion of that day. Instead of chairs for the guests, the guests sat reclining on lounges, as was customary. Well, it was just one of these repasts that our Lord sat down to, along with the wealthy Simeon and his many guests. But no sooner had He entered than this woman followed Him into the house and fell down at His feet and began to wash them with her tears. It was the custom in those days to wash one's feet on entering a house. Sandals were worn and the practice was necessary. Well, this woman had gotten into the house by some means and once inside had quietly stolen up to the feet of Jesus. And in her hands she brought a box; but her heart too, was just as full of ointment as the box she carried. And there was the sweetest perfume as she stole to His feet. And her tears started to fall down on those sacred feet; hot, scalding tears that gushed out like water. She said nothing while the tears fell, and then she took down her long, black hair and wiped His feet with the hair of her head. And after that she poured out the ointment on His feet. Then straightway the Pharisees began talking together.

How all through the New Testament these Pharisees kept whispering and talking together! They said, shaking their heads, "This man receiveth sinners"; and then, "This man, if he were a prophet, would have known who and what manner of woman this is that toucheth him: for she is a sinner." No prophet, they insisted, would allow that kind of a woman near Him but would push her away. And then the Savior read these thoughts and quickly rebuked them. He said, "Simeon, I have somewhat to say unto thee." And he said, "Master, say on." And He said, "Seest thou this woman? I entered into thine house, thou gavest me no water for my feet: but she hath washed my feet with tears, and wiped them with the hairs of her head. Thou gavest me no kiss: but this woman since the time I came in hath not ceased to kiss my feet. My head with oil thou didst not anoint: but this woman hath anointed my feet with ointment." Simeon was like a great many Pharisees nowadays, who say, "Oh, well, we will entertain that minister if we

must. We don't want to—he's a dreadful nuisance—but we will have to put up with him; it's our duty to be patronizing."

Well, the Master said more to His entertainer: "There was a certain creditor, which had two debtors; the one owed five hundred pence, and the other fifty, and when he had nothing to pay"—mark that, sinner; the debtor had nothing to pay. There is no sinner in the world that can pay anything to cancel his debt to God. The great trouble is that sinners think they can pay, some of them seventy-five cents on the dollar, some even feel able to pay ninety-nine cents on the dollar, and the one cent that they are short, they think they can make that up some way. That is not the way; it is all wrong. You must throw all the debt on God. Some few perhaps, will only claim to pay twenty-five cents on the dollar, but they are not humble enough either; they can't begin to carry out their bargain. Why, sinner, you couldn't pay one-tenth part of a single mill of the debt you are under to Almighty God.

Now it says in this parable that they could not pay him anything—they had nothing to give and the creditor frankly forgave them both. "Now, Simeon," the Master asked, "which should love that man the most?" "I suppose," was the reply, "he that was forgiven the most." "Thou hast rightly judged; this woman loves much because she hath been forgiven much," and went on to tell Simeon all about her. I suppose he wanted to make it plainer to Simeon, and he turned to the poor woman and said, "Thy sins are forgiven"—all forgiven; not part of them, not half of them, but every sin from the cradle up, every impure desire or thought was blotted out for time and eternity, and He said, "Go in peace." Yes, truly, she went out in peace, for she went out in the light of heaven. With what brightness the light must have come down to her from those eternal hills—with what beauty it must have flashed on her soul. Yes, she came to the feet of the Master for a blessing, and she got it, and if there is a poor woman here tonight who wants a blessing, she will get it.

I want to call your attention to a thought right here. You have not got the name of one of those poor women. The three women who had fallen, who had been guilty of adultery, and had been blessed by Him, not one of them has been named. It seems to me as if it had been intended that when they got to heaven we should not know them—they will just mingle with the rest. Their names have not been handed down for eighteen hundred years. They have called Mary Magdalene a fallen woman, but bear in mind there is nothing in Scripture to make us understand that she was a poor, fallen woman, and I believe if she had been, her name would not have been handed down.

Now, the next woman was altogether different from the woman in Luke. She didn't come with an alabaster box, seeking a blessing. She was perfectly indifferent; she was a careless sinner. Perhaps there are some poor fallen women who have come tonight in a careless spirit—only out of curiosity. They don't want a Savior; they don't want their sins blotted out; they don't want any forgiveness. Perhaps she had heard that at Moody and Sankey's they were going to preach repentance and that a great many fallen women were likely to be there and thought she would just come down to see how they took it.

By a Samaritan Well

Now you have a representative here. After Christ had that interview with Nicodemus, we are told He went up to Galilee by Samaria. He could have gone up to Galilee without going to Samaria, but He knew there was a fallen woman there. He got to the well and sent off His disciples to get bread. Why did He not keep one with Him? Because He knew the woman was coming that way, and she probably would not like to see so many. While He sat on the curbstone of the well, a poor fallen woman of Samaria came along for water. You know the people in those days used to come out in the morning and evening to get their water, not in the blaze of the noonday sun. No doubt she was ashamed to come out there to meet the pure and virtuous at the well, and that was the reason why she stole out at that hour.

She brought her waterpot to get water, and when she came up the Master stopped her and asked her for a drink, just to draw her out. She saw He was a Jew. (We can always tell a Jew: God has put a mark upon them.) "How is this? You a Jew and ask a Samaritan for a drink? The Jews have no dealings with the Samaritans." "Ah, you don't know Me," He replied; "if you would have asked Me for a drink I would have given you living water." "How could you give me living water? Why, you have no vessel to draw water with." "Whosoever drinketh of this water shall thirst again, but whosoever shall drink of the water that I shall give him will have a well springing up in his heart into everlasting life." "Well," probably she thought, "that is a good thing. One draft of water will give me a well—one draft of water for the rest of my days." She asked Him for this living water, and He told her, "Go, bring thy husband." He was just drawing her out, just getting her up to the point of confession. "I have no husband," she said. "For thou hast had five husbands, and he whom thou now hast is not thy husband; in that saidst thou truly." I can see that woman's astonishment. She looks all around to see who had told Him all about her. [This is] like a man who came up from Michigan lately, who came into the tabernacle and listened to the sermon which, as he told me, seemed all to be preached at him. He wondered who had told me all about him. He got Christ, and is going back to Michigan to preach the gospel of Jesus Christ.

The Word of God reached her, and she saw she was detected. "Sir, I perceive thou art a prophet"; then she went on the old religious discussion, but the Lord turned her from that and told her that the hour had come when the people must worship the Father in spirit and in truth, not in this or that particular mountain, nor yet in Jerusalem. And she said, "When the Messiah cometh He will tell us all things," and when she had said this she was ready for the truth. Then Jesus said, "I am the Messiah."

Just then she saw His disciples coming, and probably she thought these men might know who she was, and she got up her pot, and away she went to the city. The moment she got within the gates she shouted, "Come see this man I have met at the well. Is not this the Messiah? Why, He has told me all that ever I did." And you can see all the men, women, and children running out of that city up to the well. As He stands in the midst of His disciples and He sees the multitudes coming running toward them, He says, "Look yonder; look at the fields, for they are already white with the harvest; look what that poor fallen woman has done." And He went into that town as an invited guest, and many believed on account of the woman's testimony, and many more believed on account of His own.

Now, my friends, He did not condemn the poor adulteress. The Son of God was not ashamed to talk with her and tell her of that living water, those who drank of which, He said, would never die. He did not condemn her. He came to save her, came to tell how to be blessed here and blessed hereafter.

On the Temple Porch

The next case is still much worse. You may say it is like black, blacker, blackest, compared with the other two. I want to speak about this one that is in the eighth chapter of John. One woman I have spoken of was in the house of a Pharisee at a dinner party, the other by the well of Sychar, and now we come to the temple porch. They have taken a woman in adultery, have caught her in the very act. They have not gotten the man; they have held only the poor woman. While He is speaking, the Pharisees are driving this poor fallen woman right into the temple. What a commotion there would be here tonight, if such a scene should take place in the tabernacle!

She had broken the law of Moses, by which a woman caught in the act of adultery was to be put to death. The woman is brought toward Him, and now they are about to put the question of her life or death before Him. He had said that He hadn't come to condemn the world, but to save the world, and they are just going to try and condemn Him by His own words. They say to Him, "Moses in the law commandeth us, that such should be stoned: what sayest thou?" But not a word did He speak. Jesus stooped down and wrote on the ground, as though He hadn't heard them. We don't know what He wrote. Perhaps, "Grace and truth come by Jesus Christ." Perhaps He wrote that. But while He thus busied Himself they cried out the louder, demanding an answer to their question. So at length He lifted Himself up and said, "He that is without sin among you, let him first cast a stone at her." Never did an answer so completely serve its purpose; you who never were guilty of an offense, just you cast the first stone. And, amid the strangest silence He again stooped and wrought with His finger on the ground. This time, perhaps, He wrote, "I am not come to call the righteous, but sinners to repentance." And soon He rose again, but ere He did so He heard the patter of retreating feet on the pavement and when now He glanced up, He saw none but the woman. One by one they had been convicted by their own conscience, and slunk away; not one of them there could throw the stone. And the Savior looked at the woman. I can imagine the tears coming trickling down her cheeks as Jesus Christ, in kindest tones, asked her, "Woman, where are those thine accusers? hath no man condemned thee?" And for an instant she could not answer.

Who knows how that poor soul had reached her sad plight! Perhaps one of those very Pharisees who had left her had led her astray. The very man who had clamored loudest to condemn her was likely the guilty one. And there she stood alone; the betrayer was left untouched, as too often he is today—a miserable, unjust, untrue sentiment, by which the man, who is equally guilty, is received in society and the woman is condemned. But at last she gained her voice and said, "No man, my Lord," and then, perhaps, told how her parents had died when she was very young. A stepmother, perhaps, had taken her and treated her harshly, and then had turned her adrift [in] the world. Or perhaps a drunken father had turned home into darkness, and she had been driven from it almost brokenhearted; and so in her helplessness her innocent affections

were gained, and then she had been led astray. The Master knew it all, and when He heard her reply He said, "Neither do I condemn thee; go, and sin no more." She had been dragged into the temple to be stoned, but now Christ had delivered her. She came to be put to death, but she received life everlasting.

An Opportunity of New Life

My friends, the Son of God will not now condemn any poor fallen woman that leaves off her sins and just casts herself down at His feet. He will take you up just as you are. When [I was] in Philadelphia, a fallen woman came into the inquiry room and threw herself down on the floor. The Christian helpers talked and talked to her but couldn't get a word out of her; they couldn't do a thing with her. The Honorable George H. Steward came to me, and said, "We wish you would come, we don't know what to make of her." She was weeping bitterly, and, as far off as I was, I could hear her sobs all over the room. So I went and said, "What is the trouble?" At last she spoke, and the bitterness of her despairing voice went to my heart. "I have fallen from everything pure, and God cannot save me; there is no hope." I told her tenderly that God could still lift her up and save her. I said, "Are you only just willing to be forgiven? A merciful Father is waiting and longing to pardon." She said at last she could not abandon her course, as no one would give her a home. But that difficulty was gotten round by my assuring her [that] kind friends would provide for her; and then she yielded, and that same day was given a pleasant place in the home of a Presbyterian minister. But for forty-eight hours after entering her new home that poor, reclaimed woman cried, day and night, and we went for her mother, and on hearing our story the mother clasped her hands and cried, "Has my daughter really repented? Thank God for His mercy; my heart has just been breaking. I've prayed so long for her without result; take me to her." And that reformed daughter of sin has lived consistently ever since, and when I was last in Philadelphia she was one of the most esteemed members in that Presbyterian church.

And so every one of you can begin anew, and God will help and man will help you. Oh, turn, and do not die. Seven short years is the allotted life of a fallen woman. Oh, escape your early doom, escape your infamy, and hear God's voice calling you to repent. Your resolution to amend will be borne up by hosts of friends; never fear for that. Just take the decided step, and you will be helped by every good man and woman in the community. Oh, I beseech you to act right now and settle this great question for time and eternity.

I heard of a mother whose daughter was led astray, and the poor daughter tried to hide herself, thinking her mother would not forgive her. The mother went to the town where she supposed her child had gone, but she hunted and hunted unsuccessfully. The trouble with most of those girls who go astray is they go under assumed names, and this daughter had done the same thing, and that mother couldn't find her. At last she found a place where fallen women resorted to, and the mother went to the keeper of that place and begged her to let her hang up her picture in the room, and consent was granted. Hundreds of fallen women came into that room and carelessly glanced at the picture and went out. Weeks and months rolled on, until at length one night a poor fallen girl came into the room. She was going out as

carelessly as she had entered, when her eye caught the picture, and, gazing at it for a moment, she burst into a flood of tears. "Where did you get it?" she sobbed. They told her how her mother came there, heart-broken, and asked to have her picture hung up in that room, in the hope of finding her daughter. The girl's memory went back to her days of peace and purity, recalling the acts of kindness of that loved mother, and she then and there resolved to return. See how that mother sought for her and forgave her.

Oh, poor fallen ones, the Son of God is seeking for you tonight. If you haven't got a mother to pray for you, the Son of God wants to be everything to you. He wants to receive you to Himself. Let me hold Him up to you as your best Friend. He wants to take you to His loving bosom, and this very night and very hour you can be raised if you will.

There was a woman who was trying to get a poor girl to go back to her home. She said, "Neither my mother, my father, nor my brothers will forgive me. They won't permit me to go back." "Will you give me your address?" the lady asked. The address was obtained, and the very next post brought a letter marked "immediately," and it seemed as if the whole hearts of her father and mother and brothers were poured out in that letter. It was filled with kindness and urged her to come home and all would be forgotten. There is many a poor fallen girl in Chicago whose mother is praying for her, and whose heart is aching because she won't go back. Your mother will forgive you, and all your friends, if you will only show true signs of repentance. They will take you home.

O my friends, let this be the last night you will live in sin—in shame. Let this be your last night in which you will live in sin. Take those sins you have to Him, and He will forgive you. He has said, "Let the wicked forsake his ways," and pardon is ready. That is what our Lord will do. He will pardon you and make you pure. Will you let Him pardon you tonight?

Just before coming down this evening I received a letter from a fallen woman. I've received a number during the past few days. Thank God the Spirit is at work among that class! And let me say right here, if there is any person here who keeps a brothel, if you will allow Christian ladies admittance, they will go gladly and hold meetings. This idea that Christian ladies do not care for your class is false—as false as the blackest lie that ever came out of hell. Why, some of the first ladies of the city have lately been visiting these houses personally, and [they] have been trying to save their erring sisters. A few days ago, several came to me and asked if I couldn't get a list of all the brothels in the city. I went to police headquarters and got the names of the keepers and addresses and gave it to these Christian women. And since then, many houses have been visited. These charges that Christian women will not have them in their homes are equally false. The other night a lady of culture was on her knees with a poor one who told the lady that she was a fallen girl and did not know where to go if she didn't go back to her brothel. "Come and stay at my house," said the lady, "I will take care of you," and when the girl got up from her knees, the lady saw she was a poor, colored girl. That good Christian kept her till she got her a good situation. Another one not long ago received the truth, and one of our ministers wrote to her parents, got a pass and sent her home to her forgiving parents. Let me ask you not to believe that we are cruel; that we are hard-hearted; that we do not care for the fallen women but only for the abandoned men. We have a place to shelter you, and if that is not large enough, the businessmen will put up another. They will do everything for you if you are only repentant; they will not try to keep you down and cast you off. If you are sincere, there are hundreds and thousands of people in this city whose hearts will go out to you. But I want to read this letter:

CHICAGO, Dec. 14.
Mr. Moody—Many fallen women in this city would, in these days, gladly change their mode of life and seek Christ and restoration to the homes and hearts of parents and friends whom they, weakly, left many, many bitter years and months ago, if only they could see some way to an honorable living and friendly recognition and help when they should seek these.

Now, let me say here that any young woman who wants reclamation ought not to look into the future. Say to yourselves, "I will be saved tonight, come what will."

You say, "Seek first the kingdom of Christ"; but, my dear brother (for such you seem even to me), why do this if only returning shame awaits us?

I wish every fallen woman would think as this one does; why, I would be a brother to you all. Thank God, I've got a brother's heart for all of you. I wish every one of you would feel that I want to do you good—that I only want to lift you up.

Suppose a hundred fallen women of this city were at the tabernacle tonight—no doubt more than this number will be there—and that these should seek Christ and find forgiveness, for you assure us there is full forgiveness for even us, so that these scarlet stains should be "whiter than snow"—where, I ask, shall we live? What shall we do?

We must return ere the echo of the last prayer in that tabernacle has died away, to the apartments which have only known our bitter shame and again meet the devil in his chosen home.

Let me say, again, that no woman in this audience need do that. There will be homes open for you. God will provide for you if you will trust Him. I hope there will be hundreds here tonight who will say, "I will never return to that place. I will never go back to that house of shame; I will never meet the devil in those homes more; I will rather die in the poorhouse than do it; I turn my back forever upon death and hell."

No home of parent or friend, or praying Christian who joined in your prayer at the tabernacle for us, would offer our weary bodies shelter there, or our willing hands labor wherewith honest bread might be earned. No Christian's purse affords tomorrow's bread.

Dear friends, let the morrow take care of itself. Don't be looking at the future. Just walk by faith. That's what every Christian must do.

The very ones who came here to pray for us go away scorning us; and while with the virtuous wife and mother and the pure maiden we would plead a common Savior, they would thrust us from them. What can we do? Who will help us?

There remains only a life of shame and an unwept death, physical and eternal, for us. Hopelessly,
"ONE OF THEM"

This is the core of the gospel: Christ was the sacrifice for our sins. And because of His death, provision was made that all can be saved.

This sermon traces the final hours of Christ before His death on the cross. After Judas leaves the room where the last supper is taking place, Christ tells His other disciples about heaven in order to comfort them. Later we find Him praying in the darkness for the stability of His followers and for the completion of His work according to the Father's will.

His betrayal was painful for it involved Judas, a disciple whom He trusted. When we today turn our backs on Christ, He is equally hurt, for such a response is an act of rejection.

He is led away, tried, and executed, yet Jesus' execution was not final. His resurrection marked the beginning of life for those who repent. Christ died for our sins, and it is time we accepted His work on our behalf.

CHAPTER SIXTEEN

The Sacrifice of Christ

You will find my text tonight in the fifteenth chapter of First Corinthians, and part of the third verse: "Christ died for our sins according to the Scriptures." I was going to preach in the city of Dublin a few years ago, and the town was placarded giving notice of the meeting. There was one passage of Scripture at the bottom of the bill that my eye rested upon: "Christ died for our sins." I had read it a great many times, but I seemed to see it now in a new light, and that light flashed into my soul as it never did before: "Christ died for *my* sins." That's the way to put it—"for *my* sins." And I wish I could get everyone here to take it that way and just keep saying it while I preach to you tonight: "Christ died for me."

My friends, will you only make this personal and remember that He died for you? Let that little boy and girl remember that He died for you just as much as for that gray-headed man, and let those who came in to scoff at the meeting remember that the text is for them—that Christ died for you. I have often thought that if I could only make people feel this really, and could tell the story of His death as it ought to be told, I would only preach one sermon and go up and down the world and just tell this one story. I don't know anything that would break the heart of the world like this story if it could be brought before men and women and they would feel it. I know it broke my heart, and I have often thought if I could tell it as it ought to be told, I would be the happiest man in the world. I don't believe it has ever been told yet. I don't believe the man has been born who could tell it; I don't believe that the angels in heaven could tell it. Sometimes people say we have over-drawn the pictures in the Bible, but there is one story that has never been over-drawn—the story of His death. No one ever did justice to that story; no one ever made that real. I believe the heart of every man in this audience would be broken if I could make that story real.

I remember during the war how I would take up a paper and read about the great battles and loss of life; but I would lay down the paper and soon forget all about the thousands that had been slain. But I went into the war and was at the battles of Fort Donelson and Pittsburgh Landing. After I came home and began to read the papers and see the accounts of the great battles, the whole thing would come up before me. I could hear their dying groans; I could hear them crying for their mothers, their appeals for water. The whole thing was real, and the whole trouble is that most people take up this story of the Bible and don't make it real. They look upon it as the old story of eighteen hundred years ago which they have heard from their cradle. I remember I went five hundred miles to Dublin to attend a meeting, and when I got there the preacher got up and began to talk about the death of Christ. "Well," I said, "he should give us something new." But when I went home to the house where I was staying there were two old pilgrims sitting, and they were talking about the sermon and the death of Christ. The tears were trickling down their cheeks, and they spoke about the event as if Christ had died in Dublin that afternoon. I felt rebuked, ashamed at myself that those old men should speak so lovingly about this event, while I had treated it so lightly. I believe [that] if we were living as we ought to, it would be fresh every night, every hour, of our lives.

Facing the End

Now tonight I propose to take up the last hours of Christ before He went to Calvary. You know we love to hear the last words of our friends. I remember a few weeks ago, when I went to look upon the dead face of my eldest brother, how earnestly I inquired, "What were his last words?"—how I went round the places where he had been, and how for days I tried to pick up what he had said to this and that man, and how I treasured up his last words. And it seems to me every Christian ought to linger round the cross and pick up the loving words of our Savior and treasure them up. So tonight I want you just to go back nineteen hundred years. Let us forget we are living here in Chicago. Let us go back and imagine we are living in the land of Palestine—at Jerusalem; and let us just think we are walking down the streets of Jerusalem.

It is on a Thursday afternoon, and we see thirteen men coming down the street. Every eye is upon them. The boys are opening their eyes at them. Men, women, and children are running out of their houses to see those men. Let us imagine we are strangers, and we ask who these men are, and they tell us, "Why, that's the Galilean prophet and His apostles, from the city of Capernaum." We look upon them with amazement. We have heard how that man has given sight to the blind, how He has

cured the lepers, given bread to the hungry, and raised the dead. The whole land has been full of Him, and out of curiosity we follow the little band. They go along the narrow streets, and come to a common-looking house and enter and ascend a flight of stairs. Suppose we go up those stairs with them; we find them there in a guest chamber, the great Prophet seated with His twelve apostles. We are told He became exceeding sorry. He was soon to taste the bitter cup, to taste death for every man, to lay down His innocent life for the guilty, the just for the unjust, and then He is exceeding sorry. His soul is troubled, and as He sits there at that table He lets out the secret of His heart, and tells them that that night He is going to be betrayed by one of them. They look at one another, and one says, "Lord, is it I?" "No." And another says, "Master, is it I?" "No," and they one after another put the question till it comes to Judas. And that black-hearted traitor, the devil who has already been at the high priest's, turns to Him and says, "Is it I?" and the Lord says, "Thou hast said it; and what thou doest do it quickly." That ought to have broken his black heart, but it didn't; and he arose and went out of that chamber.

Hear him as he goes down those stairs and into that dark night—we are told that it was the darkest the world ever saw. That night the Son of man was to be betrayed by man. He went off to the Sanhedrin, to the chief priests, and he sold Him—sold Him very cheap, my friends—sold Him for some fifteen or twenty dollars. How many men today are selling Him as cheaply—selling him for a song! They don't want Him. A woman told me last night, "I don't want Him; I wouldn't take Him as a gift." She told me with her own lips that she would rather go to hell than heaven. Oh, what a heart! I hope if there is a hard-hearted person in this building like her, their heart will be broken tonight.

A Tender Farewell

But while Judas was out selling his Master, Jesus was speaking tender words to His disciples. What a tender parting! For three years He had been associated with that holy band; they had walked with the blessed Master, and heard those wonderful parables; they had seen Him raise people from the dead, had seen Him cure the deaf, the dumb, and the blind—they had been in His company for three years, and now they were about to be separated for a time, and it was on this occasion He uttered those memorable words: "Let not your heart be troubled."

They were now by themselves, the traitor had gone out. "Ye believe in God, believe also in me. In my Father's house are many mansions; if it were not so I would have told you. I go to prepare a place for you." There was the Master in that dark hour; in that bitter, supremely bitter hour, trying to cheer and comfort the little band. And then He uttered that wonderful prayer recorded in the seventeenth chapter of John. He poured his heart out to God in prayer. He not only prayed for His disciples, that had stood firmly by His side, but prayed for His enemies. And afterward He said, "The hour of my departure is at hand."

And then He gathered the eleven around Him and they started out of the house and went down through the streets of Jerusalem. They went out through the eastern gate, passed over through the outlying space down to the Valley of Jehoshaphat, and so to the garden of Gethsemane. And there he took Peter and James and John and went on with them a little way apart, and then [He] withdrew about a stone's throw off from them and fell on His knees and began to pray.

You can hear Him in that cold night in that garden; you can hear His piercing cry: "Father, let this cup pass from me if it be thy will." It was the prayer of agony, and He sweat, as it were, great drops of blood. Oh, the agony the Son of God passed through that night, not only physical agony, but a greater mental agony, because the sins of the world lay on Him. He bore in His person the sin of the whole world, and God the Father turned His face away from Him because God could not look upon sin. The Father had to turn His face away from Him: He could not take away the cup, but He had to leave Him drink it to the very dregs for you and me. And Peter and James and John fell asleep; they could not watch one single hour with Him.

Betrayed, Bound, and Tried

And so while they thus slept and Christ was wrestling in prayer, a band of men came on the scene. They came on with lanterns and torches, as if they were hunting for someone. Jesus well knew who they were seeking. He woke up His disciples and went to the band and said, "Whom seek ye?" And they said, "We seek Jesus of Nazareth." Then said Jesus, "I am he," and there was something so mysterious about His person, something so wonderful about His face, that they were struck with awe. They trembled and felt as dead men and could not touch Him. And then Judas stepped out from the band. We don't know but he put his arm around the Savior's neck. Ah, what a lesson to professing Christians! Judas was near enough to the Lord to put his arms around His neck, and yet he went down to hell. Ah, you are not to know true men by their making the greatest professions; that kind doesn't always stand the highest but sometimes the very lowest. Then Judas went on and carried out his bargain. He may have put his arm around His neck, but at all events he kissed Him. Christ turned and said, "Judas, betrayest thou the Son of man with a kiss?" He may have said, "Professing to be my follower, do you betray me with a kiss?" He might have asked, "What have I done that you should betray me? Was I ever unkind; have I ever been untrue; have I ever deceived you; have I ever betrayed you? Why Judas, do I receive this treatment from you?" But he merely said, "Betrayest thou the Master with a kiss? What is it that thou hast done to agree to betray thy Master with a kiss?"

And then the men seized on Him and took those innocent hands that had been raised to bless people, that had brought bread to the hungry, had touched the leprous and made them clean, touched those that were blind and made them see, touched the deaf ears and hearts and made them hear and feel—those innocent hands that had been raised only to bless people, they took and bound them. And He resisted not. He gave himself up a willing sacrifice and was obedient to their will. And after they had bound Him they started back to the city with Him.

And they took Him to Annas, the father-in-law of Caiaphas, the high priest. And they brought Him in, and instead of waiting till the morning, the Sanhedrin was gathered hastily together. They were so thirsty for His blood they couldn't wait even a few hours. They hurried Him before the assembled Senate, where the first men of the nation were gathered together. Seventy of the rulers of the Jews came into the council that night. One after another they took their seats, and Caiaphas took his place at the head of the table. There

they sat in solemn state, the highest court of the nation. And now they sought for witnesses to come and testify against Jesus. The law required that two men should agree together to establish any testimony. And at last they found two false witnesses that came and swore they heard Him talk against the holy temple, that He said they might destroy it and He could raise it up again in three days. Then, being questioned, He said, "Before Abraham was, I am." And being further questioned, He answered not a word.

At last Caiaphas raised his voice and said, "I adjure thee by the living God, that thou tell us whether thou be the Christ the Son of God." And Jesus said unto him, "Thou hast said: nevertheless I say unto you, Hereafter shall ye see the Son of man sitting on the right hand of power, and coming in the clouds of heaven." And the moment Jesus said that, Caiaphas rent his clothes and said: "He hath spoken blasphemy; what further need have we of witnesses? Behold, now ye have heard his blasphemy!" Then he hurriedly put the question, "What think ye?" And they rendered as their verdict: "He is guilty of death." How the sentence rung out in that council chamber.

It was Thursday night; it may have been midnight. Many of the citizens had retired, and it was not known until morning. The next day was a notable feast day. There were there people from all parts of the country; the whole city was crowded. Perhaps Zacchaeus was there from Jericho; perhaps many from whom He had cast out devils; perhaps blind Bartimaeus, no longer blind, was there, and that Samaritan woman Christ had met by the well of Sychar. Undoubtedly hundreds were there who, but for Jesus, could not have gotten there. Would they stand by Him? Would they cling to Him now, in this hour of

His need? And Peter—he was of course there—would he be staunch? Only a few days before he had solemnly promised to stand by his Lord to the last. "Though others might deny Him, he would die with Him." Would not Peter, at least, have moral courage to come out before all the world and own Him? Alas, no. Why, that very night as Jesus was in the judgment hall, impetuous Peter denied Him with a curse, and swore he never knew Him. It seemed there was no hand to defend Him; no hand to help Him; there He was that night in the hands of His enemy.

Before Pilate

Very early the next morning, at what hour we do not know, the officers of the governor came and bound Him and took Him away to Pilate to have Him put to death. The Romans had taken away the power of sentencing to death, and so the Jews could only put Him to death by gaining the Romans' consent. So now they brought Him to Pilate. Pilate never had such a person as that before him. He had sentenced many to death, but not like Him. He had often heard of this Galilean; His fame had long ago reached him. Strange rumors about Him had come up from Bethlehem. Perhaps Pilate had even seen Christ and talked with Him. Quite likely so, and his curiosity must have been excited by the many stories he heard about Him among his subjects. Pilate, this time, was with Christ two hours. At last he came out, after examining Him, and said, "I find no fault in this man." But the crowd cried out, "If you let this man go, you are not Caesar's friend." They knew this would touch his loyalty and ambition to be a successful politician. He could not, they argued, tolerate any rival to the Roman power, and his first duty would be to put down everything like rebellion. "If you don't condemn him, you are not Caesar's friend," rang in his ears, as the crowd insisted that Christ was a rebel and wanted to get up an insurrection in the land, and His friends wanted to make Him King. They raised their yells and ended by repeating, "You are no friend of Caesar's. We will report you at Rome, and you will lose your office." Poor Pilate! He hadn't moral courage to stand firm. And so he said, "This Jesus, is He a Galilean?" "Yes," they said, "he was brought up in Nazareth but has been living out in Galilee." So, the next thing, Pilate sent Him to Herod.

Now you can see that crowd moving through the city on their way to the Galilean's governor. When he saw Him he probably thought it was John, whom he had put to death, that had been raised from the grave, and curiosity [made him] excited to see. But when he found out who it really was, we are told he got out some cast-off garments, probably some that had belonged to one of their kings, and dressed Him in them, and, pointing their fingers in scorn at Him, [they] cried, "Hail, King of the Jews!" Then they blindfolded Him and struck Him on the head, saying in derision, "You are a prophet; tell us who struck you." Some would spit upon Him amid a torrent of scorn and contempt. Yes, my friends, they spat upon Him.

Suppose the Prince of Wales would come to this country, and someone would go up and spit upon him: why all Europe would be up about it. But when the Son of man came down to this earth they spat upon Him, and no one raised his voice against it. But with all this ignominy that bloodthirsty Herod, who took the life of John, refused to take His life, and sent Him back to Pilate. And now the crowd had increased. The whole city was excited. Everyone was talking about how the Galilean prophet had been brought before the Sanhedrin and found guilty of blasphemy, and was to die the terrible death of the cross. His friends, all the time He was on trial, not a solitary one stood up for Him. All forsook Him then. The very men who a few days before cried as He entered Jerusalem, "Hosannah, to the Son of David," now lifted up their voices and cried, "Away with Him!" "Crucify Him!"

And they brought Him back to Pilate, and undoubtedly around his house a crowd had gathered as great as that assembled here tonight. It didn't take much to rouse these Jews. They were very easily fired, and the whole city was aroused. They were clamoring—thirsty for His blood. Pilate was still anxious to release Him. His conscience told him to release Christ, and he also received a communication from his wife in which she said, "Have thou nothing to do with this just man, for I have suffered many things this day in a dream because of him." He tried to release Him, but he wanted to be on both sides. At last he said, "I've got a plan that will work, I think." It was customary, you know, to release a prisoner upon the day of the governor's feast, and he said, "I will get the vilest wretch I can, the blackest-hearted murderer and robber, and bring up this pure man and ask them which of the two they will have." But the chief priests heard what he was going to do, and went around among the crowd and told them and got their feelings worked up. And now Pilate thought he was going to get rid of the terrible responsibility of putting Him to death.

Picture the crowd standing around that governor's house. See the soldiers bringing out one with his hands dripping with the blood of his fellow man, and another who had all His life healed the sick, given life, and done good. "Which will I release unto you?" And they lift up their voices—it is the cry of the whole mob—"Barabbas, Barabbas, Barabbas," and the poor governor, disappointed, cries out, "What shall I do with Christ?" "Let Him be crucified," that was the burden of the voice that rang through the streets of Jerusalem that day.

"Away with this pestilent fellow—we don't want him. Put him to death!" Pilate turned around and washed his hands with water and said, "I am innocent of the blood of this just person." Poor, blind, deceived man. He thought that he could wash his hands of this iniquitous decision; but what a mistake. When he had said this they cried, "His blood be upon us and on our children." Would to God they had cried out, "Let His blood be upon us and our children to save them," but that wasn't the cry. "Let His blood be upon us and on our children." And look what a punishment has come upon that race—see how they've been scattered to the four winds of heaven, because they neglected Him. Only about seventy years afterwards Titus came and besieged Jerusalem, and nearly 1,100,000 people perished, and ninety-seven thousand were sold to slavery. It fell, and the Jewish people have been wanderers for eighteen hundred years.

Pain Before Death

And then Pilate gave him up to be scourged. Now, I was a great many years a Christian before I knew what the Roman custom of scourging was, but when the truth dawned upon me, when I learned what it really was, I wept for days and got down on my knees and asked Him forgiveness for not loving Him more than I had. The custom of scourging consisted in taking the wrists and binding them tightly together and then fastening them to a post or pillar. The back was bared, and a lash, composed of sharp pieces of steel plaited together, was brought down upon the back. Oh, sinner, look at the prophet Isaiah, "He was wounded for our transgressions, he was bruised for our iniquities: the chastisement of our peace was upon him; and with his stripes we are healed." He was wounded for me. Yes, with His stripes am I healed. May this be a reality to everyone here tonight. Don't let us conceal it. It was the God of heaven they scourged for us. For fifteen minutes they brought down blow upon blow on that innocent body.

O you who cast Him away; you who see no reason why you should love Him; you who cannot see why you should take your stand on His side, why you should defend His cause, think of this! And after scourging Him, instead of binding up His wounds, and bringing oil and ointment and pouring it upon those wounds, instead of doing this they put upon Him some other cast-off garments and made Him a crown of thorns, and some wretch put it on His head.

You know when Queen Victoria sits on her throne, they put a crown upon her head filled with diamonds and precious stones worth about twenty million dollars; but here they crowned God's Son with a crown of thorns, the curse of the earth. And in mockery of a king, they put a stick in His hand. You know when the Queen of England sits on her throne she has a scepter in her hand; and here in the hands of the Prince of heaven they put a stick and scoffingly shouted, "Hail, King of the Jews!" They jeered and mocked that precious Christ. At last one of the crowd took the rod out of Jesus' hand and brought it down over His defenseless head, driving those thorns into His brow.

Oh, what treatment the Son of God received! And those wounds were made for us; He bore His stripes for you and for me. You can see the blood trickle down that innocent head, down that dear face, and over His bosom. And all for us! Oh, divine, infinite compassion: "He bore our sins in his own body on the tree." And now they take off the purple robe of scorn and put His own garment upon Him, and they lift up His cross and lay it upon Him. It is not a gilded cross, such as you ladies wear about the neck; it is not a cross of polished wood, thickly set with diamonds and precious stones, but a great, rugged, heavy cross, made roughly out of a tree.

Christ's Death on the Cross

Now, I see them lift and lay it on His shoulders. And they lay crosses on two thieves who are to be led away and executed with Him. The devil wanted to blacken the name of Christ, and so He was placed between two thieves who were made to carry their own crosses. Why the cross of Jesus was taken from His shoulders after a few steps, we can easily imagine. He cannot stand up—the sins of the whole world are piled upon Him—and He cannot stand up, much less walk under the accumulated load. See Him reel and stagger! See Him fall almost fainting to the earth! The mountain weight crushes down even the Son of God! They take the cross from His shoulders and lay it upon Simon the Cyrenian. And now look, sinners, and behold your Savior, behold the Lamb of God going up to Mount Calvary, like a sheep to the slaughter. Away to Calvary they are leading Him, to crucify and put Him to death.

I see them on the way, climbing the toilsome ascent. Jesus is calling on God in prayer, praying even for His murderers. And now they have gotten Him to the summit of the hill. They've arrived; it is Golgotha, the place of the skull. And they take and lay Him down on the cross. Yonder come the soldiers with hammers and nails in their hands. You can see them take those pliant arms and stretch them out, and against those blessed, innocent hands they point the sharp spikes. You can hear that hammer come down on that nail—blow, blow— and the hands of Jesus are pierced through, fastened bleeding to the cross. Long spikes are driven through both feet, and God, the Son of the Father, lies quivering, nailed to the cross. And now they mock at Him. See, they spit on Him, hooting and laughing and yelling, "Away with him; he saved others; let him save himself if he be Christ the chosen of God."

Then the Roman soldiers lifted up the cross and placed it upright between heaven and earth, with those arms of Jesus outstretched still in blessing. The love that He had in His bosom kept those dear hands extended; they didn't need the nails. He might have come down from the cross; with one stroke of His hand He could have summoned all the angels of God against His murderers, or called down fire out of heaven to consume every one of them. But no; He willed to hang there between heaven and earth; His strength fainted not. Even "as Moses lifted up the serpent in the wilderness, even so must the Son of man be lifted up, that whosoever believeth in him should not perish but have everlasting life." O sinner, go to Calvary tonight; look on that Savior; gaze on Him between those two thieves; hear that piercing cry—does He call down fire from heaven? No, no! "Father, Father," He cries, "forgive them, for they know not what they do." Yes, I think that Christ did forgive from His heart every soul there on Calvary, even those that drove the spikes, even those that wagged their heads and reviled Him. Even the two thieves railed on Him. But at last one of them cried out, "Lord, remember

me when thou comest into thy kingdom." Oh, sinner, did Christ rebuke him, or did He keep silent? No; a benediction fell from His lips, "Today shalt thou be with me in paradise." That malefactor had but to cry and he was snatched from the brink of hell.

Oh, lost one, but cry tonight to Jesus, and He will save you. Will you not let Him? Oh, hear His gracious words to the vile malefactor, "This day shalt thou be with me in paradise." At last He cried out, "I thirst," and they gave him gall mixed with vinegar, and mocked Him again, "Hail, King of the Jews, come down from thy cross." But He patiently endured. And again He opens His lips, we hear that cry from that cross. "Father, into thy hands I commend my spirit." And then the end approaches, and He cries out in a loud voice: "It is finished." It is finished. It is finished.

What a thrill of joy must have swept through the streets of heaven. "It is finished! It is finished!" the angels cry as they strike their golden harps, and the bells of heaven, if there are any there, ring out the peal of joy. "It is finished, the whole world can now be saved. The work of the God-man is finished today on Calvary; all that man has to do is to believe and they shall be saved!"

The Son of man had triumphed; He had died to make atonement, and through Him all flesh might die and yet live eternally. The work was complete; the world was saved! Ah, I can just imagine how the black powers of hell gathered around that dying scene, and the waves of hell and death dashed upon that cross. Sometimes, down on the beach of Lake Michigan, there you see the waves coming dashing on the breakwater. They come dashing along as though they would break everything to pieces, but the waves themselves are dashed to pieces and the breakwater stands invincible. So the dark waves of death and hell come dashing up against the bosom of the Son of God. They roared and surged, but all in vain; they fell back shattered into fine spray against the Rock, Christ—Christ the destroyer of death, Christ the victor over hell. When He shouts, "It is finished," I think I see the fiend creeping back to hell and hear him whispering, "It is finished; all mankind can now be saved." They have led on the children to kill the Son of God; but they are outwitted, for God "maketh even the wrath of man to praise him."

Joseph's Bold Step

But my friends, we will not leave Him there on the cross. We are told that straightway when He yielded up the ghost, even nature owned its God. The sun refused to look longer upon the scene; darkness came over the earth for three hours; the rocks were rent, and the earth was shaken, and many that slept came forth from their graves. And when Jesus was now dead, we are told that Joseph of Arimathea, a rich man and a member of the Sanhedrin, went boldly to Pilate and begged [for] the Lord's body that he might bury it. He was a just man, he was an honorable counselor, and let me mention right here a most remarkable thing: Matthew, Mark, Luke, and John all join in telling of this pious act of Joseph's. It is not everything in this story of the last agony that all four of them bring out, but they all give this: Joseph of Arimathea, the secret disciple, was left to ask for the Lord's body. All His open disciples had forsaken Him and fled; all had forsaken Him—some had disowned Him, and Judas had betrayed Him; and it was left for Joseph of Arimathea to go to Pilate and himself alone perform the last offices for the dead Master. It was the death of Jesus that brought out Joseph of Arimathea, the secret disciple—O backward, secret Christians, shall it not touch you too? My friends, if Christ died for you on Calvary, shall you not live for Him? Shall you not speak for Him? Is not this the least you can do?

He [Joseph] went boldly into the presence of the governor and asked him for the body of Jesus. When Pilate heard He was dead he marveled. He gave orders to see that Jesus was dead. And now you can see those Roman soldiers going toward Calvary and Joseph with some of his servants behind him. See them standing at the cross and a soldier just goes up and puts a spear into the side of the Son of God, and that prophecy was brought out: "In that day there shall be a fountain opened in the house of David for sin and for uncleanness." The soldier put it in, and His blood covered the spear. Yes, Christ's blood covered sin. Yes, God, in mercy, covered sin. That act was the crowning act of indignity of earth and hell to drive that spear into the very heart of the God-man; and the crowning act of mercy and love and heaven that blood came out and covered the spear.

And now Joseph and Nicodemus take down that body. You can see them wash the blood from that head, you can see them draw those nails out carefully from His hands—from His feet, and they take that mangled and bruised body down and wash it.

(At this moment the roaring wind, which had been rising all the evening, seemed as though it would break through the roof, to which point nearly everybody's attention was attracted.)

My friends, it is only the wind. The devil doesn't want you to hear this story of Jesus' dying love for you; he doesn't want you to hear and be saved. But just give attention, and don't let him accomplish his object; let the wind go. If you don't pay attention my sermon goes for nothing.

You see them take the body down and wrap it in fine linen. You can see Joseph of Arimathea and Nicodemus, another secret disciple, anoint that body with ointment, and then a little funeral procession moving to the tomb of Joseph, hewn out of the rock, and there they lay that body away.

But, thank God, He did not rest very long. I have not time to speak about His resurrection now, but, God willing, I will speak about it before I leave. But let me ask you, are you going out of this tabernacle saying you don't want Christ—saying you would rather be without Him? Are you going out despising His love, His death, His offer of mercy? "Christ died for our sins." Will you have the benefit of His death, or send the message back to the God of heaven that you despise His love, His offer of mercy, that you despise this blessed Redeemer that came down to seek and save that which was lost?

Bailey, Faith C. *D. L. Moody.* Chicago, Moody Press, 1959.

Bennett, David. *D. L. Moody.* Minneapolis, Bethany House, 1994.

Bliss, P. P. and Ira D. Sankey. *Gospel Hymns and Sacred Songs.* New York, Bigelow and Main, 1875.

Curtis, Richard K. *They Called Him Mr. Moody.* Garden City, New York, Doubleday & Co., 1962.

Daniels, W. H. *D. L. Moody: His Words, Work and Workers.* New York, Nelson & Phillips, 1877.

Dedmon, Emmett. *Great Enterprises: 100 Years of the YMCA of Metropolitan Chicago.* Chicago, Rand McNally, 1957.

Dengler, Sandy. *D. L. Moody: God's Salesman.* (Preteen Biography Series), Chicago, Moody Press, 1986.

DeRemer, Bernard R. *Moody Bible Institute: A Pictorial History.* Chicago, Moody Press, 1960.

Findlay, James F., Jr. *Dwight L. Moody, American Evangelist, 1837–1899.* Chicago, University of Chicago Press, 1969.

Fitt, Arthur Percy. *Moody Still Lives,* New York, Fleming H. Revell, 1937.

Gericke, Paul. *Crucial Experiences in the Life of D. L. Moody.* New Orleans, Insight Press, 1978.

Goodspeed, Edgar J. *Full History of the Wonderful Career of Moody & Sankey, in Great Britain & America.* New York, AMS Press, reprint ed.

Lindsay, Gordon. *D. L. Moody.* (Men Who Changed the World Series, Vol. 7.) Dallas, Christ for the Nations, 1972.

Moody, Paul D. *My Father: An Intimate Portrait of Dwight Moody.* Boston, Little, Brown & Co., 1938.

Moody, William R. *D. L. Moody.* New York, Macmillan Co., 1930.

Pollack, John C. *Moody: A Biographical Portrait of the Pacesetter in Modern Mass Evangelism.* New York, Macmillan Co., 1963.

Powell, Emma M. *Heavenly Destiny: The Life Story of Mrs. D. L. Moody, by Her Granddaughter, Emma Moody Powell.* Chicago, Moody Press, 1943.

Sankey, Ira D. *My Life and the Story of the Gospel Hymns.* New York, Bigelow & Main, 1906.

Smith, Wilbur H. *Dwight Lyman Moody: An Annotated Biography.* Chicago, Moody Press, 1948.

Weisberger, Bernard. *They Gathered at the River: The Story of the Great Revivalists and Their Impact upon Religion in America.* Boston, Little, Brown & Co., 1958.

F. B.
MEYER

F. B. Meyer

Abridged and edited by Charles Erlandson

Contents

F. B. MEYER 1847-1929

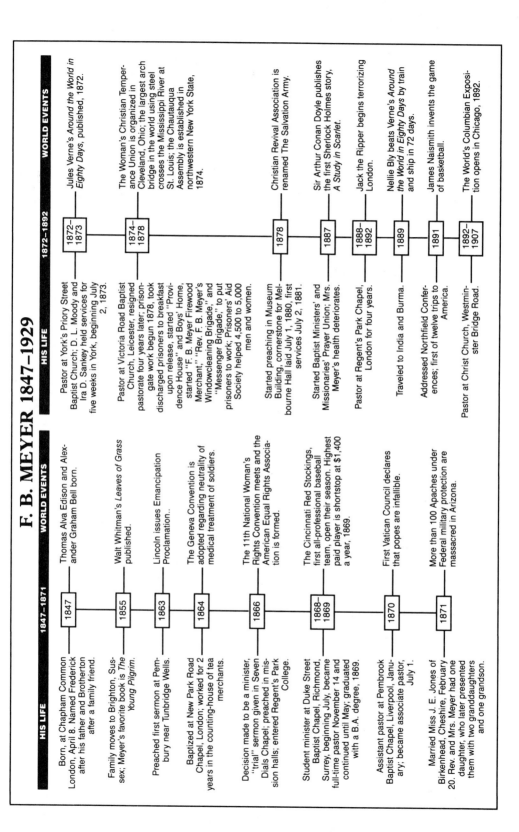

HIS LIFE — 1847-1871 — WORLD EVENTS

1847
- Born, at Chapham Common London, April 8. Named Frederick after his father and Brotherton after a family friend.
- Thomas Alva Edison and Alexander Graham Bell born.

1855
- Family moves to Brighton, Sussex; Meyer's favorite book is *The Young Pilgrim*.
- Walt Whitman's *Leaves of Grass* published.

1863
- Preached first sermon at Pembury near Tunbridge Wells.
- Lincoln issues Emancipation Proclamation.

1864
- Baptized at New Park Road Chapel, London; worked for 2 years in the counting-house of tea merchants.
- The Geneva Convention is adopted regarding neutrality of medical treatment of soldiers.

1866
- Decision made to be a minister, "trial" sermon given in Seven Dials Chapel; preached in mission halls; entered Regent's Park College.
- The 11th National Woman's Rights Convention meets and the American Equal Rights Association is formed.

1868-1869
- Student minister at Duke Street Baptist Chapel, Richmond, Surrey, beginning July; became full-time pastor November 14 and continued until May; graduated with a B.A. degree, 1869.
- The Cincinnati Red Stockings, first all-professional baseball team, open their season. Highest paid player is shortstop at $1,400 a year, 1869.

1870
- Assistant pastor at Pembrook Baptist Chapel, Liverpool, January; became associate pastor, July 1.
- First Vatican Council declares that popes are infallible.

1871
- Married Miss J. E. Jones of Birkenhead, Cheshire, February 20. Rev. and Mrs. Meyer had one daughter, who later presented them with two granddaughters and one grandson.
- More than 100 Apaches under Federal military protection are massacred in Arizona.

HIS LIFE — 1872-1892 — WORLD EVENTS

1872-1873
- Pastor at York's Priory Street Baptist Church; D. L. Moody and Ira D. Sankey held services for five weeks in York, beginning July 2, 1873.
- Jules Verne's *Around the World in Eighty Days*, published, 1872.

1874-1878
- Pastor at Victoria Road Baptist Church, Leicester, resigned pastorate four years later; prisongate work begun 1878, took discharged prisoners to breakfast upon release, started "Providence House" and Boys' Home, started "F. B. Meyer Firewood Merchant," "Rev. F. B. Meyer's Windowcleaning Brigade," and "Messenger Brigade," to put prisoners to work; Prisoners' Aid Society helped 4,500 to 5,000 men and women.
- The Woman's Christian Temperance Union is organized in Cleveland, Ohio; the largest arch bridge in the world using steel crosses the Mississippi River at St. Louis; the Chautauqua Assembly is established in northwestern New York State, 1874.

1878
- Started preaching in Museum Building, cornerstone for Melbourne Hall laid July 1, 1880, first services July 2, 1881.
- Christian Revival Association is renamed The Salvation Army.

1887
- Started Baptist Ministers' and Missionaries' Prayer Union; Mrs. Meyer's health deteriorates.
- Sir Arthur Conan Doyle publishes the first Sherlock Holmes story, *A Study in Scarlet*.

1888-1892
- Pastor at Regent's Park Chapel, London for four years.
- Jack the Ripper begins terrorizing London.

1889
- Traveled to India and Burma.
- Nellie Bly beats Verne's *Around the World in Eighty Days* by train and ship in 72 days.

1891
- Addressed Northfield Conferences; first of twelve trips to America.
- James Naismith invents the game of basketball.

1892-1907
- Pastor at Christ Church, Westminster Bridge Road.
- The World's Columbian Exposition opens in Chicago, 1892.

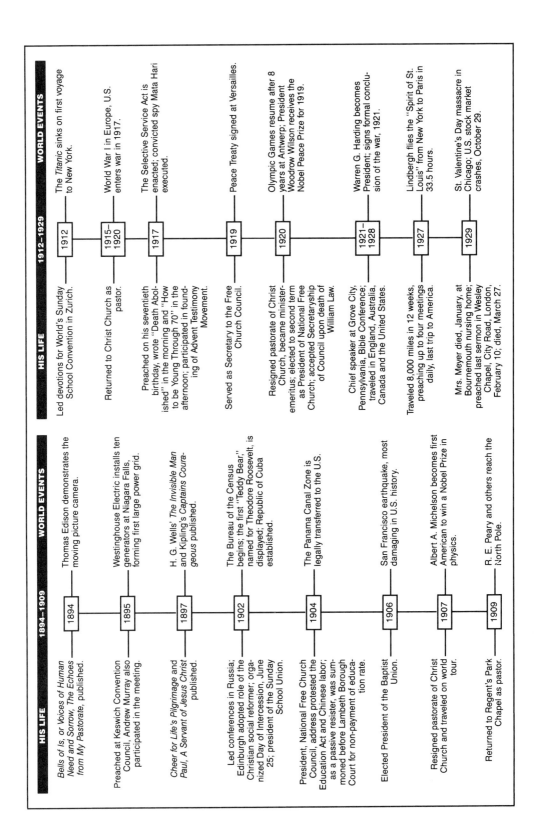

HIS LIFE	1894–1909	WORLD EVENTS
	1894	Thomas Edison demonstrates the moving picture camera.
Preached at Keswich Convention Council, Andrew Murray also participated in the meeting.	1895	Westinghouse Electric installs ten generators at Niagara Falls, forming first large power grid.
Cheer for Life's Pilgrimage and *Paul, A Servant of Jesus Christ* published.	1897	H. G. Wells' *The Invisible Man* and Kipling's *Captains Courageous* published.
Led conferences in Russia; Edinburgh adopted role of the Christian social reformer; organized Day of Intercession, June 25; president of the Sunday School Union.	1902	The Bureau of the Census begins; the first "Teddy Bear," named for Theodore Roosevelt, is displayed; Republic of Cuba established.
President, National Free Church Council, address protested the Education Act and Chinese labor; as a passive resister, was summoned before Lambeth Borough Court for non-payment of education rate.	1904	The Panama Canal Zone is legally transferred to the U.S.
Elected President of the Baptist Union.	1906	San Francisco earthquake, most damaging in U.S. history.
Resigned pastorate of Christ Church and traveled on world tour.	1907	Albert A. Michelson becomes first American to win a Nobel Prize in physics.
Returned to Regent's Park Chapel as pastor.	1909	R. E. Peary and others reach the North Pole.

WORLD EVENTS	1912–1929	HIS LIFE
The *Titanic* sinks on first voyage to New York.	1912	Led devotions for World's Sunday School Convention in Zurich.
World War I in Europe, U.S. enters war in 1917.	1915–1920	Returned to Christ Church as pastor.
The Selective Service Act is enacted; convicted spy Mata Hari executed.	1917	Preached on his seventieth birthday, wrote "Death Abolished" in the morning and "How to be Young Through 70" in the afternoon; participated in founding of Advent Testimony Movement.
Peace Treaty signed at Versailles.	1919	Served as Secretary to the Free Church Council.
Olympic Games resume after 8 years at Antwerp; President Woodrow Wilson receives the Nobel Peace Prize for 1919.	1920	Resigned pastorate of Christ Church, became minister-emeritus; elected to second term as President of National Free Church; accepted Secretaryship of Council upon death of William Law.
Warren G. Harding becomes President; signs formal conclusion of the war, 1921.	1921–1928	Chief speaker at Grove City, Pennsylvania, Bible Conference; traveled in England, Australia, Canada and the United States.
Lindbergh flies the "Spirit of St. Louis" from New York to Paris in 33.5 hours.	1927	Traveled 8,000 miles in 12 weeks, preaching up to four meetings daily, last trip to America.
St. Valentine's Day massacre in Chicago; U.S. stock market crashes, October 29.	1929	Mrs. Meyer died, January, at Bournemouth nursing home; preached last sermon in Wesley Chapel, City Road, London, February 10; died, March 27.

Bells of Is, or Voices of Human Need and Sorrow, The Echoes from My Pastorate, published.

F. B. MEYER

Introduction

Frederick Brotherton Meyer was born on April 8,1847, in Clapham, England. After taking a B.A. at London University in 1870, Meyer felt called to the ministry. In 1872 he first ministered at the Baptist Chapel in York, where he came under the deep and lasting influence of Dwight L. Moody. Until 1921, excepting the years 1879 to 1888, he continued in the pastorate. During this time he preached an estimated fifteen thousand sermons, emphasized the work of the Holy Spirit, and drew the praise of all clergymen, even those from different backgrounds.

But F. B. Meyer was never just a minister. From 1904 to 1905 and again from 1920 to 1921 he served as president of the National Free Church Council, and from 1906 to 1907 he served as president of the Baptist Union. Meyer took an active interest in social concerns and often used what some considered unorthodox methods. He established, for example, a window-cleaning brigade that provided work for men and ministered as well to released prisoners, jobless boys in danger of drifting into crime, unwed mothers, and prostitutes.

As if his work as pastor and social worker were not enough to fill a lifetime, Meyer wrote seventy volumes, which at the time of his death on March 27, 1929, had a circulation of five million copies worldwide. These volumes include expositions of Scripture, sermons, lives of Bible characters, and devotional meditations that are as relevant and as inspiring today as they were in his own day.

A contemporary of F. B. Meyer once wrote of Meyer's works: "Mr. Meyer holds in his hand the key to his reader's heart and conscience. He speaks to conscience with a kind of authority which it is not easy to analyze and yet harder to resist." Modern readers, when given the opportunity to discover the best of Meyer's writings, may find that they agree with this assessment, for the qualities that inspire Meyer's work do not go out of style.

Meyer is pre-eminently biblical. In this volume you will find some of Meyer's finest expositions of Scripture, which originally appeared as both written commentary and expository sermons. You will also experience his vivid depiction of Bible characters, such as Jonathan and Abraham. Even in his meditations whose focus is not directly a portion of Scripture, Meyer's work resounds with scriptural references and themes. One included here is even titled "How to Read Your Bible."

To his biblical nature, Meyer has added practicality. Not content to say merely "Do good," Meyer offers us "Seven Rules for Daily Living" and "The First Step Into the Blessed Life." To his practicality Meyer has also added a gift for illustration so that his message is always brought to life.

Discovering the best of F. B. Meyer, some of which has lain fallow for nearly a century, we are led to agree with C. H. Spurgeon's appraisal of Meyer: "Rev. F. B. Meyer is a great gain to the armies of evangelical truth; for his tone, spirit and aspirations are all of a fine Gospel sort. In all his books there is a sweet, holy savour."

The first five selections are all taken from Meyer's 1895 Light on Life's Duties, *a collection of his meditations. Although it is one of Meyer's briefest volumes, it is also one of his richest.*

"The Chambers of the King" presents a truly royal view of the Christian life. In this meditation Meyer demonstrates his ability to unite the entire Christian experience through a powerful and extended metaphor.

In "The Secret of Victory Over Sin" Meyer confronts what he believes is "the bitterest experience with most believers": sin. Drawing as always from Scripture, he offers practical advice about what to expect about sin and ways to keep ourselves from it.

In "The First Step Into the Blessed Life" Meyer expounds a part of the Christian life which may be found throughout his writings and which may seem foreign to contemporary readers. This is the act of consecration, an act which Meyer makes clear is not one of mere feeling but one of giving all to Christ.

In "How to Read Your Bible" Meyer presents practical and sound principles for acquiring the "holy art" of reading the Bible. For Meyer, the whole of Christian living hinges on the way we read our Bibles, which should be done as if it were a home letter and not a newspaper.

Meyer's belief that all of life is part of the divine plan is expressed in "The Common Task." Meyer teaches us here that we must do the little things in life well before we can hope to accomplish great things.

CHAPTER ONE

The Chambers of the King

Christian experience may be compared to a suite of royal apartments, of which the first opens into the second, and that again into the third, and so on. It is, of course, true that believers enter on a possession of all so soon as they are born into the royal, divine household. But, as a matter of fact, certain truths stand out more clearly to them at different stages of their history, and thus their successive experiences may be compared to the chambers of a palace, through which they pass to the throne-room and presence-chamber of their King.

And the King Himself is waiting at the threshold to act as guide. The key is in His hand, which opens, and no man shuts; which shuts, and no man opens. Have you entered the first of those chambers? If not, He waits to unlock the first door of all to you at this moment, and to lead you forward from stage to stage, till you have realized all that can be enjoyed by saintly hearts on this side of the gates of pearl. Only be sure to follow where Jesus leads the way. "Draw me, we will run after Thee" (S. of S. 1:4).

The First Chamber in the King's Holy Palace Is the Chamber of the New Birth

In some cases it is preceded by a portico, known as Conviction for Sin. But as the portico is not part of the house, and all do not pass through it, we need not stay further to describe it. Over the door of this chamber are inscribed the words: "Except a man be born again, he cannot enter" (John 3:3–5).

By nature we are destitute of life—*dead in trespasses and sins.* We need, therefore, first, not a new creed, but a new life. The prophet's staff is well enough where there is life; but it is useless on the face of a dead babe. The first requisite is *life.* This is what the Holy Spirit gives us at the moment of conversion. He comes to us through some truth of the incorruptible Word of God, and implants the first spark of the new life; and we who were dead, live. Thus we enter the first room in our Father's palace, where the new-born babes are welcomed and nursed and fed.

We may remember the day and place of our new birth, or we may be as ignorant of them as of the circumstances of our natural birth. But what does it matter that a man cannot recall his birthday, so long as he knows that he is alive?

As an outstretched hand has two sides—the upper, called *the back;* the under, called *the palm*—so there are two sides and names for the act of entrance into the Chamber of the New Birth. Angels, looking at it from the heaven side, call it *being born again.* Men, looking at it from the earth side, call it *trusting Jesus.* "Those that believe in His name are born"; "Those that receive Him have the right to become the sons of God" (John 1:12, 13). If you are born again, you will trust. And if you are trusting Jesus, however many your doubts and fears, you are certainly born again, and have entered the palace. If you go no further, you will be saved, but you will miss untold blessedness.

From the chamber of birth, where the new-born ones rejoice together, realizing for the first time the throbbing of the life of God, there is a door leading into a second chamber, which may be called

The Chamber of Assurance

And over that door of entrance, where the King awaits us with beckoning hand, these words are engraved: "Beloved, now are we the sons of God" (1 John 3:2). In many cases, of course, assurance follows immediately on conversion, as a father's kiss on his words of forgiveness to the pentitent child. But it is also true, that there are some souls, truly saved, who pass through weeks, months, and sometimes years, without being sure of their standing in Jesus, or deriving any comfort from it.

True assurance comes from the work of the Holy Spirit through the sacred Scriptures. Read the Word looking for His teaching. Think ten times of Christ for every once of yourself. Dwell much on all references to His finished work. Understand that you are so truly one with Him, that you died in Him, lay with Him in the garden tomb, rose with Him, ascended with Him back to God, and have been already welcomed and accepted in the Beloved (Eph. 2:5, 6).

Remember that His Father is your Father, and that you are a son in the Son; and as you dwell on these truths, opening your heart to the Holy Spirit, He will pervade your soul with a blessed conviction that you have eternal life, and that you are a child, not because you feel it, but because God says so (John 3:36; Rom. 8:16).

The door at the further end of this apartment leads into another chamber of the King. It is the door of consecration, leading into the

Chamber of a Surrendered Will

Above the doorway stand the words: "From henceforth let no man trouble me: for I bear branded on my body the marks of Jesus; whose I am, and whom I serve" (Gal. 6:17, RV; and Acts 27:23). Consecration is giving Jesus His own. We are His by right, because He bought us with His blood. *But, alas, He has not had His money's worth!* He paid for all, and He has had but a fragment of our energy, time, and earnings. By an act of consecration, let us ask Him to forgive the robbery of the past, and let us profess our desire to be henceforth utterly and only for Him; His slaves, His chattels, owning no master than Himself.

As soon as we say this, He will test our sincerity, as He did the young ruler's, by asking something of us. He will lay His finger on something within us which He wants us to alter, obeying some command, or abstaining from some indulgence. If we instantly give up our will and way to Him, we pass the narrow doorway into the Chamber of Surrender, which has a southern aspect, and is ever warm and radiant with His presence, because obedience is the condition of manifested love (John 14:23).

This doorway is very narrow, and entrance is only possible for those who will lay aside weights as well as sins. A weight is anything which, without being essentially wrong or hurtful to others, is yet a hindrance to ourselves. We may always know a weight by three signs: *first,* we are uneasy about it; *second,* we argue for it against our conscience; *third,* we go about asking people's advice, whether we may not keep it without harm. All these things must be laid aside in the strength which Jesus waits to give. Ask Him to deal with them for you, that you may be set in joint *in every good work* to do His will (Heb. 8:21).

At the further end of this apartment another door invites us to enter

The Chamber of the Filling of the Spirit

And above the entrance glisten the words, "Be filled with the Spirit" (Eph. 5:18). We gladly admit that the Holy Spirit is literally in the heart of every true believer (Rom. 8:9); and that the whole work of grace in our souls is due to Him, from the first desire to be saved to the last prayer breathed on the threshold of heaven. But it is also true that a period comes in our education, when we become more alive to the necessity of the Holy Spirit, and seek for more of his all-pervading heart-filling presence.

Many of us have lately been startled to find that we have been content with too little of the Holy Spirit. There has been enough throne-water to cover the stones in the river-bed, but not to fill its channel. Instead of occupying all, our gracious Guest has been confined to one or two back rooms of our hearts; as a poor housekeeper is sometimes put in to keep a mansion, dwelling in attic or cellar; while the suites of splendid apartments are consigned to dust-sheets and cobwebs, shuttered, dismantled, and locked.

Each Christian has the Holy Spirit; but each Christian needs more and more of Him, until the whole nature is filled. Nay, it would be truer to say, the Holy Spirit wants more and more of us. Let us ask our heavenly Father to give us of His Spirit in ever enlarging measures; and as we ask, let us yield ourselves incessantly to His indwelling and inworking. Then let us believe that we are filled, not because we feel it, but because we are sure that God is keeping

His word with us: "Ye shall not see wind, neither shall ye see rain; yet that valley shall be filled with water."

It is true that the filling of the Spirit involves separation, a giving up, going apart, which is keenly bitter to the flesh. The filling of Pentecost is a baptism of fire. But there is joy amid the flames as the bonds shrivel, and the limbs are free, and the Son of God walks beside.

But this chamber leads to another of exceeding blessedness.

The Chamber of Abiding in Christ

Around the doorway a vine is sculptured, with trailing branches and pendent grapes; and, entwined among the foliage, these words appear: "Abide in Me, and I in you" (John 15:4). The Holy Spirit never reveals Himself. Those who have most of His grace, "wist it not." His chosen work is to reveal the Lord. We are not conscious of the Spirit, but of Him who is the alpha and omega of our life. Christ's loveliness fills the soul, where the Spirit is in full possession, as the odor of the ointment filled the house at Bethany.

Our Lord is with us all the days; but often our eyes are holden, that we do not know Him; and if for a radiant moment we discern Him, He vanishes from our sight. There is an experience which we do not only *believe* that He is near, but we *perceive* His presence by the instinct of the heart. He becomes a living, bright reality; sitting by our hearth, walking beside us through the crowded streets, sailing with us across the stormy lake, standing beside the graves that hold our dead, sharing our crosses and our burdens, turning the water of common joys into the wine of holy sacraments.

Then the believer leans hard on the ever-present Lord, drawing on His fulness, appropriating His unsearchable riches, claiming from Him grace to turn every temptation into the means of increasing likeness to Himself. And if the branch abide constantly in the Vine, it cannot help bearing fruit; nay, the difficulty would be to keep fruit back.

We have to do with the death and not with the life part of our experience (Rom. 8:13). The oftener we sow ourselves in the clods of daily self-denial, falling into the furrows to die, the more fruit we bear. It is by always bearing about in the body the dying of the Lord Jesus, that the life of Jesus is made manifest in our mortal flesh. Prune off every bud on the old stock, and all the energy will pass up to the rare flowers and fruits grafted there by Heaven.

But see the King beckons us forward to pass onwards into

The Chamber of Victory over Sin

Above the door are the words: "Whosoever abideth in Him sinneth not" (1 John 3:6). Around the walls hang various instruments of war (Eph. 6:13); and frescoes of the over-comers receiving the fair rewards which the King hath promised (Rev. 2, 3). We must be careful of the order in which we put these things. Many seek victory over sin before yielding themselves entirely to God. But you can never enter this chamber, where the palm-branch waves, unless you have passed through the chamber of consecration.

Give yourself wholly up to Jesus, and He will keep you. Will you dare to say, that He can hold the oceans in the hollow of His hand, and sustain the arch of heaven, and fill the sun with light for millenniums, but that He cannot keep you from being overcome by sin, or filled with the impetuous rush of unholy passion? Can He not deliver His saints from the sword, His darlings from the power of the dog? Is all power

given Him in heaven and on earth, and must He stand paralyzed before the devils that possess you, unable to cast them out? To ask such questions is to answer them. "I am persuaded He is able to keep" (2 Tim. 1:12; 1 John 5:11).

We may expect to be tempted till we die. We certainly shall carry about with us an evil nature, which would manifest itself, unless kept in check by the grace of God. But if we abide in Christ, and He abide in us, if we live under the power of the Holy Spirit, temptation will excite no fascination in us, but, on the contrary, horror; the least stirring of our self-life will be instantly noticed, and met by the name and blood and Spirit of Jesus; the tides of His purity and life will flow so strongly over our being as to sweep away any black drops of ink oozing upwards from the sand.

You must, however, irrevocably shut the back door, as well as the front door, against sin. You must not dally with it as possible in any form. You must see that you are shut up to saintliness by the purpose of God (Rom. 8:29). You must definitely and forever elect the cross as the destiny of your self-life. And you will find that He will save you from all that you dare to trust Him with. "Every place that the sole of your foot shall tread upon, that have I given unto thee." And His work within is most perfect when it is least apparent; and when the flesh is kept so utterly in abeyance that we begin to think it has been altogether extracted.

Yet another door, at the far end of this chamber, summons us to advance to

The Chamber of Heart Rest

The King Himself spoke its motto-text: "Take My yoke and ye shall find rest unto your souls" (Matt. 11:29). Soft strains float on the air; the peace of God stands sentry against intruding care. Of course the soul learnt something of rest at the very outset. But those words of the Master indicate that there are at least two kinds of rest. And so the rest of forgiveness passes into the rest of surrender and satisfaction.

We lay our worries and cares where once we only laid our sins. We lose the tumultuous fever and haste of earlier days. We become oblivious to praise on the one hand and censure on the other. Our soul is poised on God, satisfied with God, seeks nothing outside God, regards all things from the standpoint of eternity and of God. The life loses the babble of its earlier course, and sweeps onward to the ocean, from which it derived its being, with a stillness which bespeaks its depth, a serenity which foretells its destiny. The very face tells the tale of the sweet, still life within, which is attuned to the everlasting chime of the land where storms come not, nor conflict, nor alarm.

Some say that the door at the end of this chamber leads into the chamber of

Fellowship in Christ's Sufferings

It may be so. All along the Christian's course there is a great and growing love for the world for which He died. But there are times when that love amounts almost to an agony of compassion and desire; and there come sufferings caused by the thorn-crown, the sneer, the mockery, the Cross, the spear, the baptism of blood and tears. All these fall to the lot of the followers of the King; and perhaps they come most plentifully to the saintliest, the likest to the Lord.

But certain it is that those who suffer thus are they who reign. Their sufferings are not for a moment to be compared to the glory revealed in their lives. And out of their bitter griefs, sweetened by the Cross, gush watersprings to refresh the weary heritage of God, like the waters of the Exodus (Ex. 15:25).

Beyond all these, and separated from them by a very slight interval, are the

Mansions of the Father's House

into which the King will lead us presently, chamber after chamber of delight, stretch after stretch of golden glory, until these natures, which are but as an infant's, have developed to the measure of the stature of our full growth, unto the likeness of the Son of God.

O soul! where have you got to? Do not linger inside the first chamber, but press on and forward. If any door seems locked, knock, and it shall be opened unto you. Never consider that you have attained, or are already perfect, but follow on to apprehend all that for which Jesus Christ apprehended you.

CHAPTER TWO

The Secret of Victory over Sin

The longer I live, and learn the experience of most Christian people, the more I long to help them and unfold glimpses of that life of peace, and power, and victory over sin, which our heavenly Father has made possible for us. There are blessed secrets in the Bible, hidden from the wise and prudent, but revealed to babes; things which eye hath not seen, nor ear heard, nor the heart of man conceived, but which God reveals by His Spirit to them that love Him; and if these were once understood and accepted, they would wipe away many a tear, and shed sunshine on many a darkened pathway.

The bitterest experience with most believers is the presence and power of sin. They long to walk through this grimy world with pure hearts and stainless garments, but when they would do good, evil is present with them. They consent to God's law that it is good; they approve it; they even delight in it after the inward man; they endeavor to keep it; but, notwithstanding all, they seem as helpless to perform it as a man whose brain has been smitten with paralysis, to walk straight.

What rivers of briny tears have fallen upon the open pages of the Penitents' Psalm (51st), shed by those who could repeat it every word from heart! And what regiments of weary feet have trodden the Bridge of Sighs, if we may so call Romans 7, which sets forth, in vivid force, the experience of a man who has not learnt God's secret!

Surely our God must have provided for all this. It would not have been like Him to fill us with hatred to sin, and longings for holiness, if there were no escape from the tyranny of the one, and no possibility of attaining the other. It would be a small matter to save us from sinning on the other side of the pearly gate; we want to be saved from sinning now, and in this dark world.

We want it for the sake of the world, that it may be attracted and convinced. We want it for our own peace, which can not be perfected whilst we groan under a worse than Egyptian bondage. We want it for the glory of God, which would be then reflected from us, with undimming brightness, as sunshine from burnished metal.

What, Then, Does the Word of God Lead Us to Expect?

Before Abraham arose to walk through the Land of Promise in its length and breadth, God bade Him "lift up his eyes and look." And before we can enter into the enjoyment of our privileges in Jesus Christ, we must know what they are, in something of their length and breadth, and depth and height.

We Must Not Expect to be Free from Temptation

Our adversary, the devil, is always going about as a roaring lion, seeking whom he may devour. He tempted our Lord, he will tempt us. He will entice us to do wrong by every avenue of sense, and will pour his evil suggestions through eye, and ear, and touch, and mouth, and mind. If he does not attack us himself, he can set on us any one of his myriad agents who will get behind us and step softly up to us and whisperingly suggest many grievous blasphemies which we shall think have proceeded from our own mind.

But temptation is not sin. A man may ask me to share the spoils of a burglary, but no one can accuse me of receiving stolen property if I indignantly refuse, and keep my doors close shut against him. Our Lord was tempted in all points as we are, yet without sin. You might go through hell itself, teeming with all manner of awful suggestions, and yet not sin. God would not allow Satan to tempt us if temptation necessarily led to sin; but temptation does not do so. There is no sin, so long as the will refuses to consent to the solicitation, or catch at the bait.

Temptation may even be a blessing to a man when it reveals to him his weakness and drives him to the almighty Savior. Do not be surprised, then, dear child of God, if you are tempted at every step of your earthly journey, and almost beyond endurance. You will not be tempted beyond what you are able to bear, and with every temptation there will be a way of escape.

We Must Not Expect to Lose Our Sinful Nature

When we are born again, a new life, the life of God, is put into us by the Holy Spirit. But the old self-life, which is called in Scripture THE FLESH, is not taken away. *"The flesh lusteth against the Spirit, and the Spirit against the flesh."*

The presence of this old self-life within our heart may be detected by its risings, rufflings, chafings, and movings toward sin, when temptation calls to it

from without. It may be as still as death before the increasing power of the new life, but it will still be present in the depths of our nature, as a Samson in the dark dungeons of Philistia; and there will be always a possibility and a fear of its strength growing again to our shame and hurt.

Do not ignore the presence of a sinful nature within you, with its tendencies and possibilities for sin. Many souls have been betrayed into negligence and unwatchfulness by the idea that the root of sin had been plucked from their hearts, and that therefore they could not sin again; and in the face of some sudden uprising of their old nature they have been filled with agony and shame, even if they have not dropped for a moment back into a sea of ink. *"If we say that we have no sin, we deceive ourselves, and the truth is not in us."*

There is a difference between *Sin*, and *sins*. Sin is the root-principle of evil, the flesh, the old self-life, the bias and tendency to sin, which may be kept down by the grace of God, but which will remain in us, though in diminishing power, till we leave this world. *Sins* are the outcome of this; the manifestations in act of the sinful nature within. From these we may be daily saved, through the grace of Jesus (Matt. 1:21). To put the matter clearly, *Sin* is not dead in us, but we may be dead to *Sin*, so that it shall not bear the deadly fruits of sins.

We Must Not Expect to be Free from Liability to Sin

What is sin? It is the "Yes" of the will to temptation. It is very difficult to express the delicate workings of our hearts, but does not something like this happen to us when we are tempted? A temptation is suddenly presented to us and makes a strong appeal. Immediately there may be a tremulous movement of the old nature, as the strings of a violin or piano vibrate in answer to any sounds that may be thrilling the air around. Some do not feel this tremulous response; others do, though I believe that it will get fainter and fainter as they treat it with continued neglect, so that at last, in the matured saint, it will become almost inaudible.

This response indicates the presence of the evil nature within, which is in itself hateful in the sight of our Holy God, and should be bemoaned and confessed, and ever needs the presence of the blood of Jesus to counteract and atone; but that tremulous movement has not as yet developed into an actual overt sin, for which we are responsible, and of which we need to repent.

Sin is the act of the will, and is only possible when the will assents to some unholy influence. The tempter presenting his temptation through the senses and emotions, makes an appeal to the will, which is our real self. If that will instantly shudders, as chickens when the hawk is hovering in the sky above them, and cries, "How can I do this great wickedness, and sin against God!" and looks at once to Jesus,—there are so far as I can understand, no sins.

If on the other hand the will begins to pelter with temptation, to dally with it, and yield to it, then we have stepped out of the light into the dark, we have broken God's Law, splashed our white robes, and brought ourselves into condemnation. To this we are liable as long as we are in this world. We may live a godly, righteous, sober life for years, but if we look away from God for only a moment, our will may be suddenly mastered, as was Louis XVIII, by the mob that invaded his palace; and we may, like David, be hurried into a sin which will blast our peace and blacken our character for all coming time.

Now what are the secrets of victory over sin?

Remember That the Blood of Jesus Is Ever at Work Cleansing You

It is sweet to notice the present tenses of Scripture. He forgiveth, healeth, redeemeth, crowneth, satisfieth, executeth judgment; but the sweetest of all is *"the blood of Jesus cleanseth from all sin."* It cleansed us when first we knelt at His cross. It will cleanse away the last remnant of sin as we cross the golden threshold. But it *does* cleanse us every hour; as the brook flows over the stones in its bed, till they glisten with lustrous beauty; and as the tear water, pouring constantly over the eye, keeps it bright and clean, in spite of all the smuts that darken the air.

The possession of a sinful nature is an evil that ever needs an antidote. The risings and stirrings of that nature beneath the appeals of temptation ever need cleansing. The permission of things in our life, which we now count harmless, but which we shall some day, amid increasing light, condemn and put away—all these need forgiveness. But for all these needs there is ample provision for us in the blood of Jesus, which is always crying to God for us. Even when we do not plead it, or remember it, or realize our need of it, it fulfils for us and in us its unceasing ministry of blessing.

Reckon Yourself Dead to the Appeals of Sin

Sin has no power over a dead man. Dress it in its most bewitching guise, yet it stirs him not. Tears and smiles and words and blows alike fail to awaken a response from that cold corpse. No appeal will stir it until it hears the voice of the Son of God.

This is our position in respect to the appeals of sin. God looks on us as having been crucified with Christ, and being dead with Him. In Him we have passed out of the world of sin and death into the world of resurrection glory. This is our position in the mind of God; it is for us to take it up and make it real by faith. We may not feel any great difference, but we must believe that there is; we must act as if there were. Our children sometimes play at make-believe; we, too, are to make believe, and we shall soon come to feel as we believe.

When, then, a temptation solicits you, say, "I am dead to thee. Spend not thine energies on one that is oblivious to thy spells and callous to thy charms. Thou hast no more power over me than over my Lord and Head." *"Reckon ye also yourselves to be dead indeed unto sin, but alive unto God through Jesus Christ our Lord"* (Rom. 6:11).

Walk in the Spirit; Keep in with the Holy Ghost

The Holy Spirit is in the heart of every believer (Rom. 8:9); but alas! too often He is shut up in some mere attic in the back of the house, whilst the world fills the rest. As long as it is so, there is one long weary story of defeat and unrest. But He is not content. *Know ye not that the Spirit, which He hath made to dwell in us, yearneth even unto jealousy envy?* (Jas. 4:5, RV). Happy are they who yield to Him. Then He will fill them, as the tide fills the harbor and lifts the barges off the banks of mud; He will dwell in them, shedding abroad the perfume of the love of Jesus; and will reveal the deep things of God.

We can always tell when we are wrong with the Spirit of God; our conscience darkens in a moment when we have grieved Him. If we are aware of such a darkness, we do well never to rest until, beneath His electric light, we have discovered the cause, and confessed it, and put it away. Besides this, if we live and walk in the Spirit, we shall find that He will work against the risings of our old nature, counteracting them as disinfecting power counteracts the germs of disease floating in an infected house, *so that we may do the things that we would* (Gal. 5:17, RV).

This is one of the most precious words in the New Testament. If you have never tried it, I entreat you to begin to test it in daily experience. *"Walk in the Spirit,"* hour by hour, by watchful obedience to His slightest promptings, and you will find that *"you will not fulfill the lust of the flesh."*

As Soon as You Are Aware of Temptation, Look Instantly to Jesus

Flee to Him quicker than a chicken runs beneath the shelter of its mother's wing when the kestrel is in the air. In the morning, ere you leave your room, put yourself definitely into His hands, persuaded He is able to keep that which you commit unto Him. Go from your room with the assurance that He will cover you with His feathers, and under His wings shall you trust. And when the tempter comes, look instantly up and say, *"Jesus, I am trusting Thee to keep me."*

This is what the Apostle Paul calls using the shield of faith. The upward glance of faith puts Jesus as a shield between the tempter and yourself. You may go through life, saying a hundred times a day, *Jesus saves me*, and He will never let those that trust in Him be ashamed. *"He is able to guard you even from stumbling"* (Jude 24, RV). You may be pressed with temptations from without, and may feel the workings of evil within, and yet your will looking earnestly to Jesus, shall remain steadfast, immovable, and unyielding. No weapon that is forged against you in the armory of hell shall prosper.

There Is Something Better Even than This

It was first taught me by a gray-haired clergyman, in the study of the Deanery, at Southampton. Once, when tempted to feel great irritation, he told us that he looked up and claimed the patience and gentleness of Christ; and since then it had become the practice of his life to claim from Him the virtue of which he felt the deficiency in himself.

In hours of unrest, "Thy peace, Lord." In hours of irritation, "Thy patience, Lord." In hours of temptation, "Thy purity, Lord." In hours of weakness, "Thy strength, Lord." It was to me a message straight from the throne. Till then I had been content with ridding myself with burdens; now I began to reach forth to positive blessing, making each temptation the occasion for the new acquisition of gold-leaf. Try it, dear reader.

When I have spoken thus in public, I have sometimes been met by the objection, "Ah, sir, it is quite true that the Lord will keep me if I look to Him, but I often forget to look *in time*." This arises from one of three causes.

Perhaps the heart and life have never been entirely surrendered to Jesus. Constant defeat always indicates that there has been failure in consecration. You must not expect Christ to keep you unless you have given your heart and life entirely over to Him, so that He is king. Christ can not be keeper if He is not king. And He will not be king at all, unless He is king in all.

Or perhaps there is a want of watchfulness. Christ will not keep us if we carelessly and wantonly put ourselves into the way of temptation. He will give His angels charge over us in every path of duty, but not to catch us every time we like to throw ourselves from the beetling height. *Watch* and pray that ye enter not into temptation.

Or perhaps there is a lack of feeding on the Word of God. No one can live a life of faith without seasons of prolonged waiting on God in the loving study of the Bible and in prayer. The man who does not make time for private devotion in the early morning can not walk with God all day. And of the two things, the devout meditation on the Word is more important to soul-health than even prayer. It is more needful for you to hear God's words than that God should hear yours, though the one will always lead to the other. Attend to these conditions, and it will become both easy and natural to trust Christ in the hour of trial.

If, notwithstanding all these helps, you should be still betrayed into a sin, and overtaken by a fault, do not lose heart. If a sheep and a sow fall into a ditch, the sow wallows in it, the sheep bleats piteously until she is cleansed. Go at once to your compassionate Savior; tell Him in the simplest words the story of your fall and sorrow; ask Him to wash you at once and restore your soul, and, whilst you are asking, believe that it is done. Then go to any one against or with whom you have sinned, and confess your faults one to another. Thus the peace of God that passeth all understanding shall return to roost in your heart, and to guard it like a sentry-angel in shining armor.

And if you thus live, free from the power of sin, you will find that the Master will begin to use you as never before and to tell you His heart-secrets, and to open to you the royal magnificence of a life hidden with Himself in God.

May this be your happy lot, dear reader.

CHAPTER THREE

The First Step into the Blessed Life

There is a Christian life, which, in comparison with that experienced by the majority of Christians, is as summer to winter, or as the mature fruitfulness of a golden autumn to the struggling promise of a cold and late spring. It is such a life as Caleb might have lived in Hebron, the city of fellowship; or the Apostle John was living when he wrote his epistles. It may be fitly termed the Blessed Life.

And the blessedness of the Blessed Life lies in this: that we trust the Lord to do in us and for us what we could not do; and we find that He does not belie His word, but that, according to our faith, so it is done to us. The weary spirit, which has vainly sought to realize its ideal by its own strivings and efforts, now gives itself over to the strong and tender hands of the Lord Jesus; and He accepts the task, and at once begins to work in it to will and to do of His own good pleasure, delivering it from the tyranny of besetting sin, and fulfilling in it His own perfect ideal.

This Blessed Life should be the normal life of every Christian; in work and rest; in the building-up of the inner life, and in the working-out of the life-plan. It is God's thought not for a few, but for all His children. The youngest and weakest may lay claim to it, equally with the strongest and oldest. We should step into it at the moment of conversion, without wandering with blistered feet for forty years in the desert, or lying for thirty-eight years with disappointed hopes in the porch of the House of Mercy.

But since many have long ago passed the moment of conversion, without entering the Blessed Life, it may be well to show clearly what the first step must be, to take us within its golden circle. Better take it late than never.

The first step into the Blessed Life is contained in the one word,

Consecration

It is enforced by the significant exhortation of the Apostle: *"Yield yourselves unto God, as those that are alive from the dead, and your members as instruments of righteousness unto God"* (Rom. 6:13).

It is not enough to give our time, or energy, or money. Many will gladly give anything, rather than *themselves*. None of these will be accounted as a sufficient substitute by Him who gave, not only His possessions, but His very Self for us. As the Lord Jesus was all for us, He asks that we should be all for Him— body, soul and spirit; one reasonable service and gift.

That consecration is the stepping-stone to blessedness, is clearly established in the experience of God's children. For instance, Frances Ridley Havergal has left us this record: "It was on Advent Sunday, December, 1873, that I first saw clearly the blessedness of true consecration. I saw it as a flash of electric light, and what you see you can never unsee. *There must be full surrender before there can be full blessedness. God admits you by the one into the other.* First I was shown that the blood of Jesus Christ, His

Son, cleanseth from all sin; and then it was made plain to me that He who had thus cleansed me, had power to keep me clean; *so I utterly yielded myself to Him and utterly trusted Him to keep me."*

The seraphic Whitfield, the brothers Wesley, the great Welsh preacher Christmas Evans, the French pastor Oberlin, and many more, have given the same testimony. And in their mouths surely this truth may be regarded as established, that we must pass through Gilgal to the Land of Rest; and that the strait gate of consecration alone leads into the Blessed Life.

The Ground of Consecration Is in the Great Scripture Statement That We Are Christ's

There is a two-fold ground of proprietorship. *We are His by purchase. "Ye are not your own, for ye are bought with a price."* Step into that slave-market where men and women are waiting like chattels to be bought. Yonder comes a wealthy planter, who, after due examination, lays down his money for a number of men and women to stock his estate. From that moment, those persons are absolutely his property, as much so as his cattle or his sheep. All they possess, all they may earn, is absolutely his.

So, the apostles reasoned, they were Christ's; and often they began their epistles by calling themselves, *"the slaves of Jesus Christ."* Paul went so far as to say that he bore in his body the brand-marks of Jesus. And are not all Christians Christ's, whether they own it and live up to it, or not, because He purchased them by His most precious blood?

We are His also by deed of gift. The Father has given to the Son all who shall come to Him. If ever you have come, or shall come, to Jesus Christ as your Sav-

ior, you show that you have been included in that wonderful donation. *"All that the Father giveth me shall come to me; and him that cometh to me I will in no wise cast out"* (John 6:37). And is it likely that the Father gave only a part of us? Nay, as utterly as He gave His Son for us, so hath He given us to His Son. And our Lord Jesus thinks much of that solemn transaction, though we, alas! often live as if it had never taken place, and were free to live as we pleased.

The Act of Consecration Is to Recognize Christ's Ownership; and to Accept It; and to Say to Him, With the Whole Heart, "Lord, I Am Thine by Right, and I Wish to Be Thine by Choice"

Of old the mighty men of Israel were willing to swim the rivers at their flood, to come to David, their uncrowned but God-appointed king. And when they met him, they cried, "Thine are we, David, and on thy side, thou son of Jesse." They were his because God had given them to him, but they could not rest content till they were his also by their glad choice.

Why then should we not say the same to Jesus Christ? "Lord Jesus, I am Thine by right. Forgive me that I have lived so long as if I were my own. And now I gladly recognize that Thou hast a rightful claim on all I have and am. I want to live as Thine henceforth, and I do solemnly at this hour give myself to Thee. Thine in life and death. Thine absolutely and for ever."

Do not try to make a covenant with God, lest you should break it and be discouraged. But quietly fall into your right attitude as one who belongs to Christ. Take as your motto the noble confession, *"Whose I am and whom I serve."* Breathe the grand old simple lines:

Just as I am,—Thy love unknown
Has broken every barrier down;
Now to be Thine, yea, Thine alone,
O Lamb of God, I come.

Consecration Is Not the Act of Our Feelings, But of Our Will

Do not try to feel anything. Do not try to make yourself fit or good or earnest enough for Christ. God is working in you to will, whether you feel it or not. He is giving you power, at this moment, to will and do His good pleasure. Believe this, and act upon it at once; and say, "Lord Jesus, I am willing to be Thine"; or, if you can not say as much as that, say, "Lord Jesus, I am willing to be made willing to be Thine for evermore."

Consecration is only possible when we give up our will *about everything.* As soon as we come to the point of giving ourselves to God, we are almost certain to become aware of the presence of one thing, if not of more, out of harmony with His will; and while we feel able to surrender ourselves in all other points, here we exercise reserve. Every room and cupboard in the house, with the exception of this, thrown open to the new occupant. Every limb in the body, but one, submitted to the practiced hand of the Good Physician. But that small reserve spoils the whole. To give ninety-nine parts and to withhold the hundredth undoes the whole transaction.

Jesus will have all or none. And He is wise. Who would live in a fever-stricken house, so long as one room was not exposed to disinfectants, air and sun? Who would undertake a case so long as the patient refused to submit one part of his body to examination? Who would become responsible for a bankrupt so long as one ledger was kept back?

The reason that so many fail to attain the Blessed Life is that there is some one point in which they hold back from God, and concerning which they prefer to have their own way and will rather than His. In this one thing they will not yield their will and accept God's, and this one little thing mars the whole, robs them of peace, and compels them to wander in the desert.

If You Can Not Give All, Ask the Lord Jesus to Take All, and Especially That Which Seems So Hard to Give

Many have been helped by hearing it put thus: Tell them to *give* and they shake their heads despondently. They are like the little child who told her mother that she had been trying to give Jesus her heart, *but it wouldn't go.* But ask them if they are willing for Him to come into their hearts and *take* all, and they will joyfully assent.

Tennyson says: "Our wills are ours to make them Thine." But sometimes it seems impossible to shape them out so as to match every corner and angle of the will of God. What a relief it is at such a moment to hand the will over to Christ, telling Him that *we are willing to be made willing* to have His will in all things, and asking him to melt our stubborn waywardness, to fashion our wills upon His anvil, and to bring us into perfect accord with Himself!

When We Are Willing That the Lord Jesus Should Take All, We Must Believe That He Does Take All

He does not wait for us to free ourselves from evil habits, or to make ourselves good, or to feel glad and happy. His one desire is that we should put our will on His side in everything. When this is done, He *instantly* enters the surrendered heart and begins His blessed work of renovation and renewal. From the very moment of consecration, though it be done in much feebleness and with slender appreciation of its meaning, the spirit may begin to say with emphasis, "I am His! I am His! Glory to God, I am His!" Directly the gift is laid on the altar, the fire falls on it.

Sometimes there is a rush of holy feeling. It was so with James Brainerd Taylor, who tells: "I felt that I needed something I did not possess. I desired it, not for my benefit only, but for that of the church and the world. I lifted up my heart that the blessing might descend. At this juncture I was delightfully conscious of giving up all to God. I was enabled in my heart to say: 'Here, Lord, take me, take my whole soul, and seal me Thine now, and Thine for ever. If Thou wilt, Thou canst make me clean.' Then there ensued such emotions as I never before experienced. All was calm and tranquil, and a heaven of love pervaded my soul. I had the witness of God's love to me, and of mine to Him. Shortly after I was dissolved in tears of love and gratitude to our blessed Lord, who came as King, and took possession of my heart."

It is very delightful when such emotions are given to us; but we must not look for them, or depend on them. Our consecration may be accepted, and may excite the liveliest joy in our Savior's heart, though we are filled with no answering ecstasy. We may know that the great transaction is done, without any glad outburst of song. We may even have to exercise faith, against feeling, as we say, many scores of times each day, "I am His." But the absence of feeling proves nothing. We must pillow our heads on the conviction that Jesus took what we gave, at the moment of our giving it, and that He will keep that which was committed to Him, against that day.

It Is Well to Make the Act of Consecration a Definite One in Our Spiritual History

George Whitfield did it in the ordination service: "I can call heaven and earth to witness that when the bishop laid his hands upon me, I gave myself up to be a martyr for Him who hung upon the cross for me. Known unto Him are all the future events and contingences. I have thrown myself blindfolded, and without reserve, into His almighty hands."

Christmas Evans did it as he was climbing a lonely and mountainous road toward Cader Idris: "I was weary of a cold heart toward Christ, and began to pray, and soon felt the fetters loosening. Tears flowed copiously, and I was constrained to cry out for the gracious visits of God. Thus I resigned myself to Christ, body and soul, gifts and labors, all my life, every day and every hour that remained to me; and all my cares I committed to Christ."

Stephen Grellet did in it the woods: "The woods are there of lofty and large pines, and my mind being inwardly retired before the Lord, He was pleased so to reveal His love to me, through His blessed Son, my Savior, that my fears were removed, my wounds healed, my mourning turned into joy; and He strengthened me to offer up myself freely to Him and to His service, for my whole life."

It matters little when and how we do it; whether by speech or in writing; whether alone or in company; but we must not be content with a general desire. We must come to a definite act, at a given moment of time, when we shall gladly acknowledge and confess Christ's absolute ownership of all we are and have.

When the Act of Consecration Is Once Truly Done, It Need Not Be Repeated

We may review with thankfulness. We may add some new codicils to it. We may learn how much more was involved in it than we ever dreamed. We may find new departments of our being, constantly demanding to be included. But we can not undo, and need never repeat it; and if we fall away from it, let us go at once to our merciful High-Priest, confessing our sin, and seeking forgiveness and restoration.

The Advantages Resulting from This Act Can Not Be Enumerated Here

They pass all count. The first and best is the special filling by the Holy Ghost; and as He fills the heart, He drives before Him the evil things which had held possession there too long; just as mercury, poured into a glass of water, sinks to the bottom, expels the water, and takes its place. Directly we give ourselves to Christ, He seals us by His Spirit. Directly we present Him with a yielded nature, He begins to fill it with the Holy Ghost. Let us not *try* to feel that it is so; let us *believe* that it is so, and reckon on God's faithfulness. Others will soon see a marked difference in us, though we wist it not.

All That We Have to Do Is to Maintain This Attitude of Full Surrender, by the Grace of the Holy Spirit

Remember that Jesus Christ offered Himself to God, *through the Eternal Spirit;* and He waits to do as much for you. Ask Him to maintain you in this attitude, and to maintain this attitude in you. Use regularly the means of medi-

tation, private prayer, and Bible study. Seek forgiveness for any failure, directly you are conscious of it; and ask to be restored. Practice the holy habit of the constant recollection of God.

Do not be eager to work for God, but let God work through you. Accept everything that happens to you as being permitted, and therefore sent by the will of Him who loves you infinitely. There will roll in upon you wave on wave, tide on tide, ocean on ocean of an experience, fitly called the Blessed Life, because it is full of the happiness of the ever-blessed God Himself.

Dear reader, will you not take this step? There will be no further difficulty about money, dress or amusements, or similar questions, which perplex some. Your heart will be filled and satisfied with the true riches. As the willing slave of Jesus Christ, you will only seek to do the will of your great and gentle Master. To spend every coin as He directs, to act as His steward, to dress so as to give Him pleasure, to spend the time only as He may approve, to do His will on earth, as it is in heaven; all this will come easy and delightful.

You are perhaps far from this at present, but it is all within your reach. Do not be afraid of Christ. He wants to take nothing from you except that which you would give up at once if you could see, as clearly as He does, the harm it is inflicting. He will ask of you nothing inconsistent with the most perfect fitness and tenderness. He will give you grace enough to perform every duty He may demand. His yoke is easy; His burden is light.

Blessed Spirit of God, by whom alone human words can be made to speak to the heart, deign to use these, to point many a longing soul to the first step into the Blessed Life, for the exceeding glory of the Lord Jesus, and for the sake of a dying world.

CHAPTER FOUR

How to Read Your Bible

The whole of Christian living, in my opinion, hinges on the way in which Christian people read the Bible for themselves. All sermons and addresses, all Bible-readings and classes, all religious magazines and books, can never take the place of our own quiet study of God's precious Word. We may measure our growth in grace by the growth of our love for private Bible study; and we may be sure that there is something seriously wrong, when we lose our appetite for the Bread of Life. Perhaps we have been eating too many sweets; or taking too little exercise; or breathing too briefly in the bracing air which sweeps over the uplands of spiritual communion with God.

Happy are they who have learned the blessed art of discovering for themselves the treasures of the Bible, which are hidden just a little below the surface, so as to test our real earnestness in finding them! No specimens are so interesting as those which the naturalist has obtained by his own exertions, and each of which has a history. No flowers are so fragrant as those which we discover for ourselves, nestling in some woodland dell, remote from the eye and step of men. No pearls are so priceless as those which we have sought for ourselves in the calm clear depths of the ocean of truth. Only those who know it can realize the joy that fills the spirit when one has made a great "find," in some hidden connection, some fresh reference, or some railway lines from verse to verse.

There are a few simple rules which may help many more to acquire this holy art, and I venture to note them down. May the Holy Spirit Himself own and use them!

Make Time for Bible Study

The Divine Teacher must have fixed and uninterrupted hours for meeting His scholars. His Word must have our freshest and brightest thoughts. We must give Him our best, and the firstfruits of our days. Hence, there is no time for Bible study like the early morning. We can not give such undivided attention to the holy thoughts that glisten like diamonds on its pages after we have opened our letters, glanced through the paper, and joined in the prattle of the breakfast table. The manna had to be gathered by the Israelites of old before the dew was off and the sun was up; otherwise it melted.

We ought, therefore, to aim at securing at least half an hour before breakfast, for the leisurely and loving study of the Bible. To some this may seem a long time in comparison with what they now give. But it will soon seem all too short. The more you read the Bible, the more you will want to read it. It is an appetite which grows as it is fed.

And you will be well repaid. The Bible seldom speaks, and certainly never its deepest, sweetest words, to those who always read it in a hurry. Nature can only tell her secrets to such as will sit still in her sacred temple till their eyes lose the glare of earthly glory, and their ears are attuned to her voice.

And shall revelation do what nature can not? Never. The man who shall win the blessedness of hearing her must watch daily at her gates and wait at the posts of her doors. There is no chance for a lad to grow, who only gets an occasional mouthful of food and always swallows that in a hurry!

Of course this season before breakfast is not possible for all. The invalid, the nurse with broken rest, the public servant, whose night is often turned into day—these stand alone, and the Lord Jesus can make it up to them, sitting with them at mid day, if needs be, beside the well.

In the case of such as can only snatch a few words of Scripture as they hasten to their work, there will be repeated the miracle of the manna. *"He that gathered much had nothing over"*; that is, all we get in our morning reading is not too much for the needs of the day; *"and he that gathered little had no lack"*; that is, when, by force of circumstances, we are unable to do more than snatch up a hasty handful of manna, it will last us all through the day; the cruse of oil shall not waste, and the barrel of meal shall not fail.

It would be impossible to name all who have traced their usefulness and power to this priceless habit. Sir Henry Havelock always spent the first two hours of each day alone with God; and if the encampment was struck at 6 A.M., he would rise at 4. Earl Cairns rose daily at 6 o'clock to secure an hour and a half for the study of the Bible and for prayer, before conducting family worship at a quarter to eight—even when the late hours of the House of Commons left him not more than two hours for his night's rest. It is the practice of a beloved friend, who stands in the front rank of modern missionaries, to spend at least three hours each morning with his Bible; and he has said that he often puts aside pressing engagements that he may not only have time but be fresh for it.

There is no doubt a difficulty in awakening and arising early enough to get time for our Bible before breakfast. But these difficulties present no barrier to those who must get away early for daily business, or for the appointments of pleasure. If we *mean* to get up, we *can* get up. Of course we must prepare the way for early rising, by retiring early to obtain our needed rest, though it be at the cost of some cozy hours by the fireside in the winter's night. But with due forethought and fixed purpose the thing can surely be done. *"All things are possible to him that believeth."*

I never shall forget seeing Charles Studd, early one November morning, clothed in flannels to protect him from the cold, and rejoicing that the Lord had awakened him at 4 A.M. to study His commands. He told me then that it was his custom to trust the Lord to call him and enable him to rise.

Might not we all do this? The weakest can do all things through Christ that strengtheneth. And though you have failed again and again when you have trusted your own resolutions, you can not fail when you are simply trusting him. *"He wakeneth morning by morning."* *"He took him by the right hand, and lifted him up; and immediately his feet and ankle bones received strength."*

Look Up for the Teaching of the Holy Spirit

No one can so well explain the meaning of his words as he who wrote them. Tennyson could best explain some of his deeper references in "In Memoriam." If, then, you want to read the Bible as you should, make much of the Holy Ghost, who inspired it through holy men. As you open the book, lift up your hearts, and say: *"Open Thou mine eyes, that I may behold wondrous things out of Thy law . . . Speak, Lord, for Thy servant heareth."*

It is marvelous what slender light commentaries cast on the inner meaning of Scripture. A simple-hearted believer, depending on the aid of the Holy Ghost, will find things in the Bible which the wisest have mistaken or missed. Well might St. John say of such, *"Ye need not that any man should teach you; but the anointing, which ye have received, teacheth you of all things."* What fire is to sympathetic ink, bringing the colorless fluid out black and clear, that the teaching of the Holy Ghost is to passages in the Bible which had seemed meaningless and bare.

We can never know too much of that literature which throws side-lights on the Bible, and which unfolds the customs of the people, difficult allusions, historical coincidences, geographical details. Geikie's *Hours with the Bible;* Kitto's *Daily Illustrations,* edited by Dr. Porter; Dr. Smith's *Bible Dictionary;* books like these are invaluable. But we should study them at another time than in the sacred morning hour, which we give to the Holy Ghost alone.

Read the Bible Methodically

On the whole there is probably no better way than to read the Bible through once every year. There is a very good plan for doing this in the life of the sainted McCheyne, who drew it up for his people. Or it may be done by taking daily, in a Bagster's Bible, three columns of the Old Testament, two of the New Testament, and one of the Psalms. This system will more than do it.

The next best plan to this is that adopted by Mr. Richardson's Bible Reading Union, which consists of tens of thousands of Christians in every part of the world, who read one chapter a day in regular rotation, and thus get through the Book in about three years.

It is wise to have a good copy of the Scriptures, strongly bound for wear and tear, of good clear print, and with as much space as possible for notes. A book of which you can make a friend and inseparable companion. But it is above all things wise at first to select one with copious marginal references, so that it may be easy to turn to the parallel passages.

For myself, this plan has invested by Bible reading with new interest. I love to have in front of me one of the Paragraph Bibles of the Religious Tract Society, which abound in well-chosen references, and a small pocket Bible in my hand, that I may easily turn to any reference I desire; and very often I get more blessing from the passages to which I refer, and those to which these lead, than from the one I may be reading.

After a while, we shall begin to make references for ourselves; and then we may not only be able to read God's Word in the most approved English rendering, which is an immense advantage, but that we may also be able to fill up the empty margins with the notes of parallel passages.

But whatever system is adopted, *be sure to read the Bible through on some system, as you would any other book.* No one would think of reading a letter, poem, or history, as many read God's Word. What wonder that they are so ignorant of its majestic prose, its exquisite lyric poetry, its massive arguments, its sublime imagery, its spiritual beauty—qualities which combine to make it the King of Books, even though the halo of inspiration did not shine like a crown about its brow!

It is sometimes well to read a book at a sitting, devoting two or three hours to the sacred task. At other times, it is more profitable to take an epoch, or an episode, or a life, and compare all that is written of it in various parts of Scripture. At other times, again, it is well to follow the plan on which Mr. Moody has so often insisted, of taking one work or thought, as Faith, or Love, or Able, and tracing it, by help of a concordance, from end to end of the inspired volume.

But in any case, let the *whole* Bible be your study; because "*All Scripture is given by inspiration of God, and is profitable.*" Even the rocky places shall gush with water springs. The most barren chapters shall blossom as the rose. "*Out of the eater shall come forth meat, and sweetness out of the strong.*"

Let us never forget that the Bible is one book; the work of one infinite Spirit, speaking through prophet and priest, shepherd and king, the old-world patriarch and the apostle who lived to see Jerusalem leveled to the ground. You may subject its words to the most searching test, but you will find they will always bear the same meaning, and move in the same direction. Let the Bible be its own dictionary, its own interpreter, its own best commentary. It is like a vast buried city, in which every turn of the spade reveals some new marvel, while passages branch off in every direction, calling for exploration.

Read Your Bible with Your Pen in Hand

Writing of F. R. Havergal, her sister says, "She read her Bible at her study table by seven o'clock in the summer, and eight o'clock in winter. Sometimes, on bitterly cold mornings, I begged that she would read with her feet comfortably to the fire, and received the reply: 'But then, Marie, I can't rule my lines neatly; just see what a find I've got!' If only one searches, there are such extraordinary things in the Bible! She res-

olutely refrained from late hours and frittering talks at night, in place of Bible searching and holy communings. Early rising and early studying were her rule through life."

None, in my judgment, have learned the secret of enjoying the Bible until they have commenced to mark it, neatly. Underlining and dating special verses, which have cast a light upon their path on special days. Drawing railway connections, across the pages, between verses which repeat the same message, or ring with the same note. Jotting down new references, or the catchwords of helpful thoughts. All these methods find plenty of employment for the pen, and fix our treasures for us permanently. Our Bible then becomes the precious memento of by gone hours, and records the history of our inner life.

Seek Eagerly Your Personal Profit

Do not read the Bible for others, for class or congregation, but for yourself. Bring all its rays to a focus on your own heart. While you are reading, often ask that some verse or verses may start out from the printed page, as God's message to yourself. Never close the book until you feel that you are carrying away your portion of meat from that hand which satisfieth the desire of every living thing. It is well, sometimes, to stop reading, and seriously ask, "What does the Holy Spirit mean *me* to learn by this? What bearing should this have on *my* life ? How can I work this into the fabric of *my* character?"

Let not the Bible be to you simply as a history, a treatise, or a poem, but as your Father's letter to yourself; in which there are some things which you will not understand till you come into the circumstances which require them; but which is also full of present help. There is a great difference between the way in which an absent child scans the parcel of newspapers, and that in which he devours the home letter, by which the beloved parent speaks. Both are interesting, but the one is general, the other is all to himself. Read the Bible, not as a newspaper, but as a home letter.

Above All, Turn from the Printed Page to Prayer

If a cluster of heavenly fruit hangs within reach, gather it. If a promise lies upon the page as a blank check, cash it. If a prayer is recorded, appropriate it, and launch it as a feathered arrow from the bow of your desire. If an example of holiness gleams before you, ask God to do as much for you. If a truth is revealed in all its intrinsic splendor, entreat that its brilliance may ever irradiate the hemisphere of your life like a star. Entwine the climbing creepers of holy desire about the lattice work of Scripture. So shall you come to say with the psalmist, *"Oh, how I love Thy law, it is my meditation all the day!"*

It is sometimes well to read over, on our knees, Psalm 119, so full of devout love for the Bible. And if any should chide us for spending so much time upon the Old Testament, or the New, let us remind them of the words of Christ, *"Man shall not live by bread alone, but by every word that proceedeth out of the mouth of God."* The Old Testament must be worth our study since it was our Savior's Bible, deeply pondered and often quoted. And the New demands it, since it is so full of what He said and did, not only in His early life, but through the medium of His holy apostles and prophets.

Advantages of a Deep Knowledge of the Bible

The advantages of a deep knowledge of the Bible are more than can be numbered here. It is the storehouse of the promises. It is the sword of the Spirit, before which temptation flees. It is the all-sufficient equipment for Christian usefulness. It is the believer's guidebook and directory in all possible circumstances. Words fail to tell how glad, how strong, how useful shall be the daily life of those, who can say with the prophet: *"Thy words were found, and I did eat them; and Thy word was unto me the joy and rejoicing of my heart."*

Practice What You Learn

But there is one thing, which may be said last, because it is most important, and should linger in the memory and heart, though all the other exhortations of this chapter should pass away as a summer brook. It is this. It is useless to dream of making headway in the knowledge of Scripture unless we are prepared to practice each new and clearly-defined duty which looms out before our view.

We are taught, not for our pleasure only, *but that we may do*. If we will turn each holy precept or command into instant obedience, through the dear grace of Jesus Christ our Lord, God will keep nothing back from us; He will open to us His deepest and sweetest thoughts. But so long as we refuse obedience to even the least command, we shall find that the light will fade from the page of Scripture, and the zest will die down quickly in our own hearts.

This book of the Law shall not depart out of thy mouth; but thou shalt meditate therein day and night, that thou mayest observe to do according to all that is written therein: for then thou shalt make thy way prosperous, and then thou shalt have good success. *Josh. 1:8*

CHAPTER FIVE

The Common Task

A young friend, richly gifted, but who is tied by inexorable necessity to an office stool, has complained to me that his life afforded no outlet for the adequate exercise of his powers.

His groan is a very common one. So many grumble about the monotony of life's dead-level, which the great majority of us have to traverse. The upland paths which give an ecstasy to tread in the bracing air and the expanding glory of the world are for the few. For most of us it is the trivial round, the common task. Each morning the bell calls to the same routine of common-place toil. Each hour brings the same program of trifles. There seems no chance for doing anything heroic, which will be worth having lived for, or will shed a light back on all past, and forward on all coming days.

But there are two or three considerations, which, if wrought into the heart, will tend to remove much of this terrible depression.

All Life Is Part of a Divine Plan

As a mother desires the best possible for her babes bending over the cradle which each occupies in turn, so does God desire to do His best for us all. He hates nothing that He has made, but has a fair ideal for each, which He desires to accomplish in us with perfect love. But there is no way of transferring it to our actual experience, except by the touch of His Spirit within, and the education of our circumstances without.

He has chosen the circumstances of our life, because they are the shortest path, if only we use them as we should, to reach the goal on which He has set His heart. He might have chosen some other country—China, India, Italy, or Mexico. He might have chosen some other age—that of the Flood, the Exodus, or of the early martyrs. He might have chosen some other lot—a royal court, a senate, a pulpit, or an author's desk. But since he chose this land, this age, and your lot (whatever it may be), we must believe that these presented the likeliest and swiftest way for realizing His purpose.

If, my brother, you could have reached your truest manhood as an emperor or a reformer, as a millionaire or a martyr, you would have been born into one of those positions; but since you are only a servant, a bank clerk, or an ordinary business man, you will find right beside you the materials and possibilities of a great life.

If, my sister, you could have attained to the loftiest development of your nature by being a mother, or a rich man's wife, or a queen, you would have found yourself placed there; but since your lot is that of a milliner's assistant, factory hand, or toiling mother, you must believe that, somewhere within your reach, if only you will search for them, you will discover the readiest conditions of a noble and useful life.

Who can wonder at the complaints of the aimlessness, the vanity, the weariness of life? People either have no plan, or they have got a wrong one. "What's the fashion?" "What do others do?"

"What's the correct thing?" How much better and wiser to believe that God has a perfect plan for each of us, and that He is unfolding it a bit at a time, by the events which He puts into our life each day!

Before Moses built the tabernacle, he saw the whole pattern of it in prophetic vision. In some secluded spot on Sinai's heights it stood before him, woven out of sunbeams; and he descended to the mountain foot to repeat it in actual curtains, gold, and wood. God does not show us the whole plan of our life at a burst, but unfolds it to us bit by bit. Each day He gives us the opportunity of weaving a curtain, carving a peg, fashioning the metal. We know not what we do, but at the end of our life the disjointed pieces will suddenly come together, and we shall see the symmetry and beauty of the divine thought. Then we shall be satisfied.

In the meantime let us believe that God's love and wisdom are doing the very best for us. In the morning ask God to show you His plan for the day in the unfolding of its events, and to give you grace to do or bear all that He may have prepared. In the midst of the day's engagements, often look up and say, "Father, is this in the plan?" At night, be still, and match your actual with God's ideal, confessing your sins and shortcomings, and asking that His will may be more perfectly done in you, even as in heaven.

Every Life Affords Opportunities for Building Up Noble Character

We are sent into this world to build up characters which will be blessed and useful in that great future for which we are being trained. There is a niche which only we can fill, a crown which only we can wear, music which only we can waken, service which only we can render. God knows what these are, and He is giving us opportunities to prepare for them. Life is our school house. Its rooms may be bare, but they are littered with opportunities of becoming fit for our great inheritance.

Knitting needles are cheap and common enough, but on them may be wrought the fairest designs in the richest wools. So the incidents of daily life may be commonplace in the extreme, but on them as the material foundation we may build the unseen but everlasting fabric of a noble and beautiful character. It does not so much matter what we do, but the way in which we do it matters greatly. What we do may or may not live; but the way in which we perform our common tasks becomes an indestructible part of our character, for better or worse, and for ever.

Suppose we meet the daily demands of life in a slovenly and careless spirit, caring only to escape blame, to earn our wage, or to preserve a decent average. Or suppose our one aim in life is to get money for our own enjoyment. Is it not clear that the meanness of the motive will react on the whole character behind it? Will it not be certain and inevitable that the soul which is always bathed in such atmosphere, confronted with such ideals, will become slovenly, careless, mercenary, and selfish? And when some great occasion arises it will call in vain for the high qualities of a noble nature.

Suppose, on the other hand, that we do the little duties of life faithfully, punctually, thoughtfully, reverently— not for the praise of man, but for the "Well done" of Christ—not for the payment we may receive, but because God has given us a little piece of work to do in His great world—not because we must, but because we choose—not as the slaves of circumstances, but as Christ's freed ones—then far down beneath the surge of common life the foundations of a character are laid, more beautiful and enduring than coral, which shall presently rear itself before the eyes of men and angels, and become an emerald islet, green with perennial beauty, and vocal with the songs of paradise.

We ought, therefore, to be very careful how we fulfill the common tasks of daily life. We are making the character in which we have to spend eternity. We are either building into ourselves wood, hay, and stubble which will have to be burnt out at great cost; or the gold, silver, and precious stones, that shall be things of beauty and joy forever.

The Great Doing of Little Things Will Make a Great Life

Let it be granted that you are a person of ordinary ability. It is as likely as not that you will never be removed into a wider sphere than the obscure one in which you have been pining, like a wood-bird in its cage. Give up your useless regret, your querulous complaint, and begin to meet the call of trivial common place, with tenderness to each person you encounter, with faith in God, as doing His best for you, with heroic courage and unswerving fidelity, with patience, thoroughness, submission.

Go on acting thus, week in and week out, year by year, with no thought of human notice, determined always to be at your best, eager only to pay out, without stint, the gold of a noble, unselfish heart. At the end of life, though you wist not that your face glistens, others will see you shining like the sun in your heavenly Father's kingdom. It will be discovered that you have unwittingly lived a great life, and you will be greeted on the threshold of heaven with the "Well done" of your Lord.

Some who are sighing for a great life

are unconsciously living it in the eye of God's angels. Those who forgo marriage that they may bring up and educate the younger children of their homes; those who deny themselves almost the necessaries of life to add some coals of comfort to the meager fire at which the chill hands of age warm themselves; those who are not only themselves pure amid temptation, but the centers of purity, shielding others; those who stand to their post of duty, though the fires, as they creep near, are scorching the skin and consuming the heart; those who meet the incessant demand of monotonous tasks with gentleness, unselfishness, and the wealth of a strong, true heart—these though they know it not, are graduating for the front ranks of heaven's nobility.

"Oh! where is the sea?" the fishes cried,
　As they swam the crystal clearness through:
"We've heard from of old of the ocean's tide,
　And we long to look on the waters blue.
The wise ones speak of the infinite sea.
Oh! who can tell us if such there be?"

The lark flew up in the morning bright,
　And sang and balanced on sunny wings;
And this was its song: "I see the light,
　I look o'er the world of beautiful things;
But flying and singing everywhere,
In vain I have searched to find the air."

It Is a Greater Thing to Do Little Things Well, Than Those Which Seem More Important

They who daily handle matters which bulk largely before the eyes of their fellows are expected to act from great motives, and to behave worthily of their great and important positions. The statesman is expected to be high-minded; the Christian lady to be virtuous; the minister to be earnest. There is no special credit to any of these for being what they profess, and are expected to be. The current is with them. Their difficulty would be to face it.

But, surely, in God's sight, it is a much greater thing when the soul conquers adverse circumstances, and rises superior to the drift of its associations. To be high-minded, when your companions are mean and degraded; to be chaste, when ease and wealth beckon you to enter the gate of vice; to be devout or zealous, when no one expects it; to do small things from great motives—this is the loftiest attainment of the soul.

It is a greater thing to do an unimportant thing from a great motive, for God, for truth, for others, than to do an important one; greater to suffer patiently each day a thousand stings, than die once as a martyr at the stake. And therefore an obscure life really offers more opportunities for the nurture of the loftiest type of character, just because it is less liable to be visited by those meaner considerations of notoriety, or applause, or money, which intrude themselves into more prominent positions, and scatter their deadly taint.

Little Things Greatly Done Prepare for the Right Doing of Great Things

We sometimes lay down the story book or the history with a groan. We have been reading of some sudden opportunity which came to a Grace Darling, reared in the obscurity of a fisherman's home, or to a Florence Nightingale, or a John Brown, living apart from the great world in the heart of the Adirondacks.

"Oh," we say, "if only such a chance would dip down into my life, and lift me out of it! I'm weary, weary of this dull level."

Ah! it is a common mistake. Men think that the occasion makes the hero; whereas it only reveals him.

The train must have been laid long before, and carefully, else the falling of a single spark would never blast the mighty rocks or shiver the frowning fortress-walls. There must be the fabric of strong and noble character, built up by patient continuance in well-doing, else the sudden appeal of the critical hour will knock vainly at the door of life, and the soul will crouch unanswering and helpless within.

If great opportunities were to come to most, we could make nothing of them. They would pass by us unnoticed or unimproved. They would go from us to those who had more nerve, or grit, or spiritual power than we. You can not, just because you will, speak a foreign language, or dash off a brilliant air upon the piano, or talk easily on the motive of one of Browning's poems. All these demand long and arduous study. That must be given first in the chamber; and then, if a sudden summons comes for any of them, on the housetop of observation, you will be ready.

You can not be brave in a crisis if you are habitually a coward. You can not be generous with a fortune if you are a miser with a limited income. You can not be unselfish in some such accident which imperils life if you are always pressing for the one vacant seat in train or omnibus, and elbowing your way to the front on every possible occasion. David must practice with sling and stone through long hours in the wilderness, or he will never bring down Goliath. Joseph must be pure in thought and strong in private self-discipline, or he will never resist the solicitations of the temptress. The Sunday School teacher must be regular, painstaking, faithful in the conduct of his class of little ragged boys, or he will never be promoted to serve his Master as a minister at home, or as a missionary abroad.

Our Behavior in Little Things Is the Truest Test of What We Are

If I were eager to secure a good employee for a responsible position, I should not attach much importance to the way in which the candidate acted on a set occasion, when he knew that he was being observed. Of course he would be on his best behavior. But give me a private window so that I can watch him in his least considered actions—how he behaves at home, how he treats his mother and sisters, how he fulfils the common duties of life. What he is then, he is really.

But if this is man's way, may it not be God's? There are great tasks to be fulfilled in eternity: angels to be judged; cities to be ruled; perhaps worlds to be evangelized. For these, suitable agents will be required: those who can rule, because they have served; those who can command, because they have obeyed; those who can save others, because they never saved themselves. Perhaps, even now our Heavenly Father is engaged in seeking those among us who can fill these posts. And He is seeking them, not amongst such as are filling high positions in the eyes of men, but in the ranks of such as are treading the trivial round and fulfilling the common task.

From the nearest fixed star the ine-

qualities of our earth, whether of Alp or molehill, are alike insignificant. We need to look at our positions from the standpoint of eternity, and probably we shall be startled at the small differences between the lots of men. The one thing for us all is to abide in our calling with God, to count ourselves as His fellow-workers, to do what we can in His grace and for His glory, never excusing ourselves, never condoning failure or misdoing, never content unless, by the help of the Blessed Spirit, we have wrought out His promptings and suggestions to the best of our power, whether in the gold of the extraordinary, or the bronze of the cheaper and more ordinary achievement.

Of course there is no saving merit in what we do. Salvation is only by simple trust in our Savior, Jesus. But when we are saved it gives new zest to life to do all for Him, as lord and master; and to know that He is well pleased in the right doing of the most trivial duties of the home or daily business.

> For what glory is it, if, when ye be buffeted for your faults, ye shall take it patiently? but if, when ye do well, and suffer for it, ye take it patiently, this is acceptable with God.
> *1 Peter 2:20.*

May each reader learn this happy art, and go through life offering all to God, as the white-stoled priests in the temple of old. Indeed, all believers have been made priests unto God; every sphere may be a holy temple; and every act done in the name of Jesus may be a spiritual sacrifice, acceptable to God through Jesus Christ.

The next three selections are taken from Life and the Way Through, *a 1913 work which is unlike Meyer's other books in that it does not consist of selections of his addresses, sermons, or expositions. It is instead a continuous account of what life in "The Way," as early Christians spoke of Christianity, is like.*

"Some Experiences on the Way" follows Meyer's discussion of what this "Way" is and how it may be entered into. In it Meyer illuminates for us some of the unpleasant events that may beset us on our way. Ultimately, he shows us how these unpleasant events are all part of God's plan and are used by God to draw us near Him.

In "Our Spending-Money" Meyer continues his discussion of life's trials and temptations, and in all of them he finds that there "is no stint in the divine provision for life." He repeats his theme, encountered in "Some Experiences on the Way," that it is through our trials that we are compelled to discover and use the source of all our resources. "Our Spending Money" has additional interest for readers of George MacDonald, for an anecdote from his daily life is briefly recounted here.

As we make our way through life we encounter "Resting-Places." Meyer finds that "Life is not all climbing, fighting, toiling." Our Guide provides us with four places of rest: nature, the day of rest, friendship, and the will of God. Meyer takes us beyond the trials we often encounter and into a vision of what our resting in "The Way" can be like.

CHAPTER SIX

Some Experiences on the Way

The way often lies for miles over the dull and irksome flats of *the commonplace*. Each dawn summons us to the same uninteresting and uninviting tasks. "The common round and daily task" are easier to sing about than practice. We feel that it is perfectly legitimate to complain of the dull, slow life we are forced to lead, the lowliness of our position, the drudgery of our toil. Surely we were made for something better than to drive the pen over reams of paper, to type out business accounts, to wait behind a counter, or travel for wares in which we have no interest. What shall we have to show for these years of obscure commonplace!

If it were not for the necessity of getting bread for ourselves and the young or aged lives that depend on us, how gladly would we renounce our homely toils, and seek some way of living more congenial and romantic, which would gain the notice of the great world, and enable us to feel at the last that we had not lived in vain. Life becomes very bitter when we allow thoughts like these to corrode it. The gnawing of the worm of remorse is only more to be feared!

Of course, the ultimate remedy for the corrosion of discontent is to get down to the bottom fact of the will of God. Every morning and evening we pray, "Thy will be done"; but of what use is it to utter this petition, unless we are content to have that will done in us? The one secret of life and peace and growth is not to devise and plan for ourselves, but to accept loyally that position which is assigned to us by divine providence, to fall in with the order of society, to be prepared to be a cogwheel so long as we are included in the great movement of the age. If the stand on which the Master of the House has placed you is a very lowly or common one, or if the room you are called to illuminate is only a cold, dark cellar, still, be content to shine your brightest, and do not repine against His decision.

Perhaps these lowly duties are the highest of which you are really capable; or perhaps they are given as the supreme test of your character; and if, like Joseph, you will be thoughtful and attentive to the poor prisoners in the gaol, you may be promoted to a high place presently, where the qualities which have been approved in the restricted sphere of the commonplace will be needed to direct the affairs of the nation. What vast numbers have never had the chance to do really big things, because they have not set themselves carefully and earnestly to do little ones. They have not been promoted to rule their ten cities because in discontented pettishness they have buried their one talent in the ground.

"He who neglects a thing which he suspects he ought to do, because it seems to him too small a thing, is deceiving himself; it is not too little, but too great for him, that he doeth it not." In point of fact, by their refusal to do little things well men are perpetually revealing their littleness. The really great will do little things greatly, and in doing them thus they show themselves of the highest quality possible. The perfect man will do common things perfectly.

Have you not noticed how the greatest artists choose the commonest incidents of life and glorify them? Take, for instance, Millet's "Angelus." What is there in that familiar picture but a potato-patch, a couple of simple peasants in the attitude of prayer, and a church steeple on the skyline in the distance! They are the most ordinary objects that he could have selected; but out of them the great artist has constructed a conception which has furnished a moving and uplifting inspiration to tens of thousands.

The fact that Wellington slept on a camp-bed, or that Nelson used such and such a common article of toilet; that Wilberforce made his vow under this tree, or that William Carey chalked his name and cobbler's trade on that board of wood, has apprised these ordinary things at a value altogether disproportionate to their actual worth. Why should the commonplace drag you down? Why should not you lift it up, so that people may even desire to be occupied in that very sphere because you once filled it? This is turning the valley of Baca into a place of watersprings.

It demands a much larger amount of virtue to do an obscure duty nobly than one that glistens in the eye of the public. Perhaps it is not so difficult to die a martyr's death, when you know that you are lighting a fire that will never be put out; but to die by inches, to starve in the absence of human love and sympathy, to plod on with no word of gratitude or recognition—this is the supreme test of character.

Besides the routine nature of our daily toil affords an opportunity for a more intensive culture of the soul. An occasional effort, on which you concentrate all your thought and prayer, may be successful in attaining the object to which you set yourself. But it is too spasmodic, too transient, to give you an opportunity of forming permanent character. The mould is broken before the metal has cooled. The wine-skin splits and the wine is spilled.

But prolonged discipline in ordinary and commonplace duty, the spirit's silence and unselfishness carried over a long track of time, the formation of a hidden habit of unassuming humility, obedience, piety, adorn the soul with a saintly beauty which can only result from the exercise of a prolonged endurance. Nothing is common or unclean unless degraded by an ignoble soul. The lowliest insect when placed beneath microscope has beauties which Solomon in all his glory could not excel. The desert bush is aflame with God, though we fail to see. The meanest flower that blows may awaken thoughts too deep for tears. The flower in a crannied wall may be a window into the infinite.

"No day," says some one, "is commonplace if we only had eyes to see its splendor. There is no duty that comes to our hand but brings with it the possibility of kingly service." Remember that the glory of Christ's nature made the poor robes He wore shine with a glory and whiteness such as no fuller on earth could attain to.

> The common problem—yours, mine, every one's
> Is not to fancy what were fair in life,
> Provided it could be—but finding first
> What may be, then find how to make it fair
> Up to our means—a very different thing.
>
> —R. Browning

Character has been said to have the power of building an edifice out of ordinary circumstances. From the same materials, common and ordinary as bricks and mortar, one man builds palaces, and another hovels, one warehouses, and another villas. Bricks and mortar are bricks and mortar until the architect makes something else. It is a good rule for an artist to mix brains with his paint, but for a Christian it is a still better rule to work character on the canvas of the commonplace until the blended materials yield a cloth of gold.

Valley of Sorrow

Sometimes the way will dip down into the shadowed valley of *great sorrow*. The Master said that He would give us a joy which no man could take from us; but He also said that our sorrow would be turned into joy. It is as though sorrow were the raw material out of which He makes joy. At Cana before He supplied the guests with wine, He had the waterpots filled with water. So you must not be surprised if now you have sorrow, for out of your present affliction He is making the eternal weight of glory, and you cannot have that without this. It worketh the far more exceeding and eternal weight of glory. There is not one tear of sorrow, humbly and resignedly shed, which is not a seed-corn cast into the desolate furrows of your life, and which shall not yield you some hundred-fold of joy when the summer has arrived.

But remember to take your sorrows from the divine permission. Even though his brethren were the obvious cause of his long suffering, Joseph refused to see their hand in it, and said: "It was not ye, God sent me hither to preserve life." If you prefer, you may make the distinction between what God permits and what He decrees. There is His decretive will that ordains, but His permission has to be sought before Satan can tempt Job, or Pilate crucify the Christ. "Thou couldst do nothing against me, except it were given thee from above."

But the ultimate fact in each case is the will of God. And the way to find sorrow's yoke both easy and light is to take it from the Father's hand, saying: "Even so, Father, for so it seemeth good in Thy sight." Then the yoke becomes wings to soar with, something as when we were children the tail of our kite helped the kite to face the wind and fly. "I asked Allah for something to ride; He gave me something to carry!"

But much depends on whether we turn to the lower or the higher help when sorrow beats down on us like a pitiless storm. If we stoop to avail ourselves of human sympathy to the exclusion of the divine, or resort to the diversion of company or travel or amusement, we shall come out of our trouble, not stronger but weaker, not greater but smaller, not richer but poorer. But if we turn Godwards, and seek to be comforted with His comfort, if we declare that we have none in heaven or earth that we desire beside Him, then will a light arise to us in the darkness, and the night shall be light about us.

"Weeping," says the psalmist, "may come in to lodge at even." (AV, marg.) We can almost see her veiled figure creeping along under the shadows of the big trees, whilst below the torrent thunders down the glen, and she seeks lodging for the night. Let us not refuse her request, for she will repay us handsomely as she leaves our house at dawn, giving place to jocund joy. Her payment will be fortitude, patience, self-control, wisdom, sympathy and faith.

Adam Bede, the great novelist tells us, did not attempt to outlive his sorrow, did not let it slip from him as a temporary burden, leaving him the same man as before. "It would be a poor result of all our anguish and wrestling," she says, "if we won nothing but our old selves at the end of it—if we could return to the same blind loves, the same self-confident frame, the same light thoughts of human suffering, the same frivolous gossip over blighted human lives, the same feeble sense of the unknown towards which we have sent forth irrepressible cries in our loneliness. Let us rather be thankful that our sorrow lives in us as an indomitable force, only changing its form, as forces do, and passing from pain into sympathy—the one poor word which includes all our best thoughts and our best love."

> Do not cheat thy heart and tell her
>   "Grief will pass away,
> Hope for fairer times in future,
>   And forget to-day."
> Tell her if you will that sorrow
>   Need not come in vain;
> Tell her that the lesson taught her
>   Far outweighs the pain.

Sorrow is necessary to the soul, as a background for the rainbow of hope to repose upon. Sorrow is the furnace that burns our bonds, so that we walk free in the fires. Sorrow is the veil flung over the cage of the songbird whilst it learns to sing. Sorrow is the excuse for God to draw nearer to us, and for Him to draw us nearer to Himself. Sorrow is God's almoner, who brings His fairest gifts packed in rough cases. But, after all, the gift which has required most packing, and comes encased in straw, and crate, and matting, however ugly the appearance, is the most valuable and precious.

In sore trouble, let us anoint our heads and wash our faces, so that we may not seem to others to be hardly used at our Father's hands. Though your heart be sad within you, let cheery words and kindly deeds go forth to others. Meet them with a gentle welcome, considerate kindness, and helpful words. There is no cure for heartache and heartbreak so sure or speedy as becoming a son or daughter of consolation, after the manner of the good Barnabas.

No trouble should be too great to make us forget to show courtesy to those around us, and especially to the poor, the timid and the oppressed. No heart-sorrow must be so engrossing as to rob us of our readiness to show kindness and sympathy. We must school ourselves to obey a code of unfaltering nobleness, whatever our inward smart; to subject ourselves to a vigorous self-discipline lest we become self-centred in our grief.

But directly we compel ourselves to take this side against ourself, we begin to recover. The heart-forces begin to rally. The tears begin to flow more quietly. A new radiance comes into our eyes, and we ask to be called not Marah, but Naomi—*pleasantness*. "I beg you," wrote Phillips Brooks, "whatever be your suffering, to learn first of all that God does not mean to take your sorrow off, but to put strength into you, that you may be able to carry it. Be sure your sorrow is not yielding you its best, unless it makes you a more thoughtful person than you have ever been before."

Perhaps the loftiest attitude to take up in the presence of some crushing sorrow is to dare to thank God for it. A lady of my acquaintance, on hearing from her doctor that her children were sickening for scarlet fever, before taking the necessary precautions, went direct to her room, and kneeling before God said: "I thank Thee, Father, for allowing this to come, because Thou couldst not have allowed so great a trouble, except for its vast revenue of gain to us all." And it was so, because through that illness salvation came to that house.

"Whatever seeming calamity happens to you," said William Law, "if you thank and praise God for it, you turn it into a blessing. Could you, therefore, work miracles, you could not do more for yourself than by this thankful spirit: for it heals with a word spoken, and turns all that it touches into happiness." Therefore,

Measure thy life by loss instead of gain.
Not by the wine drunk, but by the wine poured out.

Dangerous Places

The way becomes so precipitous and dangerous in places that it is almost impossible to keep our feet. We lose our footing and roll down the slope, carrying with us a posher of rubble, stones, and dust. In these hours of set-back and *failure*, we are sorely daunted and ashamed, especially when we can trace our mishaps to moral and spiritual defects that might and ought to have been avoided.

We are disappointed with ourselves; we become querulous and peevish because of what we fancy has been a needlessly difficult test; we lose heart and yield to the suggestion that it is useless to make any further attempt. At such times we lock ourselves up with our dark thoughts, and carefully exclude the soft warm breath of the summer which awaits us outside, the forgiving love and grace of God, which is never nearer to us than at such times.

It often seems to me that we do more to destroy our peace, and interrupt our happy relationship with God, by yielding to discouragement and pessimism, and doubting God's willingness to forgive and restore, than by our recent lapse into failure. Our sin is not so harmful in its effects, evil as they may be, as the refusal to believe that God will remember our sins and iniquities no more. At the first moment of real contri-

tion and confession, they are as absolutely wiped out as though they have never been committed. They have disappeared as a wreath of cloud in the clear heavens, or as a stone dropped into miles of ocean-water.

It is a mistake to suppose that the most successful men are those who have never failed, or that do not fail. More have succeeded through failure. The man who has never failed is less able to understand and manage his fellows, is less tactful and self-controlled, is less likely to be able to avert disaster and retrieve lost causes, than those who have learned the sources of weakness, only to guard against their recurrence, and avoid them in future.

The best teachers are they who have been warned and corrected by their own mistakes. The captain who has had an accident with his steamer, and the commander who has lost a battle, but who have deeply pondered the sharp lesson, and obtained the honey out of the carcass of the lion, are more careful and prudent than untempered success, which may become foolhardly, could make them.

Do not dwell on your faults. Notice carefully how they occurred. Analyze their inception, progress, and maturity. Learn your lesson so carefully that you may not make the same mistake again. Then forget the things that are behind, your past successes and your past failures, and "press forward to the mark of the prize of your high calling in Christ Jesus."

Listen to Carlyle's advice on this point. He says: "Never let mistakes or wrong directions, of which every man falls into many, discourage you. There is precious instruction to be got by finding we were wrong. Let a man try faithfully, manfully, to be right; he will grow daily more and more right."

The idea that prevails with so many

is to get away from their past, and begin all over again. It is natural enough; and there is a sense in which we awake each new morning to live in the freshness of new resolve; but let us never forget that the noblest men are they who make their mistakes and failures stepping-stones to a more conspicuous success, and, baffled, have learned to fight better.

> Deem not the irrevocable past
>   as wholly wasted, wholly vain,
> If, rising on its wrecks, at last
>   To something nobler we attain.
> —*Longfellow*

There is a great difference between falling with the face towards or falling with the face averted from the ideal; or, to put it bluntly, between falling up and falling *down*. There are some who, when they have lost their footing, resign themselves to the force of moral gravitation, and continually descend with an ever-increasing velocity. They despair of themselves, despair of forgiveness, despair of God. For them the one fall has so broken their self-complacency that they cannot face a repetition, and will not believe that pure virtue is unattainable in man's native strength.

Others there are, cast in a happier mold, who, while falling, keep their eyes fixed on the glistening purity above them, and have no sooner touched the ground than they spring to their feet again, and begin to climb anew. They refuse to have the great matter settled by one untoward accident. One point may be lost, but the game is not finished. Paganini once, in the face of an expectant audience, broke every string of his violin but one, and cried: "One string and Paganini!" Yes, one last string and God, will yet make music out of an almost wrecked life!

There are other setbacks, which arise not so much from moral defect or obliq-

uity, but from *errors of judgment*. We see how such and such a step led to a dissipation of energy, a waste of time, injury to ourselves and others, misunderstandings, heart-burning, and the beclouding of a fair dawn. "If only we had that chance in our hand again," we exclaim, "how differently we would act."

This confession is very tormenting. What a labyrinth of conjectures we enter upon, when we try to piece out for ourselves the happenings which might have taken place, if only we had decided and acted differently! We always seem to suppose that any course would have been better than the one we adopted, and that any other path would have brought us out on the main road.

But this is by no means certain. As likely as not, it would have landed us in a similar or worse quagmire. This incessant worry over the past is as weakening and disabling as it is absolutely useless and vain. You are not only helpless to undo what is done, but you sap the energy with which you should face the situation which has been created and requires strong handling. You discourage others by your expressions of regret.

That rude soldier, Joab, spoke admirable good sense to David when he gave way to excessive weeping over his miscreant son. "The victory that day was turned into mourning unto all the people, for the people heard say how the king was grieved for his son, and the people get them by stealth into the city, as people that are ashamed steal away when they flee in battle." And the commander-in-chief of the army, which had saved the kingdom for him, said: "Arise and go forth and speak comfortably to thy servants, for I swear by the Lord, if thou go not forth, there will not tarry a man with thee this night; and that will be worse unto thee than all the evil that hath befallen thee from thy youth until now."

On the whole, in this case also, it is wise to forget the things that are behind. It is a good maxim that if you have acted according to the best light you had at the time, what you decided on was the will of God and was the best that could be done. You had not your present experience at your side then. You could not forecast how the matter would work out. You did your best, so far as you *then* knew. If you had to make your decision again under the same conditions, it would be almost certainly identical with the one that you now deplore.

Then leave it there. Don't fret or worry. You trusted in God, when you acted; dare to believe that His hand was guiding you. This was the best way through, however difficult it is. Any other way would not only have been difficult, but impassable. The difficulties you are encountering are hard to flesh and blood, but they are as much slighter than they would have been, as the waters at the neap are lower than at the flood.

Let the past no longer debilitate you. Rise and meet the present. You did what you thought to be right when you turned back from the straight road to Canaan, and marched directly on the Red Sea. The mountains block your onward march, the sea lies all along upon your left hand, and now Pharaoh and his men of war are pressing on your track. You are in a wedge of perplexity and peril. Throw the responsibility of the position on God, whose will you have endeavored to do. Stand still and see His salvation. He will make a way in the sea and a path in the mighty waters, for none of them that trust in Him shall be desolate.

The one crucial question in all this must always be, *Am I growing?* We have had our ups and downs, our crushing defeats, our catastrophes, our hours of heartbreak and despair. Our Jabbok-brooks, with their mysterious conflicts, have left us halting in our gait. The craft of Delilah, to whom we ought never to have submitted ourselves, has deprived us of vision and brought us to grind in the prison house.

But has there been growth? After all, no man need write Ichabod on his life, if through all its various experiences he has never turned his back, but has always marched breast-forward. It is not so much a question of what we have done, but of what has accrued to our character in the doing. One battle, lost or won, seldom alone decides the fate of the campaign. Inch by inch the enemy must be driven back. Year after year the building proceeds.

The grave question is, What are the net gains of life? That we have had reverses, made bad debts, been deceived and baffled, is sure; but has the King's business prospered, and will the balance-sheet at the end show a clear and satisfactory profit? "The tired waveless" close in shore may seem no painful inch to gain; but what of that if

Far back, through creeks and inlets
  making,
Comes silent, flooding in, the main!

While writing these words, and looking out on the beautiful Carse of Gowrie, clad in its verdure of living green, stretching to the broad waters of the Tay, a slight mist is stealing upwards towards this noble pile of buildings, which commands the far-spread landscape. This mist, which may blot out the hills, and even the great Lomonds in the west, reminds one of *the questionings* and *doubts* which will sometimes overspread the soul.

Did not John the Baptist become enveloped in them? It was perhaps hardly to be wondered at. He was the child of the wide open spaces of Judah. His couch a sheltering cave, his canopy as often as not the starlit dome of the sky, his food the wild produce of nature, the winds his sisters, the giant mountains his brethren. To him it was the veriest torture to be immured in the close, sunless dungeons of the Castle of Macherus, beyond the Jordan. Hardly a breath of God's fresh air ever found its way thither, and not a ray of light. For the harmony of nature were substituted the discords of distant rioting, as when Herod gathered his captains and high estates to drunken and lascivious revelries.

Why did not He, on whose face that ray had shone, and who had been saluted as Son of God, interpose for his release? Was He unmindful, or was He impotent? In either case, He must have abdicated His throne. Was it all delusion? Had he mistaken his own longings for the semblance of that dove? Is it altogether to be wondered at that he sent messengers to Christ, saying, "Art thou He that should come, or look we for another?" A sad descent was here from his announcement, "Behold the Lamb of God!" Had he, as porter, opened the door of the sheepfold to one who was not the Shepherd after all!

Christ was not surprised. There was no rebuke in His tone, no bitterness of reproach in His reply. He only hastened to give the agreed countersign of the Messiah. "Go, tell John what ye have seen." . . . And when the messengers had gone, He affirmed John to be the greatest of woman-born. Evidently that hour of honest doubt had not, in our Lord's estimate, lowered his dignity or sullied his claim. It was almost as if our Lord took it for granted that, under such conditions of confinement on the one hand, and delayed release on the other, John's despondent questionings could hardly be wondered at.

Perhaps He judges similarly of us all. There are many incitements to similar misgivings in the present day. They arise, in part, from the comparative study of non-Christian religions; from the advance of exact scientific investigation, which leads us to demand similar exactitude in the evidences for religious statements; and in the general flux of opinion, occasioned by the decay of timeworn formularies and the slow process of substituting new ones. The old order is changing, and giving place to new; but the precise shape of the new is not yet determined, and men fail to distinguish between truth, which is immutably the same, and the forms in which it is capsuled.

There is no real reason to be disturbed by any one of these. As to the first, it would have been surprising if the old seekers after truth had not caught sight of the great panorama that lies open to God's eye, as the earth to heaven. There must have been scintillations and fragments of truth, or their words could not have satisfied such innumerable multitudes; and all truth comes ultimately through the Word of God. Mathematic truth is ever the same to every nation, kindred, and age that sets itself to its study. Always and everywhere the three angles of a triangle are equal to two right angles. Every investigator must come to that conclusion.

So when pure hearts earnestly desire to find the truth, they must come on discoveries, which remind us of the beatitudes. But outside of Christianity these scattered chippings and splinters of truth are combined into no system, set forth in no symmetrical human character, and made practicable by no sufficient dynamic. And in these three respects Christianity has nothing to fear from their rivalry. It is the one full-orbed and sufficient revelation of God to man!

Or, to take the second, is there any need to be anxious because Christianity cannot be stated in a series of clear-cut formula, or proved by such evidences as can be adduced by the astronomer or the chemist? It is "spirit and life," as the Master said. You cannot define love; you cannot give a mathematical proof of love; you cannot argue on the invariable method of love. Even the scientific man lays aside his subtle analysis and demonstration when he comes home to wife and children!

Of course religion has its evidences, just as love has, but they are not such as can be subjected to the reactions of chemistry or the investigations of the anatomist.

Or take the third source of trouble to many—the exchange of the formularies of our early religion for the views and nomenclature which are now coming into vogue. Can it be wondered at that there are discomfort, foreboding, and alarm? Can we be surprised when hands are stretched out to steady the ark of the Lord?

But there would be no anxiety if only Christian folk would distinguish between the things that can and that cannot be shaken. The statements of our belief can be shaken. Our views, we will say of inspiration by dictation, may have to be modified. Creeds which our fathers held dear, as the Athanasian, may have to be laid aside.

But none of these affect the truths which they have embodied and held. As Dr. Goulburn puts it: "It is only the principles of truth, goodness, and right which are to last for ever. The forms in which these exhibit themselves will necessarily vary with the age and state of society." That the Bible is absolutely sovereign among books, clothed with imperial splendor, echoing with the divine voice, and crowned with the halo of divine glory, is always apparent, whatever theory you have of inspiration.

There is one item of good advice which may as well be stated here. Beware not to talk about your doubts. Some people hawk their doubts about as beggars in Eastern lands hawk around their sores to extract sympathy and halfpence. If you are in doubt, there is no reason why you should not consult some one who is competent to advise you, but do not get into the way of posing as a doubter in the mistaken idea that a doubter must be an intellectualist. The only way that some people can contrive to be accounted clever is that they will not accept anything with the common herd.

When people really doubt, it is an agony too great to be talked about. It is like a family sorrow, that is only discussed when the doors are shut and the family are alone. Besides, you have no right to scatter thistledown. You may state a case or ask a question that may disturb some young soul through long years. Any fool can drive a hammer through a Murillo, or break a superb window of medieval glass; but it takes genius, patience, and laborious industry to undo the harm wrought in a thoughtless hour.

When doubts assail, it is wise to plod on in the old paths, doing what is right, and continuing to maintain the sacred habits of obedience, meditation, prayer, and service. It is always right to be good and to do right. It is always right to pray to God. It is always right to be kind and loving, generous and pure, just towards men and righteous towards God. You can always be orthodox in loving and living, whatever may happen to your orthodoxy of belief. The Lord Jesus may always be your Master. It is always right to pray to Him for help.

There may be times when in your bewilderment you cannot find help, but you can always give help. Whatever you do, refuse to allow doubt to alienate or divide you from the Father of Lights. It is not by agonizing over your difficulties, but by communion with Him that all your storms will subside and become a great calm. What you cannot understand, leave for a time and go along your way in perseverance and obedience, and some day, all unexpectedly, He will take you to His bosom, and say: "I could not explain this before, because you could not understand; but now see, it is thus and thus." In His light, we see light.

The Battle-Grounds

The travelers on the King's highway find that very often it lies directly through *the battle-grounds* of the world, that call to the soldier-element in us all, and we dare not shirk the appeal. Your lot may lie amid the green pastures and still waters! Be thankful that it is so! Yours the sweet song of the weaned child! But this is not allotted to us all. Here in the grounds of this noble residence there is a unique contrast, which will serve to illustrate this point.

We have been walking on a high ridge among the firs; suddenly, on our left, the ground slopes, and through an avenue of yews, standing at sentry-duty on either side, we descend to a lovely flower-garden, ensconced in a fine yew-hedge some five feet in depth, and except where it rears itself into arches and buttresses, some six feet high. We enter and leave through these noble arched entrances—the fitting gateways to this second Paradise.

Pursuing our way down the four successive levels of sward, on which the western sun, through the surrounding trees, is shedding shafts of light, we pass between masses of lavender, lavender-nepeta, and mignonette; and then my gentle hostess names the amazing variety of flowers before us, our voices mingling with the music of falling water and the hum of bees. One is inclined to envy these exquisite plants, thus sheltered

and shielded from the winds, and covering these banks, facing the southern sky.

But stay! Look upward to the wood behind, which shelters the garden from the north wind. Carry your eye along the ridge! Do you notice those great gaps that break the line of tree tops? They have been wrought by successive storms that have cut and torn their way, each leaving behind a deep ravine of devastation. That specially deep opening was caused by the fearful storm which wrecked the Tay Bridge and tore up in a single night, in this plantation alone, some three hundred trees.

What a contrast between these flowers and those silver, Scotch, and Australian firs and pines! Yet who would not rather be a tree fighting the hurricane in its effort to shelter the vale and plain beneath than a flower, expending its ephemeral existence in one brief summer? "The wind passeth over it, and it is gone, and the place thereof knoweth it no more."

Be thankful, then, if you are called to stand for the right against all that injures and defiles the souls of men; or if you have not yet found your regiment in the army, and your place in it, ask that you may be entrusted with some share in the great conflict, in which angels from above and demons from the pit take part, and which has swept to and fro upon the battle ground through all the Christian ages.

"Remember," says Thomas Carlyle, "now and always that life is no idle dream, but a solemn reality, based upon eternity and encompassed by eternity. Find out your task; stand to it; 'the night cometh when no man can work.'"

And Ruskin eloquently forces home on each of us his personal responsibility: "There is work," he says, "for all of us. And there is special work for each, work which I cannot do in a crowd, or as one of a mass, but as one man, acting singly, according to my gifts, and under a sense of my personal responsibilities. I have a special work to do, as one individual, who, by God's plan and appointment, has a separate position, separate responsibilities, and a separate work: a work which, if I do not do it, must be left undone."

Fight against every wrong which is blasting human purity or happiness. Do not fight for a party as such, unless you feel that its policy will better promote the well-being of others. Choose your principle first, and then ally yourself with those who think with you, for the attainment of your common purpose. To be a partisan only, and to aid and abet one party merely because it is *your* party, is liable to mislead you.

Be true to the great program of Christ, to protect the weak, to succor the wounded and crippled, to destroy the arch-enemies of man, and to witness with unfaltering voice for all that is honorable, just, pure, lovely and of good report. This will save you from expending your strength for nought. Never mind being misjudged. Confirm the feeble knees, and say to those that are of a fearful heart, Be strong!

Nay, best it is indeed,
To spend ourselves upon the
    general good;
And, oft misunderstood,
To strive to lift the limbs and
    knees that bleed;
This is the best, the fullest meed.
Let ignorance assail or hatred
    sneer;
Who loves his race he shall not
    fear;
He suffers not for long
Who cloth his soul possess in
    loving and grows strong.

Ay, labour, thou art blest,
From all the earth thy voice, a
    constant prayer,
Soars upward day and night:
A voice of aspiration after right;

A voice of effort yearning for its
    rest;
A voice of high hope conquering
    despair.

—*Lewis Morris*

But do not battle in your own might. When you come into collision with high-handed wrong; when you are called to deal with people from whom all decency and every vestige of humanity seems expunged; when you discover the Protean forms of evil, which resisted here, break out there, and evade the strokes of your good sword; or when, after a long day of fighting, you are suddenly summoned from well-earned rest to fling yourself again into the fray—amid the pressure of the fight you will certainly succumb, unless the arms of your hands are made strong by the hands of the mighty God of Jacob. Remember that in the fight you may fall in apparent failure, defeat, and death, but no effort for the right and true is ever in vain, no stroke is fruitless, no corn of wheat falls into the ground to die, but that it will spring again to yield a thousand-fold.

Oh, the pity of it, that so many amongst us, who have leisure, a competence, and even wealth, education, talent, power, are content to dream away their lives, like Tennyson's lotus-eaters, when they might be leaders and champions in the great battle against the giant evils of our time. It would be well indeed for Britain, and well for the world, if all the children of the leisured classes would consecrate themselves to these great tasks. Much of the legislation which they hate and dread would never have been proposed, if only wealth and education and opportunity had always been accepted as a trusteeship rather than a couch of ease.

Let there be a war, and our gilded youth, as in the South African campaign, will pour out in hundreds to fight beside the common soldiers in a great brotherhood of heroism! But why do not more of them hear the summons to the noblest battlefield of all, and engage in the campaign against ignorance, lust, and greed! Be it only understood that the motive must not be to discover some fresh method of killing time, or creating a diversion, but a sober consecration to a great cause, like that which Wilberforce or Shaftesbury made when they chose their life-work.

Thus the way through life moves from incident to incident, reminding us of Chaucer's *Canterbury Tales,* told by the pilgrims. For none of us do they occur in the same order. Each of us has his own series, specially adapted to his peculiar characteristics. But from time to time there are holy resting places, where we refresh ourselves, and from which we issue to meet the new experiences of a fresh piece of the road.

It is well that an almighty hand keeps the veil drawn, so that we cannot tell what may befall on the morrow. Only as we advance does the road unfold. "Now are we the sons of God, but it cloth not yet appear what we shall be." At the next turn of the road the whole secret may lie outspread like a landscape at our feet. It is of no avail to be anxious. Worry will not alter the future by a single hair. The best preparation for whatever tomorrow may bring is to do well the duty of the present hour. But whatever is hidden beneath that gauzy veil, God is there, and love, and the Golden Age, and the faces of those whom we have loved long since and lost awhile.

CHAPTER SEVEN

Our Spending-Money

We will suppose that we are about to travel on the Continent of Europe. For various reasons we are unwilling to carry any considerable sum of money on our person or in our baggage. But we arrange with one of the modern tourist agents, who has agents in every part of the world, to meet our requirements as they arise. It is specially good for those of us, who may not possess an abundance of ready cash, when some wealthy friend steps in and says that he has calculated, on a lavish scale, the amount that we shall probably require, and has deposited this with the firm. We gladly start on our journey, knowing that at each place we have only to produce our demand, and that it will be immediately and unquestioningly met.

This is a fair analogy and may be applied to the demands which are constantly being made on us by the emergencies of daily life. Its incidents, crises, and catastrophes have been so ordered as to test and reveal us to the uttermost. The telephone bell is always ringing in our soul, summoning us to answer some inquiry, or to take up some fresh case of need. How are these calls to be met?

It is not with us, as with a vessel bound for a long winter in the ice-closed polar seas, which is equipped or provisioned for a prolonged struggle with the elements and distance from ports of call. If such an arrangement were made with us, it would probably induce a self-sufficing complacency, which, in its turn, would generate an intolerable arrogance and pride.

It is well, then, what we have not the capacity to contain sufficient supplies for our life-course, even if they could be made over to us *en bloc*. There are abundant supplies; but, to use again the comparison of the Arctic voyagers, they are deposited in cairns, which are erected along the march, and which contain all that is needed to equip us for all kinds of emergency. They must be received and appropriated as the need arises. "Day by day the manna fell." The water-tanks of the locomotive engine may be filled in advance before the journey begins, but a supply of water may be caught up *in transitu* from the troughs that lie between the metals, over which it is swiftly passing. The latter is the most appropriate metaphor for our experience.

We are all familiar, of course, with the atmosphere, which enswathes and environs us. We live and move and have our being in it. It contains various elements, some of which are indispensable to human life. If they should be eliminated for five minutes all round our earth, every living creature would instantly cease to exist, and the earth would become a vast sarcophagus. We are constantly inhaling the atmosphere. By night and day, from the moment of birth, the lungs, by automatic action, are opening and compressing, to receive and exhale the air on which human life depends. Sometimes we take deeper and longer inspirations than ordinarily, but there is no cessation in the process.

But the close contact between the atmosphere of the physical world and the lungs is not so close, after all, as the subtle proximity between the spiritual atmosphere and the human spirit, when once it has become vitalized and quickened. And as there are stores of nutriment for the physical life in the natural, so are there in the spiritual, but they are unavailing unless we learn to make constant use of them.

We must avail ourselves of that spiritual, ethereal, and ineffable environment which supplies the nutriment and vigor of the religious life. Here is the fuel of the inner fire, here the bread and water of life. "Our spirits," said the late Mr. W. H. Myers, "are supported by a perpetual indrawal of this energy, and the measure of that indrawal is constantly altering."

A New Race

One of the strongest characteristics of the primitive Church was the conviction, based on experience, that it was possible for those who had accepted the Christian revelation to receive and assimilate a new quality of life, which was the very nature of the risen Christ, conveyed to the human spirit by the Divine Spirit. He was therefore described in the Nicene Creed as "the Lord and giver of life."

Christians thus formed a new race, and were members of the divine family, partaking of influences and energies which were unknown to other men. Their elder brother and exemplar was the exalted Christ. They felt, interpenetrating and supporting them, the energy of a new life, as much higher than that of the intellect as that is higher than the physical. Eucken describes it as "the living presence of an eternal and spiritual energy." Jesus described it as "the wind of God," that cometh we know not whence and goeth we know not whither.

The beginning of Christianity was, in fact, the definite emergence of a new type of humanity. Jesus Christ, by what He was, what He taught, and what He has become to those who are united with Him, has brought a new movement, a new life, a new spirit to the world. He has lifted millions to a new level. He has created a new race. "We may assume," says Harnack most justly, "what position we will in regard to Him and His message; certain it is that from His time and onward the value of our race has been enhanced."

Let us beware, then, of pressing too far our analogy between the outward atmosphere and the spiritual environment of the soul. While the former may be indicated by the neuter pronoun it, the latter is certainly a presence, a person, the presence and nature of God, as radiating from Jesus Christ, and communicated to man through the Divine Paraclete, the Comforter, the Holy Spirit.

Jesus Christ, says Paul again and again, was "a fresh creation," "the second Adam," "the first-born among many brethren." He was not only significant for what He was in Himself, but as making possible, by our sharing in His mighty dynamic, that forward leap of humanity which is the highest stage in human development. Paul saw that the spirit of man was susceptible to this dynamic. It was able, as he puts it, to receive and appropriate *grace*, which is but another name for the inflowing of transcendental vitality, with all the wisdom, strength, and love which it stands for.

To be "in Christ," in Paul's vocabulary, meant the doing away of every film of separation, so that the union of the human spirit with that transcendent personality might be unbroken and uninterrupted. Paul's one effort in all his writing is to impress on his readers that the life of the eternal God is "objectified," summed up, concentrated, in Jesus Christ. It pleased the Father that in Him all the fullness of the Godhead should dwell in an objective human form, that of that fullness all who would might receive.

John the Divine, also, knows himself to be a partaker of that divine nature, i.e. a higher kind of vitality flowing out to man through the Word of God, and passed on to man by "the Spirit that quickeneth." And the raising of Lazarus from death to life has been truly said to be the fitting close of John's great epic of the soul. The Apostle had shown us the movement of the spirit through the new birth into the spiritual world, had taught us how to draw water from the wells of the eternal, and to eat of the hidden manna, and finally the soul is brought face to face with the Resurrection and the Life to draw life from Him after such a fashion and in such a measure, as that death itself loses its power over the emancipated nature.

Now, if all this is true, and it is, does it not become more and more evident that we must learn the art of appropriating, not simply by one initial act, but perpetually, the very elixir of our religious life ? We must breathe out to God our praise and adoration, our prayer and supplication, our cries for guidance and help; but it is equally needful to breathe in the supplies of the Spirit of Jesus Christ. In prayer we give God thanks for His great goodness; but we also absorb, receive, inhale, and appropriate some of that virtue and strength which are included in the Life which was with the Father and was manifested to the world.

The various experiences of human life, to which we have referred in a former chapter, perform their highest office for us, when they convince us of our helplessness, and incline us to avail ourselves of those spiritual resources which are always within our reach. The fears that were once entertained of the approaching failure of our coal supply set science to work to discover a substitute for producing momentum and illumination.

How often temptation, trial, and the failure of human sympathy have set the soul on a quest which has finally landed it on God. Well is it when we have learned that lesson so perfectly that there has been no need for a severer taskmaster or a more rigorous discipline. In God men can find a complement for every deficiency and need.

But need it be said that it is not necessary for obtaining these things, that we should always repair to our closet, shut our door, and pray on our bended knee. We may obtain them by the instant upreach of our faith, by the opening of our being, by what may be called a long, deep, spiritual inhalation. This, as we have said, is not the whole of prayer, but it is very real prayer. It can only be exercised by those who are at one with the nature of Christ, and are accustomed to more definite and prolonged periods of devout meditation, adoration, and communion.

Toll-Gates

All along the way of our life there are what we may call toll-gates like those which used to arrest us in many parts of the country, until they were abolished. There would be fine work with those motorists whose one idea is to dash madly through the country, if they were being constantly pulled up and made to pay for the upkeep of the road! But on the way of which we are now treating there has been no abolition of the toll-gates. Indeed, they seem rather on the increase than otherwise, and they make very costly demands on the spending-money of the soul.

Your servant is late with your breakfast; or the telephone is very faint; or there is a break down in your morning train, detaining you for a precious half-hour; or a strike breaks out and delays the building of your home, or the ingathering of your hay, or the sailing of your ship. It is very stupid, very provoking; you are liable to nervous expenditure and exhaustion which threaten to consume the delicate network of your nervous system. Here is need for the exercise of patience and for the reinforcement of such patience as you have an intake of spiritual energy.

Or you have to meet some great ordeal. It is an operation on one dearer to you than life; or the necessity of detecting and dealing with defalcations and unfaithfulness which will rupture a life-friendship or compel you to dismiss an old and valued employee. You may have to sever yourself from the party with which you have been wont to act; to stand alone in your protest against an ill-judged war; to plough a lonely furrow, which will expose you to derision and hatred.

Perhaps it will be necessary to confess a delinquency, to ask forgiveness, and to lay your pride in the dust. Again you encounter the toll-gate, and have to pay its demand for courage. Almost certainly that will mean more than your own resources can meet, and again there must be a reinforcement of your overtaxed purse by an intake of that spiritual energy which shall enable you to fulfill your difficult duty.

Or you may be suddenly flung into a furnace of temptation before which the frail defenses of your soul crackle up as wood before the flame. Your blood runs fast and hot. Is it a picture, or a book, or a suggestion, or a paragraph in a newspaper? You feel that it is absolutely impossible to hold out. You must consent: your will and choice are under the sway of passion, like the last monarch of France, at the mercy of the crowd which thronged the palace, and escorted him to the Bastille. At such a time you are again at a toll-gate, and now a strong demand is made for a measure of self-control of which, again, you are not capable, and hard will be your plight unless you can obtain some reinforcement.

We need not multiply instances. So incessant and so inevitable are these demands, that none of us escape them, and most of us are perpetually on the verge of bankruptcy, as they recur. In all such cases we are in urgent need of spending-money, that we may be free to pursue our Journey.

It is said of George MacDonald, that when his family was young, he adopted the following method of teaching his children to consider one another. At the beginning of every week he put the money for the family expenditure in a common receptacle which was accessible to all the members of the household. Everyone knew that it had to last the seven days; and everyone was at liberty to take what was needed for his or her use. The housekeeper must go there for the provision of the table; the girl for her dress; the lad for his books; the father for his journeying; the child for its toys. But it was obvious that if any helped themselves unduly and extravagantly, all the others would go short.

May we not employ this analogy? Shall we not say that the resources of the Almighty have been placed in the humanity of Christ, within reach of us all, to be received by a spiritual telepathy, that none may lack anything necessary for a noble life; though the parallel fails, in that there is no limit or stint, and that the divine resources are not diminished by the heaviest drains that can be made on them? Luther may divert a vast contingent for his colossal expenditure, but the supply still brims to the lips of his little Gretchen.

It would seem as though the variety of Christ's human experiences, now that His manhood is wedded with the eternal, peculiarly fits Him to succor us in each phase of experience. Boys can make their appeal to His boyhood; young men to the strength garnered in His temptation; women to the feminine and sympathetic aspect of His nature; sufferers to His endurance of pain; the poor to His experience of hunger, thirst, and homelessness; the lonely to His memory of forsakenness; the weary to His quick recollection of the sleep in the boat and the seat by Sychar's well.

Each can get at Christ by a gate opening directly from his own house or grass-plat. Christ stands four-square to the world's need. They may come from the North of Indigence, or the South of Prosperity, from the East of Youth, and the West of Age, but they are all welcome.

Understanding Temptation

Here is the clue for the understanding of the temptations to which life exposes us. They present from some aspects problems of immense perplexity. One would have supposed that divine love would have removed every stumbling-stone from the way of our feet, but it is not so. Why? Not simply that we may learn the art of resistance and refusal, though this is much, but that we should be compelled to discover and use our resources. Some of us would never have realized what the content of Christ was, unless we had been hard driven, not only to claim His help, but to appropriate those stores of grace which will enable us to overcome evil with good.

Let that distinction be well marked. It is of immense value and significance.

We are tempted that we may learn the slenderness of our own stores, and may be compelled, like the man in the parable, to go to the big house of our rich neighbor, and say: "Friend, lend me three loaves, for a wayfaring man has come to me on his journey, and I have nothing to set before him." "Then shall He from within give as many as he needeth."

Probably, the existence of evil, as it overshadows mankind today, is due to these two great considerations. First, we cannot know a thing really and deeply, unless we are acquainted with its opposite. Second, we shall never properly appreciate or claim it, until we have been compelled to face our beggared exchequer.

You may live next door to a physician for long years, and have but a slight acquaintance. You watch him as he goes and comes; you exchange greetings when you meet in the street; you join in the common respect and goodwill of your neighbors. But let your wife or child, at dead of night, be stricken by mortal pain, and immediately that neighbor of yours assumes a new importance, and you suddenly awake to appreciate his resource, gentleness and strength. He grapples with the foe who is wrestling with the beloved life until he masters him, and restores to you your treasure. You never forget that night; and it gives you a friend, whom you have been taught by your extremity to understand.

You and I would never have known Christ, as we know Him now, had we never passed along the way of human life. We have lost many things in our journey. They have slipped out of our possession, we hardly know how. And we miss them sorely. Sweet faces, gentle presences, heirlooms of the past, treasures for which we have toiled. It is as though the bandits in the old parable have been pilfering our baggage, and appropriating what we could least have spared, and leaving us what we could quite well have surrendered. Nay, it is not bandits, but the hand of divine love that has been despoiling you, that you may seek and receive all back again from Him.

All which I took from thee I did but take,
 Not for thy harms,
But just that thou might'st seek it in my arms.
All what thy child's mistake
Fancies as lost, I have stored for thee at home;
Rise, clasp my hand, and come.

There is no stint in the divine provision for human life. If there is scarcity, it is because we have not trusted the hand that holds out its boons; or have not learned in the moment of emergency to take what we required.

How greatly do thoughts like these ennoble and sublime the lowliest life. There is always at work an interlacing of earth and heaven, of the human with the divine, of the things that press on the senses and those which eye hath not seen, nor ear heard, nor the heart of man conceived. It is charming to watch the games of gutter children, albeit that they fill the streets with chatter.

But they give such evidence of possessing the idealizing faculty. This dirty lane is a pathway through Sherwood Forest; that blind alley is a cave where the daring Robin Hood and his merry men are lying in wait for unsuspecting travelers; that slatternly girl is a princess, and on those dirty little wrists are matchless jewels! What imagination

does for the waifs and strays of our streets should be done for us by those spiritual aptitudes that weave the golden threads of eternity into the warp of very ordinary existence.

To adapt the words with which Thoreau concludes his rhapsody on Nature: "Money is not required to buy one necessity of the soul." May we not therefore accept his advice to go and live our life, whatever it may be, determined that in it there shall be a bridal of the earth and skies.

Life may be mean and hard and difficult. Let us not call it by hard names. The fault-finder would find faults in paradise itself. It looks poor because your heart is poor. The glories of the sunshine are lost on a palace if all its living-rooms face the north, while a cottage facing sunwards is healthy, sweet and glad. Do not so much trouble to alter your position—alter yourself. It is not that God, or your friends, or your circumstances are most to blame, but because you have no heaven above you, no horizon before you, no Jacob's ladder that links earth with heaven.

If you are deprived of the outward circumstances, in which so many find their satisfaction, it is that you may be compelled by a sweet compulsion to turn to those simple, holy, and soul-satisfying realities which moth cannot corrupt and thief cannot steal. "It is life near the bone that is sweetest." You, at least, cannot complain of the birdlime which keeps you from soaring. The poverty of their tiny holdings on the Scotch hills has driven many a crofter to the space, and opportunity, and wealth of lands which to his fathers were only an unattainable dream.

CHAPTER EIGHT

Resting-Places

Life is not all climbing, fighting, toiling. There are sweet vales nestling among the gaunt hills, which invite us to come apart and rest awhile. In the darkest day there are some chinks of blue. On the steepest hills there are some level places. No life is without its pause, its landings, its interspaces of rest.

Nature

First among these let us put *nature*. "If any of my readers," says Nathaniel Hawthorne, "should decide to give up civilized life, cities, houses, and whatever moral or material enormities in addition to these the perverted ingenuity of our race has contrived, then let it be in the early autumn. Then nature will love him better than at any other season, and will take him to her bosom with a more motherly tenderness."

We will not dispute with Hawthorne in his choice of the autumn for the time of wooing or being wooed; perhaps one would prefer the precise time when the later spring is merging in the early summer. But, speaking generally, what comfort, next to God's, is so wholly satisfying as nature's? How often has one thrown oneself on the sweet-smelling earth, when wearied with the clash of arms and the ceaseless conflict, saying, "Oh mother, dear mother, thy tired child comes to thy bosom for rest. Thou hast fondled and caressed millions of thy sons, but thou art as fresh and young and unworn today as though thou hadst only yesterday emerged from the Father's home, where thou west daily His delight."

We think of old Izaak Walton sitting on his primrose banks, hearing his birds sing, looking down the meadows and thinking of them as "Charles the Emperor did of the city of Florence, that they were too pleasant to be looked on, but only on holidays"; watching "here a boy gathering lilies and lady-smocks, and there a girl cropping culverkeys and cowslips, all to make garlands suitable to this present month of May."

We think, too, of Wordsworth, "the minstrel of the natural year," taking possession of his Westmorland mountains as by right of birth, that he might there exercise his vocation, and translate the language in which nature spoke to him into the tongue of ordinary folk. We think especially of Thoreau, as he reveals himself in his charming *Walden*.

We try to imagine the latter, building his little cabin beside the lakelet—"a pure white crystal in a setting of emerald," a perfect forest mirror. We smell again, as he describes it, the pungent perfume of the surrounding pines, and bathe ourselves in the golden sunlight, in which he would sit from sunrise to noon, "growing," as he says, "like corn in the night."

It is an irresistible impulse to record a snatch from one paragraph which breathes that spirit of calm restfulness that nature gives: "Every morning was a cheerful invitation to make my life of equal simplicity, and I may say innocence, with nature herself. I have been as sincere a worshipper of Aurora as the

Greeks. I got up early and bathed in the pond; that was a religious exercise, and one of the best things that I did. Morning brings back the heroic age. I was as much affected by the faint hum of a mosquito making its invisible and unimaginable tour through my apartment at earliest dawn, when I was sitting with my doors and windows open, as I could by any trumpet that ever sang of fame. . . ."

Of Thoreau, Emerson said that he saw as with a microscope, heard as with an ear-trumpet, and his memory was a photographic register of all he saw and heard. "As we read him," says Lowell, "it seems to us as if all out-of-doors had kept a diary and become its own Montagne; we look at the landscape as in a Claude Lorraine glass; compared with his, all books of similar aim seem dry as a country clergyman's meteorological almanac."

But this love of nature arose not only from hereditary endowment, but from his possession of a nature which was singularly able to detach itself from the world of men, and bring its native simplicity in contact with God's own fair world. That latter qualification is open to us all. Detachment, purity, simplicity, childlikeness, the religious soul, these are the conditions of appreciating and loving nature, as she has been courted and won by thousands who have never recorded their impressions in eloquent and burning phrase.

Nature knows her lovers, and does not hesitate to unveil her face to them. Children will always discover those who are akin to their fresh, unsophisticated natures. Even dogs and birds, squirrels and hares, discover their lovers. The brook sings its sweetest for the ear that is willing to listen and appreciate. The woods open new glades for the devotees who, tearing themselves from other loves, will give an undivided heart to their spell.

Let us tear ourselves from men and things, from the clash of politics and the strife of competition, and let that music fill our souls which nature makes in sylvan glades and beside the tiny rills that drop from level to level in the woodlands. What nature has been to the writer of these lines he will never be able to explain, because ecstasies have seized on him in mountain solitudes and in forest glades which it is not lawful to attempt to describe. It is well enough to hunt for specimens, or carry pocket microscopes, or get snapshots, but at the best these appeal to the observing and intellectual faculties, whereas there is a communion of heart to heart, which lovers know, and which defies art and speech.

Let us get away from the madding crowd, as He did whose heart was so sensitive to every voice and touch of nature, and who was so careful to adapt the natural scenery to his experiences, choosing the mountain for his temptation, the seashore for His teaching, the winepress for His agony, and the garden for His Easter.

Our Lord's sensitiveness to nature has been termed "the most charming aspect of His humanity." He watched the tall and splendid lily—not, like ours, white, but crimson—the reed quivering in the wind, the tender green of the first shoot of the fig tree. He built His teaching on the fold, the farm, the vineyard, and the whitening cornfields. The living well, the eastern glow, the ruddy hue of the stormy evening, the spate of the winter storm, and the homeward flight of the birds from their feeding grounds were objects of careful observation and enjoyment.

We like to think of Him loving the gorse and heather of the wild mountain, listening to the murmur of the waters down the hillsides, and scaling the higher reaches of the lonely hills that He might absorb the beauty of the far-spread landscape. To rest awhile amid the fairest scenes of natural beauty was His choicest recreation; and when He felt the Transfiguration glory coming on Him, He sought the moonlit slopes of Hermon. We are following His great example when we make much of those quiet resting-places that nature provides.

It is perhaps worth while to make one further addition to the restfulness which nature may secure for tired hearts and brains, and to refer to the effect that friendship with the lower animals, as we term them, may bring us. We recall the Apostle John and his domesticated pet, Cowper and his hares, Dr. John Brown in "Rate and His Friends," and Thoreau with his forest companions.

Take the two latter. The forest recluse lovingly records the mouse that sat on his hand, the partridge who brought him her brood, the moles who nested in his cellar, the red squirrels who made free of his corn which they ate before his face, the hares that came to his door at dusk; while the doctor writes graphically of his dogs—the white bull-terrier, the shepherd's dog, and the old, grey, brindled mastiff, as big as a small Highland bull, with Shakespearean dewlaps, who always reminded the doctor of the great Baptist preacher, Andrew Fuller.

It is refreshing, also, to read in one of Canon Jessopp's delightful books his disquisitions on moles and tortoises. He tells a delightful story of a tame tortoise, David, who not only came when his name was called, but exhibited something like personal attachment for his mistress, wandering into her drawing-room, climbing over the sill of the French windows, and finding his way to her feet.

Nothing could be further from our desire than to extol that excessive and culpable fondness which heaps upon dogs and cats an altogether extravagant, fastidious, and prodigal affection, bestowing on them a quite disproportionate attention, and expending on them what would suffice to redeem many a crippled existence from the direst need.

But there are opportunities of delightful intercourse between us and the dumb companions of our earthly sojourn, which need not incur reproach. On the contrary, it is altogether commendable. Mr. John Galsworthy, in an eloquent plea on the part of dogs the other day, spoke of some amongst us who are "honored" by the friendship of the lower orders of creation. The phrase is happily chosen. We are not all worthy of that honor; but where it is bestowed, it is exceedingly precious and valuable, and a great asset among the contributories to our refreshment and exhilaration.

The Christian mystics have always had this absorbing love for nature. George Fox said that "all creation gave another smell beyond what words can utter." Brother Lawrence received from the leafless tree "a high view of the providence and power of God." And it is thus written of Francis of Assisi: "As of old, the three children placed in the burning fiery furnace invited all the elements to praise and glorify God, so this man also, full of the Spirit of God, ceased not to glorify, praise, and bless in all creatures the Creator and Governor of them all. When he came to a great quantity of flowers he would preach to them, and invite them to praise the Lord, just as if they had been gifted with reason.

"So, also, cornfields and vineyards, stones, woods, and all the beauties of the fields, fountains of waters, all the verdure of gardens, earth and fire, air and wind, would he, with sincerest purity, exhort to the love and willing service of God. In short, he called all creatures by the name of brother; and in a surpassing manner, of which other men had no experience, he discerned the hidden things of creation with the eye of the heart, as one who had already escaped into the glorious liberty of the children of God."

The Rest Day

The Rest Day is, of course, another of these quiet resting-places on life's highway. Alas! Of late years, its rest has been seriously threatened, and is being threatened. The attack comes from two sides. The first is from the invasion of the motor-car, and the craze of the week-end habit. One of the daily papers remarked the other day that the motor-car had taken the place of the old family pew. The head of many a household in the present day will assemble his wife and children on Sunday morning for a run into the country with the same regularity as that with which his father used to summon them to church. In many cases, instead of spending with their young children the one day when father and mother could be at home with them, they are left to their nurses, who may be quite unworthy of the trust.

Even now, the writer of these words can recall the absolute desolation and misery of those very rare Sundays when his parents were necessarily absent from the home; and what would have been the fate of the family life, to which, under God's blessing, he owes everything, had these modern habits been in vogue, he dare not surmise.

But from the other side, the Sunday is threatened by the decay of conventional religion. The time is not so very far distant when every respectable person was expected to go to a place of worship on Sunday. That any self-respecting

people should go golfing on Sunday morning, or be seen starting for a party on the river, was unheard of. But all this is altered now, to the great detriment of society, which has surrendered one more of those sacred habits which did so much for the morality of the elder, and the proper training of the younger, members of our families.

We freely grant that, like other religious institutions, it has been perverted. To many it was irksome and tiresome, a day of heavy burdens and unnatural restraint. One example was brought under my notice of the father of a family, who was so fearful of doing wrong, that he and his children used to sit in their chairs, doing nothing whatever during the hours of the day in which they were not attending divine service. We are all familiar also with stories, not wholly unfounded, of the prohibition of hot shaving-water, and the delivery of milk.

But these are the exceptions. For myriads, through the centuries the return of the Rest Day has been fraught with untold benediction to our toiling masses, and to myriads of Christians, who, on that day, have entered into the very rest of God.

The law of septennial periodicity is written on most of the pages of natural history. Experiments on human and animal subjects yield similar results, and always establish the necessity of giving a seventh part of our time to rest, in addition to our nightly sleep. It is almost a commonplace to recall the experiment made at the French Revolution, when the Anarchists, in their desire to expunge all trace of religion, decided that the week should consist of ten days, but found it necessary to return to the older reckoning, because the nation could not endure the prolonged strain between the rest days.

It is well known that the proprietor who rests his horses and cattle on one day in the week will get more work out of them than he who keeps them at work without the seventh-day intermission. Though the same number of hours be worked in the week in each case, it is better that they should be concentrated in six days, followed by one for rest.

Deep in the constitution of the universe is engraved the law of rest. Because it is there, it is obligatory on us all. We neglect it at our peril. You cannot set yourself against the nature of things, and prosper. An inevitable Nemesis will find you out. The Rest Day is placed on a level with the other obligations of the moral law, from which we infer that its basis is to be found in the very being of God, and of man, made in His image. The increase of nervous disorders, and the multiplication of lunatic asylums, are probably directly traceable to the disregard of the weekly Rest Day.

The late Mr. Gladstone was specially careful in this matter. Anyone entering his room in Downing Street, during his tenure of the Premiership, would find that the ordinary books and periodicals of every-day use were replaced by others in keeping with the Sunday. On a Sunday evening, he writes to Mrs. Gladstone: "Although I have carelessly left at the Board of Trade, with other letters, that on which I wished to say something, yet I am going to end *this day of peace* by a few words to show that what you said did not lightly pass away from my mind." I have italicized the incidental phrase, which indicates more swiftly and emphatically than a more labored argument could do the light in which the great Christian statesman regarded the day.

And once more, among other suggestions, to one of his sons, then at Oxford, he wrote the following, which Lord Morley says was "the actual description of his own lifelong habit and unbroken practice": "There arises an important question about Sundays. Though we should, to the best of our power, avoid secular work on Sundays, it does not follow that the mind should remain idle. There is an immense field of knowledge connected with religion, and much of it is of a kind that will be of use in relating to your general studies. In these days of shallow skepticism, so widely spread, it is more than ever to be desired that we should be able to give a reason for the hope that is in us."

Parents should tax their ingenuity to make the Rest Day the most delightful of the week. Sacred music, good literature of the highest quality, the family-fellowship, the wholesome walk in the country, attendance at divine service, and the culture of the inner life, ought to be sufficient to provide a pleasant menu for the day's consumption, without resorting to the railway excursion, or the festive gathering, which leave the soul jaded and hungry, besides having entailed needless labor on those who serve us, and who deserve our consideration.

I can imagine a father who had a distinct leaning to some special line of study always reserving Sunday afternoon for the wonders of the microscope, for directing the arrangement of botanical specimens, or for discussing the fossils of a prehistoric age. What opportunities might not such an afternoon afford of driving home lessons on the traces of creative design and adaptation! Or if he were specially interested in biography, history, or geography, what vistas each of these would open! Or, when some great events were transacting on the theater of the world, or wars being fought to their issue, how much might be done by suggesting the principles on which to found right conclusions. To look out for the footsteps of God through our own age is a wholesome and elevating pursuit; and Sundays spent quietly thus in the companionship of one's family, or like-minded folk, will leave us more really rested than a long and tiring day of pleasure-seeking.

Human Affection

Another of these resting-places is in the understanding and confidence of *Human Affection*. In friendship the wearied, hunted soul finds a shelter from the windy storm and tempest. From the pitiless criticism of those who have the shallowest possible acquaintance with the sincerity and purity of our motives, we turn to our familiar friends; they, at least, will put the right construction on our actions, and will give us much credit, and more, as we give ourselves for all that is high-minded and holy. "A friend loveth at all times, and is born as a brother for adversity." In his happy-making presence we can relax ourselves, and be absolutely free and natural. The outer coat of self-repression in which we face the driving ice-cold blast of the world may be cast off, and we can assume another suit—that of tenderness, freedom of speech, and gaiety of mood.

We must choose as friends those who, in regard to religious matters at least, think as we do. There must be a point of contact, where heart absolutely and sincerely meets heart. If we do not revolve around the same pivot, the circling interests of life cannot be concentric. Do not give yourself in intimate fellowship to those who cannot sympathize with you in your holiest aspirations, and to whom you could not naturally and easily unfold your acutest pain.

It should, surely, be the subject of daily prayer to the Almighty Father that He would put the solitary into families, and bring about a fellowship of heart with some other, recalling that sweet old-time description, of which the colors can never fade, of the moment when the heart of Jonathan leapt to David's. "And it came to pass, when David had made an end of speaking to Saul, that the soul of Jonathan was knit with the soul of David, and Jonathan loved him as his own soul; and Jonathan stripped himself of the robe that was upon him, and gave it to David, and his apparel, even to his sword, and to his bow, and to his girdle."

But, after all, the home is the best place of all for shelter and rest. There are the green pastures and still waters, there the shadow of the rock in the scorching heat, there the strength of manhood at its best blended with womanhood and childhood and in their most artless and sweet endearments and faith.

The attack which is being made on the family is one of the cruelest that can be imagined. If it were to succeed, it would destroy the mightiest bulwark in human life against the hatred, opposition and criticism of the world. Our king has said, in wise and eloquent words, that "the foundations of national glory are set in the homes of the people, and that they will only remain unshaken while the family-life of our race and nation is strong, simple, and pure."

And it is true also that our homes are our best defense against the heartbreak and despair that fill asylums, jails, and dishonored graves. The Church must enter the arena and fight for our homes against the hand of the assailant. By permeating public opinion, through pulpit, press, and platform, with true ideals; by insisting on the necessity of marriage among Christians being only "in the Lord"; by her appeal for self-control, and by her advocacy of a simpler style of life and expenditure; by her insistence that husbands and wives should bring unsullied character to the marriage-altar, and that men and women should be judged by the same code—the Church may do much to preserve the sanctity of our homes.

What influence other than religion is pervasive enough, deep-seated enough, universal enough, to deal with the vast interests which are involved in this great question! Social reformers may deal with methods of segregation, science discuss the laws of blending and growth; educationists may train the young to right thoughts about their own natures and their responsibility for the hygiene of the race; moralists may urge to self-discipline and self-control, but only religion can comprehend them all, co-ordinate them with each other, and supply the breath of life. It becomes the Church to bestir herself, to give a loftier conception of wedlock and home-life, and so bring "a statelier Eden" back to man.

But our home-life cannot be left to chance. It needs culture, such as Charles Kingsley gave to it. "Home," writes his wife, "was to him the sweetest, fairest, most romantic thing in life; and there all that was best and brightest in him shone with steady and purest luster. No fatigue was too great to make him forget the courtesy of less-wearied moments, no business too engrossing to deprive him of his readiness to show kindness and sympathy. To school himself to this code of unfaltering high and noble living was the work of a self-discipline so constant that, to many people, it might appear quixotic. Justice and mercy, and that self-control which kept him from speaking a hasty word or harboring a mean suspicion, combined with a divine tenderness, were his governing principles in all his home relationship." We also must exercise such qualities, if our homes shall fulfill the highest ideal of restfulness.

The Will of God

Last is *the Will of God*. It was the olden custom in New England, as, for instance, in Lyman Beecher's family, to observe the Sabbath from Saturday night to Sunday night, when "three stars came out." Now, there are "three bright crystal laws of life," which, like pointer stars, guide the traveler's eye as he travels along the Way: To resist the tyranny of self; to recognize the rule of duty; and to live in the will of God. It is especially in the latter that the soul finds repose in the midst of the wildest storms that sweep life's ocean.

It was once said by Charles Lamb of one who had been grievously afflicted: "He gave his heart to the Purifier, and his will to the Sovereign Will of the Universe." Happy are they who have learned this art. With heart-purity they see God, and with wills submitted honestly and faithfully to His will, they have a foundation for their lives on which they may build the house of life with no fear of overthrow. Let the winds blow and the storms beat upon the structure of their character, let the waters rise and become a torrent, they cannot be moved, because they are founded on a rock.

But what can better describe the rest of the soul that has built on the will of God than those immortal lines of Dante:

> In His Will is our peace. To this all things
> By Him created, or by Nature made,
> As to a central sea, self-motion brings.

This is Mr. Gladstone's translation, and he says: "The words are few and simple, and yet they appear to me to have an inexpressible majesty of truth about them, to be almost as if they were spoken from the very mouth of God. They cannot be too deeply graven on the heart. In short, what we all want is that they should not come to us as an admonition from without, but as an instinct from within. They should not be adopted by effort or upon a process of proof, but they should be simply the translation into speech of the habitual tone to which all tempers, affections, emotions are set. In the Christian mood, which ought never to be intermitted, the sense of this conviction would return spontaneously and be the foundation of all mental thoughts and acts, and the measure to which the whole experience of life, both inward and outward, is referred."

Too often, when men speak of the will of God, they mean that they are prepared to resign themselves to it, to submit to its dealings, and accept its rulings. But more than that is demanded of the truly Christian soul—namely, that it should unite itself with it, so that God's will should become the will of the creature by a thorough and blessed interfusion and blending. This position is only possible when, on the one hand, we check and quell the inclination of our own will to act as from the center of self, and when, on the other hand, we allow God to work *in* us to will and to do of His good pleasure.

This is the great work of religion, and when we have attained union with God we retire into Him as a stronghold and sure house of defense. From all our anxieties and troubles we flee to the Rock that is higher than ourselves. We shelter under the covert of His wings. Though a host should arise against us, in this we are confident. One thing we desire of the Lord, and that we seek after, to abide in the house of the Lord all the days of our life, to behold the beauty of the Lord, and to enquire in His temple.

And thus we prepare ourselves for and seek unto that eternal union with God, when there will be no effort to say Thy will be done in earth, as in heaven,

because we shall be in heaven, and His will will be done in us, who shall then be partaking of the image of the heavenly. "Then we shall live and move with it, even as the pulse of the blood in the extremities acts simultaneously with the central movement of the heart."

Here, in point of fact, is the essence of the Atonement. Here the human comes to be at-one with the divine. We come back by the way of the Cross, which is the supreme emblem of the merging of the human will with God's, into that divine order from which we have strayed. Thomas à Kempis has rightly spoken of it as the King's high road, or as the royal pathway to Reality; and indeed there is no other method of arriving at soul-rest. "In the Cross doth all consist, and all lieth in our dying thereon; and there is none other way to life and very inward peace but the way of the Holy Cross and daily dying. Walk where thou wilt; seek whatsoever thou wilt; and thou shalt find no higher way above, nor surer way below, than the way of the Holy Cross. Turn to the heights, turn to the deeps, turn within, turn without: everywhere thou shalt find the Cross."

But, in very wonderful manner, the Cross is the gate to blessedness. The following incident shall illustrate this: A Christian man had to undergo an operation of a very painful description. He refused to take an anesthetic, lest he might die under the ordeal; and he desired, he said, to meet his Maker, if that were to be the case, with a clear mind. He cheerfully surrendered himself to the divine will and embraced it.

When laid on the operating-table, his face being downwards, over the ledge of the table he could just see the ground, and discerned two pierced, sandaled feet there. Though he could not see the upper part of the figure, he knew that Christ was keeping tryst with him, and became filled with such rapture that he had no knowledge of what was transpiring, and was quite surprised when told that the operation was over. They carried him to his bed, and he lay in a perfect ecstasy for two or three weeks till he was quite restored and returned to his ordinary avocations.

The same testimony was often given by the martyrs, who were so exalted above their physical pains as to be loath to be taken off the rack or delivered from the flame. Missionaries who passed through the Boxer riots have borne witness that they were absolutely unconscious of pain, when knives and other instruments were plunged into their flesh. They that die to themselves live unto God. While they yield to the dying side, God sees to their Easter.

Death is the stepping-stone to life and peace. "All things become new." Listen to this from Saul Kane, the converted poacher:—

The station brook, to my new eyes,
Was babbling out of Paradise;
The waters rushing from the rain
Were singing Christ has risen again.
I thought all earthly creatures knelt
From rapture of the joy I felt.

The narrow station-wall's brick ledge,
The wild hop withering in the hedge,
The lights in the huntsman's upper story
Were parts of an eternal glory,
Were God's eternal garden flowers.
I stood in bliss at this for hours.

"The All-Sufficiency of Christ" is an example of Meyer's skill as an expository preacher. Meyer contended that while only a genius could be consistently interesting and stimulating if he delivered topical sermons, an ordinary man could accomplish this if he contented himself with preaching the great paragraphs of Scripture. In "The All-Sufficiency of Christ," based on several texts from Revelation, Meyer master-fully uses the metaphor of alpha *and* omega *to represent the "alphabet of Christ's being," which spells out the answer to our every need.*

CHAPTER NINE

The All-Sufficiency of Christ

I am Alpha and Omega. (Rev. 1:8, 17; 2:8; 22:13).

It is hardly necessary to explain that these are the first and the last letters in the Greek alphabet. Obviously they represent all the intervening letters, which they enclose as in a golden clasp. On those letters was built the entire literature of that wonderful people. Plato, Socrates, Sophocles, Thucydides, and Aristotle built up their reasoning, teachings, systems, and histories on the letters contained between *alpha* and *omega*. This metaphor, as the references indicate, is in frequent use throughout the Apocalypse.

Christ's Nature

The majestic announcement at the opening of the book (chap. 1:8) refers to the eternal God. His nature underlies the whole created universe, all races of being, the entire work of redemption, the destiny of His children, the ultimate victory of righteousness, order, and peace; all that has been, is, or shall be is conditioned by His existence. It would be difficult, if not impossible, to discover a more comprehensive formulary for Him who was, and is, and is to come, than this, "Of him, and through him, and to him are all things, to whom be glory for ever and ever."

We can almost hear the unceasing chant of the four living creatures, which are before the throne, who rest not day and night, saying, both when God's purposes are evident and when they are veiled, "Holy, holy, holy, Lord God Almighty, which was, and is, and is to come." Let us worship before the immutable and eternal Lord God Almighty, joining in that ceaseless chant. He is the First and the Last, and beside Him there is no other!

In our thinking we must distinguish between that side of His ineffable nature which has revealed itself in the universe, in the creation of man, and in Jesus Christ, and that side of His nature which transcends our thought, infinite, eternal, self-existent. In the one He has revealed Himself so far as the naked spirit of man can endure the almost insufferable light. In the other is that which no man hath seen or can see, that which we can describe only by negatives, that before which angels veil their faces with their wings. "No man hath seen God at any time; the only-begotten Son, which is in the bosom of the Father, he hath revealed him."

What audacity it is to rush into His presence, without the due preparation and reverence of the heart. Even Moses was bidden to unloose his sandals when the bush burned with fire. But does it not stand to reason that, as we cannot know this great Being by the intellect, so we must give time to our fellowship with Him? We must wait before Him till the glare and noise of this clamorous world cease to monopolize our senses, and we are acclimatized to the conditions of His manifested presence.

Dr. Lyman Abbot has said truly that the profoundest truths of spiritual experience are those which are not intellectually ascertained, but spiritually discerned. They are not taught to us, but revealed. They defy definition, they transcend expression. So it must be in our fellowship with God. He is our Father. He loves us infinitely, but He is the Blessed and only Potentate, the King of kings and Lord of lords, who only hath immortality, dwelling in the light which no man can approach unto, whom no man hath seen or can see; to whom be honor and power everlasting. Such is the abyss of the Godhead for which we have no fathoming-line! We have, as Job puts it, only a whisper of Him in His works, and in Jesus a manifestation of only so much as can be translated into human speech.

Christ's Humility

In the other quotations named above, the Lord Jesus appropriates to Himself these august words, though He was meek and lowly, and emptied Himself. When the fainting disciple whom He loved fell at His feet as one dead; when the Church at Smyrna needed encouragement to remain faithful unto death; when spirits athirst for God, in this life or the next, cry out for the living water; when the way has to be opened through the gates of the city to the Tree of Life, He quotes, in part or as a whole, these majestic words, "I am Alpha and Omega, the beginning and the end, the first and the last."

The very pressing question of this hour is to ascertain whether each of us is making enough of personal contact with Christ. We hear about Him, read of Him, talk about Him, but how far do we really know Him? Might He not say rather sadly to some of us, as to Philip: "Have I been so long a time with you, and yet hast thou not known me?" On the other hand, Paul said: "I count all

things but loss for the excellency of the knowledge of Christ Jesus, my Lord . . . that I may know him!"

We may sometimes question whether we should ever have known Jesus Christ had it not been for the urgent needs forced on us by this human life. We have seen that we are tempted in order that we may know things by knowing their contrasts and opposites. To know light, we must needs know darkness; to know good, we must know evil, not by yielding to it but by resistance. Let us carry that thought further, and question whether the blessed beings in other worlds will ever appreciate the Savior as we can, who have wintered and summered with Him, during our earthly life. May not this have been in Paul's mind when he said: "I know him whom I trusted"? He trusted Christ almost before he knew Him; but having traveled with Him for thirty years, he had come to know Him.

In an Alpine village, you engage your guide to take you to the summit of Mont Blanc. He has been recommended as eminently reliable, and you trust him with your life. But during every subsequent hour you are testing him; you see how carefully he picks the path, how strong his arm and keen his eye, how quick he is to notice and prepare against the gathering avalanche. At the end of your sojourn in that mountain village you know him for yourself. You trusted in the word of another, but you now believe in him because of your personal experience. So with our Lord, we trust Him at the beginning of life on what we are told, but as the years pass we come to know Him with a certainty which asks no confirmation elsewhere.

A mathematical figure may help us here. Draw on paper a small curve. That is obviously far away from being a circle; but you can easily complete the circle, of which the curve becomes a part. So in human life Jesus Christ is the complement, or completement, of our need. He comes to us in the smallness of our patience, faith, hope, or love, and He adds Himself to our great need, and makes the perfect circle.

What God Allows

We may go further, and say that very often God allows our helplessness and failure to become extraordinarily acute in order that His grace may have a larger opportunity. It is only when we have reached our greatest extremity that we begin to realize what Jesus is prepared to be and do.

It was only when Sennacherib came against Jerusalem with scaling ladders and the full equipment for capturing a fortified city that Isaiah and Hezekiah discovered that God was prepared to be a "place of broad rivers and streams," and that there was a river—the river of His protecting care—which could make glad the city of God. Of course, there was no literal river; but God made good that lack, and Himself became all that a river could have been. He was thus the complement of their need!

It was only when Ezra, on the return of the Jews to their own land, halted at the river Euphrates, that he awoke to the peril of crossing the great wilderness, inhabited by robber tribes. But in answer to united prayer, God promised to go before the procession, and become its rear-guard. Jehovah Himself became the complement of their need! They would not have realized what He could do for them in this direction had they been fully defended by bands of soldiers.

The sisters of Bethany would never have known the Master's imperial glory as the Resurrection and the Life, had mortal sickness not overtaken Lazarus and carried him to his grave. In their dire sorrow and distress Jesus became their complement as the Resurrection and the Life. In after years they were glad to have had such a sorrow, which left them enriched forever with that unexpected revelation.

Paul himself would never have known what Jesus could be unless he had been beset by that thorn in his flesh. There was a phase in the Savior's grace which he would have never known unless that infirmity had befallen him. Then he realized that his sufferings had provided a new angle of vision, a better platform for God's saving help. Therefore he was willing rather to suffer, that the power of Christ might compensate for his deficiency; for when he was weak the strength of the Son of God was more than enough.

Let us look at some of the disabilities named in this Book; and when we have set them down, let us take the letters out of the alphabet of our Lord's nature, and spell out the word most suited to bring out salient characteristics of the saving help of his right hand.

Christ's Help

Rev. 7:17: Loneliness is an opportunity for Jesus to make Himself known. The beloved apostle was alone on the Isle of Patmos, but at the same moment he was "in the Spirit," and the Spirit revealed the Lord. There ensued that fellowship which began in what seemed at first a revelation almost too great to be borne by human flesh and blood. "I fell at his feet as one dead." Then Christ laid His hand upon him and lifted him up, and revealed to him the mystery of His own eternal life.

The ancient mystics went to the deserts in order to obtain that vision; but in quiet lonely hours, as we walk beside the ocean, or climb the mountain, or sit in our own room, He will come and manifest Himself as He does not to the world. But you must let the silt fall to the bottom; you must allow time for the glare of the world to die out from your eyes. There must also be the spirit's steadfast attention turned toward the unseen, the unwearied and loving meditation and prayer, and the atmosphere of Christian love. The failure of any of these will make it impossible to see or feel Jesus nigh.

Thomas à Kepmis says:

> Shut thy door upon thee and call unto Jesus, thy Love. When Jesus is nigh all goodness is nigh and nothing seemeth hard; but when He is not nigh all things are hard. If Jesus speaks one word, there is great comfort. To be without Jesus is a grievous hell, and to be with Jesus is a sweet Paradise. If Jesus be with thee, there may no enemy hurt thee. It is a great craft for a man to be conversant with Jesus; and to know how to hold Jesus is a great prudence.

But it must be remembered that fellowship like this is full of inspiration. The revelation given to John was instantly followed by the command to write. The soul, therefore, that is illumined by fellowship with Christ becomes, to use an ancient illustration, like the cherubim who went and came as the Lord directed. Thus holy souls, invigorated and renewed by communion with Jesus, while they wait upon Him, receive direction and instruction as to the errands they are to undertake, and they go forth to minister as He may direct. The heavenly character, seated within them, wills their movements through His loving guidance given to their hearts. He nourishes them with food celestial and enables them with grace sufficient for their day.

When, therefore, you are lonely; when, like John on the Lord's day in Patmos, you seem to hear the hymns and prayers which you can join only in spirit, turn to the Lord Himself and ask Him to bear you company. That loneliness constitutes a claim on Him. If you had not experienced it, you would not have learned what He can be and do when He draws near, saying, "Fear not." He will not leave you orphaned, He will come to you. Though lover and friend forsake, and you are passing through a dark valley unattended, the Good Shepherd will accompany you, armed with a crook to help you out of pitfalls, and a club for your foes. Therefore out of the letters of the alphabet of His being let us choose those that spell: "Unfailing Friend!"

Rev. 3:8–11: Hours of suffering give opportunities for Jesus to become known. Like the church at Smyrna, on which the first sparks of fiery trial were falling, the child of God is often called to take the way of the cross. With its suffering, its injustice, its humiliation, its bitterness, it has been trodden by millions, and has been called "the King's highway." One holy soul says: "There is none other way to life and inward peace but the way of the Cross." But nothing has brought out so much of the love and help of Jesus!

This is especially marked in the life of the Apostle Paul. Few men have come anywhere near him in the ordeal of anguish and pain. "We are made as the filth of the world, the offscouring of all things." He was always bearing about the dying of Jesus. Poverty, persecution, ill-health, the hatred of the Jewish party, these were the deep waters he was called to cross and recross. But in it all he was more than conqueror through Him that loved him. Jesus was nearer him than the chill waters. True, he suffered for Christ, but Christ suffered with him. His Lord stood by him, then who could stand against him? His spirit seems to have become full of a divine optimism as he challenges life and death, height and depth, to separate him from the love of God.

Do not let us fear suffering or pain. Do not allow yourself to shrink back when Jesus leads you into the dark chamber. He walks the furnace kindled to seven times its ordinary heat. Martyrs have asked that they might not be taken from their rack, so ecstatic were the peace and joy poured into their hearts. Sufferers for long years on beds of pain have affirmed that they would not have chosen otherwise, since the Savior has made that chamber of pain as the vestibule of heaven.

There are also experiences of suffering which are worse than most of those endured in the physical sphere, but Jesus is always standing there with the crown of life to place on the head of the overcomer. Let us not complain of our sufferings, or the lack of human sympathy, or allow people to criticize the Divine Lover; let us rather rejoice that He has trusted us with pain and disability that His power may more richly rest on us. "Be thou faithful unto death, sentry, at thy post." The First and the Last is with thee. He passed through death to a fuller life; so shalt thou!

The thousands of sick folk who were brought from every part of Galilee revealed healing qualities in Jesus that would have remained unknown had they not thronged around Him. The leper revealed His purity; the paralyzed His nervous energy; the dying His power of life. Each was a prism to break up rays of color hidden in His pure manhood. So each trial and sorrow which He comes into our lives to share reveals to us, and to the principalities and powers in the heavenlies, some new phase of that wonderful Being who is the complement of our infirmities.

Therefore, out of the alphabet of His being, let us choose the letters that spell "Wonderful Healer!"

Rev. 21:6, 7: Hours of thirst give opportunities for a more intimate knowledge of Jesus. If the woman of Sychar had not been driven by thirst, she would not have visited the well at the noon of that memorable day; and if it were not for the thirst of their souls for satisfaction, men would never say with David: "As the hart panteth for the water brooks, so panteth my soul after thee, O God." If we were perfectly supplied from ourselves, we should never know what Christ can be. We are suffered to hunger and thirst that we should not trust in ourselves, but in the living God, who gives us all things richly to enjoy. There are those among us who have an immense capacity for love, but have never been married because a suitable partner has never been forthcoming. They love children, but have none of their own. They thirst, but perhaps, like Hagar, they have never realized that a fountain is within reach; it is the personal love of Jesus.

But the special reference in this passage is not to the present, but to the future. The first heaven and the first earth have passed away! The judgment is over, and death and hades have ceased forever! The seas of division and storm are no more! The conquerors and overcomers have come into their blessed heritage, of which they have made heirs! Yet even in that beatific state there will be thirst! Jesus says, "All is over, I am Alpha and Omega, I will give to him that is athirst."

Yes, even in that life there will be need for supplies from outside ourselves. Even there we shall not be independent of Him. As the circle of light grows, the circumference of darkness will grow. As we know more, we, like Newton, shall feel we are but gathering shells on the shores of a boundless ocean. The flock will lie down in green pastures, and be led in paths of righteousness, but we shall never reach the last fountain nor be able to dispense with the presence or leadership of our Savior. When we have drunk of one set of wells, He will lead us further and more deeply into the recesses of eternity. He will still guide us to further fountains of living water. Oh, blessed absence of self-sufficiency! We shall never be self-contained, never able to dispense with Christ! But, as our nature expands, as new yearnings arise, as fresh deeps call to deeps, we shall only learn more and more of His all-sufficiency, as the way, the truth, and the life.

Therefore, out of the letters of His alphabet of being, let us choose those that spell, "Immortal Lover!"

Rev. 22:14: When we are most deeply conscious of sin it will reveal the purity and redeeming love of Jesus. In these closing verses of the Apocalypse we are back again in the earth-life, though the Master assures us that He is coming very soon. This verse contains the last beatitude that is uttered from the throne of His Ascension. The reading of the Revised Version is full of beauty, and is to be preferred to that of our Authorized Bibles. Thus, for "Blessed are they that keep his commandments," we now read, as in an earlier passage (chap. 7:14) of those who have washed their robes. It is evidently a glance back from the eternal world at an experience long past, although its blessed influence still abides. But here it is, "They are washing their robes." It is the present tense, and therefore a present experience, in a present world.

Alas! that we ever had to come to wash our robes in His most precious blood. Alas! that we need to come so often to wash them. It is a terrible thing to be a sinner! It does not seem so terrible, because this is a world of sinners, and we have never seen a sinless one. The child born in a leper colony cannot realize what leprosy is, nor what the child of noble and pure birth is like. But we know enough to repent in dust and ashes and cry, "Unclean," as did Isaiah when he beheld the glory of the Lord.

And yet! And yet!—we should never otherwise have known the love of Christ, the wonder of His forgiving grace, His patience, His tender forbearance, His fathomless humility in stooping to wash our feet. Yes, Augustine, we understand what you mean when you say, *O beata culpa,* "O blessed fault!" Yet we dare not sin that grace may abound, lest we open again His wounds. But, in our hours of contrition, we have glimpses into the heart of God in Christ, which unfallen natures cannot share. Therefore, out of the alphabet of His being, let us choose letters to spell, "The Friend of Sinners!"

Move through the flames with
     transcendent forms
  As of the Son of God, in splendor
     move!
Divide the anguish, breast with us the
     storm,
  Companion perfect grief with
     perfect Love!

"Living the Life of Jesus" is a second example of Meyer's expository preaching, based on the text of John 6:57. Taken from Meet for the Master's Use, *a collection of some of Meyer's 1898 expositions, Meyer felt they "were so evidently accompanied by the power and blessing of the Divine Spirit that it has seemed wise to put them in permanent form, in the hope that they may revive and quicken many hearts."*

In "Living the Life of Jesus" Meyer admonishes us to imitate the life of Christ, in particular His dependence on God the Father for all things. This is a truth Meyer faithfully addresses in all of his writings, so that with him we might understand Christ's words "Because I live, ye shall live also."

CHAPTER TEN

Living the Life of Jesus

As the living Father hath sent me, and I live by the Father: so he that eateth me, even he shall live by me (John 6:57).

An eastern prince was accustomed to retire for an hour every morning to a certain chamber in his palace, which was carefully reserved from every common eye, and in which he said that he found the secret of his life. When the room was entered, it was discovered that it was furnished like a shepherd's hut, for his forefathers were shepherds. There, with the most simple surroundings, he had been accustomed quietly to meditate upon his past, his present, and his future.

I want to conduct you into Christ's inner chamber in which His spirit dwelt, and the door of which He has left open for us, that we also may enter and dwell there. I desire to give you what seems to me the one secret of our Savior's life, that it may likewise become the one secret of yours and mine. From the words of our text we may infer that what the Father was to Jesus, Jesus is willing to be to you and to me. Everything that Jesus said of His relationship to the Father, we may say of our relationship to Jesus.

The Gospel of John is peculiarly the book of our Savior's inner life, and the book of our own inner life, because in the place of the Father we may substitute the Savior's name. Thus we may read the words of our text, "As the living Savior hath sent me, so I live by the Savior." If you take that Gospel according to John and substitute Christ for the Father, and hang on Christ as Christ hung on God, you will hardly ever need a book of private devotion other than that which is furnished by the golden book of the inner life, yielded in St. John's gospel.

Christ's Selflessness

The first truth to which I wish to call your attention is this: *Our Savior might have lived an independent life.*

He was the Holy One before He stooped to us and laid aside the use of the attributes of His Godhead. During His human life He might at any moment have availed Himself of His divine attributes and might have lived His human life in the power of them. Whenever He was hungry, instead of waiting for Peter or others to provide, He might have used His creative power to transform the very stones into loaves of bread.

Had He so chosen, He might have planned His own life and from the transfiguration mountain have stepped into paradise. He might have spoken His own words and have poured forth upon men such a flood of eloquence as would have shone on the pages of literature with dazzling brilliancy. He might have done His work by His own power, working His miracles merely to increase His own reputation. He might have sought His own glory as the supreme end of His life, so displaying His power and glory that His divinity should be apparent to all.

His Servant Life

Our Lord Jesus might have lived an independent life, and second, *Satan was always urging Him to do it.*

Straight from the river Jordan Jesus was led up of the Spirit into the wilderness to be tempted of the devil. You who have been baptized for service are almost certain to be led by the Spirit into the wilderness to be tempted, just because God desires to do a mighty work in your soul. The oak, which is to live for a hundred years, must be rooted and moored to stand the storm, and God, wanting you to become a strong, sturdy oak, will most certainly lead you into temptations. Temptation is not sin if the temptation is resisted. The effect of being tempted is to root us more in Christ.

The first thing the devil said to Jesus was, "Thou art the Son of God. God has just owned thee as such, as the second person of the holy Trinity. Thou hast all power. Now use that power for Thyself, and make these stones bread."

That was the crucial point in our Lord's life, and He said, "No: I am going to be a dependent human being. Inasmuch as those whom I have come to save depend upon my Father and upon me, I will learn what it is to depend by faith absolutely upon my Father. If my Father does not feed me, I will die of hunger. Man shall not live by bread alone, but by every word of God, and I am going to wait for my Father to speak."

When our Lord said that He at once definitely refused to live the independent life which would have been possible, and elected to live a life of constant dependence upon the Father.

Our Lord's Life

Look at our Lord's life. In His birth God the Father gave Him life. It was not His own life; He could not do as He liked with it, and after He had lived it for thirty-three years the Father asked again for that life. And Jesus in dying said, "Father, receive my life." It might have seemed that from the moment when He descended into the grave there was no longer any life for Him, but through the cross He came into a richer life than ever. He gave up the natural to get the eternal; He gave up the life of the flesh to receive the life of the Spirit; He gave up the life that could die, that He might receive the resurrection life of power to impart.

Jesus Christ held His life in trust,— God gave it, God maintained it, God required it, and all the time the Son said to the Father, "I live by thee." God was as much the breath of Christ's life as the air is of our natural life. It was as if His natural life kept saying to God, "May I live another hour?" and the Father said, "Live." Every minute the attitude of Christ was taking, taking, taking life from the Father. So we should live; always drawing from Christ, the fountain of life; always receiving from God life for our life. We must live because of Jesus.

So in the *plan* of our Lord's life. Sometimes He said to His disciples, "Let us go across the lake and rest." He might have chosen to pursue that plan of rest, but when the people hurried around the lake and asked to be taught and fed, in their intrusion on His quiet He saw the Father's plan. Once when He was going to Jairus' home, a woman who had an issue of blood stopped Him, I know not for how long, and in the touch of her finger He saw the intrusion of the Father's plan for the day, and He stopped His own plan to follow it.

In that wonderful fifth chapter of John, He says, "The Son can originate nothing—the Son can do nothing from Himself—but what He sees the Father doing." When He was in Joseph's shop, as a young boy of twelve or fourteen, and saw Joseph making yokes for the oxen, He studied how Joseph made them, and fashioned the yoke on which He was working like it—always copying Joseph. Then afterward when He came to live among men, He was always watching for the development of the Father's plan, and the things which God did in the unseen and eternal world, Jesus did in His earthly life. So this plan was the plan of God.

Jesus also depended on the Father for *His words*. In one of the most beautiful translations of the Revised Version in the fiftieth chapter of Isaiah we are told that God the Father came every morning to the Son and awakened Him, whispering into His ear the words which He was to say during the day, so that as Jesus went forth to teach the people day by day He did not speak His own words, but the words which the Father gave Him. On the mountain of beatitudes, when He finished one paragraph, I suppose that He would look up and say, "What next?" And that wonderful farewell discourse recorded in John consisted of the words of the Father received by Jesus as He spoke them.

Then as to *His miracles*. In that wonderful fourteenth chapter of John, Jesus says, "The words that I say unto you, I speak not from myself, but the Father abiding in me, doeth His works." We might almost say that we do not know Jesus, because He was so completely dependent upon the Father that His words were the Father's, His works were the Father's, His life was the Father's, and in Jesus we do not see Jesus but we see the Father mirrored in His words and works and life.

So also about *His will*. He had a will of His own, because He said, "Not my will." We do not understand the mystery

of His nature but we remember that He said, "Not my will but thine be done."

We know, too, how He sought *the Father's glory*. He said, "I have glorified thee on earth. It matters little what men say or think of me, I at least have given them a new thought about thyself. I have glorified thee on the earth"; and He promised to answers our prayers, "that the Father might be glorified in the Son."

Now He is there in the glory waiting to find a prayer that we have uttered that He can answer to glorify His Father; He at once answers that kind of a prayer, because He is so set on this purpose. In that last prayer He also said, "I would like to be glorified, my Father; give me glory that the Son may glorify thee." It was as if Jesus Christ was only ambitious to be well thought of in order that He might make God the Father the better considered.

What the Lord Chose

My fourth point obviously is this: If our blessed Lord chose this life of dependence out of all possible lives that He might have lived, *does it not seem wisest, most blessed, most Christlike, for you and me to give up living the independent life* in the flesh and to begin from this moment to depend upon Christ as Christ depended upon God?

If Jesus Christ held His life moment by moment in the balance at God's dictation, should not we receive the help and expend our life as Jesus wills? If Jesus Christ allowed His plan always to give way to God's plan, do you not see that instead of scheming, planning, and striving to get our own way so much, we ought always to be looking out for God's plan and to yield submissively before it? If Jesus Christ gave up His words for the words which the Father put into His lips, do we not greatly mistake in trying to elaborate our sentences and beautify them, instead of day by day waiting to receive the words our Savior gives us? If you would depend day by day on the Master for the power of His life, opening all your being, and preferring the power imparted to any power of your own, I need not say how your life would at once become divine.

Let us receive from our glorified Lord that life-power with which He is invested, that He may glorify and ennoble our daily existence. Let us so dress, so adorn our houses, so spend our time, so earn money, that men may think better of our Lord. We should not expend one hour for any other purpose than that our life might be glorifying Jesus Christ for being, or doing, or suffering, or giving,—the four departments of Christ's life.

Do you not see the beauty of having such a life that you might yield it back into the ocean from whence it came? Do you not see this great prerogative of your manhood given to you that you may give it back again? We have been so foolish in the past that we have thought that whatever gifts have been entrusted to us, must be clung to or lost; forgetting it is only those who give away what they have, who really keep and get the best.

We have clung to our money, forgetting that by giving it away we shall get something better. We have clung to sermons with their eloquence, their chastity of expression, not realizing that just as soon as we give away the human power we get the divine power. We are so afraid of giving away what was only given to us as a trust, that we fail to get what God plans to bestow. I hear my Savior singing as He goes down into the grave, "Thou wilt not leave my soul in death, nor suffer thy holy one to see corruption. Thou wilt show me the path of life. In thy presence is fulness of joy, at thy right hand are pleasures forevermore." And so He goes down into the valley of death singing, and we know that in death He finds something better than He left.

The Savior's Method

My fifth point is this: *The Savior's method may be ours.* There are two possible methods. Our Lord might always have been crucifying, as it were, His human nature; but He chose the second method and the better one—that of living a life of perfect communion with God by the Holy Ghost. "I love the Father." "That the world may know that I love the Father." Do you think that there was any difficulty, any agony except once in the supreme act of all when He was called upon to contemplate the possibility of losing the Father's smile? As the thought of being forsaken by the Father came over His soul, a dark eclipse, He said, "Save me from that"; but soon He said, "Not my will even in this, but thine be done."

Jesus loved the Father, and there is no difficulty in giving up the self-life when you are in love with the living Christ. The thing for us to do therefore is, not to dwell on the crucifixion, on the giving-up side, but to allow our whole nature to be drawn to the living Christ—not death, but life. Moreover, seek that abounding life which makes it so easy to say No to self. Make the living Jesus the reality of your whole life. Go about saying, "I live, yet not I, but Christ liveth in me."

How can Jesus become to me what the Father was to Jesus?

First: *We must be quiet; we must wait.*

In all music there are rests and sometimes whole bars of rests; so there must be in every life the sitting down quietly and allowing God by the Spirit to make Jesus dwell in us. Jesus often went up on the mountains with the thought of God the Father filling His nature, and there must be times in our life when we give an opportunity for Christ to assert Himself and impress Himself absorbingly on the vision.

Then second: *Be sure to make Jesus the first of everything.*

Remember the first words in our Bible,—"In the beginning God." The story of every day ought to be commenced with the words, In the beginning Jesus. He must be the alpha, the first, the beginning. If, before you rush into a new enterprise, my brother, you would sit quietly down and be sure Jesus Christ is first, it would save you from landing in many a quagmire. Make Jesus first of every plan, every act, every sermon, everything that can be begun, continued, and ended in Him.

Third: *Make the glory of Jesus your aim.*

You may not *feel* it to be your aim, but *choose* it to be your aim. Always remember this great principle of the Christian's life, that when you cannot feel a thing, you must choose it by act of your will, and then ask God to create in you the emotion which you have chosen to be the motive of your action. Let the glory of Jesus be your aim in every service; let His glory be the thought that animates you in making money, in your housekeeping, in your mission work. Wives often send in requests for prayer for the conversion of their husbands, but frequently they desire it not for the glory of Christ, but that the husband may no longer bring misery and disaster into the life of the wife. We must put the glory of Christ even before the conversion of men.

Then fourth: *Meet God's will in every circumstance.*

I should like to draw a circle, the circle of God's will, and then step into it, and keep in it all my life; then whatever came to me must come through the encircling will of God. If Joseph's brethren put him in the pit, it is not they who sent him into Egypt, but God. If Judas brings the cup, Jesus says, "The cup which my Father hath given me, shall I not drink it?" When I am living in the will of God, my enemy may shoot an arrow against me; by the time it reaches me it may glance aside if God wills, but if He wishes it to strike me, by the time it reaches me it has become God's will for me.

Then lastly, *reckon on God.*

Some people are constantly worrying about their faith. I have given up worrying about my faith because I think of God's faithfulness. Begin to count God faithful. It is no use worrying whether I have strength enough to believe a note of hand; the question is, whether the man who signed that check is worthy of trust. Reckon on Christ's faithfulness toward you.

Go over these steps again: Be still. Make Christ first in everything. Live absolutely for Him. Receive from Him all your words to speak, and works to do, all the power of your life; when in any emergency or need receive from Him, who sent the demand, the power to meet it. Reckon absolutely upon Christ. Meet His will in every circumstance. That is the way that Jesus lived toward His Father; live so toward Jesus.

You may ask me how it was that in the human nature of Christ He so absolutely yielded Himself to the Father. The answer comes from one of the most marvelous books in the Bible, the epistle of the Hebrews: "Who, through the eternal Spirit, offered Himself without spot to God."

I believe that that is what the baptism of Christ meant. At the moment of his baptism, Jesus did the very thing to His holy, independent life that you and I have been called to do to our natural, sinful, and debased life. The baptism of Jesus Christ, as I understand it, was His saying by symbol and metaphor, "I come to do thy will, O my God; thy law is within my heart." Then on Him there came the blessed Holy Ghost, and it was in the power of the spirit that He perpetually yielded Himself to God.

If you and I are to live toward Christ as Christ lived toward the Father, we must be baptized into the same Holy Ghost. Whatever your station or occupation may be, you may start to live that life right now, but you may lose the power to live it within twenty-four hours. The only power by which Jesus Christ can help your life is through the infilling of the Holy Ghost. Shall we not have done forever with the independent life and be able to say as never before, "The living Savior hath sent me and He lives in me"? Then you will hear Him responding, "Because I live, ye shall live also."

Meyer's expository work frequently took the form of a collection of meditations based on unrelated verses of Scripture.

One such example is The Glorious Lord, *which was published in 1896. "The Hidings of God," the first selection which appears in* The Glorious Lord, *is an exposition of Isaiah 45:15. Here Meyer deals with the difficult question of the times when God does not seem to be present in the world. Meyer concludes with a reminder of our ignorance before God and an affirmation of God's love.*

In "Christ One and Manysided," an exposition of Isaiah 27:2, Meyer discusses how although Christ fulfills our needs in all of their variety He is the one thing we require for this life and the next.

A third exposition, taken from 2 Corinthians 3:18, is "How to Become Like Christ." In it Meyer suggests that the way to become more like Christ is to recognize that we reflect His glory. Once we recognize this, we will always ask ourselves if we are acting like Him.

CHAPTER ELEVEN

The Hidings of God

Isaiah 45:15

"Thou art a God that hidest Thyself," the prophet Isaiah said, as he
looked up from his study of the processes by which God was educating His
people for their great destiny. Permitted
an insight into the ways of God's providence, he had beheld the rise and fall of
dynasty and empire, the captivity, the
exile, the restoration, the gradual elimi-
nation of idolatry and impurity, and the
fusing of the entire nation into a condition in which God could use it for His
own purpose; and now breaking away
from his long and intent scrutiny of the
ways of God, he breaks out with the cry,
"Verily thou art a God that hidest Thyself, O God of Israel, the Savior."

In Nature

It is an exclamation that often rises
to our lips *in nature*. We are always
treading in the recent footprints of God;
entering chambers that He seems just
to have left; catching the glow of light
which has just fallen from His face; but
we always miss him. We go forward, and
He is not there, and backward, but cannot perceive Him; we speak, and feel
that He hears, but there is no reply; we
look up, and know that He is looking
down, but we cannot see Him; we feel
after Him, and are conscious that His
hand is somewhere within reach, but we
never touch it. Men talk of law, and
force, but what are these expressions
save confessions that God, the mighty
worker, is hidden from our view?

The World

What thoughtful man can look upon
the state of the world without acknowledging, on the one hand, that God must
be present, and yet feeling, on the other,
that He is certainly concealed. He does
not step out of the unseen to arrest the
progress of crime and high-handed
wrong. There is no sign of His displeasure.

Though His name is constantly taken
in vain He utters no word of remon-
strance. Though His glory is constantly
trodden under foot He does not strive
nor cry. Though His help is invoked, the
heavens do not rend, or the cherub
wings become the chariot of His descent, as of old, to the psalmist's
thought. He cannot be far away; He evidently hears and observes and feels all,
but who would dare to speak or act as
bad men do unless men were wont to
calculate upon God's concealment of
Himself ?

In Life

In our own life also we have to do
with the hidings of God. Some days we
walk in the dark, unable to see His face
or to feel Him near; we sit in our deserted chambers; we puzzle over our in-
soluble problems; we ask our myriad
questions. It seems then as though a
thick veil hangs between us and Him
whom we love. We are not sensible of
any sin or inconsistency which has

caused Him to withdraw, and yet there are the hidings of His face. Why has He taken that wife, or husband, or friend from our warm embrace, when so many another life, if similarly bereaved, would have felt it less? Why this passion for love without its satisfaction? Why this hunger for knowledge and service without gratification?

From all these questions we turn, heartsick and weary, as Noah's dove from winging her flight over the restless water. We are conscious that the miracle of the gradual healing of the blind man is a parable of our experience. Our vision is but indistinct; we see men as trees walking. It will be necessary that the hand of Christ be laid again upon us ere we see all things clearly.

The Veiled View of God

And yet we cannot wonder at the mystery which veils God and His ways. We are but children. Yesterday we were in the cradle; today we are sitting on the low form of the infant school. We have not yet commenced to graduate in the higher classes, and the faculties of the wisest and best amongst us, compared with those of the youngest angel, will probably range as those of a babe, when compared with the furthest acquirements of philosophic thought.

Besides, God has to graduate His revelation. Many mysteries have been unfolded to mankind in the later pages of the Bible, which were hidden from ages and generations. The sudden blaze of uncreated glory would dazzle, blind, and kill us. We could not bear the unveiled view of God. He must needs hide His glory as He passes by, revealing only His back parts. The revelation of the majesty of our Savior was attempered to the ability of the disciples to bear it. The dawn of revelation, like that of the natural day, must by almost insensible degrees.

And then, further, it is obvious that there are reasons for God's dealings with ourselves and with others, which He cannot disclose. If He did we should not understand. How often does a parent tell a child to wait, because there are things which cannot be explained; terms, the full meaning of which cannot be understood; relations, connections with others that involve principles which lie altogether beyond the range of immature thought. God has explained as much as our human faculties can apprehend, but there is much beyond our range; we see but part of His ways, and the thunder of His power we cannot understand.

What if evil is stronger than we think? What if mere omnipotence be powerless to deal with it, and that it can only be quelled by moral and spiritual processes? What if the moral benefit of the universe can be best promoted by allowing evil slowly to work itself out? What if the redemptive purpose needs time to assert its supremacy? What if the position of all beings and all worlds is being affected by the incidents which are transpiring upon the surface of our earth? We know so little. We stand upon the rim of inexplicable mysteries; our circle of light only reveals the surrounding realm of darkness.

Moreover, God must teach us to walk by faith and not by sight; what we see we cannot hope for. Where there are no rocks we need no pilot; where the path is plain we need no guide. It often happens that God says to His child, "I must shadow from you the sensible enjoyment of My presence; I must withdraw the sunlight from your path; I must lead you from the green pastures and still waters into the darkened valley; I must deprive you of emotion, for you will grow better in the dark; but trust Me."

When God hides from us so much that we would fain know, let us believe that the same love conceals, as at other times reveals, and that shadow and sun are accomplishing our growth in grace, and in the knowledge and love of God.

The Love of God

One consideration, however, is growing precious—God is love. He that hides Himself is also the Savior. There is no question as to the essential nature of Him who is working all things after the purpose of His own will. We know what friendship is. We can trust some souls so utterly that no act of theirs, however strange it seemed, could shake our faith in their unutterable love. Instead of interpreting their heart by an isolated act, we explain the act by the tender heart behind it. We dare to believe that whatever appears to militate against love is only another way of expressing it more deeply. Thus as we think of God and know Him to be love, we stand in the sunshine of certainty, and everything settles into harmony and peace.

All attests His love. The adaptation of light to the eye, of sound to the ear, of love to the heart. Take out of human life sin and its consequences, and the residuum proclaims the beneficence of the Creator. We can account for the presence and power of much which is dark and forbidding, and for the rest we can trust. The love of kindred hearts; the rhythm and beauty of nature; the evident purpose which is leading all events and minds to a goal of glory; above all, the revelation given to us through holy men, through the Son and by the Cross—all prove to us that God is a Savior.

All His purposes emanate from His heart; all His dealings have salvation as their end; all events beneath His strong hand subserve the aims of His redeeming grace. He is saving us; He is saving the world; He is saving the universe; the Savior God is ever going forth upon His ministries of love, and whatever may daunt and bewilder is somehow consistent with a love so divine, so all-embracing, so infinite, that when the end has arrived the universe will be compelled to admit that not one act was inconsistent with its loftiest conceptions of divine tenderness.

CHAPTER TWELVE

Christ, One and Manysided

Isaiah 27:2

Life presents the same features to the toiling myriads of England as to the dwellers amid the vineyards and pasture lands of Judah, to whom Isaiah wrote when he compared it to the experiences of a caravan passing across a sandy waste. Sometimes it is the sirocco blast of temptation, burning hot; the air is laden with particles of grit that sting and irritate, and find their way through closed doors; thus all day long the devil vexes us. Sometimes the tempest of trouble rises high; the cavilings and misjudgments of men, difficulties in daily business, the overwhelming competition and strife of our time, combine to fill our lives with storm.

Now we happen on a dry place, from which human love seems to have retreated, so that no green thing breaks the monotony of our pilgrimage, no child's embrace, no tender caress, no tone or touch of love. And, again, we are traversing a weary land; we are tired, tired of the inward strife, of the daily cross, of the perpetual demand on our sympathy and self-control, longing for the evening bell, and the passage across the harbor-bar from the restless sea to the tranquil waters of the haven.

We must not take the pessimist's view of life. In every year there are more hours of sun than of rain, in all lives there are more joys than sorrows. For all grief there is an anodyne; for all loss there is compensation. Nature is always beautiful. Troops of fresh young lives are ever pouring into our world, with their merry laughter and their gay frolic. The very work of life brings zest and interest; and hope is ever painting its bright frescoes on the dark cloud that hides the future. And yet it is undeniable that there are many sad aspects to life which press themselves upon our notice, and sometimes cause heart and flesh to fail.

Men Naturally Resort to the Readiest Methods of Averting the Pressure of Anxiety and Pain

The natural man is always looking out for his hiding place, the niche in the rock which may serve as one. He resorts to a temporary expedient which serves him in pressing difficulty; but shortly after he is seeking for a covert against a tornado, which all suddenly has broken upon him. After a while he is sensible of consuming thirst, and searches in another direction for water. And again worn by fatigue he looks around for a great rock casting a sharply-defined shadow on the burning sand, in whose blue depths he may find shelter. Thus man is always seeking help in different quarters to carry him through the pressing anxieties and difficulties of his life.

The children of this world hide themselves under the golden canopy of money, which wards off many of the grosser forms of evil, but cannot satisfy the craving of the heart for love and sympathy and rest. They yield themselves to systems of philosophy that

brace men to suffer with stoical fortitude and indifference, as when the weak
and boneless animal makes for itself the
hard shell or case that shelters it from
collision and shock. Or they take refuge
in some passionate human attachment,
seeking in man or woman the covert, the
water-spring, and the shadow of a great
rock; a hope which is doomed to disappointment, because none is all-sided
enough to supply another's need in the
numberless necessities of human experience. These are broken cisterns,
clouds without rain, the mirage without
the fountain, the grate without fire.

In All True Life
There Is Education and Growth

We pass upward from *things* to human sympathy, and seek in men and
women the comforter we originally
sought in wealth, or travel, or book.
Then we pass from the outward to the
inward, from the finite to the infinite,
from the time sphere to the eternal. We
start back appalled at the insufficiency
of the tenderest human love to meet the
exhaustless hunger of our souls, and
long for the divine in human form, presented to us in the Man. Finally there
comes a great unity into our life, and
having found the Man in whom all the
fullness of the Godhead dwells, having
realized something of what He can be
to the soul that He made and redeemed,
we return again to men and things, and
find in them a beauty and fitness which
we had never realized before.

Nature wears a lovelier dress, because the Man, whom we love, arrayed
her, and her hues and scents are borrowed from His thought. Children are
lovelier, because they reflect traits of
His character. All true thoughts are
more satisfying, because we detect in
them the intonations of His voice.
Earthly friendships are transfigured,

because as we lift them to our lips they
brim with water from the fountain of
His love; and the commonest incidents
of life are invested with unwonted meaning, because all things are of Him, and
through Him, and to Him forever.

For the Christian,
Only One Being Is Needful

There is a blessed unity in his life. He
desires only the Man of whom Isaiah
spoke, the Man that trod the soil of Palestine, that died upon the cross, that
lives in the glory, the Man Christ Jesus.
Jesus is the one answer to every question, the one satisfaction of every desire.

To the apostles the Master was all in
all. In Him they found strength for spiritual conflict, defense from their foes,
tenderness amid rebuke and reproach,
rest in weariness; and Jesus Christ is
willing to be as much and more to all
who believe on Him through their word.
During His earthly life, He was the one
answer to all the aches and ills of human bodies. Blindness, paralysis, demon possession, found their antidote in
His presence, His name, His touch. And
He is still all-sufficient to meet each demand now of the spiritual, as then of
the physical life.

All We Require for This Life
and the Next Is Ours in Christ

We are, alas, too slow to possess our
possessions. Do we need a shelter from
the sirocco of temptation? We may find
it in Jesus. Hiding behind Him, taking
refuge in the pavilion of His presence,
we are secure. Put the Man Christ Jesus
between you and temptation or adverse
circumstances, as the Roman soldier his
shield between him and the fiery darts
of the foe.

In days of tempest He is the impene-
trable covert. In loneliness He is like the

murmur of waters in a dry place. In weariness He is the shadow of a great rock, beneath which we may sit with great delight. In other words Jesus Christ is the one answer of the soul to every possible circumstance, to all emergencies, to the demands and appeals of our life, like the telegraph lad with the buff-colored envelope, and its unexpected summons.

There is something more.

The Soul That Abides in Christ Extracts Blessings from the Repeated Discipline Which Reveals the Many-Sidedness of Christ

It greets sirocco and tornado; it welcomes drought and weariness; it rejoices in tribulation; because out of all these things it is acquiring an experience of qualities and attributes which otherwise had slumbered in Christ unknown.

Human need has always been the background for the revelation of God's nature, as the ailments of a child reveal the tender patience of the mother, and as the virulence of disease the resource of doctor or nurse. You asked to know Him, then be not surprised if you are placed on steep standpoints of vision whence unexpected glimpses of His nature may be obtained.

Not Unfrequently Men Teach Us What the Man Can Be

They are but broken lights of Him. Splinters from the crystal, drops from the fountain. One setting forth this trait, and another that of His character, but none of them able to combine more than one, or at the most two, of those characteristics which the prophet attributes to the Man whose praises he recites.

They are coverts, but not hiding-places; or hiding-places, but not rivers; or rivers, but not shadowing rocks. Take the best of the best of men; gather into one all the chivalry, bravery, tenderness, loveliness, which have dwelt in the fairest of our race; and all together will not suffice to depict the comprehensiveness, and glory, and sufficiency of the Son of Man.

It should be our ambition so to live that men may catch glimpses of Christ in us, so that they may say, if this man or this woman is so strong and sweet, so true and tender, what must not He be, in whom their virtues dwell as their home?

And for ourselves, such may be our fellowship with Christ, that we shall be less sensitive to the transitions and trials of our mortal life. There shall be no more sirocco, or waterless waste, or unbearable heat, because in having Him, we shall be shielded in Him. These great modern cities will become in our eyes as fair as lands of perennial spring; and sad, homeless, desolate hearts become more sensible of their possessions than of their losses, of the One Presence than of the absence of any. "Our sun shall no more go down, neither shall our moon withdraw itself, for the Lord shall be to us an everlasting light, and the days of our mourning shall be ended."

CHAPTER THIRTEEN

How to Become Like Christ

2 Corinthians 3:18

Many are seeking the true policy of life. But in all directions there is perplexity and confusion; either men are living at haphazard or are adopting a policy dictated by selfishness and worldly wisdom. On all sides the question is being asked, What is life? Whither is the hurrying current bearing us? How shall we make the best of the short interval between the cradle and the grave? What thread of all the many that offer themselves to our hand will conduct us through the labyrinth with its darkness into the light? "What shall we do?" is a question often put.

A Blessed Life

The clue to life's aims; the philosopher's stone which will turn everything into gold; the secret of a blessed useful life is to be found much rather in what we *are*, than in what we *do*. The beatitudes with which our Lord opened the great program of Christianity all turn upon character rather than upon action, and the blessedness which He promises is to the meek, the pure in heart, the peacemaker. The true policy of life, therefore, is to stay just where we are; to believe that to be what and where we are is God's will for us; and to endeavor to be the noblest, sweetest, purest, strongest possible.

Not to fret because the sphere is obscure; not to be jealous of the position occupied by others; not to allow the peace of the inner life to be broken by the feverish desire to be something else; but to be quiet, evincing all that nobility of disposition and character which the opportunity and occasion call for. For men to be strong, thoughtful, considerate of women and of the weak, tender to little children, self-controlled, able to command the tides that sweep through heart and thought. For women to be pure and devout, gentle and modest, adorned with the jewels of the meek and quiet spirit, which in God's sight is of great price; and to be this constantly, in days of fog as well as of sunshine, of illness as of buoyant strength; this surely will extract from the roughest and most toilsome path the largest amount of blessedness that this world can give.

John Stuart Mill was accustomed to say that whenever the path of his life was not clear, he was accustomed to ask what Jesus of Nazareth would probably have done under the same circumstances, and that the test never failed to indicate the true course to adopt; and for us there is surely no higher ideal of life than to ask perpetually—what would Jesus do were He in my place? Each one of us must have an ideal by which to mold our life, and there is no such ideal as that presented to us in the life of our blessed Lord. To be like Christ is to know something of the joy and peace that perennially filled His heart.

There is a great necessity that we should be all this, because knowledge depends on character; we know, only when we are willing to do His will. The light of the morning will only illumine our mind when we have followed the narrow path of obedience up the steep ascent of righteousness and truth. Many ask what is the right policy of life with the intention of being nobler and purer so soon as they clearly see how to live. Such are destined to disappointment. The only solution to life's many problems is to begin at once, just where we are, to be what God demands of us, assured that soon we shall learn all that He would teach us.

How Can We Become Christ-Like?

The answer is given in a significant text, which has been illuminated with a new beauty in the Revised Version—"We all with unveiled face, *reflecting as a mirror* the glory of the Lord, are transformed into the same image, from glory to glory."

We All

There is no monopoly in the religion of Jesus Christ. Its doors stand open for all who will enter. No inner circle, no privileged class, no school of initiates. What was possible for Moses in the old dispensation, and for him alone, is free to us all, to the rank and file of the church as well as to the apostles, to the eighteenth century as well as the first.

With Unveiled Face

We are told that Moses veiled his face, partly because the people could not stand its dazzling light, and partly because he wished to hide from them its dwindling glory (v. 13). And his veil was afterwards spread upon the hearts of the Jews, who could not see the spiritual beauty of their own law, because they were hardened. But there must be no

veil of prejudice, or unbelief, or permitted sin upon the face which is turned towards the Son of God. With the clear, undimmed gaze of purity and truth, we must look into His.

Reflecting as a Mirror

In the older version, "Beholding as in a glass," which had a helpful and deep significance; but surely this is even yet more helpful, as it is truer to the apostle's phrase. We are to reflect Jesus as the mirror does the face and movements of the person in whose apartment it stands. Silent and unobtrusive; constantly and faithfully, it reflects every gesture; so the Christian heart should live in daily, hourly fellowship with the face of Jesus Christ. As the eyes of servants are to the hand of their master, so our eyes should be directed towards, and our lives perpetually reflecting, our Lord, whom the world cannot see, but who is ever present to the eye of our faith.

As Jesus looks into our lives, in their pellucid depths He should see His own face reflected. Yea, as God the Father looks down upon us He should see a faithful reflection of His Son. And as the giddy world around casts casual glances at the people of God they should be arrested, not so much by what they say as by the features of the Master which they present.

Perhaps each unit in the Church is needed to mirror to the world some trait or feature of Emmanuel. Each believer should daily ask himself, "What do my companions and associates see of Christ in me?" and the supreme test of every action should be, "How can I so conduct myself as to reveal some trait of my Master's character?" Whatever it may cost it should be the ambition of each lover of Christ to transmit perpetually the beauty of the Lord, so that others may admire Him in them that believe.

Ask how Christ is acting; always repeat what He is doing; do nothing of yourself; whatsoever He doeth, do it likewise; make all things of the pattern shown to the eye of faith upon the Mount; act thus, not because you wish to, or like to, or feel pleasure in it, but because you ought, and thus instinctively, and unconsciously you will really become like Christ. The likeness of Christ will pass from the outward act and speech, in which there may be some effort, to the inner temper and disposition of the soul.

Put on the Lord Jesus Christ by daily appropriating the grace of His character, and that grace will become indigenous to the soil of your heart.

We Are Transformed

This is the word used of the transfiguration of Christ. We too shall have a transfiguration; not as His, a sudden and immediate change, but one that will grow on us from day to day, too gradual to be noticed save by comparisons that stretch over years. Act like Christ, and you will increasingly come to think and feel like Him.

But none of this is possible save by the grace of the Holy Spirit. He first implants the desire for the holy life, and leads us to live nearer Christ, and enables us to resemble Him, and works in us the inward temper and disposition. From beginning to end the grace of the Christian life is due to the blessed Spirit, and when once He takes the soul in hand, there is no fear that the work will retrograde or be dimmed, as the light that faded from the face of Moses; rather it will proceed, by insensible degrees, from glory to glory, and we shall see in each other more and more of the character and beauty of the Risen and Ascended Master.

But there is something yet to be said. The Lord Jesus is in the heart of each believer, by the grace of the Holy Spirit. The perfect image may be in embryo, wrapped up as a forest tree in acorn or seed, but it is certainly present. And each time we are called upon to resemble Christ, to act or speak as He would have done, to reflect Him to men, we have to deal not only with the Christ of the throne, but the Christ of the heart. Let us make way, so that the Christ in us may speak or act through us; so that the image without may be reproduced, not simply by reflection, but by indwelling and outshining.

Meyer's exposition of Scripture appeared not only as addresses, sermons, and meditations on selected verses but also as written expositions of entire books of the Bible.

"The Word as Light," taken from his Gospel of John, *is part of his exposition on what it means for Christ to be The Word and demonstrates his ability to penetrate the metaphors which Scripture uses to represent Christ.*

"The Bread Which Gives and Sustains Life," also taken from Meyer's Gospel of John, *brings the meaning of Christ as our Bread to life through keen insights into the nature of bread. Meyer's concern here, as always, is with our dependence on Christ as the giver of life. "The Bread Which Gives and Sustains Life" is representative of Meyer's entire exposition of John in its focus on the person and life of Christ.*

CHAPTER FOURTEEN

The Word As Light

That was the true Light, which lighteth every man that cometh into the world (John 1:9).

It is not for us to attempt to celebrate the praise of light. What a wonderful conception it was of the mind of God! How delicate the loom of that creative skill on which it is constructed day by day! And how complete an argument for the divine workmanship is afforded by the adaptation between the element of light and the crystalline gate of the eye by which it enters man's soul! (Luke 11:34–36).

Themes like these rather become such as our great epic bard, whose blindness made him more sensible to the value of that which he had lost, and whose lofty genius could alone find terms to describe its worth. Or, better still, light might well be the subject of a sonnet by that angel minstrel who composed the majestic Psalm of Creation which is perpetually sung before the throne (Rev. 4:11). But neither could proceed long with his task without rising from the material substance—for ethereal as light seems to be to our dull sense, it is still material—to that glorious being who made it as a parable and emblem of his divine nature. "God is light, and in Him is no darkness at all" (1 John 1:5).

But the glory of the Father's nature is of such insupportable splendor that it would be impossible for any creature that He has made to behold and enjoy it; and it is very consolatory to be told in the opening verses of the epistle to the Hebrews that our Lord Jesus is "the effulgence of his glory" (Heb. 1:3, RV). The human eye could not bear the full splendor of the sun's heart or surface of golden cloud, but it can bear the far-travelled and diluted ray; so, though we could not behold the nature of God in its direct and original manifestation, we can behold his glory in the face of Jesus Christ (2 Cor. 4:6). And for this reason we hail thankfully and adoringly the announcement that the Word is the Light.

The Characteristics of the Light

Light is pure.—It is so pure that evil cannot stain or impurity defile it. It will pass through a fetid and poisonous atmosphere without contracting taint, or carrying a germ of poison with it, as it issues forth to pursue its ministries of mercy beyond. So pure was our blessed Lord. Evil fled abashed before Him. He gauged the power of temptation, not by yielding in a hair's breadth, but by resisting and overcoming it. When He died, after thirty-three years' close contact with men, his spirit was as absolutely stainless as when He was born of a pure virgin. And the instant effect of his life within our hearts will be to kindle a purity as sweet and chaste and unearthly as his own.

Light is gentle.—With each dawn its tides revisit us after having traversed the abyss with inconceivable speed; but its waveless break so gently that they fail to shake the dewdrop from its blade of grass or the trembling petal from the overblown rose. Even the gossamer of the spider's web does not quiver as the sunbeams strike it. And how apt a symbol is here of that gentle goodness which made the shepherd-boy great, which leads the flock into the pastures of tender grass, and fans with anxious care the dull sparkle of smoking flax! And when His love is shed abroad in our hearts, it begets a corresponding gentleness in judgment, speech, and behavior. All true Christians are *gentle folk*. "The wisdom that is from above is first pure, then peaceable, *gentle*, easy to be entreated, full of mercy" (Jas. 3:17).

Light is all-pervasive.—It kindles a line of watch-fires on the pinnacles of an Alpine range; but it does not neglect the hill-slopes up which the plovers follow its last retreating beams. It gilds the golden roofs of the palace; but it glides through prison-bars to sparkle in the teardrops of the repentant prodigal. It lights the good man to his work, and the bad man to his home after the unholy revels of the night. Nor is it otherwise with the lovingkindness of Christ, which misses none in its daily ministry, however poor, and sad, and lonely; which includes the evil and the good, the just and the unjust; which "lighteth every man that cometh into the world." And it is thus with those in whom his life repeats itself. They, too, are said to be "without partiality." Their lives resemble the sun and the rain (Matt. 5:45).

Light reveals.—It revealed to Jacob the deception practiced on him by Laban under the cover of darkness. It revealed to the host of Midian the meager force before which it had fled panic-stricken, misled by the noise of the crashing pitchers and the flashing of three hundred lights. In darkness the traveller lies down to spend the night beneath the open sky, in terror lest he may stray to the brink of the ravine; but the morning, with rosy finger, reveals that he has been sleeping within a stone's cast of his home.

So does Christ reveal. He is the light of all our seeing. He not only lights up our inner sight, but He casts a light on God, and providence, and truth, and the mysteries of redemption, which, apart from Him, notwithstanding all our intelligence, had been obscure and unknown. In his light we see light. Light is whatsoever cloth make manifest. Let us lift up our souls unto Him who is light, so that we may be filled and saturated with his nature and being, and made to glow with it in this dark world; as I have seen a certain kind of diamond, which, after having been held up for some short period in sunlight, has continued to sparkle like a star when carried thence into a darkened chamber. "We all, with unveiled face beholding as in a mirror the glory of the Lord, are transformed (*i.e.*, transfigured, it is the same Greek word as in Matt. 17:2) into the same image from glory to glory, even as from the Lord the Spirit" (2 Cor. 3:18).

The Ministry of the Light

The Word was the Light of unfallen man in Paradise.—In the glades of Eden two trees were planted; the one the tree of life, the other of the knowledge of good and evil. It is impossible not to see in these a lively representation of Him who is Life and Light, and who, from the first, must have been the organ and channel of divine communication to mankind.

It was in the person of the Son that the ever-blessed God walked with our first parents in the cool of the day; conversed with them; uttered the memorable prohibition; sought them in their fall; and, with sad prevision of all that it must cost, foretold the ultimate triumph of the woman's Seed. Even then

He rejoiced in the habitable part of the earth, and his delights were with the sons of men. Even then He was the Light of man's moral nature, teaching him all he knew, and prepared to lead him on to know the deep things which lay concealed as a landscape under a morning haze. Even then the Son had commenced his favorite ministry of manifesting the name of his Father (Matt. 11:27; John 17:26).

The Word was Light in the world amid the long dark ages which preceded the Incarnation.—"The Light shineth in darkness, and the darkness comprehended it not." There are two methods by which darkness is produced. The one by absence of light; the other by loss of sight. It is dark when the sun sets, and primeval darkness resumes for a brief parenthesis its ancient sway; but it is also dark when the eye is blind. And the darkness mentioned here is not the first, but the second.

There has never been an age in which the divine Light has not shone over our world. Not gospel light, not the light of revelation, not the light as we have it; but still, Light. And whatever light existed was due to the presence and working of the Lord Jesus. *He shone* in the good He did; giving rain from heaven, and fruitful seasons, and in the food and gladness with which He filled men's hearts, so that He left not Himself without witness (Acts 14:17). *He shone* in the clear testimony given since the creation, through the works of nature, to the everlasting power and divinity of God (Rom. 1:20). *He shone* in the intuitions of truth, which we call conscience, and which are his voice in the human breast, and are so evidently referred to here as the true light, lightening every man coming into the world (Rom. 2:14, 15). *He shone* also in those great movements towards righteousness, which seem to have swept from time to time over the heathen world. Whatever of truth there was in any of these must have been due to Him. It was of the heathen that the apostle spoke when he said: "That which may be known of God is manifest in them; for God manifested it unto them" (Rom. 1:19, RV).

But the light shone amid blind and darkened hearts, which could not comprehend it. Though men knew God, they glorified Him not as God, neither were thankful; and, as the result, "they became vain in their reasonings, and their senseless heart was *darkened*" (Rom. 1:21). Since they would not believe, the god of this world was permitted to blind their eyes.

It is characteristic of this Gospel, and it well befits its theme, that so much space is given to the story of the man born blind (chap. 9), for such is really the condition of the race; and it is significant that that story is prefaced by the announcement so constantly reiterated by the Lord, "I am the Light of the world" (9:5; see also 8:12; 12:35, 46). A family born blind; a race stricken with blindness, as Saul was, and groping for someone to lead it by the hand; a vault, like that in which the dead are buried, around which the sunlight plays, whilst not one beam can enter—such is a picture of our race. "The Light shineth in darkness."

The Word was the Light of the chosen people.—Throughout their history God sent them prophets, rising up early and sending them, that they might bear witness to the coming Light. They were not that Light, but they came to bear witness to it (John 1:8); just as the moon and planets bear witness to the sun while he is absent, though every moment is bringing him nearer to close their reign. Of these John the Baptist is here cited as the greatest and last.

We need not recapitulate their names—the evangelical Isaiah; the plaintive Jeremiah; the seraphic Ezekiel; the abrupt Habakkuk; Amos the herdman; and Haggai the priest. They are not all mentioned here; but are summed up in the greatest of all, John the Baptist, of whom Christ Himself said: "Verily I say unto you, among them that are born of women there hath not risen a greater." All these were lights; John was "a burning and shining lamp"; but their light was not their own, it was derived from Him to whom they all bore witness. They spake of Him. The testimony of Jesus was the spirit of prophecy. Overtopping other men in the grandeur of their personal character, and by the gift of the Spirit of Inspiration, they saw the day of Jesus, as mountain-peaks first catch sight of the rising sun; and they declared to the world of men below what glory was on the way.

What a new interest would come into our reading of the Old Testament Scriptures, if we always remembered that they testify of Jesus, and glisten with light caught by anticipation from his life; and if we sought to discover what the Master meant when, beginning at Moses and all the prophets, "He expounded unto them in all the Scriptures the things concerning Himself."

As every dewdrop on the morning meadow glistens with the sunlight, each of them reflecting the whole sun, so do the paragraphs of the prophets flash with the presence of Jesus. They are beautiful in his beauty; strong in his strength; true in his truth. The lips may be those of man, the voice that of a prophet; but through all, the Word of God speaks, and the true Light shines. In the pages of the prophets the quick ear of love detects the accents of Him who spake as never man spake. Indeed, we are told expressly that the Spirit of Christ was in the prophets announcing

that gospel which is now preached throughout the world (1 Pet. 1:11, 12).

Finally, the Light became incarnate.— Too bright to be beheld, the Light of God curtained Himself in human flesh, as the face of Moses beneath his veil, or the Shekinah beneath the folds of the tabernacle. Such is the direct force of the word translated *dwelt* in verse 14. It might be better rendered *tabernacled.* But of this more afterwards.

And it is not possible to do more than take one brief glance at that bright world which awaits us, when, *in the ages of eternity, our blessed Lord will be still the Everlasting Light.* For it is written that the heavenly city will not need sun nor moon to shine in it, because the Lamb is the light thereof (Rev. 21:23). And so, from the first creation of man till the new creation; from the garden of innocence to the city of matured and tested holiness; from the origin of the race in its lonely and single representative to the untold myriads of his progeny who shall stand in the unsullied purity of robes washed white—always and everywhere, the Word of God is the Light of men, the *true* light, that is the archtypal light, of which all other lights are types and illustrations.

The Reception of the Light

(1) *Before his Incarnation.*—"He was in the world." In every spring, in every sunbeam, in every God-breathed thought, in every providence; walking up and down the aisles of his own temple; brooding over the teeming myriads of mankind. In Him they lived and moved and had their being. He was not an absentee from his own creation. In Him all things consisted and were maintained (Acts 17:28; Col. 1:17).

"And the world was made by Him." Mark this touching repetition of *the world;* we shall often meet with it again.

It is used repeatedly, as when a bereaved parent, brooding over the sin or misfortune of some beloved child, repeats his name again and again. "O my son Absalom! my son, my son Absalom! O Absalom, my son, my son!" And see how the Holy Spirit emphasizes the fact that our Lord was the organ through whom creation was wrought.

"And the world knew Him not." As though a man might build a splendid mansion—with frescoes on its walls, fountains splashing in marble wells, luxuriant furniture, exquisitely-planned grounds—put it in trust for the sick or destitute, go away for years, and on returning be denied admittance, or watched as an intruder; until, touching some secret spring, he showed such knowledge and power as to compel recognition of his claims.

It was a sorrowful confession, extorted from our Lord, by all his experiences, both before and after his Incarnation—"the world hath not known Thee." And it is confirmed by the Holy Ghost when He says, in the wisdom of God, "the world by wisdom knew not God." Alas for the poor world, vaunting its science and its pride, but not knowing that glorious being who was in it from the first!

(2) *At his Incarnation.*—"He came unto his own, and his own received Him not." Throughout the Old Testament the Jews are spoken of as God's peculiar treasure; but here they are described as Christ's, because Christ is God. They were his by the calling of Abram; by the covenant of circumcision; by the passage of the Red Sea; by the desert discipline; by the education of history: but when He came to them, they cried, "We will not have this man to reign over us."

"They received Him not." This is a note which we shall hear again; but in the meanwhile, the word seems carefully chosen to suggest that it was not a case of ignorance, but of wilfulness. They knew, or might have known, who He was; but they deliberately refused to enquire into his credentials, and they shut the door resolutely in his face. This is why they are a nation of weary-footed wanderers, bronzed by the sun of every clime, having everywhere a recognition, but nowhere a home.

(3) *Since the Incarnation.*—There has been no longer a dealing with nations, but with individuals. Many have received Him, rising above the general indifference around. Mary in the highlands of Nazareth; Elisabeth in the hill-country of Judea: Simeon in the temple; Hannah the prophetess; and Zachariah the priest, are representatives of untold multitudes beside. And to as many as have thus received Him He has given the right to become the sons of God.

Stepping across the humble threshold of their hearts, He has suddenly thrown aside the garments of his great humility, which He had worn as a disguise and test. Then, rising in the full stature of his divine manhood, He has taken from out his skirts a parchment patent of sonship and heirship, and, handing it to the recipient and astonished spirit, has declared that from henceforth it may dare to reckon itself, without presumption, a child of God, and an inheritor of the Kingdom of Heaven.

And for lineage, it is revealed that all such may trace their descent past earthly parentage—"not of blood"; past natural instinct or desire—"not of the will of the flesh"; past human volition—"not of the will of man": to the thought, and purpose, and grace of the Eternal Father, to whom be glory for ever and ever.

CHAPTER FIFTEEN

The Bread Which Gives and Sustains Life

As the living Father hath sent Me, and I live by the Father: so he that eateth Me, even he shall live by Me (John 6:57).

This verse may fairly be said to be the pivot around which our Lord's words about Himself revolve. It certainly gives the secret of his inner life. And it excites our deepest wonder as we read it over and over, trying vainly to explore and understand its wealth of significance. It furnishes a clue also to the interpretation of those other words with which He met the devil, on his first assault, and told him that "Man doth not live by bread alone, but by every word that proceedeth out of the mouth of God." But here He takes a further step, and says that He lives not only by the words of God, but by God Himself.

And there is a further interest in this verse, that it not only affords the clue to the inner life of the Son of man, but contains an admonition for each one of us to do as He did; exercising towards Himself the same dependence of spirit and attitude as he did towards his Father.

There was a sense, of course, in which, as the Second Person in the holy Trinity, all power was his in heaven and on earth. But of this, to use the expressive phrase of the Apostle, "He emptied Himself" (Phil. 2:7, RV), and voluntarily took up a life of momentary dependence on his Father; living on his plan, by his strength, for his glory; losing Himself utterly in his all-sufficiency, and appealing to Him in every episode and emergency of his daily life. His spirit was as dependent on Him as his body was on bread; and clung to Him as the vine to the trellis-work on which it is reared. Such is the character of the life which He bids us live towards Himself. "He that eateth Me shall live by Me."

Our Lord As Bread

We might discover many ingenious analogies to please the fancy and delight the mind, but be diverted from the main conception pressed on us, with repeated emphasis, in this discourse.

Bread contains life.—It is made of fine flour, but in the grinding of the flour the life-germs of the wheat are not destroyed, and it is their presence which makes bread the life of our life, the true fuel of our fire. In bread, the life of nature, that living principle which underlies all vegetable growth, and which is due to the direct operation of the living God, is reduced to such a form that it can conveniently become the raw material out of which we weave the texture of our being. And in the human nature of the Lord Jesus there is stored the very life of God. "As the Father hath life in Himself, He gave to the Son to have life in Himself"; so that the Son has brought to our world, incarnated in his wondrous nature, the underived, infinite, and ever-blessed life of the Eternal.

It is the presence of life in bread which causes it to sustain physical life;

it is the presence of life in the words of the Bible which renders it a book for all ages and of endless application; it is the presence of life in Jesus Christ which makes Him the food of men. Hearken to his majestic words: "I am the life"; "I am the Resurrection and the Life"; "I am the living One" (14:6; 11:25; Rev. 1:18).

Bread is all-sufficient for life.—It contains in itself all the elements needed for nutrition. Though a man have an unlimited supply of flesh, he cannot find in such a diet, however plentiful, certain qualities required to build up his frame. But on a bread-diet man will thrive and he will thrive in proportion to the number of original elements left when the processes of its preparation are complete.

Nor is it otherwise with Jesus. In Him there is everything that we need "for life and godliness." He is a hiding-place in a storm of wind; a covert from the tempest; rivers of water in drought; the shadow of a great rock in scorching heat. For the polluted, He is purity; for the irritable, He is patience; for the faint, He is courage; for the weak, He is strength; for the ignorant, He is wisdom. God, who knew the needs of our bodies, stored all nutritive qualities in the corn for us to assimilate as we need. And knowing the needs of our spirits, He stored all the elements required for our spiritual nutrition in our blessed Lord, leaving us to appropriate them as we will.

We cannot understand that wonderful inner mechanism, in virtue of which each part of our nature comes to the bread as soon as eaten, and carries off from it the special particles it requires. But we may all learn the lesson of their participation, and take to ourselves just those things in the blessed Lord which we want most.

Bread must be appropriated ere it becomes life-giving.—However much bread lies around, it avails not to appease hunger, or to do its work of nutrition, unless it is masticated and digested. And what digestion is to food, assimilating it with our bodies, *that* devout and loving meditation on the words and life and work of the Lord Jesus is to our spirits. By the one process there is brought about a union between our bodies and the bread; by the other a union between our spirits and the risen Jesus. In the one we extract the principle of physical life from bread; in the other the principle of spiritual life from the Lord of life.

No figure can unfold the meaning of all this. The only true clue is to be found in the personal experience of believers. They know what is meant, though they cannot tell the art of it to others. But it is a living fact with them, that by turning hearts and thoughts towards Jesus they are able to get strength to suffer and act in ways which, as they look back on them, appear almost past believing. O weak and suffering ones, the greater your need, the more imperative the necessity to eat his flesh! Deliberate eating and mastication are essential to good health; but not less so, after a spiritual sort, to all who would live in soul-health before God.

Yet we may illustrate what feeding on Christ is. A whole family may be fed by the words, and gentleness, and patience, of a single invalid, who thinks herself useless lumber. A generation of young men may be fed by the heroism, or intellect, or example of some chosen leader. An expedition may feed, through long privation and bitter disappointments, on the undaunted courage and inspiring hope of some chivalrous captain. A nation may feed on the deeds or words of a Pitt, a Fox, or a Wellington. And so, in the higher sphere, we may all feed our spirits on Him who offers Himself as the true Bread of man.

The great need for us all is to feed more constantly on Christ. We are so fitful and irregular in our dealings and fellowship with Him. We do not sufficiently "handle the Word of Life." We pray in a kind of despairing way for help, but do not take Him by acts of assimilating, appropriating faith; going forth from fellowship with Him, not gauging by our emotions the amount of benefit received, but by the faith which knows that it cannot look to Christ for aught, without receiving that and more also.

But there are times in every life when, all unexpectedly and unannounced, there steals into our hearts some rich experience of the love and presence of Jesus. It is sent by One who forecasts a coming trial, and prepares us to meet it as He did; who gave his apostles a rich banquet and an evident token of his power, ere He thrust them forth with his own hand into the very heart of the storm, which was even then gathering about the hills. They had been ill-prepared to meet the toils of that arduous night, had they not been previously so well fed by their Master's royal bounty. And often amid their perils they must have cheered each other by recalling their Master's power. Surely He who brake the loaves into food for thousands could hush the storm into a calm! God sends no crews to sea without first provisioning them. The miracle of the feeding of the multitudes preceded the terror of the storm.

The Teaching of the Manna

The manna, of course, contained all the elements of true bread; but there was this peculiarity in it, that it was not produced by any natural process, nor did it grow from the soil of earth: as it is written, "He gave them bread from heaven to eat." How it came, and when, no one knew; but each morning, beneath the hoar frost, round about the camp, lay the small round thing which angels might have made their food, and which heaven had dropped for the sustenance of the chosen hosts.

This is the food to which our Lord specially alludes. For purity and sweetness and sufficiency, the manna was a fitting emblem of Himself; but much more, because it came down, as He had done, from heaven (32, 33, 38, 42, 50, 51, 58).

What a marvellous tribute is here to the heavenly origin of man! His nature is fallen and degraded; but it refuses to be satisfied with anything less than that which comes down from heaven. Men try to content the hunger of their souls by husks from the swine trough and garbage from the dog-kennel, but in vain. And the fact that man, of all the living things on this earth, fails to find his satisfaction in the products of earth, proves that his origin must be sought outside the bounds of the earthsphere. He whose nature craves heavenly food must himself be of heavenly origin. And God who made him what he is could not fail to provide the nature which He has given with the food of its native sphere.

There was, therefore, special reason why our Lord so repeatedly affirmed that He came down from heaven. He was something more than a son of man. His body might be an earthen vessel, but it held a heavenly treasure. He came down from heaven, and in those words lie the glory of his pre-existence, and the mystery of his incarnation. He came from God, and went to God. Heaven was his home, as, indeed, it had been the creation of his power in ages that lie beyond time's bourne or human vision.

Life-giving Through Death

It is impossible for any one illustration to convey all God's thoughts to us.

And though bread is only possible through the death of myriads of corns of wheat, yet this is not the primary thought which bread suggests to us. And, therefore to emphasize the truth, that the power to communicate life can only be acquired through death, our Lord speaks of the bread which He would give, as *his flesh*, which He would give for the life of the world. Obviously flesh is that which has passed through death.

These are the words that proved so great a stumblingblock to some of his disciples. They said it was a hard saying, and they would not hear it. It was distasteful to them to hear their Master speak of an inevitable death, instead of the thrones of glory on which they had set their hearts. "From that time forth many of his disciples went back, and walked no more with Him."

How little did they realize that the crown is only reached by the path of the cross, and that the only life which can be communicated is that which has passed through the grave! There is an evident allusion in these words to that approaching death, which was never far from our Savior's thoughts, the death of propitiation and atonement. But He did not fail to see that what He was to suffer would be as the breaking of the shrine to let forth the imprisoned spirit of life to bless the world.

Death and resurrection and ascension must precede Pentecost. He must first descend, if He would afterwards ascend to fill all hearts, all lives, all worlds, with the aroma and power of his endless life. The life He had before his death was fair, but not communicable; that which he won in death and its defeat is fairer still, and capable of being given to all who hear and obey his invitation to come.

Doubly precious then is that life which He has given, and gives in unceasing supplies to those who feed on Him in loving lowly trust! It is a life which is death-proof; which has passed through Hades unscathed; which has acquired in the ordeal a virtue that renders it unique; and which, while it deals death to all that is of the flesh, enters us to abide, and to lift us to share his glorious life and endless reign.

The Distribution of the Bread

How significant the lesson of the miracle which served as the text for this discourse! It was the Passover at Jerusalem; but He had kept a royal Passover on those hillsides which teemed with spiritual significance. To do all things decently and in order (10); to begin each meal by giving thanks (11); to expect something more than the bare necessaries of life at the hands of God (11); to guard against waste (12); to learn that giving is the true means of increase (13); these and other lessons were taught, as the words and vales were being carpeted with the first sweet green of spring.

But two lessons stood out conspicuously—first, that there was enough for all; and secondly, that the fainting crowds must be fed through the ministry of his disciples. "He distributed to his disciples, and the disciples to them which were set down."

In all our Lord's miracles there is a marvelous economy of power. The servants must fill the water-pots with water before He makes it wine. Jairus and the mother must give their daughter something to eat when the Master has given her back to them. Others must roll away the stone, though only He can throw the life-giving word into the tomb. So here. He used the lad's loaves and fishes as the basis of the miracle; and, instead of distributing the food by miraculous agency, He passed it through the hands of his disciples, giving them a memorable share in the joyous work.

Nor is it otherwise today. There is enough in our dear Lord to meet the demands of all that are in heaven and on the earth; no man, or woman, or child, need go unfed. But if the precious Bread of Life, for lack of which men are famishing, is to be brought to them, it can only be by our hands, who stand around the Lord as a kind of inner circle. Oh, shame on us that we are so apt to feed ourselves, neglectful of the cry of the perishing; and that we content ourselves with giving again and again to the same few ranks immediately around us, till they are surfeited, and the rest left without a crumb! What wonder that we cease to enjoy the provisions we misuse; and that they fail before our eyes, leaving no basketfuls of fragments for coming days!

Say not that your knowledge of Christ is too small and fragmentary to be of any avail. Take to Him; beneath his touch a wondrous transformation will ensue; and, as you give away your all, you will find it grow beneath your hand, because it has passed from his hand to yours, and the slender provision, which threatened to be too little for yourself, shall avail for multitudes.

In The Directory of the Devout Life, *a 1904 work, Meyer presents a series of meditations on the Sermon on the Mount as found in Matthew's gospel.*

"Silent Influence" begins with Meyer's piece of wisdom "Being is doing." Meyer recognizes that placing personal piety over the calling to be light to the world is an unhealthy extreme but asserts that living a good life among men is still our greatest work.

"Simplicity in Speech" takes a hard look at our patterns of speech and concludes that often our speech is not what God would have it to be because we are not true, profound, and unselfish. Speech, according to Meyer, "is the utterance of the soul."

In "The Second Mile" Meyer provides a sensible account of what it means for us to obey Christ's hard commands to walk the second mile and not resist evil.

CHAPTER SIXTEEN

Silent Influence

Matthew 5:13–16

Being is doing. Our greatest work for God and man is to be. The influence of a holy life is our greatest contribution to the salvation and blessing of the world. Though you cannot preach, or teach, or engage in some sphere of Christian service, do not be greatly moved, if only you can live the life of God amongst men. Our Lord for thirty years was content to live an absolutely holy life, as the Lamb of God without blemish and without spot; and His supreme work in the world was not only to give His life as a ransom, but to live His life that He might leave us an example that we should follow in His steps.

Too many Christians seem to suppose that the main object of life is to engage in a sphere of direct service, whilst they leave their personal character to take care of itself, and to develop almost at haphazard; whereas our main thought and care should be that Christ should be formed in us, and be revealed in every look and gesture, every word and act. Out of that will come naturally, inevitably, and blessedly, our direct Christian service. The best work is that which arises out of the simplicity and beauty of our witness for truth and love.

We must, of course, guard against extremes. On the one hand, we may attempt so much service as to neglect that inner culture which is priceless in its effect on service, and our personal inconsistencies will neutralize the effect of our Christian activities. On the other hand, we may sincerely believe that we

are cultivating our character, when, in fact, we are sinking into a dreamy lethargy, from which we need to be aroused by the trumpet-call of duty to a dying world. We are apt to forget that the development of the inner life is not perfect, unless it issue in such going about doing good, as was the flower and fruit of our Savior's thirty years.

Though Persecuted

Our Lord had been describing the reception which the type of character that He had come to implant would certainly encounter. Instead of attracting men by its heavenly beauty, it would certainly repel them. Instead of commendation and welcome, it would arouse dislike and rebuff. The great world of men would not appreciate the poor in spirit, the mourner, the meek and merciful, the pure in heart or maker of peace—but would reproach, and persecute, and say all manner of evil falsely. But, notwithstanding all, He insisted that they should continue to bless the world by the silent and gracious influence of holy lives. Reviled, they must bless; persecuted, they must endure; defamed, they must entreat; threatened with death, they must still be as salt to their persecutors, and as light to their defamers.

However men receive our testimony, whatever they may say and do against us, notwithstanding the unreasonableness of their dislike, we must continue to be what our Lord would have us be, nay, we must *let* Him who is within us shine forth through us, so that men may be compelled to admit that the unearthly beauty of our lives is the supreme proof of the divinity and glory of our religion.

You ask what is the good of being good. Your detractors and oppressors vaunt themselves over you, take every advantage of your quiet, unresisting gentleness, and misinterpret your self-restraint. It would almost appear that they are driven to greater extremes of wickedness because of the provocation of your goodness. The soldiers of the Roman governor probably never mocked one of their ordinary victims as they did the holy, unresisting Savior. The gentle and loving wife will sometimes extract the most malignant and bitter hatred of her husband, such as he would show to no other.

But you do not know how your behavior is beginning to thaw that iron-frozen soil, how often and deeply compunction is at work, or how nearly the hatred of your oppressor is being overcome by love. The spring warmth may seem to fall on the frozen masses of snow and ice in vain, but every hour of sunshine is sapping the reign of the ice-king, and hastening the inevitable break-up of his supremacy.

That workingman who has borne the insults of his shopmates for Christ will presently have the ringleader come to beg his pardon, and with tears in his eyes ask him to pray for him. That oppressed wife will have the pleasure of leading her penitent husband to the cross. That sister will be won by her sister, who has borne contumely and reproach with unswerving gentleness. Be of good cheer, your sufferings will have their most blessed result in overcoming evil by good, as we have said. Remember, the apostle speaks of "the kingdom and patience of Jesus," which means that pa-

tient suffering ultimately secures a blessed supremacy, a royalty, an over-mastery of hardness and unkindness by gentleness, truth, and love.

When the Forth Bridge was in making, the workmen came to a crucial point, where two of the most important iron girders refused by some inches to come together for the bolts to be driven through—a process which was absolutely essential to their union and the stability of the whole fabric. Every mechanical method to bring them together was tried with no purpose; and finally, in despair, all further efforts were abandoned for the night. It was summer weather, and the sunshine of the following morning was very hot, so much so that the great masses of metal expanded beneath the genial rays, and the results were achieved by the silent touch of the sun which had defied the utmost efforts of force. So in human life. Consistency of character, purity, gentleness, sweetness, such holy living as issues from the qualities which our Lord has enumerated, will avail when the keepers of the house shall tremble, and the strong men will bow themselves.

The World's Corruption

The Lord knew well *the condition of the world*. To His holy and unerring judgment it was a carcass slowly rotting to putrefaction, and sorely needing some influence to stay its corruption. There was never an epoch in the world's history fuller of dazzling genius than that in which He was born. Some of the most brilliant names of history were shining still in the midnight sky when the bright and morning star arose over Bethlehem. But the grossness of the age was unparalleled and indescribable. The allusions made to it in the Epistles are sufficiently terrible, but the whole truth is only revealed in classic literature itself, which survives to show that the earth was corrupt before God, and that every imagination of the thoughts of man's heart was only evil continually.

In our Lord's eyes, also—to advert to the other metaphor—the world lay under the power of thick darkness. In its wisdom it knew not God. Professing themselves wise, men had become fools. The god of this world had blinded the eyes of those who believed not, and they groped in the noontide as in the murky midnight. Such has been, is, and will be, the condition of men without the gospel. The history of the human family is always repeating itself.

We cannot be surprised either at the description given by missionaries of the awful condition of heathen countries, or at the outbreaks of lawlessness and crime in nations which are only nominally Christian. Our inventions, organizations, and boasted civilization, may affect the exterior of our society, but if it were not for the presence of the Church of the Lord Jesus, and the witness borne by the lives and words of her members, there would be nothing to save it from the pit of corruption, which has swallowed up every great nation that has risen to lead the race.

Men rage against "Exeter Hall," and revile what is called "the Nonconformist Conscience," as they did against the Puritans in bygone centuries, not realizing that they evince the antagonism of corruption to the salt, and of darkness to the light, and that the very existence of our society is more largely due than they suppose to the very elements they so much dislike.

Salt

Our consistent holy living will act as an antiseptic to arrest the corruption around us. It is said that the presence of a little child, with its blue-eyed sim-

plicity and purity, has often arrested the commission of dark crimes; and as much should be said of the influence of our own daily living. A sudden silence should fall on certain kinds of conversation when we enter the room. This or the other form of worldly amusement, which has entered professedly Christian homes, should be felt out of place when we are staying there. And right through the society in which we move there should be a consciousness that there is an incongruity between our character and all that savors of impurity, falsehood, or selfishness.

We do not want to impose a sense of restraint and gloom on social gatherings when we enter. Our presence should be an incentive to the merriment of the children, the cheer of the depressed, the gladness of young and old. Flowers should burst into beauty at our steps, songs should overflow in our paths, and innocent laughter should be our accompaniment. The mountains and the hills should break forth before us into singing, and all the trees of the field should clap their hands. Instead of the thorn should come up the fir-tree, and instead of the briar the myrtle-tree. But to all that is unseemly and unworthy our presence should act as an antiseptic.

A young boy, fresh from his mother's teaching and prayers, was plunged suddenly into a large lawyer's office, where he was articled. At first he was bewildered by his strange surroundings, then the crimson mantled his cheek, and tears brimmed in his eyes. "What's the matter with you, youngster?" said a coarse voice. "Do you want to go back to your mother's apron-strings?" "No," was the reply, "but we never said such things in my mother's home as you say here." The answer elicited a burst of laughter, but the head of the office said: "Gentlemen, this lad is right, and as long as he stays with us I must request that you modify your speech." And from that moment the whole tone of that office was altered. The lad's presence acted as salt.

We may easily lose our savor. Salt left in contact with a damp soil ceases to be salty, and is good for nothing but to be trodden under foot. It is neither fit for the ground nor the dunghill. Lot lost his savor. Sodom went on its way, regardless of his presence in its midst. The Seven Churches of Asia lost their savor, and, with those of Northern Africa, were trodden down by the Moslem.

Nothing is so useless and worthless as an inconsistent and powerless Christian (Ezek. 15:3–5). Oh, break your heart if sin is as shameless and reckless in your presence as in your absence! What have you done to forfeit the power you should exert? Repent, and do the first works! Yea, ask the Lord Jesus to infuse into you His own strong, sweet, pure nature, before whom the demons were driven forth, and by whose presence, through His Church in the world, an arrest has been placed on many of those grosser forms of sin which disgraced the world of His time, and still hold sway in countries where His name is not known.

CHAPTER SEVENTEEN

Simplicity in Speech

Matthew 5:33–37

Speech! What is it? The vibration of the air set in motion by vocal chord, tongue, and lip. Apparently mechanical, yet how spiritual. Enriched from the voices of nature, the dash of the breaker, the murmur of the breeze, the song of the bird, and cry of beast, yet in its original fountains the evident gift of the Creator.

Speech is the utterance of the soul, and more, because the soul dyes and impregnates speech with its emotions and inspirations, so that they are communicated to others as by spiritual magnetism. Even when the words themselves are unintelligible we catch the divine afflatus, or our steps are quickened by the clarion appeal.

God spake, and the visible creation emerged from the realm of thought into realized fact. By speech the Law was promulgated from Sinai; and by speech He who spake as never man spake, and who was the Word of God incarnate, left us thoughts that can never die. Speech has burned with the vehemence of Demosthenes, flashed with the eloquence of Cicero, trembled with the pathos of Chrysostom, thundered with the emphasis of Luther, rung with the high note of Pitt, glittered with the brilliance of Sheridan, and poured like a torrent from the lips of Burke. What a wonderful gift is this of human speech. To what heights it may rise, to what depths descend. "Therewith bless we the Lord and Father, and therewith curse we men, which are made after the likeness of God. Out of the same fountain proceeds sweet water and bitter."

Noble Speech

The noblest form of speech is the reflection in simple and natural words of great and good thoughts which have been occupying the speaker's mind. Then language becomes strong in its simplicity and majestic in its unadorned truth. There is small need for nicely-balanced sentences or highly-flavored speech when the soul of patriot, orator, or preacher is aglow with exalted and inspiring conceptions. The volcanic fires that are burning within vent themselves in burning syllables, which plough their way into the hearts of men. When the speaker is deeply moved, his manuscript is crumpled in his hand, the precise words which he had carefully prepared are forgotten, and he makes a fresh way for himself in words that leap red-hot and alive from his lips.

The yeas and nays of Christ have been sufficient to revolutionize the ages, not because of their eloquence (as judged by human standards), but because they are weighted with the wisdom and life of God. Terse, unadorned, and simple sentences—such, for instance, as Abraham Lincoln was wont to utter—are sufficient when far-reaching and profound principles of personal conduct or public policy have to be announced.

If then we would obey this command

of our Lord as to speech, and confine ourselves to pure and simple language, we must begin to think more deeply, to love more tenderly, to cultivate our souls to nobler issues, and to amass spiritual treasure. We can safely leave our words to take care of themselves if our inner life is pure, and sweet, and strong. Let us only imbibe our Master's spirit, and love God first and our neighbors as ourselves—then from the pure fountain will flow pellucid streams like those that issue from the throne of God and of the Lamb.

Extravagant Language

It must, however, be sorrowfully confessed that for the most part the thinking of ourselves and of others is not of that order. Men are not true, or deep, or unselfish, in their innermost hearts, and they know it and therefore in all ages they have endeavored to atone for the poverty of their thought by the extravagance of their language.

Men are not *true*. To compensate, therefore, for their lack of veracity, and to induce others to think that they were neither lying nor deceiving, they have linked their words with the awful name of God, daring the All-True to step out of His silence to confound them if it were not as they said.

Men are not *profound*. To compensate, therefore, for their lack of deep and original thoughts, and to turn public attention from their threadbare and impoverished souls, they employ extravagant and exaggerated speech, like that with which a frivolous girl of the period is accustomed to express herself when for the first time she stand in the presence of the solemn majesty of the Alps at flush of dawn or under the touch of the silver moon.

Men are not *unselfish*. To compensate, therefore, for their conscious lack of that love which forgets itself in its devotion to the interests of others they will fill their speech with extravagant expressions, which may impress the ear and heart of those that hear them for the first time, but fall vain and insipid on those who know that the love which vaunts itself most passionately is more than likely to be scheming for its personal advantage.

It is common enough for us to hide our nakedness, our untruthfulness, our selfishness, under strong asseverations and protestations, which call in the Supreme Being to witness against us if it be not as we affirm.

God's Silence

The remarkable thing is that God keeps silent. Though His verdict be invoked by the habitual liar and blasphemer who swears that black is white, and calls on God to strike him dead, or in some other way to prove that his words are false, yet Heaven makes no sign. No voice speaks out of the silence; no thunderbolt hurtles through the air; no sign is given that God is not mocked. Indeed it might seem as though God had not heard, or that He was perfectly indifferent.

But such is not the case. There are many examples on record, like that, for instance, of Ananias and Sapphira, where, in answer to some blasphemous appeal, God has interposed to vindicate the truth which had been shamefully misstated. God is not indifferent. He is not careless of the interest of truth and righteousness. He hides Himself under the slow working of immutable laws. But He is never appealed to without sooner or later answering the appeal, vindicating innocence and exposing the liar and the profane. With slow, silent, and inexorable precision the divine government deals with all exaggerations, lies, and blasphemies, showing their hollowness, exposing their futility, and casting them up on the beach of the universe, to the derision of all pure and righteous souls.

In order to avoid using the name of God in their protestations, men have introduced into their speech expressions which, in fact, derived all the significance they possessed from their association with Him. It has been a mean subterfuge. They have not liked to say, *By God,* or *By the life of God,* and therefore they have substituted the phrase, *By Heaven.* They have scrupled to say, *May God strike me dead if I lie,* and therefore they have slightly modified their speech, and said, *By my life,* or *By my head,* though they know perfectly well that life and death are ultimately only at the disposal of the Almighty.

In our own speech we inherit some of these subterfuges, and apparently employ them without thought.

"Zounds," is a contraction of "By the wounds of Christ."

"My dear," or *"Dear me,"* is an English form of the Italian, *Dia mia,* my goddess.

"Good gracious," or *"My gracious,"* are clearly abbreviations of "My gracious God."

"By Jove" is, of course, the Latin name for divinity.

"Begad" is "By God."

Many similar expressions will occur to the minds of my readers, and they all savor of the attempt to give the impression of solemnity and reliableness to statements which have no other claim for consideration except that they are associated with the awful name and being of God.

No Excuses for Extravagance

The Jews, like all Oriental nations, were especially given to these exple-tives, and sheltered themselves with the excuse that, so long as they did not mention the Divine Being, they might be excused. They said "Thou shalt perform *to the Lord* thine oaths" meant that oaths which were not definitely made to the Lord, or by the invocation of the name of God, were not binding.

Our Lord shows the fallacy of this reasoning. He says that, whatever emphasis the allusions to Heaven, or Jerusalem, or the head, may give to our speech, is derived from their association with God; and that, therefore, if we would avoid the charge of blasphemy, we must cease to interlard our speech with such expressions. They are needless when our hearts are pure and our words sincere; they are objectionable, and worse, when introduced to give a false and unnatural emphasis to our speech.

As the disciples of Jesus, we must avoid, in dress, in expenditure, in our household equipment, whatever savors of extravagance. In all our behavior, as well as in our speech, there must be the simplicity and beauty of Jesus.

Perhaps there is more truth than we would care to admit in the following minute of an old Friends' meeting: "It is the judgment of Friends that we should refrain from having fine tea-tables set with fine china, seeing it is more for sight than service, and it's advised that Friends should not have so much china or earthenware sett on their mantel-pieces or on their chests of drawers, but rather sett them in their closets until they have occasion to use them. And we desire an alteration in those things that Truth's testimony is gone out against, viz., the Friends' gowns made indecently, one part over long and the other too short, with lead in the sleeves, and that Friends should come to a stability and be satisfied in the shape and compas that Truth leads into without changing as the world changes, all so that Friends' cloaths may be of a decent modest colour, not hair cut or powdered, and neither coives to be made with gathers on the forehead, bordering on the fashion of the world."

Swear Not at All

This prohibition of our Lord, "Swear not at all," does not, in my judgment, touch on the subject of taking an oath in a court of law or on the assumption of high office. He is simply dealing with the use of expletives in ordinary speech. In His own trial He did not scruple to be put upon His oath. When the high priest said unto Him, "I adjure Thee by the Living God, that Thou tell us whether Thou be the Christ, the Son of God," Jesus said, "Thou hast said."

And on one solemn occasion the Apostle Paul deliberately called God to witness that he spoke the truth in Christ, "his conscience bearing witness in the Holy Ghost."

It is not admissible that on occasions of high and solemn importance we should bare our heads as we stand before God and solemnly ask Him to stand with us in attesting the truth of the words we speak and the vows we make. But there is a vast difference between this and the incessant and thoughtless appeal to God on every small and frivolous occasion.

Treat God as the Great King

The true and holy soul finds God everywhere and in everything. Heaven above is God's throne; earth beneath, His footstool; Jerusalem, the holy city, the residence of the Great King. Note these closing words—"the Great King." We are reminded of the sublime words

with which the last of the prophets rebuked the lax and slovenly worship of the chosen people: "From the rising of the sun even unto the going down of the same My name is great among the Gentiles; and in every place incense is offered unto My name, and a pure offering, for I am a great King, saith the Lord of hosts, and My Name is terrible among the Gentiles" (Mal. 1:11, 14).

Let us cultivate this thought, that God is not only our Father, but a great King, and with all the familiarity of little children will be mingled reverential awe. Wherever we go we shall recollect the presence of God, and this will prevent us from the spirit which is betrayed into extravagant speech. We shall not dream of using words which come within the scope of our Lord's condemnation when we remember that every word is spoken in the presence of our Judge, and that of every idle word that we may speak we shall be called to give an account.

All harsh judgments of other people, who are God's creatures; all flippant reference to Scripture to spice our conversation, and suggest witticisms and conundrums; all light remarks on God's dealings with men, as in a book once published, called "The Comic History of England"; all trifling with sacred subjects, or exposing them to ridicule—will be impossible to those who invest them with the thought that God is great, and greatly to be feared, and to be had in reverence by all that are about Him.

The reverent use of the Day of God; the entrance with devout and sacred thoughts into His House; the wary and careful participation in the Lord's Supper; the loving handling of Scripture, and even of the Book which contains it; the honor with which parent and friend, old and young, are treated—all these admirable and beautiful traits, so necessary to the perfecting of character, are due to the same origin and source. When God is treated as the Great King, the whole life falls into symmetry and order, and becomes a prolonged *Yea* to truth, a profound *Nay* to falsehood and error, to the glory of Him who is God's Yea and Amen to all the needs of the human soul.

CHAPTER EIGHTEEN

The Second Mile

Matthew 5:38–42

It is the second mile that tests our character. About the first there is no controversy. We must traverse it whether we will or not.

Our Lord refers to the usage of the East in the transmission of the royal messages. They are carried forward by relays of messengers, much in the fashion of the Fiery Cross in the Highlands, as Sir Walter Scott describes it in "The Lady of the Lake." But the messengers were pressed men, *i.e.*, each village or township was bound to forward the message to the next, and the first man that was happened on, however pressing his own business, was obliged to afford the use of his horses or mules, and go forward with the royal courier, giving him a mount and accompanying him.

In the same way emergencies are continually happening to us all. We leave our homes in the morning not expecting any demand for help or any other circumstance to interfere with the regular routine of the day's engage meets; and then, all suddenly and unexpectedly, there are the sounds of horses' hoofs. A great demand has burst in on our lives, and we are obliged to go off in a direction which we never contemplated. We have no option. We are compelled to go one mile, and then the question will arise: Now you have performed what you were bound to perform, and given what any other man would have given, what are you going to do? The next mile is of prime necessity; it is in your option to go or not to go, and your action will

determine whether or not you have entered into the inner heart of Christ, and are His disciple, not in word only, but "in deed and in truth."

What as to the *left* cheek? That the right should have been struck is an incident which has happened to you altogether apart from your choice. It does not reveal your character in one way or the other, but your behavior with respect to the left cheek will show immediately what you are.

What as to your *cloak?* Apparently your creditor can claim your tunic, and there is no merit in giving this up—any must have done as much; but when that is gone, what will you do about your cloak? This is the test of what you really are.

Does Our Lord Mean That We Should Do Literally as He Says?

Are we really to go the second mile, and turn the left cheek, and let our cloak go in the wake of our coat? These questions have been asked all along the ages, and answered as we answer them still. Each questioner must be fully persuaded in his own mind; and according to your faith, so it will be done unto you.

Many saintly souls have yielded a literal obedience to these precepts. It is recorded of the eccentric but devoted Billy Bray that in going down into the pit, shortly after his remarkable conversion, an old companion gave him a stinging blow on the cheek. "Take that," he said, "for turning Methodist." In former times such an insult would never have been attempted, for the whole country knew that Billy Bray was an inveterate pugilist. All the answer that he gave, however, was, "The Lord forgive thee, lad, as I do, and bring thee to a better mind; I'll pray for thee." Three or four days after his assailant came to him under the deepest conviction of sin and asked his forgiveness.

The head of the constabulary in a great district in India told me that when he became a Christian he found it necessary to withdraw from the Gymkana (which is the European club and society rendezvous in most Indian cities), and his action in this matter aroused very strong feeling against him amongst his former associates. One day, as he was driving on the high-road, a well-known society man, driving past him in the other direction, rose up in his dog-cart and cut at him a tremendous blow with his whip, saying as he swore, "Take that, you. . . ." My friend, who is a very powerful man and of commanding presence, took it quietly, waited his opportunity of doing this man a kindness, and I believe it was the means of his conversion also.

In connection with a missionary society working among the tribes on the Congo, in which I am deeply interested, one of the missionaries resolved that he would teach a literal obedience to these words of our Lord, lest any evasion of them might lessen their authority over the hearts and lives of His people. His hearers were greatly interested and excited, and were not slow in putting the missionary to the test. On one memorable day they gathered around his house, and began asking for the articles which excited their cupidity, and which he had brought at such cost from home. In an hour or two his house was literally stripped, and his wife and he betook themselves to prayer, for, of course, it is impossible for Europeans to live in that climate without many accessories which are needless for the natives. But, in the evening, under the shadow of the night, one after another stole back bringing the articles which he had taken away, and confessing that it was impossible to retain it in his possession, because of the burden which had come upon his heart.

Many such instances are probably occurring every day, and compel us to believe that there is a range of laws which should govern our dealings with our fellows, and which are only unfolded to those who live not by sight, but by faith in the Son of God. Faith has been called the sixth sense, and lays its hands on a third keyboard of the great organ of existence.

Far be it from us, therefore, to judge any who feel it to be their duty to obey these words of the Master in all literality.

How Do We Apply His Words?

But even if to be taken literally there must be some reserves. For instance, when our Lord says, *Resist not evil*, it is impossible to apply His words universally. Suppose, for instance, as we pass along a road, we encounter a brutal man grossly maltreating a woman or a little child, or a gang of roughs assaulting a fellow traveler, it cannot be that we are forbidden to resist the wrongdoer to utmost of our power. The whole machinery of the eternal and invisible world is continually being called into requisition to succor us against "foul fiends," as Spencer puts it, and surely we may do much in these scenes of human existence. Clearly our Lord only forbids us to strike for purposes of private retaliation and revenge; we are not to be avengers in our personal quarrels, we are to guard against taking the law into our own hands lest our passion should drift us outside the warm zone of the love of God.

It is the *personal* element in the resistance of wrong that our Lord forbids; but He would surely never arrest the soldier, policeman, or even the private citizen, from stopping, so far as possible, deeds of wrong and acts of criminal assault. If thieves break into your home, or wicked men should try to injure wife or child; or you should come on some poor Jew who is set on by robbers which strip him of his property, and beat him almost to death, you are bound to interfere with a prayer to God that He would succor you.

And when the wrong has been done, as the Lord teaches us by His own behavior, we may reprimand and remonstrate and appeal to the conscience and heart. When one of the officers of the court struck Jesus with his hand, Jesus answered him, "If I have spoken evil, bear witness of the evil; but if well, why smitest thou Me?" But there we must stop. We must not say in our heart, "I will be even with thee, and give thee as much as thou hast given me."

It is equally our duty, as it seems to me, to take measures to arrest and punish the wrongdoer. Supposing that a man has wronged you, and that you have good reason to believe that he is systematically wronging others; if you have an opportunity of having him punished, you are absolutely obliged, as it seems to me, to take such action against him as will make it impossible for him to pursue his career of depredation. If your lot should be cast in a mining-camp in the Far West, which was dominated by some swaggering ruffian, and he assaulted you, I do not think that you would be contravening the law of Christ if you were to give him so strong a

handling that his power for evil would be arrested from that hour.

It being clearly understood that you put out of your heart all private revenge, all personal malice, and are living in a land where it is impossible to bring the wrongdoer before judge or jury, you may be compelled to act in a judicial capacity, doing for society what society could not do through its legalized officers and methods. Expostulation, argument, appeals to reason, might be employed first; but if these failed there would be necessity to use the only other argument that might be available.

It is clear, also, that we cannot literally obey the Lord's injunction to give to everyone that asks. Else the world would become full of sturdy beggars, who lived on the hard-earned wages of the thrifty. And this would result in the undoing of society, and of the beggars themselves. Does God give to all who ask Him? Does He not often turn aside from the borrower? He knows what will hurt or help us; knows that to many an entreaty His kindest answer is a rebuff; knows that if He were to give us all we ask we should repent of having asked so soon as we awoke in the light of eternity.

So when the drunkard or the drone asks me for money I steadfastly refuse. It is even our duty not to give money indiscriminately, and without full acquaintance with the applicant and his circumstances, for we may be giving him the means of forging more tightly the fetters by which he is bound to his sins. A piece of bread is the most we may bestow upon the mendicant until we have some knowledge of his character, his mode of life, and his real intentions. If only Christian people would resist the impulse to give money to beggars of all kinds, and reserve themselves for the more modest poor who suffer without making appeals, how much of the evil and sorrow of our time would be remedied!

What Does the Lord Require of Us?

(1) *Do not take the law into your own hands.* In the old Mosaic legislation it was enacted that as a man had done, so it should be done to him. "Eye for eye, tooth for tooth"—"hand for hand, foot for foot, burning for burning, wound for wound, strife for strife" (Exod. 21:24, 25). But in the time of our Lord this had been interpreted as conferring on a man the right to retaliation and revenge. The Jews conveniently ignored Leviticus 19:17, 18, which expressly forbade the private infliction of punishment.

When we are wronged we must refer the wrong to the great organized society of which we are part. Society will lay its hand on the wrongdoer. The judge who sits on the bench is not an individual, but the embodiment of society, the representative of law and order; and if he condemns a fellow-creature to penal servitude for life there is no kind of malice or vindictive feeling in his breast.

(2) *Turn retaliation into redemption.* When struck on the cheek the instant impulse of the natural man is to strike back on the cheek of the smiler. There should be a second blow. But the Master says if there be a second blow, let it fall on your other cheek. Instead of inflicting it, suffer it. Instead of avenging yourself on the wrongdoer, compel yourself to suffer a second blow, in the hope that when you oppose your uncomplaining patience to his brutality you may effect his redemption. The first blow was of his malice, the second blow will be of your love, and this will set new looms at work within his heart, weaving the fabric of a new life.

Thus the wrongs that men have done to God led Him to present the other cheek to them, when He sent them His only begotten Son, who, when He was reviled, reviled not again; when He suffered, He threatened not, but committed Himself to Him that judgeth righteously. The patient sufferings of our Lord have melted the hearts of men; and, as in His case, so in a lesser extent it will be in ours.

(3) *Be large-hearted.* "Freely ye have received, freely give." Do not be stingy and niggard in your behavior towards men. You are obliged to yield the coat, give the cloak; you are compelled to go for one mile at least, now, out of sincere desire to serve the purposes of the commonwealth, go another. The law compels you to give your cabman a shilling for two miles; but give him an extra sixpence if you go to the extreme margin of that distance. The law compels you to pay your debts; but if you have incurred them, and they are rightfully due, pay them without haggling.

There are certain duties in the home which fall to our lot to be performed: do them with a smile; *that is the second mile.* The husband must give the needed money to his wife for household expenditure; let him do it without grudging; *that is his second mile.* The employee must render certain services to his employer. If he renders these with a grudging spirit, doing only what he is paid to do, not entering into the spirit of his work, or doing it to the utmost of his power, he is like an impressed laborer, carrying the messages against his will; but as soon as he does his duty with alacrity and eagerness, even staying overtime to finish a piece of necessary service, *that is his second mile.*

(4) *The Master insists that we should cultivate an ungrudging, unstinting, and generous spirit.* "God loveth a cheerful giver." Think of God in His incessant giving. Giving His sun and His rain; giving to the Church and the miser, the thank-

less and heartless, equally as to the loving and prayerful. That is to be our great model. We are to be stars, ever pouring our light on the vault of night; flowers, shedding fragrance, though on the desert air; fountains, though we rise in the lonely places of the world, where only the wild things of nature come to drink. Always giving love and help to this thankless and needy world, because so sure that as we give, we shall get; as we break our barley loaves and small fishes, our hands will be filled, and filled again, out of the storehouses of God. Freely ye have received, freely give; and in what measure ye mete, it shall be measured to you again.

I want to add my testimony to the literal truth of these words. In my life I have found repeatedly that in proportion as I have given I have gotten, and that men have given into my bosom, according to heaven's own measure, pressed down, heaped up, and running over.

For all this we need to have a new baptism of love. The love of God must be poured into our hearts by the Holy Spirit, who is given unto us. We must learn to unite ourselves with our Father's redemptive purpose, looking at the wrong done to us, not so much from our standpoint, but from that of the wrongdoer, with an infinite pity for all the poisonous passion which is filling his heart, and an infinite desire to deliver and save him. One thought for his welfare will thus overmaster all desire for our personal revenge, and we shall heap on his head the hot coals of our love, to melt his heart and save him from himself.

Psalm 23, what Meyer termed "The Psalm of psalms," was so special to Meyer that he devoted an entire volume of exposition to it. He titled it The Shepherd Psalm, *published in 1895.*

In "The Shepherd Lord" Meyer applies the imagery of the psalm to Jesus as our Good Shepherd.

In "The Banquet" Meyer shows how it is not just pastoral imagery which makes this psalm so rich but also its images of our sitting down at the table with our Lord. Ultimately, he finds the fulfillment of this portion of the psalm in the Lord's Supper.

CHAPTER NINETEEN

The Shepherd Lord

The Lord is my Shepherd;
I shall not want (Ps. 23:1).

Three thousand years have passed away since the sweet singer of Israel first sang this psalm about the shepherd care of God. Thirty centuries! It is a long time. And in that vast abyss all the material relics of his life, however carefully treasured, have moldered into dust.

The harp, from the strings of which his fingers swept celestial melody; the tattered banner, which he was wont to uplift in the name of the Lord; the well-worn book of the law, which was his meditation day and night; the huge sword, with which he slew the giant; the palace chamber, from which his spirit passed away to join the harpers harping with their harps—all these lie deep amid the debris of the ages.

But this psalm—though old as the time when Homer sang or Solon gave his laws, and though trodden by the myriads of men in every succeeding age—is as fresh today as though it were just composed. Precious words! They are the first taught to our children, and perhaps the Holy Child Himself first learned to repeat them in the old Hebrew tongue beside His mother's knee in Nazareth; and they are among the last that we whisper in the ear of our beloved ones, standing in the twilight between the darkening day of earth and the breaking day of heaven. The sufferer in the sick-chamber; the martyr at the stake; the soldier on his sentry duty; the traveler amid many perils; the Cove-nanter; the Huguenot; the Vaudois—these, and a multitude which no man can number, have found in these words a lullaby for fear, an inspiration to new life and hope. "The Lord is my Shepherd; I shall not want."

"The Lord"

It is printed in small capital letters, and wherever that is the case we know that it stands for the mystic word JEHOVAH. And so much in awe did the Jews stand of that awful name that they substituted for it some lesser word for God wherever it occurred in their public reading of sacred Scripture. Only once a year was it pronounced, and that on the great Day of Atonement, by the high priest in the most holy place.

Jehovah means the Living One, the self-existent Being, the I AM; He who was and is and is to come, who inhabiteth eternity, who hath life in Himself. All other life, from the aphid on the rose-leaf to the archangel before the throne, is dependent and derived. All others waste and change and grow old; He only is unchangeably the same. All others are fires, which He supplies with fuel; He alone is self-sustained. This mighty being is our Shepherd. Lift up your heart to Him in lowly adoration, and say, "Give ear, O Shepherd of Israel, Thou that leadest Joseph like a flock; Thou that dwellest between the cherubim, shine forth."

But as we travel in thought down the ages we meet a gentle, weary Man on whom the shadow of coming sorrow hangs darkly. He is speaking within a few miles of the spot where these words had been first uttered some twelve hundred years before. Is it treason? Is it blasphemy? Is it the raving of lunacy? No; with all the marks of self-possession and sober truth He takes up these very words, and applying them to Himself, He says, "I AM THE GOOD SHEPHERD."

Combine these two—the august word for the everlasting God and the tender word for the Savior—and we have a worthy title for our Lord, *Jehovah-Jesus.* Let us read it into our psalm, and say, with a new appreciation of its meaning, "Jehovah-Jesus is my Shepherd." What need can we have which may not be met by this twofold nature? As Jehovah He has all power; as Jesus all sympathy. As Jehovah He sustains all worlds; as Jesus He ever liveth to make intercession. As Jehovah He is sovereign Lord of all; as Jesus He still treads the pathways of this world by our side, whispering sweetly and softly in our ears, "Fear not, little flock."

"Shepherd"

That precious word for God was uttered first by Jacob—himself once a shepherd—as he lay a-dying in his hieroglyphed chamber, and with the long thoughts of old age went back to the imagery of his early life, speaking of God as having "shepherded him all his life long." All through the Bible the golden thread runs, until in its closing pages we read of the Lamb who leads His flock to the river of water of life.

The Eastern shepherd occupied quite a unique position toward his flock, and a friendship sprang up between him and the dumb creatures of his care to which there is no counterpart among ourselves. Let us think ourselves into that relationship. In the early morning he would lead his flock from their fold to the pasture-lands. All day he must closely watch, lest harm should come to them from prowling beasts of prey or robber hordes. To the still waters he must lead them, that they may drink where no current shall frighten or endanger them. And at night he must conduct them back to the security of the fold. At a certain season of the year he must lead them yet farther afield, far away from his own home and the haunts of men, where he will live among them, scorched by the heat at noon and drenched by the dews at night.

Should one of the lambs be unable to keep pace with the rest of the flock he must carry it in his bosom. Should one of his flock go astray he must search for it until he finds it, tracking it by the tufts of wool left in the briers and thorns. Should danger assail he must be prepared to risk his life. Shepherds in the East look like warriors armed for fight—the gun slung over the shoulder, pistols at the belt, and club in hand.

Living on such terms, the shepherd and his flock are almost friends. They know him and answer to their names. Some always follow close behind him, as his especial favorites, sure of his love. He can do almost as he wills with any of them, going freely in and out among them without exciting the slightest symptom of alarm.

Now all this is true of our Lord Jesus, that Great Shepherd of the sheep. He has a shepherd's *heart,* beating with pure and generous love that counted not His lifeblood too dear a price to pay down as our ransom. He has a shepherd's *eye,* that takes in the whole flock, and misses not even the poor sheep wandering away on the mountains cold. He has a shepherd's *faithfulness,* which will never fail nor forsake, nor leave us comfortless, nor flee when He seeth the wolf coming. He has a shepherd's *strength,* so that He is well able to deliver us from the jaw of the lion or the paw of the bear. He has a shepherd's *tenderness*—no lamb so tiny that He will not carry it; no saint so weak that He will not gently lead; no soul so faint that He will not give it rest. He pities as a father. He comforts as a mother. His gentleness makes great. He covers us with His feathers, soft and warm and downy; and under His wings do we trust.

Ah, He has done more! "All we like sheep have gone astray; we have turned every one to his own way." Punishment and disaster were imminent; but Jesus, from His throne in eternity, saw the danger and was filled with compassion for the multitudes which were as sheep not having a shepherd. Therefore, because He was the Shepherd, He offered to give His own life as the substitute; and God laid on Him the iniquity of us all. Then was heard the terrible summons, "Awake, O sword, against My Shepherd, and against the Man that is My fellow, saith the Lord of hosts: smite the Shepherd." "He laid down His life for the sheep," and thus redeemed the flock by the blood of the everlasting covenant. Praise Him! Praise Him!

"My"

What a difference comes in with that little word *my!* "The child is dead!" said one of the farm-servants who had carried the sick boy to his mother; "*My* child is dead!" said the mother. "This estate is well known to me; I have trodden every mile of it from childhood," so speaks the gray-headed bailiff; "This is *my* estate," thus speaks the heir.

So in religion the difference between knowledge and appropriation is simply infinite. It makes all the difference between being saved or lost whether you say, "Jesus is a Savior" or "Jesus has saved me"; whether you say, "The Lord is a Shepherd" or "The Lord is *my* Shepherd; I shall not want." Even if, like Thomas, you could see the Savior in the clear light of reality, and have every doubt removed, and His hands offered to your touch, yet it would avail you but little unless you could appropriate Him by saying, "*My* Lord and *my* God."

Jesus waits to be appropriated. He is not content to be a Shepherd, a Good Shepherd, the Shepherd of the holy angels, the Shepherd and Bishop of countless redeemed ones. His travail over you will not be satisfied till you put your hand on Him and say, "*My* Shepherd." And you may do that if you will. There is nothing to hinder you. Do not tarry to inquire if you are one of His sheep; look away from yourself to Him, and see if He be not well qualified to be your Shepherd. And the first cry of "MINE!" on your part will be a certain indication that you are included in that flock which He is leading through many a tangled brake to the one fold of heaven. "The Lord is my Shepherd; I shall not want."

"I Shall Not Want"

Amid all the sorrow and want of the world the Lord's sheep are well supplied. The cry of the worldling is contained in the weary confession. "I perish with hunger." But the boast of the saint rings through the glad assurance, "My God shall supply all your need according to His riches in glory by Christ Jesus." His hired servants have bread enough and to spare; how much more His own! "The young lions do lack, and suffer hunger: but they that seek the Lord shall not want any good thing."

Your experiences may seem to contradict that glad announcement; but perhaps you have not by faith sought and appropriated the supplies which have been placed ready to your hand; or you have not made your requests known unto God with prayer and supplication; or your hour of need has not yet fully come; or you have misunderstood your real need, and are asking for something which would do you harm. In one of these directions you must seek the reason of the apparent disparity between these glad, triumphant words and your experience. For it is true forevermore that "there is no want to them that fear him." He is able to make all grace abound, and He does make all grace abound. To Him be the glory for ever and ever!

Oh, bind this bright assurance to your heart; and whatever perils may menace and threaten you, whatever wants may assail, go forward, stepping out into the dark, encouraging your heart by this sweet refrain: "The Lord is my Shepherd; I shall not want."

CHAPTER TWENTY

The Banquet

Thou preparest a table before me
In the presence of mine enemies (Ps. 23:5).

At first it seems difficult to catch the exact sequence of the psalmist's thought, as he turns from the sheep-cotes to the festal board. And yet the demands of the spiritual life so far transcend all earthly analogies as to demand that more than one metaphor should be employed, one supplying what the other lacks, so that the true conception of our relationship to God may be complete.

Now it is of course very helpful to think of one's self as a sheep, and of Christ as a Shepherd; but there can be no fellowship between the dumb animals and their watchful keeper. The little child that comes from the shepherd's shearing to meet its father has more intimate fellowship with him, though it can hardly articulate its words, than the dumb creatures of his care.

The psalmist, therefore, seems to say, "I am more than Jehovah's sheep; I am Jehovah's guest." It is a mark of great intimacy to sit with a man at his table; in the East it is essentially so. It is not only a means of satisfying hunger, but of intimate and affectionate love. Hence the aggravation of the psalmist's sorrow, as he said, "He that breaketh bread with me is he that lifteth up his heel against me." Nor was it possible for our Lord to give any more touching proof of His love for His wayward follower than to dip a sop and pass it to his hands. Here, then, arises before us a rich theme for meditation while we compare life to a seat at God's banquet-table, eating the things which He has prepared.

We Sit at the Table of God's Daily Providence

Our Heavenly Father has a great family. He is weighted with the concerns of a universe. All sentient things depend upon His sustaining power. Not a seraph cleaves the air but what derives his power of obedience from his sovereign Lord; and not a mote of life floats in the sunbeam, flashing in the light, but it is dependent upon the light and life of the central Sun, before whom angels veil their faces.

And yet, amid all the infinite variety of nature which God is supplying constantly, He is surely most attentive to the needs of those who, in an especial sense, call Him "Our Father." We are His pensioners; nay, better—we are His children! All the stores of His divine provision must fail before He can suffer us to want. He may sometimes keep us waiting until His hour has struck; but just as He will never be one moment too soon, so He will not be a moment too late. He will cause a widow woman to sustain us with the barrel of meal, which, however often scraped, will yield a fresh supply. He will rain bread from heaven, so that man may eat angels' food. He will multiply the slender store of the boy's wallet, so that present need may be met, and stores accumulated for the future.

On a recent Sunday evening a sick member of a congregation, debarred from attending her customary place of worship, intrusted to the hand of the minister a two-shilling piece, which he was to hand to a poor widow known to them both. It so happened that he encountered her slowly making her way to the church, and at once handed to her the coin. But he was hardly prepared for the immediate response: "I did not think that He would have sent it so soon."

On further inquiry he discovered that she had placed her last coin that day in the collection, and was entirely dependent upon such answer as her Heavenly Father might send to her trustful prayer that He would provide for her next meal. Evidently she had been accustomed to close dealings with God, and had learned that His deliverance is timed to arrive "when the morning breaks"—the morning of direst need; the hour when pride and self-sufficiency have expired, but when faith and hope stand expectant at the portals of the soul, looking for the deliverance which cannot be long delayed.

I never shall forget the story of an old man discovered sitting in one of the seats of York Minster, within a short period of closing-time, and who had been sitting there since the early morning, waiting. He had come to the city to find his daughter; but, having missed her, had found himself without friends or food, and with his last coin spent. Not knowing whither to turn, he had found his way into the splendid minster, and had sat there the livelong day; because, as he said, he thought the likeliest place to find his Father's table was in his Father's house. Need I add that his need was fully satisfied?

God's children seem to think that they are no better off than men of the world. And according to their faith, so it is done unto them. If we do not exercise faith and claim God's provisions, ought we to be surprised when we do not receive them? If, on the other hand, we would dare to put our finger upon His promises, which bind Him to meet His children's need, though the young lions lack and suffer hunger, we should find that our God would be equal to all our emergencies, and that not one good thing would fail of all His promises.

When men indicate certain cases in which God's children have pined to death, it is always wise to inquire whether they were living in believing fellowship with Him, and whether they had claimed the fulfillment of His specific pledges. It is very unbecoming, to say the least, that God's children should be as fretful about their daily bread, supposing they are using all lawful methods to obtain it, as the children of men. Was it not with a tone of reproach that our Lord said, "After all these things do the Gentiles seek"? What could be more assuring than His own words, backed by the experience of His own life?—"Your Heavenly Father knoweth that ye have need of all these things."

What would you say if, when schooltime came tomorrow morning, your little boy, before he started with unwilling feet to school, entered your larder and busied himself in examining its contents, with especial reference to your provision for dinner? Would he not legitimately incur your displeasure? Would you not say, "Be off to school, and leave me to care while you are gone!" Would you not rebuke him for his want of simple trust?

Oh that we might learn lessons from our babes, and believe that life is one long residence in one of the mansions of our Father's home; and that the time can never come when the table is quite bare, and when there is nothing for our need! He may suffer you to hunger, because there are some devils which will only go forth by prayer and fasting; but, sooner or later, His angel will touch you, saying, "Arise and eat"; and on the desert floor you will find, spread by angel hands, a banquet, though it be nothing more than a cruse of water at your head, and cakes baked on the hot stones of the wilderness, for your repast.

God Also Prepares the Table of Spiritual Refreshment

Can we ever forget that episode—among the most charming incidents in the forty days—in which, as the weary fishers emerged with empty boats from a long, toilsome night, they found a banquet spread for them, by the tender thoughtfulness of their Lord, upon the strand of the lake? As soon as they touched land they saw a fire of coals, and fish laid thereon, and bread. And is not this an emblem of our Lord's perpetual treatment of His children? Tired, disappointed with fruitless toils, agitated by conflicting hopes and fears, we often pull to the shore trodden by His blessed feet; nor do we ever approach Him without finding that He has anticipated our spiritual requirements, and that "His flesh is meat indeed, and His blood drink indeed."

Writing to the Corinthian Christians, the Apostle Paul said that, inasmuch as Christ had been slain as our Passover Lamb, we must imitate the children of Israel, who, with closed doors and girded loins and sandaled feet, stood around the table eating of the flesh of the lamb, whose blood on the exterior of their houses demanded their deliverance. "Christ our Passover is sacrificed for us: therefore let us keep the feast."

The life of the church between the first and second advents is symbolized by the feast on that memorable night. With joy in our voices and triumph in our mien, we stand around the table where Christ's flesh is the nourishment of all true hearts, straining our ear for the first clarion notes which will tell that the time of our exodus has come. Christian people are very much too thoughtless of the necessity of feeding off God's table for the nourishment of spiritual life. There is plenty of work being done; much attendance at conferences and special missions; diligent reading of religious books; but there is a great and fatal lack of the holy meditation upon the person, the words, and the work of the Lord Jesus Christ.

Will each reader of these lines stay here for a moment and ask if he knows anything of the interior life of meditation which is ever deriving fresh sustenance from a consideration of the Lord?

It was only the other day that I was rebuked by the habit of a well-known Roman Catholic bishop of whom it is said: "The first point of his rule was early rising, which he faithfully practiced to the last day of his life, and often recommended to others. He was the first on foot at his palace, and began his prayers and meditation between four and five o'clock in the morning, and never spent less at them than an hour. He often did this with his memoranda in his hand, so as to recall past graces and thus rekindle the flame. Nor did it seem as if any hour passed in his crowded and stirring life without by some direct act refreshing his soul by communion with God."

And, in addition to this daily practice, he set apart one or two weeks in every year that he might quietly meditate more patiently upon the great mysteries of redemption. This is what he said: "One must, by constant meditation on the great mysteries of incarnation and the redemption, plunge one's self more and more in the love of God, which is the greatest grace of one's life. I will occupy myself more and more with our Lord, with His earthly and divine life, with His hidden, suffering, and glorious life. May my own be hidden in God in Jesus Christ!"

We May Specially Apply These Words Also to the Table of the Lord's Supper

This is emphatically a table which God has prepared; which not only perpetuates the memory of the night in which our Lord was betrayed, but which enables us to raise our wandering thoughts, and to fix them on Him where He is now seated. There is no mystic change made in the bread or in the wine. The bread remains bread, and the wine wine, to the end of the simple feast; and yet, at the moment of partaking of these elements, the pious heart does realize that, by its faith and holy thought, a distinct blessing is communicated to its invigoration and comfort. It is well, of course, at that solemn moment to recall the agony and bloody sweat, the cross and passion, the precious death and burial; but it is equally incumbent to look through the azure depths and to follow the Master through their parted folds, so as to feed upon His resurrection life and to participate in the perpetual Easter-tide of His existence.

It is very helpful, where possible, to communicate at least once a week, that we may clearly learn to lift all life to the level of the Lord's table, to be at every meal as at a sacrament, and to use all the emblems of nature as means of holy fellowship with Him. How can we enough thank God that in this sense also He has prepared a table before us?

There is much comfort in the three words "prepared for me," because it would seem to indicate the *anticipatory care of God*. He does not allow us to be taken by surprise. He does not let His children ask for anything the need of which He has not foreseen. Just as He has prepared beforehand the good works in which we are to walk, so has He prepared beforehand the food by which His workers shall be nourished.

All our life's path is lined by cairns beneath which our Forerunner has placed the victuals which we shall require. "Thou presentest me with the blessings of Thy goodness." The table is spread before the hunger comes. The spring is bubbling in the shade before mother and child sink fainting on the sand. The angel of the Lord's host has not only taken possession of the hostile country, but has provided of the old corn of the land. God provisions His castles before they are besieged. "Thou *preparest* a table before me."

That is a very significant addition— *in the presence of mine enemies*. We surely are to understand by it that all around us may stand our opponents— pledged to do us harm; to cut off our supplies; to starve us out. See that ring of hostile faces, darting fierce glances and chafing to rush upon the beleaguered soul!

But they cannot cut off the supplies that come hourly from above. They cannot hinder the angel ministers who spread the table and heap it up, and then form themselves into an inner ring of defense. They may gnash their teeth at the vanity and futility of their rage; but when God elects to feed a soul, fed that soul shall be, though all hell attempt to say it nay! Many a time in David's life he ate his food in quietness and confidence, while Saul's hostile bands swept down the valleys and searched the caves to find him. As it was with David, so it has been often since.

Yes, soul, God bids thee feast; "Eat, O beloved; yea, eat and drink abundantly." The King doth bring thee into His banqueting-house, and His banner over thee is love. Thou shalt eat of the hidden manna, and drink of the secret spring which bubbles up in the beleaguered city, enabling it to defy the encircling lines of its foes. Nor is the time far distant when we shall sit with Christ in His kingdom; and as the far-traveled, footsore brethren of Joseph ate with the prince who once lay in the pit, so shall we sit down at the prepared table of the marriage supper, and Christ will gird Himself and come forth to serve us, and the festivities of an eternity, which shall never know penury or want, shall obliterate the memory of the sorrows of time.

Meyer's 1890 Abraham: or, The Obedience of Faith *is one of many works Meyer devoted to the lives of the heroes of the Bible.*

"He Obeyed," the title of one of the selections, is a phrase which epitomizes the life of Abraham. Meyer shows that although Abraham's obedience was only partial at first, it finally became complete.

"Gathered to His People," the final chapter, is a summary of Abraham's life of faith which Meyer has sketched in the entire volume. Meyer presents his summary in a unique and effective way: he tests Abraham's faith (and ours along with Abraham's) by comparing its fruits to those catalogued in 2 Peter.

CHAPTER TWENTY-ONE

He Obeyed

*By faith Abraham, when he was called to go out into a place which he should
after receive for an inheritance, obeyed* (Heb. 11:8).

Ah, how much there is in those
two words! Blessedness in heart, and
home, and life; fulfilled promises;
mighty opportunities of good—lie along
the narrow, thorn-set path of obedience
to the word and will of God. If Abraham
had permanently refused obedience to
the voice that summoned him to sally
forth on his long and lonely pilgrimage,
he would have sunk back into the obscurity
of an unknown grave in the land of
Ur, like many an Eastern sheikh before
and since. So does the phosphorescent
wave flash for a moment in the wake of
the vessel ploughing her way by night
through the southern seas; and then it
is lost to sight for ever. But, thank God,
Abraham obeyed, and in that act laid the
foundation-stone of the noble structure
of his life.

It may be that some will read these
words whose lives have been a disappointment,
and a sad surprise; like some
young fruit-tree, laden in spring with
blossom, but which, in the golden autumn
stands barren and alone amid the
abundant fruitage of the orchard. You
have not done what you expected to do.
You have not fulfilled the prognostications
of your friends. You have failed to
realize the early promise of your life.
And may not the reason lie in this, that
away back in your life, there rang out a
command which summoned you to an
act of self-sacrifice from which you
shrank? And *that* has been your one fatal
mistake. The worm at the root of the

gourd. The little rot within the timber.
The false step, which deflected the life-
course from the King's highway into a
blind alley.

Would it not be well to ascertain if
this be not so, and to hasten back to
fulfil even now the long-delayed obedience,
supposing it to be possible? Oh,
do not think that it is now too late to
repair the error of the past; or that the
Almighty God will now refuse, on account
of your delay, that to which He
once summoned you in the young, glad
years, which have taken their flight for
ever. "He is merciful and gracious, slow
to anger, and plenteous in goodness and
truth." Do not use your long delay as
an argument for longer delay, but as a
reason for immediate action. "Why tarriest
thou?"

Abraham, as the story shows, at first
met the call of God with a mingled and
partial obedience; and then for long
years neglected it entirely. But the door
stood still open for him to enter, and that
gracious Hand still beckoned him; until
he struck his tents, and started to cross
the mighty desert with all that owned
his sway. It was a partial failure, which
is pregnant with invaluable lessons for
ourselves.

At First, Then, Abraham's
Obedience Was Only Partial

He took Terah with him; indeed, it is
said that "Terah took Abram his son,

and Lot the son of Haran, and Sarai his daughter-in-law; and they went forth with them from Ur of the Chaldees" (Gen. 11:31). How Terah was induced to leave the land of his choice, and the graves of his dead, where his son Haran slept, we cannot tell. Was Abraham his favorite son, from whom he could not part? Was he dissatisfied with his camping grounds? Or, had he been brought to desire an opportunity of renouncing his idols, and beginning a better life amid healthier surroundings?

We do not know. This, at least, is clear, that he was not whole-hearted; nor were his motives unmixed; and his presence in the march had the disastrous effect of slackening Abraham's pace, and of interposing a parenthesis of years in an obedience which, at first, promised so well. Days which break in sunlight are not always bright throughout; mists, born of earth, ascend and veil the sky: but eventually the sun breaks out again, and, for the remaining hours of daylight, shines in a sky unflecked with cloud. It was so with Abraham.

The clan marched leisurely along the valley of the Euphrates, finding abundance of pasture in its broad alluvial plains, until at last Haran was reached; the point from which caravans for Canaan leave the Euphrates to strike off across the desert. There they halted, and there they stayed till Terah died. Was it that the old man was too weary for further journeyings? Did he like Haran too well to leave it? Did heart and flesh fail, as he looked out on that far expanse of level sand, behind which the sun set in lurid glory every night? In any case, he would go no farther on the pilgrimage, and probably for as many as fifteen years, Abraham's obedience was stayed; and for that period there were no further commands, no additional promises, no hallowed communings between God and His child.

It becomes us to be very careful as to whom we take with us in our pilgrimage. We may make a fair start from our Ur; but if we take Terah with us, we shall not go far. Take care, young pilgrim to eternity, to whom you mate yourself in the marriage-bond. Beware, man of business, lest you find your Terah in the man with whom you are entering into partnership. Let us all beware of that fatal spirit of compromise, which tempts us to tarry where beloved ones bid us to stay. "Do not go to extremes," they cry; "we are willing to accompany you on your pilgrimage, if you will only go as far as Haran! Why think of going farther on a fool's errand—and whither you do not know?" Ah! this is hard to bear, harder far than outward opposition. Weakness and infirmity appeal to our feelings against our better judgment. The plains of Capua do for warriors what the arms of Rome failed to accomplish. And, tempted by the bewitching allurements, which hold out to us their syren attractions, we imitate the sailors of Ulysses, and vow we will go no farther in quest of our distant goal.

"When his father was dead, He removed him into this land" (Acts 7:4). Death had to interpose, to set him free from the deadly incubus which held him fast. Terah must die ere Abraham will resume the forsaken path. Here we may get a solution for mysteries in God's dealings with us, which have long puzzled us; and understand why our hopes have withered, our schemes have miscarried, our income has dwindled, our children have turned against us. All these things were hindering our true development; and, out of mercy to our best interests, God has been compelled to take the knife in hand, and set us at liberty. He loves us so much that He dares to bear the pain of inflicting pain. And thus death opens the door to life, and through the grave we pass into the glad world of hope and promise which lies upon its farther side.

Glory to God, "to God," he saith.
Knowledge by suffering entereth,
And life is perfected through death.

Abraham's Obedience Was Rendered Possible by His Faith

"So Abram departed, as the Lord had spoken unto him. And he took Sarai his wife, and Lot, his brother's son, and all their substance that they had gathered, and the souls that they had gotten in Haran, and they went forth" (Gen. 12:5). No easy matter that! It was bitter to leave the kinsfolk that had gathered around him; for Nahor seems to have followed his old father and brother up the valley to their new settlement at Haran, and we find his family living there afterwards.[1] There was no overcrowding in those ample pastures. And to crown the whole, the pilgrim actually did not know his destination, as he proposed to turn his back on the Euphrates, and his face towards the great desert. Do you not suppose that Nahor would make this the one subject of his attack?

"What do you want more, my brother, which you cannot have here?"

"I want nothing but to do the will of God, wherever it may lead me."

"Look at the dangers: you cannot cross the desert, or go into a new country without arousing the jealousy of some, and the cupidity of others. You would be no match for a troop of robbers, or an army of freebooters."

"But He who bids me go must take all the responsibility of that upon Himself. He will care for us."

"Tell me, only, whither you are going, and where you propose to settle."

"That is a question I cannot answer; for, indeed, you know as much about it as I do myself. But I am sure that if I take one day's march at a time, that will be made clear—and the next—and the next—until at last I am able to settle in the country which God has selected for me somewhere."

This surely was the spirit of many a conversation that must have taken place on the eve of that memorable departure. And the equivalents to our words, "Enthusiast," "Fanatic," "Fool," would be freely passed from mouth to mouth. But Abraham would quietly answer: "God has spoken; God has promised; God will do better for me than ever He has said." At night, as he walked to and fro beneath the stars, he may have sometimes been inclined to give up in despair; but then that sure promise came back again on his memory, and he braced himself to obey. "By FAITH Abraham, when he was called to go out into a place which he should after receive for an inheritance, *obeyed*" (Heb. 11:8). Whither he went, he knew not; it was enough for him to know that he went with God. He leant not so much upon the promise as upon the Promiser: he looked not on the difficulties of his lot—but on the King eternal, immortal, invisible, the only wise God; who had deigned to appoint his course, and would certainly vindicate Himself.

And so the caravan started forth. The camels, heavily laden, attended by their drivers. The vast flocks mingling their bleatings with their drovers' cries. The demonstrative sorrow of Eastern women mingling with the grave farewells of the men. The forebodings in many hearts of imminent danger and prospective disaster. Sarah may even

---

1. Compare Gen. 11:29; 22:20–23; 24:10; 27:43

have been broken down with bitter regrets. But Abraham faltered not. He staggered not through unbelief. He "knew whom he had believed, and was persuaded that He was able to keep that which he had committed to Him against that day." "He was fully persuaded that what God had promised, He was able also to perform."

Moreover, the sacred writer tells us that already some glimpses of the "city which hath foundations," and of the "better country, the heavenly," had loomed upon his vision; and that fair vision had loosened his hold upon much which otherwise would have fascinated and fastened him.

Ah, glorious faith! this is thy work, these are the possibilities!—contentment to sail with sealed orders, because of unwavering confidence in the love and wisdom of the Lord High Admiral: willinghood to arise up, leave all, and follow Christ, because of the glad assurance that earth's best cannot bear comparison with heaven's least.

Abraham's Obedience Was Finally Very Complete

"They went forth to go into the land of Canaan, *and into the land of Canaan they came*" (Gen. 12:5). For many days after leaving Haran, the eye would sweep a vast monotonous waste, broken by the scantiest vegetation; the camels treading the soft sand beneath their spreading, spongy feet; and the flocks finding but scanty nutriment on the coarse, sparse grass.

At one point only would be travellers arrest their course. In the oasis, where Damascus stands today, it stood then, furnishing a welcome resting-place to weary travellers over the waste. A village near Damascus is still called by the patriarch's name. And Josephus tells us that in his time a suburb of Damascus was called "the habitation of Abraham." And there is surely a trace of his slight sojourn there in the name of his favorite and most trusted servant, Eliezer of Damascus, of whom we shall read anon.

But Abraham would not stay here. The luxuriance and beauty of the place were very attractive; but he could not feel that it was God's choice for him. And, therefore, ere long he was again on the southern track, to reach Canaan as soon as he could. Our one aim in life must ever be to follow the will of God, and to walk in those ways in the which He has pre-ordained for us to walk. Many a Damascus oasis, where ice-cold waters descending from mountain ranges spread through the fevered air a delicious coolness, and temper the scorching heat by abundant verdure, tempts us to tarry. Many a Peter, well-meaning but mistaken, lays his hand on us, saying, "This shall not be unto thee: spare thyself." Many a conspirator within the heart counsels a general mutiny against the lonely, desolate will. And it is well when the pilgrim of eternity refuses to stay short, in any particular, of perfect consecration and obedience to the extreme demands of God. When you go forth to go into the land of Canaan, do not rest until into the land of Canaan you come. Anything short of complete obedience nullifies all that has been done. The Lord Jesus must have all or none; and His demands must be fulfilled up to the hilt. But they are not grievous.

What a glorious testimony was that which our Master uttered when He said, "The Father hath not left Me alone; for I do always those things that please Him." Would that it might be true of each of us! Let us henceforth give to Christ our prompt and unlimited obedience; sure that, even if He bids us ride into the valley of death, it is through no blunder or mistake, but out of some sheer necessity, which forbids Him to treat us otherwise and which He will ere long satisfactorily explain.

Ours not to make reply,
Ours not to reason why,
Ours but to do and die.

CHAPTER TWENTY-TWO

Gathered to His People

These are the days of the years of Abraham's life which he lived; an hundred, threescore, and fifteen years. Then Abraham gave up the ghost, and died in a good old age, an old man, and full of years; and was gathered to his people (Gen. 25:8).

No human name can vie with Abraham's for the widespread reverence which it has evoked amongst all races and throughout all time. The pious Jew looked forward to reposing, after death, in the bosom of father Abraham. The fact of descent from him was counted by thousands sufficient to secure them a passport into heaven. Apostles so opposite as Paul and James united in commending his example to the imitation of primitive Christians, in an age which had seen the Lord Jesus Himself. The medieval Church canonized Abraham alone among Old Testament worthies, by no decree, but by popular consent. Devout Mohammedans reverence his name as second only to that of their prophet. What was the secret of this widespread renown? It is not because he headed one of the greatest movements of the human family; nor yet because he evinced manly and intellectual vigor; nor because he possessed vast wealth. It was rather the remarkable nobility and grandeur of his religious life that has made him the object of veneration to all generations of mankind.

At the basis of his character was a mighty Faith.—"Abraham believed God." In that faith he left his native land, and travelled to one which was promised, but not clearly indicated. In that faith he felt able to let Lot choose the best he could for himself; because he was sure that none could do better for himself than God was prepared to do for the one who trusted Him. In that faith he waited through long years, sure that God would give him the promised child. In that faith he lived a nomad life, dwelling in tents, and making no attempt to return to the settled country from which he had come out. Indeed, his soul was consumed with the passionate expectancy of the city of God. In that faith he was prepared to offer Isaac, and buried Sarah.

Do not suppose that his faith dwelt alone. On the contrary, it bore much fruit; for if we test him by those catalogues of the fruits of faith which are provided in the New Testament, we shall find that he manifested them each and all. Take, for instance, that chain of linked graces enumerated in the second epistle by the apostle Peter; a kind of golden ladder, stretched across the chasm between heaven and earth, and uniting them.

To Faith he added Virtue, or Manly Courage.—What could have been more manly than the speed with which he armed his trained servants; or than the heroism with which he, with a train of undisciplined shepherds, broke on the disciplined bands of Assyria, driving them before him as the chaff before the whirlwind, and returning victorious down the long valley of the Jordan?

And to Manly Courage he added Knowledge.—All his life he was a student in God's college of divinity. Year by year fresh revelations of the character and attributes of God broke upon his soul. He grew in the knowledge of God and the divine nature, which at the first had been to him a *terra incognita.* An unknown country grew beneath his gaze; as he climbed through the years into closer fellowship with God, and from the summit looked down upon its lengths and breadths, its depths and heights, its oceans, mountain-range, and plains.

And to Knowledge he added Temperance, or Self-Control.—That he was master of himself is evident from the way in which he repelled the offer of the King of Sodom; and curbed his spirit amid the irritations caused by Lot's herdsmen. The strongest spirits are those which have the strongest hand upon themselves, and are able, therefore, to do things which weaker men would fail in. There is no type of character more splendid than that of the man who is master of himself, because he is the servant of God; and who can rule others rightly because he can rule himself well.

And to Temperance, Patience.—Speaking of him, the voice of New Testament inspiration affirms that he "patiently endured" (Heb. 6:15). No ordinary patience was that which waited through the long years, not murmuring or complaining, but prepared to abide God's time; weaned from the breasts of earthly consolation and help, and quieted after the manner of the Psalmist who said, "I have quieted myself as a child that is weaned of his mother: my soul is even as a weaned child. Let Israel hope in the Lord from henceforth and for ever" (Ps. 131:2, 3).

And to his Patience he added Godliness.—One of his chief characteristics was his piety—a constant sense of the presence of God in his life, and a love and devotion to Him. Wherever he pitched his tent, there his first care was to rear an altar. Shechem, Hebron, Beersheba—alike saw these tokens of his reverence and love. In every time of trouble he turned as naturally to God as a child to its father; and there was such holy intercourse between his spirit and that of God, that the name by which he is now best known throughout the East is "THE FRIEND"—a name which he holds *par excellence,* and which has almost overshadowed the use of that name by which we know him best.

And to Godliness he added Brotherly Kindness.—Some men who are devoted towards God are lacking in the tenderer qualities towards those most closely knit with them in family bonds. Not so was it with Abraham. He was full of affection. Beneath the calm exterior and the erect bearing of the mighty chieftain there beat a warm and affectionate heart. Listen to that passionate cry, "Oh that Ishmael might live before Thee!" Remember God's own testimony to the affection he bore towards Isaac—"Thy son, shine only son, whom thou loves." Abraham's nature therefore may be compared to those ranges of mighty hills, whose summits rear themselves above the region of storms, and hold converse with the skies; while their lower slopes are clothes with woods and meadows, where homesteads nestle and bright children string their necklaces of flowers with merry laughter.

And to Brotherly Kindness he added Charity, or Love.—In his dealings with men he could afford to be generous, open-hearted, open-handed; willing to pay down the large price demanded for Machpelah's cave without haggling or complaint; destitute of petty pride; affable, courteous, able to break out into sunny laughter; right with God, and therefore able to shed upon men the rays of a genial, restful noble heart.

All these things were in him and abounded, and they made him neither barren nor unfruitful; they made his calling and election sure; they prepared for him an abundant entrance into the everlasting kingdom of God our Savior. The thought that underlies the expression in the Greek (πλουσίως ἡ ἔισοδος) is richly significant. The words denote the welcome given by choral songs and joyous greetings to the conqueror who, laden with spoils, returned to his native city; and they indicate that for some favored souls, at least, there is waiting on the threshold of the other world a welcome so exuberant, so boisterous in its unutterable joy, so royally demonstrative, as to resemble that given in all times to those who have conferred great benefits, or who have learned the art of stirring the loyal devotion of their fellows. If such an entrance could be accorded to any one, certainly it would be to Abraham, when, stooping beneath the weight of one hundred threescore and fifteen years, "he gave up the ghost, and died at a good old age, an old man, full of years, and was gathered to his people."

"Abraham gave up the ghost."—there was no reluctance in his death; he did not cling to life—he was glad to be gone; and when the angel-messenger summoned him, without a struggle, nay, with the readiness of glad consent, his spirit returned to God who gave it.

He was gathered to his people.—This cannot refer to his body; for that did not sleep beside his ancestors, but side by side with Sarah's. Surely then it must refer to his spirit. The world's grey fathers knew little of the future; but they felt that there was somewhere a mustering place of their clan, whither devout and holy souls were being gathered, one by one, so that each spirit, as it passed from this world, went to rejoin its people; the people from which it had sprung; the people whose name it bore; the people to which by its tastes and sympathies it was akin.

What a lovely synonym for death! To DIE is to rejoin our people; to pass into a world where the great clan is gathering, welcoming with shouts each new-comer through the shadows. Where are your people? I trust they are God's people; and if so, those that bear your name, standing on the other shore, are more numerous than the handful gathered around you here; many whom you have never known, but who know you; many whom you have loved and lost awhile; many who without you cannot be made perfect in their happiness. There they are, rank on rank, company on company, regiment on regiment, watching for your coming. Be sure you do not disappoint them! But remember, if your people are God's people, you cannot be gathered to them unless first in faith and love you are gathered to Him.

Little doubt had this noble man of the recognition of saintly spirits in the other world; and indeed, it is an untrue conception which has filled the future with strange spirits, unknowing and unknown. Heaven is not a prison with tier on tier of cells; but a HOME. And what is home without the recognition and love of fond hearts? So long as we read of David going to his child; of Paul anticipating the pleasure of meeting again his converts; of the women and disciples being able to recognize the appearance and the love of the Savior amid the glory of the resurrection body—we may be prepared to believe, with the patriarch, that dying is re-union with those to whom in the deepest sense we are related. Spiritual affinities are for all time and for eternity, and will discover themselves through all worlds.

"And his sons, Isaac and Ishmael, bur-

ied him in the cave of Machpelah."— There were great differences between these two. Ishmael, the child of his slave: Isaac, of the wedded wife. Ishmael, the offspring of expediency: Isaac, of promise. Ishmael, wild and masterful, "the wild ass"; strongly marked in his individuality; proud, independent, swift to take an insult, swift to avenge it: Isaac, quiet and retiring, submissive and meek, willing to carry wood, to be kept in the dark, to be bound, to yield up his wells, and to let his wife govern his house. And yet all differences were wiped out in that moment of supreme sorrow; and coming from his desert fastnesses, surrounded by his wild and ruffian freebooters, Ishmael united with the other son of their common father, who had displaced him in his inheritance, and who was so great a contrast to himself; but all differences were smoothed out in that hour.

Many ancient chieftains may have been gathered by that ancient cave, to join in one last act of respect to the mighty prince who had dwelt amongst them for so long. Amid the wail of the women, and the dirge which even to this day tells of sorrow for departed worth in Eastern lands—borne by a band of his trusted retainers, while a vast concourse of the camp stood wrapped in reverent silence around—the remains of the man who had dared to trust God at all costs, and who with pilgrim steps had traversed so many weary miles, were solemnly laid beside the dust of Sarah, his faithful wife. There, in all probability, they rest even to this day, and thence they will be raised at the coming of the King.

Out of materials which were by no means extraordinary, God built up a character with which He could hold fellowship as friend with friend; and a life which has exerted a profound influence on all after-time. It would seem as if He can raise any crop He chooses, when the soil of the heart and life are entirely surrendered to Him. Why should not we henceforth yield ourselves utterly to His divine husbandry, asking Him to fulfill in us the good pleasure of His goodness, and the work of faith with power? Only let us trust Him fully, and obey Him instantly and utterly; and as the years pass by, they shall witness results which shall bring glory to God in the highest, while they fill us with ceaseless praise.

David: Shepherd, Psalmist, King *(1895) is a second example of Meyer's skill in depicting the lives of biblical heroes.*

Meyer studies the origin and temper of David's faith in "The Faith of God's Elect" and shows how that faith which was developed in solitude was able to stand the public tests it faced.

While David is, of course, the focus of Meyer's work, Meyer animates David's intimate friend in "Jonathan" through a careful consideration of Jonathan's character. Meyer is also careful to enumerate the qualities of love and true friendship and shows us how such a friendship can mold character as Jonathan did David.

CHAPTER TWENTY-THREE

The Faith of God's Elect

1 Samuel 17

Who the line
Shall draw, the limits of the power define
That even imperfect faith to man affords?
—Wordsworth

In the valley of Elah today the traveler finds the remains of an immense terebinth. Perhaps this gave it its name, "the valley of the terebinth." Starting from the neighborhood of the ancient city of Hebron, the valley runs in a northwesterly direction toward the sea; it is about a mile across, and in the middle there is a deep ravine, some twenty feet across, with a depth of ten or twelve feet. Winter torrents have made this their track.

Having recovered from the chastisement inflicted on them by Saul and Jonathan at Michmash, the Philistines had marched up the valley of Elah, encamping on its western slope between Shochoh and Ephes-dammim; a name with an ominous meaning—"the boundary of blood"—probably because on more than one occasion it had been the scene of border forays. Saul pitched his camp on the other side of the valley; behind them the Judean hills, ridge on ridge, to the blue distance where Jerusalem lay, as yet in the hands of the Jebusite. That valley was to witness an encounter which brought into fullest contrast the principles on which God's warriors are to contend—not only with flesh and blood, but against the principalities and powers of darkness. Three figures stand out sharply defined on that memorable day.

First, *the Philistine champion.* He was tall—nine feet six inches in height; he was heavily armed, for his armor fell a spoil to Israel, was eagerly examined and minutely described; they even weighed it, and found it five thousand shekels of brass, equivalent to two hundredweight; he was protected by an immense shield, borne by another in front of him, so as to leave his arms and hands free; he wielded a ponderous spear, while sword and javelin were girt to his side; he was apt at braggadocio, talked of the banquet he proposed to give to the fowls and beasts, and defied the armies of the living God.

Second, *Saul*—a choice young man and a goodly. There was not among the children of Israel a goodlier person than he; from his shoulders and upward he was higher than any of the people. He had also a good suit of armor, a helmet of brass, and a coat of mail. In earlier days, when he had blown the trumpet, its notes had run throughout the land, stirring all hearts with anticipations of certain victory. Even now the formula of his former faith and fervor came easily to his lips, as he assured the young shepherd that the Lord would certainly be with him; but he dared not adventure himself in conflict with what he reckoned were utterly overwhelming odds. He was near daunting David with his materialism and unbelief: "Thou art not able to go against this Philistine to fight with him: for thou art but a youth, and he a man of war from his youth."

Third, *David*. He was but a youth, and ruddy, and withal of a fair countenance. No sword was in his hand; he carried a staff—probably his shepherd's crook; no armor had he on, save the breastplate of righteousness and the helmet of salvation; no weapon but a sling in his hand, and five smooth stones, which he had chosen out of the torrent bed, and put in the shepherd's bag which he had, even in his scrip.

But he was in possession of a mystic spiritual power, which the mere spectator might have guessed, but which he might have found it difficult to define. The living God was a reality to him. His countrymen were not simply, as Goliath insinuated, servants to Saul; they were the army of the living God. When he spake of armies, using the plural as of more than one, he may have been thinking of Jacob's vision of the host of angels at Mahanaim; or of Joshua's, when the Angel of the Covenant revealed himself as Captain of the Lord's host that waited unseen under arms, prepared to cooperate with that which Israel's chieftain was about to lead across the Jordan. As likely as not, to the lad's imagination the air was full of horses and chariots of fire; of those angel hosts which in after days he addressed as strong in might, harkening unto the voice of God, and hastening to do his pleasure in all places of his dominion. At least he had no doubt that the Lord would vindicate his glorious name, and deliver into his hands this uncircumcised Philistine.

Let us study the origin and temper of this heroic faith.

It Had Been Born in Secret and Nursed in Solitude

As day after day he considered the heavens and earth, they appeared as one vast tent, in which God dwelt. Nature was the material dwelling place of the eternal Spirit, who was as real to his young heart as the works of his hands to his poet's eyes. God was as real to him as Jesse or his brothers or Saul or Goliath. His soul had so rooted itself in this conception of God's presence that he bore it with him, undisturbed by the shout of the soldiers as they went forth to the battle, and the searching questions addressed to him by Saul.

This is the unfailing secret. There is no short cut to the life of faith, which is the all-vital condition of a holy and victorious life. We must have periods of lonely meditation and fellowship with God. That our souls should have their mountains of fellowship, their valleys of quiet rest beneath the shadow of a great rock, their nights beneath the stars, when darkness has veiled the material and silenced the stir of human life, and has opened the view of the infinite and eternal, is as indispensable as that our bodies should have food. Thus alone can the sense of God's presence become the fixed possession of the soul, enabling it to say repeatedly, with the psalmist, "Thou art near, O God."

It Had Been Exercised in Lonely Conflict

With a beautiful modesty David would probably have kept to himself the story of the lion and the bear, unless it had been extracted from him by a desire to magnify Jehovah. Possibly there had been many conflicts of a similar kind; so that his faith had become strengthened by use, as the sinews of his wiry young body by exertion. In these ways he was being prepared for this supreme conflict.

What we are in solitude we shall be in public. Do not for a moment suppose, O self-indulgent disciple, that the stimulus of a great occasion will dower thee with a heroism of which thou betrayest no trace in secret hours. The crisis will only reveal the true quality and temper of the soul. The flight at the Master's arrest will make it almost needless for the historian to explain that the hour which should have been spent in watching was squandered in sleep. It is the universal testimony of holy men that lonely hours are fullest of temptation. It is in these we must conquer if we would be victorious when the eyes of some great assembly are fastened upon us.

It Stood the Test of Daily Life

There are some who appear to think that the loftiest attainments of the spiritual life are incompatible with the grind of daily toil and the friction of the home. "Emancipate us from these," they cry; "give us nothing to do except to nurse our souls to noble deeds; deliver us from the obligations of family ties, and we will fight for those poor souls who are engrossed with the cares and ties of the ordinary and commonplace."

It was not thus with David. When Jesse, eager to know how it fared with his three older sons, who had followed Saul to the battle, bade David take them rations, and a present to the captain of their division, there was an immediate and ready acquiescence in his father's proposal: "He rose up early in the morning, and took, and went, as Jesse had commanded him." And before he left his flock he was careful to intrust it with a keeper.

We must always watch not to neglect one duty for another; if we are summoned to the camp, we must first see to the tendance of the flock. He that is faithful in the greater must first have been faithful in the least. It is in the home, at the desk, and in the Sunday-school that we are being trained for ser-

vice at home and abroad. We must not forsake the training-ground till we have learned all the lessons God has designed it to teach, and have heard his summons.

It Bore Meekly Misconstruction and Rebuke

Reaching the camp, he found the troops forming in battle array, and ran to the front. He had already discovered his brothers, and saluted them, when he was arrested by the braggart voice of Goliath from across the valley, and saw, to his chagrin, the men of Israel turn to flee, stricken with sore affright. When he expressed surprise, he learned from bystanders that even Saul shared the general panic, and had issued rewards for a champion. So he passed from one group to another of the soldiery, questioning, gathering further confirmation of his first impressions, and evincing everywhere the open-eyed wonder of his soul that "any man's heart should fail because of him."

Eliab had no patience with the words and bearing of his young brother. How dare he suggest that the behavior of the men of Israel was unworthy of themselves and their religion! What did he mean by inquiring so minutely after the particulars of the royal reward? Was he thinking of winning it? It was absurd to talk like that! Of course it could only be talk; but it was amazing to hear it suggested that he too was a soldier and qualified to fight.

Evidently something should be said to thrust him back into his right place, and minimize the effect of his words, and let the bystanders know who and what he was. "Why are thou come down? With whom," he said with a sneer, "hast thou left those few sheep in the wilderness?" Ah, what venom, as of an asp, lay in those few words! David, however, ruled his spirit, and answered softly. "Surely," said he, "my father's wish to learn of your welfare was cause enough to bring me here." It was there that the victory over Goliath was really won. To have lost his temper in this unprovoked assault would have broken the alliance of his soul with God, and drawn a veil over his sense of his presence. But to meet evil with good, and maintain an unbroken composure, not only showed the burnished beauty of his spirit's armor, but cemented his alliance with the Lamb of God.

To bear with unfailing meekness the spiteful attacks of malice and envy; not to be overcome by evil, but to overcome evil with good; to suffer wrong; to possess one's soul in patience; to keep the mouth with a bridle when the wicked is before us; to pass unruffled and composed through a very cyclone of unkindliness and misrepresentation—this is only possible to those in whose breasts the dove-like Spirit has found an abiding-place, and whose hearts are sentineled by the peace of God; and these are they who bear themselves as heroes in the fight. A marvelous exhibition was given that day in the valley of Elah that those who are gentlest under provocation are strongest in the fight, and that meekness is really an attribute of might.

It Withstood the Reasonings of the Flesh

Saul was very eager for David to adopt his armor, though he dared not don it himself. He was taken with the boy's ingenious earnestness, but advised him to adopt the means. "Don't be rash; don't expect a miracle to be wrought. By all means trust God, and go; but be wise. We ought to adopt ordinary precautions."

It was a critical hour. Had David turned aside to act on these suggestions he would certainly have forfeited the divine alliance, which was conditioned by his guileless faith. There is no sin in using means; but they must come second, not first; they must be such as God suggests. It is a sore temptation to adopt them as indicated by the flesh, and hope that God will bless them, instead of waiting before him to know what he would have done, and how. Many a time has the advice of wordly prudence damped the eager aspiration of the spirit, and hindered the doing of a great deed.

But an unseen hand withdrew David from the meshes of temptation. He had already yielded so far to Saul's advice as to have donned his armor and girded on the sword. Then he turned to Saul and said, "I cannot go with these"; and he put them off him. It was not now Saul's armor *and* the Lord, but the Lord alone; and he was able, without hesitation, to accost the giant with the words, "The Lord saveth not with sword and spear."

His faith had been put to the severest tests and was approved. Being more precious than silver or gold, it had been exposed to the most searching ordeal; but the furnace of trial had shown it to be of heavenly temper. Now let Goliath do his worst; he shall know that there is a God in Israel.

CHAPTER TWENTY-FOUR

Jonathan

1 Samuel 28:1

Souls that carry on a blest exchange
Of joys they meet with in their heavenly range,
And with a fearless confidence make known
The sorrows sympathy esteems its own,
Daily derive increasing light and force
From such communion in their pleasant course;
Feel less the journey's roughness and its length;
Meet their opposers with united strength;
And one in heart, in interest and design,
Gird up each other to the race divine.

—Cowper

In heaven's vault there are what are known as binary stars, each probably a sun, with its attendant train of worlds, revolving around a common center, but blending their rays so that they reach the watcher's eye as one clear beam of light. So do twin souls find the center of their orbit in each other; and there is nothing in the annals of human affection nobler than the bond of such a love between two pure, high-minded, and noble men, whose love passes that of women. Such love was celebrated in ancient classic story, and has made the names of Damon and Pythias proverbial. It has also enriched the literature of modern days in the love of a Hallam and a Tennyson. But nowhere is it more fragrant than on the pages that contain the memorials of the love of Jonathan and David.

David was in all probability profoundly influenced by the character of Jonathan, who must have been considerably older than himself. It seems to have been love at first sight. "When David had made an end of speaking unto Saul, the soul of Jonathan was knit with the soul of David, and Jonathan loved him as his own soul." He did not, however, avow it on the spot; but that night, as the young shepherd was sitting amid a group of soldiers, recounting with them the events of the memorable day, a royal messenger may have summoned him to Jonathan's pavilion, on entering which he was amazed to be greeted with the warm embrace of a brotherly affection which was never to wane.

He had lost Eliab in the morning; but at nightfall he had won a friend that would stick closer than a brother. The boy soldier must have shrunk back as unworthy; he must have ruefully looked down at his poor apparel as unbefitting a royal alliance. But all such considerations were swept away before the impetuous rush of Jonathan's affection, as he stripped himself of robe and apparel, of sword and bow and girdle, and gave them all to David. "Then Jonathan and David made a covenant, because he loved him as his own soul."

A True Friend

Consider the qualities of this friend whom Jehovah chose for the molding of the character of his beloved, and then be prepared to surrender to his care the choice of your most intimate associates. He knows what your temperament needs, and where to find the companion who shall strengthen you when weak, and develop latent unknown qualities.

He was every inch a man. In true friendship there must be a similarity of tastes and interests. The prime condition of two men walking together is that they should be agreed. And the bond of a common manliness knit these twin souls from the first. Jonathan was every inch a man; as dexterous with the bow as his friend with his sling. Able to flash with indignation, strong to bear without quailing the brunt of his father's wrath, fearless to espouse the cause of his friends at whatever cost, he was capable of inspiring a single armor-bearer with his own ardent spirit of attacking an army; of turning the tide of invasion; and of securing the admiration and affection of the entire people, who, standing between him and his father, refused to let him die. When Jonathan fell on Gilboa it was no fulsome flattery that led his friend, in his pathetic elegy, to exclaim:

Thy glory, O Israel, is slain upon
  thy high places!
How are the mighty fallen!

He was withal very sensitive and tender. It is the fashion in some quarters to emphasize the qualities supposed to be specially characteristic of men—those of strength, courage, endurance—to the undervaluing of the tenderer graces more often associated with women. But in every true man there must be a touch of woman as there was in the ideal man, the Lord Jesus. In him there is neither male nor female, because there is the symmetrical blending of both; and in us, too, there should be strength and sweetness, courage and sympathy; the oak

and the vine, the rock and the moss that covers it with its soft green mantle.

Jonathan had a marvelous power of affection. He loved David as himself; he was prepared to surrender without a pang his succession to his father's throne, if only he might be next to his friend; his was the love that expresses itself in tender embraces and tears, that must have response from the object of its choice.

I am distressed for thee, my
  brother Jonathan!
Very pleasant has thou been unto
  me:
Thy love to me was wonderful,
Passing the love of women.

We judge a man by his friends, and the admiration he excites in them. Any man whom David loved must have been possessed of many of those traits so conspicuous in David himself. Much is said of the union of opposites, and it is well when one is rich where the other is poor; but the deepest love must be between those whose natures are close akin. As we, therefore, review the love that united these two, now forever joined in the indissoluble bonds of eternity, we must attribute to Jonathan the poetic sensitiveness, the tender emotion, the heroism of that courage, the capacity for those uprisings of the soul to all that was pure and lovely and noble, which were so conspicuous in David.

He was distinctly religious. When first introduced to us, as, accompanied by his armor-bearer, he climbs single-handed to attack the Philistine garrison, strongly entrenched behind rocky crags, he speaks as one familiar with the ways of God, to whom there is no restraint "to save by many or by few"; and when the appointed sign is given it is accepted as a presage of the victory which the Lord is about to give (1 Sam. 14).

As he stands beside his father on the

hillside, and sees the stripling descend to slay Goliath and win a great victory for Israel, he discerns the hand of the Lord working a great victory for Israel, and his soul lifts itself in holy thought and thanksgiving (1 Sam. 19:5).

When the two friends are about to be torn from each other, with little hope of renewing their blessed intercourse, Jonathan finds solace in the fact of the divine appointment, and the Lord being between them. Between them, not in the sense of division, but of connection; as the ocean unites us with distant lands, whose shores she raves, whose freights she bears to our wharves. However far we are parted from those we love, we are intimately near in God, whose presence infills and inwraps us; thus streams mingle in the ocean to which they pour tributary tides.

And when, in the last interview the friends ever had, they met by some secret arrangement in a wood, "Jonathan came to David there, and strengthened his hand in God." All that those words imply it is not easy to write; our hearts interpret the words, and imagine the stream of holy encouragement that poured from that noble spirit into the heart of his friend. He must be strong who would strengthen another; he must have God, and be in God, who would give the consolations of God to his brother; and we can easily understand how the anguish of Jonathan's soul, torn between filial devotion to his father and his love to his friend, must have driven him back on those resources of the divine nature which are the only solace of men whose lives have been cast in the same fiery crucible.

Consider the Conflict of Jonathan's Life

He was devoted to his father. He was always found associated with that strange dark character, melancholy to madness, the prey of evil spirits, and yet so keenly susceptible to music, and so quick to respond to the appeal of chivalry, patriotism, and generous feeling; resembling some mountain lake, alternately mirroring mountains and skies, and swept by dark storms. Father and son were together in life, as they were "undivided in death."

When his father first ascended the throne of Israel the Lord was with him, and Jonathan knew it (1 Sam. 20: 13). It must have been an exceeding delight to him to feel that the claims of the father were identical with the claims of God, and the heart of the young man must have leaped up in a blended loyalty to both. But the fair prospect was soon overcast. The Lord departed from Saul; and immediately his power to hold the kingdom waned, the Philistines invaded his land, his weapons of defense failed him, his people followed him trembling, and Samuel told him that his kingdom could not continue. Then followed that dark day when Saul intruded on the priestly office in offering sacrifice. The ominous sentence was spoken: "The Lord hath sought him a man after his own heart, and the Lord hath appointed him prince unto his own people."

From that moment Saul's course was always downward; but Jonathan clung to him as if he hoped that by his own allegiance to God he might reverse the effects of his father's failure and still hold the kingdom for their race.

At first this was not so difficult. There was no one to divide his heart with his father; it was not, therefore, a hardship for him to imperil his life in unequal conflict with the Philistines; and his heart must have been fired with the gladdest anticipations as, through the woods where honey dropped, he pursued the Philistines, with all Israel at his heel, smiting them from Michmash to Aijalon.

His hopes, however, were destined to

disappointment; for, instead of the revival which he had pictured to himself, he saw his father drifting further down the strong tide that bore him out from God. Saul's failure in the matter of the destruction of the Amalekites, the dark spirit which possessed and terrified him, the alienation of Samuel—these things acted as a moral paralysis on that brave and eager heart. What could he do to reverse the decisions of that fated soul; how stem the torrent; how turn the enemy from the gate?

Surely it was this hopelessness of being able to alter any of these things that made him unable to meet Goliath. Many a time, as he heard the terrible roar of the giant's challenge, he must have felt the uprisings of a noble impulse to meet him, slay him, or die. But there came over his soul the blight of despair. What could he do when the destiny of the land he loved seemed already settled?

When he woke up to find how truly he loved David, a new difficulty entered his life. Not outwardly, because, though Saul eyed David with jealousy, there was no open rupture. David went in and out of the palace, was in a position of trust, and was constantly at hand for the intercourse for which each yearned. But when the flames of hostility, long smoldering in Saul's heart, broke forth, the true anguish of his life began. On the one hand, his duty as son and subject held him to his father, though he knew his father was doomed, and that union with him meant disaster to himself; on the other hand, all his heart cried out for David.

His love for David made him eager to promote reconciliation between his father and his friend. It was only when repeated failure had proved the fruitlessness of his dream that he abandoned it; and then the thought must have suggested itself to him: Why not extricate yourself from this sinking ship while there is time? Why not join your fortunes with his whom God hath chosen? The new fair kingdom of the future is growing up around him—identify yourself with it, though it be against your father.

The temptation was specious and masterful, but it fell blunt and ineffectual at his feet. Stronger than the ties of human love were those of duty, sonship, loyalty to God's anointed king; and in some supreme moment he turned his back on the appeal of his heart, and elected to stand beside his father. From that choice he never flinched. When David departed whither he would, Jonathan went back to the city. His father might sneer at his league with the son of Jesse, but he held his peace; and when finally Saul stated for his last battle with the Philistines, Jonathan fought beside him, though he knew that David was somehow involved in alliance with them.

It was one of the grandest exhibitions of the triumph of principle over passion, of duty over inclination, that the annals of history record. Jonathan died as a hero; not only because of his prowess in battle with his country's foes, but because of his victory over the strongest passion of the human heart, the love of a strong man, in which were blended the strands of a common religion, a common enthusiasm for all that was good and right.

Conflicts like these await us all—when the appointment of God says one thing and the choice of the heart says another; when the wind sets in from one quarter and the tide from the opposite one. Whenever this befalls thee, may God's grace enable thee to follow as straight a course, as true to the loftiest dictates of conscience, as Jonathan, the son of Saul!

Never content with his present state before his Lord, Meyer constantly sought ways to progress into the blessed life. In "Seven Rules for Daily Living," the last meditation found in Light on Life's Duties, *Meyer briefly formulates rules by which earnest Christians may do this. In a sense, inasmuch as "Seven Rules for Daily Living" represents a condensation of Meyer's wisdom, it stands as a summary of his thought.*

CHAPTER TWENTY-FIVE

Seven Rules for Daily Living

These brief and simple words are intended for many earnest Christians who are dissatisfied with their present life, and long to enter that more blessed state of rest and peace of which they catch occasional glimpses; as white-plumaged sea-birds flash for a moment, far away over the breakers, and then are lost to sight.

Now out of my own experience I would suggest these seven rules to my fellow-Christians:

Make a Definite Consecration of Yourselves to God

Dr. Doddridge has left in his diary a very beautiful form of self-consecration. With most it would be sufficient to write out Miss Havergal's hymn, and to sign their names at the foot.

Take my life and let it be
Consecrated, Lord, to Thee.

Take my hands and let them move
At the impulse of They love.

Take my feet and let them be
Swift and beautiful for Thee.

Take my voice and let me sing
Always—only—for my King.

Take my lips and let them be
Filled with messages from Thee.

Take my silver and my gold,
Not a mite would I withhold.

Take my moments and my days,
Let them flow in endless praise.

Take my intellect and use
Every power as Thou shalt
  choose.

Take my will and make it Thine,
It shall be no longer mine.

Take my heart, it is Thine own,
It shall be Thy royal throne.

Take my love, my God, I pour
At Thy feet its treasure store.

Take myself, and I will be
Ever, only, all for Thee.

But in any case it is well to write down some record of the act, to keep for future reference.

Of course when we have really given ourselves once, we can not give ourselves a second time. We may renew the consecration vows, we may review the deed of gift, we may insert any new clauses we like; and if we have gone astray, we may ask the Lord to forgive the foul wrong and robbery which we have done Him, and to restore our souls into the position from which we have fallen. Oh, how sweet the promise, *"He restoreth my soul!"* Dear Christian reader, seek some quiet spot, some still hour, and yield yourself to God.

Tell God That You Are Willing to be Made Willing about All

A lady was once in great difficulties about certain things which she felt eager to keep under her own control. Her friend, wishful to press her into the better life of consecration, placed before her a blank sheet of paper, and pressed her to write her name at the foot, and then to lay it before God in prayer. She did so, and at once entered this blessed life.

Are you willing to do this? Are you prepared to sign your name to a blank sheet of paper and then hand it over to God, for Him to fill in as He please? If not, ask Him to make you willing and able to do this and all things else. You never will be happy until you let the Lord Jesus keep the house of your nature, closely scrutinizing every visitor and admitting only His friends. He must reign. He must have all or none. He must have the key of every closet, of every cupboard, and of every room. Do not try to make them fit for Him. Simply give Him the key. He will cleanse and renovate and make beautiful.

Reckon on Christ to Do His Part Perfectly

Directly you give, He takes. Directly you open the door, He enters. Directly you roll back the floodgates, He pours in a glorious tide of fulness; fulness of wealth, of power, of joy. The clay has only to be plastic to the hand of a Palissy. The marble has only to be pliant to the chisel of a Michael Angelo. The organ has only to be responsive to the slightest touch of a Handel. The student has only to follow the least hint of a Faraday or a Whewell. And there will be no failure in results. Oh, to be equally susceptible to the molding influences of Christ! We shall not fail in realizing the highest ideal of which we are capable, if only we will let Him do His work unhindered.

Confess Sin Instantly

If you allow acid to drop and remain on your steel fenders, it will corrode them; and if you allow sin to remain on your hearts unconfessed, it will eat out all peace and rest.

Do not wait for the evening to come, or until you can get alone, but *there* in the midst of the crowd, in the very rush of life, with the footprints of sin still fresh, lift up your heart to your merciful and ever-present Savior, and say, "Lord Jesus, wash me now from that sin, in they precious blood, and I shall be whiter than snow." The blood of Jesus is ever at work, cleansing us from unconscious sin; but it is our part to apply for it to cleanse from conscious and known sins so soon as we are aware of their presence in our lives.

Hand over to Christ Every Temptation and Care

When you feel temptation approaching you, as a bird by some quick instinct is aware that the hawk is hovering near, then instantly lift your heart to Christ for deliverance. He can not rebuff or fail you. *"He will gather you under His feathers, and under His wings shall you trust."* And when any petty annoyance or heavier worry threatens to mar your peace, in the flash of a moment, hand it over to Jesus, saying, "Lord, I am oppressed; undertake this for me."

"Ah!" you sigh, "I wish indeed I could live like this, but in the moment of need I forget to look." Then do this: trust in Christ to keep you trusting. Look to Him so to abide in you as to keep you abiding. In the early morning entrust to Him the keeping of your soul, and then as hour succeeds to hour expect Him to keep that which you have committed unto Him.

Keep in Touch with Christ

Avoid the spirit of fault-finding, criticism, uncharitableness, and anything inconsistent with His perfect love. Go where He is most likely to be found, either where two or three of His children are gathered, or where the lost sheep is straying. Ask Him to wake you morning by morning for communion and Bible-study. Make other time in the day, especially in the still hour of the evening twilight, between the work of the day and the avocations of the evening, when you shall get alone with Him, telling Him all things, and reviewing the past under the gentle light which streams from His eyes.

Expect the Holy Ghost to Work in, with, and for You

When a man is right with God, God will freely use him. There will rise up within him impulses, inspirations, strong strivings, strange resolves. These must be tested by Scripture and prayer, and if evidently of God they must be obeyed.

But there is this perennial source of comfort: God's commands are enablings. He will never give us a work to do without showing exactly how and when to do it, and without giving us the precise strength and wisdom we need. Do not dread to enter this life because you fear that God will ask you to do something you can not do. He will never do that. If He lays aught on your heart, He will do so irresistibly; and as you pray about it, the impression will continue to grow, so that presently, as you look up to know what He wills you to say or do, the way will suddenly open, and you will probably have said the word, or done the deed, almost unconsciously.

There may be failures in this life, but they will arise on the human side, not the divine. Well will it be if we can instantly discover the cause of failure, and confess it, and seek restoration to the old peace and joy. After all, the sheep does not keep the shepherd. The shepherd keeps the sheep, and feeds it, and leads it, and makes it to lie down. What then may we not expect from our Good Shepherd? and who can paint the verdure of the green pastures, or the crystal beauty of those unfailing springs, to which He will lead the docile and trustful spirit?

Be that spirit thine, dear reader, and mine.

FOR ADDITIONAL INFORMATION

Bryant, Al, ed. *Daily Meditations with F. B. Meyer.* Waco, Texas, Word Books, 1979.

Demaray, Donald E. *Pulpit Giants: What Made Them Great.* Chicago, Moody Press, 1973.

Fullerton, William. *F. B. Meyer, A Biography.* London, Marshall, Morgan & Scott, Ltd., n.d.

Lotz, Philip Henry. *Founders of Christian Movements.* Freeport, New York, Books for Libraries Press, 1970.

Mann, A. Chester. *F. B. Meyer, Preacher, Teacher, Man of God.* New York, Revell, 1929.

Meyer, F. B. *Bells of Is, or Voices of Human Need and Sorrow, The: Echoes from My Pastorate.* New York, Revell, 1894.

———. *Call and Challenge of the Unseen, The.* New York, Revell, 1928.

———. *Christ in Isaiah.* London, Marshall, Morgan and Scott, 1950.

———. *Christian Living.* New York, H. M. Caldwell, 1890.

———. *Expository Preaching.* New York, Hodder, 1910.

———. *F. B. Meyer.* Introduction by Robert G. Lee, New York, Revell, 1950.

———. *Joseph: Beloved, Hated. Exalted.* New York, Revell, n.d.

———. *Paul: A Servant of Jesus Christ.* New York, Revell, 1897.

———. *Peter: Fisherman, Disciple, Apostle.* New York, Revell, 1920.

———. *Way into the Holiest Expositions of the Epistle to the Hebrews.* New York, Revell, 1893.

Rawlyk, George and Mark A. Noll, eds. *Amazing Grace: Evangelicalism in Australia, Britain, Canada and the United States.* "F. B. Meyer in Britain & America," Grand Rapids, Michigan, Baker Books, 1993.

Zylstra, Cornelius, ed. *The Best of F. B. Meyer.* Grand Rapids, Michigan, Zondervan, 1984.

TOPICAL INDEX

BIBLICAL INDEX